T0321935

# Research Anthology on Business Aspects of Cybersecurity

Information Resources Management Association
*USA*

Published in the United States of America by
  IGI Global
  Information Science Reference (an imprint of IGI Global)
  701 E. Chocolate Avenue
  Hershey PA, USA 17033
  Tel: 717-533-8845
  Fax:  717-533-8661
  E-mail: cust@igi-global.com
  Web site: http://www.igi-global.com

Library of Congress Cataloging-in-Publication Data

Names: Information Resources Management Association, editor.
Title: Research anthology on business aspects of cybersecurity /
  Information Resources Management Association, editor.
Description: Hershey, PA : Information Science Reference, [2022] | Includes
  bibliographical references and index. | Summary: "This reference book
  considers all emerging aspects of cybersecurity in the business sector
  including frameworks, models, best practices, and emerging areas of
  interest, discussing items such as audits and risk assessments that
  businesses can conduct to ensure the security of their systems, training
  and awareness initiatives for staff that promotes a security culture and
  software and systems that can be used to secure and manage cybersecurity
  threats"-- Provided by publisher.
Identifiers: LCCN 2021040445 (print) | LCCN 2021040446 (ebook) | ISBN
  9781668436981 (hardcover) | ISBN 9781668436998 (ebook)
Subjects: LCSH: Data protection. | Computer security. | Computer
  crimes--Prevention. | Business enterprises--Security measures.
Classification: LCC HF5548.37 .R47 2022  (print) | LCC HF5548.37  (ebook) |
  DDC 005.8--dc23
LC record available at https://lccn.loc.gov/2021040445
LC ebook record available at https://lccn.loc.gov/2021040446

British Cataloguing in Publication Data
A Cataloguing in Publication record for this book is available from the British Library.

The views expressed in this book are those of the authors, but not necessarily of the publisher.

For electronic access to this publication, please contact: eresources@igi-global.com.

# List of Contributors

# Table of Contents

### Section 3
### Securing and Managing Cybersecurity Threats

# Preface

There have been numerous cases in which businesses have had to reveal to their consumers that their networks have been hacked and personal data stolen. Unfortunately, while these cases are no longer rare, they can still be debilitating for the business as consumers lose their trust in the organization and their ability to safeguard information. Cybersecurity is an area that concerns a number of fields and is a vital aspect to keep company information secure and protected. Businesses in every sector must remain up to date on the current strategies, research, and practices in order to train employees appropriately, avoid unnecessary risks online, and maintain a secure organization overall. There are endless potential pitfalls and dangers businesses must consider to protect themselves, and maintaining a working knowledge of cybersecurity is essential for continued safety and to ensure the trust of their stakeholders.

Thus, the *Research Anthology on Business Aspects of Cybersecurity* seeks to fill the void for an all-encompassing and comprehensive reference book covering the latest and emerging research, concepts, and theories for those working in business. This one-volume reference collection of reprinted IGI Global book chapters and journal articles that have been handpicked by the editor and editorial team of this research anthology on this topic will empower businesses, managers, executives, entrepreneurs, security analysts, cybersecurity professionals, business professionals, IT consultants, programmers, systems engineers, researchers, academicians, and students with an advanced understanding of critical issues and advancements of the current trends, risks, and best practices of cybersecurity in business.

The *Research Anthology on Business Aspects of Cybersecurity* is organized into three sections that provide comprehensive coverage of important topics. The sections are:

1. Cybersecurity Audits and Risk Assessment;
2. Organizational Awareness and Cybersecurity Training; and
3. Securing and Managing Cybersecurity Threats.

The following paragraphs provide a summary of what to expect from this invaluable reference tool.

Section 1, "Cybersecurity Audits and Risk Assessment," examines audits of organizational systems and security practices in order to help uncover risks and provides emerging research on risk assessments and management. The opening chapter in this section, "Audits in Cybersecurity," by Prof. Regner Sabillon of the Universitat Oberta de Catalunya, Spain, provides a comprehensive literature review of the most relevant approaches for conducting cybersecurity audits, including auditing perspectives for specific scopes and the best practices that many leading organizations are providing for security and auditing professionals to follow. Another opening chapter, "Auditor Evaluation and Reporting on Cybersecurity Risks," by Prof. Jeffrey S. Zanzig of Jacksonville State University, USA and Prof. Guillermo A. Francia III from the University of West Florida, USA, considers how cybersecurity guidance from COBIT, the National Institute of Standards and Technology, and the Center for Internet Security can be mapped into five cyber infrastructure domains to provide an approach to evaluate a system of cybersecurity. The next chapter, "The NIST Cybersecurity Framework," by Profs. Gregory B. White and Natalie Sjelin from CIAS, The University of Texas at San Antonio, USA, discusses the National Institute of Standards and Technology (NIST) developed the Cyber Security Framework (CSF) to assist critical infrastructures in determining what they need in order to secure their computer systems and networks. The following chapter, "A Hybrid Asset-Based IT Risk Management Framework," by Profs. Baris Cimen, Meltem Mutluturk, Esra Kocak, and Bilgin Metin of Bogazici University, Turkey, proposes a hybrid risk management framework using both qualitative and quantitative methods to analyze risk within organizations and reduce them with practical countermeasures. Another chapter, "The CyberSecurity Audit Model (CSAM)," by Prof. Regner Sabillon of the Universitat Oberta de Catalunya, Spain, presents the outcome of two empirical research studies that assess the implementation and validation of the cybersecurity audit model (CSAM), designed as a multiple-case study in two different Canadian higher education institution. A concluding chapter, "The Two-Dimensional CCSMM," by Profs. Gregory B. White and Natalie Sjelin from CIAS, The University of Texas at San Antonio, USA, discusses the community cybersecurity maturity model (CCSMM) which defines four dimensions and five implementation mechanisms in describing the relative maturity of an organization or an SLTT's cybersecurity program. The final chapter in this section, "Threat and Risk Assessment Using Continuous Logic," by Profs. Aristides Dasso and Ana Funes of the Universidad Nacional de San Luis, Argentina, presents a method to help assesses threats and risks associated with computer and networks systems and integrates the Framework for Improving Critical Infrastructure Cybersecurity—developed by the National Institute of Standards and Technology—with a quantitative method based on the use of a Continuous Logic, the Logic Scoring of Preference (LSP) method.

Section 2, "Organizational Awareness and Cybersecurity Training," examines strategies that businesses may use to ensure employee awareness and security training, and addresses the struggles associated with maintaining a secure organization. The opening chapter in this section, "Interdisciplinary Training and Mentoring for Cyber Security in Companies," by Prof. Ileana Hamburg of the Institute of Work and Technology, Germany, proposes an interdisciplinary training program in cybersecurity curriculum and an interdisciplinary mentoring program to be included in entrepreneurial learning. The following chapter, "SETA and Security Behavior: Mediating Role of Employee Relations, Monitoring, and Accountability," by Dr. Peace Kumah of Ghana Education Service, Ghana and Profs. Daniel Okyere Walker and Winfred Yaokumah from Pentecost University College, Ghana, proposes and tests a causal model that estimates the direct effect of employee security training on security behavior as well as its indirect effects as mediated by employee relations, monitoring, and accountability. Another opening chapter, "Factors Influencing Information Security Policy Compliance Behavior," by Prof. Kwame Simpe Ofori of the University of Electronic Science and Technology of China, China; Prof. Hod Anyigba from Nobel International Business School, Ghana; Profs. George Oppong Appiagyei Ampong and Eli Fianu of Ghana Technology University College, Ghana; Prof. Osaretin Kayode Omoregie from Pan-Atlantic University, Nigeria; and Prof. Makafui Nyamadi of the University of Ghana, Ghana, seeks to examine information security compliance from the perspective of the general deterrence theory (GDT) and information security climate (ISC) in order to discuss the implications, limitations, and directions for future research. The next section, "Achieving a Security Culture," by Prof. Adéle Da Veiga of the University of South Africa, South Africa, aims to give organizations an overview of the concept of security culture, the factors that could influence it, an approach to assess the security culture, and to prioritize and tailor interventions for high-risk areas. The following chapter, "Cyber Security Competency Model Based on Learning Theories and Learning Continuum Hierarchy," by Prof. Winfred Yaokumah of Pentecost University College, Ghana, proposes a cybersecurity competency model that integrates learning theories (cognitive, affective, and psychomotor), learning continuum hierarchy (awareness and training), and cybersecurity domain knowledge. Another section, "The Role of Education and Awareness in Tackling Insider Threats," by Prof. Nigel McKelvey of the Letterkenny Institute of Technology, Ireland and Profs. Kevin Curran and Shaun Joseph Smyth from Ulster University, UK, examines those who fall into the category which can be referred to as insiders and highlights the activity of outsourcing which is employed by many organizations and defines the term insider threat while pointing out what differentiates an accidental threat from a malicious threat. An additional chapter, "The Role of Human Resource Management in Enhancing Organizational Information Systems Security," by Dr. Peace Kumah of Ghana Education Service, Ghana, examines the role of HRM in enhancing organizational information systems security using importance-performance map analysis. The next chapter in this section, "Identifying HRM Practices for Improving Information Security Performance: An Importance-Performance Map Analysis," by Profs. Winfred Yaokumah and Charles Buabeng-Andoh of Pentecost University College, Ghana and Dr. Peace Kumah from Ghana Education Service, Ghana, focuses on identifying key human resource management (HRM) practices necessary for improving information security performance from the perspective of IT professionals. The next chapter, "Assessing the Value of Executive Leadership Coaches for Cybersecurity Project Managers," by Prof. Darrell Norman Burrell of Florida Institute of Technology, USA, explores the values and potential benefits of executive coaching as a leadership development tool for information technology and cybersecurity project managers. A concluding chapter, "Towards a Student Security Compliance Model (SSCM): Factors Predicting Student Compliance Intention to Information Security Policy," by Prof. Felix Nti Koranteng of the University of Education, Winneba, Ghana, proposes a students' security compliance model (SSCM) that attempts to explain predictive factors of students' ISP compliance intentions and encourages further research to confirm the proposed relationships using qualitative and quantitative techniques. The next chapter, "Internal Marketing Cybersecurity-Conscious Culture," by Prof. Gordon Bowen of Northumbria University, UK and Prof. Atul Sethi from Ulster University, UK, discusses the idea that internal marketing is a tool of which there are many to embed a culture to combat cybersecurity threats. Another concluding chapter, "Raising Information Security Awareness in the Field of Urban and Regional Planning," by Prof. Margit Christa Scholl of Technische Hochschule Wildau, Germany, provides a review of the scientific literature of leading academic journals in the area of IS and the transfer of scientific knowledge for practical purposes and presents Serious Games as a way to achieve a deeper understanding of how to promote sustainable ISA using creative methods. The final chapter in this section, "A Comparative Study in Israel and Slovenia Regarding the Awareness, Knowledge, and Behavior Regarding Cyber Security," by Profs. Moti Zwilling and Galit Klein of Ariel University, Israel and Prof. Dušan Lesjak of International School for Social and Business Studies, Slovenia, explores the connection between cybersecurity awareness, cyber knowledge, and cybersecurity behavior by measuring the behaviors among students in two similar countries: Israel and Slovenia.

Section 3, "Securing and Managing Cybersecurity Threats," discusses the current threats to security that businesses face in the modern era as well as ways to combat them. The opening chapter in this section, "Enterprise Security: Modern Challenges and Emerging Measures," by Manish Shukla, Harshal Tupsamudre, and Dr. Sachin Lodha of Tata Consultancy Services, India, describes the changing cyber ecosystem due to extreme digitalization and then its ramifications that are plainly visible in the latest trends in cyber-attacks. The next chapter, "Practical Align Overview of the Main Frameworks Used by the Companies to Prevent Cyber Incidents," by Prof. Rogério Yukio Iwashita of the University of São Paulo, Brazil and Prof. Luiz Camolesi Junior from University of Campinas, Brazil, helps information security professionals compare the information security maturity level within companies and between the companies using benchmarks and helps them decide where they should focus their efforts. Another opening chapter, "National Cybersecurity Strategies," by Prof. Regner Sabillon of the Universitat Oberta de Catalunya, Spain, studies the phases to unify our national cybersecurity strategy model (NCSSM) in any nation cyber strategy that is either under development or improvement stages. An additional chapter, "Network and Data Transfer Security Management in Higher Educational Institutions," by Prof. Winfred Yaokumah of Pentecost University College, Ghana and Prof. Alex Ansah Dawson from Kwame Nkrumah University of Science and Technology, Ghana, explores communications security through the use of an empirical survey to assess the extent of network and data transfer security management in Ghanaian higher educational institutions. The next chapter, "Conceptualizing the Domain and an Empirical Analysis of Operations Security Management," by Prof. Winfred Yaokumah of Pentecost University College, Ghana, conducts an in-depth review of scholarly and practitioner works to conceptualize the domain of operations security management and classifies operations security management into 10 domains. The following chapter, "Challenges in Securing Industrial Control Systems Using Future Internet Technologies," by Prof. Mirjana D. Stojanović of University of Belgrade, Serbia and Prof. Slavica V. Boštjančič Rakas from Mihailo Pupin Institute, University of Belgrade, Serbia, explores challenges in securing industrial control systems (ICS) and Supervisory Control And Data Acquisition (SCADA) systems using future internet technologies. Another chapter, "Security Framework for Supply-Chain Management," by Prof. Kathick Raj Elangovan of Concordia University, Canada, talks about the security framework for cyber threats in supply chain management and discusses in detail the implementation of a secure environment through various controls. A concluding chapter, "Cybersecurity Incident Response and Management," by Prof. Regner Sabillon of the Universitat Oberta de Catalunya, Spain, presents a systematic literature review on best practices regarding cybersecurity incident response handling and incident management and identifies incident handling models that are used worldwide when responding to any type of cybersecurity incident. Another chapter in this section, "Lawful Trojan Horse," by Prof. Bruce L. Mann of Memorial University, Canada, discusses how several news outlets, for example, reported that Germany's Federal Criminal Police Office (BKA) was using a Trojan Horse to access the smartphone data of suspected individuals before the information was encrypted. The following chapter, "Modeling a Cyber Defense Business Ecosystem of Ecosystems: Nurturing Brazilian Cyber Defense Resources," by Profs. João Mello da Silva, Edison Ishikawa, Eduardo Wallier Vianna, Jorge Henrique Cabral Fernandes, Paulo Roberto, and Ricardo Zelenovsky of the University of Brasília, Brazil, proposes a cyber defense business ecosystem of ecosystems (BEoE) model with two ecosystems that must be created or fostered, the human resources training ecosystem and the product and service homologation and certification ecosystem. The final chapter in this section, "The Challenges and Solutions of Cybersecurity Among Malaysian Companies," by Prof. Puteri Fadzline Tamyez of the University Malaysia Pahang, Malaysia, analyzes the challenges faced by Malaysian companies in cybersecurity and determines solutions for Malaysian companies to overcome challenges in cybersecurity.

Although the primary organization of the contents in this work is based on its three sections offering a progression of coverage of the important concepts, methodologies, technologies, applications, social issues, and emerging trends, the reader can also identify specific contents by utilizing the extensive indexing system listed at the end. As a comprehensive collection of research on the latest findings related to business aspects of cybersecurity, the *Research Anthology on Business Aspects of Cybersecurity* provides businesses, business professionals, managers, IT consultants, programmers, researchers, academicians, students, and all audiences with a complete understanding of the challenges that face those working in business. Given the need for a better understanding of cybersecurity within businesses, such as the risks, threats, and frameworks, this extensive book presents the latest research and best practices to address these challenges and provide further opportunities for improvement.

# Section 1
# Cybersecurity Audits and Risk Assessment

# Chapter 1
# Audits in Cybersecurity

**Regner Sabillon**
*Universitat Oberta de Catalunya, Spain*

## ABSTRACT

*The objective of this chapter is to provision a comprehensive literature review of the most relevant approaches for conducting cybersecurity audits. The study includes auditing perspectives for specific scopes and the best practices that many leading organizations are providing for security and auditing professionals to follow. The chapter reviews relevant features for auditing approaches in the following order: ISO/IEC 27001:2013, ISO/IEC 27002:2013, Control Objectives for Information and Related Technology (COBIT) 2019, Information Technology Infrastructure Library (ITIL) 4, AICPA, ISACA, NIST SP 800-53, NIST CSF v1.1, IIA, PCI DSS, ITAF, COSO, ENISA, NERC CIP, and CSAM.*

## INTRODUCTION

This study reviews the most important standards, frameworks, methodologies, guidelines, best practices and models that are used worldwide for planning, execution, reporting and follow-up audit phases in the areas of information security (InfoSec), cybersecurity and information technology.

The chapter reviews relevant features for auditing approaches in the following order: ISO/IEC 27001:2013; ISO/IEC 27002:2013; Control Objectives for Information and Related Technology (COBIT) 2019; Information Technology Infrastructure Library (ITIL) 4, AICPA; ISACA; NIST SP 800-53; NIST CSF v1.1; IIA; PCI DSS; ITAF; COSO; ENISA; NERC CIP and CSAM. Some methodologies have a specific purpose and others provide the audit approaches for certain institutions that have global impact.

## ISO/IEC 27001: 2013

This international standard was designed and is maintained by the International Organization for Standardization (ISO). ISO standards are reviewed every five years, previous edition was published in 2005 and the second edition was released in 2013. The ISO/IEC 27001:2013 known as *Information technology - Security techniques – Information security management systems - Requirements*. It is based on the Information Security Management System (ISMS). ISO/IEC 27001:2013 can be used by organizations

DOI: 10.4018/978-1-6684-3698-1.ch001

to establish, implement, maintain and continually improve the ISMS. ISO/IEC 27001:2013 consists of 7 clauses (Table 1), control objectives and controls are aligned with ISO/IEC 27002:2013, which contains 14 control clauses, 35 security categories and 114 controls. Terminology is based on ISO/IEC 27000: *Information technology - Security techniques – Information security management systems – Overview and vocabulary.*

Clauses 9 and 10 provide guidelines for:

1.   Monitoring, measurement, analysis and evaluation
2.   Internal audit
3.   Management review
4.   Nonconformity and corrective action
5.   And Continual Improvement of the ISMS

*Table 1. ISO/IEC 27001:2013 Information Security Management Systems Clauses*

| ISO/IEC 27001: Security Control Clauses |
|---|
| 1. Clause 4: Context of the organization<br>2. Clause 5: Leadership<br>3. Clause 6: Planning<br>4. Clause 7: Support<br>5. Clause 8: Operation<br>6. Clause 9: Performance Evaluation<br>7. Clause 10: Improvement |

## ISO/IEC 27002: 2013

This international standard was designed and is maintained by the International Organization for Standardization (ISO). ISO standards are reviewed every five years, previous edition was published in 2005 and the second edition was released in 2013. The ISO/IEC 27002:2013 known as *Information technology - Security techniques – Code of practice for information security controls.* It is based on the Information Security Management System (ISMS) from the ISO/IEC 27001. ISO/IEC 27002:2013 can be used by organizations to select controls with any ISMS implementation, implement universally accepted information security controls and to develop information security management guidelines for their specific business environments.

ISO/IEC 27002:2013 contains 14 control clauses (Table 2), 35 security categories (Table 3) and 114 controls.

In terms of audits, *ISO/IEC 27002:2013* highlights two specific controls for planning and conducting audits:

12.7.1 Information system audit controls: Requirements and activities are to be planned without causing impact to business processes. A guidance implementation is provided that includes 7 guidelines.

*Table 2. ISO/IEC 27002:2013 Security Control Clauses*

| ISO/IEC 27002: Security Control Clauses |
|---|
| 8. Clause 5: Information Security Policies |
| 9. Clause 6: Organization of Information Security |
| 10. Clause 7: Human Resource Security |
| 11. Clause 8: Asset Management |
| 12. Clause 9: Access Control |
| 13. Clause 10: Cryptography |
| 14. Clause 11: Physical and Environmental Security |
| 15. Clause 12: Operations Security |
| 16. Clause 13: Communication Security |
| 17. Clause 14: System Acquisition, Development and Maintenance |
| 18. Clause 15: Supplier Relationships |
| 19. Clause 16: Information Security Incident Management |
| 20. Clause 17: Information Security Aspects of Business Continuity Management |
| 21. Clause 18: Compliance |

*Table 3. ISO/IEC 27002:2013 Security Categories*

| ISO/IEC 27002: Security Categories |
|---|
| 1. Category 5.1: Management direction for information security |
| 2. Category 6.1: Internal organization |
| 3. Category 6.2: Mobile devices and teleworking |
| 4. Category 7.1: Prior to employment |
| 5. Category 7.2: During employment |
| 6. Category 7.3: Termination and change of employment |
| 7. Category 8.1: Responsibilities of assets |
| 8. Category 8.2: Information classification |
| 9. Category 8.3: Media handling |
| 10. Category 9.1: Business requirements of access control |
| 11. Category 9.2: User access management |
| 12. Category 9.3: User responsibilities |
| 13. Category 9.4: System and application access control |
| 14. Category 10.1: Cryptographic controls |
| 15. Category 11.1: Secure areas |
| 16. Category 11.2: Equipment |
| 17. Category 12.1: Operational procedures and responsibilities |
| 18. Category 12.2: Protection from malware |
| 19. Category 12.3: Backup |
| 20. Category 12.4: Logging and monitoring |
| 21. Category 12.5: Control of operational software |
| 22. Category 12.6: Technical vulnerability management |
| 23. Category 12.7: Information systems audit considerations |
| 24. Category 13.1: Network security management |
| 25. Category 13.2: Information transfer |
| 26. Category 14.1: Security requirements of information systems |
| 27. Category 14.2: Security in development and support processes |
| 28. Category 14.3: Test data |
| 29. Category 15.1: Information security in supplier relationships |
| 30. Category 15.2: Supplier service delivery management |
| 31. Category 16.1: Management of information security incidents and improvements |
| 32. Category 17.1: Information security continuity |
| 33. Category 17.2: Redundancies |
| 34. Category 18.1: Compliance with legal and contractual requirements |
| 35. Category 18.2: Information security reviews |

18.2.3 Technical compliance review: This controls states that systems should be reviewed constantly to verify compliance with information security policies. This control provides an implementation guidance covering expertise from auditors, appropriate planning of penetration testing and vulnerability assessments and it also includes scope for technical compliance reviews and recommends to use *ISO/IEC TR 27008: Information technology – Security techniques – Guidelines for auditors on information security controls* for conducting technical compliance reviews.

# CONTROL OBJECTIVES FOR INFORMATION AND RELATED TECHNOLOGY (COBIT) 2019

Control Objectives for Information and Related Technology (COBIT) is a framework for governance and management of enterprise information and technology for any organization. The COBIT 2019 Core documentation is organized as follows:

1. Framework: Introduction and Methodology
2. Framework: Governance and Management Objectives
3. Design Guide: Designing an Information and Technology Governance Solution
4. Implementation Guide: Implementing and Optimizing an Information and Technology Governance Solution

COBIT 2019 provides inputs to the COBIT Core where section AP013 is exclusive for Managed Security, then the Core framework publications, adding Design Factors and Focus Areas which result in a tailored enterprise governance system for Information and Technology.

ISACA and ITAF guidelines and procedures can be utilized for planning COBIT audits.

# INFORMATION TECHNOLOGY INFRASTRUCTURE LIBRARY (ITIL) 4

ITIL is a framework created to standardize the selection, planning, delivery and maintenance of Information Technology services within any company. The main goal is to improve efficiency and achieve predictable service delivery. ITIL is the global standard for the Information Technology Service Management (ITSM) industry. AXELOS in the United Kingdom (UK), is responsible for maintaining ITIL and all its publications. ITIL is mapped in ISO 20000 Part 1 and its certification scheme can be tailored to adopt and adapt ITIL in alignment with business specific needs.

The core publications map the entire ITIL service lifecycle and are:

1. ITIL Service Strategy
2. ITIL Service Design
3. ITIL Service Transition
4. ITIL Service Operation
5. ITIL Continual Service Improvement

Information Security Management is included in the Service Design (Section 4.6) and contains purpose, goal, objective, scope, value, policies, principles, basic concepts, the Information Security Management System (ISMS) of ISO 27001, ISMS activities/methods/techniques, security controls, management of security breaches and incidents, triggers/inputs/outputs/interfaces of the Information Security Management (ISM), Key Performance Indicators (KPIs), information management and Challenges/Critical Success Factors (CSFs) and risks of the ISM.

The Continual Service Improvement (CSI) publication provides principles (Section 3), processes (Section 4) and methods and techniques (Section 5).

ITIL can use a series of different criteria for assessment that is presented in Table 4.

*Table 4. ITIL assessment criteria*

| Resource | Description |
| --- | --- |
| ITIL Maturity model | A set of 4,000 questions in 30 different questionnaires, that cover 26 processes and 4 functions |
| ISO/IEC 20000 | The ISO standard for service management |
| COBIT Process Assessment Model | Assessment aligned between COBIT 5 and ISO/IEC 15504 (Standard for IT process assessment) |
| CMMI-SVC | Capability Maturity Model for services |
| AXELOS skills framework | Assessment for project and program management, ITSM, leadership and personal management |
| SFIA | Skills Framework for the Information Age to review the capabilities of IT personnel |
| European e-Competence Framework | Assessments of IT staff capabilities |

# AMERICAN INSTITUTE OF CERTIFIED PUBLIC ACCOUNTANTS (AICPA)

According to AICPA (2017), its Cybersecurity risk management program is a *"Set of policies, processes and controls designed to protect information and systems from security events that could compromise the achievement of the entity's cybersecurity objectives and to detect, respond to, mitigate, and recover from, on a timely basis, security events that are not prevented."*

The Cybersecurity Risk Management Reporting Framework verifies the effectiveness of existing security controls between organization and its stakeholders. The framework consists of the following components:

- Description criteria for management's description of any entity's cybersecurity risk management program
- Trust services control criteria for security, availability and confidentiality
- AICPA Guide reporting on an entity's cybersecurity risk management program

System and Organization Controls (SOCs) are categorized as follows:

- SOC for Cybersecurity guide that includes organization-wide reporting
- SOC 1 Guide that supports controls reporting at service organizations that impact internal controls over financial reporting

- SOC 2 Guide that supports reporting for controls related security, availability, processing integrity, confidentiality and privacy and for restricted-use reporting
- SOC 3 for general-use reporting

Assessments are conducted as audit engagements or engagements for different SOCs (1,2 or 3).

## INFORMATION SYSTEMS AUDIT AND CONTROL ASSOCIATION (ISACA)

According to ISACA (2017), cybersecurity is really important to many members of the Board of Directors in part to the fact that bad publicity can be generated once one organization is victim of a major data breach or cyberattack. To invest in proper measures, Companies need to evaluate their current and emerging risks and to audit existing or future controls in order to protect information assets. Control investments should cover awareness, policy, Intrusion Detection Systems (IDS), event logging, incident response, vulnerability scanning, classification of information and cyber assets, forward intelligence and technology/architecture/systems hardening. Cybersecurity audits are organized in three lines of defense:

1. Management: Control Self-Assessments (CSAs), Pen testing, Technical testing, Social testing and Regular Management review
2. Risk Management: Threats/Vulnerabilities/Risks, Risk evaluation, Business Impact Analysis (BIA) and Emerging risk
3. Internal Audit: Internal controls testing, Cybersecurity compliance, Risk acceptance and Digital Forensics investigations

Cybersecurity audits are more complex than any general audit, planning and scoping is shown in Table 5.

*Table 5. ISACA's cybersecurity audits by areas and types*

| Areas | Types of Cybersecurity Audits |
| --- | --- |
| Governance | Cybersecurity policy, Technical key operating procedures |
| Risk | Cybersecurity risk register update, risk treatment, risk reporting |
| Management | Cybersecurity incident reviews |
| Assurance | Cybersecurity risk management process |

Cybersecurity audits should have specific goals that ought to be aligned with objectives and enterprise outcomes (Table 6).

*Table 6. ISACA's cybersecurity audit goals aligned with business outcomes*

| Cybersecurity goals | Business outcomes |
|---|---|
| Proper and effective cybersecurity documentation (Policies, Standards and Procedures) | Audit will review governance, controls for effective and adequate documents |
| Emerging risk is properly identified, evaluated and treated | Cybersecurity audits will focus on processes, tools and methods |
| Cybersecurity processes are defined, deployed and measured during business transformation | Cybersecurity reviews will cover transforming processes |
| Cybersecurity incident response addresses cyberattacks and breaches that are identified and treated appropriately | Cybersecurity (in-depth technical) audits to seek early recognition and identification of cyberattacks in timely and appropriate fashion as specified by corporate documentation |

# NIST SPECIAL PUBLICATION 800-53

The NIST Special Publication 800-53 Revision 5 is the "Security and Privacy Controls for Information Systems and Organizations", the publication includes a catalog for security and privacy controls. These controls are flexible, customizable and can be implemented fully or partially in any organization seeking managing security risks. The controls are addressed from a functionality and an assurance perspective.

NIST SP 800-53 provides 20 different security controls (Table7). Each control has objectives, supplemental guidance, related controls, control enhancements and references to other NIST Special Publications. Controls are categorized as common controls, system-specific controls and hybrid controls.

*Table 7. Security and Privacy Controls in NIST Special Publication 800-53 v5*

| NIST Special Publication 800-53 v5: Security and Privacy Control Families |
|---|
| 1. Access control |
| 2. Awareness and training |
| 3. Audit and accountability |
| 4. Assessment, authorization and monitoring |
| 5. Configuration management |
| 6. Contingency planning |
| 7. Identification and authentication |
| 8. Individual participation |
| 9. Incident response |
| 10. Maintenance |
| 11. Media protection |
| 12. Privacy authorization |
| 13. Physical and environmental protection |
| 14. Planning |
| 15. Program management |
| 16. Personnel security |
| 17. Risk assessment |
| 18. System and services acquisition |
| 19. System and communications protection |
| 20. System and information integrity |

The Audit and accountability family includes the following controls:

1. Audit and accountability policy and procedures
2. Audit events
3. Content of audit records
4. Audit storage capacity
5. Response to audit processing failures
6. Audit, review, analysis and reporting
7. Audit reduction and report generation
8. Time stamps
9. Protection of audit information
10. Non-repudiation
11. Audit record retention
12. Audit generation
13. Monitoring for information disclosure
14. Session audit
15. Alternate audit capability
16. Cross-organizational auditing

## NIST CYBERSECURITY FRAMEWORK (CSF) VERSION 1.1

The NIST Cybersecurity Framework (CSF) version 1.1 focuses on business drivers linked to cybersecurity activities and risks. The framework has three main components:

1. Framework Core: Desired cybersecurity outcomes are properly identified
2. Implementation Tiers: Qualitative measure of the organization's cybersecurity risks management
3. Framework Profiles: Alignment between the Framework Core and the organization's requirements, objectives, risk appetite and resources

The main functions of the Framework Core are identified as Identify, Protect, Detect, Respond and Recover. Each function contains categories, subcategories and informative references. The NIST CSF consists of 5 functions, 23 categories, 108 subcategories and 6 informative references (COBIT 5, ISA 62443-2-1:2009, ISA 62443-3-3:2013, ISO/IEC 27001: 2013, NIST SP 800-53 Rev 4 and Center for Internet Security - Top 20 Critical Security Controls (CIS CSC). The framework can be implemented as the foundation of a new cybersecurity program, new cybersecurity risk management, combine with other cybersecurity framework or standard either partially or in a full implementation.

The NIST CSF follows a continuous lifecycle which covers planning, designing, building, deploying, operating and decommissioning phases.

Audits are specified for many subcategories of the core functions of the NIST CSF.

# THE INSTITUTE OF INTERNAL AUDITORS (IIA)

According to the Institute of Internal Auditors (IIA), cybersecurity is defined as the technologies, processes and practices designed to protect the information assets of any organization. Like ISACA, the IIA also considers the "Three Lines of Defense Roles and Responsibilities" to protect cybersecurity related to management, controls and governance. Furthermore, IIA adds roles and responsibilities to the "Three Lines of Defense":

1. First Line of Defense: Chief Technology Officer (CTO), Chief Security Officer (CSO), Chief Information Security Officer (CISO), Chief Information Officer (CIO), Chief Executive Officer (CEO) and other members of Upper Management
2. Second Line of Defense: IT risk management and IT compliance managers and officers
3. Third Line of Defense: Chief Audit Executive (CAE) and Internal Audit activity

IIA utilizes the Cybersecurity Risk Assessment Framework for planning and conducting cybersecurity audits (Table 8).

*Table 8. IIA's Cybersecurity Risk Assessment Framework*

| Components | Framework Activities |
|---|---|
| Cybersecurity Governance | • Risk appetite<br>• Cybersecurity policy<br>• Risk assessment and monitoring<br>• Training<br>• Examination of third-party vendors |
| Inventory of Information Assets: Data, Infrastructure and Applications | • Data inventory<br>• Device inventory<br>• Software inventory |
| Standard Security Configurations | • Secure configurations for hardware and software<br>• Secure configurations for networking devices |
| Information Access Management | • Controlled use of administrative privileges<br>• Account monitoring and control<br>• Controls on *Need to know* access<br>• Population of users |
| Prompt Response and Remediation | • Continuous improvements<br>• Assessment of vulnerabilities, threat intelligence and gap identification<br>• Performance metrics<br>• Inventory of knowledge, skills and abilities |
| Ongoing Monitoring | • Malware defenses<br>• Limitation and controls for network ports, protocols and services<br>• Application security<br>• Wireless access controls<br>• Boundary defense<br>• Penetration testing, phishing tests and red teaming exercises<br>• Change event management<br>• Data protection and data loss prevention |

IIA also recommend specific publications for planning and conducting cybersecurity audits (Table 9).

*Table 9. IIA's publications for cybersecurity audits*

| IIA publication guidance for cybersecurity audits |
|---|
| 1. Practice Guide, "Business Continuity Management – Crisis Management" |
| 2. Practice Guide, "Auditing Privacy Risks, 2nd Edition" |
| 3. Global Technology Audit Guide (GTAG), "Change and Patch Management Controls: Critical for Organizational Success, 2nd Edition" |
| 4. Global Technology Audit Guide (GTAG), "Management of IT Auditing, 2nd Edition" |
| 5. Global Technology Audit Guide (GTAG), "Information Technology Outsourcing, 2nd Edition" |
| 6. Global Technology Audit Guide (GTAG), "Identity and Access Management" |
| 7. Global Technology Audit Guide (GTAG), "Developing the IT Audit Plan" |
| 8. Global Technology Audit Guide (GTAG), "Information Security Governance" |
| 9. Global Technology Audit Guide (GTAG), "Auditing IT Governance" |
| 10. Position Paper, "The Three Lines of Defense in Effective Risk Management and Control" |

## PAYMENT CARD INDUSTRY DATA SECURITY STANDARD (PCI DSS)

PCI DSS is the global standard for the payment industry that involves the major payment cards like American Express, Discover Financial Services, JCB International, Mastercard, Visa Inc and Visa Europe. Compliance with PCI DSS protects merchants and cardholders for the storage, processing and transmission of transaction data. The PCI DSS compliance is a continuous process that includes major phases for assessing, remediating and reporting.

The standard has specific goals and requirements that are presented in Tables 10 and 11.

*Table 10. PCI DSS's Goals*

| PCI DSS Goals |
|---|
| 1. Build and maintain a secure network |
| 2. Protect cardholder data |
| 3. Maintain a vulnerability management program |
| 4. Implement strong access control measures |
| 5. Regularly monitor and test networks |
| 6. Maintain an information security policy |

The PCI DSS Council is responsible for maintaining the set of standards but each payment card brand is responsible for setting the compliance programs, validation and enforcement. The Council maintains approved

Qualified Security Assessors (QSAs) and Approved Scanning Vendors (ASVs) to audit PCI DSS compliance of merchants and the Self-Assessment Questionnaire (SAQ) is another tool to help organizations to self-validate PCI DSS compliance but are not required to submit a Report on Compliance (ROC).

*Table 11. PCI DSS's Requirements*

| Goal alignment | PCI DSS Requirements |
|---|---|
| 1 | 1. Install and maintain a firewall configuration to protect cardholder data<br>2. Do not use vendor-supplied defaults for system passwords and other security parameters |
| 2 | 3. Protect stored cardholder data<br>4. Encrypt transmission of cardholder data across open, public networks |
| 3 | 5. Use and regularly update anti-virus software or programs<br>6. Develop and maintain secure systems and applications |
| 4 | 7. Restrict access to cardholder data by business need to know<br>8. Assign a unique ID to each person with computer access<br>9. Restrict physical access to cardholder data |
| 5 | 10. Track and monitor all access to network resources and cardholder data<br>11. Regularly test security systems and processes |
| 6 | 12. Maintain a policy that addresses information security for all personnel |

The audit compliance process is generally defined by the following stages:

1. PCI DSS Scoping: Define the audit scope based on risk levels that are determined by the payment card brand. To be conducted at least annually and prior to the annual assessment
2. Assessing: To evaluate compliance in alignment with the audit scope. To be audited once a year
3. Compensating Controls: Qualified Security Assessor (QSA) validate alternative control technologies and processes
4. Reporting: Qualified Security Assessor (QSA) or entity submits the required documentation on an annual basis
5. Clarifications: Qualified Security Assessor (QSA) or entity provides clarifications/updates upon request from the acquiring bank or payment card brand. As required

## INFORMATION TECHNOLOGY ASSURANCE FRAMEWORK (ITAF)

The Information Technology Assurance Framework (ITAF) provides standards, guidelines and tools for conducting Information Systems audits and assurance assessments. ITAF also provisions guidance, techniques and tools to plan, design, conduct, report related to any Information Systems (IS) audits and assurance engagements. ITAF standards are mandatory, guidelines are optional, tools and techniques are presented as supplementary material that could be discussion documents, technical directions, white papers, audit programmes or books.

Table 12 presents the ITAF architecture:

The ITAF section 3630.7 Information Security Management provides important guidelines for auditing, the same applies for other ITAF sections like:

- 3450: IT processes
- 3630: Auditing IT General Controls

*Table 12. ITAF architecture*

| ITAF: IS Audit and Assurance Standards and Guidelines (Third Edition) | | | |
|---|---|---|---|
| **Standards** | | **Guidelines** | |
| General Standards | 1001-1008 | General Guidelines | 2001-2008 |
| Performance Standards | 1201-1207 | Performance Guidelines | 2201-2208 |
| Reporting Standards | 1401-1402 | Reporting Guidelines | 2401-2402 |

## COMMITTEE OF SPONSORING ORGANIZATIONS (COSO)

The Committee of Sponsoring Organizations of the Treadway Commission (COSO) Enterprise Risk Management (ERM) Integrated Framework is *"A process, effected by an entity's board of directors, management and other personnel, applied in strategy setting and across the enterprise, designed to identify potential events that may affect the entity, and manage risks to be within its risk appetite, to provide reasonable assurance regarding the achievement of entity objectives."*

Table 13 presents the components of COSO ERM Integrated Framework. These components are used to plan and conduct IT and assurance audits.

*Table 13. COSO ERM Integrated Framework*

| ERM Integrated Framework |
|---|
| **Internal Environment**: The internal environment encompasses the tone of an organization, and sets the basis for how risk is viewed and addressed by an entity's people, including risk management philosophy and risk appetite, integrity and ethical values, and the environment in which they operate. |
| **Objective Setting**: Objectives must exist before management can identify potential events affecting their achievement. Enterprise risk management ensures that management has in place a process to set objectives and that the chosen objectives support and align with the entity's mission and are consistent with its risk appetite. |
| **Event Identification**: Internal and external events affecting achievement of an entity's objectives must be identified, distinguishing between risks and opportunities. Opportunities are channeled back to management's strategy or objective-setting processes. |
| **Risk Assessment**: Risks are analyzed, considering the likelihood and impact, as a basis for determining how they could be managed. Risk areas are assessed on an inherent and residual basis. |
| **Risk Response:** Management selects risk responses—avoiding, accepting, reducing or sharing risk—developing a set of actions to align risks with the entity's risk tolerances and risk appetite. |
| **Control Activities:** Policies and procedures are established and implemented to help ensure the risk responses are effectively carried out. |
| **Information and Communication:** Relevant information is identified, captured and communicated in a form and time frame that enable people to carry out their responsibilities. Effective communication also occurs in a broader sense, flowing down, across and up the entity. |
| **Monitoring:** The entirety of enterprise risk management is monitored and modifications are made as necessary. Monitoring is accomplished through ongoing management activities, separate evaluations or both. |

# EUROPEAN UNION AGENCY FOR NETWORK AND INFORMATION SECURITY (ENISA)

According to ENISA (2018), information security audits are independent reviews and examinations of system records, activities and related documentation that are intended to improve the level of information security, by avoiding improper designs and by optimizing the efficiency of security processes and safeguards.

ENISA has published and is enforcing specific guidelines for planning and conducting information security audits followed by Operators providing Essential Services (OES), Digital Service Providers (DSP) and National Competent Authorities (NCA) of European Union (UE) Member States.

The information security audit guidelines include forms of information security audit, scope, process, outcomes, objectives, EU policy context, methodology, target audience, goals, principles, good practices, recommendations, relevant information security self-assessment, management frameworks and alignment to control frameworks.

*Table 14. Security Measures to be reviewed during Information Security audits*

| Parts | Sub-parts | Security Measures |
|---|---|---|
| 1. Governance and Ecosystem | 1.1 Information system security governance & risk management | 1. Information system security risk analysis<br>2. Information system security policy<br>3. Information system security accreditation<br>4. Information system security indicators<br>5. Information system security audit<br>6. Human resource security<br>7. Asset management |
| | 1.2 Ecosystem management | 1. Ecosystem mapping<br>2. Ecosystem relations |
| 2. Protection | 2.1 IT Security architecture | 1. Systems configuration<br>2. System segregation<br>3. Traffic filtering<br>4. Cryptography |
| | 2.2 IT Security administration | 1. Administration accounts<br>2. Administration information systems |
| | 2.3 Identity and Access management | 1. Authentication and identification<br>2. Access rights |
| | 2.4 IT Security maintenance | 1. IT security maintenance procedure<br>2. Industrial control systems |
| | 2.5 Physical and environmental security | 1. Physical and environmental security |
| 3. Defence | 3.1 Detection | 1. Detection<br>2. Logging<br>3. Log correlations and analysis |
| | 3.2 Computer security incident management | 1. Information system security incident response<br>2. Incident response<br>3. Communication with Competent Authorities and CSIRTs |
| 4. Resilience | 4.1 Continuity of operations | 1. Business continuity management<br>2. Disaster recovery management |
| | 4.2 Crisis management | 1. Crisis management organization<br>2. Crisis management process |

The EU information security audit lifecycle for National Competent Authorities (NCA) consists of three phases:

Pre-audit/planning phase, Audit execution/fieldwork phase and Post-execution phase.

Security measures for Operators providing Essential Services (OES) are highlighted in Table 14.

To facilitate the information security audit processes, ENISA provides the audit methodology for Digital Service Providers (DSP) that presents a mapping of the five elements in Table 15.

*Table 15. Digital Service Providers (DSP) audit methodology during Information Security audits*

| Implementing Regulation Elements | Security Measures |
|---|---|
| 1. Security of systems and facilities | – Physical and environmental security<br>– Access control to network and information systems<br>– Integrity of network components and information systems<br>– Change management<br>– Asset management<br>– Security of data at rest |
| 2. Incident handling | – Security incident detection & response<br>– Security incident reporting |
| 3. Business continuity management | – Business continuity<br>– Disaster recovery capabilities<br>– Secure of supporting utilities |
| 4. Monitoring, auditing and testing | – Monitoring and logging<br>– System tests<br>– Security assessments<br>– Interface security<br>– Software security<br>– Customer monitoring and log access |
| 5. Compliance with (Inter)national Standards | – Compliance<br>– Interoperability and portability |

## NORTH AMERICAN ELECTRIC RELIABILITY CORPORATION FOR CRITICAL INFRASTRUCTURE PROTECTION (NERC CIP)

The North American Electric Reliability Corporation (NERC) is a not-for-profit international regulatory authority responsible to assure the effective and efficient reduction of risks to the reliability and security of the grid. NERC develops and enforces Reliability Standards; annually assesses seasonal and long-term reliability. NERC's area of responsibility spans the continental United States, Canada, and the northern portion of Baja California, Mexico.

NERC Reliability Standards define all requirements for planning and operation of the bulk power system in North America. The NERC Standards are based on a results-based approach that includes targeting required actions and results. Each NERC Standard utilizes a defense-in-depth methodology by covering *Performance, Risk and Competency.*

In terms of cybersecurity compliance, NERC Standards for Critical Infrastructure Protection (CIP) define a compliance enforcement authority, evidence retentions guidelines, processes for compliance and monitoring assessment that cover:

- Compliance audit
- Self-certification
- Spot checking
- Compliance investigation
- Self-reporting
- Complaint

Severity of compliance elements is categorized in Violation Severity Levels (VSL) that integrate lower, moderate, high and severe VSLs. The NERC CIP Standards are in Table 16.

*Table 16. NERC Reliability Standards for Critical Infrastructure Protection (CIP)*

| NERC CIP Standards |
| --- |
| 1. CIP-002-5.1a Cyber Security – Bulk Electric System (BES) Cyber System Categorization |
| 2. CIP-003-7 Cyber Security – Security Management Controls |
| 3. CIP-004-6 Cyber Security – Personnel & Training |
| 4. CIP-005-5 Cyber Security – Electronic Security Perimeter(s) |
| 5. CIP-006-6 Cyber Security – Physical Security of BES Cyber Systems |
| 6. CIP-007-6 Cyber Security – System Security Management |
| 7. CIP-008-5 Cyber Security – Incident Reporting and Response Planning |
| 8. CIP-009-6 Cyber Security – Recovery Plans for BES Cyber Systems |
| 9. CIP-010-2 Cyber Security – Configuration Change Management and Vulnerability Assessments |
| 10. CIP-011-2 Cyber Security – Information Protection |
| 11. CIP-014-2 Cyber Security – Physical Security |

## THE CYBERSECURITY AUDIT MODEL (CSAM)

The CyberSecurity Audit Model (CSAM) is a new exhaustive model that encloses the optimal assurance assessment of cybersecurity in any organization and it can verify specific guidelines for Nation States that are planning to implement a National Cybersecurity Strategy (NCS) or want to evaluate the effectiveness of its National Cybersecurity Strategy or Policy already in place. The CSAM can be implemented to conduct internal or external cybersecurity audits, this model can be used to perform single cybersecurity audits or can be part of any corporate audit program to improve cybersecurity controls. Any audit team has either the options to perform a full audit for all cybersecurity domains or by selecting specific domains to audit certain areas that need control verification and hardening. The CSAM has 18 domains; domain 1 is specific for Nation States and domains 2-18 can be implemented at any organization. The organization can be any small, medium or large enterprise, the model is also applicable to any Non-Profit Organization (NPO).

The aim of this model is to introduce a cybersecurity audit model that includes all functional areas, in order to guarantee an effective cybersecurity assurance, maturity and cyber readiness in any organization or any Nation State that is auditing its National Cybersecurity Strategy (NCS). This model was envisioned as a seamless and integrated cybersecurity audit model to assess and measure the level of cybersecurity maturity and cyber readiness in any type of organization, no matter in what industry or sector the organization is positioned. Moreover, by adding guidelines assessment for the integration of a national cybersecurity policy, program or strategy at the country level. Many cybersecurity frameworks are mostly oriented towards a specific industry like the *"PCI DSS"* for credit card security, the *"NERC CIP Cyber Security"* for the bulk power system or the *"NIST Cybersecurity Framework"* for protecting national critical infrastructure. Hence, all the existing frameworks do not provide a one-size fits all for planning and conducting cybersecurity audits. The necessity to mapping against specific cybersecurity frameworks is because of regulatory requirements, to satisfy the demands of industry regulators, to comply with internal or external audits, to satisfy business purposes and customer requirements or simply by improving the enterprise cybersecurity strategy.

The CyberSecurity Audit Model (CSAM) contains overview, resources, 18 domains, 26 sub-domains, 87 checklists, 169 controls, 429 sub-controls, 80 guideline assessment and an evaluation scorecard shown in Figure 1.

*Figure 1. The CyberSecurity Audit Model (CSAM)*

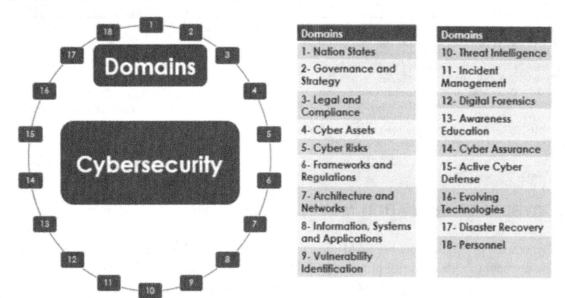

## CONCLUSION

This chapter provides a comprehensive literature review for standards, frameworks, methodologies, guidelines, best practices and models for information security, cybersecurity and information technology auditing and assurance. In this study, we selected the material based on current practices in the areas of compliance, audit engagements, governance, security risk management, assessments, audits and control verifications. Most methodologies do not cover all cybersecurity domains for auditing planning and execution. In many instances, it is required to combine more than one framework to cover many areas in information security and cybersecurity.

Furthermore, the existing information security/ cybersecurity standards, frameworks, methodologies, guidelines, best practices and models will constantly need to be updated, as the cyberthreat landscape keeps evolving and cybercriminals find more sophisticated ways to launch their cyberattacks against companies and individuals.

# REFERENCES

AICPA. (2017). *Trust Services Criteria*. American Institute of Certified Public Accountants, Inc.

AICPA. (2020). *SOC for Cybersecurity*. Retrieved from https://www.aicpa.org/interestareas/frc/assuranceadvisoryservices/aicpacybersecurityinitiative.html

AXELOS. (2016). *ITIL Practitioner Guidance*. The Stationary Office.

AXELOS. (2019). *ITIL Foundation: ITIL* (4th ed.). The Stationary Office.

European Union Agency for Network and Information Security – ENISA. (2018). *Guidelines on assessing DSP and OES compliance to the NISD security requirements: Information Security Audit and Self-Assessment/Management Frameworks*. Retrieved from www.enisa.europa.eu

International Standardization Organization – ISO. (2013). *International Standard ISO/IEC 27002: Information technology – Security techniques – code of practice for information security controls* (2nd ed.). International Standardization Organization – ISO.

International Standardization Organization – ISO. (2013). *International Standard ISO/IEC 27002: Information technology – Security techniques – Information security management systems - Requirements* (2nd ed.). International Standardization Organization – ISO.

ISACA. (2010). *Information Security Management Audit/Assurance Program*. Retrieved from www.isaca.org

ISACA. (2014). *ITAF 3rd Edition: A Professional Practices Framework for IS Audit/Assurance*. Retrieved from www.isaca.org

ISACA. (2017). *Auditing Cyber Security: Evaluating Risk and Auditing Controls*. Retrieved from www.isaca.org

ISACA. (2018). *COBIT 2019 Design Guide: Designing an Information and Technology Governance Solution*. Retrieved from www.isaca.org

ISACA. (2018). *COBIT 2019 Framework: Governance and Management Objectives*. Retrieved from www.isaca.org

ISACA. (2018). *COBIT 2019 Framework: Introduction and Methodology*. Retrieved from www.isaca.org

ISACA. (2018). *COBIT 2019 Implementation Guide: Implementing and Optimizing an Information and Technology Governance Solution*. Retrieved from www.isaca.org

Lachapelle, E., & Bislimi, M. (2016). *Whitepaper: International Standard ISO/IEC 27002: Information technology – Security techniques – code of practice for information security controls, PECB/ Parabellum Cyber Security*. Retrieved from www.pecb.com

National Institute of Standards and Technology - NIST. (2017). *NIST Special Publication 800-53 Revision 5*. U.S. Department of Commerce. Retrieved from https://csrc.nist.gov/publications/detail/sp/800-53/rev-5/draft

National Institute of Standards and Technology - NIST. (2018). *Framework for Improving Critical Infrastructure Cybersecurity Version 1.1.* U.S. Department of Commerce. doi:10.6028/NIST.CSWP.04162018

North American Electric Reliability Corporation. (2020). *NERC CIP Reliability Standards*. Retrieved from https://www.nerc.com/pa/Stand/Pages/CIPStandards.aspx

Office of Government Commerce. (2007). *ITIL Continual Service Improvement*. The Stationary Office.

Office of Government Commerce. (2007). *ITIL Service Design*. The Stationary Office.

Payment Card Industry Security Standards Council. (2010). *PCI DSS Quick Reference Guide: Understanding the Payment Card Industry Data Security Standard version 2.0*. Retrieved from www.pcisecuritystandards.org

Payment Card Industry Security Standards Council. (2018). *Payment Card Industry (PCI) Data Security Standard: Requirements and Security Assessment Procedures Version 3.2.1*. Retrieved from www.pcisecuritystandards.org

Sabillon, R., Serra-Ruiz, J., Cavaller, V., & Cano, J. (2017). A Comprehensive Cybersecurity Audit Model to Improve Cybersecurity Assurance: The CyberSecurity Audit Model (CSAM). *Proceedings of Second International Conference on Information Systems and Computer Science (INCISCOS)*. 10.1109/INCISCOS.2017.20

The Institute of Internal Auditors - IIA (2016). *Assessing Cybersecurity Risk: Roles of the Three Lines of Defense. Supplemental Guidance - Global Technology Audit Guide (GTAG)*. IIA.

## ADDITIONAL READING

Choi, Y. (2018). *Selected Readings in Cybersecurity*. Cambridge Scholars Publishing.

## KEY TERMS AND DEFINITIONS

**Cybersecurity Audit:** Methodology to verify cybersecurity controls effectiveness and weaknesses.

**Cybersecurity Framework:** Particular set of rules to plan, implement, validate and audit cybersecurity controls in different organizational areas.

*Previously published in Cyber Security Auditing, Assurance, and Awareness Through CSAM and CATRAM; pages 126-148, copyright year 2021 by Information Science Reference (an imprint of IGI Global).*

# Chapter 2
# Auditor Evaluation and Reporting on Cybersecurity Risks

**Jeffrey S. Zanzig**
*Jacksonville State University, USA*

**Guillermo A. Francia III**
 https://orcid.org/0000-0001-8088-2653
*University of West Florida, USA*

## ABSTRACT

*Tremendous improvements in information networking capabilities have brought with them increased security risks resulting from the deterioration of the ability of a physical layer of computer security to protect an organization's information system. As a result, audit committees have had to deal with new security issues as well as the need to understand the cyber perpetrator and ensure the proper training of employees to consider cybersecurity risks. Standard setters including the Institute of Internal Auditors and the American Institute of Certified Public Accountants have issued guidance about lines of defense and reporting on an entity's cybersecurity risk management program and controls, respectively. Each of these topics is considered along with how cybersecurity guidance from COBIT, the National Institute of Standards and Technology, and the Center for Internet Security can be mapped into five cyber infrastructure domains to provide an approach to evaluate a system of cybersecurity.*

## INTRODUCTION

Just a few decades ago information systems consisted primarily of mainframe computers with what were commonly referred to as "dumb terminals" that granted access into a mainframe computer which performed an organization's information processing. The risk of intruders accessing such systems was significantly less and physical security measures such as locked doors and security guards served as an effective approach in protecting information systems from outsiders. Substantial information processing

DOI: 10.4018/978-1-6684-3698-1.ch002

capabilities were then added with the widespread use of the Internet, company networks, and the distribution of computing power to the end user. Unfortunately, it also resulted in an immense increase in the danger of outsiders hacking into company information systems gaining access to sensitive information and causing various types of malicious behavior.

A recent cybersecurity attack at the Marriott hotel chain illustrates what can happen when cybersecurity incidents occur and are not thoroughly resolved. In 2015, Marriott Hotels acquired another hotel, known as Starwood Hotels and Resorts Worldwide, as part of a $13.6 billion deal which made Marriott the No. 1 hotel chain in the world. Four days after the announcement of this 2015 merger, Starwood stated that credit card information had been stolen in some of its hotel restaurants and gift shops as a result of malware that attackers installed on point-of-sale systems in 2014. In December 2018, The Wall Street Journal reported the theft of personal information for up to 500 million customers as a result of a hack of Marriott's customer database for its Starwood properties. Although Marriott claimed that the 2018 discovery was unrelated to the prior incident, security experts believe that a more thorough investigation of the initial intrusion would have identified a second intruder who was able to stay in the Marriott reservation system for the more than three years following the initial security breach (McMillan, 2018).

The objectives of this research are to provide an overview of some of the considerations that are involved in an assessment of an organization's system of cybersecurity including: lines of defense, audits and reporting, and standards and frameworks for evaluation. This article begins by considering challenges facing today's audit committees, the need to understand the common profile of the cyber perpetrator, and the necessity of employee training to overcome complacency in dealing with cybersecurity risks. This is followed by guidance from both the Institute of Internal Auditors (IIA) and the American Institute of Certified Public Accountants (AICPA). A thought-provoking discussion based on IIA literature considers what the IIA refers to as "three lines of defense" to address risks in today's cyber environment. Guidance from the AICPA describes reporting on an entity's cybersecurity risk management program and controls. In the audit of security systems to address cybersecurity risks, it is also essential to make use of standards and frameworks to facilitate a proper evaluation. This is also addressed by considering how guidance from COBIT, the National Institute of Standards and Technology, and the Center for Internet Security can be mapped into five cyber infrastructure domains.

## BACKGROUND

A primary focus of an audit committee is to provide an independent oversight function to ensure that the processing and storage of information is performed in a secure and reliable manner to meet the needs of information users. Although the birth of the Internet and extensive networking capabilities has substantially increased the ability of organizations to process and disseminate information, it has also opened the door to allow greater access to information systems by unauthorized and many times malicious intruders. It is certainly a difficult task to address these security issues due to the constantly changing availability of technology that is both within and outside of an organization's control. This section discusses challenges faced by audit committees as a result of cybersecurity issues. It also considers common profiles of the cyber perpetrator and how noncompliance with information security policy by well-meaning organizational personnel can allow unauthorized access into an organization's information system.

## Challenges Facing Today's Audit Committee

Lanz (2014) points out that today's audit committee faces challenges in their governance of cybersecurity, including:

- Organizations must reconcile between the availability of products and services to enable business in cyberspace and protecting information in accordance with business and regulatory requirements.
- The periodic briefings that information security professionals provide to audit committee members may not be relevant enough for them to properly perform governance duties.
- Lack of cybersecurity training for organization personnel can serve as a weak link despite large investments in information security technology.
- Organization's that rely on third parties to provide information processing services should ensure that a vendor management program exists to provide evidence that the vendor follows due diligence to protect sensitive information.

## Common Profiles of the Cyber Perpetrator

Galligan and Rau (2015) stress the importance of having a risk assessment process that considers the cyber risk profile(s) most likely to pose a threat to an organization. They point out that certain industries may be more susceptible to a specific type of cyberattack. They describe the following broad categories of perpetrators:

- **Nation-states and Spies**: Involve hostile foreign nations looking to obtain trade secrets and intellectual property to achieve competitive and military advantages.
- **Organized Criminals**: Involve persons seeking to steal money and private information such as through identify theft of an organization's customers.
- **Terrorists**: Involve persons who want to launch cyberattacks against important infrastructure such as banks.
- **Hacktivists**: Involve persons who desire to make a political or social statement through the theft or publication of sensitive organization information.
- **Insiders**: Involve persons who are trusted members of an organization that want to sell or share sensitive information.

## Organizational Noncompliance

Although the ability of an organization to deal with the malicious behavior of persons is certainly an issue that must be considered, another significant threat arises from insiders who intend no harm to the information system but simply fail to understand and follow appropriate security policies. Stafford, Deitz, and Li (2018) posed the research question: "How can auditors identify and contribute to the correction of non-malicious insider threats to cybersecurity in the firm?" Through two specific case studies and depth interviews with trained auditors, these researchers defined and considered the following types of non-malicious insider threats:

- **CyberComplacency:** Computer users who are less concerned about cybersecurity diligence than their company would like because they believe they are working with invulnerable platforms.
- **Cybersecurity Loafing**: technically competent employees who take unauthorized steps to bypass specific security policies in order to achieve greater workgroup efficiency.

The results of the research concluded that applying sanctions against employees for these non-malicious threats is less effective than having information system auditors consult with system users to better educate them regarding system vulnerabilities and the importance of following established information security policy.

## FOCUS OF THE ARTICLE

Auditing standard setters from the Institute of Internal Auditors and the American Institute of Certified Public Accountants have issued guidance about lines of defense and reporting on an entity's cybersecurity risk management program and controls, respectively. Standards and frameworks from COBIT, the National Institute of Standards and Technology, and the Center for Internet Security can be used in the evaluation of a system of cybersecurity.

### Internal Audit and Cybersecurity

The Institute of Internal Auditors (IIA) (2016) defines cybersecurity as "the technologies, processes, and practices designed to protect an organization's information assets – computers, networks, programs, and data – from unauthorized access." They also point out that the risks of cybersecurity extend well beyond the general and application controls that internal audit has traditionally assessed in regard to information technology. This increased risk is largely attributable to global connectivity that allows persons outside of the organization to access information. To address this additional risk, the IIA suggests that organizations have in place three lines of defense.

### The First Line of Defense

The IIA (2013) states that "operational management naturally serves as the first line of defense because controls are designed into systems and processes under the guidance of operating management." The key aspect of the first line of defense is to ensure that appropriate positions of responsibility are established and staffed with qualified talent to address current and emerging cybersecurity issues. The IIA (2016) includes the following examples of key operating management positions that can be established:

- **Chief Technology Officer (CTO)**: Responsible for supplying knowledge and direction regarding the availability of technologies to guide the organization's mission. The CTO is often responsible for protecting the intellectual property of the organization.
- **Chief Information Security Officer (CISO)**: Serves as a foundation in the identification and understanding of cyber threats. The CISO often takes a lead role in the development of oversight programs to ensure the protection of organization assets and stakeholder data.

- **Chief Information Officer (CIO)**: Acts to drive an organization's competitive advantage and strategic change. The CIO is often responsible for developing an information cybersecurity program and implementing entity-wide cybersecurity training.

In situations where it may be impractical to establish the above positions, the assignment of the various cybersecurity responsibilities can be approached through "a council of business and information technology (IT) managers who have a stake in responding to cybersecurity risk." The IIA (2016) also identifies some specific examples of activities in the first line of defense including:

- Administration of security procedures, testing, and training.
- Putting in place intrusion detection systems and handling penetration testing.
- Maintenance of an inventory of technology devices, information assets, and associated software.
- Recruiting and retaining appropriately certified IT talent.

## The Second Line of Defense

The IIA (2013) explains the second line of defense as being what management does to set up "various risk management and compliance functions to help build and/or monitor the first line of defense controls." The IIA (2016) mentions the following three points in describing the responsibilities of the second line of defense:

- An assessment of cybersecurity risks and exposures to evaluate whether they are in line with the risk appetite of the organization.
- Monitoring the organization for changes in legal requirements and risks.
- Working with the functions established in the first line of defense to make certain that suitable controls are designed.

The second line of defense therefore involves the specific activities that operating management implements to ensure cybersecurity risk control and compliance (IIA 2013).

## The Third Line of Defense

The IIA (2013) defines the third line of defense as having an organization's "internal auditors provide the governing body and senior management with comprehensive assurance based on the highest level of independence and objectivity within the organization. This high level of independence is not available within the second line of defense." The IIA (2016) uses the following points to illustrate some of the activities of the third line of defense:

- Provide regular independent evaluations of preventive and detective measures regarding cybersecurity issues.
- Track the diligence with which remediation takes place to address identified cybersecurity concerns.
- Work with the second lines of defense to perform cybersecurity risk assessments of various third parties including service organizations and suppliers.

## The Cybersecurity Risk Management Examination

In May 2017, the American Institute of Certified Public Accountants (AICPA) issued an attestation guide entitled "Reporting on an Entity's Cybersecurity Risk Management Program and Controls" ("Cybersecurity Guide"). In contrast to a CPA's evaluation of internal accounting controls that is integrated with an audit of a public company's financial statements, which focuses exclusively on objectives of external financial reporting, a more detailed examination is required for a CPA to attest to whether an entity's cybersecurity risk management program achieves an organization's overall business objectives.

## The Standard Examination Report

The cybersecurity risk management report can cover a specific point in time or be for a period of time. Three major components of the report include:

1. Management's description of the entity's cybersecurity risk management program consists of a narrative that describes how an organization identifies its information assets, defines management's approach to dealing with the cybersecurity risks faced by those assets, and describes the primary security policies and processes that have been put into operation to protect its information assets.
2. Management's assertion addressing whether (i) "the description is presented in accordance with the description criteria and," (ii) "the controls within the entity's cybersecurity risk management program were effective to achieve the entity's cybersecurity objectives based on the control criteria." (See section on "Assessing Cybersecurity Objectives").
3. Practitioner's report stating separate opinions on whether the components of management's assertion described above have been met. (See section on "Forming the Opinion").

   It should be recognized that due to the high likelihood of security events or breaches, a cybersecurity risk management program is considered effective if the program can detect security events in a timely manner and recover from them with a minimum amount of disruption to company operations.

## Assessing Cybersecurity Objectives

One of the first issues in dealing with an evaluation of an organization's Cybersecurity Risk Management Program involves an evaluation of whether management's description of the program includes appropriate cybersecurity objectives that address specific cybersecurity risks that the organization faces. The Committee of Sponsoring Organizations of the Treadway Commission (COSO) framework points out criteria that can be used to evaluate whether cybersecurity objectives are appropriate, including that they:

- **Specifically explain** cybersecurity risks that need to be lessened;
- **Are measurable or observable** so that it can be determined whether the objective has been met;
- **Are attainable** in that controls can be implemented that if suitably designed and complied with can achieve each objective;
- **Are relevant** in that they support the organization's overall objectives including the availability of system processing, confidentiality of information, and the integrity of both system data and processing;

- **Are time bound** to represent the desired functioning of cybersecurity controls over time.

If a practitioner were to conclude that management's cybersecurity objectives were either incomplete or not suitable, the issues should be brought to management's attention so that they can be addressed. A lack of willingness on the part of management to make appropriate revisions could result in either the practitioner's refusal to accept the engagement or restricting the use of the report to those who understand the risks not addressed.

## Forming the Opinion

The opinion that the practitioner expresses in a cybersecurity risk management examination covers two different but related subject matters:

1. Description of the entity's cybersecurity risk management program, and
2. The effectiveness of controls within the program to achieve the entity's cybersecurity objectives.

An unmodified report is a report in which the auditor feels that the above subject matters have been appropriately addressed. Table 1 taken from the Cybersecurity Guide presents some other opinion possibilities.

*Table 1. Other opinion possibilities*

| Nature of Matter Giving Rise to the Modification | Practitioner's Professional Judgment About the Pervasiveness of the Effect or Possible Effects on the Description or on the Effectiveness of Controls | |
| --- | --- | --- |
| | **Material but Not Pervasive** | **Material and Pervasive** |
| **Scope limitation**<br>· **The practitioner is unable to obtain sufficient appropriate evidence.** | Qualified opinion | Disclaimer of opinion |
| **Material misstatements**<br>· **Subject Matter 1:**<br>**The description is materially misstated.**<br>**Or**<br>· **Subject Matter 2:**<br>**The controls were not effective to achieve the entity's cybersecurity objectives.** | Qualified opinion | Adverse opinion |
| It is possible for different opinions to be issued regarding the two subject matters. | | |

## The Design-Only Examination

In situations where an organization has either a very young or significantly changed cybersecurity risk management program, it may be appropriate to temporarily bypass forming an assertion about the effectiveness of controls to accomplish cybersecurity objectives until the program has had more time to actually function. In such situations, the Cybersecurity Guide points out that the design-only report would just address:

1. "The description of the entity's cybersecurity risk management program and
2. The suitability of the design of the controls implemented within that program to achieve the entity's cybersecurity objectives."

Practitioners should consider restricting the use of a design-only report to the client's board members, organizational personnel, and specific third parties likely to understand it.

## Examining a Portion of the Cybersecurity Program

Although the Cybersecurity Guide addresses an entity-wide evaluation, it also points out that management may elect to have only a portion of the program evaluated. The determination of the acceptability of this limited evaluation depends on whether the subject matters of the engagement are expected to appropriately address the needs of the intended users. For example, such a situation could exist if an organization intends to sell off a portion of their operations and intends to examine only the independent program issues of that segment to address the needs of the prospective buyers. In any case involving a partial examination, a practitioner should evaluate whether it is appropriate to restrict report usage to a limited group of users.

## Standards and Frameworks for Auditing Cybersecurity

Standards provide a set of rules that can be monitored for compliance by a specialized field's authoritative bodies and related professionals. The grouping of rules and related concepts into appropriate frameworks furnishes the basic building blocks to identify and decide upon appropriate courses of action to address complex problems. Although the enumeration of an exhaustive set of standards and frameworks appropriate for a cybersecurity audit is beyond the scope of this article, this section presents standards and frameworks selected from four prominent and published works including contributions from the ISACA (formerly known as Information Systems Audit and Control Association), the National Institute of Standards and Technology (NIST), and the Center for Internet Security (CIS). These published works cover, in an overlapping manner, the Risk Management Framework (RMF) as set out by the NIST.

## COBIT® 2019

*COBIT® 2019* is a framework for the governance and management of enterprise information and technology whose purpose is to facilitate the achievement of the enterprises' goals (ISACA, 2019). It provides control objectives with which the effectiveness of Information Technology (IT) controls can be evaluated. While the governance objectives of COBIT ® 2019, are grouped into the three domains: Evaluate, Direct and Monitor; the management objectives are group into the following four domains (ISACA, 2019):

1. **Align, Plan, and Organize (APO)**: Addresses the overall organization, strategy and supporting activities for Information and Technology (I&T).
2. **Build, Acquire and Implement (BAI):** Deals with the definition, acquisition, and implementation of I&T solutions for the enterprise.
3. **Deliver, Service and Support (DSS):** Is concerned with the delivery of secure operations and support of I&T services.

4. **Monitor, Evaluate and Assess (MEA):** Addresses the performance monitoring and conformance of I&T with performance targets, internal control objectives and external requirements.

## NIST SP 800-37

The *National Institute of Standards and Technology (NIST) Special Publication (SP) 800-37, Revision 2* (also known as *Risk Management Framework for Information Systems and Organizations A System Life Cycle Approach for Security and Privacy*) (NIST, 2018) describes the Risk Management Framework (RMF) and provides guidelines for applying the framework to information systems within an organization with the intent of helping the organization manage its security and privacy risks. The RMF promotes real-time risk management and common control authorization through a continuous security monitoring process. The seven steps of RMF are as follows:

1. **Prepare:** Requires the establishment of context and priorities in preparation for the management of security and privacy risks.
2. **Categorize:** The systems and information are properly triaged based on the analysis of the impact of loss.
3. **Select:** In order to properly mitigate the identified risks, initial sets of controls are selected.
4. **Implement:** The controls are implemented and described.
5. **Assess:** The implemented controls are assessed and evaluated.
6. **Authorize:-** The system and the common acceptable controls are authorized.
7. **Monitor:** The system and controls are continuously monitored, documented, evaluated, and improved.

## NIST SP 800-53

*National Institute of Standards and Technology (NIST) Special Publication (SP) 800-53 Revision 4* (also known as *Security and Privacy Controls for Federal Information Systems and Organizations*) *(NIST, 2015)* describes a set of standards and guidelines to help federal agencies and partners meet the requirements set by the Federal Information Security Management Act (FISMA), which was signed into law as part of the Electronic Government Act of 2002. The law applies to any component of an information system that stores, processes, or transmits information. The security controls specified in this set are divided into 18 families of controls that are categorized according to severity as being: Low-impact, Moderate-impact and High-impact.

## Center for Internet Security Controls

*Center for Internet Security (CIS)* Controls (CIS, 2019) are best practice guidelines for computer security that were initially developed and introduced by the SANS Institute in 2008 and later transferred to the Center for Internet Security (CIS) in 2015. The 20 CIS Controls, also known as CIS Critical Security Controls, are delineated into three groups: Basic, Foundational and Organizational. These controls are developed by leading security experts and, if correctly implemented, could reduce security risks and operational costs and thereby, significantly improve an organization's defensive posture. The 20 CIS Controls (CIS, 2019), grouped into Basic (**B**), Foundational (**F**), and Organizational (**O**), are as follows:

1.  **(B)** Inventory and Control of Hardware Assets
2.  **(B)** Inventory and Control of Software Assets
3.  **(B)** Continuous Vulnerability Management
4.  **(B)** Controlled Use of Administrative Privileges
5.  **(B)** Secure Configuration for Hardware and Software on Mobile Devices, Laptops, Workstations and Servers
6.  **(B)** Maintenance, Monitoring and Analysis of Audit Logs
7.  **(F)** Email and Web Browser Protections
8.  **(F)** Malware Defenses
9.  **(F)** Limitation and Control of Network Ports, Protocols and Services
10. **(F)** Data Recovery Capabilities
11. **(F)** Secure Configuration for Network Devices (Firewalls, Routers and Switches)
12. **(F)** Boundary Defense
13. **(F)** Data Protection
14. **(F)** Controlled Access Based on the Need to Know
15. **(F)** Wireless Access Control
16. **(F)** Account Monitoring and Control
17. **(O)** Implement a Security Awareness and Training Program
18. **(O)** Application Software Security
19. **(O)** Incident Response and Management
20. **(O)** Penetration Tests and Red Team Exercises

## SOLUTIONS AND RECOMMENDATIONS

The previously presented cybersecurity guidance from COBIT, the National Institute of Standards and Technology, and the Center for Internet Security can be mapped into five cyber infrastructure domains to provide an approach to evaluate a system of cybersecurity.

### Cyber Infrastructure Requirements and Controls

The cyber infrastructure is the backbone of the information technology (IT) enterprise. In this research, the authors' based their study on five cyber infrastructure domains--a departure from the more granular seven domains found in a typical IT infrastructure. Figure 1 presents the five cyber infrastructure domains showing that all domains fall within the realm of the Physical Domain.

For each domain, the authors' examined it, specified its predominant requirements, identified the controls to satisfy the requirements, and mapped those controls to the standards and frameworks that are described in the previous section of this article. The remainder of this section illustrates the application of the standards and frameworks to the requirements and controls that are found in each of the cyber infrastructure domains.

*Figure 1. The five cyber infrastructure domains*

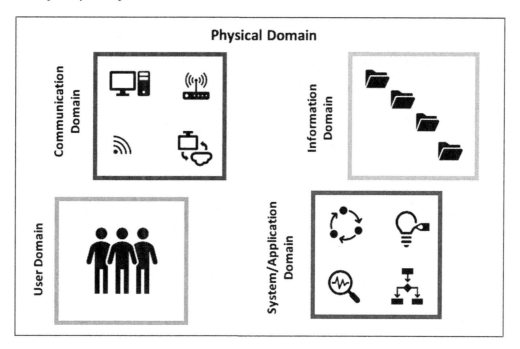

## Physical Domain

The *Physical Domain* includes the equipment, devices, mechanisms, policies, and controls that are used to physically secure the cyber assets. Examples of these are locks, gates, fences, alarm systems, computing devices and storage, and badges, among others. The four critical security requirements of the physical domain are as follows:

1. **Security of Physical Access to Assets:** Requires the protection of physical assets through the implementation and monitoring of secure access mechanisms.
2. **Training of Physical Security Personnel:** Involves the periodic training of personnel on both physical and cybersecurity.
3. **Facility Management**: Entails the implementation and enforcement of safety and health policies, the maintenance of facilities to enable smooth operations, the creation of contingency plans including power and data backups, and the record keeping of physical incidents and assets.
4. **Asset Management**: Includes the safeguarding and handling of information assets. It also involves the proper transfer, backup, and destruction of information storage systems and devices.

The mapping of the requirements and controls with the frameworks and standards for the physical domain is depicted in Table 2.

*Table 2. The Physical Domain Requirements and Controls*

| Requirements | Controls | Frameworks and Standards |
|---|---|---|
| Secure physical access to assets | · Physical asset and activity monitoring<br>· Event Logs<br>· Physical access mechanism | COBIT 2019: *DSS 01.03*<br>CIS: *1, 12, 14*<br>NIST 800-37 Rev 2: *Task P-10*<br>NIST 800-53 Rev 4: *AC-3, PE-6,*<br>   *PS-1* |
| Physical security personnel adequately trained | · Periodic cybersecurity awareness training | COBIT 2019: *APO 07.03*<br>CIS: *17*<br>NIST 800-37 Rev 2: *Task P-17*<br>NIST 800-53 Rev 4: *AT-2, AT-3,*<br>   *AT-4* |
| Facility management | · Regular monitoring and testing of uninterruptible power supplies<br>· Records of facility incidents<br>· Maintained compliance with safety and health regulations | COBIT 2019: *DSS 01.05*<br>CIS: *9, 17*<br>NIST 800-37 Rev 2: *Task P-15*<br>NIST 800-53 Rev 4: *AC-3, PE-2,*<br>   *PE-3, PE-6* |
| Asset management | · Formal process of disposition, transfer, and removal of IT assets | COBIT 2019: *BAI 09.03*<br>CIS: *1*<br>NIST 800-37 Rev 2: *Task M-7*<br>NIST 800-53 Rev 4: *MP-2, MP-3,*<br>   *MP-4, MP-5, MP-6, PE-20* |

## User Domain

The *User Domain* includes the various users that maintain and interact with the cyber assets. It also includes the access and authorization mechanisms whose purpose is to protect the cyber system from unauthorized access. The four critical security requirements of the user domain are as follows:

1. **Identification and Management of Users:** Entails the documentation and delineation of user responsibilities.
2. **User Training:** It is imperative that all users undergo periodic security awareness security training.
3. **Identity Management, Authentication and Access Control:** The management of user credentials and the provision for user access, authentication and authorization mechanisms.
4. **Continuous Security Monitoring:** Entails the continuous and persistent monitoring of user activities.

The mapping of the requirements and controls with the frameworks and standards for the user domain is depicted in Table 3.

## Communication Domain

The *Communication Domain* includes the network systems and peripherals that facilitate the transfer of information from one cyber endpoint to another. It also includes the various communication media, such as fiber optics, copper cables, and radio waves. In addition, this domain considers mechanisms that facilitate secure data transmissions. The five critical security requirements of the communication domain are as follows:

*Table 3. The user domain requirements and controls*

| Requirements | Controls | Frameworks and Standards |
|---|---|---|
| Identify and manage users | · Documented cybersecurity roles and responsibilities | COBIT 2019: *APO 01.02, 07.06, DSS 06.03*<br>CIS: *17, 19*<br>NIST 800-37 Rev 2: *Task S-4*<br>NIST 800-53 Rev 4: *AC-1, AC-2, AC-5, AC-6* |
| Train users on cybersecurity awareness | · Periodic cybersecurity personnel awareness training | COBIT 2019: *APO 07.03, BAI 05.07*<br>CIS: *17*<br>NIST 800-37 Rev 2: *Task P-17*<br>NIST 800-53 Rev 4: *AT-2, AT-3, AT-4* |
| Identity management, authentication and access control | · Managed identities and credentials for users<br>· Managed access and authorizations for users<br>· Authentication of users | COBIT 2019: *DSS 05.04, 05.10, 06.03*<br>CIS: *1, 5, 12, 14, 15, 16*<br>NIST 800-37 Rev 2: *Task M-1*<br>NIST 800-53 Rev 4: *AC-1, AC-3, CM-5, CM-10, IA-5* |
| Continuous monitoring of user activities | · Monitored personnel cyber activity for potential cyber incidents | COBIT 2019: *DSS 05.07*<br>CIS: *5, 7, 14, 16, 17*<br>NIST 800-37 Rev 2: *Task M-2*<br>NIST 800-53 Rev 4: *AC-6, AC-7, AC-8* |

1.  **Management of Communication Assets**: Communication assets must be managed and secured. Controls for this requirement include the mapping and tracking of communication flow and a periodic vulnerability assessment of communication assets.
2.  **Manage Device Authentication and Access Control**: Entails the provision for device authentication and access control for the protection of system and data integrity and confidentiality.
3.  **Network Defense**: Includes securing the network and all its peripherals.
4.  **Continuous Monitoring of Network Behavior**: Similar to the constant monitoring of user behavior, network traffic must also be monitored for abnormal behavior.
5.  **Incident Response and Recovery:** Entails the creation and maintenance of the organization's incident response and recovery plans.

The mapping of the requirements and controls with the frameworks and standards for the communication domain is depicted in Table 4.

## Information Domain

The *Information Domain* includes the data that is either transmitted, processed, or stored. Depending on its purpose, it may be presented on various forms: plain, compressed, encrypted, digital, or analog. The four critical security requirements of the information domain are as follows:

1.  **Data Protection**: Entails the provision to protect the confidentiality and integrity of information that are critical to the organization.

*Table 4. The communication domain requirements and controls*

| Requirements | Controls | Frameworks and Standards |
|---|---|---|
| Manage communication assets | · Mapped organizational communication and data flows<br>· Vulnerability assessment | COBIT 2019: *DSS 05.02*<br>CIS: *12, 16*<br>NIST 800-37 Rev 2: *Task A-3*<br>COBIT 2019: *APO 12.01, 12.02, 12.03*<br>CIS: *3*<br>NIST 800-53 Rev 4: *CA-2, RA-5* |
| Manage device authentication and access control | · Managed remote access<br>· Protected network integrity<br>· Authenticated network devices | COBIT 2019: *APO 13.01, DSS 01.04*<br>COBIT 2019: *DSS 01.05, 05.02*<br>CIS: *9, 14, 15, 18*<br>NIST 800-37 Rev 2: *Task P-11*<br>COBIT 2019: *DSS 05.04, 05.10, 06.10*<br>CIS: *16*<br>NIST 800-53 Rev 4: *AC-17, AC-18, IA-3, SC-40, SC-41* |
| Network Defense | · Protected communication and control networks | COBIT 2019: *DSS 05.02, APO 13.01*<br>CIS: *8, 9, 12, 14, 15*<br>NIST 800-37 Rev 2: *Task R-2*<br>NIST 800-53 Rev 4: *PE-9, SC-8, SC-10, SC-41* |
| Continuous monitoring of network behavior | · Monitored network for potential cyber incidents<br>· Periodic network vulnerability scan | COBIT 2019: *DSS 01.03, 03.05, 05.07*<br>CIS: *1, 7, 8, 9, 12, 14, 15,16*<br>COBIT 2019: *BAI 03.01, DSS 05.01*<br>CIS: *3, 20*<br>NIST 800-37 Rev 2: *Task S-5*<br>NIST 800-53 Rev 4: *CA-7, SI-4* |
| Incident response and recovery | · Incident response plan<br>· Recovery plan | COBIT 2019: *APO 12.06, BAI 01.10 DSS 01.03, 02.02, 03.04*<br>CIS: *19*<br>NIST 800-37 Rev 2: *Task A-5*<br>COBIT 2019: *APO 12.06, DSS 02.05, 03.04*<br>CIS: *10* |

2. **Data Availability**: The availability of information is an important factor in day-to-day operations of an enterprise and thereby, should always be enabled.
3. **Data Backup**: Demands that provisions must be in place for data to be stored, monitored, reviewed, and restored whenever necessary.
4. **Manage Data Assets**: The management of data assets must include the policy to store, dispose, share, transmit and destroy information as needed.

The mapping of the requirements and controls with the frameworks and standards for the information domain is depicted in Table 5.

*Table 5. The information domain requirements and controls*

| Requirements | Controls | Frameworks and Standards |
|---|---|---|
| Data protection | · Stored data protection mechanisms<br>· Transmitted data protection mechanism<br>· Data leak prevention mechanism | COBIT 2019: *APO 01.06, BAI 02.01, 06.01*<br>CIS: *13*<br>COBIT 2019: *APO 01.06, DSS 05.02 06.06*<br>CIS: *5, 13, 14, 15*<br>COBIT 2019: *APO 01.06, BAI 04.04*<br>CIS: *1, 2, 13, 16*<br>NIST 800-37 Rev 2: *Task P-10*<br>NIST 800-53 Rev 4: *AC-21, MP-2, MP-4, MP-6, MP-7, SC-8* |
| Data availability | · Mechanism to ensure data availability | COBIT 2019: *APO 13.01, BAI 04.04*<br>CIS: *1, 2, 13*<br>NIST 800-37 Rev 2: *Task P-11*<br>NIST 800-53 Rev 4: *SC-5, SC-6* |
| Data backup | · Process for maintaining and testing data backup | COBIT 2019: *APO 13.01, DSS 01.01, 04.07*<br>CIS: *10*<br>NIST 800-37 Rev 2: *Task P-13*<br>NIST 800-53 Rev 4: *CP-6, CP-9, MP-4* |
| Manage data assets | · Managed data repository, asset removal, transfer and disposition | COBIT 2019: *BAI 09.03*<br>CIS: *13, 14, 16*<br>NIST 800-37 Rev 2: *Task P-12*<br>NIST 800-53 Rev 4: *PE-19, SC-8* |

## System and Application Domain

The *System and Application Domain* includes the software, categorized as either system or application. The system software manages the operations of the cyber devices and provides the platform for the application software to operate. Examples of system software are the various operating systems such as Mac OS, Windows, Linux, and Solaris. The application software performs specific tasks for the users. Examples of application software are database management systems, web browsers, image processing software, and other productivity software. The four critical security requirements of the system and application domain are as follows:

1. **Software Asset Management**: Entails the provision for the inventory, prioritization, proper utilization, legitimate acquisition, transfer, and disposal of software assets.
2. **Software Risk Assessment**: Requires the periodic vulnerability assessment and threat evaluation of software assets.
3. **Software and System Security**: Entails establishing security baseline and integrity checking of software assets.
4. **Protection Processes and Procedures**: Entails the provision for processes and procedures for software change/patch management, secure software and system development and maintenance of software/system audit log.

The mapping of the requirements and controls with the frameworks and standards for the system and application domain is depicted in Table 6.

*Table 6. The system and application domain requirements and controls*

| Requirements | Controls | Frameworks and Standards |
|---|---|---|
| Software asset management | · Inventory of system and application software<br>· Formal process of disposition, transfer, and removal of software assets<br>· Process to prioritize software asset based on criticality and value to business | COBIT 2019: *BAI 09.01, 09.02, 09.05*<br>CIS: *2*<br>NIST 800-37 Rev 2: *Task P-10*<br>COBIT 2019: *BAI 09.01, 09.02*<br>CIS: *2, 13*<br>COBIT 2019: *APO 03.03, 03.04 12.01*<br>CIS: *4, 13, 14*<br>NIST 800-53 Rev 4: *AC-1, AC-3, CM-11, MA-1* |
| Software risk assessment | · Software and system assessment for vulnerabilities<br>· Identification and documentation of software and system threats | COBIT 2019: *APO 12.01, 12.02, 12.03*<br>CIS: *3*<br>NIST 800-37 Rev 2: *Task R-2*<br>COBIT 2019: *APO 12.01, 12.02, 12.03*<br>CIS: *3, 4, 18*<br>NIST 800-53 Rev 4: *CA-8, PL-2, SI-4* |
| Software and system security | · Software and system integrity checking mechanism<br>· Established and documented system and software baseline configuration | COBIT 2019: *APO 01.06, BAI 06.01, DSS 06.02*<br>CIS: *2, 3*<br>COBIT 2019: *BAI 10.01, 10.02, 10.03*<br>CIS: *3, 9, 11, 12, 14, 16*<br>NIST 800-37 Rev 2: *Task P-4*<br>NIST 800-53 Rev 4: *AC-20, CM-10, SI-7* |
| Protection processes and procedures | · Implementation of a secure system and software development life cycle<br>· Process for configuration change control<br>· Maintained and documented software and system audit/log records | COBIT 2019: *APO 13.01, BAI 03.01, 03.02, 03.03*<br>CIS: *18*<br>COBIT 2019: *BAI 01.06, 06.01*<br>CIS: *3, 11*<br>COBIT 2019: *APO 11.04, BAI 03.05, DSS 05.04, 05.07*<br>CIS: *6*<br>NIST 800-37 Rev 2: *Task C-2*<br>NIST 800-53 Rev 4: *AU-1, AU-2, AU-3, AU-4, AU-9* |

## FUTURE RESEARCH DIRECTIONS

The complexity of the cyber threat and risk landscape portends the difficulty of developing and implementing an audit model that is robust, efficient, and adaptable to the rapid changes and advancements in cyber technologies. Adherence to established standards and frameworks provides guidelines and best practices with which the cybersecurity audit process could depend on. However, there are issues related to the process that remain unresolved or in need of some improvement. In this regard, the authors propose that following research directions:

- Investigate the use of blockchain technology to promote the validation and verification of internal controls;
- Design and develop digital transactions that are recorded on a digital and distributed ledger;
- Develop and implement metrics for cybersecurity audit; and
- Develop and implement a process for mapping cybersecurity controls with regulatory compliance.

## CONCLUSION

The integration of cyber infrastructure into the enterprise compels organizations to judiciously build and develop a sound organizational culture on cybersecurity and a set of mechanisms to defend against cyberattacks. To this end, an organization must enable an independent entity with an oversight function to ensure that the cyber related activities are securely performed, and information resources are protected.

This article presents three risk mitigation defenses suggested by the Institute of Internal Auditors, which include suggestions for establishing appropriate positions and policies to address cyber risks, along with regular independent evaluations by internal auditors. To allow for even greater independence, the AICPA provides a reporting framework in which external Certified Public Accountants can be engaged to conduct a cybersecurity risk management examination. Any system of attestation requires an appropriate set of audit objectives upon which to base the evaluation. This research considers criteria for the assessment of cybersecurity objectives that were created by cybersecurity auditing standards and frameworks from four prominent authoritative bodies. It posits a cyber infrastructure that is composed of five domains and the cybersecurity requirements of each domain. Subsequently, internal controls are suggested to satisfy the cybersecurity requirements and mapped to the auditing standards and frameworks that cover the Risk Management Framework (RMF). Lastly, the article illustrates the invaluable benefit of using the standards and frameworks towards the development and implementation of internal controls for cybersecurity.

## REFERENCES

American Institute of Certified Public Accountants. (2017). *Reporting on an Entity's Cybersecurity Risk Management Program and Controls*. Author.

Center for Information Security. (2019). *CIS Controls™*. Author. Retrieved June 14, 2019, from https://www.cisecurity.org/controls/

Galligan, M. E., & Rau, K. (2015). *COSO in the Cyber Age. Committee of the Sponsoring Organizations of the Treadway Commission (COSO)*. Retrieved April 6, 2019, from https://www.coso.org/documents/COSO%20in%20the%20Cyber%20Age_FULL_r11.pdf

Institute of Internal Auditors. (2013). *IIA Position Paper: The Three Lines of Defense in Effective Risk Management and Control*. Altamonte Springs, FL: Author.

Institute of Internal Auditors. (2016). *Global Technology Audit Guide (GTAG) Assessing Cybersecurity Risk: Roles of the Three Lines of Defense.* Altamonte Springs, FL: Author. Retrieved April 6, 2019, from https://www.aicpa.org/content/dam/aicpa/interestareas/frc/assuranceadvisoryservices/downloadabledocuments/cybersecurity/gtag-assessing-cybersecurity-risk.pdf

ISACA. (2019). *COBIT 2019 Framework: Introduction and Methodology.* Author. Retrieved June 12, 2019, from https://www.isaca.org/Knowledge-Center/Academia/Pages/Model-Curriculum-for-IS-Audit-and-Control-3rd-Edition.aspx

Lanz, J. (2014). Cybersecurity Governance: The Role of the Audit Committee and the CPA. *The CPA Journal, 84*(11), 6–10.

McMillan, R. (2018, December 3). Marriott Faulted on Earlier Hack. *Wall Street Journal*, p. B.1. Retrieved March 18, 2019, from http://lib-proxy.jsu.edu/login?url=https://search-proquest-com.lib-proxy.jsu.edu/docview/2140801768?accountid=11662

National Institute of Standards and Technology. (2018). *Risk Management Framework for Information Systems and Organizations: A System Life Cycle Approach for Security and Privacy. SP 800-37 Rev. 2.* Author. Retrieved June 12, 2019, from https://csrc.nist.gov/publications/detail/sp/800-37/rev-2/final

National Institute of Standards and Technology (NIST). (2015). *Security and Privacy Controls for Federal Information Systems and Organizations. SP 800-53 Rev. 4.* Author. Retrieved June 17, 2019, from https://nvlpubs.nist.gov/nistpubs/SpecialPublications/NIST.SP.800-53r4.pdf

Retrieved April 6, 2019, from https://www.theiia.org/3-Lines-Defense

Stafford, T., Deitz, G., & Li, Y. (2018). The Role of Internal Audit and User Training in Information Security Policy Compliance. *Managerial Auditing Journal, 33*(4), 410–424. Retrieved April 7, 2019, from. doi:10.1108/MAJ-07-2017-1596

## ADDITIONAL READING

Al-Moshaigeh, A., Dickins, D., & Higgs, J. L. (2019). Cybersecurity risks and controls: Is the AICPA's SOC for cybersecurity a solution?: Certified public accountant. *The CPA Journal, 89*(6), 36–41. http://lib-proxy.jsu.edu/login?url=https://search-proquest-com.lib-proxy.jsu.edu/docview/2239575100?accountid=11662

Bozkus Kahyaoglu, S., & Caliyurt, K. (2018). Cyber security assurance process from the internal audit perspective. *Managerial Auditing Journal, 33*(4), 360–376. doi:10.1108/MAJ-02-2018-1804

Brazina, P. R., Leauby, B. A., & Sgrillo, C. (2019). Cybersecurity Opportunities for CPA Firms. *Pennsylvania CPA Journal*. Retrieved from https://www.picpa.org/articles/picpa-news/2019/04/24/pa-cpa-journal-cybersecurity-opportunities-for-cpa-firms

Chang, Y. T., Chen, H., Cheng, R. K., & Chi, W. (2019). The impact of internal audit attributes on the effectiveness of internal control over operations and compliance. *Journal of Contemporary Accounting & Economics*, *15*(1), 1–19. doi:10.1016/j.jcae.2018.11.002

Drew, J. (2018). Paving the way to a new digital world. *Journal of Accountancy*, *225*(6), 18–22. http://lib-proxy.jsu.edu/login?url=https://search-proquest-com.lib-proxy.jsu.edu/docview/2135522857?accountid=11662

English, D. B. M. (2019). Rise of the (Accounting) Machines? Blockchain and AI: The Changing Face of the Profession. *California CPA*, (9), 12. Retrieved from http://search.ebscohost.com.ezproxy.lib.uwf.edu/login.aspx?direct=true&db=edsgao&AN=edsgcl.585801546&site=eds-live

Mintchik, N., & Riley, J. (2019). Rationalizing fraud: How thinking like a crook can help prevent fraud: Certified public accountant. *The CPA Journal*, *89*(3), 44–50. http://lib-proxy.jsu.edu/login?url=https://search-proquest-com.lib-proxy.jsu.edu/docview/2195794728?accountid=11662

Mylrea, M., & Dourisetti, S. N. G. (2018). Blockchain for Supply Chain Cybersecurity, Optimization and Compliance. *2018 Resilience Week (RWS), Resilience Week (RWS)*, 2018: 70-76. Retrieved from https://doi.org.ezproxy.lib.uwf.edu/10.1109/RWEEK.2018.8473517

Nickerson, M. A. (2019). Fraud in a world of advanced technologies: The possibilities are (unfortunately) endless: Certified public accountant. *The CPA Journal*, *89*(6), 28–34. http://lib-proxy.jsu.edu/login?url=https://search-proquest-com.lib-proxy.jsu.edu/docview/2239576995?accountid=11662

Wertheim, S. (2019). Auditing for Cybersecurity Risk. *The CPA Journal*, *89*(6), 68–71. http://search.ebscohost.com.ezproxy.lib.uwf.edu/login.aspx?direct=true&db=bth&AN=136901855&site=eds-live

## KEY TERMS AND DEFINITIONS

**Audit Committee:** A committee composed of outside members of a company's board of directors, that is responsible for oversight involving a company's internal controls and information reporting.

**Blockchain:** A digital register or ledger which embodies a permanent, time stamped, and cryptographically validated record of transactions.

**Cyber Infrastructure:** A collection of information technology systems and software, physical and information assets, processes, and people that enables an organization to efficiently and securely function on cyberspace.

**Cybersecurity:** A set of processes, practices, and technologies designed to protect, on the realm of cyberspace, the three tenets of information security: confidentiality, integrity, and availability.

**Frameworks:** A grouping of rules and related concepts into a logical approach that can be used to identify complex problems and decide upon appropriate courses of action to address them.

**Internal Audit:** A group of professionals who work within an organization to perform an independent appraisal activity to achieve efficiency and effectiveness in regard to both operating activities and information reporting.

**Regulatory Compliance:** The state of being in conformance to the requirements of a relevant law, policy, or regulation.

**Security Metric:** A quantitative, repeatable, accurate, and scalable measurement of an organization's security posture.

**Security Monitoring:** A process of data collection, analysis, and detection with the goal of proactively securing an organization.

**Standards:** A set of rules that can be monitored for compliance by a specialized field's authoritative bodies and related professionals.

*Previously published in the Encyclopedia of Organizational Knowledge, Administration, and Technology; pages 1194-1211, copyright year 2021 by Business Science Reference (an imprint of IGI Global).*

# Chapter 3
# The NIST Cybersecurity Framework

**Gregory B. White**
*CIAS, The University of Texas at San Antonio, USA*

**Natalie Sjelin**
*CIAS, The University of Texas at San Antonio, USA*

## ABSTRACT

*With the increase in cybercrimes over the last few years, a growing realization for the need for cybersecurity has begun to be recognized by the nation. Unfortunately, being aware that cybersecurity is something you need to worry about and knowing what steps to take are two different things entirely. In the United States, the National Institute of Standards and Technology (NIST) developed the Cyber Security Framework (CSF) to assist critical infrastructures in determining what they need in order to secure their computer systems and networks. While aimed at organizations, much of the guidance provided by the CSF, especially the basic functions it identifies, are also valuable for communities attempting to put together a community cybersecurity program.*

## INTRODUCTION

It is a common problem among individuals attempting to secure an organization's critical computer systems and networks to struggle with where to begin. With limited budgets, where can the funds be used most wisely? Can an incremental plan be developed to ultimately arrive at the security posture desired but over a period of time that takes into consideration the need to work within budgets?

The CCSMM introduced in this text is a plan to help guide communities in the creation and maturation of their cybersecurity program. A geographic community, however, is made up of a number of organizations and individuals all of whom will contribute to the security, or insecurity, of the community. This text focuses on the overall community's program and does not delve deeply into a plan for any one type of organization or sector. This is where the NIST Cyber Security Framework (CSF) enters the picture.

DOI: 10.4018/978-1-6684-3698-1.ch003

The CSF was designed to provide guidance to the critical infrastructures on how to organize their security efforts based on a plan to manage cybersecurity risk in a cost-effective way.

The CSF contains a lot of great information and guidance. Unfortunately for many organizations, in particular smaller organizations, the amount of information contained in the CSF can be overwhelming leaving people in a similar position to where they were before reading the CSF. Recognizing this, NIST produced another document, *Small Business Information Security: The Fundamentals*, which discusses much of what is introduced in the basic core of the CSF without the overwhelming list of sub-categories and references that the CSF contains. This allows small businesses to focus their efforts in an organized manner as they go about securing their systems and networks.

For communities, the CSF also contains much information that will not be immediately useable at the community level although it will pertain to many of the individual organizations within the community. Instead, the topics introduced in the companion document for small businesses that NIST produced can help focus a community's efforts providing an extra level of guidance that will enable the community to organize their efforts. Thus, the CCSMM and the CSF can go hand-in-hand within a community to help the community address cybersecurity from different angles.

## BACKGROUND

Since the 1990's, the federal government has been keenly aware of the dangers cyber events posed to the various critical infrastructures and thus focused considerable attention on securing these infrastructures. PDD 63 issued in 1998 and discussed earlier in the text was a big step forward in organizing the efforts of the various critical infrastructure sectors so that they could collectively work together to solve the challenges they each faced. Then in 2013 the White House issued Executive Order 13636 (2013) *Improving Critical Infrastructure Cybersecurity* which continued the focus on the critical infrastructures and attempted to keep things moving in a direction that would lead to more secure infrastructures. Besides addressing information sharing as was discussed in a previous chapter, EO 13636 also directed NIST to "lead the development of a framework to reduce cyber risks to critical infrastructure."

In 2014 the Cybersecurity Enhancement Act (CEA) of 2014 was signed into law. One of the things that this act did was to expand the role of NIST to "identify a prioritized, flexible, repeatable, performance-based, and cost-effective approach, including information security measures and controls, that may be voluntarily adopted by owners and operators of critical infrastructure to help them identify, assess, and manage cyber risks". (CEA, 2014) This in essence expanded upon the previous guidance in EO 13636 provided additional guidance to NIST for the creation of a framework.

In 2014 NIST released version 1.0 of the *Framework for Improving Critical Infrastructure Cybersecurity*. In 2016 revision 1 of the *Small Business Information Security: The Fundamentals* document was released which incorporated much of the basic framework from the CSF but made it more useable for small businesses. In 2017 a draft of CSF version 1.1 was released for public comment and in April of 2018 version 1.1 was officially released. This new version was compatible with the original in that it did not change the basic framework but instead expanded upon it to take into account things outside of the critical infrastructures such as their supply chains.

NIST and the federal government have been encouraging not only the critical infrastructures but government agencies to adopt the framework as part of their cybersecurity programs. They have also encouraged industry to use it as well and several large government contractors have done so and published papers on how well it has worked for them. The framework has taken hold in this government enclave but has not really caught on as well outside of government circles. This is actually somewhat disappointing as there is much useful guidance in the various NIST documents concerning the CSF. This is also true for communities. The NIST CSF can provide additional guidance beyond the steps outlined in the CCSMM that will allow communities to develop a more coordinated approach to establishing their cybersecurity program.

## THE NIST CYBER SECURITY FRAMEWORK (CSF)

Before jumping into how the CSF applies to community cybersecurity programs, it will be useful to have a better understanding of what the CSF entails. The CSF was initially created for organizations that are part of the various critical infrastructures. The CSF is made up of three parts: the Framework Core, the Implementation Tiers, and the Framework Profiles. Not all of these are going to be equally as important to a community cybersecurity program but they will be important to organizations within the community. What is involved in each of these parts is as follows:

- **Framework Core:** a set of cybersecurity activities, outcomes, and informative references that are common across sectors and critical infrastructure. Elements of the Core provide detailed guidance for developing individual organizational Profiles
- **Implementation Tiers:** provide a mechanism for organizations to view and understand the characteristics of their approach to managing cybersecurity risk, which will help in prioritizing and achieving cybersecurity objectives.
- **Framework Profiles:** will help an organization to align and prioritize its cybersecurity activities with its business/mission requirements, risk tolerances, and resources. (NIST, 2018)

A deeper investigation of each of these will be covered starting with the Framework Core. The Framework Core is the part of the CSF that people are most familiar with. As described in the CSF, the core is:

*a set of cybersecurity activities, desired outcomes, and applicable references that are common across critical infrastructure sectors. The Core presents industry standards, guidelines, and practices in a manner that allows for communication of cybersecurity activities and outcomes across the organization from the executive level to the implementation/operations level. The Framework Core consists of five concurrent and continuous Functions—Identify, Protect, Detect, Respond, Recover. When considered together, these Functions provide a high-level, strategic view of the lifecycle of an organization's management of cybersecurity risk. The Framework Core then identifies underlying key Categories and Subcategories – which are discrete outcomes – for each Function and matches them with example Informative References such as existing standards, guidelines, and practices for each Subcategory. (NIST, 2018)*

The functions mentioned are especially important to any effort to establish a community cybersecurity program. As mentioned above, the CSF core consists of Functions, Categories, Subcategories, and references as shown in the diagram below.

*Figure 1. The NIST Cybersecurity Framework core. (NIST, 2018)*

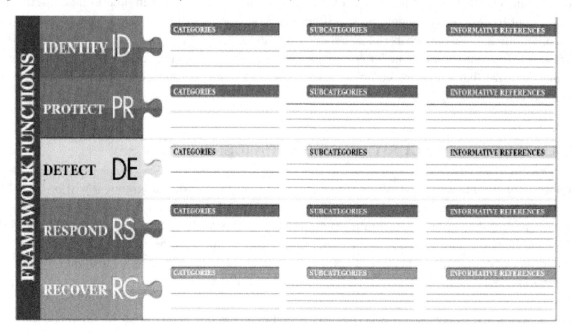

The key to the core from the perspective of a community's program are the five functions: Identify, Protect, Detect, Respond, and Recover. **Identify** simply means that an organization needs to know what resources it has, what valuable data it needs to protect, what defenses it has in place, and what remaining vulnerabilities and risks may still be present and that have been deemed an acceptable risk to an organization. It is important that organizations know what they have in order to understand what they need to be concerned with. A simple example of this might be a new vulnerability that has been discovered and that has been exploited in a specific operating system. If the organization knows what resources it has (which includes hardware and software) it will know if it should be concerned or if this is something that will not impact them because they don't have any systems running this particular operating system.

**Protect** means exactly what one might expect. What measures has an organization taken in order to protect its resources, data, and people? This includes not just cybersecurity but physical security, personnel security, and operational security. It includes all measures that are taken in order to maintain the security of the organization's valuable resources and data. It is interesting to note that in the earliest days of computing, computer security was primarily an issue of physical security. You controlled access to the computing device and only allowed authorized individuals to use the system. This remained the primary focus of security through the 1970's as computer systems were mostly mainframe computers with remote terminal rooms. Organizations simply controlled access to the system and the terminals in order to protect the data. Passwords were used, often not only to control access but to also control the amount of time a specific user was allowed on the system. It wasn't until the 1980's with the introduction of the IBM PC that things changed dramatically. Initially userids and passwords were still the primary means to enforce security but with the introduction of these cheap (relatively) computing devices there was a movement towards establishing networks and connecting these networks to other networks and the birth of what we now know as the Internet occurred. It is also interesting to note that the protocols used in the ARPANET, from which the Internet arose, were not devised with security in mind and this led to many security issues that were experienced in the 1980's and 1990's. Eventually in the late 1980's an operational model of cybersecurity was developed by the U.S. Air Force which promoted more than protection – it added Detection and Response.

The **Detect** function is first a realization that the security community has never been able to produce an absolutely secure computer system that works in all environments. Either a new vulnerability may be discovered in an application or an operating system, a user may make a mistake (such as providing their userid and password to somebody who asks for it), or a system may be misconfigured. Whatever the case, the ultimate result is that protection mechanisms will have failed. When this happens, the organization should have technology and processes in place to be able to detect the loss of security and what the impact of the loss has been (e.g. loss of intellectual property, theft of services, or loss of sensitive information).

When some aspect of security has been lost, the **Respond** function includes the technology and actions that an organization will take in order to react effectively to the incident. The immediate focus should be on gaining control of the system or network and preventing the loss of any additional data or services. An analogy for several of these functions might be the measures an organization takes to prevent fires in their facility, but they will also have smoke/fire detection equipment in case one occurs despite their prevention measures. When a fire is detected the immediate concern is to prevent loss of life and resources by evacuating individuals and initiating fire suppression equipment. Often this may involve the efforts of trained individuals who have practiced in advance so that they know what to do when a fire occurs. They also want to act quickly so that the fire doesn't spread to additional parts of the facility. The same is true when speaking of cybersecurity. After the incident has been contained, the focus can then shift to recovery.

The **Recovery** function involves the technology and processes that will allow the organization to first engage in its most important activities and to eventually (and hopefully shortly) return to its normal business activities. The recovery function is critical in cybersecurity as it is in other aspects of security. Processes and technology need to be identified that will allow for the rapid return to normal processing. Plans need to be in place for this to occur so that everybody knows what part they will play in recovery and to ensure the most critical activities are returned to operational status as quickly as possible.

These five functions are items that everybody involved in cybersecurity should be familiar with, no matter what their scope – organization, city, state, or nation. Categories are subdivisions within the Functions where outcomes tied to programmatic needs are grouped. The diagram below shows the list of categories associated with each of the individual functions.

Subcategories continue to further divide the categories into technical and management activities. For each one of these subcategories, a number of informative references are provided. Informative References are pointers to specific standards, guidelines, best practices, or other documents where more information can be found as to how to achieve the particular subcategory outcome. A table showing the subcategories and informative references for one category (Asset Management) in one function (Identify) is shown below.

There are a lot of similar references contained in the CSF which is one of the drawbacks to it from a small business perspective. There are simply too many subcategories and references to be able to deal with them. For the various critical infrastructures this information is very important, and it can be argued that they would be for small businesses as well, but providing somebody an encyclopedia's worth of knowledge when they are actually looking for a "how-to" guide is not going to help them and will thus probably not be used. This is why the CSF is most often being used by critical infrastructures, government agencies, and large government contractors.

*Figure 2. NIST CSF Functions and Categories*

| Function Unique Identifier | Function | Category Unique Identifier | Category |
|---|---|---|---|
| ID | Identify | ID.AM | Asset Management |
| | | ID.BE | Business Environment |
| | | ID.GV | Governance |
| | | ID.RA | Risk Assessment |
| | | ID.RM | Risk Management Strategy |
| | | ID.SC | Supply Chain Risk Management |
| PR | Protect | PR.AC | Identity Management and Access Control |
| | | PR.AT | Awareness and Training |
| | | PR.DS | Data Security |
| | | PR.IP | Information Protection Processes and Procedures |
| | | PR.MA | Maintenance |
| | | PR.PT | Protective Technology |
| DE | Detect | DE.AE | Anomalies and Events |
| | | DE.CM | Security Continuous Monitoring |
| | | DE.DP | Detection Processes |
| RS | Respond | RS.RP | Response Planning |
| | | RS.CO | Communications |
| | | RS.AN | Analysis |
| | | RS.MI | Mitigation |
| | | RS.IM | Improvements |
| RC | Recover | RC.RP | Recovery Planning |
| | | RC.IM | Improvements |
| | | RC.CO | Communications |

As previously mentioned, there are two other parts to the CSF – the Implementation Tiers and the Framework Profiles.

*Implementation Tiers provide context on how an organization views cybersecurity risk and the processes in place to manage that risk. Tiers describe the degree to which an organization's cybersecurity risk management practices exhibit the characteristics defined in the Framework (e.g., risk and threat aware, repeatable, and adaptive). The Tiers characterize an organization's practices over a range, from Partial (Tier 1) to Adaptive (Tier 4). These Tiers reflect a progression from informal, reactive responses to approaches that are agile and risk-informed. During the Tier selection process, an organization should consider its current risk management practices, threat environment, legal and regulatory requirements, business/mission objectives, and organizational constraints. (NIST, 2018)*

*Figure 3. A sample of NIST CSF subcategories and Informative References*

| Function | Category | Subcategory | Informative References |
|---|---|---|---|
| IDENTIFY (ID) | Asset Management (ID.AM): The data, personnel, devices, systems, and facilities that enable the organization to achieve business purposes are identified and managed consistent with their relative importance to organizational objectives and the organization's risk strategy. | ID.AM-1: Physical devices and systems within the organization are inventoried | CIS CSC 1<br>COBIT 5 BAI09.01, BAI09.02<br>ISA 62443-2-1:2009 4.2.3.4<br>ISA 62443-3-3:2013 SR 7.8<br>ISO/IEC 27001:2013 A.8.1.1, A.8.1.2<br>NIST SP 800-53 Rev. 4 CM-8, PM-5 |
| | | ID.AM-2: Software platforms and applications within the organization are inventoried | CIS CSC 2<br>COBIT 5 BAI09.01, BAI09.02, BAI09.05<br>ISA 62443-2-1:2009 4.2.3.4<br>ISA 62443-3-3:2013 SR 7.8<br>ISO/IEC 27001:2013 A.8.1.1, A.8.1.2, A.12.5.1<br>NIST SP 800-53 Rev. 4 CM-8, PM-5 |
| | | ID.AM-3: Organizational communication and data flows are mapped | CIS CSC 12<br>COBIT 5 DSS05.02<br>ISA 62443-2-1:2009 4.2.3.4<br>ISO/IEC 27001:2013 A.13.2.1, A.13.2.2<br>NIST SP 800-53 Rev. 4 AC-4, CA-3, CA-9, PL-8 |
| | | ID.AM-4: External information systems are catalogued | CIS CSC 12<br>COBIT 5 APO02.02, APO10.04, DSS01.02<br>ISO/IEC 27001:2013 A.11.2.6<br>NIST SP 800-53 Rev. 4 AC-20, SA-9 |
| | | ID.AM-5: Resources (e.g., hardware, devices, data, time, personnel, and software) are prioritized based on their classification, criticality, and business value | CIS CSC 13, 14<br>COBIT 5 APO03.03, APO03.04, APO12.01, BAI04.02, BAI09.02<br>ISA 62443-2-1:2009 4.2.3.6<br>ISO/IEC 27001:2013 A.8.2.1<br>NIST SP 800-53 Rev. 4 CP-2, RA-2, SA-14, SC-6 |
| | | ID.AM-6: Cybersecurity roles and responsibilities for the entire workforce and | CIS CSC 17, 19<br>COBIT 5 APO01.02, APO07.06, APO13.01, DSS06.03 |

There are four Tiers defined in the CSF from Tier 1 to Tier 4. Each higher tier describes an increasing degree of thoroughness and intricacy. NIST stresses that the Tiers do not represent maturity levels and recommends that organizations obtain guidance from other sources such as ISAOs, other maturity models, and Federal government departments. The target Tier selected by an organization should reflect its goals and considers their threat environment, risk management practices, legal and regulatory requirements, and what is feasible for the organization. The four identified tiers and their characteristics are:

- *Tier 1: Partial*
  - *Risk Management Process – Organizational cybersecurity risk management practices are not formalized, and risk is managed in an ad hoc and sometimes reactive manner.*
  - *Integrated Risk Management Program – There is limited awareness of cybersecurity risk at the organizational level. The organization implements cybersecurity risk management on an irregular, case-by-case basis due to varied experience or information gained from outside sources.*
  - *External Participation – The organization does not understand its role in the larger ecosystem with respect to either its dependencies or dependents. The organization does not collaborate with or receive information such as threat intelligence, best practices, and technologies, from other entities.*

- *Tier 2: Risk Informed*
  - *Risk Management Process – Risk management practices are approved by management but may not be established as organizational-wide policy.*
  - *Integrated Risk Management Program – There is an awareness of cybersecurity risk at the organizational level, but an organization-wide approach to managing cybersecurity risk has not been established.*
  - *External Participation – Generally, the organization understands its role in the larger ecosystem with respect to either its own dependencies or dependents, but not both.*
- *Tier 3: Repeatable*
  - *Risk Management Process – The organization's risk management practices are formally approved and expressed as policy.*
  - *Integrated Risk Management Program – There is an organization-wide approach to manage cybersecurity risk. Risk-informed policies, processes, and procedures are defined, implemented as intended, and reviewed.*
  - *External Participation – The organization understands its role, dependencies, and dependents in the larger ecosystem and may contribute to the community's broader understanding of risks.*
- *Tier 4: Adaptive*
  - *Risk Management Process – The organization adapts its cybersecurity practices based on previous and current cybersecurity activities, including lessons learned and predictive indicators.*
  - *Integrated Risk Management Program – There is an organization-wide approach to managing cybersecurity risk that uses risk-informed policies, processes, and procedures to address potential cybersecurity events.*
  - *External Participation – The organization understands its role, dependencies, and dependents in the larger ecosystem and contributes to the community's broader understanding of risks.* (NIST, 2018)

The above is an abbreviated description of the Tiers from the CSF. It is not intended to be a tutorial or how-to document for selecting a Tier but rather as an introduction to the topic so that the concepts are understood. The term "community" is used several times in the descriptions which may be confusing. Community in this text refers to a city or town or similar geographic region. Community as it was used in the NIST CSF generally is used to mean a "community of interest" which means a group of organizations that all have something in common such as a sector (e.g. power, water, telecommunications) or it could actually mean a city though there is not a clean translation of the concepts to a city. The reason is that a city is made up of many different organizations without a single entity that controls them. The mayor of a city may suggest, recommend, or encourage organizations in the city to act in a certain way but mayors ultimately do not control all organizations within the city boundaries.

The last part of the CSF is the Framework Profile. There are actually two profiles – the Current Profile and the Target Profile. A description of what a profile is according to the NIST CSF is as follows:

*A Framework Profile represents the outcomes based on business needs that an organization has selected from the Framework Categories and Subcategories. The Profile can be characterized as the alignment of standards, guidelines, and practices to the Framework Core in a particular implementation scenario.*

*Profiles can be used to identify opportunities for improving cybersecurity posture by comparing a "Current" Profile (the "as is" state) with a "Target" Profile (the "to be" state). To develop a Profile, an organization can review all of the Categories and Subcategories and, based on business/mission drivers and a risk assessment, determine which are most important; it can add Categories and Subcategories as needed to address the organization's risks. The Current Profile can then be used to support prioritization and measurement of progress toward the Target Profile, while factoring in other business needs including cost-effectiveness and innovation. Profiles can be used to conduct self-assessments and communicate within an organization or between organizations. (NIST, 2018)*

Tiers address the organization's risk management goals while the Profiles will address the specific categories and subcategories that the organization will be addressing. These two parts go together and are part of the overall plan to help an organization develop a cybersecurity program or to improve an existing program. Notice how the description states the organization needs to determine which categories and subcategories are most important to the organization. This is a simple statement but a big challenge. Sometimes regulatory requirements may help to dictate which categories are important for the organization but in the absence of such additional guidance, determining which categories and subcategories are most important is more of a challenge – especially for smaller businesses with no full-time security personnel. The CSF goes on to describe seven steps in outlining how it can help an organization with their program.

**Step 1:** Prioritize and Scope. The organization identifies its business/mission objectives and high-level organizational priorities.

**Step 2:** Orient. Once the scope of the cybersecurity program has been determined for the business line or process, the organization identifies related systems and assets, regulatory requirements, and overall risk approach.

**Step 3:** Construct a hypothesis, Create a Current Profile. The organization develops a Current Profile by indicating which Category and Subcategory outcomes from the Framework Core are currently being achieved.

**Step 4:** Conduct a Risk Assessment. The organization analyzes the operational environment in order to discern the likelihood of a cybersecurity event and the impact that the event could have on the organization.

**Step 5:** Create a Target Profile. The organization creates a Target Profile that focuses on the assessment of the Framework Categories and Subcategories describing the organization's desired cybersecurity outcomes. Organizations also may develop their own additional Categories and Subcategories to account for unique organizational risks.

**Step 6:** Determine, Analyze, and Prioritize Gaps. The organization compares the Current Profile and the Target Profile to determine gaps. Next, it creates a prioritized action plan to address gaps – reflecting mission drivers, costs and benefits, and risks – to achieve the outcomes in the Target Profile.

**Step 7**: Implement Action Plan. The organization determines which actions to take to address the gaps, if any, identified in the previous step and then adjusts its current cybersecurity practices in order to achieve the Target Profile. (NIST, 2018)

Again, the goal of presenting these steps is not to provide guidance on exactly how to implement the CSF but rather to provide a basic introduction to the Framework and its various parts so that a discussion of how the Framework may apply to a community will become more apparent. The CSF is designed for organizations and any organization desiring to implement the CSF should consult the actual document for more guidance – see (NIST, 2018)

## APPLYING THE FRAMEWORK TO COMMUNITIES

The Cyber Security Framework is designed to help individual organizations improve their cybersecurity programs. Even very large organizations can use the guidance it presents – in fact it can be argued that it is more applicable to at least medium-sized businesses due to the amount of information it contains and the steps an organization will have to go through to incorporate it. A community is not made up of a single organization nor even a group of similar organizations in a given sector. It also does not have management control over all entities within its boundaries. This means the creation of a community cybersecurity program is going to be fundamentally different in what it can accomplish.

One of the big differences for a community is that it can't simply mandate certain cybersecurity activities be taken by all members of the community. There may be some basic things that can be mandated by government such as breach notification laws that have been implemented by many states, but the community can't, for example, simply require all organizations to conduct user-level awareness training for the private sector. What the community has to do is to encourage organizations to conduct certain activities and to show the benefit of doing so to the organizations if they accomplish them. In certain unique instances the community may also be able to provide incentives for accomplishing specific activities such as working with an insurance company to offer members of the community reduced rates on cyber insurance if the organization accomplishes certain steps. Another potential incentive is the possible ability to use cybersecurity as a business advantage. Should an organization be faced with making a decision between two vendors, one of which has reached a certain level of cybersecurity maturity while the other has not, the organization may choose to select the organization with the proven security program. They may decide that by doing so the likelihood of a third-party security breach will be reduced which may be enough of an incentive to choose that organization. In a similar manner, the DoD, and potentially other organizations, has elected to place certain requirements on its vendors before the DoD will do business with them. Because the DoD values security so highly, and cybersecurity in particular in this case, it has elected to require its vendor to follow certain processes and procedures if the vendor wants to do business with the DoD. Obtaining compliance certificates or conducting assessments to prove that an organization has met some level of security will certainly involve a cost to that organization. In the end, however, it will be a business decision that organizations will make in deciding what cybersecurity activities to be involved in or to embrace.

Since a community is not a single, large organization, developing a cybersecurity program for a community is a challenge. In the previous chapters the phases identified activities that could be performed by the community when its organizations work together. There are a few items listed in the CCSMM levels that can be accomplished by a single organization, generally a part of the city government. An example of this would be the creation of a cybersecurity annex for the city's emergency response plans. Many items, however, will simply be things that the community as a whole will have to cooperate together on and to encourage other members of the community to join with them. An example of this would be the creation of an ISAO. Thus, the list of informative references from the CSF will have little applicability to the community as an entity but will be invaluable for organizations within the community.

What then is the community's role in terms of the CSF? As has been suggested, the role of the community will be that of encouraging its members to consider the use of the CSF, or other models or guidelines, in order to improve the cybersecurity program for individual organizations. Since many of the members of the community, in fact most of the members of the community, will not be part of the government (at any level), or the critical infrastructures, the detailed CSF may not be so easy to apply. Instead, the NIST document *Small Business Information Security: The Fundamentals* publication (Paulsen & Toth, 2016a) can serve as a tool the community can use in helping all organizations develop their individual cybersecurity programs.

As stated, the community's role will mostly be in the encouragement of its organizations. The obvious question to ask is "Who will be doing this encouraging?" In order for the CCSMM to be adopted in a community there will need to be a champion for community cybersecurity. This champion can be a city official or it can be an industry leader, but a champion is needed in order to ensure the program keeps moving forward until it is firmly rooted within the community. At the lower levels, Level 1 and Level 2, the champion may at times feel alone in their efforts to encourage the community as a whole to move forward. The list of activities previously provided in the chapters on the various dimensions should help the champion in terms of the type of things that should be encouraged at first. Once the community ISAO is created and firmly entrenched, the ISAO can become the champion for the community and can be the one that leads many of the efforts mentioned for the levels in each of the dimensions.

As organizations begin to establish their programs it can be quite daunting. For the same reason that the CCSMM was established for communities – to provide a yardstick and a roadmap – organizations need something similar to help them. The full CCSMM includes an organizational level and this is the part of the model that will most closely align with the CSF. From the whole community perspective, however, there are two essential elements that programs should consider, and that the community champion can discuss to help the members of the community. These are described in the CSF and in the companion fundamental guide for small businesses. The first of these are the six security measures outlined in the small business fundamental guide and that are shown in the diagram below

The six security measures shown in this diagram are areas of security that should be considered when any organization builds its security program. Cybersecurity is just one of these concerns. Missing any one of these measures can lead to a security event that can adversely impact the organization. When an organization embarks on the development of its security program, it should ask "what am I doing in each of these areas?" Several of these may already be in place in the organization, such as Physical Security and Personnel Security, because we are already used to thinking about them in our society. Whether the others have been considered will depend on the organization though if they are implementing the organizational scope of the CCSMM, they will be covering some of the others as well.

The second essential area was discussed in the CSF. It is the five functions which were broken down into categories and subcategories. Previously these functions were briefly described. It is time to look at them in a little greater detail.

- *Identify: Develop an organizational understanding to manage cybersecurity risk to systems, people, assets, data, and capabilities.*
  - *The activities in the Identify Function are foundational for effective use of the Framework. Understanding the business context, the resources that support critical functions, and the related cybersecurity risks enables an organization to focus and prioritize its efforts, consistent with its risk management strategy and business needs. Examples of outcome Categories*

*within this Function include: Asset Management; Business Environment; Governance; Risk Assessment; and Risk Management Strategy.*

- *Protect: Develop and implement appropriate safeguards to ensure delivery of critical services.*
  - ◦ *The Protect Function supports the ability to limit or contain the impact of a potential cybersecurity event. Examples of outcome Categories within this Function include: Identity Management and Access Control; Awareness and Training; Data Security; Information Protection Processes and Procedures; Maintenance; and Protective Technology.*
- *Detect: Develop and implement appropriate activities to identify the occurrence of a cybersecurity event.*
  - ◦ *The Detect Function enables timely discovery of cybersecurity events. Examples of outcome Categories within this Function include: Anomalies and Events; Security Continuous Monitoring; and Detection Processes.*

*Figure 4. The six security measures (Paulson & Toth, 2016a)*

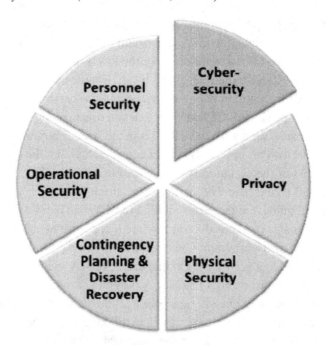

- **Physical Security** – the protection of property, e.g. using fences and locks;
- **Personnel Security** – e.g. using background checks;
- **Contingency Planning and Disaster Recovery** – how to resume normal operations after an incident, also known as Business Continuity Planning;
- **Operational Security** – protecting business plans and processes, and
- **Privacy** – protecting personal information.[2]

- *Respond: Develop and implement appropriate activities to take action regarding a detected cybersecurity incident.*
  - *The Respond Function supports the ability to contain the impact of a potential cybersecurity incident. Examples of outcome Categories within this Function include: Response Planning; Communications; Analysis; Mitigation; and Improvements.*
- *Recover: Develop and implement appropriate activities to maintain plans for resilience and to restore any capabilities or services that were impaired due to a cybersecurity incident.*
  - *The Recover Function supports timely recovery to normal operations to reduce the impact from a cybersecurity incident. Examples of outcome Categories within this Function include: Recovery Planning; Improvements; and Communications.* (NIST, 2018)

As an organization builds the cybersecurity portion of its overall security program, it is important for it to ask what it is doing in each of these functions. It is not enough to implement Respond and Recover activities to be prepared when a cybersecurity event occurs, the organization should be hopefully conducting activities to prevent the event from occurring in the first place. Likewise, it is not enough to perform the Identify and Protect functions because, as too many organizations have learned, no matter what you do, you need to be prepared to detect when your protection activities fail and have in place response and recovery capabilities. All five of these functions are required for a viable and sustainable organizational cybersecurity program.

These five functions are also important at the community level. As the community champion at first, and later the community ISAO, oversees the creation of the community cybersecurity program, all five of these functional areas apply to the community as well – though in a little different manner. For example:

- **Identify**: what cybersecurity resources does the community have? Who might be able to help others should an event occur? What are the potential targets in the community and who are the possible threat actors that may target them? What other resources exist in the state or nation that might be able to help when a cyber event occurs?
- **Protect**: What are the high value targets in the community doing to protect their cyber infrastructures? What processes and procedures has the community established to share information of attacks on one member that may impact another? Are organizations in the community sharing best practices to help each other protect their assets? Has the community established chapters of professional cybersecurity networking organizations (such as ISSA and ISACA)? Does the community sponsor a cybersecurity workshop or seminar on at least an annual basis that is open to all members of the community?
- **Detect**: What is the community doing to look for and share indicators of compromise? What other information sharing efforts are underway? Who else is the community communicating with in order to obtain other potential indicators of compromise? Has the community established a SOC or has it contracted with another entity to provide SOC services?
- **Respond**: What has the community done in order to enable a cooperative response to a cyber event impacting a significant portion of the community? What has the community done to be able to come together to continue functioning in the event of a cyber event? Do organizations and individuals know who to contact in the event of a cyber incident and when this contact should be made? Does the community have a Disaster Recovery Plan that includes cyber events? Has a community cyber event response plan been developed and incorporated into its overall emergency

response plan? Do all individuals and organizations identified in the response plan know what their responsibilities are? Does the community examine and practice their cyber event response plan at least annually through functional or tabletop exercises?

- **Recover**: What agreements and processes are in place in the community to work together to bring the community back to its pre-event posture? Are backups made of important data to ensure that the community and individual organizations can return to normal operations as quickly as possible? Do organizations keep backup copies of data in a secure location separate from the system that is used to normally process the data? Are cooperative agreements in place to help organizations work with other organizations to speed the recovery process?

Each community will be different in terms of how they carry out plans to create a cybersecurity program but they all need to consider and include the five functional areas when making their plans. Up to this point, organizations within a community have been treated similarly and it has been stated that all organizations need to consider the five functional areas. While this is true, not all organizations need to cover the functional areas to the same level. For a community to reach a specific level in the CCSMM, organizations within the community will also have to be implementing their own cybersecurity programs. It will be hard for the community to have, for example, a viable information sharing program unless organizations within the community have reached a level of maturity that will enable them to participate in the information sharing program. This does not mean, however, that all organizations in the community must be at the same level of maturity for the community to be considered to have reached that same level. While every organization within the community should be considering cybersecurity as it applies to them, not all will need to be as mature. Small organizations that do not store personal information on the citizens in the community may not need to maintain as high of a level of cybersecurity as others that do store this sort of information. They may not be as big of a target for cyber-attacks. Still, they need to consider what would happen to their employees, customers, or the community should they suffer a cyber-attack that impacts their operations. At the same time, other organizations, such as those in the financial services sector, will need to maintain a high level of security because of the possibility of attacks on their systems. The various infrastructures that the community relies on as well as local government systems will also need to be at a higher level of security.

So, what is the relationship between the level of maturity for the community and the level of security of individual organizations within the community? This is not an easy question to answer as it should be clear by now that the level that individual organizations should attain depends on the specific organization. In general, organizations related to the individual infrastructures, their vendors, the critical city government offices and those they are connected to, and major employers in the community should be at the same level of security as the community is targeting. As for the rest of the organizations within the community, they should be at a level of security that allows them to participate in the security programs in the community (such as information sharing efforts and community cybersecurity exercises and informational events) that are part of the level of security the community is targeting.

The focus has been on the NIST *Cyber Security Framework* and its companion document, the NIST *Small Business Information Security: The Fundamentals* documents. There are a number of other documents that may be useful for both communities and the organizations within them. NIST Special Publication 800-171 titled *Protecting Controlled Unclassified Information in Nonfederal Systems and Organizations* introduces 14 families of security requirements as shown in the diagram below:

*Figure 5. Security Requirements Families (Ross et el. 2016b)*

| FAMILY | FAMILY |
|---|---|
| Access Control | Media Protection |
| Awareness and Training | Personnel Security |
| Audit and Accountability | Physical Protection |
| Configuration Management | Risk Assessment |
| Identification and Authentication | Security Assessment |
| Incident Response | System and Communications Protection |
| Maintenance | System and Information Integrity |

Each family of security requirements includes a number of requirements related to the topic of the family. Each family has both basic security requirements and derived security requirements. The *basic security requirements* provide high-level and fundamental security requirements for that family. The derived security requirements supplement the basic security requirements and come from NIST Special Publication 800-53. NIST SP 800-171 includes a detailed discussion of both the basic and derived security requirements. The purpose of NIST SP 800-53 is to "provide guidelines for selecting and specifying security controls for organizations and information systems supporting the executive agencies of the federal government". (NIST, 2013) Neither of these documents provide step-by-step guidance for securing systems but they both provide valuable information that can be used by organizations wanting to implement a cybersecurity program. From the community's perspective, these documents provide additional information to better understand the bigger picture of what organizations need to be doing within the community and can be areas that the community's champion helps to publicize to members of the community.

## CONCLUSION

The NIST Cybersecurity Framework is a valuable document containing a lot of very useful information including a number of references that will point a security professional to additional documents on a variety of security topics. It is not designed for communities or for all of the organizations within a community. Instead, it was designed to address critical infrastructure cybersecurity and has been used by them as well as government departments and agencies. Large government contractors have also utilized the information within the CSF. The CSF introduces five functions – Identify, Protect, Detect, Respond, and Recover – all of which should be part of every organization's cybersecurity program, no matter what the size. The companion publication from NIST, *Small Business Information Security: The Fundamentals*, was designed for small businesses who would not be able to address all that is found in the CSF publication. This document is also more applicable to a community as a whole. It introduces six security measures – Cybersecurity, Physical Security, Personnel Security, Operational Security, Privacy, and Contingency Planning & Disaster Recovery – all of which are pertinent to both organizational and community cybersecurity programs. A community needs to consider all six of these security measures as well as the five functions of the CSF when developing their program and when encouraging organizations within the community to improve their own cybersecurity programs.

The tie between the CSF and the CCSMM is simply that the CCSMM defines a variety of characteristics that should be part of a cybersecurity program at various levels. It is not specific in terms of identifying what has to be done for each of the five functions identified in the CSF or the six security measures in the small business document. Instead, a community or an organization that has determined it wants to attain a specific level in the model should look at the characteristics identified at that level and then determine what it can do in the five functional areas to obtain that characteristic. The CSF then can be used as a reference to find specific guidance on the variety of areas that the community has identified it needs to work on.

While this text is focused on communities, it is important for a community attempting to attain a specific maturity level as outlined in the CCSMM to ensure that organizations within the community attain a certain level of maturity as well. Not all organizations need to be at the same level as the community, it will depend on the type of organization, what assets they control, and what data they store. Essential local government offices such as law enforcement and emergency services will need to be at the same level as the community. The organizations that provide the essential services such as water, power, and communications will also need to be at the same level. Financial services, because of the information they process, will be a natural target and should be at the same level as the community as well. Employers with a large number of employees or customers as well as organizations with large financial assets, because they too will be a natural target for cyber-attacks, should also be at the same level as the community. Smaller businesses that do not control the same type of assets, are not a vendor for any of the critical community organizations, and that do not maintain a large amount of personnel information on citizens may not need to be at the same level.

# REFERENCES

Executive Order 13636: Improving Critical Infrastructure Cybersecurity. (2013). Retrieved from https://www.govinfo.gov/content/pkg/FR-2013-02-19/pdf/2013-03915.pdf

Joint Task Force Transformation Initiative. (2013). *NIST Special Publication: 800-53 Rev. 4. Security and privacy controls for federal information systems and organizations.* Retrieved from https://nvlpubs.nist.gov/nistpubs/SpecialPublications/NIST.SP.800-53r4.pdf

NIST, National Institute of Standards and Technology. (2018). *Framework for improving critical infrastructure cybersecurity version 1.1.* Retrieved from https://nvlpubs.nist.gov/nistpubs/CSWP/NIST.CSWP.04162018.pdf

Paulsen, C., & Toth, P. (2016). *NISTIR 7621 Rev. 1: Small business information security: The fundamentals.* Retrieved from NIST website: https://nvlpubs.nist.gov/nistpubs/ir/2016/NIST.IR.7621r1.pdf

Ross, R., Viscuso, P., Guissanie, G., Dempsey, K., & Riddle, M. (2016). *NIST Special Publication 800-171 Rev. 1: Protecting controlled unclassified information in nonfederal systems and organizations.* Retrieved from NIST website: https://nvlpubs.nist.gov/nistpubs/SpecialPublications/NIST.SP.800-171r1.pdf

S.1353 - Cybersecurity enhancement act (CEA) of 2014. (2014). Retrieved from congress.gov website: https://www.congress.gov/bill/113th-congress/senate-bill/1353/text

*Previously published in Establishing Cyber Security Programs Through the Community Cyber Security Maturity Model (CC-SMM); pages 171-192, copyright year 2021 by Information Science Reference (an imprint of IGI Global).*

# Chapter 4
# A Hybrid Asset–Based IT Risk Management Framework

**Baris Cimen**
 https://orcid.org/0000-0002-2445-6235
*Department of Management Information Systems, Bogazici University, Turkey*

**Meltem Mutluturk**
 https://orcid.org/0000-0001-5666-594X
*Department of Management Information Systems, Bogazici University, Turkey*

**Esra Kocak**
 https://orcid.org/0000-0002-4808-830X
*Department of Management Information Systems, Bogazici University, Turkey*

**Bilgin Metin**
 https://orcid.org/0000-0002-5828-9770
*Department of Management Information Systems, Bogazici University, Turkey*

## ABSTRACT

*Information security has become one of the most important responsibilities of all organizations due to increasing cyber threats. Attackers take advantage of systems vulnerabilities; therefore, system administrators should be aware of potential threats to take necessary actions to protect their organizations and stakeholders. At this point, a risk assessment is needed to discover possible threats for vulnerable systems of the organization and to implement strategies for the business goals. This study proposes a hybrid risk management framework using both qualitative and quantitative methods to analyze risk within organizations and reduce them with practical countermeasures. Based on this framework, case studies have been carried out considering three hypothetical companies identifying possible information security risks, and these risks have been reduced to an acceptable level by applying the proposed risk analysis methodology.*

DOI: 10.4018/978-1-6684-3698-1.ch004

## INTRODUCTION

Cyber-attacks have confounded information technology infrastructure of organizations and posed significant threats to their valuable information resources that have been valued as extremely important assets in cyberspace. Business managers need to be savvy to possible threats, aware of and prepared for both internal and external elements in order to manage cybersecurity risks. Hence, risk analysis procedure assists managers through evaluating possible threats or risks imposed on organizations, measuring the probability and impact of those risks and finally implementing strategies that create additional value to business operations by means of protecting their most precious information assets. Although, the most established risk analysis methodologies give great attention to technical risks, in recent, business organizations need risk analysis that incorporates social and organizational elements of complex systems with technical aspects in order to correctly evaluate and manage those risks. Within this context, the main objective of this paper is to address information risk management concepts considering possible threats and important organizational assets.

Drawing upon BS 7799 (Biery, 2006) information security risk management guidelines, in addition, by contributing additional possible threats, three hypothetical companies have been examined in terms of their business and organizational priorities. To that end, a strategic framework was proposed in order to identify critical business operations and relevant threats along with asset valuation for these three companies. Finally, a summary of evaluations and solutions were proposed to the identified threats for these companies. This study proposes a hybrid risk management framework via using both qualitative and quantitative methods to analyze risks within three hypothetical companies with the aim of incorporating social and organizational aspects alongside technical ones to overcome incompetencies of methods that previous studies did not. The remainder of the paper is structured as follows. The extant literature on cybersecurity risk analysis and management was reviewed and followed by presenting the proposed risk management framework. The paper concludes by providing a summary of the results and an overview of solutions and evaluations.

## BACKGROUND

Business Impact Analysis (BIA) has been defined as the process of conducting risk and gap assessment along with the implementation of global security standards considering people, process and technology in an organization (Sikdar, 2017). Business landscape renders a need for BIA within the context of business continuity management plan as a result of the latest trends such as globalization, e-commerce, enterprise resource planning, outsourcing business operations and legal and regulatory norms (Sikdar, 2017). Moreover, companies have developed BIA programs to cope with crisis events such as technological failures, natural events and deliberate disasters (Păunescu et al., 2018). While performing BIA, it is crucial to think in an organizational context and to understand relationships and dependencies throughout the enterprise including customers, business partners, stakeholders, supply chain vendors along with legal and regulatory institutions (Sikdar, 2017). According to Bjerga and Aven (2016), BIA estimates the possible damages that an enterprise might suffer without taking into consideration recovery methods. Although BIA and risk analysis have been often treated as separate activities, they are linked to each other by basic premises such as, what can happen, what will be affected and what are the resulting effects and impact (Hiles, 2002). Within this context, risk analysis refers to the study of evaluating possible threats and risks. The main objective of a risk analysis is to understand the existing environment and identify risks through analysis of several types of information such as security requirements and objectives, system and network architecture and infrastructure, physical assets, operating systems, data repository, etc. (Schmittling, 2010). According to Patel et al. (2008) risk assessment methods can be either qualitative or quantitative. While qualitative methodologies have used a common approach based on threat, vulnerability, and probability through generally using verbal hazard scales such as low, medium, high (Ghazouani et al., 2014), quantitative risk analysis methods have incorporated into what the literature refers to as probabilistic risk assessment (PRA) including mathematical procedures for risk evaluation (Henriques de Gusmão et al., 2018). Information systems (IS) risk literature contains a compilation of various risk models and conceptualization of risk factors along with risk components. On the other hand, one of the early studies by Rainer (1991) proposed a risk analysis process that uses a combination of qualitative and quantitative methodologies including steps for identifying IT assets, assigning value to these assets, stating possible threats to IT assets along with vulnerability of them to potential threats, and finally determining IT risk exposure for the organization. On the other hand, Alter and Sherer (2004) presented a broadly adaptable model of system-related risks including risk management, possible outcomes and their probabilities, impacts on other systems, and resulting financial gains and losses. Another study by Karabacak and Sogukpinar (2005) adopted a survey-based quantitative approach to analyze the security risks of information technologies by using the method named as Information Security Risk Analysis Method (ISRAM) consisting of seven steps. Moreover, they conducted a case study to exemplify these steps to analyze the risk arising from computer viruses. Furthermore, Sun, Srivastava, and Mock (2006) developed an alternative methodology for the risk analysis of information security systems (ISS) by adopting the Dempster-Shafer theory. They presented a cost-benefit analysis of control measures to reduce information security risk under belief functions. Moreover, Khambhammettu et al. (2013) described a framework for risk assessment including four different approaches to conducting a threat assessment. Although this study contributed, it didn't cover unexpected threats such as insider threats. Another study by Ghazouani et al. (2014) presented an overview of the previous risk methodologies through conducting comparative analysis and then proposed an integrated qualitative approach based on ISO 27005 along with a mathematical formulation of risk. They recommended developing an alternate IS risk management tool by using COBIT standards. Furthermore, Roldan-Molina et al. (2017) compiled different risk assessment tools for information and communication technology (ICT) infrastructure and in the cybersecurity domain.

Recently, Pate-Cornell et al. (2018) conducted a quantitative risk analysis and presented a probabilistic risk analysis framework for cybersecurity in an organization. In this study, three illustrative examples were described to exemplify decision support by quantifying the cyber risk and the risk reduction benefits of a spectrum of countermeasures such as encryption, reduction of the number of entry points, or modification of the operation software (Paté-Cornell et al., 2018). Another recent study by De Gusmao et al. (2018) adopted a fault tree analysis (FTA) approach to determine the vulnerability of cybersecurity and identify potential consequences of cyber-attacks. In this study, they proposed a structured model to measure cyber-attack scenarios that consider the risk of financial losses and analysis of restoration time analysis via fuzzy theory decision (Henriques de Gusmão et al., 2018).

Many methods have been incorporated into the field such as monte-carlo simulation as this method is used in cases with high uncertainty such as finance. In this setting, such a method can come in handy as risk assessment of information security is a complex structure with many parameters and a change in one project on its outcome and probability. Therefore, Monte-Carlo can simulate many possible outcomes according to the given parameters.

Another method frequently used within this field of research is Bayesian Networks (Holm et al., 2005; van der Veeken et al., 2016). This method can help with the likelihood estimations of risk assessment. Other methods used are Agent-based Simulation used in studies such as that of Weimer et al. (2016) and Niazi and Hussein (2011), which can simulate different agents (human or other) given their characteristics as well as their interactions, the game theory approach, fuzzy decision models and social network analysis such as has been used in the study of Yin and Chen (2012).

This paper proposed a framework for how to perform a risk analysis for data centers within enterprises by adopting a hybrid risk analysis methodology including both qualitative and quantitative norms. Based on this framework, case studies have been carried out considering three hypothetical companies identifying possible information security risks, and these risks have been reduced to an acceptable level by applying the proposed risk analysis methodology.

## RISK ASSESSMENT METHODS

### Qualitative Methods

### Conflicting Incentives Risk Analysis (CIRA)

CIRA models risks by way of conflicting incentives among stakeholders. The primary focus of this method is the stakeholders' actions and perceived outcomes of these actions. This method is similar to game theory and can be applied to the scenario analysis of human-agent interaction and incentives (Rajbhandari, 2013).

### CORAS

This method is model-based used to conduct a risk analysis. It is a 7-step method for information security risk analysis using its own language built on UML. CORAS models threat scenarios to assets. Although the risk analysis uses qualitative values, quantification can be accomplished (Den Braber et al., 2007).

### CCTA Risk Analysis Management Method (CRAMM)

CRAMM first identifies and evaluates assets subsequently assessing the threats and vulnerabilities towards these assets and lastly combines the risk estimation and assessment into a single analysis. This method also proposes a risk management method (Yazar, 2002).

### OCTAVE Allegro

The primary focus of this method is threat profiling assets. This method identifies and profiles assets, identifies threats and vulnerabilities to these assets and provides risk mitigation according to the threat information. This method incorporates threat trees into its process (Caralli et al., 2007).

## Factor Analysis of Information Risk (FAIR)

This method is based on risk assessment and as the name implies, it has 4 pre-defined factors for every loss and probability calculation. This method also provides a way to obtain quantitative results from the analysis (Freund & Jones, 2014).

## Quantitative Methods

## Information Security Risk Analysis Method (ISRAM)

The ISRAM method is a quantitative method that analyses the security risks of information technologies by way of the manager and employee participation. It also complies with the ISO 177999 and ISO 13335 standards. The input is obtained from a discussion among the risk analysis team. From this discussion, the important factors thought to affect the probability and outcome of a breach are found and each factor is given a weight. The outcome of the analysis is a quantitative value that is calculated using a risk formula (Karabacak & Soğukpınar, 2005).

## RISK ANALYSIS FRAMEWORK

Risk Analysis is a process to identify and manage potential problems that may create a threat to key enterprise activities or projects. For a successful Risk Analysis, it is necessary to identify potential threats that may be encountered first and then to estimate the likelihood of these threats. Once the risks are identified, they are analyzed to identify the qualitative and quantitative impact of the risk on the company so that appropriate steps can be taken to mitigate them.

## Risk Analysis Plan

The risk analysis plan includes these definitions and guidelines:

- Threat Identifications
- Risk Assessment
- Risk Mitigation

## Threat Identifications

A more systematic process involves the use of threats checklists and examining possible threats in the company. Some companies have been developing threat checklists based on their experience from past events. These checklists can help the IT team and managers both to identify specific threats in the checklist and to expand team thinking. The past experience of the company's IT consultants and managers and experts in the industry can be important resources to identify the potential risks.

Identifying the sources of threats by category is another method for exploring potential threats. Some examples of categories for potential threats include the following *Table 1*.

*Table 1. Example Thread Categories*

| Thread Category | Extended Categories |
|---|---|
| Technical | Extended categories Requirements, Technology, Interfaces, Performance, Quality, etc. |
| External | Custom, Contract, Market, Snooker, etc. |
| Organizational | Project Dependencies, Logistics, Resources, Budget, etc. |
| Managerial | Planning, Schedule, Estimation, Controlling, Communication, etc. |

## Risk Assessments

Once potential threats are identified, they are assessed based on the likelihood of occurrence of threat and possible losses accompanying the threat. Not all threats are equal. Some threats are more harmful than others, so the cost of a threat incident can vary greatly. After the threats and their possible effects and the likelihood of occurrence are identified, the impact values of the risks can be calculated by using the following formulas:

*Total Impact Value of Risk = Busines Impact of Asset × (Vulnerability level × Likelihood of Threat)*

*Threat Impact = Vulnerability Level × Likelihood of Threat*

The Business Impact, Likelihood of Threat and Vulnerability Level can be explained as below:

## Business Impact of an Asset

Information Security Asset Classification is one of the key necessities because it lets a company assess the value of its information assets and to assign resources to protect them. The business impact from the loss of Confidentiality, Integrity and Availability of the Information Asset is considered. Business impact depends on asset value. Business Impact of the asset is taken as between 1 and 2 in our study.

## Likelihood of Threat

Some threats are expected to occur than others because an information asset is extensively exposed in the system or the number of potential attacks or incidents is high. The likelihood of a threat shows the probability of a potential threat for a vulnerability. Likely of threat can be derived from annual reports on cyber incident frequency. The likelihood percentages and corresponding likelihood values used in risk calculation is given in *Table 2*. In this study, the most significant 35 vulnerability sources are chosen given in *Table 3*. Also related countermeasures and/or controls for these vulnerability sources given in *Table 4*.

Our methodology depends on choosing a proper threat likelihood value in *Table 2* for each vulnerability source for the risk calculation. In our methodology, five of the threat likelihood for vulnerability controls are chosen as Very High, nine of them are accepted as high, nine of them are selected as Medium, and 12 of them are chosen as Low likelihood.

*Table 2. Classification of threat likelihood*

| Likelihood (Percentage range) | Corresponding Likelihood Value |
|---|---|
| Low likelihood – $\left(0\% < x < 30\%\right)$ | 1 |
| Medium likelihood – $\left(30\% \leq x < 60\%\right)$ | 4 |
| High likelihood – $\left(60\% \leq x < 80\%\right)$ | 8 |
| Very High likelihood – $\left(80\% \leq x \leq 100\%\right)$ | 16 |

## Vulnerability Level

A vulnerability is a weakness that can be exploited by possible threats such as data breaches, unexpected system failures or natural disasters. In this study 35 potential vulnerability sources are given as shown in Table 3. In Table 4, the related controls and/or countermeasures are presented as courses of actions to reduce these vulnerabilities. An adopted course of action corresponds to a vulnerability level between 1 and 5.

## Threat Impact

The Threat Impact indicates how seriously a potential threat affects a specific vulnerability source in the total system risk. Threat Impact is related with both the security controls and the likelihood of a threat. It shows which vulnerability source is much more exposed to threats for the information asset.

The following list shows the degrees of the Threat Impact given in *Figure 1*.

1. Informational
2. Low
3. Medium
4. High
5. Critical

*Figure 1. Threat Impact Degree*

| Percentage | Value | Vulnerability Level 1 | 2 | 3 | 4 | 5 |
|---|---|---|---|---|---|---|
| (1-29)% | 1 | Ideal | Informational | Informational | Low | Medium |
| (30-59)% | 4 | Informational | Informational | Low | Medium | High |
| (60-79)% | 8 | Informational | Low | Medium | High | Critical |
| (80-100)% | 16 | Low | Medium | High | Critical | Critical |

(Likelihood)

Having criteria to determine high impact risks can help narrow the focus on a few critical risks that require mitigation. For example, suppose that high-impact risks could cause $100,000 or more losses. Only a few potential risk events meet these criteria. These are the critical few potential risk events that the IT experts and managers should focus on when developing risk mitigation or management plan. Risk assessment is about developing an understanding of which potential risks have the greatest possibility of occurring and can have the most significant negative impact. In *Table 3* some potential threat sources are given.

After defining the potential threat/vulnerability sources table, the total impact value of risk can be represented by *Figure 2*.

*Figure 2. Total Impact Value of the Risk*

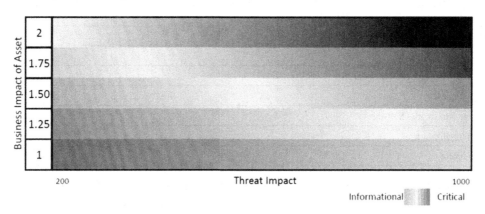

## Risk Mitigation

Risk Mitigation is to take reasonable action to minimize the amount of the possible loss suffered. The ways of managing them are investigated. A risk mitigation plan is developed to reduce the impact of a risk. The risks may be mitigated by the following ways:

- Risk avoidance
- Risk sharing
- Risk reduction
- Risk transfer

Each of these abatement techniques can be an effective means of reducing the risks assessed. The risk mitigation plan covers risk mitigation approaches for all identified risk events and actions that IT professionals and managers will take to mitigate these risks.

## Risk Avoidance

Risk avoidance refers to preferring lower-risk alternatives to high-risk ones. It can usually be costlier.

*Table 3. Potential Vulnerability Sources*

| 1 | Physical Location |
|---|---|
| 2 | UPS Availability |
| 3 | Generator Availability |
| 4 | Environmental ThreatSense Prevention Management System Availability |
| 5 | Internet Connection |
| 6 | Where data is stored |
| 7 | The environment in which backups are stored |
| 8 | Fire Prevention |
| 9 | Maintenance Agreement |
| 10 | Patch Tracking |
| 11 | Can it be replaced easily? (Replaceability) |
| 12 | Network protection (Firewall, IPS, WAF, DDOS, DNS Firewall, …….) |
| 13 | Maintenance Firms Access |
| 14 | Qualification of Authorized Personnel |
| 15 | Backup frequency |
| 16 | Clustering (Hardware / Software) |
| 17 | Server Virtualization |
| 18 | Log Monitoring |
| 19 | Response to Detected Incidents |
| 20 | Network Segmentation |
| 21 | The malicious software detection system |
| 22 | Air Conditioner Availability |
| 23 | Technical team coordination |
| 24 | Insurance for cyber threats |
| 25 | Hardware / Software support team availability (per week) |
| 26 | Cybersecurity Vulnerability Assessment |
| 27 | TEMPEST |
| 28 | Root / Administrator Password Change Frequency |
| 29 | Password Delivery Method |
| 30 | Data Loss Prevention Application |
| 31 | Physical strength of the structure |
| 32 | Compliance with industrial standards |
| 33 | Budget for replacement |
| 34 | Protection of Sensitive Data |
| 35 | Access control of Sensitive Data |

## Risk Sharing

Risk-sharing involves partnering with others to share responsibility for the risk activities. Many organizations often try to reduce political, legal, labor, and other risk types by developing a joint venture with another company.

## Risk Reduction

Risk reduction is the investment to reduce the risk in a company. For example, by making necessary expenditures for a situation that is considered as high risk, the risk can be reduced to an acceptable level.

## Risk Transfer

Risk transfer is a risk reduction method that shifts the risk from the company to another party. The purchase of insurance on certain items is a risk transfer method. The risk is transferred from the company to the insurance company.

# RISK ASSESSMENT CASE STUDY OF ABC HOLDING

In this paper, risk analysis of three companies' data centers is uncovered through case studies.

## ABC Holding

ABC holding is a multinational company that mainly produces construction materials. The holding has investments in paint production, fast food and cleaning sectors. The holding has more than 5,000 employees.

All three companies below belong to ABC Holding. All of them basically have air conditioning systems, UPS, Environmental ThreatSense prevention management system, high-speed symmetrical internet connection, fire prevention, patch tracking system, clustering, and log monitoring in their data centers.

### Company A (Headquarters of ABC Holding)

The headquarters of ABC holding facility has a 30 square meter room in the building which is used as a data center. In addition to the properties listed above, there are power generators, high-speed internet connection with a failover link and SLA agreement upon 99.99% availability, firewall, Intrusion Prevention System (IPS), and network-based attack monitoring facilities in the data center. The data center has 5 cabins and 42 physical servers. The data center door is locked and only 5 people who are responsible for the data center have the physical key. Many services, especially an Enterprise Resource Planning (ERP) system and e-mail and Customer Relationship Management (CRM) applications are hosted in this data center.

## Company B (Branch Office #1 of ABC Holding)

Company B is the branch office of the ABC holding. It is responsible for the middle east region. It operates in a 500 square meter office in a plaza with 25 employees. The information technology infrastructure of the branch office is provided from the 16 square meter data center in the office. The data center has a total of 50 physical server computers in 7 server cabins. In addition to the properties listed above, there are RAID, Firewall, Network-based attacks monitoring system, and DLP software in the data center. The file storing and sharing services, regional information databases, e-mail servers and other service applications are hosted from this data center. The entrance to the data center is made by RFID cards. Only 5 people in charge of servers are allowed to access the data center.

## Company C (Branch Office #2 of ABC Holding)

Company C is another branch office of ABC holding. It is responsible for the Europe region. It operates in a 200 square meter office in a trade center with 10 employees. The information technology infrastructure of the branch office is provided from the 10 square meter data center in the office. The data center has a total of 15 physical server computers in 2 server cabins. In addition to the properties listed above, there are RAID, maintenance agreement, Firewall, WAF, IPS, and Malicious software detection system in the data center. File storing and sharing services, regional information databases, e-mail servers and other service applications are hosted from this data center. Entrance to data centers are made by fingerprint readers. Only 2 people in charge of servers are allowed to access the data center.

## Risk Analysis Plan

In this step, the data centers of these 3 companies are examined by experts who have worked in the IT sector for many years and 35 sources of potential threats are found, as shown in *Table 3*.

## Threat Assessment Case Study

In this section, the identified threats of the three companies are assessed based on the likelihood of occurrence of the threat and possible impact of the threat.

In *Table 4*, threat assessments and calculated risk impact values are shown.

## Risk Mitigation

After determining the value of the identified risks, this step attempts to find ways to manage them. First, the minimum and maximum values of the risk assessment table are calculated and the overall risk ranges according to these values are determined. According to *Table 4*, the minimum impact value of risk is 200, and the maximum is 2000. In *Table 5*, overall risk ranges are demonstrated from informational to critical based on the minimum and the maximum values.

*Table 4. Threat Assessment Table*

| # | Vulnerability Level | Likelihood Value of Threat | Threat Impact | | |
|---|---|---|---|---|---|
| | The Vulnerability Level: 1 (Lowest), 5 (Highest) <br> Likelihood Value of Threat: 1 (Lowest), 16 (Highest) <br> Business Impact: 1 (Lowest), 2 (Highest) <br> Total Impact Value of Risks: max. 2000 points, min. 200 points | | **COMPANY ASSETS** | | |
| | | | A <br> Business Impact of the asset <br> 2 | B <br> Business Impact of the asset <br> 1.75 | C <br> Business Impact of the asset <br> 1.25 |
| **1** | **Physical Location** | | | | |
| | Fingerprint or Retina Reader Entry Section two way authentication (1) Card Entry Section (2) - Key Section / Only Officials can enter (3) - Switching Department / Other staff can enter or Keyless Section (4) - in Outdoor Environment Service (5) | 1 | 3 | 2 | 1 |
| **2** | **UPS Availability** | | | | |
| | More than one UPS (1) Only one UPS (3), Not available (5) | 16 | 16 | 80 | 16 |
| **3** | **Generator** | | | | |
| | Available (1), Not available (5) | 1 | 1 | 5 | 1 |
| **4** | **Environmental ThreatSense prevention management (e.g., long term power failure, pollution, chemicals, liquid leakage, moisture, smoke, heat vs.)** | | | | |
| | Excellent (1) Good (2) Normal (3), Poor (4), Worst (5) | 1 | 2 | 4 | 2 |
| **5** | **Internet Connection** | | | | |
| | SLA and Failover Link (1), SLA or Failover Link (3), Neither SLA nor Failover Link (5) | 1 | 1 | 5 | 3 |
| **6** | **Where data is stored** | | | | |
| | Both SAN/NAS and cloud (1), SAN/NAS or cloud (2), A virtualized server with RAID (3), A virtualized server (4), Server without virtualization (5) | 8 | 40 | 40 | 8 |
| **7** | **Environment in which cold backups are stored** | | | | |
| | Separate Building/Private Section/Cloud/Datacenter (1), Separate building (3), In the same building/Fireproof safe (4), In the same building (5) | 8 | 16 | 40 | 8 |
| **8** | **Fire Prevention** | | | | |
| | Alarm / Auto Fire Suppression (1), Manual extinguishing / Fire extinguisher (3), No Measure (5) | 4 | 12 | 12 | 12 |
| **9** | **Maintenance Agreement** | | | | |
| | Yes (1), No (5) | 1 | 5 | 5 | 1 |
| **10** | **Patch Tracking Is** | | | | |
| | Automatic but try first (1), Automatic (2), Periodic / Warning As it grows (3), Not Followed (5) | 16 | 48 | 80 | 16 |
| **11** | **Can it be replaced easily?** | | | | |
| | Can be purchased with money (1), available for purchase, very expensive (3), information / prestige will be lost even if purchased (5) | 1 | 5 | 5 | 3 |
| **12** | **Network protection (Firewall, IPS, WAF, DDOS, DNS Firewall, .......)** | | | | |
| | 3+ assets (1), 2 assets (3), 1 (5) | 16 | 48 | 80 | 16 |

*continues on following page*

*Table 4. Continued*

| # | Vulnerability Level | Likelihood Value of Threat | Threat Impact A (2) | Threat Impact B (1.75) | Threat Impact C (1.25) |
|---|---|---|---|---|---|
| | The Vulnerability Level: 1 (Lowest), 5 (Highest)<br>Likelihood Value of Threat: 1 (Lowest), 16 (Highest)<br>Business Impact: 1 (Lowest), 2 (Highest)<br>Total Impact Value of Risks: max. 2000 points, min. 200 points | | **COMPANY ASSETS** | | |
| | | | A<br>Business Impact of the asset<br>2 | B<br>Business Impact of the asset<br>1.75 | C<br>Business Impact of the asset<br>1.25 |
| **1** | **Physical Location** | | | | |
| 13 | **Maintenance firms Access with** | | | | |
| | VPN with two way authentication (1), VPN (2), rlogin (3), 3ʳᵈ party desktop sharing apps (4), without VPN (5) | 4 | 12 | 16 | 4 |
| 14 | **Qualification of Authorized Personnel** | | | | |
| | Advanced Level (1), Intermediate Level (3), Not sufficient (5) | 4 | 12 | 16 | 4 |
| 15 | **Backup frequency** | | | | |
| | Daily (1), Weekly (2), Monthly (3), Once in 3 Month s (4), Yearly (5) | 8 | 24 | 32 | 8 |
| 16 | **Clustering (Hardware / Software)** | | | | |
| | Two or more hardware with load balancer active/active (1), Two hardware one active one backup active passive (3), No cluster (5) | 8 | 8 | 40 | 8 |
| 17 | **Server Virtualization** | | | | |
| | Yes (1), No (5) | 16 | 16 | 80 | 16 |
| 18 | **Log Monitoring** | | | | |
| | SIEM and Real-time Alarms (1), Logging and log backup (3), No log monitoring (5) | 4 | 12 | 20 | 4 |
| 19 | **Response to Detected Incidents** | | | | |
| | in Real-time (1) Within 30 mins (2) Within 2 hours (3) Within 6 hours (4), uncertain (5) | 4 | 16 | 20 | 8 |
| 20 | **Network Segmentation** | | | | |
| | Firewall between VLANs (1), Servers in DMZ (2), VLAN (3), Not available (5) | 1 | 1 | 5 | 5 |
| 21 | **Malicious software detection system** | | | | |
| | Both EDR and corporate anti-virus (1), Corporate anti-virus (3), Personal anti-virus (4), Not available (5) | 8 | 40 | 40 | 8 |
| 22 | **Air Conditioner Availability** | | | | |
| | Available with back up (1), Only one (3), Not available (5) | 4 | 4 | 4 | 4 |
| 23 | **Technical team coordination** | | | | |
| | Excellent (1), Good (2), Normal (3), Poor (4), Worst (5) | 4 | 16 | 20 | 4 |
| 24 | **Insurance for cyber threats** | | | | |
| | Available (1), Not available (5) | 4 | 20 | 20 | 4 |
| 25 | **Hardware / Software support team availability (per week)** | | | | |
| | 168 hours (1), 168 - 84 hours (2), 84 - 42 hours (3), 42- 16 (4), <16 (5) | 4 | 12 | 20 | 4 |

*continues on following page*

*Table 4. Continued*

| | | | COMPANY ASSETS | | |
|---|---|---|---|---|---|
| | | | **A** | **B** | **C** |
| The Vulnerability Level: 1 (Lowest), 5 (Highest)<br>Likelihood Value of Threat: 1 (Lowest), 16 (Highest)<br>Business Impact: 1 (Lowest), 2 (Highest)<br>Total Impact Value of Risks: max. 2000 points, min. 200 points | | | **Business Impact of the asset** | **Business Impact of the asset** | **Business Impact of the asset** |
| | | | **2** | **1.75** | **1.25** |
| **#** | **Vulnerability Level** | **Likelihood Value of Threat** | **Threat Impact** | | |
| **1** | **Physical Location** | | | | |
| **26** | **Cybersecurity Vulnerability Assessment** | | | | |
| | Weekly (1), Monthly (2), Yearly (3), Never (5) | 1 | 3 | 5 | 2 |
| **27** | **TEMPEST** | | | | |
| | Available (1), Not available (5) | 1 | 5 | 5 | 1 |
| **28** | **Root / Administrator Password Change Frequency** | | | | |
| | Every day (1), Every week (2), Every 3-4 months (3), Yearly (4), When required or never (5) | 8 | 32 | 40 | 16 |
| **29** | **Password Delivery Method** | | | | |
| | Hard to solve (1), Haphazard, easy to solve password (3), More than one-person, unprotected passwords (5) | 8 | 24 | 40 | 24 |
| **30** | **Data Loss Prevention Application** | | | | |
| | DLP policy and software data classification (1), Data classification software (3), Manual data classification (4), Not available (5) | 8 | 40 | 40 | 40 |
| **31** | **Physical strength of the structure (building)** | | | | |
| | Excellent (1), Good (2), Normal (3), Poor (4), Worst (5) | 1 | 2 | 5 | 3 |
| **32** | **Compliance with industrial standards** | | | | |
| | Yes (1), No (5) | 1 | 1 | 5 | 1 |
| **33** | **Budget for replacement** | | | | |
| | Available (1), Not available (5) | 1 | 5 | 5 | 1 |
| **34** | **Protection of Sensitive Data** | | | | |
| | Tokenization Encryption with key management (1), Tokenization Encryption without key management (3), No Tokenization Encryption (5) | 16 | 48 | 80 | 16 |
| **35** | **Access control of Sensitive Data** | | | | |
| | Both blocking, masking (1), Masking (2), Blocking (3), No access control (5) | 8 | 16 | 40 | 8 |
| | **TOTAL RISK IMPACT VALUE** | | 1132 | 1687 | 350 |

*Table 5. Overall Risk Ranges Table*

| Risk Range | Risk Level |
|---|---|
| (1640-2000) | Critical |
| (1280-1640) | High |
| (920-1280) | Moderate |
| (560-920) | Low |
| (200-560) | Informational |

According to *Table 3*, the total risk impact values of A, B, and C companies are 1132, 1687, 350 respectively. This means that the risk range of company A is moderate, company B is critical while company C is informational. In the next step, it is necessary to look at what needs to be done to reduce the risk range of companies A and B to an acceptable range (low or informational). The following ways can be used to reduce risks:

- Eliminating the risk source
- Lowering the likelihood of risk occurrence
- Lowering the impact of the risk

In the specified case, eliminating the risk source and lowering the likelihood of the risk occurrence are not possible, the third way should be used. As the likelihood of the threat, which is planned to be reduced, increases, the impact on the overall risk value of the company also increases. *Table 5* shows the threat assessments and re-calculated risk impact values of the three companies after the risk mitigation process has been conducted.

As shown in *Table 6*, the overall risk impact values of companies A and B have been reduced to a low level and the risk range of company C has also decreased.

## CONCLUSION

In this paper, three hypothetical companies have been taken into consideration by identifying their possible information security risks and these risks have been reduced to an acceptable level through deploying constructed risk analysis methodology. The proposed method is a hybrid method, which is a combination of qualitative and quantitative parts. In the quantitative part, survey results and risk tables were used to analyze information security risks. In this manner, the proposed method is simple and does not include mathematical procedures or software tools. In the qualitative part, subjective evaluations are made based on IT experts' experiences in this research area.

The main advantage of the proposed framework is to provide guidance for companies that will perform information security risk analysis for their data centers. Furthermore, this study contributes to the existing literature on how to perform risk analysis for data centers. The framework proposes an information risk analysis within an organizational context and from a business-oriented perspective. In this manner, the framework has gratified both organizational and technical requirements regarding trends in the recent business landscape.

*Table 6. Threat Assessment Table (after mitigation)*

| # | Vulnerability Level | Likelihood Value of Threat | COMPANY ASSETS | | |
|---|---|---|---|---|---|
| | The Vulnerability Level: 1 (Lowest), 5 (Highest)<br>Likelihood Value of Threat: 1 (Lowest), 16 (Highest)<br>Business Impact: 1 (Lowest), 2 (Highest)<br>Total Impact Value of Risks: max. 2000 points, min. 200 points | | A | B | C |
| | | | Business Impact of the asset | Business Impact of the asset | Business Impact of the asset |
| | | | 2 | 1.75 | 1.25 |
| | | Likelihood Value of Threat | Threat Impacts | | |
| **1** | **Physical Location** | | | | |
| | Fingerprint or Retina Reader Entry Section two way authentication (1) Card Entry Section (2) - Key Section / Only Officials can enter (3) - Switching Department / Other staff can enter or Keyless Section (4) - in Outdoor Environment Service (5) | 1 | 3 | 2 | 1 |
| **2** | **UPS Availability** | | | | |
| | More than one UPS (1) Only one UPS (3), Not available (5) | 16 | 16 | **16*** | 16 |
| **3** | **Generator** | | | | |
| | Available (1), Not available (5) | 1 | 1 | 5 | 1 |
| **4** | **Environmental ThreatSense prevention management (e.g., long term power failure, pollution, chemicals, liquid leakage, moisture, smoke, heat vs.)** | | | | |
| | Excellent (1) Good (2) Normal (3), Poor (4), Worst (5) | 1 | 2 | 4 | 2 |
| **5** | **Internet Connection** | | | | |
| | SLA and Failover Link (1), SLA or Failover Link (3), Neither SLA nor Failover Link (5) | 1 | 1 | 5 | 3 |
| **6** | **Where data is stored** | | | | |
| | Both SAN/NAS and cloud (1), SAN/NAS or cloud (2), A virtualized server with RAID (3), A virtualized server (4), Server without virtualization (5) | 8 | **8*** | **8*** | 8 |
| **7** | **Environment in which cold backups are stored** | | | | |
| | Separate Building/Private Section/Cloud/Datacenter (1), Separate building (3), In the same building/Fireproof safe (4), In the same building (5) | 8 | **8*** | **8*** | 8 |
| **8** | **Fire Prevention** | | | | |
| | Alarm / Auto Fire Suppression (1), Manual extinguishing / Fire extinguisher (3), No Measure (5) | 4 | 12 | 12 | 12 |
| **9** | **Maintenance Agreement** | | | | |
| | Yes (1), No (5) | 1 | 5 | 5 | 1 |
| **10** | **Patch Tracking Is** | | | | |
| | Automatic but try first (1), Automatic (2), Periodic / Warning As it grows (3), Not Followed (5) | 16 | **16*** | **16*** | 16 |
| **11** | **Can it be replaced easily?** | | | | |
| | Can be purchased with money (1), available for purchase, very expensive (3), information / prestige will be lost even if purchased (5) | 1 | 5 | 5 | 3 |
| **12** | **Network protection (Firewall, IPS, WAF, DDOS, DNS Firewall, .......)** | | | | |
| | 3+ assets (1), 2 assets (3), 1 (5) | 16 | **16*** | **16*** | 16 |

*continues on following page*

## Table 4. Continued

| | The Vulnerability Level: 1 (Lowest), 5 (Highest)<br>Likelihood Value of Threat: 1 (Lowest), 16 (Highest)<br>Business Impact: 1 (Lowest), 2 (Highest)<br>Total Impact Value of Risks: max. 2000 points, min. 200 points | | COMPANY ASSETS | | |
| | | | A | B | C |
| | | | Business Impact of the asset | Business Impact of the asset | Business Impact of the asset |
| | | | 2 | 1.75 | 1.25 |
| # | Vulnerability Level | Likelihood Value of Threat | Threat Impacts | | |
| 1 | **Physical Location** | | | | |
| 13 | **Maintenance firms Access with** | | | | |
| | VPN with two way authentication (1), VPN (2), rlogin (3), 3rd party desktop sharing apps (4), without VPN (5) | 4 | 12 | 16 | 4 |
| 14 | **Qualification of Authorized Personnel** | | | | |
| | Advanced Level (1), Intermediate Level (3), Not sufficient (5) | 4 | 12 | 16 | 4 |
| 15 | **Backup frequency** | | | | |
| | Daily (1), Weekly (2), Monthly (3), Once in 3 Month s (4), Yearly (5) | 8 | 8* | 8* | 8 |
| 16 | **Clustering (Hardware / Software)** | | | | |
| | Two or more hardware with load balancer active/active (1), Two hardware one active one backup active passive (3), No cluster (5) | 8 | 8 | 8* | 8 |
| 17 | **Server Virtualization** | | | | |
| | Yes (1), No (5) | 16 | 16 | 16* | 16 |
| 18 | **Log Monitoring** | | | | |
| | SIEM and Real-time Alarms (1), Logging and log backup (3), No log monitoring (5) | 4 | 12 | 20 | 4 |
| 19 | **Response to Detected Incidents** | | | | |
| | in Real-time (1) Within 30 mins (2) Within 2 hours (3) Within 6 hours (4), uncertain (5) | 4 | 16 | 20 | 8 |
| 20 | **Network Segmentation** | | | | |
| | Firewall between VLANs (1), Servers in DMZ (2), VLAN (3), Not available (5) | 1 | 1 | 5 | 5 |
| 21 | **Malicious software detection system** | | | | |
| | Both EDR and corporate anti-virus (1), Corporate anti-virus (3), Personal anti-virus (4), Not available (5) | 8 | 8* | 8* | 8 |
| 22 | **Air Conditioner Availability** | | | | |
| | Available with back up (1), Only one (3), Not available (5) | 4 | 4 | 4 | 4 |
| 23 | **Technical team coordination** | | | | |
| | Excellent (1), Good (2), Normal (3), Poor (4), Worst (5) | 4 | 16 | 20 | 4 |
| 24` | **Insurance for cyber threats** | | | | |
| | Available (1), Not available (5) | 4 | 20 | 20 | 4 |
| 25 | **Hardware / Software support team availability (per week)** | | | | |
| | 168 hours (1), 168 - 84 hours (2), 84 - 42 hours (3), 42- 16 (4), <16 (5) | 4 | 12 | 20 | 4 |

*continues on following page*

*Table 4. Continued*

| | | | COMPANY ASSETS | | |
|---|---|---|---|---|---|
| | | | A | B | C |
| | The Vulnerability Level: 1 (Lowest), 5 (Highest)<br>Likelihood Value of Threat: 1 (Lowest), 16 (Highest)<br>Business Impact: 1 (Lowest), 2 (Highest)<br>Total Impact Value of Risks: max. 2000 points, min. 200 points | | Business Impact of the asset | Business Impact of the asset | Business Impact of the asset |
| | | | 2 | 1.75 | 1.25 |
| # | Vulnerability Level | Likelihood Value of Threat | Threat Impacts | | |
| 1 | Physical Location | | | | |
| 26 | Cybersecurity Vulnerability Assessment | | | | |
| | Weekly (1), Monthly (2), Yearly (3), Never (5) | 1 | 3 | 5 | 2 |
| 27 | TEMPEST | | | | |
| | Available (1), Not available (5) | 1 | 5 | 5 | 1 |
| 28 | Root / Administrator Password Change Frequency | | | | |
| | Every day (1), Every week (2), Every 3-4 months (3), Yearly (4), When required or never (5) | 8 | 8* | 8* | 8* |
| 29 | Password Delivery Method | | | | |
| | Hard to solve (1), Haphazard, easy to solve password (3), More than one-person, unprotected passwords (5) | 8 | 8* | 8* | 8* |
| 30 | Data Loss Prevention Application | | | | |
| | DLP policy and software data classification (1), Data classification software (3), Manual data classification (4), Not available (5) | 8 | 8* | 8* | 8* |
| 31 | Physical strength of the structure (building) | | | | |
| | Excellent (1), Good (2), Normal (3), Poor (4), Worst (5) | 1 | 2 | 5 | 3 |
| 32 | Compliance with industrial standards | | | | |
| | Yes (1), No (5) | 1 | 1 | 5 | 1 |
| 33 | Budget for replacement | | | | |
| | Available (1), Not available (5) | 1 | 5 | 5 | 1 |
| 34 | Protection of Sensitive Data | | | | |
| | Tokenization Encryption with key management (1), Tokenization Encryption without key management (3), No Tokenization Encryption (5) | 16 | 16* | 16* | 16 |
| 35 | Access control of Sensitive Data | | | | |
| | Both blocking, masking (1), Masking (2), Blocking (3), No access control (5) | 8 | 8* | 8* | 8 |
| | TOTAL RISK IMPACT VALUE | | 620 | 679 | 280 |
| *indicates mitigated threats and re-calculated impact values of risks | | | | | |

## LIMITATIONS

The data and information provided in this study were created by experts working in the IT industry for many years. Each industry can have its own data security challenges and risks. For this reason, it is aimed to present an inclusive case study as much as possible. Also, the mitigation step did not take cost into account, therefore mitigation strategies may change to incorporate cost into the equation.

## REFERENCES

Alter, S., & Sherer, S. A. (2004). A General, But Readily Adaptable Model of Information System Risk. *Communications of the Association for Information Systems, 14*(1). Advance online publication. doi:10.17705/1CAIS.01401

Biery, K. J. (2006). Aligning an information risk management approach to BS 7799-3:2005. SANS Reading Room.

Bjerga, T., & Aven, T. (2016). Some perspectives on risk management: A security case study from the oil and gas industry. *Proceedings of the Institution of Mechanical Engineers, Part O: Journal of Risk and Reliability, 230*(5), 512–520. doi:10.1177/1748006X16654589

Caralli, R. A., Stevens, J. F., Young, L. R., & Wilson, W. R. (2007). *Introducing octave allegro: Improving the information security risk assessment process* (No. CMU/SEI-2007-TR-012).

Den Braber, F., Hogganvik, I., Lund, M. S., Stølen, K., & Vraalsen, F. (2007). Model-based security analysis in seven steps—A guided tour to the CORAS method. *BT Technology Journal, 25*(1), 101–117. doi:10.100710550-007-0013-9

Freund, J., & Jones, J. (2014). *Measuring and managing information risk: a FAIR approach*. Butterworth-Heinemann.

Ghazouani, M., Faris, S., Medromi, H., & Sayouti, A. (2014). Information Security Risk Assessment A Practical Approach with a Mathematical Formulation of Risk. *International Journal of Computers and Applications, 103*(8), 36–42. doi:10.5120/18097-9155

Henriques de Gusmão, A. P., Mendonça Silva, M., Poleto, T., Camara e Silva, L., & Cabral Seixas Costa, A. P. (2018). Cybersecurity risk analysis model using fault tree analysis and fuzzy decision theory. *International Journal of Information Management, 43*, 248–260. doi:10.1016/j.ijinfomgt.2018.08.008

Hiles, A. (2002). *Enterprise Risk Assessment and Business Impact Analysis: Best Practices*. Rothstein Associates Inc.

Holm, H., Korman, M., & Ekstedt, M. (2015). A bayesian network model for likelihood estimations of acquirement of critical software vulnerabilities and exploits. *Information and Software Technology, 58*, 304–318. doi:10.1016/j.infsof.2014.07.001

ISO/IEC 27005:2008, "Information technology -- Security techniques-Information security risk management

Karabacak, B., & Sogukpinar, I. (2005). ISRAM: Information security risk analysis method. *Computers & Security*, *24*(2), 147–159. doi:10.1016/j.cose.2004.07.004

Khambhammettu, H., Boulares, S., Adi, K., & Logrippo, L. (2013). A framework for risk assessment in access control systems. *Computers and Security, 39*(A), 86–103.

Niazi, M. A., & Hussain, A. (2011). A novel agent-based simulation framework for sensing in complex adaptive environments. *IEEE Sensors Journal*, *11*(2), 404–412. doi:10.1109/JSEN.2010.2068044

Paté-Cornell, M. E., Kuypers, M., Smith, M., & Keller, P. (2018). Cyber Risk Management for Critical Infrastructure: A Risk Analysis Model and Three Case Studies. *Risk Analysis*, *38*(2), 226–241. doi:10.1111/risa.12844 PMID:28679022

Patel, S. C., Graham, J. H., & Ralston, P. A. S. (2008). Quantitatively assessing the vulnerability of critical information systems: A new method for evaluating security enhancements. *International Journal of Information Management*, *28*(6), 483–491. doi:10.1016/j.ijinfomgt.2008.01.009

Păunescu, C., Popescu, M. C., & Blid, L. (2018). Business impact analysis for business continuity: Evidence from Romanian enterprises on critical functions. *Management and Marketing*, *13*(3), 1035–1050. doi:10.2478/mmcks-2018-0021

Rainer, R. K. Jr, Snyder, C. A., & Carr, H. H. (1991). Risk analysis for information technology. *Journal of Management Information Systems*, *8*(1), 129–147. doi:10.1080/07421222.1991.11517914

Rajbhandari, L. (2013). *Risk Analysis Using "Conflicting Incentives" as an alternative notion of Risk* (Ph.D. thesis). Gjøvik University College.

Roldán-Molina, G., Almache-Cueva, M., Silva-Rabadão, C., Yevseyeva, I., & Basto-Fernandes, V. (2017). A Comparison of Cybersecurity Risk Analysis Tools. *Procedia Computer Science*, *121*, 568–575. doi:10.1016/j.procs.2017.11.075

Schmittling, R. A. M. (2010). Performing a Security Risk Assessment. *ISACA Journal*, *1*, 1–7.

Sikdar, P. (2017). Practitioner's Guide to Business Impact Analysis. Practitioner's Guide to Business Impact Analysis. doi:10.1201/9781315187884

Sun, L., Srivastava, R. P., & Mock, T. J. (2006). An information systems security risk assessment model under the Dempster-Shafer theory of belief functions. *Journal of Management Information Systems*, *22*(4), 109–142. doi:10.2753/MIS0742-1222220405

Van der Veeken, P., Van Schooten, S., Shinde, R., Dunnewind, M., & van den Berg, J. (2016, December). Applying Bayesian game theory to analyse cyber risks of bank transaction systems. In *2016 International Conference on Computing, Analytics and Security Trends (CAST)* (pp. 84-89). IEEE. 10.1109/CAST.2016.7914945

Weimer, C. W., Miller, J. O., & Hill, R. R. (2016, December). Agent-based modeling: An introduction and primer. In *Winter Simulation Conference (WSC)*, (pp. 65-79). IEEE.

Yazar, Z. (2002). A qualitative risk analysis and management tool–CRAMM. *SANS InfoSec Reading Room White Paper, 11*, 12-32.

Yin, Q., & Chen, Q. (2012, January). A Social Network Analysis Platform for Organizational Risk Analysis—ORA. In *2012 Second International Conference on Intelligent System Design and Engineering Application (ISDEA)*, (pp. 760-763). IEEE. 10.1109/ISdea.2012.546

## KEY TERMS AND DEFINITIONS

**Residual Risk:** It is the risk that cannot be reduced to the acceptable level after risk processing.

**Risk:** It is a measure of how open assets are against potential threats.

**Risk Analysis:** Evaluation of possible threats and possible risks.

**Risk Processing:** As a result of risk analysis, it is a package/plan of measures to reduce the risks to an acceptable level and maintain this level.

**Threat:** Potential hazard that can partially or totally interrupt the operation of systems, processes and other information system components.

**Threat Impact:** The threat Impact indicates how seriously a potential threat affects a vulnerability in the system.

**Vulnerability:** Weakness leading to a threat.

*Previously published in Advanced Models and Tools for Effective Decision Making Under Uncertainty and Risk Contexts; pages 236-253, copyright year 2021 by Business Science Reference (an imprint of IGI Global).*

# Chapter 5
# The CyberSecurity Audit Model (CSAM)

**Regner Sabillon**
*Universitat Oberta de Catalunya, Spain*

## ABSTRACT

*This chapter presents the outcome of two empirical research studies that assess the implementation and validation of the cybersecurity audit model (CSAM), designed as a multiple-case study in two different Canadian higher education institution. CSAM can be applied for undertaking cybersecurity audits in any organization or nation state in order to evaluate and measure the cybersecurity assurance, maturity, and cyber readiness. The architecture of CSAM is explained in central sections. CSAM has been examined, implemented, and established under three research scenarios: (1) cybersecurity audit of all model domains, (2) cybersecurity audit of numerous domains, and (3) a single cybersecurity domain audit. The chapter concludes by showing how the implementation of the model permits one to report relevant information for future decision making in order to correct cybersecurity weaknesses or to improve cybersecurity domains and controls; thus, the model can be implemented and sufficiently tested at any organization.*

## INTRODUCTION

Organizations try to protect cyber assets and put into effect cybersecurity measures and programs, however in spite of this continuing effort it is far unavoidable to avert cybersecurity breaches and cyberattacks.

A recent study from Hiscox (2017) highlights that prevalence of cyberattacks is high in British, American and German Companies from unique industries and sectors together with technology, financial, enterprise services, manufacturing, professional services, retail, construction, transport, food and drinks, healthcare, leisure, telecommunication, real estate, media, energy and pharmaceutical and starting from small organizations to large corporations; 57% of the corporations have experienced as a minimum one and 42% of those corporations have dealt with two or more cyberattacks within a year. Most businesses (62%) usually get over a cyber incident in much less than 24 hours; a quarter (26%) usually takes less than an hour to get back to business while some groups spend days or more to recover

DOI: 10.4018/978-1-6684-3698-1.ch005

from a cyberattack. A current trend covers greater spending in cybersecurity budgets, companies that already experienced a cyberattack are willing to put money into acquiring prevention technologies (24%) and detection technologies (23%). Smaller organizations incur with higher economic effect because of cyberattacks in comparison with larger corporations, most companies that participated in this study are taken into consideration as "cyber novices" in relation with the cyber readiness test (Hiscox, 2017) – the gap analysis indicates that investing money or having huge cybersecurity budgets do not help corporations to attain a "Cyber Experts" level. On the contrary, a major financial outlay isn't always the solution but enforcing other strategy and process measures like upper management involvement, cybersecurity awareness training, systematic monitoring and documentation. The costs of a cyberattack vary by geographic zones, for instance with corporations with more than 1,000 employees the financial impact will cost $ 53,131 in Germany, $ 84,045 in the UK and $ 102,314 in the USA.

Meulen et al. (2015) indicate that stakeholders need to comprehend the threat landscape in order to prepare for potential cyberattacks and at the same time to enforce defensive measures for protection. They summarized that there are not unique standards for classifying cyberthreats, the existing evidence suggests that is uncertain when it comes to defining threat assessments; they identified states, cyber-criminals and hacktivists as the main threat actors and they also perceived cyberthreats linked to access, disclosure, manipulation of information, obliteration and denial of service.

In spite of enough cybersecurity measures, employees continue to be the weakest link in cybersecurity. Personnel are directly connected to financial losses related to data breaches and cybersecurity incidents (Pendergast, 2016).

IT audits are being redefined to include cybersecurity however there aren't clear guidelines or unison to which areas, sub-areas, domains or sub-domains to incorporate in a cybersecurity audit. The CyberSecurity Audit Model (CSAM) was designed to address the limitations and inexistence of cybersecurity controls to handle comprehensive cybersecurity or domain-specific cybersecurity audits. An comprehensive cybersecurity audit model is needed to support the information security function. Furthermore, a model to deliver cybersecurity awareness training based on company roles is also necessary to change the traditional awareness programs.

We present the results of two empirical studies that assessed the implementation and validation of the CSAM through extensive cybersecurity audits. These studies were motivated by the lack of universal guidelines to conduct comprehensive cybersecurity audits and the existing weaknesses of general programs to deliver cybersecurity awareness training.

Our multi-case studies were conducted to answer the following questions:

How can we evaluate and measure the cybersecurity assurance, maturity and cyber readiness in any organization or Nation State?

Why it is necessary to increase cyber awareness at the organizational and personal levels?

## BACKGROUND

This chapter look into an innovative model for creating, developing, planning, delivering and maintaining a CyberSecurity Audit (CSA) methodology or program that was corroborated in two different Canadian Higher Education organizations under unrelated projects and schedules. The implementations in both organizations were part of a multi-case study research along with the Cybersecurity Awareness TRAining Model (CATRAM); another innovative model to conduct and deliver cybersecurity awareness training.

The CyberSecurity Audit Model (CSAM) was conceived distinctively to conduct partial or complete cybersecurity audits classified by a specific domain, selected domains or the full audit of all domains within any organization. CSAM was designed to be functional for any type of organization, no matter the size nor the industry or sector where the organization is positioned.

In this chapter, CSAM was endorsed as the foundational model of our target organizations. These organizations did not have any policy in place for cybersecurity audits and CSAM was validated to introduce cybersecurity audits for their security domains and existing security controls. These days, CSAM is being adopted to develop the future cybersecurity audit programs for these higher education organizations.

## LITERATURE REVIEW

Whenever a team of auditors might be participating in an IT, Information Security or compliance audit, there will be constant phases like planning, defining objectives and scope, clarifying engagement boundaries, running the audit, confirming evidence, assessing risks, presenting the audit findings and book follow up tasks. Planning any cybersecurity assessment is not different than any type of audit but can take countless resources due to the complexity of many cybersecurity domains.

ISACA points out the relevance of incorporating security controls as part of a complete framework and strategy, cyber assurance might be accomplished by management reviews, cyber risk assessments and cybersecurity controls audits. Hollingsworth recapitulated from his cybersecurity audit study, that the integral audit process produced evidence and remediation requirements to develop better cybersecurity controls; the involved audit team was able to remediate system documentation and nonconformities during the pre-audit phase and he concluded that upper management support and attention to cybersecurity audits turn into a standard for organizations.

Cybersecurity is located as the premier technology challenge for Information Technology (IT) audit managers and professionals; thus, companies should consider reviewing on a continuously their IT audit plans to address the cybersecurity threats and emerging technologies (Protiviti, 2017a). This research shows that managing cybersecurity audits are more important in certain geographic areas than others – North America (70%), Europe (58%), Latin America (56%), Oceania (53%), Middle East (50%), Africa (49%) and Asia (35%). However, North America is the only area where overseeing cybersecurity audits are within the Top 3 priorities when it comes to auditing. It is also revealed several imperative key considerations for directors including culture, competitiveness, compliance and cybersecurity (Protiviti, 2017b). Cybersecurity internal audits can support board of directors and senior management in these particular ways:

Evaluation of corporate processes to measure the attention to high-value information and systems

More effectively awareness of the cyberthreat landscape

Appraisal of the organizational cyber incident response readiness

The significance of conducting internal audits to verify the cybersecurity control's effectiveness, cyber risk management is based on roles and responsibilities (Deloitte, 2015):

First Line of defense: Business and Information Technology operations

Second Line of defense: Information and technology risk management

Third Line of defense: In-house audits

Deloitte's cybersecurity framework entitles that a few cybersecurity domains may be assessed through current IT audits, however the majority of cyber capabilities are not assessed by using the internal audits' scope. This framework includes risk and compliance management, development cycle, security program, third-party vendor management, information/asset control, access control, threat/vulnerability control, data control and protection, risk analytics, crisis control and resiliency, safety operation and security awareness and training. Moreover, Deloitte's framework is aligned with industry frameworks just like the National Institute of Standards and Technology (NIST), Information Technology Infrastructure Library (ITIL), Committee of Sponsoring Organizations of the Treadway Commission (COSO) and International Organization for Standardization (ISO).

ISACA (2016) designed an audit and assurance program primarily based on the NIST Cybersecurity Framework (CST) for comparing cybersecurity controls. This sort of audit program will review configuration management, incident management processes, networks, servers, awareness, enterprise continuity management, information security, governance administration practices for any company, its departments and relationships with third party vendors. The converting nature of cyberthreats demands businesses to develop cyber resilience and versatility as far as possible, by imposing cyber-by-layout in all their initiatives together with continuous assessments and cyber risks re-evaluations (ICAEW, 2016). Cybersecurity training and awareness are very important, but cybersecurity/InfoSec practices should be a component of any organizational culture.

A cybersecurity survey conducted by means of Deloitte and the National Association of State Chief Information Officers (NASCIO) highlights that the most important cybersecurity tasks for 2016 had been training and awareness, cybersecurity monitoring, strategy, governance, cybersecurity operations, risk assessments, cybersecurity metrics, regulatory and legislative compliance and access management. Additionally, cybersecurity budgets went through an increase from 37% in 2014 to 48% in 2016 respectively for the cybersecurity audit costs and the recurrent evaluation activities had been code reviews, cyber risk assessments, penetration testing, application safety vulnerability testing, cyberthreat intelligence analytics, privacy impact assessments, wargaming, business continuity exercises, disaster recovery exercises, protection tracking and operations center tasks (Deloitte University Press, 2016). The 2017 version covers vital cybersecurity adoptions together with frameworks based on countrywide standards, awareness education, InfoSec culture, strategic plans, metrics to measure applications and cyber insurance (NASCIO, 2017).

For example, one global assignment in reviewing cybersecurity preparedness is the absence of standards to execute cybersecurity audits (Ross, 2015). Simple, precise and substantial approaches need to be targeted to deal with measures against cyberattacks, to make clear cybersecurity audit processes, to affirm that sensitive information is encrypted and to ensure patch management best practices.

Furthermore, there aren't any metrics to determine cybersecurity audits and the cybersecurity audit topic is badly understood as it renews really quickly. In order to cover a meaningful scope for planning a cybersecurity audit, the auditors must include all relevant areas in any organization; these areas are customer operations, finance, human resources, IT systems and applications, legal, purchasing, regulatory affairs, physical security and all applicable third parties that have relationships with the business (Khan, 2016).

Audit reporting isn't always about generating more than one report about information security weaknesses with out recommending the adequate solutions (Messier, 2016). The IT auditor team does not forget tips as a mandatory section when drafting the final audit report, but it is really useful that consists of corrective, preventive or immediate actions for the subsequent audit or a follow-up audit. The intention of cybersecurity audits should grasp on providing real evaluations of cybersecurity controls, standards, frameworks, procedures, strategies and recommendations to management.

Leidos (2017) designed the "Cyber Defense Maturity Evaluation (CDME)" that evaluates 13 key process areas and these areas must reach an *"ideal state/level 4.0"* for the domains:

- Organization and Mission
- Executive Support
- Architecture and Engineering
- Security Technology
- Enterprise User Awareness
- Enterprise Visibility and Monitoring
- Malware Analysis
- Response and Mitigations
- Analysis Process and Skills
- Defender Operations
- Intelligence Management
- Metrics and Measuring Success
- Supporting Programs

This comprehensive enterprise defense framework was conceived on "how" approach instead of focusing on the basic "what", the framework itself is helping organizations to defend, sustain and outpace evolving cyber attackers. Leidos (2017) also enabled the Core Security Framework (CSF) assessment that evaluates cybersecurity implementations including 5 functions and 22 categories based on the Commerce Department's National Institute of Standards and Technology (NIST) security framework. The CSF utilizes metrics for risk management principles and best practices for cybersecurity.

Conducive to cyber readiness studies, Hathaway et al. (2015) established the leading comprehensive methodology that has been applied to 125 countries and available in 6 languages; Arabic, Chinese, English, French, Russian, and Spanish. Furthermore, the authors developed unique Cyber Readiness Index (CRI) country profiles for France, Germany, India, Italy, Japan, the Netherlands, Saudi Arabia, United Kingdom and United States of America. The Cyber Readiness Index 1.0 was originally disseminated in November 2013 and is now superseded by The Cyber Readiness Index 2.0 edition of November 2015. This methodology stresses that *"No country is cyber ready"* and evaluates the nation's level of preparedness to deal with cyber risks, the identification of critical areas related to the cyber domain and the focus to implement certain initiatives to protect their economy and connectivity in terms of cybersecurity.

In terms of financial and cybersecurity audits, financial auditors have been engaged for many years by assessing IT controls since 1974 (SAS3), 1982 (SAS 44), 1992 (SAS70), 1997 (WebTrust), 1999 (SysTrust), 2003 (Trust Services Principles & Criteria - TSPC), 2010 (SSAE 16), 2011 (SOC1), 2016 (SSAE 18) and most recently in 2017; following the criteria from the Cybersecurity Risk Management Reporting Framework and Examination. The Center for Audit Quality recommends these cybersecurity frameworks as foundations to implement and assess a corporate cybersecurity risk management program including NIST Framework for improving critical infrastructure cybersecurity, ISO/IEC 27001/27002, US Securities and Exchange Commision (SEC) Cybersecurity Guidelines and Trust Services Criteria (TSC), (CAQ, 2017).

Moreover, the American Institute of Certified Public Accountants (AICPA) developed its own cybersecurity framework – the Cybersecurity Reporting Framework is an entity-level cybersecurity risk management framework focused towards upper management's description, upper management's assertion and the opinions of Certified Public Accountants (CPAs).

## THE CYBERSECURITY AUDIT MODEL (CSAM)

The CyberSecurity Audit Model (CSAM) is a new exhaustive model that encloses the optimal assurance assessment of cybersecurity in any organization and it can verify specific guidelines for Nation States that are planning to implement a National Cybersecurity Strategy (NCS) or want to evaluate the effectiveness of its National Cybersecurity Strategy or Policy already in place. The CSAM can be implemented to conduct internal or external cybersecurity audits, this model can be used to perform single cybersecurity audits or can be part of any corporate audit program to improve cybersecurity controls. Any audit team has either the options to perform a full audit for all cybersecurity domains or by selecting specific domains to audit certain areas that need control verification and hardening. The CSAM has 18 domains; domain 1 is specific for Nation States and domains 2-18 can be implemented at any organization. The organization can be any small, medium or large enterprise, the model is also applicable to any Non-Profit Organization (NPO).

The aim of this model is to introduce a cybersecurity audit model that includes all functional areas, in order to guarantee an effective cybersecurity assurance, maturity and cyber readiness in any organization or any Nation State that is auditing its National Cybersecurity Strategy (NCS). This model was envisioned as a seamless and integrated cybersecurity audit model to assess and measure the level of cybersecurity maturity and cyber readiness in any type of organization, no matter in what industry or sector the organization is positioned. Moreover, by adding guidelines assessment for the integration of a national cybersecurity policy, program or strategy at the country level. Many cybersecurity frameworks are mostly oriented towards a specific industry like the *"PCI DSS"* for credit card security, the *"NERC CIP Cyber Security"* for the bulk power system or the *"NIST Cybersecurity Framework"* for protecting national critical infrastructure. But, all the existing frameworks do not provide a one-size fits all for planning and conducting cybersecurity audits. The necessity to mapping against specific cybersecurity frameworks is because of regulatory requirements, to satisfy the demands of industry regulators, to comply with internal or external audits, to satisfy business purposes and customer requirements or simply by improving the enterprise cybersecurity strategy.

The CyberSecurity Audit Model (CSAM) contains overview, resources, 18 domains, 26 sub-domains, 87 checklists, 169 controls, 429 sub-controls, 80 guideline assessment and an evaluation scorecard shown in Figure 1.

## Overview

This section introduces the model organization, the working methodology and the possible options for implementation.

*Figure 1. The CyberSecurity Audit Model (CSAM)*

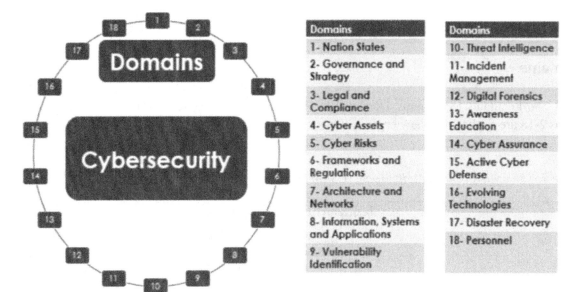

## Resources

This component provides links to additional resources to help understanding some of the cybersecurity topics:

Cybersecurity: NIST Computer Security Resource Center, Financial Industry Regulatory Authority (FINRA) cybersecurity practices and Homeland Security cybersecurity.

National Cybersecurity Strategy (NCS): North Atlantic Treaty Organization (NATO) cybersecurity strategy, European Union Agency for Network and Information Security (ENISA) cybersecurity strategy and Organisation for Economic Co-operation and Development (OECD) comparative analysis of national cybersecurity strategies.

Governance: PricewaterhouseCoopers Board cybersecurity governance and MITRE cybersecurity governance.

Cyber Assets: NERC critical cyber assets.

Frameworks: Foresite common cybersecurity frameworks, United States Computer Emergency Readiness Team (US-CERT) framework and ISACA's implementing the NIST cybersecurity framework.

Architecture: Trusted Computer Group (TCG) architect's guide and US Department of Energy's IT security architecture.

Vulnerability Management: SANS vulnerability assessment and Homeland Security vulnerability assessment and management.

Cyber Threat Intelligence: SANS – Who's using cyberthreat intelligence and how?

Incident Response: Computer Security Incident Response Team (CSIRT) frequent asked questions.

Digital Forensics: SANS forensics whitepapers.

Awareness: National Cyber Security Alliance – Stay safe online and PCI DSS -Best practices for implementing security awareness program.

Cyber Defense: SANS- The sliding scale of cybersecurity.

Disaster Recovery: Financial Executives International (FEI) Canada – Cybersecurity and business continuity.

Personnel: Kaspersky – Top 10 tips for educating employees about cybersecurity.

## Domains

The CSAM contains 18 domains. Domain 1 has been designed specifically for Nations States and domains 2-18 are applicable to any organization as illustrated in Table 1.

*Table 1. The CyberSecurity Audit Model (CSAM) domains*

| The CyberSecurity Audit Model (CSAM) domains | |
|---|---|
| | **Domains** |
| **The CyberSecurity Audit Model (CSAM)** | 1. Nation States<br>2. Governance and Strategy<br>3. Legal and Compliance<br>4. Cyber Assets<br>5. Cyber Risks<br>6. Frameworks and Regulations<br>7. Architecture and Networks<br>8. Information, Systems and Applications<br>9. Vulnerability Identification<br>10. Threat Intelligence<br>11. Incident Management<br>12. Digital Forensics<br>13. Awareness Education<br>14. Cyber Assurance<br>15. Active Cyber Defense<br>16. Evolving Technologies<br>17. Disaster Recovery<br>18. Personnel |

## Sub-Domains

All domains have at least one sub-domain but in certain cases there might be several sub-domains per domain.

The sub-domains are:

- Cyberspace
- Governance
- Strategy
- Legal and Compliance
- Cyber Asset Management
- Cyber Risks
- Frameworks and Regulations
- Architecture
- Networks

- Information
- Systems
- Applications
- Vulnerability Management
- Threat Intelligence
- Incident Management
- Digital Forensics
- Awareness Education
- Cyber Insurance
- Active Cyber Defense
- Evolving Technologies
- Disaster Recovery
- Onboarding
- Hiring
- Skills
- Training
- Offboarding

## Controls

Each domain has sub-domains that are assigned a reference number. Controls are identified by clause numbers and an assigned checklist. In order to verify the control evaluation, the cybersecurity control is either in place or inexistent.

## Checklists

Each checklist is linked to a specific domain and the subordinated sub-domain. The checklist verifies the validity of the cybersecurity sub-controls in alignment with a control clause. The cybersecurity auditors have the option to collect evidence to verify the sub-control compliance.

## Guideline Assessment

The guideline assessment only applies to the Nation States domain. The guidelines are evaluated for cybersecurity culture, National Cybersecurity Strategy (NCS), cyber operations, critical infrastructure, cyber intelligence, cyber warfare, cybercrime and cyber diplomacy.

## Evaluation Scorecard

The control, guideline and sub-control evaluation is calculated after the audit has been completed. The evaluation consists in assigning scores and ratings for each control, guideline and sub-control.

We calculate the final cybersecurity maturity rating of the Nation States domain by using the following criteria. The score can be mapped to a specific maturity level:

Immature (I): 0-30

The Nation State does not have any plans to manage its cyberspace. A National Cybersecurity Strategy (NCS) or Policy is inexistent.

Developing (D): 31-70

The Nation State is starting to focus on national cybersecurity. If technologies are in place, the Nation State needs to focus on key areas to protect cyberspace.

Mature (M): 71-90

While the Nation State has a mature environment. Improvements are required to the key areas that have been identified with weaknesses.

Advanced (A): 91-100

Nation State has excelled in national cybersecurity and cyberspace practices. There is always room for improvement. Nation State could become an international leader and help other Nation States with cybersecurity and cyberspace matters.

And for domains 2-18, we calculate the final cybersecurity maturity rating of any organization by using the following criteria:

The score can be mapped to a specific maturity level:

Immature (I): 0-30

The organization does not have any plans to manage its cybersecurity. Controls for critical cybersecurity areas are inexistent or very weak. The organization has not implemented a comprehensive cybersecurity program.

Developing (D): 31-70

The organization is starting to focus on cybersecurity matters. If technologies are in place, the organization needs to focus on key areas to protect cyber assets. Attention must be focused towards staff, processes, controls and regulations.

Mature (M): 71-90

While the organization has a mature environment. Improvements are required to the key areas that have been identified with weaknesses.

Advanced (A): 91-100

The organization has excelled in implementing cybersecurity best practices. There is always room for improvement. Keep documentation up-to-date and continually review cybersecurity processes through audits.

## METHODOLOGY

The goal of this study was to investigate and provide comprehensive models for the challenges that may arise when planning and delivering cybersecurity audits along with deploying cybersecurity awareness training.

Case studies are considered the most relevant of observational studies, any case study results are limited in generalizability and broader applications (Edgard and Manz, 2017). Some authors prefer to design their case studies using the research methodology provided by Yin (2009). Bartnes and Brede (2016) presented their research using data collection, data analysis, scenario and case content sections. Meszaros and Buchalcevova (2016) designed the Online Services Security Framework (OSSF) and their research methods were organized in a process with the following activities:

1. Problem identification and motivation
2. Define the objectives for a solution
3. Design and development
4. Demonstration
5. Evaluation
6. Communication

On a different approach, the case study of Bartnes et al. (2016) compiled the research method in an industrial case context, data collection and analysis and privacy and confidentiality issues sections. According to Yin (2014), a definition of a case study encloses the following:

*A case study investigates a contemporary phenomenon in a real-world context, a case study will have more variables of interest than data points, the main research questions are "how" or "why", case studies can include single or multiple cases, case studies are limited to quantitative evidence and are useful methods for evaluation. (Yin, 2014)*

Following this statement, we designed, implemented and validated a multiple-case study based on Yin (2018) of three exercises - A cybersecurity audit and a cybersecurity awareness training in a Canadian higher education institution and cybersecurity audit in a second Canadian higher education institution. We cannot disclose further details to protect the confidentiality and anonymity of our target organizations and its participants, that allowed us to complete this multi-case study research. We conducted our multi-case study following the research methodology proposed by Yin (2018).

We recognized that the main problems are linked to conduct cybersecurity audits in a comprehensive and timely fashion by including the proper domains to be audited. Furthermore, how to deliver the appropriate cybersecurity awareness training to target different corporate groups in conjunction with topics that are aligned with the current cyberthreat landscape. Our motivation aimed to design a model that included an all in one approach to plan and conduct cybersecurity audits at any organization with the ability to assess national cybersecurity strategies as well. In addition, we discovered that it was necessary to deal with the lack of knowledge to face cyberattacks and cyberthreats, as a result we ended up designing an organizational cybersecurity awareness training model that can be implemented to create the foundations of any cybersecurity awareness program.

We designed two theoretical cybersecurity models (CSAM & CATRAM) in order to be functional for any type of organization, no matter the size nor the industry or sector where the organization is positioned. The case study research proposition was to validate the execution of our models. The case involved the active participation of all levels of staff in our target organization in order to benefit by the case study research outcomes. The lessons learned from our study may help other organizations for further testing and implementations of our models.

Once we designed our cybersecurity models, we approached upper management of our initial target organization and presented our case study research proposal. We decided to conduct a cybersecurity pre-assessment to understand the organizational cybersecurity function and from there, plan to implement CSAM (Sabillon et al., 2017) while simultaneously delivering our cybersecurity awareness training based on CATRAM (Sabillon et al., 2018), and the results of the model's validation will be instrumental to understand the current cybersecurity status of the organization. The target organization management felt that this case study research was a win-win opportunity for the institution and for the researchers.

The first author conducted interviews, observations, online surveys and collected documentation pertinent to the scope of the case study. The same approach was followed for our second target institution.

During the pre-assessment stage, the first author collected data using online surveys from IT staff, the IT manager and the registrar director. While delivering the cybersecurity training based on CATRAM, we collected survey data from all different groups including the board of directors, executives, managers, IT staff and end users. Thus, we collected evidence when conducting the cybersecurity audits based on CSAM (Sabillon, 2018) and organized by cybersecurity domains. The data collection phase allowed us to gather evidence from multiple sources like documents, policies, archival records, open-ended interviews, observations, structured interviews, structured surveys, multiple site visits, presentations, meetings, and computer and server logs. Data collection was similar in our second target institution.

The authors utilized a variety of approaches for data analysis. For the CATRAM dataset, we created flowcharts, charts, graphics and tabulated the data provided from the cybersecurity awareness training sessions. On the other hand, the biggest dataset came from the CSAM audit where the data was recorded in our control forms, sub-control forms and checklists for each cybersecurity domain and sub-domain that we audited.

We focused the dissemination of our multi-case study research, its results and our cybersecurity models to academic audiences, IT audit teams, cybersecurity audit teams and IT auditors. We presented a final report of our case study research to the executives of our target organizations, by highlighting the results and providing recommendations to address existing cybersecurity weaknesses. The authors designed a linear-analytic structure for this exploratory multi-case study research.

## RESULTS

The CSAM was implemented and validated using three different scenarios at two different Canadian higher education institutions. In order to implement and validate the CSAM, we also designed the CATRAM that was simultaneously implemented along with the CSAM in our first target organization.

### Scenario I: Cybersecurity audit of all model domains

The following tables provide a series of results to present the findings in the research scenario I. We illustrate the assessment of the CSAM cybersecurity domains and its main controls. Table 2 and Table 3 summarize the results and domain ratings for the research scenario where all CSAM cybersecurity domains were audited in our target organization 1 and target organization 2.

### Scenario II: Cybersecurity Audit of Several Domains (Governance and Strategy, Legal and compliance, Cyber Risks, Frameworks and Regulations, Incident Management, Cyber Insurance and Evolving Technologies)

The following tables provide a series of results to present the findings in the research scenario II. We illustrate the assessment of seven cybersecurity domains and its main controls. Table 4 and Table 5 summarize the results and domain ratings for the research scenario II where multiple cybersecurity domains were audited in our target organization 1 and target organization 2.

*Table 2. Multiple Cybersecurity domain score (Scenario I) for Target Organization 1*

| No. | Domain | Ratings | | | | Score |
|---|---|---|---|---|---|---|
| | | I | D | M | A | |
| 2 | Governance and Strategy | ☐ | ☒ | ☐ | ☐ | 35% |
| 3 | Legal and Compliance | ☐ | ☐ | ☒ | ☐ | 90% |
| 4 | Cyber Assets | ☒ | ☐ | ☐ | ☐ | 30% |
| 5 | Cyber Risks | ☐ | ☒ | ☐ | ☐ | 60% |
| 6 | Frameworks and Regulations | ☒ | ☐ | ☐ | ☐ | 30% |
| 7 | Architecture and Networks | ☐ | ☒ | ☐ | ☐ | 67% |
| 8 | Information, Systems and Apps. | ☐ | ☒ | ☐ | ☐ | 55% |
| 9 | Vulnerability Identification | ☒ | ☐ | ☐ | ☐ | 30% |
| 10 | Threat Intelligence | ☐ | ☒ | ☐ | ☐ | 60% |
| 11 | Incident Management | ☒ | ☐ | ☐ | ☐ | 10% |
| 12 | Digital Forensics | ☒ | ☐ | ☐ | ☐ | 30% |
| 13 | Awareness Education | ☐ | ☒ | ☐ | ☐ | 60% |
| 14 | Cyber Insurance | ☐ | ☐ | ☒ | ☐ | 90% |
| 15 | Active Cyber Defense | ☒ | ☐ | ☐ | ☐ | 5% |
| 16 | Evolving Technologies | ☐ | ☐ | ☐ | ☒ | 100% |
| 17 | Disaster Recovery | ☒ | ☐ | ☐ | ☐ | 30% |
| 18 | Personnel | ☐ | ☐ | ☒ | ☐ | 77% |
| **Multiple Domain -Cybersecurity Maturity Rating** | | | | | | |
| Developing (D): 31-70<br>The organization is starting to focus on cybersecurity matters. If technologies are in place, the organization needs to focus on key areas to protect cyber assets. Attention must be focused towards staff, processes, controls and regulations. | | ☐ | ☒ | ☐ | ☐ | **51%** |

## Scenario III: A single cybersecurity domain audit (Awareness Education)

Before conducting our case study research, our target organization did not have any cybersecurity awareness model or any cybersecurity awareness education program whatsoever. The CATRAM delivery allowed the organization, to build a strong foundation for a future implementation of a comprehensive cybersecurity awareness training program. The cybersecurity audit of the awareness education domain was conducted after the successful delivery and implementation of CATRAM.

We provide a series of tables to present the findings in the research scenario III for both organizations. Table C1 illustrates the assessment of the main cybersecurity awareness education controls. Table 6 and 7 summarize the results and domain rating for awareness education in our target organization 1 and target organization 2.

*Table 3. Multiple Cybersecurity domain score (Scenario I) for Target Organization 2*

| No. | Domain | Ratings | | | | Score |
|---|---|---|---|---|---|---|
| | | **I** | **D** | **M** | **A** | |
| 2 | Governance and Strategy | ☐ | ☒ | ☐ | ☐ | 42% |
| 3 | Legal and Compliance | ☐ | ☐ | ☐ | ☒ | 100% |
| 4 | Cyber Assets | ☐ | ☐ | ☒ | ☐ | 80% |
| 5 | Cyber Risks | ☐ | ☒ | ☐ | ☐ | 70% |
| 6 | Frameworks and Regulations | ☐ | ☐ | ☒ | ☐ | 90% |
| 7 | Architecture and Networks | ☐ | ☐ | ☒ | ☐ | 80% |
| 8 | Information, Systems and Apps. | ☐ | ☐ | ☒ | ☐ | 87% |
| 9 | Vulnerability Identification | ☐ | ☐ | ☐ | ☒ | 100% |
| 10 | Threat Intelligence | ☐ | ☐ | ☐ | ☒ | 95% |
| 11 | Incident Management | ☐ | ☐ | ☐ | ☒ | 92% |
| 12 | Digital Forensics | ☐ | ☐ | ☒ | ☐ | 85% |
| 13 | Awareness Education | ☐ | ☐ | ☐ | ☒ | 95% |
| 14 | Cyber Insurance | ☐ | ☐ | ☒ | ☐ | 85% |
| 15 | Active Cyber Defense | ☐ | ☒ | ☐ | ☐ | 60% |
| 16 | Evolving Technologies | ☐ | ☐ | ☒ | ☐ | 80% |
| 17 | Disaster Recovery | ☐ | ☐ | ☒ | ☐ | 89% |
| 18 | Personnel | ☐ | ☐ | ☒ | ☐ | 85% |
| **Multiple Domain -Cybersecurity Maturity Rating** | | | | | | |
| **Mature (M): 71-90** <br> While the organization has a mature environment. Improvements are required to the key areas that have been identified with weaknesses. | | ☐ | ☒ | ☐ | ☐ | **83%** |

*Table 4. Multiple Cybersecurity domain score (Scenario II) for Target Organization 1*

| No. | Domain | Ratings | | | | Score |
|---|---|---|---|---|---|---|
| | | **I** | **D** | **M** | **A** | |
| 2 | Governance and Strategy | ☐ | ☒ | ☐ | ☐ | 35% |
| 3 | Legal and Compliance | ☐ | ☐ | ☒ | ☐ | 90% |
| 5 | Cyber Risks | ☐ | ☒ | ☐ | ☐ | 60% |
| 6 | Frameworks and Regulations | ☒ | ☐ | ☐ | ☐ | 30% |
| 11 | Incident Management | ☒ | ☐ | ☐ | ☐ | 10% |
| 14 | Cyber Insurance | ☐ | ☐ | ☒ | ☐ | 90% |
| 16 | Evolving Technologies | ☐ | ☐ | ☐ | ☒ | 100% |
| **Multiple Domain -Cybersecurity Maturity Rating** | | | | | | |
| **Developing (D): 31-70** <br> The organization is starting to focus on cybersecurity matters. If technologies are in place, the organization needs to focus on key areas to protect cyber assets. Attention must be focused towards staff, processes, controls and regulations. | | ☐ | ☒ | ☐ | ☐ | **59%** |

*Table 5. Multiple Cybersecurity domain score (Scenario II) for Target Organization 2*

| Cybersecurity Audit Model (CSAM) | | | | | | |
|---|---|---|---|---|---|---|
| No. | Domain | Ratings | | | | Score |
| | | I | D | M | A | |
| 2 | Governance and Strategy | ☐ | ☒ | ☐ | ☐ | 42% |
| 3 | Legal and Compliance | ☐ | ☐ | ☐ | ☒ | 100% |
| 5 | Cyber Risks | ☐ | ☒ | ☐ | ☐ | 70% |
| 6 | Frameworks and Regulations | ☐ | ☐ | ☒ | ☐ | 90% |
| 11 | Incident Management | ☐ | ☐ | ☐ | ☒ | 92% |
| 14 | Cyber Insurance | ☐ | ☐ | ☒ | ☐ | 85% |
| 16 | Evolving Technologies | ☐ | ☐ | ☒ | ☐ | 80% |
| **Multiple Domain -Cybersecurity Maturity Rating** | | | | | | |
| **Mature (M): 71-90**<br>While the organization has a mature environment. Improvements are required to the key areas that have been identified with weaknesses. | | ☐ | ☐ | ☒ | ☐ | **80%** |

*Table 6. Overall Cybersecurity domain rating (Scenario III) in Target Organization 1*

| Cybersecurity Audit Model (CSAM) | | | |
|---|---|---|---|
| Domain | 13-Awareness Education | | |
| Control Evaluation | Ratings | | Score |
| | Immature | ☐ | |
| | Developing | ☒ | **60%** |
| | Mature | ☐ | |
| | Advanced | ☐ | |
| **Developing (D): 31-70**<br>The organization is starting to focus on cybersecurity matters. If technologies are in place, the organization needs to focus on key areas to protect cyber assets. Attention must be focused towards staff, processes, controls and regulations.<br>The Awareness Education domain is developing. The organization has a foundation model for cybersecurity awareness and additional efforts are required to develop a complete cybersecurity awareness program. | | | |

## DISCUSSION

This study presents the architecture and the dual validation of the CyberSecurity Audit Model (CSAM). The aim of this model is to introduce a cybersecurity audit model that includes all functional areas, in order to guarantee an effective cybersecurity assurance, maturity and cyber readiness in any organization or any Nation State that is auditing its National Cybersecurity Strategy (NCS). This model was designed as a seamless and integrated cybersecurity audit model to assess and measure the level of cybersecurity maturity and cyber readiness in any type of organization, no matter in what industry or sector the organization is positioned. Moreover, by adding guidelines assessment for the integration of a national cybersecurity policy, program or strategy at the country level.

*Table 7. Overall Cybersecurity domain rating (Scenario III) in Target Organization 2*

| Cybersecurity Audit Model (CSAM) | | | |
|---|---|---|---|
| **Domain** | **13-Awareness Education** | | |
| **Control Evaluation** | **Ratings** | | **Score** |
| | Immature | ☐ | |
| | Developing | ☐ | |
| | Mature | ☐ | |
| | Advanced | ☒ | **95%** |
| **Advanced (A): 91-100** The organization has excelled in implementing cybersecurity best practices. There is always room for improvement. Keep documentation up-to-date and continually review cybersecurity processes through audits. The Awareness Education domain is advanced. The organization has a foundation model for cybersecurity awareness and additional efforts are required to develop a complete cybersecurity awareness program that includes all staffing level and customers. | | | |

Several cybersecurity frameworks are mostly oriented towards a specific industry like the *"PCI DSS"* for credit card security, the *"NERC CIP Cyber Security"* for the bulk power system or the *"NIST Cybersecurity Framework"* for protecting national critical infrastructure. Hence, all the existing frameworks do not provide a one-size fits all for planning and conducting cybersecurity audits. The needs for mapping against specific cybersecurity frameworks is because of regulatory requirements, to satisfy the demands of industry regulators, to comply with internal or external audits, to satisfy business purposes and customer requirements or simply by improving the enterprise cybersecurity strategy.

We compared our model in Table 8, to emphasize the main features against *"The Cybersecurity Framework (CSF) Version 1.1: NIST (2017)"* and *"The Audit First Methodology: Donaldson et al. (2015)"*. The CSAM is not for a specific industry, sector or organization – On the contrary, the model can be utilized to plan, conduct and verify cybersecurity audits everywhere. The CSAM has been conceived to conduct partial or complete cybersecurity audits either by a specific domain, several domains or the comprehensive audit for all domains.

## CONCLUSION

The main objectives of this multi-case study were to design and validate two cybersecurity models; the CyberSecurity Audit Model (CSAM) along with the Cybersecurity Awareness TRAining Model (CATRAM) to address the challenges to conduct comprehensive cybersecurity audits and to deliver cybersecurity awareness training based on staff roles respectively. The cybersecurity models including all its components were successfully validated by a multiple case study performed in two Canadian higher education institutions.

The CSAM is not for a specific industry, sector or organization – On the contrary, the model can be utilized to plan, conduct and verify cybersecurity audits everywhere. The CSAM has been designed to conduct partial or complete cybersecurity audits either by a specific domain, several domains or the comprehensive audit for all domains. Likewise, the CATRAM can support the implementation of a foundation for consolidating a cybersecurity awareness training program at any organization.

*Table 8. Comparison of some cybersecurity audit models*

| Audit Model or Framework | Description |
|---|---|
| The Cybersecurity Framework (CSF) Version 1.1: NIST (2017) | The first version was conceived in 2014 to improve cybersecurity of critical infrastructure. The version 1.1 manages cybersecurity risks for critical infrastructure. It includes of the Framework Core, the Framework Implementation Tiers and the Framework profiles.<br>The Framework Core includes five functions – Identify, Protect, Detect, Respond and Recover; then each of these functions have categories and subcategories. In addition, the Core contains Informative resources like cybersecurity standards, guidelines and best practices.<br>The Tiers define cybersecurity context organized from partial to adaptive tier.<br>The Profile presents the outcomes based on organizational needs. The current profile can later be compared with a target profile. |
| The Audit First Methodology: Donaldson et al. (2015) | This approach considers other cybersecurity controls and leaves preventive control execution until the end. This audit includes five different stages:<br>1. Threat analysis: This phase identifies Confidentiality, Integrity and Availability (CIA) threats that may impact IT and corporate data. Threat impact and indicators are defined.<br>2. Audit controls: It includes the design of threat audit controls.<br>3. Forensic controls: This phase helps to implement the required forensic controls for the enterprise cybersecurity functional areas:<br>1) Systems administration<br>2) Networks<br>3) Applications<br>4) Endpoints, servers and devices<br>5) Identity, authentication and access<br>6) Data protection and cryptography<br>7) Monitoring, vulnerabilities and patch management<br>8) Availability, disaster recovery and physical protection<br>9) Incident management<br>10) Supply chain and asset management<br>11) Policy, audit, e-Discovery and training<br>4. Detective controls: Detective controls are designed to alert, detect, stop and repel cyberattacks.<br>5. Preventive controls: These controls block undesired activities and stop them from occurring. |
| The CyberSecurity Audit Model (CSAM): Sabillon et al. (2017) | The CSAM includes overview, resources, 18 domains, 26 sub-domains, 87 checklists, 169 controls, 429 sub-controls, 80 guideline assessments and an evaluation scorecard. Domain 1-Guideline assessment are specific for Nation States and domains 2-18 are applicable to any type of organization. Several domains have specific sub-domains where controls are evaluated. Then the checklists verify compliance about specific sub-controls based on domain/sub-domain.<br>The scorecard results determine the domains rating and score that will produce the overall cybersecurity maturity rating. |

The results of this study show that cybersecurity audits conducted by domains can be very effective to evaluate controls and responses to cyberthreats. Thus, the delivery of cybersecurity training based on organizational roles and responsibilities tend to motivate personnel to create and maintain awareness in their workplaces as well in their personal lives.

The limitation of our study is that both models were validated in a single organization, time constraints, lack of interest for the topics and lack of engagement were some of the challenges that we have to overcome from some of the participants. For that reason, CSAM was also valiudated in second organization. Hence, future testing will enhance the model results by engaging more organizations.

The case study findings have implications for our target organizations but at the same time, implications for future research to review and expand our proposed cybersecurity models.

# REFERENCES

Alotaibi, F., Furnell, S., Stengel, I., & Papadaki, M. (2016). A review of Using Gaming Technologies for Cyber-Security Awareness. *International Journal of Information Security Research*, 6(2), 660–666. doi:10.20533/ijisr.2042.4639.2016.0076

Axelos. (2015). *Cyber Resilience Best Practices*. Norwich: Resilia.

Beyer, M., Ahmed, S., Doerlemann, K., Arnell, S., Parkin, S., Sasse, A., & Passingham, N. (2015). *Awareness is only the first step: A framework for progressive engagement of staff in cyber security*. Hewlett Packard Enterpise.

Beyer, R., & Brummel, B. (2015). *Implementing Effective Cyber Security Training for End Users of Computer Networks*. Society for Human Resource Management and Society for Industrial and Organizational Psychology.

Cano, J. (2016). La educación en seguridad de la información. Reflexión pedagógicas desde el pensamiento de sistemas. *Memorias 3er Simposio Internacional en "Temas y problemas de Investigación en Educación: Complejidad y Escenarios para la Paz"*.

Cano, J. (2016). Modelo de madurez de cultura organizacional de seguridad de la información. Una visión desde el pensamiento sistémico-cibernético. Actas de la XIV Reunión Española sobre Criptología y Seguridad de la Información, 24-29.

Cyber, X. (2019). 2019 Global ICS & IIoT Risk Report. A data-driven analysis of vulnerabilities in our industrial and critical infrastructure. *CyberX Labs*. Retrieved from https://cyberx-labs.com/resources/risk-report-2019/

ESET. (2017). *ESET Cybersecurity Awareness Training*. ESET Canada. Retrieved from https://www.eset.com/ca/cybertraining/

Fujitsu. (2017). *The Digital Transformation PACT*. Retrieved from https://www.fujitsu.com

Gartner. (2016). *2016 Gartner Magic Quadrant for Security Awareness Computer-Based Training Vendors*. Gartner, Inc.

Gartner. (2018). *How to Build an Enterprise Security Awareness Program*. Gartner, Inc.

Gartner. (2018). *How to Secure the Human Link*. Gartner, Inc.

Gartner. (2018). *Magic Quadrant for Security Awareness Computer-Based Training*. Gartner, Inc.

Hayden, L. (2016). *People-Centric Security: Transforming your Enterprise Security Culture*. Mc Graw Hill.

Hollingsworth, C. (2016). Auditing fro FISMA and HIPAA: Lessons Learned Performing an In-House Cybersecurity Audit. *ISACA Journal*, 5, 1–6.

International Organization for Standardization - ISO. (2005). *ISO/IEC 27001:2005 – Information Technology – Security Techniques – Information Security Management Systems – Requirements*. ISO.

International Organization for Standardization -ISO. (2012). *ISO/IEC 27032:2012 – Information Technology – Security Techniques – Guidelines for Cybersecurity*. ISO.

ISACA. (2017). *Auditing Cyber Security: Evaluating Risk and Auditing Controls*. ISACA.

LeClair, J., Abraham, S., & Shih, L. (2013). An Interdisciplinary Approach to Educating an Effective Cyber Security Worforce. *Proceedings of Information Security Curriculum Development Conference*, 71-78.

MediaPro. (2017). *A Best Practices Guide for Comprehensive Employee Awareness Programs*. MediaPro.

MITRE. (2010). *The Importance of Using EARNEST*. The MITRE Corporation. Retrieved from https://www.mitre.org/sites/default/files/pdf/mitre_earnest.pdf

MITRE. (2017). *Cybersecurity Awareness & Training*. The MITRE Corporation.

Monahan, D. (2014). *Security Awareness Training: It's not just for Compliance-Research Report Summary. Enterprise Management Associates*. EMA.

National Institute of Standards and Technology – NIST. (2003). *Building an Information Technology Security Awareness and Training Program*. NIST Special Publication 800-50.

National Institute of Standards and Technology – NIST. (2017). *An Introduction to Information Security*. NIST Special Publication 800-12 Revision 1.

Nguyen, T.N., Sbityakov, L., & Scoggins, S. (2018). *Intelligence-based Cybersecurity Awareness Training- an Exploratory Project*. CoRR, abs/1812.04234.

NTT Group. (2017). *Embedding cybersecurity into digital transformation - a journey towards business resilience*. NTT Security. Retrieved from https://www.nttsecurity.com

PCI Security Standards Council - PCI DSS. (2014). *Best Practices for Implementing a Security Awareness Program*. PCI DSS.

Penderdast, T. (2016). How to Audit the Human Element and Assess Your Organization's Security Risk. *ISACA Journal, 5*, 1–5.

PhishMe. (2017). PhishMe CBFree. *PhishMe Headquarters*. Retrieved from https://phishme.com/resources/cbfree-computer-based-training/

Ponemon Institute. (2018). Assessing the DNS Security Risk. Research report sponsored by Infoblox. Ponemon Institute LLC.

Sabillon, R., Serra-Ruiz, J., Cavaller, V., & Cano, J. (2017). A Comprehensive Cybersecurity Audit Model to Improve Cybersecurity Assurance: The CyberSecurity Audit Model (CSAM). *Proceedings of Second International Conference on Information Systems and Computer Science (INCISCOS)*. 10.1109/INCISCOS.2017.20

Sabillon, R., Serra-Ruiz, J., Cavaller, V., Jeimy, J., & Cano, M. (2019). An Effective Cybersecurity Training Model to Support an Organizational Awareness Program: The Cybersecurity Awareness TRAining Model (CATRAM). A Case Study in Canada. *Journal of Cases on Information Technology, 21*(3), 26–39. doi:10.4018/JCIT.2019070102

SANS Institute. (2017). 2017 Security Awareness Report: It's time to communicate. *SANS Security Awareness.* Retrieved from https://securingthehuman.sans.org/media/resources/STH-SecurityAwarenessReport-2017.pdf

Security Awareness, S. A. N. S. (2017). *2017 Security Awareness Report*. SANS Institute.

Symantec. (2014). *Symantec Security Awareness Program: Mitigate information risk by educating your employees*. Symantec Corporation.

Ward, M. (2016). *Security Awareness and Training: Solving the unintentional insider threat*. Cyber Safe Worforce LLC.

Whitman, M. E., & Mattord, H. J. (2019). *Management of Information Security* (6th ed.). Cengage Learning, Inc.

Yin, R. K. (2014). *Case Study Research: Design and Methods* (5th ed.). Sage Publications.

Yin, R. K. (2018). *Case Study Research and Applications* (6th ed.). Sage Publications.

## ADDITIONAL READING

Choi, Y. (2018). *Selected Readings in Cybersecurity*. Cambridge Scholars Publishing.

## KEY TERMS AND DEFINITIONS

**Cybersecurity Audit:** Audit to be conducted to verify cybersecurity controls.
**Cybersecurity Domains:** Cybersecurity areas that support a cybersecurity program in any organization.
**Cybersecurity Maturity:** Level of experience that an organization has implemented and acquired for cybersecurity practices.

*Previously published in Cyber Security Auditing, Assurance, and Awareness Through CSAM and CATRAM; pages 149-232, copyright year 2021 by Information Science Reference (an imprint of IGI Global).*

# APPENDIX 1

## Template for Overall Cybersecurity Rating for Domain 1 (Nation States)

*Table 9. Overall Cybersecurity Rating for Domain 1 (Nation States)*

| Cybersecurity Audit Model (CSAM) | | | | | |
|---|---|---|---|---|---|
| **Domain** | **1-Nation States** | | | | |
| **Sub-Domain: 1.1 Cyberspace** | **Ratings** | | | | **Score** |
| | **I** | **D** | **M** | **A** | |
| 1.1.1 Cybersecurity Culture | ☐ | ☐ | ☐ | ☐ | |
| 1.1.2 National Cybersecurity Strategy | ☐ | ☐ | ☐ | ☐ | |
| 1.1.3 Cyber Operations | ☐ | ☐ | ☐ | ☐ | |
| 1.1.4 Critical Infrastructure | ☐ | ☐ | ☐ | ☐ | |
| 1.1.5 Cyber Intelligence | ☐ | ☐ | ☐ | ☐ | |
| 1.1.6 Cyber Warfare | ☐ | ☐ | ☐ | ☐ | |
| 1.1.7 Cybercrime | ☐ | ☐ | ☐ | ☐ | |
| 1.1.8 Cyber Diplomacy | ☐ | ☐ | ☐ | ☐ | |
| **Final Cybersecurity Maturity Rating** | ☐ | ☐ | ☐ | ☐ | |

## Rating

If your score is:

Immature (I): 0-30

The Nation State does not have any plans to manage its cyberspace. A National Cybersecurity Strategy or Policy is inexistent.

Developing (D): 31-70

The Nation State is starting to focus on national cybersecurity. If technologies are in place, the Nation State needs to focus on key areas to protect cyberspace.

Mature (M): 71-90

While the Nation State has a mature environment. Improvements are required to the key areas that have been identified with weaknesses.

Advanced (A): 91-100

Nation State has excelled in national cybersecurity and cyberspace practices. There is always room for improvement. Nation State could become an international leader and help other Nation States with cybersecurity and cyberspace matters.

## Template for Overall Cybersecurity Rating for Domains 2-18

*Table 10. Overall Cybersecurity Rating for Domains 2-18*

| Cybersecurity Audit Model (CSAM) | | | | | | |
|---|---|---|---|---|---|---|
| **No.** | **Domain** | **Ratings** | | | | **Score** |
| | | **I** | **D** | **M** | **A** | |
| 2 | Governance and Strategy | ☐ | ☐ | ☐ | ☐ | |
| 3 | Legal and Compliance | ☐ | ☐ | ☐ | ☐ | |
| 4 | Cyber Assets | ☐ | ☐ | ☐ | ☐ | |
| 5 | Cyber Risks | ☐ | ☐ | ☐ | ☐ | |
| 6 | Frameworks and Regulations | ☐ | ☐ | ☐ | ☐ | |
| 7 | Architecture and Networks | ☐ | ☐ | ☐ | ☐ | |
| 8 | Information, Systems and Apps. | ☐ | ☐ | ☐ | ☐ | |
| 9 | Vulnerability Identification | ☐ | ☐ | ☐ | ☐ | |
| 10 | Threat Intelligence | ☐ | ☐ | ☐ | ☐ | |
| 11 | Incident Management | ☐ | ☐ | ☐ | ☐ | |
| 12 | Digital Forensics | ☐ | ☐ | ☐ | ☐ | |
| 13 | Awareness Education | ☐ | ☐ | ☐ | ☐ | |
| 14 | Cyber Insurance | ☐ | ☐ | ☐ | ☐ | |
| 15 | Active Cyber Defense | ☐ | ☐ | ☐ | ☐ | |
| 16 | Evolving Technologies | ☐ | ☐ | ☐ | ☐ | |
| 17 | Disaster Recovery | ☐ | ☐ | ☐ | ☐ | |
| 18 | Personnel | ☐ | ☐ | ☐ | ☐ | |
| **Final Cybersecurity Maturity Rating** | | ☐ | ☐ | ☐ | ☐ | |

## Rating

If your score is:

Immature (I): 0-30

The organization does not have any plans to manage its cybersecurity. Controls for critical cybersecurity areas are inexistent or very weak. The organization has not implemented a comprehensive cybersecurity program.

Developing (D): 31-70

The organization is starting to focus on cybersecurity matters. If technologies are in place, the organization needs to focus on key areas to protect cyber assets. Attention must be focused towards staff, processes, controls and regulations.

Mature (M): 71-90

While the organization has a mature environment. Improvements are required to the key areas that have been identified with weaknesses.

Advanced (A): 91-100

The organization has excelled in implementing cybersecurity best practices. There is always room for improvement. Keep documentation up-to-date and continually review cybersecurity processes through audits.

# APPENDIX 2

We have included all CSAM checklists in this appendix. Appendix 2 contains checklists for all sub-domains:

- Cyberspace
- Governance
- Strategy
- Legal and Compliance
- Cyber Asset Management
- Cyber Risk
- Frameworks and Regulations
- Architecture
- Networks
- Information
- Systems
- Applications
- Vulnerability Management
- Threat Intelligence
- Incident Management
- Digital Forensics
- Awareness Education
- Cyber Insurance
- Active Cyber Defense
- Evolving Technologies
- Disaster Recovery
- Personnel Onboarding
- Personnel Hiring
- Personnel Skills
- Personnel Training
- Personnel Offboarding

# Cybersecurity Audit Checklist: CSAM-Cyberspace: 1.1.1 (Cybersecurity Culture)

*Table 11. Domain: 1-Nation States*

| Clause | No. | Guidelines Assessment | Findings | | | Supporting Evidence | Comments |
|---|---|---|---|---|---|---|---|
| | | | Compliant | Minor Nonconformity | Major Nonconformity | | |
| 1.1.1 | 1 | Does the Nation State promote the adoption of a national cybersecurity culture for the society and its citizens? | ☐ | ☐ | ☐ | | |
| 1.1.1 | 2 | Does the Nation State have involved all sectors of the society to create and develop a national cybersecurity culture? | ☐ | ☐ | ☐ | | |
| 1.1.1 | 3 | Does the Nation State have cybersecurity awareness training programs for its citizens? | ☐ | ☐ | ☐ | | |
| 1.1.1 | 4 | Does the Nation State have involved academia with cybersecurity research and development initiatives? | ☐ | ☐ | ☐ | | |
| 1.1.1 | 5 | Does the Nation State have involved the private sector with cybersecurity research and development initiatives? | ☐ | ☐ | ☐ | | |
| 1.1.1 | 6 | Does the Nation State have incentive mechanisms to encourage new cybersecurity products and services? | ☐ | ☐ | ☐ | | |
| 1.1.1 | 7 | Does the Nation State have government incentives to encourage cybersecurity education, knowledge sharing and skills development? | ☐ | ☐ | ☐ | | |
| 1.1.1 | 8 | Does the Nation State have introduced mechanisms to reduce the digital divide? Do Internet and Telecommunication services will be improved? | ☐ | ☐ | ☐ | | |

# Cybersecurity Audit Checklist: CSAM-Cyberspace: 1.1.2 (NCSS)

*Table 12. Domain: 1-Nation States*

| Clause | No. | Guidelines Assessment | Findings | | | Supporting Evidence | Comments |
|---|---|---|---|---|---|---|---|
| | | | Compliant | Minor Nonconformity | Major Nonconformity | | |
| 1.1.2 | 1 | Is the NCSS regularly reviewed? Are there any mechanisms to review and audit the NCSS? | ☐ | ☐ | ☐ | | |
| 1.1.2 | 2 | Does the NCSS involve the participation of all related national main agencies, industries, sectors, military, police and academia? | ☐ | ☐ | ☐ | | |
| 1.1.2 | 3 | Does the Nation State have designated an agency to deal with all national cybersecurity matters? | ☐ | ☐ | ☐ | | |
| 1.1.2 | 4 | Does the Nation State have a national CSIRT to monitor and protect cyberspace? | ☐ | ☐ | ☐ | | |
| 1.1.2 | 5 | Does the Nation State have clear coordination and communication procedures for all its agencies in case of different levels of cyberattacks? | ☐ | ☐ | ☐ | | |
| 1.1.2 | 6 | Does the Nation State have designated a military unit in charge of developing military cyber capabilities? | ☐ | ☐ | ☐ | | |
| 1.1.2 | 7 | Is the NCSS integrated with the Nation State security strategies? | ☐ | ☐ | ☐ | | |
| 1.1.2 | 8 | Does the NCSS include a secure, resilient and reliable cyberspace? | ☐ | ☐ | ☐ | | |
| 1.1.2 | 9 | Is the NCSS evaluating all possible risks that may affect national information and communication technologies? | ☐ | ☐ | ☐ | | |
| 1.1.2 | 10 | Is the NCSS continually identifying various stakeholders to develop cyber offensive and defensive capabilities? | ☐ | ☐ | ☐ | | |

## Cybersecurity Audit Checklist: CSAM-Cyberspace: 1.1.3 (Cyber Operations)

*Table 13. Domain: 1-Nation States*

| Clause | No. | Guidelines Assessment | Findings | | | Supporting Evidence | Comments |
|--------|-----|----------------------|-----------|-----------------------|-----------------------|---------------------|----------|
| | | | Compliant | Minor Nonconformity | Major Nonconformity | | |
| 1.1.3 | 1 | Does the Nation State have a national cyber operations center? | ☐ | ☐ | ☐ | | |
| 1.1.3 | 2 | Is the Nation State continually implementing and enhancing cyber defensive operations? | ☐ | ☐ | ☐ | | |
| 1.1.3 | 3 | Is the Nation State continually implementing and enhancing cyber offensive operations? | ☐ | ☐ | ☐ | | |
| 1.1.3 | 4 | Does the Nation State have recruited qualified staff to operate and manage the national cyber operations center? | ☐ | ☐ | ☐ | | |
| 1.1.3 | 5 | Does the Nation State have monitoring capabilities for cyberspace? | ☐ | ☐ | ☐ | | |
| 1.1.3 | 6 | Does the Nation State have all the required tools and technologies at the national cyber operations center? | ☐ | ☐ | ☐ | | |
| 1.1.3 | 7 | Does the Nation State have case management capability at the national cyber operations center? | ☐ | ☐ | ☐ | | |
| 1.1.3 | 8 | Does the Nation State have detection, analysis, and response operations at the national cyber operations center? | ☐ | ☐ | ☐ | | |
| 1.1.3 | 9 | Does the Nation State have clear standard operating procedures and policies to run the national cyber operations center? | ☐ | ☐ | ☐ | | |
| 1.1.3 | 10 | Does the Nation State have a metric program to measure the effectiveness of the national cyber operations? Are Cyber Red/White/Blue Team exercises planned and executed? | ☐ | ☐ | ☐ | | |

## Cybersecurity Audit Checklist: CSAM-Cyberspace: 1.1.4 (Critical Infrastructure -CI)

*Table 14. Domain: 1-Nation States*

| Clause | No. | Guidelines Assessment | Findings | | | Supporting Evidence | Comments |
|--------|-----|----------------------|-----------|-----------------------|-----------------------|---------------------|----------|
| | | | Compliant | Minor Nonconformity | Major Nonconformity | | |
| 1.1.4 | 1 | Does the Nation State have identified all its national critical infrastructure/ critical infrastructure information, systems, cyber assets, data and capabilities? | ☐ | ☐ | ☐ | | |
| 1.1.4 | 2 | Does the Nation State have developed plans to protect all its national critical infrastructure services? | ☐ | ☐ | ☐ | | Anomalies, events, incidents, 24/7 monitoring, detection processes |
| 1.1.4 | 3 | Does the Nation State have implemented measures to detect cybersecurity events? | ☐ | ☐ | ☐ | | |
| 1.1.4 | 4 | Does the Nation State have implemented plans to respond to specific cybersecurity incidents? | ☐ | ☐ | ☐ | | |
| 1.1.4 | 5 | Does the Nation State have implemented resilience and recovery plans after the impact of a cybersecurity incident? | ☐ | ☐ | ☐ | | |

| Clause | No. | Guidelines Assessment | Findings | | | Supporting Evidence | Comments |
|--------|-----|----------------------|----------|---|---|---------------------|----------|
| | | | Compliant | Minor Nonconformity | Major Nonconformity | | |
| 1.1.4 | 6 | Does the State Nation is following a specific cybersecurity framework to protect CI? | ☐ | ☐ | ☐ | | |
| 1.1.4 | 7 | Does the State Nation have implemented *Information Exchange* to protect CI? | ☐ | ☐ | ☐ | | |
| 1.1.4 | 8 | Does the State Nation have defined clear roles and responsibilities for all CI stakeholders? | ☐ | ☐ | ☐ | | |
| 1.1.4 | 9 | Does the State Nation have defined communication procedures in case of any incident affecting CI? | ☐ | ☐ | ☐ | | |
| 1.1.4 | 10 | Does the State Nation review and audit its cybersecurity program to protect CI? | ☐ | ☐ | ☐ | | |

## Cybersecurity Audit Checklist: CSAM-Cyberspace: 1.1.5 (Cyber Intelligence)

*Table 15. Domain: 1-Nation States*

| Clause | No. | Guidelines Assessment | Findings | | | Supporting Evidence | Comments |
|--------|-----|----------------------|----------|---|---|---------------------|----------|
| | | | Compliant | Minor Nonconformity | Major Nonconformity | | |
| 1.1.5 | 1 | Does the Nation State have Cyber Intelligence capabilities? | ☐ | ☐ | ☐ | | |
| 1.1.5 | 2 | Does the Nation State have Cyber Counter Intelligence capabilities? | ☐ | ☐ | ☐ | | |
| 1.1.5 | 3 | Does the Nation State have Cyber Intelligence services to address cyberthreats? | ☐ | ☐ | ☐ | | Information collection, verification, aggregation, analysis and intelligence sharing |
| 1.1.5 | 4 | Does the Nation State Cyber Intelligence support operational, tactical and strategic environments? | ☐ | ☐ | ☐ | | |
| 1.1.5 | 5 | Does the Nation State Cyber Counter Intelligence support operational, tactical and strategic environments? | ☐ | ☐ | ☐ | | |
| 1.1.5 | 6 | Does the Nation State assign resources to increase the Cyber Intelligence capabilities? | ☐ | ☐ | ☐ | | |
| 1.1.5 | 7 | Does the Nation State assign resources to increase the Cyber Counter Intelligence capabilities? | ☐ | ☐ | ☐ | | |
| 1.1.5 | 8 | Do national intelligence agencies collaborate gathering cybersecurity intelligence? | ☐ | ☐ | ☐ | | |
| 1.1.5 | 9 | Does the Nation State collect intelligence related to the latest APTs and cyber-espionage? | ☐ | ☐ | ☐ | | |
| 1.1.5 | 10 | Does the Nation State analyze the current cyber threat landscape? Are there any collaboration with international agencies? | ☐ | ☐ | ☐ | | Five eyes, NSA, 9 eyes, 14 eyes, 41 eyes |

# Cybersecurity Audit Checklist: CSAM-Cyberspace: 1.1.6 (Cyber Warfare)

*Table 16. Domain: 1-Nation States*

| Clause | No. | Guidelines Assessment | Findings | | | Supporting Evidence | Comments |
|--------|-----|----------------------|----------|---------------------|---------------------|---------------------|----------|
| | | | Compliant | Minor Nonconformity | Major Nonconformity | | |
| 1.1.6 | 1 | Is the Nation State prepared to protect its cyber domain? | ☐ | ☐ | ☐ | | |
| 1.1.6 | 2 | Is the Cyber domain strategy aligned with the NCSS? | ☐ | ☐ | ☐ | | |
| 1.1.6 | 3 | Does the Nation State include cyber defense to protect its cyberspace? | ☐ | ☐ | ☐ | | Cyber defensive and offensive operations |
| 1.1.6 | 4 | Does the Nation State include strategic cyber operations? | ☐ | ☐ | ☐ | | |
| 1.1.6 | 5 | Does the Nation State have specific battlefield cyber capabilities? | ☐ | ☐ | ☐ | | |
| 1.1.6 | 6 | Does the Nation State have a tactical military cybersecurity unit? | ☐ | ☐ | ☐ | | |
| 1.1.6 | 7 | Does the Nation State have organized cyber warrior forces? | ☐ | ☐ | ☐ | | |
| 1.1.6 | 8 | Does the Nation State have formal programs to recruit, train and hire cybersecurity specialists? | ☐ | ☐ | ☐ | | Either military and/or civilian personnel |
| 1.1.6 | 9 | Is the Nation State able to apply cyber retaliation and cyber deterrence in order to prevent or stop full scale-neutralize cyber attacks? | ☐ | ☐ | ☐ | | |
| 1.1.6 | 10 | Does the Nation State have the ability to measure the effectiveness any cyber scenario? | ☐ | ☐ | ☐ | | Briefing and Debriefing, Present reports |

# Cybersecurity Audit Checklist: CSAM-Cyberspace: 1.1.7 (Cybercrime)

*Table 17. Domain: 1-Nation States*

| Clause | No. | Guidelines Assessment | Findings | | | Supporting Evidence | Comments |
|--------|-----|----------------------|----------|---------------------|---------------------|---------------------|----------|
| | | | Compliant | Minor Nonconformity | Major Nonconformity | | |
| 1.1.7 | 1 | Does the Nation State have laws to prosecute cybercrime? | ☐ | ☐ | ☐ | | |
| 1.1.7 | 2 | Does the Nation State have several organizations that are fighting national and international cybercrime? | ☐ | ☐ | ☐ | | |
| 1.1.7 | 3 | Does the Nation State have national cybersecurity awareness programs to prevent cybercrime? | ☐ | ☐ | ☐ | | |
| 1.1.7 | 4 | Does the Nation State have a multi-angled program with government agencies and private sector to prevent and report cybercrime? | ☐ | ☐ | ☐ | | |
| 1.1.7 | 5 | Does the police have cybercrime units to investigate and prosecute cybercrime? Do these cybercrime units have the required training and tools to tackle the modus operandi of cybercriminals? | ☐ | ☐ | ☐ | | |
| 1.1.7 | 6 | Does the national police have cross-links and information exchanges with foreign cybercrime police units? Are these programs part of bilateral collaborations or exchange between international police organizations? | ☐ | ☐ | ☐ | | Interpol, Europol |

| Clause | No. | Guidelines Assessment | Findings | | | Supporting Evidence | Comments |
|---|---|---|---|---|---|---|---|
| | | | Compliant | Minor Nonconformity | Major Nonconformity | | |
| 1.1.7 | 7 | Does the national judiciary system cover prosecution of new forms of cybercrime? | ☐ | ☐ | ☐ | | |
| 1.1.7 | 8 | Do digital investigations are protected by the national civil, criminal and judiciary systems? | ☐ | ☐ | ☐ | | |
| 1.1.7 | 9 | Does the Nation State regulate ISPs and telecommunication carriers in order to inform of any actor that may incur in cybercrime operations? | ☐ | ☐ | ☐ | | |
| 1.1.7 | 10 | How is the Nation State dealing with jurisdiction, sovereignty and international cooperation issues to fight cybercrime? | ☐ | ☐ | ☐ | | |

# Cybersecurity Audit Checklist: CSAM-Cyberspace: 1.1.8 (Cyber Diplomacy)

*Table 18. Domain: 1-Nation States*

| Clause | No. | Guidelines Assessment | Findings | | | Supporting Evidence | Comments |
|---|---|---|---|---|---|---|---|
| | | | Compliant | Minor Nonconformity | Major Nonconformity | | |
| 1.1.8 | 1 | Does the Nation State participate actively in global Internet governance initiatives? | ☐ | ☐ | ☐ | | IAB, IETF, ICANN, ITU, IGF, IEEE |
| 1.1.8 | 2 | Does the Nation State participate actively in cyber diplomacy to improve global cybersecurity? | ☐ | ☐ | ☐ | | |
| 1.1.8 | 3 | Does the Nation State participate in bilateral agreements to reduce tensions in cyberspace? | ☐ | ☐ | ☐ | | |
| 1.1.8 | 4 | Does the Nation State participate in multilateral agreements to reduce tensions in cyberspace? | ☐ | ☐ | ☐ | | |
| 1.1.8 | 5 | Does the Nation State participate in pro action initiatives related to cyber diplomacy? | ☐ | ☐ | ☐ | | |
| 1.1.8 | 6 | Does the Nation State participate in prevention initiatives related to cyber diplomacy? | ☐ | ☐ | ☐ | | |
| 1.1.8 | 7 | Does the Nation State participate in preparation initiatives related to cyber diplomacy? | ☐ | ☐ | ☐ | | |
| 1.1.8 | 8 | Does the Nation State participate in response initiatives related to cyber diplomacy? | ☐ | ☐ | ☐ | | |
| 1.1.8 | 9 | Does the Nation State participate in recovery initiatives related to cyber diplomacy? | ☐ | ☐ | ☐ | | |
| 1.1.8 | 10 | Does the Nation State participate in after care initiatives related to cyber diplomacy? | ☐ | ☐ | ☐ | | |

# Cybersecurity Audit Checklist: CSAM-Governance

*Table 19. Domain: 2-Governance and Strategy*

| Clause | No. | Checklist Questions | Findings | | | Supporting Evidence | Comments |
|---|---|---|---|---|---|---|---|
| | | | Compliant | Minor Nonconformity | Major Nonconformity | | |
| 2.1.1 | 1 | Is there a valid metric framework in place? | ☐ | ☐ | ☐ | | |
| 2.1.2 | 2 | Are the roles and responsibilities for each line of defense clearly described? | ☐ | ☐ | ☐ | | |
| 2.1.4 | 3 | The organization has defined a taxonomy for cybersecurity risks? | ☐ | ☐ | ☐ | | |
| 2.1.2 | 4 | Have the organization clearly defined responsibilities to support cybersecurity governance? | ☐ | ☐ | ☐ | | |
| 2.1.4 | 5 | Management actions are in accordance with the organization's governance? | ☐ | ☐ | ☐ | | |
| 2.1.2 | 6 | Do staff support the organization's strategy and objectives? | ☐ | ☐ | ☐ | | |
| 2.1.3 | 7 | Does management encourage periodical cybersecurity reviews? | ☐ | ☐ | ☐ | | |
| 2.1.4 | 8 | Are the external contracting practices evaluated based on the organization's strategies and objectives? | ☐ | ☐ | ☐ | | |
| 2.1.1 | 9 | Do the organization's policies, standards and procedures support the governance and strategy? | ☐ | ☐ | ☐ | | |
| 2.1.5 | 10 | Are the cybersecurity risk management practices properly managed? | ☐ | ☐ | ☐ | | |

# Cybersecurity Audit Checklist: CSAM-Strategy

*Table 20. Domain: 2-Governance and Strategy*

| Clause | No. | Checklist Questions | Findings | | | Supporting Evidence | Comments |
|---|---|---|---|---|---|---|---|
| | | | Compliant | Minor Nonconformity | Major Nonconformity | | |
| 2.2.1 | 1 | The organization has established a cybersecurity policy? | ☐ | ☐ | ☐ | | |
| 2.2.2 | 2 | Is the organization implementing a cybersecurity strategy aligned with IT and InfoSec strategies? | ☐ | ☐ | ☐ | | |
| 2.2.2 | 3 | The scope of the cybersecurity strategy reflects the size and the sector/industry of the organization? | ☐ | ☐ | ☐ | | |
| 2.2.1 | 4 | Is the cybersecurity strategy aligned with the organization governance? | ☐ | ☐ | ☐ | | |
| 2.2.1 | 5 | Is the cybersecurity strategy linked to other relevant organizational policies? | ☐ | ☐ | ☐ | | |
| 2.2.5 | 6 | Has the organization defined strategic, tactical and operational plans for cybersecurity initiatives? | ☐ | ☐ | ☐ | | |
| 2.2.4 | 7 | The organization encourages monitoring and reporting of preventive, detective and corrective measures | ☐ | ☐ | ☐ | | |
| 2.2.1 | 8 | Do you ensure that cybersecurity is incorporated with the organization's values and objectives? | ☐ | ☐ | ☐ | | |
| 2.2.1 | 9 | Does your organization adopt cybersecurity governance rules? | ☐ | ☐ | ☐ | | |
| 2.2.3 | 10 | Does cybersecurity governance include continual improvement practices and progress monitoring? | ☐ | ☐ | ☐ | | |

## Cybersecurity Audit Checklist: CSAM-Legal and Compliance

*Table 21. Domain: 3-Legal and Compliance*

| Clause | No. | Checklist Questions | Findings | | | Supporting Evidence | Comments |
|--------|-----|---------------------|-----------|-------------------------|------------------------|---------------------|----------|
| | | | Compliant | Minor Nonconformity | Major Nonconformity | | |
| 3.1.1 | 1 | The organization is complying with statutory, regulatory and contractual requirements? | ☐ | ☐ | ☐ | | |
| 3.1.2 | 2 | What legislations are applicable to your institution? | ☐ | ☐ | ☐ | | |
| 3.1.3 | 3 | What are the measures to protect your business records? | ☐ | ☐ | ☐ | | |
| 3.1.4 | 4 | Provide proof of protection controls for data and privacy of personal information | ☐ | ☐ | ☐ | | |
| 3.1.5 | 5 | List controls to avoid misuse of information and premises | ☐ | ☐ | ☐ | | |
| 3.1.6 | 6 | What methodologies of cybersecurity frameworks are you following? | ☐ | ☐ | ☐ | | |

## Cybersecurity Audit Checklist: CSAM-Cyber Assets

*Table 22. Domain: 4-Cyber Assets*

| Clause | No. | Checklist Questions | Findings | | | Supporting Evidence | Comments |
|--------|-----|---------------------|-----------|-------------------------|------------------------|---------------------|----------|
| | | | Compliant | Minor Nonconformity | Major Nonconformity | | |
| 4.1.1 | 1 | Does your organization have identified primary assets that support cybersecurity? | ☐ | ☐ | ☐ | | |
| 4.1.1 | 2 | Does your organization have identified secondary assets that support cybersecurity primary assets? | ☐ | ☐ | ☐ | | |
| 4.1.2 | 3 | Does the organization keeps track of physical asset inventory? | ☐ | ☐ | ☐ | | |
| 4.1.2 | 4 | Does the organization keeps track of software asset inventory? | ☐ | ☐ | ☐ | | |
| 4.1.5 | 5 | Does the organization have information classification guidelines to ensure protection? | ☐ | ☐ | ☐ | | |
| 4.1.4 | 6 | Has the organization adopted procedures to label and handle information? | ☐ | ☐ | ☐ | | |

## Cybersecurity Audit Checklist: CSAM-Cyber Risks

*Table 23. Domain: 5-Cyber Risks*

| Clause | No. | Checklist Questions | Findings | | | Supporting Evidence | Comments |
|---|---|---|---|---|---|---|---|
| | | | Compliant | Minor Nonconformity | Major Nonconformity | | |
| 5.1.1 | 1 | Does the organization define risk scope and boundaries? | ☐ | ☐ | ☐ | | |
| 5.1.1 | 2 | What criteria is used to assess cyber risks? | ☐ | ☐ | ☐ | | |
| 5.1.1 | 3 | What methodology is used to deal with identified risks? | ☐ | ☐ | ☐ | | |
| 5.1.3 | 4 | How do you manage residual risks? | ☐ | ☐ | ☐ | | |
| 5.1.4 | 5 | What procedures are in place to manage risk acceptance? | ☐ | ☐ | ☐ | | |
| 5.1.1 | 6 | Are there any risk communication and consultation processes? | ☐ | ☐ | ☐ | | |
| 5.1.1 | 7 | Do you have procedures for risk monitoring? | ☐ | ☐ | ☐ | | |
| 5.1.1 | 8 | How often do you review your risk management processes? | ☐ | ☐ | ☐ | | |
| 5.1.2 | 9 | What criteria was used to define your cyber asset classification? | ☐ | ☐ | ☐ | | |
| 5.1.5 | 10 | What are the goals and objectives of your cyber risk management? | ☐ | ☐ | ☐ | | |

## Cybersecurity Audit Checklist: CSAM-Frameworks

*Table 24. Domain: 6-Frameworks*

| Clause | No. | Checklist Questions | Findings | | | Supporting Evidence | Comments |
|---|---|---|---|---|---|---|---|
| | | | Compliant | Minor Nonconformity | Major Nonconformity | | |
| 6.1.1 | 1 | Is your organization following one or more best practices from an IT, information security or cybersecurity framework? | ☐ | ☐ | ☐ | | |
| 6.1.2 | 2 | Is your organization certified on a specific cybersecurity framework? If not, do you consider this approach will be useful to your business? | ☐ | ☐ | ☐ | | If the organization is certified or planning to certify on a specific framework, then a separate framework audit must be conducted. |
| 6.1.3 | | Are you interested or planning to implement either partially or completely best practices from the following frameworks? | ITIL ☐ | ISO 27001 ☐ | NIST SP800-53 ☐ | ISC2 CBK ☐ | |
| | | | NIST Cybersecurity ☐ | COBIT ☐ | SANS 20 ☐ | DHS CRR ☐ | |
| | | | Australian DSD ☐ | PCI DSS ☐ | HIPAA ☐ | HITRUST CSF ☐ | |
| | | | NERC CIP ☐ | ISO 27032 ☐ | ISACA audit and assurance ☐ | NERC ☐ | |
| | | | ITAF ☐ | COSO ☐ | ISF ☐ | Other: _____ | |

## Cybersecurity Audit Checklist: CSAM-Architecture: 7.1.1 (Data Centres)

*Table 25. Domain: 7-Architecture and Networks*

| Clause | No. | Checklist Questions | Findings | | | Supporting Evidence | Comments |
|--------|-----|---------------------|----------|--------------------|--------------------|---------------------|----------|
| | | | Compliant | Minor Nonconformity | Major Nonconformity | | |
| 7.1.1 | 1 | Does the organization control physical access to data centres and server rooms? Do you keep an access log? | ☐ | ☐ | ☐ | | |
| 7.1.1 | 2 | Does the organization have proper equipment hosting requirements? | ☐ | ☐ | ☐ | | Water-cooled equipment, weight, electrical supply, receipt of new equipment, diagrams, maintenance, decommissioning |
| 7.1.1 | 3 | Is Power management adequate to the facilities? | ☐ | ☐ | ☐ | | |
| 7.1.1 | 4 | Do you monitor environmental conditions and alert systems? | ☐ | ☐ | ☐ | | Temperature, humidity, air quality |
| 7.1.1 | 5 | Are the facilities in compliance with safety standards and legislation? | ☐ | ☐ | ☐ | | |
| 7.1.1 | 6 | Do you coordinate routine maintenance accordingly? | ☐ | ☐ | ☐ | | |

## Cybersecurity Audit Checklist: CSAM-Architecture: 7.1.2 (IT Operations)

*Table 26. Domain: 7-Architecture and Networks*

| Clause | No. | Checklist Questions | Findings | | | Supporting Evidence | Comments |
|--------|-----|---------------------|----------|--------------------|--------------------|---------------------|----------|
| | | | Compliant | Minor Nonconformity | Major Nonconformity | | |
| 7.1.2 | 1 | Do you incorporate security measures in all your IT Operations? | ☐ | ☐ | ☐ | | |
| 7.1.2 | 2 | Do you keep up-to-date documentation for critical processes or functions? | ☐ | ☐ | ☐ | | Standard Operating Procedures (SOPs), Operation logs, Operations schedules |
| 7.1.2 | 3 | Do you monitor events, incidents, routine operational activities and status/performance of systems? | ☐ | ☐ | ☐ | | |
| 7.1.2 | 4 | Do you manage job scheduling accordingly? | ☐ | ☐ | ☐ | | |
| 7.1.2 | 5 | Do you have a backup management plan? Are your backup tapes or media stored outside the main building? Are you able to restore any specific data based on corrupt data, lost data, disaster recovery or historical data? | ☐ | ☐ | ☐ | | |
| 7.1.2 | 6 | Do you have a Print management plan? Have you changed the default settings/passwords on your printers? Have you implemented secure printing for confidential printouts? | ☐ | ☐ | ☐ | | |

## Cybersecurity Audit Checklist: CSAM-Architecture: 7.1.3 (Servers)

*Table 27. Domain: 7-Architecture and Networks*

| Clause | No. | Checklist Questions | Findings | | | Supporting Evidence | Comments |
|---|---|---|---|---|---|---|---|
| | | | Compliant | Minor Nonconformity | Major Nonconformity | | |
| 7.1.3 | 1 | Do you restrict physical and logical access to servers to authorized technical staff? | ☐ | ☐ | ☐ | | |
| 7.1.3 | 2 | Do you keep a patch management plan for all your servers? Do you follow approved change management for new updates and patches? | ☐ | ☐ | ☐ | | |
| 7.1.3 | 3 | Do you have configuration and alerts in place to monitor server uptime/downtime? | ☐ | ☐ | ☐ | | |
| 7.1.3 | 4 | Do you inspect/review your servers regularly in order to hardening security? | ☐ | ☐ | ☐ | | |
| 7.1.3 | 5 | Have you implemented virtualization? Do you keep inventory of your virtual servers and host machines? Have you encrypted server communications (SSL or IPSec)? Do you restrict access to the virtual server management console and hypervisors? | ☐ | ☐ | ☐ | | |
| 7.1.3 | 6 | Do you perform regular maintenance on all your physical/virtual servers? | ☐ | ☐ | ☐ | | |
| 7.1.3 | 7 | Do you have procedures for old server decommissioning and disposal? | ☐ | ☐ | ☐ | | |

## Cybersecurity Audit Checklist: CSAM-Architecture: 7.1.4 (Storage)

*Table 28. Domain: 7-Architecture and Networks*

| Clause | No. | Checklist Questions | Findings | | | Supporting Evidence | Comments |
|---|---|---|---|---|---|---|---|
| | | | Compliant | Minor Nonconformity | Major Nonconformity | | |
| 7.1.4 | 1 | Have you defined a data storage policy for all your storage devices? | ☐ | ☐ | ☐ | | HDDs, NAS, SANs, DAS, CAS |
| 7.1.4 | 2 | Have you implemented a storage naming convention and hierarchy? | ☐ | ☐ | ☐ | | |
| 7.1.4 | 3 | Are you enforcing freedom of information, data protection and IT governance regulations for your stored data? | ☐ | ☐ | ☐ | | |
| 7.1.4 | 4 | Do you have an archiving policy? | ☐ | ☐ | ☐ | | |
| 7.1.4 | 5 | Are you able to retrieve archived data as necessary? | ☐ | ☐ | ☐ | | |

## Cybersecurity Audit Checklist: CSAM-Architecture: 7.1.5 (Defense-in-Depth)

*Table 29. Domain: 7-Architecture and Networks*

| Clause | No. | Checklist Questions | Findings | | | Supporting Evidence | Comments |
|--------|-----|---------------------|----------|--------------------|--------------------|---------------------|----------|
| | | | Compliant | Minor Nonconformity | Major Nonconformity | | |
| 7.1.5 | 1 | Have you implemented cybersecurity defense-in-depth? | ☐ | ☐ | ☐ | | |
| 7.1.5 | 2 | Which type of defense have you implemented? | ☐ | ☐ | ☐ | | Concentric rings, overlapping redundancy, segregation or a combination |
| 7.1.5 | 3 | What vulnerabilities are you addressing per layer? | ☐ | ☐ | ☐ | | |
| 7.1.5 | 4 | How are the layers weakening the vulnerabilities? | ☐ | ☐ | ☐ | | |
| 7.1.5 | 5 | What kind of interactions exist between layers? | ☐ | ☐ | ☐ | | |

## Cybersecurity Audit Checklist: CSAM-Architecture: 7.1.6 (Physical Security)

*Table 30. Domain: 7-Architecture and Networks*

| Clause | No. | Checklist Questions | Findings | | | Supporting Evidence | Comments |
|--------|-----|---------------------|----------|--------------------|--------------------|---------------------|----------|
| | | | Compliant | Minor Nonconformity | Major Nonconformity | | |
| 7.1.6 | 1 | Do you have policies and procedures to limit unauthorized access to restricted facilities? | ☐ | ☐ | ☐ | | |
| 7.1.6 | 2 | Do you have methods in place to control access to your secure areas? | ☐ | ☐ | ☐ | | |
| 7.1.6 | 3 | Is your computing area physically secured? | ☐ | ☐ | ☐ | | |
| 7.1.6 | 4 | Do you have a screen saver policy? Do screens automatically lock after inactivity? | ☐ | ☐ | ☐ | | Via GPO |
| 7.1.6 | 5 | Have you implemented procedures to avoid laptop or equipment theft? | ☐ | ☐ | ☐ | | Cable locks, secure storage |

## Cybersecurity Audit Checklist: CSAM-Architecture: 7.1.7 (Third Party Products and Services)

*Table 31. Domain: 7-Architecture and Networks*

| Clause | No. | Checklist Questions | Findings | | | Supporting Evidence | Comments |
|---|---|---|---|---|---|---|---|
| | | | Compliant | Minor Nonconformity | Major Nonconformity | | |
| 7.1.7 | 1 | Do you have strict processes for selecting suppliers, vendors and consultants? | ☐ | ☐ | ☐ | | |
| 7.1.7 | 2 | Do you limit access to suppliers, vendors and consultants? | ☐ | ☐ | ☐ | | |
| 7.1.7 | 3 | Do you monitor unauthorized changes or systems reconfiguration related to your infrastructure and architecture? | ☐ | ☐ | ☐ | | |

## Cybersecurity Audit Checklist: CSAM-Architecture: 7.1.8 (Frameworks)

*Table 32. Domain: 7-Architecture and Networks*

| Clause | No. | Checklist Questions | Findings | | | Supporting Evidence | Comments |
|---|---|---|---|---|---|---|---|
| | | | Compliant | Minor Nonconformity | Major Nonconformity | | |
| 7.1.8 | 1 | Do you follow a specific security architecture framework? | ☐ | ☐ | ☐ | | SABSA, TOGAF |
| 7.1.8 | 2 | Do you follow architecture process models or framework models? | ☐ | ☐ | ☐ | | |
| 7.1.8 | 3 | Do you have a centralized, decentralized or hybrid IT architecture? | ☐ | ☐ | ☐ | | |

## Cybersecurity Audit Checklist: CSAM-Architecture: 7.1.9 (OSI model)

*Table 33. Domain: 7-Architecture and Networks*

| Clause | No. | Checklist Questions | Findings | | | Supporting Evidence | Comments |
|---|---|---|---|---|---|---|---|
| | | | Compliant | Minor Nonconformity | Major Nonconformity | | |
| 7.1.9 | 1 | Have you taken measures to ensure smooth flowing of data throughout the OSI layers? | ☐ | ☐ | ☐ | | |
| 7.1.9 | 2 | Have you implemented security solutions for all seven OSI layers? | ☐ | ☐ | ☐ | | |
| 7.1.9 | 3 | Have you enforced network port security for TCP and UDP? | ☐ | ☐ | ☐ | | |

## Cybersecurity Audit Checklist: CSAM-Architecture: 7.1.10 (Interconnection devices)

*Table 34. Domain: 7-Architecture and Networks*

| Clause | No. | Checklist Questions | Findings | | | Supporting Evidence | Comments |
|--------|-----|---------------------|----------|--------------------|--------------------|---------------------|----------|
| | | | Compliant | Minor Nonconformity | Major Nonconformity | | |
| 7.1.10 | 1 | Have you enforced security measures for hubs, repeaters and NICs? | ☐ | ☐ | ☐ | | |
| 7.1.10 | 2 | Have you enforced security measures for layer 2 switches, bridges and Wireless Access Points (WAPs)? | ☐ | ☐ | ☐ | | |
| 7.1.10 | 3 | Have you enforced security measures for layer 3 switches and routers? | ☐ | ☐ | ☐ | | |
| 7.1.10 | 4 | Have you enforced security measures for layer 4 switches? | ☐ | ☐ | ☐ | | |
| 7.1.10 | 5 | Have you enforced security measures for gateways? | ☐ | ☐ | ☐ | | |
| 7.1.10 | 6 | Have you enforced security measures for modems? | ☐ | ☐ | ☐ | | |
| 7.1.11 | 7 | Have you enforced security measures for PBXs? | ☐ | ☐ | ☐ | | |

## Cybersecurity Audit Checklist: CSAM-Architecture: 7.1.11 (Network Segmentation)

*Table 35. Domain: 7-Architecture and Networks*

| Clause | No. | Checklist Questions | Findings | | | Supporting Evidence | Comments |
|--------|-----|---------------------|----------|--------------------|--------------------|---------------------|----------|
| | | | Compliant | Minor Nonconformity | Major Nonconformity | | |
| 7.1.11 | 1 | Have you implemented isolation and segmentation to hardening network security? | ☐ | ☐ | ☐ | | |
| 7.1.11 | 2 | Have you implemented secure VLANs? | ☐ | ☐ | ☐ | | |
| 7.1.11 | 3 | Have you implemented server isolation? | ☐ | ☐ | ☐ | | |
| 7.1.11 | 4 | Have you implemented domain isolation? | ☐ | ☐ | ☐ | | |
| 7.1.11 | 5 | Have you implemented a Demilitarized Zone (DMZ) | ☐ | ☐ | ☐ | | |

## Cybersecurity Audit Checklist: CSAM-Architecture: 7.1.12 (Encryption)

*Table 36. Domain: 7-Architecture and Networks*

| Clause | No. | Checklist Questions | Findings | | | Supporting Evidence | Comments |
|--------|-----|---------------------|-----------|-------------------|-------------------|---------------------|----------|
| | | | Compliant | Minor Nonconformity | Major Nonconformity | | |
| 7.1.12 | 1 | Do you protect data/information using encryption techniques? | ☐ | ☐ | ☐ | | |
| 7.1.12 | 2 | Have you implemented VPNs? | ☐ | ☐ | ☐ | | |
| 7.1.12 | 3 | Have you implemented symmetric key encryption? | ☐ | ☐ | ☐ | | |
| 7.1.12 | 4 | Have you implemented asymmetric key encryption? | ☐ | ☐ | ☐ | | |
| 7.1.12 | 5 | Have you implemented PKI? | ☐ | ☐ | ☐ | | |
| 7.1.12 | 6 | Have you implemented SSL and TLS? | ☐ | ☐ | ☐ | | |
| 7.1.12 | 7 | Have you implemented digital signatures? | ☐ | ☐ | ☐ | | |

## Cybersecurity Audit Checklist: CSAM-Architecture: 7.1.13 (Monitoring and Detection)

*Table 37. Domain: 7-Architecture and Networks*

| Clause | No. | Checklist Questions | Findings | | | Supporting Evidence | Comments |
|--------|-----|---------------------|-----------|-------------------|-------------------|---------------------|----------|
| | | | Compliant | Minor Nonconformity | Major Nonconformity | | |
| 7.1.13 | 1 | Do you monitor ingress, egress and data loss prevention (DLP) in your organization? | ☐ | ☐ | ☐ | | |
| 7.1.13 | 2 | Have you configured and monitored corporate antivirus? | ☐ | ☐ | ☐ | | |
| 7.1.13 | 3 | Have you configured and monitored corporate anti-malware or security suite? | ☐ | ☐ | ☐ | | |
| 7.1.13 | 4 | Do you have an IDS in place? Do you monitor it? | ☐ | ☐ | ☐ | | |
| 7.1.13 | 5 | Do you have an IPS in place? Do you monitor it? | ☐ | ☐ | ☐ | | |
| 7.1.13 | 6 | Do you have a SIM, SIEM or SEM in place? Do you monitor it? | ☐ | ☐ | ☐ | | |
| 7.1.13 | 7 | Do you have a firewall in place? Do you monitor it? | ☐ | ☐ | ☐ | | |

## Cybersecurity Audit Checklist: CSAM-Networks: 7.2.1 (Connectivity)

*Table 38. Domain: 7-Architecture and Networks*

| Clause | No. | Checklist Questions | Findings | | | Supporting Evidence | Comments |
|--------|-----|---------------------|----------|--|--|---------------------|----------|
| | | | Compliant | Minor Nonconformity | Major Nonconformity | | |
| 7.2.1 | 1 | Do you enforce security on your wired and Wi-Fi networks connectivity? | ☐ | ☐ | ☐ | | |
| 7.2.1 | 2 | Have you implemented security on your Internet nodes? | ☐ | ☐ | ☐ | | |
| 7.2.1 | 3 | Have you implemented security on your Intranet nodes? | ☐ | ☐ | ☐ | | |
| 7.2.1 | 4 | Have you implemented security on your Extranet nodes? | ☐ | ☐ | ☐ | | |
| 7.2.1 | 5 | Have you considered a security assessment for your IoT devices? | ☐ | ☐ | ☐ | | |

## Cybersecurity Audit Checklist: CSAM-Networks: 7.2.2 (Telecom carriers and ISPs)

*Table 39. Domain: 7-Architecture and Networks*

| Clause | No. | Checklist Questions | Findings | | | Supporting Evidence | Comments |
|--------|-----|---------------------|----------|--|--|---------------------|----------|
| | | | Compliant | Minor Nonconformity | Major Nonconformity | | |
| 7.2.2 | 1 | Does your carrier and/or ISP offer security on your dedicated private channel and Internet link? | ☐ | ☐ | ☐ | | |
| 7.2.2 | 2 | Does your carrier and/or ISP offer monitoring tools for your upload link? | ☐ | ☐ | ☐ | | |
| 7.2.2 | 3 | Does your carrier and/or ISP offer monitoring tools for your download link? | ☐ | ☐ | ☐ | | |

## Cybersecurity Audit Checklist: CSAM-Networks: 7.2.3 (Pen Testing)

*Table 40. Domain: 7-Architecture and Networks*

| Clause | No. | Checklist Questions | Findings | | | Supporting Evidence | Comments |
|---|---|---|---|---|---|---|---|
| | | | Compliant | Minor Nonconformity | Major Nonconformity | | |
| 7.2.3 | 1 | Do you plan your pen testing accordingly? | ☐ | ☐ | ☐ | | |
| 7.2.3 | 2 | Do you define a clear scope when performing a pen test? | ☐ | ☐ | ☐ | | |
| 7.2.3 | 3 | Do you approve a written permission for any pen test? | ☐ | ☐ | ☐ | | |
| 7.2.3 | 4 | Do you ensure that your pen tests include **"Do not harm"** procedures? | ☐ | ☐ | ☐ | | |
| 7.2.3 | 5 | Do you verify that your pen testers are highly qualified to conduct the work? | ☐ | ☐ | ☐ | | |
| 7.2.3 | 6 | Do you release communication and escalation plans to your organization during the tests? | ☐ | ☐ | ☐ | | |

## Cybersecurity Audit Checklist: CSAM-Networks: 7.2.4 (Fault Management)

*Table 41. Domain: 7-Architecture and Networks*

| Clause | No. | Checklist Questions | Findings | | | Supporting Evidence | Comments |
|---|---|---|---|---|---|---|---|
| | | | Compliant | Minor Nonconformity | Major Nonconformity | | |
| 7.2.4 | 1 | Have you implemented fault management to detect, log, alert and fix network issues? | ☐ | ☐ | ☐ | | |
| 7.2.4 | 2 | Does your network management include network discovery and topology mapping features? | ☐ | ☐ | ☐ | | |
| 7.2.4 | 3 | Have you configured properly your networks to discover events related to fault detection? | ☐ | ☐ | ☐ | | |

## Cybersecurity Audit Checklist: CSAM-Networks: 7.2.5 (Configuration Management)

*Table 42. Domain: 7-Architecture and Networks*

| Clause | No. | Checklist Questions | Findings | | | Supporting Evidence | Comments |
|---|---|---|---|---|---|---|---|
| | | | Compliant | Minor Nonconformity | Major Nonconformity | | |
| 7.2.5 | 1 | Have you implemented configuration management so you can easily track network/systems configuration linked to hardware and software? | ☐ | ☐ | ☐ | | |
| 7.2.5 | 2 | Are you able to discover your network devices using a specific tool? | ☐ | ☐ | ☐ | | |
| 7.2.5 | 3 | Are you able to discover software and firmware versions in order to schedule future network updates? | ☐ | ☐ | ☐ | | |

## Cybersecurity Audit Checklist: CSAM-Networks: 7.2.6 (Accounting Management)

*Table 43. Domain: 7-Architecture and Networks*

| Clause | No. | Checklist Questions | Findings | | | Supporting Evidence | Comments |
|---|---|---|---|---|---|---|---|
| | | | Compliant | Minor Nonconformity | Major Nonconformity | | |
| 7.2.6 | 1 | Have you implemented accounting management in order to measure network utilization parameters? | ☐ | ☐ | ☐ | | |
| 7.2.6 | 2 | Are you measuring the utilization of all your network resources? | ☐ | ☐ | ☐ | | |
| 7.2.6 | 3 | Are you analyzing data gathered to detect usage patterns? | ☐ | ☐ | ☐ | | |

## Cybersecurity Audit Checklist: CSAM-Networks: 7.2.7 (Performance Management)

*Table 44. Domain: 7-Architecture and Networks*

| Clause | No. | Checklist Questions | Findings | | | Supporting Evidence | Comments |
|---|---|---|---|---|---|---|---|
| | | | Compliant | Minor Nonconformity | Major Nonconformity | | |
| 7.2.7 | 1 | Have you negotiated with your carrier or ISP a SLA to include metrics to evaluate the performance level of network services? | ☐ | ☐ | ☐ | | |
| 7.2.7 | 2 | Are you evaluating input queue drops, output queue drops and ignored packets? | ☐ | ☐ | ☐ | | |
| 7.2.7 | 3 | Are you evaluating CPU utilization, buffer allocation and memory allocation? | ☐ | ☐ | ☐ | | Device level: Relationship between network protocols and buffer availability |
| 7.2.7 | 4 | Are you evaluating performance for any WAN? | ☐ | ☐ | ☐ | | |

## Cybersecurity Audit Checklist: CSAM-Networks: 7.2.8 (Network Security)

*Table 45. Domain: 7-Architecture and Networks*

| Clause | No. | Checklist Questions | Findings | | | Supporting Evidence | Comments |
|---|---|---|---|---|---|---|---|
| | | | Compliant | Minor Nonconformity | Major Nonconformity | | |
| 7.2.8 | 1 | Have you hardening network authentication security? | ☐ | ☐ | ☐ | | |
| 7.2.8 | 2 | Have you hardening network firewalls security? | ☐ | ☐ | ☐ | | |
| 7.2.8 | 3 | Have you hardening network authorization security? | ☐ | ☐ | ☐ | | |
| 7.2.8 | 4 | Have you hardening network segmentation security? | ☐ | ☐ | ☐ | | |
| 7.2.8 | 5 | Have you hardening IDS/IPS security? | ☐ | ☐ | ☐ | | |
| 7.2.8 | 6 | Have you implemented alert notification and remediation for attempted cyberattacks? | ☐ | ☐ | ☐ | | |

# Cybersecurity Audit Checklist: CSAM-Networks: 7.2.9 (Endpoints)

*Table 46. Domain: 7-Architecture and Networks*

| Clause | No. | Checklist Questions | Findings | | | Supporting Evidence | Comments |
|--------|-----|---------------------|----------|--------------------|--------------------|---------------------|----------|
| | | | Compliant | Minor Nonconformity | Major Nonconformity | | |
| 7.2.9 | 1 | Are you regularly running inventories of authorized and unauthorized devices in your organization? | ☐ | ☐ | ☐ | | |
| 7.2.9 | 2 | Are you regularly running inventories of authorized and unauthorized software in your organization? | ☐ | ☐ | ☐ | | |
| 7.2.9 | 3 | Do you keep master images of laptops, mobile devices, laptops, workstations and servers? Are these images stored on a secure server? | ☐ | ☐ | ☐ | | |
| 7.2.9 | 4 | Have you implemented continuous vulnerability assessment and remediation for your endpoints? | ☐ | ☐ | ☐ | | |

# Cybersecurity Audit Checklist: CSAM-Networks: 7.2.10 (Firewalls)

*Table 47. Domain: 7-Architecture and Networks*

| Clause | No. | Checklist Questions | Findings | | | Supporting Evidence | Comments |
|--------|-----|---------------------|----------|--------------------|--------------------|---------------------|----------|
| | | | Compliant | Minor Nonconformity | Major Nonconformity | | |
| 7.2.10 | 1 | What kind of firewalls do you have in place? | ☐ | ☐ | ☐ | | Hardware/ Software, Packet filtering, application systems, stateful inspection, NGFW, network layer, transport layer, context aware, proxy server, reverse proxy server, NAT, host-based |
| 7.2.10 | 2 | What kind of approach do you follow to configure your firewalls? | ☐ | ☐ | ☐ | | Block by default, allow specific traffic, etc.... |
| 7.2.10 | 3 | Do you follow specific procedures to create firewall rules? | ☐ | ☐ | ☐ | | Form, approval request |
| 7.2.10 | 4 | Do you follow the least privilege principle for granting network access through your firewalls? Do you configure access rules with minimal access rights? | ☐ | ☐ | ☐ | | |
| 7.2.10 | 5 | Do you filter ICMP messages? | ☐ | ☐ | ☐ | | |
| 7.2.10 | 6 | Do you grant mobile devices access by using MAC filtering? | ☐ | ☐ | ☐ | | |
| 7.2.10 | 7 | Have you enforced security to access firewall consoles? | ☐ | ☐ | ☐ | | Internal and external ports |
| 7.2.10 | 8 | Do you restrict network access and resources to visitors, temporary workers and consultants? | ☐ | ☐ | ☐ | | |
| 7.2.10 | 9 | Do you document all firewall rule changes? | ☐ | ☐ | ☐ | | |
| 7.2.10 | 10 | Do you perform firewall audits every semester? Do you schedule regular firewall maintenance for every firewall? Do you backup your firewall configurations? | ☐ | ☐ | ☐ | | |

# Cybersecurity Audit Checklist: CSAM-Information: 8.1.1 (Service Desk)

*Table 48. Domain: 8-Information, Systems and Applications*

| Clause | No. | Checklist Questions | Findings | | | Supporting Evidence | Comments |
|---|---|---|---|---|---|---|---|
| | | | Compliant | Minor Nonconformity | Major Nonconformity | | |
| 8.1.1 | 1 | Is your Help Desk enforcing best security practices? | ☐ | ☐ | ☐ | | |
| 8.1.1 | 2 | Are you using a ticketing system to track all security events and incidents? | ☐ | ☐ | ☐ | | |
| 8.1.1 | 3 | Is your Help Desk able to deal with cybersecurity events and incidents? | ☐ | ☐ | ☐ | | |
| 8.1.1 | 4 | Are your Help Desk analysts escalating cybersecurity issues whenever is required? | ☐ | ☐ | ☐ | | |
| 8.1.1 | 5 | Is your Help Desk creating and updating your knowledge base to deal with recurrent incidents? | ☐ | ☐ | ☐ | | |

# Cybersecurity Audit Checklist: CSAM-Information: 8.1.2 (Desktop Support)

*Table 49. Domain: 8-Information, Systems and Applications*

| Clause | No. | Checklist Questions | Findings | | | Supporting Evidence | Comments |
|---|---|---|---|---|---|---|---|
| | | | Compliant | Minor Nonconformity | Major Nonconformity | | |
| 8.1.2 | 1 | Are you enforcing desktop and laptop security policies? | ☐ | ☐ | ☐ | | |
| 8.1.2 | 2 | Do you have a desktop and laptop image program in place? | ☐ | ☐ | ☐ | | |
| 8.1.2 | 3 | Are you deploying releases, upgrades, patches and hot fixes through a release management program? | ☐ | ☐ | ☐ | | |
| 8.1.2 | 4 | Do you monitor and audit your organization's desktop and laptop computers? | ☐ | ☐ | ☐ | | |
| 8.1.2 | 5 | Are your laptops using an encryption program? | ☐ | ☐ | ☐ | | |

## Cybersecurity Audit Checklist: CSAM-Information: 8.1.3 (InfoSec Management)

*Table 50. Domain: 8-Information, Systems and Applications*

| Clause | No. | Checklist Questions | Findings | | | Supporting Evidence | Comments |
|---|---|---|---|---|---|---|---|
| | | | Compliant | Minor Nonconformity | Major Nonconformity | | |
| 8.1.3 | 1 | Do you have policies to manage and protect organizational data? | ☐ | ☐ | ☐ | | |
| 8.1.3 | 2 | Have you defined data ownership in your organization? | ☐ | ☐ | ☐ | | |
| 8.1.3 | 3 | Are you protecting sensitive information? | ☐ | ☐ | ☐ | | |
| 8.1.3 | 4 | Are you in compliance with federal and provincial legal requirements for data and information? | ☐ | ☐ | ☐ | | |
| 8.1.3 | 5 | Are you collecting personal data? Are you ensuring that personal data is protected against misuse, modification, unauthorized access and disclosure? | ☐ | ☐ | ☐ | | |

## Cybersecurity Audit Checklist: CSAM-Information: 8.1.4 (Documentation)

*Table 51. Domain: 8-Information, Systems and Applications*

| Clause | No. | Checklist Questions | Findings | | | Supporting Evidence | Comments |
|---|---|---|---|---|---|---|---|
| | | | Compliant | Minor Nonconformity | Major Nonconformity | | |
| 8.1.4 | 1 | Do you have an IT documentation policy? | ☐ | ☐ | ☐ | | |
| 8.1.4 | 2 | Are you documenting your critical processes and procedures? | ☐ | ☐ | ☐ | | |
| 8.1.4 | 3 | Have you implemented standardized documentation formats? | ☐ | ☐ | ☐ | | |
| 8.1.4 | 4 | Are you following proper version controls and retirement controls? | ☐ | ☐ | ☐ | | |

## Cybersecurity Audit Checklist: CSAM-Information: 8.1.5 (Project Management)

*Table 52. Domain: 8-Information, Systems and Applications*

| Clause | No. | Checklist Questions | Findings | | | Supporting Evidence | Comments |
|---|---|---|---|---|---|---|---|
| | | | Compliant | Minor Nonconformity | Major Nonconformity | | |
| 8.1.5 | 1 | Are you using project management methodologies and best practices for all your projects? | ☐ | ☐ | ☐ | | |
| 8.1.5 | 2 | Are you considering security for all the projects that you plan to implement in your organization? | ☐ | ☐ | ☐ | | |
| 8.1.5 | 3 | Do your PM methodologies ensure that all internal and external resources follow best cybersecurity practices? | ☐ | ☐ | ☐ | | |

## Cybersecurity Audit Checklist: CSAM-Information: 8.1.6 (Change Management)

*Table 53. Domain: 8-Information, Systems and Applications*

| Clause | No. | Checklist Questions | Findings | | | Supporting Evidence | Comments |
|---|---|---|---|---|---|---|---|
| | | | Compliant | Minor Nonconformity | Major Nonconformity | | |
| 8.1.6 | 1 | Have you implemented change management in your organization? | ☐ | ☐ | ☐ | | |
| 8.1.6 | 2 | Have you identified the change approvers in your organization? | ☐ | ☐ | ☐ | | |
| 8.1.6 | 3 | Have you defined a change impact and risk categorization matrix? | ☐ | ☐ | ☐ | | |

## Cybersecurity Audit Checklist: CSAM-Information: 8.1.7 (Records Management)

*Table 54. Domain: 8-Information, Systems and Applications*

| Clause | No. | Checklist Questions | Findings | | | Supporting Evidence | Comments |
|---|---|---|---|---|---|---|---|
| | | | Compliant | Minor Nonconformity | Major Nonconformity | | |
| 8.1.7 | 1 | Have you implemented document control and records management in your organization? | ☐ | ☐ | ☐ | | |
| 8.1.7 | 2 | Are your maintaining physical and electronic records? | ☐ | ☐ | ☐ | | |
| 8.1.7 | 3 | Have you implemented security measures to protect your physical and electronic records? | ☐ | ☐ | ☐ | | |
| 8.1.7 | 4 | Have you implemented procedures for data retention? | ☐ | ☐ | ☐ | | |
| 8.1.7 | 5 | Have you implemented procedures for data destruction? | ☐ | ☐ | ☐ | | |

## Cybersecurity Audit Checklist: CSAM-Information: 8.1.8 (Privacy)

*Table 55. Domain: 8-Information, Systems and Applications*

| Clause | No. | Checklist Questions | Findings | | | Supporting Evidence | Comments |
|---|---|---|---|---|---|---|---|
| | | | Compliant | Minor Nonconformity | Major Nonconformity | | |
| 8.1.8 | 1 | Have you taken security measures to protect privacy? | ☐ | ☐ | ☐ | | |
| 8.1.8 | 2 | Have you developed a Privacy Impact Analysis (PIA)? | ☐ | ☐ | ☐ | | Based on Technology, Processes and People |
| 8.1.8 | 3 | Do you provide notice prior to collecting personal information? | ☐ | ☐ | ☐ | | |
| 8.1.8 | 4 | Do you offer *opt-in* and *opt-out* information options? | ☐ | ☐ | ☐ | | |

## Cybersecurity Audit Checklist: CSAM-Information: 8.1.9 (Audits)

*Table 56. Domain: 8-Information, Systems and Applications*

| Clause | No. | Checklist Questions | Findings | | | Supporting Evidence | Comments |
|--------|-----|---------------------|----------|----------|----------|---------------------|----------|
| | | | Compliant | Minor Nonconformity | Major Nonconformity | | |
| 8.1.9 | 1 | Do you conduct audits to ensure that the organization is protected and controlled? | ☐ | ☐ | ☐ | | |
| 8.1.9 | 2 | Do you verify general control procedures? | ☐ | ☐ | ☐ | | |
| 8.1.9 | 3 | Do you verify preventive, detective and corrective security controls? | ☐ | ☐ | ☐ | | |
| 8.1.9 | 4 | Do you achieve assurance by continuous auditing and monitoring? | ☐ | ☐ | ☐ | | |

## Cybersecurity Audit Checklist: CSAM-Systems: 8.2.1 (Operating Systems)

*Table 57. Domain: 8-Information, Systems and Applications*

| Clause | No. | Checklist Questions | Findings | | | Supporting Evidence | Comments |
|--------|-----|---------------------|----------|----------|----------|---------------------|----------|
| | | | Compliant | Minor Nonconformity | Major Nonconformity | | |
| 8.2.1 | 1 | Do you regularly schedule operating systems maintenance and support? | ☐ | ☐ | ☐ | | |
| 8.2.1 | 2 | Do you regularly inventory and maintain your systems scripts? | ☐ | ☐ | ☐ | | |
| 8.2.1 | 3 | Do you regularly inventory and maintain your systems programs? | ☐ | ☐ | ☐ | | |
| 8.2.1 | 4 | Do you monitor interfaces to hardware and identify any failure? | ☐ | ☐ | ☐ | | |
| 8.2.1 | 5 | Are you hardening authentication security? | ☐ | ☐ | ☐ | | |
| 8.2.1 | 6 | Are you hardening authorization security? | ☐ | ☐ | ☐ | | |
| 8.2.1 | 7 | Are you hardening file system permissions security? | ☐ | ☐ | ☐ | | |
| 8.2.1 | 8 | Are you hardening access privileges security? | ☐ | ☐ | ☐ | | |
| 8.2.1 | 9 | Have you implemented Single Sign-On (SSO) to log on multiple systems? | ☐ | ☐ | ☐ | | |
| 8.2.1 | 10 | Do you regularly inventory and verify your organization's GPOs? | ☐ | ☐ | ☐ | | |

## Cybersecurity Audit Checklist: CSAM-Systems: 8.2.2 (Access Management)

*Table 58. Domain: 8-Information, Systems and Applications*

| Clause | No. | Checklist Questions | Findings | | | Supporting Evidence | Comments |
|---|---|---|---|---|---|---|---|
| | | | Compliant | Minor Nonconformity | Major Nonconformity | | |
| 8.2.2 | 1 | Have you implemented a strong password policy for systems administrators and end users? | ☐ | ☐ | ☐ | | |
| 8.2.2 | 2 | Have you implemented an access control policy? | ☐ | ☐ | ☐ | | |
| 8.2.2 | 3 | Have you implemented a formal procedure for granting and blocking user's access? | ☐ | ☐ | ☐ | | |
| 8.2.2 | 4 | Have you implemented privilege management based on the principle of least privilege? | ☐ | ☐ | ☐ | | |
| 8.2.2 | 5 | Have you implemented user rights management based on job roles and segregation of duties? | ☐ | ☐ | ☐ | | |
| 8.2.2 | 6 | Have you implemented a clear desk policy? | ☐ | ☐ | ☐ | | |
| 8.2.2 | 7 | Have you implemented a clear screen policy? | ☐ | ☐ | ☐ | | |

## Cybersecurity Audit Checklist: CSAM-Systems: 8.2.3 (Logging and monitoring)

*Table 59. Domain: 8-Information, Systems and Applications*

| Clause | No. | Checklist Questions | Findings | | | Supporting Evidence | Comments |
|---|---|---|---|---|---|---|---|
| | | | Compliant | Minor Nonconformity | Major Nonconformity | | |
| 8.2.3 | 1 | Is audit logging enabled on all your systems? | ☐ | ☐ | ☐ | | |
| 8.2.3 | 2 | Do you monitor all your systems? | ☐ | ☐ | ☐ | | |
| 8.2.3 | 3 | Have you taken security measures to protect logs against tampering and unauthorized access? | ☐ | ☐ | ☐ | | |
| 8.2.3 | 4 | Are all your systems synchronized? | ☐ | ☐ | ☐ | | |
| 8.2.3 | 5 | Is logging enabled for systems administrators and operators? | ☐ | ☐ | ☐ | | |

## Cybersecurity Audit Checklist: CSAM-Systems: 8.2.4 (Databases)

*Table 60. Domain: 8-Information, Systems and Applications*

| Clause | No. | Checklist Questions | Findings | | | Supporting Evidence | Comments |
|---|---|---|---|---|---|---|---|
| | | | Compliant | Minor Nonconformity | Major Nonconformity | | |
| 8.2.4 | 1 | Have you implemented DB standards and policies? | ☐ | ☐ | ☐ | | |
| 8.2.4 | 2 | Do you keep inventory of all your existing databases? | ☐ | ☐ | ☐ | | |
| 8.2.4 | 3 | Have you taken security measures to avoid database manipulation? | ☐ | ☐ | ☐ | | |
| 8.2.4 | 4 | Have you defined triggers that will generate alerts? | ☐ | ☐ | ☐ | | |
| 8.2.4 | 5 | Do you perform database maintenance and monitoring? | ☐ | ☐ | ☐ | | |

## Cybersecurity Audit Checklist: CSAM-Systems: 8.2.5 (Licensing)

*Table 61. Domain: 8-Information, Systems and Applications*

| Clause | No. | Checklist Questions | Findings | | | Supporting Evidence | Comments |
|--------|-----|---------------------|----------|--|--|---------------------|----------|
| | | | Compliant | Minor Nonconformity | Major Nonconformity | | |
| 8.2.5 | 1 | Do you keep track of all your software licensing? | ☐ | ☐ | ☐ | | Contracts, keys, tokens, subscriptions, upgrades, OEMs |
| 8.2.5 | 2 | Have you implemented software licensing management? | ☐ | ☐ | ☐ | | |
| 8.2.5 | 3 | Do you have processes in place for managing the software licensing phases? | ☐ | ☐ | ☐ | | Requirements, design, evaluate, procure, build, deploy, operate, optimize and retire |

## Cybersecurity Audit Checklist: CSAM-Systems: 8.2.6 (Web Management)

*Table 62. Domain: 8-Information, Systems and Applications*

| Clause | No. | Checklist Questions | Findings | | | Supporting Evidence | Comments |
|--------|-----|---------------------|----------|--|--|---------------------|----------|
| | | | Compliant | Minor Nonconformity | Major Nonconformity | | |
| 8.2.6 | 1 | Have you taken security measures to protect websites, web-based applications and Internet services? | ☐ | ☐ | ☐ | | |
| 8.2.6 | 2 | Are you able to mitigate any cyber threat that could impact your websites, web-based applications and Internet services? | ☐ | ☐ | ☐ | | |
| 8.2.6 | 3 | Do you monitor your website and web-based applications? | ☐ | ☐ | ☐ | | Availability, resilience and security |

## Cybersecurity Audit Checklist: CSAM-Systems: 8.2.7 (TPS)

*Table 63. Domain: 8-Information, Systems and Applications*

| Clause | No. | Checklist Questions | Findings | | | Supporting Evidence | Comments |
|--------|-----|---------------------|----------|--|--|---------------------|----------|
| | | | Compliant | Minor Nonconformity | Major Nonconformity | | |
| 8.2.7 | 1 | Have you taken security measures to protect TPS? | ☐ | ☐ | ☐ | | |
| 8.2.7 | 2 | Do you protect confidential information generated by TPS? | ☐ | ☐ | ☐ | | i.e. Payroll, bookstore |
| 8.2.7 | 3 | Do your flowcharts have strict security controls for the TPS? | ☐ | ☐ | ☐ | | |

## Cybersecurity Audit Checklist: CSAM-Systems: 8.2.8 (ERP)

*Table 64. Domain: 8-Information, Systems and Applications*

| Clause | No. | Checklist Questions | Findings | | | Supporting Evidence | Comments |
|---|---|---|---|---|---|---|---|
| | | | Compliant | Minor Nonconformity | Major Nonconformity | | |
| 8.2.8 | 1 | Have you taken security measures to protect ERP? | ☐ | ☐ | ☐ | | |
| 8.2.8 | 2 | Do you protect confidential information generated by ERP? | ☐ | ☐ | ☐ | | |
| 8.2.8 | 3 | Do your flowcharts have strict security controls for the ERP? | ☐ | ☐ | ☐ | | |

## Cybersecurity Audit Checklist: CSAM-Systems: 8.2.9 (e-Commerce)

*Table 65. Domain: 8-Information, Systems and Applications*

| Clause | No. | Checklist Questions | Findings | | | Supporting Evidence | Comments |
|---|---|---|---|---|---|---|---|
| | | | Compliant | Minor Nonconformity | Major Nonconformity | | |
| 8.2.9 | 1 | Have you taken security measures to protect e-Commerce? | ☐ | ☐ | ☐ | | |
| 8.2.9 | 2 | Do you protect confidential information generated by e-Commerce systems? | ☐ | ☐ | ☐ | | |
| 8.2.9 | 3 | Do your flowcharts have strict security controls for the e-Commerce systems? | ☐ | ☐ | ☐ | | |

## Cybersecurity Audit Checklist: CSAM-Systems: 8.2.10 (Systems utilities)

*Table 66. Domain: 8-Information, Systems and Applications*

| Clause | No. | Checklist Questions | Findings | | | Supporting Evidence | Comments |
|---|---|---|---|---|---|---|---|
| | | | Compliant | Minor Nonconformity | Major Nonconformity | | |
| 8.2.10 | 1 | Do you keep track of all your systems utilities? | ☐ | ☐ | ☐ | | |
| 8.2.10 | 2 | Have you implemented security measures for remote desktop connections? | ☐ | ☐ | ☐ | | |
| 8.2.10 | 3 | Have you implemented security measures for virtual desktop access? | ☐ | ☐ | ☐ | | |
| 8.2.10 | 4 | Do you regularly uninstall utilities that are no longer needed? | ☐ | ☐ | ☐ | | |

## Cybersecurity Audit Checklist: CSAM-Systems: 8.2.11 (MAM)

*Table 67. Domain: 8-Information, Systems and Applications*

| Clause | No. | Checklist Questions | Findings | | | Supporting Evidence | Comments |
|---|---|---|---|---|---|---|---|
| | | | Compliant | Minor Nonconformity | Major Nonconformity | | |
| 8.2.11 | 1 | Have you hardening security on all mobile devices through your Mobile Application Management (MAM)? | ☐ | ☐ | ☐ | | |
| 8.2.11 | 2 | Have you implemented controls to wipe data/block any stolen/lost mobile device? | ☐ | ☐ | ☐ | | |
| 8.2.11 | 3 | Have you implemented procedures to report and deal with stolen/lost mobile devices? | ☐ | ☐ | ☐ | | |

## Cybersecurity Audit Checklist: CSAM-Applications: 8.3.1 (SDLC)

*Table 68. Domain: 8-Information, Systems and Applications*

| Clause | No. | Checklist Questions | Findings | | | Supporting Evidence | Comments |
|---|---|---|---|---|---|---|---|
| | | | Compliant | Minor Nonconformity | Major Nonconformity | | |
| 8.3.1 | 1 | Have you implemented security measures during all SDLC phases? From planning to maintenance? | ☐ | ☐ | ☐ | | |
| 8.3.1 | 2 | Have you included vulnerability and control testing? | ☐ | ☐ | ☐ | | |
| 8.3.1 | 3 | Have you included security during the code review process? | ☐ | ☐ | ☐ | | |
| 8.3.1 | 4 | Have you separated system development, testing and production environments? | ☐ | ☐ | ☐ | | |
| 8.3.1 | 5 | Do you have different access controls for system development, testing and production environments? | ☐ | ☐ | ☐ | | |
| 8.3.1 | 6 | Do you stay current on application vulnerabilities? | ☐ | ☐ | ☐ | | |
| 8.3.1 | 7 | Do you have procedures for media sanitization and destruction? | ☐ | ☐ | ☐ | | |

## Cybersecurity Audit Checklist: CSAM-Applications: 8.3.2 (Cybersecurity apps)

*Table 69. Domain: 8-Information, Systems and Applications*

| Clause | No. | Checklist Questions | Findings | | | Supporting Evidence | Comments |
|--------|-----|---------------------|----------|--------------------|--------------------|---------------------|----------|
| | | | Compliant | Minor Nonconformity | Major Nonconformity | | |
| 8.3.2 | 1 | Is your antivirus program up-to-date? | ☐ | ☐ | ☐ | | |
| 8.3.2 | 2 | Is your cybersecurity program up-to-date? | ☐ | ☐ | ☐ | | |
| 8.3.2 | 3 | Is your anti-malware program up-to-date? | ☐ | ☐ | ☐ | | |
| 8.3.2 | 4 | Is your firewall program up-to-date? | ☐ | ☐ | ☐ | | |
| 8.3.2 | 5 | Is your IDS program up-to-date? | ☐ | ☐ | ☐ | | |
| 8.3.2 | 6 | Is your IPS program up-to-date? | ☐ | ☐ | ☐ | | |
| 8.3.2 | 7 | Is your SEM program up-to-date? | ☐ | ☐ | ☐ | | |
| 8.3.2 | 8 | Is your SIM program up-to-date? | ☐ | ☐ | ☐ | | |
| 8.3.2 | 9 | Is your SIEM program up-to-date? | ☐ | ☐ | ☐ | | |

## Cybersecurity Audit Checklist: CSAM-Applications: 8.3.3 (Open source)

*Table 70. Domain: 8-Information, Systems and Applications*

| Clause | No. | Checklist Questions | Findings | | | Supporting Evidence | Comments |
|--------|-----|---------------------|----------|--------------------|--------------------|---------------------|----------|
| | | | Compliant | Minor Nonconformity | Major Nonconformity | | |
| 8.3.3 | 1 | Have you installed open source software on your organization critical servers? | ☐ | ☐ | ☐ | | |
| 8.3.3 | 2 | Do you have specific requirements when selecting an open source software? | ☐ | ☐ | ☐ | | |
| 8.3.3 | 3 | When installing free software are you ensuring that code does not contain malicious instructions? | ☐ | ☐ | ☐ | | Spyware, surveillance software |
| 8.3.3 | 4 | When using freeware, shareware or any open source software, are you ensuring that is fully patched and using the latest versions? | ☐ | ☐ | ☐ | | To avoid zero day attacks |
| 8.3.3 | 5 | Do you allow your end users to install their own open source software? | ☐ | ☐ | ☐ | | |

## Cybersecurity Audit Checklist: CSAM-Applications: 8.3.4 (Merchant)*

*Table 71. Domain: 8-Information, Systems and Applications*

| Clause | No. | Checklist Questions | Findings | | | Supporting Evidence | Comments |
|--------|-----|---------------------|----------|--------------------------|--------------------------|---------------------|----------|
| | | | Compliant | Minor Nonconformity | Major Nonconformity | | |
| 8.3.4 | 1 | Do you maintain security network? | ☐ | ☐ | ☐ | | |
| 8.3.4 | 2 | Do you protect cardholder data? | ☐ | ☐ | ☐ | | |
| 8.3.4 | 3 | Do you maintain a vulnerability management program? | ☐ | ☐ | ☐ | | |
| 8.3.4 | 4 | Have you implemented access control measures? | ☐ | ☐ | ☐ | | |
| 8.3.4 | 5 | Do you monitor your networks? | ☐ | ☐ | ☐ | | |
| 8.3.4 | 6 | Do you have an information security policy? | ☐ | ☐ | ☐ | | |

*Additional security controls may apply based on PCI DSS requirements

## Cybersecurity Audit Checklist: CSAM-Applications: 8.3.5 (Social Media)

*Table 72. Domain: 8-Information, Systems and Applications*

| Clause | No. | Checklist Questions | Findings | | | Supporting Evidence | Comments |
|--------|-----|---------------------|----------|--------------------------|--------------------------|---------------------|----------|
| | | | Compliant | Minor Nonconformity | Major Nonconformity | | |
| 8.3.5 | 1 | Have you changed the default privacy settings on all your social media apps? | ☐ | ☐ | ☐ | | |
| 8.3.5 | 2 | Have you taken measures to deal with impersonation? | ☐ | ☐ | ☐ | | |
| 8.3.5 | 3 | Are your familiar with the acceptable use policies? | ☐ | ☐ | ☐ | | |
| 8.3.5 | 4 | Do you keep a strong password? | ☐ | ☐ | ☐ | | |
| 8.3.5 | 5 | Are you taking measures to keep a good online presence and reputation? | ☐ | ☐ | ☐ | | |

## Cybersecurity Audit Checklist: CSAM-Applications: 8.3.6 (Network Management)

*Table 73. Domain: 8-Information, Systems and Applications*

| Clause | No. | Checklist Questions | Findings | | | Supporting Evidence | Comments |
|---|---|---|---|---|---|---|---|
| | | | Compliant | Minor Nonconformity | Major Nonconformity | | |
| 8.3.6 | 1 | Are your network management applications up-to-date? | ☐ | ☐ | ☐ | | |
| 8.3.6 | 2 | Is your app. monitoring physical and logical access to diagnostic and configuration ports? | ☐ | ☐ | ☐ | | |
| 8.3.6 | 3 | Are you restricting networks connections? | ☐ | ☐ | ☐ | | |
| 8.3.6 | 4 | Have you configured session time-out limits? | ☐ | ☐ | ☐ | | |
| 8.3.6 | 5 | Have you implemented network routing controls? | ☐ | ☐ | ☐ | | |

## Cybersecurity Audit Checklist: CSAM-Applications: 8.3.7 (VoIP)

*Table 74. Domain: 8-Information, Systems and Applications*

| Clause | No. | Checklist Questions | Findings | | | Supporting Evidence | Comments |
|---|---|---|---|---|---|---|---|
| | | | Compliant | Minor Nonconformity | Major Nonconformity | | |
| 8.3.7 | 1 | Are you enforcing Session Initiation Protocol (SIP)? | ☐ | ☐ | ☐ | | |
| 8.3.7 | 2 | Are you provisioning on all your VoIP devices? | ☐ | ☐ | ☐ | | Disabling admin interfaces, changing default passwords, limiting network access |
| 8.3.7 | 3 | Have you disabled voice portal dialing? | ☐ | ☐ | ☐ | | |
| 8.3.7 | 4 | Do you check for weak passwords across the network? | ☐ | ☐ | ☐ | | |
| 8.3.7 | 5 | Do you check for international forwarding? | ☐ | ☐ | ☐ | | |
| 8.3.7 | 6 | Do you check for accounts without authentication? | ☐ | ☐ | ☐ | | |

## Cybersecurity Audit Checklist: CSAM-Applications: 8.3.8 (Unified Communication)

*Table 75. Domain: 8-Information, Systems and Applications*

| Clause | No. | Checklist Questions | Findings | | | Supporting Evidence | Comments |
|---|---|---|---|---|---|---|---|
| | | | Compliant | Minor Nonconformity | Major Nonconformity | | |
| 8.3.8 | 1 | Have you taken security measures to protect video, chat, email, VoIP and presence? | ☐ | ☐ | ☐ | | |
| 8.3.8 | 2 | Have you disabled unused services? | ☐ | ☐ | ☐ | | |
| 8.3.8 | 3 | Do you monitor your call logs? | ☐ | ☐ | ☐ | | |
| 8.3.8 | 4 | Do you use built-in UC security tools? | ☐ | ☐ | ☐ | | |
| 8.3.8 | 5 | Have you implemented Quality of Service (QoS)? | ☐ | ☐ | ☐ | | |

## Cybersecurity Audit Checklist: CSAM-Applications: 8.3.9 (Input controls) *

*Table 76. Domain: 8-Information, Systems and Applications*

| Clause | No. | Checklist Questions | Findings | | | Supporting Evidence | Comments |
|---|---|---|---|---|---|---|---|
| | | | Compliant | Minor Nonconformity | Major Nonconformity | | |
| 8.3.9 | 1 | Does the app have data checks and validation controls to ensure data is accurate, complete and authorized? | ☐ | ☐ | ☐ | | |
| 8.3.9 | 2 | Does the app have approval and override controls to ensure data is accurate, complete and authorized? | ☐ | ☐ | ☐ | | |
| 8.3.9 | 3 | Does the app have pended items controls to ensure data is accurate, complete and authorized? | ☐ | ☐ | ☐ | | |

*These controls can apply to any application

## Cybersecurity Audit Checklist: CSAM-Applications: 8.3.10 (Access controls) *

*Table 77. Domain: 8-Information, Systems and Applications*

| Clause | No. | Checklist Questions | Findings | | | Supporting Evidence | Comments |
|---|---|---|---|---|---|---|---|
| | | | Compliant | Minor Nonconformity | Major Nonconformity | | |
| 8.3.10 | 1 | Does the app have authorization and approval rights controls to ensure data is accurate, complete and authorized? | ☐ | ☐ | ☐ | | |
| 8.3.10 | 2 | Does the app have automated segregation of duties controls to ensure data is accurate, complete and authorized? | ☐ | ☐ | ☐ | | |
| 8.3.10 | 3 | Does the app have access rights controls to ensure data is accurate, complete and authorized? | ☐ | ☐ | ☐ | | |

**These controls can apply to any application

# Cybersecurity Audit Checklist: CSAM-Applications: 8.3.11 (Transmission controls) *

*Table 78. Domain: 8-Information, Systems and Applications*

| Clause | No. | Checklist Questions | Findings | | | Supporting Evidence | Comments |
|--------|-----|---------------------|----------|--|--|---------------------|----------|
| | | | Compliant | Minor Nonconformity | Major Nonconformity | | |
| 8.3.11 | 1 | Does the app have completeness and validity of content controls to ensure files are received from a trustful source and follow an accurate and complete processing? | ☐ | ☐ | ☐ | | |
| 8.3.11 | 2 | Does the app have data transmission controls to ensure files are received from a trustful source and follow an accurate and complete processing? | ☐ | ☐ | ☐ | | |

*These controls can apply to any application

# Cybersecurity Audit Checklist: CSAM-Applications: 8.3.12 (Processing controls) *

*Table 79. Domain: 8-Information, Systems and Applications*

| Clause | No. | Checklist Questions | Findings | | | Supporting Evidence | Comments |
|--------|-----|---------------------|----------|--|--|---------------------|----------|
| | | | Compliant | Minor Nonconformity | Major Nonconformity | | |
| 8.3.12 | 1 | Does the app have automated file identification and validation controls to ensure data is accurate and complete? | ☐ | ☐ | ☐ | | |
| 8.3.12 | 2 | Does the app have automated functionality and calculations controls to ensure data is accurate and complete? | ☐ | ☐ | ☐ | | |
| 8.3.12 | 3 | Does the app have data extraction, filtering and reporting controls to ensure data is accurate and complete? | ☐ | ☐ | ☐ | | |
| 8.3.12 | 4 | Does the app have interface balancing, aging processing and duplicate checks controls to ensure data is accurate and complete? | ☐ | ☐ | ☐ | | |

**These controls can apply to any application

# Cybersecurity Audit Checklist: CSAM-Applications: 8.3.13 (Output controls) *

*Table 80. Domain: 8-Information, Systems and Applications*

| Clause | No. | Checklist Questions | Findings | | | Supporting Evidence | Comments |
|--------|-----|---------------------|----------|--|--|---------------------|----------|
| | | | Compliant | Minor Nonconformity | Major Nonconformity | | |
| 8.3.13 | 1 | Does the app have general ledger controls to ensure data is accurate and complete? | ☐ | ☐ | ☐ | | |
| 8.3.13 | 2 | Does the app have subledger posting controls to ensure data is accurate and complete? | ☐ | ☐ | ☐ | | |

**These controls can apply to any application

## Cybersecurity Audit Checklist: CSAM-Applications: 8.3.14 (Integrity controls) *

*Table 81. Domain: 8-Information, Systems and Applications*

| Clause | No. | Checklist Questions | Findings | | | Supporting Evidence | Comments |
|---|---|---|---|---|---|---|---|
| | | | Compliant | Minor Nonconformity | Major Nonconformity | | |
| 8.3.14 | 1 | Does the app have processing data controls to ensure data is consistent and correct? | ☐ | ☐ | ☐ | | |
| 8.3.14 | 2 | Does the app have monitoring and storage controls to ensure data is consistent and correct? | ☐ | ☐ | ☐ | | |
| 8.3.14 | 3 | Does the app have update authorization controls to ensure data is consistent and correct? | ☐ | ☐ | ☐ | | |

\*\*These controls can apply to any application

## Cybersecurity Audit Checklist: CSAM-Applications: 8.3.15 (Audit trails) *

*Table 82. Domain: 8-Information, Systems and Applications*

| Clause | No. | Checklist Questions | Findings | | | Supporting Evidence | Comments |
|---|---|---|---|---|---|---|---|
| | | | Compliant | Minor Nonconformity | Major Nonconformity | | |
| 8.3.15 | 1 | Does the app have automated tracking of changes controls to ensure data is consistent and correct? | ☐ | ☐ | ☐ | | |
| 8.3.15 | 2 | Does the app have automated tracking of overrides controls to ensure data is consistent and correct? | ☐ | ☐ | ☐ | | |
| 8.3.15 | 3 | Does the app evaluate the effectiveness of other controls to ensure data is consistent and correct? | ☐ | ☐ | ☐ | | |

\*These controls can apply to any application

## Cybersecurity Audit Checklist: CSAM-Applications: 8.3.16 (e-mail)

*Table 83. Domain: 8-Information, Systems and Applications*

| Clause | No. | Checklist Questions | Findings | | | Supporting Evidence | Comments |
|--------|-----|---------------------|----------|------|------|----------|----------|
| | | | Compliant | Minor Nonconformity | Major Nonconformity | | |
| 8.3.16 | 1 | Have you implemented an antispam tool? | ☐ | ☐ | ☐ | | |
| 8.3.16 | 2 | Have you enforced the avoidance of opening attachments or clicking on suspect links? | ☐ | ☐ | ☐ | | This could trigger malware, spyware, ransomware |
| 8.3.16 | 3 | Have you enforced training on phishing techniques? | ☐ | ☐ | ☐ | | Users can become victims of identity theft or financial scams |
| 8.3.16 | 4 | Do you enforce with your end users that email is not a tool to share personal or confidential information? | ☐ | ☐ | ☐ | | |
| 8.3.16 | 5 | Are you using/encouraging personal email accounts for work purposes? | ☐ | ☐ | ☐ | | |
| 8.3.16 | 6 | Do you verify any spoofed/suspicious email before replying to it? | ☐ | ☐ | ☐ | | |
| 8.6.16 | 7 | Do you enforce with your end users to avoid connecting to public Wi-Fi's? | ☐ | ☐ | ☐ | | |

## Cybersecurity Audit Checklist: CSAM-Vulnerability Management

*Table 84. Domain: 9-Vulnerability Identification*

| Clause | No. | Checklist Questions | Findings | | | Supporting Evidence | Comments |
|--------|-----|---------------------|----------|------|------|----------|----------|
| | | | Compliant | Minor Nonconformity | Major Nonconformity | | |
| 9.1.2 | 1 | Has the organization identified where all assets reside? This applies to physical and logical assets | ☐ | ☐ | ☐ | | |
| 9.1.3 | 2 | Does your organization perform host-based vulnerability scans? List tools | ☐ | ☐ | ☐ | | |
| 9.1.3 | 3 | Does your organization perform network-based vulnerability scans? List tools | ☐ | ☐ | ☐ | | |
| 9.1.5 | 4 | Does the organization evaluate technical, process, organizational and emergent vulnerabilities? | ☐ | ☐ | ☐ | | |
| 9.1.6 | 5 | What actions do you take as part of your vulnerability remediation? | ☐ | ☐ | ☐ | | |
| 9.1.1 | 6 | Do you have proper reporting and metrics mechanisms related to vulnerability management? | ☐ | ☐ | ☐ | | |

## Cybersecurity Audit Checklist: CSAM-Threat Intelligence

*Table 85. Domain: 10-Threat Intelligence*

| Clause | No. | Checklist Questions | Findings | | | Supporting Evidence | Comments |
|--------|-----|---------------------|-----------|----------------------|----------------------|---------------------|----------|
| | | | Compliant | Minor Nonconformity | Major Nonconformity | | |
| 10.1.1 | 1 | Do you analyze information in order to identify and predict cyber capabilities and cyber threats? | ☐ | ☐ | ☐ | | |
| 10.1.1 | 2 | Do you possess the mechanisms and tools to monitor and analyze the current cyber threat landscape? | ☐ | ☐ | ☐ | | |
| 10.1.2 | 3 | Do you have measures that keep threats from exploiting vulnerabilities? | ☐ | ☐ | ☐ | | |
| 10.1.2 | 4 | Do you have measures in place to identify and isolate malware? | ☐ | ☐ | ☐ | | |
| 10.1.3 | 5 | Do you monitor logs, systems reports and security alerts? | ☐ | ☐ | ☐ | | |
| 10.1.4 | 6 | Do you have plans to develop CTI skills in-house or outsource them? | ☐ | ☐ | ☐ | | |
| 10.1.4 | 7 | Which CTI tools and tactics are you currently using? | ☐ | ☐ | ☐ | | Examples are SIEM. SIM, SEM, IDS, IPS, firewalls, Forensics tools |
| 10.1.1 | 8 | Do you gather CTI from vendors, public feeds, law enforcement, private feeds, social media or open source feeds? | ☐ | ☐ | ☐ | | |
| 10.1.5 | 9 | What best practices can you use to improve and integrate CTI into your systems? | ☐ | ☐ | ☐ | | |
| 10.1.5 | 10 | What challenges is the organization facing to develop and integrate CTI capabilities? | ☐ | ☐ | ☐ | | |

## Cybersecurity Audit Checklist: CSAM-Incident Management

*Table 86. Domain: 11-Incident Management*

| Clause | No. | Checklist Questions | Findings | | | Supporting Evidence | Comments |
|--------|-----|---------------------|-----------|----------------------|----------------------|---------------------|----------|
| | | | Compliant | Minor Nonconformity | Major Nonconformity | | |
| 11.1.1 | 1 | Do you have a cybersecurity incident response plan in place? | ☐ | ☐ | ☐ | | |
| 11.1.5 | 2 | Have you implemented processes for detection, identification, analysis and response to cybersecurity incidents? | ☐ | ☐ | ☐ | | |
| 11.1.2 | 3 | Have you established escalation and communication processes to handle incidents? | ☐ | ☐ | ☐ | | |
| 11.1.4 | 4 | Do you have formal plans to respond and document cybersecurity breaches? | ☐ | ☐ | ☐ | | |
| 11.1.2 | 5 | Have you developed processes to communicate with internal parties and external stakeholders in case of a security incident? | ☐ | ☐ | ☐ | | |
| 11.1.1 | 6 | Do you have a plan to organize and train teams to respond to cybersecurity incidents? | ☐ | ☐ | ☐ | | |

| Clause | No. | Checklist Questions | Findings | | | Supporting Evidence | Comments |
|---|---|---|---|---|---|---|---|
| | | | Compliant | Minor Nonconformity | Major Nonconformity | | |
| 11.1.5 | 7 | Do your conduct continuous reviews to your incident handling processes? | ☐ | ☐ | ☐ | | |
| 11.1.5 | 8 | Do you keep record of all cybersecurity incidents? | ☐ | ☐ | ☐ | | |
| 11.1.5 | 9 | Do you identify lessons learned and review incident response handling? | ☐ | ☐ | ☐ | | |
| 11.1.1 | 10 | Have you categorized cybersecurity and reporting time frames for your organization? | ☐ | ☐ | ☐ | | |

# Cybersecurity Audit Checklist: CSAM-Digital Forensics

*Table 87. Domain: 12-Digital Forensics*

| Clause | No. | Checklist Questions | Findings | | | Supporting Evidence | Comments |
|---|---|---|---|---|---|---|---|
| | | | Compliant | Minor Nonconformity | Major Nonconformity | | |
| 12.1.1 | 1 | Is the organization able to perform in-house digital forensic investigations? | ☐ | ☐ | ☐ | | |
| 12.1.2 | 2 | Is any third-party vendor hired for internal digital investigations? | ☐ | ☐ | ☐ | | |
| 12.1.1 | 3 | Is the technical staff familiar with all phases of digital forensics? | ☐ | ☐ | ☐ | | |
| 12.1.1 | 4 | Is the organization able to provide validation of the occurrence of a cyberattack? | ☐ | ☐ | ☐ | | |
| 12.1.3 | 5 | Can the organization gather digital evidence in case of any future prosecution? | ☐ | ☐ | ☐ | | |
| 12.1.4 | 6 | Is your technical staff proficient with evidence management? | ☐ | ☐ | ☐ | | |
| 12.1.5 | 7 | Is the organization capable of complying with any e-discovery case for litigation support? | ☐ | ☐ | ☐ | | |
| 12.1.1 | 8 | Is your technical staff proficient in the use of DF procedures, tools and methodologies? | ☐ | ☐ | ☐ | | |
| 12.1.1 | 9 | Is your technical staff able to deal with Anti-Forensics tactics, techniques and procedures(TTPs)? | ☐ | ☐ | ☐ | | |
| 12.1.3 | 10 | Have you established capabilities to investigate cyberattacks and/or any type of cybercrime that could impact your operations? | ☐ | ☐ | ☐ | | |

## Cybersecurity Audit Checklist: CSAM-Awareness

*Table 88. Domain: 13-Awareness Education*

| Clause | No. | Checklist Questions | Findings | | | Supporting Evidence | Comments |
|--------|-----|---------------------|----------|-----------------------|-----------------------|---------------------|----------|
| | | | Compliant | Minor Nonconformity | Major Nonconformity | | |
| 13.1.1 | 1 | Does your organization have a cybersecurity awareness program? | ☐ | ☐ | ☐ | | |
| 13.1.1 | 2 | Do you provide some kind of cybersecurity training to your staff? | ☐ | ☐ | ☐ | | |
| 13.1.2 | 3 | Is training delivered on a regular recurring basis? | ☐ | ☐ | ☐ | | |
| 13.1.1 | 4 | Do employees are following security policies of the organization? | ☐ | ☐ | ☐ | | |
| 13.1.1 | 5 | Are you delivering training to recognize and deal with social engineering? | ☐ | ☐ | ☐ | | |
| 13.1.1 | 6 | Do your staff know how to recognize and report a security incident? | ☐ | ☐ | ☐ | | |
| 13.1.1 | 7 | Is your personnel able to detect and respond to any cybersecurity emergency? | ☐ | ☐ | ☐ | | |
| 13.1.1 | 8 | Do you enforce privacy and confidentiality requirements in your organization? | ☐ | ☐ | ☐ | | |
| 13.1.1 | 9 | Are your employees following security procedures for data and information protection? | ☐ | ☐ | ☐ | | |
| 13.1.4 | 10 | Is your awareness training focused and delivered to specific audiences like end users, managers, IT, C-Suite executives and Board of Directors? | ☐ | ☐ | ☐ | | |
| 13.1.1 | 11 | Is your awareness training covering multidimensional topics? | ☐ | ☐ | ☐ | | |
| 13.1.1 | 12 | Does your training outline cover technical, social and user behaviour areas? | ☐ | ☐ | ☐ | | |

## Cybersecurity Audit Checklist: CSAM-Cyber Insurance

*Table 89. Domain: 14-Cyber Insurance*

| Clause | No. | Checklist Questions | Findings | | | Supporting Evidence | Comments |
|--------|-----|---------------------|----------|-----------------------|-----------------------|---------------------|----------|
| | | | Compliant | Minor Nonconformity | Major Nonconformity | | |
| 14.1.1 | 1 | What kind of cyber insurance coverage would your organization seek? Would you include first party and/or third party coverage? | ☐ | ☐ | ☐ | | Options could be cyber omissions & errors, privacy, media protection and computer networks |
| 14.1.5 | 2 | Is your organization aware that cyber insurance cannot offer coverage for weaknesses in your cybersecurity architecture or program? | ☐ | ☐ | ☐ | | |
| 14.1.3 | 3 | Are you prepared to fulfill a cybersecurity audit requirement in order to get a cyber insurance policy? | ☐ | ☐ | ☐ | | |
| 14.1.3 | 4 | Would you implement a recommended cybersecurity framework, standard or good practice in order to acquire a cyber insurance? | ☐ | ☐ | ☐ | | |
| 14.1.2 | 5 | How would you handle your current cybersecurity weaknesses in a potential cyber insurance risk assessment? | ☐ | ☐ | ☐ | | |

## Cybersecurity Audit Checklist: CSAM-Active Cyber Defense

*Table 90. Domain: 15- Active Cyber Defense*

| Clause | No. | Checklist Questions | Findings | | | Supporting Evidence | Comments |
|---|---|---|---|---|---|---|---|
| | | | Compliant | Minor Nonconformity | Major Nonconformity | | |
| 15.1.1 | 1 | Does the organization have implemented passive defense to protect its networks, architecture and systems? | ☐ | ☐ | ☐ | | |
| 15.1.1 | 2 | What ACD measures have you implemented? | ☐ | ☐ | ☐ | | |
| 15.1.3 | 3 | What controls are in place to detect and analyze cyberattacks? | ☐ | ☐ | ☐ | | |
| 15.1.4 | 4 | What controls are in place to mitigate cyberattacks? | ☐ | ☐ | ☐ | | |
| 15.1.5 | 5 | Do you have any countermeasures in place? | ☐ | ☐ | ☐ | | |

## Cybersecurity Audit Checklist: CSAM-Evolving Technologies

*Table 91. Domain: 16- Evolving Technologies*

| Clause | No. | Checklist Questions | Findings | | | Supporting Evidence | Comments |
|---|---|---|---|---|---|---|---|
| | | | Compliant | Minor Nonconformity | Major Nonconformity | | |
| 16.1.1 | 1 | Do you consider security when buying new assets for your organization? | ☐ | ☐ | ☐ | | |
| 16.1.1 | 2 | Do you evaluate cybersecurity matters with external stakeholders, outsourcing companies and vendors? | ☐ | ☐ | ☐ | | |
| 16.1.4 | 3 | Do you follow a specific procedure for acquiring/ hiring new security technologies, products or services? | ☐ | ☐ | ☐ | | |
| 16.1.4 | 4 | What measures do you adopt when implementing new digital technologies? | ☐ | ☐ | ☐ | | |
| 16.1.4 | 5 | Do you have a policy to manage mobile technology vulnerabilities, threats and risks? | ☐ | ☐ | ☐ | | |
| 16.1.4 | 6 | Do you encourage a Bring-Your-Own-Device (BYOD) policy at your workplace? | ☐ | ☐ | ☐ | | |
| 16.1.5 | 7 | Do you allow telework, work from home and digital collaborations? | ☐ | ☐ | ☐ | | |
| 16.1.4 | 8 | Do you manage any kind of cloud computing? | ☐ | ☐ | ☐ | | |
| 16.1.4 | 9 | Have you enforced policies to hardening security for social networks? | ☐ | ☐ | ☐ | | |
| 16.1.4 | 10 | Do you assess associated cybersecurity issues, vulnerabilities and risks when acquiring a new technology? | ☐ | ☐ | ☐ | | |

## Cybersecurity Audit Checklist: CSAM-Disaster Recovery

*Table 92. Domain: 17- Disaster Recovery*

| Clause | No. | Checklist Questions | Findings | | | Supporting Evidence | Comments |
|---|---|---|---|---|---|---|---|
| | | | Compliant | Minor Nonconformity | Major Nonconformity | | |
| 17.1.1 | 1 | Have you identified cyberassets that are critical to the continuous operation of your organization? | ☐ | ☐ | ☐ | | |
| 17.1.2 | 2 | Have you taken measures to protect your critical services and infrastructure? | ☐ | ☐ | ☐ | | |
| 17.1.3 | 3 | Have you taken any measures in case of a cybersecurity disaster? | ☐ | ☐ | ☐ | | |
| 17.1.1 | 4 | Do you have formal and current Business Continuity Planning (BCP) and Disaster Recovery Planning (DRP) in place? | ☐ | ☐ | ☐ | | |
| 17.1.3 | 5 | Have you followed Business Impact Analysis (BIA) to determine your critical cybersecurity processes? | ☐ | ☐ | ☐ | | |
| 17.1.4 | 6 | Do you include cybersecurity testing while reviewing your BCP? | ☐ | ☐ | ☐ | | |
| 17.1.3 | 7 | Is BCP/DRP training material content aligned with current business status? | ☐ | ☐ | ☐ | | |
| 17.1.6 | 8 | Is the backup of business-critical systems, data, applications and documentation properly managed? | ☐ | ☐ | ☐ | | |
| 17.1.1 | 9 | Has the Business Impact Analysis (BIA) covered time frames, priorities, resources and interdependencies that support key processes of the organization? | ☐ | ☐ | ☐ | | |
| 17.1.1 | 10 | Have you determined Recovery Point Objectives (RPOs) for your critical processes? | ☐ | ☐ | ☐ | | |

## Cybersecurity Audit Checklist: CSAM-Personnel Hiring

*Table 93. Domain: 18- Personnel*

| Clause | No. | Checklist Questions | Findings | | | Supporting Evidence | Comments |
|---|---|---|---|---|---|---|---|
| | | | Compliant | Minor Nonconformity | Major Nonconformity | | |
| 18.2.1 | 1 | Does the organization highlight the importance of any new hire's behaviour that is aligned with policies and standards? | ☐ | ☐ | ☐ | | |
| 18.2.2 | 2 | Does the organization have clear disciplinary actions for staff that may infringe cybersecurity policies and standards? | ☐ | ☐ | ☐ | | |
| 18.2.2 | 3 | Do disciplinary actions include security breaches committed by employees, consultants or third-party stakeholders? | ☐ | ☐ | ☐ | | |
| 18.2.3 | 4 | Does the organization provide assigned office space and computing devices to the new hire? | ☐ | ☐ | ☐ | | |
| 18.2.3 | 5 | Does the organization provide assigned telecom and wireless services to the new hire? | ☐ | ☐ | ☐ | | |
| 18.2.3 | 6 | Does the organization provide the proper permissions and access to the new hire in order to work remotely? | ☐ | ☐ | ☐ | | |

| Clause | No. | Checklist Questions | Findings | | | Supporting Evidence | Comments |
|--------|-----|---------------------|----------|--|--|---------------------|----------|
| | | | Compliant | Minor Nonconformity | Major Nonconformity | | |
| 18.2.3 | 7 | Does the organization provide any kind of building security device or physical access? | ☐ | ☐ | ☐ | | Access cards, tokens, biometric, alarm code, keys |
| 18.2.3 | 8 | Does the organization provide any kind of logical security? | ☐ | ☐ | ☐ | | Passwords, FOBs, folder access, drive access |
| 18.2.3 | 9 | Does the organization enforce Ethernet port security? | ☐ | ☐ | ☐ | | |
| 18.2.1 | 10 | Does the organization have proper procedures for 'Leave of absence request' and 'Return from Leave of absence'? | ☐ | ☐ | ☐ | | . |

# Cybersecurity Audit Checklist: CSAM-Personnel Onboarding

*Table 94. Domain: 18- Personnel*

| Clause | No. | Checklist Questions | Findings | | | Supporting Evidence | Comments |
|--------|-----|---------------------|----------|--|--|---------------------|----------|
| | | | Compliant | Minor Nonconformity | Major Nonconformity | | |
| 18.1.1 | 1 | Does the organization clearly state the job responsibilities in the job profile? | ☐ | ☐ | ☐ | | |
| 18.1.2 | 2 | Does the organization ask for criminal background check prior to any job offer? | ☐ | ☐ | ☐ | | |
| 18.1.2 | 3 | Does the organization ask for credit check prior to any job offer? | ☐ | ☐ | ☐ | | |
| 18.1.2 | 4 | Does the organization ask for security clearance prior to any high-profile job offer? | ☐ | ☐ | ☐ | | |
| 18.1.3 | 5 | Does the organization stress enough to the new hire the responsibilities when it comes to organizational cybersecurity matters? | ☐ | ☐ | ☐ | | |

# Cybersecurity Audit Checklist: CSAM-Personnel Offboarding

*Table 95. Domain: 18- Personnel*

| Clause | No. | Checklist Questions | Findings | | | Supporting Evidence | Comments |
|--------|-----|---------------------|----------|--|--|---------------------|----------|
| | | | Compliant | Minor Nonconformity | Major Nonconformity | | |
| 18.5.1 | 1 | Does the organization have a clear termination request process? | ☐ | ☐ | ☐ | | |
| 18.5.1 | 2 | Does the organization have an immediate termination request process? | ☐ | ☐ | ☐ | | |
| 18.5.1 | 3 | Does the organization have a clear change of position request process? | ☐ | ☐ | ☐ | | |

# Cybersecurity Audit Checklist: CSAM-Personnel Skills

*Table 96. Domain: 18- Personnel*

| Clause | No. | Checklist Questions | Findings | | | Supporting Evidence | Comments |
|--------|-----|---------------------|----------|--------------------|--------------------|---------------------|----------|
| | | | Compliant | Minor Nonconformity | Major Nonconformity | | |
| 18.3.1-3 | 1 | Does the organization encourage skills and competencies development based on roles? | ☐ | ☐ | ☐ | | |
| 18.3.1-3 | 2 | Are goals defined for the acquisition of cybersecurity skills and competencies? | ☐ | ☐ | ☐ | | |
| 18.3.1-3 | 3 | Does the organization know its current status for cybersecurity skills and competencies? | ☐ | ☐ | ☐ | | |
| 18.3.1-3 | 4 | Does the organization encourage cybersecurity knowledge transfer based on Good Practices? | ☐ | ☐ | ☐ | | |
| 18.3.1-3 | 5 | Which skills and competencies the organization wants its employees to develop and improve? | ☐ | ☐ | ☐ | | Governance, cybersecurity strategy, cyber risks, architecture, cyber operations, assessments, audits, testing, compliance |

# Cybersecurity Audit Checklist: CSAM-Personnel Training

*Table 97. Domain: 18- Personnel*

| Clause | No. | Checklist Questions | Findings | | | Supporting Evidence | Comments |
|--------|-----|---------------------|----------|--------------------|--------------------|---------------------|----------|
| | | | Compliant | Minor Nonconformity | Major Nonconformity | | |
| 18.4.1 | 1 | Does the organization deliver an orientation training for new hires? | ☐ | ☐ | ☐ | | |
| 18.4.2 | 2 | Does the orientation training cover basics of organizational cybersecurity? | ☐ | ☐ | ☐ | | |
| 18.4.3 | 3 | Does the organization have valid training for departmental systems, apps and controls? | ☐ | ☐ | ☐ | | |
| 18.4.4 | 4 | Does the organization have valid training for corporate systems, apps and controls? | ☐ | ☐ | ☐ | | |
| 18.4.2 | 5 | All new hires participate in a cybersecurity awareness training? | ☐ | ☐ | ☐ | | |

# Chapter 6
# The Two–Dimensional CCSMM

**Gregory B. White**

*CIAS, The University of Texas at San Antonio, USA*

**Natalie Sjelin**

*CIAS, The University of Texas at San Antonio, USA*

## ABSTRACT

*The community cyber security maturity model (CCSMM) defines four dimensions and five implementation mechanisms in describing the relative maturity of an organization or an SLTT's cybersecurity program. These are used in defining levels of maturity and the cybersecurity characteristics of an organization or SLTT at each level. In order to progress from one level to the next, a variety of activities should take place, and these are defined in terms of five different mechanisms. In between two levels are a variety of activities that should take place to help the entity to advance from one level to the next. These groups of activities describe four phases, each of which takes place between two levels. Thus, Phase 1 defines the activities that should occur for an entity to advance from Level 1 to Level 2.*

## INTRODUCTION

The Community Cyber Security Maturity Model (CCSMM) was developed as a result of the lessons learned in conducting state and community cybersecurity exercises around the nation. Exercises are an awareness tool to help people understand the issues related to a specific disaster situation. They are also a proven method to test to see if the mechanisms, processes and procedures an organization has put in place are sufficient to address a variety of different disaster scenarios. With cybersecurity, the issue was first one of awareness – state and community leaders were mostly unaware of the potential impact of a cybersecurity event and needed to be made aware that cybersecurity is an important issue for them. Community leaders needed to understand that without cybersecurity, their community could be negatively impacted in a variety of ways that could cause severe consequences for their citizens. The belief at the time was that by making leaders aware they needed to pay attention to cybersecurity they would then follow up with development of the needed processes, procedures, and technology. The reality proved to be different.

DOI: 10.4018/978-1-6684-3698-1.ch006

When the team that conducted an exercise returned to the state or community to see how well they were doing after about a year, they discovered that while the leaders were still aware that cybersecurity was something they needed to address, they had most often not taken any real steps in forming a strategy to implement a cybersecurity program. There were plenty of vendors willing to sell products and services but which of these were the most important and which needed to be accomplished first before the others? The exercise team had made the incorrect assumption that participants in the exercise would know what to do and that simply did not prove to be the case. They therefore took a step back and created guidance that could be provided to states and communities that would provide a path for them to follow – keeping in mind that most participants did not at the time have a budget to purchase cybersecurity products or services. The resulting plan that was created was the CCSMM.

## BACKGROUND

A critical factor in developing the CCSMM was that cybersecurity is not a binary issue. A state or community does not either have security or it doesn't. There are many levels of security preparedness and not every entity needs the same level of security preparedness – it should be based on the actual threats to the state, community, tribe, territory, or organization. This implies there are different levels of security that can be implemented so one of the first tasks in developing a program would be to understand the different levels, understand what is currently implemented, and know what the ultimate goal is. In other words, what security level is needed or desired by the community? The CCSMM was thus created to provide three things:

1. A "yardstick" so that SLTTs could determine where they currently are in the maturity of their cybersecurity program. What level are they currently at? How prepared is the community as a whole, or individual organizations within the community, to prevent, detect, and respond to and recover from a cyber-attack? At first the critical infrastructures in the community and the local government entities will be the primary components the model will focus on but as the community matures, it will increasingly take on a whole-community approach. There are several dimensions that will be described and a community may not be at the same level for all dimensions at the same time. In fact, it is will not be uncommon for a community to be at several different levels among the dimensions as it progresses. To be considered at a specific level overall, however, the community has to exhibit the characteristics in all of the dimensions at that level.

2. A "roadmap" to describe a path to advance from one level to the next. This would describe the various activities that need to take place in order to advance. After determining what level the community currently is at, a decision needs to be made concerning what level they aspire to. Not all communities are the same and not all communities will need to attain the highest level of security represented in the model. The level of threat to a community will be heavily dependent on what organizations reside in the community. For example, is there a military installation or a large component of the federal or state government? Is there a significant national monument or historical site that serves as a symbol for the nation? Is there a significant industry or manufacturing installation present in the community? All of these will impact the likelihood of an attack on the community as well as the potential threat actor (i.e. who might want to launch an attack on the community or organizations within the community – a nation-state, a criminal organization, a

terrorist group, or curious individuals). The roadmap will help the community and organizations within the community to determine what they need to do on their path to their desired level.

3.   A "common point of reference" so that individuals in different communities across the country could talk about their individual programs and relate them to each other. If all are working from the same model it makes it easier to discuss common issues, problems and solutions. If there is no common point of reference then it is harder for individuals to compare their program and thus to benefit from the experiences each has had in attempting to secure their own community. It is counterproductive for communities to all try to build their own programs without benefiting from the experiences of others. Communities should not all have to make the same mistakes in order to learn what they can do – they should be able to benefit from others who have been down the same path before them but for this to work the paths need to be roughly similar.

With these three goals in mind, one of the first tasks that needed to be defined was the different levels of the model. The levels SLTTs would be striving for. Each of these levels would then describe the characteristics of an SLTT at that level which would provide a description for what the SLTT was striving to obtain. It would also aid in the creation of the steps that would need to be taken to reach that level and provide a basis for different communities to share their experiences.

## DEFINING THE LEVELS

There are a number of different maturity models that have been created for a variety of different environments. In 2014 the Department of Energy (DOE) published Version 1.1 of the Cybersecurity Capability Maturity Model (C2M2). Among other things, it offered a very good definition of what a maturity model is:

*A maturity model is a set of characteristics, attributes, indicators, or patterns that represent capability and progression in a particular discipline. Model content typically exemplifies best practices and may incorporate standards or other codes of practice of the discipline. A maturity model thus provides a benchmark against which an organization can evaluate the current level of capability of its practices, processes, and methods and set goals and priorities for improvement. Also, when a model is widely used in a particular industry (and assessment results are shared), organizations can benchmark their performance against other organizations. An industry can determine how well it is performing overall by examining the capability of its member organizations. To measure progression, maturity models typically have "levels" along a scale—C2M2 uses a scale of maturity indicator levels (MILs) 0–3, which are described in Section 3.2. [of DOE 2014] A set of attributes defines each level. If an organization demonstrates these attributes, it has achieved both that level and the capabilities that the level represents. Having measurable transition states between the levels enables an organization to use the scale to:*

- *Define its current state*
- *Determine its future, more mature state*
- *Identify the capabilities it must attain to reach that future state.* (DOE 2014)

The model proposed by the DOE utilized four Maturity Indicator Levels (MIL) to describe the different levels of maturity that an organization could be at. Level MIL 0 basically represented an organization that did not perform any of the practices defined for higher levels. The practices are grouped into ten domains as follows:

- Risk Management
- Asset, Change, and Configuration Management
- Identity and Access Management
- Threat and Vulnerability Management
- Situational Awareness
- Information Sharing and Communications
- Event and Incident Response, Continuity of Operations
- Supply Chain and External Dependencies Management
- Workforce Management
- Cybersecurity Program Management

In 2015 the Software Engineering Institute (SEI) at Carnegie Mellon University (CMU) published the *Cybersecurity Capability Maturity Model for Information Technology Services (C2M2 for IT Services), Version 1.0*. This document was largely taken from the DOE C2M2 as it described in its Acknowledgements section. (SEI, 2015) In 2019 the Department of Defense announced the creation of a Cybersecurity Maturity Model Certification (CMMC) program to be implemented in 2020. The program was developed in conjunction with the Johns Hopkins University Applied Physics Laboratory and the SEI at CMU. (MeriTalk, 2019) It leaned heavily on the requirements specified in the NIST SP 800-171 publication (Edwards and Hays, 2019) and has a mapping of the Controlled Unclassified Information (CUI) security requirements in the NIST SP 800-53 publication *Security and Privacy Controls for Federal information Systems and Organizations*. (NIST 2015)

There are five notional CMMC levels which describe the maturity of the organization's security processes. These five levels are:

Level 1: Processes are ad hoc
Level 2: Processes are documented
Level 3: Processes are guided by policy
Level 4: Practices are periodically evaluated for effectiveness
Level 5: Processes are tailored and improvement data is shared

All of the more recent documents attest to the desire to help organizations develop strong security programs. The CCSMM, which was originally developed in 2008 and first discussed in 2009 (White, 2009), is obviously not based on these later documents but shares many of the same components and is also a five-level model. Since these other security related maturity models came after the creation of the CCSMM, it was actually influenced more by the original Capability Maturity Model (CMM) for software engineering which was published by the SEI at CMU in 1987. Since then there have been several other publications describing it, some with slight wording variations. It was designed to help an organization mature their software development processes to help them become more efficient and ultimately produce better and more reliable software. The CMM has five levels:

Level 1: Initial
Level 2: Repeatable
Level 3: Defined
Level 4: Managed
Level 5: Optimizing

Each level, with the exception of Level 1, has a number of Key Process Areas (KPA) that describe the basic requirements that should be met by the organizations software processes. Level 1 had no KPAs assigned to it. The levels provide a path for organizations to follow as they seek to improve their software development processes.

These are not the only maturity models in existence and new ones are periodically being developed. What is important to understand about the CCSMM is that it was initially designed to not address specific security requirements as a model such as the NIST Cybersecurity Framework does, but instead it addresses the type of requirements that are needed for a cybersecurity program. As such it allows for the specific requirements that might be required of an organization in a given sector while another organization in a different sector might have a different specific requirement. For example, the CCSMM might talk about the need for security assessments to be performed on a periodic basis. For an organization in a sector such as the Financial Services Sector this might translate to a specific type of external assessment being accomplished annually while a different organization in a different sector, say a retail shoe store, may find it adequate to accomplish an external assessment every other year. The point from the perspective of the overall CCSMM model is that entities are conducting appropriate assessments when they should be.

Like the CMM, the CCSMM also has five levels. Initially it was designed to help communities to improve the maturity of their cybersecurity processes or program. Later, it was expanded to cover more than just communities and this will be covered in the next chapter. Just like the CMM, the CCSMM provides a path for communities to follow in order to improve the maturity of their cybersecurity program. The five levels of the CCSMM are shown in Figure 1.

## CCSMM Level 1: Initial

Using the CCSMM as a framework for community cybersecurity, a Level 1 community may not have in place the processes that are needed at the higher levels. They may not even have an overall program to address cybersecurity. Communities at Level 1 may have implemented certain processes or programs but have not implemented enough to qualify for Level 2.

Figure 1 also provides a short description of the characteristics that communities should display for the four dimensions of the model. For example, at Level 1 the community and its leaders have minimal awareness of cybersecurity and the potential impact the loss of security could have on the community. They most likely do not understand the dependence the community has on cyber infrastructures. The community has either no organized cybersecurity information sharing program, or at best has a minimal one that only a few organizations are a member of. The processes that may be in place within the community are not assessed or tested on a regular basis and there is most likely no cyber part of the community's Continuity of Operations Plan (COOP). It is interesting to note, but probably not surprising, that none of the communities that the CIAS conducted community exercises for were past Level 1 in the maturity of their programs.

*Figure 1. The Five Levels of the CCSMM and the Characteristics Found in Each level*

| **LEVEL 1** Initial | **LEVEL 2** Established | **LEVEL 3** Self-Assessed | **LEVEL 4** Integrated | **LEVEL 5** Vanguard |
|---|---|---|---|---|
| • Minimal cyber awareness<br><br>• Minimal cyber info sharing<br><br>• Minimal cyber assessments and policy & procedure evaluations<br><br>• Little inclusion of cyber into Continuity of Operations Plan (COOP) | • Leadership aware of cyber threats, issues and imperatives for cyber security and community cooperative cyber training<br><br>• Informal info sharing/ communication in community; working groups established; ad-hoc analysis, little fusion or metrics; professional orgs established or engaged<br><br>• No assessments, but aware of requirement; initial evaluation of policies & procedures<br><br>• Aware of need to integrate cyber security into COOP | • Leaders promote org security awareness; formal community cooperative training<br><br>• Formal local info sharing/cyber analysis. initial cyber-physical fusion; informal external info sharing/ cyber analysis and metrics gathering<br><br>• Autonomous tabletop cyber exercises with assessments of info sharing, policies & procedures, and fusion; routine audit program; mentor externals on policies & procedures, auditing and training<br><br>• Include cyber in COOP; formal cyber incident response/recovery | • Leaders and orgs promote awareness; citizens aware of cyber security issues<br><br>• Formal info sharing/ analysis, internal and external to community; formal local fusion and metrics, initial external efforts<br><br>• Autonomous cyber exercises with assessments of formal info sharing/local fusion; exercises involve live play/metrics assessments<br><br>• Integrate cyber in COOP; mentor externals on COOP integration; formal blended incident response and recovery | • Awareness a business imperative<br><br>• Fully integrated fusion /analysis center, combining all-source physical and cyber info; create and disseminate near real world picture<br><br>• Accomplish full-scale blended exercises and assess complete fusion capability; involve/ mentor other communities/entities<br><br>• Continue to integrate cyber in COOP; mentor externals on COOP integration; formal blended incident response and recovery |

*/*-*-+-+/*

## CCSMM Level 2: Established

At Level 2: Established your community has established a basic program and has elements and processes for all four of the dimensions in place. Awareness programs (such as user cybersecurity training and training aimed specifically at community leaders) have been implemented and leaders know of the importance of cybersecurity to the community and to their individual organizations. They are also aware of the need for user training as they understand that cybersecurity is not just the responsibility of IT or security staff but is a function that all are collectively responsible for.

The community will also have established at least an informal cybersecurity information sharing program. This does not mean that a Security Operations Center (SOC) has been created with staffing around the clock, but it does mean that methods have been implemented that allow for communicating information on cybersecurity issues to organizations around the community. The community may still not be conducting assessments or other activities to test the processes, policies, and procedures but the need for these is understood and organizations may be conducting their own at this point. The community has also implemented cyber into its COOP and has created a cyber incident response plan. The community may not have conducted any exercises but plans should be in the process of development to do so in the future.

## CCSMM Level 3: Self-Assessed

Communities at Level 3: Self-Assessed have progressed far enough that they have an established, stable cybersecurity program. They understand enough about cybersecurity and what needs to be accomplished that they are capable of conducting their own assessments to determine how well the community is doing. This is not to say that there can't be improvements and additional components added to their program, but by this point they should have at least a minimal viable and sustainable program that is the goal of the CCSMM program. When participating communities reach Level 3, they should be much more aware of gaps in their current security posture. They should be establishing baselines, sharing information on a regular basis, and refining processes and procedures. They understand that performance in these areas is to be monitored and measured often. Leadership must continue to promote security awareness at all levels and training initiatives should be well underway. In the exercise realm, those at Level 3 should be conducting events at least once per year that include a cyber component and preferably have at least one exercise that is primarily cyber focused. The exercises may at first be conducted with participation from just the critical infrastructures and local government entities but should progress to a whole-community approach that will include involvement from industry. The community should incorporate the key concepts from previous levels as often as possible in the exercises. This includes information sharing, policies and procedures, and continuity of operations. Cyber incident response and recovery should be formalized by this point and will be a major focus of the exercises that are conducted. At Level 3: Self-Assessed the community will also have an understanding of the impact that individuals and organizations in the community (as well as the state and other communities) have on the community itself.

## CCSMM Level 4: Integrated

At Level 4: Integrated cybersecurity is integrated across the community wherever it should be considered. Citizens and organizations have a role in community cybersecurity and the citizens as a whole understand this. The community needs to be communicating with the state as well (assuming there is a state program, otherwise they may need to communicate directly with other communities or organizations such as the Multi-State ISAC). The message that up to this point has been largely contained within organizations should be spread to everyone within the community. Assessments of process, procedures, policies, and technology are conducted on a regular basis. There should be at least annual cyber exercises but also exercises in which cyber is blended with attacks that affect both physical and cyber assets or functions. Emergency management organizations should have a solid grasp on cybersecurity concepts and integration into normal operations is crucial. Community-centric incident response plans must directly address cyber incidents, and regular assessment of procedures associated with those plans should be conducted. The real thrust of Level 4: Integrated is that the community should be integrating its efforts with all members and organizations within the community as well as working with the state and other communities. Cybersecurity is considered an integral concern for the community and for organizations within the community.

## CCSMM Level 5: Vanguard

Attaining Level 5: Vanguard means your community is maintaining a fully-vigilant cybersecurity posture. Exercise capabilities are well-rounded and include cyber and non-cyber events. Communities and the organizations within them must continue to evaluate current policies, procedures, and plans for additional integration and refinement. This is especially true where incident response is concerned due to the highly volatile nature of the threat landscape. Cybersecurity programs include the entire population of a community at this point, and a complete sense of cybersecurity awareness is found among citizens. Exercises are routinely conducted with other communities and organizations at the local level and with the state. Exercises should also be full-scale events that are as realistic as possible, with live-fire events that incorporate as many elements to test as is appropriate. Exercises have moved beyond simple tabletop events (though these may still also be conducted) and now should include functional exercises.

At this level, information sharing is at its most advanced, where fusion and dissemination of data received from various sources occurs at an acceptable pace. Information gathered is considered "all-source", meaning it is received from all sectors within the community and is processed in near real-time. The result is what is known as "near ground truth", or what is happening at this moment in time.

It is expected that at Level 5: Vanguard, communities are actively involved in mentorship of other SLTTs for the purposes of increased cybersecurity and information sharing. Even if there aren't any additional capabilities expected after Level 5, communities should routinely re-evaluate their cybersecurity posture in accordance with the metrics for each of the CCSMM levels. This helps keep everything on track and avoids complacency among stakeholders.

There is a lot more to each of the levels described above which will be addressed later in this book. For now, however, the basic differences between the levels, and the specific focus of each level should be understood. A comparison of the descriptions of each level in the previous paragraphs or in Figure 1 will yield a number of different activities that must be accomplished as the community progresses. The specific levels are connected by the events that take place to progress between levels for each dimension. These occur in what are referred to in the model as Phases. Phase 1 contains activities that will occur between Level 1 and Level 2, Phase 2 will connect Levels 2 and 3, and so forth.

## THE PHASES

To advance from one level of the model to the next will take time as several activities will need to be performed, processes instituted, and programs developed. The term Phase is used to define the period of time between levels, and the activities performed during that period of time. There are four phases for the five levels of the CCSMM.

If the CCSMM's levels are milestones, then the phases of the model are the roadmap to achievement. Each phase must be followed in order to arrive at the next destination, and it's imperative that every phase requirement be met in order to ensure preparedness for subsequent phases. In that vein, the CCSMM's phases have been constructed with a set of requirements that are organized into five categories.

**Metrics** help communities and their citizens determine what to measure so the current security posture can be fully understood. **Technology** obviously will play a role as well so ascertaining when is the right time to purchase and deploy new technology (both hardware and software) to address a characteristic at the next level is something organizations and communities must often consider. The question of who needs what **training** should be asked as part of the program and each phase introduces new training for additional users. **Processes and procedures** are foundational to cybersecurity readiness and looking to upcoming level requirements means that each phase will address what is already documented versus what still needs to be created. Finally, **assessments** are instrumental in evaluating success and participants must decide how to best plan and conduct both as part of their CCSMM strategy. With these five categories of requirements in mind, the phases can be discussed and will be examined in more detail in later chapters.

## Phase 1: Initial to Established

Phase 1 is really just about initiating the conversation on a variety of cybersecurity topics. There is little expectation in terms of having a lot of processes and procedures in place, and minimal information sharing is expected beyond inter-departmental discussions. As organizations, communities, and states progress through Phase 1, increased awareness at high and middle level management will occur, information sharing becomes a major discussion point, and topics such as cybersecurity training and exercises are introduced.

By the end of this phase, participants must have at least a defined cybersecurity awareness program, informal but regular information sharing working groups, some level of cybersecurity training and education, assessment and planning finished, and should have conducted at least one cybersecurity exercise or be planning one. In this case the exercise will be for awareness purposes and will most likely be a tabletop exercise. In later levels, once procedures are established, the exercise can be used to evaluate the effectiveness of established processes, procedures, and programs. It should be noted that when the model was developed it was understood that most, if not all, communities that are at Level 1 will likely not have a large budget for implementing the activities in Phase 1. Budgets are generally set at least a year if not more in advance. When the community first starts on its path to cybersecurity preparedness members of the community will be learning about the things they need to do and can at that time better budget for it. This means that for the most part, activities in Phase 1 should be at no- or low-cost to the community and its organizations. As the community advances in its level of maturity there will be time for a cybersecurity budget to be introduced so that later phases will have the funding that will be required to accomplish all that will need to be done to establish a long-term, viable and sustainable program.

## Phase 2: Established to Self-Assessed

Phase 2 takes the lessons learned from implementing Phase 1 and adds additional focus on information sharing and exercises. Organizational and community leadership should be actively involved in promoting cybersecurity awareness at all levels (e.g. user, supervisor, and executive levels), showing support as often as required. If interest in cybersecurity issues is not shown by the leaders of an organization the employees will also not be interested. On the other hand, if a CEO, mayor, or head of a government department routinely asks about the cybersecurity status of the organization then it will have a positive impact on the next level of leadership which will translate to an increased interest down through all levels of the organization.

By the end of Phase 2, information sharing working groups should be well-established, meeting regularly with formal agendas and discussion topics. Whenever possible, such working groups should include a mix of public and private organizations. This helps keep conversations relevant to the entire community and leads to the whole-community focus that is desired.

Technology assessments should be conducted by this point, with the questions answered concerning what is needed and where. Basic implementation of "low hanging fruit" is strongly suggested but not necessarily required. What is meant by this is that simple, inexpensive security processes or technology (especially well documented and reviewed public domain software) that will improve some aspect of cybersecurity should be considered to advance the status of an organization or the community.

Where needed, to go along with the increased awareness of the importance of cybersecurity for all individuals in an organization, training and education should be in place to provide each group with the knowledge and skills they will need to be more secure. This could include, for example, organization-sponsored training seminars conducted by internal staff or formal training classes by a vendor. The point here is to ensure some level of training is occurring on a periodic but scheduled basis. There may also be the possibility of sharing cybersecurity training programs between organizations in the community. There may exist an organization that has developed an effective user cybersecurity training program that they may be willing to share with others in the community. Taking a look at the cybersecurity problem from a whole-community perspective makes it more likely that such sharing might take place.

Finally, exercises must incorporate incident response and recovery from a cybersecurity event. If the community's emergency management organization has annual drills or exercises, some of these should have a strong cyber element to them and in fact an annual cyber-only exercise should be planned. What communities will often find when they introduce a cyber element to a more traditional community exercise (such as a natural disaster, chemical accident, or terrorist attack), the exercise participants will gravitate toward the aspects they are comfortable with and may ignore the parts they are not as familiar with. A cyber aspect to one of these other exercises is only going to be valuable if it is considered along with all of the other issues that need to be addressed. Too often communities may find that an answer such as "we would just go back to doing it with paper and pencil like we did years ago" will be the answer and the cyber event will be swept aside. What folks who have actually experienced an event in which cyber assets were lost have seen is that going back to the old ways is not always easy and may not even be possible. Forms that used to exist and the training and processes needed to use them instead of the newer cyber processes may no longer be available and individuals, especially those who were not around in "the old days" will not know what to do. Including cyber components/events in other exercises helps introduce the broader exercise programs that are part of Phase 3 and beyond but having a cyber-only event will allow for the participants to focus on cyber issues exclusively and will not allow them to sweep cyber aside to concentrate on more familiar emergency responses.

## Phase 3: Self-Assessed to Integrated

When a community arrives at Level 3 it has advanced far enough in the CCSMM to have developed a sustainable cybersecurity program. Communities, and organizations within them, that are moving from Level 3 to Level 4 should expect a lot more emphasis on measuring success in areas such as awareness, information sharing, and processes and assessments (such as exercise planning). Phase 3 involves greatly expanding cybersecurity awareness to move beyond

Information sharing continues to be a key initiative in this phase. Communities will need to increasingly be making strides towards establishing a formal fusion center that operates on an around-the-clock basis. Fusion Centers are entities often at a state level but also may be established in larger communities which accept reports of various "observations" from around the community and "fuse" them together to determine those that may be related and that may indicate a bigger issue may be brewing. On the cybersecurity side, there are also companies that can provide assistance with the current state of cyber threats and could be a valuable addition to the community program or to individual organizations. Fusion centers are often associated with the law enforcement and intelligence communities and employ individuals with a background in one or both of these fields. Fusion centers are similar to ISAOs but have a broader focus in that they look at all hazards that occur within a community. The "organizational boundaries and into the local community at an even greater level. Citizens should be notified of preventative security measures that can be made in their daily lives, and information pertaining to cybersecurity incidents that might have an impact on them should be disseminated in a standardized manner. An annual cybersecurity day that may first be introduced at a lower level for the community should now feature an increased number of things that citizens can/should do. Public service announcements on local TV, cable, and radio stations could feature short messages on cybersecurity and short training and awareness programs could be featured on community channels on a variety of cybersecurity topics, some now even at a technical level.

fusing" of information is not an easy mission but is one that has been discussed in greater detail over the past few decades. A well-known example might be the bombing of the federal building in Oklahoma City in 1995. The individuals who detonated the bomb had in the months leading up to the attack purchased large (but not uncommon) amounts of ammonium nitrate (which can be used in bomb making but is also commonly used as a fertilizer), nitromethane and Tovex. They had attempted to purchase the nitromethane under the pretense that they needed it for fuel for motorcycle racing. The amount they wanted was unusual and the first individual they approached to make the purchase refused to sell it to them and, in fact, reported the request to the FBI. They also stole 500 blasting caps from a quarry. They then acquired seventeen bags of ANFO (ammonium nitrate/fuel oil) for use in the bomb. These items were not purchased or stolen from one community but occurred over several states. They also rented storage space and then a truck to transport the bomb. The job of a fusion center would be to note the purchase of items that could be used in bomb making, especially under suspicious circumstances as reported by the one individual to the FBI. All of these seemingly disparate events when put together provide a different possible picture of what is occurring than what might be assumed by looking at the individual events separately. This is the goal of a Fusion Center – to put the pieces together in order to prevent an attack from occurring. The difficulty in accomplishing this, however, is also evident in this same example as it occurred over more than one community and state, the individuals used an alias, and individually all of these are common transactions. To accomplish similar activity for the cyber domain, public and private partnerships should be established at this level, and clear lines of communication should be defined and developed. From a process, planning, and exercise perspective, the fusion center participants will increasingly have a very active role in identifying needed processes to be able to spot crossovers between cyber and other domains, creating plans for addressing cybersecurity incidents, and exercising those plans on a regular basis.

Assessments will increase in frequency and in detail as Level 4 is attained. The topic of assessments is receiving increased attention in the cybersecurity field. For several years, some organizations in industry have required that their vendors who access their information or connect to their networks have specific types of assessments performed before they will accept them as vendors. The topic is frequently also discussed in relationship to cyber insurance policies and branches of the federal government have also increasingly been laying requirements on any industry that wants to do business with them. It is important to explain the role of the community in assessments and what they are expected to do. Individual organizations within the community may require assessments be conducted by their vendors but this is not a community requirement but an individual organization requirement. The community will not be involved in assessment of individual organizations and their security policies except as it pertains to the whole-community cybersecurity effort. The community can, however, provide recommendations for individual organizations, especially small businesses, as to what they might want to examine in their own programs. This is another area where organizations may be willing to share what they use with others in the community and increasingly free resources can be found on the Internet to help organizations conduct assessments – especially against things like the requirements found in the NIST Cyber Security Framework. DHS/CISA also offers some forms of assessments for local governments and infrastructures.

Exercises, which are a major part of a community's assessment effort, will transition from tabletop events to more functional exercises in real or near-real time. In other words, for a functional (or partially functional) cybersecurity exercise or physical exercise with cyber elements the actual sequence of events an attacker might take will be conducted to a certain level to determine if individuals and organizations know what they should do. This level of exercise requires a lot more coordination to conduct and should incorporate as many stakeholders as possible. The key here is simulating a real event as much as possible without having to alter real-time system operations or impacting operational networks. Not impacting operational networks is a critical factor – while you want to "touch" operational networks potentially, the exercise should not unduly impact ongoing operations. When possible, exercise planners should seek input and participation from external organizations and neighboring communities for a true picture of how a cyber event may affect the region.

## Phase 4: Integrated to Vanguard

In the fourth and last phase of CCSMM implementation, all of the pieces will be combined into a comprehensive program. The result will be a community that contains full cybersecurity awareness at all levels, including public and private organizations within the community as well as local citizens. Similar to a physical crime or event, a citizen is equipped with tools for reporting cyber incidents to proper authorities for further investigation, follow-up and response. Residents will be taught how to protect themselves, their data, and their devices using low or no-cost methods. Programs that simulate in the cyber arena non-cyber programs such as Crime Stoppers and Neighborhood Watches have already been proposed and implemented at some level in some communities. "Neighborhood Cyber Watches" and "Cybercrime Stoppers" will actually begin to be introduced at a lower level but at Level 5 this aspect should be well incorporated and understood in the community. A broad "culture of cybersecurity", though started at an earlier level, should be resident throughout the community.

Information sharing will be solidified during this phase, with full, bi-directional sharing and fusion of data. As organizations and individuals begin to share information, they are generally hesitant to share their own information although they are interested in receiving information. As they become more comfortable with the information sharing program they will gradually enter into a two-way sharing effort where they will not only receive information but will also be willing to share information about things that they see and that have occurred in their own organization. In addition to gathering data from multiple sources in various sectors, the fusion center and/or the community ISAO will regularly disseminate relevant information to stakeholders. Participation in the fusion center and/or community ISAO will expand to include all major community functions, including law enforcement, emergency services, various government functions, the private sector, education, etc. The fusion center and/or community ISAO will be either supported by local government funding or will be fully self-sufficient (in the case of the ISAO model). They will be integrated into emergency response activities when needed.

Technology decisions for security will be made consistently and include the needs of the community as part of the decision-making process. Any minor improvements should have been accomplished by this point, and major projects will be initiated or scheduled to be started. Sharing of best practices in terms of tools and processes to use them will be prevalent in the community.

Training and education will include the needs of the local community and will accomplish both awareness and specialized training for professionals. This effort will expand to include K-12 schools and higher education institutions providing a robust pipeline of security savvy individuals, and the community should provide assistance where possible.

Cyber incident response and recovery will become formal, with key partnerships established and well-documented. Mutual aid agreements between organizations or surrounding communities may be necessary and will be established. A mutual aid agreement is simply a document that lays out how two or more communities will agree to assist each other should one or more of them become involved in a cybersecurity event that is having a negative impact. It may include things such as an agreement to allow the attacked community to utilize the computing resources of the supporting community while they are recovering from the event. Leadership will provide support and assistance where needed. Plans that are derived as part of the CCSMM implementation will be reviewed at least annually, and a team should be established for the purpose of approving and implementing changes.

Finally, assessment, test, and exercise activities will evolve to a more advanced and comprehensive level. All of these should now include interaction with the state and other communities. Wherever possible, all exercises, no matter what the focus, will consider including cybersecurity elements. This includes natural disaster drills, anti-terrorism exercises, and medical emergency events. Participation in such activities will evolve to become well-rounded, meaning all sectors within the community will be represented. The CCSMM does not prescribe the type of exercise for this phase and leaves that decision up to planners. However, it is strongly suggested that at least one full-scale, community-wide cyber/physical exercise be planned and conducted every year. This is really the only way to ensure that everyone knows their role during an emergency that directly or indirectly impacts cyber assets within the community.

Also remember that Level 5 is the "Vanguard" level. Efforts in this phase should begin to incorporate elements from outside of the community. Other communities should be invited to participate in cybersecurity indicators of compromise information sharing, training, sharing of best practices, and exercises. In reality, a community will not simply jump into becoming a vanguard during this phase, elements will have been introduced at lower levels, but during this phase it becomes ingrained into the planning process.

## LESSONS LEARNED: THE COMMUNITY CYBER SECURITY MATURITY MODEL

Without a model, such as the Community Cyber Security Maturity Model, to follow, cities can easily flounder in their attempt to establish a sustainable security program. An initial rise in cybersecurity awareness and a desire to do something to improve cybersecurity can quickly take a back seat to other issues that occur in the community. Even with the model, establishing a community-wide program is not an easy task. It will take time and it is easy for initial interest in it to dissipate as organizations face their day-to-day concerns and requirements. This is especially true in communities where the leadership changes on a regular basis. Elected officials have a number of concerns and cybersecurity is usually not one of the campaign points that they push. What has been shown to be a key factor in a community's ability to sustain the development of the program until it is mature enough to sustain itself is the need for a champion in the community.

It is not critical what sector the champion comes from, but it is essential that the champion remains in the community for a period of time sufficient for the community to establish the community program. In the past, champions have been individuals such as a city employee such as the city's CISO or CIO, a leader from an industry/business in the community such as a member of the local Chamber of Commerce, or an individual from an organization with sufficient support from leadership to spend time in coordinating meetings and encouraging individuals and various sectors across the community. At first the entire community may not be represented but there are a few organizations that are particularly important to have represented as early in the process of establishing a program as possible. This includes local government, the different utilities, community emergency management, law enforcement, and representatives from significant industry within the community.

It has also been shown to be helpful to have political coverage as well. A representative from Congress for the community can often pull together people in a meeting when interest may begin to dwindle due to other priorities within the community. Another item that can help is to quickly establish a Cybersecurity Day or a Culture of Security Day for the community. These events should include parts for government, industry and citizens so the level of cybersecurity in the community is raised and motivation to continue with establishing the program will be periodically rekindled.

From the beginning of the program, participants should understand that establishing a cybersecurity program will not occur overnight, nor is it something that can be done once and forgotten. It will be an ongoing effort that constantly will need to be updated as new technology is developed. Just like the police department, fire department, or emergency services, the need to maintain a high level of preparation and training in cybersecurity is essential as the "problem" is not going to go away.

## CONCLUSION

Attacks on states and communities have increased and have become almost commonplace. In order to better handle intrusions and to hopefully prevent them in the first place, an organized cybersecurity program needs to be established within organizations in a community and with the community from a whole-community perspective. Awareness is often the first step taken to establish such a program but only raising the awareness of cybersecurity as an issue to be addressed is not sufficient to maintain long-term support for cybersecurity. Awareness alone is also not enough to ensure an organized approach to developing a sustainable program.

The Community Cyber Security Maturity Model (CCSMM) provides a way for a community to determine where they are in the maturity of their program, a plan to decide what they need to do in order to progress in maturing their program, and a common lexicon to be able to discuss programs between communities in different areas of the country. Discussing and being able to compare programs provides a way for all communities to share ideas on how to implement various aspects of the model and thus for all communities to work together in creating a more secure nation.

A community will need to first evaluate where they are at in terms of the maturity of their cybersecurity program. Then they must decide at what level they believe they will need to be in order to address the threats to their community. Not all communities have to be at the same level and not all communities need to attain the highest level of the model.

The 2-dimensional model contains five levels – Initial, Established, Self-assessed, Integrated, and Vanguard. Communities all start at the Initial level which is where they start planning for their program.

When communities first recognize the importance of cybersecurity they generally do not have any budget set aside for it as budgets are established a year or more in advance. Efforts at the Initial level therefore are limited to as much as possible no- and low-cost items.

The second level is Established. As the name implies, programs at this level have been formally established and efforts to have a viable and sustainable cybersecurity program within the community are well underway. At the third level, Self-Assessed, communities have advanced far enough that their program should be sustainable and is mature enough that they are able to assess and understand their needs. Organizations within the community should be able to, and should actually be conducting efforts, to help each other. The fourth level is Integrated. At this level the community and organizations don't see cybersecurity as a separate component to their other operations but recognize that cybersecurity is cross-cutting and impacts every aspect of the community. Thus, cybersecurity needs to be considered by everyone. Finally, the fifth level is Vanguard and communities at this level are considered to be models for others to follow. A Vanguard community will be reaching out to the state and to other communities to help them with their own programs.

The CCSMM model is designed around four dimensions. At each level the characteristics for a community at that level in each of the dimensions is described. The dimensions are Awareness, Information Sharing, Policy and Planning. These will be discussed in more detail in subsequent chapters. In between each of the levels is a Phase which consists of the activities that must occur to advance the community from one level to the next. With five levels, there are four advancement phases.

Finally, it should be emphasized that it is often easy to confuse activities for individual organizations within a community and the overall whole-community cybersecurity program. While the community should be encouraging individual organizations to advance their own level of cybersecurity maturity, the community (as in the local government) is not responsible for the security of all organizations within its geographic boundaries. The CCSMM program is designed to help the whole-community to advance its level of security preparedness. It will include encouraging some organizations (such as the critical infrastructures and local government entities) to adopt certain cybersecurity practices but these are done only in relationship to how they impact the entire community. There are other models (including other parts of the CCSMM) that are designed to help individual organizations and these are discussed briefly in later chapters.

## REFERENCES

Cybersecurity capability maturity model (C2M2). (2014, February). Retrieved February 27, 2020, from Energy.gov website: https://www.energy.gov/sites/prod/files/2014/03/f13/C2M2-v1-1_cor.pdf

DoD to streamline cyber acquisition with new certification model. (2019). Retrieved from MeriTalk website: https://www.meritalk.com/articles/dod-to-streamline-cyber-acquisition-with-new-certification-model/

Edwards, S., & Hays, S. (2019). *What is the cybersecurity maturity model certification (CMMC)?* Retrieved from SUMMIT7 website: https://info.summit7systems.com/blog/cmmc

White, G. (2011). The community cyber security maturity model. *IEEE Conference on Technologies for Homeland Security*, 173-178.

White, G. (2012). A Grassroots Cyber Security Program to Protect the Nation. *45th Hawaii International Conference on System Science.* 10.1109/HICSS.2012.60

White, G., & Granado, N. (2009). Developing a Community Cyber Security Incident Response Capability. *42nd Hawaii International Conference on System Science.*

## ADDITIONAL READING

Curtis, P., Mehravari, N., & Stevens, J. (2015). *Cybersecurity capability maturity model for information technology services (C2M2 for IT services), version 1.0* (Technical Report No. CMU/SEI-2015-TR-009). Retrieved from Software Engineering Institute Carnegie Mellon University website: https://apps.dtic.mil/dtic/tr/fulltext/u2/1026943.pdf

Ross, R., Viscuso, P., Guissanie, G., Dempsey, K., & Riddle, M. (2015). NIST Special Publication: Vol. 800-171 Rev. 1. Protecting controlled unclassified information in nonfederal information systems and organizations. Retrieved from National Institute of Standards and Technology website: https://nvlpubs.nist.gov/nistpubs/SpecialPublications/NIST.SP.800-171.pdf

*Previously published in Establishing Cyber Security Programs Through the Community Cyber Security Maturity Model (CC-SMM); pages 32-54, copyright year 2021 by Information Science Reference (an imprint of IGI Global).*

# Chapter 7
# Threat and Risk Assessment Using Continuous Logic

**Aristides Dasso**
*Universidad Nacional de San Luis, Argentina*

**Ana Funes**
*Universidad Nacional de San Luis, Argentina*

## ABSTRACT

*Threat and Risk Assessment is an important area in cybersecurity. It covers multiple systems and organizations where cybersecurity is significant, such as banking, industry, SCADA, Energy Management System, among many others. The chapter presents a method to help assessing threats and risks associated with computer and networks systems. It integrates the Framework for Improving Critical Infrastructure Cybersecurity—developed by the National Institute of Standards and Technology—with a quantitative method based on the use of a Continuous Logic, the Logic Scoring of Preference (LSP) method. LSP is a method suitable for decision making that provides the guidelines to produce a model to assist the expert in the process of assessing how much a product or system satisfy a number of requirements, in this case associated to the identification, protection, detection, response and recovery of threat and risks in an organization.*

## INTRODUCTION

The chapter presents a method to help assessing threats and their associated risks. Threat and Risk Assessment encompass a wide area, ranging from building construction to network and computer security through automotive design and construction, and many others such as Supervisory Control And Data Acquisition (SCADA), Energy Management System (EMS) systems among others, many of them closely associated with computer and networks systems.

DOI: 10.4018/978-1-6684-3698-1.ch007

Assessing threats and the risks associated to them implies several tasks such as identifying threat and risks, detecting them and their level of danger to a particular organization cybersecurity system, as well as to decide what to do with a specific threat, the costs of prevention or correction, the consequences of the actual risks occurring or, alternatively, not paying any attention to them, disregarding them.

Properly identifying, recognizing, making out a possible threat is the first step in this process; consequently, to have a list of characteristics, traits, attributes or requirements can be of help in that task. Therefore, it is necessary in first place to clearly define the set of requirements that can be of use in identifying threats and their related risks. Second, it is important to have a method that using those requirements eases the building of a model that assist people in charge with the job of assessing threats and risks in order to make well informed decisions on the matter.

The method proposed here is aimed at giving help in the area of cybersecurity and it is based on the Framework for Improving Critical Infrastructure Cyber security developed by the National Institute of Standards and Technology (NIST). The proposal integrates this framework with a quantitative method based on the use of a Continuous Logic, the Logic Scoring of Preference (LSP) method. LSP is a method suitable for decision making that provides the guidelines to produce a model/tool to assist the expert in the process of assessing how much a product or system satisfy a number of requirements, in this case associated to the identification, protection, detection, response and recovery of threat and risks in an organization. More specifically, the proposal is aimed to supplement steps 3 to 5 in the NIST program (NIST, 2018) with the necessary activities to develop a quantitative LSP model for assessing threat and risks in an organization. Therefore starting from a set of requirements taken from the NIST Framework, and applying the LSP method, a decision model can be developed. The resulting model can be used as an effective tool to assist professionals in the process of assessing potential threats and risks involved in any kind of organization, be it industrial, service, utilities, etc., providing a global indicator as well as a set of partial indicators, for each system under evaluation. These indicators are values in the interval [0; 100]; the global indicator represents the stage in which a system under evaluation is with respect to the whole set of critical threat and risk requirements identified and, in the case of the partial indicators, to cohesive subgroups of requirements.

## BACKGROUND

The next two subsections discuss related work on threat and risk assessment and introduce some concepts of the LSP method necessary to understand the rest of the work.

### Threat and Risks Assessment

Threat and Risk Assessment is part of an ongoing process of identifying, assessing, and responding to risk. Threat and Risk Assessment in cyber security contexts is becoming more and more a concern for organizations of any kind, i.e. industrial, utilities, service oriented, etc., since computers and networks have penetrated nearly every activity. Organizations increasingly have the need to assess the potential threats and the risks involved in their processes and infrastructures. Not only commercial and government institutions but also utilities are aware of the potential threats to their infrastructures. Many open source and proprietary methods exist today to perform a risk and threat assessment, some focused on specific types of risk and some focused on specific business sectors. Of course the problem of threat and risk assessment is also considered in settings where security is a concern in a wider sense, for instance the threats and risks confronted in cyber terrorism, cyber war, and other similar scenarios; an overview of this can be found in Lewis, J. A. (2002). The threats and risks involved in unmanned aerial vehicles (UAVs) are also considered in Hartmann, K., Steup, C. (2013). In Ciapessoni, E. et al. (2018) the authors developed a method based on probabilities considering that threats can go from natural disasters to deliberate acts of sabotage.

There are also US patents on the subject such as Magdych et al. (2003), and Kelley, J. D., Lahann, J. S., Mackey II, D. H. (2006).

In Cherdantseva, Y. et al. (2016) there is a review of Threat and Risk assessment methods for Supervisory Control And Data Acquisition (SCADA) systems of great size and scope. It must be considered that SCADA systems are prone to attacks that can have serious consequences, e.g. Stuxnet malware (Zetter, K. 2019). Also Bayne, J. (2002) furnishes an overview of the whole process of Threat and Risk Assessment. There are also guides to risk management such as ISO 31000 (2018).

There is an extensive literature on security and network structure concerning smart grid environments, e.g. a Threat and Risk Assessment methodology, presented in Smith P. (AIT), Editor. (n.d.), where a "threat identification approach, based on attack graphs" is proposed. They use *Semantic Threat Graphs* (STGs) as "a tool to precisely determine the necessary countermeasures for the identified threats".

Also the European Network and Information Security Agency (ENISA) analyzes in ENISA (2010) the future risks in a scenario of future air travel, were Internet of Things (IoT) and Radio Frequency IDentification (RFID) technologies are used. The methodology employed is based on the standard ISO/IEC 27005:2008 Information technology — Security techniques — Information Security Risk Management. A very detailed "Vulnerabilities and Threats List" has been developed. A "Risk Identification and Assessment" is considered based on three elements, i.e. Risk = f(Asset, Vulnerability, Threat). A spread sheet was elaborated as part of the development (ENISA, n.d.).

Webb, J., Ahmad, A., Maynard, S. B., & Shanks. G. (2014) posit that they have identified deficiencies in Information Security Risk Management (ISRM), so they propose a Situation Awareness (SA) for ISRM model.

## The Logic Score of Preference (LSP) Method

The Logic Scoring of Preference (LSP) method (Dujmovic, J. J., 1996, 1997, 1997b, 2007, 2018) has been adopted in this work as an integral part of the proposed threat and risk assessment decision methodology. LSP is a method for the realization of complex criterion functions and their application in the area of decision, evaluation, optimization, comparison and selection of general complex systems.

Since it is a general decision and evaluation method, it can be applied to different scenarios, particularly to the processes involved in threat and risks evaluation and decision. Given that LSP is not a simple additive scoring method, it is especially useful where the use of complex *and/or* decisions is necessary.

As in many other methods, initially in LSP the user requirements must be clearly determined, i.e. the main attributes to be taken into consideration for the model under development, as well as their corresponding preference values must be defined. These are generally organized in the form of a hierarchical tree, where the leaves of the tree correspond to the attributes to be evaluated. These attributes are called *performance variables*. Each one of these variables is then mapped into an *elementary preference* by defining and applying the corresponding *elementary criterion*, as the schema on Figure 1 shows.

An elementary criterion is a function that transforms a performance variable (real value) into an elementary preference (value in the interval [0; 100]). An elementary preference represents the degree of fulfillment of a requirement, where 0 means that the requirement has not been fulfilled at all and 100 that it has been completely satisfied.

The elementary preferences, obtained from the transformation of each performance variable via their corresponding elementary criteria, are used as input to the LSP *Criterion Function* or *Aggregation Structure*, as Figure 1 shows. Theses preferences are iteratively aggregated until a single global indicator of the degree of fulfillment of the whole system requirements can be obtained. More specifically, the aggregation structure creation process starts by aggregating elementary preferences by means of a set of operators provided by the LSP method. Aggregating a set of elementary preferences means to replace a group of them by a single output preference, which is a partial indicator of the degree of satisfaction with respect to the group of aggregated preferences. These output preferences are then aggregated again until a single output global preference $G_0$ is obtained. During this process, not only the elementary and partial preferences must be aggregated but it is also necessary to take into account both the relative importance of each preference as well as the necessary logic relationship between them.

*Figure 1. An overview of the LSP method evaluation process*

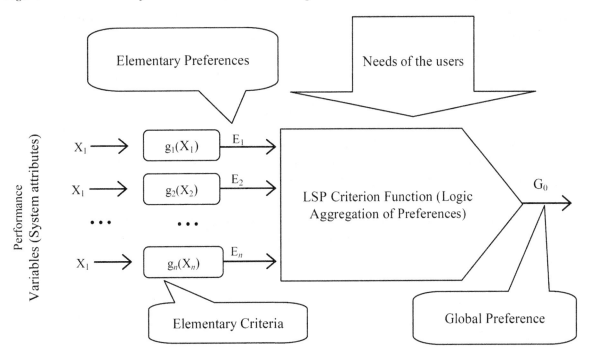

The calibration of the LSP Criterion Function represents the most complex phase in the whole process, since not only it is necessary to take into account the needs of end users but also to validate the model to preserve the representation condition, i.e. the behaviour of the measures in the model to be the same as the corresponding entities in the real world.

Once the calibration of the LSP Criterion Function has finished, the evaluation process of threat and risks can start. It means that the values corresponding to each of the performance variables of the system under evaluation must be collected and provided as input to the model to finally obtain a global performance indicator, corresponding to the degree of compliance to the threat and risks assessment requirements, as well as a series of partial indicators corresponding to each of the subcategories considered in the requirement tree.

The numbers delivered by the model point up the degree of compliance of the security implementations as well as the likelihood of risks that the organization is under. Both the partial indicators as well as the global indicator will assist stakeholders –normally, the threat and risks assessment team– on making decisions about the assessment.

## The NIST's Framework for Improving Critical Infrastructure Cybersecurity

The Cybersecurity Enhancement Act of 2014 granted The National Institute of Standards and Technology with the "role of identifying and developing cybersecurity risk frameworks for voluntary use by critical infrastructure owners and operators.". (NIST, 2018). The Framework was developed with cybersecurity for critical infrastructures in mind, but it can be used by institutions of any size, degree of risk or sophistication.

There are diverse standards, guidelines, and practices, referenced to by the Framework which allow the organizations to describe their current cybersecurity posture; depict their target state for cybersecurity; identify and prioritize opportunities for improvement within the context of a continuous and repeatable process; assess progress toward the target state and communicate among internal and external stakeholders about cybersecurity risk.

The framework can be used in different ways by organizations. A first direct application is to compare the organization's current cybersecurity activities with those outlined in the Framework Core. In this way, executives can obtain a feedback about a fundamental question: "How are we doing?" and, consequently, strengthen their cybersecurity practices where and when deemed necessary.

The framework also provides a common language to communicate requirements among stakeholders responsible for the delivery of different services to an organization.

An important use of the framework is establishing or improving a cybersecurity program. In (NIST, 2018) a number of steps to create a new cybersecurity program or improve an existing one are given, namely

**Step 1:** *Prioritize and Scope*. The organization identifies its business/mission objectives and high-level organizational priorities. With this information, the organization makes strategic decisions regarding cybersecurity implementations and determines the scope of systems and assets that support the selected business line or process.

**Step 2:** *Orient*. Once the scope of the cybersecurity program has been determined for the business line or process, the organization identifies related systems and assets, regulatory requirements, and overall risk approach. The organization then consults sources to identify threats and vulnerabilities applicable to those systems and assets.

**Step 3:** *Create a Current Profile*. The organization develops a current profile by indicating which category and subcategory outcomes from the Framework Core are currently being achieved. If an outcome is partially achieved, noting this fact will help support subsequent steps by providing baseline information.

**Step 4:** *Conduct a Risk Assessment.* This assessment could be guided by the organization's overall risk management process or previous risk assessment activities. The organization analyzes the operational environment in order to discern the likelihood of a cybersecurity event and the impact that the event could have on the organization. It is important that organizations identify emerging risks and use cyber threat information from internal and external sources to gain a better understanding of the likelihood and impact of cybersecurity events.

**Step 5:** *Create a Target Profile.* The organization creates a Target Profile that focuses on the assessment of the Framework Categories and Subcategories describing the organization's desired cybersecurity outcomes. Organizations also may develop their own additional Categories and Subcategories to account for unique organizational risks. The organization may also consider influences and requirements of external stakeholders such as sector entities, customers, and business partners when creating a Target Profile. The Target Profile should appropriately reflect criteria within the target Implementation Tier.

**Step 6:** *Determine, Analyze, and Prioritize Gaps.* The organization compares the Current Profile and the Target Profile to determine gaps. Next, it creates a prioritized action plan to address gaps – reflecting mission drivers, costs and benefits, and risks – to achieve the outcomes in the Target Profile. The organization then determines resources, including funding and workforce, necessary to address the gaps. Using Profiles in this manner encourages the organization to make informed decisions about cybersecurity activities, supports risk management, and enables the organization to perform cost-effective, targeted improvements.

**Step 7:** *Implement Action Plan.* The organization determines which actions to take to address the gaps, if any, identified in the previous step and then adjusts its current cybersecurity practices in order to achieve the Target Profile. For further guidance, the Framework identifies example Informative References regarding the Categories and Subcategories, but organizations should determine which standards, guidelines, and practices, including those that are sector specific, work best for their needs.

Any or all of these steps should be repeated as needed to assess and improve cybersecurity in an organization.

The method proposed here is intended to be of help especially in steps 3 to 5. Building the requirement tree and the LSP Criterion Function provides the organization with a model that reflects the organization needs and the desired cybersecurity requirements, i.e. an ideal target profile. At the same time, its application to the actual practices makes available a current profile and the possibility of assessing the potential risk, creating action plans and achieving new evaluations in a future.

## THE THREAT AND RISKS ASSESMENT MODEL DEVELOPMENT PROCESS

As assessing the threats and the associated risks is of crucial importance to organizations, making the right decisions in that assessment is also important for those involved in the decisions. What are the possible threats?; have we identified all the possible threats?, what is the degree of danger of an identified threat?; can it safely be ignored, since the probability of its occurrence is very low and the cost of taken it in consideration is too high?; is the risk of a threat very low?; have the organization the means to recovery given the occurrence of a specific risk?. These and many more questions are confronted by that people concerned with threat and risk assessment. It is not easy to answer them without resorting to some kind of tools, to recognize possible threats and the risks involved and what to do about them.

Having this motivation in mind, the authors propose the adoption of the method presented here for the development of an assessment model, which is based on requirements taken from the Framework for Improving Critical Infrastructure Cybersecurity by the National Institute of Standards and Technology Version 1.1 (NIST, 2018), and the guidelines of the Logic Scoring of Preference (LSP) method, a soft computing method suitable to help in evaluation and decision making. The NIST Framework is used to identify the requirements associated to threats and risks identification, protection, detection, response and recovery, while the LSP method provides the activities and techniques for the development of a quantitative model built on the basis of NIST Framework requirements.

The following subsections describe the Threat and Risk Assessment model development process that can be adopted when conducting a risk assessment phase in a cybersecurity program.

## Threat and Risks Assessment Requirements

An important point when building a model is determining the organization needs. In the first place, the organization must determine the scope of the systems to be evaluated since different business lines or processes within an organization may have different business needs and associated risk tolerances. The same occurs when using the NIST Framework: "To account for the unique cybersecurity needs of organizations, there are a wide variety of ways to use the Framework. The decision about how to apply it is left to the implementing organization." (NIST, 2018, p. vi). Besides that, NIST establishes that "Because each organization's risks, priorities, and systems are unique, the tools and methods used to achieve the outcomes described by the Framework will vary." (NIST, 2018, p. 2). These considerations and other similar ones also apply to the Threat and Risk Assessment model presented here.

Therefore, the first activity when developing an assessment model will be to determine the user´s needs and build a requirement model. Also the LSP method prescribes it as the initial activity, resulting in a hierarchical structure named *requirement tree* as main artifact, which will hold all the non functional requirements, i.e. the characteristics, sub-characteristics and attributes considered for the evaluation process.

A computable characteristic is one that cannot be measured in a direct way and whose value is obtained from other sub-characteristics or attributes that define it, i.e. they represent high level abstraction concepts. A sub-characteristic is also a computable characteristic, while an attribute or performance variable corresponds to a leaf of the requirement tree and can be measured in a direct way or by applying a specific metric.

To develop the threat and risks requirement tree, the five Functions of the NIST Framework Core (NIST, 2019) (Identify, Protect, Detect, Respond, Recover) can be considered as the top level characteristics in the requirement tree. "The Framework Core then identifies underlying key Categories and Subcategories – which are discrete outcomes – for each Function, and matches them with example Informative References such as existing standards, guidelines, and practices for each Subcategory." (NIST, 2018, p.3). The categories and subcategories mentioned above will form part of the tree as sub-characteristics or performance variables. They are presented in (NIST, 2018, p.3) in table format and have a hierarchical arrangement with four items (columns): Functions, Categories, Subcategories and Informative References.

When adopting the whole NIST Framework Core, the resulting requirement tree model will consist of five Functions, twenty three Categories, one hundred and eight Subcategories, and five hundred and four Informative References, some of these last ones sometimes subdivided as well. Informative References seem to be the obvious choice for the performance variables in the requirement tree model. They could be a great help in assigning the values needed during the evaluation process.

Table 1 shows only the first two levels of the requirement model based on the Framework Core, while Table 2 shows all the requirements for the Category Communications (RC.CO), under the top level function RECOVER (RC). RC.CO contains three subcategories and seven Informative References that are as well subdivided, which for reasons of space are shown abbreviated.

*Table 1. The first two levels in the Framework Core (NIST, 2019)*

| Function | Category |
|---|---|
| IDENTIFY (ID) | Asset Management (ID.AM): |
| | Business Environment (ID.BE): |
| | Governance (ID.GV): |
| | Risk Assessment (ID.RA): |
| | Risk Management Strategy (ID.RM): |
| | Supply Chain Risk Management (ID.SC) |
| PROTECT (PR) | Identity Management, Authentication and Access Control (PR.AC) |
| | Awareness and Training (PR.AT) |
| | Data Security (PR.DS) |
| | Information Protection Processes and Procedures (PR.IP) |
| | Maintenance (PR.MA) |
| | Protective Technology (PR.PT) |
| DETECT (DE) | Anomalies and Events (DE.AE) |
| | Security Continuous Monitoring (DE.CM) |
| | Detection Processes (DE.DP) |
| RESPOND (RS) | Response Planning (RS.RP) |
| | Communications (RS.CO) |
| | Analysis (RS.AN) |
| | Mitigation (RS.MI) |
| | Improvements (RS.IM) |
| RECOVER (RC) | Recovery Planning (RC.RP) |
| | Improvements (RC.IM) |
| | Communications (RC.CO) |

*Table 2. Subcategories and Informative References of Category Communications (RC.CO) of Function RECOVER (RC). (NIST, 2019)*

| Function | Category | Subcategory | Informative References | | |
|---|---|---|---|---|---|
| **RECOVER (RC)** | **Communications (RC.CO):** | **RC.CO-1** | **COBIT 5** (COBIT® 5. 2012, pp39, 40) | EDM03.02 | Activity 1 |
| | | | | | to |
| | | | | | Activity 6 |
| | | | **ISO/IEC 27001:2013** | A.6.1.4 (ISO/IEC 27001. 2013, p. 10) | Appropriate contacts |
| | | | | Clause 7.4 (ISO/IEC 27001. 2013, p. 6) | Comm. a) |
| | | | | | to |
| | | | | | Comm. e) |
| | | **RC.CO-2** | **COBIT 5** (COBIT® 5. 2012, p 214). | MEA03.02 | Activity 1 |
| | | | | | Activity 2 |
| | | | **ISO/IEC 27001:2013** (ISO/IEC 27001. 2013, p. 6) | Clause 7.4 | Comm. a) |
| | | | | | to |
| | | | | | Comm. e) |
| | | **RC.CO-3** | **COBIT 5** (COBIT® 5. 2012, p 111) | APO12.06 | Activity 1 |
| | | | | | to |
| | | | | | Activity 4 |
| | | | **ISO/IEC 27001:2013** (ISO/IEC 27001. 2013, p. 6) | Clause 7.4 | Comm. a) |
| | | | | | to |
| | | | | | Comm. e) |
| | | | **NIST SP 800-53 Rev. 4** | CP-2 (NIST, 2013, pp. F-129, F-131) | CP-2(1) |
| | | | | | to |
| | | | | | CP-2(8) |
| | | | | IR-4 (NIST, 2013, pp. F-177, F-181) | IR-4(1) |
| | | | | | to |
| | | | | | IR-4(10) |

## Elementary Criteria for the NIST Framework's Informative References

The next activity, prescribed by the LSP method, consists in the definition of an *Elementary Criterion* for each attribute in the requirement tree, in this case for each informative reference considered. An elementary criterion is a metric that returns a value in the Real interval [0; 100], which represents the fulfillment degree of the respective attribute in the system under evaluation and is referred to as *elementary preference*. During the evaluation process, the performance variables are transformed into elementary preferences by means of the application of their corresponding elementary criteria.

The definition of adequate elementary criteria is part of the work to be done when a model is developed. During the model calibration, sometimes elementary criteria must be modified if it proves necessary to fine-tune the model and preserve the representation condition.

During the process of elementary criteria definition, NIST Framework's Informative References must be taken into consideration. Many of the defined metrics will be direct, i.e. a resulting elementary preference takes the same value assigned to the corresponding performance variable, which sometimes can be obtained from expert's opinions or by simple observation. In other cases, an indirect metric will be necessary, e.g. the Informative Reference MEA03.02 (*IT compliance and support for business compliance with external laws and regulations*) shown in Table 2, which is part of the subcategory RC.CO-2 in COBIT 5, has two Activities. Activity 2 instructs to "Communicate new and changed requirements to all relevant personnel." (COBIT® 5, 2012). This implies that whoever is in charge should produce a list of new and changed requirements and a list of the relevant personnel to whom that should be communicated. Equation 1 shows the elementary criterion $MEA03.02_{A2}$ defined for Activity 2 as the mean value between the percentage of changed requirements effectively received by the relevant personnel and the percentage of new requirements effectively received by the relevant personnel. In Equation 1, *#New* denotes the total number of new requirements; *#Changed* the total number of changed requirements; *NP* the total number of relevant personnel to whom the new requirements should be communicated; *#NewRec$_i$* the total number of new requirements effectively received by the relevant personnel *i*. *CP* the total number of relevant personnel to whom the changed requirements should be communicated; *#ChRec$_i$* total number of changed requirements effectively received by the relevant personnel *i*.

$$MEA03.02_{A2} = \left( \frac{\sum_i^{NP} \# NewRec_i \times 100}{\# New} + \frac{\sum_i^{CP} \# ChRec_i \times 100}{\# Changed} \right) / 2 \qquad (1)$$

To properly evaluate $MEA03.02_{A2}$, the threat and risks assessment team will have to gather the necessary data for applying the elementary criteria shown in Equation 1, i.e. consulting the appropriate personnel to verify whether the task prescribed in informative reference $MEA03.02$ has been completed, so as to obtain a correct estimation of the functioning of the involved personnel.

## Aggregation of Preferences

Once the requirement tree has been constructed, a new activity can start: the construction of a quantitative threat and risk model. This model consists of an *aggregation structure* referred to as *LSP Criterion Function*, which is the result of a logic aggregation of preferences by means of an iterative process. The process starts with the aggregation of groups of related elementary preferences using GCD (Generalized Conjunction Disjunction) operators, provided by the LSP method, to obtain a group of partial preferences. These partial preferences are then iteratively aggregated by means of appropriated GCD operators until a single global indicator is finally obtained. Therefore, each partial indicator is the result of the aggregation of at least two partial or elementary preferences. In this way, step by step and applying this aggregation procedure, the partial indicators can be conveniently arranged to produce a single global indicator that represents the degree of fulfillment of all the requirements arranged into the requirement tree.

More specifically, to aggregate *n* elementary preferences $E_1, ..., E_n$ in a single preference $E_0$, i.e. the resulting preference $E_0$ interpreted as the percentage of satisfaction of the *n* requirements, is expressed by a function that has the following two properties:

1.   The relative importance of each elementary preference $E_i$ ($i = 1...n$) is expressed by a weight $W_i$,
2.   $min(E_1, ..., E_n) \le E_i \le max(E_1, ..., E_n)$ .

The GCD operators are obtained from the instantiation of the weighted power mean (Equation 2).

$$E(r) = (W_1 E^r_1 + W_2 E^r_2 + ... + W_n E^r_n)^{1/r}, \tag{2}$$

where $0 < W_i < 100$, $0 \le E_i \le 100$, $i = 1, ..., n$, $W_1 + ... + W_n = 1$, $-\infty \le r \le +\infty$

The choice of $r$ determines the location of $E(r)$. For $r = -\infty$ the weighted power mean reduces to the pure conjunction and for $r = +\infty$ to the pure disjunction, giving place to a Continuous Preference Logic. The range between pure conjunction and pure disjunction is usually covered by a sequence of equidistantly located GCD operators named: C, C++, C+, C+−, CA, C−+, C−, C−−, A, D−−, D−, D−+, DA, D+−, D+, D++, D. For a more detailed description of the technique see Dujmovic, J. J. (1997), Dujmovic, J. J. (2007), Dujmovic, J.J. (2018).

As a result of the application of the proposed method, a threat and risk model can be developed and adapted to the particular needs of a given organization. Seven GCD operators have been mainly employed in the aggregation structures shown in this work: CA, C−+, C−, C−, A, DA y D++. Typically, strong simultaneity operators are used for aggregating mandatory inputs, while weak simultaneity operators are adopted in presence of desirable attributes, meaning that the presence of a value of 0 (zero) in any of the inputs do not produce a zero in the output as it happens when a strong conjunction operator is applied. Therefore, in these cases, operators as C− or C−− can be adopted since they represent weak quasi-conjunctions. Operators A, DA and D++ are adopted in presence of optional attributes. In conclusion, the chosen operators should become more and more conjunctive as more mandatory the characteristics aggregated are.

Figure 2 shows a possible final aggregation of the five top level preferences resulting from the aggregation of the five top level categories (IDENTIFY (ID), PROTECT (PR), DETECT (DE), RESPOND (RS), and RECOVER (RC)). These five partial preferences have been aggregated by the operator CA since they all have been judged to be mandatory, meaning none of them should be with a very low value. Note that the rounded rectangles on the lef of the figure depict the top level preferences, which serve as inputs to the operator CA; each of them represent the abstraction of a partial aggregation structure.

The weights associated to each elementary preference should be assigned by the person or persons in charge of threat and risk decision making. They must reflect the importance that each preference has in the decision model being constructed. This is also illustrated by Figure 3 and Figure 4, where different parts of the whole aggregation structure built for the requirement tree of Table 2 are shown. In these figures, circles represent GCD operators, rectangles correspond to elementary preferences and the weights are shown over the edges (arrows). Rounded rectangles in light grey do not form part of LSP method notation, they have been introduced to indicate partial preferences corresponding to the abstraction of the aggregation of a set of preferences in the requirement tree.

On Figure 3 a partial aggregation structure for Function RECOVER (RC) is presented. Only the labels of the corresponding categories and subcategories are shown. No Informative References are displayed.

*Figure 2. Aggregation structure for the five top level functions*

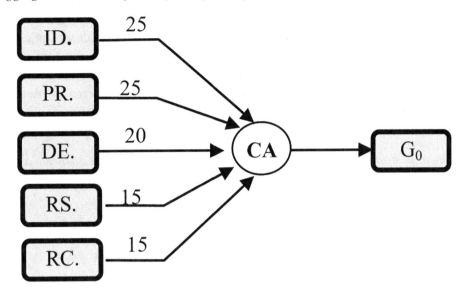

*Figure 3. Partial aggregation structure for Function RECOVERY (RC)*

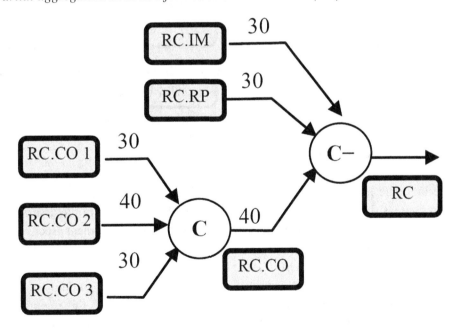

In Figure 4 the aggregation structure built for subcategory RC.CO 3 (*Recovery activities are communicated to internal and external stakeholders as well as executive and management teams*) is shown. Since aggregation structures allow discriminating between mandatory or non mandatory preferences, they permit to graduate how mandatory a given preference is considered by using the adequate GCD operators. However, sometimes there are features considered optional and whose absence should not penalize the result of the whole evaluation. In this situation a particular LSP structure, referred to as *partial absorption*, can be used. This structure is useful when aggregating a mandatory preference with optional preferences. Hence, if the mandatory preference is equal to zero the result of the partial absorption will be zero whatever the values of the optional preferences are. In any other case, the output corresponds to a mean value in a given range (see Dujmovic (1985) for more details on this). In Figure 4 a partial absorption structure can be seen. It corresponds to the aggregation of the Informative Reference for COBIT 5 APO 12.06 and it is shown in the rectangle with a dotted line. In this structure, both preferences "Act. 1" and "Act. 4" have been considered mandatory, while preferences "Act. 2" and "Act. 3" have been deemed optional.

*Figure 4. Aggregation structure for Subcategory RC.CO 3, showing a Partial Absorption for COBIT 5*

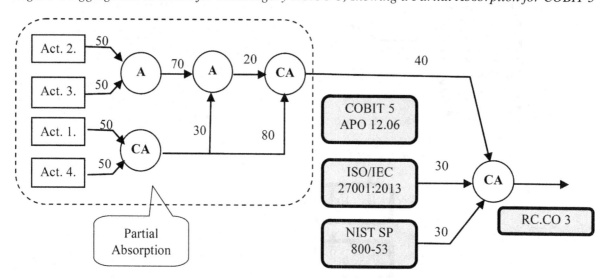

## SOLUTIONS AND RECOMMENDATIONS

There is a wide literature having to do with threat and risk assessment since the subject cuts across many and different areas. In multiple cases not only methodologies to use in the assessment but also procedures and techniques dealing with the decisions to be taken in the assessment process can be found. There is also a substantial amount of guidelines and recommendations such as the one being used here, namely NIST Framework, or COBIT, ISO/IEC, etc.; however, although they are very thorough, they are not enough by themselves to make assessment decisions and many of those guidelines are in need of a complementary model that helps in making decisions on the assessment. In this regard, the proposed method in this chapter can be used to assist in the process of building a model for the assessment of threat and risks and then forming the right decisions.

It is important to note that the method proposed here allows the development of a model, that can be adapted to specific needs and at the same time refined by adopting recommendations of other frameworks, not only from NIST. For example, standards such as COBIT, ISO/IEC, could also be used to refine the scope of the requirements considered for building the quantitative model. Therefore, the final aggregation structure can be adapted to different organization requirements and particular needs, as well as the weights and GCD operators employed can be changed to better reflect the necessities of an organization.

## FUTURE RESEARCH DIRECTIONS

The requirements and the aggregation structure shown in this chapter can, of course, be changed to be adapted to different needs and demands that are specific to an organization or area. Therefore, the possibility of applying the proposed method to create a new model for other areas of cybersecurity, such as Supervisory Control And Data Acquisition (SCADA), systems that are widely used in assorted environments, or power distribution, construction, etc., should also be possible.

Therefore, potential avenues to explore in future research directions can be found in considering other requirements and in changing the resulting aggregation structure, by taking into account different proposals for cybersecurity according to new fields or different needs.

## CONCLUSION

Assessing threats and risks implies making decisions, i.e. identifying threats, what is and what is not a threat, what is the potential of an identified threat, can it be avoided or not, what are the risks associated with a given threat, how can those risks be confronted, what are the costs of them and many other aspects have to be considered when evaluating threats and risks. Every one of these questions –and of course several other– require to figure out, to decide how important the threat is as well as its associated risk. So having methodologies and tools supporting these decisions is of outstanding significance.

Every human organization is prone to be subject to threats and risks and suffer their consequences. Having a flexible and reliable method that help in identifying and making right decisions about threats and risks is of paramount importance for the organization.

The threat and risk assessment method proposed in the chapter can be of great help for those people whose task in an organization is to assess the possible threats and risks confronted by their institution. The method presented makes use of a list of requirements. These requirements are of help in identifying the threats and risks that are likely to be faced up to by an organization dealing with cybersecurity. So this list of requirements is crucial and should be taken into consideration when building a method that can be of help in recognizing possible threats and the risks to be come up against by a cybersecurity installation. The proposal presented has considered the requirements taken from the Framework for Improving Critical Infrastructure Cybersecurity of the National Institute of Standards and Technology. (NIST, 2018). As part of the proposed method, these requirements have been used as input for building a quantitative model by following the directions given by the Logic Score of Preference (LSP) method, a method based on a continuous logic for the evaluation and comparison of complex systems. The model resulting from the integration of the NIST framework and the LSP method returns a series of quantitative indicators that are suitable for discerning and detecting security flaws at different levels, therefore providing insight for the decision making processes involved in determining the possible actions to be done to improve whatever would be necessary in the security and possible mitigation of threats and their associated risks.

The combination of the NIST Framework with the LSP method provides a powerful tool to help in the assessment of the current status of the organization and also a starting point for adopting a decision on the course of action to be taken.

# REFERENCES

Bayne, J. (2002). *An Overview of Threat and Risk Assessment.* Version 1.2f. SANS Institute, Information Security Reading Room.

Cherdantseva, Y., Burnap, P., Blyth, A., Eden, P., Jones, K., Soulsby, H., & Stoddart, K. (2016). A review of cyber security risk assessment methods for SCADA systems. *Computers & Security, 56*(February), 1–27. doi:10.1016/j.cose.2015.09.009

Ciapessoni, E., Cirio, D., Pitto, A., Marcacci, P., Lacavalla, M., Massucco, S., Silvestro, F., & Sforna, M. (2018). A Risk-Based Methodology and Tool Combining Threat Analysis and PowerSystem Security Assessment. *Energies, 11*(1), 83. doi:10.3390/en11010083

COBIT® 5. (2012). *Enabling Processes.* ISACA.

Dujmovic, J. J. (1996). A Method for Evaluation and Selection of Complex Hardware and Software Systems. *The 22nd International Conference for the Resource Management and Performance Evaluation of Enterprise Computing Systems. CMG96 Proceedings, 1,* 368-378.

Dujmovic, J. J. (1997). Quantitative Evaluation of Software. *Proceedings of the IASTED International Conference on Software Engineering,* 3-7.

Dujmovic, J. J. (2007, December). Continuous Preference Logic for System Evaluation. *IEEE Transactions on Fuzzy Systems, 15*(6), 1082–1099. doi:10.1109/TFUZZ.2007.902041

Dujmović, J. (2018). *Soft Computing Evaluation Logic. The LSP Decision Method and Its Applications.* Hoboken, NJ: John Wiley & Sons.

Dujmovic, J. J., & Bayucan, A. (1997). Evaluation and Comparison of Windowed environments. *Proceedings of the IASTED Interna Conference Software Engineering (SE'97),* 102-105.

Dujmovic, J. J., & Elnicki, R. (1982). A DMS Cost/Benefit Decision Model: Mathematical Models for Data management System Evaluation, Comparison, and Selection. National Bureau of Standards.

European Network and Information Security Agency (ENISA). (2010). *Flying 2.0 Enabling automated air travel by identifying and addressing the challenges of IoT & RFID technology* (IoT/RFID Scenario Risk Assessment). European Network and Information Security Agency (ENISA).

European Network and Information Security Agency (ENISA). (n.d.). *Annex II - Risk Assessment Spreadsheet.* https://www.enisa.europa.eu/publications/flying-2.0-enabling-automated-air-travel-by-identifying-and-addressing-the-challenges-of-iot-rfid-technology-1

Hartmann, K., & Steup, C. (2013). *The Vulnerability of UAVs to Cyber Attacks - An Approach to the Risk Assessment".2013 5th International Conference on Cyber Conflict.* NATO CCD COE Publications.

ISO 31000. (2018). Risk Management – Guidelines. Second Edition 2018-02. Reference number ISO31000:2018(E).

ISO/IEC 27001. (2013). Information technology - Security techniques - Information security management systems – Requirements. Second edition. 2013-10-01. Reference number ISO/IEC 27001:2013(E).

Kelley, J. D., Lahann, J. S., Mackey II, D. H. (2006). *Network threat risk assessment tool.* United States, Patent Application Publication. Pub. No.: US 2006/0064740 A1, US 2006O064740A1.

Lewis, J. A. (2002). *Assessing the Risks of Cyber Terrorism, Cyber War and Other Cyber Threats.* Center for Strategic and International Studies. https://www.csis.org/

Magdych. (2003). *System, method and computer program product for risk assessment scanning based on detected anomalous events.* United States Patent. Patent No.: US 6,546,493 B1.

NIST, National Institute of Standards and Technology. (2018). *Framework for Improving Critical Infrastructure Cybersecurity. Version 1.1 April 16, 2018.* NIST.

NIST, National Institute of Standards and Technology. (2019). *NIST - 2018-04-16_framework_v1.1_core1. xlsx.* https://www.nist.gov/document/2018-04-16frameworkv11core1xlsx

NIST Special Publication 800-53, Revision 4. (2013). *Security and Privacy Controls for Federal Information Systems and Organizations.* NIST.

Smith, P. (Ed.). (n.d.). D2.2 Threat and Risk Assessment Methodology. SPARKS Consortium.

Webb, J., Ahmad, A., Maynard, S. B., & Shanks, G. (2014). A situation awareness model for information security risk management. *Computers & Security, 44,* 1–15. doi:10.1016/j.cose.2014.04.005

Zetter, K. (2019). *How Digital Detectives Deciphered Stuxnet, the Most Menacing Malware in History.* https://www.wired.com/2011/07/how-digital-detectives-deciphered-stuxnet/

## ADDITIONAL READING

Bajpayee, J., Mathias, D., Aftosmis, M., Dotson, J., & Stern, E. (2017). *Asteroid Threat Assessment Project (ATAP). NASA Ames Research Center, Small Bolide Advisory Group.* SBAG.

Blanchard, D. C., Griebel, G., Pobbe, R., & Blanchard, R. J. (2010). *Risk assessment as an evolved threat detection and analysis process.* Neuroscience and Biobehavioral Reviews. Published by Elsevier Ltd.

Chockalingam, S., Hadžiosmanović, D., Pieters, W., Teixeira, A., & van Gelder, P. (2017). Integrated Safety and Security Risk Assessment Methods: A Survey of Key Characteristics and Applications. In G. Havarneanu, R. Setola, H. Nassopoulos, & S. Wolthusen (Eds.), Lecture Notes in Computer Science: Vol. 10242. *Critical Information Infrastructures Security. CRITIS 2016.* Springer. doi:10.1007/978-3-319-71368-7_5

Macher, G., Armengaud, E., Brenner, E., & Kreiner, C. (2016). A Review of Threat Analysis and Risk Assessment Methods in the Automotive Context. In A. Skavhaug, J. Guiochet, & F. Bitsch (Eds.), Lecture Notes in Computer Science: Vol. 9922. *Computer Safety, Reliability, and Security. SAFECOMP 2016.* Springer. doi:10.1007/978-3-319-45477-1_11

Reid Meloy, J., & Hoffmann, J. (2014). *International handbook of threat assessment.* Oxford University Press.

Schneier, B. (2015). *Secrets and Lies: Digital Security in a Networked World. Print.* Online., doi:10.1002/9781119183631

Stergiopoulos, G., Gritzalis, D., & Kouktzoglou, V. (2018, April). Using formal distributions for threat likelihood estimation in cloud-enabled IT risk assessment. *Computer Networks, 134*(7), 23–45. doi:10.1016/j.comnet.2018.01.033

Turner, J. T., & Gelles, M. (2012). *Threat Assessment, A Risk Management Approach.* Routledge. doi:10.4324/9780203725375

Vossekuil, B., Fein, R. A., & Berglund, J. M. (2015). Threat assessment: Assessing the risk of targeted violence. *Journal of Threat Assessment and Management, 2*(3-4), 243–254. doi:10.1037/tam0000055

## KEY TERMS AND DEFINITIONS

**Continuous Logic:** A logic whose truth values can take continuous values in a given range (i.e. [0, 1], [0, 100]) instead of values like Truth or False.

**Decision Method:** A procedure, technique or planned way of arriving to a decision. Normally it could be said the decision is the process of making up one´s mind. There are several decision methods ranging from very simple ones to more formal or axiomatic methods.

**Decision Theory:** The study of choices that a given agent can take.

**Risk Assessment:** Documenting the evaluation done of the possibility of occurrence of a risk as well as the damage associated and the measures to avoid it or at least mitigate the outcomes from the risk. Closely related with Risk Management.

**Risk Management:** Identify, evaluate, and assign priority to the potential risks with the goal of defining the methods, resources to minimize or mitigate the outcomes from the risk. Closely related with Risk Assessment.

**Threat and Risk Assessment:** Assessing risks is closely associated with a corresponding threat. Nearly any human endeavour has a potential threat and a risk correlated with it. Assessing both is mandatory in some areas, e.g. building construction, country security, network security, etc.

**Threat Assessment:** The manner of devising the possibility and importance of a potential threat.

*Previously published in the Encyclopedia of Organizational Knowledge, Administration, and Technology; pages 1212-1227, copyright year 2021 by Business Science Reference (an imprint of IGI Global).*

# Section 2
# Organizational Awareness and Cybersecurity Training

# Chapter 8
# Interdisciplinary Training and Mentoring for Cyber Security in Companies

**Ileana Hamburg**

*Institute of Work and Technology, Germany*

## ABSTRACT

*Cyber security is interdisciplinary, and it is to expect that security professionals and other employees working with computers to have suitable knowledge. In this chapter an interdisciplinary training program in cyber security curriculum and an interdisciplinary mentoring program to be included in entrepreneurial learning will be proposed. It helps to produce synergy in groups and generates ideas to solve complex problems. Entrepreneurial learning is a basis for education of entrepreneurs, and it should also include such interdisciplinary programs. The author explained the advantages of interdisciplinary training and mentoring programs in this context particularly in the field of cyber security. Such programs are missing both in education as well as in companies. Two examples of European projects with the participation of the author will be done to improve entrepreneurial education and training and encourage SMEs to be innovative. The programs are supported by digital learning platforms, and interdisciplinary trainers and mentors help the learners. The main method is interdisciplinary problem-based learning (IPBL).*

## INTRODUCTION

Cyber security which historically was technical a subfield of computer science gained importance in fields like law and business management, as well as areas of technology such as smart grids, cars, and other cyber-physical systems (also due to pervasive computing technology).

The study field Ethics helps to distingue right from wrong, and good from bad. It analyzes the morality of human behaviors, policies, laws and social structures (Brey, 2005; Bynum, 2003; Hamburg & Grosch, 2017).Computer/Information ethics focuses on questions of responsibility for defects in the work of software, on preventing access to private information stored in computer databases, centralization and decentralization of power in computerized environments, as well as copy right, intellectual prop-

DOI: 10.4018/978-1-6684-3698-1.ch008

erty, and commercial confidentiality issues. The ethical right and responsibility referring information technology are related with legal responsibility and legal rights. Legal acts tend to be assessed on their ethical merits, while amendments to existing laws or legal acts or introduction of new ones increasingly require ethical grounding.

Ethics should be is a critical part of every cyber security defense strategy in organizations because without clear ethical standards and rules, employees cannot protect systems and data.

Due to their connections to computer systems and the Internet, all these areas must consider unanticipated security vulnerabilities (https://www.interpol.int/Crimeareas/Cybercrime/Cybercrime). Necessary quickly protecting measurements against cyber-crime requires collaboration between disciplines but at the same time, the field of cyber security is still relatively new and certain aspects cannot be standardized.

Literature study shows that traditional technological research in cyber security is not connected with companies´, public and private sectors' nontechnical tasks dealings with cyber security (Ramirez, 2017).

Based on literature review Ramirez (https://www.semanticscholar.org/paper/Making-cyber-security-interdisciplinary-%3A-for-a-and-Ramirez/6dbd08f328672d8cc3ac0fc164a7212c4b0888cf) summarized follow categories of cyber security research:

- The Public category includes issues of concern to governments: work regarding laws, international norms, and national security. Global technical standards produced by bodies like W3C, while often specifying norms, are in the Infrastructure category.
- The Business category includes most of the articles that address technological problems of cyber security; specifically, those problems referring the actual infrastructure of cyberspace.
- The Infrastructure category includes papers that discuss various aspects of cyber security of critical infrastructure, as well as security issues concerning the operation of cyberspace, such as cryptography.
- The General category contains all papers with issues which pervade the entire realm of cyber security, as well as descriptions of the field in general, and characterizations of cyberspace and humans' interactions with it and includes also most articles from social sciences.

This disconnect between traditional technological research in cyber security and the public and private sectors' nontechnical dealings with cyber security results from neither technical researchers nor management in business or government reaching out to communicate to the other parties, but there is also a communication problem between researchers in the same category (Ramirez, 2017). Communication among researchers and between research fields and other sectors of society should be improved. In order to facilitate cross-disciplinary communication, Ramirez recommended authors to harmonize their jargon usage. This change would improve idea flow between authors from different disciplines, who work solutions, but who write for separate audiences in their publications. To identify areas in this context of harmonization, Ramirez (https://www.semanticscholar.org/paper/Making-cyber-security-interdisciplinary-%3A-for-a-and-Ramirez/6dbd08f328672d8cc3ac0fc164a7212c4b0888cf) examined the extent of differences used keywords in articles from each the four security sub disciplines, analyzed time-series trends of terminology in cyber security journal articles, and developed a methodology for authors or standards bodies to use when deciding whether a word or phrase is appropriately interdisciplinary, or has been accepted by the general cyber security community. Because security is inherently interdisciplinary (Dalal & Tetrick, 2016) it is to expect every security professionals and other employees working with computers to have knowledge in many other domains and understand fields that refer their careers but it does not exist. It is necessary that employees also in other fields have knowledge in connection with security. NIST's National Initiative for Cybersecurity Education (NICE) underlines that it should be done a crucial step toward remedying shortage of "people with the knowledge, skills, and abilities to perform the tasks required for cybersecurity work." Such a workforce will include "technical and nontechnical roles that are staffed with knowledgeable and experienced people." But it is difficult to produce a workforce with these interdisciplinary skills and to solve the problem of communication among researchers and between many research fields and other sectors of society. Collaboration and communication between these fields is lacking, due also to different terminology between these fields and few interdisciplinary journal publications.

One solution could be an interdisciplinary training program in cyber security which can encourage employees to understand more cyber security and researchers to serve as an example for other institutions (Ramirez, 2017; Scandura & Pellegrini, 2010).

The World Economic Forum (2009) states, "Entrepreneurship education is essential for developing the human capital necessary for the society of the future. It is not enough to add entrepreneurship on the perimeter – it needs to be core to the way education operates."

The European definition of entrepreneurial learning includes the development of entrepreneurial attitudes, skills and knowledge that enable the individual to turn creative ideas into action also referring cyber security.

Mentoring in education has been gaining importance in the last decade mainly due to worldwide educational reforms, internationalization and the need of new literacies.

Interdisciplinary mentoring has become more important also because science and research are increasingly multidisciplinary and because interdisciplinary mentorship help produce synergy in groups. It generates ideas and to solve complex problems. Interdisciplinary mentoring require the building of community of diverse scientists/experts with mentoring, education/work experience, which will create opportunities to establish collaborations and work in an interdisciplinary mode. However, there is a lack of research on interdisciplinary mentoring in cyber security particularly for small and medium sized companies (SMEs). Promoting mentoring relationships can be an alternative/help to education training courses and workshops, which have often a decontextualized nature and their response to learners' actual needs are not satisfactory.

In this chapter the author explained the advantages of interdisciplinary training and mentoring programs particularly in the field of cyber security. An example of an interdisciplinary training program is given which will be adapted and used in European projects. It is intended to apply this program later in entrepreneurial learning in vocational education and training (VRT) institutions together with interdisciplinary mentoring.

The skills of interdisciplinary mentors will be shortly described. Research shows that there not exist interdisciplinary cyber security seminars in education programs at European Universities and technical schools and not interdisciplinary training programs for employees in companies. The benefits of a cyber security program that is specifically interdisciplinary are more complex than the benefits of existing single-department cyber security education/training programs. By allowing cyber security to be an accessible field of study to anyone, workers in companies and students can anticipate and avoid vulnerabilities more effectively than if, they were trained on an as-needed basis in the workforce. Examples of European projects in this context with contribution of the author will be done.

## INTERDISCIPLINARY TRAINING PROGRAM IN CYBER SECURITY EMBEDDED IN ENTREPRENEURIAL LEARNING

Cyber security is a growing market and one of the faster growing subdisciplines of computer science; cyber security landscape represents a patchwork.

Cyber security:

- is a multidisciplinary issue, with an often misunderstood definition, requiring input from computer science, business, political science, management, mathematics, ethics, physics, engineering, and economics
- professionals have little interaction with workers in the other areas.

Most current courses at universities and vocational training institutions (VET) do not allow diversity in a substantive amount; and most students remain unaware of the extent of this problem and cannot decide to pursue it independently (http://www.cs.rpi.edu/research/pdf/12-03.pdf).

Cyber security operations involve core technologies, processes and practices designed to protect networks, computers, programs, people and data from attack, damage, injury or unauthorized access. Due to cyber threat environments like hacker attacks, effective systems must also involve employee end users of computer systems to manage them, because nearly all employees with access to computers or networks play a cyber security role in their organizations whether they know it or not (VanDerwerken & Ubell, 2011).

Organizations offer training opportunities for in-house cyber security experts to ensure the integrity of internal and client systems, but they must provide training that prepares also end users to circumvent increasing cyber threats (West, 2008).

SMEs are not organizations which failed as large organizations but many aspects are considered similar to larger organizations. In fact, qualitatively they are very different and have to be managed differently from large organizations (Hamburg et al., 2018). Often they lack of information and resources (as it does they do not have the economies of scale when investing in these), have no a clear vision of sustainability (as they are concerned with survival), have a patriarchal thinking (as often there is only one investor and it is in their best interest for the company to succeed) and insufficient mechanisms of learning (due to lack of time and resources). They do not have the time and resources to invest in long term strategies and are concerned with short term survival if they are to compete. On the other hand they are more flexible than large organizations as they do not have a large amount of stakeholders in decision making and once a decision is made they can implement the outcome very quickly.

In many cases SMEs are slow to undertake new forms of training or ones referring to new domains like cyber security despite the fact that some of them been proven to maintain employee productivity improving a firm's competitive advantage (Hamburg et al., 2018).

For optimum effectiveness, SMEs must identify the cyber security competencies required for user job success, determine gaps in security expertise, and develop gap-closing strategies.

The nature of employee cyber security roles varies. Required competencies may range from technical basic awareness to business process skills (Wagner, 2008). These may include skills to mitigate technical risks, capacity to develop policies and governance, and specific practices to achieve regulatory compliance. To evaluate and strengthen cyber defense, SMEs must define roles within the job and security architecture. Then it is possible to evaluate training needs and organize cyber security training in the broader system (Brummel et al., 2005).

The World Economic Forum's educating the Next Wave of Entrepreneurs report (2008) states, "Not everyone needs to become an entrepreneur to benefit from entrepreneurship education, but all members of society need to be more entrepreneurial. It is necessary to create the types of environments that are conducive to encouraging entrepreneurial ways of thinking and behaving." The report emphasizes the need to mainstream entrepreneurship across all disciplines and expose all students and all faculty to entrepreneurial thought and processes (O'Brien & Hamburg, 2014, 2019). When faculties from all disciplines are engaged in entrepreneurial thinking, entrepreneurship will be moved from the perimeter to the core of education.

Entrepreneurial learning is:

- An observable phenomenon, something entrepreneurs engage in or are associated with,
- A concept that has started to receive increasingly explicit articulation in academic literature in the past decade and which has been implicit in the literature since Schumpeter (1950),
- A core policy objective in developed Western countries implemented through funded programs targeted at entrepreneurs (https://www.researchgate.net/publication/228419882_The_Matter_of_Entrepreneurial_Learning_A_Literature_Review).

Entrepreneurial learning is still a relatively new area of study, presenting more interests since it was associated it i.e. with globalization, the spread of new ICTs, and the revival of small business. The entrepreneurship studies and organizational learning literature (Dierkes, 2001; Easterby-Smith & Lyles, 2003), which was done parallel during the past decade, raised the interest in entrepreneurial learning.

Entrepreneurial learning has emerged as an important area of inquiry in relation to both the academic studies of entrepreneurship and the practical development of new entrepreneurs also in companies. Theoretical approaches that focus on diverse aspects of entrepreneurial learning are divided into two main groups, referring to analyzing object: those focusing on the individual entrepreneur and those focusing on the organizational context (https://www.researchgate.net/publication/228419882_The_Matter_of_Entrepreneurial_Learning_A_Literature_Review).

The first approach has as object the personal learning experience and the cognitive capabilities of the „entrepreneurial individuals" the second refer entrepreneurship „as a collective activity and at various scales, from the single firm and its immediate network until the national system of innovation". Entrepreneurial learning can be considered a type of management learning to build an entrepreneur and to set up new business; Kolb (1984) uses the theory of experiential learning to describe how entrepreneurs learn from experience; entrepreneurship is a behavior that is learned through experience. Some authors (i.e. Gibb, 1997) try to use Learning organization in SME context.

In order to improve the practical character of education and training for entrepreneurs to be prepared also for avoid later cyber-attacks it is necessary to (Gibb, 1997):

- Support understanding of entrepreneurial learning,
- Integrate it into teacher/trainer education,
- Create strong cooperation between higher education, research and business life,
- Develop a basic interdisciplinary education according to digital transformation.

A starting point should be to integrate interdisciplinary programs for cyber security in entrepreneurial learning. It:

- stimulates innovation and capacities to deal with digital change and globalization,
- engages and motivates students through relevant learning experiences for education, life and work,
- empowers people to create value for society and deal also with security challenges.

In the following, we propose a training program combining cyber security and the basis for development of law and policy as well as ethic rules to be included also in entrepreneurial learning. It is based on a thorough understanding of the technology that underlies the current and future cyber security in the company (education institutions). Engineers who develop products and solve problems can improve policies choices if they evaluate policy needs and legal/compliance requirements, including those that are inefficient. Rules of computer ethics are important not only for cyber security professionals but also for all people using computer to protect moral rights.

This training aims to bring the relevant technology, the current legal landscape and ethical problems together, for a richer understanding of each. Some included cyber security topics are (Wilson & Bowen, 2011):

- Understand threat, vulnerability and risk,
- Achieving basic concepts of security - confidentiality, integrity and availability,
- Basic concepts about Internet: how it works, packet switching, routing, DNS, etc.
- Anonymity within on-line communication what to do when attacks is difficult;
- Problems related to identity, authentication and decision-making.

Key cybersecurity laws and policy concepts included are:

- Rules referring cyber security and who makes them – legislators, regulators and private groups
- Responsibilities of companies in protecting networks and tasks;
- Rules referring information-sharing (public/private and private/private);
- Regulation and private civil litigation within cybersecurity measures;
- Obligations to provide information
- Data privacy regulation in the EU and its impact on cybersecurity (e.g. insider heat monitoring).

Ethical aspects (Brey, 2005; Bynum & Rogerson, 2003) should:

- get clear about interests, rights, and moral values that are at stake in computer security,
- recognize ethical questions and dilemmas in their work,
- balance different moral principles in resolving such ethical issues.

Some topics are:

- Actions to take if and when an incident occurs,
- How much information (and which information) should be shared with others,
- Steps to take to prevent such a breach in the future,

- Roles and what are the responsibilities associated with each of those roles referring internet and cyber security,
- Problems in connection with, copyright, trade secrets, and sabotage.

Interdisciplinary groups of students (employees) to tackle problems from technical, legal/policy and ethical angles are necessary to be organized. Difficulties in cross training could be different for different profiles. It is easier to provide engineering students with instruction in law and policy than it is to provide law students will little or no technical background with technical instruction.

Efforts at the graduate level should not ignore the large cybersecurity workforce already in place. Steps must be taken to provide existing cybersecurity professionals and other employees with interdisciplinary training to achieve the knowledge they need in their jobs.

## Interdisciplinary Mentoring Program at Work and Learning

Digitalization and other new developments require for employees and employers as well as for student new knowledge and changes in their education, training and work methods (O'Brien & Hamburg, 2019; Ragins & Cotton, 1999). Mentoring could become a bridge to promote more individual learning and an option to support more individuals to achieve personal and career competences, gain new professional development as self-knowledge, and commit themselves to their personal and professional development in today's rapid pace of change https://www.researchgate.net/publication/279515191_Constructing_an_Interdisciplinary_Mentoring_Framework_for_ELT_Teacher_Education_and_Teacher_Development.

There is difference in education, training and work between mentoring and coaching: mentoring related to long-term professional development, whereas coaching has been associated with a specific goal in a teaching, learning or working context aimed at improving performance in a task in a short-term framework (Delaney, 2012). Referring mentoring at work Kram (1985) published a study giving a theoretical foundation for understanding developmental relationships at work in both man and woman. Other studies have contributed to the understanding of mentorship relationships, the participants, the context of the relationships and methodological research issues.

Differences exist referring mentoring functions within and across relationships (Hamburg et al.,2018; Ragins & Kram, 2007): the distinction between career functions, psychosocial functions and psychological attachments in the relationship have been studied (Kram, 1985). Both career and psychosocial functions influence mentees' job and career satisfaction (Allen et al., 2008).

Mentoring could be initiated formally or informally. Baugh and Fagenson-Eland (Baugh & Fagenson, 2007) underlines that due to the characteristics of formal programs (expectations, time among others) long term relationships are less likely to occur in these programs than in informal mentoring relationships.

According to Ragin's and Cotton (see also Hamburg and Grosch, 2017) formal and informal mentoring "may differ on multiple dimensions. One key difference is the way the relationship is formed. Informal relationships occur naturally...formal relationships are often the result of some type of matching process initiated within the context of a company-sponsored mentoring program."

The first one has a definitive structure and purpose, the second does not specify the means or process and for a lack of a better phrase "goes with the flow" and allows the mentor and protégé flexibility to meet whatever needs or circumstances that may arise in the relationship (https://scholarworks.waldenu. edu/dissertations/2446/

According to Scandura and Pellegrini (2010) e-mentoring "is the process of mentoring a protégé (mentee) over the Internet by a mentor usually not physically present at the protégés site or location.

Mentoring relationships are dynamic and complex; they can be different during different phases of the relationship and evolve through phases that reflect different experiences and patterns of interactions. Kram (1985) identified 4 phases: initiation, cultivation, separation, and redefinition. The process by which these relationships influence personal development and change have been studied, i.e. McGowan, Stone, and Kegan (2007) examine how mentee development is influenced by mentoring relationships. Some of these relations enable both mentors and mentees to transition through increasingly complex stages of adult development.

The mentoring partnership must be established so that both mentor and mentee feel safe to express their thoughts and feelings, and to take risks and fulfill some requirements. They should show interest being committed and invested in the mentoring partnership.

The addressed issues should be done openly being straightforward and honest about perceived areas of need. Collaboration between mentor and mentee should be fostered. It can include reinforcing brainstorming, creativity, and learning together. It is necessary that mentor and mentee try to understand the other's point of view and accept another person's ideas.

A set of duration is not required for the mentoring relationship but it is recommended that mentors and mentees interact frequently during the first months. Both should be encouraged to meet at least once per month and keep in touch through phone or email.

After first months, they can decide if it is necessary to continue the mentoring relationship, and if so, if the frequency of meetings should change. During the mentoring process, if a mentor or mentee feels that the relationship is not productive or compatible, the Mentor Program Coordinator should be informed so that a change can be made.

Referring feedback mentors and mentees will be checked in with periodically and requested to provide it so that the program can be evaluated and improved.

Suggested mentoring activities are:

- Discuss short term and long-term career goals and professional interests.
- Discuss effective instructional strategies, training development and curricular issues.
- Explore funding opportunities.
- Discuss student issues such as advising, motivating, and handling.
- Share experiences on managing time, handling stress, and balancing workload effectively.
- Explore professional development opportunities
- Address special needs or questions and help in troubleshooting difficult situations.
- Matches with mentees should be made based on intake forms that identified common areas of interest.

Overall the mentee's main role in the relationship is accepting guidance from someone who is knowledgeable and experienced. The mentee needs to look for and target a mentor who is a good fit for them. Concerning this, a mentee should also not be afraid to ask for advice. Once advice is given by the mentor, it is recommended on the mentee to follow up, do the advised research and "do their homework".

Risk taking is important for a mentee as well - this could be starting off in a position not familiar with.

Mentoring offers a number of benefits for SMEs. Research has shown a positive influence on mentee performance (Dierkes, 2001; Hamburg et al., 2018). Mentoring can address SMEs needs for timely, relevant training content, does not require significant personal and cost resources. The most important benefits for companies are a quickly introduction of new employees and support of integration of staff with special needs.

Mentors for SMEs have different backgrounds having general business/management competences, technical ones or sectoral specific experience. Within SMEs, that already use mentoring, business mentors can play general roles across all areas of company business to a specific focus role, i.e., in the sales or marketing areas. Mentors can help to carry out an analysis including existing knowledge gaps and staff skills needs. Often SMEs need to strengthen their current market position before entering international markets with new products or strategies and need help in this transition.

Particularly important are mentors for first-time SME entrepreneurs in assembling teams, developing business plans, product development or sales/marketing and security strategies. They can help companies to prepare an investment plan and guide them in implementing this.

Mentoring can support sustainable development by allowing SMEs to acquire knowledge from internal and external sources that will allow them to achieve their current strategies and create relationships that may help them in the future.

Also at work it is necessary to study the wide range of developmental relationships that occur within and outside institutions. They can be organized as the classic mentoring relationship or in peer, group or network relationships and have different characteristics such as formal, informal or e-mentoring.

Of special note to mentoring researchers is the work who refer to various types of capital being created and exchanged in the workplace mentoring relationship and process. These include human capital, movement capital, social/political capital and signaling, (d) path-goal clarity, values clarity, and relational gains.

Referring the cyber-security mentors in companies, they represent a wide diversity of age, experience and personality types within the industry. Sure not everybody is the right fit to be a mentor but security cyber security professionals who have been in the industry long enough have knowledge and experience to offer.

A cyber professional should seek out these characteristics for a mentor: someone who is willing to share knowledge, skills, and experience and demonstrates a positive attitude. They should be willing to respond quickly to a potential mentee's questions, and provide straightforward advice. It needs to be a win-win relationship, where the mentor also gains value from the "fresh eyes" of the mentee.

Overall the mentor's main role is to provide guidance for the mentee. The mentor should motivate, encourage and change the mentee's mindset to think cybersecurity throughout their whole career.

The key is establishing a program that empowers mentors, along with guidelines and training for effectiveness.

A successful mentoring program in cyber security not only helps mentees with their career aspirations, but can have a positive impact on company's security culture as well. Cyber-security and other professionals who have been successfully mentored not only have a more positive view of their team and company, but will certainly have a higher retention rate as well. Today's job market for qualified cyber security and other technical professionals demand the establishing a strong mentoring program and this will can be an attractive project for any organization or education/training organization.

Mentees should research the various cybersecurity career options. Cybersecurity is a wide area, so the mentee should understand what area of cyber intrigues them most (for instance, red team, blue team or a mix of both). The mentee must continue to discover and learn with continuing education in the form of a degree, certification, or self-teaching. The mentee must be prepared to do the hard work, as mentors want motivated mentees willing to roll up their sleeves and dive in.

Once a cyber-professional finds a mentor, the mentor needs to help the mentee extend their professional network. A mentor with lots of valuable connections they are willing to share will greatly benefit the mentee.

Some tasks for mentoring cyber security:

- Help bridging the gap between experience and a transition into cybersecurity - Most people that are interested in this field have a hard time linking their experience into cybersecurity.
- Assist the mentee to change their mindset to best highlight and leverage past experience to land a cybersecurity job or use cyber knowledge within own work.

Interdisciplinary mentoring has become more important in the last years. Research and different developments and fields are increasingly multidisciplinary and based upon a large amount of crosstalk. So it is necessary that mentoring follow this trend. Interdisciplinary mentorship is the tool of scientists and educators to help produce synergy in groups, and to generate multifocal ideas and complex solutions to complex challenges. The outcome of interdisciplinary mentoring is that a community of diverse scientists can be unified by mentoring connections. These connections will create opportunities to establish collaborations and work in an interdisciplinary fashion.

Some qualities of an interdisciplinary Mentor (https://www.mrs.org/docs/default-source/programs-and-outreach/diversity-resources/interdisciplinary-mentoring.pdf?sfvrsn=4630f411_0) are i.e.:

1. **Know yourself**. Being more connected to ourselves helps to facilitate the connection to others, improves perceptions about others, and aids in identification of the talents of the mentee.
2. **Pay it forward**. Many of us have had a mentor in some form or another during our careers. So, now it is time to give that same experience to others, who in turn will do the same.
3. **See the best in others**. Probably the most important talent in a mentor is the ability to identify the best skills and qualities in the individuals they are mentoring. Conversely, they need to see weaknesses and have the ability to help change or control these traits.
4. **Open-minded**. Be able to find common ground with whomever they work. 5. Flexibility. Role shifting happens often as we move between groups. Being able to contribute in diverse roles is an essential talent.

## Examples

The author worked within the Erasmus+ European project Cyber Security *(www.cybersecurityplus.org)* with partners from Education, Research, and Industry/Business (Hamburg et al., 2018; Hamburg, 2019).

The project supports the Cyber Security Strategy prepared by European Commission in order to take precautions against the cyber-attacks which are performed continuously to the organizations and strategically important offices.

Within the context of this strategy, it is decided that training in cyber security field must be increased in education and training.

The aims of the project were the followings

- Disseminating cyber security issues within formal and non-formal education,
- Adding cyber security to the curriculum of VET,

- Raising awareness about secure use of internet and secure internet services,
- Improving and disseminating the service in this sector,
- Fostering research-development activities in this context,
- Broadening the pool of skilled workers capable of supporting a cyber-secure nation,
- Fostering development and skills of teachers/trainers, mentors and founding partnership by focusing on the education of company trainers and partners in multidisciplinary organized training in schools and companies,
- Supporting strong partnerships in business community and educational institutions.

Some outputs of the project are:

- Development of a road map about cyber security research in European Practices and Education
- Development of a curriculum in cyber security education and training
- Organizing interdisciplinary seminars and conferences
- Development and distribution of a Book about cyber security

The partners of the project from Germany, Turkey, Spain, Portugal, Italy, and Lithuania developed studies about cyber security strategies including training in their countries and are preoccupied to develop European measures as the sum of all national and international ones to protect the availability of information and communications technology and the integrity, authenticity and confidentiality of data in cyberspace [Hamburg, 2019; Hamburg & Bucksch, 2016].

Topics of the studies were:

- Cyber security strategy in project partner counters based on its Importance
- Examples of cyber security /information security syllabus for students
- Research of interdisciplinary education and training methods, mentoring and Innovative technologies to practical teaching and learning of cyber security
- Conclusions to be included in the development of Cyber Security Curriculum within the project

One difficult existing aspect in all project partner countries is the missing of cyber security experts and preparing of future ones as well as other organization members for cyber security. Referring cyber security education particularly in VET, the project partner countries also Germany do not have any body responsible for educational and professional training programs for raising awareness with the general public, promoting cyber security courses and communication in this field. There are no cyber security courses in vocational schools and in company training. Also cyber security courses are not included in entrepreneurial learning.

So, one of the objectives of ERASMUS + Project Cyber Security is beside to disseminate cyber security issues in formal and non-formal education and organizations and fostering the development and skills of teachers, trainers from VET and to contribute to create a cyber-security culture and communication strategies in organizations.

The next actual steps are the continuation of the work and the partners started to develop an interdisciplinary training program in cyber security first for vocational schools and then to adapt it to higher education and to SMEs. It is intended to improve entrepreneurial learning in partner countries in this context.

The German partner works now with SMEs and is in the test phase of a such program. 20 German SMEs have been contacted and interviews have been organized to know the existing cyber security training and the willingness to organize a multidisciplinary mentoring program. An e-handbook for interdisciplinary mentoring is in the development.

Also a multidisciplinary training will be organized at the beginning at a VET school in Germany and later in companies.

The European cooperation with the project partner and other new ones will be continued.

So, the project will contribute in improving knowledge and skills of people in avoiding cyber-attacks. It will be done also through integrated the adapted interdisciplinary program in entrepreneurial learning at all levels. The cooperation with industry assures a practical character of the next project outcomes (Hamburg & Grosch, 2017) A platform for communication and training is in development and cloud computing will be used for this tool.

Another project Reinnovate with partners from Germany, Ireland, Spain, Lithuania and Romania, which will be presented, supports the SMEs to improve their knowledge and skills also in cyber security and the use of internal and external data and information. It is known that new economy bring with it many challenges for SMEs. They are more productive than larger organizations, they often remain stagnant (European Commission, 2015). In a recent project Archimedes, SMEs identified the burden of workload trying to sustain business and security. They emphasized the need for staff to take initiative and develop new business strategies including a cyber-security one. In 2018, the author started the work within Reinnovate, aimed to translate policies to support entrepreneurship into practice by focusing on cultivating an entrepreneurial culture in small companies (Hamburg et al., 2018; Hamburg and Bucksch, 2016).

Prior to the starting the project, the REINNOVATE consortium conducted a survey to determine the challenges and needs of 142 SMEs in Europe in order to be innovative, to grow and to cope with digital changes and existing dangers like cyber-attacks. It was found that 97% of asked companies want to become more innovative but corresponding competences are missing. Other barriers to innovation are resources (60%) i.e. specialized equipment, unprepared staff in cyber security rules. The survey explored the potential of SME collaboration with Higher Education institutes in order to help them to be more innovative. The hypothesis was that leveraging from public research organizations would address the resourcing issues SMEs faced regarding innovation. One of the main concerns SMEs had was that higher education does not understand SMEs business needs or take too long to design and implement solution SMEs can use.

Research skills were seen as significantly important with, 87% of SME identifying research skills as important or very important to their organization, however there is a significant skills gap with 62% of SMEs having no research skills. To address such missing skills gaps the Reinnovate consortium with higher education institutes and research organizations, chamber of commerce and SME representative bodies started to develop research skills to stimulate the employees' ability to systematically identify new digital opportunities and manage the implementation of these to improve the performance of the company (Hamburg, 2019). Four interdisciplinary learning modules have been developed and offered to SME staff to help them

- to use workplace-oriented research to identify opportunities from national & international perspectives incorporating digital transformations and including cyber security gaps.
- to gather and analyze the relevant data to allow them to implement a business opportunity or an innovative idea in connection with digital transformation.

- to manage an own research project about a business model including cyber security measures and evaluate it.

The training program is supported by an ICT learning platform, interdisciplinary trainers and mentors. The main used method is interdisciplinary problem-based learning (IPBL) a student-centered pedagogy, combining two different teaching methods: Problem-based Learning (O´Brien & Hamburg, 2019) and Interdisciplinary Learning. Fostering a multi-perspective approach to highly complex problems like cyber security ones and corruption, students work in interdisciplinary teams.

A mentoring program for entrepreneurs online and face-to face started within Reinnovate with mentors from university and research, which collaborate within the project, and mentees entrepreneurs. Mentees should be taken from the SMEs and are learners who would like to follow the training within Reinnovate. The mentoring program aims particularly to develop workplace research skills of mentees which will enhance the absorptive capacity of SMEs by encouraging employees to source new ideas and opportunities and apply them to their organization. Due to Corona Crisis the training program started only virtually as well as by using the e-mentoring.

## CONCLUSION

Solutions to cyber security training and education challenges require an interdisciplinary approach.

The benefits of a cyber-security interdisciplinary education/training program are different from the benefits of existing single-department cyber security education programs i.e. the problem of the human factor can be better solved by achieving practical knowledge of security at more people (Ramirez, 2017). Available education in the early years can avoid the problem of computer vulnerabilities affecting previously unaffected disciplines, like medicine and mechanical engineering. This fact is inevitable with the spreading of the Internet - Internet of Things. By allowing cyber security to be an accessible field of study to anyone, security situation of organizations will be improved, workers and students can anticipate and avoid vulnerabilities more effectively than if they were received training for current tasks on an as-needed basis in the workforce.

In order to make possible to all members of society need to be more entrepreneurial, innovative and having security knowledge it is necessary to create interdisciplinary learning environments to encourage entrepreneurial ways of thinking and behaving and adapt to digital environments and events like cyber-attacks. Entrepreneurship should be treated across all disciplines and expose all students and all faculty to entrepreneurial thought and processes.

SMEs must collaborate to optimize employee-focused cyber defense safeguards and identify end user knowledge gaps. Some cyber security specialists are aware of the cyber fraud types plaguing their organizations and where vulnerabilities exist. A training needs analysis approach facilitates ascertaining strengths, weaknesses, training needs, learning objectives and performance outcomes of all employees (Beyer et al., 2014).

Practitioners have to understand the role of computer-using employees and cyber risk mitigation, organize support for end user training, mobilize SMEs to achieve competencies to match the challenge and broker integrated solutions. Psychologists from companies can measure whether training is well designed, role specific, and effective and has achieved desired outcomes. The cooperation research - SMEs play an integral role in the solution. The importance of knowledge transfer between researcher, education institutions and companies is recognized by EU members and is reflected in their national programmers developed under the Lisbon strategy. Efforts to support public research institutions to improve this situation have been done within the Committee for Scientific and Technical Research (CREST). Education-industry cooperation is associated with the transfer of knowledge and technology, this collaboration is important because helps companies to become more competitive. To ensure that the achievements of the academic sector also benefit industry, and in order to put academic research and knowledge to work specifically for industry it is necessary to strength their cooperation.

Many interactions between research institutions and companies involve large firms, being considered more durable and regular than with SMEs. Other reasons for this situation i.e. lack of interest from research and education institutions to support companies, poor capabilities of SMEs to recognize the importance of innovation for their businesses and competitiveness and to engage in knowledge transfer activities, existing of practical approaches that support research abut not the transfer of research results to SMEs. One of the future work of the author is to continue to initiate and work in projects strengthening the cooperation with SMEs also within an interdisciplinary cyber domain.

# REFERENCES

Allen, T. D., Eby, L. T., O'Brien, K. E., & Lentz, E. (2008). The state of mentoring research: A qualitative review of current research methods and future research implications. *Journal of Vocational Behavior*, *73*(3), 343–357. doi:10.1016/j.jvb.2007.08.004

Baugh, G., & Fagenson-Eland, E. (2007). Formal mentoring programs: A "poor cousin" of informal relationships. In B. R. Ragins & K. E. Kram (Eds.), *The handbook of mentoring at work: Theory, research and practice* (pp. 373–399). Sage.

Baugh, S., & Scandura, T. (1999). The effect of multiple mentors on protégé attitudes toward the work setting. *Journal of Social Behavior and Personality*, *14*(4), 503.

Beyer, R., Mol, M., Haney, M., Staggs, J., Brummel, B., & Hale, J. (2014). Organizational cybersecurity. *Education and Training: Best Practices and Future Trends*.

Brey, P. (2005). The Importance of Privacy in the Workplace. In S. Hansson & E. Palm (Eds.), *The Ethics of Privacy in the Workplace* (pp. 97–118). Peter Lang.

Brummel, B., Hale, J., & Mol, M. (in press). Training cyber security personnel. In Introduction to Homeland Security. Heinemann.

Bynum, T., & Rogerson, S. (Eds.). (2003). *Computer Ethics and Professional Responsibility: Introductory Text and Readings*. Blackwell.

Dalal & Tetrick. (Eds.). (2003). The Psychosocial Dynamics of Cyber Security. Taylor & Francis.

Delaney, Y. A. (2012). Research on mentoring language teachers: Its role in language education. *Foreign Language Annals*, *45*(1), 184–202. doi:10.1111/j.1944-9720.2011.01185.x

Dierkes, M. (2001). *Handbook of Organizational Learning and Knowledge*. Oxford University Press.

Easterby-Smith, M., & Lyles, M. A. (2003). *The Blackwell Handbook of Organizational Learning and Knowledge Management*. Blackwell.

Gibb, A. A. (1997). Small firms Training and Competitiveness: Building Upon the Small Business as a Learning Organisation. *International Small Business Journal, 15*(3), 13–29. doi:10.1177/0266242697153001

Hamburg, I. (2019). Implementation of a digital workplace strategy to drive behavior change and improve competencies. In *Strategy and behaviors in the digital economy strategy and behaviors in the digital economy*. IntechOpen.

Hamburg, I., & Bucksch, S. (2016). Approaches for bridging research an industry. Archives of Business Research, 4(1), 209-215. doi:10.14738/abr.41.1845

Hamburg, I., & Grosch, K. R. (2017). Ethical aspects in cyber security. Archives of Business Research, 5(10), 199-206. doi:10.14738/abr.510.3818

Hamburg, I., O'Brien, E., & Vladut, G. (2018). Workplace-oriented research and mentoring of entrepreneurs: cooperation university - industry. *Archives of Business Research, 6*, 243-25.

Kolb, D. A. (1984). *Experiential Learning: Experience as the Source of Learning and Development*. Prentice-Hall.

Kram, K. (1985). *Mentoring at work: Developmental relationships in organizational life*. Scott, Foresman.

McGowan, E. M., Stone, E. M., & Kegan, R. (2007). A Constructive-Developmental Approach to Mentoring Relationships. In *The handbook of mentoring at work: theory, research, and practice* (pp. 401–426). Sage Publications.

O'Brien, E., & Hamburg, I. (2014). Supporting sustainable strategies for SMEs through training, cooperation and mentoring. In Higher education studies 4, no. 2, (p. 61-69). Academic Press.

O'Brien, E., & Hamburg, I. (2019): A critical review of learning approaches for entrepreneurship education in a contemporary society. European Journal of Education: Research, Development and Policy. doi:10.1111/ejed.12369

Ragins, B., & Cotton, J. (1999). Mentor functions and outcomes: A comparison of men and women in formal and informal mentoring relationships. *The Journal of Applied Psychology, 84*(4), 529–550. doi:10.1037/0021-9010.84.4.529 PMID:10504893

Ragins, B., & Kram, K. E. (Eds.). (2007). *The handbook of mentoring at work: Theory, research, and practice*. Sage. Publications.

Ramirez, R. (2017). *Making Cyber Security Interdisciplinary: Recommendations for a Novel Curriculum and Terminology Harmonization*. https://www.researchgate.net/publication/318987341_Making_Cyber_Security_Interdisciplinary_Recommendations_for_a_Novel_Curriculum_and_Terminology_Harmonization

Scandura, T., & Pellegrini, E. (2010). Workplace mentoring: Theoretical approaches and methodological issues. In L. Allen & T. Eby (Eds.), *The Blackwell handbook of mentoring: A multiple perspectives approach* (pp. 71–92). John Wiley & Sons Ltd.

Van Derwerken, J., & Ubell, R. (2011). Training on the Cyber Security Frontlines. *T + D, 65*(6), 4650.

Wagner, T. (2008). *Even our "best" schools are failing to prepare students for 21st-century careers and citizenship.* Retrieved from https://www.tonywagner.com/rigorredefined/

West, R. (2008). The psychology of security. *Communications of the ACM, 51*(4), 34–40. doi:10.1145/1330311.1330320

Wilson, M., Stine, K., & Bowen, P. (2011). National Institute of Standards and Technology (NIST) Special Publication 800–16: Information technology security training requirements: A role-and performance-based model (Draft): Nov.

World Economic Forum. (2009). *Executive summary: Educating the next wave of entrepreneurs.* Geneva: World Economic Forum.

## KEY TERMS AND DEFINITIONS

**Cyber Security:** Cyber security is an umbrella term and includes technologies, processes, and practices to protect networks, devices, programs and data from attack, damage, or unauthorized access. Ccyber security encompasses different types of security. Cyber security gained importance in many fields like law and business management, smart grids, cars, and other cyber-physical systems.

**E-Mentoring:** E-mentoring means providing guided mentoring relationship by using online software or email. It has advantages by allowing participants to communicate at their own convenience and beyond time zones and they do not need to be in the same physical location. It is very useful i.e. during the periods like Corona crisis one.

**Entrepreneurial Learning:** The European definition of entrepreneurial learning includes development of entrepreneurial attitudes, skills and knowledge that enable the individual to turn creative ideas into action. Their role is to engage and motivate students/entrepreneurs through relevant learning experiences for education, life and work. Entrepreneurial learning is a basis for education of entrepreneurs, and it should also include interdisciplinary learning/training programs

**Entrepreneurship:** Entrepreneurship refers to designing, launching, and running a new business. Entrepreneurship is "a process of new value creation" and the formation of the entrepreneur as a person also for transformations like digital ones. It can be understood also as capacity and willingness to develop, organize, and manage a business venture taking also its risks to make a profit.

**Interdisciplinary Mentoring:** Interdisciplinary mentoring can be seen as the mentoring of the future. Scientists use it to produce synergy in groups, to generate multifocal ideas and complex solutions to complex challenges. It has many advantages by using it in education also in entrepreneurial one.

**Interdisciplinary Training:** Interdisciplinary training involves the combining of training in two or more disciplines and use knowledge from these disciplines. It requires thinking across boundaries.

**IPBL:** Interdisciplinary problem-based learning (IPBL) combines two teaching methods: problem-based learning (PBL) and interdisciplinary learning. The students are guided to follow seven steps to problem solving and are assigned different roles in their interdisciplinary groups.

**SME:** An SME means a "small to medium enterprise", and there are various parameters to measure an SME. European Commission distinguish within SMEs small-medium, small, and micro enterprises.

*Previously published in the Handbook of Research on Cyber Crime and Information Privacy; pages 356-371, copyright year 2021 by Information Science Reference (an imprint of IGI Global).*

# Chapter 9
# SETA and Security Behavior:
## Mediating Role of Employee Relations, Monitoring, and Accountability

**Winfred Yaokumah**
*Pentecost University College, Accra, Ghana*

**Daniel Okyere Walker**
*Pentecost University College, Accra, Ghana*

**Peace Kumah**
*Ghana Education Service, Accra, Ghana*

## ABSTRACT

*This article contends that information security education, training and awareness programs can improve employee security behavior. Empirical studies have analyzed the direct effects of employee security training on security behavior without taking into account the mediating role of employee relations, monitoring, and accountability. Based on employee relations and accountability theories, this study proposes and tests a causal model that estimates the direct effect of employee security training on security behavior as well as its indirect effects as mediated by employee relations, monitoring, and accountability. The empirical analysis relies on a survey data from a cross section of employees from five major industry sectors and a structural equation modeling approach via SmartPLS 3.0. The results show that employee security training has indirect and significant effects on security behavior through its influence on employee relations, monitoring, and accountability. However, the result does not indicate direct and significant effect of security training on employee security behavior.*

DOI: 10.4018/978-1-6684-3698-1.ch009

## INTRODUCTION

Organizations rely on information systems to enhance productivity and performance, thereby gaining competitive advantage and achieving strategic goals. Users of information systems are, however, prone to intentional and unintentional security risks. Users tend to be the major contributing factor in many information security breaches (Abawajy, 2014). As such, an increasing amount of attention is being paid to the human side of information security (Marett, 2015). According to Ponemon Institute (2012), employees are the main causes of many data breaches in organizations. Information security breaches often occur in organizations due to employees' ignorance or careless behaviors (Abawajy, 2014). For instance, employee negligence or maliciousness account for 78% of data breaches in organizations (Ponemon Institute, 2012). As a result, organizational leaders are seeking behavioral solutions to effect a positive change in employee behavior toward the security of information resources (Pattinson et al., 2016).

An important aspect of managing employee security behavior in organizations is through security education, training, and awareness. Information security education is the organizational effort at making employees aware of the security environment, policies, and security manuals of the organization (D'Arcy et al., 2009). A growing body of evidence suggests that information security training can be used to improve employee information security behavior (Chen, Ramamurthy & Wen, 2015; Helkala & Bakås, 2014; Tsohou et al., 2015). The main reason organizations provide security education, training, and awareness programs is to change employees' behavior and to reduce employees' undesirable security behavior toward organizational information resources (Abawajy, 2014). Through the use of effective training techniques, employees can be educated on how to make safe information security decisions (Kennedy, 2016).

Employee information security education, training and awareness programs and security behavior continue to be strong themes in the human aspects of information security literature (Boss et al., 2015; Chu & Chau, 2014; Pattinson & Anderson, 2007). However, little attention is being paid to human factors that can influence employee security behavior. Many organizations have established SETA and security monitoring programs to safeguard information resources (Chen, Ramamurthy & Wen, 2015). But the current methods of training employees about information security are apparently failing as the number of employee-related breaches is increasing each year (Kennedy, 2016). Lacey (2010) believes that lack of proper training and supervision are the contributing factors behind many information security breaches. However, Slusky and Partow-Navid (2012) argue that failure of employees to comply with security measures is not due to lack of security training and awareness. Even individuals with security knowledge are unable to draw the necessary conclusions about digital risks when browsing the web (Bennett & Bertenthal, 2016). Thus, there is a significant gap between employee information security training and security behavior (Stanciu & Tinca, 2016). Parsons et al. (2014) suggest that organizations should assess the impact of information security training programs on addressing organizational information security challenges.

According to Meso, Ding and Xu (2013), there is the need for a broader and better training of employees to be able to effectively deal with information security risks. Organizations need to incorporate into security education, training and awareness programs three key interventions (mediators), including establishing closer employee relations, monitoring employees' security behavior, and making employees accountable for security. Employee relations, monitoring, and accountability are core human resource (HR) management activities that can improve employee behavior. Human resource management plays an important role by coordinating the activities (policies and procedures) of the organization, which are consistent with the overall business goals and objectives. Employee relations are identified as social exchange relationship between an employer and the employees in the organization (Sivalogathasan & Hashim, 2013). Monitoring is the activities undertaken by one party to gain information about another party's level of compliance (Ferrin et al., 2007) to specified requirements. Accountability is a "process in which a person has a potential obligation to explain his or her actions to another party who has the right to pass judgment on those actions and to administer potential positive or negative consequences in response to them" (Vance, Lowry & Eggett, 2015, p. 347).

Based on the accountability and employee relations theories, this study develops and examines the influence of employee information security training on employee information security bahavior mediated through the organizational security activities of creating employee relations, security monitoring, and accountability. Yaokumah and Kumah (2018) explore the effect of security policy on compliance. D'Arcy, Hovav, and Galletta (2009) investigate perceived certainty and severely of sanctions as the major mediating factors between security policies; security education, training, and awareness (SETA) programs; computer monitoring, and information systems misuse intention. Both certainty and severely of sanctions explain only 30% of the variations in information systems misuse intention. This suggests that other factors can account for information systems misuse intention, and for that matter employee security behavior. Thus, the extent of the impact training, employee relations, monitoring, and accountability have on improving employee information security behavior has not been adequately researched from theoretical and empirical perspectives. For improving employee information security behavior, this paper proposes that employee relations, monitoring, and accountability should directly improve employee information security behavior or act as the vital link or mediators between employee information security training and the employee information security behavior.

## BACKGROUND AND HYPOTHESES

### Theoretical Background and Conceptual Model

Two theories were used in this study to explain how security training could improve security behavior: the accountability theory (Vance, 2013; Vance, Lowry & Eggett, 2015) and the employee relations theory (Coleman, 2017; Ross & Bamber, 2009; The Great Soviet Encyclopedia, 1979). Accountability theory comprised of four main constructs: identifiability, expectation of evaluation, awareness of monitoring, and social presence (Vance, Lowry & Eggett, 2015). Identifiability is a person's knowledge that his activities could be linked to him and thus revealed his/her true identity (Vance, Lowry & Eggett, 2015). Expectation of evaluation is the belief that one's "performance would be assessed by another according to some normative ground rules and with some implied consequences" (Lerner & Tetlock, 1999, p. 255). Awareness of monitoring is a user's state of active cognition that his or her system-related work is being monitored (Vance, Lowry, & Eggett 2015). Social presence is the awareness that there are other users in the system (Vance, Lowry, & Eggett 2015).

The employee relations theory proposed that humans are socio-psychological beings and have moral qualities - including goals, motivation, and values (The Great Soviet Encyclopedia, 1979). To increase productivity, a method of dealing with employees should take into consideration human moral needs. The theory focused on factors fostering a positive or negative attitude toward employees, the influence of the work group on the individual, the effectiveness of forms and methods of supervision, and the improvement of conditions for work, relaxation, and leisure (The Great Soviet Encyclopedia, 1979). The unitarist theory of employee relations emphasized co-dependency of employers and employees in which the organization is viewed the as an integrated, friendly and collaborative whole (Coleman, 2017). The employers and employees regard the organization as a happy family with a common purpose and mutual co-operation (Ross & Bamber, 2009) towards the achievement of organizational goals. Unitarist focussed on increased employee loyalty in the attainment of organizational goals.

Based on these theories, the current study proposed that an employee with the knowledge that his or her identity could not be hidden and his activities are being monitored would be more likely to engage in desirable security behavior. The fundamental assumption in our theoretical use of accountability theory is that accountability and monitoring would change employees' behavior toward information security policies. For employee relations theory, our assumption is that when employees' moral needs are addressed there would be the tendency of positive behavior toward information security. Our conceptual model proposed that employee' information security training, mediated by employee accountability, employee relations, and employee monitoring would improve employee desirable information security behavior (see Figure 1). The conceptual model suggested that employees who had security training would have increased perception of accountability, which in turn would influence their behavior toward information security.

Given the above explanation of the mediating effect of accountability, employee relations, and employee monitoring, the study posited that employees who had security training would have desirable security behaviors that would improve information security. Moreover, the model suggested that security training would directly improve employees' security behavior without the mediators (accountability, employee relations, and employee monitoring).

*Figure 1. Conceptual model of employee security training on security behavior*

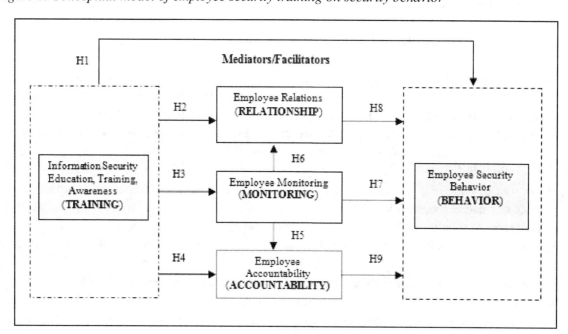

## Employee Security Behavior

Literature on employee security behavior provided diverse and sometimes inconsistent findings. A recent study suggested that the level of user security behavior is low (Das & Khan, 2016). According to Safa et al. (2015), user security behavior such as user negligence, ignorance, lack of awareness, mischievous, apathy and resistance were usually the reasons for security breaches. Applying structural equation modelling techniques, Safa et al. (2015) found that information security awareness and attitude towards information security had positive effect on users' behavior, while perceived behavioral control did not significantly affect user behaviour. However, in an earlier and a related study, Zhang et al. (2009) examined the factors affecting end-user security behavior and found that perceived behavioral control had significant impact on intention to comply with security policy. Chen and Li (2014) distinguished between formal control (deterrence and punishment) and informal control (misperception of social norms). Formal control mechanisms effectively reduced employee's omission behaviors whereas informal control mechanisms contributed to the dissemination of omission behaviors among employees (Chen & Li, 2014). Considering these contradictory findings, the current study proposed that security training, monitoring, accountability, and employee relations could have significant influence on employee security behavior.

## Security Training, Education, Awareness

Information security education, training, and awareness are three inter-related activities organizations employ to foster employees' understanding and compliance with information security policies and guidelines. According to NIST Special Publication 800-16 (1998), user education, training, and awareness are important aspects when addressing human factors and competencies in information security. Security education is a means of providing adequate information security awareness amongst employees (Kaspersky & Furnell, 2014). Information security awareness is the level of comprehension that users have about the importance of information security best practices (Abawajy, 2014). Security awareness is a primary pillar of security for any organization to avoid major security breaches (Dahbur, Bashabsheh, & Bashabsheh, 2017) and the most cost-effective means of enhancing security (Albrechtsen & Hovden, 2010).

Previous studies reported inconsistent findings with regard to whether security training and awareness programs have direct influence on employee security behavior. For example, Zhang and McDowell (2009) noted that security education alone is of little value to changing user behavior. However, according to McCrohan, Engel and Harvey (2010), information security awareness and training initiatives would improve security behavior. McCrohan, Engel, and Harvey (2010) found that cyber threat education and awareness intervention could change user security behavior. Helkala and Bakås (2014) also demonstrated that education is necessary in changing people's security behaviour. This suggested that the more information security knowledge employees' have, the better their behavior toward information security. Based on this notion the following hypothesis was proposed:

**Hypothesis 1:** There is a direct, positive, and significant relationship between employee information security training, education and awareness (TRAINING) and employee's information security behavior (BEHAVIOR).

Moreover, the dependency on humans in protecting information resources necessitated an information security awareness program to make people conscious of their roles and responsibilities toward information security (Kruger, Drevin, & Steyn 2010). An important aspect of security training is to made employee responsible and accountable for security. Kruger, Drevin, and Steyn (2010) found a significant relationship between knowledge of concepts and behavior. But McCrohan, Engel and Harvey (2010) doubted whether simple admonition of security threats can change behavior. A global security survey confirmed that security education, training and awareness programs are not working as well as they could be (Tsohou et al., 2012), hence the need for accountability, monitoring, and employee relations.

Accountability theory proposed that user's active cognitive ability is enhanced when they are made aware that their activities are being monitored (Vance, Lowry, & Eggett 2015). Employees monitoring produces fruitful outcomes when the employee is aware that they are being monitored (Vance, Lowry, & Eggett 2015). Thus, when employees participated in security training and awareness programs, they should be monitored to ascertain whether the training goals have been achieved. With respect to the relationship between training and accountability, Burley (2017) noted that training has significant impact on employee accountability. For example, a well-designed security training program would include how the employee should create an action plan. This would include how to apply what has been learned when the employee returned to work. Based on these concepts, the following hypotheses were put forth:

**Hypothesis 2:** There is a positive and a significant relationship between employee information security training, education and awareness (TRAINING) and improvement in employee relations (RELATIONSHIP).

**Hypothesis 3:** There is a positive and a significant relationship between employee information security training, education and awareness (TRAINING) and improvement in information security monitoring (MONITORING).

**Hypothesis 4:** There is a positive and a significant relationship between employee information security training, education and awareness (TRAINING) and employee information security accountability (ACCOUNTABILITY).

## Employee Monitoring

Systematic monitoring and evaluation of employees' security behavior are of great importance (Albarrak, 2011). Employee monitoring is an important component of organizational efforts to maintain employee productivity and to manage employee misconduct (Ford et al., 2015). Lack of security evaluation method might expose organizations to several risky situations (Rigon et al., 2014). To enhance employee performance, many organizations are increasingly using electronic performance monitoring systems (Bhave, 2014). Technology allows for extensive monitoring of employees with video, phones, internet, social media, application logs, and other methods with which employee behaviors can be tracked (Ford et al., 2015). Another emerging form of employee monitoring is through global positioning system (GPS) (Bhave, 2014). However, employee monitoring has been contended as it could be considered a breach of privacy (Towns & Cobb, 2012) and close monitoring might result in negative employee reactions (Jeske & Santuzzi, 2015). Similarly, Whalen and Gates (2010) suggested that voluntary monitoring should be made a condition of employment in order to yield positive results.

One key construct of accountability theory is social presence. Social presence suggested that users are aware of the presence of other users in the system (Vance, Lowry & Eggett, 2015) who might observe their activities. The awareness that others are observing (monitoring) their activities might compel employees to comply with policies. Monitoring could influence accountability in two ways. Dishonest employees might fear disciplinary actions and those complying with security requirements might expect acknowledgment. Also, employee relations theory focused on meeting the social and psychological needs of the employees. Through monitoring, an organization would ascertain the needs of the employees. Knowing the needs and addressing those needs would create closer employee relations (Coleman, 2017).

Moreover, when people are being monitored they would put up acceptable behavior (Vance, Lowry, & Eggett 2015). Monitoring employees gives the organization the opportunity to watch for mistakes and errors. A monitoring system enables the organization to identify strength and weaknesses of employees on regular bases. Employees' strength and weaknesses would be exposed. When employees' strengths are acknowledged their behavior toward work might change (Ross & Bamber, 2009). Also, pointing out employees' weaknesses and mistakes might improve security behaviors (Ford et al., 2015). A previous study found that a frequent supervisory use of electronic performance monitoring was associated with better task performance and organizational citizenship behaviors (Bhave, 2014). Thus, the following hypotheses were proposed:

**Hypothesis 5:** There is a positive and a significant relationship between security monitoring (MONITORING) and employee information security accountability (ACCOUNTABILITY).

**Hypothesis 6:** There is a positive and a significant relationship between security monitoring (MONITORING) and improvement in employee relations (RELATIONSHIP).

**Hypothesis 7:** There is a positive and a significant relationship between security monitoring (MONITORING) and employee's information security behavior (BEHAVIOR).

## Employee Relations

Gennard and Judge (2002) defined employee relations as the study of rules, regulations, and agreements which are employed to manage employees individually and collectively with the aim of gaining employee commitment to the realization of an organization's goals and objectives. To ensure security in information systems, it is necessary to address human behavior and organisation-related issues (Trcek et al., 2007). Employee relations are human resource strategies designed to manage relationships between employers and employees (Andrea Rea, n.d). Employee relations programs are aimed at providing fair and consistent treatment to all employees, prevent and resolve problems arising from situations at work, and addressing issues affecting employees such as pay and benefits, supporting work-life balance, and safe working conditions (Andrea Rea, n.d). Employee relations programs ensure the most effective use of employees to accomplish the organization's objectives (Andrea Rea, n.d.). The strength of an employee's identification with and involvement in an organization has a significant effect on behavioral intention (Lebek et al., 2014). This is because disgruntled employees can expose valuable business trade secrets or engage in corporate espionage or sabotage (Ford et al., 2015). The social exchange relationship between the employer and the employee determined the employee work outcomes (Sivalogathasan & Hashim, 2013). Therefore, employee relations could influence employee security behavior. The following hypothesis was proposed:

**Hypothesis 8:** There is a positive and a significant relationship between employee relations (RELATIONSHIP) and employee's information security behavior (BEHAVIOR).

## Employee Accountability

While organizations invest significant funds to ensure that buildings and computing systems are secured, the responsibility that the employees have for maintaining information systems security is often overlooked (Hazari, Hargrave & Clenney, 2008). Responsibility and accountability could change the behaviors of users who accesses systems and applications to perform tasks. Accountability is seen as a quality in which a person displays a willingness to accept responsibility (Vance, 2013). It is regarded as a process in which a person has a potential obligation to explain his or her actions to another party who has the right to pass judgment on the actions as well as to subject the person to potential consequences (Vance, 2013). One promising means of modifying the behaviors of employees is through accountability (Tadmor & Tetlock, 2009). Accountability theory suggested that a person's expectation that he or she would be held accountable for an action or inaction reduces the likelihood of behaving in socially unacceptable way (Sedikides et al., 2002). Zaman and Saif (2016) found that perceived accountability has a significant positive relationship with job performance as it could change the behaviors while performing tasks. According to Styles and Tryfonas (2009), employees are responsible for and are duty-bound to secure computing resources they operate and interact with. Based on this notion, the following hypothesis was proposed:

**Hypothesis 9:** There is a positive and a significant relationship between employee information security accountability (ACCOUNTABILITY) and employee's information security behavior (BEHAVIOR).

## METHODOLOGY

The accessible population was the organizations located within Greater Accra municipal area of Ghana. A total of 49 organizations were selected from within industry sectors involving 650 respondents (15 participants from each organization within the 5 main industry sectors and 80 participants from other organizations) were invited to take part in the study. Details of the sample includes: (a) ten (2 public and 8 private) universities (150 participants); (b) ten licensed banks (150 participants); (c) six public utility companies (water, electricity, telecommunication) (90 participants); (d) seven government public service institutions (105 participants); (e) five healthcare institutions (75 participants); and (f) eleven others (IT, Manufacturing, Oil and Gas, etc.) (80 participants). These organizations were selected because they are mandated by law and regulations such as the Electronic Transactions Act 772 (2008) and Bank of Ghana Act 612 (2002) (Bank of Ghana, 2011) to maintain the confidentiality and integrity of customers' information.

A simple random sampling method was employed to select participants from the organizations. A structured questionnaire was used to gather information from the respondents. The questions on the questionnaires were modified such that it could be relevant to the context of the study. The modification was done as a result a field test conducted, with comments received from a panel of experts (two information security practitioners, two HR practitioners, and one senior academic faculty) to establish the validity the instrument. The questionnaires were then self-administered to the respondents through post and by email.

The first part of the questionnaire was designed to reflect the profile of the respondents. The second part contained the questions which reflected four independent (exogenous) latent variables and one dependent (endogenous) variable. The questions were 40 indicator variables from the five constructs (see Figure 2 and Table 2). The questionnaire comprised of 11 measurement items relating to *information security education, training and awareness* (Hwang et al., 2017), *5 items on employee relations* (Bumgarner & Borg, 2007), 4 items on *security monitoring* (Al-Omari, El-Gayar & Amit Deokar, 2012), 11 items on *accountability* (Bumgarner & Borg, 2007), and 9 items on *security behavior* (Siponen et al., 2014). Ratings were done on a Likert scale of 1 (strongly disagree) to 5 (strongly agree). Respondents were asked to rate the extent to which each of the variables that could influence their behavior toward information security.

Out of the 650 questionnaires sent to the respondents, 318 were completed and used in the data analysis. This represented a response rate of 48.9 percent. Table 1 showed the sample characteristics of the respondents. The Partial Least Square (PLS) structural Equation Modelling (SEM) path modeling was adopted in analyzing the data. The study first analyzed the measurement model to test the reliability and validity of the measurement model. SmartPLS 3.0 (Ringle, Wende, & Becker, 2015) was used to perform path analysis and test the research hypotheses. Moreover, the study used bootstrapping with 5000 re-samples (Goodhue, Lewis, & Thompson, 2007) for obtaining t-statistics between constructs of the research model.

*Table 1. Sample characteristics*

| Respondents | No. of Questionnaire Received | Percent (%) |
|---|---|---|
| **Industry Sector** | | |
| Education Institution | 74 | 23.3 |
| Public Utility Company | 38 | 11.9 |
| Financial Institution | 68 | 21.4 |
| Government | 36 | 11.3 |
| Health Care | 38 | 11.9 |
| Others (IT Companies, Oil and Gas, Manufacturing) | 64 | 20.1 |
| **Experience (Years)** | | |
| 1-5 | 46 | 14.5 |
| 6-10 | 114 | 35.8 |
| 11-15 | 138 | 43.4 |
| 16-20 | 18 | 5.7 |
| 21 and above | 2 | 0.6 |

$N = 318$

# DATA ANALYSIS

This study employed a two-step structural equation modelling (SEM) approach: a) assessment of the measurement model and b) the analysis of the structural model. The assessment of the measurement model measured the adequacy of the model with respect to the relationship between the latent variables and the items measuring them (Hair et al., 2014). Thus, the measurement model was used to confirm the reliability and validity of the measures. The structural model was employed to determine the influence of employee security training on security behavior by testing a set of hypotheses.

## Assessment of the Measurement Model

The assessment of the model was to ascertain the relationship between the constructs and their indicators. The assessment model was evaluated for the a) individual item reliability (factor loading), b) internal consistency reliability (composite reliability and Cronbach's alpha), and c) construct validity (convergent validity and discriminant validity).

The individual item reliability (factor loading) indicated the correlations of the items with their respective latent variables (Hulland, 1999). The standardized loadings were assessed in order to evaluate individual item reliability. The items with low loadings must be dropped and should not be used in further analysis as they provided very little explanatory power to the model and therefore biasing the estimates of the parameters linking the latent variables (Nunnally, 1978). For the cut-off point, a rule of thumb was to accept items with loadings of 0.7 or more (Fornell & Larcker, 1981). A loading of 0.7 indicated that about 50% of the variance in the observed variables was due to the latent variable (Hulland, 1999). According to Chin (1998), where scales were adapted from other settings, a loading of 0.5 might be used as the cut-off point (Chin, 1998). However, items with loadings of less than 0.4 (a threshold commonly used for factor analysis results) or 0.5 should be dropped (Hulland, 1999). In this study, all items having a loading less than 0.7 were dropped. Twenty items were used in the analysis of the structural model while the rest were dropped for not attaining the loadings cut-off point of 0.7.

Furthermore, the study ascertained the Cronbach's alpha and composite reliability scores to determine the reliability of the measured constructs (Fornell, & Larcker, 1981). Cronbach's alpha represented the coefficient of reliability (or consistency). It denoted how well a set of items (or variables) measured a single one-dimensional latent construct (Hair et al., 2011). Composite reliability (CR) score was considered superior to Cronbach's Alpha as it used the item loadings obtained within the theoretical model (Fornell, & Larcker, 1981). However, both composite reliability and Cronbach's Alpha could be acceptable with scores of 0.7 and above (Nunnally, 1978). Applying the benchmark of 0.7 for Cronbach's Alpha and composite reliability ((Nunnally, 1978), the five constructs (security training, employee relations, employee monitoring, accountability, security behavior) in this study exceeded the minimum requirements for reliability measures (Hair et al., 2014). Thus, all the constructs demonstrated acceptable level of reliability (see Table 3).

When multiple items were used to measure individual latent variables, attention should be paid not only to the reliability of the individual measurement items, but also to the extent to which the measures demonstrated convergent validity (Hulland, 1999). Convergent validity represented the measure of internal consistency. It was estimated to ensure that the items measure each latent variable it measured and not measuring another latent variable. The average variance extracted (AVE) (Fornell & Larcker, 1981) was used to assess the convergent validity of the latent variables. AVE measured the amount of variance that a latent variable captured from its measurement items relative to the amount of variance due to measurement errors (Hair et al., 2014). Fornell and Larcker ((1981) stated that AVE should be higher than 0.5. This meant that at least 50% of measurement variance was captured by the latent variables. In this study, the estimates of AVEs (Table 3) were above 50% for all the latent variables. After assessing the individual item reliability and convergent validity of the measurement model, the discriminant validity of the measurement was also evaluated. Discriminant validity indicated the extent to which a given latent variable was different from other latent variables in the model (Hulland, 1999).

To assess discriminant validity, two tests were conducted: a) analysis of cross-loadings and b) analysis of average variance extracted (AVE). The analysis of cross-loading was conducted by following the rule that items should have a higher correlation with the latent variable that they were supposed to measure than with any other latent variable in the model (Chin, 1998). Convergent validity was initially assessed through indicator reliability. The rule of thumb was that standardized indicator outer loadings must be 0.708 or higher (Hair et al., 2014). Two indicators were removed from accountability construct. All other indicators were above 0.708. The average variance extracted (AVE) was also a measure of convergent validity and it exceeded 0.60 for all the constructs in the model; the cut-off was 0.50 (Hair et al., 2014). The Fornell and Larcker (1981) criterion for assessing discriminant validity was applied. The squared interconstruct correlations were all below the construct AVEs, thus indicating discriminant validity. Finally, all indicator loadings were higher than their cross-loadings, providing further evidence that all the criteria for discriminant validity were met (Table 3).

## Assessment of the Structural Model

On the basis of the analyzed results from the assessment of the measurement model, the questionnaire used was considered valid and reliable in assessing the model. Following, the quality of the structural model was assessed to determine its ability to predict endogenous constructs. This was achieved by using the cross-validated redundancy $Q^2$, coefficient of determination $R^2$ (Sarstedt et al., 2014; Urbach & Ahlemann, 2010), and the strength of the path coefficients (Hair et al., 2011). The Stone-Geiser $Q^2$ (Geisser, 1975; Lee et al., 2011) assessed the predictive accuracy of the proposed model (Hair et al., 2011; Hair et al., 2012). It measured how accurately the PLS-SEM model predicted the observed data points (Hair et al., 2014). The $Q^2$ was a nonparametric measure obtained using the blindfolding procedure with values larger than zero indicating predictive relevance (Hair et al., 2011). SmartPLS automatically provided the $Q^2$ value for each endogenous latent variable. The analysis yielded a $Q^2$ value of 0.289 for accountability, 0.149 for employee relations, 0.188 for monitoring, and 0.272 for security behavior (Table 4). Therefore, each factor had a high predictive capability in predicting employee information security behavior.

The $R^2$ denoted the measure of the variance of each of the endogenous constructs explained by exogenous constructs, thus measuring the predictive power of the exogenous constructs (Chin, 2010; Urbach & Ahlemann, 2010). The $R^2$ measure ranged from 0 to 1, with values closer to 1 indicating greatest degree of predictive power. For variance explained by the endogenous variables to have practical and statistical significance, it was recommended that $R^2$ values be greater than 0.10 (Hair et al., 2014). As a guideline for assessing $R^2$, 0.67, 0.33 and 0.19 represented substantial, moderate, and weak respectively (Lee et al., 2011). A more stringent assessment with $R^2$ value of 0.75 representing substantial; value of 0.5 and 0.25 represented moderate and weak $R^2$ respectively (Hair et al., 2014).

*Table 2. Factor loading*

| Constructs | Indicators | Loading > 0.7 |
|---|---|---|
| SECURITY EDUCATION, TRAINING AND AWARENESS | | |
| ST01 | My organization provides employees with appropriate security education before giving them authorized access to the corporate network. | 0.748 |
| ST02 | My organization provides employees with education on the proper usage of technologies associated with information. | 0.811 |
| ST03 | My organization provides employees with proper security education on risks associated with internet usage. | 0.780 |
| ST04 | Employees in my organization are made not to store passwords in insecure places. | 0.717 |
| ST06 | My organization utilizes various communication methods in order to improve the information security awareness of employees. | 0.718 |
| ST07 | My organization provides employees with education on their responsibility for information security exposure. | 0.740 |
| ST10 | My organization provides education to promote employees' awareness of information security issues. | 0.727 |
| ST11 | All employees are periodically tested on their knowledge of security procedures, including their knowledge of newly emerging threats. | 0.765 |
| EMPLOYEE MONITORING | | |
| BC02 | I am aware that my organization monitors any modification or altering of computerized data by employees | 0.823 |
| BC03 | I am aware that my organization monitors employees' computing activities and conducts periodic audits to detect the use of unauthorized software on its computers. | 0.896 |
| BC04 | I am aware that my organization reviews logs of employees' computing activities on a regular basis. | 0.851 |
| EMPLOYEE RELATIONS | | |
| ER01 | My organization makes fairness and good faith in the treatment of employees a priority. | 0.837 |
| ER02 | My organization provides adequate mechanisms for employees to express their grievances without penalty and for them to see those grievances being conscientiously addressed. | 0.793 |
| ER03 | My organization handles re-deployment/down-sizing in a manner that minimizes hostile feelings on the part of former employees. | 0.818 |
| ER04 | My organization offers a procedure which would allow employees to report attempts by outsiders to extort their organization in circumventing security. | 0.733 |
| ER05 | If an employee is going through a period of great difficulties in his or her personal life, there is a policy for temporarily reducing that employee's responsibilities for critical systems and access to critical systems. | 0.761 |
| ACCOUNTABILITY | | |
| SA02 | All employees are required to sign confidentiality and intellectual property agreements. | 0.744 |
| SA06 | Information security policies defined the proper use of e-mail, internet access, and instant messaging by employees. | 0.846 |
| SA11 | Employees are given adequate incentives to report security breaches and bad security practices. | 0.776 |
| INFORMATION SECURITY BEHAVIOR | | |
| BEC06 | I comply with information security policies (e.g. secure password, clear desk/screen policy, classification and handling of information). | 0.819 |
| BEC07 | I assist others in complying with information security policies. | 0.802 |
| BEC08 | I recommend that others comply with information security policies. | 0.795 |
| BEC09 | I do not access social networking websites during work time. | 0.716 |

*Table 3. Results of the measurement model evaluation*

| | Construct | 1 | 2 | 3 | 4 | 5 | AVE (> 0.5) | CA (> 0.7) | CR (> 0.7) |
|---|---|---|---|---|---|---|---|---|---|
| 1 | ACCOUNTABILITY | **0.790** | | | | | 0.624 | 0.701 | 0.833 |
| 2 | BEHAVIOR | 0.584 | **0.784** | | | | 0.615 | 0.790 | 0.864 |
| 3 | MONITORING | 0.591 | 0.575 | **0.857** | | | 0.734 | 0.818 | 0.892 |
| 4 | RELATIONSHIP | 0.560 | 0.556 | 0.479 | **0.789** | | 0.623 | 0.849 | 0.892 |
| 5 | TRAINING | 0.641 | 0.480 | 0.522 | 0.410 | **0.752** | 0.565 | 0.890 | 0.912 |

Note: Discriminant validity - Square roots of average variances extracted (AVEs) shown on diagonal in bold. CR – Composite reliability, CA – Cronbach's Alpha.

From Table 4 and Figure 2, $R^2$ for accountability was 0.501, indicating that about 50.1% of the variance in accountability was explained by security training and monitoring. The $R^2$ for monitoring was 0.273, revealing that about 27.3% of the variance in monitoring was accounted for by security training. The $R^2$ for employee relations was 0.265, showing that about 26.5% of the variance in employee relations were accounted for by security training and monitoring. Finally, the $R^2$ for employee security behavior was 0.468, revealing that about 46.8% of the variance in employee security behavior was accounted for by employee relations, security training (not significant), monitoring, and accountability. Consequently, the results were a sign of adequate model fit between the proposed research model and the empirical data.

*Table 4. $R^2$ and $Q^2$ coefficients*

| Constructs | $R^2$ | $R^2$ Adjusted | $Q^2$ |
|---|---|---|---|
| ACCOUNTABILITY | 0.501 | 0.498 | 0.289 |
| MONITORING | 0.273 | 0.270 | 0.188 |
| RELATIONSHIP | 0.265 | 0.260 | 0.149 |
| BEHAVIOR | 0.475 | 0.468 | 0.272 |

## Hypotheses Testing

Table 5 and Figure 2 disclosed the standardized path coefficients of the structural model under investigation. The path coefficients indicated the strength of the direct relationship between constructs. Security training has no direct and significant influence on security behavior ($\beta_1 = 0.091, p = 0.0.065$), indicating that H1 was not supported. Security training, however, had positive and significant influence on employee relations ($\beta_2 = 0.219, <0.001$), monitoring ($\beta_3 = 0.522, <0.001$), and accountability ($\beta_4 = 0.457, p < 0.001$); inferring that hypotheses H2, H3 and H4 were all supported. Moreover, employee monitoring had a positive and significant influence on accountability ($\beta_5 = 0.353, p < 0.001$), employee relations ($\beta_6 = 0.364, p < 0.001$), and on security behavior ($\beta_7 = 0.271, p < 0.001$); inferring that hypotheses H5, H6 and H7 were also supported. Finally, employee relations had positive and significance influence on security behavior ($\beta_8 = 0.269, p < 0.001$), showing support for hypothesis H8. Also, accountability had a positive and significant influence on employee security behavior ($\beta_9 = 0.215, p < 0.001$), supporting

H9. As could be observed from Figure 2, the paths through the mediators (employee relations, monitoring, and accountability) showed the highest significant path coefficients to security behavior. This suggested that employee relations, monitoring, and accountability played a vital role between security training and improvement in employees' security behavior.

*Table 5. Hypotheses testing results*

| Hypotheses | | Path Coefficients ($\beta$) | Sample Mean (M) | Standard Deviation (SD) | Effect Size ($f^2$) | t-Statistics | p-Values | Result |
|---|---|---|---|---|---|---|---|---|
| H1 | TRAINING -> BEHAVIOR | 0.091 | 0.092 | 0.049 | 0.009 | 1.852 | 0.065 | Not Supported |
| H2 | TRAINING -> RELATIONSHIP | 0.219 | 0.223 | 0.056 | 0.048 | 3.904 | 0.000 | Supported |
| H3 | TRAINING -> MONITORING | 0.522 | 0.527 | 0.035 | 0.375 | 14.788 | 0.000 | Supported |
| H4 | TRAINING -> ACCOUNTABILITY | 0.457 | 0.452 | 0.051 | 0.304 | 8.973 | 0.000 | Supported |
| H5 | MONITORING -> ACCOUNTABILITY | 0.353 | 0.357 | 0.053 | 0.181 | 6.620 | 0.000 | Supported |
| H6 | MONITORING -> RELATIONSHIP | 0.364 | 0.370 | 0.061 | 0.131 | 5.984 | 0.000 | Supported |
| H7 | MONITORING -> BEHAVIOR | 0.271 | 0.272 | 0.064 | 0.082 | 4.252 | 0.000 | Supported |
| H8 | RELATIONSHIP -> BEHAVIOR | 0.269 | 0.271 | 0.057 | 0.090 | 4.722 | 0.000 | Supported |
| H9 | ACCOUNTABILITY -> BEHAVIOR | 0.215 | 0.213 | 0.073 | 0.039 | 2.938 | 0.003 | Supported |

The effect size ($f^2$) was another measure that verified whether the effects indicated by the path coefficients were low (0.02), moderate (0.15), or high (0.35) (Cohen, 1988). Effect size showed whether the effect of a specific independent latent variable on a dependent latent variable was substantial (Chin, 2010). Table 5 indicated that the effect size of security training on monitoring was the highest 0.375, whereas that of security training on security behavior was the lowest (0.009). Other effect sizes ranged between low and moderate.

## DISCUSSION

Previous research emphasized the use of SETA programs to improve employee security behavior (Helkala, & Bakås, 2014; McCrohan, Engel & Harvey, 2010). Regarding the direct effect of SETA on security behaviour, our current study did not find direct and significant effect of SETA on security behavior. This contradicted earlier findings that SETA programs were the most effective means of influencing employee security behavior (Kennedy, 2016; Mani, Choo, & Mubarak, 2014). The results of the current study showed no direct and significant effect of employee security education, training and awareness

*Figure 2. Structural model of security training on security behavior*

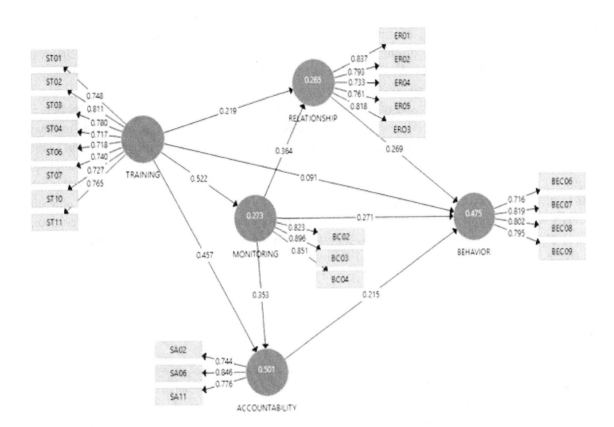

on improving employee security behavior. This is in consonance with an earlier study that did not find a significant change in users' security behavior between those who had completed a training program and those who did not have any security training on information security (Chin, Etudo & Harris, 2016). Thus, security education alone is of little value to changing user behavior (Zhang & McDowell, 2009). This suggested that security education, training and awareness programs are least effective in themselves if organizations fail to include other mediating factors.

With respect to the effect of the mediators (employee monitoring, employee relations, and accountability) on security behavior, our results found that employee relations, employee monitoring, and accountability were the most important factors that could shape employee behavior toward information security. This was clearly demonstrated in the total effects they had on security behavior (Table 5). In order of the predicative values of their influence on security behavior were: employee monitoring, employee relations, and accountability. Thus, in particular, employee monitoring played the most crucial role in enhancing employee behaviour, followed by employee relations. Evidently, the pathway from security training, monitoring, employee relations, through to security behavior appeared to be the most significant based on their path coefficients. Thus, security education, training and awareness programs should include stronger employee monitoring system. Contrary to the argument that employee would object to monitoring (Jeske & Santuzzi, 2015), monitoring can create employee relations which would then improve security behavior. As can be observed from the findings, security monitoring has direct influence on employee relations which then influence employees' desirable security behavior. Much attention has not been paid to employee relations in earlier studies. However, its influence on employee behavior is crucial in protecting information resources. For example, disgruntled employees can expose valuable business trade secrets or engage in corporate espionage or sabotage (Ford et al., 2015). Accordingly, Sivalogathasan & Hashim (2013) believed that the social exchange relationship between the employer and the employee would determine the employee work outcomes.

Though significant, accountability contributed the least to improving employee security behavior among the three mediators. Overall, the significant influence of employees' accountability on employees' behavior toward information security offered another important opportunity for information security management practices. Although earlier studies have reported that accountability and deterrent factors might not be very effective in altering employee behavior (Siponen & Vance, 2010; Hu et al., 2011), our results suggested that when employees undergo security training and are made accountable, their security behaviors improve. Therefore, accountability plays a crucial role in making employees behave in acceptable manner (Tadmor & Tetlock, 2009). Accordingly, similar to a previous finding (D'Arcy, Hovav, & Galletta, 2009), accountability is required to enhancing employee security behavior. Thus, organizations should also pay attention to accountability when implementing security training programs.

## CONCLUSION

The current study examined the extent of the influence information security education, training and awareness (SETA) programs has on employee information security behavior. The study argued that failure of employees to apply with security measures is not mainly due to lack of security training and awareness (Slusky & Partow-Navid, 2012). For organizations to improve employees' security behavior, organizational leaders should not only focus resources on security training programs, but also pay an equal attention to creating employee relations, monitoring employee security behavior, and make employee accountable for security behavior. SETA made the most significant impact on security behavior through monitoring, followed by employee relations, and then accountability. This suggested that security training designers should implement security monitoring systems after security training has been conducted. This would help evaluate any changes in employees' security behavior. Information gathered on employees should provide the bases for accountability in the form of reward and punishment. However, our findings revealed significant role of employee relations on security behavior. Thus, instead on melting out instant punishment as a way of accountability, HR managers should develop policies to address employees' social and moral needs.

This research fills an important gap in the literature on employees' information security behavior from two perspectives: theoretical and methodological. This study developed and empirically tested a five-construct model that examined the influence of employee information security training experience on employees' information security behavior, mediated via employee relations, monitoring, and accountability. From theoretical perspective, the study brought together two theories - the employee relations theory and the accountability theory - that have not been combined in the context of employee information security behavior. The study tested the model using partial least squares structural equation modelling (PLS-SEM).

From methodological perspective, prior studies related to employee information security behavior focussed on univariate quantitative approach and qualitative research methods. Multivariate techniques are recommended to encourage diverse approaches, along with methodological rigor. The result provides one of the few empirical validations of employee security behavior. It recognizes its multidimensional nature as conceptualized through security training, employee relations, monitoring, and accountability. In particular, it extends security behavior research by considering the influence of employee relations, monitoring and accountability drawn from the organizational behavior theories. The findings of this study also have important implications for information security program management practices. Management could use the finding of this study as a guide in developing and implementing information security policy by paying critical attention not only to security training, but also putting in place monitoring, accountability, and employee relations to improve employee security behavior.

This study is limited to a developing country. There would be the need to test the model in different contexts for possible refinement of the model, thus providing a better understanding of the influence of security training on employee security behavior in different settings. Future work would consider important-performance analysis to identify the key indicators for improving employee security behavior, which would be beneficial for management decision-making. Also, the current study did not consider the influence of the control variables - industry sector differences and the experience of the participants. Information security practices might differ from one industry to the other due to various laws and regulation compliance. Therefore, future work would examine different structural models for each industry sector and compare the results. Multi-group analysis would provide useful information by obtaining differences and similarities in inter-sector security practices.

## REFERENCES

Abawajy, J. (2014). User preference of cyber security awareness delivery methods. *Behaviour & Information Technology*, *33*(3), 237–248. doi:10.1080/0144929X.2012.708787

Al-Omari, A., El-Gayar, O., & Deokar, A. (2012). Security policy compliance: User acceptance perspective. In *45th Hawaii International Conference on System Sciences*. doi:10.1109/HICSS.2012.516

Albarrak, A. I. (2011). Evaluation of Users Information Security Practices at King Saud University Hospitals. *Global Business & Management Research*, *3*(1).

Albrechtsen, E., & Hovden, J. (2010). Improving information security awareness and behaviour through dialogue, participation and collective reflection: An Intervention Study. *Computers & Security*, *29*(4), 432–445. doi:10.1016/j.cose.2009.12.005

Andrea Rea (n.d) What Is Employee Relations? - Definition & Concept Retrieved from http://study.com/academy/lesson/what-is-employee-relations-definition-lesson-quiz.html

Bank of Ghana. (2011). Preamble for the Legal and Regulatory framework. Retrieved from https://www.bog.gov.gh/supervision-a-regulation/regulatory-framework

Bhave, D. P. (2014). The Invisible Eye? Electronic Performance Monitoring and Employee Job Performance. *Personnel Psychology*, *67*(3), 605–635. doi:10.1111/peps.12046

Boss, S. R., Galletta, D. F., Lowry, P. B., Moody, G. D., & Polak, P. (2015). What do systems users have to fear? Using fear appeals to engender threats and fear that motivate protective security behaviors. *Management Information Systems Quarterly*, *39*(4), 837–864. doi:10.25300/MISQ/2015/39.4.5

Bumgarner, J., & Borg, S. (2007). US-CCU Cyber-Security Check List (2007). US-CCU (Cyber Consequences Unit) Cyber-Security Check. Retrieved from www.usccu.us

Burley, K. (2017). Employee Accountability Training Activities. Retrieved from https://bizfluent.com/info-8407188-employee-accountability-training-activities.html

Chen, H., & Li, W. (2014). Understanding organization employee`s information security omission behavior: An integrated model of social norm and deterrence. In *PACIS 2014 Proceedings*. Retrieved from http://aisel.aisnet.org/pacis2014/280

Chen, Y., Ramamurthy, K., & Wen, K. (2015). Impacts of comprehensive information security programs on information security culture. *Journal of Computer Information Systems*, *55*(3), 11–19. doi:10.1080/08874417.2015.11645767

Chin, A. G., Etudo, U., & Harris, M. A. (2016). On Mobile Device Security Practices and Training Efficacy: An Empirical Study. *Informatics In Education*, *15*(2), 235–252. doi:10.15388/infedu.2016.12

Chin, W. W. (1998). *The partial least squares approach for structural equation modeling*. In G. A. Marcoulides (Ed.), *Modern methods for business research* (pp. 295–336). London: Lawrence Erlbaum.

Chin, W. W. (2010). How to write up and report PLS analyses. In V. Esposito Vinzi, W.W. Chin, J. Henseler et al. (Eds.), Handbook of Partial Least Squares: Concepts, Methods and Applications (pp. 655-690). London. UK: Springer.

Chu, A. M., & Chau, P. Y. (2014). Development and validation of instruments of information security deviant behavior. *Decision Support Systems*, *66*(C), 93–101. doi:10.1016/j.dss.2014.06.008

Coleman, Q. (2017). What Are the Different Theories of Industrial Relations? Retrieved from https://bizfluent.com/facts-6323679-different-theories-industrial-relations-.html

D'Arcy, J., Hovav, A., & Galletta, D. (2009). User awareness of security countermeasures and its impact on information systems misuse: A deterrence approach. *Information Systems Research*, *20*(1), 79–98. doi:10.1287/isre.1070.0160

Dahbur, K., Bashabsheh, Z., & Bashabsheh, D. (2017). Assessment of Security Awareness: A Qualitative and Quantitative Study. *International Management Review*, *13*(1), 37–58.

Das, A., & Khan, H. U. (2016). Security behaviors of smartphone users. *Information & Computer Security*, *24*(1), 116–134. doi:10.1108/ICS-04-2015-0018

Ferrin et al., (2007). Can I Trust You to Trust Me? A Theory of Trust, Monitoring, and Cooperation in Interpersonal and Intergroup Relationships. *Group & Organization Management*, *32*(4), 465-474.

Ford, J., Willey, L., White, B. J., & Domagalski, T. (2015). New concerns in electronic employee monitoring: Have you checked your policies lately? *Journal of Legal, Ethical & Regulatory Issues*, *18*(1), 51–70.

Fornell, C., & Larcker, D. F. (1981). Evaluating structural equation models with unobservable variables and measurement error. *JMR, Journal of Marketing Research, 18*(1), 39–50. doi:10.2307/3151312

Geisser, S. (1975). The predictive sample reuse method with applications. *Journal of the American Statistical Association, 70*(350), 320–328. doi:10.1080/01621459.1975.10479865

Gennard, J., & Judge, G. (2002). *Employee Relations*. London: CIPD.

Goodhue, D., Lewis, W., & Thompson, R. (2007). Statistical power in analyzing interaction effects: Questioning the advantage of PLS with product indicators. *Information Systems Research, 18*(2), 211–227. doi:10.1287/isre.1070.0123

Hair, J. F., Hult, G. T. M., Ringle, C. M., & Sarstedt, M. (2014). *A primer on partial least squares structural equation modeling (PLS-SEM)*. Thousand Oaks, CA: Sage.

Hair, J. F., Ringle, C., & Sarstedt, M. (2011). PLS-SEM: Indeed a silver bullet. *Journal of Marketing Theory and Practice, 19*(2), 139–151. doi:10.2753/MTP1069-6679190202

Hair, J. F., Sarstedt, M., Ringle, C., & Mena, J. A. (2012). An assessment of the use of partial least squares structural equation modeling in marketing research. *Journal of the Academy of Marketing Science, 40*(3), 414–433. doi:10.100711747-011-0261-6

Hazari, S., Hargrave, W., & Clenney, B. (2008). An empirical investigation of factors influencing information security behavior. *Journal of Information Privacy and Security, 4*(4), 3–20. doi:10.1080/2333696X.2008.10855849

Helkala, K., & Bakås, T. H. (2014). Extended results of Norwegian password security survey. *Information Management & Computer Security, 22*(4), 346–357. doi:10.1108/IMCS-10-2013-0079

Hu, V. C., & Scarfone, K. (2012). Guidelines for Access Control System Evaluation Metrics. *National Institute of Standards and Technology Interagency Report, NISTIR, 7874*. doi:10.6028/NIST.IR.7874

Hulland, J. (1999). Use of partial least squares (PLS) in strategic management research: A review of recent studies. *Strategic Management Journal, 20*(2), 195–204. doi:10.1002/(SICI)1097-0266(199902)20:2<195::AID-SMJ13>3.0.CO;2-7

Hwang, I., Kim, D., Kim, T., & Kim, S. (2017). Why not comply with information security? An empirical approach for the causes of non-compliance. *Online Information Review, 41*(1), 2–18. doi:10.1108/OIR-11-2015-0358

Jeske, D., & Santuzzi, A. M. (2015). Monitoring what and how: Psychological implications of electronic performance monitoring. *New Technology, Work and Employment, 30*(1), 62–78. doi:10.1111/ntwe.12039

Kaspersky, E., & Furnell, S. (2014). A security education Q&A. *Information Management & Computer Security, 22*(2), 130–133. doi:10.1108/IMCS-01-2014-0006

Kelley, T., & Bertenthal, B. I. (2016). Attention and past behavior, not security knowledge, modulate users' decisions to login to insecure websites. *Information & Computer Security, 24*(2), 164–176. doi:10.1108/ICS-01-2016-0002

Kennedy, S. E. (2016). The pathway to security – mitigating user negligence. *Information & Computer Security, 24*(3), 255–264. doi:10.1108/ICS-10-2014-0065

Kent Marett, K. (2015). Checking the manipulation checks in information security research. *Information & Computer Security, 23*(1), 20–30. doi:10.1108/ICS-12-2013-0087

Kruger, H., Drevin, L., & Steyn, T. (2010). A vocabulary test to assess information security awareness. *Information Management & Computer Security, 18*(5), 316–327. doi:10.1108/09685221011095236

Lacey, D. (2010). Understanding and transforming organizational security culture. *Information Management & Computer Security, 18*(1), 4–13. doi:10.1108/09685221011035223

Lebek, B., Markus, J. N., Hohler, B., & Breitner, M. H. (2014). Information security awareness and behavior: A theory-based literature review. *Management Research Review, 37*(12), 1049–1092. doi:10.1108/MRR-04-2013-0085

Lee, L., Petter, S., Fayard, D., & Robinson, S. (2011). On the use of partial least squares path modeling in accounting research. *International Journal of Accounting Information Systems, 12*(4), 305–328. doi:10.1016/j.accinf.2011.05.002

Mani, D., Choo, K. R., & Mubarak, S. (2014). Information security in the South Australian real estate industry. *Information Management & Computer Security, 22*(1), 24–41. doi:10.1108/IMCS-10-2012-0060

McCrohan, K. F., Engel, K., & Harvey, J. W. (2010). Influence of awareness and training on cyber security. *Journal of Internet Commerce, 9*(1), 23–41. doi:10.1080/15332861.2010.487415

Meso, P., Ding, Y., & Xu, S. (2013). Applying protection motivation theory to information security training for college students. *Journal of Information Privacy and Security, 9*(1), 47–67. doi:10.1080/15536548.2013.10845672

National Institute of Standards and Technology (NIST). (1998). *Information technology training requirements: A role- and performance-based model (NIST Special Publication 800-16).* Washington, DC: U.S. Department of Commerce.

NCA. (2008). Electronic Transactions Act 772. Retrieved from https://nca.org.gh/assets/Uploads/NCA-Electronic-Transactions-Act-773.pdf

Nunnally, J. C. (1978). *Psychometric theory* (2nd ed.). New York: McGraw-Hill.

Parsons, K., McCormac, A., Pattinson, M., Butavicius, M., & Cate Jerram, C. (2014). A study of information security awareness in Australian government organisations. *Information Management & Computer Security, 22*(4), 334–345. doi:10.1108/IMCS-10-2013-0078

Pattinson, M., Parsons, K., Butavicius, M., McCormac, A., & Calic, D. (2016). Assessing information security attitudes: A comparison of two studies. *Information & Computer Security, 24*(2), 228–240. doi:10.1108/ICS-01-2016-0009

Pattinson, M. R., & Anderson, G. (2007). How well are information risks being communicated to your computer end-users? *Information Management & Computer Security, 15*(5), 362–371. doi:10.1108/09685220710831107

Ponemon Institute. (2012). *The human factor in data protection*. Retrieved from http://www.trendmicro. com/cloud-content/us/pdfs/security-intelligence/reports/rpt_trend-micro_ponemon-survey–2012.pdf

Rigon, E. A., Westphall, C. M., dos Santos, D. R., & Westphall, C. B. (2014). A cyclical evaluation model of information security maturity. *Information Management & Computer Security, 22*(3), 265–278. doi:10.1108/IMCS-04-2013-0025

Ringle, C. M., Wende, S., & Becker, J.-M. (2015). SmartPLS 3. Boenningstedt: SmartPLS GmbH. Retrieved from http://www.smartpls.com

Ross, P., & Bamber, G. J. (2009). Strategic choices in pluralist and unitarist employment relations regimes: A study of Australian telecommunications. *Industrial & Labor Relations Review, 63*(1), 24–41. doi:10.1177/001979390906300102

Safa, N. A., Sookhak, M., Von Solms, R., Furnell, S., Ghani, N. A., & Herawan, T. (2015). Information security conscious care behavior formation in organizations. *Computers & Security, 53*, 65–78. doi:10.1016/j.cose.2015.05.012

Sarstedt, M., & Mooi, E. A. (2014). *A Concise Guide to Market Research: The Process, Data, and Methods Using IBM SPSS Statistics*. Berlin: Springer. doi:10.1007/978-3-642-53965-7

Sedikides, C., Herbst, K. C., Hardin, D. P., & Dardis, G. J. (2002). Accountability as a deterrent to self-enhancement: The search for mechanisms. *Journal of Personality and Social Psychology, 83*(3), 592–605. doi:10.1037/0022-3514.83.3.592 PMID:12219856

Siponen, M., Mahmood, A., & Pahnila, S. (2014). Employees' adherence to information security policies: An exploratory field study. *Information & Management, 51*(2), 217–224. doi:10.1016/j.im.2013.08.006

Siponen, M., & Vance, A. O. (2010). Neutralization: New Insights into the Problem of Employee Systems Security Policy Violations. *Management Information Systems Quarterly, 34*(3), 487–502. doi:10.2307/25750688

Sivalogathasan, V., & Hashim, A. (2013). changes in employee relations: Impact of perceived organizational support on social exchange of the outsourcing industry in Sri Lanka. *Skyline Business Journal, 9*(1), 43–49.

Slusky, L., & Partow-Navid, P. (2012). Students information security practices and awareness. *Journal of Information Privacy and Security, 8*(4), 3–6. doi:10.1080/15536548.2012.10845664

Stanciu, V., & Tinca, A. (2016). Students' awareness on information security between own perception and reality – an empirical study. *Accounting & Management Information Systems, 15*(1), 112–130.

Styles, M., & Tryfonas, T. (2009). Using Penetration Testing Feedback to Cultivate an of Proactive Security amongst End-users. *Information Management & Computer Security, 17*(1), 44–52. doi:10.1108/09685220910944759

Tadmor, C., & Tetlock, P. E. (2009). Accountability. In D. Matsumoto (Ed.), *The Cambridge Dictionary of Psychology* (p. 8). Cambridge: Cambridge University Press.

The Gale Group, Inc. (1970). *The Great Soviet Encyclopedia(1970-1979)* (3rd ed.). Retrieved from http://encyclopedia2.thefreedictionary.com/Human+Relations+Theory

Towns, D., & Cobb, L. (2012). Notes on: GPS technology; employee monitoring enters a new era. *Labor Law Journal, 63*(3), 203–208.

Trcek, D., Trobec, R., Pavešic, N., & Tasic, J. F. (2007). Information systems security and human behaviour. *Behaviour & Information Technology, 26*(2), 113–118. doi:10.1080/01449290500330299

Tsohou, A., Karyda, M., Kokolakis, S., & Kiountouzis, E. (2012). Analyzing trajectories of information security awareness. *Information Technology & People, 25*(3), 327–352. doi:10.1108/09593841211254358

Tsohou, A., Karyda, M., Kokolakis, S., & Kiountouzis, E. (2015). Managing the introduction of information security awareness programmes in organisations. *European Journal of Information Systems, 24*(1), 38–58. doi:10.1057/ejis.2013.27

Urbach, N., & Ahlemann, F. (2010). Structural equation modeling in information systems research using partial least squares. *Journal of Information Technology Theory and Application, 11*(2), 5–40.

Vance, A., Lowry, P. B., & Eggett, D. (2013). Using accountability to reduce access policy violations in information systems. *Journal of Management Information Systems, 29*(4), 263–290. doi:10.2753/MIS0742-1222290410

Vance, A., Lowry, P. B., & Eggett, D. (2015). A new approach to the problem of access policy violations: Increasing perceptions of accountability through the user interface. *Management Information Systems Quarterly, 39*(2), 345–366. doi:10.25300/MISQ/2015/39.2.04

Whalen, T., & Gates, C. (2010). Watching the watchers: "voluntary monitoring" of infosec employees. *Information Management & Computer Security, 18*(1), 14–25. doi:10.1108/09685221011035232

Yaokumah, W., & Kumah, P. (2018). Exploring the Impact of Security Policy on Compliance. In *Global Implications of Emerging Technology Trends* (pp. 256–274). Hershey, PA: IGI Global.

Zaman, U., & Saif, M. I. (2016). Perceived accountability and conflict management styles as predictors of job performance of public officials in Pakistan. *Gomal University Journal of Research, 32*(2), 24–35.

Zhang, J., Reithel, B. J., & Li, H. (2009). Impact of perceived technical protection on security behaviors. *Information Management & Computer Security, 17*(4), 330–340. doi:10.1108/09685220910993980

Zhang, L., & McDowell, W. C. (2009). Am I really at risk? Determinants of online users' intentions to use strong passwords. *Journal of Internet Commerce, 8*(3–4), 180–197. doi:10.1080/15332860903467508

*Previously published in the Journal of Global Information Management (JGIM), 27(2); pages 102-121, copyright year 2019 by IGI Publishing (an imprint of IGI Global).*

# Chapter 10
# Factors Influencing Information Security Policy Compliance Behavior

**Kwame Simpe Ofori**
https://orcid.org/0000-0001-7725-9756
*School of Management and Economics, University of Electronic Science and Technology of China, China*

**Hod Anyigba**
*Nobel International Business School, Ghana*

**George Oppong Appiagyei Ampong**
*Department of Management, Ghana Technology University College, Ghana*

**Osaretin Kayode Omoregie**
*Department of Finance, Lagos Business School, Pan-Atlantic University, Nigeria*

**Makafui Nyamadi**
*Department of Operations and Information Systems, Business School, University of Ghana, Ghana*

**Eli Fianu**
*Ghana Technology University College, Ghana*

## ABSTRACT

*One of the major concerns of organizations in today's networked world is to unravel how employees comply with information security policies (ISPs) since the internal employee has been identified as the weakest link in security policy breaches. A number of studies have examined ISP compliance from the perspective of deterrence; however, there have been mixed results. The study seeks to examine information security compliance from the perspective of the general deterrence theory (GDT) and information security climate (ISC). Data was collected from 329 employees drawn from the five top-performing banks in Ghana and analyzed with PLS-SEM. Results from the study show that security education training and awareness, top-management's commitment for information security, and peer non-compliance behavior affect the information security climate in an organization. Information security climate, punishment severity, and certainty of deterrent were also found to influence employees' intention to comply with ISP. The implications, limitations, and directions for future research are discussed.*

DOI: 10.4018/978-1-6684-3698-1.ch010

# INTRODUCTION

*"Data breaches keep happening. So why don't you do something? – The New York Times"*

Worldwide IT security spending was poised to increase to $124 billion dollars in 2019 from $71.1 billion in 2017 (Gartner, 2018; Hwang et al., 2017). Big ticket cases of data breaches in 2017 and 2018 more than ever, highlighted the need for better systems and controls to curtail and contain data protection contraventions. Both small and large companies like Yahoo, AT&T Citi Bank, JP Morgan, and Equifax have all fallen prey to data protection problems, internally (New York Times, 2018). Data compliance has become a key competitive resource employed by firms to outpace their competitors – typically involving the adoption and use of security policy initiatives (Kim & Kim, 2017). It is therefore by no means an understatement when reiterated that information security and its application is pivotal to the firms growth and success (Doherty et al. 2009). Furthermore, clarity has been established that the human element is major cause of information security breachesin organizations. In other words information security policy behavior is key to improving information security levels in organizations (Balozian & Leidner, 2017).

Prior research has attempted to explain information security policy breaches through the General Deterrence Theory (Chan et al., 2005; Donalds & Osei-Bryson, 2020; C. Lee et al., 2016; S. M. Lee et al., 2004), Theory of Planned Behavior, Protection Motivation Theory and Organizational Theory (Rajab & Eydgahi, 2019). While organizational theory focuses on the effect of security climate on security policy compliance (Chan et al., 2005), deterrence theory highlights the effect of user awareness of IS security countermeasures on perceived certainty and severity of organizational sanctions (D'Arcy et al., 2009). According to the literature, one key way to encourage and motivate employees to comply with Information Security Policy (ISP) is the enforcement of sanctions under the general deterrence theory framework (GDT) (Aurigemma & Mattson, 2017). The GDT framework embraces disinsentives that match appropriate sanctions to violators of the ISP (Wall et al., 2013). In other words, if employees perceive that there are harsh penalties once they are caught violating information systems security policy; they are less likely to violate information systems security policy (Cheng et al., 2013). Further, Diver (2007) opines that understanding and interpreting the effects of sanctions are critical because employee non-compliance is typically the mainspring of all ISPs. This therefore almost certainly addresses the relevance of the GDT in enforcing ISP. As maintained by the literature, another major compliance attribute – information security climate – has been found to have significant impact on compliance because workplace quality devoid of anti-compliance behavior is driven by the nature of peer socialization in the organization (Yazdanmehr & Wang, 2016). Although studies on GDT and security climate have laid solid foundation in the field, they have largely been inconclusive with respect to compliance (Chen et al., 2018; D'Arcy et al., 2009; Herath et al., 2018; Herath & Rao, 2009; Safa et al., 2019).

Clearly, there is a lack of coherence on the integration of general deterrence theory (GDT) – a theory that speaks to compliance bahavior and organizational Information Security Climate (ISC). In this study, we use the GDT as a foundation to build an integrated information security policy compliance behavior model that incorporates critical turnaround factors: Information Security Climate (ISC), Intention to Comply (INT) and GDT constructs. This research attempts to provide a systematic insight of the factors affecting information security policy compliance. In particular, an attempt to highlight key antecedent factors affecting policy compliance behavior in order to enhance organizational capabilities of safeguarding systems to enhance productivity and security. Specifically, these factors can contribute to enhanced employee awareness creation, creating a conducive environment for security alertness and adoption and increasing employees' ability to comply with policies.

First, the research approaches security compliance behavior with a new approach. Although the GDT has been previously used to understand the reasons why employees will or will not comply with policy instruments in a given situation, it has yet to be used to interpret the security climate of organizations in management information systems (MIS) research. Second, components of information security policy compliance behavior perceived under the GDT is integrated with security climate to understand antecedent factors affecting policy compliance. It is expected that this study will provide a comprehensive understanding of how organizations need to effectively implement security compliance policies in today's dynamic business environment.

## BACKGROUND

## Background on Information Security Compliance

The ever-increasing use of information systems (IS) and its tools, the affordability of computers coupled with the level of dependency of today's world on information creates the need to secure data and enhance IS security at all times. The security of organizations IS largely depends on the type of IS policies in place as well as the degree to which these policies are implemented within the organization (Aurigemma & Panko, 2011; Hina & Dominic, 2018; Hu et al., 2012; Kolkowska et al., 2017; Sohrabi Safa et al., 2016). The extent to which IS policies support IS security have been proved to rely on the extent to which employees within the firm comply with these policies (Cram et al., 2017; D'Arcy & Herath, 2011). This need has raised concerns for research in the area of IS compliance by stakeholders in organizations; thus, the focus for this study.

The main aim for IS security in firms is to protect them from hackers and other external threats to getting the information from the client and from firms that can use this piece of stolen information unethically (Hina & Dominic, 2018; Kim & Kim, 2017; Nasir et al., 2018; Von Solms, 2005). To avoid the threats posed by these hackers, firms try to empower their employees through training provided by security experts in their information technology (IT) department to help them form an unbreakable link in their security chain (Alshare et al., 2018; Bansal et al., 2016; C. Lee et al., 2016). These security trainings take varied forms as individual employees have different levels of knowledge and understanding of IS security issues, thus, specified comprehensive guidelines are provided. These guidelines are referred to as IS security policies. It is always expected that all employees comply with these IS security policy guidelines at all times to foster strength in the firm's IS structure. Once any of these policies are broken or compromised, the firm becomes vulnerable to IS breaches and attacks from outside or from within, leading to 'insider threat' to IS security (Hina & Dominic, 2018; Siponen et al., 2014; Sommestad et al., 2014; Van Niekerk & Von Solms, 2010). Increasingly, apart from the usual external threats, internal threats are have seen sharp increases – growing in appetite.

For a completely assured IS security, there is the need for individuals to practise all the guidelines spelt out in the IS policy. Some of these policies may be seen as negligible to others but this may be very costly, considering the labor and logistics involved in undertaking them.This is termed as 'willful noncompliance' in the IT industry which comes with diverse repercussions (Aurigemma & Panko, 2011; Hardy, 2006; Hina & Dominic, 2018; Kolkowska et al., 2017; Sohrabi Safa et al., 2016; Vroom & Von

Solms, 2004). To avert these repercussions, it is prudent that firms enforce security compliance in all cases and at all times. These ISPs help firms lower and effectively manage IS risks, foster good corporate governance and information technology (IT) through security compliance (Da Veiga & Eloff, 2007; Moulton & Coles, 2003; Rocha Flores et al., 2014; Thomson & Von Solms, 2005; Von Solms, 2005).

## Organizational Information Security Climate

Studies have revealed that firm's information security climate develops in a similar way just as organizational culture (Alhogail, 2015; Alnatheer, 2015; Lacey, 2010; Van Niekerk & Von Solms, 2010). This usually starts with the firm's board approving the firms IS strategy for effective management of the firm's IS and its tools in the short to long term. The board is also responsible for the provision of the intent and direction for the utmost protection of its database and information through established IS policies in place. A case in point is that, the board can state in its IS security policy the value it places on its information as an asset to the business, thus the need for its confidentiality, integrity and preservation throughout its information lifecycle (Dhillon et al., 2016). In this regard, employees are expected to comply with the set of IS security policy of the firm at all times as influenced by intrinsic and extrinsic factors. This implies that the type of information security climate that materializes in firms is prudent to foster or hamper IS protection within firms. This need has caused firms to assess the information security climate at play in respective firms to determine whether this climate falls in line with the firm's strategy and vision in maintaining information security in the short to long term (D'Arcy & Greene, 2014; Da Veiga & Martins, 2015; Hina & Dominic, 2018).

Some studies have revealed that the presence and type of security culture in firms are crucial in individual employees' compliance with information security policies (Da Veiga & Eloff, 2010; Da Veiga, 2016; Hina & Dominic, 2018; Karlsson et al., 2018). Another study also posits that the establishment of an information security climate in firms has a positive impact on the way employees perceive and behave towards information security issues to guard against information breaches and other unethical security issues from internal or external sources (Parsons et al., 2010). Some critical success factors to information security climate in firms include: the support received from top management on information security, the establishment of an effective information security policy and its awareness creation, the training of staff on compliance with this information security policy, the assessment and analysis of risks of information security, the firm's organizational culture, and compliance with information security policy with ethical conducts (Alshare et al., 2018; Parsons et al., 2010). Among these factors, top management support stands out as a noteworthy predictor of firms' information security climate.

Employees are largely influenced by their peers based on the organizational norms they follow. To buttress this point, Venkatesh et al. (2003) find a significant relationship between social influence and intention to use information systems. Similarly, employees tend to copy the behavior of their peers and grow confident over their actions with time. Thompson et al. (1994, p. 173) also reiterates that "individuals with little experience will have their beliefs about job fit influenced by advertising, opinions expressed by peers, and current practices in the organization". An inexperienced employee may hold unrealistic beliefs about how senior colleagues may perceive their actions or inactions which makes them susceptible to social pressure. In practice, employees accomplish task and routines based on peer practices in order to minimize the fear of non-compliance. A non-compliance behavior in the context of information security refers to some degree of belief or ideas that peers are not rule following (Hwang et al., 2017). For example, Lee & Lee (2002) found that enhanced occupational subjective norms and the willingness to comply will decrease the misuse of secutity systems. This directly implies that employee's security compliance are predetermined by peers (Padayachee, 2012).

Studies have revealed that for top management to provide significant support in the establishment of good information security climate, there is the need for them to be educated and trained on information security issues (Chan et al., 2005; Goo et al., 2014; Shih, 2015; Yazdanmehr & Wang, 2016). The education and training of top management translate into a positive influence on building the right information security climate to help guard against insider and outsider security threats that arise in the course of business operations. From the above arguments, we propose that:

$H_1$: *Security Education, Training and Awareness has a significant positive influence on Information Security Climate.*

$H_2$: *Top-Management Commitment to Information Security positively affects Information Security Climate.*

$H_3$: *Information Security Climate positively affects employees' intention to comply with information security policy*

$H_4$: *Peer Non-Compliance Behavior has a negative effect Information Security Climate.*

## General Deterrence Theory

This study employs the General Deterrence Theory (GDT) in explaining the factors influencing information security policy compliance behavior. According to the GDT, people will generally weigh the pros and cons before they engage in any act of crime (Cameron, 1988; Stafford, 2015). They will only choose crime when they perceive the benefits associated with it pays. If the individuals come to the conclusion that there is a great chance of them being caught and a severe punishment meted-out accordingly, there is a higher chance that such individuals will not engage in these acts. Based on this theory, Herath & Rao (2009) posit that as the certainty and severity of punishment increases, the rate of unacceptable behavior in society or in firms will decrease. Thus, the severity and certainty of punishment will lead to a positive effect on the intent of individuals to engage in security compliance with information security policies of organizations (Siponen et al., 2014). Their study further revealed that the certainty to detect unacceptable behavior in firms has a positive impact on employees' intentions to comply with IS security policies at all times (Siponen et al., 2014).

Once the crime detection system of firms breaks down the intentions not to comply with IS security policy will increase (Milgrom & Roberts, 1982; Quackenbush, 2011; Sitren & Applegate, 2012; Stafford, 2015; Watling et al., 2010). Their study also revealed that deterrent severity had a greater impact on compliance than deterrent certainty (Stafford, 2015). Another study also revealed that sanctions which consisted severity, of social pressure from direct supervisors, colleagues and expert IS security staff, detection probability, social pressure and swiftness of legal sanctions have impact on the likelihood of compliance with IS policies (Cheng et al., 2014; D'Arcy et al., 2009; Johnson et al., 2015; Paternoster & Piquero, 1995; Williams & Hawkins, 1986; Zagare & Kilgour, 2000). These stands as countermeasures and strong disincentives that dissuade people from committing antisocial acts. In line with the arguments above, we therefore hypothesize that:

$H_5$: *Punishment Severity has a positive effect on employees' intention to comply with information security policy.*

$H_6$: *Deterrent Certainty has a positive effect on employees' intention to comply with information security policy.*

$H_7$: *Employees' intention to comply with the information security policy has a positive effect on employees' actual compliance behavior.*

*Figure 1. Hypothesized model*

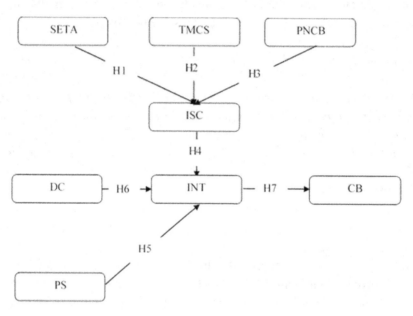

## METHODOLOGY

### Instrument Development

The measurement items for the latent variables in the current study were adopted from previous studies to improve content validity (Straub et al., 2004). In all, there were eight constructs, each of which were measured with multiple items. The items were, however, re-worded to reflect the context of the study environment. The resulting questionnaire was pretested with 25 experienced MIS professionals in the banking industry and senior researchers with expertise on the subject matter to review, give comments and make suggestions to improve the questions. Their comments were incorporated to make the questionnaire more comprehensible. Further, a pilot study was conducted with 85 employees to validate the instruments. Results from an exploratory factor analysis showed that the instrument had good validity.

### Measurement Instrument

Security Education, Training and Awareness was measured with five items adopted from D'Arcy, Hovav, and Galletta (2009). The three items used to measure Top management commitment to security (TMCS) was adopted from D'Arcy and Greene (2014). Peer Non-Compliance Behavior was measured with three items adopted from Hwang et al. (2017) while Information Security Climate was measured with five items adopted from Chan et al. (2005) and Goo et al. (2014). Perceived Severity of punishment was measured with three items adopted from Herath and Rao (2009) and Son (2011). The three items used to measure Deterrent Certainty was adopted from Son (2011) while Compliance Intention was measured with four items derived from Ifinedo (2012). Lastly, Compliance behavior was measured with four items derived from Siponen, Mahmood, and Pahnila (2014) and Humaidi and Balakrishnan (2017). All the measurement items were presented in English and measured using a five-point Likert scale anchored between strongly disagree (1) and strongly agree (5).

## Sample And Data Collection

In order to test the hypothesized research model, the researchers adopted a survey research methodology to collect data. Due to the nature of the study, permission had to be sought from top management of the banks considered in the survey. High level and mid-level information systems managers in the 5 topmost performing banks in Ghana were considered for the study. The researchers explained the importance of the research to the managers and assured them that the data collected will be treated with the utmost confidentiality. The researchers also promised to share a summary of their findings with the managers. Having convinced the managers to allow us to perform our study with their banks, we shared a link to our web-based survey which they in turn sent to their employee mailing list. A total of 1235 employees at various levels were contacted via email to fill the web-based questionnaire. After two weeks, 213 employees had responded. The managers resent the link to the web-based questionnaire after two weeks and reminded employees who had not previously completed the questionnaire to do so in the next two weeks of grace period. In the next two weeks, 116 more employees responded. Since the web-based questionnaire was configured to force respondents to answer all questions, none of the responses were discarded. A total of 329 respondents participated in the survey. Of this number, 172 were males and 157 were females.

## Common Method Bias

Common method bias could pose a threat to the conclusions drawn from the hypothesized relationships since the study adopts a cross-sectional design and also because both dependent and independent variables are collected from the same respondents (Podsakoff, Mackenzie, and Podsakoff, 2003). Suggestions by Mackenzie and Podsakoff (2012) were followed to address any issues of common method bias. First of all, some items were reversed to guarantee that all responses do not correspond to a larger effect. Secondly, items were randomly arranged in the questionnaire in order to reduce floor effect that may force respondents to provide monotonous responses from participants. Finally, the Harman's one factor test was employed to check the potential existence of common method bias. The first factor accounts for only 25.23%, which shows that common method bias is not likely to pose a significant problem in this study.

## RESULTS AND ANALYSIS

Data collected from the survey was analysed using the Partial Least Square approach to Structural Equation Modeling (PLS-SEM) on SmartPLS Version 3. Structural Equation Modeling (SEM) allowed the researchers to test causal relationships between latent variables in the proposed research model. There are two approaches to SEM (Hair et al., 2014); the covariance-based SEM that requires the data to exhibit multivariate normality and the variance-based approach PLS-SEM which does not require multivariate normality. A preliminary study of the data collected showed that the data was non-normal, hence our choice of PLS-SEM. In line with the two-step approach to evaluating Structural Equation Models recommended by Chin (1998) the reliability and validity of the measurement model was first tested and then the significance of structural paths between the latent constructs in the hypothesized model were also assessed.

### Measurement Model Assessment

The measurement model was assessed based on reliability, convergent validity and discriminant validity. The reliability of the constructs was assessed with Cronbach's alpha and composite reliability. From Table 1 it can be seen that both Cronbach's alpha and Composite reliability values for all constructs are compellingly higher than 0.7 threshold recommended by Henseler, Hubona, and Ray (2016). Convergent validity of the measurement model was assessed using the Average Variance Extracted. Hair et al. (2014) recommend that AVE should be greater than 0.5 for convergent validity to be assured. From Table 1 it can be seen that AVE values for all constructs are greater than the 0.5 threshold, indicative of good convergent validity.

Discriminant validity is assured when the following three conditions are met: (a) the loadings of each construct is greater than the cross loadings with other constructs (Chin, 1998); (b) the square root of the AVE for each construct is greater than the correlation between that construct and any other construct (Fornell & Larcker, 1981); (c) the heterotrait-monotrait ratio of correlations (HTMT) values are less than 0.85. From Table 2 it can be seen that the loadings of each construct are greater than the cross-loadings. The results in Table 2 shows that the square root of the AVE for each construct is greater than the cross correlation with other constructs. Finally, results of the more recent $HTMT_{0.85}$ criterion presented in Table 3 also proves discriminant validity has been achieved. In all, the results showed that the psychometric properties of the measures used in the study were adequate.

### Structural Model Assessment

Having verified the measurements model, the structural model was assessed to determined whether the structural relations in the model being tested are meaningful. A bootstrap resampling procedure (with an iteration of 5000 sub-samples drawn with replacements from the initial sample of 329) was used to determine the significance of the path coefficients in the structural model. The explanatory power of the structural model was assessed by its ability to predict endogenous construct using the coefficient of determination $R^2$. Results for the assessment of the structural model are presented in Table 4 and Figure 2.

*Table 1. Factor loadings and reliability statistics*

|  | CB | INT | DC | ISC | PNCB | PS | SETA | TMCS | α | C.R | A.V.E |
|---|---|---|---|---|---|---|---|---|---|---|---|
| CB1 | **0.856** | 0.584 | 0.390 | 0.368 | -0.155 | 0.308 | 0.387 | 0.285 | 0.857 | 0.902 | 0.700 |
| CB2 | **0.847** | 0.555 | 0.461 | 0.386 | -0.220 | 0.347 | 0.346 | 0.254 | | | |
| CB3 | **0.887** | 0.537 | 0.400 | 0.288 | -0.180 | 0.317 | 0.238 | 0.244 | | | |
| CB4 | **0.750** | 0.428 | 0.218 | 0.288 | -0.162 | 0.274 | 0.250 | 0.252 | | | |
| INT1 | 0.482 | **0.838** | 0.533 | 0.301 | -0.197 | 0.519 | 0.275 | 0.224 | 0.887 | 0.922 | 0.747 |
| INT2 | 0.538 | **0.886** | 0.574 | 0.372 | -0.165 | 0.538 | 0.367 | 0.260 | | | |
| INT3 | 0.550 | **0.882** | 0.581 | 0.364 | -0.166 | 0.487 | 0.233 | 0.203 | | | |
| INT4 | 0.616 | **0.851** | 0.524 | 0.387 | -0.219 | 0.482 | 0.356 | 0.285 | | | |
| DC1 | 0.437 | 0.594 | **0.889** | 0.309 | -0.197 | 0.502 | 0.361 | 0.226 | 0.848 | 0.908 | 0.768 |
| DC2 | 0.415 | 0.561 | **0.901** | 0.307 | -0.194 | 0.496 | 0.403 | 0.274 | | | |
| DC3 | 0.319 | 0.524 | **0.837** | 0.241 | -0.153 | 0.421 | 0.250 | 0.135 | | | |
| ISC1 | 0.371 | 0.349 | 0.313 | **0.842** | -0.412 | 0.242 | 0.390 | 0.520 | 0.865 | 0.908 | 0.712 |
| ISC2 | 0.336 | 0.390 | 0.291 | **0.845** | -0.385 | 0.177 | 0.332 | 0.439 | | | |
| ISC3 | 0.364 | 0.354 | 0.259 | **0.873** | -0.372 | 0.162 | 0.420 | 0.461 | | | |
| ISC4 | 0.269 | 0.298 | 0.236 | **0.813** | -0.333 | 0.163 | 0.368 | 0.414 | | | |
| PNCB1 | -0.173 | -0.193 | -0.204 | -0.466 | **0.936** | -0.123 | -0.229 | -0.160 | 0.913 | 0.945 | 0.851 |
| PNCB2 | -0.203 | -0.178 | -0.163 | -0.370 | **0.918** | -0.099 | -0.216 | -0.090 | | | |
| PNCB3 | -0.223 | -0.227 | -0.206 | -0.390 | **0.914** | -0.106 | -0.240 | -0.076 | | | |
| PS1 | 0.285 | 0.539 | 0.494 | 0.215 | -0.146 | **0.880** | 0.245 | 0.129 | 0.847 | 0.907 | 0.765 |
| PS2 | 0.320 | 0.471 | 0.419 | 0.118 | -0.042 | **0.862** | 0.189 | 0.137 | | | |
| PS3 | 0.376 | 0.522 | 0.501 | 0.243 | -0.117 | **0.881** | 0.321 | 0.168 | | | |
| SETA1 | 0.293 | 0.252 | 0.306 | 0.394 | -0.262 | 0.177 | **0.801** | 0.291 | 0.846 | 0.889 | 0.617 |
| SETA2 | 0.319 | 0.274 | 0.308 | 0.358 | -0.174 | 0.233 | **0.760** | 0.269 | | | |
| SETA3 | 0.317 | 0.322 | 0.326 | 0.358 | -0.189 | 0.268 | **0.813** | 0.342 | | | |
| SETA4 | 0.308 | 0.298 | 0.289 | 0.254 | -0.090 | 0.278 | **0.774** | 0.230 | | | |
| SETA5 | 0.222 | 0.267 | 0.293 | 0.363 | -0.221 | 0.205 | **0.777** | 0.201 | | | |
| TMCS1 | 0.260 | 0.220 | 0.154 | 0.381 | -0.036 | 0.119 | 0.244 | **0.809** | 0.821 | 0.893 | 0.735 |
| TMCS2 | 0.238 | 0.220 | 0.194 | 0.476 | -0.080 | 0.174 | 0.287 | **0.874** | | | |
| TMCS3 | 0.295 | 0.281 | 0.264 | 0.529 | -0.176 | 0.131 | 0.338 | **0.888** | | | |

Note: CB – Cmpliance Behavior, INT – Compliance Intention, DC – Deterent Certainty, ISC – Information Security Climate, PNCB – Peer Non-Compliance Behavior, PS – Punishment Severity, SETA – Security Education, Training and Awareness, TMSC – Top Management Commitment for Information Security, α – Cronbach's alpha, C.R – Composite Reliability, AVE – Average Variance Extracted

In support of hypotheses H1, Security Education, Training and Awareness (SETA) was found to have a significant positive effect on Information Security Climate (β = 0.216, p = 0.000). Top Management Commitment to Information Security (TMCS) was found to have the most significant effect on Information Security Climate (β = 0.430, p = 0.000). Peer Non-Compliance Behavior (PNCB) was also found to have a significant negative effect on Information Security Climate (β = -0.341, p = 0.000), providing support for H3. This result implies that as Peer Non-Compliance behavior increase it is expected that a non-favorable information security climate would be formed. As expected, Information Security Climate was found to have a significant positive impact on employee' Intention to comply with information security policy ($\beta = 0.212$, $p = 0.000$). Deterrent Certainty was found to have the most significant effect on employees Intention to comply with Information Security Policy ($\beta = 0.395$, $p = 0.000$). Punishment Severity was also found to have a significant effect on employees Intention to comply with information security policy ($\beta = 0.324$, $p = 0.000$), providing support for H6. As expected employees' Intention to comply with information security policy was found to have a significant positive effect on Actual Compliance Behavior ($\beta = 0.634$, $p = 0.000$). In all 40.2% of the variance in Compliance behavior was explained by the model. The overall fitness of the model was assessed using the SRMR composite factor model. The composite model SRMR value for the model was 0.055, below the 0.08 threshold recommended by Hu and Bentler (1999). This is an indication that the proposed model presents a good model fit.

*Table 2. Testing discriminant validity using Fornell-Larcker criterion*

|  | CB | INT | DC | ISC | PNCB | PS | SETA | TMCS |
|---|---|---|---|---|---|---|---|---|
| CB | **0.837** |  |  |  |  |  |  |  |
| INT | 0.634 | **0.864** |  |  |  |  |  |  |
| DC | 0.448 | 0.640 | **0.876** |  |  |  |  |  |
| ISC | 0.400 | 0.413 | 0.327 | **0.844** |  |  |  |  |
| PNCB | -0.214 | -0.216 | -0.208 | -0.447 | **0.923** |  |  |  |
| PS | 0.373 | 0.585 | 0.541 | 0.222 | -0.119 | **0.875** |  |  |
| SETA | 0.370 | 0.357 | 0.388 | 0.448 | -0.247 | 0.290 | **0.785** |  |
| TMCS | 0.309 | 0.282 | 0.243 | 0.546 | -0.121 | 0.166 | 0.342 | **0.857** |
| Note: Square root of the AVEs are shown in bold on the diagonal | | | | | | | | |

*Table 3. Testing discriminant validity using the HTMT ratio*

|  | CB | INT | DC | ISC | PNCB | PS | SETA | TMCS |
|---|---|---|---|---|---|---|---|---|
| CB |  |  |  |  |  |  |  |  |
| INT | 0.720 |  |  |  |  |  |  |  |
| DC | 0.512 | 0.736 |  |  |  |  |  |  |
| ISC | 0.459 | 0.469 | 0.378 |  |  |  |  |  |
| PNCB | 0.245 | 0.240 | 0.234 | 0.496 |  |  |  |  |
| PS | 0.438 | 0.674 | 0.634 | 0.254 | 0.131 |  |  |  |
| SETA | 0.431 | 0.413 | 0.454 | 0.513 | 0.271 | 0.346 |  |  |
| TMCS | 0.368 | 0.327 | 0.282 | 0.636 | 0.127 | 0.198 | 0.401 |  |

*Table 4. Hypotheses testing*

| Hypotheses | Path | Path Coefficient | T Statistics | P Values | Result |
|---|---|---|---|---|---|
| H1 | SETA →ISC | 0.216 | 4.189 | 0.000 | Supported |
| H2 | TMCS →ISC | 0.430 | 8.332 | 0.000 | Supported |
| H3 | PNCB→ ISC | -0.341 | 7.687 | 0.000 | Supported |
| H4 | ISC →INT | 0.212 | 4.565 | 0.000 | Supported |
| H5 | PS → INT | 0.324 | 4.950 | 0.000 | Supported |
| H6 | DC →INT | 0.395 | 5.545 | 0.000 | Supported |
| H7 | INT → CB | 0.634 | 12.617 | 0.000 | Supported |
| Model Fit | | | | | |
| SRMR | 0.055 | | | | |

*Figure 2. Estimated structural model*

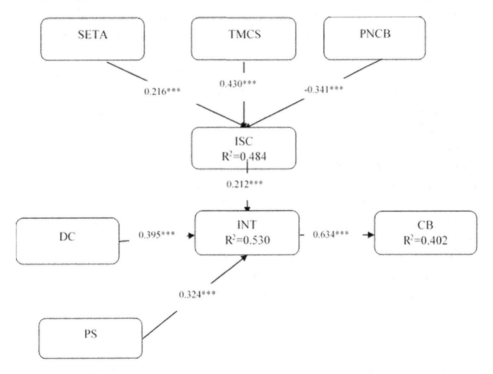

## SOLUTIONS AND RECOMMENDATIONS

Following the model of this study based on integrated Information Security Climate and the General Deterrence Theory, seven hypotheses were stated to be tested. Findings from the analysis using the Partial Least Square approach to Structural Equation Modeling (PLS-SEM) suggest that all the relationships stated are all supported empirically. This suggests that all the constructs of information security climate and general deterrence theory are significant in explaining information security compliance behavior of employees in Ghana. By implication, security climate and deterrence influence information security policy compliance behavior.

Findings from our analysis confirmed the positive influence of security education, training and awareness on information security climate as did the hypothesis that stated that security education, training and awareness have a significant positive influence on information security climate. This suggests that security education, training and awareness inherent in an organization would improve the security climate of the organization. Also, the management of information systems must invest in education, training and awareness programmes for employees over time. The practice will become institutionalized over time as everyone in the organization will become conscious of information security and as a result most employees will be willing to follow the rules guiding the use of the information system. This finding is evident in studies such as (D'Arcy et al. 2009; Thomson & van Niekerk, 2012; Hwang et al. 2017; D'Arcy & Greene, 2014), who submitted that efforts by organizations that improve the awareness, training and education of employees have significant influence on information security climate.

In the same vein, the statement that top-management commitment for information security positively affects information security climate is upheld. The implication of this is that favorable behavior of top managers toward information security policy (in terms of compliance, supervision, education, training, procedures, regulations and awareness, behavior, and investment in security system) improves employees' perception of information security climate towards compliance behavior. In other words, when employees observe commitment to information security by top managers, their perception of information security climate improve and are motivated to comply with information security policies. Findings from Chan et al (2005); Hu et al. (2012), D'Arcy & Greene (2014) support this finding as they share the opinion that top-managers behavior toward information security policy influence information security climate.

Similarly, the third hypothesis of this study stating that peer non-compliance behavior has a negative effect on information security climate was supported statistically (t=7.69, $p<0.05$) with a path coefficient of -0.341. This suggests that observed non-compliance behavior of fellow workers in an organization will negatively impact the perception of the information security climate which might influence other employees in the organization to behave in an illicit manner. This finding is as well supported by existing literature (see Chan et al. 2005; Goo et al. 2013; Cheng et al. 2013; Hwang et al. 2017)

Security education, training and awareness, top-management commitment and peer behavior was found to impact information security climate significantly. It is further revealed that information security climate significantly affect intentions to comply with information security policy (t=4.57, $p<0.05$) as presented in the fourth hypothesis of this study with a path coefficient of 0.212. The result suggests that favorable perception of the information security climate of an organization positively influence employees' intention to comply with information security policy. The implication here is that, when an employee develops a security climate with compliance behavior, the intention to follow information security guidelines is motivated within him/her. This finding also follows from existing literature such as Goo et al. (2014), Chan et al. (2005) and D'Arcy and Greene (2014) who report findings that suggest the positive influence of information security climate on the compliance behavior of employees towards information security policies.

In terms of deterrence, the hypothesis that "punishment severity has a positive effect employees' intention to comply with information security policy" is statistically supported. This finding suggests that the perception of severity of punishment positively influences information security system compliance intention which implies that as the perception of severity and cruelty of punishment for committing illicit act with the information system increases there is increased intention to follow security rules of the organization. Likewise, this finding is consistent with the those of Hareth & Rao (2009), Cheng et al. (2013), D'Arcy et al. (2009), Ifinedo (2012, 2016) and Siponen et al (2014).

Moreover, findings on the deterrent certainty confirm the argument that certainty of sanction will motivate employees' compliance intention. Finding from the analysis support our argument as stated in the fifth hypothesis. This finding as against the submissions of most studies in the literature (for example see Cheng et al. (2013), Hareth & Rao (2009), Klien & Luciano (2016) and Ifinedo (2016)) suggest insignificance of certainty of punishment to compliance behavior shows that deterrence certainty is even important that severity of deterrence as the observed coefficient is greater than that of severity. By implication, when the perception of certainty of being caught or detected is high, employees are demotivated to violate security system instructions and thereby motivate the intentions to comply with security policy. This is also corroborated by D'Arcy et al. (2009) who found positive effect of certainty of sanction on compliance behavior towards information security policy.

All the factors of interest of this study that influence compliance intention have been upheld by the analysis. The result from the analysis further supports the positive influence of intentions to comply with information security policy on actual information security policy compliance behavior. It suggests that information security policy compliance intention strongly and positively affects actual information security compliance behavior. This finding is also evident in the works of Sponen et al. (2014), Siponen et al (2010) and Sommestad et al. (2015).

## FUTURE RESEARCH DIRECTIONS

As evidenced by most research, our own research has some limitations. First of all, the study was based on data collected from employees of only the five top-performing banks in Ghana. Care should be taken when generalizing the findings to the whole banking sector of the financial services sector in Ghana or elsewhere. In the future, researchers could replicate the study to cover other sectors of the economy or other financial institutions outside the banking sector. Even though a number of precautionary measures, such as safeguarding the anonymity of the participants and use of hypothetical scenarios of the company were taken to prevent the possibility of evaluation apprehension bias, some participants in our survey may still have provided responses that are socially desirable instead of how they actually feel. The study was also based on the general deterrence theory, which deals more with coercive controls. In future studies, it would be interesting to explore remunerative factors too.

## CONCLUSION

Though recent studies are emphasizing the adoption factors that are intrinsic to employees in order to encourage compliance behavior, this study presents some fundamental findings that may benefit information system managers. Organizations are established to achieve preconceived goals and as such are unwilling to allow some callous behavior from deviant employees to truncate the successful achievement of these set goals. Findings from this study revealed that contextual variables are important to motivating compliance with information security policy. Therefore, information system managers are adviced to ensure that top managers lead by example in following information security policy. Top managers also ought to put in place measures that will encourage compliance behavior in their organizations – in this context, banks. More so, continual awareness and training should be initiated to better acquaint employees of the dangers of non-compliance and the existence of punishment for violation of laid down security policies.

In addition, the study presented findings concerning deterrence. Severity and certainty of sactions are revealed to significantly influence compliance behavior. Additionaly, this study places more importance on certainty than severity of sanctions. Therefore, information system managers are advised to implement a deterrent framework that will be swift and certain to detect non-compliance with information security policy. More so, the punishment to such act should be severe enough to serve as example and deterrent for other employees.

Some studies have downplayed the importance of General Deterrence theory based on the some intrinsic arguments. However, this study has come to uphold the importance of the deterrence construct on information security compliance. Moreover, contrary to studies that have upheld only the severity of punishment and suggested that certainty of punishment is not important, this study has posited that certainty of deterrence is more important. This finding cannot be adjudged to be erroneous. Logically, a very severe punishment can only be implemented when the certainty of deterrent is high. It becomes useless when the certainty of the punishment or deterrent is low. This study further justifies the use of environmental or contextual factors as important factors in explaining information security policy compliance behavior as all the considered constructs are revealed to be influential on compliance. Therefore, this study provides an empirical validation of the General Deterrence theory and the Security Climate framework of information security compliance behavior.

# REFERENCES

Alhogail, A. (2015). Design and validation of information security culture framework. *Computers in Human Behavior*, 49(1), 567–575. doi:10.1016/j.chb.2015.03.054

Alnatheer, M. A. (2015). Information Security Culture Critical Success Factors. 12th International Conference on Information Technology - New Generations, 37–86. 10.1109/ITNG.2015.124

Alshare, K. A., Lane, P. L., & Lane, M. R. (2018). Information security policy compliance: A higher education case study. *Information and Computer Security*, 26(1), 91–108. doi:10.1108/ICS-09-2016-0073

Aurigemma, S., & Mattson, T. (2017). Deterrence and punishment experience impacts on ISP compliance attitudes. *Information and Computer Security*, 25(4), 421–436. doi:10.1108/ICS-11-2016-0089

Aurigemma, S., & Panko, R. (2011). A composite framework for behavioral compliance with information security policies. *Proceedings of the Annual Hawaii International Conference on System Sciences*, 3248–3257. 10.1109/HICSS.2012.49

Balozian, P., & Leidner, D. (2017). Review of IS Security Policy Compliance. *ACM SIGMIS Database: The DATABASE for Advances in Information Systems*, 48(3), 11–43. doi:10.1145/3130515.3130518

Bansal, G., Green, W., Hodorff, K., & Marshall, K. (2016). *Moral Beliefs and Organizational Information Security Policy Compliance : The Role of Gender*. Academic Press.

Cameron, S. (1988). The Economics of Crime Deterrence: A Survey of Theory and Evidence. *Kyklos*, *41*(2), 301–323. doi:10.1111/j.1467-6435.1988.tb02311.x

Chan, M., Woon, I., & Kankanhalli, A. (2005). Perceptions of information security at the workplace : Linking information security climate to compliant behavior. *Journal of Information Privacy and Security*, *1*(3), 18–41. doi:10.1080/15536548.2005.10855772

Chen, X., Wu, D., Chen, L., & Teng, J. K. L. (2018). Sanction severity and employees' information security policy compliance: Investigating mediating, moderating, and control variables. *Information & Management*, *55*(8), 1049–1060. doi:10.1016/j.im.2018.05.011

Cheng, L., Li, W., Zhai, Q., & Smyth, R. (2014). Understanding personal use of the Internet at work: An integrated model of neutralization techniques and general deterrence theory. *Computers in Human Behavior*, *38*, 220–228. doi:10.1016/j.chb.2014.05.043

Cheng, L., Li, Y., Li, W., Holm, E., & Zhai, Q. (2013). Understanding the violation of IS security policy in organizations: An integrated model based on social control and deterrence theory. *Computers & Security*, *39*, 447–459. doi:10.1016/j.cose.2013.09.009

Chin, W. W. (1998). The partial least squares approach to structural equation modeling. In G. A. Marcoulides (Ed.), *Modern Methods for Business Research* (Vol. 295, pp. 295–336). Lawrence Erlbaum Associates, Publisher; doi:10.1016/j.aap.2008.12.010

Cram, W. A., Proudfoot, J. G., & D'Arcy, J. (2017). Organizational information security policies: A review and research framework. *European Journal of Information Systems*, *26*(6), 605–641. doi:10.105741303-017-0059-9

D'Arcy, J., & Greene, G. (2014). Security culture and the employment relationship as drivers of employees' security compliance. *Information Management & Computer Security*, *22*(5), 474–489. doi:10.1108/IMCS-08-2013-0057

D'Arcy, J., & Herath, T. (2011). A review and analysis of deterrence theory in the IS security literature: Making sense of the disparate findings. *European Journal of Information Systems*, *20*(6), 643–658. doi:10.1057/ejis.2011.23

D'Arcy, J., Hovav, A., & Galletta, D. (2009). User awareness of security countermeasures and its impact on information systems misuse: A deterrence approach. *Information Systems Research*, *20*(1), 79–98. doi:10.1287/isre.1070.0160

Da Veiga, A. (2007). An information security governance framework. *Information Systems Management*, *24*(4), 361–372. doi:10.1080/10580530701586136

Da Veiga, A. (2016). Comparing the information security culture of employees who had read the information security policy and those who had not Illustrated through an empirical study. *Information and Computer Security*, *24*(2), 139–151. doi:10.1108/ICS-12-2015-0048

Da Veiga, A., & Eloff, J. H. P. (2010). A framework and assessment instrument for information security culture. *Computers & Security*, *29*(2), 196–207. doi:10.1016/j.cose.2009.09.002

Da Veiga, A., & Martins, N. (2015). Information security culture and information protection culture: A validated assessment instrument. *Computer Law & Security Review*, *31*(2), 243–256. doi:10.1016/j.clsr.2015.01.005

Dhillon, G., Syed, R., & Pedron, C. (2016). Interpreting information security culture: An organizational transformation case study. *Computers & Security*, *56*, 63–69. doi:10.1016/j.cose.2015.10.001

Diver, S. (2007). Information security policy –adevelopment guide for large and small companies, Sans Institute.

Doherty, N., Anastasakis, L., & Fulford, H. (2009). Institutional repository the information security policy unpacked : A critical study of the content of university policies. *International Journal of Information Management*, *29*(6), 449–457. doi:10.1016/j.ijinfomgt.2009.05.003

Donalds, C., & Osei-Bryson, K. M. (2020). Cybersecurity compliance behavior: Exploring the influences of individual decision style and other antecedents. *International Journal of Information Management*, *51*, 102056. doi:10.1016/j.ijinfomgt.2019.102056

Fornell, C., & Larcker, D. F. (1981). Evaluating structural equation models with unobservable variables and measurements error. *JMR, Journal of Marketing Research*, *18*(1), 39–50. doi:10.1177/002224378101800104

Gartner. (2018, August). Gartner forecasts worldwide information security spending to exceed $124 billion in 2019. *Gartner Newsroom*.

Goo, J., Yim, M. S., & Kim, D. J. (2014). A path to successful management of employee security compliance: An empirical study of information security climate. *IEEE Transactions on Professional Communication*, *57*(4), 286–308. doi:10.1109/TPC.2014.2374011

Hair, J. F., Hult, T. M., Ringle, C., & Sarstedt, M. (2014). *A Primer on Partial Least Squares Structural Equation Modeling (PLS-SEM)*. Sage Publications. doi:10.1016/j.lrp.2013.01.002

Hardy, G. (2006). Using IT governance and COBIT to deliver value with IT and respond to legal, regulatory and compliance challenges. *Information Security Technical Report*, *11*(1), 55–61. doi:10.1016/j.istr.2005.12.004

Henseler, J., Hubona, G., & Ray, P. A. (2016). Using PLS path modeling in new technology research : Updated guidelines. *Industrial Management & Data Systems*, *116*(1), 2–20. doi:10.1108/IMDS-09-2015-0382

Herath, T., & Rao, R. H. (2009). Protection motivation and deterrence: A framework for security policy compliance in organisations. *European Journal of Information Systems*, *18*(2), 106–125. doi:10.1057/ejis.2009.6

Herath, T., Yim, M. S., D'Arcy, J., Nam, K., & Rao, H. R. (2018). Examining employee security violations: Moral disengagement and its environmental influences. *Information Technology & People*, *31*(6), 1135–1162. doi:10.1108/ITP-10-2017-0322

Hina, S., & Dominic, P. D. D. (2018). Information security policies ' compliance : A perspective for higher education institutions. *Journal of Computer Information Systems*, 1–11. doi:10.1080/08874417.2018.1432996

Hu, L., & Bentler, P. M. (1999). Cutoff criteria for fit indexes in covariance structure analysis: Conventional criteria versus new alternatives. *Structural Equation Modeling*, 6(1), 1–55. doi:10.1080/10705519909540118

Hu, Q., Dinev, T., Hart, P., & Cooke, D. (2012). Managing Employee Compliance with Information Security Policies: The Critical Role of Top Management and Organizational Culture. *Decision Sciences*, 43(4), 615–660. doi:10.1111/j.1540-5915.2012.00361.x

Humaidi, N., & Balakrishnan, V. (2017). Indirect effect of management support on users' compliance behaviour towards information security policies. *The HIM Journal*, 47(1), 17–27. doi:10.1177/1833358317700255 PMID:28537207

Hwang, I., Kim, D., Kim, T., & Kim, S. (2017). Why not comply with information security? An empirical approach for the causes of non-compliance. *Online Information Review*, 41(1), 2–18. doi:10.1108/OIR-11-2015-0358

Ifinedo, P. (2012). Understanding information systems security policy compliance: An integration of the theory of planned behavior and the protection motivation theory. *Computers & Security*, 31(1), 83–95. doi:10.1016/j.cose.2011.10.007

Johnson, J. C., Leeds, B. A., & Wu, A. (2015). Capability, Credibility, and Extended General Deterrence. *International Interactions*, 41(2), 309–336. doi:10.1080/03050629.2015.982115

Karlsson, M., Denk, T., & Åström, J. (2018). Perceptions of organizational culture and value conflicts in information security management. *Information and Computer Security*, 26(2), 213–229. doi:10.1108/ICS-08-2017-0058

Kim, S. S., & Kim, Y. J. (2017). The effect of compliance knowledge and compliance support systems on information security compliance behavior. *Journal of Knowledge Management*, 21(4), 986–1010. doi:10.1108/JKM-08-2016-0353

Kolkowska, E., Karlsson, F., & Hedström, K. (2017). Journal of Strategic Information Systems Towards analysing the rationale of information security non-compliance : Devising a Value-Based Compliance analysis method. *The Journal of Strategic Information Systems*, 26(1), 39–57. doi:10.1016/j.jsis.2016.08.005

Lacey, D. (2010). Understanding and transforming organizational security culture. *Information Management & Computer Security*, 18(1), 4–13. doi:10.1108/09685221011035223

Lee, C., Lee, C. C., & Kim, S. (2016). Understanding information security stress: Focusing on the type of information security compliance activity. *Computers & Security*, 59, 60–70. doi:10.1016/j.cose.2016.02.004

Lee, J., & Lee, Y. (2002). A holistic model of computer abuse within organizations. *Information Management & Computer Security*, 10(2), 57–63. doi:10.1108/09685220210424104

Lee, S. M., Lee, S. G., & Yoo, S. (2004). An integrative model of computer abuse based on social control and general deterrence theories. *Information & Management*, 41(6), 707–718. doi:10.1016/j.im.2003.08.008

Mackenzie, S. B., & Podsakoff, P. M. (2012). Common method bias in marketing : Causes, mechanisms, and procedural Remedies. *Journal of Retailing*, 88(4), 542–555. doi:10.1016/j.jretai.2012.08.001

Milgrom, P., & Roberts, J. (1982). Predation, reputation, and entry deterrence. *Journal of Economic Theory, 27*(2), 280–312. doi:10.1016/0022-0531(82)90031-X

Moulton, R., & Coles, R. S. (2003). Applying information security governance. *Computers & Security, 22*(7), 580–584. doi:10.1016/S0167-4048(03)00705-3

Nasir, A., Arshah, R. A., & Hamid, M. R. A. (2018). The Significance of Main Constructs of Theory of Planned Behavior in Recent Information Security Policy Compliance Behavior Study : A Comparison among Top Three Behavioral Theories. *IACSIT International Journal of Engineering and Technology, 7*(29), 737–741. doi:10.14419/ijet.v7i2.29.14008

Padayachee, K. (2012). Taxonomy of compliant information security behavior. *Computers & Security, 31*(5), 673–680. doi:10.1016/j.cose.2012.04.004

Parsons, K., Mccormac, A., Butavicius, M., & Ferguson, L. (2010). *Human factors and information security : Individual, culture and security environment.* Science And Technology. doi:10.14722/ndss.2014.23268

Paternoster, R., & Piquero, A. (1995). Reconceptualizing deterrence: An empirical test of personal and vicarious experiences. *Journal of Research in Crime and Delinquency, 32*(3), 251–286. doi:10.1177/0022427895032003001

Podsakoff, P. M., Mackenzie, S. B., & Podsakoff, N. P. (2003). Common method biases in behavioral research: A critical review of the literature. *The Journal of Applied Psychology, 88*(5), 879–903. doi:10.1037/0021-9010.88.5.879 PMID:14516251

Quackenbush, S. L. (2011). Deterrence theory: Where do we stand? *Review of International Studies, 37*(2), 741–762. doi:10.1017/S0260210510000896

Rajab, M., & Eydgahi, A. (2019). Evaluating the explanatory power of theoretical frameworks on intention to comply with information security policies in higher education. *Computers & Security, 80,* 211–223. doi:10.1016/j.cose.2018.09.016

Rocha Flores, W., Antonsen, E., & Ekstedt, M. (2014). Information security knowledge sharing in organizations: Investigating the effect of behavioral information security governance and national culture. *Computers & Security, 43*(1), 90–110. doi:10.1016/j.cose.2014.03.004

Safa, N. S., Maple, C., Furnell, S., Azad, M. A., Perera, C., Dabbagh, M., & Sookhak, M. (2019). Deterrence and prevention-based model to mitigate information security insider threats in organisations. *Future Generation Computer Systems, 97,* 587–597. doi:10.1016/j.future.2019.03.024

Shih, S. P., & Liou, J. Y. (2015). Investigate the Effects of Information Security Climate and Psychological Ownership on Information Security Policy Compliance. In PACIS (p. 28).

Siponen, M., Adam Mahmood, M., & Pahnila, S. (2014). Employees' adherence to information security policies: An exploratory field study. *Information & Management, 51*(2), 217–224. doi:10.1016/j.im.2013.08.006

Sitren, A. H., & Applegate, B. K. (2012). Testing Deterrence Theory with Offenders: The Empirical Validity of Stafford and Warr's Model. *Deviant Behavior, 33*(6), 492–506. doi:10.1080/01639625.201 1.636685

Sohrabi Safa, N., Von Solms, R., & Furnell, S. (2016). Information security policy compliance model in organizations. *Computers & Security, 56*, 1–13. doi:10.1016/j.cose.2015.10.006

Sommestad, T., Hallberg, J., Lundholm, K., & Bengtsson, J. (2014). Variables influencing information security policy compliance. *Information Management & Computer Security, 22*(1), 42–75. doi:10.1108/IMCS-08-2012-0045

Son, J. Y. (2011). Out of fear or desire? Toward a better understanding of employees' motivation to follow IS security policies. *Information & Management, 48*(7), 296–302. doi:10.1016/j.im.2011.07.002

Stafford, M. C. (2015). Deterrence Theory: Crime. In International Encyclopedia of the Social & Behavioral Sciences: Second Edition (pp. 18–168). doi:10.1016/B978-0-08-097086-8.45005-1

Straub, D., Boudreau, M.-C., & Gefen, D. (2004). Validation guidelines for IS positivistic research. *Communications of the Association for Information Systems, 13*(1), 380–427.

Thompson, R. L., Higgins, C. A., & Howell, J. M. (1994). Influence of experience on personal computer utilization: Testing a conceptual model. *Journal of Management Information Systems, 11*(1), 167–187. doi:10.1080/07421222.1994.11518035

Thomson, K. L., & Von Solms, R. (2005). Information security obedience: A definition. *Computers & Security, 24*(1), 69–75. doi:10.1016/j.cose.2004.10.005

Van Niekerk, J. F., & Von Solms, R. (2010). Information security culture: A management perspective. *Computers & Security, 29*(4), 476–486. doi:10.1016/j.cose.2009.10.005

Venkatesh, V., Morris, M. G., Davis, G. B., & Davis, F. D. (2003). User acceptance of information technology: Toward a unified view. *Management Information Systems Quarterly, 27*(3), 425–478. doi:10.2307/30036540

Von Solms, S. H. (2005). Information Security Governance - Compliance management vs operational management. *Computers & Security, 24*(6), 443–447. doi:10.1016/j.cose.2005.07.003

Vroom, C., & von Solms, R. (2004). Towards information security behavioural compliance. *Computers & Security, 23*(3), 191–198. doi:10.1016/j.cose.2004.01.012

Wall, J. D., Palvia, P., & Lowry, P. B. (2013). Control-Related Motivations and Information Security Policy Compliance: The Role of Autonomy and Efficacy. *Journal of Information Privacy and Security, 9*(4), 52–79. doi:10.1080/15536548.2013.10845690

Watling, C. N., Palk, G. R., Freeman, J. E., & Davey, J. D. (2010). Applying Stafford and Warr's reconceptualization of deterrence theory to drug driving: Can it predict those likely to offend? *Accident; Analysis and Prevention, 42*(2), 452–458. https://www.ncbi.nlm.nih.gov/entrez/query.fcgi?cmd=Retrieve&db=PubMed&list_uids=20159066&dopt=Abstract doi:10.1016/j.aap.2009.09.007 PMID:20159066

Williams, K. R., & Hawkins, R. (1986). Perceptual research on general deterrence: A critical review. *Law & Society Review, 20*(4), 545–572. doi:10.2307/3053466

Yazdanmehr, A., & Wang, J. (2016). Employees' information security policy compliance: A norm activation perspective. *Decision Support Systems, 92*, 36–46. doi:10.1016/j.dss.2016.09.009

Zagare, F. C., & Kilgour, D. M. (2000). Perfect deterrence. *Cambridge Studies in International Relations, 24*(1), 15–25.

## KEY TERMS AND DEFINITIONS

**Compliant Information Security Behavior:** Refers to the set of core information security activities that need to be carried out by individuals to maintain information security as defined by information security policies.

**Deterrence:** Is defined as the preventative effect that actual or threatened punishment has on potential offenders.

**General Deterrence Theory (GDT):** Originates from criminology. It proposes that severe, swift, and certain sanctions result in deterring individuals from engaging in particular behaviours.

**Information Security Climate:** Is defined as the employee's perception of the current organizational state in terms of information security as evidenced through dealings with internal and external stakeholders.

**Information Security Culture:** Is defined as a natural aspect in the daily activities of every employee.

**Information Security Education:** Refers to a program or efforts to make employees aware of the environment, policy and manual of an organization's security.

**Perceived Severity of Punishment:** Is defined as actor's subjective judgment of how costly to himself the penalty he expects would be.

# Chapter 11
# Achieving a Security Culture

**Adéle Da Veiga**

(iD) https://orcid.org/0000-0001-9777-8721

*University of South Africa, South Africa*

## ABSTRACT

*A security culture can be a competitive advantage when employees uphold strong values for the protection of information and exhibit behavior that is in compliance with policies, thereby introducing minimal incidents and breaches. The security culture in an organization might, though, not be similar among departments, job levels, or even generation groups. It can pose a risk when it is not conducive to the protection of information and when security incidents and breaches occur due to employee error or negligence. This chapter aims to give organizations an overview of the concept of security culture, the factors that could influence it, an approach to assess the security culture, and to prioritize and tailor interventions for high-risk areas. The outcome of the security culture assessment can be used as input to define security awareness, training, and education programs aiding employees to exhibit behavior that is in compliance with security policies.*

## INTRODUCTION

The protection of information in an organization is a combined effort of technological, procedural as well as human-related controls (ENISA, 2017). Management that understands the behavioral and cultural aspects of their organization can use it to reduce the risk end-users could pose to information protection (Whittman & Mattord, 2012). One of the human or behavioral controls that organizations can focus on is to inculcate a strong security culture (AlHogail, 2015; ENISA, 2017; Geeling, Brown, & Weimann, 2016). A strong security culture is a culture where information is protected throughout its lifecycle when employees process and interact with it, introducing minimal risk from accidental or ignorant behavior as part of everyday practice in the organization (Da Veiga & Martins, 2015a).

DOI: 10.4018/978-1-6684-3698-1.ch011

A strong or positive security culture in an organization is essential to mitigate risk from a human perspective in order to secure information (AlHogail, 2015; ENISA, 2017). This will contribute to reducing the risk of employee misbehavior, increase the overall security policy and regulatory compliance, improve the organization's security stance and aim to minimize financial loss due to security incidents or breaches related to employee behavior (Mahfuth, Yussof, Baker & Ali, 2017; Van Niekerk & Von Solms, 2010; Verizon, 2017). It is critical to evaluate the security culture continuously and to address identified gaps to improve employees' compliance with security policies and requirements. Organizations can achieve this by regularly conducting an assessment of the security culture, monitoring the change and implementing corrective actions to influence the culture positively (Da Veiga & Martins, 2015a).

This chapter defines the concept of a security culture in the context of an information security and cybersecurity culture. An overview of the development of it in an organization is discussed, focusing on the internal factors that could potentially influence the security culture. A security culture assessment approach is discussed with practical advice to roll out such an assessment in an organization. The emphasis is on understanding what the as-is security culture is in order to implement corrective actions to influence it positively. Examples are given of how to analyze the data, which management can use to define change management plans using methods such as awareness, training and education.

## Defining a Security Culture

A security culture can be seen as the unconscious manner in which things are done in an organization to secure information. Every organization has a security culture, which is a subculture of the wider organizational culture (Da Veiga & Martins, 2017; Hayden, 2016; Schlienger & Teufel, 2003; Van Niekerk & Von Solms, 2005). The security culture can be explained as the "way things are done" in the organization to secure information. The way things are done by employees are underpinned by their assumptions, values, beliefs and attitudes (Schein, 1985, Van Niekerk & Von Solms, 2005), which is described as, "the way an organization functions as a sort of collective unconscious for the organization" (Hayden, 2016, pp. 44).

The manner in which employees undertake to protect information when they process it, is based on their shared tacit assumptions, as formed by their beliefs and values, and relates to the motivation for their decisions (Da Veiga & Eloff, 2010; Van Niekerk & Von Solms, 2006). The espoused values such as honesty and fairness form over time and relate to what employees believe should be done to protect information (Da Veiga & Martins, 2015b; Van Niekerk & Von Solms, 2006). The security culture of an organization is visible in tangible aspects of the organization, which are referred to as artifacts, underlined by the values of the organization. These tangible aspects could relate to the security policies and related training sessions, an incident-reporting or helpline, monthly awareness e-mails, the use of technology such as digital certificates for e-mail and so on (Okere, Van Niekerk, & Carroll, 2012; Schein, 1985; Schlienger & Teufel, 2003).

# SECURITY CULTURE IN AN ORGANIZATIONAL CONTEXT

## The Difference Between a Security Culture and a Cybersecurity Culture

The concepts of cybersecurity culture and information security culture both refer to the concept of a culture related to security, but from a different context. Cybersecurity can be seen as a subset or a component of information security (ISACA, 2017; B. von Solms & R. von Solms, 2018). In the same manner a cybersecurity culture is a subset of an information security culture. The distinguishing factors are the format of the information, the technology and the human element involved, as explained below.

Cybersecurity is concerned with the safeguards that must be implemented to protect information in a digital format from threats that emanate from a global network, like the internet (ISACA, 2017). Information security, on the other hand, includes threats to information across the architecture and in various formats, including hardcopy documents as well as verbal or visual communications (ISACA, 2017, C. P. Pfleeger, S. L. Pfleeger, & Margulies 2015). The cybersecurity culture is therefore described as the way things are done by users to protect information in cyberspace, whereas the information security culture is the way users do things to protect information throughout its lifecycle and in various formats, typically in the context of an organization or entity. From an organizational perspective the cybersecurity culture forms part of the wider information security culture in an organization. For example, the risk that employees introduce by downloading malicious files from the internet will pertain to the cybersecurity culture as well as the information security culture, whereas leaving confidential client documents in open office areas relates only to the context of information security culture.

A cybersecurity culture has been defined formally as, "the knowledge, beliefs, perceptions, attitudes, assumptions, norms and values of people regarding cybersecurity and how they manifest in people's behavior with information technologies" (ENISA, 2017, pp. 5). This definition is in line with the aim of cybersecurity culture being, "to instill a certain way to 'naturally behave' in daily life, a way that subscribes to certain [cybersecurity] assumptions" (Gcaza et al., 2015, pp. 3). The definition of cybersecurity includes three distinct concepts, namely the protection of digital information and information system resources in cyberspace as well as the protection of the end user using cyberspace (Da Veiga, 2016b; Von Solms & Van Niekerk, 2013). A cybersecurity culture can therefore not be confined to people in organizations, but extends to the individual in his/her work and home environment, the national and international context which includes organizations and even governments (Da Veiga, 2016b) who should define action plans and strategies on all levels to mitigate risks from cyberspace (Luiijf, Besseling & De Graaf, 2013). In contrast, an information security culture focuses on the organizational environment and what the organization, as the accountable party, should do to protect organizational information, which includes a focus on the behavior of employees who process the information.

The information security culture includes what employees do on a routinely basis that is accepted as the norm when processing information across the security architecture of an organization. The information security culture also extends to the behavior of employees relating to physical security, disaster recovery and business continuity (Da Veiga & Eloff, 2010). The scope of information security culture therefore focuses specifically on the culture of employees of an organization, which could include permanent staff, contractors, temporarily staff, consultants and third parties. In the context of this chapter the term "security culture" will be used when referring to an "information security culture", which is inclusive of a cybersecurity culture in the context of an organization.

## Dominant and Sub Security Cultures in Organizations

The security culture in an organization often manifests in a dominant security culture with related sub security cultures (Da Veiga & Martins, 2017). The dominant security culture reflects the common perceptions of the majority of the employees of how information should be secured in line with the fundamental information security requirements. The subcultures are reflected in groups of employees that have common perceptions as a result of residing in a certain region, being in different departments or having different demographical traits related to age, gender, race or educational backgrounds (Da Veiga & Martins, 2017; E. C. Martins & N. Martins, 2016). A subculture might transpire in a department where employees believe the protection of the confidentiality of information is less important and where the emphasis is on meeting deadlines and sharing information quickly. The dominant security culture can be leveraged to influence the sub security cultures and to aid in directing beliefs and behavior of a sub security culture with the aim of aligning it with the dominant culture (E. C. Martins & N. Martins, 2016). Having a dominant security culture and various sub security cultures in one organization has the result that the same approach cannot be followed to change or influence the security culture, as the perceptions and non-compliance behavior across the subcultures might vary. A tailored and focused approach for the dominant and sub security cultures is therefore required to institute effective change in each. A security culture assessment can aid management to understand the security culture across the organization and to match the interventions to the needs.

## The Desired Security Culture

The information security culture in an organization can be compared with an ethics culture as defined by Rossouw and Van Vuuren (2013). They name four categories of strategies for an ethical culture, namely reactive, compliance, integrity and totally aligned, which can also be applied to a security culture, figure 1. Management should aim for a totally aligned strategy for a security culture. In such a security culture management proactively engages with employees and deploys resources to direct the security culture. The organization's strategy and vision accommodate security, and positive reinforcement is used to reward compliance behavior. The totally aligned security culture can be seen as a strong or positive culture where employees value information and process it securely throughout its lifecycle. The incidents related to employee errors and negligence are minimized in the totally aligned security culture and employees have a thorough understanding of what is expected of them when processing information.

A reactive strategy towards security culture is the opposite of the aligned strategy. Organizations that are reactive focus on equipping employees on an ad-hoc basis, often after data breaches or security incidents occurred. An organization has an integrity strategy towards the security culture when it proactively implements strategies to minimize incidents, such as employee training and awareness, and data-loss prevention strategies; however, the approach is neither proactive nor integrated with the overall strategy of the organization. A compliance strategy focuses on compliance with regulatory and industry standards, as well as on the organization's policies and procedures. In this environment management typically performs self-assessments, monitoring and audits. For the compliance strategy the approach is rule-based and not an integral part of the operations across the organization.

Figure 1. Security culture strategies

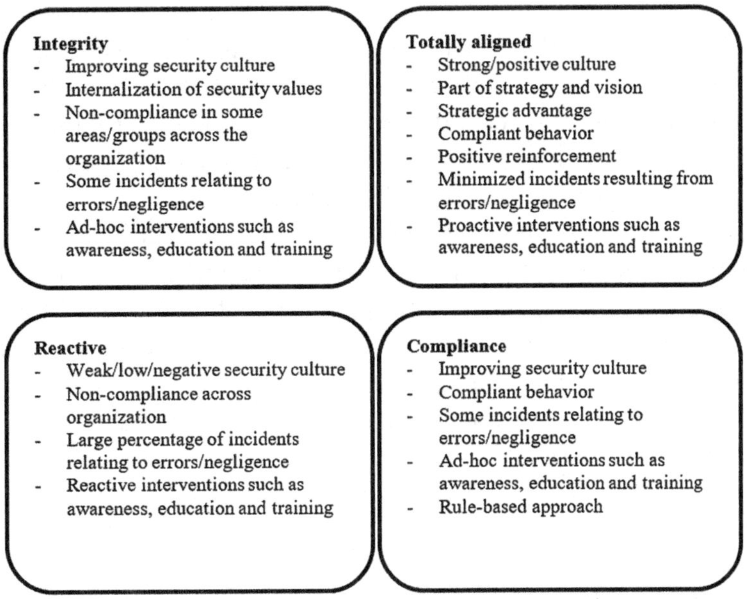

## Security Culture and Small and Medium-Size Enterprises

A security culture applies to large organizations as well as small- and medium-size (SMEs) enterprises (organizations). In the same way that an organization has an organizational culture, each organization has a unique security culture. While the concept also applies to SMEs, one needs to take cognizance of the fact that SMEs might not process the same volumes of information, have the same governance structures or level of information security policies in place, but are exposed to the same information security and cyber risks as large organizations. SMEs experience different challenges to large organizations in that they often do not have sufficient resources to invest in information security such as having a lack of skills, budget and time (Dojkovski, Lichtenstein & Warren, 2010). It is, however, also important for SMEs to ensure that they have a strong security culture to aid them in mitigating the risk from a human perspective. SMEs should also concentrate on addressing the factors discussed in the next section that influence a security culture as it is part of the foundational elements to implement information security. Whilst it is important to assess the security culture in SMEs, it is important to ensure that SMEs use their resources to implement the necessary technology and process controls for information security and progress to focus on training, awareness and education of employees to further strengthen the security culture.

## FACTORS THAT INFLUENCE A SECURITY CULTURE

Security culture is regarded as a subset of the organizational culture (Schlienger & Teufel, 2003; Van Niekerk & Von Solms, 2005). One can therefore refer to the development of an organizational culture to understand what influences the development of a security culture has in an organization. Hellriegel,

Slocum and Woodman (1998) explain the development of an organizational culture as a process over time, initiated by the strategy and vision of senior management in an organization. Their direction is conveyed through policies and procedures in the organization, which influence employee behavior. Over time the employee behavior becomes part of the organizational culture and as such also the way in which information is processed and secured, being the security culture. Figure 2 illustrates the development of a security culture with the embedded cybersecurity culture and related dominant or subcultures. The security culture is not rigid and can be influenced by a number of external and internal factors.

Factors external to the employee and organization play a role in influencing the security culture in an organization, such as regulation (AlHogail, 2015) and the national culture (G. Hofstede, G. J. Hofstede & Minkov, 2010). Internal factors such as the personality of the employees and their perceptions can also contribute to influence their behavior and in turn influence the security culture (Padayachee, 2012). Organizations need to ensure that the external and internal factors are considered as part of the security program to ensure that a holistic approach is followed to promote compliance in a consistent and effective manner.

*Figure 2. Developing and influencing a security culture*
*(adapted from Da Veiga & Martins, 2017)*

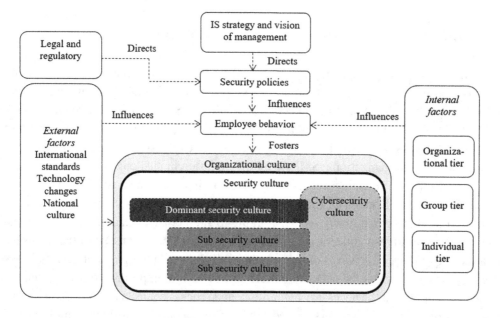

## Internal Influences

The internal influences refer to factors internal to the organization. They can be grouped under the organizational tier where formal structures are defined, the group tier where employees operate in groups and the individual tier where individuals each have a unique personality, background and traits. The next section gives an overview of each.

## Organizational Tier

Formal structures that influence employee attitude and behavior are added on the organizational tier (Robbins, 2001). These could relate to formal roles assigned to the board of directors, executive management, senior management and security practitioners to govern security in an organization (ISACA, 2017). Executive management defines the manner in which security is managed in the organization, with top management leading by example to enable employees to follow (ISACA, 2017; Mohelska & Sokolova, 2015). According to ISACA (2017) top management should endorse security requirements and follow through on disciplinary action where employees do not comply. Their expectations should be communicated through various channels, including awareness and education programs. To further direct the security culture, executive management should provide the necessary resources such as cybersecurity practitioners with sufficient skills and experience as well as sufficient financial resources to implement security requirements and to educate employees.

## Group Tier

There are various compositions of groups in organizations, each with unique views and ways of functioning (Robbins, Odendaal & Roodt, 2003). These groups relate to the composition of subcultures that are evident in organizations and could include members of a group in a department, a committee, a certain age group, gender or educational background (Robbins, 1997). The Chief Security Officer (CSO) should ensure that awareness programs specifically target groups of employees that exhibit behavior that are not in compliance with the security policy or that is not aligned with the expected security culture.

## Individual Tier

Employees (individuals) have various characteristics that vary in terms of their demographics, background, nationality, age, personalities, attitudes and assumptions (Robbins, 2001). The characteristics of individuals could influence the manner in which they behave and comply with security requirements in an organization (Robbins et al., 2003). The security awareness programs of organizations should therefore also make provision for individual training and education.

## External Influences

External influences on the organization relate to factors that can influence the security culture from outside the organization such as competitors, changes in the economy, new technological developments, national culture, industry standards and legal requirements. For example, organizations with offices in jurisdictions with data protection regulation have to implement controls to protect personal information and ensure compliance with the processing requirements of the respective privacy laws. Employees will be expected to process personal information according to the organization's privacy policies and necessary legal requirements. Offices in jurisdictions without data protection legislation will not be required to adhere to the same strict legal requirements for the processing of personal information and as such the culture towards privacy might vary from highly, moderated to low, across jurisdictions (DLA Piper, 2018). New technology also influences the manner in which employees share and process information that could either contribute to the protection of information or introduce risk. New technology like the

Internet of Things (IoT), Bring Your Own Device (BYOD), cloud computing, and social media usage introduce new risks to the integrity, confidentiality and availability of information. Employees have, for example, been found to share too much information over social media and in some cases confidential information, which can lead to litigation (He, 2012). While external factors emanate from outside the organization, it often has an impact on a strategic and operational level in an organization where internal policies have to be formulated to minimize risks from external factors.

As the focus is on the security culture from within the organization and what management can do to direct it purposefully, the next section will discuss the internal factors – referred to as the foundational elements – that form the cornerstone of a desired security culture in an organization.

## THE FOUNDATIONAL ELEMENTS FOR A DESIRED SECURITY CULTURE

Figure 3 outlines the foundational elements of a security culture. While all these elements and external factors play a role to influence and direct the security culture, it should be noted that security training, education and awareness are among the most critical elements. The security culture of employees who have attended or who have been exposed to either security training or awareness has been found to be higher or more positive compared to those employees who were not (Da Veiga, 2016a). However, the elements such as the role of leadership and change management are also critical to embed security values in the organization.

*Figure 3. Foundational elements of a security culture*

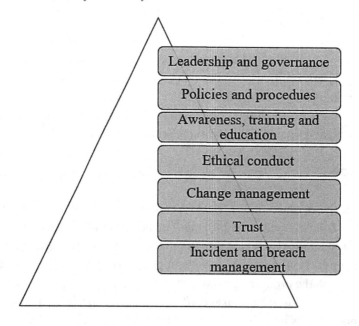

## Leadership and Governance

Management and leadership in security are required to cultivate a strong security culture (Glaspie & Karwowski, 2018). Management should set the strategic direction, policy principles, lead by example, provide the necessary resources to implement security across the organization, and implement appropriate governance structures to support the security culture on the organizational level (Glaspie et al., 2018). Top management support, buy-in and direction can positively influence the security culture (Alnatheer, 2012; Dojkovski et al., 2010; Kraemer & Carayon, 2005). Top management also plays a role in creating awareness amongst employees regarding what is expected to protect information in line with the desired security culture (Dojkovski et al., 2010). Their expectations are typically documented in the security policies as the "overall intention and direction as formally expressed by management" (ISO/IEC, 2013 pp.13). To further govern security in the organization, management should display their commitment by giving clear direction and explicitly assigning roles and responsibilities while also acknowledging their security responsibilities (ISO/IEC, 2013).

## Policies and Procedures

Security policies and procedures are regarded as critical success factors for an information security program (ISO/IEC, 2013). However, creating a security policy alone neither ensures employee awareness nor compliance (Glaspie et al., 2018). The ISO/IEC 17799 (2013) international standard includes the distribution of guidance about the policies as well as appropriate awareness, training and education as critical success factors to implement information security in an organization. The positive impact of being aware of the security policy contents is illustrated by research that have found that the security culture is more positive (or stronger) for employees who have read the security policy, as opposed to those who have not (Da Veiga, 2016b).

Encouragement to comply with the security policies have also been found to improve security across the organization (Tang, Li & Zhang, 2015). It has been found that compliance levels to policies are influenced by rewards as well as punishment for non-compliance (Chen, Ramamurthy & Wen, 2015; Whittman & Mattord, 2012). The same approach can however not be used for all organizations as each organization's security culture is unique. For example, in a security culture case study conducted in a bank, only 55.4% of employees indicated that security requirements should be part of their performance appraisal; however, in an audit and tax firm, 79.3% of employees were comfortable with incorporating security requirements in their performance appraisal with the aim of improving security policy compliance.

## Awareness, Training, and Education

Security awareness, training and education (SETA) are aimed at empowering employees through knowledge, skills and guidance to protect information (Whitman & Mattord, 2017). Awareness activities focus on ensuring that employees remain conscious of information security requirements (Whitman & Mattord, 2019). Security education focuses on a formal delivery of security requirements while security training is training tailored for employees to use the organizational resources in the context of their job role (Whitman & Mattord, 2019).

Security education (Al Hogail, 2015) and training (Glaspie et al., 2018) are critical to creating a security culture (Chen & Wen, 2015). Similarly, security awareness is regarded as one of the most important factors to create a strong security culture (Al Hogail, 2015; ENISA, 2017; Ruighaver, Maynard, & Chang, 2007), which has also been emphasized by the Organization for Economic Cooperation and Development (OECD, 2002). Security awareness is regarded as focusing on "what" as opposed to "how", which relates to training (Herold, 2011). Security awareness is typically less formal than training, with a variety of delivery methods (e.g. posters, e-mails, newsletters, speakers, logos, banners, promotional items) and is conducted on a continuous basis by the organization to update employees about security policy requirements (Herold, 2011).

Targeted SETA programs are required to address the "human error or failure" effectively (Whitman & Mattord, 2019, pp. 268). A security culture assessment can be used to identify the job levels or departments that require SETA as well as the most preferred method of delivery. This can aid management to direct the SETA programs effectively to match the needs of the employees and to address the gaps identified. While the security culture assessment can inform SETA programs, it is key to use a holistic approach whereby the effectiveness of SETA programs is also assessed by using different techniques. Whitman and Mattord (2019) recommend an approach whereby awareness outcomes can typically be assessed with true/false or multiple-choice scales, training outcomes can be assessed through applied learning, and educational outcomes can be assessed through essay-style questions relating to interpretive learning. It is important to note that a security culture assessment does not measure the learning outcomes of SETA programs, but rather the perception and attitudes of employees towards security in the organization.

## Ethical Conduct

In the information security field, information security professionals are guided by codes of ethics such as those of the Association for Computing Machinery (ACM, 2018), the Information Systems Security Association (ISSA, 2018) and the Information Systems Audit and Control Association (ISACA, 2018). All employees are not necessarily guided by these codes of ethics. They will typically be guided by the ethics code of the organization. However, employees from different nationalities or countries could have different perceptions towards ethics (Whitman & Mattord, 2012). To complicate the matter even more it has been found that attitudes towards ethics in the use of computer resources differ among individuals in the same country or even in one organization (Whitman & Mattord, 2012). Whitman and Mattord (2012) emphasize that education can be used to overcome the challenge of diverse ethical attitudes. It is therefore critical for the organization to understand the perceptions and attitude of their workforce in order to identify employee groups whose attitudes and perceptions are not in line with the organization's code of ethics and security policies. The information security culture assessment as discussed in this chapter can be used to identify such groups and to establish what interventions are required.

## Change Management

Change management is important to instill a strong information security culture (Ashenden & Sasse, 2013; Ruighaver et al., 2007). A formal change management approach should be followed to direct the security culture purposefully. Change can only be initiated through a formal process during which the security culture is assessed to gain an understanding of it (Berry & Houston, 1993; Byars & Rue,

1997; Herold, 2011). The assessment serves as an organizational diagnosis to identify the as-is security culture and any prevailing issues or risks in the dominant culture or subcultures with the objective of improving or directing the culture. The data can be used to "stimulate and guide desirable changes" (Martins, 2017, pp. 1) in the security culture. Security culture changes should be implemented in such a manner that the changes are embedded and over time become part of the overall organizational culture. Change management approaches such as Prosci's ADKAR (Hiatt, 2006) change management model have been applied successfully in projects (Kazmi & Naarananoja, 2014; Kiani & Shah, 2014; Sheperd, Harris, Chung & Himes, 2014) and can also be applied to conduct the security culture assessment and to implement related changes.

The ADKAR change management model includes five phases, namely awareness (about the necessity for change), desire (to be part of and to support the change), knowledge (of how to bring about the change), ability (to be capable of implementing changes) and reinforcement (to maintain the implemented changes). These phases can be used to implement the change management actions as identified from the security culture assessment. Knowledge of the survey data and findings can be used to create awareness amongst stakeholders and employees for the need to change, which will also support the desire to change. Knowledge of how to change can be derived from the survey data by focusing on the most negative concepts and groups as identified in the data. The ability to change should be supported by management resources that also extend to a follow-up assessment to monitor the change and impact of the actions, which can be used to reinforce changes. Interestingly, in the security culture case studies conducted employees indicated their willingness to change and preparedness to accept some inconvenience to change. For example, in one of the financial organizations, 96% of employees indicated that they were prepared to change their working practices in order to secure information assets, with another 97% indicating that they were willing to accept inconvenience to secure important information. This might, however, not be the case in all organizations and a structured change program can aid management to implement security changes in a constructive manner.

## Trust

When implementing security in an organization, a trusting relationship should be in place between management and employees so that compliance with security policies is facilitated and commitment to information security is illustrated by management – especially, as trust is regarded as one of the fundamental characteristics of leadership (Robbins, 1997; Flowerday and Von Solms, 2006). Trust is necessary in organizations to facilitate the sharing of knowledge (Rossouw & Van Vuuren, 2013), which also relates to knowledge of how to secure information. To facilitate an environment of knowledge-sharing through security training, education and awareness, a trusting relationship should be in place to contribute to the development of a strong security culture. Trust as a construct is also assessed during the security culture assessment to establish if it could be hampering the development of a totally aligned security culture.

## Incident and Breach Management

Incident and breach management relates to the plan of the organization to respond in the event of a security incident or data breach in terms of the detection, reaction and recovering (Whitman & Mattord 2019). From the employees' perspective it is important that they know what a security incident is, who to report it to and what to do in the event of such an incident. In previous security culture assessments conducted in organizations, employees indicated in many of the case studies that they did not know who to report security incidents to and also did not know what an incident is. Table 1 portrays the results of one of these case studies in which employees were asked who they should report security incidents to. In this case study the majority believed they should report to the Group Information Security Officer, followed by their manager, where in actual fact they were required to report security incidents to the Helpdesk. In this same case study 72.1% of employees knew what a security incident is. In the follow-up surveys this improved to 87.6%, following targeted interventions.

*Table 1. Reporting security incidents responses*

| Response Option | Frequency | Percentage of Responses |
|---|---|---|
| Helpdesk | 206 | 9.5% |
| Immediate manager | 1 287 | 59.6% |
| Group information security officer | 1 596 | 73.9% |
| Human Resources | 61 | 2.8% |
| Information Technology | 225 | 10.4% |
| I don't know | 92 | 4.3% |
| Whistle-blowing process | 138 | 3.6% |

# A PROCESS TOWARDS CHANGING THE SECURITY CULTURE IN AN ORGANIZATION

There are various reasons why organizations might want to conduct a security culture assessment. They might need data to prove a suspicion that the behavior of employees in a certain department or biographical group is not in line with the expected culture. The organization might want to identify aspects of risk in the security culture to prioritize and tailor interventions, or to monitor the impact and success of change after the implementation of interventions. One benefit of the security culture assessment is that the data can be used to inform the content and focus of awareness, training and education programs. Follow-up assessments can provide management with data to benchmark and compare progress to further identify awareness, training and education needs.

## The Security Culture Assessment Approach

Organizations that embark on a security culture assessment project can use the approach outlined in figure 4 as a guideline to conduct the assessment. This approach has four phases to conduct the assessment in a planned, structured and organized manner with the objective of obtaining valid and reliable data that management can use for strategic decisions to improve the security culture. It is a quantitative approach whereby a questionnaire is deployed in an organization by using a survey strategy. Questionnaires work well when deployed to assess attitude towards and opinions about an organizational practice (Saunders, Lewis & Thornhill, 2016), such as the security culture. The results can be generalized across the organization if a statistical representative sample is used and surveys are also a cost-effective approach (Saunders et al., 2016). A mixed method approach can also be used, such as incorporating documentary research where communications, contents of security policies and audit reports are reviewed. More in-depth information can be obtained if interviews or focus groups are used to confirm data from the security culture survey, for example to explore reasons for certain answers provided by the various demographical groups. The steps in each of the four phases are discussed below to give organizations a high-level overview of how to conduct the security culture assessment.

*Figure 4. Security culture assessment approach*

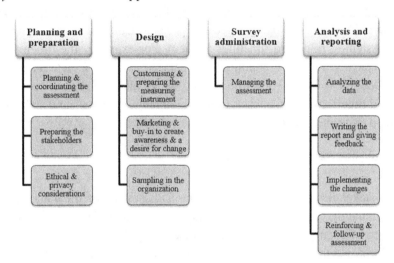

## Planning and Coordinating the Assessment

There are a number of aspects to consider when planning the security culture assessment, such as the objective of the assessment, the scope, data protection legislation and project management. Firstly, management should identify the objective of conducting a security culture assessment. Usually, the two most common reasons for assessments are to measure and to change (Borg & Mastrangelo, 2008). The objective could relate to understanding the current security culture to integrate the findings as part of the risk profile of the organization, or to follow up on audit findings in certain business units or regions where employee behavior resulted in security incidents or breaches, or to identify what the content and focus of the security awareness program should be for various departments. Ultimately, the objective is to purposefully change the security culture to the desired culture in which less incidents and data breaches are occurring owing to employees' behavior.

Management should also agree on the scope of the project, such as whether all the organization's offices in the various regions and countries should be included. It should also be determined whether all employees have access to computers to be able to access and complete the questionnaire electronically, and/or whether paper-based questionnaires will be required. Another factor to consider is whether the questionnaire should be translated into more than one language, especially if offices in other countries are included.

Many organizations prefer to host the survey internally, while others make use of third parties or consultants. When third parties or consultants are used, organizations usually have to engage in a third-party contract process and agree on the privacy and security requirements of the data. This could take some time to negotiate and agree on, especially if different data protection regulations are to be considered for cross-border transfer of the data. For example, if the offices of the organization are located across the United States as well as Europe, the employees' biographical data, as captured in the questionnaires, will be saved in the third-party database, which could reside in the United States. The General Data Protection Regulation (GDPR) (European Parliament, 2016) requirements for cross-border transfer of European citizens' data must then be considered and applied in the survey process.

The assessment process does not only relate to sending out the questionnaire and analyzing the data. The project should be managed using aspects of project management principles, such as defining specific tasks and assigning roles and timelines to them. For example, the timeline of activities; the survey timeframe (typically not during a holiday or year-end as the response rates will be lower); the stakeholders to include; the different roles; the budget; which tasks can run concurrently; planning the feedback method and timeframe for feedback to management, employees and stakeholders; and so on should be determined (Martins, 2017).

## Preparing the Stakeholders

The management of stakeholders in the security culture assessment is critical and often impacts on the success of organizational diagnoses projects. Ledimo (2017) emphasizes that the stakeholders should be identified upfront and engaged with to manage resistance and concerns. A number of stakeholders, which include the Information Security Officer (ISO) or Chief Information Officer (CIO) and departments in the organization, such as training or human resources, should be part of the team to increase the success of the project (ENISA, 2017).

The ISO or CIO is often the security culture assessment project sponsor that either drives the project or allocates the responsibility to someone in his or her team. When an organization conducts an assessment, the output will result in change plans that have to be implemented (Ledimo, 2017). The stakeholders tasked with implementing the change should therefore be involved from the start. These stakeholders could relate to the marketing and communications team that designs and delivers awareness material, the training team that might need to compile and deliver customized and focused training based on the results, the Information Technology Department that might need to work with the training team to assist in defining the training content or to implement/revise technological controls, and the risk and compliance team that might need to follow up on high-risk departments or integrate the findings in their reports. In some instances, trade union representatives should be included as they might need to give input for the planning and should receive feedback on the results as it could impact their members.

The stakeholders comprising individuals or committees (e.g. Risk and Compliance Committee) should be identified upfront and their buy-in should be obtained. This could be done by presenting the project to them and discussing the benefits and potential use of the results to institute change. The board or executive representation might also be required to support the security culture assessment project (ENISA, 2017).

## Ethical and Privacy Considerations

Questionnaires usually include a section where demographical data is collected in order to segment the data for comparison purposes and to identify priority groups across the organization to target interventions. While the questionnaires should be anonymous, personal identifiable data such as department name, age, job level, language, years of employment and gender is still collected. When these data fields are combined, it might be possible to identify individuals especially in demographical groups in which there are only a few staff members. Ethical and privacy requirements should therefore be considered, as listed below in alphabetic order (Da Veiga, 2017):

- **Autonomy:** Employees' decision to participate or not to participate in the security culture assessment should be respected (Mitchell & Jolley, 2007; Oates, 2012; Saunders et al., 2016).
- **Best Interest:** The participants should be informed of the security culture assessment through a proper communication channel such as a meeting, e-mail of informed consent agreement where their interests and role are described (HPCSA, 2008).
- **Benevolence:** A risk assessment can be conducted to evaluate the type of personal identifiable information and attitude, or opinion information that will be collected to ensure that the rights of participants are respected, and that confidentiality and privacy requirements are met. Ultimately the benefits should outweigh the risk of the assessment (Miller & Brewerton, 2003, Saunders et al., 2016).
- **Compassion:** The organizations should illustrate compassion if participants from vulnerable groups, such as those with disabilities, are included. Measures should be implemented to enable them to participate (HPCSA, 2008).
- **Confidentiality:** The personal identifiable information and all responses should be treated as confidential by all parties, including any third parties involved in the planning, hosting, data cleansing, statistical analysis and report writing (Miller & Brewer, 2003; HSRC, 2017; Oates, 2012; Saunders et al., 2016). Adequate security measures should be in place to protect the electronic survey data when sent across the organizational or third-party networks, in the database as well as when being e-mailed or statistically analyzed.
- **Consent:** Employees should give consent for their data being transferred cross-border, or if their data will be used for other purposes (European Parliament, 2016; Oates, 2012; Saunders et al.; 2016).
- **Excellence and Competence:** The questionnaire should be validated statistically to ensure that the data and findings are reliable and valid (ISACA, 2016; HPCSA, 2008; HSRC, 2017).
- **Honesty:** The project team should ensure that the data used in reports and feedback sessions is reported on in an honest and accurate manner (Miller & Brewerton, 2003; Singapore Statement, 2010, Saunders et al., 2016).
- **Human Rights:** The human rights of all participants and stakeholders should be considered, for example to have fair selection criteria representing all groups across the organization when defining the selection criteria if a sampling approach is used (HPCSA, 2008).
- **Impartiality and Independence:** The stakeholders involved must declare any conflicts of interest, such as being a shareholder of the company that will host the data (ALLEA, 2017).

- **Integrity:** The assessment must be conducted in line with the organizational values considering fairness, honesty and quality of the data collection, analysis and reporting (Singapore Statement, 2010; HPCSA, 2008).
- **Justice:** The project team and stakeholders must treat all the participating employees with respect, sensitivity and fairness, especially if the employees are compensated to participate (HSRC, 2017; HPCSA, 2008).
- **Objectivity and Independence:** The project team should conduct the assessment in line with their organizational codes of ethics and professional codes of ethics (Babie, 2004; ALLEA, 2017; ISACA, 2016). If the project is audited or monitored, the reviews should be conducted independently from the project team. Objective decisions should be made based on the data and facts and not on opinions.
- **Transparency:** The participants must be informed of the survey objective, any possible risks and expectations. Results should be communicated to the relevant stakeholders to ensure transparency (Mitchell & Jolley, 2007).

## Customizing and Preparing the Measuring Instrument

There are a number of security culture questionnaires available, which can be used for the assessment of security culture. The most prominent ones are listed below in alphabetical order:

- AlHogail (2015) proposed the Information Security Culture Framework (ISCF), which comprises five dimensions, namely strategy, technology, organization, people and environment (STOPE). Four domains of human behavior factors (preparedness, responsibility, management, and society and regulations) are assessed in each of the dimensions. This questionnaire has a reliability score (Cronbach alpha) of 0.619 to 0.928.
- The Information Security Culture Assessment (ISCA) questionnaire has been designed to assess the as-is security culture in an organization (Da Veiga & Eloff, 2010). The questionnaire is based on the Information Security Culture Framework (Da Veiga & Eloff, 2010) and comprises ten dimensions, namely change management, information asset management, information security leadership, information security management, information security policies, information security program, trust, user management, training and awareness, and privacy perception. The reliability score (Cronbach alpha) is between 0.764 and 0.877 (Da Veiga & Martins, 2015b). This questionnaire was used successfully in five financial institutions in South Africa, in a mining organization as well as consumer market organization. In one of the financial institutions the questionnaire was deployed across twelve countries at four different occasions during a period of eight years to monitor the impact of the interventions and change on the information security culture (Da Veiga & Martins, 2015a, 2015b, 2017) and in another it was deployed twice. Furthermore, it was implemented in a government parastatal and in an audit, tax and advisory firm. The results obtained from these assessments were found to be valid and reliable to facilitate changes in employee attitude and related behavior, and to inculcate a positive information security culture.
- In a book Lance Haydon (2016) published he included a security culture survey with ten questions to measure security culture. He proposes that a security culture can be defined as the Competing Security Cultures Framework (CSCF), being either a process culture (with tight control and internal focus), a compliance culture (with tight control and external focus), a trust culture (with loose

control and internal focus) or an autonomy culture (with loose control and external focus). The objective is to assess and identify the cultural traits and values relating to security in the organization in order to map the culture in one of the four quadrants of the CSCF. This approach follows a survey method.

- Schienger (Schlienger & Teufel, 2003; 2005) developed an information security culture questionnaire and corresponding tool. He defined questions focusing on the individual's attitude, the organization's attitude and the possible solution where after the results are triangulated. The questionnaire is currently available in German as part of Schlienger's consulting services of Tree Solution (2018).

In this chapter the ISCA questionnaire is used for illustration purposes as it is statistically validated and produced positive results in case studies, which were published. The full questionnaire is available in a 2018 publication by Da Veiga, titled "An approach to information security culture change combining ADKAR and the ISCA questionnaire to aid transition to the desired culture" in the Information and Computer Security Journal.

The theoretical questionnaire dimensions (constructs) are as follows (Da Veiga & Martins 2015a, Da Veiga & Martins 2015b):

1. **Information Asset Management:** Assesses users' perceptions of the protection of information assets
2. **Information Security Management:** Assesses management's perceptions of information security management
3. **Change Management:** Assesses the perceptions about change and the willingness of users to change in order to protect information
4. **User Management:** Assesses user awareness and training with regard to the requirements to protect information
5. **Information Security Policy:** Assesses whether users understand the information security policy and whether communication thereof was successful
6. **Information Security Program:** Assesses the effectiveness of investing in information security resources
7. **Trust:** Assesses the perceptions of users regarding the safekeeping of private information and their trust in the communications of the organization
8. **Information Security Leadership:** Assesses users' perceptions of information security governance (e.g. monitoring) to minimize risks to information
9. **Training and Awareness:** Assesses employees' perception of additional needs for information security training
10. **Privacy Perception:** Assesses employees' perception of privacy principles

While this questionnaire's questions are defined, it is important to customize the terminology and perhaps add or remove one or two questions that might be relevant/not relevant in the background section of the questionnaire, and include specific biographical questions relating to the structure of the organization and profile of the employees. It is advisable not to change too much of the questionnaire as it affects its reliability and validity. Should this be the case, statistical analysis, such as the Cronbach Alpha and factor analysis should be conducted to validate the questionnaire again (Martins & Ledimo, 2017).

The questionnaire can be developed in an online tool such as SurveyTracker (Scantron, 2018), SurveyMonkey (2018) or Qualtrics (2018). These tools include electronic distribution of the questionnaire, automatic data capturing and also the analysis and exporting of the data.

## Marketing and Buy-in to Create Awareness and a Desire for Change

It is important to market the security culture survey to the employees and stakeholders in order to get enough responses for the survey across the organization. The questionnaire can be accompanied by an invitation or cover letter from management such as the Chief Information Officer or the Chief Information Security Officer, explaining the objective, why to participate, how long it will take, confidentiality and anonymity and any further instructions. This is typically sent via e-mail with the hyperlink to the electronic questionnaire. Regular reminder emails help to obtain responses; so do incentives such as receiving a small gift on completion, or standing a change to win a prize (Martins & Ledimo, 2017b).

## Sampling in the Organization

Various sampling techniques, such as simple random, stratified, clustered, convenience or snowball sampling can be used (Cresswell, 2014; Oates, 2012; Saunders, Lewis, & Thornhill, 2016). If the objective is to obtain insight into the dominant and subcultures, all employees can be invited to participate, thereby including the entire organization as the sample. The method of Krejcie and Morgan (1970) can be applied to obtain a 95% confidence that the results can be generalized across the organization. Using this method an organization can calculate how many responses are required for the overall results, as well as per biographical group such as a department, as long as the organization can determine the number of employees in each department. For example, an organization with 100 employees requires a response rate of 80, an organization with 500 employees requires a response rate of 217, an organization with 1 000 employees require a response rate of 278 and an organization with 10 000 employees require a response rate of 370. If an organization with 10 000 employees calculate the response rate per job level or department, the overall responses required will be more than 370 as the responses should be calculated separately per department, which will add up to more than the overall figure. Where sufficient responses are not obtained, the results can be validated with interviews or focus groups.

## Managing the Assessment

The security culture assessment should be managed by tracking the responses received on a weekly basis, identifying departments or groups with insufficient responses, sending out reminders and establishing if additional communication is required to motivate employees to respond. The various stakeholders, such as the technical team hosting the survey, the communication team that might post notices on the intranet or that sends out reminders require updates on the progress. The process for the completion of paper-based questionnaires should also be planned and managed, for example if facilitators will be used and for data capturing.

## Analyzing the Data

It is advisable to use a statistical analysis program such as IBM SPSS Statistics (IBM Analytics 2018) to analyze the data. A Likert scale is used for the ISCA questions. Scores below a mean of 4.00 (Da Veiga & Martins 2015a) can be flagged for improvement, as indicated in figure 5.

*Figure 5. Likert scale application for the ISCA*

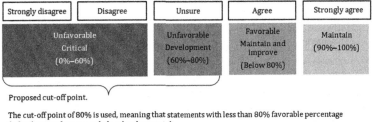

Proposed cut-off point.

The cut-off point of 80% is used, meaning that statements with less than 80% favorable percentage (4 for the mean) are regarded as developmental.

The security culture data can be analyzed by conducting the following as a minimum:

- The number of responses (frequencies) for each of the biographical groups should be calculated, as well as whether a representative response rate was obtained. Table 2 gives an example of the responses received per job level in one of the security culture assessments. In the last column the means for all the security culture questions are listed, showing a close resemblance between the job levels.
- The means of each of the statements in the ISCA can be calculated. These can be listed from the highest to the lowest to identify the most positive and most negative statements to prioritize interventions. Scores below a mean of 4.00 can be flagged for improvement where actions plans should be defined. Table 3 illustrates the top five results of a security culture assessment comparing the means for four of the surveys conducted. The "*" indicates a significant improvement from the 2010 to 2013 data.
- The means of each of the ten dimensions can be calculated. The dimensions with the lowest mean score should be prioritized for interventions.
- T-tests and analysis of variance (ANOVA) tests can be conducted to identify significant differences among biographical groups such as departments or age groups. This will give management an indication of which group to prioritize for the interventions as well as how to customize interventions for each group based on the specific aspects that scored low as identified in the data. Figure 6 presents the data of one of the security culture assessments where the data was segmented among employees in the Information Technology (IT) department, compared with employees who are not working in IT. The t-tests indicated that there was a significant difference between the means of these groups. For example, in 2013 the IT group, with a mean of 4.15, was significantly more positive than the non-IT group with a mean of 4.09. The implication is that the non-IT group should be prioritized if management plans interventions, which would typically be defined where means are below 4 for the mean.

*Table 2. Responses and means per job level*

| Response | Percentage of Responses | Means |
|---|---|---|
| Executive | 2.4% | 3.94 |
| Manager | 20.8% | 3.90 |
| Non-managerial employee | 76.5% | 3.89 |
| No response | 0.3% | N/A |

*Table 3. Five most positive statements*

| Statements | Dimension | 2013 | 2010 | 2007 | 2006 |
|---|---|---|---|---|---|
| It is important to understand the threats (e.g. theft of equipment, alterations or misuse of information) to the information assets in my division. | Information asset management | * 4.53 | 4.48 | 4.48 | 4.43 |
| I accept that some inconvenience (e.g. changing my password regularly, locking away confidential documents or making back-ups) is necessary to secure important information. | Change | 4.43 | 4.40 | 4.43 | 4.37 |
| I am aware of the information security aspects relating to my job function (e.g. how to choose a password or handle confidential information). | User management | * 4.44 | 4.36 | 4.36 | 4.22 |
| I believe it is necessary to commit people to information security. | Information security program | * 4.38 | 4.33 | 4.33 | 4.26 |
| I am prepared to change my working practices in order to ensure the security of information assets (e.g. computer systems and information in paper or electronic format). | Change | 4.30 | 4.29 | 4.25 | 4.20 |

*Figure 6. Means for IT and non-IT employees*

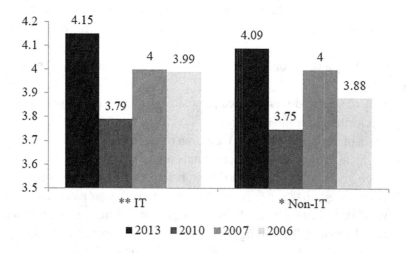

T-tests can also be used to identify significant improvements from one survey to the next as indicated in table 4. The "*" indicates that the means of the 2013 statements were significantly more positive when compared with the 2010 means.

*Table 4. Significant differences for individual statements*

| Statements | Dimension | 2013 | 2010 |
|---|---|---|---|
| My division clearly outlines what is expected of me with regard to information security. | Information security leadership | * 3.82 | 3.66 |
| I believe employees adhere to the information security policy. | Information security leadership | * 3.81 | 3.66 |
| The contents of the information security policy were effectively communicated to me. | User management | 3.73 | 3.69 |
| I am informed in a timely manner as to how information security changes will affect me. | Change | 3.75 | 3.71 |
| The contents of the information security policy are easy to understand. | Information security policies | * 3.81 | 3.76 |

- If the survey was repeated, comparison analysis can be done to identify improvement or changes from the previous results. The means per dimension for each of the years when the survey was conducted can be displayed on a radar chart as depicted in figure 7. The overall mean for 2013, 4.10, indicates an improvement from the 2010 overall mean, 3.76. The ten dimensions of the ISCA questionnaire, used in this specific case study, are displayed with the means of the questions for each dimension. For most of the dimensions, the same trend is visible with awareness and training being the dimension where the most intervention and improvement is required compared to the information access management dimension that remained one of the most positive dimensions. The privacy dimension was only included in the 2010 and 2013 survey and hence no data is available for the other two years.

The advantage of the longitudinal analysis is to track and monitor the change over time to establish if interventions were successful and where corrective action is required. This type of analysis can be done per department, job level or office area to also track over time whether the security culture is improving or if not, and where intervention is required. The data can also aid management to motivate for budget aimed at awareness, training and education initiatives or to showcase success of corrective actions.

## Writing the Report and Giving Feedback

Once the data analysis is complete, the next step is to compile a report of the results with the recommendations. Typically the report should include aspects such as the security culture assessment (survey) objective, the methodology followed, the number of responses received compared to the sample sizes required, the overall results per dimensions, the results per statement, the results per biographical group (positive and negative results), recommended action plans and an implementation plan (Martins, 2017). The report can also be summarized in PowerPoint to be presented to the various stakeholder groups. Feedback should also be given to employees to ensure transparency and for employees to understand the necessity to change where improvement is required.

Table 5 gives an extract of recommendations that were made in one of the security culture assessments. For more examples please refer to the article "Defining dominant and sub security cultures", in *Computers & Security* by Da Veiga and Martins published in 2017.

*Figure 7. Means per dimension for four assessments*

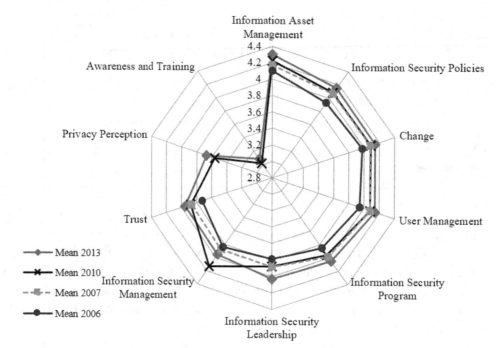

*Table 5. Example of recommendations*

| Intervention | ISCA Finding | Recommendation |
|---|---|---|
| Communication about the sharing of passwords | Employees believe they can share their passwords with (2010):<br>Helpdesk<br>Managers<br>Secretaries<br>Colleagues | **Action:** Communicate to employees that no passwords should be shared<br>**Demographical group:** Non-IT employees and non-managerial<br>**Method:** E-mail, presentation and web-based training (in order of method preferred by employees) |
| Communication of the security policy | 31.9% of respondents believe that the security policy was not explained and communicated to them effectively<br>38.9% of respondents have not read the security policy<br>32.2% of respondents do not know where to get a copy of the security policy | **Action:** Conduct additional policy communication and awareness<br>**Demographical groups:** Non-IT department, South Africa, United Kingdom and Australia<br>**Method:** Develop a security policy brochure with content overview and link<br>Send out monthly e-mails with policy content messages<br>Conduct face-to-face policy overview presentations |

## Implementing the Changes

The security culture assessment results provide management with a view of the security culture and which aspects or groups require change to improve the culture. A change management process such as that of ADKAR can typically be used to implement the change. Awareness about the change can be created through the feedback to stakeholders, focusing on the offices or groups that scored the lowest. The desire to change can be motivated by illustrating aspects that require improvement which, for example, can be discussed in focus groups. This can be reinforced through the use of role models, change agents in departments, incorporating security aspects in performance appraisals or incentives. The transition phase includes the focus of education, training and awareness for employees in the aspects identified in the ISCA assessment, starting with the priority audiences. Organizations should ensure that they have the necessary resources and ability to change, such as training the ISO and CISOs, or making use of external consultants to implement some of the changes required. Reinforcing the change can be facilitated by conducting a follow-up ISCA survey.

## Reinforcing and Follow-up Assessment

The follow-up ISCA assessment can be used to monitor the implemented changes and to identify where the results improved. Additional data in the organization can also be used, for example to track the number of incidents related to employee error and negligence prior to and after interventions.

## CONCLUSION

In this chapter the concept of a security culture was discussed as being the unconscious manner in which things are done in an organization to secure information. The security cultures vary among organizations and even within an organization with dominant and sub security cultures that emerge. The intrinsic and extrinsic factors that influence a security culture are discussed in this chapter, emphasizing the importance of education, training and awareness.

This chapter further outlined a process to assess the security culture by discussing the key aspects to consider – from identifying the stakeholders to the report writing and feedback phase. The Information Security Culture Assessment (ISCA) instrument was discussed as a questionnaire that can be used to establish the level of the security culture with the objective of identifying biographical groups or areas, such as business units or age groups in the organization where intervention is required to direct the security culture purposefully through interventions that can be conveyed by training, awareness and education.

The importance of focusing on the human element is emphasized to aid with security policy compliance and ultimately to establish a strong security culture. An information security culture will be evident in employees that exhibit compliance behavior and have coherent values towards protecting information, thereby minimizing the threat the human element poses to the protection of information. The aim is to achieve a totally aligned security culture.

## REFERENCES

AlHogail, A. (2015). Design and validation of information security culture framework. *Computers in Human Behavior*, *49*, 567–575. doi:10.1016/j.chb.2015.03.054

AlHogail, A. (2015). Cultivating and Assessing an Organizational Information Security Culture: An Empirical Study. *International Journal of Security and Its Applications*, *9*(7), 163–178. doi:10.14257/ijsia.2015.9.7.15

All European Academics (ALLEA). (2017). *The European Code of Conduct for Research Integrity.* Retrieved from https://ec.europa.eu/research/participants/data/ref/h2020/other/hi/h2020-ethics_code-of-conduct_en.pdf

Alnatheer, M. (2012). Understanding and Measuring Information Security Culture in Developing Countries: Case of Saudi Arabia. In *Proceedings of the Pacific Asia Conference on Information Systems (PACIS).* Ho Chi Minh City, Vietnam: Association of Information Systems.

Ashenden, D., & Sasse, A. (2013). CISOs and organizational culture: Their own worst enemy? *Computers & Security, 39*, 396–405. doi:10.1016/j.cose.2013.09.004

Association for Computing Machinery (ACM). (n.d.). *ACM code of ethics and professional conduct.* Retrieved from www.acm.org/about/code-of-ethics

Babie, E. (2004). *The practice of social research* (10th ed.). Belmont, CA: Thomson Wadsworth.

Berry, M. L., & Houston, J. P. (1993). *Psychology at work.* Brown and Benchmark Publishers.

Borg, I., & Mastrangelo, P. M. (2008). *Employee surveys, tools and practical applications. Employee surveys in management: theories, tools and practical applications.* Cambridge, MA: Hogrefe.

Byars, L. L., & Rue, L. W. (1997). *Human resource management* (5th ed.). Boston: McGraw-Hill.

Chen, Y., Ramamurthy, K., & Wen, K. (2015). Impacts of comprehensive information security programs on information security culture. *Journal of Computer Information Systems, 55*(3), 11–19. doi:10.1080/08874417.2015.11645767

Cresswell, J. W. (2014). *Research design – Qualitative, quantitative, and mixed methods approaches* (4th ed.). Los Angeles, CA: SAGE Publications.

Da Veiga, A. (2016a). Comparing the information security culture of employees who had read the information security policy and those who had not: Illustrated through an empirical study *Information &. Computers & Security, 22*(24), 139–155. doi:10.1108/ICS-12-2015-0048

Da Veiga, A. (2016b). A cybersecurity culture research philosophy and approach to develop a valid and reliable measuring instrument. In *Proceedings of 2016 Science and Information Computing Conference* (SAI2016) (pp. 1006-1115), London: IEEE. 10.1109/SAI.2016.7556102

Da Veiga, A. (2017). Ethical and privacy considerations for research. In N. Martins, E. Martins, & R. Viljoen (Eds.), *Organizational Diagnosis: A guide for practitioners* (pp. 273–298). Randburg, South Africa: Knowledge Resources.

Da Veiga, A., & Eloff, J. H. P. (2010). A framework and assessment instrument for information security culture. *Computers & Security, 29*(2), 196–207. doi:10.1016/j.cose.2009.09.002

Da Veiga, A., & Martins, N. (2015a). Improving the information security culture through monitoring and implementation actions illustrated through a case study. *Computers & Security, 49*, 162–176. doi:10.1016/j.cose.2014.12.006

Da Veiga, A., & Martins, N. (2015b). Information security culture and information protection culture: A validated assessment instrument. *Computer Law & Security Review, 31*(2), 243–256. doi:10.1016/j.clsr.2015.01.005

Da Veiga, A., & Martins, N. (2017). Defining and identifying dominant information security cultures and subcultures. *Computers & Security, 70*, 72–94. doi:10.1016/j.cose.2017.05.002

DLA PIPER. (2018). *Data protection laws of the world*. Retrieved from https://www.dlapiperdataprotection.com/index.html

Dojkovski, S., Lichtenstein, S., & Watten, M. J. (2010). Enabling information security culture: Influences and challenges for Australian SMEs. *Proceedings of the Australasian Conference on Information Systems, (ACIS)*.

European Union Agency for Network and Information Security (ENISA). (2017). *Cyber security culture in organizations*. Retrieved from doi:10.2824/10543

Flowerday, S., & Von Solms, R. (2006). Trust an element of information security. In *Proceedings of Security and Privacy in Dynamic Environments (IFIP/SEC2005)* (pp. 87–98). Boston: Kluwer Academic Publishers. doi:10.1007/0-387-33406-8_8

Gcaza, N., & Von Solms, R. (2017). A strategy for a cybersecurity culture: A South African perspective. *The Electronic Journal on Information Systems in Developing Countries, 80*(1), 1–17. doi:10.1002/j.1681-4835.2017.tb00590.x

Geeling, S., Brown, I., & Weimann, P. (2016). Information systems and culture – a systematic hermeneutic literature review. In *Proceedings of the International Conference on Information Resource Management (CONF-IRM)* (paper 40). South Africa, Cape Town: Association for Information Systems.

Glaspie, H. W., & Karwowski, W. (2018). Human Factors in Information Security Culture : A Literature Review Human Factors in Information Security Culture : A Literature Review. In *Proceedings of Advances in Intelligent Systems and Computing* (pp. 269–280). Springer.

Haydon, L. (2016). *People centric security – Transforming your enterprise security culture*. McGraw-Hill Education.

He, W. (2012). A review of social media security risks and mitigation techniques. *Journal of Systems and Information Technology, 14*(2), 171–180. doi:10.1108/13287261211232180

Health Professions Council of South Africa (HPCSA). (2008). *General Ethical Guidelines for the Health Professions Council of South Africa, Annexure 12*. Retrieved from http://www.hpcsa.co.za/conduct/Ethics

Hellriegel, D., Slocum, J. W. Jr, & Woodman, R. W. (1998). *Organizational behavior* (8th ed.). Cincinnati, OH: South-Western College.

Herold, R. (2011). *Managing an information security and privacy awareness and training program* (2nd ed.). Boca Raton, FL: Taylor and Francis Group.

Hiatt, J. M. (2006). *ADKAR: A Model for Change in Business, Government and our Community*. Loveland, CO: Library of Congress.

Hofstede, G., Hofstede, G. J., & Minkov, M. (2010). *Cultures and Organizations: Software of the mind* (3rd ed.). The McGraw-Hill Companies.

Human Sciences Research Council (HSRC). (2018). *Code of Research Ethics*. Retrieved from http://www.hsrc.ac.za/en/about/research-ethics/code-of-research-ethics

IBM Analytics. (2018). *IBM SPSS Statistics*. Retrieved from https://www.ibm.com/analytics/data-science/predictive-analytics/spss-statistical-software

Information Systems Audit and Control Association (ISACA). (2017). *Cybersecurity Fundamentals Study Guide* (2nd ed.). ISACA.

Information Systems Audit and Control Association (ISACA). (2018). *Code of Professional Ethics*. Retrieved from http://www.isaca.org/certification/code-of-professional-ethics/pages/default.aspx

ISO/IEC. (2013). *ISO/IEC 27002: Information technology – security techniques – code of practice for information security management*. BSI.

Kazmi, S. A., & Naarananoja, M. (2014). Collection of change management models – an opportunity to make the best choice from the various organizational transformational techniques. *GSTG International Journal on Business Management*, *3*(3), 71–79.

Kiani, A., & Shah, M. H. (2014). An application of ADKAR change model for the change management competencies of school heads in Pakistan. *Journal of Managerial Sciences*, *VIII*(1), 77–95.

Kraemer, S., & Carayon, P. (2005). Computer and Information Security Culture: Findings from two Studies. In *Proceedings of the Human Factors and Ergonomics Society Annual Meeting* (pp. 1483-1487). Orlando, FL: Human Factors and Ergonomic Society. 10.1177/154193120504901605

Krejcie, R. V., & Morgan, D. W. (1970). Determining Sample Size for Research Activities. *Educational and Psychological Measurement*, *30*(3), 607–610. doi:10.1177/001316447003000308

Ledimo, O. (2017). Preparing and involving all stakeholders. In N. Martins, E. Martins, & R. Viljoen (Eds.), *Organizational Diagnosis: A guide for practitioners* (pp. 25–38). Randburg, South Africa: Knowledge Resources.

Luiijf, E., Besseling, K., & De Graaf, P. (2013). Nineteen national cyber security strategies. *International Journal of Critical Infrastructures*, *9*(1/2), 2–31. doi:10.1504/IJCIS.2013.051608

Mahfuth, A., Yussof, S., Baker, A. A., & Ali, N. (2017). A systematic literature review: Information security culture. In *Proceedings of the International Conference on Research and Innovation in Information Systems* (ICRIIS) (pp. 456-463). Langkawi, Kedah, Malaysia: IEEE. 10.1109/ICRIIS.2017.8002442

Martins, E. C. (2017). Planning and coordinating an organizational diagnosis. In N. Martins, E. Martins, & R. Viljoen (Eds.), *Organizational Diagnosis: A guide for practitioners* (pp. 1–23). Randburg, South Africa: Knowledge Resources.

Martins, E. C., & Ledimo, O. (2017). Developing and sourcing assessment instruments. In N. Martins, E. Martins, & R. Viljoen (Eds.), *Organizational Diagnosis: A guide for practitioners* (pp. 39–83). Randburg, South Africa: Knowledge Resources.

Martins, E. C., & Ledimo, O. (2017b). Survey administration process. In N. Martins, E. Martins, & R. Viljoen (Eds.), *Organizational Diagnosis: A guide for practitioners* (pp. 85–112). Randburg, South Africa: Knowledge Resources.

Martins, E. C., & Martins, N. (2016). Organizational culture. In S. P. Robbins, A. Odendaal, & G. Roodt (Eds.), *Organizational Behaviour* (3rd ed.; pp. 606–641). Cape Town, South Africa: Pearson Education.

Martins, N. (2017). Survey administration process. In N. Martins, E. Martins, & R. Viljoen (Eds.), *Organizational Diagnosis: A guide for practitioners* (pp. 1810–202). Randburg, South Africa: Knowledge Resources.

Miller, R. L., & Brewerton, J. D. (2003). *The A-Z of Social Research*. London: Sage Publications. doi:10.4135/9780857020024

Mitchell, M. L., & Jolley, J. M. (2007). *Research design explained* (6th ed.). London: Thomson Wadsworth.

Mohelska, H., & Sokolova, M. (2015). Organizational culture and leadership – joint vessels? *Procedia: Social and Behavioral Sciences*, *171*, 1011–1016. doi:10.1016/j.sbspro.2015.01.223

Oates, B. J. (2012). *Researching Information Systems and Computing*. London: SAGE Publications, Inc.

Okere, I., Van Niekerk, J., & Carroll, M. (2012). Assessing Information Security Culture: A Critical Analysis of Current Approaches. In *Proceedings of the Information Security for South Africa Conference (ISSA)* (pp. 136-143). IEEE. 10.1109/ISSA.2012.6320442

Organization for Economic Co-Operation and Development (OECD). (2002). *Guidelines for the security of information systems and networks. Towards a culture of security*. Retrieved from http://www.oecd.org/internet/ieconomy/15582260.pdf

Padayachee, K. (2012). Taxonomy of compliant information security behavior. *Computers & Security*, *31*(5), 673–680. doi:10.1016/j.cose.2012.04.004

Pfleeger, C. P., Pfleeger, S. L., & Margulies, J. (2015). *Security in Computing* (5th ed.). Upper Saddle River, NJ: Prentice Hall.

Qualtrics. (2018). *Qualtrics Research Core*. Retrieved from https://www.qualtrics.com/research-core/

Robbins, S. P. (1997). *Essentials of Organizational behavior* (5th ed.). Upper Saddle River, NJ: Prentice Hall.

Robbins, S. P. (2001). *Organizational behaviour* (9th ed.). Prentice Hall.

Robbins, S. P., Odendaal, A., & Roodt, G. (2003). *Organizational behaviour – Global and Southern African perspectives*. Cape Town, South Africa: Pearson Education.

Rossouw, D., & Van Vuuren, L. (2013). *Business ethics* (5th ed.). Oxford University Press.

Ruighaver, A. B., Maynard, S. B., & Chang, S. (2007). Organizational security culture: Extending the end-user perspective. *Computers & Security*, *26*(1), 56–62. doi:10.1016/j.cose.2006.10.008

Saunders, M., Lewis, P., & Thornhill, A. (2016). *Research methods for business students* (7th ed.). Pearson Education Limited.

Scantron. (2018). *SurveyTracker*. Retrieved from http://www.scantron.com/software/survey/surveytracker-plus/overview

Schein, E. H. (1985). *Organizational culture and leadership*. San Francisco: Jossey-Bass Publishers.

Schlienger, T., & Teufel, S. (2003). Analyzing information security culture: Increased trust by an appropriate information security culture. In *Proceedings of the International Workshop on Trust and Privacy in Digital Business (TrustBus 2003) in conjunction with the 14th International Conference on Database and Expert Systems Applications (DEXA 2003)*. Prague: IEEE. 10.1109/DEXA.2003.1232055

Schlienger, T., & Teufel, S. (2005). Tool supported management of information security culture. In *Proceedings of IFIP 20th International Information Security Conference proceedings* (pp.65-77). Springer. 10.1007/0-387-25660-1_5

Sheperd, M. L., Harris, M. L., Chung, H., & Himes, E. M. (2014). Using the Awareness, Desire, Knowledge, Ability, Reinforcement Model to build a shared governance culture. *Journal of Nursing Education and Practice*, *6*(4), 90–104.

SurveyMonkey. (2018). Retrieved from http://www.surveymonkey.com

Tang, M., Li, M., & Zhang, T. (2015). The impacts of organizational culture on information security culture: A case study. *Information Technology Management*, *17*(2), 1–8.

The European Parliament. (2016). *The European Council. General Data Protection Regulation (GDPR), Regulation (EU) 2016/679*. Official Journal of the European Union.

The Information Systems Security Association (ISSA). (2018). *ISSA code of ethics*. Retrieved from www.issa.org/?page=codeofethics

The Singapore Statement on Research Integrity. (2010). Retrieved from www.singaporestatement.org

Tree Solution. (2018). *Sicherheitskultur*. Retrieved from http://www.treesolution.ch/10-0-Smart-Tools-fuer-mehr-Sicherheit.html

Van Niekerk, J. F., & Von Solms, R. (2010). Information security culture: A management perspective. *Computers & Security*, *29*(4), 476–486. doi:10.1016/j.cose.2009.10.005

Verizon. (2017). *Data breach investigations report* (10th ed.). Retrieved from http://www.verizonenterprise.com/verizon-insights-lab/dbir/2017/

Von Solms, B., & Von Solms, R. (2018). Cybersecurity and information security – what goes where? *Information and Computer Security*, *26*(1), 2–9. doi:10.1108/ICS-04-2017-0025

Von Solms, R., & Van Niekerk, J. (2013). From information security to cyber security. *Computers & Security*, *38*, 97–102. doi:10.1016/j.cose.2013.04.004

Whitman, M. E., & Mattord, H. J. (2012). *Principles of information security* (4th ed.). Course Technology Cengage Learning.

Whitman, M. E., & Mattord, H. J. (2017). *Management of information security* (5th ed.). Course Technology Cengage Learning.

Whitman, M. E., & Mattord, H. J. (2019). *Management of information security* (6th ed.). Course Technology Cengage Learning.

## ADDITIONAL READING

Da Veiga, A. (2018). An approach to information security culture change combining ADKAR and the ISCA questionnaire to aid transition to the desired culture. *Information and Computer Security Journal, 2018*(5). doi:10.1108/ICS-08-2017-0056

Geert Hofstede. (2018). *Geert Hofstede*. Retrieved September 14, 2018, from https://geerthofstede.com/

Hofstede, G., Hofstede, G. J., & Minkov, M. (2010). *Cultures and Organizations - Software of the Mind*. New York, USA: McGraw-Hill.

Hofstede Insights. (2018). *Hofstede Insights*. Retrieved September 14, 2018, from https://www.hofstede-insights.com/

Keil Centre. (2018). *Keil centre*, chartered psychologists and ergonomists, Retrieved September 14, 2018, from http://www.keilcentre.co.uk/products-services/safe-people/safety-culture/safety-culture-maturity-model/

Minkov, M., & Hofstede, G. (2013). *Cross-cultural analysis – The science and art of comparing the world's modern societies and their cultures*. California, USA: Sage Publications. doi:10.4135/9781483384719

## KEY TERMS AND DEFINITIONS

**Cybersecurity Culture:** The cybersecurity culture is the unconscious way things are done by users to protect information in cyberspace. This culture extends to home users, employees in organizations or entities, users in communities as well as users from a national or international context.

**Information Security Culture:** The information security culture is the unconscious way things are done by employees to protect information throughout its life cycle and in various formats, typically in the context of an organization or entity. The information security culture includes cybersecurity culture in the context of an organization.

**Information Security Culture Assessment (ISCA):** A validated security culture questionnaire with ten constructs to assess the security culture in an organization.

**Security Culture:** A security culture can be seen as the unconscious manner in which things are done in an organization to secure information. The security culture is synonymous with the information security culture and includes cybersecurity culture in the context of an organization.

*Previously published in Cybersecurity Education for Awareness and Compliance; pages 72-100, copyright year 2019 by Information Science Reference (an imprint of IGI Global).*

# Chapter 12

# Cyber Security Competency Model Based on Learning Theories and Learning Continuum Hierarchy

**Winfred Yaokumah**

https://orcid.org/0000-0001-7756-1832

*Pentecost University College, Ghana*

## ABSTRACT

*There is an urgent need for transformative changes in cyber security awareness and training programs to produce individuals and the workforce that can deal with business risks emanating from the prevailing and emerging cyber-attacks. This chapter proposes a cyber security competency model that integrates learning theories (cognitive, affective, and psychomotor), learning continuum hierarchy (awareness and training), and cyber security domain knowledge. Employing literature search of scholarly and practitioner works, together with cyber security standards from governmental and non-governmental organizations, the chapter integrates cyber security domain knowledge, learning theories, and learning continuum hierarchy to design a model of cyber security competencies suitable for use in educating individuals and the general workforce. This theoretical-based approach to designing cyber security awareness and training programs will produce skillful individuals and workforce that can mitigate cyber-attacks in the global business environment.*

## INTRODUCTION

Cyber security is a global concern owing to the increasing reliance on the Internet (Dahbur, Bashabsheh, & Bashabsheh, 2017). It is one of the most serious economic and national security challenges faced by governments (Moskal, 2015), developed and developing nations (Stoddart, 2016), and public and the private businesses (Gunzel, 2017). National and international businesses are at risk as the Internet facilitates both business transactions and cyber-attacks across geographical boundaries. Cyber threats

DOI: 10.4018/978-1-6684-3698-1.ch012

come from numerous sources, including hostile governments, terrorist groups, disgruntled employees, and malicious intruders (Nunez, 2017). The attacks can range from stealing of employees' personal information (Office of Personnel Management, 2015) to attacks on critical infrastructure such as derailment of passenger trains, contamination of water supplies, and shutting down of power grid (Palmer, 2014).

Dealing with cybercrime becomes necessary because of the high cost of cybercrime on the societies, governments, and individuals (Wiederhold, 2014). For instance, the loss of revenue due to cyber attacks is estimated at US$240,000 per day among business organizations and can be more than US$100,000 per hour for retailers (Hui, Kim, & Wang, 2017; Neustar 2012). The Center for Strategic and International Studies estimates that an average annual cost of cybercrime to the global economy is $400 billion (McAfee, 2014); whereas Eubanks (2017) predicts that an average approximate cost of cybercrime will reach US$6 trillion by 2021.

Cyber threats pose danger to national security, financial security, and undermine individuals' privacy. Cyber security has become a top national priority (Proclamation 9508, 2016). It is an important institutional and community responsibility that requires an effective partnership between institutions and the entire community (Oblinger, 2015), including individuals and the general workforce. Thus, to effectively deal with cyber attacks, action is needed at national and global levels requiring individuals, society, and private businesses to better understand and to deal with cyber threats (Stoddart, 2016). The workforce and individuals need competencies and skills, including behavioural, management, and technical expertise to handle cyber attacks in the dynamic cyber threats environment (Singapore Increases Cyber security Training for Youths, 2014).

However, there seems to be a problem of inadequate knowledge and skill among individuals and the general workforce as to how to appropriately maintain cyber safety and respond to cyber attacks. Individuals and the current workforce apparently lack how to effectively apply cyber security measures. According to Russell (2017), public awareness of cyber threats is growing. However, evidence suggests that there are rapid increases in cyber related crimes in the recent years. For example, Global Economic Crime Survey records a high rise of cybercrime from 4th to 2nd position on the global economic crimes list (Global Economic Crime Survey, 2016).

Therefore, there is an urgent need for transformative changes in the current cyber security education to produce individuals and workforce to deal with business risks emanating from the prevailing and emerging cyber attacks. These changes are necessary because of the multifaceted nature of cyber security, the scope of cyber attacks and activities, and the targets of cyber attacks (businesses, government, individual users, and ICT service providers).

Cyber security awareness and training underpinned by relevant learning theories are needed for individuals in the society and the workforce to produce people that are capable of mitigating the current and future cyber attacks (Moskal, 2015). Thus, there will be improvement in cyber security if the individuals and the workforce are aware and properly trained to apply necessary safeguards to deal with issues related to digital privacy and security (Rohrer & Hom, 2017).

The purpose of this chapter is to propose a Cyber Security Competency Model for the current workforce and individuals aimed at developing cyber security knowledge and skills needed to address current global cyber security labor shortage (ITU, 2017). The study includes adding learning theories to cyber security body of knowledge and the learning continuum hierarchy (awareness and training) to support cyber security instructional design and development activities. Efforts at strengthening cyber defences warrant a solid theoretical research foundation (Ortiz & Reinerman-Jones, 2015). However, too often, theory and practice are separated from one another in training programs (ACM, 2014). A cyber security domain knowledge that is underpinned by learning theories (Bloom, 1956; Krathwohl, Bloom, & Masia, 1973; Simpson, 1972), mapped to learning continuum hierarchy will have greater impact. The proposed model will provide a reference and an understanding of how educators should design and manage cyber security awareness and training programs.

In order to achieve the purpose of this chapter, a review of literature of prior practitioner and scholarly works was conducted. The review examines contents of cyber security awareness and training programs from international standards (ISO/IEC 27032, 2012; NIST Special Publication 800-16, 2003), professional training institutes and manuals (Laudon & Traver, 2014; QS TopUniversities, 2018; Sans Technology Institute, 2018), and governmental cyber awareness campaigns (Proclamation 9648, 2017; Proclamation 9508, 2016), and scholarly works (Abawajy, 2014; Affisco, 2017; Poboroniuc et al., 2017; Porter (2016).

The cyber security domain areas relating to cyber security awareness and training were classified using a simple sorting tool to ascertain the number of occurrences of common themes. The themes with higher scores were used to illustrate the matching of learning continuum hierarchy and the learning theories (cognitive, psychomotor, and affective).

## BACKGROUND

### Cyber Attack Targets and Threats Environment

The literature discusses cyber threats and their influence on businesses, governments, individuals, and other stakeholders. Australian Cyber Security Centre Threat Report (ACSC, 2017) classifies the targets for cyber attacks into four: Businesses, Governments, Home users, and ICT Providers. The Australian Cyber Security Centre is an important Australian Government initiative to ensure that Australian cyber networks are amongst the hardest in the world to compromise (ACSC, 2017). Figure 1 shows the targets of cyber attacks. Among others, businesses are targets for trade secrets, personal sensitive information, and client information. Governments are targeted for national security information, communications among politicians, and for sensitive legal documents. Home users or individuals are the target of cyber attacks with respect with individual's banking information and personal identifiable information, while ICT providers' networks are targeted for clients' data.

A recent study finds that 24% of cyber attacks target banks, 23% target telecommunications companies, while 20% target financial services organizations (Hui, Kim, & Wang, 2017). Cyber related offences are of many forms, including malware and ransom ware infection, misuse of personal data (Bergmann et al., 2017), advanced persistent threats, social engineering attacks, insider threats, attacks on network assets (Happa & Goldsmith, 2017), and distributed denial of service (DDOS) attacks. For example, a survey of IT professionals from 38 countries finds 50% of the respondents having experienced business disruptions due to DDOS attacks (Kaspersky Lab 2015). According to Hui, Kim, and Wang (2017), the motives for cybercrime consist of disrupting business operations (28%), distracting the business to make way for main attacks to take place (18%), holding the companies to ransom (17%), and political motivations (11%).

*Figure 1. Targets of cyber attacks*

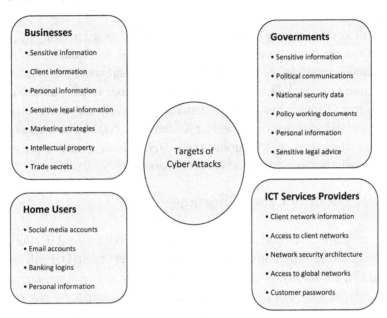

## Business Risk and Cyber Security Labor Landscape

A major risk that businesses across all sectors are facing today is the threat of cyber-attacks (Russell, 2017). Cyber violence and the antidote to cybercrime are fast becoming a global concern for businesses (Hanewald, 2008). Recent years have witnessed cyber attacks on businesses, government agencies, schools, hospitals, and critical public infrastructure, threatening public safety and national security (Proclamation 9648, 2017). Engle (2017) predicts that cyber security threats will represent the third highest risk businesses will face in 2018. Therefore, cyber security concerns are shared responsibilities (Proclamation 9508, 2016) requiring individuals in the society, general workforce, and cyber security professionals to promote cyber security education to defend the cyberspace (McDuffie & Piotrowski, 2014).

Currently, there is an increasing demand for cyber security workforce (Yang & Wen, 2017). Cyber security and safety are seriously challenged by shortages of skilled cyber security personnel (VanDerwerken & Ubell, 2011), trained cyber security workforce, and knowledgeable cyber security individuals who use the cyberspace for their everyday activities. There are currently 2 million shortages of cyber security personnel worldwide (Bell, 2016). According to the U.S. Bureau of Labor Statistics, there is a growing need for cyber security personnel and it is expected that by 2022 information security analyst jobs would grow by 37 percent (Patel, 2014).

Bell (2016) emphasizes that having the workforce with the skills and experience in cyber security is the most critical for business success. Organizations should provide cyber security training for their entire workforce to avoid cyber vulnerabilities. Locasto et al. (2011) suggest training of new information security workers through education rather than mass certification of the existing cyber security workforce. The need to develop cyber security talent from within the organization is important (Bell, 2016). Teaching both technical and societal aspects of cyber security is of critical importance (Vishik

& Heisel, 2015). This may begin from developing fundamental skills and knowledge for individuals and general workforce.

Thus, the problem of a cyber security labor shortage should be tackled not only by producing technical professionals to handle cyber crime because cyber safety involves individuals, businesses, society, and governments. For example, individuals interact with businesses and government information systems in the cyber space and need to know how to safely navigate the cyber space. Additionally, the workforce who are professionals from different disciplines are unable to actively keep themselves updated with the latest information related to cyber security (Tan Kar & Ramaiah, 2007). This makes them vulnerable to cyber attacks, thereby putting their organizations at risk. Hence, collective awareness and training of all peoples will improve resilience to cyber threats (Proclamation 9648, 2017).

## Addressing Cyber Security Labor Shortage

Information security program developed and run by training and educational institutions can contribute immensely to making organizational environment more secure and efficient (DePaolis and Williford; 2015; Eyadat, 2015; Bicak, Liu, & Murphy, 2015). Cyber security awareness and training play a major role in mitigating cyber attacks. Security awareness is a primary pillar of security for any organization to avoid major security breaches (Dahbur, Bashabsheh, & Bashabsheh, 2017). For instance, Porter (2016) notes the importance public education in mitigating cyber deception.nMcCrohan, Engel, and Harvey (2010) examine the impact of cyber threat education and awareness intervention on changes in user security behavior and find that when users are educated of the threats and trained about proper security practices, their behaviors can enhance online security for themselves and the firms where they are employed.

Abawajy (2014) also finds that information security awareness using combined delivery methods of text-based, game-based and video-based are needed in security awareness programs. Information sharing can strengthen the maturity of cyber security program (Korte, 2017). Consequently, Affisco (2017) suggests expanding of cyber security learning in the business programs. Security programs, among others, should address modern technical needs of the individuals, workforce, industry, and academics (Poboroniuc et al., 2017).

## MAIN FOCUS OF THE CHAPTER

The proposed Cyber Security Competency Model provides learning strategies for individuals and the workforce who will help reduce business risks emanating from cyber attacks. The model is composed of three components: Learning continuum hierarchy, cyber security domain knowledge, and learning theories. In the following sections, the chapter discusses and establishes the relationships among the components.

## Component 1: Learning Continuum Hierarchy

This section describes the stages of learning (awareness, training, and education) referred to as the learning continuum hierarchy (NIST Special Publication 800-16, 2003). Learning is a continuum, which starts with awareness, builds on to training, and evolves into education (NIST Special Publication 800-16, 2003). The first and the lowest level (Stage 1) of learning continuum hierarchy is *awareness*. At this level, users need to know about how cyber security affects them, their work, their home, and which methods to use to defend themselves against the threats. Awareness stage aims at allowing individuals to recognize IT security concerns and respond accordingly (NIST Special Publication 800-16, 2003). Cyber security awareness seeks to focus an individual's attention on security issues. The second level (Stage 2) of the learning continuum hierarchy is *training*.

Training strives to produce relevant and needed skills and competencies within an area of practice. Training is learning by doing, which is a well-planned program to develop specific skills and knowledge (Surbhi, 2015). Training aims at improving the performance, productivity, and competency of learners (Surbhi, 2015). The third level (Stage 3) is *education*. Education is a means of learning which develops an individual's sense of reasoning, understanding, judgement and intellectual abilities (Surbhi, 2015). It aims at delivering knowledge about facts, events, values, beliefs, general concepts, and principles (Surbhi, 2015).

*Table 1. Stages of cyber security learning continuum*

| Stages of Learning | Learning Continuum | Focus/Objective | Target Group |
|---|---|---|---|
| Stage 1 | Awareness | • Knowledge of a situation or fact<br>• Focus attention on an issue<br>• Change behaviour<br>• Reinforce best practices | Users of IT Systems (Individuals in the Society) |
| Stage 2 | Training | • Inculcate specific skills<br>• Develop specific skills<br>• Practical application<br>• Hands-on experience<br>• Narrow<br>• Job experience<br>• Short term<br>• Present job<br>• Improve performance and productivity<br>• How to do specific task | General Workforce |
| Stage 3 | Education | • Produces theoretical knowledge<br>• Theoretical oriented<br>• Develop a sense of reasoning and judgement<br>• Teaches general concepts<br>• Wide<br>• Comparatively long term<br>• Future job<br>• General concepts | IT Professionals and Related Discipline |

## Component 2: Cyber Security Domain Knowledge

A review of literature reveals several themes that form cyber security domain knowledge in terms of security training and awareness. Secondary data were gathered from scholarly sources, practitioner sources, training manuals and programs in cyber security (Laudon & Traver, 2014; Sans Technology Institute, 2018), and international governmental and non-governmental organizations (ISO/IEC 27032, 2012; NIST Special Publication 800-50, 2003) championing cyber security. ISO/IEC 27032:2012 is an international standard that provides guidance for improving the state of cyber security. The standard describes cyber security practices and the roles of stakeholders in the cyberspace, guideline for resolving common cyber security issues, and a framework for stakeholders to collaborate to resolve cyber security issues (ISO/IEC 27032, 2012).

The standard identifies the following major domains: (a) Information security, (b) Network security, (c) Internet security, and (d) Critical information infrastructure protection. In addition, NIST Special Publication 800-50 (2003) provides a list of cyber security awareness themes. Sans Technology Institute is a major professional cyber security training provider and provides in-depth cyber security training contents. About 175 items were retrieved from the literature search. The core competencies associated with cyber security training and awareness themes were grouped using a simple sorting program and manual inspection of similar themes. The number of occurrences of each theme were derived and presented in Table 2.

*Table 2. Cyber security training and awareness themes*

| Cyber Security Training and Awareness Theme | N |
|---|---|
| Malware | 15 |
| Phishing | 12 |
| Hacking | 9 |
| Spoofing | 8 |
| Pharming | 3 |
| Identity fraud | 17 |
| Denial-of-Service (DOS) | 5 |
| Sniffing | 3 |
| Password protection | 9 |
| Email protecting | 11 |
| Data backup | 9 |
| Incident response | 7 |
| Handheld device security | 13 |
| Encryption | 5 |
| System patches | 4 |
| Software licensing | 2 |
| Access control | 6 |
| Privacy protecting | 8 |
| File sharing | 10 |
| Social engineering | 12 |
| Shoulder surfing | 7 |

N=175 (N= number of occurrence of similar themes)

## Component 3: Learning Theories

Theories are organized and systematic articulation of a set of statements in a particular discipline or subject area, communicated in a meaningful way that describe, explain, predict, and prescribe conditions under which some phenomena occur (Ingelse, 1997). Learning theories are often used when designing educational, training, and learning processes (Bloom, et al. 1956). Here, the chapter employs three learning theories (cognitive, affective, and psychomotor) to explain cyber security awareness and training program development. The choice of the three theories is as a result of their various focuses that fall in line with the core cyber security controls (technical, administrative, and physical).

Figure 2 shows the three learning theories and their sub domains. Cognitive domain is mental skills often referred to knowledge (Bloom, 1956) and is more closely related to technical control. Affective domain is the growth in feelings or emotional area often known as attitude or self (Krathwohl, Bloom, & Masia, 1973), which is closely linked to the administrative control. The psychomotor domain is the manual or physical skills, generally referred to as skills (Simpson, 1972), which is also related to the physical control.

*Figure 2. Learning theories (three domains of learning)*

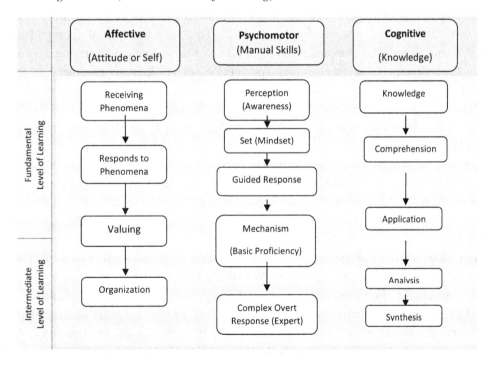

## Cognitive Theory

This is mental skills often referred to as knowledge (Bloom, 1956). The cognitive domain involves knowledge and the development of intellectual skills (Bloom, 1956; Anderson et al., 2000). This comprises of recall or recognition of specific facts, procedural patterns, and concepts that serve in the development of intellectual abilities and skills. There are six major categories (remembering, understanding, applying, analyzing, evaluating, and creating) of cognitive processes. The categories can be thought of as degrees of difficulties. That is, the first one must normally be mastered before the next one can occur.

In chronological order, *remembering* involves recall or retrieval of previously learned information. *Understanding* involves comprehension of the meaning and interpretation of instructions and problems (Anderson et al., 2000). This stage helps the learner to state a problem in one's own words. *Applying* involves the use of a concept in a new situation. For example, applying what was learned in the classroom in novel situation at the work place. *Analyzing* involves separation of information or concepts into component parts so that its organizational structure may be understood.

It includes drawing distinction between facts and inferences (Anderson et al., 2000). *Evaluating* makes judgments about the value of ideas or information. Lastly, *creating* builds a structure or pattern from diverse elements and puts parts together to form a whole, with emphasis on creating a new meaning or structure.

## Psychomotor Theory

This is the manual or physical skills, generally referred to as skills (Simpson, 1972). The psychomotor domain includes physical movement, coordination, and use of the motor-skill areas (Simpson, 1972). Development of these skills requires practice and is measured in terms of speed, precision, distance, procedures, or techniques in execution (Simpson, 1972). Thus, psychomotor skills rage from manual tasks, such as fixing a computer component, to more complex tasks, such as operating a complex piece of machinery. Psychomotor has seven constructs (perception, set, guided response, mechanism, complex overt response, adaptation, and origination). *Perception* (awareness) gives the individual the ability to use sensory cues to guide motor activity (Simpson, 1972). This ranges from sensory stimulation, through cue selection, to translation. *Set* (mindset) makes individuals ready to act. It includes mental, physical, and emotional sets.

These three sets are dispositions that predetermine a person's response to different situations sometimes called mindsets (Simpson, 1972). *Guided Response* is the early stages in learning a complex skill that includes imitation and trial and error. At this stage adequacy of performance is achieved by practicing. *Mechanism* (basic proficiency) is the intermediate stage in learning a complex skill. Learned responses have become habitual and tasks can be performed with some confidence and proficiency.

In addition, *Complex Overt Response* (expert) is the skilful performance of motor acts that involves complex movement patterns (Simpson, 1972). *Proficiency* indicates by a quick, accurate, and highly coordinated performance, requiring a minimum of energy (Simpson, 1972). This category includes performing without hesitation – an automatic performance. *Adaptation* skills are well developed and the individual can modify movement patterns to fit special requirements. Lastly, *Origination* is the creating of new movement patterns to fit a particular situation or specific problem (Simpson, 1972). At this stage, learning outcomes emphasize creativity based upon highly developed skills.

## Affective Theory

This is the growth in feelings or emotional area often known as attitude or self (Krathwohl, Bloom, & Masia, 1973). Affective domain has five constructs (receiving phenomena, responds to phenomena, valuing, organization, and internalizes values). *Receiving Phenomena* is the awareness, willingness to hear, selected attention. *Responds to Phenomena* is an active participation on the part of the learners (Krathwohl, Bloom, & Masia, 1973). The learner attends and reacts to a particular phenomenon. Learning outcomes may emphasize compliance in responding, willingness to respond, or satisfaction in responding. *Valuing* is the worth or value a person attaches to a particular object, phenomenon, or behaviour (Krathwohl, Bloom, & Masia, 1973).

This ranges from simple acceptance to the more complex state of commitment. Valuing is based on the internalization of a set of specified values, while clues to these values are expressed in the learner's overt behavior which is often identifiable. *Organization* organizes values into priorities by contrasting different values, resolving conflicts between them, and creating a unique value system (Krathwohl, Bloom, & Masia, 1973). Here, the emphasis is on comparing, relating, and synthesizing values. Finally, *Internalizes Values* (characterization) is a value system that controls behaviour (Krathwohl, Bloom, & Masia, 1973). The behavior is pervasive, consistent and predictable, which are the most important characteristics of the learner.

## SOLUTIONS AND RECOMMENDATIONS

### Proposed Cyber Security Competency Model

The section presents the basic components of the proposed Cyber Security Competency Model (see Figure 3). This is followed by the detailed Cyber Security Competency Model (see Table 3). The model integrates all the components (Learning Continuum Hierarchy, Cyber Security Domain Knowledge, and Learning Theories) presented in the previous sections. Figure 3 shows the major parts of the model by mapping the Learning Continuum Hierarchy (awareness & training) to Cyber Security Domain Knowledge and Learning Theories in order to achieve cyber security awareness and training objectives. In its basic form, the model suggests that the foundation of getting the desired result from cyber security efforts depends on the following theoretical perspectives:

1. Changing perception and building user's interest (affective theory – such as valuing and internalizing values.
2. Recognizing the threats (cognition theory – such as knowledge and comprehension).
3. Employing practical techniques and methods (psychomotor theory – such as perception and mindset).

Firstly, affective theory can be used to build users' interest in cyber security because users tend to retain facts better when they are personally identified with or use the information personally. Secondly, users are more inclined to follow procedures they have good understanding of. Therefore, cognitive theory (knowledge, comprehension) should form the foundation of user's recognition of threats and attacks. Thirdly, psychomotor theory of makes users adept to practically deal with cyber attacks.

The detailed model (see Table 3) has two cyber security competency levels: Level 1 (Cyber Security Awareness for individuals and general public) and Level 2 (Cyber Security Training for the general workforce). The third level, which is outside the scope of this chapter, addresses Cyber Security education for IT technical and professional workers.

*Figure 3. Basic components of cyber security competency model for individuals and general workforce*

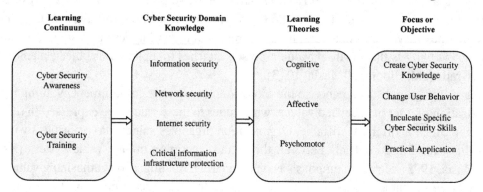

## Level 1: Cyber Security Awareness for Individuals and General Public

This cyber security awareness level of competency mainly focuses on individuals and the general public. The model suggests that cyber security awareness will encourage safe usage habits, change user perceptions of cyber security, inform users about how to recognize potential cyber threats and attacks, and educate users about cyber security techniques to be used to mitigate cyber threats. *At the awareness level, remembering, understanding*, and *applying* of *cognitive theory can be linked to cyber security themes.* For example, at the *remembering* level individuals will be made to describe or recall the types of malware. At the *understanding* stage individuals can explain the steps involved in scanning malware. Also at the *applying* stage the individual will be expected to follow cyber security best practices to mitigate identity fraud and phishing attacks. *Psychomotor theory can also be used to explain individual awareness of cyber safety.*

For instance, cyber security awareness at the *perception* (awareness) stage, individuals can learn to physically protect their mobile devices. At the *set* (mindset) stage, individuals may show desire to learn a new process, such as how to use antimalware to scan viruses on their mobile devices. *Guided response* makes individuals, for example, to follow instructions to configure anti-virus software or assemble a portable computing device. Also, *mechanism* (basic proficiency) enables individuals to use personal computers or repair a computer. Also, affective theory can be applied to cyber security awareness. For example, *receiving phenomena* can explain individuals' listening and remembering of cyber security awareness messages on hacking, password protection and identity theft. *Responds to phenomena* involves compliance with cyber safety rules and practicing them.

## Level 2: Cyber Security Training for the General Workforce

This cyber security training level of competency mainly focuses on the general workforce. Cognitive theory again explains how the workforce should be trained to mitigate cyber attacks. For example, at the *analyzing* stage the workforce is able to analyze the performance of a laptop computer and deploy security patches. At the *evaluating* stage, the workforce will justify the choice of anti-malware or encryption method. Additonally, at the training stage, psychomotor theory can explain the workforce's ability to deal with cyber attacks. For instance, *complex overt response* (expert) makes individuals to response quickly to cyber incidents.

Moreover, the *adaptation* stage underpins individuals' ability to modify email protection instructions to meet the current needs of dynamic cyber environment. Moreover, affective theory explains the effectiveness of cyber security training. For example, an employee's valuing of cyber security measure will inform management on matters that she feels strongly about (such as cyber security non-compliance among employees). *Organization* may involve recognizing the need for cyber privacy or acceptance of professional cyber ethical standards.

*Table 3. Cyber security competency model for individuals and general workforce*

| Cyber Security Competency Level | Component 1 Cyber Security Learning Hierarchy | Component 2 Awareness and Training Themes | Component 3: Learning Theories | | | Focus/Objective |
|---|---|---|---|---|---|---|
| | | | Cognitive Domain | Affective Domain | Psychomotor Domain | |
| Level 1 (Every Individual/ General Public) | Cyber Security Awareness | Malware Spoofing Phishing Hacking Identity fraud Shoulder surfing Protect mobile device Password protection | Knowledge Comprehension Application | Receiving phenomena Responding to phenomena | Perception Set (Mindset) Guided response Mechanism | Knowledge of a situation or fact Focus attention on an issue Change user behavior Reinforce best practices |
| Level 2 (General Workforce) | Cyber Security Training | Encryption Data backup System patches Privacy protecting Email protection Identity fraud Handheld device security Incident response Ethical standards | Comprehension Application Analysis Synthesis | Responding to phenomena Valuing Organize values into priorities | Guided response Mechanism Complex response Adaptation | Inculcate specific skills Develop specific skills Practical application Hands-on experience On-the-job experience Improve performance and productivity Perform specific task |

## Recommendations

Cyber security is a global phenomenon that requires attention of governments, businesses, service providers, and individuals. Several stakeholders are needed to help improve cyber security and business risks, decrease cyber security risks, and reduce cyber security labor shortages. The role of international organizations, the role of governments to establish cyber security community training centers and to embark on awareness programs, and the role of the businesses community and training institutions to undertake research and develop instructional manuals. Weiser and Conn (2017) suggest that to avoid data breaches there is the need to integrate cyber security into business curriculum.

At the global level, international organizations and governments should lead the way of sponsoring cyber security awareness, training, and education programs in both developed and developing nations. There is an urgent need for the government and training institutions to establish several training centers to train individuals and the current workforce, including workers from both government agencies and private companies. There is the need for government grants and private companies' investment in cyber security education. As there is insufficient number of available courses in the cyber security related area in colleges (Namin, Hewett, & Inan, 2014), educators should promote cyber security education by introducing new course modules (Namin, Hewett, & Inan, 2015). Thus, there is also the need to support cyber security researchers and educators who are developing the skills, tools, and workforce required for a safer technology future (Proclamation 9335, 2015).

While there is a general shortage of cyber security skills, the cyber security instructors at training centers and faculty teaching at colleges should be thoroughly trained through workshops so that they can be more competent in developing cyber security programs to train the workforce. These workshops should focus on theoretical basis of cyber security to practical application of measures to curb cyber attacks. The cyber security competency model proposed in this chapter can be a reference point. Development of learning centers, community of practice, and online learning portals will be effective means of cyber security education (Pittman & Pike, 2016). International organizations, governments, and businesses should support cyber security training and research centres. When grants are available, individuals and the workforce will be encourage to undertake training in cyber security, leading to reduction in cyber security business risks and vulnerabilities.

## FUTURE RESEARCH DIRECTIONS

Research in cyber security is emerging. Because of the breadth and multi-disciplinary nature of cyber security, training and educational institutions are constantly attempting to improve curricula to address rapid changes in cyber crime environment and attack strategies. The current chapter addresses a model of cyber security awareness and training for individuals and the general workforce. However, two issues have not been adequately addressed in the chapter. First, there is an issue with the mapping cyber security domain knowledge to learning hierarchy (awareness and training). This is because some of the themes are overlapping. For instance, a topic on malware scanning may overlap, falling under awareness as well as training. In order to deal with this concern, future work will involve an empirical primary research to investigate this classification. Second, the proposed model is based on learning theories only. The study did not examine the theories behind individual cyber security topics, for example a topic on cryptography, penetration testing and compliance.

Future work will examine theoretical underpinning of each topic so as to provide better understanding of the topics (themes) when they are being taught. Thirdly, the current model addresses only individuals and the general workforce. Future work will focus on developing and designing cyber security curricula, based on sound theories, for IT professionals and cyber security personnel.

## CONCLUSION

This chapter propose cyber security competency model to be use in cyber security awareness and training programs for individuals and the general workforce. The model combined three learning models with cyber security awareness and training domain knowledge identified in the literature. The three theories have different theoretical perspectives. Combining theories in training and awareness programs is important. However, too often, theory and practice are separated from one another in training programs (ACM, 2014). A cyber security domain knowledge that is underpinned by learning theories, mapped to learning continuum hierarchy (awareness and training) is important. It will enable individuals and the workforce to effectively deal with cyber vulnerabilities and attacks within their domain.

Virtually everybody uses the cyberspace. Therefore, depending on only few individuals (cyber professional) to protect cyber space and curb cyber crime can be challenging. Accordingly, this chapter proposed a holistic approach to learning that involves individuals (every individual that uses the cyber space) and the general workforce. Teaching cyber security at the two stages of learning (awareness and training) that includes the theoretical domains of learning (cognitive, affective, and psychomotor) and mapped to appropriate cyber security domain knowledge is expected to have a greater impact on cyber workforce development. Moreover, the proposed cyber security competency model provided a reference and an understanding of how educators and trainers should manage cyber security awareness and training programs to prepare individuals and the workforce to minimize cyber security risks.

## REFERENCES

Abawajy, J. (2014). User preference of cyber security awareness delivery methods. *Behaviour & Information Technology*, *33*(3), 236–247. doi:10.1080/0144929X.2012.708787

ACM. (2014). Toward Curricular Guidelines for Cybersecurity. Report of a Workshop on Cybersecurity Education and Training. *Proceedings of the 45th ACM technical symposium on Computer Science education*. doi: 10.1145/2538862.2538990

Affisco, J. F. (2017). Expanding cyber security learning in the business curriculum. *Proceedings for the Northeast Region Decision Sciences Institute (NEDSI)*, 420-435.

Australian Cyber Security Centre ACSC. (2017). *ACSC threat report 2017*. Retrieved on August 4, 2017, from: https://www.acsc.gov.au/publications/ACSC_Threat_Report_2017.pdf

Bell, R. (2016). Cybersecurity: It's mission critical for business. *Workforce*, *95*(10), 12.

Bicak, A., Liu, M., & Murphy, D. (2015). Cybersecurity curriculum development: Introducing specialties in a graduate program. *Information Systems Education Journal*, *13*(3), 99–110.

Chowdhury, W. (2015). Are warnings from online users effective?: An experimental study of malware warnings influencing cyber behaviour. *International Journal of Cyber Behavior, Psychology and Learning*, *5*(2), 44–58. doi:10.4018/IJCBPL.2015040104

Dahbur, K., Bashabsheh, Z., & Bashabsheh, D. (2017). Assessment of security awareness: A Qualitative and quantitative study. *International Management Review*, *13*(1), 37–58.

DePaolis, K., & Williford, A. (2015). The nature and prevalence of cyber victimization among elementary school children. *Child and Youth Care Forum, 44*(3), 377–393. doi:10.100710566-014-9292-8

Engle, P. (2017). Key business risks for 2018. *Industrial Engineer: IE, 49*(12), 20.

Eyadat, M. S. (2015). Higher education administrators roles in fortification of information security program. *Journal of Academic Administration in Higher Education, 11*(2), 61–68.

Gunzel, J. A. (2017). Tackling the cyber threat: The impact of the DOD'S network penetration reporting and contracting for cloud services rule on DOD contractor cybersecurity. *Public Contract Law Journal, 46*(3), 687–712.

Hanewald, R. (2008). Confronting the pedagogical challenge of cyber safety. *Australian Journal of Teacher Education, 33*(3). doi:10.14221/ajte.2008v33n3.1

Ingelse, K. (1997). *Theoretical frameworks. Northern Arizona University NAU OTLE Faculty Studio.* Retrieved on June 2, 2017, from: http://www.ljemail.org/reference/ReferencesPapers.aspx?ReferenceID=799515

ISO27032 (ISO 27032). (n.d.). *Guidelines for cybersecurity information technology -- Security techniques -- Guidelines for cybersecurity.* Retrieved on August 15, 2017, from: https://www.iso.org/standard/44375.html

ITU. (2017). *Global Cybersecurity Index 2017.* Retrieved on December 22, 2017, from: https://www.itu.int/en/ITU-D/Cybersecurity/Pages/GCI-2017.aspx

Korte, J. (2017). Mitigating cyber risks through information sharing. *Journal of Payments Strategy & Systems, 11*(3), 203–214.

Laudon, K. C., & Traver, C. G. (2014). *E-Commerce – Business, Technology, and Society* (10th ed.). Upper Saddle River, NJ: Pearson Education, Inc.

Leung, L. (2015). A panel study on the effects of social media use and internet connectedness on academic performance and social support. *International Journal of Cyber Behavior, Psychology and Learning, 5*(1), 1–16. doi:10.4018/ijcbpl.2015010101

Locasto, M. E., Ghosh, A. K., Jajodia, S., & Stavrou, A. (2011). Virtual extension the ephemeral legion: Producing an expert cyber-security work force from thin air. *Communications of the ACM, 54*(1), 129–131. doi:10.1145/1866739.1866764

McCrohan, K. F., Engel, K., & Harvey, J. W. (2010). Influence of awareness and training on cyber security. *Journal of Internet Commerce, 9*(1), 23–41. doi:10.1080/15332861.2010.487415

McDuffie, E. L., & Piotrowski, V. P. (2014). The Future of Cybersecurity Education. *Computer, 47*(8), 67-69. doi:10.1109/MC.2014.224

MIT. (2013). *Cyber security and human psychology.* Retrieved on November 11, 2015, from: http://cybersecurity.mit.edu/2013/11/cyber-security-and-humanpsychology

Moskal, E. J. (2015). A model for establishing a cybersecurity center of excellence. *Information Systems Education Journal, 13*(6), 97–108.

Namin, A. S., Hewett, R., & Inan, F. A. (2014). Building Cyber Security Instructional Plans Through Faculty Development Program. *Annual International Conference On Infocomm Technologies In Competitive Strategies*, 91-100. doi:10.5176/2251-2195_CSEIT14.22

Namin, A. S., Hewett, R., & Inan, F. A. (2015). Faculty Development Programs on Cybersecurity for Community Colleges. *Annual International Conference On Computer Science Education: Innovation & Technology*, 19-28. doi:10.5176/2251-2195_CSEIT15.9

NIST. (2014). *NIST Cybersecurity Framework*. Retrieved on May 19, 2017, from: https://www.nist.gov/sites/default/files/documents/cyberframework/cybersecurity-framework-021214.pdf

Nunez, K. A. (2017). Negotiating in and around critical infrastructure vulnerabilities: Why the department of defense should use its other transaction authority in the new age of cyber attacks. *Public Contract Law Journal*, *46*(3), 663–685.

Office of Personnel Management (OPM). (2015). *Notify employees of cybersecurity incident*. Retrieved on July 3, 2017, from: https://www.opm.gov/news/releases/2015/06/opm-to-notify-employees-of-cybersecurity-incident

Ortiz, E. C., & Reinerman-Jones, L. (2015). Theoretical Foundations for Developing Cybersecurity Training. Lecture Notes in Computer Science, 9179, 480-487. doi:10.1007/978-3-319-21067-4_49

Palmer, R. K. (2014). *Critical Infrastructure: Legislative Factors for Preventing*. Retrieved on October 7, 2016, from: http://archive.defense.gov/transcripts/transcript.aspx? transcript-id=5136

Parry, M. (2009). Community Colleges Mobilize to Train Cybersecurity Workers. *The Chronicle of Higher Education*, 14.

Patel, P. (2014). Defense against the dark arts (of Cyberspace) universities are offering graduate degrees in cybersecurity. *IEEE Spectrum*, *51*(6), 26. doi:10.1109/MSPEC.2014.6821610

Pittman, J. M., & Pike, R. E. (2016). An observational study of peer learning for high school students at a cybersecurity camp. *Information Systems Education Journal*, *14*(3), 4–13.

Poboroniuc, M. S., Naaji, A., Ligusova, J., Grout, I., Popescu, D., Ward, T., & Jackson, N. (2017). ICT security curriculum or how to respond to current global challenges. *World Journal on Educational Technology*, *9*(1), 40–49.

Porter, C. (2016). Toward practical cyber counter deception. *Journal of International Affairs*, *70*(1), 161–174.

Prichard, J. J., MacDonald, L. E., & Hunt, L. (2004). Cyber terrorism: A study of the extent of coverage in computer security textbooks. *Journal of Information Technology Education*, 3279–3289.

Proclamation 9335. (2015). Proclamation 9335--National Cybersecurity Awareness Month, 2015. *Daily Compilation Of Presidential Documents*, 1-2.

Proclamation 9508. (2016). National Cybersecurity Awareness Month, 2016. *Daily Compilation of Presidential Documents*, 1-2.

Proclamation 9648. (2017). National Cybersecurity Awareness Month, 2017. *Daily Compilation Of Presidential Documents*, 1-2.

QS TopUniversities. (2018). *QS World University Rankings by Subject 2016 - Computer Science & Information Systems*. Retrieved on February 2, 2018, from: https://www.topuniversities.com/university-rankings/university-subject-rankings/2016/computer-science-information-systems

Rohrer, K. K., & Hom, N. (2017). Where do we start with cybersecurity? *Strategic Finance*, 62-63.

Ruiz, R., Winter, R., Kil Jin Brandini, P., & Amatte, F. (2017). The leakage of passwords from home banking sites: A threat to global cyber security? *Journal of Payments Strategy & Systems*, *11*(2), 174–186.

Russell, G. (2017). Resisting the persistent threat of cyber-attacks. *Computer Fraud & Security*, *2017*(12), 7–11. doi:10.1016/S1361-3723(17)30107-0

Sans Technology Institute. (2018). *Master's Degrees - Information Security*. Retrieved on April 2, 2018, from: https://www.sans.edu/academics/degrees/msise

Singapore Increases Cybersecurity Training for Youths. (2014). *Information Management Journal*, *48*(1), 17.

Stoddart, K. (2016). UK cyber security and critical national infrastructure protection. *International Affairs*, *92*(5), 1079–1105. doi:10.1111/1468-2346.12706

Surbhi, S. (2015). *Difference Between Training and Education*. Retrieved on September 22, 2017, from: https://keydifferences.com/difference-between-training-and-education.html

Tan Kar, P., & Ramaiah, C. K. (2007). Awareness of cyber laws in young Singaporeans. *DESIDOC Bulletin of Information Technology*, *27*(6), 41–53. doi:10.14429/djlit.27.6.144

Vishik, C., & Heisel, M. (2015). *Cybersecurity Education snapshot for workforce development in the EU Network and Information Security (NIS) Platform*. Retrieved on January 6, 2017, from: https://resilience.enisa.europa.eu/nis-platform/shared-documents/wg3-documents/cybersecurity-education-snapshot-for-workforce-development-in-the-eu/view

Weiser, M., & Conn, C. (2017). Into the Breach: Integrating Cybersecurity into the Business Curriculum. *Bized*, *16*(1), 36–41.

Wiederhold, B. K. (2014). The role of psychology in enhancing cybersecurity. *Cyberpsychology, Behavior, and Social Networking*, *17*(2). doi:10.1089/cyber.2014.1502 PMID:24592869

Yang, S. C., & Wen, B. (2017). Toward a cybersecurity curriculum model for undergraduate business schools: A survey of AACSB-accredited institutions in the United States. *Journal of Education for Business*, *92*(1), 1–8. doi:10.1080/08832323.2016.1261790

## KEY TERMS AND DEFINITIONS

**Cyber Competency:** The ability, skill, and knowledge by individuals to protect themselves and their organization's cyberspace.

**Denial of Service (DoS):** This happens when hackers flood a server with useless traffic to inundate and overwhelm the network, often degrading the server's performance and causing it to shut down with the intent of damaging the organization's reputation and customer relationships.

**Hacking:** An intentional disruption, defacing, or even destroying an information resources normally carried out on the internet.

**Identity Fraud:** This is an unauthorized use of another person's personally identifiable information, such as social security, driver's license, credit card numbers, user names, and passwords for illegal financial benefit.

**Pharming:** This involves redirecting a web link to an address different from the intended one, with the fake site appearing as the intended destination.

**Phishing:** A deceptive normally online attempt by an attacker to obtain user's confidential information for financial gain.

**Sniffing:** This is a program that monitors information travelling over a network, enabling hackers to steal proprietary and sensitive information from anywhere on a network.

**Spoofing:** This occurs when hackers attempt to hide their true identities or misrepresent themselves by using fake e-mail addresses or masquerading as someone else.

*Previously published in Global Cyber Security Labor Shortage and International Business Risk; pages 94-110, copyright year 2019 by Business Science Reference (an imprint of IGI Global).*

# Chapter 13
# The Role of Education and Awareness in Tackling Insider Threats

**Shaun Joseph Smyth**
*Ulster University, UK*

**Kevin Curran**
*Ulster University, UK*

**Nigel McKelvey**
*Computer Science Department, Letterkenny Institute of Technology, Ireland*

## ABSTRACT

*Insider threats present a major concern for organizations worldwide. As organizations need to provide employees with authority to access data to enable them to complete their daily tasks, they leave themselves open to insider attacks. This chapter looks at those who fall into the category which can be referred to as insiders and highlights the activity of outsourcing which is employed by many organizations and defines the term insider threat while pointing out what differentiates an accidental threat from a malicious threat. The discussion also considers various methods of dealing with insider threats before highlighting the role education and awareness plays in the process, the importance of tailoring awareness programs, and what the future holds for insider threats within organizations.*

## INTRODUCTION

In the early 1990s the United States saw a drive in the growth of business because of telecommunications networks and the Internet. Despite this growth, the dependency placed upon these networks placed the U.S. in a precarious position as it also increased their vulnerability to cyber exploitation and by the end of the twentieth century the U.S. had become the most vulnerable nation to cyber-attacks aiming to disrupt or interfere with essential services (McConnell, 2002).

DOI: 10.4018/978-1-6684-3698-1.ch013

Organizations, worldwide regardless of their size or form have all accepted that an increase in the development of their existing services is essential if they are to improve and gain a much-needed advantage over their fellow competitors. In their quest to achieve this goal organizations understand that a greater dependence is placed upon the need for information technology (IT) for them to compete successfully in the world of modern-day business (Abawajy, 2014). Businesses are already connected with the bulk of transactions taking place in an electronic format the consequence of which is a constant rise in the quantity of both personal and sensitive data produced and later collected. Sensitive data is looked upon as one of the many assets of any organization as many appreciate its significance, considering it to be the lifeblood of the processes and procedures which take place within their business (Sarkar, 2010). As many of today's organizations compete in lively and fast-moving environments which are constantly developing, they produce a large volume of sensitive data in a bid to achieve their goals which include lower prices, higher quality of products and services and a rapid development. However, the provision of new opportunities coupled with the globalization of activities in both businesses and organizations combined with the swift growth of ICT has given rise to a new problem in the form of threats (Stavrou et al. 2014).

Organizations can find themselves on the receiving end of threats as their information security is susceptible to dangers from a wide variety of sources which present in many different formats varying from the less complicated spam emails to the more structured and complex form of attack such as malwares (malicious software) which can steal or contaminate data and ultimately produce enough damage to leave systems in a condition where they are inoperable (Abawajy, 2014).

One such threat includes that caused as a direct result of online social networking (OSN) which has recently experienced a sudden rise. Certain employees within organizations are accountable for information and are later responsible for the leakage of this same information to outside parties. Careless use of social media has a harmful influence on organizations placing networks and systems at risk of malware which can result in many negative issues including copyright and defamation issues, reduced productivity which significantly affect the organization's reputation and future income (Molok et al. 2011).

Modern-day information systems are challenged by a wide range of threats and even though attacks which are started from outside such as viruses and hacking receiving much publicity the insider threat however, presents a considerably higher level of danger (Theoharidou et al. 2005). This view is shared by Baracaldo and Joshi (2012), McCormac et al. (2012), and Warkentin and Willison (2009) who all point out that Insider attacks are still one of the most dangerous threats organizations can face today.

The insider threat comes from the trusted organizational member and they can cause the greatest harm as they have access to the organization's greatest asset 'information'. Those individuals employed within an organization have the capability to either damage or destroy sensitive information using uncomplicated noncompliance of security policies, negligence, the absence of motivation in the protection of sensitive data, careless actions within the workplace or insufficient training. Including reduced productivity and revenue such actions result in the failure to protect the confidentiality of the organization, its associates, customers and ultimately the reputation of the organization's information system. This problem is often referred to as the 'endpoint security problem' as the employee is the last point of contact or endpoint of the information system (IS) and its network. It is often said that the weakest link or greatest security problem within a network lies between the keyboard and the chair (Warkentin, and Willison, 2009).

Organizations are faced with an ever-growing task in relation to computer security and face persistent attacks from both external and internal sources as there are many different threats which are all keen to breach organizational security defenses with a noticeable increase in the vulnerability to threats posed by the insider because of the worryingly high increase in the possession of privileged access to the network which they enjoy and require to carry out their jobs (Nurse et al. 2014; Martinez-Moyano et al.2008).

This view is also expressed by Claycomb and Nicoll (2012) as they highlight that insider threats are both a constant and ever-increasing problem. The insider attack presents a much greater risk to organizations, the main reason for this however is not solely due to the advantage which the insider currently enjoys by already holding secure access to the network but it is also due to the fact that the majority of network security procedures direct their attention to the prevention of external attacks from those who are outside the network perimeter the consequence of which is a reduction in the importance assigned to the safeguarding of network components against malicious access internally from within the actual network itself from management/employees who already have network access and certain privileges inside the network itself (Nurse et al.2014; McCormac et al. 2012). Martinez-Moyano et al (2008) also emphasize that the growing dependence of organizations on technological infrastructures has placed organizations in a position where they are exposed to an increased vulnerability from insider threats.

The rest of this chapter looks at those individuals who can be classed as insiders and offers a definition for the term 'insider threat' looking at their frequency of occurrence and the different causes. The practice of non-compliance within the workplace is examined highlighting some reported breaches of security by organizational employees and the reported damage caused to those organizations due to the practice of insider threats. Also covered within this chapter are the roles which both education and awareness can play in dealing with the growing problem of the insider threat within an organizational setting including the possibility of reducing the issue or eradicating it completely as organizations now place more emphasis on external threats and their prevention than they do on the insider threat which can be equally if not more dangerous to an organization.

## BACKGROUND

The cost incurred to businesses worldwide due to security breaches and computer viruses has been a total of $1.6 trillion a year and 39,363 human years of productivity (Ula and Fuadi, 2017). This highlights the importance placed in the ability for organizations to protect their assets and why the security of information is such a major concern in organizations. The potential for attacks from hackers is such a worry that many are forced to employ services in a bid to protect against viruses and malware and the likelihood of an attack from an outsider. However, although protection from external attacks is an important concern it is also essential not to dismiss the possibility of attacks which occur closer to home as much evidence suggests that internal breaches have been the cause of many significant, costly attacks and security incidences in both government and organizational sectors (Sarkar, 2010). A similar view is shared by Chinchani et al. (2005) as they highlight that many organizations concentrate solely on external attacks as techniques and tools are now available to help in finding and fixing such weaknesses, unlike the internal threat which is not yet fully understood, difficult to calculate and there is an absence of available tools and techniques which are able to help with such a situation.

Insider attacks are a well-recognized problem with the threat they offer being acknowledged as far back as the 1980s (Chinchani et al. 2005). However, for years organizations have wrestled with this internal issue of defending themselves from individuals which they should trust in the day-to-day running of their business. Such individuals are referred to as 'insiders' which include employees, freelance workers, consultants and others who have the privilege of having access to vital areas within an organization which ultimately enables them to access important organizational information. Individuals in such positions however may exploit the trust bestowed upon them for their own personal gain and pose as a serious threat to confidentiality within the organization, the organization's significant assets and ultimately the organization's reputation (Liu et al. 2008).

Insiders worldwide are accountable for many such incidents with reports of insider threats by those granted the privilege of access to information within organizations where they have been employed. Many such incidents however, go unreported to protect the reputation and good name of the organization yet many still make the headlines such as the following:

- Over a period of months in 1996 two credit union employees working together altered credit reports for monetary gain. Both employees had authorization as part of their normal duties to update information received by the company however these two individuals misused their authorization by removing negative credit indicators and adding fabricated indicators of positive credit in exchange for money. The total amount of fraud because of these activities surpassed $215,000 however, the risk associated with the credit union as a result was immense (Randazzo et al. 2005).
- Sarkar (2010) highlights how the UK government hit the headlines in 2008 when a Home Office contractor lost a USB stick which held details of all 84,000 prisoners within Wales and England resulting in the end of a £1.5 million contract with a management consultancy firm.
- An international financial services company fell victim to a logic bomb in 2002 deleting 10 billion files in the company and affecting servers of over 1300 companies throughout the United States. The company suffered losses totaling $3million needed to repair damage and recreate the deleted files. Investigations later revealed that the logic bomb was planted by a frustrated employee who quit the company over a dispute regarding the amount of his annual bonus (Randazzo et al. 2005).

The incentive to work on insider threats varies from country to country as the U.S. interest appears to be centered more around events which cause damage to national security such as the case of Robert Hanssen, an FBI insider who was arrested in 2001 for stealing and selling secrets to the Russians and more recently, the case of Bradley Manning an American soldier and insider who revealed many confidential U.S. government documents. When compared to the $7billion fraud committed against the French bank Societe Generale by one of its own traders, Jerome Kerviel the difference is obvious (Hunker and Probst, 2011).

## WHO ARE INSIDERS?

A reliable definition of an insider is difficult to obtain and as such it hampers the detection of threats from this group of individuals. The assumption of a perimeter around an organization such that those within the perimeter can referred to as insiders is not practical with the increase in mobile computing and outsourcing (Bishop and Gates, 2008). Similarly, an insider can have wireless connectivity and have a physical presence far away from an organization while likewise individuals can be physically present within an organization but have no authorization to use the computation infrastructure (Chinchani et al. 2005). Despite the arguments which surround an insider's physical location, many descriptions of what constitutes an insider are however offered. One such definition includes that proposed by Magklaras and Furnell (2005) who explain that the insider is an individual who has legitimately been given the ability to access one or several elements of the IT infrastructure using one or more authentication mechanisms. It is the use of the word legitimately which differentiates between the insider who enjoys a certain level of trust and advantages in comparison to the external hacker who must spend extra time and effort in obtaining a point of entry to the computer system an advantage which the insider already enjoys. As Sarkar (2010) highlights the insider can be an employee who has the required privileges such as keys, log on details for the network and suitable network access to enable them to fulfil his/her duties in their place of work on a day-to-day basis. This is a view which is shared by Greitzer et al. (2008) who define the insider as a person who is now or was on some earlier occasion granted the authority to access the organization's information system, data or network and such authorization is indicative of a high level of trust in that individual.

Hayden (1999) who also explains that insiders who can be employees, contractors or service providers or somebody with valid access to a system however, stresses that the issue of trust is an important factor regarding insiders as the more privileges they enjoy on the system, the greater will be their level of knowledge and access on the system and ultimately, they pose a higher potential threat.

Probst et al. (2010) describe an insider as the following:

- An insider is an individual who has rightful access to resources.
- An insider is an individual or company which the organization trust.
- An insider is the user of a system who can use their privileges for the wrong purpose.
- An insider is an individual who despite having authorized access may use this benefit to damage or remove organizational assets or help outsiders in carrying out such acts.

Probst et al. also highlight how the following definition for an insider has been proposed:

*An insider is a person that has been legitimately empowered with the right to access, represent, or decide about one or more assets of the organization's structure. (Probst et al. 2010)*

Despite this proposed definition of insiders, there are however, insiders which are not necessarily always friendly in nature helping organizations in their day-to-day functions as some may present as threats posing a danger to organizations and their resources namely their private data/information (Park and Ho, 2004). In defining the insider Anderson (1999) looks at the intent of the insider classifying them into three categories which include Normal – Abnormal – Malevolent. Anderson (1999) explains each of these three categories further highlighting the intent of each of three insider types as follows:

- **Normal:** This category of insider is likely to carry out insider activity which is unlikely to present a threat.
- **Abnormal:** The insider activity by this group may consist of routine errors which may cause issues in a weak system causing private information to be accidentally revealed
- **Malevolent:** This includes insider activity which presents a threat as it is carried out with mischievous intent.

McConnell (2002) highlights that everybody connected to the Internet is a possible insider within an organization and ordinarily in an environment which is non-computing the authority to access information is based upon distinct roles which relates to users and the access privileges they have. However, within the modern computing environment roles often change and, in many instances, are less well-defined.

The greatest threat to computer security is symbolized by insiders as these individuals understand fully the commercial side of their organization and the workings of the computer system and they possess confidentiality and the legitimate access to the network which enables them to carry out insider attacks (Nguyen et al. 2003)

## THE INSIDER THREAT

The subject of the insider threat is not a new issue as documented reports of this problem date as far back as the 1980s (Chinchani et al. 2005) and as Miller and Maxim (2015) stress it is the responsibility of organizations to face up to the fact that insider threats pose a significant threat and are increasing in difficulty. The task of achieving a conclusive definition for the insider threat is both challenging and complex as so many varied opinions on this subject exist (Humphreys, 2008). Despite this fact there are however, many different definitions presented on this subject some of which including the following:

Cappelli et al. define the insider threat as:

*Individuals who were, or previously had been, authorized to use the information systems they eventually employed to perpetrate harm. (Cappelli et al. 2004)*

Bishop and Gates explain how the insider threat can be defined with respect of these two primitive actions:

1. *violation of a security policy using legitimate access violation of a security policy using legitimate access*
2. *violation of an access control policy by obtaining unauthorized access* (Bishop and Gates, 2008)

Finally, the definition offered by Greitzer et al. differs again as they say:

*The insider threat is manifested when human behavior departs from compliance with established policies, regardless of whether it results from malice or a disregard for security policies. (Greitzer et al. 2008)*

Greitzer and Frincke (2010) also highlight that despite the vast amount of research which has been carried out on the insider threat, especially in the studies of both the psychology and motivation of insiders, the prediction of insider attacks however still proves exceedingly difficult. The insider threat has commanded a serious amount of attention and it is referred to as the most difficult security problem to deal with because the insider has information which is unknown to outside hackers and as a result, they are able to inflict serious damage (Hunker and Probst, 2011). Internal attacks take place when authorized individuals including trusted employees within an organization execute specific actions in the organization abusing the trust and privileges, they have thus causing harm to the organization (Baracaldo and Joshi, 2012; Chinchani et al. 2005; Greitzer et al. 2008; Blackwell, 2009). As Greitzer et al. (2008) point out insider threats begin when the behavior of humans deviates from compliance with established policies whether it is a result of malicious intent or just a complete disregard for security policies

Trying to escape such threats from insiders is a frightening task as it is essential that employees receive privileges to enable them to carry out their jobs in an efficient manner. However, the provision of too many privileges to an employee can have detrimental effects if they are misused in either an intentional or unintentional fashion (Baracaldo and Joshi, 2012). Greitzer and Frincke (2010) claim that only a small number of employees take part in the type of behavior which could be described as that of an insider threat as the rest of the working population is made up of individuals who are classed as both honest and hard-working. Worryingly however, they also highlight that a report by the U.S. Department of Defense in 1997 confirmed that 87% of those intruders into the Department of Defense which were recognized included either employees or others who were internal to that organization.

The main motivational factor behind many insider attacks is pure and simple financial gain as highlighted by Cappelli et al. (2004) as they claim that carrying out insider attacks for any other purpose is simply not worth the risk. Financial gain can be achieved through different formats depending on the type of organization in which the insider threat takes place. In financial establishments such as banks, the value lies in customer account records and company accounts which give a direct route to funds while other types of organizations such as software companies do not offer such immediate financial rewards as the real value lies in the branded software code (Chinchani et al. 2005). Monetary losses incurred because of insider attacks range in value from five hundred dollars to tens of million dollars with approximately 75% of organizations experiencing a negative impact to their business and 28% reporting a negative influence on their reputations (Baracaldo and Joshi, 2012). All commercial sectors are troubled by the insider threat for several reasons including the following:

- Personal gain and profit (scams, fraud or theft of information and other assets).
- Taking part in reckless behavior whether it was intended to cause harm or not.
- Malicious damage/sabotage which was intended to inflict harm.

Martinez-Moyano et al. (2008) clarifies that data analysis carried out by CERT/CC (coordination center for the computer emergency response team) stresses that the three different insider threats which organizations face include 1) Long term, 2) Sabotage, 3) Espionage or information threat. Franqueira et al. (2010) also highlights that other classifications of the insider threat concentrate solely on the intentions of the insider and likewise organizes them into three separate categories which include the following:

- Theft of information also referred to as espionage when individuals steal private or personal from the organization.
- IT sabotage which occurs when somebody damages the organization or any individual within it.
- Finally, the third category refers to fraud which occurs when someone acquires unwarranted services or property from the organization.

Franqueira et al. (2010) point out however, that there is a connection between these three classifications as impersonators are in a better position to execute fraud while trespassers or those who carry out a lawful action in an illegal or improper manner are in a better place for the execution of sabotage and espionage. According to Greitzer and Frincke (2008) there are many different types of crimes associated with insider threats include Espionage, Sabotage, Terrorism, Embezzlement, Extortion, Bribery and Corruption. Even though insider threats have a higher success rate, they occur less often than outsider attacks as displayed in table 1. They pose a greater risk than their counterparts and have an immediate advantage by having legitimate access to the system (Chinchani et al. 2005).

*Table 1. Percentage of Insider attacks against outsider attacks*

| Year | 2004 | 2005 | 2006 | 2007 | 2008 | 2010 |
|---|---|---|---|---|---|---|
| **Insider Attacks** | 29% | 20% | 32% | 31% | 34% | 27% |
| **Outsider Attacks** | 71% | 80% | 68% | 69% | 66% | 73% |

(Zawalge et al. 2013)

## MALICIOUS/ACCIDENTAL THREATS

The very mention of an insider threat invokes the image of an unhappy employee who is planning to take revenge or a malicious employee who is looking to achieve financial gain. Every organization is afflicted by employees who unintentionally put their employers and the organization itself in danger. Such insider threats however, are not deliberate and take place due to basic unfamiliarity or inexperience (Sarkar, 2010). All insider threats are not the same, as highlighted by Miller and Maxim (2015). There are several different types of insider threats which include the malicious insiders who are current or former employees or even trusted partners of the organization who abuse their positions and their legitimate access to the organization's network system/data making decisions fully aware that their actions will cause damage to the organization and have a full understanding that their actions will have a negative effect on the organization they attack. Such actions include - but are not restricted to - theft of information, fraud and sabotage. In comparison to this there are the insiders who are exploited by outside groups and influenced into carrying out actions which they see as reasonable but will result in damage to the organization. Finally, there is the category of insiders who, despite having privileges, are careless in security responses or cause a security breach through incorrect handling of the organization's main asset, 'information' on the network (Miller and Maxim, 2015; Cole, 2015; Glasser and Lindauer, 2013). Since few employees take part in insider threat activities the task of predicting insider attacks is made more difficult and experts have realized that a character who is despondent in his or her place of work and current job situation signifies the characteristics displayed by a would-be insider threat (Greitzer and Frincke, 2010).

Sarkar (2010) highlights that the largest security threat comes from those individuals with extended privileges and authorized access as great emphasis is placed on the importance of understanding the psychology of those individuals who are involved in insider activity, both malicious and non-malicious. Hunker and Probst (2011) list that there are psychosocial signs which highlight that an individual has the potential to be a malicious insider, some of which include the following:

- Disgruntled
- Accepting feedback
- Anger management
- Disengagement
- Disregard for authority

- Performance issues

The detection of malicious insiders presents an enormous task as Azaria et al. (2014) explain that initially the quantity of malicious insiders who have been exposed inside any given organization is normally very small, normally only amounting to a mere handful over the space of a decade thus creating an imbalanced data set of more than 99.9% honest users and less than 0.1% of malicious insiders which is not ideal for machine learning algorithms as they naturally assume data is balanced and the use of imbalanced data usually results in high accuracy for the majority class. Azaria et al. (2014) are also keen to point out that detection of malicious insiders is hindered further due to the lack of a publicly available data set for the insider threat as many companies are unwilling to share such data to protect their reputation.

Colwill (2009) emphasizes that the insider threat is constantly present revealing itself in many different formats and that the malicious insider can cause more harm to an organization as it has more advantages than the outside attacker. Colwill (2009) also highlights that those individuals who carry out malicious insider actions have a casual experience or mechanism which influences their motivation and ultimately leads to betrayal. Such experiences can be classified into three main sources which include:

- Rising, intensified or unaddressed dissatisfaction with their role or worth within an organization.
- Recruitment by unfriendly outside individuals or groups.
- The penetration of a malicious threat actor to a trusted position.

Neumann (2010) points out that despite the vast amount of attention which the intentional malicious misuse achieves it would however be considered irresponsible to overlook the acceptable accidental misuse as there is a likelihood that once this type of activity is accepted it could encourage malicious misuse later.

## OUTSOURCING

Worldwide communications offer the chance to outsource tasks which were previously carried out within the organization in the home country to sites almost anywhere in the world. Such moves can involve transporting organizational activities to areas which have a favorable taxation structure which is more profitable with lower labor and set-up costs involving companies abroad which offer services at prices which are inexpensive and can deliver skills which are in limited supply. As a result, the move by organizations to outsourcing has become such an attractive proposition that the practice of outsourcing has become universal throughout the public and private sectors (Jones and Colwill, 2008). The quantity of third-party employees who are granted the privilege of long-term access to company systems and information comparable to that of full-time employees is increasing rapidly and as such the position of large volumes of outsider third party personnel is changed to insiders creating confusion over the difference between full-time company employees and third-party personnel (Jones and Colwill, 2008; Munshi et al. 2012).

While the subcontracting and outsourcing of certain tasks offers many benefits such as leading to improvements in efficiency, monetary gains, cheaper labor costs and other potential advantages it does however present the issue of the movement of organizational boundaries where security defenses could have been placed (Gollmann, 2011). As the growing tendency within organizations favors the use of mobile computing, working from home and outsourcing it also increases the probability of insider attacks. Outsourcing increases the possibility of confidential data being breached as information is moved beyond the organization's control and this data is made available to these third parties (Ophoff et al. 2014).

Despite the obvious difficulty of organizations ensuring that the confidential information they share while outsourcing stays confidential and no data breaches occur, outsourcing is however, not without its own difficulties. As highlighted by Colwill (2009) who firstly explains that the language differences can present issues such as misinterpretation misunderstanding at all stages and secondly outsourcing approaches can create further complications as many permanent staff witness roles being outsourced leading to feelings of alienation within the organization and employees are fearful of job security in case their roles within the organization are next in line for outsourcing. Colwill (2009) also highlights that provision of effective education in outsourced locations to the same level as it can be delivered within an organization is difficult due to the numbers of employees hired each month and due their physical location.

With many companies outsourcing many functions to external service providers, possibly in other countries allowing them to avail of the financial benefits, technical issues such as auditing the part of a business process which is being outsourced become difficult. Data protection and collection laws vary from country to country and outsourcing the task of auditing itself can be challenging as protection of the valuable confidential data already collected is of supreme importance and data should be as anonymous as possible so that it does not relate back to a particular individual revealing only the required data which the auditor needs to get results but prevents them from access to data they do not require and as a results prevents them from drawing unwanted conclusions from the data they have access to (Probst et al. 2010).

## STOPPING INSIDER THREATS

An extensive and successful insider threat mitigation approach must include the motivational factors and behavior of humans beside organizational factors such as policies, procedures, hiring, training practices and technical weaknesses along with the best practices for avoidance or the early detection of unauthorized insider activity (Greitzer et al. 2008). Most mitigation strategies concentrate on how incidents are performed, detected and how the insider's identification is revealed. Even though such methods are successful in stopping insiders and their activity this occurs only when significant damage has already happened. Monitoring networks, email accounts and the log in activity of employees and their everyday work pattern may find irregularities here or there without causing suspicion. However, by the time these irregularities begin to add up and it is time to act on these findings it is in many cases too late as the insider has already acted and the damage has already been performed (Puleo, 2006).

As organizations develop, they become reliant on information technology with growing importance placed upon information security which was initially viewed as a technology problem which could be tackled using complex hardware and software solutions. However, the increasing number of security breaches has since disproved this theory, proving that it is in fact mainly a people problem as failure by the end users to recognize and follow the technological controls creates a concern as systems are compromised as a result (Yayla. 2011). With the issue of the insider threat growing in difficulty Sarkar (2010) also highlights that technical solutions are not adequate for this issue as insider threats are essentially a people issue while Whitman (2003) emphasizes that technologists often ignore the human solutions opting instead for technology solutions when in fact it is essential that the human factor must firstly be discussed and incorporate technology for support when needed to achieve the required human behaviors. Colwill (2009) highlights that there is no disputing that the least technical controls for the prevention of insider attacks should include the following:

1. Encryption;
2. Access control;
3. Smallest possible privilege;
4. The use of monitoring, auditing and reporting

Colwill (2009) also points out that standard security policies and procedures are needed, and organizations must enforce said policies showing clearly what is expected of their employees. One method employed is the strict enforcement of company policies and excluding the personal use of any company assets within the workplace. As Colwill (2009) however, highlights that for such a measure to be successful it would need networks to be closed to all but essential business applications thus avoiding access to websites which are not work related and prevent time wasting and the risk of malware infections.

One method of detecting insider misbehavior is to adopt the use of monitoring as a suitable system can substantially reduce the potential of insider attacks and give an alert for the presence any suspicious behavior on the system so that the user's privileges can be restricted and prevent a possible insider attack (Baracaldo and Joshi, 2012). Even though research revealed that 70% of fraud is an insider issue 90% of security controls and monitoring are still focused on the external threat (Colwill, 2009). However, Greitzer and Frincke (2010) point out that although monitoring employees is an important activity in the fight against the prevention of possible insider threats they also highlight that employees could take offence when they learn that the very organization they work hard for each day is monitoring their very activity as only a minority of employees actually engage in insider activity which could possibly harm the organization.

As Flynn, et al. (2003) however, points out the use of monitoring should not just limit itself to individuals within the organization as the growing trend is leaning towards an increase in a mobile workforce who have the potential to cause an insider threat through the malicious use of the many mobile devices which this section of the workforce employ has also increased the potential for malicious use. Organizations need to be aware of the functionality of these mobile devices and in some cases the use of privately-owned mobile devices can be prohibited completely as they could be used to seize sensitive information and remote access to privileged data should be limited to a certain number and keep a log of when users use remote access for further inspection.

The Implementation of strong passwords is strongly recommended as is the practice of precise account management policies (Greitzer and Frincke, 2010; Randazzo et al. 2005). Even though the practice of good password management is strongly recommended within organizations, Randazzo et al. (2005) point out however that active practices such as compulsory password protection and change policies and the use of password-protected screen savers should be encouraged as this reduces the opportunity of insiders carrying out an attack using a fellow employee's computer or account. The importance of effective password practice is also highlighted by Cappelli et al. (2009) who explain that however vigilant an organization is in trying to prevent insider threats, if there is a possibility that their computer accounts can be compromised then the opportunity to side-step manual and automated controls exists and for this reason, password management practices and policies should apply to all employees to ensure that all the activity on any account is attributed to the account holder and only the account holder. If for any reason an employee's employment, consulting or contracting contract needs to be stopped then the immediate deactivation should take place of all their computer accounts, authorization on the system, remote access and privileges within the organization (Randazzo et al. 2005; Flynn et al. 2003)

Organizations should apply separate policies which privileged users should sign as they can cause the most harm having the greatest access to systems, networks and applications and they can log into the system as another user and have greater technical ability. Organizations should also employ techniques which only enable online activity to be attributed to one single employee thus disabling the privileged user from carrying out online activity under the guise of another employee. As with other employees if the privileged user's contract had to be ended then the organization should disable their access to the system at once to prevent an insider attack from a former employee (Flynn et al. 2003).

Organizations should investigate methods by which employees feel they can report suspicious behavior. Occurrences such as the sharing of passwords, trying to access information which an employee does not need to fulfil their duties or trying to gain access to unauthorized information or showing a complete disregard for the organization's safety policies and noncompliance with policies which are in place to protect the organization and the information it safeguards. Encouraging employees to engage in this type of practice will alert security personnel to the noncompliance with policies, thus providing them with the opportunity to investigate the issue before it becomes a major problem (Randazzo et al. 2005).

## EDUCATION AND AWARENESS

In many organizations, the bulk of their security budget and time is devoted to placing defenses at the system boundary to protect the information and assets stored from outsiders including thieves and hackers who were engaged in the practice of economic espionage and other illegal activities. The everchanging environment has resulted in major technological advances offering employees the ability to make the most of the opportunity to communicate with the organization's network while still enjoying better mobility and this growth in remote working, home working and the decision to include outsourcing further complicates the issue with an increase in the number of personnel who have access to insider privileges resulting in organizations being exposed to an increased number of insider threats (Jones and Colwill, 2008). Appropriate employee education is a significant contributor to improving the durability of an organization and essential for the effective management of insider threats (Eggenschwiler et al. 2016). In the world of cybercrime Insiders have become one of the most extensively mentioned offenders as numbers increased with the past decade alone seeing a steady rise in the volume of attacks which have been reported as a direct result of insider activity (Eggenschwiler et al. 2016).

Technical solutions can offer valuable protection against security threats in the form of technology which offers a method for both the regulation and control of access to information and helps with the monitoring and detection of malicious activity. They are however unable to deliver a complete solution to the problem as it is the working environment and the human element which deliver the true foundations for success as the activities of cyber criminals takes on many different formats. It is for this very reason that the practice of user awareness and ongoing education are both recognized activities considered crucial in the mitigation of cyber threats (Colwill, 2009; Choo, 2011). Colwill (2009) also points out that the greatest non-technical methods accessible for both human issues and security are possibly education, training and awareness. Eggenschwiler et al. (2016) also emphasize the importance of educational measures, employee training and awareness campaigns highlighting the crucial part they play in the quest for insider threat recovery as they stress that encouragement of relevant education for employees within organizations is essential as the practice of such behavior not only contributes greatly to the strength of an organization but it is vital as it contributes considerably to the provision of an effective insider threat management.

Probst et al. (2010) highlight that employing the use of suitable training and awareness-building education will inspire the preferred security culture which an organization is looking for, while Furnell and Clarke (2005) emphasize that both awareness and understanding of security are prerequisites for the establishment of an effective security culture within an organization. Hunker and Probst (2011) highlight the importance of staff security awareness as they emphasize that it should be regarded as an essential factor for any comprehensive plan and the three levels of user awareness which should exist include the following:

- **Perception:** The user can detect treats in the environment.
- **Understanding:** The user can combine information from different sensors, understand them and the resulting knowledge allowing them decrease risks in the environment.
- **Prediction:** The user can predict future attacks and alter their own behavior to reduce or remove the risk completely.

The roles of awareness, training and education are also recognized by Whitman (2003) who highlights that one of the essential roles performed by an organization's security should be the implementation of a security education, training and awareness (SETA) program. Such programs seek to inform employees of the significance of security and its application in the day-to-day operation of an organization and by pairing this education program with a successful awareness program the desired result can be achieved, namely that employees will be able to recall the information provided, remembering organizational security and be conscious of this security as they deal with important information as they carry out their daily tasks in the workplace.

It is through the implementation or non-implementation of security countermeasures such as technology for monitoring purposes and SETA programs that organizations can prove their level of commitment to security. The awareness of employees along with the identification of the level of commitment shown by organizations will ultimately influence behavioral intent (Aurigemma and Panko, 2012). Siponen (2000) points out that information security awareness refers to a state where employees are aware and truly committed to the organization's security mission and although increased awareness should in theory decrease user related faults and improve the effectiveness of security techniques and procedures. This however is not always the case as in many instances despite creating security awareness amongst employees the true effectiveness of information security techniques and procedures is however lost as many end-users either misuse, misunderstand or simply do not employ the end-user security guidelines. Siponen et al. (2006) highlights that since the main threat to IS (information system) security is created by employees, alternative measures need to be adopted to deal with this issue as it is not enough for employees to be aware of IS security principles but there is a need for them to learn the IS procedures. The use of training sessions, presentations, newsletters, emails and screen savers in the promotion of IS security awareness in organizations is strongly supported as is the use of posters, brochures and newsletters in increasing the IS security messages within organizations. Kyobe (2005) emphasizes the importance of both education and awareness, highlighting that in order to achieve a better understanding of both security principles and application of technology policies in an organization it is fundamental to educate, train and generate security awareness.

Jones and Colwill, (2008) point out that security and awareness programs should be utilized to generate a better understanding of threats which exist both from insiders and outsiders emphasizing the methods employed to gain information or data access including malicious attacks and the direct consequences which can be suffered by an organization as a direct result of failure of controls. Such programs may also have an influence in creating a better level of trust between the employee and their employer as they offer the employee a better understanding and reason for the security policies and protocols which have been put in place as highlighted by Jones and Colwill (2008) and (Colwill, 2009). Employing such training updates also helps increase staff awareness of the organization's security cultural values and an improved staff awareness should realize a reduction in the probability of accidental breaches and a rise in the volume of malicious activity which is detected and reported (Jones and Colwill, 2008). A similar opinion is shared by Anderson (1999) who claims that in many cases the simple employment of measures such as security awareness, education, detection and reaction measures will often help with the insider problem which plagues many organizations.

## TAILORING AWARENESS PROGRAMS

The recommendation for organizations whether large or small is the implementation of a security, education, training and awareness program to achieve an effective insider threat management. Although many ideas within cybersecurity awareness are common worldwide each organization should however tailor the training programs appropriately to specifically deal with the policies and meet the needs of their own organization (Cone et al. 2007). Each employee is an individual and when commencing an awareness program within an organization this should be taken into consideration as their different personalities will govern how they deal with compliance in relation to cybersecurity policies and when dealing with SETA programs a one size fits all approach should not be adopted as it is recommended that organizations instead provide a cybersecurity training and influential messages which are modified accordingly to meet the distinctive elements of each employee's personalities (Mc Bride et al. 2012).

Third parties are usually present at some point within processes as outsourcing is commonplace within many of today's organizations and as such, they may need education which is equivalent to that of the organization's full-time employees. It is important to offer solutions which not only develop but also preserve trust and relationships over time with the focus fixed on education and the creation of a better attention to security and support for employees and third parties. Delivering an effective education also presents a difficult hurdle which must be conquered, and ongoing education and awareness should support changes to meet the needs of employees especially in outsourced environments as providers are constantly increasing in numbers and many new employees are hired each month (Colwill, 2009). While the continuation of ongoing awareness programs is necessary especially in settings which have large turnovers of staff, Colwill (2009) expresses that finding out the success of programs in such areas can however prove difficult.

## FUTURE RESEARCH DIRECTIONS

The insider threat is a problem which has the potential to cause significant damage, has been increasing in frequency in earlier years and it is a problem which is expected to grow in years to come. Many organizations are not fully aware of the seriousness of the problem that the insider threat poses, and it is essential that the future needs to ensure that all organizations are fully aware of the situation and apply company-wide policies to guarantee that all assets stay protected from the risks that they are constantly facing (Humphreys, 2008). With the increased number of organizations outsourcing tasks it is necessary that those carrying out outsourced tasks are receiving efficient education and awareness training like that of full-time insider employees as those in outsourced environments are regarded in many cases as insiders as they are offered the same privileges and access to information to enable them to carry out their duties.

Cone et al. (2007) highlights that an organization which receives effective security awareness training can greatly improve the confidence an organization has in their information although keeping the attention of a trainee for a satisfactory time span which is long enough to convey the required information is a challenge especially when the targeted audience view the topic as unexciting. New methods of delivering information in awareness training exercises are needed in the future and one such method which engages the target audience is the use of video games as they are involving and keep the attention of those for whom it is designed for (Cone et al. 2007).

Previous studies have concentrated on insider attacks which have already occurred and reactive issues such as what happens post insider attack and as Azaria et al. (2014) points out the detection of past attacks is not a serious problem and interest should be placed on what type of attack will be used in the future if the situation should arise where insider threats are prevented completely. Sarkar (2010) highlights that many professionals refer to the insider threat as a time bomb and the belief is that insider threats are more extensive than the figures which are recorded as many organizations do not divulge figures on the frequency of breaches and how often they occur as it could ultimately damage the reputation of the organization.

## CONCLUSION

While awareness and education can both prepare the groundwork, the actual alteration in the behavior of individuals however, involves ceasing the practice of old habits and forming new ones through targeted training. To obtain the greatest benefit this needs to involve more than simply repeating security policies and veer towards building understanding along with development of knowledge of circumstances which cause security risks and the behaviors and reactions which are needed (Colwill, 2009). The insider threat is a well-established security issue and without adequate techniques, there is little that can be done to counteract the problem of the insider threat (Chinchani et al. 2005) and Hunker and Probst (2011) point out that the insider is already present within the system in some shape or form. The threat from insiders physically exists and is increasing in size and according to Miller and Maxim (2015) it is the duty of organizations to come to the reality that the insider threat could strike at any time and they should adopt a more aggressive standpoint in fighting the insider threat and avoid 'the run for cover' attitude.

The issue of the insider threat is an exclusive dilemma which can never be completely eradicated (Miller and Maxim, 2015; Sarkar, 2010; Hunker and Probst, 2011; Chinchani et al. 2005) and it can only be managed by employing mitigation strategies although due to the complexity of employees, contractors, suppliers, consultants outsourcing and the mobility of workforces this is an ongoing challenge for organizations (Sarkar, 2010). The worrying aspect is that although employees should be made aware of the difference between acceptable and unacceptable behavior in the workplace and from firms surveyed only 20% propose to increase awareness in the future and only 40% now offer constant awareness training to employees (Colwill, 2009).

# REFERENCES

Abawajy, J. (2014). User preference of cyber security awareness delivery methods. *Behaviour & Information Technology*, *33*(3), 237–248. doi:10.1080/0144929X.2012.708787

Anderson, R. H. (1999). *Research and Development Initiatives Focused on Preventing, Detecting, and Responding to Insider Misuse of Critical Defense Information Systems (No. RAND-CF-151-OSD)*. Rand Corp.

Aurigemma, S., & Panko, R. (2012). January. A composite framework for behavioral compliance with information security policies. In *45th Hawaii International Conference on System Science (HICSS)* (pp. 3248-3257). IEEE.

Azaria, A., Richardson, A., Kraus, S., & Subrahmanian, V. S. (2014). Behavioral analysis of insider threat: A survey and bootstrapped prediction in imbalanced data. *IEEE Transactions on Computational Social Systems*, *1*(2), 135–155. doi:10.1109/TCSS.2014.2377811

Baracaldo, N., & Joshi, J. (2012). A trust-and-risk aware RBAC framework: tackling insider threat. In *Proceedings of the 17th ACM symposium on Access Control Models and Technologies* (pp. 167-176). ACM. 10.1145/2295136.2295168

Bishop, M., & Gates, C. (2008). Defining the insider threat. In *Proceedings of the 4th annual workshop on Cyber security and information intelligence research: developing strategies to meet the cyber security and information intelligence challenges ahead* (p. 15). ACM.

Blackwell, C. (2009). A security architecture to protect against the insider threat from damage, fraud and theft. In *Proceedings of the 5th Annual Workshop on Cyber Security and Information Intelligence Research: Cyber Security and Information Intelligence Challenges and Strategies* (p. 45). ACM. 10.1145/1558607.1558659

Cappelli, D., Moore, A., Trzeciak, R., & Shimeall, T. J. (2009). *Common sense guide to prevention and detection of insider threats 3rd edition–version 3.1*. Published by CERT, Software Engineering Institute, Carnegie Mellon University. Retrieved from http://www. cert. org

Chinchani, R., Iyer, A., Ngo, H. Q., & Upadhyaya, S. (2005). Towards a theory of insider threat assessment. In *Proceedings. International Conference on Dependable Systems and Networks, 2005 (DSN 2005)* (pp. 108-117). IEEE. 10.1109/DSN.2005.94

Choo, K. K. R. (2011). *Cyber threat landscape faced by financial and insurance industry. Trends & issues in crime and criminal justice No. 408*. Canberra: Australian Institute of Criminology.

Claycomb, W. R., & Nicoll, A. (2012). Insider threats to cloud computing: Directions for new research challenges. In *IEEE 36th Annual Computer Software and Applications Conference (COMPSAC)* (pp. 387-394). IEEE.

Cole, E. (2015). *Insider threats and the need for fast and directed response.* SANS Institute InfoSec Reading Room, Tech. Rep.

Colwill, C. (2009). Human factors in information security: The insider threat–Who can you trust these days? *Information Security Technical Report, 14*(4), 186–196. doi:10.1016/j.istr.2010.04.004

Cone, B.D., Irvine, C.E., Thompson, M.F., & Nguyen, T.D. (2007). A video game for cyber security training and awareness. *Computers & Security, 26*(1), 63-72.

Eggenschwiler, J., Agrafiotis, I., & Nurse, J. R. (2016). Insider threat response and recovery strategies in financial services firms. *Computer Fraud & Security, 2016*(11), 12–19. doi:10.1016/S1361-3723(16)30091-4

Flynn, L., Huth, C., Trzeciak, R., Buttles, P., & Nations, A. (2013). *Best Practices Against Insider Threats in All Nations. Technical Note CMU/SEI-2013-TN-023.* Software Engineering Institute.

Franqueira, V. N., van Cleeff, A., van Eck, P., & Wieringa, R. (2010). External insider threat: A real security challenge in enterprise value webs. In *International Conference on Availability, Reliability, and Security 2010 (ARES'10)* (pp. 446-453). IEEE. 10.1109/ARES.2010.40

Furnell, S., & Clarke, N. (2005). Organisational security culture: Embedding security awareness, education and training. *Proceedings of the 4th World Conference on Information Security Education*, 67-74.

Glasser, J., & Lindauer, B. (2013). Bridging the gap: A pragmatic approach to generating insider threat data. In IEEE Security and Privacy Workshops (SPW), 2013 (pp. 98-104). IEEE. doi:10.1109/SPW.2013.37

Greitzer, F. L., & Frincke, D. A. (2010). Combining traditional cyber security audit data with psychosocial data: towards predictive modeling for insider threat mitigation. In *Insider threats in cyber security* (pp. 85–113). Boston, MA: Springer. doi:10.1007/978-1-4419-7133-3_5

Greitzer, F. L., Moore, A. P., Cappelli, D. M., Andrews, D. H., Carroll, L. A., & Hull, T. D. (2008). Combating the insider cyber threat. *IEEE Security and Privacy, 6*(1), 61–64. doi:10.1109/MSP.2008.8

Hayden, M. (1999). *The Insider Threat to U.S. Government Information Systems* (NSTISSAM-INFOSEC/1-99). National Security Agency.

Humphreys, E. (2008). Information security management standards: Compliance, governance and risk management. *Information Security Technical Report, 13*(4), 247–255. doi:10.1016/j.istr.2008.10.010

Hunker, J., & Probst, C. W. (2011). Insiders and Insider Threats-An Overview of Definitions and Mitigation Techniques. *Journal of Wireless Mobile Networks, Ubiquitous Computing and Dependable Applications, 2*(1), 4–27.

Jones, A., & Colwill, C. (2008). Dealing with the malicious insider. *Australian Information Security Management Conference*, 52.

Kyobe, M. (2005). Addressing e-crime and computer security issues in homes and small organizations in South Africa. *European management and technology conference on the integration of management and technology*, 1-13.

Liu, D., Wang, X., & Camp, J. (2008). Game-theoretic modeling and analysis of insider threats. *International Journal of Critical Infrastructure Protection, 1*, 75–80. doi:10.1016/j.ijcip.2008.08.001

Magklaras, G. B., & Furnell, S. M. (2005). A preliminary model of end user sophistication for insider threat prediction in IT systems. *Computers & Security, 24*(5), 371–380. doi:10.1016/j.cose.2004.10.003

Martinez-Moyano, I. J., Rich, E., Conrad, S., Andersen, D. F., & Stewart, T. R. (2008). A behavioral theory of insider-threat risks: A system dynamics approach. *ACM Transactions on Modeling and Computer Simulation, 18*(2), 7. doi:10.1145/1346325.1346328

McBride, M., Carter, L., & Warkentin, M. (2012). *Exploring the role of individual employee characteristics and personality on employee compliance with cybersecurity policies*. RTI International-Institute for Homeland Security Solutions.

McConnell, M. (2002). Information assurance in the twenty-first century. *Computer, 35*(4), supl16-supl19.

McCormac, A., Parsons, K., & Butavicius, M. (2012). *Preventing and profiling malicious insider attacks (No. DSTO-TR-2697). Defence Science and Technology Organisation Edinburgh*. Command Control Communications And Intelligence Div.

Miller, R., & Maxim, M. (2015). *I Have to Trust Someone.... Don't I?* CA Technologies.

Molok, N. N. A., Ahmad, A., & Chang, S. (2011). Information leakage through online social networking: Opening the doorway for advanced persistence threats. *Journal of the Australian Institute of Professional Intelligence Officers, 19*(2), 38.

Neumann, P. G. (2010). Combatting insider threats. In *Insider Threats in Cyber Security* (pp. 17–44). Boston, MA: Springer. doi:10.1007/978-1-4419-7133-3_2

Nguyen, N., Reiher, P., & Kuenning, G. H. (2003). Detecting insider threats by monitoring system call activity. In *Information Assurance Workshop*, 2003. *IEEE Systems, Man and Cybernetics Society* (pp. 45-52). IEEE. 10.1109/SMCSIA.2003.1232400

Nurse, J. R., Legg, P. A., Buckley, O., Agrafiotis, I., Wright, G., Whitty, M., ... Creese, S. (2014). A critical reflection on the threat from human insiders–its nature, industry perceptions, and detection approaches. In *International Conference on Human Aspects of Information Security, Privacy, and Trust* (pp. 270-281). Springer. 10.1007/978-3-319-07620-1_24

Park, J. S., & Ho, S. M. (2004). Composite role-based monitoring (CRBM) for countering insider threats. In *International Conference on Intelligence and Security Informatics* (pp. 201-213). Springer. 10.1007/978-3-540-25952-7_15

Probst, C. W., Hunker, J., Gollmann, D., & Bishop, M. (2010). Aspects of insider threats. In *Insider Threats in Cyber Security* (pp. 1–15). Boston, MA: Springer. doi:10.1007/978-1-4419-7133-3_1

Puleo, A. J. (2006). *Mitigating insider threat using human behavior influence models (No. AFIT/GCE/ENG/06-04)*. Air Force Inst Of Tech Wright-Patterson Afb Oh School of Engineering And Management.

Randazzo, M.R., Keeney, M., Kowalski, E., Cappelli, D.M., & Moore, A.P. (2005). *Insider threat study: Illicit cyber activity in the banking and finance sector.* Academic Press.

Sarkar, K. R. (2010). Assessing insider threats to information security using technical, behavioural and organisational measures. *Information Security Technical Report, 15*(3), 112–133. doi:10.1016/j.istr.2010.11.002

Siponen, M., Pahnila, S., & Mahmood, A. M. (2006). A new model for understanding users' is security compliance. PACIS 2006 Proceedings, 48.

Siponen, M. T. (2000). A conceptual foundation for organizational information security awareness. *Information Management & Computer Security, 8*(1), 31–41. doi:10.1108/09685220010371394

Stavrou, V., Kandias, M., Karoulas, G., & Gritzalis, D. (2014). Business Process Modeling for Insider threat monitoring and handling. In *International Conference on Trust, Privacy and Security in Digital Business* (pp. 119-131). Springer. 10.1007/978-3-319-09770-1_11

Theoharidou, M., Kokolakis, S., Karyda, M., & Kiountouzis, E. (2005). The insider threat to information systems and the effectiveness of ISO17799. *Computers & Security, 24*(6), 472–484. doi:10.1016/j.cose.2005.05.002

Ula, M., & Fuadi, W. (2017). A Method for Evaluating Information Security Governance (ISG) Components in Banking Environment. *Journal of Physics: Conference Series, 812*(1), 012031. doi:10.1088/1742-6596/812/1/012031

Warkentin, M., & Willison, R. (2009). Behavioral and policy issues in information systems security: The insider threat. *European Journal of Information Systems, 18*(2), 101–105. doi:10.1057/ejis.2009.12

Whitman, M. E. (2003). Enemy at the gate: Threats to information security. *Communications of the ACM, 46*(8), 91–95. doi:10.1145/859670.859675

Yayla, A. A. (2011). Controlling insider threats with information security policies. *European Conference on Information Systems*, 242.

## KEY TERMS AND DEFINITIONS

**Compliance:** The certification or confirmation that the person performing an action such as an employee does so in a manner which meets company rules and policies and the activity is carried out meeting standards and guidelines as per the conditions of a contract.

**Cyber-Attacks:** A cyber-attack refers to an assault against a computer system, network, or internet-enabled application or device. Hackers employ a wide range of devices to carry out such attacks. They include malware, ransomware and many other approaches.

**Cybercrime:** This refers to any illegal activity involving a computer, networked device or a network. Many cybercrimes take place purely for financial gain although some take place against computers or devices to impair them or disable them and others use computers to spread malware, illegal information, images, or other types of data.

**Espionage:** This is the act of acquiring private information without the authorization from the owner of the confidential information and it is often referred to as spying or obtaining secret information which can be political, military, or industrial in format.

**Fraud:** This refers to deception, wrongful or criminal misdoings which are solely intended to result in either financial or personal gain.

**Malware:** This is short for malicious software which is designed purposely with the focus of initiating damage on a computer, server, or computer network. Malware causes damage once it is implanted or introduced in some manner to the target computer in the form of executable code, active content or other software while the user is still unaware that their system has been compromised.

**Mitigation:** This is the action involved in reducing the force, severity, intensity or painfulness of something and as a result the seriousness or grief experienced from something unpleasant is therefore decreased.

**Organizations:** This refers to a group of people such as that found in an institution or association who collectively work together in an organized way to achieve a shared purpose or to successfully undertake and achieve collective goals.

**Outsider:** This is a person or individual who does belong to or who is not involved or included within a specific group of people or organization.

**Sabotage:** This is a deliberate action whose goal is to weaken an organization by causing disruption, obstruction or destruction. Those that engage in this process are referred to as saboteurs and they usually hide their identities due to the result of the penalties inflicted because of their actions.

**Spam:** Unwanted or inappropriate messages sent via the Internet normally to a large volume of Internet users usually for advertising purpose or to entice individuals to reveal personal information or spreading malware.

*Previously published in Cybersecurity Education for Awareness and Compliance; pages 33-52, copyright year 2019 by Information Science Reference (an imprint of IGI Global).*

# Chapter 14
# The Role of Human Resource Management in Enhancing Organizational Information Systems Security

**Peace Kumah**

*Ghana Education Service, Ghana*

## ABSTRACT

*Emerging human resource management (HRM) practices are focusing on background checks, training and development, employer-employee relations, responsibility and accountability, and monitoring of information systems security resources. Information systems security ensures that appropriate resources and adequate skills exist in the organization to effectively manage information security projects. This chapter examined the role of HRM in enhancing organizational information systems security. Using importance-performance map analysis, the study found training, background checks, and monitoring as crucial HRM practices that could enhance organizational information systems security. Moreover, four indicators, consisting of training on mobile devices security; malware management; background checks; and monitoring of potential, current, and former employees recorded high importance but with rather low performance. Consequently, these indicators should be improved. On the contrary, the organizations placed excessive focus on responsibility, accountability, and employee relations.*

## INTRODUCTION

Human resource management (HRM) practices are day-to-day activities including recruitment and selection, performance appraisal (Khan, 2010), training and development (Katuo & Budhwar, 2006), career planning management, compensation (Ahmad & Schroeder, 2003), and internal communication (Oladipo & Adbulkadir, 2011). Human resource management plays a vital role in organizations through performance of administrative HR functions such as recruitment, training, promotion, welfare services, performance appraisal, salary administration, and collective bargaining, and retention of employees

DOI: 10.4018/978-1-6684-3698-1.ch014

(Asare-Bediako, 2011). HRM practices are strategic tools for gaining higher employee performance (Khan, 2010). For organizations to achieve their set goals, strategic plans to invest in employee knowledge, skills and abilities are crucial (Battaglio et al., 2017). Human resource management practices must be strategic in measuring current workforce capacities (Goodman et al., 2015) and in assessing the prudent use of human resources (Selden, 2009). Therefore, it is important for organizations to incorporate human capital into the organization's strategic planning by investing in the workforce (Selden, 2009).

Without strong security controls, businesses risk the possibility of financial loss, legal liability, reputation harm (Amarachi, Okolie & Ajaegbu, 2013), and the effect on national security (Okewu et al., 2018). Therefore, emerging information systems security research is discovering ways to improve organizational security by motivating employees to engage in more secure security behaviors using HRM practices (Boss et al., 2015). Information security management system is a collection of policies concerned with information technology related risks (Amarachi, Okolie & Ajaegbu, 2013). Information security management system aims at implementing the appropriate measures in order to eliminate or minimize the impact that various security related threats and vulnerabilities might have on an organization (Amarachi, Okolie, & Ajaegbu, 2013).

Human resource management practices can address the problem of the human-oriented factors. Human resource management practices of employee recruitment and selection, training and development, performance monitoring and appraisals are very important to improve organisational performance (Naz, Aftab, & Awais, 2016). Investing in training and development can motivate staff and support the growth of the organisation (Leidner & Smith, 2013). Information systems security and data privacy training can serve as critical controls for safeguarding organisation's information resources (Baxter, Holderness, & Wood, 2016). Safa et al. (2018) identify lack of employees' awareness, negligence, resistance, disobedience, apathy and mischievousness as the root causes of information security incidents in organisations. As a result, Odun-Ayo et al. (2017) propose a framework for enhancing human resources in addressing information security. Thus, to achieve the best results, security training and awareness programs should be regularly evaluated so that corrective actions can be taken (Rantos, Fysarakis & Manifavas, 2012).

In addition, employee relations are seen by employers as critical in achieving job performance through employee involvement, commitment and engagement (Radhakrishna & Raju, 2015). Moreover, employee monitoring is a significant component of employers' efforts to maintain employee productivity (Ford et al., 2015). Employee background checks are important to ascertain criminal records, character, and fitness of the employee (Sarode & Deore, 2017). Furthermore, employee's accountability can improve information security (Vance, Lowry, & Eggett, 2013). However, accountability can have both positive and negative effect on work behavior (Ossege, 2012). Enhancing information systems security by focusing on human resource management practices has not received much attention by researchers. Using Importance-Performance Map Analysis (IPMA) (Ringle & Sarstedt, 2016), this chapter aims at exploring the role of HRM practices in improving organizational information systems security. In particular, the chapter (a) discusses the use of IPMA, (b) identifies the HRM practices that can improve the performance of organisational information systems security and (c) the specific HRM indicators that can enhance organisational information systems security

## BACKGROUND

## Information Systems Security

Information systems security is a global concern (Ikenwe, Igbinovia, & Elogie, 2016; White, Hewitt, & Kruck, 2013). It involves protection of information assets from unauthorized access, accidental loss, destruction, disclosure, modification, or misuse (Tassabehji, 2005). Information security involves managing risks related to the use, processing, storage, transmission of information or data and the systems and processes used for those purposes (Yalman & Yesilyurt, 2013). Information security is a multi-disciplinary area involving professional activity of developing and implementing technical, organisational, human-oriented security mechanisms in order to keep information systems free from threats (Cherdantseva & Hilton, 2013). As a result of increasing dependency on information technology (IT) systems and emerging security threats and vulnerabilities relating to privacy, identity theft, and cybercrime, the role of IT professionals become crucial for maintaining security of information resources (Khao, Harris, & Hartman, 2010).

Information systems security breaches may result in loss of sensitive information and productivity which may lead to huge financial liabilities, adversely affecting the reputation of the organisation (Abawajy, 2014). Information security needs to become an organisation-wide and strategic issue, taking it out of the IT domain and aligning it with the corporate governance approach (Amarachi, Okolie, & Ajaegbu, 2013). Au and Fung (2019) suggested that IT Governance practices can improve knowledge dissemination of information security within organizations. Balozian, Leidner and Warkentin (2019) suggested that managers' participation in the information systems policy decision-making process could motivate lower-level employees toward policy compliance.

Information technology professionals are facing challenging tasks analysing, designing, and deploying solutions to protect information resources. Notwithstanding, previous studies acknowledge that human factors are the major sources of many security failures (Abawajy, 2014; Driscoll & McKee, 2007; Furnell & Thomson, 2009; Komatsu, Takagi, & Takemura, 2013). Human beings are vulnerable to a wide range of security attacks, which range from deliberate violation of security policy to circumvention of physical and technical security controls (Stewart, Tittel, & Chapple, 2005). Moreover, people underestimate the likelihood of the occurrence of security breaches (Herath & Rao, 2009). It is important to understand the employees' personal attitudes, norms and beliefs and the link between compliance and rewards/punishment (Cram, D'Arcy & Proudfoot, 2019).

One of the key challenges in information security management is to understand how human factors affect the outcomes of information security in an organisation (Hu et al., 2012). Organisations are taking measures to ensure the security of information (Yalman & Yesilyurt, 2013). However, organisations invest inefficiently in information technology security measures (Zhao, Xue, & Whinston, 2013), while human attitude was identified as having significant impact on compliance with security policy (Zhang, Reithel, & Li, 2009). Thus, technological security solutions alone are ineffective at reducing security breaches. According to Angst, Block, D'Arcy and Kelley (2017), information technology (IT) security investments are effective at reducing the incidence of data security breaches when they are balanced with institutional factors. According to Herath and Rao (2009), organisational commitment, social influence, and threat perceptions about the severity of breaches effect employees' attitudes toward policy compliance.

Burns et al. (2017) established the relationship between organisational insiders' psychological capital with information security threat and coping appraisals. Self-control is a major factor influencing individual behaviour towards information security (Hu, West, & Smarandescu, 2015). Moreover, suspicion plays a role between users' normal working behaviors and their ability to change that behavior to detect and react to cyber attacks (Hirshfield et al., 2019). Khan and AlShare (2019) found significant difference in employees' information security policy violation with respect to perceived privacy, subjective norms, perceived severity of penalty, and organizational security culture.

Organisations should measure their information security performance in order to make the right decisions (Bernik & Prislan, 2016) and channel resources to areas of high importance that will lead to high security performance. A recent study showed that a high level of information security performance is mostly dependent on measures aimed at managing employees (Bernik & Prislan, 2016). Managing employees' security behaviors for better information security performance will require security training and development programs, creating employee relations, background checks and monitoring, and accountability.

## Security Training and Development

Training and development is a planned process and the most important tool that exposes employees to new knowledge, higher level of skills and technologies for higher performance (Subramaniam, Shamsudin, & Ibrahim, 2011). Blair (2007) emphasized the importance of investment into training and development as it can give competitive advantage to organizations. According to (AL-Qudah, Osman, Ab Halim, and Al-Shatanawi (2014), training and development can be used to improve the capabilities of employees and to promote organizational commitment towards the attainment of organizational goals. Furthermore, Hassan (2016) concluded that training and development plays significant role in organizational performance. Also, Saifalislam, Osman and AlQudah (2014) and Sattar, Ahmad and Hassan (2015) proposed positive and significant relation between training and development and employee performance. Koh (2018) examined the Influence of Human Resource Management Practices on Employee Performance in the Manufacturing Sector in Malaysia. Data was collected through survey from 161 manufacturing sector in Malaysia. The regression analysis indicated significant positive relationship between training and development and employee performance. The study, therefore, suggested that training and development is the most critical factor that influences employee performance.

Misra and Khurana (2018) stressed the need for enhancing the employability skills of information technology professionals. Investing in training and development can motivate staff and support the growth of the organisations (Leidner & Smith, 2013). While lack of security training often lie behind many contemporary breaches (Lacey, 2010), security education enables skilled professionals and ensures adequate security awareness among end users (Kaspersky & Furnell, 2014). Abawajy (2014) evaluated the effects of various information security awareness delivery methods that could improve end-users' information security awareness and behavior. By conducting experiments on information security awareness using three different methods: text-based, game-based and video-based, the study suggested that a combined delivery methods of improving end-users' information security awareness and behaviour are better than individual security awareness delivery method (Abawajy, 2014). A related study determined the impact of cyber threat education and awareness intervention on changes in user security behaviour (McCrohan, Engel, & Harvey, 2010). The study was based on protection motivation theory and an experimental was performed by using undergraduate business school students. McCrohan, Engel and Harvey (2010) found that when users are educated of the threats to e-commerce and trained about proper security practices, their behavior could be changed to enhance information security. Hence, security and assurance should be a core component of the curriculum for all information security and business students (White, Hewitt, & Kruck, 2013).

Moreover, a survey conducted on 196 undergraduate students in a business college to investigate students' understanding and attitudes toward information security suggested that when universities provide easily accessible security training programs to students, information security improves (Kim, 2014). In a related study, Da Veiga (2016) determined the influence information security policy had on the information security culture by comparing the security behavior of employees who read the policy to those who did not. An empirical study was conducted at four intervals over eight years across 12 countries using a validated information security culture assessment (ISCA) questionnaire. The overall information security culture was significantly more positive for employees who had read the information security policy compared with employees who had not. Employees' information security training can improve adherence to security policies when employees are shown the reasons behind the written policies (Ramakrishna & Figueroa, 2017). Accordingly, organisational security education, training and awareness efforts influence employees' threat and coping appraisals (Posey, Roberts & Lowry, 2015).

## Employer-Employee Relationship

The most critical asset in organizations is the people. It is therefore important for organizations to have keen interest in managing employer-employee relationships. Employer- employee relationship enhances commitment, job satisfaction and engagement that eventually improve organizational outcome employer-employee relationships employer-employee relationships (Klaas, Olson-Buchanan & Ward, 2012; Bashshur & Oc, 2015). For example, Bhattacharya, Trehan and Kaur (2018) established the importance of psychological contract amongst the employer and employees. Bhattacharya et al. (2012) stated the need to pay attention to employer-employee relationship to enable their businesses to grow. Empirical studies on the impact of employer-employee relationships on business growth revealed positive relationship between employer-employee relationships and business growth (Dumisani, Chux, Andre & Joyc, 2014).

Employee relations are seen by employers as critical in achieving job performance through a focus on employee involvement, commitment and engagement. The emphasis of employee relations is now focussed on relationship with individual employees (Radhakrishna & Raju, 2015). Organisational commitment is a means by which information security threats become personally relevant to employees (Posey, Roberts, & Lowry, 2015). A previous study revealed that IT employees were treated with only moderate fairness/justice by the organisations, however, their commitment to their organisation was fairly high (Patrick, 2012). It was found that organisational justice significantly influenced organisational commitment of IT employees. The results of this study provided considerable insight into the IT employees' perceptions of fairness could promote commitment (Patrick, 2012). Also, D'Arcy and Greene (2014) examined the influence of security-related and employment relationship factors on employees' security compliance decisions. Data were collected using two online surveys that were administered at separate points in time. The study found that security culture is a driver for employees' security compliance in the workplace and that employee's feeling of job satisfaction influences security compliance intention (D'Arcy & Greene, 2014).

## Background Checks and Monitoring

According to Stringer (2009), recruitment remains a critical element for effective implementation of HRM practices. The role of HRM in every organization is to identify, select and recruit suitable employees. The Society for Human Resource Management (SHRM) indicated that background checks are important tool that employers must use to reduce the risk of a negligent hiring (SHRM, 2012). Sarode and Deore (2017) emphasized that it is critical for HR mangers to conduct background checks on potential employees to avoid recruiting wrong people. Background checks for the IT professionals and every individual in other sectors is crucial for all organizations (Valentine, 2014). Freeman (2013) concluded that background check gives great advantage to employers as people who may engage in workplace violence, defraud, steal or unreliable and untrustworthy are eliminated. Furthermore, a meta-analysis of some studies revealed significant correlation between background check and employee behavior (Aamodt, 2015).

Background checks of potential employee have become essential task for HR personnel so that the organisation could avoid recruiting the wrong persons (Sarode & Deore, 2017). Hughes, Keller, & Hertz (2010) discussed issues of higher education institutions' policies and procedures with regard to background checks for students, staff, and faculty in light of homeland security concerns. Brody and Cox (2015) emphasized the need for thoroughness and accuracy of background checks and security clearance investigations. Brody (2010) explored the various methods available when conducting a pre-employment screening investigation in attempt to hire honest employees, those less likely to commit fraud against their organisation. Using interviews with experts in the area of background investigation services, the study recommended that organisations should consider performing other screening techniques before hiring an employee. Brody (2010) cautioned that merely relying on the most basic background check may lead to the hiring of the wrong employee, one likely to commit fraud. Besides, employees are increasingly monitored concerning their behaviors and actions. The use of monitoring systems has been advocated for improved performance, increased productivity, and reduced costs (Holt, Lang, & Sutton, 2017). Without effective monitoring disgruntled employees can expose valuable business trade secrets or engage in corporate espionage or sabotage (Ford et al., 2015). They may render the organisation to several risky situations (Rigon et al., 2014). Therefore, it is importance to analyse the strength, weakness, opportunity and threat in service delived by employees (Misra & Adewumi, 2015).

Sreejith and Mathirajan (2016) developed criteria for continuous employee performance evaluation of Information Technology organizations. Monitoring an employee's behaviors and actions is an essential HR practice. Monitoring improves employee-employer relationships, enhances employee competence, ensures that employees comply with safety regulations, improves performance and increases production rates (Durden, 2019). Monitory system ensures accountability, enhances planning and organizational performance. Without effective monitoring employees will lose focus by engaging in illegal activities (Alampay & Hechaniya, 2010) and discontented employees can reveal trade secrets or sabotage projects (Ford et al., 2015).

## Responsibility and Accountability

Employees should be accountable to and be responsibility for preventing security breaches. According to Styles and Tryfonas (2009), employees are duty-bound to consider the security of the computing and information resources they interact with. Accountability makes employees answerable for accomplishing a goal or assignment (U.S. Office of Personnel Management, n.d). It often connotes punishment or negative consequences of punishing employees, creating fear and anxiety in the work environment. But accountability can produce positive and valuable results. When used constructively, it can improve employee performance, enhance participation and involvement, increase feelings of competency, enhance commitment to the work, improve creativity and innovation, and produce higher employee morale and satisfaction with the work (U.S. Office of Personnel Management, n.d). Accountability should focus not only on punishment but also reward. Parker (2008) remarked that without security rewards and sanctions in all employee job performance appraisals, any attempt to secure information assets in an organisation is purely cosmetics. Thus, those who control security, those who are constrained by it, and those who use and possess the assets must be sufficiently motivated to make it work (Parker, 2008).

In a recent study, Zaman and Saif (2016) found that perceived accountability has a significant positive relationship with job performance. Thomson and van Niekerk (2012) showed how employee apathy towards information security can be addressed through the use of existing theory in social sciences. Based on goal-setting theory, the study suggested that employees' performance of their roles and responsibilities can contribute towards organisational culture of information security (Thomson & van Niekerk, 2012). To understand security behaviour by developing a security behaviour typology based on the concepts of discipline and agility, Harnesk and Lindström (2011) undertook a case study to analyze security behaviors. The study found that security behaviour can be shaped by discipline and agility and that both can exist collectively if organisations consider the constitutional and existential aspects of information security (IS) management. Vance, Lowry, and Eggett (2013) presented a new approach for reducing access policy violations. Drawing from the theory of accountability, the study identified four system mechanisms that heighten an individual's perception of accountability: identifiability, awareness of logging, awareness of audit, and electronic presence (Vance, Lowry, & Eggett, 2013). Safa et al. (2019) proposed deterrence as the mitigating factor for reducing insider threat to information systems resources. Deterrence discourages employees from engaging in information security misbehaviour and the severity of sanctions significantly influence individuals' attitudes from information security misconduct (Safa et al., 2019).

## MAIN FOCUS OF THE CHAPTER

### Explaining Importance-Performance Map Analysis

The chapter explains the principles underlying and procedures involved in using IPMA. The first step in creating an importance-performance map (IPM) requires selecting the target construct of interest in the PLS path model (Ringle & Sarstedt, 2016). Reviewing studies on the use of partial least squares structured equation modelling (PLS-SEM) (Hair et al., 2012; Ringle et al., 2012; Sarstedt et al., 2014) reveals that information security researchers basically rely on the standard PLS path model analysis, ignoring the Importance-Performance Map Analysis (IPMA). IPMA provides guidance for the prioritization of managerial activities of high importance but require performance improvements (Ringle & Sarstedt, 2016). It is particularly useful for generating additional findings and conclusions from the standard PLS-SEM. Thus, in this study IPMA is used to evaluate the level of importance organisations attach to each of the HRM factors and indicators, which can improve information security performance.

Consider the PLS path model in Figure 1 with five constructs ($C_1$ to $C_5$). In PLS path model in Figure 1, $C_5$ represents the key target construct. $C_5$ is directly predicted by $C_1$ to $C_4$. Also, $C_1$ has indirect effect on $C_5$ via $C_2$, $C_3$, and $C_4$. To perform Importance-Performance Map Analysis, the PLS path model in

Figure 1 will be transformed into IPMA grid as shown in Figure 2 with two dimensions – importance and performance dimensions. The addition of the predecessor constructs' ($C_1$ to $C_4$) direct and indirect effects yields their total effects on $C_5$. This represents the importance dimension in the IPMA (Ringle & Sarstedt, 2016). On the other hand, the constructs' average latent variable scores represent the performance dimension in IPMA. The higher values indicate a greater performance and vice versa (Ringle & Sarstedt, 2016). Also in Figure 1, $x_{ij}$ (for example $x_{11}$, $x_{22}$, $x_{42}$) represents the indicators of the constructs $C_i$ and $p_i$ ($p_1$ to $p_9$) represents the path coefficients.

Now, the two dimensions can be plotted graphically by placing the total effects (Importance dimension) on the x-axis and the rescaled latent variable scores (re-scaled on a range from 0 to 100), representing the Performance dimension on the y-axis. This results in an Important-Performance Map in Figure 2. Moreover, the two dimensional IPMA model is further divided into four quadrants. To achieve this, two lines are drawn on the Importance-Performance Map. The vertical line is the mean importance value and the horizontal line is the mean performance value of the constructs. Thus, these two lines divide the Importance-Performance Map into four areas with importance and performance values below and above the average (Figure 2). Generally, when analyzing the Importance-Performance Map, constructs appearing in the lower right area (i.e. Quadrant I) are of the highest interest to achieving improvement in the target construct ($C_5$), followed by the higher right (i.e. Quadrant II), lower left (i.e. Quadrant III) and, finally, the higher left areas (i.e. Quadrant IV) (Ringle & Sarstedt, 2016).

*Figure 1. Concept of path model of IPMA*

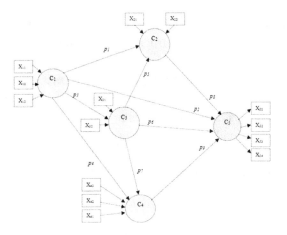

The four quadrants (Figure 2) are generally referred to as *concentrate here (Quadrant I)*, *keep up the good work (Quadrant II)*, *low priority (Quadrant III)*, and *possible overkill (Quadrant IV)*. The constructs and indicators that fall within the quadrants can be interpreted as below (Ringle & Sarstedt, 2016).

*Quadrant I* (High Importance/Low Performance). The constructs or indicators that fall within this quadrant represent key areas that need to be improved with top priority.

*Quadrant II* (High Importance/High Performance). All constructs or indicators that fall within this quadrant are the strength of the organisations.

*Quadrant III* (Low Importance/Low Performance). Any of the constructs or indicators that falls within this quadrant is not important to the organisations.

*Quadrant IV* (Low Importance/High Performance). This denotes constructs or indicators that are overly emphasized by the organisations. Organisations, instead of continuing to focus in this quadrant, should allocate more resources to deal with constructs or indicators that fall within *Quadrant I*.

*Figure 2. Relative importance-performance regions*

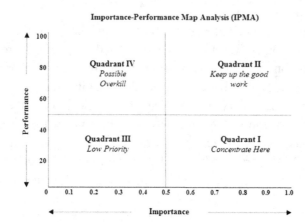

## Importance-Performance Map Analysis (IPMA)

Specifically, to further explain the concept, Figure 3 and Figure 4 demonstrate IPM for both constructs and indicators respectively. In Figure 3, $C_1$ is particularly important to improve the performance of the target construct $C_5$, as it falls within the *Quadrant I* (High Importance/Low Performance). More precisely, a one-unit point increase in $C_1$'s performance increases the performance of $C_5$ by the value of $C_1$'s total effect on $C_5$. Thus, in Figure 3, the performance of $C_1$ is relatively low; there is therefore substantial room for improvement, making this construct particularly relevant for managerial actions. Moreover, to generate IPM for indicators, individual data points in the Importance-Performance Map are derived from indicator mean values and their total effect on a particular target construct, $C_5$. As can be observed in Figure 4, $x_{11}$, $x_{23}$ have the highest importance but low performance values (Quadrant I). Thus, these indicators will require management attention to improve their performance in order to enhance the performance of the target construct, $C_5$.

## Assessing HRM and Information Systems Security Model

A structured survey questionnaire was used to collect data from Information Security Officers, Chief Information Officers, IT Managers, IT Specialists, and other IT staff in organizations in assessing the model. When using IPMA, three requirements must be met (Ringle & Sarstedt, 2016). Firstly, the latent variable scores should be re-scaled on a range of 0 and 100, thus requiring that all indicators in the PLS path model should use a metric or quasi-metric scale (Sarstedt & Mooi, 2014). Secondly, all the indicator coding must have the same scale direction. The minimum value of an indicator must represent the worst outcome and the maximum value must represent the best outcome of the indicator (for instance 1 represents *strongly disagree* and 5 *strongly agree*). Otherwise, conclusion cannot be drawn that the higher latent variable scores represent better performance. Accordingly, the current study used a metric with 5 likert scale which can be scaled between 0 and 100. Thirdly, regardless of the measurement model being formatively or reflectively, the outer weights estimates must be positive. Negative outer weights might be a result of high indicator collinearity and these indicators should be removed from the analysis (Hair et al., 2017). To meet this requirement, all the items whose outer weights were negative have been removed (see Table 1).

*Figure 3. Constructs - IPMA on the target construct, C5*

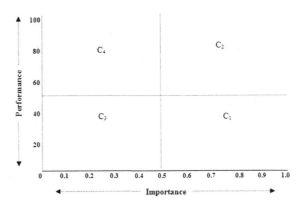

*Figure 4. Indicators - IPMA on the target construct, $C_5$*

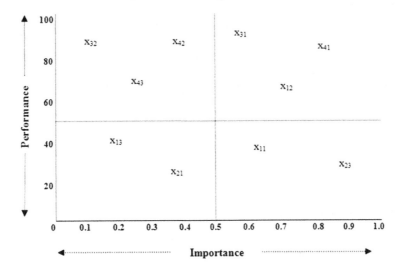

Moreover, the blindfolding and bootstrapping techniques were used. The blindfolding procedure was used in assessing the predictive relevance (Stone-Geisser's $Q^2$ value) of the structural model (Geisser, 1974; Stone, 1974). According to Hair et al. (2014), a $Q^2$ value larger than zero for the reflective endogenous latent variable indicates the path model's predictive relevance. Table 2 showed the structural model's predictive relevance. Also, bootstrapping was performed. It is a nonparametric procedure that allows testing the statistical significance of various PLS-SEM results, such as path coefficients, Cronbach's alpha, and $R^2$ values (Hair et al., 2017). The results from bootstrapping with 5,000 samples using the no sign change option and the 95 percent confidence intervals showed that all the path coefficients were statistically significant (Table 3). More specifically, TRAINING, MONITORING, ACCOUNTABILITY, and RELATIONSHIP each has significant and positive effects on INFORMATION SECURITY. Thus, the bootstrapping results demonstrated that all total effects on the target construct, INFORMATION SECURITY, were significant.

Observably, in Table 1, Table 2, and Table 3, the requirements of the measurement model assessment have been met. The outer weights were above zero. Those items below zero were removed from further analysis. The instrument validity and reliability requirements were fulfilled. The predictive relevance via blindfolding technique was also fulfilled. Through the bootstrapping results, the structural model also showed that all the constructs had significant effect on the target construct. Instrument reliability and validity were also tested via Cronbach's alpha and outer loadings. According to Hair et al. (2017), items with outer loading less than zero should be removed from further analysis. Consequently, items whose outer loadings were less than zero were removed from the study (see Table 1). Moreover, the Cronbach's alpha shows the reliability coefficients of the measures: Security Training and Awareness (.778), Employer-Employee Relationship (.849), Background Checks and Monitoring (.811), Responsibility and Accountability (.696), and Information Security (.790) (see Table 1). Apart from Responsibility and Accountability, all the measures were all found to be far above the threshold of 0.7 (or higher) and were considered acceptable according to Nunally's (1978) guidelines. Based on these, the study proceeded to create Importance-Performance Map.

*Table 1. Validity, reliability and descriptive statistics*

| Constructs | Indicators | Outer Weight > 0 | Mean | SD | Cronbach Alpha |
|---|---|---|---|---|---|
| SECURITY TRAINING AND AWARENESS | | | | | |
| ST01 | Employees are given periodic training on security policies. | 0.272 | 3.95 | .997 | |
| ST02 | Employees are trained to keep mobile devices secured. | 0.362 | 3.53 | .925 | |
| ST06 | Employees are trained to be suspicious of any software that arrives in the mail, even though it may appear to be packaged and sent by trusted persons or vendors. | 0.290 | 3.25 | .984 | .778 |
| ST10 | Employees have been made aware of the fact that mass produced and mass distributed software could still contain targeted malware. | 0.361 | 3.40 | .954 | |
| EMPLOYER-EMPLOYEE RELATIONSHIP | | | | | |
| ER01 | The organisation makes fairness and good faith in the treatment of employees a priority. | 0.732 | 3.87 | .803 | |
| ER02 | The organisation provides adequate mechanisms for employees to express their grievances without penalty and for them to see those grievances being conscientiously addressed. | 0.017 | 3.60 | .755 | |
| ER03 | The organisation handles re-deployment/down-sizing in a manner that minimizes hostile feelings on the part of former employees. | 0.117 | 3.64 | .774 | .849 |
| ER04 | The organisation offers a procedure which allows employees to report attempts by outsiders to extort their organisation in circumventing security. | 0.251 | 3.72 | .718 | |
| ER05 | If an employee is going through a period of great difficulties in his or her personal life, there is a policy for temporarily reducing that employee's responsibilities for critical systems and access to critical systems. | 0.053 | 3.73 | .815 | |

*continues on following page*

*Table 1. Continued*

| Constructs | Indicators | Outer Weight > 0 | Mean | SD | Cronbach Alpha |
|---|---|---|---|---|---|
| BACKGROUND CHECKS AND MONITORING | | | | | |
| BC02 | If an employee is promoted to a considerably higher level of responsibility and access, a new background check is carried out. | 0.477 | 3..35 | .973 | .811 |
| BC03 | Background screening is carried out for of potential and third parties. | 0.359 | 3.18 | .845 | |
| BC04 | An effort is made to track the current whereabouts of former employees who were deeply acquainted with critical systems and procedures. | 0.333 | 3.25 | 1.045 | |
| RESPONSIBILITY AND ACCOUNTABILITY | | | | | |
| SA02 | All employees are required to sign confidentiality and intellectual property agreements. | 0.291 | 3.34 | .862 | .696 |
| SA06 | Information security policies defined the proper use of e-mail, internet access, and instant messaging by employees. | 0.689 | 3.53 | 1.058 | |
| SA11 | Employees are given adequate incentives to report security breaches and bad security practices. | 0.237 | 3.51 | .817 | |
| INFORMATION SECURITY | | | | | |
| BEC06 | Information is generally disseminated throughout the organisation on a need-to-know basis. | 0.298 | 3.75 | .692 | .790 |
| BEC07 | Areas of responsibility are distributed among employees in such a way that a single employee cannot carry out a critical operation without the knowledge of other employees. | 0.329 | 3.47 | .768 | |
| BEC08 | The employee's physical and electronic access logs are periodically reviewed to identify access patterns that are not motivated by normal work responsibilities. | 0.301 | 3.73 | .725 | |
| BEC09 | Employees are required to take periodic vacations, so that ongoing activities they might otherwise be able to conceal would be noticed by their temporary replacements. | 0.346 | 3.70 | .808 | |

*Table 2. Stone-Geisser's $Q^2$ value*

| Constructs | SSO | SSE | $Q^2$ (=1-SSE/SSO) |
|---|---|---|---|
| ACCOUNTABILITY | 954 | 672.471 | 0.295 |
| INFORMATION SECURITY | 1,272 | 920.981 | 0.276 |
| MONITORING | 954 | 742.136 | 0.222 |
| RELATIONSHIP | 1,590 | 1,352.801 | 0.149 |
| TRAINING | 1,272 | 1,272.000 | - |

## Determining HRM Practices for Enhancing Information Systems Security

The IPMA technique produced the structural model and Important-Performance Map (Figure 5) to identify the important HRM practices that can improve the performance of organisational information security. Table 4 and Figure 5 show the path coefficients and the performance values of the constructs. Table 5 shows the direct, indirect, and the total effects (the Importance dimension) together with the Performance values (re-scaled between 0 and 100). These values were used to create the graphical representation of the Importance-Performance Map (Figure 6). The Important-Performance Map utilises unstandardized total effects for the importance-dimension (x-axis) and the re-scaled performance values of the latent and manifest variables on the performance dimension (y-axis).

Figure 6 reveals that two direct predecessors of INFORMATION SECURITY, MONITORING and TRAINING, have a particularly high importance but relatively low performance (Quadrant I). Observably, TRAINING construct has considerably higher importance than the MONITORING construct. Managerial actions should therefore prioritize improving the performance of security TRAINING. Moreover, the importance of MONITORING was relatively high but its performance was relatively low. Attention also needs to be paid on improving the performance of MONITORING, which can be achieved by focusing on the predecessor construct of MONITORING, which is TRAINING. On the other side, the result showed that too much attention has been paid to RELATIONSHIP (Quadrant IV). This denoted

*Table 3. Path coefficients and statistical significance*

| Constructs | Sample Mean | Standard Deviation | Path Coefficients | T Statistics | *p*-values |
|---|---|---|---|---|---|
| ACCOUNTABILITY -> INFORMATION SECURITY | 0.180 | 0.077 | 2.333 | 2.333 | 0.020 |
| MONITORING -> ACCOUNTABILITY | 0.334 | 0.059 | 5.713 | 5.713 | 0.000 |
| MONITORING -> INFORMATION SECURITY | 0.242 | 0.064 | 3.804 | 3.804 | 0.000 |
| MONITORING -> RELATIONSHIP | 0.383 | 0.067 | 5.691 | 5.691 | 0.000 |
| RELATIONSHIP -> INFORMATION SECURITY | 0.290 | 0.054 | 5.280 | 5.280 | 0.000 |
| TRAINING -> ACCOUNTABILITY | 0.485 | 0.056 | 8.718 | 8.718 | 0.000 |
| TRAINING -> INFORMATION SECURITY | 0.135 | 0.054 | 2.501 | 2.501 | 0.012 |
| TRAINING -> MONITORING | 0.576 | 0.035 | 16.461 | 16.461 | 0.000 |
| TRAINING -> RELATIONSHIP | 0.247 | 0.062 | 3.856 | 3.856 | 0.000 |

*Table 4. Performance / index values and path coefficients*

| Constructs | LV Index Values | Performances | ACCOUNTABILITY | INFORMATION SECURITY | MONITORING | RELATIONSHIP |
|---|---|---|---|---|---|---|
| ACCOUNTABILITY | 3.477 | 61.933 | | 0.134 | | |
| INFORMATION SECURITY | 3.660 | 66.499 | | | | |
| MONITORING | 3.261 | 56.537 | 0.323 | 0.178 | | 0.313 |
| RELATIONSHIP | 3.801 | 70.015 | | 0.252 | | |
| TRAINING | 3.516 | 62.904 | 0.507 | 0.106 | 0.616 | 0.214 |

LV – Latent Variable

that RELATIONSHIP constructs was overly emphasized by the organisations. Instead of continuing to focus on RELATIONSHIP, organisations should allocate more resources to increase the performance of TRAINING and MONITORING. Surprisingly, ACCOUNTABILITY fell within Quadrant III, indicating low importance and performance.

*Figure 5. Structural model of importance-performance analysis*

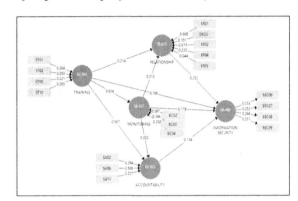

*Table 5. Direct, indirect, and total effects of importance-performance construct values*

| Predecessor Construct | Direct Effect on Security | Indirect Effect on Security | Total effect on Security/ Importance | Performance |
|---|---|---|---|---|
| ACCOUNTABILITY | 0.134 | - | 0.134 | 61.933 |
| MONITORING | 0.131 | 0.169 | 0.300 | 56.537 |
| RELATIONSHIP | 0.252 | - | 0.252 | 70.015 |
| TRAINING | 0.023 | 0.390 | 0.413 | 62.904 |
| Average | | | 0.275 | 62.847 |

Notes: All effects denote unstandardized effects.

*Figure 6. IPM constructs on information security*

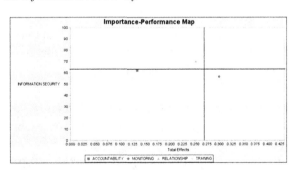

## Determining HRM indicators for Enhancing Information Systems Security

In the previous section, TRAINING and MONITORING were identified as very important for improving information security performance. However, to gain more specific information as to which key training and monitoring indicators will increase the performance of organisational information security, the indicator level Importance-Performance Map Analysis was performed. Table 6 shows the total effects (Importance dimension) and the information security (performance dimension) values at the indicator level. These values were used to create the indicator level Importance-Performance Map, as shown in Figure 7. The four quadrants on the IPM is made possible using the mean level of importance of 0.073 and the mean level of performance of 63.051, indicated by the vertical and the horizontal lines on the map.

In Quadrant I, *Concentrate Here*, the respondents perceived the attributes within this region as highly important, but their performance was very low. From the map (Figure 7), six key indicators/attributes were found that could improve information security performance. These are classified under the two constructs:

### Security Training

- ST02 Employees are trained to keep mobile devices secured.
- ST06 Employees are trained to be suspicious of any software that arrives in the mail, even though it may appear to be packaged and sent by trusted persons or vendors.
- ST10 Employees have been made aware that mass distributed software could contain targeted malware.

### Monitoring

- BC02 If an employee is promoted to a considerably higher level of responsibility and access, a new background check is carried out.
- BC03 Background screening is carried out for potential and third parties (suppliers, contractors, building maintenance personnel).
- BC04 An effort is made to track the current whereabouts of former employees who were deeply acquainted with critical systems and procedures.

Moreover, the following two indicators fell within Quadrant II (High Importance/High Performance). These indicators are the strength of the organisations. The indicated that the organisation must "keep up good works" in these areas to maintain security performance.

- ST01 Employees are given periodic training on security policies.
- ER01 The organisation makes fairness and good faith in the treatment of employees a priority.

On the contrary, seven indicators of EMPLOYEE RELATIONS and EMPLOYEE ACCOUNTABIL-ITY constructs were categorised as low importance but high performance, as they fell within Quadrant III and Quadrant IV respectively. The indicators are listed below.

## Employee Relations

- ER02 The organisation provides adequate mechanisms for employees to express their grievances without penalty and for them to see those grievances being conscientiously addressed.
- ER05 If an employee is going through a period of great difficulties in his or her personal life, there is a policy for temporarily reducing that employee's responsibilities for critical systems and access to critical systems.
- ER03 The organisation handles re-deployment and down-sizing in a manner that minimizes hostile feelings on the part of former employees.
- ER04 The organisation offers a procedure which would allow employees to report attempts by outsiders to extort their organisation in circumventing security.

## Accountability

- SA02 All employees are required to sign confidentiality and intellectual property agreements.
- SA06 Information security policies defined the proper use of e-mail, internet access, and instant messaging by employees.
- SA11 Employees are given adequate incentives to report security breaches and bad security practices.

*Table 6. Importance-performance indicator values*

| Indicators | Total Effect (Importance) | Information Security (Performance) |
|---|---|---|
| BC02 | 0.119 | 58.648 |
| BC03 | 0.103 | 54.403 |
| BC04 | 0.077 | 56.132 |
| ER01 | 0.153 | 71.698 |
| ER02 | 0.004 | 64.937 |
| ER03 | 0.025 | 65.881 |
| ER04 | 0.059 | 68.082 |
| ER05 | 0.011 | 68.239 |
| SA02 | 0.035 | 58.491 |
| SA06 | 0.068 | 63.365 |
| SA11 | 0.030 | 62.736 |
| ST01 | 0.084 | 73.742 |
| ST02 | 0.121 | 63.208 |
| ST06 | 0.091 | 56.132 |
| ST10 | 0.117 | 60.063 |
| Average | 0.073 | 63.051 |

*Figure 7. IPM indicators on information security*

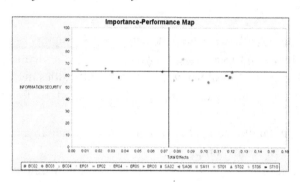

## SOLUTIONS AND RECOMMENDATIONS

The study identified security training, background checks and monitoring as the major HRM practices that can improve the performance of information security in organisations. Managerial actions should therefore prioritize improving training, background checks and monitoring. While lack of security training often lie behind many contemporary breaches (Lacey, 2010), investing in training and development can motivate staff and support the growth of the organisation (Leidner & Smith, 2013). HRM practices on security policy compliance found training for career development as positively associated with employees' behavioral intent to comply with security policy (Youngkeun Choi, 2017). Hence, information security training effectively reduces employees' non-compliance (Hwang et al., 2017). Security training, at the indicator level, ST02 ("Employees are trained to keep mobile devices secured") has a relatively high importance when focusing on information security, but required some room for performance improvement. Hence, performance improvements can focus on offering high-quality security trainings to provide users with the skills and knowledge they need to protect the mobile devices (Yaokumah, 2016). Similarly, other indicators, ST06 and ST10, focussed on employee training on malware. This should be given particular attention regarding improving the information security performance.

Moreover, the background checks and monitoring of the current employees, third parties, and former employees were found as important HRM practices that can improve the performance of organisational information security. A thorough and accurate background checks and security clearance investigations (Brody & Cox, 2015) can help an organisation to hire honest employees, those less likely to commit fraud against the organisation (Brody, 2010). Likewise, employee monitoring systems can improve performance, increase productivity, and reduce costs (Holt, Lang, & Sutton, 2017). In particular, at the indicator level, BC02 ("If an employee is promoted to a considerably higher level of responsibility and access, a new background check is carried out") has a relatively high importance but required performance improvement. Similarly, the BC03 ("Background screening is carried out for potential employees and third parties - suppliers, contractors, building maintenance personnel") and BC04 ("An effort is made to track the current whereabouts of former employees who were deeply acquainted with critical systems and procedures") required performance improvement. Thus, further improvement efforts should be concentrated on mobile devices security, malware, monitoring and background screening of current and former employees, including third party contractors.

Two indicators were found to be the strength of the organisations as they have attained the highest importance and performance levels in the organisations. These are ST01 ("Employees are given periodic training on security policies") and ER01 ("The organisation makes fairness and good faith in the treatment of employees a priority"). Accordingly, the organisations should continue to provide regular security training on security policies to the employees. Employees' information security training enhances adherence to security policies (Ramakrishna & Figueroa, 2017) and influences employees' threat and coping appraisals (Posey, Roberts, & Lowry, 2015). Besides, fairness in treating employees positively influences information security behaviour. Employees' perceptions of fairness promote commitment (Patrick, 2012).

On the contrary, two HRM practices, Employee Relations and Accountability were found to be of low importance but with high performance. This signified that these two constructs were overly emphasized by the organisations. Thus, accountability might not have remarkable impact on employees' security compliance behavior (Abed & Roland, 2016). Rather, instead of continuing to focus in employee relations and accountability, organisations should allocate more resources for security training programs, background checks and employee monitoring.

## FUTURE RESEARCH DIRECTIONS

The significance importance of security training, background checks and monitoring on improving information security offer an important opportunity for information security management practices. Organisations can improve information security by channelling resources from less important activities and invest them in security training, background checks and monitoring. Besides, before applying IPMA, this study demonstrated the concept and the use of importance-performance map analysis. By combining the analysis of the importance and performance dimensions of the IPMA, the study allowed the IT and HR leaders to identify and prioritize HRM practices and indicators that were most important for improving the performance of the organisations' information security. The study also provided guidance for the formulation of information security strategy that could accurately allocate resources to maximise a high return on security investment.

The findings extended information security research literature by showing how HRM practices (training, background checks and monitoring) can play a major role in improving information security. Our results provided one of the few empirical validations of information security to be recognized as a multi-disciplinary issue as conceptualized through HRM practices. In addition, the study extended information security research by considering the role of employee relations and accountability from the HRM literature. However, some HRM practices were not included in the current study. For example, including remuneration and rewards might further enhance information security literature. Moreover, because HRM practices may differ among the organisations, future research using a multi-group analysis that allows for contrasting group results might produce an insightful finding.

## CONCLUSION

In this chapter, the IPMA technique was discussed and applied to measure HRM practices from the perspective of IT professionals to identify priority areas for the allocation of resources to improve the performance of organisational information security. A survey was conducted on the IT professionals' perceptions to identify areas of importance and performance of HRM practices. Using IPMA technique, the study identified security training, background checks and monitoring as highly important that needed to be improved in order to enhance organisational information security performance. Two indicators (periodic training in adherence to security policy and fairness in treating employees) were found to have attained the highest importance and performance levels in the organisations. In terms of key indicators for specific management actions, attention needed to be paid to: (a) training to keep mobile devices secured, b) training on malware, (c) tracking of the whereabouts of former employees who were deeply acquainted with critical systems and procedures, and d) background checks on employee promoted to a considerably higher level of responsibility and system access. Organisations need to consider allocating resources to training, background check and monitoring.

# REFERENCES

Aamodt, M. G. (2015). Using background checks in the employee selection process. In C. Hanvey & K. Sady (Eds.), *Practitioner's Guide to Legal Issues in Organizations*. New York: Springer. doi:10.1007/978-3-319-11143-8_4

Abawajy, J. (2014). User preference of cyber security awareness delivery methods. *Behaviour & Information Technology*, *33*(3), 237–248. doi:10.1080/0144929X.2012.708787

Abed, J., & Roland, W. H. (2016). Understanding deterrence theory in security compliance behavior: A quantitative meta-analysis approach. *SAIS 2016 Proceedings*. Retrieved from http://aisel.aisnet.org/sais2016/28

Ahmad, S., & Schroeder, R. G. (2003). The impact of human resource management practices on operational performance: Recognising country and industry differences. *Journal of Operations Management*, *21*(1), 19–25. doi:10.1016/S0272-6963(02)00056-6

AL-Qudah, M. K. M., Osman, A., Ab Halim, M. S., & Al-Shatanawi, H. A. (2014). The effect of human resources planning and training and development on organizational performance in the government sector in Jordan. *International Journal of Academic Research in Business and Social Sciences*, *4*(4).

Alampay, E. A., & Hechanova, R. M. (2010). Monitoring employee use of the internet in Philippine organizations. *The Electronic Journal on Information Systems in Developing Countries*, *40*(5), 1–20. doi:10.1002/j.1681-4835.2010.tb00287.x

Amarachi, A. A., Okolie, S. O., & Ajaegbu, C. (2013). Information security management system: Emerging issues and prospect. *IOSR Journal of Computer Engineering.*, *12*(3), 96–102. doi:10.9790/0661-12396102

Angst, C. M., Block, E. S., D'Arcy, J., & Kelley, K. (2017). When do IT security investments matter? Accounting for the influence of institutional factors in the context of healthcare data breaches. *Management Information Systems Quarterly*, *41*(3), 893–916. doi:10.25300/MISQ/2017/41.3.10

Asare-Bediako, K. (2011). *Human resource management in Ghana lacks strategic focus*. Ghana News Agency. Retrieved from http://www.ghananewsagency.org/social/human-resource-management-in-ghana-lacks-strategic-focus—27174

Au, C. H., & Fung, W. S. (2019). Integrating knowledge management into information security: From audit to practice. *International Journal of Knowledge Management, 15*(1), 37–52. doi:10.4018/IJKM.2019010103

Balozian, P., Leidner, D., & Warkentin, M. (2019). Managers' and employees' differing responses to security approaches. *Journal of Computer Information Systems, 59*(3), 197–210. doi:10.1080/08874417.2017.1318687

Bashshur, M. R., & Burak, O. C. (2015). When voice matters: A multilevel review of the impact of voice in organizations. *Journal of Management, 41*(5), 1530–1554. doi:10.1177/0149206314558302

Battaglio, P., Goodman, D., & French, P. E. (2017). Contracting out for municipal human resources: Analyzing the role of human capital in the make or buy decision. *Public Administration Quarterly, 41*(2), 297–333.

Baxter, R. J., Holderness, D. K. Jr, & Wood, D. A. (2016). Applying basic gamification techniques to it compliance training: Evidence from the lab and field. *Journal of Information Systems, 30*(3), 119–133. doi:10.2308/isys-51341

Bernik, I., & Prislan, K. (2016). Measuring Information Security Performance with 10 by 10 model for holistic state evaluation. *PLoS One, 11*(9), 1–33. doi:10.1371/journal.pone.0163050 PMID:27655001

Bhattacharya, C. B., Sen, S., & Korschun, D. (2012). Using corporate social responsibility to win the war for talent. *MIT Sloan Management Review, 49*, 37–44.

Bhattacharya, S., Trehan, G., & Kaur, K. (2018). Factors Determining Psychological Contract of IT Employees in India. *International Journal of Human Capital and Information Technology Professionals, 9*(1), 37–52. doi:10.4018/IJHCITP.2018010103

Blair, D., & Sisakhti, R. (2007). Sales training: what makes it work? *T & D Magazine*. Retrieved from www.astd.org/astd/Publications/TD_Magazine/2007_pdf/August/0708ExecSum.htm

Boss, S. R., Galletta, D. F., Lowry, P. B., Moody, G. D., & Polak, P. (2015). What do systems users have to fear? Using fear appeals to engender threats and fear that motivate protective security behaviors. *Management Information Systems Quarterly, 39*(4), 837–864. doi:10.25300/MISQ/2015/39.4.5

Brody, R. G. (2010). Beyond the basic background check: Hiring the "right" employees. *Management Research Review, 33*(3), 210–223. doi:10.1108/01409171011030372

Brody, R. G., & Cox, V. L. (2015). Background investigations a comparative analysis of background checks and federal security clearance investigations. *Business Studies Journal, 7*(1), 84–94.

Bumgarner, J., & Borg, S. (2007). *US-CCU Cyber-Security Questionnaire*. US-CCU (Cyber Consequences Unit) Cyber-Security Check. Retrieved from www.usccu.us

Burns, A. J., Posey, C., Roberts, T. L., & Lowry, P. B. (2017). Examining the relationship of organisational insiders' psychological capital with information security threat and coping appraisals. *Computers in Human Behavior, 68*, 190–209. doi:10.1016/j.chb.2016.11.018

Cherdantseva, Y., & Hilton, J. (2013). Information security and information assurance. The discussion about the meaning, scope and goals. In F. Almeida & I. Portela (Eds.), *Organisational, Legal, and Technological Dimensions of Information System Administrator*. IGI Global Publishing.

Choi, Y. (2017). Human resource management and security policy compliance. *International Journal of Human Capital and Information Technology Professionals, 8*(3), 14. doi:10.4018/IJHCITP.2017070105

Cram, W. A., D'Arcy, J., & Proudfoot, J. G. (2019). Seeing the Forest and the Trees: AMeta-Analysis of the Antecedents to Information Security Policy Compliance. *Management Information Systems Quarterly, 43*(2), 1–24. doi:10.25300/MISQ/2019/15117

Cybercrime Unit. (2016). *Government will fight Cyber Crime*. Retrieved from http://cybercrime.gov. gh/?p=313

D'Arcy, J., & Greene, G. (2014). Security culture and the employment relationship as drivers of employees' security compliance. *Information Management & Computer Security, 22*(5), 474–489. doi:10.1108/IMCS-08-2013-0057

Da Veiga, A. (2016). Comparing the information security culture of employees who had read the information security policy and those who had not: Illustrated through an empirical study. *Information & Computer Security, 24*(2), 139–151. doi:10.1108/ICS-12-2015-0048

Driscoll, C., & McKee, M. (2007). Restorying a culture of ethical and spiritual values: A role for leader storytelling. *Journal of Business Ethics, 73*(2), 205–217. doi:10.100710551-006-9191-5

Dumisani, X., Chux, G. I., Andre, S., & Joyce, N. (2014). The Impact of Employer-Employee Relationships on Business Growth. *Journal of Economics, 5*(3), 313–324. doi:10.1080/09765239.2014.11885007

Durden, O. (2019). *The advantages of monitoring employees*. Retrieved from https://smallbusiness.chron. com/advantages-monitoring-employees-18428.html

EEOC vrs Freeman (2013). *Court Slams EEOC on Background Check Lawsuit No. 09-CV-2573*. Retrieved from https://www.employmentlawspotlight.com/2013/08/court-slams-eeoc-on-background-check-lawsuit/

Ford, J., Willey, L., White, B. J., & Domagalski, T. (2015). New concerns in electronic employee monitoring: Have you checked your policies lately? *Journal of Legal, Ethical & Regulatory Issues, 18*(1), 51–70.

Furnell, S., & Thomson, K. L. (2009). From culture to disobedience: Recognizing the varying user acceptance of IT security. *Computer Fraud & Security, 2*(2), 5–10. doi:10.1016/S1361-3723(09)70019-3

Geisser, S. (1974). A Predictive Approach to the Random Effects Model. *Biometrika, 61*(1), 101–107. doi:10.1093/biomet/61.1.101

Goodman, D., French, P. E., & Battaglio, R. P. Jr. (2015). Determinants of local government workforce planning. *American Review of Public Administration, 45*(2), 135–152. doi:10.1177/0275074013486179

Hair, J. F., Hult, G. T. M., Ringle, C. M., & Sarstedt, M. (2014). *A primer on partial least squares structural equation modeling (PLS-SEM)*. Thousand Oaks, CA: Sage.

Hair, J. F., Hult, G. T. M., Ringle, C. M., & Sarstedt, M. (2017). *A primer on partial least squares structural equation modeling (PLS-SEM)*. Thousand Oaks, CA: Sage.

Hair, J. F., Sarstedt, M., Ringle, C., & Mena, J. A. (2012). An assessment of the use of partial least squares structural equation modeling in marketing research. *Journal of the Academy of Marketing Science*, *40*(3), 414–433. doi:10.100711747-011-0261-6

Herath, T., & Rao, H. R. (2009). Protection motivation and deterrence: A framework for security policy compliance in organisations. *European Journal of Information Systems*, *18*(2), 106–125. doi:10.1057/ejis.2009.6

Hirshfield, L., Bobko, P., Barelka, A. J., Costa, M. R., Funke, G. J., Mancuso, V. F., & Knott, B. A. (2019). The role of human operators' suspicion in the detection of cyber attacks. Cyber Law, Privacy, and Security: Concepts, Methodologies, Tools, and Applications, 1482-1499.

Holt, M., Lang, B., & Sutton, S. G. (2017). Potential employees' ethical perceptions of active monitoring: The dark side of data analytics. *Journal of Information Systems*, *31*(2), 107–124. doi:10.2308/isys-51580

Hu, Q., Dinev, T., Hart, P., & Cooke, D. (2012). Managing employee compliance with information security policies: The critical role of top management and organisational culture. *Decision Sciences Journal*, *43*(4), 615–659. doi:10.1111/j.1540-5915.2012.00361.x

Hu, Q., West, R., & Smarandescu, L. (2015). The Role of Self-Control in Information Security Violations: Insights from a Cognitive Neuroscience Perspective. *Journal of Management Information Systems*, *31*(4), 6–48. doi:10.1080/07421222.2014.1001255

Hughes, S., Keller, E. W., & Hertz, G. T. (2010). Homeland security initiatives and background checks in higher education. *New Directions for Institutional Research*, *2010*(146), 51–62. doi:10.1002/ir.342

Hwang, I., Kim, D., Kim, T., & Kim, S. (2017). Why not comply with information security? An empirical approach for the causes of non-compliance. *Online Information Review*, *41*(1), 2–18. doi:10.1108/OIR-11-2015-0358

Ikenwe, I. J., Igbinovia, O. M., & Elogie, A. A. (2016). Information Security in the Digital Age: The Case of Developing Countries. *Chinese Librarianship*, *42*, 16–24.

Javad, A., & Weistroffer, H. R. (2016). Understanding Deterrence Theory in Security Compliance Behavior: A Quantitative Meta-Analysis Approach. *SAIS 2016 Proceedings*. Retrieved from http://aisel.aisnet.org/sais2016/28

Karlsson, F., Åström, J., & Karlsson, M. (2015). Information security culture – state-of-the-art review between 2000 and 2013. *Information & Computer Security*, *23*(3), 246–285. doi:10.1108/ICS-05-2014-0033

Kaspersky, E., & Furnell, S. (2014). A security education Q&A. *Information Management & Computer Security*, *22*(2), 130–133. doi:10.1108/IMCS-01-2014-0006

Katuo, A., & Budhwar, P. (2006). Human resource management systems andorganizational performance: A test of a mediating model in the Greek manufacturing context. *International Journal of Human Resource Management*, *17*(7), 1223–1253. doi:10.1080/09585190600756525

Khan, H. U., & AlShare, K. A. (2019). Violators versus non-violators of information security measures in organizations - A study of distinguishing factors. *Journal of Organizational Computing and Electronic Commerce*, *29*(1), 4–23. doi:10.1080/10919392.2019.1552743

Khan, M. A. (2010). Effects of human resource management practices on organizational performance - An empirical study of oil and gas industry in Pakistan. European Journal of Economics. *Finance and Administrative Sciences, 24*, 157–175.

Khao, B., Harris, P., & Hartman, S. (2010). Information security governance of enterprise information systems: An approach to legislative compliant. *International Journal of Management and Information Systems, 14*(3), 49–55.

Kim, E. B. (2014). Recommendations for information security awareness training for college students. *Information Management & Computer Security, 22*(1), 115–126. doi:10.1108/IMCS-01-2013-0005

Klaas, B. S., Olson-Buchanan, J. B., & Anna-Katherine, W. (2012). The determinants of alternative forms of workplace voice: An integrative perspective. *Journal of Management, 38*(1), 314–345. doi:10.1177/0149206311423823

Koh, R. J. (2018). The Influence of human resource management practices on employee performance in the manufacturing sector in Malaysia. *International Journal of Human Resource Studies, 8*(2).

Komatsu, A., Takagi, D., & Takemura, T. (2013). Human aspects of information security: An empirical study of intentional versus actual behavior. *Information Management & Computer Security, 21*(1), 5–15. doi:10.1108/09685221311314383

Lacey, D. (2010). Understanding and transforming organisational security culture. *Information Management & Computer Security, 18*(1), 4–13. doi:10.1108/09685221011035223

Leidner, S., & Smith, S. M. (2013). Keeping potential job-hoppers' feet on the ground. *Human Resource Management International Digest, 21*(1), 31–33. doi:10.1108/09670731311296492

McCrohan, K. F., Engel, K., & Harvey, J. W. (2010). Influence of awareness and training on cyber security. *Journal of Internet Commerce, 9*(1), 23–41. doi:10.1080/15332861.2010.487415

Miller, D. (2017). *Importance of School Monitoring And Evaluation Systems*. Retrieved from http://leansystemssociety.org/importance-of-school-monitoring-and-evaluation-systems/

Misra, R. K., & Khurana, K. (2018). Analysis of Employability Skill Gap in Information Technology Professionals. *International Journal of Human Capital and Information Technology Professionals, 9*(3), 53–69. doi:10.4018/IJHCITP.2018070104

Misra, S., & Adewumi, A. (2015). An Analysis of the Suitability of Cloud Computing Services in the Nigerian Education Landscape. *Proceeding of IEEE International Conference on Computing, Communication and Security*, 1-4. 10.1109/CCCS.2015.7374203

Naz, F., Aftab, J., & Awais, M. (2016). Impact of Human Resource Management Practices (HRM) on Performance of SMEs in Multan, Pakistan. *International Journal of Management. Accounting & Economics, 3*(11), 699–708.

Nunnally, J. C. (1978). *Psychometric theory* (2nd ed.). New York, NY: McGraw-Hill.

Odun-Ayo, I., Misra, S., Omoregbe, N., Onibere, E., Bulama, Y., & Damasevičius, R. (2017). *Cloud-Based Security Driven Human Resource Management System. In Frontiers in Artificial Intelligence and Applications* (Vol. 295, pp. 96–106). Advances in Digital Technologies.

Okewu, E., Misra, S., Sanz, L. F., Maskeliūnas, R., & Damaševičius, R. (2018). An e-Environment System for Socio-economic Sustainability and National Security. *Problemy Ekorozwoju, 13*(1), 121–132.

Oladipo, J. A., & Abdulkadir, D. S. (2011). Strategic human resource management and organizational performance in the Nigerian manufacturing sector: An empirical investigation. *International Journal of Business and Management, 6*(9), 46–56.

Ossege, C. (2012). Accountability – are we better off without it? *Public Management Review, 14*(5), 585–607. doi:10.1080/14719037.2011.642567

Overseas Security Advisory Council (OSAC). (2012). *Ghana 2012 OSAC crime and safety report*. Retrieved from https://www.osac.gov

Parker, D. B. (2008). Security accountability in job performance. *Information Systems Security, 3*(4), 16–20. doi:10.1080/10658989509342474

Patrick, H. A. (2012). Commitment of information technology employees in relation to perceived organisational justice. *IUP Journal of Organisational Behavior, 11*(3), 23–40.

Posey, C., Roberts, T. L., & Lowry, P. B. (2015). The impact of organisational commitment on insiders' motivation to protect organisational information assets. *Journal of Management Information Systems, 32*(4), 179–214. doi:10.1080/07421222.2015.1138374

Radhakrishna, A., & Raju, S. R. (2015). A study on the effect of human resource development on employment relations. *IUP Journal of Management Research, 14*(3), 28–42.

Ramakrishna, A., & Figueroa, N. (2017). Is seeing believing? Training users on information security: Evidence from Java Applets. *Journal of Information Systems Education, 28*(2), 115–122.

Rantos, K., Fysarakis, K., & Manifavas, C. (2012). How effective is your security awareness program? An evaluation methodology. *Information Security Journal: A Global Perspective, 21*(6), 328-345.

Rigon, E. A., Westphall, C. M., dos Santos, D. R., & Westphall, C. B. (2014). A cyclical evaluation model of information security maturity. *Information Management & Computer Security, 22*(3), 265–278. doi:10.1108/IMCS-04-2013-0025

Ringle, C. M., & Sarstedt, M. (2016). Gain more insight from your PLS-SEM results: The importance-performance map analysis. *Industrial Management & Data Systems, 116*(9), 1865–1886. doi:10.1108/IMDS-10-2015-0449

Safa, N. S., Maple, C., Furnell, S., Azad, M. A., Perera, C., Dabbagh, M., & Sookhak, M. (2019). Deterrence and prevention-based model to mitigate information security insider threats in organisations. *Future Generation Computer Systems, 97*, 587–597. doi:10.1016/j.future.2019.03.024

Safa, N. S., Maple, C., Watson, T., & Von Solms, R. (2018). Motivation and opportunity based model to reduce information security insider threats in organisations. *Journal of Information Security and Applications, 40,* 247-257.

Saifalislam, K. M., Osman, A., & AlQudah, M. K. (2014). Human resource management practices: Influence of recruitment and selection, and training and development on the organizational performance of the Jordanian Public University. *Journal of Business and Management, 16*(5), 43-46.

Sarode, A. P., & Deore, S. S. (2017). Role of third party employee verification and background checks in HR management: An overview. *Journal of Commerce & Management Thought, 8*(1), 86–96. doi:10.5958/0976-478X.2017.00005.2

Sattar, T., Ahmad, K., & Hassan, S. M. (2015). The role of human resource practices in employee performance and job satisfaction with mediating effect of employee engagement. *Pakistan Economic and Social Review, 53*(1), 81–96.

Selden, S. C. (2009). *Human capital: Tools and strategies for the public sector.* Washington, DC: CQ Press. doi:10.4135/9781483330754

Sreejith, S. S., & Mathirajan, M. (2016). Identifying Criteria for Continuous Evaluation of Software Engineers for Reward and Recognition: An Exploratory Research. *International Journal of Human Capital and Information Technology Professionals, 7*(4), 61–78. doi:10.4018/IJHCITP.2016100105

Stewart, J. M., Tittel, E., & Chapple, M. (2005). *Certified Information Systems Security Professional (Study Guide)* (3rd ed.). San Francisco: Sybex.

Stone, M. (1974). Cross-Validatory Choice and Assessment of Statistical Predictions. *Journal of the Royal Statistical Society. Series A (General), 36*(2), 111–147.

Styles, M., & Tryfonas, T. (2009). Using penetration testing feedback to cultivate proactive security amongst end-users. *Information Management & Computer Security, 17*(1), 44–52. doi:10.1108/09685220910944759

Subramaniam, C., Shamsudin, F. M., & Ibrahim, H. (2011). Linking human resource practices and organisational performance: Evidence from small and medium organizations in Malaysia. *Journal Pengurusan, 32,* 27–37. doi:10.17576/pengurusan-2011-32-04

Syamala, D. B., & Dasaraju, S. R. (2014). *A suggested conceptual framework for employee background Check.* ICBPEM, Knowledge Partner.

Tassabehji, R. (2005). Information security threats: From evolution to prominence. In *Evcyclopedia of Multimedia Technology and Networking (Margherita Pagani).* Idea Group Inc. doi:10.4018/978-1-59140-561-0.ch058

Thomson, K., & van Niekerk, J. (2012). Combating information security apathy by encouraging prosocial organisational behaviour. *Information Management & Computer Security, 20*(1), 39–46. doi:10.1108/09685221211219191

U.S. Office of Personnel Management. (n.d.). Retrieved from https://www.opm.gov

Valentine, R. L. (2014). *Human Resource Management. Stanford, CA: Cengage Learning. SHRM.*

Vance, A., Lowry, P. B., & Eggett, D. (2013). Using accountability to reduce access policy violations in information systems. *Journal of Management Information Systems, 29*(4), 263–290. doi:10.2753/MIS0742-1222290410

White, G. L., Hewitt, B., & Kruck, S. E. (2013). Incorporating global information security and assurance in I.S. education. *Journal of Information Systems Education, 24*(1), 11–16.

Yalman, Y., & Yesilyurt, M. (2013). Information Security Threats and Information Assurance. *TEM Journal, 2*(3), 247–252.

Yaokumah, W. (2016). The influence of students' characteristics on mobile device security measures. *International Journal of Information Systems and Social Change, 7*(3), 44–66. doi:10.4018/IJISSC.2016070104

Zaman, U., & Saif, M. I. (2016). Perceived accountability and conflict management styles as predictors of job performance of public officials in Pakistan. *Gomal University Journal of Research, 32*(2), 24–35.

Zhang, L., & McDowell, W. C. (2009). Am I really at risk? Determinants of online users' intentions to use strong passwords. *Journal of Internet Commerce, 8*(3–4), 180–197. doi:10.1080/15332860903467508

Zhao, X., Xue, L., & Whinston, A. B. (2013). Managing interdependent information security risks: Cyberinsurance, managed security services, and risk pooling arrangements. *Journal of Management Information Systems, 30*(1), 123–152. doi:10.2753/MIS0742-1222300104

*Previously published in the Handbook of Research on the Role of Human Factors in IT Project Management; pages 278-303, copyright year 2020 by Business Science Reference (an imprint of IGI Global).*

# Chapter 15

# Identifying HRM Practices for Improving Information Security Performance:
## An Importance–Performance Map Analysis

**Peace Kumah**
*Ghana Education Service, Accra, Ghana*

**Winfred Yaokumah**
 https://orcid.org/0000-0001-7756-1832
*Department of Information Technology, Pentecost University College, Accra, Ghana*

**Charles Buabeng-Andoh**
 https://orcid.org/0000-0003-3781-684X
*Pentecost University College, Ghana*

## ABSTRACT

*This article focuses on identifying key human resource management (HRM) practices necessary for improving information security performance from the perspective of IT professionals. The Importance-Performance Map Analysis (IPMA) via SmartPLS 3.0 was employed and 232 samples were collected from information technology (IT) professionals in 43 organizations. The analysis identified information security training, background checks and monitoring as very important HRM practices that could improve the performance of organizational information security. In particular, the study found training on mobile devices security and malware; background checks and monitoring of potential, current and former employees as of high importance but with low performance. Thus, these key areas need to be improved with top priority. Conversely, the study found accountability and employee relations as being overly emphasized by the organisations. The findings raised some useful implications and information for HR and IT leaders to consider in future information security strategy.*

DOI: 10.4018/978-1-6684-3698-1.ch015

## INTRODUCTION

Securing sensitive and critical information is a global concern (Ikenwe, Igbinovia, & Elogie, 2016; White, Hewitt, & Kruck, 2013). It involves protection of information assets from unauthorized access, accidental loss, destruction, disclosure, modification, or misuse (Tassabehji, 2005). Information security is a multi-disciplinary area involving professional activity of developing and implementing technical, organisational, human-oriented security mechanisms in order to keep information systems free from threats (Cherdantseva & Hilton, 2013). As a result of increasing dependency on information technology (IT) systems and emerging security threats and vulnerabilities relating to privacy, identity theft, and cybercrime, the role of IT professionals become crucial for maintaining security of information resources (Khao, Harris, & Hartman, 2010). Information security breaches may result in loss of sensitive information and productivity which may lead to huge financial liabilities, adversely affecting the reputation of the organisation (Abawajy, 2014). Information technology professionals are facing challenging tasks analysing, designing, and deploying solutions to protect information resources. Notwithstanding, previous studies acknowledge that human factors are the major sources of many security failures (Abawajy, 2014; Driscoll & McKee, 2007; Furnell & Thomson, 2009; Komatsu, Takagi, & Takemura, 2013). Human beings are vulnerable to a wide range of security attacks, which range from deliberate violation of security policy to circumvention of physical and technical security controls (Stewart, Tittel, & Chapple, 2005). Moreover, people underestimate the likelihood of the occurrence of security breaches (Herath & Rao, 2009).

A key area in information security research is discovering ways to motivate employee to engage in more secure behaviors (Boss et al., 2015). Human resource management (HRM) practices can address the problem of the human-oriented factors. Human resource management practices of employee recruitment and selection, training and development, performance monitoring and appraisals are very important to improve organisational performance (Naz, Aftab, & Awais, 2016). Investing in training and development can motivate staff and support the growth of the organisation (Leidner & Smith, 2013). IT security and data privacy training can serve as critical controls for safeguarding organisation's information resources (Baxter, Holderness, & Wood, 2016). However, to achieve the best results, security training and awareness programs should be regularly evaluated so that corrective actions can be taken (Rantos, Fysarakis & Manifavas, 2012). In addition, employee relations are seen by employers as critical in achieving job performance through employee involvement, commitment and engagement (Radhakrishna & Raju, 2015). Moreover, employee monitoring is a significant component of employers' efforts to maintain employee productivity (Ford et al., 2015). Employee background checks are important to ascertain criminal records, character, and fitness of the employee (Sarode & Deore, 2017). Furthermore, employee's accountability can improve information security (Vance, Lowry, & Eggett, 2013). However, accountability can have both positive and negative effect on work behavior (Ossege, 2012).

Improving information security by focusing on human resource management practices has not received much attention by researchers. From the perspective of IT professionals, this current study focuses on identifying key HRM practices that can improve information security performance using Importance-Performance Map Analysis (IPMA) (Ringle & Sarstedt, 2016). Specifically, the study identifies the HRM practices that IT professionals perceive as important and whose performance is necessary to improve information security in organisations. The study answers the following research questions:

1.  What are the important HRM practices (factors) that can improve the performance of organisational information security?
2.  What are the important indicators for enhancing the performance of organisational information security?

Reviewing studies on the use of partial least squares structured equation modelling (PLS-SEM) (Hair et al., 2012; Ringle et al., 2012; Sarstedt et al., 2014) reveals that information security researchers basically rely on the standard PLS path model analysis, ignoring the Importance-Performance Map Analysis (IPMA). IPMA provides guidance for the prioritization of managerial activities of high importance but require performance improvements (Ringle & Sarstedt, 2016). It is particularly useful for generating additional findings and conclusions from the standard PLS-SEM. Thus, in this study IPMA is used to evaluate the level of importance organisations attach to each of the HRM factors and indicators, which can improve information security performance.

## BACKGROUND

### Concept of Importance-Performance Map Analysis

The study first explains the principles underlying and procedures involved in using IPMA. The first step in creating an importance-performance map (IPM) requires selecting the target construct of interest in the PLS path model (Ringle & Sarstedt, 2016). Consider the PLS path model in Figure 1 with five constructs ($C_1$ to $C_5$). In PLS path model in Figure 1, $C_5$ represents the key target construct. $C_5$ is directly predicted by $C_1$ to $C_4$. Also, $C_1$ has indirect effect on $C_5$ via $C_2$, $C_3$, and $C_4$. To perform Importance-Performance Map Analysis, the PLS path model in Figure 1 will be transformed into IPMA grid as shown in Figure 2 with two dimensions – importance and performance dimensions. The addition of the predecessor constructs' ($C_1$ to $C_4$) direct and indirect effects yields their total effects on $C_5$. This represents the importance dimension in the IPMA (Ringle & Sarstedt, 2016). On the other hand, the constructs' average latent variable scores represent the performance dimension in IPMA. The higher values indicate a greater performance and vice versa (Ringle & Sarstedt, 2016). Also, in Figure 1, $x_{ij}$ (for example $x_{11}$, $x_{22}$, $x_{42}$) represents the indicators of the constructs $C_i$ and $p_i$ ($p_1$ to $p_9$) represents the path coefficients.

Now, the two dimensions can be plotted graphically by placing the total effects (Importance dimension) on the x-axis and the rescaled latent variable scores (re-scaled on a range from 0 to 100), representing the Performance dimension on the y-axis. This results in an Important-Performance Map in Figure 2. Moreover, the two dimensional IPMA model is further divided into four quadrants. To achieve this, two lines are drawn on the Importance-Performance Map. The vertical line is the mean importance value and the horizontal line is the mean performance value of the constructs. Thus, these two lines divide the Importance-Performance Map into four areas with importance and performance values below and above the average (Figure 2). Generally, when analyzing the Importance-Performance Map, constructs appearing in the lower right area (i.e. Quadrant I) are of the highest interest to achieving improvement in the target construct ($C_5$), followed by the higher right (i.e. Quadrant II), lower left (i.e. Quadrant III) and, finally, the higher left areas (i.e. Quadrant IV) (Ringle & Sarstedt, 2016).

*Figure 1. Concept of path model of IPMA*

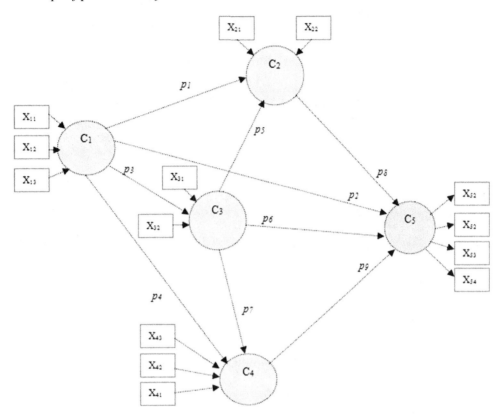

The four quadrants (Figure 2) are generally referred to as *concentrate here (Quadrant I)*, *keep up the good work (Quadrant II)* *low priority (Quadrant III)*, and *possible overkill (Quadrant IV)*. The constructs and indicators that fall within the quadrants can be interpreted as below (Ringle & Sarstedt, 2016).

*Quadrant I* (High Importance/Low Performance). The constructs or indicators that fall within this quadrant represent key areas that need to be improved with top priority.

*Quadrant II* (High Importance/High Performance). All constructs or indicators that fall within this quadrant are the strength of the organisations.

*Quadrant III* (Low Importance/Low Performance). Any of the constructs or indicators that falls within this quadrant is not important to the organisations.

*Quadrant IV* (Low Importance/High Performance). This denotes constructs or indicators that are overly emphasized by the organisations. Organisations, instead of continuing to focus in this quadrant, should allocate more resources to deal with constructs or indicators that fall within *Quadrant I*.

In particular, to further explain the concept, Figure 3 and Figure 4 demonstrate IPM for both constructs and indicators respectively. In Figure 3, $C_1$ is particularly important to improve the performance of the target construct $C_5$, as it falls within the *Quadrant I* (High Importance/Low Performance). More precisely, a one-unit point increase in $C_1$'s performance increases the performance of $C_5$ by the value of $C_1$'s total effect on $C_5$. Thus, in Figure 3, the performance of $C_1$ is relatively low; there is therefore

*Figure 2. Relative importance-performance regions*

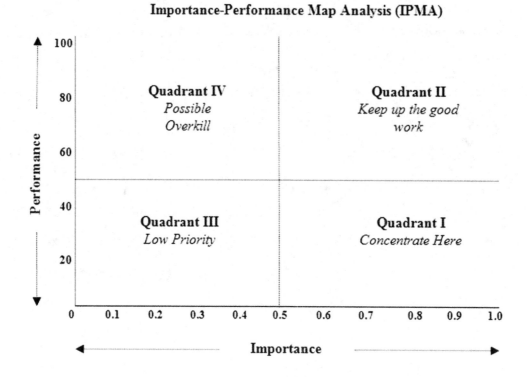

substantial room for improvement, making this construct particularly relevant for managerial actions. Moreover, to generate IPM for indicators, individual data points in the Importance-Performance Map are derived from indicator mean values and their total effect on a particular target construct, $C_5$. As can be observed in Figure 4, $x_{11}$, $x_{23}$ have the highest importance but low performance values (Quadrant I). Thus, these indicators will require management attention to improve their performance in order to enhance the performance of the target construct, $C_5$.

## Empirical Background

### Information Security

Information security involves managing risks related to the use, processing, storage, transmission of information or data and the systems and processes used for those purposes (Yalman & Yesilyurt, 2013). One of the key challenges in information security management is to understand how human factors affect the outcomes of information security in an organisation (Hu et al., 2012). Organisations are taking measures to ensure the security of information (Yalman & Yesilyurt, 2013). However, organisations invest inefficiently in information technology security measures (Zhao, Xue, & Whinston, 2013), while human attitude was identified as having significant impact on compliance with security policy (Zhang, Reithel, & Li, 2009). Thus, technological security solutions alone are ineffective at reducing security breaches. Accordingly to Angst, Block, D'Arcy and Kelley (2017), information technology (IT) security investments are effective at reducing the incidence of data security breaches when they are balanced with institutional factors. According to Herath and Rao (2009), organisational commitment, social influence, and threat perceptions about the severity of breaches affect employees' attitudes toward policy compliance. Burns et al. (2017) established the relationship between organisational insiders' psychological capital with information security threat and coping appraisals. Self-control is a major factor influencing individual behaviour's towards information security (Hu, West, & Smarandescu, 2015).

Organisations should measure their information security performance in order to make the right decisions (Bernik & Prislan, 2016) and channel resources to areas of high importance that will lead to high security performance. A recent study showed that a high level of information security performance is mostly dependent on measures aimed at managing employees (Bernik & Prislan, 2016). Managing employees' security behaviors for better information security performance will require security training and development programs, creating employee relations, background checks and monitoring, and accountability.

*Figure 3. Constructs - IPMA on the target construct, $C_5$*

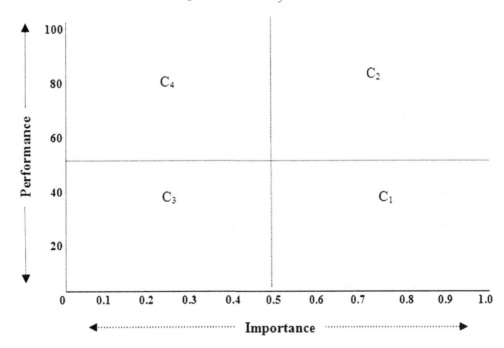

## Security Training and Development

Investing in training and development can motivate staff and support the growth of the organisations (Leidner & Smith, 2013). While lack of security training often lies behind many contemporary breaches (Lacey, 2010), security education enables skilled professionals and ensures adequate security awareness among end users (Kaspersky & Furnell, 2014). Abawajy (2014) evaluated the effects of various information security awareness delivery methods that could improve end-user information security awareness and behavior. By conducting experiments on information security awareness using three different methods: text-based, game-based and video-based, the study suggested that combined delivery methods of

*Figure 4. Indicators - IPMA on the Target Construct, $C_5$*

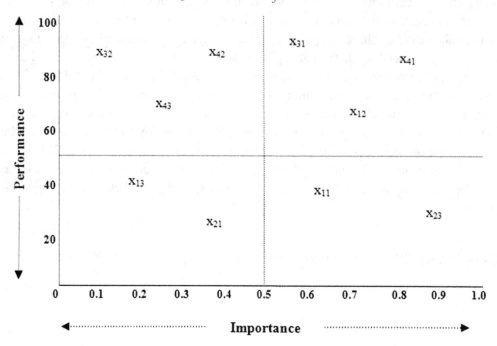

improving end-users' information security awareness and behaviour are better than individual security awareness delivery method (Abawajy, 2014). A related study determined the impact of cyber threat education and awareness intervention on changes in user security behaviour (McCrohan, Engel, & Harvey, 2010). The study was based on protection motivation theory and an experimental was performed by using undergraduate business school students. McCrohan, Engel and Harvey (2010) found that when users are educated of the threats to e-commerce and trained about proper security practices, their behavior could be changed to enhance information security. Hence, security and assurance should be a core component of the curriculum for all information security and business students (White, Hewitt, & Kruck, 2013).

Moreover, a survey conducted on 196 undergraduate students in a business college to investigate students' understanding and attitudes toward information security suggested that when universities provide easily accessible security training programs to students, information security improves (Kim, 2014). In a related study, Da Veiga (2016) determined the influence information security policy had on the information security culture by comparing the security behavior of employees who read the policy to those who did not. An empirical study was conducted at four intervals over eight years across 12 countries using a validated information security culture assessment (ISCA) questionnaire. The overall information security culture was significantly more positive for employees who had read the information security policy compared with employees who had not. Employees' information security training can improve adherence to security policies when employees are shown the reasons behind the written policies (Ramakrishna & Figueroa, 2017). Accordingly, organisational security education, training and awareness efforts influence employees' threat and coping appraisals (Posey, Roberts, & Lowry, 2015).

## Employer-Employee Relationship

Employee relations are seen by employers as critical in achieving job performance through a focus on employee involvement, commitment and engagement. The emphasis of employee relations is now focussed on relationship with individual employees (Radhakrishna & Raju, 2015). Organisational commitment is a means by which information security threats become personally relevant to employees (Posey, Roberts, & Lowry, 2015). A previous study revealed that IT employees were treated with only moderate fairness/justice by the organisations, however, their commitment to their organisation was fairly high (Patrick, 2012). It was found that organisational justice significantly influenced organisational commitment of IT employees. The results of this study provided considerable insight into the IT employees' perceptions of fairness could promote commitment (Patrick, 2012). Also, D'Arcy and Greene (2014) examined the influence of security-related and employment relationship factors on employees' security compliance decisions. Data were collected using two online surveys that were administered at separate points in time. The study found that security culture is a driver for employees' security compliance in the workplace and that employee's feeling of job satisfaction influences security compliance intention (D'Arcy & Greene, 2014).

## Background Checks and Monitoring

Background checks of potential employee have become essential task for HR personnel so that the organisation could avoid recruiting the wrong persons (Sarode & Deore, 2017). Hughes, Keller, & Hertz (2010) discussed issues of higher education institutions' policies and procedures with regard to background checks for students, staff, and faculty in light of homeland security concerns. Brody and Cox (2015) emphasized the need for thoroughness and accuracy of background checks and security clearance investigations. Brody (2010) explored the various methods available when conducting a pre-employment screening investigation in attempt to hire honest employees, those less likely to commit fraud against their organisation. Using interviews with experts in the area of background investigation services, the study recommended that organisations should consider performing other screening techniques before hiring an employee. Brody (2010) cautioned that merely relying on the most basic background check may lead to the hiring of the wrong employee, one likely to commit fraud. Besides, employees are increasingly monitored concerning their behaviors and actions. The use of monitoring systems has been advocated for improved performance, increased productivity, and reduced costs (Holt, Lang, & Sutton, 2017). Without effective monitoring disgruntled employees can expose valuable business trade secrets or engage in corporate espionage or sabotage (Ford et al., 2015). They may render the organisation to several risky situations (Rigon et al., 2014).

## Security Responsibility and Accountability

Employees should be accountable to and be responsibility for preventing security breaches. According to Styles and Tryfonas (2009), employees are duty-bound to consider the security of the computing and information resources they interact with. Accountability makes employees answerable for accomplishing a goal or assignment (U.S. Office of Personnel Management, n.d.). It often connotes punishment or negative consequences of punishing employees, creating fear and anxiety in the work environment. But accountability can produce positive and valuable results. When used constructively, it can improve employee performance, enhance participation and involvement, increase feelings of competency, enhance commitment to the work, improve creativity and innovation, and produce higher employee morale and satisfaction with the work (U.S. Office of Personnel Management, n.d.). Accountability should focus not only on punishment but also reward. Parker (2008) remarked that without security rewards and sanctions in all employee job performance appraisals, any attempt to secure information assets in an organisation is purely cosmetics. Thus, those who control security, those who are constrained by it, and those who use and possess the assets must be sufficiently motivated to make it work (Parker, 2008).

In a recent study, Zaman and Saif (2016) found that perceived accountability has a significant positive relationship with job performance. Thomson and van Niekerk (2012) showed how employee apathy towards information security can be addressed through the use of existing theory in social sciences. Based on goal-setting theory, the study suggested that employees' performance of their roles and responsibilities can contribute towards organisational culture of information security (Thomson & van Niekerk, 2012). To understand security behaviour by developing a security behaviour typology based on the concepts of discipline and agility, Harnesk and Lindström (2011) undertook a case study to analyze security behaviors. The study found that security behaviour can be shaped by discipline and agility and that both can exist collectively if organisations consider the constitutional and existential aspects of information security (IS) management. Vance, Lowry, and Eggett (2013) presented a new approach for reducing access policy violations. Drawing from the theory of accountability, the study identified four system mechanisms that heighten an individual's perception of accountability: identifiability, awareness of logging, awareness of audit, and electronic presence (Vance, Lowry, & Eggett, 2013).

## METHODOLOGY

A structured survey questionnaire was used to collect data from IT professionals (Information Security Officers, Chief Information Officers, IT Managers, IT Specialists, other IT staff) in forty three organisations within five main industry sectors (government public service institutions, public utility companies - water, electricity, and telecommunication, financial institutions, educational institutions, healthcare institutions, and others - manufacturing, oil and gas, IT) in Ghana. The human aspects of US-CCU (United States Cyber Consequences Unit) Cyber-security Questionnaire (Bumgarner & Borg, 2007) were adapted. The questionnaire was developed to be used to assess an organisation's personnel security management. The items on the questionnaire were modified to address the context of the study. In general, the awareness of cyber related crimes among employees in Ghanaian organisations is below the minimum cyber security threshold and most businesses and government organisations lagged behind in the implementation of information security measures to mitigate security threats and vulnerabilities (Cybercrime Unit, 2016). Overseas Security Advisory Council (OSAC, 2011) of the U.S. Department of State reported that there are increasing numbers of people who become victims to credit card fraud in Ghana.

Some items on the questionnaire were slightly altered as a result a field test conducted, with comments received from experts (two information security practitioners, two HR practitioners, and one senior academic faculty) to establish the validity of the instrument. The questionnaires were administered to the respondents through post and by email. The first part of the questionnaire was designed to reflect the profile of the respondents. The second part contained questions that reflect the four independent constructs and one dependent target construct. The questionnaire comprised of measurement items relating to information security training (11-items), employee relations (5-items), background checks and monitoring (4-items), accountability (11-items), and information security (9-items). Ratings were done on a Likert scale of 1 (strongly disagree) to 5 (strongly agree). Respondents were asked to rate the extent to which each variable could improve the performance of information security in their organisations. Out of the five hundred questionnaires sent to the respondents, 232 were completed and used in the data analysis. This represents a response rate of 46.4 percent.

Importance-Performance Map Analysis within the context of partial least squares structural equation modeling (PLS SEM) via SmartPLS 3.0 was used to identify the key determinants (factors and indicators) for improving the performance information security. Instrument reliability and validity were tested via Cronbach's alpha and outer loadings. According to Hair et al. (2017), items with outer loading less than zero should be removed from further analysis. Consequently, items whose outer loadings were less than zero were removed from the study (see Table 1). Moreover, the Cronbach's alpha shows the reliability coefficients of the measures: Security Training and Awareness (.778), Employer-Employee Relationship (.849), Background Checks and Monitoring (.811), Responsibility and Accountability (.696), and Information Security (.790) (see Table 1). Apart from Responsibility and Accountability, all the measures were all found to be far above the threshold of 0.7 (or higher) and were considered acceptable according to Nunally's (1978) guidelines.

## DATA ANALYSIS

The data analysis follows the procedure recommended by Ringle and Sarstedt (2016). These are 1) requirements checking, 2) computation of the performance values, 3) computation of the importance values, 4) Importance-Performance Map creation, and 5) ascertaining the factors and indicators on the Importance-Performance Map. These will be done under two sections: a) assessment of the measurement model and b) evaluation of the importance-performance map analysis.

### Assessment of the Measurement Model

When using IPMA, three requirements must be met (Ringle & Sarstedt, 2016). Firstly, the latent variable scores should be re-scaled on a range of 0 and 100, thus requiring that all indicators in the PLS path model should use a metric or quasi-metric scale (Sarstedt & Mooi, 2014). Secondly, all the indicator coding must have the same scale direction. The minimum value of an indicator must represent the worst outcome and the maximum value must represent the best outcome of the indicator (for instance 1 represents strongly disagree and 5 strongly agree). Otherwise, conclusion cannot be drawn that the higher latent variable scores represent better performance. Accordingly, the current study used a metric with 5 likert scale which can be scaled between 0 and 100. Thirdly, regardless of the measurement model being formatively or reflectively, the outer weights estimates must be positive. Negative outer weights might be a result of high indicator collinearity and these indicators should be removed from the analysis (Hair et al., 2017). To meet this requirement, all the items whose outer weights were negative have been removed (see Table 1).

*Table 1. Validity, reliability and descriptive statistics*

| Constructs | Indicators | Outer Weight > 0 | Mean | SD | Cronbach Alpha |
|---|---|---|---|---|---|
| **SECURITY TRAINING AND AWARENESS** | | | | | |
| ST01 | Employees are given periodic training on security policies. | 0.272 | 3.95 | .997 | |
| ST02 | Employees are trained to keep mobile devices secured. | 0.362 | 3.53 | .925 | |
| ST06 | Employees are trained to be suspicious of any software that arrives in the mail, even though it may appear to be packaged and sent by trusted persons or vendors. | 0.290 | 3.25 | .984 | .778 |
| ST10 | Employees have been made aware of the fact that mass produced and mass distributed software could still contain targeted malware. | 0.361 | 3.40 | .954 | |
| **EMPLOYER-EMPLOYEE RELATIONSHIP** | | | | | |
| ER01 | The organisation makes fairness and good faith in the treatment of employees a priority. | 0.732 | 3.87 | .803 | |
| ER02 | The organisation provides adequate mechanisms for employees to express their grievances without penalty and for them to see those grievances being conscientiously addressed. | 0.017 | 3.60 | .755 | |
| ER03 | The organisation handles re-deployment/down-sizing in a manner that minimizes hostile feelings on the part of former employees. | 0.117 | 3.64 | .774 | .849 |
| ER04 | The organisation offers a procedure which allows employees to report attempts by outsiders to extort their organisation in circumventing security. | 0.251 | 3.72 | .718 | |
| ER05 | If an employee is going through a period of great difficulties in his or her personal life, there is a policy for temporarily reducing that employee's responsibilities for critical systems and access to critical systems. | 0.053 | 3.73 | .815 | |
| **BACKGROUND CHECKS AND MONITORING** | | | | | |
| BC02 | If an employee is promoted to a considerably higher level of responsibility and access, a new background check is carried out. | 0.477 | 3..35 | .973 | |
| BC03 | Background screening is carried out for of potential and third parties. | 0.359 | 3.18 | .845 | .811 |
| BC04 | An effort is made to track the current whereabouts of former employees who were deeply acquainted with critical systems and procedures. | 0.333 | 3.25 | 1.045 | |
| **RESPONSIBILITY AND ACCOUNTABILITY** | | | | | |
| SA02 | All employees are required to sign confidentiality and intellectual property agreements. | 0.291 | 3.34 | .862 | |
| SA06 | Information security policies defined the proper use of e-mail, internet access, and instant messaging by employees. | 0.689 | 3.53 | 1.058 | .696 |
| SA11 | Employees are given adequate incentives to report security breaches and bad security practices. | 0.237 | 3.51 | .817 | |
| **INFORMATION SECURITY** | | | | | |
| BEC06 | Information is generally disseminated throughout the organisation on a need-to-know basis. | 0.298 | 3.75 | .692 | |
| BEC07 | Areas of responsibility are distributed among employees in such a way that a single employee cannot carry out a critical operation without the knowledge of other employees. | 0.329 | 3.47 | .768 | .790 |
| BEC08 | The employee's physical and electronic access logs are periodically reviewed to identify access patterns that are not motivated by normal work responsibilities. | 0.301 | 3.73 | .725 | |
| BEC09 | Employees are required to take periodic vacations, so that ongoing activities they might otherwise be able to conceal would be noticed by their temporary replacements. | 0.346 | 3.70 | .808 | |

Furthermore, the blindfolding and bootstrapping techniques were used. The blindfolding procedure was used in assessing the predictive relevance (Stone-Geisser's $Q^2$ value) of the structural model (Geisser, 1974; Stone, 1974). According to Hair et al. (2014), a $Q^2$ value larger than zero for the reflective endogenous latent variable indicates the path model's predictive relevance. Table 2 showed the structural model's predictive relevance. Also, bootstrapping was performed. It is a nonparametric procedure that allows testing the statistical significance of various PLS-SEM results, such as path coefficients, Cronbach's alpha, and $R^2$ values (Hair et al., 2017). The results from bootstrapping with 5,000 samples using the no sign change option and the 95 percent confidence intervals showed that all the path coefficients were statistically significant (Table 3). More specifically, TRAINING, MONITORING, ACCOUNTABILITY, and RELATIONSHIP each has significant and positive effects on INFORMATION SECURITY. Thus, the bootstrapping results demonstrated that all total effects on the target construct, INFORMATION SECURITY, were significant.

As has been observed in Table 1, Table 2, and Table 3, the requirements of the measurement model assessment have been met. The outer weights were above zero. Those items below zero were removed from further analysis. The instrument validity and reliability requirements were fulfilled. The predictive relevance via blindfolding technique was also fulfilled. Through the bootstrapping results, the structural model also showed that all the constructs had significant effect on the target construct. Based on these, the study proceeded to create Importance-Performance Map.

*Table 2. Stone-Geisser's $Q^2$ values*

| Constructs | SSO | SSE | $Q^2$ (=1-SSE/SSO) |
|---|---|---|---|
| ACCOUNTABILITY | 954 | 672.471 | 0.295 |
| INFORMATION SECURITY | 1,272 | 920.981 | 0.276 |
| MONITORING | 954 | 742.136 | 0.222 |
| RELATIONSHIP | 1,590 | 1,352.801 | 0.149 |
| TRAINING | 1,272 | 1,272.000 | - |

## HRM Factors for Improving Information Security Performance

The IPMA technique produced the structural model and Important-Performance Map (Figure 5) to identify the important HRM practices that can improve the performance of organisational information security. Table 4 and Figure 5 show the path coefficients and the performance values of the constructs. Table 5 shows the direct, indirect, and the total effects (the Importance dimension) together with the Performance values (re-scaled between 0 and 100). These values were used to create the graphical representation of the Importance-Performance Map (Figure 6). The Important-Performance Map utilises unstandardized total effects for the importance-dimension (x-axis) and the re-scaled performance values of the latent and manifest variables on the performance dimension (y-axis).

Figure 6 reveals that two direct predecessors of INFORMATION SECURITY, MONITORING and TRAINING, have a particularly high importance but relatively low performance (Quadrant I). Observably, TRAINING construct has considerably higher importance than the MONITORING construct. Managerial actions should therefore prioritize improving the performance of security TRAINING. Moreover, the importance of MONITORING was relatively high but its performance was relatively low. Attention also needs to be paid on improving the performance of MONITORING, which can be achieved by focusing on the predecessor construct of MONITORING, which is TRAINING. On the other side, the result showed that too much attention has been paid to RELATIONSHIP (Quadrant IV). This denoted that RELATIONSHIP constructs was overly emphasized by the organisations. Instead of continuing to focus on RELATIONSHIP, organisations should allocate more resources to increase the performance of TRAINING and MONITORING. Surprisingly, ACCOUNTABILITY fell within Quadrant III, indicating low importance and performance.

*Table 3. Path coefficients and statistical significance*

| Constructs | Sample Mean | Standard Deviation | Path Coefficients | T Statistics | *p*-values |
|---|---|---|---|---|---|
| ACCOUNTABILITY -> INFORMATION SECURITY | 0.180 | 0.077 | 2.333 | 2.333 | 0.020 |
| MONITORING -> ACCOUNTABILITY | 0.334 | 0.059 | 5.713 | 5.713 | 0.000 |
| MONITORING -> INFORMATION SECURITY | 0.242 | 0.064 | 3.804 | 3.804 | 0.000 |
| MONITORING -> RELATIONSHIP | 0.383 | 0.067 | 5.691 | 5.691 | 0.000 |
| RELATIONSHIP -> INFORMATION SECURITY | 0.290 | 0.054 | 5.280 | 5.280 | 0.000 |
| TRAINING -> ACCOUNTABILITY | 0.485 | 0.056 | 8.718 | 8.718 | 0.000 |
| TRAINING -> INFORMATION SECURITY | 0.135 | 0.054 | 2.501 | 2.501 | 0.012 |
| TRAINING -> MONITORING | 0.576 | 0.035 | 16.461 | 16.461 | 0.000 |
| TRAINING -> RELATIONSHIP | 0.247 | 0.062 | 3.856 | 3.856 | 0.000 |

*Table 4. Performance / index values and path coefficients*

| Constructs | LV Index Values | Performances | ACCOUNTABILITY | INFORMATION SECURITY | MONITORING | RELATIONSHIP |
|---|---|---|---|---|---|---|
| ACCOUNTABILITY | 3.477 | 61.933 | | 0.134 | | |
| INFORMATION SECURITY | 3.660 | 66.499 | | | | |
| MONITORING | 3.261 | 56.537 | 0.323 | 0.178 | | 0.313 |
| RELATIONSHIP | 3.801 | 70.015 | | 0.252 | | |
| TRAINING | 3.516 | 62.904 | 0.507 | 0.106 | 0.616 | 0.214 |

LV – Latent Variable

*Figure 5. Structural model of importance-performance analysis*

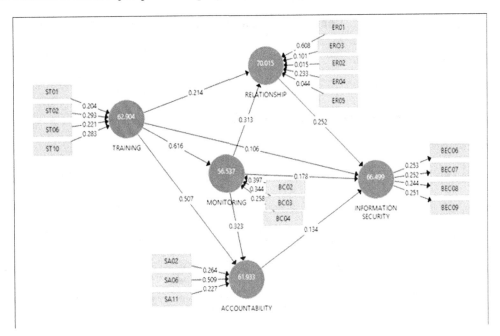

## Key Indicators for Improving Information Security Performance

In the previous section, TRAINING and MONITORING were identified as very important for improving information security performance. However, to gain more specific information as to which key training and monitoring indicators will increase the performance of organisational information security, the indicator level Importance-Performance Map Analysis was performed. Table 6 shows the total effects (Importance dimension) and the information security (performance dimension) values at the indicator level. These values were used to create the indicator level Importance-Performance Map, as shown in Figure 7. The four quadrants on the IPM is made possible using the mean level of importance of 0.073 and the mean level of performance of 63.051, indicated by the vertical and the horizontal lines on the map.

*Table 5. Direct, indirect, and total effects of importance-performance construct values*

| Predecessor Construct | Direct Effect on Security | Indirect Effect on Security | Total effect on Security/ Importance | Performance |
|---|---|---|---|---|
| ACCOUNTABILITY | 0.134 | - | 0.134 | 61.933 |
| MONITORING | 0.131 | 0.169 | 0.300 | 56.537 |
| RELATIONSHIP | 0.252 | - | 0.252 | 70.015 |
| TRAINING | 0.023 | 0.390 | 0.413 | 62.904 |
| Average | | | 0.275 | 62.847 |

Notes: All effects denote unstandardized effects.

*Figure 6. IPM Constructs on Information Security*

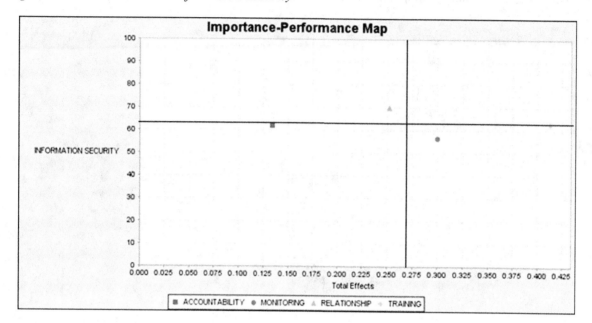

In Quadrant I, *Concentrate Here*, the respondents perceived the attributes within this region as highly important, but their performance was very low. From the map (Figure 7), six key indicators/attributes were found that could improve information security performance. These are classified under the two constructs:

## Security Training

- ST02: Employees are trained to keep mobile devices secured.
- ST06: Employees are trained to be suspicious of any software that arrives in the mail, even though it may appear to be packaged and sent by trusted persons or vendors.
- ST10: Employees have been made aware that mass distributed software could contain targeted malware.

## Monitoring

- BC02: If an employee is promoted to a considerably higher level of responsibility and access, a new background check is carried out.
- BC03: Background screening is carried out for potential and third parties (suppliers, contractors, building maintenance personnel).
- BC04: An effort is made to track the current whereabouts of former employees who were deeply acquainted with critical systems and procedures.

Moreover, the following two indicators fell within Quadrant II (High Importance/High Performance). These indicators are the strength of the organisations. The indicated that the organisation must "keep up good works" in these areas to maintain security performance.

- ST01: Employees are given periodic training on security policies.
- ER01: The organisation makes fairness and good faith in the treatment of employees a priority.

Conversely, seven indicators of EMPLOYEE RELATIONS and EMPLOYEE ACCOUNTABILITY constructs were categorised as low importance but high performance, as they fell within Quadrant III and Quadrant IV respectively. The indicators are listed below.

## Employee Relations

- ER02: The organisation provides adequate mechanisms for employees to express their grievances without penalty and for them to see those grievances being conscientiously addressed.
- ER05: If an employee is going through a period of great difficulties in his or her personal life, there is a policy for temporarily reducing that employee's responsibilities for critical systems and access to critical systems.
- ER03: The organisation handles re-deployment and down-sizing in a manner that minimizes hostile feelings on the part of former employees.
- ER04: The organisation offers a procedure which would allow employees to report attempts by outsiders to extort their organisation in circumventing security.

*Table 6. Importance-performance indicator values*

| Indicators | Total Effect (Importance) | Information Security (Performance) |
|---|---|---|
| BC02 | 0.119 | 58.648 |
| BC03 | 0.103 | 54.403 |
| BC04 | 0.077 | 56.132 |
| ER01 | 0.153 | 71.698 |
| ER02 | 0.004 | 64.937 |
| ER03 | 0.025 | 65.881 |
| ER04 | 0.059 | 68.082 |
| ER05 | 0.011 | 68.239 |
| SA02 | 0.035 | 58.491 |
| SA06 | 0.068 | 63.365 |
| SA11 | 0.030 | 62.736 |
| ST01 | 0.084 | 73.742 |
| ST02 | 0.121 | 63.208 |
| ST06 | 0.091 | 56.132 |
| ST10 | 0.117 | 60.063 |
| Average | 0.073 | 63.051 |

## Accountability

- SA02: All employees are required to sign confidentiality and intellectual property agreements.
- SA06: Information security policies defined the proper use of e-mail, internet access, and instant messaging by employees.
- SA11: Employees are given adequate incentives to report security breaches and bad security practices.

*Figure 7. IPM indicators on information security*

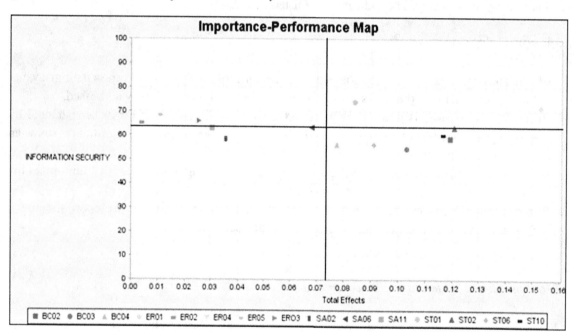

## DISCUSSION

The study identified security training, background checks and monitoring as the major HRM practices that can improve the performance of information security in organisations. Managerial actions should therefore prioritize improving training, background checks and monitoring. While lack of security training often lie behind many contemporary breaches (Lacey, 2010), investing in training and development can motivate staff and support the growth of the organisation (Leidner & Smith, 2013). HRM practices on security policy compliance found training for career development as positively associated with employees' behavioral intent to comply with security policy (Youngkeun Choi, 2017). Hence, information security training effectively reduces employees' non-compliance (Hwang et al., 2017). Security training, at the indicator level, ST02 ("Employees are trained to keep mobile devices secured") has a relatively high importance when focusing on information security but required some room for performance improvement. Hence, performance improvements can focus on offering high-quality security trainings to provide users with the skills and knowledge they need to protect the mobile devices (Yaokumah, 2016).

Similarly, other indicators, ST06 and ST10, focused on employee training on malware. This should be given particular attention regarding improving the information security performance.

Moreover, the background checks and monitoring of the current employees, third parties, and former employees were found as important HRM practices that can improve the performance of organisational information security. A thorough and accurate background checks and security clearance investigations (Brody & Cox, 2015) can help an organisation to hire honest employees, those less likely to commit fraud against the organisation (Brody, 2010). Likewise, employee monitoring systems can improve performance, increase productivity, and reduce costs (Holt, Lang, & Sutton, 2017). In particular, at the indicator level, BC02 ("If an employee is promoted to a considerably higher level of responsibility and access, a new background check is carried out") has a relatively high importance but required performance improvement. Similarly, the BC03 ("Background screening is carried out for potential employees and third parties - suppliers, contractors, building maintenance personnel") and BC04 ("An effort is made to track the current whereabouts of former employees who were deeply acquainted with critical systems and procedures") required performance improvement. Thus, further improvement efforts should be concentrated on mobile devices security, malware, monitoring and background screening of current and former employees, including third party contractors.

Two indicators were found to be the strength of the organisations as they have attained the highest importance and performance levels in the organisations. These are ST01 ("Employees are given periodic training on security policies") and ER01 ("The organisation makes fairness and good faith in the treatment of employees a priority"). Accordingly, the organisations should continue to provide regular security training on security policies to the employees. Employees' information security training enhances adherence to security policies (Ramakrishna & Figueroa, 2017) and influences employees' threat and coping appraisals (Posey, Roberts, & Lowry, 2015). Besides, fairness in treating employees positively influences information security behaviour. Employees' perceptions of fairness promote commitment (Patrick, 2012).

On the contrary, two HRM practices, Employee Relations and Accountability were found to be of low importance but with high performance. This signified that these two constructs were overly emphasized by the organisations. Thus, accountability might not have remarkable impact on employees' security compliance behavior (Abed & Roland, 2016). Rather, instead of continuing to focus in employee relations and accountability, organisations should allocate more resources for security training programs, background checks and employee monitoring.

## CONCLUSION

In this study, the IPMA technique was discussed and applied to measure HRM practices from the perspective of IT professionals to identify priority areas for the allocation of resources to improve the performance of organisational information security. A survey was conducted on the IT professionals' perceptions to identify areas of importance and performance of HRM practices. Using IPMA technique, the study identified security training, background checks and monitoring as highly important that needed to be improved in order to enhance organisational information security performance. Two indicators (periodic training in adherence to security policy and fairness in treating employees) were found to have attained the highest importance and performance levels in the organisations. In terms of key indicators for specific management actions, attention needed to be paid to: (a) training to keep mobile devices secured, b) training on malware, (c) tracking of the whereabouts of former employees who were deeply acquainted with critical systems and procedures, and d) background checks on employee promoted to a considerably higher level of responsibility and system access. Organisations need to consider allocating resources to training, background check and monitoring.

Practically, the significance importance of security training, background checks and monitoring on improving information security offer an important opportunity for information security management practices. Organisations can improve information security by channelling resources from less important activities and invest them in security training, background checks and monitoring. Besides, before applying IPMA, this study demonstrated the concept and the use of importance-performance map analysis. By combining the analysis of the importance and performance dimensions of the IPMA, the study allowed the IT and HR leaders to identify and prioritize HRM practices and indicators that were most important for improving the performance of the organisations' information security. The study also provided guidance for the formulation of information security strategy that could accurately allocate resources to maximise a high return on security investment.

Theoretically, the findings extended information security research literature by showing how HRM practices (training, background checks and monitoring) can play a major role in improving information security. Our results provided one of the few empirical validations of information security to be recognized as a multi-disciplinary issue as conceptualized through HRM practices. In addition, the study extended information security research by considering the role of employee relations and accountability from the HRM literature. However, some HRM practices were not included in the current study. For example, including remuneration and rewards might further enhance information security literature. Moreover, because HRM practices may differ among the organisations, future research using a multi-group analysis that allows for contrasting group results might produce an insightful finding.

## REFERENCES

Abawajy, J. (2014). User preference of cyber security awareness delivery methods. *Behaviour & Information Technology*, *33*(3), 237–248. doi:10.1080/0144929X.2012.708787

Abed, J., & Roland, W. H. (2016). Understanding deterrence theory in security compliance behavior: A quantitative meta-analysis approach. In *SAIS 2016 Proceedings*. Retrieved from http://aisel.aisnet.org/sais2016/28

Angst, C. M., Block, E. S., D'Arcy, J., & Kelley, K. (2017). When do IT security investments matter? Accounting for the influence of institutional factors in the context of healthcare data breaches. *Management Information Systems Quarterly*, *41*(3), 893–916. doi:10.25300/MISQ/2017/41.3.10

Baxter, R. J., Holderness, D. K. Jr, & Wood, D. A. (2016). Applying basic gamification techniques to it compliance training: Evidence from the lab and field. *Journal of Information Systems*, *30*(3), 119–133. doi:10.2308/isys-51341

Bernik, I., & Prislan, K. (2016). Measuring Information Security Performance with 10 by 10 model for holistic state evaluation. *PLoS One*, *11*(9), 1–33. doi:10.1371/journal.pone.0163050 PMID:27655001

Boss, S. R., Galletta, D. F., Lowry, P. B., Moody, G. D., & Polak, P. (2015). What do systems users have to fear? Using fear appeals to engender threats and fear that motivate protective security behaviors. *Management Information Systems Quarterly, 39*(4), 837–864. doi:10.25300/MISQ/2015/39.4.5

Brody, R. G. (2010). Beyond the basic background check: Hiring the "right" employees. *Management Research Review, 33*(3), 210–223. doi:10.1108/01409171011030372

Brody, R. G., & Cox, V. L. (2015). Background investigations a comparative analysis of background checks and federal security clearance investigations. *Business Studies Journal, 7*(1), 84–94.

Bumgarner, J., & Borg, S. (2007). US-CCU Cyber-Security Questionnaire. US-CCU (Cyber Consequences Unit) Cyber-Security Check. Retrieved from www.usccu.us

Burns, A. J., Posey, C., Roberts, T. L., & Lowry, P. B. (2017). Examining the relationship of organisational insiders' psychological capital with information security threat and coping appraisals. *Computers in Human Behavior, 68*, 190–209. doi:10.1016/j.chb.2016.11.018

Cherdantseva, Y., & Hilton, J. (2013). Information security and information assurance. The discussion about the meaning, scope and goals. In F. Almeida & I. Portela (Eds.), *Organisational, Legal, and Technological Dimensions of Information System Administrator*. IGI Global.

Choi, Y. (2017). Human resource management and security policy compliance. *International Journal of Human Capital and Information Technology Professionals, 8*(3), 14. doi:10.4018/IJHCITP.2017070105

Cybercrime Unit. (2016). Government will fight Cyber Crime. Retrieved from http://cybercrime.gov.gh/?p=313

D'Arcy, J., & Greene, G. (2014). Security culture and the employment relationship as drivers of employees' security compliance. *Information Management & Computer Security, 22*(5), 474–489. doi:10.1108/IMCS-08-2013-0057

Da Veiga, A. (2016). Comparing the information security culture of employees who had read the information security policy and those who had not: Illustrated through an empirical study. *Information & Computer Security, 24*(2), 139–151. doi:10.1108/ICS-12-2015-0048

Driscoll, C., & McKee, M. (2007). Restorying a culture of ethical and spiritual values: A role for leader storytelling. *Journal of Business Ethics, 73*(2), 205–217. doi:10.100710551-006-9191-5

Ford, J., Willey, L., White, B. J., & Domagalski, T. (2015). New concerns in electronic employee monitoring: Have you checked your policies lately? *Journal of Legal. Ethical & Regulatory Issues, 18*(1), 51–70.

Furnell, S., & Thomson, K. L. (2009). From culture to disobedience: Recognizing the varying user acceptance of IT security. *Computer Fraud & Security, 2*(2), 5–10. doi:10.1016/S1361-3723(09)70019-3

Geisser, S. (1974). A Predictive Approach to the Random Effects Model. *Biometrika, 61*(1), 101–107. doi:10.1093/biomet/61.1.101

Hair, J. F., Hult, G. T. M., Ringle, C. M., & Sarstedt, M. (2014). *A primer on partial least squares structural equation modeling (PLS-SEM)*. Thousand Oaks, CA: Sage.

Hair, J. F., Hult, G. T. M., Ringle, C. M., & Sarstedt, M. (2017). *A primer on partial least squares structural equation modeling (PLS-SEM)*. Thousand Oaks, CA: Sage.

Hair, J. F., Sarstedt, M., Ringle, C., & Mena, J. A. (2012). An assessment of the use of partial least squares structural equation modeling in marketing research. *Journal of the Academy of Marketing Science*, *40*(3), 414–433. doi:10.100711747-011-0261-6

Herath, T., & Rao, H. R. (2009). Protection motivation and deterrence: A framework for security policy compliance in organisations. *European Journal of Information Systems*, *18*(2), 106–125. doi:10.1057/ejis.2009.6

Holt, M., Lang, B., & Sutton, S. G. (2017). Potential employees' ethical perceptions of active monitoring: The dark side of data analytics. *Journal of Information Systems*, *31*(2), 107–124. doi:10.2308/isys-51580

Hu, Q., Dinev, T., Hart, P., & Cooke, D. (2012). Managing employee compliance with information security policies: The critical role of top management and organisational culture. *Decision Sciences Journal*, *43*(4), 615–659. doi:10.1111/j.1540-5915.2012.00361.x

Hu, Q., West, R., & Smarandescu, L. (2015). The Role of Self-Control in Information Security Violations: Insights from a Cognitive Neuroscience Perspective. *Journal of Management Information Systems*, *31*(4), 6–48. doi:10.1080/07421222.2014.1001255

Hughes, S., Keller, E. W., & Hertz, G. T. (2010). Homeland security initiatives and background checks in higher education. *New Directions for Institutional Research*, *2010*(146), 51–62. doi:10.1002/ir.342

Hwang, I., Kim, D., Kim, T., & Kim, S. (2017). Why not comply with information security? An empirical approach for the causes of non-compliance. *Online Information Review*, *41*(1), 2–18. doi:10.1108/OIR-11-2015-0358

Ikenwe, I. J., Igbinovia, O. M., & Elogie, A. A. (2016). Information Security in the Digital Age: The Case of Developing Countries. *Chinese Librarianship*, *42*, 16–24.

Javad, A., & Weistroffer, H. R. (2016). Understanding Deterrence Theory in Security Compliance Behavior: A Quantitative Meta-Analysis Approach. In *SAIS 2016 Proceedings*. Retrieved from http://aisel.aisnet.org/sais2016/28

Karlsson, F., Åström, J., & Karlsson, M. (2015). Information security culture – state-of-the-art review between 2000 and 2013. *Information & Computer Security*, *23*(3), 246–285. doi:10.1108/ICS-05-2014-0033

Kaspersky, E., & Furnell, S. (2014). A security education Q&A. *Information Management & Computer Security*, *22*(2), 130–133. doi:10.1108/IMCS-01-2014-0006

Khao, B., Harris, P., & Hartman, S. (2010). Information security governance of enterprise information systems: An approach to legislative compliant. *International Journal of Management and Information Systems*, *14*(3), 49–55.

Kim, E. B. (2014). Recommendations for information security awareness training for college students. *Information Management & Computer Security*, *22*(1), 115–126. doi:10.1108/IMCS-01-2013-0005

Komatsu, A., Takagi, D., & Takemura, T. (2013). Human aspects of information security: An empirical study of intentional versus actual behavior. *Information Management & Computer Security, 21*(1), 5–15. doi:10.1108/09685221311314383

Lacey, D. (2010). Understanding and transforming organisational security culture. *Information Management & Computer Security, 18*(1), 4–13. doi:10.1108/09685221011035223

Leidner, S., & Smith, S. M. (2013). Keeping potential job-hoppers' feet on the ground. *Human Resource Management International Digest, 21*(1), 31–33. doi:10.1108/09670731311296492

McCrohan, K. F., Engel, K., & Harvey, J. W. (2010). Influence of awareness and training on cyber security. *Journal of Internet Commerce, 9*(1), 23–41. doi:10.1080/15332861.2010.487415

Naz, F., Aftab, J., & Awais, M. (2016). Impact of Human Resource Management Practices (HRM) on Performance of SMEs in Multan, Pakistan. *International Journal of Management. Accounting & Economics, 3*(11), 699–708.

Nunnally, J. C. (1978). *Psychometric theory* (2nd ed.). New York, NY: McGraw-Hill.

Ossege, C. (2012). Accountability – are we better off without it? *Public Management Review, 14*(5), 585–607. doi:10.1080/14719037.2011.642567

Overseas Security Advisory Council (OSAC). (2012). Ghana 2012 OSAC crime and safety report. Retrieve from https://www.osac.gov

Parker, D. B. (2008). Security accountability in job performance. *Information Systems Security, 3*(4), 16–20. doi:10.1080/10658989509342474

Patrick, H. A. (2012). Commitment of information technology employees in relation to perceived organisational justice. *IUP Journal of Organisational Behavior, 11*(3), 23–40.

Posey, C., Roberts, T. L., & Lowry, P. B. (2015). The impact of organisational commitment on insiders' motivation to protect organisational information assets. *Journal of Management Information Systems, 32*(4), 179–214. doi:10.1080/07421222.2015.1138374

Radhakrishna, A., & Raju, S. R. (2015). A study on the effect of human resource development on employment relations. *IUP Journal of Management Research, 14*(3), 28–42.

Ramakrishna, A., & Figueroa, N. (2017). Is seeing believing? Training users on information security: Evidence from Java Applets. *Journal of Information Systems Education, 28*(2), 115–122.

Rantos, K., Fysarakis, K., & Manifavas, C.(2012). How effective is your security awareness program? An evaluation methodology. *Information Security Journal: A Global Perspective, 21*(6), 328-345.

Rigon, E. A., Westphall, C. M., dos Santos, D. R., & Westphall, C. B. (2014). A cyclical evaluation model of information security maturity. *Information Management & Computer Security, 22*(3), 265–278. doi:10.1108/IMCS-04-2013-0025

Ringle, C. M., & Sarstedt, M. (2016). Gain more insight from your PLS-SEM results: The importance-performance map analysis. *Industrial Management & Data Systems, 116*(9), 1865–1886. doi:10.1108/IMDS-10-2015-0449

Sarode, A. P., & Deore, S. S. (2017). Role of third party employee verification and background checks in HR management: An overview. *Journal of Commerce & Management Thought, 8*(1), 86–96. doi:10.5958/0976-478X.2017.00005.2

Stewart, J. M., Tittel, E., & Chapple, M. (2005). *Certified Information Systems Security Professional (Study Guide)* (3rd ed.). San Francisco: Sybex.

Stone, M. (1974). Cross-Validatory Choice and Assessment of Statistical Predictions. *Journal of the Royal Statistical Society. Series A (General), 36*(2), 111–147.

Styles, M., & Tryfonas, T. (2009). Using penetration testing feedback to cultivate proactive security amongst end-users. *Information Management & Computer Security, 17*(1), 44–52. doi:10.1108/09685220910944759

Tassabehji, R. (2005). Information security threats: From evolution to prominence. In *Encyclopedia of Multimedia Technology and Networking*. Hershey, PA: IGI Global. Retrieved from http://encyclopedia.jrank.org doi:10.4018/978-1-59140-561-0.ch058

Thomson, K., & van Niekerk, J. (2012). Combating information security apathy by encouraging prosocial organisational behaviour. *Information Management & Computer Security, 20*(1), 39–46. doi:10.1108/09685221211219191

U.S. Office of Personnel Management. (n.d.). Retrieved from https://www.opm.gov

Vance, A., Lowry, P. B., & Eggett, D. (2013). Using accountability to reduce access policy violations in information systems. *Journal of Management Information Systems, 29*(4), 263–290. doi:10.2753/MIS0742-1222290410

White, G. L., Hewitt, B., & Kruck, S. E. (2013). Incorporating global information security and assurance in I.S. education. *Journal of Information Systems Education, 24*(1), 11–16.

Yalman, Y., & Yesilyurt, M. (2013). Information Security Threats and Information Assurance. *TEM Journal, 2*(3), 247–252.

Yaokumah, W. (2016). The influence of students' characteristics on mobile device security measures. *International Journal of Information Systems and Social Change, 7*(3), 44–66. doi:10.4018/IJISSC.2016070104

Zaman, U., & Saif, M. I. (2016). Perceived accountability and conflict management styles as predictors of job performance of public officials in Pakistan. *Gomal University Journal of Research, 32*(2), 24–35.

Zhang, L., & McDowell, W. C. (2009). Am I really at risk? Determinants of online users' intentions to use strong passwords. *Journal of Internet Commerce, 8*(3–4), 180–197. doi:10.1080/15332860903467508

Zhao, X., Xue, L., & Whinston, A. B. (2013). Managing interdependent information security risks: Cyberinsurance, managed security services, and risk pooling arrangements. *Journal of Management Information Systems, 30*(1), 123–152. doi:10.2753/MIS0742-1222300104

*Previously published in the International Journal of Human Capital and Information Technology Professionals (IJHCITP), 9(4); pages 23-43, copyright year 2018 by IGI Publishing (an imprint of IGI Global).*

# Chapter 16
# Assessing the Value of Executive Leadership Coaches for Cybersecurity Project Managers

**Darrell Norman Burrell**
https://orcid.org/0000-0002-4675-9544
*Florida Institute of Technology, USA*

## ABSTRACT

*With the complex nature of impacts of cybersecurity breaches, it is critical that organizational have cybersecurity project managers that can make sound managerial and leadership decisions. Often cybersecurity project managers act quickly with managerial decisions at work. When time is of the essence, strategic thinking, strategic communication, and strategic decision making are critical to organizational effectiveness and productivity. Decision making and strategic communications are just a few skills that executive leadership coaches can teach. This article explores the values and potential benefits of executive coaching as a leadership development tool for information technology and cybersecurity project managers.*

## INTRODUCTION

Currently, career development, primarily professional and leadership development remains a low priority for cybersecurity and information technology professionals (Oltsik, 2017). According to (Oltsik, 2017), another disquieting data point is that cybersecurity and information technology professionals need more business training to enhance the technicians' career and business development. Lester and Parnell (2006) outline that many organizations promote technical personnel into management positions believing that technical expertise transfers directly into leadership competencies. However, the professional capacities required of high performing technical experts might not be the same skills required in leadership roles

DOI: 10.4018/978-1-6684-3698-1.ch016

(Lester and Parnell, 2006). Technical competence does not transfer into managerial competence as technical skills involve analytical and design whereas the managerial role requires people skills, decision-making, and team building competencies (Goldberg, 2006; Rothenberger, 2016; Dzameshie, 2012). As an information technology executive with firsthand experience of transitioning from a technical role to a leadership position, the learning curve is steep and extremely challenging. In fact, this practice is customary due to the lack of leadership development programs (Burrell, Nobles, & Aridi, 2018). The adage of leadership is leadership is not a one fits all, especially in cybersecurity (Burrell, Nobles, & Aridi, 2018). There needs to be considerable thought and methodical decision-making in designing leadership development programs for those leaders working in cybersecurity because of the interdisciplinary vastness of the field accompanied by mandating requirements for Board of Directors and corporate officers (Burrell, Nobles, & Aridi, 2018). These obligatory provisions are enforced to safeguard critical information, systems and networks, and customers' financial and informational properties—yet, leadership development remains an afterthought (Burrell, Nobles, & Aridi, 2018).

According to Boyd (2018) being successful as a cybersecurity manager requires more than just understanding technology. Effective leadership in cybersecurity requires managers at all level to develop some soft skills related to communication, strategic decision making, and employee management (Boyd, 2018). Cybersecurity project managers need the communication, writing, and strategic thinking skills more than ever because they are often required to justify equipment and software purchases that can run from hundreds of thousands to millions of dollars (Boyd, 2018). This requires an ability to understand and communicate strategically so that senior leaders in their language (Boyd, 2018). This communications with leaders outside of the cyber realm requires the ability to understand the value and gracefully articulate organizational importance of needed resources (Boyd, 2018). Most technical degree programs or certifications do not teach these skills to cybersecurity leaders, hence induction and growth of executive coaching as a leadership development tool.

The popularity of coaching as a practice to attain projects' success is increasing worldwide (Lebian, 2011, McCarhty, 2011). Researches conforming effective interrelation between coaching and successful project management (McCarthy, 2011). Organizations spend a year 2 billion dollars, globally, in procurement of coaching services (Walker-Fraser, 2011).

The purpose of this paper is to explore coaching as a developmental practice to investigate the effectiveness of executive coaching as an integrated intervention that enhances leadership competencies and project management success through the lens of growing volume of literature on the value and benefits of executive coaching through exploration of the following questions:

- How effective is executive coaching to achieve project management success?
- How effective is coaching on organizational productivity?
- What is the role of executive coaching practice on building business-oriented skills and competencies?
- Can any business implement the coaching to serve productivity and effectiveness, or implementing coaching requires special characteristics?

## EXECUTIVE COACHING HISTORY AND DEFINITION

Recently, the executive coaching developed to become the trendiest practice to construct the organizational effectiveness and efficiency (Newsome & Dent, 2011). Further, coaching emerged to become the most reputable business methods to construct leadership development and business sustainability (Kampa- Kokesh & Anderson, 2005; Newsome & Dente, 2011).

According to Kampa- Kokesh and Anderson (2005), the executive coaching practice appeared in the late 1940s. The practice started to operate as an affiliation of the consulting profession and psychologist's science. Thus, researching the literature to explore the history of the coaching intervention leads to discover six important topics including: a) definitions and interpretations; (b), objectives and goals; (c) methodologies; (d) relevance to psychology; (e) therapy and coaching skills; (f) recipients and advantages of users (Kampa- Kokesh & Anderson, 2005).

## DEFINITION AND CONCEPTUAL UNDERSTANDING

As its broadest status, coaching is primarily defined as "process of equipping people with tools, knowledge, and opportunities they need to develop them and become more effective" (Peterson & Hicks, 1995, p: 41). The coaching was technically was classified as a technique or a tool that management can utilize to increase performance as factor to achieve projects' success and business sustainability. Further, in the 1990 executive coaching emerged urgently in the business industry as an intervention to change the management conduct of managers, project managers and leaders in the middle and senior-level to improve the technical perception of project selection and quality management (Peterson & Hicks, 1995).

In the leadership literature, (Feldman, 2001) specified the three major basis factors of executive coaching profession including: (a) one-on-one training and mentoring; (b) it requires the implementation of 360- feedback on managers; (c) coaching target to enhance executives, leaders, and project managers competencies and effectiveness. Similarly, the consulting psychology literature referred to the same factors as Feldman identification to construct the definition and understanding of executive coaching (2001). Furthermore, Definitions and understanding of executive coaching vary in accordance with perspectives, philosophy, approach, and professional and contextual objective and reason for coaching (Newsome and Dent, 2011).

In this section, the literature pertaining coaching imposes the necessity to provide a theoretical insight and explanation about leadership and collateral theories in order to present an academic and empirical vision about coaching practice. Nevertheless, leadership has attracted the interest and curiosity of academic researchers and scholars worldwide. Further, a wide academic literature and research with different theoretical methods implemented to analyze and explain the arduousness complexity of leadership practice (Northouse, 2013). Literature review and books implemented many definitions and interpretations about leadership.

Vugat, Hogan, and Kaiser discussed the abroad and different approaches that researchers utilized to define leadership. Researchers expressed continuously that leadership has a long developing history. Vugat et.al argued that leadership may emerge as a therapy and solution to group and people and communication and collaboration challenges and difficulties (2008).

Senge in his book The Fifth Discipline: The Art of & Practice of Learning Organization quoted a statement for Confucius that had said more than twenty-five years ago, "To become a leader, you must first become a human being", Confucius created a developmental theory dealing with the seven "meditative spaces" (2006). Senge (2006) delivered and explained Confucius's vision of the collateral connection between leadership and wisdom, and assuring that wisdom is one of the oldest competencies of leadership. Unfortunately, the leadership perspective has almost lost the compass of the art of leading in today's business industry. The concept and logic about leadership have lost and suffered technical and contextual confusion under the harsh parturition of innovation and technology (Senge, 2006).

Vugat, Hogan, and Kaiser (2008) discuss the misconception of the leadership phenomenon in today's perception of leading people. Further, Vugat, Hogan, and Kaiser (2008) argued that the misunderstanding based on the tendency to perceive leadership from the authority and power point of view. The Vugat, Hogan, and Kaiser (2008) study analyzed Leadership from three different perceptions of the conventional wisdom. First, leadership must be assessed in an equation that composed of leadership and followership (Vugat, Hogan, & Kaiser, 2008). Seconds, leadership must be studied from a psychological basis of both leaders and followers who might not always converge (Vugat, Hogan, & Kaiser, 2008). Third, the modern leadership evaluation must take into consideration the recent technological and international factors and changes that played a role to evolve the perception of leadership (Vugat, Hogan, & Kaiser, 2008).

However, evaluation of leadership coaching is significantly different from other approaches to leadership development. Leadership coaching is widely defined in the perception of the developmental relationship between a coach and a client which required enhancing the client's leadership competencies to be an effective manger (Ely, Boyce, Nelson, Zaccaro, Broome, and Whyman, 2010).

## THE INTERRELATION BETWEEN COACHING AND PERFORMANCE AND PROJECT MANAGEMENT

In the literature investigating the interrelation between coaching and the success of project management and increasing business performance, the coaching illustrated as a tool that serves strategically the interest of project managers to achieve projects success and increase the employees' performance (Walker-Fraser, 2011). However, despite the popularity of coaching as an intervention to increase the business productivity, yet, the empirical studied concerning the validity of coaching as a practice is scarce (CIPD, 2010). The Chartered Institute of Personnel and Development (CIPD) investigated the dimensions of coaching as a learning to develop the performance that leads to a major factor of the success of project management success (CIPD, 2010). Moreover, CIPD established an investigation to verify the impact of coaching a developmental tool for leadership and project management. The survey implemented an investigation of 729 HR managers and representatives that reported the positive impact of coaching a developmental technique to achieve project management success (CIPD, 2010; Saowalux, & Peng (2007).

In the literature involving the examination of coaching as an emerging intervention to accomplish project management success, many researchers tried to verify the aspects of coaching as a leadership integrated development phenomenon. Therefore, the aspects that is presented in the literature to study coaching as a project management practice including: (a) credentials or skills for choosing a coach; (b) personal and professional attributes for effective executive coach; (d), pros and cons for internal and external executive coach; (e), the perception of the engagement of executive coaching; (f), specifications of coaching techniques and tools; (f) signs of executive coaching success; (g), learning, conduct, and culture change resulted from executive coaching (Kampa- Kokesh & Anderson, 2005; Newsome & Dente, 2011).

## METHODOLOGIES TO THE COACHING PROCESS IN PROJECT MANAGEMENT

Despite the fact that the standards of the coaching process are fairly the same among all, however, the approaches implemented by coaches to implement changes through executives, project managers and organizational leadership culture mainly depend on the professional and technical background of coaches and their intellectual and academic philosophes. Hence, there are five main approaches for executive coaching that were presented by Pltier (2001) which was updated by Newsome and Dente (2011), the five approaches are: psychodynamic, behaviorist, person-centered, cognitive therapeutic, and system-oriented (Newsome and Dente, 2011).

### Psychodynamic Approach

In this approach, psychologists are utilized to help executives obtain a psychological scientific background and competencies to increase their ability to understand the way their people think, feel, and react in the workplace (Pltier, 2001; Lebian, 2011). Additionally, with this approach, psychologists help executives and leaders to improve their vision of themselves and other and how to manage their employees effectively in accordance with this vision (Labian, 2011). Gary et.al presented an argument in his research claimed that psychologists are the most qualified to be coaches (2011).

However, the qualifications of the coaching profession as a developmental tool are not regulated with a disciplinary competency frame (Vugat, Hogan, Kaiser, 2008) Therefore, some researchers stated that psychologists are the most qualified for the coaching practice. Thus, the characteristics and skills of the psychologists are the qualifications required to the executive coaching role, such as, professionalism, communication and listening skills, understanding the psychology of human-inner are the characteristics that a coach should attain. Feldman & Lankau achieved a study that tested 87 executive coaching participants and presented their findings of the necessary qualifications of executive coaching are identical to the psychologists' attributes and expertise in order to create the reorganizational development and change towards success and sustainability (Feldman & Lankau, 2010, Journal of Management, 2005).

### Behaviorist Approach

In this approach, the focus on changing the behavior through observation rather than through inner-status of the coach (Macarthey, Milner, 2011). The practitioners suggested two leadership approaches to represent the behavioral approach including transformational and transactional (Khan et.al, 2012). According to Khan et.al (2012), the transformational and the transactional are the best leadership style that executive coaches must implement to achieve the behavioral coaching approach. A survey was implemented by Khan Et.al to prove this vision; a number of 280 questionnaires were established to confirm this hypothesis.

### Cognitive Therapy Approach

This approach based on the theory of the cognitive psychology that executive coaches must learn to their own thoughts and visions to be able to change their employees (Pettier, 201; Strange, 2011). Strange confirmed that the cognitive psychology approach is an effective managerial development technique to achieve project management success. However, the validity of this approach requires executing a supportive mentoring strategy and a special organizational culture (2011).

## System-Oriented Approach

In this approach, the coach required to understand the work atmosphere and the factors that might affect the executives and employees behavior (Peltier, 2001; Strange, 2011). In this approach, the coach needs to know the whole organizational system with its complexities, challenges, stakeholders, culture, and market requirements in order to be able to create effective mentoring strategies that are system-oriented (Peltier 2001; Strange, 2011).

## EXECUTIVE COACHING COMPETENCIES IMPACT ON STRATEGIC PROJECT MANAGEMENT EFFECTIVENESS

The popularity of coaching is emerging worldwide in business and academia (Lebian, 2011). The Chartered Institute of Personnel and Development (CIPD) (2011) survey regarding the prevalence of coaching as a practice to increase organizational effective reflected that % 90 of participants claimed that coaching is a recommended tool for individual and organizational development (Candis & Magnolia, 2010). Researchers and scholars are in constant debate about the strategic credentials and attributes that coaching must possess to help achieve project management effectiveness and organizational sustainability. Therefore, the International Federation raised a deep concern regarding the unregulated system of competencies and skills for the executive coaching profession (McCarthy &Miller, 2011). Nevertheless, in the strategic project management, Laufer (2012) established nine managerial practices to support the guidance of the operational and strategic organizational development and to help systemize the executive coaching professional basis. The Laufer's nine leadership practices are embraced by executive coaches in the strategic coaching process to improve the organizational effectiveness and performance (Hannafy & Vitulano, 2013). The nine Laufer (2012) leadership practices that are considered by researchers as key strategic practices for executive coaching process (Hannafy & Vitulano, 2013). The nine leadership practices are: 1) Embrace the living order; 2) challenge the status quo; 3) Fit the project activities to the proper context; 4) Recruiting the right people is a priority; Create the productive culture; 5) Concentrate on effective communication skills, 6) Planning and monitoring are daily strategies; 8) Focus on results, and 9) lead by example in order to manage successfully. Additionally, many researchers suggested a systematic coaching approach as a strategy to create a systematical change in organizations (Feldman & Lankau, 2010; Journal of Management, 2005). The systematic coaching change could be managed by executives and top management; however, they must execute a framework that including systematic managerial practices to achieve the targeted change (Feldman & Landau). The Laufer's managerial practices are tools and techniques that coaches might utilize to lead organizational systematic and organizational change (Laufer, 2012). Thus, the systematic change process is a strategic brand that refers to systemize logical integration through a coaching framework (Wood, 2011).

Nevertheless, the systematic coaching process requires the executive coaches to possess keen managerial skills in order to be able to implement the necessary coaching framework that Laufer suggested as a leadership strategic plan to create systematic change (2012). Further, the requirements for leaders and executive coaches to implement the systematic change in organizations are multi-facet as a result of challenges and complexities (ICF, 2011; McCarthy &Miller, 2011). In addition, Luntz (2011) presented nine principles to the project management profession "leading to manage" including: people-centeredness; (b) paradigm-breaking; (c), passion; (d) perfection; (e) prioritization; (f) persistence; (g) persuasion; (h) partnership; and (g) principled-action (Luntz, 2011). Luntz's principles are factors for strategic project management to lead organizations to winning market positioning (Luntz, 2011, Ely, 2010). The nine principles of Lutz can be implemented by executive coaches to clarify the vision of the daily operational activities and dues. Additionally, in the coaching process of project management development, the executives are required to construct a special coaching model that correlates with the internal organizational vision, mission, goals, and cultures; and that interact with the external opportunities, weakness and challenges of the market (Mayfield & Mayfield, 2012; Feldman, 2010). The luntz's leadership principles might help identifies a systematic culture to organizational learning (Walker-Frazer, 2011). For organizations, the value of coaching and mentoring exists in the quality culture that carries the organizational values, norms, and principles (Freedman &Perry, 2010).In other words, the Lutz leadership principles and Laufer practices are a strategic and effective coaching framework for organizational culture to enhance the organizational learning of project management (Laufer, 2012; Lutz, 2011; Freedman & Perry, 2010).

## COACHING AS AN ORGANIZATIONAL BEHAVIOR AND SYSTEM THINKING

The latest researches documented effective outcomes of the success on the nature of the relationship between the behavioral system approach and executive coaching (Visser, 2010). The studies stated productive organizational operational outcomes on performance and sustainability (Visser, 2010). According to Skinner, the behavioral system approach includes the behavioral of an organization and the system approach under the guidance of the coaching practice (2007). Skinner implemented a comprehensive theoretical framework includes the explanation and illustration of the development of the system approach under the practice of the executive coaching (2007).

Effective organizational behavior is a strategic and operational activity that requires a behavioral transition in the business perception of its vision, goals, objectives, and culture to accomplish the targeted connectivity with organizational productivity and performance (Visser, 2010). In viewing the relating basis of the coaching process and behavioral system; researchers state the executive coaching as a systemic behavioral practice. The behavioral system supported coaches with three systematic developmental lessons (Wasylyshyn, 2003). The first lesson reflects the importance of the daily interaction between the coach and the employees to change the thinking status and mental states (Wasylyshyn, 2003). Further, mentoring the daily operational interaction helps in polishing the human system thinking (Visser, 2010). The psychodynamic and cognitive approaches concentrate on the importance of coaching the personal needs, desires, and attitude toward steering the success and productivity of a project (Wasylyshyn, 2003). The second, this lesson concentrates on the philosophy that the coach must give attention and mentoring to the present time and setting behavior rather than building assumptions and judgments of the past behavior (Thomas et al., 2007; Westerman, 1998). However, the psychodynamic and many other humanitarian approaches suggest the importance of analyzing the past causes and motives of the inner-psychic to solve the present conflicts. Thus, the behavioral system approach that coach must pay attention to the "now- and –here "theory in dealing with the present complexities and challenges (Thomas et al., 2007; Westerman, 1998).

The third lesson states that the coach is allowed to be manipulative in order to achieve the success of behavioral system approach (Thomas et al., 2007; Westerman, 1998). Further, the behavioral system suggests manipulation as a coaching technique to improve and develop many organizational gaps (Thomas et al., 2007; Westerman, 1998). However, psychodynamic and cognitive approaches object to the usage of the manipulation as a strategic tool to solve an operational problem and develop organizational and individual strategic gaps (Visser, 2010). Additionally, the cognitive psychodynamic approaches classified the manipulative tool as unethical and against the professional and ethical values (Visser, 2010).

## ORGANIZATIONAL CHANGE TO EFFECTIVENESS THROUGH EXECUTIVE COACHING

Many organizations and industries are in a time of rapid change and progress caused by the emergence of technology. The development and progress that occurred in the communications and networking technology have changed the management styles and philosophies (Dey, 2009). However, to compete in this dynamic, many organizations are implementing technology and innovation to manage and empower its effectiveness. Increasingly, organizations are utilizing Project Support Office (PSO) as an organizational entity to assist project managers in implementing the project management techniques, methodologies, and tools to coach and mentoring the project management success. According to Wysocki (2014), PSO can help the coaching process by providing administrative and operational support in according with projects' goals and objectives. The managers can utilize the six functions of POS to support the success of the coaching process to achieve the organizational effectiveness goal. The POS six functions are: project support, coaching and mentoring, standards and methods, development and staffing, decision-making, performance-enhancement, and measurement-reporting (Wysocki, 2014). The POS is established primarily to foster the processes, techniques, and practices of project management (Pellegrinelli, 2011). Furthermore, the PSO is a challenge for many companies and requires a status of suitability to be incorporated into its system (Pellegrinelli, 2011). The challenges including lack of leadership support, lack of compelling business status, the involvement of strict performance standards for program suitability and effectiveness (Wysocki, 2014). The POS has a maturity version which is called PMMM that provides the project managers and executive coaches with ten valuable administrative, operational, and technical practices to reflect management maturity including communication management, procurement management, risk management, and integration management (Pellegrinelli, 2011); Wysocki, 2014). Kaleshovaska (2014) states that most organizations have found PSO and PMMM as a valuable project management asset for effective and efficient organizations that enable them to respond to the dynamic environment and challenging and changing markets. Additionally, executive coaches and leaders who are interested to attain sustainable growth and achieve a competitive edge in the market must pay a serious attention to incorporating technology and innovation in their organizational leadership and management (Kaleshovaska, 2014).

In this section, an illustration of the impact of executive coaching on improving the portfolio management with its selection, performance, and evaluation is implemented. To explain, the organizational core has shifted to the usage the management of variable projects. The shift of the streamline in the management line of organizations requires the implementation of new technological tools, techniques, and development portfolio product (Wysocki, 2014). Furthermore, the necessity for developing an efficient portfolio project system is a demandingly emerging as the science of portfolio management. In lieu of this demand, the project management institute (PMI) strived nearly for the last ten decades to provide the required knowledge, studies, tools, programs, researches, Coaching and mentoring, and technology to satisfy the needs of the project management field and business area (Wysocki, 2014). Nevertheless, the PMI institute involved in issuing a coaching and mentoring programs that support the project and portfolio management discipline (Wysocki, 2014). The PMI programs concentrate on coaching professional training, issues PM certificates, lectures for PM tests through media interaction, and executive coaching training for executives and project managers (PMI, 2013). Hence, organizations are motivated to train its executives and top management to be qualified for executive coaching and professional project managers to achieve the effectiveness and the competitive management quality in the market.

In accordance with Artto and Dietrich (2014), the program project managers are responsible to execute the strategies to help the organizational objectives to be linked to operational goals. The linkage programs are implemented through a professional coaching program process that begins with initiation and moving to planning, executing and controlling until the closing date of the process (Artto and Dietrich, 2014).

The coaching professional programs that organizations implement with the supervision of either a contracted external trained coach certified by PMI or an internal trained executive coach, lead the firm to mentor the achievement of the five project portfolio management stages including:

1. **Process Initiation:** Put a clear work plan including the projects' schedules, recruiting the qualified staff, staffing the working teams, assigning responsibilities and decision-making authorities, setting the proper standards and principles for the working culture (Artto and Dietrich 2014);
2. **The planning stage:** This stage documents all the details of project management process such as stating the project process dates, signing the experts and experienced staff, and a comprehensive budgeting plan;
3. **Executing process:** In this stage a, execution for strategies to manage challenges, performance objectives, analyzing and operating risks, and addressing all the dimensions of the accomplishment of the project and the interest of the stakeholder;
4. **Controlling and Maintaining Stage:** A clear plan to maintain the time schedule, budget, and financial plan, and the closing constraints of the project;
5. **The Closing Stage:** Thus, the PMI model of the project management and portfolio management presents a mentoring guidance to the executive coach to successfully and efficiently complete the project with international quality standards and a competitive international management scope (Artto and Dietrich 2014).

## Coaching and Organizational Resistance Change

Organizational change is the strategy of an organization to target a future movement toward the desired goal to increase its productivity, effectiveness, and operational and market development away from its present condition (Lunerburge, 2010). Further, organizations are urged to change as a result of many global and national economic, technological and market competitiveness pressure and challenges (Lunerburge, 2010). In this process, the role of executive coaching is strategically intense and divers (Creemers, 2011). According to Creemer, there are many reasons that cause organizational resistance to change such as: 1) Dislike of change, 2) the concern about the new system, 3) lack of capability of leaders to prepare organizations to change, and, 4) lack of leadership's competencies to prepare for the future required as operational strategies and planes (2011). Thus, the resistance to change can be reduced dramatically by implementing a therapy program that clarifies all the internal and external factors that cause and effect the change transition and educate employees about the process (Creemer, 2011).

Moreover, leaders and executive coaches' role is to initiate change and decrease the organizational resistance to change (Creemers, 2011). In addition, the PMI initiated a guidance program to help executive coaching implement to overcome organizational resistance to change (Creemers, 2011). The PMI program includes the following items to develop an organization through resistance to change stated by Duke (2011) and Anderson (2011) including:

1. **Learning and Communication:** Organizational resistance to change can be eliminated from an intensive coaching effort to educate employees about change and the factors behind and benefits from it (Duke, 2011). Executive coaches must communicate with people in the firm and assure their readiness and recognition of the change process including causes and effects (Duke, 2011);
2. **Participation and Involvement:** Executive coaching process must include the involvement of employee and staff in the changing making and implementation process. The involvement and participation of organizational employee through specify problems and the plans to solving them reduce organizational resistance to change (Anderson, 2011; Lunerburge, 2010);
3. **Organizing and Support:** The executive coach must issue a strategic plan stating the leadership behavior and the organizational culture to organize the operational transition to change. This program of leaders' behavior reduces transitional tension which helps will organizational resistance to change (Anderson, 2011);
4. **Negotiation, Cooptation and settlement process:** Executive coaching process includes the negotiation process with the managers and experts to help lead the changing process and be part of the future staff of the organization. The cooptation involves choosing a group of leaders that have a decision-making authority to manage the organizational change transition (Anderson, 2011; Lunerburge, 2010).

Hence, the executive coaching is a strategic factor to assure organizational change success and effectiveness (Spector, 2011). The executive coaching is a prominent basis and the operational backbone for the change initiative and accomplishment especially as it relates to cybersecurity project managers.

## Leadership Complexities and Challenges

The Burrell Leadership Intricacy Model (2017) outlines eleven critical themes that make leading today and the future so challenging to such a level that investment in leadership development interventions is not an organizational luxury it is a paramount operations strategy. These themes were developed through several focus group interviews with members technical managers that attended the 2017 International Studying Leadership Conference at the University of Richmond in Richmond VA, USA (see Table 1).

According to Elkins (2015), data from 21 CEOs and 21 promising middle managers from various companies indicated that across a range of leadership measures; there is a distinct correlation between increased levels of critical thinking and decision-making skills with higher levels of managerial effectiveness for managing financial, human, and organizational resources. Elkins (2015) indicates that managers with higher levels of cognition perform more efficiently when tasked with managing multiple complex projects. Kouzes and Posner (2017) postulate the significance of increasing higher-level leadership thinking and decision-making, which are critical capabilities for senior leaders. Business cycles in the

*Table 1. Burrell leadership intricacy model*

| Intricacy Variables | Burrell Leadership Intricacy Model (2017) |
|---|---|
| Theme 1 | Managerial retrospection does not lead to foresight since the variables and conditions of internal and external environment can be in unremitting instability, which make adaptability and change management skills precious. |
| Theme 2 | Exchanges and engagements between system elements are nonlinear and interconnected in such a way that small alterations can manufacture inexplicably sizeable impacts and consequences. |
| Theme 3 | Information in both the international and external environment is often exceedingly overloaded, uncertain, incomplete, or indecipherable. |
| Theme 4 | Innovations, breakthroughs, and solutions can be developed from the congruent dynamics within the organizational system and cannot be imposed by external forces with inevitable and predictable outcomes. |
| Theme 5 | New technologies are disrupting mature work practices, shifting the nature of old communication approaches, and taxing elderly collaboration approaches. |
| Theme 6 | Expertly comprehending the most effective and efficient ways to leverage organizational strengths and industry best practices is one of the most critical duties of leadership. |
| Theme 7 | Traditional organizational boundaries are dissolving in ways that necessitate unlocked transparency, flexible hierarchies, dispersed resources, distributed decision-making, loosening of centralized controls to foster the development of an organizational learning culture at every level of the organization. |
| Theme 8 | Increased globalization and enlarged employee diversity will require fresh levels of cooperation, pioneering ways of thinking, modern ways of comprehension that require respect, learning-centered curiosity, sympathy, and empathy. |
| Theme 9 | The ability to tap into the organization's expertise talent and collective intelligence is the most valuable organizational asset. |
| Theme 10 | Social capital and the ability to tap into expertise and knowledge networks are very critical because they provide access to data and information that is essential to complex problem solving and effectual decision-making, |
| Theme 11 | The need to create and support cultures in which it is safe to take the type of risks and tolerance and appreciation for what can be learned from failure to improve both business process and organizational strategy. |

current corporate environment are shorter and more complicated; hence, mandating for leaders to possess above average leadership thinking and decision-making abilities to quickly align efforts with strategic objectives while leading in a multifaceted environment (Burrell, Nobles, & Aridi, 2018). The volatile nature of cybersecurity challenges corporate executives, cybersecurity professionals, and information technologists due to constant threat changes, risk management, regulatory implementation, and resource constraints (Burrell, Nobles, & Aridi, 2018).

Organizations consistently integrate new technologies to aid in the decision-making process to reduced risk; yet, the impact of the continuous changes on leaders remain underexplored (Burrell, Nobles, & Aridi, 2018). The need for leadership development through executive coaching for cybersecurity professionals should be a top priority given the rate that new technologies are integrated to prevent leaders from leveraging outdated practices and methods through the customization of leader programs for cybersecurity professionals and information technologists (Burrell, Nobles, & Aridi, 2018).

# REFERENCES

Anderson, A. (2011). *Engaging resistance: How ordinary people successfully champion Change*. Palo Alto, CA: Stanford University Press.

Artto, A. K., & Dietrich, P. H. (2014). Strategic business management through multiple projects. Hoboken, NJ: Wiley.

Boyd, A. (2018, March). It Takes More Than Tech Skills To Be a Strong Cyber Leader. *NextGov*. Retrieved from: https://www.nextgov.com/cybersecurity/2018/03/it-takes-more-tech-skills-be-strong-cyber-leader/146520/

Burrell, D. N., Nobles, C., & Aridi, A. S. (2018). The critical need for formal leadership development programs for cybersecurity and information technology professionals. In *Proceedings of the 2018 International Conference on Cyber Warfare and Security* (pp. 82-91). Academic Conferences International Limited.

Candis, B. (2010, February). Assessing Leadership Readiness Using Developmental Personality Style: A tool for leadership coaching. *International Journal of Evidence Based Coaching and Mentoring*, 8(1).

Chartered Institute of Personnel and Development. (2010). *Learning and Development 2010*. Survey report. London: CIPD. Retrieved from: http://www.cipd.co.uk/binaries/5215_learning_talent_development%20survey_report.pdf

Creemers, B. (2010). *Improving the quality of education: Dynamic Approaches to school Improvement*. New York, NY: Routledge.

Cunningham, L., & McNally, K. (2003). *Improving Organizational and Individual Performance through Coaching*. A Case Study by Mosby, Inc. 1067-991x/2003/doi:10.1067/nrsi.2003.90

Duke, D. L. (2011). *The challenge of school district leadership*. New York, NY: Routledge.

Elkins, R. (2015). *Business: Golden Nugget Methods for High Effectiveness - Leadership, Management & Communication*. Seattle, WA: CreateSpace Independent Publishing Platform.

Ely, K., Boyce, L. A., Nelson, J. K., Zaccaro, S. J., Hernez-Broome, G., & Whyman, W. (2010). Evaluating Leadership Coaching: A review and integrated framework. *The Leadership Quarterly*. Retrieved from: Journal homepage: www.elsevier.com/locate/leaqua

Feldman, D. C. (2001). Career coaching: What HR professionals and managers need to know. *Human Resources Planning, 24*, 26–35.

Feldman, D. C., & Lankau, M. J. (2010). Executive Coaching: A review and Agenda for Future Research. *Journal of Management*. doi:10.1177/0149206305279599

Fenwick, F. J. & Gayle, C. A. (2008). Missing Links in Understanding the Relationship Between Leadership and Organizational Performance. *International Business & Economics Research Journal, 7*.

Freeman, A. M., & Perry, J.A. (2010). Executive coaching under pressure: A case stud. *Consulting Psychology Journal: Practice and Research, 6*, 189-202.

Gray, E. D., Ekinci, Y., & Goregaokar, H. (2011). Coaching SME managers: business development or personal therapy? Faculty of management and law, University of Surrey. Doi:10.108/09585

Hannafey, T., & Vitulano, L. A. (2013). Ethics and Executive Coaching: An Agency Theory Approach. *Journal of Business Ethics, 115*(3), 599–603. doi:10.100710551-012-1442-z

Kampa-Kokesh, S., Anderson, M., (2005). *Executive Coaching: A comprehensive Review of the Literature.* Educational Publishing Foundation and the Society of Consulting Psychology. DOI doi:10.1037//1061-4087.53.4.2O5

Khan, V., Hafeez, M., Rizfi, S. M., Hasanain, A., Maria, A. (2012). The relationship of leadership styles, employees commitment, and organization. Performance. *European Journal of Economics, Finance and Administrative*, 49.

Kouzes, J., & Posner, B. (2017). *The Leadership Challenge: How to Make Extraordinary Things Happen in Organizations.* Boston, MA: Harvard Business Review Publishing.

Lebihan, R. (2011). *Business schools tap coaching trend.* Australian Financial Review.

Lester, D. L. & Parnell, J. A. (2006). The Desktop Manager. S.A.M. *Advanced Management Journal, 71*(4), 43-49.

Lunenburg, F. C., & Ometein, A. O. (2010). *Educational administration: Concepts and practices.* Thousand Oaks, CA: Wadsworth/Cengage Learning.

Mayfield, J., & Mayfield, M. (2012). the leadership relation between leader Motivating language and employee self-efficacy. A partial least squares model analysis. *Journal of Business Communication.* doi:10.1177/0021943612456036

McCarthy, G., & Milner, J. (2012). Managerial coaching: challenges, opportunities and Training. Sydney Business School, University of Wollongong, School of Psychology, Deakin University. DOI doi:10.1108/JMD-11-2011-0113

Newsom & Dent. (2011). A Work Behavior Analysis of Executive Coaches. *International Journal of Evidence Based Coaching and Mentoring, 9*(2), 1.

Northouse, P. G. (2013). *Leadership Theory and Practice* (6th ed.). Western Michigan University.

Obiwuru, T. C., Okwu, A. T., Akpa, V. O., & Nwankwere, I. A. (2011). Effects of leadership style on organizational performance: A survey of selected small scale enterprise in Ikosia-Ketu counsil development area of Lagos state, Nigeria. Academic Press.

Oltsik, J. (2017). *The life and times of cybersecurity professionals.* ESG and ISSA: Research Report. Available at: https://www.esg-global.com/hubfs/issa/ESG-ISSA-Research-Report-Life-of-Cybersecurity-Professionals-Nov-2017.pdf?hsCtaTracking=a63e431c-d2ce-459d-8787-cc122a193baf%7Ce74f0327-0bbc-444a-b7a8-e2cd08d1999e

Paul, G. W., & Berry, D. M. (2013). *The Importance of Executive Leadership in Creating a Post-Merged Organizational Culture Conducive to Effective Performance Management.* SA Journal of Human Resources Management/SA.

Pellegrinelli, S., (2011). What's in a name? Project and program? *International Journal of Project Management, 29*(2), 232-240.

Peltier, B. (2001). *The psychology of executive coaching: Theory and Application.* Ann Arbor, MI: Sheridan Books.

Peterson, D. B., & Hicks, M. D. (1995). *The leader as coach: Strategies for coaching and Developing others*. Minneapolis, MN: Personnel Decisions.

Saowalux, P. & Peng, C. (2007). *Impact of Leadership Style on Performance: A Study of Six Sigma Professionals in Thailand*. International DSI/Asia and Pacific DSI.

Senge, P. M. (2006). The Fifth Discipline: The Art and Practice of the Learning Organization. Academic Press.

Spector, B. (2011). *Implementing organizational change: theory into practice-international edition*. Upper Saddle River, NJ: Prentice Hall.

Strang, K. D. (2011). Leadership substitute and personality impact on time and quality in virtual new product development project. *Project Management Journal*, *42*(1), 73–90. doi:10.1002/pmj.20208

Thomas, F. N., Waits, R. A., & Hartsfield, G. L. (2007). The influence of Gregory Bateson: Legacy or vestige? *Kybernetes*, *36*(7/8), 871–883. doi:10.1108/03684920710777397

Visser, M. (2007b). System dynamics and group facilitation: Contributions from communication Theory. *System Dynamics Review*, *23*(4), 453–463. doi:10.1002dr.391

Vugt, M. V., Hogan, R., & Kaiser, R. (2008). *Leadership, Followership, and Evolution*. 2008 American Psychologist Association 0003-066X/08. Doi:10.1037/0003-066x.63.3.182

Walker-Fraser, A. (2011, August). An HR perspective on executive coaching for organizational Learning. *International Journal of Evidence Based Coaching and Mentoring*, *9*(2).

Wasylyshyn, K. M. (2003). Coaching and executive character: Core problems and basic approaches. *Consulting Psychology Journal: Practice and Research*, *55*(2), 94–106. doi:10.1037/1061-4087.55.2.94

Wenson, E. (2010, November). After-coaching leadership skills and their impact on direct reports: Recommendations for organizations. *Human Resource Development International*, *13*(5), 607–616. doi:10.1080/13678868.2010.520485

Wysocki, R. K. (2014). Effective Project Management: Traditional, agile, extreme (7th ed.). Academic Press.

*Previously published in the International Journal of Human Capital and Information Technology Professionals (IJHCITP), 10(2); pages 20-32, copyright year 2019 by IGI Publishing (an imprint of IGI Global).*

# Chapter 17
# Towards a Student Security Compliance Model (SSCM):
## Factors Predicting Student Compliance Intention to Information Security Policy

**Felix Nti Koranteng**

https://orcid.org/0000-0001-5917-381X

*University of Education, Winneba, Kumasi Campus, Ghana*

## ABSTRACT

*Users are considered the weakest link in ensuring information security (InfoSec). As a result, users' security behaviour remains crucial in many organizations. In response, InfoSec research has produced many behavioural theories targeted at explaining information security policy (ISP) compliance. Meanwhile, these theories mostly draw samples from employees often in developing countries. Such theories are not applicable to students in educational institutions since their psychological orientation with regards to InfoSec is different when compared with employees. Based on this premise, the chapter presents arguments founded on synthesis from existing literature. It proposes a students' security compliance model (SSCM) that attempts to explain predictive factors of students' ISP compliance intentions. The study encourages further research to confirm the proposed relationships using qualitative and quantitative techniques.*

## INTRODUCTION

Secured management of Information Security (InfoSec) continues to be one of the most relevant issues within organizations. This is because they thrive on intense use of information, hence there is no ambiguity that InfoSec is core to its activities. Traditionally, InfoSec has focused mostly on technological solutions (Öugütçü, Testik, & Chouseinoglou, 2016). However, the need for end-user behaviour has gained attention in recent times (Safa, Von Solms, & Furnell, 2016). This is because of the inability to monitor user behaviour at all times regardless of the increased sophistication of Information and Technology infrastructure and software development. Practitioners and researchers in InfoSec have come to realize

DOI: 10.4018/978-1-6684-3698-1.ch017

that there is a need for Information Systems security solutions to cover a wider range of activities and give equal attention to all. This is because, technology alone cannot be effective for addressing information security issues (Herath & Rao, 2009). Accordingly, research in InfoSec now addresses issues in three main areas namely; people, process and technology. With regard to technology, research work targets the introduction of infrastructure and cryptographic algorithms that enhance methods for prevention, detection, and response to security breaches. Similarly, security processes within the organization have been improved to ensure minimal compromise on confidentiality, integrity, and availability of information. Research on the psychological aspect and behaviour of users has also explored users' compliance with Information Security Policies (ISPs). Consequently, a number of factors have been identified to impact security compliance.

Even though this approach has proven to be somehow effective, majority of the existing studies that have empirically evaluated factors that impact InfoSec behaviour tend to draw their samples from employees of various organizations with little attention to academic institutions. Yet, these factors cannot be generalized and thus it is expected that they may not impact especially students in the manner in which they impact employees. It is however imperative to turn attention to InfoSec issues within higher education institutions considering their high consumption, usage, and knowledge of technology (Öugütçü et al., 2016). This raises further concerns given the increased risk that is associated with cyberspaces. Worriedly, studies that analyze the factors that impact student's compliance with ISPs in developing communities such as Africa. There is enough evidence that students in such areas pay less attention to information security issues (Gross & Acquisti, 2005). Hence this study seeks to present a literature analysis on the factors that impact compliance to information security with a particular focus on African students. It is expected that the findings will provide meaningful information to researchers and practitioners on how to promote information security policy compliance among students. This study, therefore, seeks to provoke thinking and argue for the need for a tailor-made model specific to explaining students' ISP compliance.

## LITERATURE REVIEW

The importance of organizations' information security cannot be overemphasized. Hence, technological as well as behavioural measures are often initiated to curb the adverse effects of improper use and policy non-conformity. However, behavioural issues top the approaches in safeguarding information (Safa et al., 2016). Therefore, scholars have explored various avenues in an attempt to explain information security behaviour. Considering that human behaviour is complex and difficult to understand (Wiafe, Nakata, Moran, & Gulliver, 2011). Mostly, the factors that determine adherence to policies meant to guide security behaviour has been explored. Extant studies agree that deterrent mechanisms such as fear appeal, threat, certainty of and severity of punishment are effective in guiding people to comply with security policies (Cheng, Li, Li, Holm, & Zhai, 2013; Herath & Rao, 2009; Safa et al., 2019). Other studies have argued that concepts such as habit strength, security support, prior experiences, self-efficacy, and perceived vulnerability are more effective in explaining information security compliance (Ifinedo, 2012; Johnston & Warkentin, 2010; Tsai et al., 2016).

As already mentioned, majority of these existing studies tend to focus on information security issues within organizations with less attention on higher education institutions. Yet, students of higher education do not have the same psychological contract as compared to employees in organizations. This is because as employees of an organization find the need to protect vital documents of their organization, students, on the other hand, may not see themselves to be obliged in doing so. Consider a situation within an academic institution and issues regarding the protection of students' grades. Both faculty and staff may deem it as a responsibility to ensure that these scores are kept safe and, in an event where they see loopholes that leads to the leakage of such information, they may take appropriate actions. However, a student in this circumstance will not consider the same. Relatedly, Yoon and Kim (2012) demonstrated that students do not have similar information risk perception when compared to employees. This is much evident in many educational institutions including African (Ngoqo & Flowerday, 2015). Ngoqo & Flowerday (2015) suggest that many African students lack requisite conscious care on information security. Hence, their actions intentionally or unintentional subject institutions' IS resources to various risks. This lack of concern can be attributed to a lack of adequate IT skills, awareness of security policy and experience in dealing with possible and imminent threats on IS resources (Chandarman & Van Niekerk, 2017; Ngoqo & Flowerday, 2014).

Amidst these, studies on the determinants of InfoSec compliance behavior among students is scarce. It has thus become imperative for investigations to be conducted to determine the factors that contribute to student's compliance with ISPs. Students are the largest users of information systems infrastructure in all higher education institutes (Rhode, Richter, Gowen, Miller, & Wills, 2017) and they also form the largest populations within these institutions. As such, they can serve as an asset when they are provided with the appropriate skills. The relevance of InfoSec activities within higher education cannot be under-estimated, especially considering that higher education encompasses a number of vital documents (transcripts, certificates, examinations papers, etc.). In addition, students are the next generation of hackers, employees, and employers, and their understanding of InfoSec activities and the ability to comply is key to a successful future organization. It is therefore imperative to understand students' InfoSec behavior within the perspective of existing behavioral theories

# BEHAVIORAL THEORIES AND INFOSEC ACTIVITIES

## Theory of Planned Behavioral and Security Compliance

The Theory of Planned Behaviour (TPB) (Ajzen, 1991) is a prominent framework for explaining technology use behaviour. The theory is an upgrade of the Theory of Reasoned Action (Fishbein & Ajzen, 1977). TPB argues that a person's behaviour is influenced by their behavioural Intentions (INT). However, these effects are not direct but rather moderated by Actual Behavioural Control. Although this moderation effect is existent, many scholars have sort to adopt Perceived Behavioural Control (PBC) due to the difficulty in measuring Actual Behavioural Control. Aside from this, PBC along with Attitude (ATT) and Subjective Norm (SN) have been identified to influence Intentions (Shin & Hancer, 2016). Attitude is an individual's positive or negative judgment about a behaviour whereas Subjective Norm is a person's perceived expectations of relevant others.

There is evidence that these constructs are relevant in explaining security compliance behaviour. For instance, Ifinedo (2012) adopted the TPB to investigate IS security compliance of a group of employees. The study found significant effects of Subjective Norm and Attitude on Compliance Intention. Similarly, using the theory as a foundation, Kim, Yang, & Park (2014) concluded that, the variables in TPB is effective in predicting compliance behaviour. Other literature reviews have also pointed out that TPB constructs are the most relevant in explaining compliance intention and behaviour (Nasir, Arshah, & Ab Hamid, 2018; Sommestad & Hallberg, 2013). This suggests that the theory is adequate for assessing students' information security compliance behaviour. Nonetheless, it is imperative to extend existing models and methods to complement the rapid changes in information security landscape. This paper therefore argues for the modification of TPB. It argues that the introduction of deterrence, information security awareness and information security knowledge sharing into TPB will facilitate the understanding of ISP compliance intention within the context of students of higher education. This is because some studies have found significant relationships between these constructs and security behaviour (Bulgurcu, Cavusoglu, & Benbasat, 2010; Safa et al., 2016).

The original theory (TPB) does not highlight the ordering of constructs with regards to their importance. Conversely, some scholars believe that the potency of some of the constructs reduces in different scenarios and environments. For instance, in the case where technology behavior and use is completely voluntary, Perceived Behavioural Control is of lesser value (Sommestad & Hallberg, 2013). The activities of students in ensuring information security compliance may be largely voluntary, thus, Perceived Behavioural Control can be omitted from the model under such circumstance. Meanwhile, new concepts (Deterrence, Information Security Awareness, and Information Security Knowledge Sharing) have been integrated with Attitude and Subjective Norm to form Students' Security Compliance Model (SSCM). Consequently, this chapter argues that Deterrence, Information Security Awareness, and Information Security Knowledge Sharing are direct predictors of Attitude and Subjective Norm. In addition, Attitude and Subjective Norm predicts students' compliance Intentions to information security. Figure 1 is a diagrammatic representation of the conceptualization of factors that influence students' information security compliance in higher education.

*Figure 1. Students' Security Compliance Model*

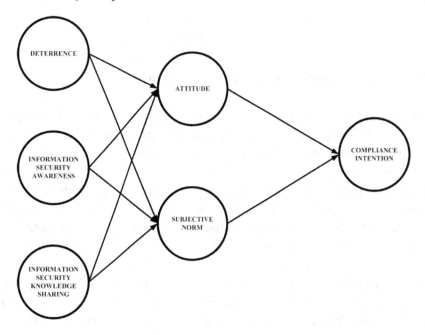

## Deterrence Theories and Policy Conformity

As inferred earlier, information security policies enlist acceptable guidelines for ensuring information security. They also contain repercussions for non-compliance. The concepts originate from the General Deterrence Theory (GDT) which posits that an individual's decision to commit or abstain from crime is rational (Higgins, Wilson, & Fell, 2005). Thus, people compare the benefits and costs before committing a crime. In other words, a person will perpetuate a crime when he/she perceives that the benefits outweigh the cost and vice. As a result, several studies have found a nexus between willingness to comply with ISPs and perceived benefit/cost.

For instance, according to Parsons et al., (2015) employees in organizations with severe sanctions for non-compliance possess favorable attitudes towards information security. Similarly, Rajab and Eydgahi, (2019) and Safa et al., (2019) confirm that when people are certain that their non-compliance behavior will be detected and will lead to severe punishments, they tend to positively relate to ISP. In a study by Shreeve et al., (2002), students confirmed that penalties are effective in guiding behavior and that schools with penalty systems record higher conformance behavior from students. Recently, Patchin and Hinduja (2018) also found that student is deterred by threats of punishment. That is, in the absence of clear and consistent consequences for unacceptable security behavior, deviant behavior will fester. Deterrent approaches thus provide an effective alternative for guiding students' Attitude and behavior towards ISP.

## Information Security Awareness

Information Security Awareness is important in improving students' affect towards complying with ISP. For students' to appropriately handle data and interact with information systems, they must be equipped with the requisite skills. Indeed, proper knowledge and skills improve security behavior (Yaokumah, Walker, & Kumah, 2019). Badie and Lashkari (2012) contend that regardless of the sophisticated technologies and protection mechanisms, unaware users remain a viable vector for attacks. That is to say that, the lack of awareness and proper skills may lead individuals to commit intentional or unintentional errors that could be detrimental to information security. Jones, Chin, and Aiken (2014) assert that students lack proper education, training, and awareness and thus contributes to the growing security problems. Moreover, Farooq, Isoaho, Virtanen, and Isoaho (2015) found that more than 75% of students lack security training. Studies attribute this to the lack of comprehensive security programs available for students (Kim, 2014; Slusky & Partow-Navid, 2012). Meanwhile, institutions can provoke ISP compliance when programs aimed at training and increasing students' awareness of their roles and responsibilities with regards to InfoSec are implemented (Adams & Makramalla, 2015). This is because students who are better informed on information security will be better informed about the relevance of appropriate data handling techniques as well as the prevalence of imminent threats. Moreover, well-trained students exhibit a positive attitude toward information security policy (Parsons et al., 2015). Bulgurcu, Cavusoglu, and Benbasat (2010) provide empirical evidence for this assertion. Although their study sampled employees, it is possible similar results will be found among students.

## Information Security Knowledge Sharing

Knowledge is a crucial asset in organizations. It provides the theoretical understanding, facts, and information for learning and experience (Safa et al., 2016). Knowledge sharing is the willingness of students to share the information they have acquired (Koranteng & Wiafe, 2019). Effective knowledge sharing has been established to help solve problems and enable the creation of new ideas. Knowledge, when shared evenly across the organizational structure improves efficiency, reduces cost and mitigates risks (Lee, Lee, & Sanford, 2011). Therefore, InfoSec knowledge sharing is an effective approach to mitigating the risks associated with information systems. For instance, if experts are challenged with a security problem, they could disseminate information on how it was solved and others could also implement proactive measures for similar future attacks. This reduces the time and money for developing duplicate solutions for similar attacks (Feledi, Fenz, & Lechner, 2013). Relevant studies have confirmed that InfoSec knowledge sharing thwarts security risks such as phishing (Arachchilage & Love, 2014; Tamjidyamcholo, Baba, Shuib, & Rohani, 2014). However, it continues to be one of the major challenges that hinder the progress of information security compliance among employees (Tamjidyamcholo et al., 2014). This situation may not be experienced among students because it has been demonstrated that students are motivated to share knowledge by taking advantage of advancement in modem technologies (Koranteng, Wiafe, & Kuada, 2019). Koranteng, Wiafe, Katsriku, and Apau (2019) posits that students have a high norm of reciprocity which positively affects their frequency of interactions. Due to the strong interaction ties among students, they willingly share knowledge and learn from each other (Eid & Al-Jabri, 2016). This is also corroborated by Aslam, Shahzad, Syed, and Ramish (2013). To this regard, students in higher education may share their knowledge on information security practices and this will impact the security behavior.

## Attitude

As already indicated, Attitude refers to an individual's affect toward ISP (Ajzen, 1991). It describes a person's overall judgment on InfoSec and it is manifested in a person or entity. It originates from previous experiences, ideas or activities (Hepler, 2015). Extant studies have established a positive correlation between Attitude and compliance intention (Safa & Von Solms, 2016; Safa et al., 2016). In a related study, Safa et al., (2019) found that Attitude is a significant predictor of ISP compliance. That is, when users positively relate to ISPs, there is a high probability of compliance (Ifinedo, 2014). The new generation of students often referred to as Millennials are highly abreast of the issues surrounding InfoSec (Parker, Ophoff, Van Belle, & Karia, 2015). They experience or encounter multiple threats when using their personal devices such as mobile phones. Hence, many students understand the negative effects caused by such threats and are poised to have favorable opinions on InfoSec (Stanciu & Tinca, 2016). Yoon et al., (2012) contend that students exhibit a good InfoSec habit. Similarly, Hajli and Lin (2016) conclude that students possess a positive Attitude towards InfoSec. Likewise, Cordova, Eaton, Greer, and Smith (2017) also regard students' Attitude towards computer security threat as favourable. Although, Wiafe, Nakata, and Gulliver (2014) insists that Attitude do not always predict behavioural intentions, the authors also admit that there is relationship between. Indeed, Mayer, Kunz, and Volkamer (2017) confirms that Attitude remains a reliable factor for predicting compliance intention. Consequently, students' Attitude toward ISP compliance may predict compliance behavior.

## Subjective Norm

Subjective Norm reflects the probability to perform a behavior due to the expectations of relevant others (Ajzen, 1991). An individual may perform a behavior because they perceived that people important to them deem it appropriate. Relevant research asserts that social pressure from significant others such as lecturers and supervisors may lead students to behave in a particular way (Safa et al., 2015). In other words, students occasionally want approval from respected colleagues and authorities, hence they seek to behave in ways they perceive to be in accordance with the expectations of these authorities. Some scholars assert that Subjective Norm is very influential in predicting technology behavior (Binyamin, Rutter, & Smith, 2018). For instance, Arpaci (2016) found that students accepted the use of mobile cloud storage services because of influences from significant others. Gong, Han, Li, Yu, and Reinhardt (2019) also concluded that students' behavioral intention to adopt online services is informed by perceptions of relevant others. Other scholars have also confirmed this relationship (Yeap, Ramayah, & Soto-Acosta, 2016). According to Halder, Pietarinen, Havu-Nuutinen, Pöllänen, and Pelkonen (2016), this relationship is stronger in developing countries. This is because, students in such countries tend to appreciate authorities and mostly conform to their expectations (Hofstede, 2001). As a result, findings from Buabeng-Andoh, Yaokumah, and Tarhini (2019) confirm that Subjective Norm is relevant in predicting students' behavioral intentions. Within the scope of ISP compliance, Cheng et al., (2013) have suggested that Subjective Norm influences ISP compliance. Similarly, findings from Foltz, Newkirk, and Schwager (2016) confirm that students' behavioral intentions on social networking sites security is impacted by Subjective Norm. Given these backgrounds, students may be likely to conform to security policy requirement due to the expectations of relevant other.

## FUTURE RESEARCH DIRECTIONS

The chapter has reviewed extant empirical studies that provide a strong foundation on the factors that account for security compliance behavior among students. As earlier indicated, human elements in an organization remain key in ensuring the safety of information. People are considered the weakest link in InfoSec. Therefore, without a particular focus on how to improve information security behavior, institutions continue to be at risk. Eisenhardt, Gioia, and Langley (2016) believe that qualitative research is aimed at theory building since it aids researchers in defining the relationships between observed variables. To confirm or advance the proposed relationships in this chapter, future studies are encouraged to adopt different qualitative techniques to synthesize the relationships espoused. Based on the study's conceptual model and others derived from relevant qualitative reasoning, additional studies can focus on using quantitative techniques to empirically test the relationships proposed.

Moreover, the arguments in this chapter present a worrying trend that suggests a lack of educational programs and courses on information and computer security. While the focus of this chapter is not to assess the state of InfoSec education, it highlights the need for further investigations into the status of InfoSec related programs and training existent particularly in developing countries. This is because aside from the security of institutions' information, other studies have attributed the rapid rise in cybercrime incidents such as online fraud to the lack of relevant educational programs (Apau, Koranteng, & Adu, 2019). Finally, studies are also encouraged to examine the implications of the assertions delivered by this chapter and explore the possible and relevant policy directions that stakeholders could undertake to achieve desirable results.

# CONCLUSION

Breaches in an organization's Information Systems (IS) security does not only cause financial losses but also loss of trust and reputation. Therefore, the protection of organizational information is very crucial. Institutions tend to channel huge investments into technology to safeguard ISs. However, this is inadequate, as attackers target people and not technology. However, to make users robust to techniques adopted by attackers, security policy compliance is key. Therefore, scholars have extensively explored the determinants of security policy compliance. This is aimed at developing frameworks that enhance users' compliance with information security. While these studies provide relevant recommendations, many of them draw samples from employees with very few focusing on students. Meanwhile, research has shown that the psychological disposition of students differs from employees as students readily disregard security policies. This chapter, therefore, performed a literature synthesis and developed a Students' Security Compliance Model (SSCM) aimed at explaining students' security policy compliance behavior. In SSCM, Attitude and Subjective Norm are dependent on Deterrence, Information Security Awareness, and Information Security Knowledge Sharing. In addition, Attitude and Subjective Norm predict students' compliance Intentions to information security. Future studies are encouraged to empirical test the proposed relationships in the model.

# REFERENCES

Adams, M., & Makramalla, M. (2015). Cybersecurity skills training: an attacker-centric gamified approach. *Technology Innovation Management Review, 5*(1).

Ajzen, I. (1991). The theory of planned behavior. *Organizational Behavior and Human Decision Processes, 50*(2), 179–211. doi:10.1016/0749-5978(91)90020-T

Apau, R., Koranteng, F. N., & Adu, S. (2019). Cyber-crime and its effects on e-commerce technologies. *Journal of Information, 5*(1), 39–59. doi:10.18488/journal.104.2019.51.39.59

Arachchilage, N. A. G., & Love, S. (2014). Security awareness of computer users: A phishing threat avoidance perspective. *Computers in Human Behavior, 38*, 304–312. doi:10.1016/j.chb.2014.05.046

Arpaci, I. (2016). Understanding and predicting students' intention to use mobile cloud storage services. *Computers in Human Behavior, 58*, 150–157. doi:10.1016/j.chb.2015.12.067

Aslam, M. M. H., Shahzad, K., Syed, A. R., & Ramish, A. (2013). Social capital and knowledge sharing as determinants of academic performance. *Journal of Behavioral and Applied Management, 15*(1), 25–42.

Badie, N., & Lashkari, A. H. (2012). A new evaluation criteria for effective security awareness in computer risk management based on AHP. *Journal of Basic and Applied Scientific Research, 2*(9), 9331–9347.

Binyamin, S. S., Rutter, M. J., & Smith, S. (2018). The Influence of Computer Self-Efficacy and Subjective Norms on the Students' Use of Learning Management Systems at King Abdulaziz University. *International Journal of Information and Education Technology (IJIET), 8*(10), 693–699. doi:10.18178/ijiet.2018.8.10.1124

Buabeng-Andoh, C., Yaokumah, W., & Tarhini, A. (2019). Investigating students' intentions to use ICT: A comparison of theoretical models. *Education and Information Technologies*, *24*(1), 643–660. doi:10.100710639-018-9796-1

Bulgurcu, B., Cavusoglu, H., & Benbasat, I. (2010). Information security policy compliance: An empirical study of rationality-based beliefs and information security awareness. *Management Information Systems Quarterly*, *34*(3), 523–548. doi:10.2307/25750690

Chandarman, R., & Van Niekerk, B. (2017). Students' cybersecurity awareness at a private tertiary educational institution. *African Journal of Information and Communication*, *20*(20), 133–155. doi:10.23962/10539/23572

Cheng, L., Li, Y., Li, W., Holm, E., & Zhai, Q. (2013). Understanding the violation of IS security policy in organizations: An integrated model based on social control and deterrence theory. *Computers & Security*, *39*, 447–459. doi:10.1016/j.cose.2013.09.009

Cordova, J., Eaton, V., Greer, T., & Smith, L. (2017). A comparison of CS majors and non-CS majors attitudes regarding computer security threats. *Journal of Computing Sciences in Colleges*, *33*(2), 4–10.

Eid, M. I. M., & Al-Jabri, I. M. (2016). Social networking, knowledge sharing, and student learning: the case of university students. *Computers & Educationand Education*, *99*, 14–27. Retrieved from http://ssrn.com/abstract=2780765

Eisenhardt, K. M., Gioia, D. A., & Langley, A. (2016). Theory-Method Packages: A Comparison of Three Qualitative Approaches to Theory Building. In Academy of Management Proceedings (Vol. 2016, p. 12424). Academic Press.

Farooq, A., Isoaho, J., Virtanen, S., & Isoaho, J. (2015). *Information security awareness in educational institution: An analysis of students' individual factors. In 2015 IEEE Trustcom/BigDataSE/ISPA* (Vol. 1, pp. 352–359). IEEE.

Feledi, D., Fenz, S., & Lechner, L. (2013). Toward web-based information security knowledge sharing. *Information Security Technical Report*, *17*(4), 199–209. doi:10.1016/j.istr.2013.03.004

Fishbein, M., & Ajzen, I. (1977). *Belief, attitude, intention and behavior: An introduction to theory and research*. Reading, MA: Addison-Wesley.

Foltz, C. B., Newkirk, H. E., & Schwager, P. H. (2016). An empirical investigation of factors that influence individual behavior toward changing social networking security settings. *Journal of Theoretical and Applied Electronic Commerce Research*, *11*(2), 1–15. doi:10.4067/S0718-18762016000200002

Gong, Z., Han, Z., Li, X., Yu, C., & Reinhardt, J. D. (2019). Factors influencing the adoption of online health consultation services: The role of subjective norm, trust, perceived benefit and offline habit. *Frontiers in Public Health*, *7*, 286. doi:10.3389/fpubh.2019.00286 PMID:31637229

Gross, R., & Acquisti, A. (2005). Information revelation and privacy in online social networks. In Workshop On Privacy In The Electronic Society (pp. 71–80). doi:10.1145/1102199.1102214

Hajli, N., & Lin, X. (2016). Exploring the security of information sharing on social networking sites: The role of perceived control of information. *Journal of Business Ethics, 133*(1), 111–123. doi:10.100710551-014-2346-x

Halder, P., Pietarinen, J., Havu-Nuutinen, S., Pöllänen, S., & Pelkonen, P. (2016). The Theory of Planned Behavior model and students' intentions to use bioenergy: A cross-cultural perspective. *Renewable Energy, 89*, 627–635. doi:10.1016/j.renene.2015.12.023

Hepler, J. (2015). A good thing isn't always a good thing: Dispositional attitudes predict non-normative judgments. *Personality and Individual Differences, 75*, 59–63. doi:10.1016/j.paid.2014.11.016

Herath, T., & Rao, H. R. (2009). Encouraging information security behaviors in organizations: Role of penalties, pressures and perceived effectiveness. *Decision Support Systems, 47*(2), 154–165. doi:10.1016/j.dss.2009.02.005

Higgins, G. E., Wilson, A. L., & Fell, B. D. (2005). An application of deterrence theory to software piracy. *The Journal of Criminal Justice and Popular Culture, 12*(3), 166–184.

Hofstede, G. J. (2001). Adoption of communication technologies and national culture. *Information Systems Management, 6*(3), 55–74. doi:10.9876im.v6i3.107

Ifinedo, P. (2012). Understanding information systems security policy compliance: An integration of the theory of planned behavior and the protection motivation theory. *Computers & Security, 31*(1), 83–95. doi:10.1016/j.cose.2011.10.007

Ifinedo, P. (2014). Information systems security policy compliance: An empirical study of the effects of socialisation, influence, and cognition. *Information & Management, 51*(1), 69–79. doi:10.1016/j.im.2013.10.001

Johnston & Warkentin. (2010). Fear Appeals and Information Security Behaviors: An Empirical Study. *Management Information Systems Quarterly, 34*(3), 549. doi:10.2307/25750691

Jones, B. H., Chin, A. G., & Aiken, P. (2014). Risky business: Students and smartphones. *TechTrends, 58*(6), 73–83. doi:10.100711528-014-0806-x

Kim, E. B. (2014). Recommendations for information security awareness training for college students. *Information Management & Computer Security, 22*(1), 115–126. doi:10.1108/IMCS-01-2013-0005

Kim, S. H., Yang, K. H., & Park, S. (2014). An integrative behavioral model of information security policy compliance. *TheScientificWorldJournal, 2014*, 2014. doi:10.1155/2014/463870 PMID:24971373

Koranteng, F. N., & Wiafe, I. (2019). Factors that Promote Knowledge Sharing on Academic Social Networking Sites: An Empirical Study. *Education and Information Technologies, 24*(2), 1211–1236. doi:10.100710639-018-9825-0

Koranteng, F. N., Wiafe, I., Katsriku, F. A., & Apau, R. (2019). *Understanding trust on social networking sites among tertiary students: An empirical study in Ghana*. Applied Computing and Informatics. doi:10.1016/j.aci.2019.07.003

Koranteng, F. N., Wiafe, I., & Kuada, E. (2019). An Empirical Study of the Relationship Between Social Networking Sites and Students ' Engagement in Higher Education. *Journal of Educational Computing Research, 57*(5), 1131–1159. doi:10.1177/0735633118787528

Lee, G., Lee, W. J., & Sanford, C. (2011). A motivational approach to information providing: A resource exchange perspective. *Computers in Human Behavior, 27*(1), 440–448. doi:10.1016/j.chb.2010.09.006

Mayer, P., Kunz, A., & Volkamer, M. (2017). Reliable behavioural factors in the information security context. In *Proceedings of the 12th International Conference on Availability, Reliability and Security* (pp. 1–10). 10.1145/3098954.3098986

Nasir, A., Arshah, R. A., & Ab Hamid, M. R. (2018). The Significance of Main Constructs of Theory of Planned Behavior in Recent Information Security Policy Compliance Behavior Study: A Comparison among Top Three Behavioral Theories. *International Journal of Engineering & Technology, 7*(2.29), 737–741.

Ngoqo, B., & Flowerday, S. (2014). Linking student information security awareness and behavioural intent. In HAISA (pp. 162–173). Academic Press.

Ngoqo, B., & Flowerday, S. V. (2015). Exploring the relationship between student mobile information security awareness and behavioural intent. *Information & Computer Security, 23*(4), 406–420. doi:10.1108/ICS-10-2014-0072

Öugütçü, G., Testik, Ö. M., & Chouseinoglou, O. (2016). Analysis of personal information security behavior and awareness. *Computers & Security, 56*, 83–93.

Parker, F., Ophoff, J., Van Belle, J.-P., & Karia, R. (2015). Security awareness and adoption of security controls by smartphone users. In *2015 Second international conference on information security and cyber forensics (InfoSec)* (pp. 99–104). 10.1109/InfoSec.2015.7435513

Parsons, K. M., Young, E., Butavicius, M. A., McCormac, A., Pattinson, M. R., & Jerram, C. (2015). The influence of organizational information security culture on information security decision making. *Journal of Cognitive Engineering and Decision Making, 9*(2), 117–129. doi:10.1177/1555343415575152

Patchin, J. W., & Hinduja, S. (2018). Deterring teen bullying: Assessing the impact of perceived punishment from police, schools, and parents. *Youth Violence and Juvenile Justice, 16*(2), 190–207. doi:10.1177/1541204016681057

Rajab, M., & Eydgahi, A. (2019). Evaluating the explanatory power of theoretical frameworks on intention to comply with information security policies in higher education. *Computers & Security, 80*, 211–223. doi:10.1016/j.cose.2018.09.016

Rhode, J., Richter, S., Gowen, P., Miller, T., & Wills, C. (2017). Understanding Faculty Use of the Learning Management System. *Online Learning, 21*(3), 68–86. doi:10.24059/olj.v21i3.1217

Safa, N. S., Maple, C., Furnell, S., Azad, M. A., Perera, C., Dabbagh, M., & Sookhak, M. (2019). Deterrence and prevention-based model to mitigate information security insider threats in organisations. *Future Generation Computer Systems, 97*, 587–597. doi:10.1016/j.future.2019.03.024

Safa, N. S., Sookhak, M., Von Solms, R., Furnell, S., Ghani, N. A., & Herawan, T. (2015). Information security conscious care behaviour formation in organizations. *Computers & Security, 53*, 65–78. doi:10.1016/j.cose.2015.05.012

Safa, N. S., & Von Solms, R. (2016). An information security knowledge sharing model in organizations. *Computers in Human Behavior, 57*, 442–451. doi:10.1016/j.chb.2015.12.037

Safa, N. S., Von Solms, R., & Furnell, S. (2016). Information security policy compliance model in organizations. *Computers & Security, 56*, 70–82. doi:10.1016/j.cose.2015.10.006

Shin, Y. H., & Hancer, M. (2016). The role of attitude, subjective norm, perceived behavioral control, and moral norm in the intention to purchase local food products. *Journal of Foodservice Business Research, 19*(4), 338–351. doi:10.1080/15378020.2016.1181506

Shreeve, A., Boddington, D., Bernard, B., Brown, K., Clarke, K., Dean, L., ... Shiret, D. (2002). Student perceptions of rewards and sanctions. *Pedagogy, Culture & Society, 10*(2), 239–256. doi:10.1080/14681360200200142

Slusky, L., & Partow-Navid, P. (2012). Students information security practices and awareness. *Journal of Information Privacy and Security, 8*(4), 3–26. doi:10.1080/15536548.2012.10845664

Sommestad, T., & Hallberg, J. (2013). A review of the theory of planned behaviour in the context of information security policy compliance. In *IFIP International Information Security Conference* (pp. 257–271). 10.1007/978-3-642-39218-4_20

Stanciu, V., & Tinca, A. (2016). Students' awareness on information security between own perception and reality--an empirical study. *Accounting and Management Information Systems, 15*(1), 112–130.

Tamjidyamcholo, A., & Baba, M. S. (2014). Evaluation model for knowledge sharing in information security professional virtual community. *Computers & Security, 43*, 19–34. doi:10.1016/j.cose.2014.02.010

Tsai, H. S., Jiang, M., Alhabash, S., LaRose, R., Rifon, N. J., & Cotten, S. R. (2016). Understanding online safety behaviors: A protection motivation theory perspective. *Computers & Security, 59*, 138–150. doi:10.1016/j.cose.2016.02.009

Wiafe, I., Nakata, K., & Gulliver, S. (2014). Categorizing users in behavior change support systems based on cognitive dissonance. *Personal and Ubiquitous Computing, 18*(7), 1677–1687. doi:10.100700779-014-0782-3

Wiafe, I., Nakata, K., Moran, S., & Gulliver, S. R. (2011). Considering user attitude and behaviour in persuasive systems design: the 3d-rab model. In ECIS (p. 186). Academic Press.

Yaokumah, W., Walker, D. O., & Kumah, P. (2019). SETA and Security Behavior: Mediating Role of Employee Relations, Monitoring, and Accountability. *Journal of Global Information Management, 27*(2), 102–121. doi:10.4018/JGIM.2019040106

Yeap, J. A. L., Ramayah, T., & Soto-Acosta, P. (2016). Factors propelling the adoption of m-learning among students in higher education. *Electronic Markets, 26*(4), 323–338. doi:10.100712525-015-0214-x

Yoon, C., Hwang, J.-W., & Kim, R. (2012). Exploring factors that influence students' behaviors in information security. *Journal of Information Systems Education*, *23*(4), 407–415.

## KEY TERMS AND DEFINITIONS

**Attitude:** A student's positive or negative affect towards information security policy.

**Deterrence:** An action of discouraging improper security behavior by instilling fear of punishment.

**Information Security Awareness:** The degree to which students are conscious of acceptable security behavior.

**Information Security Knowledge Sharing:** The probability that students will willingly share the information security knowledge they have acquired.

**Information Security Policies (ISPs):** It denotes acceptable guidelines for ensuring institutions' information security.

**Information Systems (IS):** An integrated set of digital products for collecting, processing, and storing institutions' informational resources.

**Subjective Norm:** The likehood that a student will perform security behaviour because of the expectation of relevant others.

*Previously published in Modern Theories and Practices for Cyber Ethics and Security Compliance; pages 204-216, copyright year 2020 by Information Science Reference (an imprint of IGI Global).*

# Chapter 18
# Internal Marketing Cybersecurity– Conscious Culture

**Gordon Bowen**
*Northumbria University, London, UK*

**Atul Sethi**
*Ulster University, London, UK*

## ABSTRACT

*The chapter is putting forward the idea that internal marketing is a tool of which there are many to embed a culture to combat cybersecurity threats. This conceptual paper is suggesting that cybersecurity threats are multi-facet and although internal marketing is a major contributing factor in reducing the threats, other factors are in play. The shape of the organisation (i.e., bureaucratic or organic) has an important bearing on the implementation of a marketing-oriented culture, including that of internal marketing and, thus, the success of a cybersecurity-conscious organisational culture. Another significant factor in creating a cybersecurity-conscious organisational culture is the management willingness to empower and employees and their willingness to accept the responsibility to make decisions and be accountable, which requires acceptance of the authority.*

## INTRODUCTION

Cybercrime will cost societies $6 trillion annually by 2019, which is twice the cost of what was paid in 2015. Escalating at this rate requires serious action to be taken by organisations, society, and governments. To combat cybercrime currently, $1 trillion is spent on cybersecurity (radiusits.com). The focus of this paper is on the internal environment of the firm from the perspective of internal marketing to combat the internal threat of cybercrime and improve awareness of cybersecurity by using an internal marketing lenses.

DOI: 10.4018/978-1-6684-3698-1.ch018

The organisational landscape has a bearing on the effectiveness of combatting cybersecurity issues (Nye, 2017). Cybersecurity combines "public good" attributes, frequently associated with governmental responsibilities for private market goods and services, and private organisations with non-market, non-governmental resources, and information sharing. Management of governmental responsibilities requires a robust governance structure (Kuerbis & Badiei, 466, 2017). The paper suggests that not only governments and nations have responsibility for cybersecurity, but the organisation and employees have ownership of the governance structures internally to mitigate the effects of cybercrime. Furthermore, some of the responsibilities of government need to be cascaded down to organisations to gain the organisational commitment necessary for organisations to defend their organisation and employees against cybercrime. Shackelford & Kastelic, (2015) suggest there is a growing agreement that nations need to take responsibility for enhancing cybersecurity. Ultimately, governments and nations will require to engage organisations in cybersecurity, and organisations must shoulder more of the burden of cybersecurity. To ensure firms are ready to engage with the responsibilities of governance and activities related to cybersecurity, the paper contends that an internal marketing approach is necessary, because cybersecurity is everyone's responsibility, and employee responsibility is a key driver to guarantee cybersecurity safeguarding of the organisation.

## THEORETICAL CONCEPTS

### Determinants of internal marketing

"Market orientation", "market-driven" or "customer orientation" are used interchangeably and have a component of internal marketing orientation (IMO) (Naude´, Desai & Murphy,:1205, 2003). There is no agreed definition of the internal marketing construct (Rafiq & Ahmad, 2000). The use of marketing approaches within the organisation to create and publicise overall corporate values is an integral part of internal marketing (Hogg & Carter, 2000). The paper is positioning IMO as an important factor to embed a positive factor to embed employee engagement in detecting and preventing cybercrime within the organisation.

Schneider, (1990) and James el (1979) consider the perception of organisational climate is based on "person" and "situation" variables. Person x situation = perception of organisational climate. The Table 1 identifies the variables (Person and Situational) and the perception of the organisation (situation x person) (see *Table 1*).

Naude´, Desai & Murphy, (2003) develop the following hypotheses for the variables in Table 1:

1.  IMO will vary by age – younger age groups and generations will have stronger attitudes and transfer the expectations to the organisation. A significant factor is an age as a determinant of IMO. This implies that younger people's attitudes would need moulding to the organisational cybersecurity policies and procedures to ensure consistency in the operational requirements.
2.  IMO results from males (gender) will be positive. The results bear this out that there is a positive outcome between males and IMO. Females tend to be more critical than men. This particular variable is not significant as a determinant of IMO.

*Table 1. Possible determinants of internal marketing (Naude´, Desai & Murphy, 2003)*

| Variables | | |
|---|---|---|
| **Person** | **Situation** | **Person x situation** |
| 1 Age | 4. Location | 7. Organisational socialisation |
| 2. Gender | 5. Tenure | 8. Involvement |
| 3. Level of education | 6. Function | 9. Commitment |
| | | 10. Organisational satisfaction |
| | | 11. Communication |
| | | 12. Evaluation of local management |
| | | 12. Evaluation of direct manager |
| | | 13. Evaluation of colleagues |

3.  IMO results will correlate to education i.e. the higher the level of education the more critical the individual. The higher the level of education the more negative the perception of the organisation. This particular variable was not significant as an influencer of IMO.

4.  Different locations will view the organisation's IMO differently. This hypothesis is significant. This could be due to the different tasks being undertaken at different sites. This requires organisations to ensure the culture of cyber-security is consistent, so employees that locate from different locations with the firm will have a consistent approach to the threat of cybersecurity.

5.  The length of tenure correlates positively with IMO. The length of service correlates positively with IMO and is thus significant. Once a cybersecurity culture is in place, then from an IMO perspective those with long tenure under this culture could be more critical of the new culture and become less vigilant on cyber-security threats, than new employees.

6.  Different functions evaluate IMO differently. This is not a significant determinant of IMO.

7.  Reviewing the person and situation variables only age, tenure and locations are significant determinants of IMO.

8.  Organisational socialisation correlates positively to IMO. Organisational socialisation is defined " as the process by which an individual comes to appreciate the values, abilities, expected behaviours, and social knowledge essential for assuming an organisational role and for participating as an organisational member" (Louis, 1980, 229 -230). There is a correlation between IMO and organisational socialisation. However, higher levels of socialisation depend on the ability of the employees to cope positively with their work. The implication for cybersecurity is that employees that are less able to cope with their work, would be less able to exhibit the cybersecurity values and behaviours expected.

9.  There is a positive relationship between the degree of involvement and a respondent's IMO. This appears to be the case that involvement has a high significance on IMO. Engaged and involved employees are more willing to exhibit the necessary behaviour expected in a cybersecurity environment.

10. Commitment is positively related to the perception of IMO. This hypothesis is significant in its effect on IMO. Commitment is related to organisational goals and the individual acceptance of the goals. Also, a sense of belonging is an attribute of commitment.

11. Organisational satisfaction is linked to three dimensions i.e. reward satisfaction, stimulation from work and workload. The three factors are positively related to IMO.

12. Communications construct has two dimensions openness and information accuracy, which are positively related to IMO. Accuracy of information is slightly more significant than openness.

13. Employees' perception of local management's IMO correlates positively to their overall perception of the organisation's IMO. The employees' perception of local management market orientation is positively linked to IMO scores.

14. Employees' perception of supervisors' level of IMO correlates positively with the individual's perception of the organisation's IMO. The employees' perception of their supervisors' market orientation is positively linked to IMO scores.

15. Employees' overall perception of the company's IMO correlates positively with their relationship to co-workers and their perception of their colleagues' market-oriented behaviour. The perceived level of market orientation of colleagues does influence other employees own perceived level of IMO.

The most influential variables on IMO are the location (which depends on job function), length of tenure and age. The person x situation variables show that local and direct management, socialisation and satisfaction factors are important contributors to IMO.

## Internal Marketing Tools

In any organisations, it is important that all departments act as integrated systems, so that they achieve the organisational goals in a coordinated way. this requires interdepartmental exchange of ideas, knowledge, activities and internal services. services are acts of performances that one party offers to other, and the activities are essentially intangible, non-ownable, non-storable, heterogenous, perishable and variable. The unique characteristics of services requires, a three-dimensional marketing approach. The three dimensions of service marketing are illustrated by service marketing triangle (see Figure 1), that argues for External Marketing, Internal Marketing and Interactive Marketing (Dabhade & Yadav, 2013).

The external marketing efforts are directed by the organisation towards understanding and exceeding its customers' expectations, the Internal marketing are the activities the organisation must carry on to train, motivate, and reward its employees m so the employees are able and willing to deliver the customer services to the customers; and the interactional marketing incudes those activities that involves interaction between the employees with the customers (Dabhade & Yadav, 2013). Unless the organisations market the ideas, knowledge, practices and procedures related to wide range of activities including that related to cyber security; it will not be possible to offer secure services to the customers.

Understanding internal marketing in terms of marketing principles and the context of employees has been researched for more than 30 years (Berry et al, 1976). Traditional communication techniques of promotion, such as advertising and personal selling are common approaches to promote products to external customers. These techniques are also used to communicate with employees (Berry, 1981). Berry et al, (1976) related internal marketing to employees (internal customers) and jobs as products. Munir (2015) suggests that internal marketing is not just about communications tactics, such as employee commitment, workplace posters, and employee meetings. Internal communication is a significant component of internal marketing. Furthermore, internal communication is a new employer-employee contract (Varey

*Figure 1. Service marketing triangle*

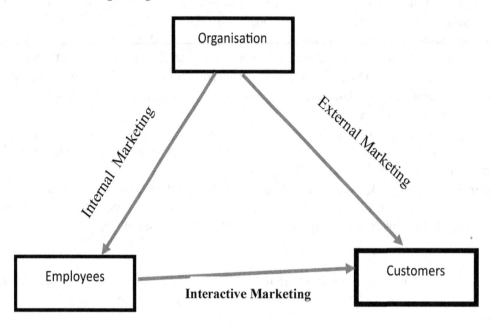

& Lewis, 1999). Effective management of internal communications could bring many organisational benefits (Piercy & Morgan, 1995).

Internal marketing in many parts of the literature is associated with marketing techniques in a human resource management resource context to continuously improve employer-employee relationship to satisfy employees and customers (Kotler & Armstrong, 1991; Wildes & Parkes, 2005). Abzari, Ghorbani & Madani (2011) consider internal marketing as part of the human resource function.

Furthermore, research suggests that training is an underpinning dimension of internal marketing, which can be sub-divided into four categories, namely service standards, training, development programmes and rewards (Papasolomou & Vrontis, 2006). Lee & Chen (2005), further conceptualised that internal marketing as having five functions, namely recruitment, training, incentives, communications and retaining employees, all are human resource functions. 11 of the 42 internal marketing definitions focus on training apart from customer focus (Huang & Rundle-Thiele, 2015). Implementation of internal marketing requires employees with skills and information (Paraskevas, 2001). Internal marketing requires employee know-how and autonomy to meet their wants and needs (Ballantye, 1997).

Internal marketing research is an important starting point, which will be survey-based on internal marketing practices measurements (Huang & Rundle-Thiele, 2015). The type of data that could be collected include:

Supervisors clearly state their expectations of others (Bearden & Niemeyer, 1999); Receiving feedback from supervisors that informs the employees' progress (Bearden & Niemeyer, 1999); Supervisor clearly states expectations of me (Bearden & Niemayer, 1999); Supervisors do a good job of sharing information (Bearden & Niemayer, 1999; Naude´, Desai & Murphy, 2003; Tsai & Tang, 2008); Communication is weak between departments and employees (Peltier & Scovotti, 2005); Employees can reach managers easily (Chang & Chang, 2008); Employees have a solid understanding of the ways the organisation evaluates their work (Karasa et al, 2008; Chang & Chang, 2008); and Employees at all levels understand the direction and key priorities of the organisation (Huang & Rundle-Thiele, 2015).

In order to embed cybersecurity practices and governance, an internal marketing approach requires engagement with employees to create dialogue and understanding of the organisation and management expectations from the process and practices. Dialogue between employees and ensuring information is relevant and accurate will underpin the success of embedding cybersecurity practices. The model to embed cybersecurity practices includes internal communications, training and internal research. Although all dimensions are significant, training is the most important. Worth noting is that the model is based on western culture, and differences are likely to occur in eastern culture.

## Internal Marketing And Cybersecurity Environment

Data security and privacy are pressing issues facing marketing today (Ferrell, 2017). The domains that are suggested as important to marketers are related to consumers, organisational, ethical, and legal (Martin & Murphy, 2017). Consumers, organisations and regulators are important stakeholders. Organisations collect and use consumer data for marketing activities, which are required for marketing activities. Consumers sacrifice privacy so that marketers can understand their wants and needs, which is necessary for competitiveness (Romanosky, 2016). Organisations have a responsibility and opportunity to protect consumer data. The organisational culture should press for increase cybersecurity internally (opportunity for internal marketing and its ability to influence organisational culture) and externally. Consequently, organisations need to carry out a risk assessment on the use and protection of the data. Marketing research needs to investigate the interface between using and acquiring data. Marketing requirements for big data and data analytics suggest that most organisations are at risk (Ferrell, 2017). This suggests that cybersecurity is the responsibility both legally and ethically for organisations and they have a responsibility to develop and implement governance rules and processes for handling data internally.

Understanding the nature and properties of privacy ethic is a step in the right direction to prevent cybersecurity issues. Organisations interact with regulatory and legal bodies to ensure and develop compliance, but this interaction could lead to conflict (Martin & Murphy, 2017).

Decisions on cybersecurity are a strategic decision. Ferrell (2017) state that ethics form part and parcel of every strategic decision in the digital environment. Understanding the risks digital systems put on consumers is important. The systems contain diverse and sensitive information, such as credit card details and national insurance numbers. Understanding the risks associated with holding this data is paramount. Donaldson & Dunfee (1994) suggest research around stakeholder norms and based on integrative stakeholder theory using ethical perspectives and social contract theory is a requirement. However, the organisation may accept or comply with stakeholder norms, but they may also not wish to do so. Hypernorms (help to evaluate lower level norms that are applied to develop the roots of ethical acceptability) for stakeholders may be areas organisations may wish to avoid. Organisational norms will decide, which stakeholders are important and if data privacy is a top priority. Also, do they have the resources to protect consumers (Maignan & Ferrell, 2004)? Internal marketing or an internal marketing orientation culture cannot protect against cybersecurity issues if the organisation does not put the necessary resources in place and the nature of cybersecurity issues means resources must be sustained and developed and updated.

As stated earlier social contracts is an avenue to protect privacy but social contracts (all contracts) are based on fairness. Research on the harm an act or practice can cause, which gives rise to unfairness is document by Ohlhausen (2014). Unfairness could be applied to data privacy risk assessment and the prevention of data breaches (Ferrell, 2017). Frameworks suggested to reduce unfairness is justice theory and power responsibility equilibrium. The frameworks would be able to express fairness expectations (Martin & Murphy, 2017). Ferrell & Gresham (1985) developed a descriptive model for understanding ethical decisions in an organisation. Privacy decisions the model indicate individual values, and attitudes, organisational factors (impact of significant others) and opportunities (policies and compliance requirements). Specialised code of ethics for top financial and accounting officers improve the integrity of financial reporting (Ahluwalia et al, 2016). Specialised data privacy codes should help organisations develop a more effective data privacy culture thatsupports ethical decisions. Importantly, is an understanding of the risks to the organisation and consumers and the development of effective cybersecurity (Ferrell, 2017).

All organisations should have a privacy crisis management or a backup plan to minimise the risks from data breaches. The plan needs embedding in an ethic and compliance programme for data privacy and security. Those that think social contracts, values, policies, and norms can be an effective deterrent in cybersecurity has not consider external risk, which requires collaboration with other organisations (Ferrell, 2017).

Possibly one the greatest risk is complacency by the organisation and the consumer in protecting their data and privacy. Akhter (2014) found the self-efficacy influenced privacy concerns negatively. Privacy concerns impacts the frequency of online transactions, reasons why organisations must protect consumer privacy and data. Ferrell (2017) suggest that marketing research should evolve to include frameworks to address and raise awareness of issues that influence cybersecurity. The impact on cybersecurity on brand image, erosion of consumer trust and organisations reputation. Cybersecurity is an external threat and is uncontrollable making trust difficult to secure. Internal marketing is not a panacea to cybersecurity issues but is a stepping stone along with new techniques not yet developed.

## Internal Marketing and Firm's Performance

The empirical evidence gives limited support that is positive correlation exists between internal marketing practices, organisational effectiveness and organisational performance (Ahmed, Rafiq & Saad, 2003). Galpin (1997) coined the phrase "organisational influencer systems" are required to implement business strategy internally. The framework identified a number of factors to embed business strategy internally and could be designated the internal marketing mix. The factors are identified below:

- Strategic rewards;
- Internal communications;
- Training and development;
- Organisational structure;
- Senior leadership;
- Physical environment;
- Staffing, selection, and recruitment;
- Interfunctional coordination;
- Incentive systems;
- Empowerment; and
- Operational/process changes.

There is much similarity between this framework and others already discussed. It is worth noting that strategic rewards and incentive systems serve different purposes. Incentive systems are a basic requirement to motivate individuals' actions such as organisational culture, values and business activities behaviour (Pfeiffer, 1998), whilst strategic rewards are linked to motivating future performance to achieve business goals (Hale, 1998). Incentive systems are backward looking and strategic rewards is a forwarding looking factor. The previous discussion has linked cybersecurity to strategic decisions, which implies it is important for the future prosperity of the organisation. This, in turn, suggests that to influence cybersecurity behaviour the internal marketing factor of strategic rewards has an important part to play.

The paper by Ahmed, Rafiq & Saad, (2003) is proposing that the internal marketing mix developed by Galpin (1997) will lead to improved individual and organisational performance, by managing the interdependent elements in the internal marketing mix.

Organisational competitive advantage is discussed in two contexts, namely competitive forces (Porter, 1980; 1985) and resource-based view (Barney, 1991; Prahalad & Hamel, 1990). Supporters of the Porter view of strategy is that competitive advantage comes from analysis and understanding the industry environment to determine a unique position, which is known as "strategic position". Counter to this strategy is the resource-based view (RBV), which relies on "core competencies" or "distinctive competences" to develop a competitive strategy (Prahalad & Hamel, 1990). Core competences are organisational based capability according to Prahalad & Hamel (1990). Taking an RBV approach to strategy the organisational competencies that will improve a firm's performance is based on the three internal marketing constructs are Ahmed, Rafiq & Saad, (2003):

- Customer/market orientation;
- Employee satisfaction; and
- Specific/individual competencies.

The external marketing philosophy (market/customer oriented) and marketing tools will also mediate the relationship between internal marketing and the organisational competence constructs and the firm's performance (Ahmed, Rafiq & Saad, 2003). The research postulates the following:

There is a significant and positive relationship between the internal marketing mix and business performance.

Organisational competences mediate the relationships of internal marketing mix with business performance.

Application of marketing-like philosophy and application of marketing-like tools moderates the relationship between the internal marketing mix and organisational competencies.

All the above hypotheses were supported. The internal marketing mix is a method to support and facilitate organisational competencies. The results support the role of top management as the initiator of internal marketing (Barnes, 1989), and it requires continuous support (George, 1990). Gro¨nroos (1981) states make the point that internal management should be part of strategic management. The results are also supportive of the notion that senior management is an important driver of market orientation (Kohli & Jaworski, 1990).

## SKILLS TO REDUCE CYBERSECURITY ATTACKS

Skills are a combination of knowledge, experience, and abilities that the user can apply to be successful (Levy, 2005; Boyatzis & Kolb, 1991). The acquisition of skills is a multi-stage process and is a learning process linked to incremental stages (Gravill, Compeau, & Marcolin, 2006). Stage 1 is the initial acquisition of the skills (declarative knowledge). This type of knowledge is given by instruction and information to the recipient of the knowledge. The recipient receives fundamental knowledge (Gravill, Compeau, & Marcolin, 2006). Stage 2 is practicing the declarative knowledge to convert it into procedural knowledge (Neves & Anderson, 1981). In this stage, knowledge is organised and users can the knowledge to accomplish activities (Gravill, Compeau, & Marcolin, 2006). Stage 3 is the final stage and is characterized by autonomous and efficiency by practicing activities and gaining more experience. This improves skills further. Experience is a positive influence on computer usage, which reinforces the need for skills (Gravill, Compeau, & Marcolin, 2006). A generalisation of procedural knowledge and increase performance comes throughout the stages (Gravill, Compeau, & Marcolin, 2006). Skills honed over time become competences (Eschenbrenner & Nah, 2014).

Competence is a high level of skill that can be certified or allow a person to practice in a profession (Levy & Ramin, 2015). Maturing knowledge of a person improves skills, which develops the user's competency (Eschenbrenner & Nah, 2014). Competency (knowledge, experience, and abilities) is acquired once a skill is practiced over time (Levy & Ramin, 2015).

According to Goode & Levy (2017), IT (information technology) skills are those skills that relate to software, hardware, and programming in order to develop technical skills in IS (information systems). IT skills are becoming the norm in the work environment, as IT becomes a fixture in the workplace (Weigel & Hazen, 2014). Competence in IT empower users and has an impact on the users' workplace productivity and leadership effectiveness (Marcolin, et al, 2000).IT skills are essential for organisations to gain competitive parity, butthe management of those IT skills that enables the organisation to sustain a competitive advantage (Downey & Smith, 2000). The ability of a firm to have competences in cybersecurity, over and above current IT skills would enhance an organisation's sustain competitive advantage. Cybersecurity would move from an exclusively IT role to an organisation-wide responsibility, thus becoming part of the strategic decision making process in the organisation. Verizon Enterprise Solutions (2014) carried out a survey and the results suggested that data breaches are found by users armed with the necessary identification and reporting skills. The implication is that technology alone cannot guarantee security (Carlton, Levy & Ramim, 2018). Users' failure to take countermeasures when a breach is perceived to be responsible for interference in productivity (Choi, Levy, & Hovav, 2013). The most recurring data breaches since 2003 can be classified as miscellaneous errors, crimeware, insider misuse, and physical theft/loss. All are due to human error or misuse (Verizon Enterprise Solutions, 2015). Social engineering is a continuing cause for concern, "unfortunately, even the best security mechanisms can be bypassed through social engineering" (Winkler & Dealy, 1995:1). Social engineering is seen as a greater threat to organisations and people (Kvedar, Nettis, & Fulton, 2010). However, the top three security issues are namely, malware, use of stole personal information, and phishing (Verizon Enterprise Solutions, 2016).

Organisational competencies show a partial correlation as a mediator of organisational performance. However, marketing-oriented behaviour is an important mediator between internal marketing mix and business performance (Ahmed, Rafiq & Saad, 2003; Kohli & Jaworski, 1990; Narver & Slater, 1990). The internal marketing mix is a strong predictor of employee satisfaction, but employee satisfaction is not a significant mediator for internal marketing mix- performance relationship. The literature identifies that job satisfaction and customer perceptions of quality for UK financial advisers that no relationship exists (Ahmed, Rafiq & Saad, 2003; Herrington & Lomax, 1999). Market-oriented philosophy has a moderating influence on the internal marketing mix and organisational competences (Ahmed, Rafiq & Saad, 2003; Quester & Kelly, 1999).

Concluding from the research by Ahmed, Rafiq & Saad, (2003), firstly, improving organisational competencies improves business performance. Undoubtedly, improved cybersecurity is an organisational competence that has become more and more pressing due to the prevalence of the internet, and consequently, business performance will move forward. Market and customer orientation and individual and specific competencies are strong influencers on business performance. From their research job, satisfaction does not receive much support. Nevertheless, job satisfaction is an important factor. Secondly, the elements that build organisational competencies are empowerment, top management support, strategic rewards, physical environment, internal communication, interfunctional co-ordination and training, and development. Finally, managers can enhance the variables in the internal marketing mix that influence organisational competencies by adopting a marketing-centric philosophy towards human resource issues and use market type tools such as market research, segmentation, etc. for implementing human resource strategies.

## A Framework to Assess Cybersecurity

One cannot eliminate risk entirely so one needs to mitigate risk. Cybersecurity risk is associated with a disruption to the business and instantaneous loss caused by a malicious cyber situation (NIST, 2014). National Institute of Standards and Technology (NIST, 2014, 8 - 9) created a framework to assess cybersecurity with the following functions:

**Step 1. Identity:** Develop organisational understanding in these areas (assets, systems, data, and capability) to manage cybersecurity risks in asset management, business environment, governance, risk assessment, and risk management;

**Step 2. Protect:** Develop and implement appropriate safeguards to ensure delivery of critical infrastructure services, i.e. access control, awareness and training, data security, information protection processes and procedures, maintenance and protective technology;

**Step 3. Detect:** Development and implement the appropriate activities to identify the occurrence of a cybersecurity event, i.e. anomalies and events, security continuous monitoring and detection processes;

**Step 4. Respond:** Develop and implement the appropriate activities to identify to take action regarding a cybersecurity event, i.e. response planning, communications, analysis, mitigation, and improvements;

**Step 5. Recover:** Develop and implement the appropriate activities to maintain plans for resilience and restore any capabilities or services that were impaired due to a cybersecurity event, i.e. recovery planning, improvements, and communications.

The 5 functions are continuous cyclical and current in nature.

Research by Carlton, Levy and Ramim (2018) suggests non-IT professional should have opportunities to develop appropriate cybersecurity skills and to use a tool (Cybersecurity Index) to assess the cybersecurity skill level in the organisation. Application of the tool enables management to identify skill gaps in relation to cybersecurity and moves away from the survey approach to determine deficiencies. Gender, hours accessing the internet, job function, or other demographic determinants were not found to be significant factors in influencing the level of cybersecurity skills. Individual skills found to minimise cybersecurity threat are the following:

- Preventing the leaking of confidential digital information to unauthorized individuals Sk1;
- Preventing malware via non-secure websites Sk2;
- Preventing personally identifiable information theft via access to non-secure websites Sk3;
- Preventing personally identifiable information theft via email phishing Sk4;
- Preventing malware via email Sk5;
- Preventing credit card theft by purchasing from non-secure websites Sk6;
- Preventing information system compromise via USB or storage device exploitations Sk7;
- Preventing unauthorised information system access via password exploitations Sk8;
- Preventing personally identifiable information theft via social networks Sk9.
- The skills are categorised as follow leading to Cybersecurity Skills Index:
- Work Information Systems (Sk1, Sk7 & Sk8)
- Malware (Sk2, Sk5 & Sk6)
- Personal identifiable information (Sk3, Sk4, & Sk9)
- Overall Cybersecurity Skills Index based on the above categories.

Skills relating to reduction in unauthorised leakage of confidential information were significantly improved as a result of increased age, advanced education level and use of IT systems during the course of employment. Preventing personally identifiable information theft on social media improved with time spent on the internet, which is not unsurprising.

Cybersecurity awareness is a short-term solution that only provides employees with exposure. However, cybersecurity training and education that includes hands-on cybersecurity activities with scenario-building exercises, deliver knowledge, skills and deeper understanding that enable employees to develop the right cybersecurity skills (Whitman Mattord, 2018).

## Internal Marketing Implementation

Although internal marketing is a growing and important area of marketing for academic, there are few models that deal with its implementation (Ballantyne, 2003; Gilmore & Carson, 1995). The different approaches to the implementation of internal marketing include Woodruffe (1995) argues the principal elements of internal marketing programme are training and personnel development, effective internal communications, integration technique, and motivational programmes to increase knowledge and understanding of market orientation. Ballantyne (1996) suggests that a bank approach to internal marketing by focusing on customer orientation is an appropriate approach. The bank launched a "customer service improvement programme", with the desire to change staff attitudes by the use of formal communications and engagement of staff in policy and procedures changes. There are only a few internal marketing models on implementation (Papasolomou, 2006).

Implementation of internal marketing requires a supportive board of directors, chief executive and other top senior executives (Felton, 1959). Unless the organisation receives clear signals from top-management internal marketing will find it challenging to take root in the organisation culture. Coupled with this is the need for interfunctional co-ordination support, especially between marketing and HRM departments (Rafiq & Ahmed, 1993; Ahmed, Rafiq & Saad, 2003). Interaction between departments also facilitates information sharing, leading to responsiveness to customer needs in relation to quality, products, and services (Kohli & Jaworski, 1990; Narver & Slater, 1990). Another benefit of implementing internal marketing will improve the overall business process in the organisation (Ahmed, Rafiq & Saad, 2003; Varey, 1995).

Organisational structure influences how organisations adapt to changes in the external environment. Two organisational structures developed for two different environments developed by (Burns & Stalker, 1961):

1.  The mechanistic model is suitable for stable and unchanging external environments. The emphasis is on rules, procedures, and dominated by a hierarchy of authority; and
2.  The organic model is suitable for uncertain external environments. The emphasis is on free-flowing, decentralised, and more adaptive organisational system (Buchanan & Huczynski, 1991).

The mechanistic model of organisational design is associated with bureaucracy, which implies extensive departmentalism, high formalisation, a limited information network (downward communication), and not much participation by lower ranked employees in decision making (Robins, 1996).

Employee empowerment is the link to successful internal marketing. A formal marketing plan for an internal market is of little value if customer contact staff are not motivated and empowered to deliver the level of service quality required (Payne, 1993: 37). Gilmore & Carson (1995) state that the involvement and empowerment of employees to enable them to make decisions relating to customers is part of the internal marketing activities. Employee empowerment is paramount for service organisations. Pushing decision lower in the organisation and empowering people close to the customer is a crucial factor for internal marketing (French & Bell, 1995). One could argue that employees that are not empowered and cannot make decisions relating to customers they interact could lower morale and deliver inferior service to customers. Empowered employees are more committed, more productive, more competent, more satisfied and innovative, while they create high-quality products and service than non-empowered employees (Whetten, Cameron & Wood (1996); Greenberger & Strasser, 1991 & Spreitzer, 1992). A contrary view is that employee empowerment will result in higher labour costs, which could result in slower or inconsistent service delivery, and bad decisions on the part of employees (Bowen & Lawler, 1996). Consequently, it could lead to dissatisfied customers, negative word of mouth communications, and higher prices, which no organisation can afford.

An organisation's structure can facilitate or inhibit empowerment. Rigid organisational structures will limit empowerment, to minimise the effect of this type of organisation elimination of bureaucratic rules and in its place organisational support systems that encourage empowerment (Peters, 1988). Freedom to take risks, flexibility, and to make mistakes need embedding in the organisation structure so it becomes part of the market orientation culture. Implementation of internal marketing is to change the organisational culture and leverage the dimensions of internal marketing (image of the internal customer, training and development, internal performance standards, and rewards systems). Results from a bank that used the above dimensions to improve service quality and customer satisfaction led to dissatisfied customers and divisiveness amongst staff and ambiguity. In the background the bank is engaging in compulsory redundancy, the prospects for promotion or job rotation is stagnant and lack of employee empowerment in terms of decision making and organisational rigidities that stop staff from meeting expectations of internal and external customers. Bureaucratic and mechanistic structures in banks hinder the benefits of internal marketing and they need to move to organic structures that are supportive of marketing oriented environments. Empowerment alone cannot create a marketing oriented culture if employees are not given decision-making powers and are willing to take responsibility and authority (Papasolomou, 2006).

## IMPLICATION TO MANAGEMENT

Cybersecurity is a major threat to the internal workings of an organisation. The ability of the organisation to respond to the threat of cybersecurity depends on the organisational structure and how it engages and empowers its employees. In business, we tend to think of security issues as external i.e. keeping them out of the organisation, but cybersecurity is an internal threat that have entered the organisation from the external environment (outside the organisation). Cybersecurity issues can also be introduced by employees (Carlton, Levy & Ramim, 2018). The underlying assumption in this paper is that cybersecurity enters from the external environment and internal marketing is a tool to manage the internal/external interface of the threat. Effective management of the interface requires senior management support and facilitation and an organisational mind-set that puts the customer at the centre of the organisation, a customer-centric organisation. Internal marketing is a technique to manage the boundary between the external and internal environments. Senior management involvement is imperative, because cybersecurity decisions are strategic and require the right decision makers to be fully cognisant of the issues and have the strategic leverage to allocate the resources required in the implementation process. Cybersecurity makes internal marketing an organisational-wide activity, thus linking into the strategic planning process. However, the internal marketing technique and the management of interface might vary dependent on the organisational structure. A bureaucratic organisation will find a marketing orientation approach more demanding to implement than an adaptive organisation, the so-called organic model. One significant issue is to ensure the organisation is cybersecurity ready, which requires understanding where the deficiencies in cybersecurity knowledge and understanding lay within the organisation. This is the subject of the next paragraph.

Cybersecurity issues are not a constant and will mutate, which will require the organisation to adopt a flexible and nimble organisational structure. The organic structure would appear to be more adaptable to cybersecurity threats, but not all organisations can adopt such a structure due to the nature of the business. Firms that require a procedural approach to decision making may find it challenging to adopt an organic structure. Cybersecurity decision making requires an approach that is decentralised and autonomous approach to enable threats to be dealt with swiftly and in a timely manner. Cybersecurity threats as stated earlier is an organisational threat and internal marketing techniques must permeate across the organisation. Collaboration between different functions is an imperative and detection and prevention techniques shared continuously across the organisation. Sharing knowledge and information on cybersecurity internally solves the problem reactively. There is a need for collaboration across industries and other firms even competitors so that cybersecurity threats take on a proactive stance. This will enable organisations to alert others to new threats, sharing best practice improving internal marketing techniques by applying and developing models such as CSI, develop common training and development programmes and develop governance systems that integrate not only within the organisation, but across different organisations. Adoption of the collective approach to fighting cybersecurity means more resources are being marshalled and there is an economies of scale advantage for the participating organisations. More eyes watching cybersecurity activities helps to minimise the effect of social engineering, which is still the biggest threat to undermining cybersecurity governance. Bureaucratic organisation with the centralised approach to decision making may have to deploy autonomous cybersecurity groups that can make cybersecurity decisions proactively. These groups would have to be organisation-wide and communications between them seamless to share information and update programmes and activities. The cybersecurity grouping in a bureaucratic organisation must have a market orientation approach, which is the glue to make organisations become cybersecurity proof.

Internal marketing is an important determinant for detecting and defeating cybersecurity threats. Employee engagement is an important factor, which will lead to employee empowerment, but the organisational structure, procedures, and policies might inhibit this process. Research on inhibitors to employee engagement and market orientation will be a prerequisite to a successful cybersecurity strategy. The governance structure for cybersecurity should link to the strategic planning process and will influence HRM strategy in relation to IT skillsets, recruitment, retention, and strategic rewards. Awareness of cybersecurity issues will be sufficient for some staff, but to be effective engagement in training and development will be the only convincing way to give the organisation and employees the skills required to guard against cyber-threats. However, this will require additional expense, which not all organisations can afford or are willing to pay. There will need to be a trade-off, which will vary with the organisation. Cybersecurity needs to be recognised by the organisation as a team effort, so that strategic rewards are for the whole team and not for individual performance. The implementation of internal marketing will play an important role in achieving the desired objectives.

Cybersecurity tends to be the preserve of computing. Nevertheless, marketing needs to engage with research in this area, because it affects consumers in many ways from their behaviour, perception of the organisation and employees, brand integrity, customer satisfaction, customer relations to product and service quality. Marketing may be required to adopt appropriate governance procedures and policies on cybersecurity on how they deal with customers that have been compromised by cybersecurity threat. The TSB bank is returning money to customers taken from their bank account via cybersecurity action(s). Will more organisations have to relax customer rules and policies to offset and minimise the impact of cybersecurity threats?

## CONCLUSION

Cybersecurity cannot be departmentalised and communications localised. All staff must be engaged in cybersecurity activities and awareness training is not sufficient. Development training from training course to scenario activities to give the hands-on are necessary components to bring staff to the appropriate skillset to minimise the cybersecurity threat. Given the nature of cybersecurity requirements, it will not be a cheap exercise, and hence the strategic imperative needs to be factored in. Cybersecurity implementation will incur many costs from ensuring there is an internal marketing culture of market orientation, awareness training to extensive training and development in cybersecurity. To ensure there is value for the organisation cybersecurity needs to be more prominent in organisations so it has an effective governance system and is embedded the corporate strategy process, thus it becomes part of the strategic decision-making process. This will help to elevate its status to senior management, drive the necessary organisational and human resource management changes. Importantly, internal marketing alone cannot fix the cybersecurity threat, and the internal and external environments will be significant influencers. Cybersecurity safety is a multi-dimensional problem and requires many actors to come together to formulate an overarching strategy.

# REFERENCES

Abzari, M., Ghorbani, H., & Madani, F. A. (2011). The effect of internal marketing on organizational commitment from market-orientation viewpoint in hotel industry in Iran. *International Journal of Marketing Studies*, *3*(1), 147–155. doi:10.5539/ijms.v3n1p147

Ahluwalia, S., Ferrell, O. C., Ferrell, L., & Rittenburg, T. (2016). BSarbanes-Oxley 406 Code of Ethics for Senior Financial Officers and Firm Behavior. *Journal of Business Ethics*, *151*(3), 693–705. doi:10.100710551-016-3267-7

Ahmad, P. K., Rafiq, M., & Saad, N. M. (2003). Internal marketing and the mediating role of organisational competences. *European Journal of Marketing*, *37*(9), 1221–1241. doi:10.1108/03090560310486960

Akhter, S. H. (2014). Privacy concern and online transactions:the impact of internet self-efficiency and internet involvement. *Journal of Consumer Marketing*, *31*(2), 118–125. doi:10.1108/JCM-06-2013-0606

Ballantyne, D. (1996). Internal networks for internal marketing. In *Proceedings of 4th International Colloquium in Relationship Marketing*. Swedish School of Economics.

Ballantyne, D. (1997). Relationship marketing of services-perspectives from 1983 and 2000. *Journal of Marketing Management*, *13*(5), 343–366. doi:10.1080/0267257X.1997.9964479

Ballantyne, D. (2003). A relationship-mediated theory of internal marketing. *European Journal of Marketing*, *37*(9/10), 1242–1260. doi:10.1108/03090560310486979

Barnes, J. G. (1989). The role of internal marketing: If the staff won't buy it, why should the customer? *Irish Marketing Review*, *4*(2), 11–21.

Barney, J. B. (1991). Firm resources and sustained competitive advantage. *Journal of Management*, *17*(1), 99–120. doi:10.1177/014920639101700108

Bearden, W. O., & Netemeyer, R. G. (1999). *Handbook of Marketing Scales: Multi-Item Measures for Marketing and Consumer Behavior Research* (2nd ed.). SAGE Publications. doi:10.4135/9781412984379

Berry, L. L. (1981). The employee as customer. *Journal of Retail Banking*, *3*(1), 25–28.

Berry, L. L., Hensel, J. S., & Burke, M. C. (1976). Improving retailer capability for effective consumerism response. *Journal of Retailing*, *52*(3), 3–14.

Bowen, D.E. & Lawler, E.E. III. (1992). The empowerment of service workers: what, why, how, and when. *Sloan Management Review*, *8*(1), 31-9.

Boyatzis, R. E., & Kolb, D. A. (1991). Assessing individuality in learning: The learning skills profile. *Educational Psychology*, *11*(3/4), 279–295. doi:10.1080/0144341910110305

Buchanan, D., & Huczynski, A. (1991). *Organisational Behaviour: An Introductory Text* (2nd ed.). Englewood Cliffs, NJ: Prentice-Hall.

Burns, T., & Stalker, G. M. (1961). *The Management of Innovation*. London: Tavistock.

Carlton, M., Levy, Y., & Ramim, M. (2019). Mitigating cyber attacks through the measurement of non-IT professionals' cybersecurity skills. *Technology Information & Computer Security*, *27*(1), 101–121. doi:10.1108/ICS-11-2016-0088

Chang, C. S., & Chang, H. C. (2008). Perceptions of internal marketing. *Journal of Advanced Nursing*, *8*(87), 92–100. PMID:19120584

Choi, M. S., Levy, Y., & Hovav, A. (2013), The role of user computer self-efficacy, cybersecurity countermeasures awareness, and cybersecurity skills influence on computer misuse. *Proceedings of the Pre-International Conference of Information Systems (ICIS) SIGSEC – Workshop on Information Security and Privacy (WISP) 2013*. Available at: http://aisel.aisnet.org/wisp2012/29

Donaldson, T., & Dunfee, T. W. (1994). Toward a Unified Conception of Business Ethics: Integrative Social Contracts Theory. *Academy of Management Review*, *19*(2), 252–284. doi:10.5465/amr.1994.9410210749

Downey, J. P., & Smith, L. A. (2011). The role of computer attitudes in enhancing computer competence in training. *Journal of Organizational and End User Computing*, *23*(3), 81–100. doi:10.4018/joeuc.2011070105

Eschenbrenner, B., & Nah, F. F.-H. (2014). Information systems user competency: A conceptual foundation. *Communications of the Association for Information Systems*, *34*, 1363–1378. doi:10.17705/1CAIS.03480

Felton, A. P. (1959, July). Making the marketing concept work. *Harvard Business Review*, 55–65.

Ferrell, O. C. (2017). Broadening marketing's contribution to data privacy. *Journal of the Academy of Marketing Science*, *5*(2), 160–163. doi:10.100711747-016-0502-9

Ferrell, O. C., & Gresham, L. G. (1985). A Contingency Framework for Understanding Ethical Decision Making in Marketing. *Journal of Marketing*, *49*(3), 87–96. doi:10.1177/002224298504900308

French, W. L., & Bell, C. H. Jr. (1995). *Organisational Development* (5th ed.). Englewood Cliffs, NJ: Prentice-Hall.

Galpin, T. J. (1997). Making strategy work. *The Journal of Business Strategy*, *18*(1), 12–14. doi:10.1108/eb039824

George, W. R. (1977). The retailing of services – a challenging future. *Journal of Retailing*, *53*(3), 85–98.

Gilmore, A., & Carson, D. (1995). Managing and marketing to internal customers. In W. J. Glynn & J. G. Barnes (Eds.), *Understanding Services Management* (pp. 295–321). Chichester, UK: John Wiley & Sons.

Goode, J., & Levy, Y. (2017). Towards empirical exploration of employee's cybersecurity countermeasures awareness and skills: differences in training delivery method and program type. *Proceeding of the Knowledge Management (KM) 2017 Conference, Faculty of Information Studies (FiS)*, 18-30.

Gravill, J. I., Compeau, D. R., & Marcolin, B. I. (2006). Experience effects on the accuracy of self-assessed user competence. *Information & Management*, *43*(3), 378–394. doi:10.1016/j.im.2005.10.001

Greenberger, D. B., & Strasser, S. (1991). The role of situational and dispositional factors in the enhancement of personal control in organisations. *Research in Organizational Behavior*, *13*, 111–145.

Hale, J. (1998). Strategic rewards: Keeping your best talent from walking out the door. *Compensation and Benefits Management, 14*(3), 39–50.

Herrington, G., & Lomax, W. (1999). Do satisfied employees make customers satisfied? An investigation into the relationship between service employee job satisfaction and customer perceived service quality. In *Marketing and Competition in the Information Age, Proceedings of the 28th EMAC Conference*. Humboldt University.

Hogg, G., & Carter, S. (2000). Employee attitudes and responses to internal marketing. In R. Varey & B. Lewis (Eds.), *Internal Marketing: Directions for Management* (pp. 109–124). London: Routledge. doi:10.4324/9780203207352.ch7

Huang, Y.-T., & Rundle-Thiele, S. (2015). A holistic management tool for measuring internal marketing activities. *Journal of Services Marketing, 29*(6/7), 571–584. doi:10.1108/JSM-03-2015-0112

James, L., Gent, M., Hater, J., & Coray, K. (1979). Correlates of psychological influence: An illustration of the psychological climate approach to work environment perceptions. *Personnel Psychology, 32*(3), 563–588. doi:10.1111/j.1744-6570.1979.tb02154.x

Karasa, A., & Akinci, F., EsatoElu, A.E., Parsons, A.L., & Sarp, N. (2008). An evaluation of the opinions of hospital employees regarding the contribution of internal marketing to the application of total quality management in Turkey. *Health Marketing Quarterly, 24*(3), 167–187. PMID:19042534

Kohli, A., & Jaworski, B. (1990). Market orientation: The construct, research propositions, and managerial implications. *Journal of Marketing, 54*, 1–18. doi:10.1177/002224299005400201

Kotler, P., & Armstrong, G. (1991). *Principles of Marketing* (5th ed.). Englewood Cliffs, NJ: Prentice-Hall.

Kuerbis, B., & Badiei, F. (2017). Mapping the cybersecurity institutional landscape. *Digital Policy. Regulation & Governance, 19*(6), 466–492. doi:10.1108/DPRG-05-2017-0024

Kvedar, D., Nettis, M., & Fulton, S. P. (2010). The use of formal social engineering techniques to identify weaknesses during a computer vulnerability competition. *Journal of Computing Sciences in Colleges, 26*(2), 80–87.

Lee, C., & Chen, W. J. (2005). The effects of internal marketing and organisational culture on knowledge management in the information technology industry. *International Journal of Management, 22*(4), 661–672.

Levy, Y. (2005). A case study of management skills comparison in online MBA programs. *International Journal of Information and Communication Technology Education, 1*(3), 1–20. doi:10.4018/jicte.2005070101

Levy, Y., & Ramim, M. M. (2015). An assessment of competency-based simulations on e-learners' management skills enhancements. *Interdisciplinary Journal of E-Learning and Lifelong Learning, 11*, 179-190. Available at: www.ijello.org/Volume11/IJELLv11p179-190Levy1958.pdf

Louis, M. (1980). Surprise and sense making: What newcomers experience in entering unfamiliar organisational settings. *Administrative Science Quarterly, 25*(2), 226–249. doi:10.2307/2392453 PMID:10247029

Maignan, I., & Ferrell, O. C. (2004). CorporateSocialResponsibilityand Marketing: An Integrative Framework. *Journal of the Academy of Marketing Science, 32*(1), 3–19. doi:10.1177/0092070303258971

Marcolin, B. L., Compeau, D. R., Munro, M. C., & Huff, S. L. (2000). Assessing user competence: Conceptualization and measurement. *Information Systems Research, 11*(1), 37–60. doi:10.1287/isre.11.1.37.11782

Martin, K., & Murphy, P. (2017). The Role of Data Privacy in Marketing. *Journal of the Academy of Marketing Science, 45*(2), 135–155. doi:10.100711747-016-0495-4

Munir, Z. A., Othman, A. A., Shukur, S. A. M., Ithnin, R., & Rusdi, S. D. (2015). Practices of internal marketing in small and medium industry. *International Journal of Social Science and Humanity, 5*(4), 358–361. doi:10.7763/IJSSH.2015.V5.480

Narver, J. C., & Slater, S. F. (1990). The effect of market orientation on business profitability. *Journal of Marketing, 54*(4), 20–35. doi:10.1177/002224299005400403

National Institute of Standards and Technology (NIST). (2014). *Framework for improving critical infrastructure cybersecurity (version 1.0).* Available at: www.nist.gov/cyberframework/upload/cybersecurity-framework-021214.pdf

Naude´, P., Desai, J., & Murphy, J. (2003). Identifying the determinants of internal marketing orientation. *European Journal of Marketing, 37*(9), 1205–1220. doi:10.1108/0390560310486951

Nye, J. S. Jr. (2017). Deterrence and dissuasion in cyberspace. *International Security, 41*(3), 44–71. doi:10.1162/ISEC_a_00266

Ohlhausen, M. K. (2014). Privacy Challenges and Opportunities: The Role of the Federal Trade Commission. *Journal of Public Policy & Marketing, 33*(1), 4–9. doi:10.1509/jppm.33.1.4

Papasolomo, I. (2006). Can internal marketing be implemented within bureaucratic organisations? *Journal of Bank Marketing, 24*(3), 194–212. doi:10.1108/02652320610659030

Papasolomou, I., & Vrontis, D. (2006). Using internal marketing to ignite the corporate brand: The case of the UK retail bank industry. *Brand Management, 14*(1/2), 177–195. doi:10.1057/palgrave.bm.2550059

Paraskevas, A. (2001). Internal service encounters in hotels: An empirical study. *International Journal of Contemporary Hospitality Management, 13*(6), 285–292. doi:10.1108/09596110110400481

Payne, A. (1993). *The Essence of Services Marketing.* Hemel Hempstead, UK: Prentice-Hall.

Peltier, J. W., & Scovotti, C. (2005). Relationship marketing and disadvantaged health care segments. *Health Marketing Quarterly, 22*(2), 69–90. doi:10.1300/J026v22n02_05 PMID:15914375

Peters, T. (1988). *Thriving on Chaos.* New York, NY: Alfred A. Knopf.

Pfeiffer, J. (1998, May). Six dangerous myths about pay. *Harvard Business Review,* 108–109. PMID:10179647

Piercy, N. F., & Morgan, N. (1995). Internal marketing – the missing half of the marketing programme. *Long Range Planning, 24*(2), 82–93. doi:10.1016/0024-6301(91)90083-Z

Prahalad, C. K., & Hamel, G. (1990). The core competence of the corporation. *Harvard Business Review*, (May/June): 79–91.

Rafiq, M., & Ahmed, P. (2000). Advances in the internal marketing concept: Definition, synthesis and extension. *Journal of Services Marketing*, *14*(6), 449–462. doi:10.1108/08876040010347589

Rafiq, M., & Ahmed, P. K. (1993). The scope of internal marketing: Defining the boundary between marketing and human resource management. *Journal of Marketing Management*, *9*(3), 219–232. doi:10.1080/0267257X.1993.9964234

Robins, S. P. (1996). *Organisational Behavior: Concepts, Controversies, Applications* (7th ed.). Englewood Cliffs, NJ: Prentice-Hall.

Romanosky, S. (2016). Examing the Costs and Causes of Cyber Incidents. *Journal of Cybersecurity*, *0*(0), 1–15.

Schneider, B. (1990). *Organizational Climate and Culture*. San Francisco, CA: Jossey-Bass Publishers.

Shackelford, S. J. (2014). Managing Cyber Attacks in International Law, Business, and Relations. In *Search of Cyber Peace*. Cambridge, UK: Cambridge University Press. doi:10.1017/CBO9781139021838

Spreitzer, G. M. (1992). *When organisations dare: the dynamics of individual empowerment in the workplace* (PhD dissertation). University of Michigan, Ann Arbor, MI.

Tsai, Y. F., & Tang, T. W. (2008). How to improve service quality: Internal marketing as a determining factor. *Total Quality Management*, *19*(11), 1117–1126. doi:10.1080/14783360802323479

Varey, R. J. (1995). Internal marketing: A review and some interdisciplinary research challenges. *International Journal of Service Industry Management*, *6*(1), 40–63. doi:10.1108/09564239510078849

Varey, R. J., & Lewis, B. R. (1999). A broadened conception of internal marketing. *European Journal of Marketing*, *33*(9), 926–944. doi:10.1108/03090569910285869

Verizon Enterprise Solutions. (2014). *Verizon 2014 data breach investigations report*. Available at: www.verizonenterprise.com/DBIR/2014/

Verizon Enterprise Solutions. (2015). *Verizon 2015 data breach investigations report*. Available at: www.verizonenterprise.com/DBIR/2015/

Verizon Enterprise Solutions. (2016). *Verizon 2016 data breach investigations report*. Available at: www.verizonenterprise.com/verizon-insights-lab/dbir/2016/

Weigel, F. K., & Hazen, B. T. (2014). Technical proficiency for IS success. *Computers in Human Behavior*, *31*, 27–36. doi:10.1016/j.chb.2013.10.014

Whetten, D., Cameron, K., & Woods, M. (1996). *Effective Empowerment and Delegation*. London: HarperCollins.

Whitman, M. E., & Mattord, H. J. (2018). *Principals of Information Security* (6th ed.). Boston, MA: Cengage Learning.

Wildes, V. J., & Parks, S. C. (2005). Internal service quality. *International Journal of Hospitality & Tourism Administration*, 6(2), 1–27. doi:10.1300/J149v06n02_01

Winkler, S., & Dealy, B. (1995). Information security technology? Don't rely on it: a case study in social engineering. *Proceedings of the Fifth USENIX UNIX Security Symposium*. Available at: www. usenix. org/legacy/publications/library/proceedings/security95/full_papers/winkler.pdf

Woodruffe, H. (1995). *Services Marketing*. London: Pitman. Retrieved from www.radiusits.com/5-startling-statistics-about-cybersecurity-in-2018/

*Previously published in the Handbook of Research on Innovations in Technology and Marketing for the Connected Consumer; pages 135-154, copyright year 2020 by Business Science Reference (an imprint of IGI Global).*

# Chapter 19

# Raising Information Security Awareness in the Field of Urban and Regional Planning

Margit Christa Scholl
*Technische Hochschule Wildau, Wildau, Germany*

## ABSTRACT

*IT is being increasingly used in most areas of life. With the IoT, this technology is set to be in a state of continuous evolution in urban and regional settings. The ongoing development of digitalization processes also increases the possibilities of abuse—both at the technical and interpersonal level. Better information security (IS) awareness (ISA) and knowledge about the dangers that accompany digitalization and the corresponding protective measures are important in private and work life. However, ISA is often overlooked. Training the relevant awareness and skills should also be included in urban and regional planning for citizens. This article thus provides a review of the scientific literature of leading academic journals in the area of IS and the transfer of scientific knowledge for practical purposes. The article presents Serious Games as a way to achieve a deeper understanding of how to promote sustainable ISA using creative methods. Furthermore, ideas of how to apply the Fun Theory and its practice to integrate awareness into modern urban and regional planning will be discussed.*

## 1. INTRODUCTION

Nowadays, we increasingly depend on information technology (IT) in our work and private lives. In the modern information society, computers and computer networks are becoming more and more important to business processes and for performing specialized tasks. IT transmits, electronically processes, and stores large amounts of data and a wide variety of information (BAköV, 2009). However, previous IT security mechanisms have reached their limits, and reliability and controllability cannot be assumed as the norm (BSI 2015). Government digital agendas—such as that of the Federal Government of Germany[1] or the European Digital Agenda[2]—seek to keep abreast of digital networking and the digital changes in society.

DOI: 10.4018/978-1-6684-3698-1.ch019

However, at the same time cybersecurity is creating new challenges. The term information security, as used in (inter)national standards, consists of more than just IT security. The goal of information security (IS) is to protect information of all types and origins (BAköV, 2009). Risk management in cyberspace must become part of national efforts. In this sense, all cities and regions face major challenges in terms of promoting digitalization on the one hand and responsibility towards their citizens on the other.

Digitalization is a core aspect of the "smartness" of the Internet of Things (IoT), smart homes, smart grids, and the smart city. Nevertheless, as summarized in Scholl and Scholl (2014), a smart city as an urban space would have the characteristics of a culture of innovation, a high quality of life—also referred to as "liveability"—global competiveness and attractiveness, security and safety, and economic and environmental sustainability. A smart city would have a smart municipal government managing and implementing policies towards those ends by leveraging ICT and institutions and by actively involving and collaborating with stakeholders (Al Awadhi et al., 2012). As the current *CIP Report* points out, smart-city projects are increasingly dominating the conversation around the future of urban environments and have also introduced a range of security challenges (Gordon & McAleese, 2017). To achieve trust in the development of smart cities, IS must be an integral part of the initiatives. Because both individuals and organizations are affected by IS challenges and information security awareness (ISA), these trainings (ISAT) should be provided for everyone on an ongoing daily basis. Von Solms and von Solms (2018) are working on simplifying the terminology to be used in the governance of cybersecurity and IS in order to explain to the boards of directors and executive management their responsibilities and accountability in this regard.

The results of a survey conducted in 2014 among EU and German citizens show that about 33 per cent of those questioned said that they were very concerned about becoming victims of identity theft.[3] To overcome this, values like integrity, honesty, and trust are required at the individual level, as well as professional and business competency accompanied by management and leadership skills: these include maintaining a positive attitude, team building, empowerment, coaching and training others, and influencing decision makers to embrace new standards of achievement and social behaviour that lead to appropriate IS and organizational resilience (Sullivant, 2016). Once damage has occurred to businesses, public administrations, and governmental or other institutions (see figure 1), it can trigger a chain of events with adverse effects for smart cities and electronic government (e-government) or future smart government.

But what does this mean for urban and regional planning processes in more concrete terms? In the opinion of the author, responsibility for the ISA of employees falls not only to companies but also to cities and municipalities, which should provide education for their inhabitants. This means establishing a general programme to provide information about threats and risks, vulnerabilities (which are gaps in the security of a system or a software or in the organization itself), the various kinds of attacks, and possible damage: this programme should be implemented creatively through urban and regional planning (see Figure 1). Moreover, the cybersecurity authorities and intelligence services around the world would, in principle, have to cooperate with one another to track down perpetrators. The demand coming from authorities and companies for comprehensive digitalization must go hand in hand with IS—which in turn must be accompanied by awareness. ISA affects everyone in society.

The research questions in this paper are:

**RQ #1:** What are the main current scientific findings from the field of occupational ISA and ISAT that can be used in practice?

*Figure 1. How threats become risks (own documentation)*

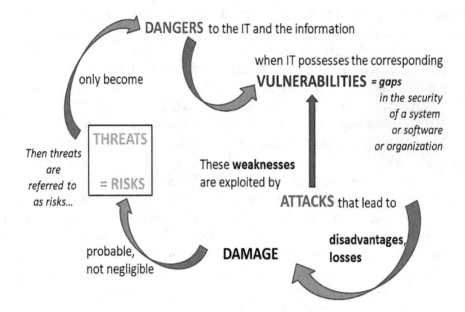

**RQ #2:** How can we transfer these findings to the urban and regional planning processes of an entire society?

**RQ #3:** How can we achieve sustainability in IS sensitization and societal resilience?

The objective of this paper is a systematic compilation of past scientific insights into IS, ISA, and ISAT and the possible transfer of these insights into practical implementation for urban and regional planning because of the importance of smart cities in the future. The next section of the paper will give a brief overview of IS and human actors. Section three shows the results of comprehensive literature reviews and examines the relevant scientific information relating to aspects of ISA, IS culture, and ISA measurements, theories, and trainings. After this scientific round-up, section four is a discussion of the RQ, further research results relating to game-based learning scenarios and the Fun Theory, and the consequences for practice in the field of urban and regional planning, e.g. smart cities. The conclusions and future work are presented in section five.

## 2. BACKGROUND TO DIGITIZATION, IS, AND HUMAN ACTORS

Smart, cost-effective, scalable, innovative solutions that can address the problems of urbanization are needed. There are six components that underpin most smart-city models: government, economy, mobility, environment, liveability, and people. All these components help a smart city achieve multiple benefits (Kathoun & Zeadally 2017). Yet factors such as natural disasters, climate change, energy crises, political instability, financial crises, food security, and terrorist attacks may threaten future urban development (Spaans & Waterhout 2017). Moreover, cyberattacks, a lack of IS, and the insufficient protection of sensitive data also make smart cities vulnerable. As Kitchin and Dodge (2017) have pointed out, smart-city technologies are promoted as an effective way to counter and manage uncertainty and urban risks through the efficient delivery of services, yet paradoxically they create new vulnerabilities and threats, including making city infrastructure and services insecure, brittle, and open to extended forms of criminal activity. This paradox has largely been ignored or underestimated by commercial and governmental interests or tackled through a technically mediated mitigation approach. Kitchin and Dodge (2017) identify the following vulnerabilities to cyberattacks inherent in smart-city technologies and systems:

1. Weak software security and data encryption;
2. The use of insecure legacy systems and poor maintenance;
3. The size, sophistication, and diversity of smart-city systems, which have many interdependencies and large and complex attack surfaces;
4. Human error and the deliberate malfeasance of disgruntled (ex-)employees.

The first of these points reflects the fact that we cannot have 100 percent security. There are a number of different encryption methods based on different mathematical principles—however, the key length specified in bits and used in the procedure must be continuously increased to match computer performance (BAköV, 2009). Modern encryption methods offer adequate security based on the quality of the particular algorithm,[4] a sufficiently long key, and suitable key management.[5] Unfortunately, this security often fails as a result of incorrect implementation or incorrect use of the procedures as well as faulty programming—a prominent example in Germany is the electronic mailbox system for lawyers.[6] Likewise, in practice, old and vulnerable methods are used instead of current developments. Thus, we often have to deal with badly designed and unsafe/unsecure systems.

The second point relates to the fact that there are still many old devices in use with operating systems whose support has expired. In addition, a data backup strategy and software and patch management with version control and updates are a general requirement. Systems engineers and IT professionals in institutions need a clear understanding of security configurations and countermeasures so that secure software and hardware can be deployed to prevent cyberattacks and to maintain system functionality by patching vulnerabilities and updating systems. The current analysis of Ho et al. (2017) in their ongoing study using Activity Theory (AT) to examine the interactions between Systems Engineers and Penetration Testers suggests that as these subjects interact and learn, the insitutions also benefit through an evolving culture of security awareness.

The third point—the interdependencies between smart-city technologies or systems—has the potential to create cascade effects. By understanding the interdependencies not only within ICT but also of technology and infrastructure with water, electricity, and food (WEF) systems, cities can anticipate and avoid these knock-on effects (Romero-Lankao et al., 2018). Tøndel et al. (2017) refer to mutual dependencies too, in this case for the smart-grid vision of power systems. To ensure the effective reliability of a power system, the interdependencies between power and ICT systems need to be properly understood and consideration given to old damage scenarios, such as hidden failures in protection systems, as well as new threats like cyberattacks (Tøndel et al., 2017). As Sarwat et al. (2018) note, the current literature does not properly emphasize the challenges posed by the interconnectedness of the different smart-city networks. They point to the critical need to design solutions that take these interdependencies between networks into account by applying realistic examples and scenarios (Sarwat et al., 2018).

The final point suggests that technical exploitation can be significantly aided by human error. It is assumed that this aspect can also apply to the actions of citizens using smart-city technologies in public spaces. Hwang and Choi (2017) suggest that because cultural manifestations and artefacts reflect the social environment, governments should diagnose those that are operative in communication, storytelling about e-government information system security (ISS), formal and informal discourses about ISS, leaders' implicit and explicit support for ISS, and rituals and physical symbols embodying the awareness of the importance of ISS among members of an organization.

A summary of these points is outlined in an interview with Rob Kitchin (Schechtner, 2017), which suggests that the various complex issues that citizens and city managers face could be neatly taken apart to isolate well-defined technical problems that can be adequately addressed by technology. A technical approach thus reduces city systems and people to relatively simple components and agents, and this mostly ignores the metaphysical aspects of human life, subjectivity, and the role of politics, ideology, soft values, social and institutional structures, capital, and culture in shaping everyday life and urban development and governance (Schechtner, 2017).

## 3. RESULTS OF LITERATURE REVIEWS

The originally more intensive literature research conducted in 2016 had the following criteria: the search would be limited to scientific publications from the past ten years, i.e. starting from the year 2006—some ten scientific journals were used, including *Information Systems Quarterly*, *Information Systems Research*, *European Information Systems*, *Information Security & Information Security Journal: A Global Perspective*, and *International Journal of Information Security*; the keywords "information security", "awareness", and "human factor" were chosen as a starting point—however, the special area healthcare was not considered; the investigation was not directed toward a specific type of attack such as phishing but set out to adopt a broad-based approach. In line with this primary research, the following topics have been grouped: awareness raising and training and applied awareness measures; security-awareness measures and factors influencing information behaviour and IS culture; human factors influencing the vulnerability of information security; knowledge, attitudes, and behavior; social engineering (SE) methods; the role of information security managers; the measurement of information security awareness; history and theories. In addition, there were some articles with a more particular focus on measures relating to the effectiveness of awareness trainings and scientific literature on psychological aspects as well as game-based learning methods. In mid-2016, around 150 scientific articles were identified, some 80 of which were used more intensively for references. With a view to examining these findings for transferability to society in general, the author continued to study the scientific literature. In addition, tracking the publication market for the above topics combined with literature from the network "URBAN e-PLANNING RESEARCH NETWORK (UEP_NET)" and the topic "smart cities" is an ongoing process, so that further and current scientific publications are included in this article.

Starting with the final point highlighted by Kitchin and Dodge (2017)—human error—cybersecurity professionals agree that security depends on people more than on technical controls and countermeasures (Benson et al. 2018). Nonetheless, a distinction should always be made between victims and perpetrators. The lack of ISA, ignorance, negligence, apathy, mischief, and resistance are at the root of user mistakes (Safa et al. 2016). Herath and Rao (2009) find that employees in their sample underestimate the probability of security breaches. In several publications it is pointed out that in cybercrime phishing, human ignorance, and inattention are exploited to steal information from users. Benson et al. (2018) argue that what all the rather different economy sectors have in common is that current attacks by cybercriminals start with SE as the weakest link in the security chain. A lack of understanding of security issues coupled with the pervasive use of computers makes employees a "critical factor" in the IS equation (Choi et al. 2008). This idea of considering the user as the "weakest link" in IS can be found in the large number of studies that try to explain employee adherence to or non-compliance with IS.

However, as Dark (2006) points out, knowledgeable human beings are better at preventing IS breaches that occur due to negligence or accident as well as those that stem from malicious activity and the anomalous behaviour of systems. They can efficiently and effectively respond to incidents by reporting them promptly, quarantining problems, and diagnosing and treating these problems correctly (Dark, 2006). The systematic literature review by Mahfuth et al. (2017) on IS culture in organizations also shows that there is a positive correlation between the level of knowledge and the behaviour of workers. According to Al-Daeef et al. (2017), user training as a non-technical solution to security threats is thought to complement and enhance the performance of technical tools. Thus, technology solutions alone are not sufficient to ensure IS countermeasures. And IS is more comprehensive than simple IT security (Hagen et al. 2008). However, building a corporate IS culture in organizations is itself a diverse and complex process (see Sullivant 2016). If one transfers these ideas to the design of smart cities, then trust-promoting interactions should be planned and developed in public places.

Security awareness has been defined in many different ways. Most of the studies are empirical and concerned with the human factors influencing IS, which are the main reason for considering and defining ISA. As can be seen, different studies produce different definitions in terms of the amount and variety of aspects involved. Nevertheless, there is overall support for the KAB model, which originally comes from the social sciences and covers the three dimensions of knowledge, attitude, and behaviour (Kruger & Kearney, 2006). Al-Daeef et al. (2017) have combined several literatures in their current definition: ISA is "the security knowledge that has been gradually acquired through a continuous and updated catchy training manner to influence trainees' behaviour".

There is no easy linear way to explain human behaviour. For example, in contrast to a previous study, the analyses of Liang et al. (2013) reveal that punishment expectancy is a strong determinant of compliance behaviour, whereas the effects of reward expectancy are not significant. Pattinson et al. (2016) find a strong correlation with ISA for the measure relating to the three behaviours "Internet use," "mobile computing," and "email use." Hu et al. (2012) find that the participation of high-level managers in IS initiatives has a significant direct and indirect influence on employees' attitudes toward, subjective norms of, and perceived behavioural control over compliance with IS policies. Workman (2007), who investigates SE attacks, also recommends that managers assist employees in recognizing and discriminating appropriate commitment targets. Warkentin et al. (2011) indicate that certain social conditions within the organizational setting contribute to an informal learning process. Kirlappos et al. (2013) conclude that effective problem detection and the adaptation of security measures need to be decentralized, and employees should be the principal agents deciding how to implement security in specific contexts.

The results produced by Sun et al. (2011) revealed a non-linear relationship between security levels and "information security readiness" (ISR)—this means that for data with high criticality, enhancing security levels had a positive impact on ISR, but only up to the point perceived as appropriate by the participants; for data with low criticality, the enhancement of security levels was perceived as unnecessary (Sun et al. 2011). Moreover, Willison and Warkentin (2013) commented that little attention has been paid to the motivation of those internal staff members who perpetrate deliberate and malicious computer abuse, while numerous studies have focused on the security behaviour of employees without regard to the motivational factors. The study of Dang-Pham et al. (2017) shows that favourable security attitudes and engagement in daily activities have positive impacts on security advice sharing, whereas the perception of excessive social pressure makes employees deliberately refuse to share security advice.

As the reviewed literature shows, an important factor influencing IS is not necessarily insufficient knowledge but rather a lack of compliance with ISA and IS behaviour (Slusky & Partow-Navid, 2012). Using the vocabulary of the KAB model, this is the attitude or the will and ability to convert their knowledge into IS-compliant behaviour. This is supported by current research: "Information security awareness changes are associated with a wide range of interrelated alterations at the organisational, technological and individual level" (Tsohou et al., 2015; see also Shaw et al., 2009). As a result, an organization needs to roll out a series of ISA programmes oriented toward perception, comprehension, and projection (Shaw et al., 2009). Awareness is a crucial part of any IS programme at either the personal or organizational level (Al-Daeef et al., 2017).

Following Cone et al. (2006), training and awareness are generally accomplished using a combination of several techniques: formal training sessions, which can be instructor-led, brown-bag seminars, or video sessions; passive computer-based and web-based training (CBT/WBT), representing a centralized approach with the flexibility of self-paced training; strategic placement of awareness messages; and interactive computer-based training, such as video games, which can be divided into two kinds—first-person interaction games or resource management simulations (Cone et al., 2006). Since personal, classroom trainings often seem to be elaborate and costly, many rely on online/offline trainings like WBT. However, there is the risk that "a monotonous slide show fails to challenge the user and provides no dialogue for further elaboration" (Cone et al., 2006). As a comprehensive example, Kim et al. (2017) developed an Internet-based cyberinformation security education & training and monitoring & reporting system to address the security breaches of malicious email and the attachment of documents commonly found in public institutions and private companies. As a result, the security education rate of 78 percent was raised throughout the system, and the user sense of security has been strengthened (Kim et al., 2017). However, the participation rate does not say anything about the sustainability of the measure.

CyberCIEGE, an interactive video game, has been made available to US government organizations, schools, and universities as a safety-awareness tool for free and successful use, engaging users in the adventure-storytelling approach to making security-relevant decisions (Cone et al., 2007). Significant demand for skilled cybersecurity personnel in the US led to funding for the GenCyber programme[7], which successfully leveraged game-based learning to increase the interest of high-school students in cybersecurity and boost their awareness of cybersecurity and safe online behaviour. Chun et al. (2016) present the SLOB (Security Learning by Ontology Browsing) Web Portal that brings together many multimedia data and learning resources for college-level cybersecurity classes at one central location in a unified framework. According to the evaluation of Jin et al. (2018), "learning through these activities provided high school students with an immersive, learner-centered experience, which has been proven very effective on cybersecurity awareness training and practical skill acquisition for learners from diverse backgrounds". The need for situational awareness training is also present in other hazard areas with sophisticated and specially designed simulation environments and visualization of surgical procedures (see, for example, Sanfilippo, 2017).

Since patent applications have already reached a high level of practicability, three further examples of tools and training systems are mentioned here. Firstly, under the rubric "Context-aware Training Systems, Apparatuses and Systems", computer-implemented systems are being developed for sensing a user action and selecting a training action from a range of options; the action is then delivered to the user if it indicates a need for the user to be trained and the cost or benefit of exposing the user to the action indicates that exposure to it is warranted (Sadeh-Koniecpol et al., 2017a). Secondly, a programme entitled "Mock Attack Cybersecurity Training System and Methods" assesses the susceptibility of an electronic device user to a cybersecurity threat by identifying user-related information, selecting a mock attack, and—when a sensor detects that the user has interacted with the electronic device in response to this attack—recording the action, which is used to determine the susceptibility of the user to a cybersecurity threat (Sadeh-Koniecpol et al., 2017b). Thirdly, a cybersecurity training system with automated application of branded content uses lures and training actions to help the user of an electronic device recognize and act appropriately in situations that could compromise electronic device security (Sadeh-Koniecpol et al., 2016).

As Vaidya et al. (2014) point out, the use of an interactive approach is necessary for teaching a complex subject such as privacy. The primary tools used by these authors are that of case studies and gaming scenarios and should be designed to present privacy concepts in a manner that makes them accessible to a variety of disciplines of study (Vaidya et al., 2014). Also, Beyer et al. (2016) describe that the secret is to engage people in the right way, so they can convert learning into tangible action and new behaviour. For that, we need communication between, collaboration with, and the active participation of people. In order to achieve this with online-based simulations in an optimal way, high levels of investment are necessary for digital games. ISAT as an effective training and educational experiment should help learners to acquire new knowledge, practice this knowledge for a longer period of time, and apply it to other related activities (see Al-Daeef et al., 2017). The training should also be embedded in a context the users are familiar with and understood as an ongoing activity (Al-Daeef et al., 2017). The success of such simulations of real-world situations, which could be digital or analogue, can be confirmed by the author through her own experience. The advantage of such embedded trainings is that the knowledge they convey can be retained for a longer time and transferred to other related areas and retrieved in real situations.

The results of Kirlappos and Sasse (2012) also point to the need for a change of direction in safety/security awareness, education, and training by not overloading users with warnings and not telling them what experts think the behaviour of the user should be. Rather, effective security awareness begins with the perspective and decision-making processes of users who do not master them perfectly (Kirlappos & Sasse 2012). Further research shows that besides the theoretical approach of knowledge transfers and the promotional approach of emotionality, a systematic communicational approach in the form of team-based applications is needed to achieve lasting ISA that results in the intention and behaviour to protect confidential information (Pokoyski, 2009; Khan et al., 2011). The combination of these three approaches is called ISAT 3.0 (Scholl et al., 2016). This corresponds to the idea that ISA is role-based learning, detailing the roles and responsibilities of a user vis-à-vis ICT systems within their organization, and may be based on situational learning as an effective user-centred approach that improves the ability to secure one's surroundings. Systemic sensitization measures—Learning 3.0 as per Scholl et al. (2016)—therefore rely on a correlation that is constantly changing rather than a static and superficial cause-and-effect principle. It is thus concerned with conflict between people, communication, the formation of community, shared work, and the realization of the individual power of action through "allies". Without this emotional and motivational way of raising awareness, both the actual know-how transfer, Learning 1.0 (Scholl et al., 2016), and advertising "for security", Learning 2.0 (Scholl et al., 2016), seem ineffective.

# 4. DISCUSSION OF THE RQ AND CONSEQUENCES FOR PRACTICE IN THE FIELD OF URBAN AND REGIONAL PLANNING

Recent reviews of the cybersecurity threat landscape show that no industry segment is immune to cyberattacks and the public sector tops the list for targeted security incidents (Benson, 2017). Citizens of the twenty-first century live in a world where they are more connected than ever before, are exposed to an unprecedented amount of information, and have a greater awareness of social, political, and environmental complexities. Thus, engaging citizens in the urban planning process is a complex and divisive issue not only because of people's busy lifestyles and competing priorities but also as a result of top-down government approaches and the current tools and techniques for engagement that are used. Head (2007) argues that more effective dialogue between governments and citizens encourages discussion between stakeholders in the decision-making process, too. Such a dialogue should include public information security policies and public trainings designed to raise awareness of the vulnerabilities of city infrastructures and systems.

## 4.1. Main Current Scientific Findings of ISA and ISAT

All the studies investigated include the aspect of knowledge. Sometimes this refers to knowledge about the consequences of cyberattacks or security breaches and the protection of information or data, and sometimes to knowledge about the organizational security policy. But without knowledge, there seems to be no awareness. The next important defining aspect that most studies agree on is attitude. This is associated with the need for employees to understand the subject of IS and to see themselves as an important component in it and hence feel responsible for it. Finally, there are some studies which see the actual behaviour of employees or users as part of the concept of ISA. At the very least, the common goal is to achieve a change in human behaviour to create more IS through trainings for raising awareness.

However, the findings of Kirlappos and Sasse (2012) suggest that "advice given in current user education is largely ignored because it focuses on indicators users do not understand or trust. To help users, we need to explain how and why the indicators of trustworthiness they use successfully in the real world fail them online." (Kirlappos & Sasse, 2012). ISAT itself is overlooked in most implemented information security programmes (Al-Daeef et al., 2017). Although many of the ISAT concepts are universal, they must typically be tailored to address the policies and requirements of a particular organization. In addition, many forms of ISAT fail because they are rote and do not require users to think about and apply security concepts (Cone et al., 2006). The first step toward effective user education about ISA is to recognize that awareness, education, and training are three distinct steps in a process to improve user competence (Kirlappos & Sasse, 2012).

In smart cities, several technologies are connected to each other at different levels (devices, connected spaces, smart infrastructures, connected citizens) to provide seamless communication and contextual services. Digital technologies in smart cities can capture personally identifiable information as well as household-level data about citizens—characteristics, location and movements, activities. They can link this data to create recombined data and use this to produce profiles of citizens and places as a decision-making tool, which—according to Head (2007)—also involves building institutional bridges between governmental leaders and citizens, often termed "community engagement." Moreover, the security of smart-city technologies and the data they generate are vulnerable to hacking and theft, which raises questions about the uncertainties and implications of a data breach for citizens. However, citizens in smart cities are frequently unaware of the risks of the smart devices they use or the security implications of certain usage habits.

With regard to RQ#1 it can be argued that there is no simple linear cause-and-effect relationship for ISA between knowledge and attitudes, and certainly not with regard to the real IS behaviour practised by people. Although scientific research indicates a general need for (cyberthreat) education, trainings, and awareness (see, for example, McCrohan et al., 2010; Shaw et al., 2009; Kim, 2014; Jones et al., 2014), the review of the scientific literature shows that the design of ISA trainings has not been a main subject of significant research. However, a major problem for human actors seems to be the application of IS knowledge in real-world situations. Besides situational target orientation, ISAT needs individual emotionality and team-based communication and exchange as a means to create motivation. To achieve 1) emotionalization and 2) motivation, creative techniques and, in particular, digital and analogue serious games are becoming more important in the field of IS, ISA, and ISAT (Scholl et al., 2016).

Extensive Awareness courses have been developed, and employees drilled to make IS part of their, and the company's, culture (Von Solms, 2010). Deterrence approaches to reduce employee abuse have also been recommended by Willison and Warkentin (2013), who would like research to be more focused on the social artefact. "What needs to be done … is to consider how users make decisions in their everyday activities (both in business and personal settings) and try to tailor newly-proposed security solutions based on this, accommodating their work or personal goals when interacting with technology and the folk models they form on the virtual world based on their real-world experiences" (Kirlappos & Sasse 2012). Building on the findings of Van Niekerk and Von Solms (2010) on the necessity of a joint learning process, Beyer et al. (2016) see responsibility, trust, communication, and cooperation as the four cornerstones of an engaging IS culture. On the one hand, transferring responsibility to governments and shifting the onus to administrative action make it clear that IS needs to be integrated in all areas, and, on the other, that measures and assistance must be defined and implemented in line with concrete target groups and the requirements of cultural diversity. The results of Chen et al. (2008) indicate the importance of people's cultural backgrounds, suggesting that the analogue and digital learning scenarios within the ISAT should be varied accordingly.

## 4.2. Transfer Into Urban and Regional Design

Zhang and Li (2018) refer to the dominant role of social factors such as urban governance in the process of urban adjustment and adaptation as a means to foster development that is both sustainable and resilient. In their opinion, the establishment of an urban rational development mechanism could help improve the capacity of cities to cope more effectively with the various crises involved (Zhang & Li, 2018). In line with Collier et al. (2013), emerging and challenging areas—such as geospatial ICT, green infrastructure planning, novel design using collaborative responses, climate planning, limiting urban sprawl, and short-circuit economic approaches—are explored as viable facets for devising and sustaining urban transition strategies. While it may be possible to develop practical solutions and guidelines, the process of transition may be much more problematic and may not suit policy timescales, and considerable differences and conflicting approaches may arise (Collier et al., 2013).

As Zhang and Li (2018) have pointed out, a city is the most complex and typical socio-ecological system shaped by human beings. Rob Kitchin asked in an interview (Schechtner, 2017) how architects, planners, and electronics and computer scientists understand cities differently and how this gap can be closed. His impression is that electronics engineers and computer scientists see the city more as a group of recognizable and manageable systems that are largely rational, mechanical, linear, and hierarchical (Schechtner, 2017). In addition, urban systems are largely treated as generic analytical categories with some typical deviations, meaning that a solution developed for a city can be transferred and replicated elsewhere. Because of this instrumental rationality and the associated criticism of technology-based solutions to urban issues, city planners and city managers are sometimes cautious about accepting them. They see a city as a complex, multifaceted, contingent, open, and relational entity with contradictory and complex problems. Following Kitchin and Dodge (2017), they typically see cities as places, not systems. From this position, cities have different histories, cultures, social and community relationships, economies, governmental and institutional structures, politics, legacy infrastructures, political and administrative geographies, links and interdependencies with other places, and different, often competing actors and stakeholders.

One should also differentiate between the sensitization and training of people. The general objective of raising everybody's awareness of IS is to sharpen their perception in this respect, create emotional concern, and thus motivate deeper understanding and involvement. The aim of IS trainings, which should be specific to the target groups and the tasks they perform as well as to the roles in the specific organization (Beyer et al., 2016), is to provide the necessary knowledge and competencies for security-conscious behaviour. To reduce the degree of uncertainty and lack of awareness, the author recommends applying games for sensitization with didactic purposes.

Serious-game design combines learning design with game features. Rather than concentrating on gaming as entertainment, the serious-games approach is grounded in educational need and theory. In contrast to recreational games, serious games are more complex and contain not just a story, art, and software development but also pedagogical strategies that discern learning theory, teaching and learning approaches, assessment, and feedback (Zyda, 2005; Cornillie et al., 2012; Raybourn, 2014). Serious games have been applied in numerous fields including military contexts, education, well-being, advertising, cultural heritage, interpersonal communication, and health (Laamarti et al., 2014). With an experimental co-design process, the serious game "Energy Safari" supports the integration of "real world" components and thus provides a safe learning space and open environment that invites exploration and experimentation (Gugerell & Zuidema, 2017). Their analysis of the game co-design process itself illustrates that co-designers are quite capable of experimenting with serious-game components to create a meaningful and recognizable regional narrative that deeply embeds regional challenges and instigates civic learning (Gugerell & Zuidema, 2017).

The use of serious games in participatory design activities in architecture and planning is an alternative way of representing and communicating information and has the potential to make the learning process more interesting, playful, and hence even more effective. This approach can also establish a dialogue between designers and citizens and raise awareness of the urban environment and its architectural representation using a game engine (Di Mascio & Dalton, 2017). The rapid developments in smart-city implementation have led researchers to focus on the design of serious games to simulate various other aspects of smart cities. A further example, Urban Data Game (UDG), aims to motivate the learning of data skills for big, live data sets—this game relies on the principles of narrative, game-based learning, inquiry, collaborative learning, and challenge (Wolff et al., 2015). The paper by Wolff et al. (2015) proposes an approach to teaching data literacy in the context of urban innovation tasks, using a version of UDG: the games "are supported by a set of training data and resources that will be used in school trials for exploring the problems people have when dealing with large data and trialling novel approaches for teaching data literacy" (Wolff et al., 2015).

The research into learning activities conducted by Kangas (2010) extended from the classroom to a playful learning environment (PLE) for children with game co-creation, play, and computer games: the results show that this is a way to foster activity, creativity, imagination, and group work skills (Kangas 2010). For adults, games are used to describe many different activities involving people. New forms of participation, collaboration, co-production, and innovative technical solutions with Web 2.0 are also used for public participatory GIS (PP GIS) research (see Poplin, 2012). However, previous research results in this area do not indicate that citizens are automatically empowered (Moody, 2007; Krek, 2005; Gunning, 2003; Buchanan & Gordon, 1962)—possibly another indication that different target groups and generations need to be specifically addressed. The aim of Poplin's paper is to study the implementation of serious games to encourage online public participation in urban planning, a new research field in which (2D/3D) spatial representations that are close to reality were integrated within the concept of the game (Poplin, 2012). The developed concept of playful public participation in urban planning included playful elements such as storytelling, walking and moving, sketching, drawing, and games (Poplin, 2012). Research has shown that for a serious game to be successful, the overall structure of the game and the instructions provided to play it should be kept simple to minimize the time spent learning the rules of the game (Mitchell & Savill-Smith, 2004). Effective serious games must provide feedback to encourage focus on the process at hand as well as the performance achieved (Poplin, 2012; Cornillie et al., 2012; Raybourn, 2014).

The paper by Hendrix et al. (2016) investigates whether games can be effective cybersecurity training tools. The authors conclude that there is not yet enough evidence to draw any definite conclusions. Their results indicate that products and studies mostly work over a short period, while it is known that short-term interventions are not particularly effective at prompting behavioural change (Hendrix et al., 2016). Cybersecurity consists of a number of different aspects, from digital equipment, software, and cryptography to human processes and psychology. As identified in the paper by Anderson et al. (2013), which investigates games as effective cybersecurity training tools, better training in this area is required for both the general public and businesses themselves. Moreover, Hendrix et al. (2016) found that most of the academic studies target the end user, and that there is a clear lack of games that target IT infrastructure and especially management decisions around IT infrastructure.

Nevertheless, Ersoy (2017) argues for cities as centres of innovation with integrated infrastructures. Here, three elements emerge as important factors posing major challenges: ensuring collaboration, inclusion, and institutional capacity in the context of mobilizing collective learning and transforming city infrastructure (Ersoy, 2017). Lee et al. (2013) use an integrated road-mapping process for the services, devices, and technologies of smart cities to show how different types of road maps can be coordinated to provide a clear picture of the technological changes and uncertainties associated with the strategic planning of complex innovations (Lee et al., 2013). Collaboration, communication, and exchange between different actors with different objectives are also urgently needed in addressing the requirements of IS and ISA.

With respect to RQ#2 and the question "How can we transfer these findings into the urban and regional planning processes of an entire society?" it is important to bear in mind the research finding that the learning process (in organizations) must be based on a user-centred approach, paying attention to target groups, gender, and culture—this relies on individual knowledge and skills as well as on concrete (work) connections. Sensitization and security training are a promising approach to raising user awareness and thus minimizing the negative impact of user mistakes and misconduct, which cannot be addressed only with technical solutions (Al-Daeef et al., 2017). Transferring this to urban and regional planning processes means building up game-based playground areas with awareness games focused on interaction, communication, and sensitization with different backgrounds and at different knowledge levels.

## 4.3. Gamification in Urban and Regional Planning

Although urban orders are normally generated via a top-down hierarchy, they may sometimes be generated by bottom-up spontaneity (Zhang & Li, 2018). Top-down hierarchical processes tend to be passive and more objective, while bottom-up spontaneity is active and more subjective. In order to consider alternative smart-city perspectives, Moustaka et al. (2017) propose a model-based smart-city profiling that incorporates local needs and challenges and integrates them into future design and implementation ideas. Gamification might be a method to empower citizens and involve them in urban and regional planning processes. Moreover, as Pokoyski (2018) argues, "playing is learning—literally from childhood". There are different examples of games in cities and environments for adults who like to play in their free time, as the following pictures show (see Figures 2–4). Playing in public places is therefore also a great way for adults to integrate the formal and informal mechanisms of communication and can help enhance interactions between citizens.

*Figure 2. Chess game on the go in Chicago, USA (2017, June)*

One of the most famous examples of game-based citizen "education" was the piano staircase created in 2009 at Odenplan Metro in Stockholm, Sweden, using an idea based on the Fun Theory (TheFunTheory.com). The goal is long-term behavioural change (see Peeters et al., 2013). With the Fun Theory, developers believe that the easiest way to change people's behaviour for the better is by shaping it (see Figure 3). As a result of the intervention, 66 per cent more people than normal chose the stairs over the escalator. More examples can be found on YouTube:

- The world's deepest bin (https://www.youtube.com/watch?v=qRgWttqFKu8);
- The bottle tree (https://www.youtube.com/watch?v=tjCCa6VaxuA);
- The doodle jump stairs (https://www.youtube.com/watch?v=CWwee62DW3U);
- The colour clean toilet (https://www.youtube.com/watch?v=uCEgjeV9t8I).

The Fun Theory would thus suggest that fun can clearly change behaviour for the better. According to the Gartner IT Glossary, "Humans are 'hard-wired' to enjoy games and have a natural tendency to interact more deeply in activities that are framed in a game construct."8 Gamification is seen as the most important enabler of change processes in organizations, too. Using game-typical elements involves serious thinking about game-design principles and game mechanics in a non-game context. Moreover, with its empathy-based, discursive approach, it can be seen as a customer loyalty tool that can be used to introduce, transform, or operate systems, processes, and complexity, and encourage the adoption of desired behaviours.

*Figure 3. Piano stairs – TheFunTheory.com – Rolighetsteorin.se, October 7, 2009 https://www.youtube. com/watch?v=21Xh2n0aPyw*

Information security concerns require more than just electronic learning or traditional communication à la marketing. Gamification is considered a trigger for awareness-raising activities (Helisch & Pokoyski, 2009). It thrives on role models (leadership) and social team processes as well as constant exchange in the context of dynamic change. According to Helisch & Pokoyski (2009), there are three elements to promote:

- Knowledge, in the sense of "I have recognized the problem, understood and know what to do!"
- Intention, in the sense of "I want to act in accordance with safety (because it benefits my organization and thus myself!)"

- Ability, in the sense of "In my (organizational) environment safety-compliant action is basically possible."

Cognition, motivation/loyalty, and organization/culture are addressed through the play-based promotion of these three elements (Helisch & Pokoyski, 2009). The user-centred approach needs to include the main topics of interest to raise ISA and should also enable exchange in informal learning processes in certain social conditions within the urban and regional setting. Playing is often equated with freedom of action, and by allowing players to make mistakes in relation to certain rules, almost every game becomes a simulation of reality (Pokoyski, 2018). Because people are interested in participating in games and performing activities that might otherwise be considered too complex or boring, gamification can create the first steps toward freedom of choice and a mature and consolidated relationship with IS. We need to look for solutions that pick up on and promote dialogues based on discursive principles. This works very well in analogue learning scenarios. It can also work digitally but requires much smarter tool development than the WBT that have so far been implemented.

The next example (Figure 4) shows real game-based analogue learning scenarios in urban and regional spaces and their possible applicability for IS-related themes. Figure 4's game-based analogue learning of tree species and their fruits provides inspiration for building up an urban game with sentences relating to data security, as shown in Figure 5. The game "Security on the go" from the "Security Arena" established at the TUAS Wildau with fourteen situations at the airport (see Figure 6) can be easily transferred to a smart-city situation and could be developed as a training path.

*Figure 4. Initial inspiration for game-based analogue learning (2017, April)*

Game-based analogous learning of tree species and their fruits in the urban forest of the town Marktheidenfeld (Germany), April 2017.

*Figure 5. First transposition into a sentence data security game ("Data Security" is part of the "Information Security Arena". These notes for the digital world were defined withing the project "SecAware4job" of the TUAS Wildau.)*

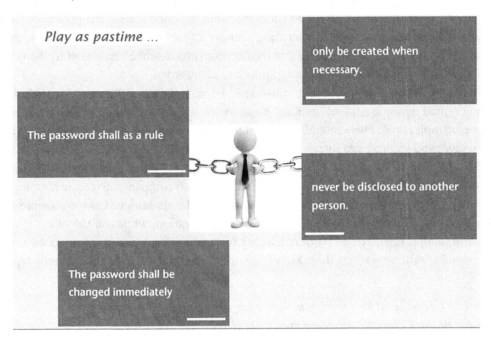

*Figure 6. Game "Security on the go" with 14 situations at the airport that can be transferred to a smart-city or company situation ("Security on the go" is part of the "Information Security Arena", specified within the project SecAware4job for the TUAS Wildau, see http://secaware4job.wildau.biz)*

The themes in this security case (Figure 6) are abandoned documents and dumpster diving, encryption, unprotected Wi-Fi, theft, insufficient updates, risk countries, loss, interception and recording using mobile phones, social engineering, opportunistic crimes, eavesdropping, shoulder surfing, control-copy confiscation, and open Internet access. The game rules are as follows: first, the person or team should jointly assign the fourteen risk cards by matching scenarios that are presented on the learning map (or along a path). The second task is to place fourteen appropriate defence cards next to the relevant risk cards. If you play the game as a competition, points can be awarded.

In many places, such games can help to raise ISA, because people often connect with the existing public, unencrypted network without thinking about IS. However, nothing is private in an open Wi-Fi network! For example, smart cities shouldn't support open Wi-Fi hotspots. Citizens have a right to education, information, and security and safety. The urban and regional design of a city square should not just include free public Wi-Fi but also possibilities for analogue communication about the risks involved or gamification as a means to raise ISA. Cities can collaborate with companies to create learning scenarios in urban spaces and squares. For that, we should combine digital and analogue learning scenarios because, on the one hand, life is more and more supported by digitalization, while, on the other, it will always be analogue in nature. Figures 7 to 9 offers another inspiration for creating urban space for analogue communication in learning stations (here sketched with old bathtubs) geared to different aspects of IS.

*Figure 7. Second inspiration for creating urban space for analogue communication within a workshop/ training in the Berlin Centre for Higher Education (2016)*

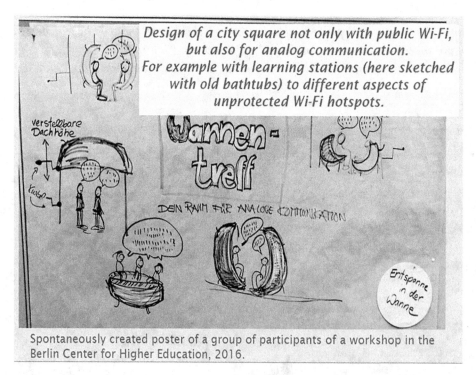

*Figure 8. Third inspiration for creating urban space for analogue communication. Examples from Chicago, USA: left, a moving picture of a woman performing an action at a specific moment, and right, the corrspoinding picture of a man (2017, April).*

*Figure 9. Fourth inspiration for creating urban space for analogue communication. Examples from Chicago, USA: left, a board game, and right, a throwing game (2017, April).*

## 4.4. Sustainability in IS Sensitization and Societal Resilience

The extent to which the twenty-first-century world will be "sustainable" depends in large part on the sustainability of cities (Ahern, 2011). As Kitchin & Dodge (2017) have pointed out, there are two key security risks with respect to the emergence of smart cities. The first is the security of newly installed "intelligent" technologies and "smart" upgrades to existing infrastructures and systems and the extent to which these are vulnerable to being hacked (Kitchin & Dodge, 2017). The second is the security of the data generated, stored, and shared across such technologies and infrastructures (Kitchin & Dodge, 2017). The latter is directly related to the former as improper access to data is often achieved via security weaknesses in a system's components, architecture, and operation. Moreover, vulnerabilities in city infrastructures and systems are exacerbated by a number of factors in relation to urban management. In addition, many smart-city vendors have little or no experience of embedding security features into their products, and cyberattacks on important urban infrastructure and city management systems have been increasing, with implications for human safety and security.

The increasing pressure on cities and local councils to make year-on-year "efficiency" savings affects security in three ways (Kitchin & Dodge, 2017):

- First, there is long-term underinvestment in infrastructure maintenance and an over-reliance on legacy systems;
- Second, the depression of salaries in most public sector organizations makes it more difficult to recruit and retain skilled and motivated IT staff who can properly implement and maintain smart-city technologies, which often leads to a lack of continuity, coordination, and responsibility;
- Third, there is a lack of investment in dedicated cybersecurity personnel and leadership in city governments. So, cybersecurity expertise is usually limited to a handful of personnel, and training across the wider workforce is limited or non-existent (increasing the likelihood of human error).

Following Kitchin, the technical approach frames urban issues in an instrumental and practical sense and not within a broader normative framework (Schechtner, 2017). Therefore, in Kitchin's opinion, it is necessary to be open to the goals, principles, practices, and policies of the smart-city initiatives and to think critically about how technologies, for example, influence city administrations. While an app could help manage homeless services or traffic flow more effectively, it does not address underlying structural causes (Schechtner, 2017). Intelligent urban technologies aim to solve questions like traffic optimization: developers might, for example, say that technology can make a system more sustainable without saying what it means to be "sustainable" beyond instrumental goals. However, there are many ideas of sustainability, and adopting the principles of different positions could lead to the development of alternative solutions.

Zhang and Li (2018) studied the difference between urban resilience (UR) and urban sustainability (US), because UR and US studies contrast not only in their different theoretical bases but also, to an even greater degree, in their empirical work. They indicate that a "concept of rational urban development" can be achieved only when it is both resilient and sustainable (Zhang & Li, 2018). According to this concept, UR is the passive process of monitoring, facilitating, maintaining, and recovering a virtual cycle between ecosystem services and human well-being through a concerted effort contingent on external influencing factors; US, on the other hand, is an active process of synergetic integration and co-evolution between the subsystems making up a city that does not compromise the possibilities for developing the surrounding areas, thus helping to mitigate the harmful effects of development on the biosphere (Zhang & Li, 2018).

Urban rational development should be seen as a process-oriented rather than an outcome-oriented action (Zhang & Li, 2018). Experimenting and learning are increasingly seen as a means to develop innovative governance approaches in the pursuit of a more sustainable society (Gugerell & Zuidema, 2017). With regard to RQ#3, "How can we achieve sustainability in IS sensitization and societal resilience?", we know for sure that raising ISA is an ongoing process. This means that if city planners consider the multiple aspects of IS from the beginning of the planning process, actually design game-based public ISAT, and integrate them into leisure activities for citizens, this should not just be done once but continuously. Changes in technology will be accompanied by new vulnerabilities and dangers, including cyberattacks. Moreover, Gugerell & Zuidema's analysis in 2017 shows that prototypes need a nuanced balance between generic and specific to allow experimentation and generate an open learning space that is, however, deeply rooted in a regional narrative and can subsequently trigger a rich variety of civic learning activities (Gugerell & Zuidema, 2017). As a consequence, city and regional planners will themselves have to experiment with public awareness training areas to create this balance.

Although smart cities have the potential to make a significant contribution to the urban sustainability agenda, so far this has not been achieved, and even with the new Urban Agenda,[9] ways to achieve urban sustainability remain, broadly speaking, unclear (Sengupta et al., 2017). As is the case in the general relationship between environmentally friendly behaviour and quality of life (see Venhoeven et al., 2017), the transition to a sustainable society in terms of IS and ISA is also an important goal: to achieve this, transition awareness and individual behavioural change will be necessary in the coming years. Emotional engagement through game-based learning (GBL) is one milestone; others include the integrative participation of citizens in urban and regional planning and a holistic approach to the development of cities.

## 5. CONCLUSION AND OUTLOOK

Digitization and the IoT will continue to build up huge networks, resulting in great changes in urban development and our lives as a whole (private, work, social). According to Rob Kitchin, the technical approach assumes that technology can solve all the problems of a city instead of recognizing that some problems can best be solved through political or social interventions, collective action, public policy, infrastructure investment, or citizen-oriented deliberative democracy (Schechtner, 2017). Moreover, technology itself leads to new challenges. Our existence within the present fifth wave category proposed by Von Solms (2010) means living with malware, phishing, spoofing, and other techniques used by criminals, which makes things extremely risky for any Internet user. There is no doubt that the increasing, technically supported mobility in all sociopolitical and economic areas is leading to an increase in the importance of IS, especially IT security, data protection, and data security. The increasing deployment of ICT in the infrastructure of cities has increased interest in smart cities with the long-term objective of enhancing the quality of services provided to citizens and ultimately improving their quality of life (Khatoun & Zeadally, 2017). However, the proliferation of digitalization leads to various IS risks and privacy issues, which should feature in urban and regional planning processes for educating citizens. Security solutions, recommendations, and standards for Internet technologies and their services should not only be discussed but also trained in the context of our private, working, and social lives.

Serious games can mimic real-world issues and thus provide a safe and open environment that invites exploration, experimentation, and learning (Gugerell & Zuidema, 2017). ISA needs knowledge, emotional concern, and team-based interaction (Helisch & Pokoyski, 2009; Scholl et al., 2016). Gamification is the key to developing IS sensitization, and many people also love games in public areas. Therefore, urban spaces should include learning areas with gamification to help raise everyone's ISA. Moreover, learning and experimenting can unfold in different formats, such as games or co-design processes (Gugerell & Zuidema, 2017). Research could further be embedded into practical (smart city) projects providing fast and systematic IS learning.

The process of transferring this into the social sphere should be scientifically substantiated in practical projects. There are two aspects to consider here: on the one hand, the society—the place where IS is to be lived—which is characterized by guidelines, procedures, and structures; on the other, the citizens—actors whose knowledge, attitudes, and behaviour make it possible to create an authentic security culture. Both sides need a common learning process that can be delineated as follows: citizens in the society and government and administration as a whole acquire IS-relevant knowledge and awareness and practise appropriate behaviour so that security culture is lived actively. However, more research on ISA is necessary in urban and regional contexts, and this requires increased public funding. Finally, these challenges will demand a higher level of inter- or transdisciplinary collaboration in both research and practice than is presently the case (Ahern, 2011). The current state of research on IS, ISA, and ISAT shows that there is no uniform framework and, more specifically, that further interdisciplinary research and comprehensive evaluations of real-life situations are necessary.

## REFERENCES

Ahern, J. (2011). From fail-safe to safe-to-fail: Sustainability and resilience in the new urban world. *Landscape and Urban Planning*, *100*(4), 341–343. doi:10.1016/j.landurbplan.2011.02.021

Al-Daeef, M. M., Basir, N., & Saudi, M. M. (2017). Security Awareness Training: A Review. In *Proceedings of the World Congress on Engineering* (Vol. 1, pp. 5-7).

AlAwadhi, S., Aldama-Nalda, A., Chourabi, H., Gil-Garcia, R. J., Leung, S., Mellouli, S., . . . Walker, S. (2012). Building Understanding of Smart City Initiatives. In H. J. Scholl, M. Janssen, M. Wimmer et al. (Eds.), Electronic Government (pp. 40-53). Springer. doi:10.1007/978-3-642-33489-4_4

Anderson, R., Barton, C., Böhme, R., Clayton, R., Van Eeten, M. J., Levi, M., . . . Savage, S. (2013). Measuring the cost of cybercrime. In *The economics of information security and privacy* (pp. 265-300). Springer Berlin Heidelberg. Retrieved from http://www.econinfosec.org/archive/weis2012/presentation/Moore_presentation_WEIS2012.pdf

BAköV [Bundesakademie für öffentliche Verwaltung im Bundesministerium des Innern]/Federal Academy of Public Administration in the Federal Ministry of Interior. (2009). IT Security Officer in the Public Administration (version 3.0, edition 2009) [Manual]. BAköV & BSI in co-operation with the Fraunhofer Institute for Secure Information Technology (SIT).

Benson, V. (2017). *The State of Global Cyber Security: Highlights and Key Findings*. London, UK: LT Inc. doi: Retrieved from https://www.researchgate.net/publication/318310907_THE_STATE_OF_GLOBAL_CYBER_SECURITY_HIGHLIGHTS_AND_KEY_FINDINGS doi:10.13140/RG.2.2.22825.49761

Benson, V., McAlaney, J., & Frumkin, L. A. (2018). Emerging Threats for the Human Element and Countermeasures in Current Cyber Security Landscape. In Psychological and Behavioral Examinations in Cyber Security (pp. 266-271). Hershey, PA: IGI Global.

Beyer, M., Ahmed, S., Doerlemann, K., Arnell, S., Parkin, S., Sasse, A., & Passingham, N. (2016). *Awareness is only the first step. A framework for progressive engagement of staff in cyber security* [white paper]. Hewlett Packard.

Bundesamt für Sicherheit in der Informationstechnik/Federal Office for Information Security (BSI). (2015). Knowing risks, accepting challenges, designing solutions: Preface. In *Conference Proceedings for the 14th German IT Security Conference*, Bonn, Germany.

Buchanan, J., & Gordon, T. (1962). *The calculus of consent: Logical foundations of a constitutional democracy*. Ann Arbor, MI: University of Michigan Press. doi:10.3998/mpub.7687

Chen, C. C., Medlin, B. D., & Shaw, R. S. (2008). A cross-cultural investigation of situational information security awareness programs. *Information Management & Computer Security*, 16(4), 360–376. doi:10.1108/09685220810908787

Choi, N., Kim, D., Goo, J., & Whitmore, A. (2008). Knowing is doing. An empirical validation of the relationship between managerial information security awareness and action. *Information Management & Computer Security*, 16(5), 484–501. doi:10.1108/09685220810920558

Chun, S. A., Geller, J., Taunk, A., Sankaran, K., & Swaminathan, T. (2016). Slob: security learning by ontology browsing: comprehensive cyber security learning resources in a web portal. *Journal of Computing Sciences in Colleges*, 31(5), 95–101.

Collier, M. J., Nedović-Budić, Z., Aerts, J., Connop, S., Foley, D., Foley, K., ... Verburg, P. (2013). Transitioning to resilience and sustainability in urban communities. *Cities (London, England)*, 32, 21–28. doi:10.1016/j.cities.2013.03.010

Cone, B. D., Irvine, C. E., Thompson, M. F., & Nguyen, T. D. (2007). A Video Game for Cyber Security Training and Awareness. *Computers & Security*, 26(1), 63–72. doi:10.1016/j.cose.2006.10.005

Cone, B. D., Thompson, M. F., Irvine, C. E., & Nguyen, T. D. (2006). Cyber security training and awareness through game play. In *IFIP International Information Security Conference*, Boston, MA (pp. 431-436). Springer. 10.1007/0-387-33406-8_37

Cornillie, F., Clarebout, G., & Desmet, P. (2012). The role of feedback in foreign language learning through digital role playing games. *Procedia: Social and Behavioral Sciences*, 34, 49–53. doi:10.1016/j.sbspro.2012.02.011

Dang-Pham, D., Pittayachawan, S., & Bruno, V. (2017). Why employees share information security advice? Exploring the contributing factors and structural patterns of security advice sharing in the workplace. *Computers in Human Behavior*, 67, 196–206. doi:10.1016/j.chb.2016.10.025

Dark, M. J. (2006). Security Education, Training and Awareness from a Human Performance Technology Point of View. In M. E. Whitman & H. J. Mattord (Eds.), *Readings and Cases in Management of Information Security* (pp. 86–104). Course Technology, Mason.

Di Mascio, D., & Dalton, R. (2017). Using Serious Games to Establish a Dialogue Between Designers and Citizens in Participatory Design. In *Serious Games and Edutainment Applications* (pp. 433–454). Springer International Publishing. doi:10.1007/978-3-319-51645-5_20

Ersoy, A. (2017). Smart cities as a mechanism towards a broader understanding of infrastructure interdependencies. *Regional Studies, Regional Science, 4*(1), 26–31.

Gordon, L. W., & McAleese, G. W. (2017). Resilience and Risk Management in Smart Cities. *The CIP Report.*

Gugerell, K., & Zuidema, C. (2017). Gaming for the energy transition. Experimenting and learning in co-designing a serious game prototype. *Journal of Cleaner Production, 169*, 105–116. doi:10.1016/j.jclepro.2017.04.142

Gunning, J. P. (2003). *Understanding democracy: an introduction to public choice.* Nomad Press.

Hagen, J. M., Albrechtsen, E., & Hovden, J. (2008). Implementation and effectiveness of organizational information security measures. *Information Management & Computer Security, 16*(4), 377–397. doi:10.1108/09685220810908796

Head, B. W. (2007). Community engagement: Participation on whose terms? *Australian Journal of Political Science, 42*(3), 441–454. doi:10.1080/10361140701513570

Helisch, M., & Pokoyski, D. (Eds.). (2009). Security Awareness. Neue Wege zur erfolgreichen Mitarbeiter-Sensibilisierung. Vieweg+Teubner.

Hendrix, M., Al-Sherbaz, A., & Victoria, B. (2016). Game based cyber security training: are serious games suitable for cyber security training? *International Journal of Serious Games, 3*(1), 53-61/2384-8766.

Herath, T., & Rao, H. R. (2009). Encouraging information security behaviors in organizations: Role of penalties, pressures and perceived effectiveness. *Decision Support Systems, 47*(2), 154–165. doi:10.1016/j.dss.2009.02.005

Ho, S. M., Von Eberstein, A., & Chatmon, C. (2017). In S. Goel (Ed.), *Expansive Learning in Cyber Defense: Transformation of Organizational Information Security Culture.*

Hu, Q., Dinev, T., Hart, P., & Cooke, D. (2012). Managing employee compliance with information security policies: The critical role of top management and organizational culture. *Decision Sciences, 43*(4), 615–660. doi:10.1111/j.1540-5915.2012.00361.x

Hwang, K., & Choi, M. (2017). Effects of innovation-supportive culture and organizational citizenship behavior on e-government information system security stemming from mimetic isomorphism. *Government Information Quarterly, 34*(2), 183–198. doi:10.1016/j.giq.2017.02.001

Jin, G., Tu, M., Kim, T. H., Heffron, J., & White, J. (2018). Game based Cybersecurity Training for High School Students. In *Proceedings of the 49th ACM Technical Symposium on Computer Science Education* (pp. 68-73). ACM. 10.1145/3159450.3159591

Jones, B. H., Chin, A. G., & Aiken, P. (2014). Risky business: Students and smartphones. *TechTrends*, *58*(6), 73–83. doi:10.100711528-014-0806-x

Kangas, M. (2010). Creative and playful learning: Learning through game co-creation and games in a playful learning environment. *Thinking Skills and Creativity*, *5*(1), 1–15. doi:10.1016/j.tsc.2009.11.001

Kathoun, R., & Zeadally, S. (2017). *Cybersecurity and Privacy Solutions in Smart Cities. IEEE Communications Magazine, 55(3),* 51–59. doi:10.1109/MCOM.2017.1600297CM

Khan, B., Alghathbar, K. S., Nabi, S. I., & Khan, M. K. (2011). Effectiveness of information security awareness methods based on psychological theories. *African Journal of Business Management*, *5*(26), 10862–10868.

Kim, B. H., Kim, K. C., Hong, S. E., & Oh, S. Y. (2017). Development of cyber information security education and training system. *Multimedia Tools and Applications*, *76*(4), 6051–6064. doi:10.100711042-016-3495-y

Kim, E. B. (2014). Recommendations for information security awareness training for college students. *Information Management & Computer Security*, *22*(1), 115–126. doi:10.1108/IMCS-01-2013-0005

Kirlappos, I., Beautement, A., & Sasse, M. A. (2013). 'Comply or Die' Is Dead: Long Live Security-Aware Principal Agents. In A. A. Adams, M. Brenner, & M. Smith (Eds.), *Financial Cryptography and Data Security, FC 2013* (pp. 70–82). Springer. doi:10.1007/978-3-642-41320-9_5

Kirlappos, I., & Sasse, M. A. (2012). Security education against phishing: A modest proposal for a major rethink. *IEEE Security and Privacy*, *10*(2), 24–32. doi:10.1109/MSP.2011.179

Kitchin, R., & Dodge, M. (2017). The (in)security of smart cities: vulnerabilities, risks, mitigation and prevention. Retrieved from https://osf.io/preprints/socarxiv/f6z63

Krek, A. (2005). Rational ignorance of the citizens in public participatory planning. In *10th symposium on Information-and communication technologies (ICT) in urban planning and spatial development and impacts of ICT on physical space, CORP.*

Kruger, H. A., & Kearney, W. D. (2006). A prototype for assessing information security awareness. *Computers & Security*, *25*(4), 289–296. doi:10.1016/j.cose.2006.02.008

Laamarti, F., Eid, M., & El Saddik, A. (2014). An Overview of Serious Games. *International Journal of Computer Games Technology*, 11.

Lee, J. H., Phaal, R., & Lee, S. H. (2013). An integrated service-device-technology roadmap for smart city development. *Technological Forecasting and Social Change*, *80*(2), 286–306. doi:10.1016/j.techfore.2012.09.020

Liang, H., Xue, Y., & Wu, L. (2013). Ensuring Employees' IT Compliance: Carrot or Stick? *Information Systems Research*, *24*(2), 279–294. doi:10.1287/isre.1120.0427

Mahfuth, A., Yussof, S., Baker, A. A., & Ali, N. A. (2017). A systematic literature review: Information security culture. In *2017 International Conference on Research and Innovation in Information Systems (ICRIIS)*, (pp. 1-6). IEEE. 10.1109/ICRIIS.2017.8002442

McCrohan, K. F., Engel, K., & Harvey, J. W. (2010). Influence of Awareness and Training on Cyber Security. *Journal of Internet Commerce*, *9*(1), 23–41. doi:10.1080/15332861.2010.487415

Mitchell, A., & Savill-Smith, C. (2004). The use of computer and video games for learning: A review of the literature. Retrieved from http://dera.ioe.ac.uk/5270/7/041529_Redacted.pdf

Moody, R. (2007). Assessing the role of GIS in e-government: A tale of e-participation in two cities. In Electronic Government (pp. 354-365).

Moustaka, V., Vakali, A., & Anthopoulos, L. G. (2017). CityDNA: Smart City Dimensions' Correlations for Identifying Urban Profile. In *Proceedings of the 26th International Conference on World Wide Web Companion* (pp. 1167-1172). 10.1145/3041021.3054714

Pattinson, M., Parsons, K., Butavicius, M., McCormac, A., & Calic, D. (2016). Assessing information security attitudes: A comparison of two studies. *Information & Computer Security*, *24*(2), 228–240. doi:10.1108/ICS-01-2016-0009

Peeters, M., Megens, C., van den Hoven, E., Hummels, C., & Brombacher, A. (2013, April). Social stairs: taking the piano staircase towards long-term behavioral change. In *International Conference on Persuasive Technology* (pp. 174-179). Springer. 10.1007/978-3-642-37157-8_21

Pokoyski, D. (2009). Security Awareness: Von der Oldschool in die Next Generation – eine Einführung. In M. Helisch & D. Pokoyski (Eds.), *Security Awareness. Neue Wege zur erfolgreichen Mitarbeiter-Sensibilisierung* (pp. 1–8). *Vieweg+Teubner*. doi:10.1007/978-3-8348-9594-3_1

Pokoyski, D. (2018). Zählen oder erzählen – was zählt? Security und Gamfication: Awareness you can touch and feel. *Datakontext*, (2), 12-18.

Poplin, A. (2012). Playful public participation in urban planning: A case study for online serious games. *Computers, Environment and Urban Systems*, *36*(3), 195–206. doi:10.1016/j.compenvurbsys.2011.10.003

Raybourn, E. M. (2014). A new paradigm for serious games: Transmedia learning for more effective training and education. *Journal of Computational Science*, *5*(3), 471–481. doi:10.1016/j.jocs.2013.08.005

Romero-Lankao, P., Bruns, A., & Wiegleb, V. (2018). From risk to WEF security in the city: The influence of interdependent infrastructural systems. *Environmental Science & Policy*, *90*, 213–222. doi:10.1016/j.envsci.2018.01.004

Sadeh-Koniecpol, N., Wescoe, K., Brubaker, J., & Hong, J. (2017). U.S. Patent No. 9,547,998. Washington, DC: U.S. Patent and Trademark Office.

Sadeh-Koniecpol, N., Wescoe, K., Brubaker, J., & Hong, J. (2017b). U.S. Patent No. 9,558,677. Washington, DC: U.S. Patent and Trademark Office.

Sadeh-Koniecpol, N., Wescoe, K., & Ferrara, J. A. (2016). U.S. Patent No. 9,398,029. Washington, DC: U.S. Patent and Trademark Office.

Safa, N. S., Von Solms, R., & Furnell, S. (2016). Information security policy compliance model in organizations. *Computers & Security, 56*, 70–82. doi:10.1016/j.cose.2015.10.006

Sanfilippo, F. (2017). A multi-sensor fusion framework for improving situational awareness in demanding maritime training. *Reliability Engineering & System Safety, 161*, 12–24. doi:10.1016/j.ress.2016.12.015

Sarwat, A. I., Sundararajan, A., Parvez, I., Moghaddami, M., & Moghadasi, A. (2018). Toward a Smart City of Interdependent Critical Infrastructure Networks. In *Sustainable Interdependent Networks* (pp. 21–45). Cham: Springer. doi:10.1007/978-3-319-74412-4_3

Schechtner, K. (2017). Bridging the Adoption Gap for Smart City Technologies: An Interview with Rob Kitchin. *IEEE Pervasive Computing, 16*(2), 72–75. doi:10.1109/MPRV.2017.38

Scholl, H. J., & Scholl, M. (2014). Smart Governance: A Roadmap for Research and Practice. In Kindling & E. Greifeneder (Eds.), iConference 2014 Proceedings (pp. 163-176). Illinois: iSchools.

Scholl, M., Fuhrmann, F., & Pokoyski, D. (2016). Information Security Awareness 3.0 for Job Beginners. In J.E. Quintela Varajão, M.M. Cruz-Cunha, & R. Martinho et al. (Eds.), *Conference on ENTERprise Information Systems (CENTERIS)* (pp. 433-436). Porto, Portugal.

Sengupta, U., Doll, C. N., Gasparatos, A., Iossifova, D., Angeloudis, P., da Silva Baptista, M. D. S., … Oren, N. (2017). Sustainable Smart Cities: Applying Complexity Science to Achieve Urban Sustainability. Retrieved from https://abdn.pure.elsevier.com/en/publications/sustainable-smart-cities-applying-complexity-science-to-achieve-u

Shaw, R. S., Chen, C. C., Harris, A. L., & Huang, H.-J. (2009). The impact of information richness on information security awareness training effectiveness. *Computers & Education, 52*(1), 92–100. doi:10.1016/j.compedu.2008.06.011

Slusky, L., & Partow-Navid, P. (2012). Students Information Security Practices and Awareness. *Journal of Information Privacy and Security, 8*(4), 3–26. doi:10.1080/15536548.2012.10845664

Spaans, M., & Waterhout, B. (2017). Building up resilience in cities worldwide – Rotterdam as participant in the 100 resilient cities programme. *Cities (London, England), 61*, 109–116. doi:10.1016/j.cities.2016.05.011

Sullivant, J. (2016). *Building a Corporate Culture of Security: Strategies for Strengthening Organizational Resiliency*. Oxford: Butterworth-Heinemann.

Sun, J., Ahluwalia, P., & Koong, K. S. (2011). The more secure the better? A study of information security readiness. *Industrial Management & Data Systems, 111*(4), 570–588. doi:10.1108/02635571111133551

Tøndel, I. A., Foros, J., Kilskar, S. S., Hokstad, P., & Jaatun, M. G. (2017). Interdependencies and Reliability in the Combined ICT and Power System: An overview of current research. *Applied Computing and Informatics*. Retrieved from https://www.sciencedirect.com/science/article/pii/S2210832716300552

Tsohou, A., Karyda, M., Kokalakis, S., & Kiountouzi, E. (2015). Managing the introduction of information security awareness programmes in organisations. *European Journal of Information Systems, 24*(1), 38–58. doi:10.1057/ejis.2013.27

Vaidya, J., Lorenzi, D., Shafiq, B., Chun, S., & Badar, N. (2014, October). Teaching privacy in an interactive fashion. In *Proceedings of the 2014 Information Security Curriculum Development Conference* (p. 7). ACM.

Van Niekerk, J. F., & Von Solms, R. (2010). Information security culture: A management perspective. *Computers & Security*, *29*(4), 476–486. doi:10.1016/j.cose.2009.10.005

Venhoeven, L., Steg, L., & Bolderdijk, J. W. (2017). Can Engagement in Environmentally-Friendly Behavior Increase Well-Being? In Handbook of Environmental Psychology and Quality of Life Research (pp. 229-237). Springer International Publishing. doi:10.1007/978-3-319-31416-7_13

Von Solms, B., & Von Solms, R. (2018). *Cyber security and information security–what goes where? Information & Computer Security, (just-accepted)*. Emerald Publishing Limited. doi:10.1108/ICS-04-2017-0025

Von Solms, S. H. (2010). The 5 Waves of Information Security – From Kristian Beckman to the Present. In K. Rannenberg, V. Varadharajan, & C. Weber (Eds.), *SEC 2010, IFIP International Federation for Information Processing AICT 330* (pp. 1–8). doi:10.1007/978-3-642-15257-3_1

Warkentin, M., Johnston, A. C., & Shropshire, J. (2011). The influence of the informal social learning environment on information privacy policy compliance efficacy and intention. *European Journal of Information Systems*, *20*(3), 267–284. doi:10.1057/ejis.2010.72

Willison, R., & Warkentin, M. (2013). Beyond deterrence: An expanded view of employee computer abuse. *Management Information Systems Quarterly*, *37*(1), 1–20. doi:10.25300/MISQ/2013/37.1.01

Wolff, A., Kortuem, G., & Cavero, J. (2015). Urban Data Games: creating smart citizens for smart cities. In *Proceedings of IEEE 15th International Conference on Advanced Learning Technologies* (pp. 164–165). IEEE. 10.1109/ICALT.2015.44

Workman, M. (2007). Gaining Access with Social Engineering: An Empirical Study of the Threat. *Information Systems Security*, *16*(6), 315–331. doi:10.1080/10658980701788165

Zhang, X., & Li, H. (2018). Urban resilience and urban sustainability: What we know and what do not know? *Cities (London, England)*, *72*, 141–148. doi:10.1016/j.cities.2017.08.009

Zyda, M. (2005). From visual simulation to virtual reality to games. *Computer*, *38*(9), 25–32. doi:10.1109/MC.2005.297

## ENDNOTES

[1]    https://www.digitale-agenda.de/Webs/DA/DE/Home/home_node.html

[2]    https://ec.europa.eu/digital-single-market/.

[3]    https://de.statista.com/statistik/daten/studie/295485/umfrage/besorgnis-der-eu-buerger-opfer-eines-identitaetsdiebstahls-im-internet-zu-werden

[4]    https://www.bsi.bund.de/DE/Themen/ITGrundschutz/ITGrundschutzKataloge/Inhalt/_content/m/m04/m04034.html

5    https://www.bsi.bund.de/DE/Themen/ITGrundschutz/ITGrundschutzKataloge/Inhalt/_content/m/
m02/m02046.html?nn=6610622

6    https://www.heise.de/newsticker/meldung/Besonderes-elektronisches-Anwaltspostfach-Schaden-
ersatzforderung-und-Vertroestungen-3976424.html

7    https://www.gen-cyber.com

8    https://www.gartner.com/it-glossary/gamification-2/

9    http://habitat3.org/the-new-urban-agenda/

*Previously published in the International Journal of E-Planning Research (IJEPR), 8(3); pages 62-86, copyright year 2019 by IGI Publishing (an imprint of IGI Global).*

# Chapter 20
# A Comparative Study in Israel and Slovenia Regarding the Awareness, Knowledge, and Behavior Regarding Cyber Security

**Galit Klein**
*Ariel University, Israel*

**Moti Zwilling**
*Ariel University, Israel*

**Dušan Lesjak**
*International School for Social and Business Studies, Slovenia*

## ABSTRACT

*With the COVID-19 pandemic, many organizations and institutions moved to e-learning and to e-working from home. With the increase in internet usage, the rate of cyber-attacks have also increased, and this was followed by the request for more cyber security behaviors from employees and students. In the current study, the authors explore the connection between cyber security awareness, cyber knowledge, and cyber security behavior. The authors measured the behaviors among students in two similar countries: Israel and Slovenia. Results show that students felt they had adequate awareness on cyber threat but apply only a few protective measures to protect their devices, usually relatively common and simple ones. The study findings also show that awareness to cyber threats mediate the connection between knowledge and protection behaviors, but only in the case that the knowledge is specific with regard to IT protection courses. Results, implications, and recommendations for effective cyber security training programs for organizations and academic institutions are presented and discussed.*

DOI: 10.4018/978-1-6684-3698-1.ch020

## INTRODUCTION

As the usage of internet increases, cyber security became one of the main concern for private individuals, companies and governments. Cyber threats include various malwares and cybercrime activities, such as the usage of trojan horses, worms, ransomware and spyware malware to perform attacks, collect information, bypass an unauthorised access to data assets and other kinds of hateful behaviours (Srinivas, Kumar Das & Kumar, 2019). These malicious attacks harming and causing disruption to business operations, financial loss but also reduce the trust between computer users and their companies services. In order to response to this problem government legislated several regulation that are aim to protect private and public sectors from crime behaviours, such as the 1996 Health Insurance Portability and Accountability Act (HIPAA) or the Federal Information Security Management Act (FISMA) (Srinivas et al., 2019).

Legislating regulation is just one solution, among others, that increases awareness to cyber hazards among others, including education and training programs. While education process and interactions is not considered as a new idea and has been introduced for several years (Dunn, 2012)[1] the new pandemic accelerated this process. Today, more than ever, children, students, teachers and lecturers are learning through the internets. According to Dunn (2012) the ability to access into unlimited amounts of data, cause them to expand their learning and knowledge horizons, but also to add to their dynamic educational experiences (Dunn, 2012). With that, moving to e-learning environment and relying on cyber technologies which are improved rapidly (from a technological perspective) had yield an increasingly difficult challenges to protect the users from malicious activities and cyber-attacks. As the potential for cyber-attacks became lucid, researches (e.g. Al-Janabi, S., & Al-Shourbaji, 2016; McDaniel, 2013) argue that educational institution should apply cyber awareness programs for cyber protection and cyber security methods. Awareness programs should provide cyber awareness program, cyber knowledge and cyber security active training for users and employees. The programs should be instrumental in developing and spreading security awareness among cyber users, employing proper physical access controls, obeying the security policies and rules as laid down by the institution and the firm in order to achieve the best security outcomes (McDaniel, 2013).

Several cyber security awareness training programs had been presented in the literature affiliated with the awareness program itself (Shaw et al., 2009). Other studies (Lehto, 2015) emphasized the need to understand the factors that motivate or suppress cyber hazard awareness among users. In the current study we will address another angel, and try to reveal *if there is a connection between cyber knowledge, cyber awareness and cyber security behaviours*. To measure these connections we conducted a comparison study in which we compare collected data by Israeli and Slovenian students from the department of Economics & Business Administration, in both countries. The data was defined by the following variables: cyber knowledge, cyber behaviour and the cyber security awareness. Implications and results are farther discussed.

## LITERATURE REVIEW

### Cyber Security Risks and Solutions

Since the end of the 20th century cyber online transactions has become integral part of our life. As cyber usage becomes more and more prominent, amongst individuals with different levels of knowledge of information technology (IT), there also has been an escalating in the number of cyber-attacks. Cyber threats range from a simple attack, such as spam mails, to a more complicated attacks, such as those conducted by organized cyber-crime groups that use malicious software to steal, corrupt and destroy data stored in people's and organization's devices (Lehto, 2015). For example, in the year 2016, 65% of the UK large businesses reported of being a victim to viruses, spyware or malware. Since this number is only represent companies that reported on a cyber-attack incident we can only assume that the "real" number is much higher (Sharf, 2016). Form individual perspective scholars found that the rate of cyber bullying victimization increased from 18.8% in 2007 to 27.32% in 2010 (Hinduja and Patchin, 2014). Similarly Rek and Milanovski, (2017) reported that most of the secondary school pupils admit to share personal information regarding their life in the networks without having enough aware of the potential exploitation of this information.

According to Srinivas et al. (2019) cyber-attacks are various and include different behaviors that are aimed for different instruments, that have some connection to the networkers. For example attacks can be executed by an implementation of viruses and various attack methodologies, such as the usage of infected programs; phishing attacks, which aim to steal important information from the users, such as information regarding their banking accounts; Planting Trojan horses, which are composed of lines of codes that are directed to execute some harmful function in the users' cyber instruments or portable devices; Worms, which are defined as programs that are actively seek for more instruments in the network to infect them and delete and or utilize important data and files in the system; Spyware which is defined as a program that tracks after crucial and confidential information; Ransomware and Crypto-Ransomwares, which are malwares that prevents or limits the users from accessing their system until a requested payment of money, mostly in cryptocurrency, will be delivered by them (i.e. a ransom money); Unauthorized access, that includes the access by unauthorized person in order to grab crucial information from the system, including important credentials and passwords. These example are part of a wide range of malicious behaviors that evolve as the usage of computers and the networks increase. Unfortunately this is an arms race where companies that act to produce cyber defense tools against cyber-attacks find themselves facing with new techniques of attacks by new malicious tools which are managed and operated by malicious attackers (adversary).

Understating that the increase in the cyber usage escalate the problem of cyber-attacks leads to requirement for solutions in manner of cyber security standards. Cyber security standards are defined as methods and processes that are implemented and used in an attempt to protect the users or the organizations' cyber environments (Srinivas et al., 2019). These policies and affiliated operational mitigation programs are aimed to reduce and minimize various attacks, and are diversified from macro to micro solutions: from national strategies to individual education programs. The national strategy to secure the cyberspace include among others: legislation of laws, rules and regulations. For example The National Strategy to Secure Cyberspace in the USA is aiming for prevention cyber-attacks against America's critical infrastructures, reducing national system's and infrastructure's vulnerabilities to cyber-attacks and the derived damage as well as the recovery time reduction from cyber-attacks that do acquire[2]. Many companies and individuals search for solutions that can defend themselves from cybersecurity incidents. The solutions are aim to detect and identify cybersecurity incidents before they occur, respond and defend the company's assets or individual's devices from the attack or minimize the damage if the attack already carried out and perform recovery activities in their networks and their systems from the cybersecurity incidents when the attack is detected by IDS (Intrusion Detection Systems) applications. These response categories to cyber threats can also be divided into the following technical solutions: I)

Anti-viruses programs or cyber security requirements or procedures, and II) to non-technical solutions, such as cyber security awareness training programs.

## Security Awareness Training and Educating Programs

Cyber security behaviors' mapping indicated that individuals are often perform minimum efforts to protect themselves from cyber-attacks. For example, Lukanovič (2017) reported that 40% of the responders in his study argue that they did not know how to install or did not install a protection software on their Internet-connected devices (computer, phone, etc.). The author also report that around 85% of the correspondents admit their computer was infected by virus. While in this study the responders indicated on high percentage of cybersecurity incidents, around one-half of the responders felt that they hold enough information to protect themselves from the misuse of their personal data. These examples highlight the gap between knowledge and behaviors.

One of the approaches to mitigate cyber security incidents is to develop specific programs that are aim to increase the awareness among cyber and network users in an effective way (Kumaraguru et al.,2007). According to the Information Security forum (ISF), security awareness is considered as a "continual process of learning by which, trainees realize the importance of information security issue, the security level required by the organization, and individuals' security duties"[3] . This definition emphasize the role of learning and the length of lessons taken by the trainees, however Al-Daeef, Basir and Saudi (2017) also highlight the role of behaviors that should also be taken into account. The authors argue that learning should be considered as the first phase, that must be accompanied by a change in the behaviors of the users. Thus they defined cyber security awareness as "the security knowledge that has been gradually acquired through a continuous and catchy training manner to influence trainees' behavior" (p. 6).

In addition, Dodge (2007), highlight the need for cyber awareness training in organizations since, for his opinion, most of the recent cyber breaches were caused due to direct involvement of human factors, such as negligent of technology operations or inside intruders. Dodge (2007) and Shaw et al., (2009) also suggested that many users are unaware of the cyber risks that council in usage of applications, during the delivery process of information by social networks or that are conceal during the process of web pages surfing along the internet. The scholars suggested that hackers, either individual or organized cyber-crime groups, usually search for the vulnerable squad related to information and networks security which the user is not aware to. The squad is often based on an application, known as a "Software application Bug", (also known as CVE [Common Vulnerability Exploit] or due to a security breach which was created by the users themselves unintentionally. Therefore, increasing the users awareness to these vulnerabilities can increase their readiness to protect the networks from cyber-hazards and cybersecurity incidents.

Over the years scholars explored types of cyber security awareness programs that suggested to students as well as to organizations. For example, Abawajy (2014) explored user preferences regarding cyber security awareness training techniques and methods. Abawajy indicated that cyber education/training can be categories to different methods depending on delivery technique which contains: online training, contextual training and embedded training. Pawlowski & Yoonhyuk (2015) examined students' regard to cyber security threats. The scholars succeed to identified 23 concepts that are forming the cyber security understandings. Based on their findings they suggested that cyber security courses most concern as a problem centered, during which the course should include case studies that are tailored to students' level of awareness. In addition they advise to use this taxonomy and alter security issues from higher-level courses to intermediate and lower ones. Son et al. (2015) also suggested to make differentiation between the programs suggested by the institution. With that, they advise that the program must include some practice plans, such as security labs, to strength the success of the programs.

Although several cyber awareness program are recommended for education institutions there are still existing questions regarding the effect of cyber awareness programs and cyber security behaviors. Dodge (2007) found that phishing scam victims level has dropped among students who were exposed to a program illustrating phishing attacks. McCrohan, Engel., & Harvey (2010) examined the awareness of users to passwords and evaluated ways of securing computers pre and post cyber security training and found that the cyber education/training internet experience created a change in their behaviors. As such the scholars emphasized the need for an appropriate security practices that will change the online behavior in their day-to-day practice. Eminağaoğlu, Uçar., & Eren (2009), showed that awareness campaigns can play as a positive effect in reducing cyber risks among individuals. The authors found that the level of exposure and the extension of training program have forced students to use complex passwords for their own computer during time. The authors argue that providing security awareness to individuals influence the complete reaction toward information security management among employees and individuals. However, changing the password is one of the approaches students can apply to protect their devices. There are many additional means that may not be trivial for the laymen users. In the current study we postulate that *cyber knowledge increases cyber awareness to cyber security problem*s. We also intend to explore whether *cyber knowledge will increase cyber awareness to hazard, which will effect the protection behaviors* that the students will carry out to protect their devices from being infected by malicious software. Since Israel and Slovenia have similar GDP values as both considered as developed countries the behaviors of students in both countries was compared.

## METHODOLOGY

### Sample

A paper-based survey was distributed, among BA students from the department of Economics and Business Administration at Ariel University in Israel (n= 81), and BA and MBA students at the International School for Social and Business Studies from Celje, in Slovenia (n=35). The subjects were located through convenience sampling. Overall the sample included 116 subjects who participated in the survey. Table 1 exhibits the demographic characteristic of the total sample and for each of the respondents within the countries

Around 46% of the responders were male, but most of them came from Israel, while the number of females was much higher in the Slovenian group compared to the number of the males in Slovenia. The majority of the students were full-time students, both in Israel and in Slovenia. Most of the Israeli responders, majored in economics, while the Slovenian responders were divided between economic and business administration.

*Table 1. demographic Characteristics of the sample*

| Characteristics of participants | Israel | | Slovenia | | Total | |
|---|---|---|---|---|---|---|
| | # | % | # | % | # | % |
| Total | 81 | 100 | 35 | 100 | 116 | 100 |
| Male | 43 | 53.1 | 10 | 28.6 | 53 | 45.7 |
| Female | 38 | 46.9 | 25 | 71.4 | 63 | 54.3 |
| **Type of students** | | | | | | |
| Bachelor | 67 | 82.7 | 11 | 31.4 | 78 | 67.2 |
| Master | 10 | 12.3 | 24 | 68.6 | 34 | 29.3 |
| Ph.D. | 4 | 4.9 | | | 4 | 3.4 |
| **Type of study** | | | | | | |
| Part-time | 24 | 29.6 | 9 | 25.7 | 33 | 28.4 |
| Full-time | 57 | 70.4 | 26 | 74.3 | 83 | 71.6 |
| **Study field** | | | | | | |
| Economics | 33 | 40.7 | 15 | 42.9 | 48 | 41.4 |
| Business & Management | 24 | 29.6 | 20 | 57.1 | 44 | 37.9 |
| ICT & Logistics & Other | 24 | 29.6 | | | 24 | 20.7 |

## Instruments

### Survey Study

To measure our assumptions we developed a new questionnaire that aimed to test familiarity of the subjects to cyber in general as well as to test the level of awareness to cyber security risks[4] specifically. Table 2 present the questions and scale that measured the different variables. Each respondent was being asked about former knowledge in cyber, internet usage and cyber security experience. The classification to different categories was conducted according to the level of respondent's knowledge to cyber security and cyber threats (*Knowledge*), their cyber security awareness (*Awareness*), their familiarity with cyber security incidents, and their attempts to control and prevent cyber-attack (*Behavior*).

### Fuzzy Logic Study

A fuzzy testing concept, or more specifically, fuzzy hypothesis testing is a considered as a verification-based method in machine learning. The fuzzy hypothesis test is used to determine the truth (or falsity) of a proposed hypothesis. The fuzzy model is executed on the fuzzy data and produce a value on [0,1] indicates on the degree to which the hypothesis is considered as valid for a given sample data.

A fuzzy set, as defined by Zadeh (1965) is composed of several elements: Inputs that are connected to outputs through member functions. The model used is comprised of three steps as described by Zwilling (2020):

- "The first step of Fuzzification is executed as the transformation of numerical values into ordinary language, if necessary. For example, the inputs hold linguistic values such as Low, Medium, and High. Each variable usually contains three to seven terms (Attributes)."

- "The second step is expressed in a "Fuzzy Inference" which defines the system behavior by means of the rules such as <if>, <and>, <then>, <with>. The conditional clauses create rules, which evaluate the input variables. These conditional clauses were designed as follows:

- <if> $x_1$ is value $x'1$ <and> $x'_2$ is value $x'_2$ … <and> $x'_N$ is value $x'_N$ <then> $y_1$ is value $y'_1$ <WITH> probability s, where $x_i$ are inputs, $y_j$ are outputs, $x'_i$ are values of inputs, $y'_j$ are values of outputs and s is a degree of support".

- "The third step ("Defuzzification") is expressed by transformation of linguistic values into numerical ones, if necessary. The outputs also use linguistic values and various types and shapes of membership functions".

"The fuzzy logic was described by the following terminology: A fuzzy set A is defined as (U, μA), where U is the relevant universal set and μA: U ® 0,1 is a membership function, which assigns each element from U to the fuzzy set A. The membership of the element x Î U of a fuzzy set A is indicated as μA(x). We define F(U) as the set of all fuzzy set. Then the "classical" set A is the fuzzy set where: μA: U ®{0, 1}. Thus x Î A, μA(x) = 0 and x ÎA, μA(x) = 1. Let Ui, i = 1, 2, …, n, be universals. Then the fuzzy relation R on U = U1 x U2 x … x Un is a fuzzy set R on the universal U".

A fuzzy model based questionnaire data for hypothesis testing validation was used for the first study (Figure 1). The Sav data was transformed into a csv file. In order to create the mapping functions for each fuzzy hypothesis, the fuzzy sets corresponding to "Country", "Awareness", "Attendance" and "Protection" have been determined. The member functions were chosen with a triangle function and the set of rules was set according to the appropriate scale (Figure 2). Finally the output was analyzed by the following code:

1. fis = ('Slovenia2.fis')
2. input = readmatrix('Slo.csv')
3. Output = evalfis(fis, input)

*Figure 1. Fuzzy Logic Model Design.*

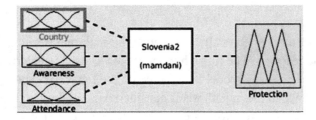

*Figure 2. Fuzzy Logic Rules*

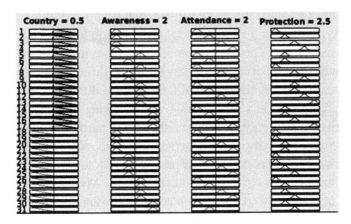

## RESULTS

## Descriptive Analysis

Descriptive analysis was initially conducted to capture the amount of awareness, knowledge and behaviors toward cyber-attacks. The results of the mean and standard deviation scores, for the total countries and in each country alone, are presented in the Table 2.

*Table 2. Descriptive statistics*

| Variables' name | Description/Question | Descriptive Statistics | | IL (n=89) | SI (n=35) | |
|---|---|---|---|---|---|---|
| | | Mean (Sd.) | Yes * | Mean (St.) | Mean (St.d) | T/ Chi² |
| Awareness | Are you familiar with the term cyber security (1- no knowledge to 4- very good | 2.44 (.81) | | 2.39 (.84) | 2.57 (.60) | T= 1.10 p>0.05 |
| Familiarity | Familiarity of different sources – total score (range from 0 through 9 sources) | 3.98 (.81) | | 3.56 (1.91) | 4.85 (2.36) | T= 3.83** |
| IT_past · | Attendance in IT security training in the past | | 21.8% | 23.6 | 17.1 | X²=.647 |
| IT future | Would like to attend in IT security training. (1- definitely not to 5- definitely yes). | 3.74 (.97) | | 3.65 (1.0) | 3.97 (.85) | T=1.66· |
| Threats | The main cyber security threats are-( 1- strongly disagrees to 5- strongly disagree) | 4.04 (.87) | | 4.06 (.88) | 4.00 (.86) | T= -.35, p>0.05 |
| Effect of Education on awareness | The extend in which the current education influenced their cyber-security awareness (1- definitely not affected to 5- strongly affected) | 3.22 (.98) | | 3.15 (.90) | 3.40 (.95) | T=1.29, p>0.05 |
| Recognition | I usually recognize and know the differences between http and https protocol | | 51.6% | 52.8% | 48.6% | X²= .18 |
| Provide | Total sum of the amount of information that the responders provide in the web (1-strongly disagree to 5- strongly disagree) | 2.42 (.93) | | 2.54 (.90) | 2.13 (.95) | T= -2.19* |
| Computer knowledge | Self-evaluation of skills and knowledge in using computer application (range from 1-no skills to 5- very high skills) | 3.22 (.67) | | 3.25 (.70) | 3.16 (.60) | T=.62, p>0.05 |
| Behavioral | I know how to behave in case of cyber-attack (1- definitely no to 5-rather yes.) | 3.10 (1.19) | | 3.07 (1.19) | 3.17 (1.20) | T=.66, p>0.05 |
| Choice | Is the use of technology products coming from your desire or by coercion (1-definitely by coercion to 5- definitely by choice) | 3.22 (1.00) | | 3.40 (.98) | 3.11 (1.02) | T=1.46, p>0.05 |
| Protection | Sum of the score in the usage that the responders make to protect their instrument (ranged from 0 to 11) | 4.09 (2.23) | | 3.50 (1.87) | 5.60 (2.39) | T=5.16*** |
| Length | The average length of your standard password (minimum 0 to maximum -14) | 9.43 (5.27) | | 8.99 (5.72) | 10.49 (3.85) | T=1.41, p>0.05 |
| Password | Do you use the same password for different portals, system and application | | 54.8% | 63 | 34.3 | X²=8.31** |
| Finish | Sum of the activities that the responders are acting when finish working on the computer (range from 0 to 4) | 1.37 (.73) | | 1.32 (.67) | 1.48 (.88) | T=1.08, p>0.05 |

*Note:* ' = standard deviation appears in the parentheses; ᵃ yes represent the percentage of people that were argue they agree with the sentence. It is relevant for dichotomy questions (i.e. yes/no questions). ᵇ for the categorical variables, the results indicate the percentage of respondents who agree with the item from the corresponding country.
'p< 0.10; *p<0.05; **p<0.01

The result indicate that responders have medium level of awareness to cyber security (M=2.44), but it was a somewhat higher among the Slovenian students compared to the Israeli values (M=2.59 and M=2.39 respectively). The overall knowledge ranged between lower to low knowledge, across the different knowledge measurement. The responders felt they have medium level amount of computer knowledge (M=3.22) and half of them argue that they know the differences between http and https protocol. However, when we asked about the degree of familiarity to different cyber protection tools out of optional 9 tools they were familiar in average with 4. When asking them about their involvement and participation in IT security courses, only 21% answered that they participate in such courses. Analysis of their behaviors regarding cyber security reveals that the subjects made some efforts to protect their tools, but it wasn't ultimate. The responders defend their password with longer length (around 9 characters), and felt that they know how to behave in the case of cyber-attack (M=3.22). On the other hand only few protection activities when finishing working on their computers were reported. Therefore it appears that the subjects are aware of the hazards in the web and make some attempts to defend themselves from cybersecurity incidents.

## The Connection Between Cyber Security Knowledge, Cyber Security Awareness and Cyber Security Behaviors

Our main concern was to assess the factors that affect cyber security behaviors and whether cyber security awareness mediate the connection between cyber knowledge and cyber security behaviors. Particularly we wanted to explore and understand if attendance in cyber security courses are related to more hazard behaviors. To analyze our assumption we conducted a path analysis by the Amos™ software with two independent variables: *computer knowledge*, indicating general knowledge regarding the usage of computer (model 1-2) and *attendance in IT courses in the past* (model 3-4). We also measured independent behaviors with two variables: *Protection*, representing the amount of measurement that the subject use to protect their devices from cyber security incidents. In addition we measured the *provide* variable which represent the amount of information that the responders are willing to share on the web. Higher result indicate on less secure behavior. Lastly, we control the students country. Table 3 exhibits the result of the path analysis.

We first measured general computer knowledge as our independent variables. We wondered if computer knowledge raise awareness which lead to more cyber *protection* behaviors. The results, as appear in table 3 model 1, indicate that the model fit was not adequate: $\chi2= 16.14$, df=2 p<0.05, TLI=.36, CFI=.79, RMSEA=.24.

In the second analysis we measured whether computer knowledge is connected to higher readiness to provide information through the web via the mediation of cyber awareness. The results, as appear in table 3 model 1, indicate that the model fit was not adequate: $\chi2= 16.08$, df=2 p<0.05, TLI= -.11, CFI=.63, RMSEA=.24. Based on the two analyses we can conclude that the awareness for cyber security does not affect the connection between computer knowledge and cyber security behaviours[5].

Next we measured the connection of attending in IT security courses with cyber security behaviors via the mediation effect of the awareness to cyber security. Table 3 exhibits model 3 fit results. The model is illustrated in Figure 3.

*Figure 3. Connection between attendance in IT course in the past, cyber security awareness and protection behaviors.*
Boldface arrows indicate structural component. e = error.

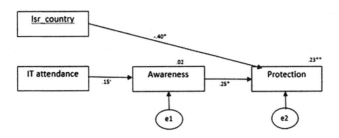

*Table 3. The results of path analysis*

| Model | Root | χ2 | df | CFI | NFI | TLI | RMSEA | χ2/df | 95%CI |
|---|---|---|---|---|---|---|---|---|---|
| Model2 | Computer knowledge--- awareness---protection | 16.14 | 2 | .79 | .78 | .36 | .24 | 8.07 | -.03, .11 |
| Model2 | Computer knowledge--- awareness---provide | 16.08 | 2 | .63 | .63 | -.11 | .24 | 8.04 | -.08, .02 |
| Model3 | IT_attendance--- awareness---protection | 1.28 | 2 | 1.00 | .96 | 1.07 | .00 | .64 | .07, .18 |
| Model4 | IT_attendance--- awareness---provide | 1.33 | 2 | 1.00 | .85 | 1.65 | .00 | .69 | -.02, -.00 |

Overall the fit of model 3 measurement was adequate: χ2= 1.28, df=2, TLI=1.07, CFI=1.00, RM-SEA=.00. The result shows that attendance in IT security in the past was close to significant with the awareness to cyber security (β=.15, p <0.10). Awareness was also connected with cyber protection behaviours (β=.25, p <0.01). In addition the bootstrap results showed that the indirect effect of attendance in IT security courses and protection behaviours via to cyber security awareness was significant (.11, B-CCI=.07-.018, p<0.00). We also found that the connection between the country and protection behaviour was significant (β=-.40, p <0.01) indicating that the Slovenian students make more cyber protections behaviors.

*Figure 4. Connection between attendance in IT course in the past, cyber security awareness and the readiness to provide information in the web.*
Boldface arrows indicate structural component. e = error.

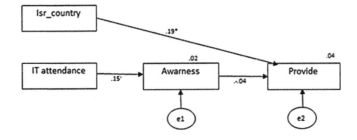

Lastly, we analysed if the connection between attendance in IT security course in the past is connected to the readiness to provide information, via the mediation of the cyber security awareness. Figure 4 illustrated the result of path analysis and table 3 exhibits model 4 fit results.

Overall the fit of model 4 measurement was adequate: $\chi2= 1.33$, df=2, TLI=1.65, CFI=1.00, RMSEA=.00. The result shows that the attendance in IT security in the past was close to significant related with the awareness of cyber security ($\beta$=.15, p <0.10), but awareness was not connected with the readiness to provide information on the web ($\beta$=-.04, p>0.05). The bootstrap results showed that the indirect effect of attendance in IT security courses and the readiness to provide information via the awareness to cyber security was significant (.09, B-CCI=-.02-.001, p<0.00). We also found that the connection between the country and protection behaviour was significant ($\beta$=.19, p <0.05) indicating that the Israeli students have more willingness to provide information through the web networks, indicating on more hazard behaviors.

The results indicate that while general knowledge may not affect the awareness to cyber security or to cyber security behaviors, attending in IT security courses do connect through the mediation of awareness to cyber knowledge.

## Conformation of the Statistical Model Based on Fuzzy Logic Model

The fuzzy logic model was found as supporting the study findings. It was found that Slovenian students who attended IT Training courses in the past, have more awareness to cyber threats and their cyber protection behavior is influenced by these two variables, so as they are less exposed to cyber threats then their Israeli students. The Surface output is shown in Figures 5.

*Figure 5. Output of Fuzzy Logic Surface related to the fit model*

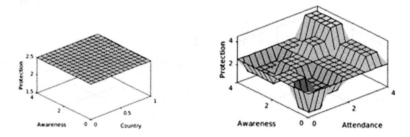

## CONCLUSION

The current study results show that internet users aware to the term "cyber security". The majority of the participates in our study felt they had adequate awareness to cyber hazard. However, being aware of a problem does not means that people are taking means to prevent them from being attacked. Similar to former studies (e.g. Imgraben, Engelbrecht, & Choo, 2014; Rek & Milanovski, 2017) we found that responders made basic and not sufficient activities. For example they used long password, and tried not to provide many information on the web. On the other hand, when they had to do active behaviors, such as conducting different procedures, when finishing using the computer, we found that the readiness to protect their device decrease. As such we can found a gap between active and passive behaviors. Since long password are mostly mandatory by the institution, we recommend that more protection action should be implant as mandatory action, to protect organizational tools.

We also found that awareness mediate the connection between knowledge and cyber security behaviors. With that, the result were somewhat surprising. Cyber hazard awareness did not affect the connection between general cyber knowledge and cyber security behaviors. On the other hand, awareness to cyber hazard mediate the connection between attendance in IT security courses and cyber security behaviors. E.g. students that participants in IT security courses in the past had higher awareness to cyber hazards, therefore conducted more protection action and provide less information on the web. These results is in congruent with former studies that indicated on the role of cyber security education programs in promoting security behaviors (Abawajy, 2014; Al-Daeef et al., 2017; Dodge, 2007). Our research reinforces the previous claims and suggests that one of the reason for the connection between cyber hazard knowledge and cyber protection behavior stems from an awareness to the potential threats in the web.

The connection between knowledge and behaviors can be explained through the Theory of Planned Behavior (TPB) (Fishbein & Ajzen, 2010). According to the theory, intention is the best predictor of planned behavior. Thus if users are aware of the threat of using computers highly it will motivate them to take multiple action to protect their computer. With that, behavior is also affected from other elements, such as the amount of self-efficacy and controllability. Therefore, when the responders perceived themselves as being able to control the situation by their behaviors, their motivation to take actions increases. This may explain why participants tend to conduct behaviors that were mandatory or required simple computer knowledge, but fail to apply more sophisticated actions to protect their devices from being abused. The results highlight the importance role of cyber security programs to motivate the cyber users for proactive behaviors. It also highlight the need to implant simple protection method that will compensate on the lack of cyber knowledge.

Lastly, we found a connection between the responder's country and the cyber security behaviors. Israeli students tend to make fewer protection behaviors and delivered more information on the web, compare to Slovenian students. One explanation is that Israelis feels that they live in a leading high-tech technology country, which is perceived as a cyber country or cyber nation (Tabansky, 2013). Thus, they may rely on their organization and country to implement protective method that will secure their devices. As individuals, they do not feel that they need to be active in protecting their devices or their organizational assets. Indeed, in his study, Tabansky (2013), describes Israel as a country that continuously strive to develop cyberspace solutions according to the change in opportunity and risks. The systematic perception of Israeli as facing against global cyber threats lead many high-tech firms in Israel to develop cyber defense technologies and invest in cyber protection R&D. Based on this assumption we believe that the more the country is developed in their substantial GDP value and tend to invest in cyber security protections measurements (such as in the case of Israel), the less the citizens make effort to conduct active protection behaviors and rely on outsiders entities to protect them. Therefore, more efforts should be invested in educating and increasing the awareness among the citizens of these countries. The result also indicated that the awareness, knowledge and especially behaviors are effected by cultural defense, values and demographic characteristic. more research should explore effects of psychological factors, such as self-efficacy and national-cultural values (Hofstede, 2001; Klein et al., 2016; Klein & Shtudiner, 2016; Shtudiner et al., 2019) on Internet user behaviors. future studies are needed to explore the active actions from senior management in the evaluated countries and may be considered as a follow up research.

During the last decades, the need to mitigate cyber risks awareness among employees and individuals had increased. Based on the results of the current study we present several recommendation that we believe will assist to increase cyber security awareness and protect personal and organizational devices.

- Organizations should provide risk management framework or internal polices, similar to the framework provided by The National Institute Standards and Technology (NIST)[6]. The cybersecurity framework (CSF) offers free guidance, based on existing regulation, standards, guidelines and practices. This framework intend to aid the organizations to better protect themselves from cyber security threats. E.g. The NIST framework indicate five core functions: Identify, Protect, Detect, Respond and Recover from attacks. However, organizations will need to customize the cybersecurity framework so it will suit the specific threats that firms is more vulnerable to. For example, universities must protect their students' and lecturers' information, while financial institutions face more extreme hazards concerning the privacy and financial threats. Therefore while the framework is general, each firm should tailor a specific protection method according to its aims and processes.

- Organizations, especially educational institutions, need to provide cyber security and cyber protection training courses. These courses duration can be either long (e.g. semester) or given as a workshop and modules (i.e. short ones), similar to the NIST courses[7]. In any case, these courses should be mandatory for the employees and students. We also recommend that students and employees will need to undergo training session on cyber threats and on cyber protection's tools on a regulatory bases, since the world of cyber hazard and cyber protection changes rapidly.

- Organizations need to oblige employees and students to implement methods that will protect organizational and individual devices. For example, to set a password that will be long enough and multi-character, so it will reduce the chance of cracking the password by Brute Force technique, for example. Organization can provide protection tools, such as antivirus software, that will be appealing for implementation by the workers and students.

- In countries that have higher awareness to high-tech and cyber R&D, similarly to Israel, organizations should explore more thoroughly the level of awareness and behaviors of their employees concerning cyber threats and cyber protection. They also should make specific courses that will highlight the gap between the national protection programs and individuals protection behaviors. As we found in our study, Israeli students made less protection behaviors compare to the Slovenian counterparts even though the country is well recognize and perceived by its high-tech development in cyber within High-Tech companies.

- Organization must rely on themselves and obtain a reliable network protection tools. Organization should not rely on the voluntary behaviors of their employees, not yet alone students. As such, they need to determine clear standards, policy and protection measurements. If the organization has number of branches or cooperation with other institution (resemble to university and research centers) standards and protection methods should be set in all of organizational branches and centers.

To conclude, with the new decade and the Covid-19 pandemic, more organizations and institutions converted to e-learning and working from home procedures (e-working). With the increase usage of internet and internet tools usage, so is the growth in the risk of being a victim to cyber-attack. Future work should focus on exploring how specific training programs based on the study findings improve the level of cyber knowledge and skills. We believe that knowledge is the basic for behavioral changes. Therefore cyber security education can assist in preventing cyber-attacks and reduction of damages caused to networks, databases and network-components due to cyber-attacks performed by organized-cybercrime groups or cybercrime individuals.

# REFERENCES

Abawajy, J. (2014). User preferences of cyber security awareness delivery methods. *Behavior & Information Technology, 33*(3), 236-247.

Al-Daeef, M. M., Basir, N., & Saudi, M. M. (2017, July). Security awareness training: A review. In *Proceedings of the World Congress on Engineering* (*Vol. 1*, pp. 5-7). Academic Press.

Al-Janabi, S., & Al-Shourbaji, I. (2016). A study of cyber security awareness in educational environment in the middle east. *Journal of Information & Knowledge Management, 15*(1). doi:10.1142/S0219649216500076

Dodge, R. C. Jr, Carver, C., & Ferguson, A. J. (2007). Phishing for user security awareness. *Computers & Security, 26*(1), 73–80. doi:10.1016/j.cose.2006.10.009

Dunn, J. (2012). *The importance of internet access in schools.* Available at http:// www.edudemic.com/2012/12/the-importance-of-internet-access-in-schools/

Eminağaoğlu, M., Uçar, E., & Eren, S. (2009). The positive outcomes of information security awareness training in companies – A case study. *Information Security Technical Report, 14*(4), 223–229. doi:10.1016/j.istr.2010.05.002

Fishbein, M., & Ajzen, I. (2011). *Predicting and Changing Behavior: The reasoned Action Approach.* Psychology Press. doi:10.4324/9780203838020

Hinduja, S., & Patchin, J. W. (2014). *Cyberbullying.* Cyberbullying Research Center. Retrieved September, 7, 2015 retrieved from https://cyberbullying.org/Cyberbullying-Identification-Prevention-Response.pdf

Hofstede, G. (2011). Dimensionalizing cultures: The Hofstede model in context. *Online Readings in Psychology and Culture, 2*(1), 2307–2319. doi:10.9707/2307-0919.1014

Imgraben, J., Engelbrecht, A., & Choo, K. (2014). Always connected, but are smart mobile users getting more security savvy? A survey of smart mobile device users'. *Behaviour & Information Technology, 33*(12), 1347–1360. doi:10.1080/0144929X.2014.934286

Klein, G. (2016). Trying to make rational decisions while employing intuitive reasoning: A Look at the due-diligence process using the dual-system reasoning model. *International Journal of Entrepreneurship and Innovation Management, 20*(3/4), 214–234. doi:10.1504/IJEIM.2016.077962

Klein, G., & Shtudiner, Z. (2016). Trust in others: Does it affect investment decisions? *Quality & Quantity, 50*(5), 1949–1967. doi:10.100711135-015-0245-6

Kumaraguru, P., Acquisti, A., Rhee, Y., & Nunge, E. (2007). Protecting people from phishing: The design and evaluation of an embedded training email system. *Conference on Human Factors in Computing Systems – Proceedings*, 905-914. 10.1145/1240624.1240760

Letho, M. (2015), Cyber Security Competencies - Cyber Security Education and Research in Finnish Universities. *14th European Conference on Cyber Warfare and Security (ECCWS)*, 179-188.

Lukanović, L. (2017). *Računalniška kriminaliteta in varstvo osebnih podatkov: diplomska naloga.* Available at: http://www.ediplome.fm-kp.si/Lukanovic_Lea_20171017.pdf

McCrohan, K., Engel, K., & Harvey, J. (2010). Influence of awareness and training on cyber security. *Journal of Internet Commerce*, *9*(1), 23–41. doi:10.1080/15332861.2010.487415

McDaniel, E. (2013, July). Securing the information and communications technology global supply chain from exploitation: Developing a strategy for education, training, and awareness. In *Proceedings of the Informing Science and Information Technology Education Conference* (pp. 313-324). Informing Science Institute. 10.28945/1813

Pawlowski, S., & Yoonhyuk, J. (2015). Social representations of cyber security by university students and implications for instructional design. *Journal of Information Systems Education*, *26*(4), 281–294.

Rek, M., & Milanovski, B.K. (2017). *Slovenija, Ljubljana: Fakulteta za medije* [izdelava]. Slovenija, Ljubljana: Univerza v Ljubljani, Arhiv družboslovnih podatkov [distribucija], IDNo: MPSS16.

Sharf, E. (2016). Information exchanges: regulatory changes to the cyber-security industry after Brexit: Making security awareness training work. *Computer Fraud & Security*, *2016*(7), 9–12. doi:10.1016/S1361-3723(16)30052-5

Shaw, R. S., Chen, C. C., Harris, A. L., & Huang, H.-J. (2009). The impact of information richness on information security awareness training effectiveness. *Computers & Education*, *52*(1), 92–100. doi:10.1016/j.compedu.2008.06.011

Shtudiner, Z., Klein, G., Zwilling, M., & Kantor, J. (2019). The value of souvenirs: Endowment effect and religion. *Annals of Tourism Research*, *74*, 17–32. doi:10.1016/j.annals.2018.10.003

Srinivas, J., Das, A. K., & Kumar, N. (2019). Government regulations in cyber security: Framework, standards and recommendations. *Future Generation Computer Systems*, *92*, 178–188. doi:10.1016/j.future.2018.09.063

Tabansky, L. (2013). Critical Infrastructure Protection Policy: The Israeli Experience. *Journal of Information Warfare*, *12*(3), 78–86.

Zadeh, L. A. (1965). Fuzzy sets. *Information and Control*, *8*(3), 338–353. doi:10.1016/S0019-9958(65)90241-X

Zwilling, M., Levy, S., Gvili, Y., & Dostal, P. (2020). Machine learning as an effective paradigm for persuasive message design. *Quality & Quantity*, *54*(3), 1–23. doi:10.100711135-020-00972-0

## ENDNOTES

[1]    Acknowledgment: The research was funded by the Ariel Cyber Innovation Center.

[2]    https://georgewbush-whitehouse.archives.gov/pcipb/

[3]    Information Security Forum (ISF): The Standard of Good Practice for Information Security. Security Standards. 2007.

[4]    Detail information regarding the instruments can be found in Zwilling, M., Klein, G., Lesjak, D., Wiechetek, L., Faith, C., Hamdullah, N.B. (2020). Cyber security knowledge, cyber threat awareness and cyber user behavior: A comparative behavioral study of Israel, Poland, Slovenia and Turkey. *Journal of Computer Information System.* 1-16 https://www.tandfonline.com/eprint/PX76PBVGPDYKV8VNYZYS/full?target=10.1080/08874417.2020.1712269

[5]    We also measured a direct connection between computer knowledge and cyber security behaviours. The model fit was still not adequate ($\chi2= 21.56$, df=2 $p<0.05$, $\chi2= 22.31$, df=2 $p<0.05$).

[6]    https://www.nist.gov/cyberframework

[7]    https://www.nist.gov/cyberframework/online-learning

*Previously published in Responsible AI and Ethical Issues for Businesses and Governments; pages 128-147, copyright year 2021 by Engineering Science Reference (an imprint of IGI Global).*

# Section 3
# Securing and Managing Cybersecurity Threats

# Chapter 21
# Enterprise Security:
## Modern Challenges and Emerging Measures

**Manish Shukla**
*TCS Research, Tata Consultancy Services, India*

**Harshal Tupsamudre**
*TCS Research, Tata Consultancy Services, India*

**Sachin Lodha**
*TCS Research, Tata Consultancy Services, India*

## ABSTRACT

*As we increasingly depend on technology, cyber threats and vulnerabilities are creating trust issues for businesses and enterprises, and cybersecurity is being considered as the number one threat to the global economy over the next 5-10 years. In this chapter, the authors explain this phenomenon by first describing the changing cyber ecosystem due to extreme digitalization and then its ramifications that are plainly visible in the latest trends in cyber-attacks. In the process, they arrive at five key implications that any modern enterprise needs to be cognizant of and discuss eight emerging measures that may help address consequences of those implications substantially. It is hoped that these measures will play a critical role in making enterprise security more proactive, cognitive, automated, connected, invisible, and risk aware.*

## INTRODUCTION

Due to the extensive digitalization in the last decade, the cost of entry into cyberspace has rapidly come down. Importantly, it has induced major changes in the enterprise and in its operating environment as manual and paper oriented processes are being replaced with software. Large scale digitalization has also made it possible for enterprises to better analyze their performance, cost drivers, customer behavior and associated risks. With the emergence of Internet of Things (IoT), there is now an explosion of interconnectivity that has led to the rapid blurring of the boundaries between virtual and physical worlds.

DOI: 10.4018/978-1-6684-3698-1.ch021

Information flows that originally were within the digital spaces are now flowing into physical spaces, leading to numerous benefits and several concerns, especially with regards to safety, security and privacy.

Indeed, a cyber threat is a possibility of an attack, via cyberspace, targeting the cyberspace of an organization for the purpose of disrupting, disabling, destroying, maliciously controlling a computing environment or stealing sensitive information (Kissel, 2011). According to 'The Global Risk Report 2019' by World Economic Forum, cyber threat is ranked 5th in terms of likelihood and ranked 7th with respect to overall impact (World Economic Forum, January 15, 2019). A large majority of respondents (82%) expect increased risk of data and money theft, and disruption in critical services (80%). The survey results clearly show the perception of new risks due to increased digitalization. This belief is substantiated by the fact that cyber threats can come from any direction, as shown by a massive distributed denial of service (DDoS) attack by IoT devices which were infected by Mirai botnet starting in 2016 (Antonakakis et al., 2017). Similarly, Meltdown (Lipp et al., 2018) and Spectre (Kocher et al., 2018) hardware vulnerabilities in modern processors allow malicious programs to steal data which is being processed on the vulnerable computer. Additionally, there are threats which are equally applicable to software and hardware, for example, ransomware attacks (Shukla, Mondal, & Lodha, 2016). The current generation of cyber threats are getting more sophisticated and have the ability to spread rapidly due to high interconnectivity between systems.

## CHANGING CYBER ECOSYSTEM

To better understand the explosion of cyber-attacks, we have to look at the changes in the cyber ecosystem due to digitalization and hyper interconnectivity.

1. **Increase in Attack Surface:** Traditionally, attack surface of a system is defined as the exposure of an application, its interfaces and objects to an attacker (Heumann, Keller, & Turpe, 2010). However, from an enterprise perspective, a system consists of a combination of hardware and software assets and the humans using them.

It has been demonstrated multiple times that even if the software is bug free, yet it is possible to steal personal and sensitive data by exploiting hardware vulnerabilities (Lipp et al., 2018; Kocher et al., 2018). In a recent paper, researchers have shown systematic degradation in deep-neural-networks (DNN) under bitwise errors that are induced by hardware fault attacks (S. Hong, Frigo, Kaya, Giuffrida, & Dumitras, 2019). According to (Ornes, 2016), only 5 million IoT devices went online in 2016 and it is estimated that 20-50 billion devices will be online by 2020. Thus, the hardware part of attack surface is growing at a rapid pace, and, that too, without security bedded into it.

Typically, software creation process involves multiple people with varying level of skills in information security, which results in buggy software. Attacks on software can be broadly divided in two classes: a) exploitation of benign software, and b) threat from malicious software. Both of these classes are fairly prominent, for example, authors in (Evtyushkin, Ponomarev, & Abu-Ghazaleh, 2016) have shown an attack on branch predictors to bypass address space layout randomization (ASLR). Similarly, authors have demonstrated exploitation of web-applications for mounting cross-site scripting (XSS) attacks and performing parasitic computation on victim's system (Eskandari, Leoutsarakos, Mursch, & Clark, 2018; Steffens, Rossow, Johns, & Stock, 2019). The other class of attacks using software is well-known, for example, ransomware (a class of malware), which sabotages the system and extort money from the user (Shukla et al., 2016). In 2018 30% data breaches were due to vulnerability in the system (Verizon, 2019).

According to researchers, human behavior is not consistent, irrational at times, and is influenced by multiple factors (Evans, Maglaras, He, & Janicke, 2016). Further, people willingly perform risky activities even if the consequences are known. Due to this, humans are considered as the weakest link in any security chain. Therefore, there is a long history of attackers exploiting human behavior (Mann, 2017). The data breach report (Verizon, 2019) mentions that 34% of breaches in 2018 happened because of insiders and 15% users misused their privileges.

2. **Scalable Attack:** A process, software or system is said to be scalable if it adapts to increasing demands or change in operational environment. With that respect, cyber-attacks are inherently scalable as they just have to exploit the resources on a computational device. One of the major reasons for their scalability is the continuous growth in the attack surface. This situation is further augmented by the lack of proper patching of buggy software or the lack of knowledge about the benefits of the regular patching of system. Often enterprise does not know the worth of a system, and hence, the associated risk to it (Shukla, Manjunath, Saxena, Mondal, & Lodha, 2015). It leads to poor prioritization of the vulnerabilities that needs to be patched and how it will affect the stability of the overall network (Abraham & Nair, 2015).

Cyber-attacks on IoT devices are more prominent as there are no good agreed upon security standards in the community (Ornes, 2016). Mirai botnet had shown that in IoT ecosystem even the basic cybersecurity hygiene of changing the default password is not followed, which enabled the botnets rapid spread (Antonakakis et al., 2017). According to a latest study (Abolhassan, 2017), the chances of finding a victim and the success of an attack improve steadily with time for a slight variation in the attack pattern. One variant of Mirai botnet caused crashing of 900 thousand routers and affected over 20 million users in Germany (Wang et al., 2017).

There is an emergence of newer attacks where the attacker tries to directly monetize the victim's compute resources for mining cryptocurrency on each affected node (Eskandari et al., 2018). The JavaScript based mining attack is highly scalable as it is executed inside a browser. Spam is another classic example of highly scalable attack as real email addresses are cheaply available in the underground markets. In an even simpler scenario, a dictionary based spam attack is sufficient to target large number of individuals as people tend to have 'firstname.lastname' as their email id.

Certain classes of attacks are usually harder to detect because they are indistinguishable from their benign lookalike, for example, ransomware is indistinguishable from a benign process (Shukla et al., 2016). Due to this, the detection of an ongoing attack takes some time, which is sufficient for the attack to spread.

3. **Accessible Attack:** Due to the extensive digitalization in the last decade, the cost of entry into cyberspace has rapidly come down. The underground economy related to cyber threats is seeing positive growth (Lusthaus, 2019). For example, attack vectors like malicious programs, also known as malwares, are easily available as a paid service. In this business model, also called Malware-as-a-Service, the malware is advertised and distributed like a normal commercial software (Gutmann, 2007). For example, Trojans like Locky can be purchased for as low as three-figure sum (Abolhassan, 2017). This has lowered the barrier for a naive attacker as extensive computer expertise is not al-

ways necessary, although it could help in generating strategic effect in and from cyberspace. The similar trend is observed for ransomware (Shukla et al., 2016) where it is offered as a service and for phishing campaigns where easy entry is possible through phishing kits (Ramzan, 2010). These underground shops either provide the malware as a service, where they take cut for each successful attack, or accept one-time payment for their exploit kits. In both the cases, they lower the expertise needed to mount a cyber-attack and make them easily accessible (Abolhassan, 2017).

Also, source-code of multiple malwares are openly and freely available on internet which can be used for creating new variants, for example, Mirai botnet and its variants (Wang et al., 2017). The availability of free SSL certificates from Certificate Authorities like 'Let's Encrypt' (Ma et al., 2019) makes the malware, phishing sites and malicious advertisements look more authentic and harder to detect. Additionally, certain hacker groups also release the unknown vulnerabilities in public for exploitation, for example, WannaCry ransomware utilized the vulnerability in the Server Message Block (SMB) protocol, which was initially discovered by a well-known security agency of the US government, and later disclosed by the 'Shadow Broker' group (Shao, Tunc, Satam, & Hariri, 2017).

4.  **Desired Impact:** In cyberspace, the action and reactions can affect the entire global community by just a click of button, that is, cyber-threats have the potential to be far more widespread and in far less amount of time (Leon, 2015). As the cost of entry into cyberspace is also lowered due to digitalization, it is easier to have a desired impact by launching a cyber-attack. The main motivating factors for a threat actor to launch a cyber-attack are:

    a.  **Personal Gains:** The attacker utilizes the confidential information of a victim for self-benefit, for example, credit card number of the victim for online shopping, or intellectual property of an enterprise for monetary gains (Homoliak, Toffalini, Guarnizo, Elovici, & Ochoa, 2019; Verizon, 2019).

    b.  **Revenge:** The attacker is driven by a desire to harm the victim, for example, a disgruntled employee leaking customer information in public domain (Homoliak et al., 2019; Verizon, 2019).

    c.  **Fame/Ego/Vanity:** The attacker tries to establish or show-off their intellectual capabilities. Mirai botnet is a typical example of this kind of attack (Antonakakis et al., 2017).

    d.  **Sabotage:** The goal here is to bring down the operations of an enterprise or a state or an industrial internet of things (IIoT) by compromising their cyberspace, or physically damaging their infrastructure (Langner, 2011; Giles, 2019). Sabotage is different from the 'Revenge' motive as the latter has emotional motivations, whereas the same might not be the case with the former. These attacks are mostly sponsored by nation states for their own good and typically show high level of sophistication, for example, Stuxnet and WannaCry.

    e.  **Extortion:** The attacker asks for favor in lieu of returning or restoring something important to the victim. It is similar to the 'Personal Gain' motive, but more direct and coercive in nature. For example, a ransomware which encrypts the user files on a system and then asks for ransom for decrypting it (Shukla et al., 2016).

    f.  **Political and Social Justice:** The attacker tries to get vigilante justice against the unjust and powerful. A well cited example is 'Anonymous Collective', a hacktivist group which hacks websites or computer networks in order to convey social or political messages (George & Leidner, 2019).

g. **Patriotism and Ideology:** The attacker's sole motivation is to help own country by crippling another country's cyberspace, or spy on someone, or install a backdoor (Vacca, 2019).

5. **Attribution is Difficult:** In case of cyber-attack it is hard to determine who initiated the attack and who is responsible for it (Finlay & Payne, 2019). Attribution is difficult, as more than often attacks are complicated and they are not physically observable. Also, attackers use sophisticated tools to hide their digital traces. Detection and damage assessment of a cyber-attack usually takes time, which in turn delays the attribution of attack (Langner, 2011; Giles, 2019). Further, it requires coordination between multiple independent affected or unaffected entities, and might require analysis of classified information that participating entities would not prefer to reveal (Finlay & Payne, 2019). Thus, making attribution of a cyber-attack even harder task. The risk of misattribution is even greater as it can create diplomatic or military conflict between the victim and the falsely accused entity. Certain nations promote and follow 'hack back' as a possible countermeasure to cyber-attacks. It gives the victim of a cyber-attack a chance to hunt down the suspected attackers (Messerschmidt, 2013). This is, however, a problematic countermeasure when attack attribution is hard, and also quite drastic if a third party utilizes it for deteriorating relations between two entities. For example, in 2014 Microsoft obtained ex parte order for controlling 22 domains for stopping two botnet networks. However, this also reportedly blocked 5 million valid users of Vitalwerks (Hiller, 2014). Cyber-attacks flourish due to multi-dimensional, hard and time consuming nature of the attack attribution.

## Latest Trends in Cyber-Attacks

The cyber-attacks are getting increasingly more sophisticated, and involve malware, artificial intelligence, cryptocurrency and social engineering. This has put the data, software, hardware and human assets of an enterprise, government and nation at a constant risk. According to a latest Data Breach Report (Verizon, 2019), 52% breaches were due to hacking, 33% involved social engineering and 28% involved malware. Following is the list of trending cyber-Attacks:

1. **Attrition**: An attack which tries to degrade, destroy or disable the network based services of an enterprise by flooding it. For example, a botnet utilizes a number of internet connected devices for mounting a distributed denial-of-service (DDoS) attack. As mentioned earlier, Mirai botnet (Antonakakis et al., 2017) is one such instance wherein the attacker used the IoT devices for performing DDoS.

2. **Social Engineering Attacks** - In this, the attacker first harvests the personal information of the user from social networking sites like Facebook and Linkedin. He either tries to get additional information from the user either through phone, or by spear-phishing campaign, or by defrauding the user. The following are two well-known examples of social engineering attack:

    a. **Web Phishing:** It is one the most prevalent web based attack. The attacker tries to fool the user in clicking a link, embedded in an email or SMS, to a malicious website. The website in turn may have a form for capturing personal and sensitive information of the user, or try to launch a drive-by download attack (J. Hong, 2012). Here, drive-by-download is an exploitation technique which takes advantage of the browser vulnerabilities to automatically download a dropper (an application which in turn downloads the malware) or an actual malware.

However, to use this technique, the attacker needs to take control over the legitimate websites for automating downloads.

b.   **Email Phishing:** The attacker sends a fake email to the victim and tricks her into sharing private and sensitive data or execution of malware (J. Hong, 2012). A more advanced form of phishing is known as 'spear phishing' which targets specific individuals and uses specific knowledge about them. That way, the attacker appears more legitimate and increases the success rate of the attack. If the 'spear phishing' attack is used against a high level target within an enterprise, then it is known as 'whaling' (J. Hong, 2012).

3.   **Cryptojacking**: In this exploit, the user's browser downloads a JavaScript while visiting a website, which then uses the CPU cycles of the user's system for mining crypto-currency. Often this happens without the user's consent or knowledge, however, the owner of the website may or may not have the knowledge about this parasitic computing (Eskandari et al., 2018).

4.   **Spam**: This is an attack in which the attacker abuses or manipulates the email ecosystem by injecting or producing undesired content for changing the behavior of the user or the system for long term self-gains (Ferrara, 2019). As per (Nahorney, 2017), it continues to represent the bulk of email traffic (more than 50%) in 2017. Without proper filtering at email gateway, an enterprise has to assign two employees for every hundred employees just for filtering the spam emails. Spam can be effectively utilized for unsolicited sales, political manipulation, dispersing incorrect information on public health, swaying stock markets and data leaks (Ferrara, 2019).

5.   **Malware**: According to Data Breach Report (Verizon, 2019), 28% data breach happened due to malware. This involved losses due to usage of Trojans, ransomware, worms and viruses. Email is the most abused medium for malware delivery and quite a serious one for enterprises (Nahorney, 2017), wherein the attacker lures the user by carefully crafted subject and message into clicking on an embedded link or malicious attachment. The embedded link usually leads to a compromised website for drive-by-download attack. In case of an attachment, it could be a malicious binary or a benign downloader for downloading the malware in a separate process.

6.   **Business Email Compromise (BEC)**: This attack is continuously growing and has huge impact on enterprises and small businesses in terms of monetary losses (Nahorney, 2017). In 2018 alone, Internet Crime Complaint Center (IC3) received 20,373 BEC complaints with total losses amounting to over 1.2 billion USD (FBI, 2018). In this attack, the victim receives a fake email purportedly from a person in authority requesting some urgent data, money transfer or validation of details on some embedded link in email. If the victim hastily follows to fulfil the request, then it could result in financial losses, data leakage or drive-by-download attack. IC3 further classifies the BEC attack based on the impersonation level and the requested data.

7.   **Hacking the Human**: The attacker either manipulates the human emotion or is motivated by the emotions. Based on that, this attack can be further divided into two subcategories:

a.   **As Targets:** Humans are the weakest link in any security chain, therefore there is a long history of attackers exploiting people (Mann, 2017). They are susceptible to social engineering attacks and render the most secure system useless, for example, Stuxnet was able to get into an air-gapped system due to an individual using an infected USB drive. Like any computer system, humans are hackable (Mann, 2017) who have their own vulnerabilities (unique at times), behavioral traits, and they are prone to fatigue. A large workforce translates into a larger attack surface for the attackers.

b. **As Attacker:** Insider-threat is attributed as one of the key threats to the enterprises (Homoliak et al., 2019). This is particularly worrisome and hard to detect as insiders are the individuals associated with the enterprise who misuse their access rights and internal working of the enterprise, knowingly or unknowingly (mostly through social engineering).

8. **Adversarial Machine Learning**: Cyber attackers are finding newer ways of exploiting artificial intelligence as more and more safety, security and privacy critical systems are starting to use it. For example, the authors in (Eykholt et al., 2017) demonstrated an attack on deep-neural-network (DNN) of an autonomous vehicle by perturbing the physical objects that reliably caused classification errors in DNN based classifiers. Further, researchers (Ferrara, 2019) describe a possible future scenario consisting of an AI fueled multimedia spam which uses real-time reenactment of a video sequence. This is an example of abusing AI based systems for generating fake content, also known as Deep Fake (Blitz, 2018). It is a worrying trend as the generated fake content seems indistinguishable from the real content. Fredrikson et al (Fredrikson, Jha, & Ristenpart, 2015) describe a model inversion attack wherein the attacker could extract the recognizable image of an individual's face from the model. Another kind of attack is presented by Biggio et al (Biggio, Nelson, & Laskov, 2012), wherein they poisoned the input data to machine learning algorithm and caused degradation in its predictive ability. Authors in (Yuan, He, Zhu, & Li, 2019) have shown multiple such security and privacy attacks on AI based systems.

## Impact of Cyber-Attack

More than often, the impact of cyber-attack on a victim is multi-dimensional and has a temporal nature. The most common impact of a successful cyber-attack is economic. It is observed that post attack, the stock price of the victim organization suffers losses in the following days. The effect is even worse when the breach is not disclosed by the organization, but later discovered by the investors (Amir, Levi, & Livne, 2018). This is accompanied by a drop in daily excess return, increase in trading volume and deterioration of liquidity after the public disclosure (Bianchi & Tosun, 2019). As a side effect, there is also a negative impact on the organization's reputation and customer base (Cashell, Jackson, Jickling, & Webel, 2004; Bianchi & Tosun, 2019; Smith, Jones, Johnson, & Smith, 2019). Also, the estimated cost of downtime itself is between $6.3 million and $8.4 million a day (Leon, 2015).

The cyber-attack may also result in loss of intellectual property, critical business secrets, personal information and customer data. This is in addition to the decreased productivity, damage to physical infrastructure, regulatory fines and legal fees (Cashell et al., 2004; Leon, 2015; Ausherman, 2018).

In rare cases, a cyber-attack could prove fatal to the human life, for example, the Triton malware (Giles, 2019) attack on petrochemical plants could disable safety systems designed to prevent catastrophic industrial accidents. Authors in (Yan, Xu, & Liu, 2016) demonstrated a contactless attack on the sensor system of the autonomous vehicle and caused malfunction. Similarly, researchers (Gaukstern & Krishnan, 2018) have discussed the cyber-attacks targeting networked critical medical devices, for example, pacemakers and insulin pumps.

In general, cyber-attacks also increase the operating cost of a business as they either have to maintain some surplus for recovering from a cyber-attack or they have to get insurance as a financial protection against the inevitable threat (Watkins, 2014).

## Implications

Cyber threats are continuously evolving and there exists no silver-bullet solution to address them all. Therefore, the enterprise should have at its disposal a repertoire of tools and techniques to guard data, software, hardware and human assets against the evolving cyber threats. In particular, enterprise should select and implement measures by taking into considerations the following things:

1. *Defend against the best attacker*, with sophisticated malicious programs such as malware and ransomware becoming easily accessible as a paid service, it is now easy even for a naive attacker to launch state-of-the-art attacks against any target of their choice.
2. *Compliance oversight is growing*, since enterprises rarely think about security and privacy first, governments across the globe are intervening and enforcing strict regulations (e.g., GDPR), failing to which the enterprise could incur hefty fines and reputation loss.
3. *Compliance is not substitute for security*, being compliant with regulations and policies do not shield enterprises from security breaches.
4. *Security is everyone's responsibility*, defending hardware and software assets is must, however there exists a possibility of attacks penetrating the enterprise network and reaching its employees and partners. Hence, it is equally important to strengthen the weakest link in the security chain, that is, humans.
5. *Security can never be 100%*, one can only increase the levels of deterrence, thereby making the existing cyber-attacks more costly.

## MEASURES

Security is inherently an asymmetric game between an attacker and a defender, where the attacker has to find a *single* exploit in the defense and the defender has to guard against *all* types of attacks. Traditional security measures such as network firewalls and end-point protection are not enough to address modern security threats. The deluge of cyber-attacks sweeping across the world has enterprises and governments thinking about new ways to protect their digital assets, and the corporate and state secrets stored within. As malicious actors continue to push the boundaries and discover new frontiers to exploit, enterprises need to be on the cutting edge and ensure their critical assets are protected.

In this section, we describe various emerging measures to counter cyber threats, discuss their benefits and highlight their pitfalls.

### Bug Bounty Programs

Bug bounty programs are a modern way for enterprises to identify security vulnerabilities in their systems by harvesting the efforts and knowledge of security researchers and ethical hackers across the globe in exchange for monetary rewards. These programs have become the new norm, with organizations big and small, private and government, offering lucrative incentives to encourage hacker community to disclose high value software bugs in their systems. The adoption of bug bounty programs by prominent government agencies such as the U.K.'s National Cyber Security Centre, Singapore's Ministry of Defense, and the U.S. Department of Defense may have set a new standard for the future of cybersecurity practice.

Bug bounty programs are also on the rise in risk-averse and highly regulated industries such as financial services, banking, insurance, healthcare and education (Hackerone, 2019). There even exists a bug-bounty program for improving the security of the internet (Internet Bug Bounty, 2019).

Benefits of bug bounty programs are two-fold. First, bug bounty programs offer a unique opportunity for organizations to employ a large and diverse population of security researchers and ethical hackers to examine their software products and hence offer protection against the best attacker. Secondly, the public nature of these programs indicates to their users that the organization is committed towards security improvements. As organizations benefit from the best security researchers around the globe, conversely, security researchers also benefit from searching for bugs in multiple bug bounty programs. Elite hackers can earn more than a million USD per year searching for security bugs as internet-scale companies e.g., Dropbox, GitHub, Google, Intel, and Twitter shell out thousands of dollars for high severity bugs (Hackerone, 2019). Fortunately, enterprises can use bug bounty programs to incentivize security researchers and ethical hackers to find security bugs or vulnerabilities before the public becomes aware of them.

The crowdsourcing platforms such as HackerOne and Bugcrowd enable organizations to launch bounty programs and connect with a global force of hundreds of thousands of hackers. The platforms are impressively effective as 77% of the public bug bounty programs receive their first valid vulnerability within the 24 hours of its launch (Hackerone, 2019). In 2018 alone, hackers had earned more than 19 million USD for valid results. However, the work is still in progress, as 93 percent of the Forbes Global 2000 companies still do not have known vulnerability disclosure policies. Google with its Project Zero has started an altogether different trend of finding vulnerabilities not only in their own products but also in the products of other vendors on which their own products rely. Interestingly, Project Zero has a policy of making the bug report public if the vendor fails to release the security patch within 90 days after bug disclosure.

Bug bounty programs also present a challenge since anyone can participate, and submit a low quality bug reports (Laszka, Zhao, & Grossklags, 2016). In fact, the key challenge many bug-bounty programs face is managing noise, or the proportion of low quality reports they receive. These low quality reports include spam (i.e., completely irrelevant reports), false positives (i.e., security issues that do not actually exist), and out-of-scope reports. Bug bounties are becoming a popular tool to mitigate software vulnerabilities; however, it is still unclear how to design mechanism and incentive structures to influence the long-term success of bounty programs. In a phenomenon known as front-loading effect, newly launched programs attract researchers at the expense of older programs since the probability of finding bugs decays after the launch of a program, even though bugs found later yield on average higher rewards (Thomas Maillart & Chuang, 2016). Further, current bounty programs lack rigorous techniques for setting bounty amounts and attract economically rational hackers. Rather than claim bounties for serious bugs, hackers often sell or exploit them. A majority of bug bounty programs are private, where a set of elite hackers is selected and invited to find bugs. One major challenge in the private bug bounties is to solve a matching problem involving bug bounty programs and specialized people based on various factors such as experience, reputation, skills, availability and rewards. The problem is computationally hard if the preference lists of both the parties is bounded and contain ties (Gharote, Phuke, Patil, & Lodha, 2019).

## Cloud Computing

Cloud computing is an on-demand, cost-efficient and fault-tolerant delivery of compute, storage, databases, analytics, networking, mobile, developer tools, management tools, IoT (Internet of Things), security and enterprise applications. With the cloud, businesses no longer need to plan for infrastructure capacity needs; instead, they can instantly scale up and down as required in minutes and deliver results faster. Cloud computing allows enterprises, start-ups, small and medium-sized businesses, and companies in the public sector to access the resources they need to respond quickly to evolving business requirements.

The main benefit of cloud infrastructure is that it allows enterprises to scale and innovate, while maintaining a secure environment and paying only for the services that are required. Cloud is particularly beneficial for small and medium scale enterprises that cannot afford to keep up with a rapidly evolving regulatory landscape. Cloud providers typically have many compliance-enabling features that enterprises can use to achieve a higher level of security at scale (LMark Judd, Joerg Fritsch, 2018). Cloud providers engage globally with governments, regulators, standards bodies, and non-governmental organizations to ensure that they are compliant. Cloud environments are regularly audited, and cloud infrastructure and services are approved to operate under several compliance standards and industry certifications across geographies and industries, including PCI DSS, ISO 27001 and HIPAA. In most of the cases, cloud providers also allow enterprises to choose the country where their data can reside in order to be compliant with data residency regulations of different countries. Cloud vendors equip enterprises with tools that allow them to determine where their content will be stored, secure their content in transit or at rest, and manage access to services and resources. However, *being compliant with industry regulations and policies do not shield enterprises from security breaches.*

Cloud vendors also provide several security capabilities and services to increase privacy and control network access. These include DDoS mitigation, data encryption, monitoring and logging, identity and access control, and penetration testing. Therefore, enterprises can retain the control of the security to protect their content, platform, applications, systems, and networks. While security of the cloud is the responsibility of the cloud vendor, the security in the cloud is the responsibility of the enterprise. Much like an on-premises data center, the enterprise is responsible for managing the operating system (including installing updates and security patches), application software, and the configuration of the firewall. Enterprise should carefully consider the services they choose, as their responsibilities vary depending on the services they use, the integration of those services into their IT environments, and applicable laws and regulations. In addition, when using cloud services enterprises are responsible for managing the security of content, including:

- The cloud services that are used with the content,
- The country where their content is stored,
- The format and structure of their content whether it is masked, anonymized, or encrypted and
- The management of access rights.

As companies continue to adopt more cost efficient cloud-based solutions, attackers are adapting their tactics to locate and steal the data they find to be of most value. Consequently, there has been a corresponding increase in hacking cloud-based email servers via the use of phishing attacks and credential theft (Verizon, 2019). Further, the loss of information caused by misconfigurations is unprecedented. According to a research report by McAfee, 99% of misconfigurations in the public cloud go unreported, suggesting there are numerous companies around the world unwittingly leaking data (McAfee, 2019).

Although enterprises can encrypt sensitive data and store it securely on cloud, it is infeasible for many business organizations to adopt cloud if they need to perform operations on sensitive data. Historically, encrypted data has been impossible to operate on without first decrypting them. To address this gap, homomorphic cryptosystems were invented that could perform unlimited chaining of algebraic operations in the cipher space, which means that an arbitrary number of additions and multiplications can be performed on the encrypted data (Gentry, 2009). However, the technology in its current form is too slow for practical applications.

## Privacy by Design

Almost every enterprise is now data driven, that is, they gather data about their customers for operational and analytical purposes. This data-driven approach helps them in better decision making, investments, improving information technology usage, and providing tailored services and other benefits to their customers. However, the customer data often includes sensitive and personally identifiable information, which can lead to significant exposure of sensitive information when used in the business processes of the enterprise. Further, enterprises are now adopting cloud for lowering their costs and product development life-cycle. In the last few years, the cloud computing ecosystem has changed significantly. There are more cloud providers offering more features and value added services (Varghese & Buyya, 2018). Enterprises leverage this heterogeneity in the cloud ecosystem by utilizing resources from different providers, however this also increases the attack surface for the enterprise.

In the last decade, users are getting more concerned about their privacy rights. This behavior is clearly reflected in the 2014 landmark decision of the top European court in favor of 'right to be forgotten' plea from Mario Costeja Gonzalez against Google. The court directed Google to delete 'inadequate, irrelevant or no longer relevant' data from its result on request from an individual (Travis & Arthur, 2014). In a more recent scandal, personal data of millions of Facebook users was harvested without their consent and then used for political advertising (Cadwalladr & Graham-Harrison, 2018). 'Cambridge Analytica' achieved this by exploiting Facebook's Open API for gathering friends' data of users who permitted it to access their profile (Isaak & Hanna, 2018). Incidents like this tarnish the reputation of the enterprises and has long lasting operational and financial impact on them. For example, post scandal Facebook's share prices went down, governments got suspicious of Facebook's operating procedure and there was a delete Facebook accounts movement (Gonzalez, Yu, Figueroa, Lopez, & Aragon, 2019).

Also, regulations like, General Data Protection Regulation (GDPR) empower consumers by obligating enterprises for anonymizing data, notification of breach, across border data transfer and consent requirement from the user for any data processing. Failure to comply may result in legal and monetary penalties. For example, for severe violations, GDPR penalty is maximum of 20 million euros or 4% of total global turnover of the enterprise in preceding fiscal year.

There is a statutory requirement in GDPR for 'Privacy by Design' (PbD), which means 'data protection through technology means'. In other words, privacy should not be considered after the product is developed, rather, privacy requirement and controls should be considered in the design and implementation phase (Bird, 2016). The 'California Consumer Privacy Act' also recommends that enterprise should consider PbD. It is a system engineering approach which prescribes that privacy must be considered during all phases of the engineering process. It was developed as a framework to assimilate privacy into information technology, networked infrastructure and actual designs (Cavoukian, 2010). However, PbD became a necessity in sectors where data privacy concerns persist. Further, PbD compliance is mandatory under newer regulations (Romanou, 2018). The seven core features of PbD are as follows (Cavoukian, 2010):

1. **Proactive not Reactive; Preventative not Remedial**: The privacy must be proactive rather than reactive, that is, instead of a post facto measure, PbD prevent them from occurring.
2. **Privacy as the Default**: The privacy of an individual should not be affected if she does nothing, that is, privacy rules should be embedded with default privacy rules.
3. **Privacy Embedded into Design**: Privacy should not be an add-on or patch up work after the product development, rather it should be considered during all phases of the engineering.
4. **Full Functionality**. Positive-Sum, not Zero-Sum. Unnecessary trade-offs should not be considered while embedding privacy, rather include all legitimate requirements in a 'win-win' manner.
5. **End-to-End Security**: Life Cycle Protection. Data should be securely acquired, retained and then destroyed in a timely fashion when it is no longer required.
6. **Visibility and Transparency**: Assure stakeholders that data is being used according to prior stated promises and objectives and could be audited later on.
7. **Respect for User Privacy**: Architect and data users must respect an individual's preferences by providing strong privacy defaults, suitable notifications and usable options.

However, the recommendations in PbD should be considered with a pinch of salt. Researchers and practitioners have pointed out that PbD is vague, it is difficult to adopt, difficult to apply in certain domains, values corporate interests over consumer's interests and does not stress on restriction on data collection (Gurses, Troncoso, & Diaz, 2011; van Rest, Boonstra, Everts, van Rijn, & van Paassen, 2012; Rubinstein & Good, 2013). For example, according to (van Rest et al., 2012), the original PbD guidelines fail to say anything about legacy systems, and there is a trust deficit with respect to consumers' adoption of PbD. Furthermore, researcher described the seven principles of PbD as more aspirational than practical since they do not offer any design guidance and appear impractical or repetitive in some scenarios (Rubinstein & Good, 2013).

## DevSecOps

DevOps is a conceptual and operational blend of development and operations (Myrbakken & Colomo-Palacios, 2017). It suggests practices that help in streamlining of software delivery process, inclusion of feedback from production to development, and reducing the overall time from inception to delivery. DevOps promotes the four principals consisting of culture, automation, measurement and sharing (Myrbakken & Colomo-Palacios, 2017). DevSecOps is a natural extension to DevOps which prescribes bringing operations and development together with security functions (Bird, 2016). DevSecOps is a proactive approach to cybersecurity where secure practices are embedded into the entire lifecycle of software development. It is an improvement over the older security model for continuous integration and delivery models provided by the modern agile frameworks. Additionally, DevSecOps promote communication and collaboration within the team and ensures that everyone is responsible for security. Further, it is easier to plan and execute integration of security controls early in development life-cycle by involving security experts. Additionally, this also reduces delays and issues while incorporating security controls as compared to implementing security once the system is developed. This early inclusion of security experts in the design and development phase is known as 'Shift Security Left' (Bird, 2016). Figure 1, shows the comparison between a 'waterfall' cycle and 'DevOps' cycle. It can be seen that DevOps prescribes iterative, incremental and automated inclusion of security into the development cycle, which makes the process more efficient, repeatable, and easy to use (Bird, 2016).

*Figure 1. The waterfall cycle versus the DevOps cycle, adapted from (Bird, 2016).*

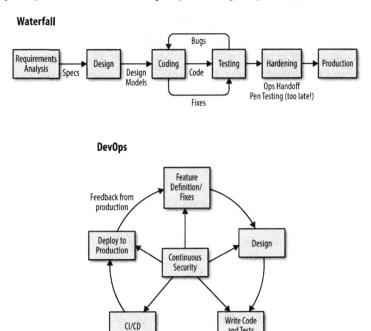

DevOps does not prescribe cloud as a requirement to run a system, although following DevOps practices on cloud may greatly help in continuous integration and delivery of the application. It also provides security and other important services, for example, account management, auditing, encryption, key management and monitoring. Even though a success enabler, the 'Cloud Security Alliance' lists down 12 major security and privacy threats to cloud and its users (Bird, 2016). Apart from this, the other major aspects of DevOps also increase the threat to enterprise and its assets. For example, microservices allow designing of self-contained isolated functions which can be tested, deployed and managed independently, however they also increase the attack surface, implementation complexity and other issues. Similarly, there are issues pertaining to separation of duties, change control and inherent issues in software container (LXC or Docker) (Bird, 2016). All of this makes the security as a vital component that must be included in agile methodology like DevOps.

## Isolation

In cybersecurity, isolation is a conceptual solution in which a software operates within a very restrictive environment with no impact on the application providing the isolation, system or platform on which it is run. It guarantees about what a piece of code can or cannot do irrespective of the input parameters (Shu et al., 2016). There are different types and levels of isolation which are possible to restrict a software, for example, application sandboxing is one such technique for application isolation. Isolation is a useful method to evaluate software which are not trusted (security isolation) or expected to have some bug or vulnerability which might affect the rest of the system (fault isolation) (Shu et al., 2016). The idea of isolation is particularly important as most of the applications utilize one or more third party libraries which may have unknown vulnerability (Kula, German, Ouni, Ishio, & Inoue, 2018). Isolation limits the damage and, therefore, is a useful defense against the best attacker.

**Network Isolation.** Perfect cybersecurity is not possible due to multiple reasons and all enterprises experience a breach at some point in time. Network isolation is used for hardening the systems with large attack surface and running trusted programs, for example, web server, domain name server and email server (Shu et al., 2016). Isolating network components makes it difficult for the attacker to damage the entire network of the victim as we limit communication throughout the network, thereby reducing the attack options available to the attacker. However, moving from a flat network model to a segmented network has some side-effects, for example, it increases the complexity of the overall system and reduces the system performance. An extreme example of network isolation is an 'air gapped' network, wherein a secure network is physically isolated from an unsecured network or a network which connects to an unsecured network (Kim Zetter, 2014). However, an air-gapped does not offer any guarantees of being 100% secure (Guri, Zadov, & Elovici, 2019). Virtual Private Network (VPN) is another network isolation method, which enables a user to send and receive data on a shared or public network by extending a private network across a public network.

Network isolation or segmentation is a very useful concept and it is used for enabling other security architectures. For example, 'Zero Trust Architecture' is based on the principal of 'never trust, always verify' to protect network resources. It leverages network segmentation as one of the key enablers for separating a trusted 'protect surface' from the rest of the resources (Kindervag, 2010). Further, understanding the users, application and their access patterns with respect to the 'protect surface' helps in putting appropriate access controls as close to the 'protect surface' as possible. The 'Cloud Security Alliance' defines the Software Defined Perimeter (SDP) which enforces a need-to-know based access model that verifies the posture and the identity of the device before granting access to the application infrastructure.

**OS Level Isolation:** Here the operating system (OS) kernel allows multiple instances of the user-space. It decouples applications from the OS so that individual applications execute in their own virtualized environment commonly known as containers. An application running inside a container has access to devices and data which are assigned to the container. OS level virtualization is different from hardware level virtualization as the later virtualizes the hardware architecture by implementing a virtual machine monitor and decouples the OS from the hardware. Additionally, OS virtualization allows more control over individual processes, which is more beneficial than hardware virtualization, for example, OS level virtualization allows an easy migration of individual applications as compared to the complete OS migration. However, there are few security problems with OS level isolation that need to be considered before its adoption, for example, kernel exploits, denial of service attacks, container breakouts, poisoned images and compromising secrets (Bird, 2016).

**Compute Isolation:** Intel introduced a set of security related instructions for some of its new central processing units (CPU), called Software Guard Extension (SGX). These instructions allow the user and OS code to create private regions of memory called *enclaves*. The content in the enclave is encrypted and it is inaccessible for reading and writing by any process (irrespective of their privilege level) outside the enclave. As and when needed, the CPU decrypts the content only for the code which is running within the enclave. This way the enclave isolates the computation from rest of the system and avoids any data exfiltration attack by enabling secure computation. However, it is also possible to use the SGX in a cyber-attack, which makes their detection very hard, for example, botnet creation or malware operating in enclave (Davenport & Ford, 2014). Recently, researchers have shown an attack based on SGX and return-oriented-programming (ROP) which bypassed ASLR, stack canaries, and address sanitizer to mount a code-reuse attack (Schwarz, Weiser, & Gruss, 2019). The SGX-ROP attack in turn could invoke arbitrary system calls from the host process to gain arbitrary code execution. Similarly, SGX is also shown to conceal a malware attack (Schwarz, Weiser, Gruss, Maurice, & Mangard, 2017). Apart from this, there are well known side channel attacks on SGX, for example, cache attacks (Brasser et al., 2017).

**Sandboxing:** It is a technique of isolating one process from the rest of the system. The isolation can limit access to benign OS from a malicious process or access to an application from a malicious OS (Li et al., 2014). A sandbox is a heavily restricted environment with access to tightly controlled set of resources. A less restrictive sandbox is also known as process compartmentalization (Gudka et al., 2015). Sandbox environment is quite useful for evaluating an untrusted software or for fault isolation (Shu et al., 2016). For example, Chrome Web Browser uses a sandbox for rendering untrusted web-pages with JavaScript code (Barth, Jackson, Reis, Team, et al., 2008).

## Security Operations Center

*Figure 2. The core building blocks of a SOC, adapted from (Torres, 2015).*

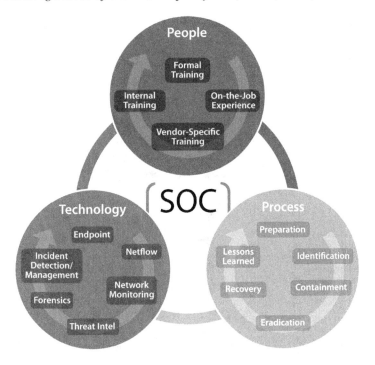

From an enterprise perspective, Security Operations Center (SOC) is a facility that is responsible for its information security issues like: a) securing its cyberspace, b) monitoring and analyzing incidents and events, c) proactively and appropriately handling incidents, and, d) assessing regulatory compliance (Kowtha, Nolan, & Daley, 2012). As the volume of data and attacks have gone up in the recent past (Verizon, 2019), it is imperative to have a specialized facility like SOC to handle cyber incidents and gather threat intelligence. This helps an enterprise in proactively taking more informed decisions in a short duration against their adversaries and reduce the number of possible breaches. It has been shown that SOC benefits from coordinated and collaborative handling of incidents. For a successful SOC the coordination and collaboration must exist between people, technology and processes (Torres, 2015), as shown in Figure 2. Technology aspect of SOC usually deals with data collection, aggregation, analytics, detection, reporting and mitigation. The processes aspect of SOC prescribes repeatable incident management workflows, clear responsibilities of team members and appropriate actions for each incident. This helps in proper resource allocation and investigation procedures. Finally, people aspect mandates suitable skill set for analyzing the incidents. Further, the team working in a SOC should consistently update their skills by attending the necessary training to deal with constantly changing cyber-attack ecosystem. As shown in Figure 3, for an effective SOC, the data gathered from the continues monitoring should be aggregated, processed and analyzed for investigating and reviewing suspicious activities that caused the incident (Torres, 2015).

*Figure 3. Data aggregation and compatible technologies aid detection, adapted from (Torres, 2015).*

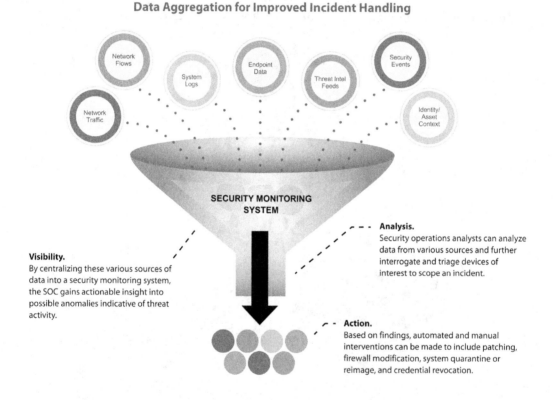

However, the SOC operations are often marred with too many false positives. This is either due to a stretched workforce, lack of additional contexts to help the analyst, large volume of events or incomplete analysis, which eventually leads to human 'alert fatigue' (Torres, 2015). It is an information overload problem in which true alerts are missed due to large number of false alarms. Another major problem is the lack of skilled information security professionals in enterprise. It is estimated that by 2019 there will be a shortage of over 1 million cybersecurity professionals. To counter the shortage, enterprises invest substantially in cybersecurity technologies (Nobles, 2018). To a certain extent, automation of SOC can help in alleviating fatigue related issues as it minimizes the human-in-the-loop and, hence, fatigue related issues (Hassan et al., 2019). Similarly, enterprise can leverage the large amount of data that is available to SOC for building an effective machine learning system for reducing the false positives and remediating the skilled workforce issue.

## Awareness and Training

Humans are the weakest link in the security chain. More than 50% of data breaches in enterprises involve social attacks or human error (Verizon, 2019). While the majority of employees do not set out to cause harm, many of them do it inadvertently through bad password habits, visiting phishing websites or opening malicious attachments. Therefore, in addition to strengthening organizational defenses against cyber threats, it is equally important to provide security training to employees. The most important factor in effective information security is to make the users aware of the different risks, and equip them with a proper training to counter those risks. Awareness is not the same as training as highlighted in NIST Special Publication 800-16 (Wilson & Hash, 2003):

*Awareness is not training. The purpose of awareness presentations is simply to focus attention on security. Awareness presentations are intended to allow individuals to recognize IT security concerns and respond accordingly. In awareness activities, the learner is the recipient of information, whereas the learner in a training environment has a more active role. Awareness relies on reaching broad audiences with attractive packaging techniques. Training is more formal, having a goal of building knowledge and skills to facilitate the job performance. Training strives to produce relevant and needed security skills and competencies.*

Security awareness and training for enterprise users is a rapidly growing market. According to Gartner, the security awareness computer-based training (CBT) market will grow to over 1.1 billion USD by 2020 (Kish & Carpenter, 2019). Enterprises are spending more energy and money to create what is termed as human firewall by training people on the best practices to prevent breaches. Enterprises are using innovative ways to simplify complex cybersecurity topics such as phishing (Figure 4). Further, they are moving away from traditional non-interactive video-based teaching methods to more dynamic gamification based techniques. The benefits of gamification include improved engagement, increased motivation, immediate feedback and long-term retention (Jin, Tu, Kim, Heffron, & White, 2018; CJ et al., 2018; Tupsamudre et al., 2018). Additionally, leading security education vendors provide a facility to launch simulated attacks to trigger employee behavior and measure the effectiveness of training over time (Huisman, 2019). Enterprises that treat security education as an inherently unproductive investment are a diminishing group, and training companies are increasingly focusing on security education that is effective as well as efficient at driving enterprise security performance.

The world of cyber security is constantly evolving as attackers learn new information and sophisticated techniques to attack enterprise systems. Therefore, it is necessary to keep up with cyber criminals and rejuvenate the cybersecurity training program of an enterprise at regular intervals. It is equally important to keep employees in charge of enterprise security up-to-date with the constantly evolving security guidelines and practices. For instance, once an ardent supporter of password composition policy and password expiry, NIST now recommends organizations to banish password composition rules and password expiry in favor of long passwords (Grassi et al., 2019).

*Figure 4. Enterprises are using graphical ways to teach employees about complex cybersecurity topics (Credit: Tata Consultancy Services Ltd. 2019).*

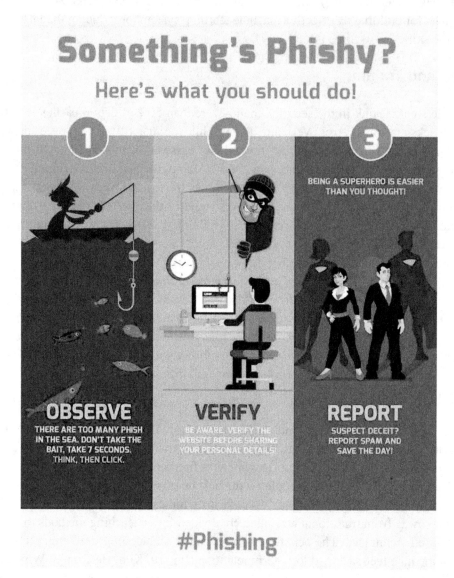

Another challenge is to design effective games that will resonate with diverse audience of an enterprise ranging from HR to technical personnel. Training should be relevant and continuous so that everybody understands that security is everyone's responsibility. It is also important to customize the content as per the needs of particular roles or responsibilities. For instance, training for sales team should be different from the training aimed at executives. Further, the interactive learning experience has to be delivered on computing devices of different shapes and sizes, such as laptop computers, tablets and smartphones, and developed in different languages for geographically distributed organizations.

## Cyber Range

Cyber ranges are interactive, simulated representations of an organization's local network, system, tools, and applications that are connected to a simulated Internet level environment (NIST, 2018). A cyber range provides a controlled environment to practice computer network operations skills related to real-world network attack and defense scenarios by simulating large-scale complex networks. The training aspect focuses on evaluating attack scenarios by isolating the environment from other networks in order to contain live malicious activity, to better understand the gaps in the security posture, and implement the best security practices. The evaluation aspect allows a cyber-range to offer a commercial incentive as organizations evaluate the security of their products/services, experience real-attack scenarios in a safe environment, and measure and improve their attack response time against the best attacker.

Cyber ranges are in use and provided by organizations across the government, private industry, and academia. The cyber range efforts in academics are primarily dedicated for research and training purposes. The Lincoln Laboratory at MIT has created Cyber Systems Assessments Group that focuses on analyzing, understanding, and assessing cyber-containing systems by involving in activities including red teaming, system exploitation, building of cyber range infrastructure and evaluations of cyber capabilities. Defense Advanced Research Projects Agency (DARPA) has built a National Cyber Range (NCR) by partnering with Johns Hopkins University and Lockheed Martin (a global security and aerospace company headquartered in Maryland) to protect and defend US's critical information assets. By size and capacity, it has Global Information Grid or Internet scale testing (Davis & Magrath, 2013). Being part of the Comprehensive National Cyber security Initiative (CNCI), in addition to serving the US military, the NCR is open to government, industry, and academia to carry out tests on both classified and unclassified technologies (Ferguson, Tall, & Olsen, 2014).

A cyber range would immensely help enterprises with a critical ability to evaluate the security of their infrastructure in view of ever growing cyber threats before their live adoption at onsite. A cyber range can closely bring the reality of cyber ecosystem into a controlled lab environment and gradually helps enterprise to adopt strong security practices. A dedicated and custom-oriented cyber range would help enterprises test the resilience of their critical technologies and commercial infrastructures. It provides a secure ecosystem with the latest tools, techniques and malware to integrate and test technologies, networks and systems by exposing them to a wide range of cyber threats. The desired experimental network topology and software configuration are mapped onto the physical infrastructure of the cyber range. While the actual infrastructure may consist of a cluster of machines, through emulation the enterprises can configure the cluster to behave as per the desired experiment topology including routing and WAN links. The costs associated with the set up and on-going maintenance of dedicated computer and network resources can be partially compensated through virtualization which allows a smaller physical network to emulate a larger network. Using a cyber-range is indicative of extreme maturity for an organization's security stance.

However, there are several disadvantages to this approach as well (IXIA, 2016). In a purely virtualized environment, it is not possible to model certain attacks scenarios that are prevalent in the real world, purely because of physical performance constraints of virtual architectures. A great example of this is realistic distributed denial-of-service (DDoS) attacks. In many cyber range environments, DDoS analysis mitigation by a response team can work only at low-scale because of the limits of virtualization. Two more examples of why pure virtualization can cause issues are network throughput, which is always lower in a virtualized environment, and firewall IPS/IDS performance, which are greatly constrained in terms of performance when those elements are purely virtualized. Other challenge is that cyber ranges simulate large environments consisting of thousands of machines and network nodes. Therefore, creation, deployment, control and maintenance of these environments is a lot of work. These overheads add-up when the organization is deploying multiple diverse cyber range scenarios to train their workforce.

## Cyber Insurance

There is no such thing as foolproof security. Cyber-attacks are likely to occur and can cause moderate to severe losses for enterprises large and small. As part of a risk management plan, organizations routinely must decide which risks to avoid, accept, control or transfer. Transferring risk is where cyber insurance comes into play. Cyber insurance is a risk management and mitigation strategy having a corollary benefit of improving the adoption of preventive measures (products, services, and best practices), thus, helping improve the cyber security posture of organizations as well as country (DSCI, 2019). Cyber Insurance is designed to guard businesses from the potential effects of cyber-attacks. It helps an organization mitigate risk exposure by offsetting costs, after a cyber-attack/breach has happened. To simplify, cyber insurance is designed to cover the fees, expenses and legal costs associated with cyber breaches that occur after an organization has been hacked or from theft or loss of client/employee information.

Digitization of businesses have increased threat surface and vulnerabilities. Further, attacks are becoming more complex, menacing, and stealthy causing heavy financial losses to the enterprises. Moreover, the danger of insider threat makes it extremely difficult for enterprises to ensure a foolproof protection from attacks. Apart from the monetary loses, the hidden costs of a data breach, which includes lost businesses, partnerships, and reputation could be even more damaging, necessitating a better risk management strategy. While most enterprises highlight the adequacy of their spending on cyber security products and solutions as a means to safeguard businesses, none can really assure complete security, as attacks are getting more sophisticated with each passing day. Further, newly enacted regulations such as EU GDPR impose hefty fines (up to 20 million Euros or 4% of global turnover whichever is higher) on enterprises for non-compliance. Cyber insurance cannot protect an enterprise from cyber-attacks, but it can keep its business on stable financial footing should a significant security event occur (Lindros & Tittel, 2016).

One major challenge that inhibits robust risk assessment and, hence, cyber insurance is the shortage of data on cyber-attacks. This problem is further aggravated by enterprises' reluctance on sharing data that can help insurance providers evaluate risks. It is difficult to quantify comprehensiveness and adequacy of cover damages owing to cyber extortion, reputational loss, and rapidly evolving data and privacy landscape. Some of the cyber-attacks seen in the wild are not just from random hackers, but from state actors or quasi-state actors operating directly or indirectly at the behest of governments. Further, there are hackers working for criminal enterprises financially connected to terror organizations. Many cyber insurance contracts state that the insurer does not have to pay for incidents caused by an act of war or act of terror. If insurers attempt to use this exception to avoid paying for damages caused by malware suspected of being tied to state actors or terrorist organizations, cyber insurance could become virtually worthless. Despite all these challenges, cyber insurance market is set to grow (Souter, 2019). The total value of premiums is forecasted to reach 7.5 billion USD by 2020. According to PwC, about one-third of U.S. companies currently purchase some type of cyber insurance (PWC, 2019).

# Blockchain

A blockchain is an open, distributed ledger that can record transactions between two parties efficiently and in a verifiable and permanent way (Blockchain, 2019). Each block contains transaction data, time-stamp and a link (cryptographic hash) to its previous block. The linked blocks form a chain and, hence the name blockchain. Once recorded, the data in any given block cannot be altered without alteration of all subsequent blocks, which requires consensus of the network majority. Blockchain is becoming increasingly popular and is used in a wide range of applications including cybersecurity. There are three types of blockchains – public blockchain, private blockchain and hybrid blockchain. While a public blockchain has absolutely no access restrictions and anyone with an Internet connection can join the network, a private blockchain is permissioned; only a restricted set of users have the rights to decide what will be recorded in the blockchain. Permissioned blockchains have a number of advantages over public blockchains (Scherer, 2017). Most notable is the ability to split the network into segments where only a subset of nodes needs to validate transactions to a particular application, allowing the use of parallel computing and better scaling. Public blockchains can only process a couple of transaction per second and is therefore far from usable.

Blockchain is emerging as a viable technology when it comes to protecting businesses and other entities from cyber-attacks. Recently, NASA implemented permissioned blockchain technology in order to boost cybersecurity, and prevent denial of service and other attacks on air traffic services (Reisman, 2019). The traditional Domain Name System (DNS) that maps network node names into IP addresses depends on a centralized trust model, and it is highly regulated. Blockchain based DNS on the other hand is decentralized and cannot be controlled or manipulated by a single central authority (Barret, 2019). Decentralized DNS offers many benefits such as countering censorship by authorities, or preventing DNS spoofing, where attackers can corrupt DNS data so that the name server returns an incorrect IP address and redirects traffic to an attacker computer. However, decentralized DNS can also be abused by attackers for malicious purposes (Amado, 2018). Blockchain based solutions have also been proposed for IoT security and privacy (Dorri et al., 2017).

Blockchains allow entities who do not trust one another to share valuable data in a secure, tamperproof way. Blockchains employs cryptography and innovative software rules to store data that are extremely difficult for attackers to manipulate. However, implementing blockchain in practice is harder. Even when developers use tried-and-tested cryptographic tools, it is easy to accidentally put them together in ways that are not secure or make mistakes while setting them up (Orcutt, 2018). Creating blockchain-based bug bounty programs and incentivizing people to report flaws could be a way forward.

# Quantum Computing

Quantum computing harnesses quantum mechanical phenomena, such as superposition and entanglement, to perform information processing in ways not possible or not practical by classical computing (Chiu, 2019). Classical computers operate on bits which can have one of two states - 0 or 1, whereas quantum computers operate on quantum bits (or *qubits*) which can be in both 0 and 1 states simultaneously. A qubit operation exploits this quantum superposition by allowing many computations to be performed in parallel - a two-qubit system performs the operation on 4 values, a three-qubit system on 8, and so on. Quantum computers have the potential to revolutionize computation by solving certain types of intractable problems that would take millions of years on classical computers. Therefore, the realization of quantum computers could achieve new breakthroughs in medicine, artificial intelligence, optimization and many others. John Preskill coined the term quantum supremacy (Preskill, 2018) to characterize computational tasks performable by quantum devices, which classical devices could not. Despite the reports of quantum supremacy (Tavares, 2019), a practical quantum computer may not emerge for another decade or more (Gwynne, 2018), nevertheless organizations must prepare for cybersecurity threats in the post-quantum era.

Quantum computer have capabilities to break existing asymmetric key cryptosystems, which protects internet and powers global e-commerce. Symmetric encryption and asymmetric encryption are two cornerstones of modern cryptography. While symmetric encryption employs a single key for encryption as well as decryption (e.g., AES), asymmetric encryption employs a key-pair, one (public key) for encryption and the other (private key) for decryption (e.g., RSA). The development of a quantum computer may affect symmetric key encryption and asymmetric key encryption differently. For instance, Grover's algorithm provides a quadratic speedup on a quantum computer, which has the effect of cutting the encryption strength of AES in half (Grover, 1996). Whereas, Shor's algorithm provides an exponential speedup on a quantum computer enabling one to crack RSA (Rivest-Shamir-Adleman) cryptosystem, which is based on the hard mathematical problem of large, prime number factorization (Shor, 1994). The quantum speedup also yields many other mainstream cryptographic algorithms such as Digital Signature Algorithm (DSA), Elliptic-curve Diffie–Hellman (ECDH), etc. vulnerable to attack. The implication is that, while AES can be made robust against a quantum computer by increasing the key size, asymmetric cryptosystems are vulnerable to quantum attack, and there is no alternative but to replace them by quantum-resistant ones. The potential negative consequences are severe given the ubiquity of asymmetric encryption schemes in securing internet, IoT and cloud computing.

In response to the emerging quantum threats, in 2016 NIST called upon cryptographers for submissions for quantum-resistant public-key algorithms as part of its Post-Quantum Cryptography project. NIST received sixty-plus cryptographic algorithms from around the world during the first round of submissions of which 26 algorithms were shortlisted for the second round for further analysis (NIST, 2019). Unlike the factorization of large prime numbers used by RSA - which is vulnerable to quantum attack - these algorithms are based on different mathematical classes (lattice, code, multivariate and hash schemes) not known to be susceptible to quantum attack. The standardization process is in progress and the draft standard is expected to be available between 2022 and 2024.

## CONCLUSION

Trust is essential to cooperation as it produces positive-sum outcomes that strengthen society and benefit its individual members. However, as we increasingly depend on technology, cyber threats and vulnerabilities are creating trust issues for businesses and enterprises. As per the latest 2019 CEO Imperative study (Yonge, 2019), CEOs see cybersecurity as the number one threat to the global economy over the next five to ten years.

This should not be surprising to the reader based on the early discussion we had in this chapter on the changing cyber ecosystem, latest trends in cyber-attacks and their impact. We then delved into their five key implications that any modern enterprise need to be cognizant of and described eleven emerging measures that may help address consequences of those implications substantially. For each measure, we also highlighted some open issues and challenges that need attention from both researchers' and practitioners' communities. If anything, it simply confirmed 'no free lunch' nature of cybersecurity.

Decades ago, enterprise security was predominantly audit driven, based on static defenses with controls centered on passwords and perimeter security. It then evolved into more of reactive security that was rule and signature based, with focus on protection and detection. It now needs to be more proactive, risk aware, cognitive, automated and connected. It has to be baked into processes, systems, and new digital channels with the intent to manage risk across the entire business ecosystem of customers, suppliers, and other third parties. Moreover, it has to be largely invisible, that is, it should enable protection, governance and control without impacting usability or hindering operations and at the same time providing assurance of delivering on aspects of data protection and privacy.

Different measures that we brought up in this chapter can help in this mission, for example, Bug Bounties, Cyber Range, Privacy by Design can help enterprise with being more proactive, Cloud Computing, Cyber Insurance and Isolation can play their part in managing risks, Security Operations Center provides ample play ground to be cognitive, automated and leverage connectedness. These are not solved problems by any imagination, and offer a fertile ground for contributing to both theory and practice of cybersecurity and privacy research.

## REFERENCES

Abolhassan, F. (2017). *Cyber security. Simply. Make it happen*. Springer. doi:10.1007/978-3-319-46529-6

Abraham, S., & Nair, S. (2015). *A predictive framework for cyber security analytics using attack graphs*. arXiv preprint arXiv:1502.01240

Amado, R. (2018). *How Cybercriminals are using Blockchain DNS: From the Market to the Bazar*. Retrieved December 5, 2019, from https://www.digitalshadows.com/blog-and-research/how-cybercriminals-are-using-blockchain-dns-from-the-market-to-the-bazar/

Amir, E., Levi, S., & Livne, T. (2018). Do firms underreport information on cyber-attacks? Evidence from capital markets. *Review of Accounting Studies*, 23(3), 1177–1206. doi:10.100711142-018-9452-4

Antonakakis, M., April, T., Bailey, M., Bernhard, M., Bursztein, E., Cochran, J., . . . Zhou, Y. (2017). Understanding the Mirai Botnet. In *26th USENIX Security Symposium (USENIX Security 17)* (pp. 1093-1110). USENIX.

Ausherman, N. (2018). *Dealing with Cyber Attacks - Steps You Need to Know*. NIST.

Barret, T. (2019). *Blockchain, IoT and DNS*. Retrieved December 5, 2019, from https://ccnso.icann.org/sites/default/files/field-attached/presentation-blockchain-iot-dns-11mar19-en.pdf

Barth, A., Jackson, C., Reis, C., Team, T., & Google Team. (2008). *The Security Architecture of the Chromium Browser*. Technical report. Stanford University.

Bianchi, D., & Tosun, O. K. (2019). *Cyber Attacks and Stock Market Activity*. Available at SSRN 3190454

Biggio, B., Nelson, B., & Laskov, P. (2012). *Poisoning Attacks Against Support Vector Machines*. arXiv preprint arXiv:1206.6389

Bird, J. (2016). *DevOpsSec: Securing Software Through Continuous Delivery*. Academic Press.

Blitz, M. J. (2018). Lies, Line Drawing, and Deep Fake News. *Oklahoma Law Review, 71*, 59.

Blockchain. (2019). *Wikipedia - Blockchain*. Retrieved December 5, 2019, from https://en.wikipedia.org/wiki/Blockchain

Brasser, F., Müller, U., Dmitrienko, A., Kostiainen, K., Capkun, S., & Sadeghi, A. R. (2017). Software Grand Exposure: SGX Cache Attacks are Practical. In *11th USENIX Workshop on Offensive Technologies*. USENIX.

Cadwalladr, C., & Graham-Harrison, E. (2018). Revealed: 50 Million Facebook Profiles Harvested for Cambridge Analytica in Major Data Breach. *Sat, 17*, 22–03.

Cashell, B., Jackson, W. D., Jickling, M., & Webel, B. (2004). The Economic Impact of Cyber-attacks. Congressional Research Service Documents, CRS RL32331.

Cavoukian, A. (2010). Privacy by Design: The Definitive Workshop. A Foreword by Ann Cavoukian, ph.d. *Identity in the Information Society, 3*(2), 247–251. doi:10.100712394-010-0062-y

Chiu, E. (2019). *Preparing Enterprises for the Quantum Computing Cybersecurity Threats*. Retrieved December 5, 2019, from https://cloudsecurityalliance.org/artifacts/preparing-enterprises-for-the-quantum-computing-cybersecurity-threats/

CJ, G., Pandit, S., Vaddepalli, S., Tupsamudre, H., Banahatti, V., & Lodha, S. (2018). Phishy - A Serious Game to Train Enterprise Users on Phishing Awareness. In *Proceedings of the 2018 annual symposium on computer-human interaction in play companion extended abstracts* (pp. 169-181). New York: ACM.

Davenport, S., & Ford, R. (2014). SGX: the Good, the Bad and the Downright Ugly. *Virus Bulletin, 14*.

Davis, J., & Magrath, S. (2013). *A survey of cyber ranges and testbeds (Tech. Rep.). Defence Science And Technology Organisation Edinburgh*. Cyber And Electronic Warfare Div.

Dorri, A., Kanhere, S. S., Jurdak, R., & Gauravaram, P. (2017). *Blockchain for IoT security and privacy: The case study of a smart home. In 2017 IEEE international conference on pervasive computing and communications workshops (PerCom workshops)* (pp. 618–623). IEEE. doi:10.1109/PERCOMW.2017.7917634

DSCI. (2019). *Cyber Insurance in India*. Retrieved October 3, 2019, from https://www.dsci.in/sites/default/files/documents/resourcecentre/Cyber%20Insurance%20In%20India.pdf

Eskandari, S., Leoutsarakos, A., Mursch, T., & Clark, J. (2018). A First Look at Browser-Based Cryptojacking. In *2018 IEEE European Symposium on Security and Privacy Workshops (EuroS&PW)* (pp. 58-66). IEEE.

Evans, M., Maglaras, L. A., He, Y., & Janicke, H. (2016). Human Behaviour as an Aspect of Cybersecurity Assurance. *Security and Communication Networks, 9*(17), 4667–4679. doi:10.1002ec.1657

Evtyushkin, D., Ponomarev, D., & Abu-Ghazaleh, N. (2016). Jump Over ASLR: Attacking Branch Predictors to Bypass ASLR. In *The 49th Annual IEEE/ACM International Symposium on Microarchitecture* (p. 40). IEEE.

Eykholt, K., Evtimov, I., Fernandes, E., Li, B., Rahmati, A., Xiao, C., . . . Song, D. (2017). *Robust Physical-World Attacks on Deep Learning Models.* arXiv preprint arXiv:1707.08945

FBI. (2018). *Internet crime report.* Retrieved September 20, 2019, from https://pdf.ic3.gov/2018IC3Report.pdf

Ferguson, B., Tall, A., & Olsen, D. (2014). National cyber range overview. In *Proceedings of the 2014 IEEE Military Communications Conference* (pp. 123-128). Washington, DC: IEEE. 10.1109/MIL-COM.2014.27

Ferrara, E. (2019). The History of Digital Spam. *Communications of the ACM, 62*(8), 82–91. doi:10.1145/3299768

Finlay, L., & Payne, C. (2019). The Attribution Problem and Cyber Armed Attacks. *AJIL Unbound, 113*, 202–206. doi:10.1017/aju.2019.35

Fredrikson, M., Jha, S., & Ristenpart, T. (2015). Model Inversion Attacks that Exploit Confidence Information and Basic Countermeasures. In *Proceedings of the 22nd ACM SIGSAC Conference on Computer and Communications Security* (pp. 1322-1333). ACM. 10.1145/2810103.2813677

Gaukstern, E., & Krishnan, S. (2018). Cybersecurity Threats Targeting Networked Critical. *Medical Devices (Auckland, N.Z.).*

Gentry, C. (2009). *A Fully Homomorphic Encryption Scheme* (Unpublished Doctoral Dissertation). Stanford University. crypto.stanford.edu/craig

George, J. J., & Leidner, D. E. (2019). From Clicktivism to Hacktivism: Understanding Digital Activism. *Information and Organization, 29*(3), 100249. doi:10.1016/j.infoandorg.2019.04.001

Gharote, M., Phuke, N., Patil, R., & Lodha, S. (2019). Multi-objective Stable Matching and Distributional Constraints. *Soft Computing, 23*(9), 2995–3011. doi:10.100700500-019-03763-4

Giles, M. (2019). *Triton is the World's Most Murderous Malware, and it's Spreading. MIT Technology Review.*

González, F., Yu, Y., Figueroa, A., López, C., & Aragon, C. (2019). *Global Reactions to the Cambridge Analytica Scandal: An Inter-Language Social Media Study.* Academic Press.

Grassi, P. A., Fenton, J. L., Newton, E. M., Perlner, R. A., Regenscheid, A. R., Burr, W. E., & Richer, J. P. (2019). Digital Identity Guidelines. *NIST Special Publication, 800*, 63–3.

Grover, L. K. (1996). *A fast quantum mechanical algorithm for database search.* arXiv preprint quant-ph/9605043

Gudka, K., Watson, R. N., Anderson, J., Chisnall, D., Davis, B., Laurie, B., ... Richardson, A. (2015). Clean Application Compartmentalization with SOAAP. In *Proceedings of the 22nd ACM SIGSAC Conference on Computer and Communications Security* (pp. 1016-1031). ACM.

Guri, M., Zadov, B., & Elovici, Y. (2019). Odini: Escaping Sensitive Data from Faraday-Caged, Air-Gapped Computers via Magnetic Fields. *IEEE Transactions on Information Forensics and Security.*

Gürses, S., Troncoso, C., & Diaz, C. (2011). Engineering Privacy by Design. *Computers. Privacy & Data Protection, 14*(3), 25.

Gutmann, P. (2007). The Commercial Malware Industry. *DEFCON Conference.*

Gwynne, P. (2018). *Practical quantum computers remain at least a decade away.* Retrieved December 5, 2019, from https://physicsworld.com/a/practical-quantum-computers-remain-at-least-a-decade-away/

Hackerone. (2019). *The Hacker Powered Security Report 2010.* Retrieved October 3, 2019, from https://www.hackerone.com/sites/default/files/2019-08/hacker-powered-security-report-2019.pdf

Hassan, W. U., Guo, S., Li, D., Chen, Z., Jee, K., Li, Z., & Bates, A. (2019). Nodoze: Combatting Threat Alert Fatigue with Automated Provenance Triage. NDSS.

Heumann, T., Keller, J., & Türpe, S. (2010). *Quantifying the Attack Surface of a Web Application. Sicherheit 2010.* Sicherheit, Schutz und Zuverlassigkeit.

Hiller, J. S. (2014). Civil cyberconflict: Microsoft, Cybercrime, and Botnets. *Santa Clara Computer and High-Technology Law Journal, 31,* 163.

Homoliak, I., Toffalini, F., Guarnizo, J., Elovici, Y., & Ochoa, M. (2019). Insight into Insiders and it: A Survey of Insider Threat Taxonomies, Analysis, Modeling, and Countermeasures. *ACM Computing Surveys, 52*(2), 30. doi:10.1145/3303771

Hong, J. (2012). *The Current State of Phishing Attacks.* Academic Press.

Hong, S., Frigo, P., Kaya, Y., Giuffrida, C., & Dumitras, T. (2019). *Terminal Brain Damage: Exposing the Graceless Degradation in Deep Neural Networks under Hardware Fault Attacks.* arXiv preprint arXiv:1906.01017

Huisman, J. (2019). *Magic Quadrant for Security Awareness Computer-Based Training.* Retrieved October 3, 2019, from https://www.gartner.com/en/documents/3950454/magic-quadrant-for-security-awareness-computer-based-tra

Internet Bug Bounty. (2019). *The Internet Bug Bounty.* Retrieved October 3, 2019, from https://internetbugbounty.org/

Isaak, J., & Hanna, M. J. (2018). User Data Privacy: Facebook, Cambridge Analytica, and Privacy Protection. *Computer, 51*(8), 56–59. doi:10.1109/MC.2018.3191268

IXIA. (2016). *Cyber Range: Improving Network Defense and Security Readiness.* Retrieved October 3, 2019, from https://www.testforce.com/testforce files/newsletter/Aug 2016/ixia.pdf

Jin, G., Tu, M., Kim, T.-H., Heffron, J., & White, J. (2018). Game Based Cybersecurity Training for High School Students. In *Proceedings of the 49th ACM Technical Symposium on Computer Science Education* (pp. 68-73). New York, NY: ACM. 10.1145/3159450.3159591

Judd, M., & Fritsch, J. (2018). *Comparing Security Controls and Paradigms in AWS, Google Cloud Platform and Microsoft Azure.* Retrieved October 3, 2019, from https://www.gartner.com/en/documents/3877942/comparing-security-controls-and-paradigms-in-aws-google-

Kim Zetter. (2014). *Hacker Lexicon: What is an Air Gap?* Retrieved September 20, 2019, from https://www.wired.com/2014/12/hacker-lexicon-air-gap/

Kindervag, J. (2010). *Build Security Into Your Network's DNA: The Zero Trust Network Architecture.* Forrester Research Inc.

Kish, D., & Carpenter, P. (2017). *Forecast Snapshot: Security Awareness Computer-based Training, Worldwide, 2017.* Retrieved October 3, 2019, from https://www.gartner.com/en/documents/3629840/forecast-snapshot-security-awareness-computer-based-trai

Kissel, R. (2011). *Glossary of key information security terms.* Diane Publishing. doi:10.6028/NIST.IR.7298r1

Kocher, P., Genkin, D., Gruss, D., Haas, W., Hamburg, M., Lipp, M., . . . Yarom, Y. (2018). *Spectre Attacks: Exploiting Speculative Execution.* arXiv preprint arXiv:1801.01203

Kowtha, S., Nolan, L. A., & Daley, R. A. (2012). Cyber Security Operations Center Characterization Model and Analysis. *IEEE Conference on Technologies for Homeland Security*, 470-475. 10.1109/THS.2012.6459894

Kula, R. G., German, D. M., Ouni, A., Ishio, T., & Inoue, K. (2018). Do developers update their library dependencies? *Empirical Software Engineering*, 23(1), 384–417. doi:10.100710664-017-9521-5

Langner, R. (2011). Stuxnet: Dissecting a cyberwarfare weapon. *IEEE Security and Privacy*, 9(3), 49–51. doi:10.1109/MSP.2011.67

Laszka, A., Zhao, M., & Grossklags, J. (2016). *Banishing Misaligned Incentives for Validating Reports in Bugbounty Platforms.* Computer Security-ESORICS.

Leon, A. D. (2015). *Impacts of Malicious Cyber Activities* (Unpublished Doctoral Dissertation). Johns Hopkins University.

Li, Y., McCune, J., Newsome, J., Perrig, A., Baker, B., & Drewry, W. (2014). Minibox: A Two-way Sandbox for x86 Native Code. *USENIX Annual Technical Conference*, 409-420.

Lindros, K., & Tittel, E. (2016). *What is Cyber Insurance and Why You Need It.* Retrieved October 3, 2019, from https://www.cio.com/article/3065655/what-is-cyber-insurance-and-why-you-need-it.html

Lipp, M., Schwarz, M., Gruss, D., Prescher, T., Haas, W., Mangard, S., . . . Hamburg, M. (2018). *Meltdown.* arXiv preprint arXiv:1801.01207

Lusthaus, J. (2019). Beneath the Dark Web: Excavating the Layers of Cybercrime's Underground Economy. *IEEE European Symposium on Security and Privacy Workshops*, 474-480. 10.1109/EuroSPW.2019.00059

Ma, Z., Reynolds, J., Dickinson, J., Wang, K., Judd, T., Barnes, J. D., ... Bailey, M. (2019). The Impact of Secure Transport Protocols on Phishing Efficacy. *USENIX Workshop on Cyber Security Experimentation and Test.*

Maillart, T., Zhao, M., Grossklags, J., & Chuang, J. (2016). Given Enough Eyeballs, All Bugs are Shallow? Revisiting Eric Raymond with Bug Bounty Programs. *Journal of Cybersecurity*, 3(2), 81–90. doi:10.1093/cybsec/tyx008

Mann, I. (2017). *Hacking the Human: Social Engineering Techniques and Security Countermeasures*. Routledge. doi:10.4324/9781351156882

McAfee. (2019). *Cloud-native: The Infrastructure-as-a-service Adoption and Risk*. Retrieved October 3, 2019, from https://cloudsecurity.mcafee.com/cloud/en-us/forms/white-papers/wp-cloud-adoption-risk-report-iaas.html

Messerschmidt, J. E. (2013). Hackback: Permitting Retaliatory Hacking by Non-state Actors as Proportionate Countermeasures to Transboundary Cyberharm. *Colum. J. Transnat'l L.*, *52*, 275.

Myrbakken, H., & Colomo-Palacios, R. (2017). Devsecops: A Multivocal Literature Review. *International Conference on Software Process Improvement and Capability Determination*, 17-29. 10.1007/978-3-319-67383-7_2

Nahorney, B. (2017). *ISTR Email Threats 2017*. An ISTR Special Report.

NIST. (2018). *Cyber Ranges*. Retrieved October 3, 2019, from https://www.nist.gov/sites/default/files/documents/2018/02/13/cyber ranges.pdf

NIST. (2019). *Post-Quantum Cryptography – Project Overview*. Retrieved December 5, 2019, from https://csrc.nist.gov/projects/post-quantum-cryptography/

Nobles, C. (2018). Botching Human Factors in Cybersecurity in Business Organizations. *HOLISTICA-Journal of Business and Public Administration*, *9*(3), 71–88. doi:10.2478/hjbpa-2018-0024

Orcutt, M. (2018). *How secure is blockchain really?* Retrieved December 5, 2019, from https://www.technologyreview.com/s/610836/how-secure-is-blockchain-really/

Ornes, S. (2016). Core Concept: The Internet of Things and the Explosion of Interconnectivity. *National Academy of Sciences*, *113*(40), 11059-11060.

Preskill, J. (2018). Quantum Computing in the NISQ era and beyond. *Quantum*, *2*, 79. doi:10.22331/q-2018-08-06-79

PWC. (2019). *Insurance 2020 & Beyond: Reaping the Dividends of Cyber Resilience*. Retrieved October 3, 2019, from https://www.pwc.com/gx/en/industries/financial-services/publications/insurance-2020-cyber.html

Ramzan, Z. (2010). Phishing Attacks and Countermeasures. In Handbook of Information and Communication Security (pp. 433-448). Academic Press.

Reisman, R. J. (2019). *Air Traffic Management Blockchain Infrastructure for Security*. Authentication, and Privacy.

Romanou, A. (2018). The Necessity of the Implementation of Privacy by Design in Sectors where Data Protection Concerns Arise. *Computer Law & Security Review*, *34*(1), 99–110. doi:10.1016/j.clsr.2017.05.021

Rubinstein, I. S., & Good, N. (2013). Privacy by Design: A Counterfactual Analysis of Google and Facebook Privacy Incidents. *Berkeley Technology Law Journal*, *28*, 1333.

Scherer, M. (2017). *Performance and Scalability of Blockchain Networks and Smart Contracts* (Dissertation). Retrieved from http://urn.kb.se/resolve?urn=urn:nbn:se:umu:diva-136470

Schwarz, M., Weiser, S., & Gruss, D. (2019). Practical Enclave Malware with Intel SGX. In *International Conference on Detection of Intrusions and Malware, and Vulnerability Assessment* (pp. 177-196). 10.1007/978-3-030-22038-9_9

Schwarz, M., Weiser, S., Gruss, D., Maurice, C., & Mangard, S. (2017). Malware Guard Extension: Using SGX to Conceal Cache Attacks. In *International Conference on Detection of Intrusions and Malware, and Vulnerability Assessment* (pp. 3-24). 10.1007/978-3-319-60876-1_1

Shao, S., Tunc, C., Satam, P., & Hariri, S. (2017). Real-time IRC Threat Detection Framework. In IEEE 2nd International Workshops on Foundations and Applications of Self Systems (pp. 318-323). IEEE.

Shor, P. W. (1994, November). Algorithms for quantum computation: Discrete logarithms and factoring. In *Proceedings 35th annual symposium on foundations of computer science* (pp. 124-134). IEEE. 10.1109/SFCS.1994.365700

Shu, R., Wang, P., Gorski, S. A. III, Andow, B., Nadkarni, A., Deshotels, L., ... Gu, X. (2016). A Study of Security Isolation Techniques. *ACM Computing Surveys*, *49*(3), 50. doi:10.1145/2988545

Shukla, M., Manjunath, S., Saxena, R., Mondal, S., & Lodha, S. (2015). Poster: Winover Enterprise Dark Data. In *Proceedings of the 22nd ACM SIGSAC Conference on Computer and Communications Security* (pp. 1674-1676). ACM.

Shukla, M., Mondal, S., & Lodha, S. (2016). Poster: Locally Virtualized Environment for Mitigating Ransomware Threat. In *Proceedings of the 2016 ACM SIGSAC Conference on Computer and Communications Security* (pp. 1784-1786). 10.1145/2976749.2989051

Smith, K. T., Jones, A., Johnson, L., & Smith, L. M. (2019). Examination of Cybercrime and its Effects on Corporate Stock Value. *Journal of Information. Communication and Ethics in Society*, *17*(1), 42–60.

Souter, G. (2019). *Cyber Insurance Market Set to Grow Despite Challenges: Panel*. Retrieved October 3, 2019, from https://www.businessinsurance.com/article/20190924/NEWS06/912330822/Cyber-insurance-market-set-to-grow-despite-challenges-Panel

Steffens, M., Rossow, C., Johns, M., & Stock, B. (2019). Don't Trust the Locals: Investigating the Prevalence of Persistent Client-side Cross-site Scripting in the Wild. *Network and Distributed System Security Symposium*. 10.14722/ndss.2019.23009

Tavares, F. (2019). *Google and NASA Achieve Quantum Supremacy*. Retrieved December 5, 2019, from https://www.nasa.gov/feature/ames/quantum-supremacy/

Torres, A. (2015). *Building a World-Class Security Operations Center: A Roadmap*. SANS Institute.

Travis, A., & Arthur, C. (2014). EU Court Backs 'Right to be Forgotten': Google Must Amend Results on Request. *The Guardian*. Retrieved October 3, 2019, from https://www.theguardian.com/technology/2014/may/13/right-to-be-forgotten-eu-court-google-search-results

Tupsamudre, H., Wasnik, R., Biswas, S., Pandit, S., Vaddepalli, S., Shinde, A., ... Lodha, S. (2018). GAP: A Game for Improving Awareness about Passwords. In *Joint Conference on Serious games* (pp. 66-78). 10.1007/978-3-030-02762-9_8

Vacca, J. R. (2019). *Online Terrorist Propaganda, Recruitment, and Radicalization.* CRC Press. doi:10.1201/9781315170251

van Rest, J., Boonstra, D., Everts, M., van Rijn, M., & van Paassen, R. (2012). Designing Privacy-by-design. In *Annual Privacy Forum* (pp. 55-72). Academic Press.

Varghese, B., & Buyya, R. (2018). Next Generation Cloud Computing: New Trends and Research Directions. *Future Generation Computer Systems, 79,* 849–861. doi:10.1016/j.future.2017.09.020

Verizon. (2019). *Data Breach Investigations Report.* Retrieved September 20, 2019, from https://enterprise.verizon.com/resources/reports/dbir/

Wang, A., Liang, R., Liu, X., Zhang, Y., Chen, K., & Li, J. (2017). An Inside Look at IOT Malware. In *International Conference on Industrial IOT Technologies and Applications* (pp. 176-186). 10.1007/978-3-319-60753-5_19

Watkins, B. (2014). *The Impact of Cyber Attacks on the Private Sector. Briefing Paper.* Association for International Affair.

Wilson, M., & Hash, J. (2003). Building an Information Technology Security Awareness and Training Program. *NIST Special Publication, 800*(50), 1–39. doi:10.6028/NIST.SP.800-50

World Economic Forum. (2019). *The Global Risks Report 2019.* Retrieved September 20, 2019, from https://www.weforum.org/reports/the-global-risks-report-2019

Yan, C., Xu, W., & Liu, J. (2016). *Can You Trust Autonomous Vehicles: Contactless Attacks against Sensors of Self-driving Vehicle.* DEFCON.

Yonge, J. d. (2019). *For CEOs, Are the Days of Sidelining Global Challenges Numbered?* Retrieved September 20, 2019, from https://www.ey.com/en gl/growth/ceo-imperative-global-challenges

Yuan, X., He, P., Zhu, Q., & Li, X. (2019). Adversarial Examples: Attacks and Defenses for Deep Learning. *IEEE Transactions on Neural Networks and Learning Systems, 30*(9), 2805–2824. doi:10.1109/TNNLS.2018.2886017 PMID:30640631

# Chapter 22
# Practical Align Overview of the Main Frameworks Used by the Companies to Prevent Cyber Incidents

**Rogério Yukio Iwashita**
*University of São Paulo, Brazil*

**Luiz Camolesi Junior**
*University of Campinas, Brazil*

## ABSTRACT

*Among the biggest cybercrime or information security challenges, the information security professionals must be up to date with the new risks, cases, and different ways of attacks. Being up to date in this complex and aggressive scenario is a huge challenge and is a necessity to the security professional to fight against the cybercriminals. Additionally, based on this standard of requisites to start an information security program, an immature professional may be confused on the different frameworks used by the industries, mainly ISO/IEC 27000 family, NIST 800-53, NIST Cybersecurity Framework, COBIT, etc. This chapter will help the information security professional to decide where is important to focus efforts, to decide what is feasible and which control does not demand any additional investment. Additionally, this grade helps the InfoSec professionals to compare the information security maturity level within the companies and between the companies, comparing with benchmarks.*

## INTRODUCTION

Probably the most known standard used by most companies to improve the information or cyber Security program is the ISO/IEC 27000 family. This standard which is derived from a British standard of 1999 is commonly used due the international certification which provides to external entities, a holistic view of the company security level. Today, the ISO/IEC 27000 family is composed by more than 40 standards,

DOI: 10.4018/978-1-6684-3698-1.ch022

normalizing diverse topics, since the Information technology – Security Techniques – Information security management systems – Requirements (ISO/IEC 27001), Network security (ISO/IEC 27033), Incident investigation (ISO/IEC 27043), among other topics. Nowadays, the newest ISO/ IEC 27000 standard is the ISO/IEC 27701, which propose a set of controls to the Information Security management systems focusing on the data privacy, which may reply to the nowadays demand of data privacy requirements, mostly to respond to the new European laws (GDPR) and many other similar privacy policies around the world.

The National Institute of Standards and Technology (NIST) of the U.S. Department of Commerce maintains the known publication NIST Special Publication 800-53 Revision 4 since 2013 (last revision was on 2015) which is a set of security controls, including the description of and a suggestion on how to measure, implement and administer these controls. Although this publication describes the how-to, it also helps to delimiter the customization of these controls, explaining in details the reasons, risks and key points to success on the main goal: protect the assets of the company, but most providing the reader the ability to improve or optimize it for their own purpose and goals.

More recently, in 2014, due a USA Executive Order, a Cybersecurity framework (CSF) were created consolidating the best practices of different industry sectors and government. As the consequence, this framework is aimed to the security focused on the business and also on the privacy of the people. The components of a Cybersecurity framework are the "Framework Implementation Tiers" topic which may provide a holist view of the implementation of each control, grading from 1 (Tier 1) to 4 (Tier 4).

This chapter will demonstrate that these standards, even with more than twenty years they still must be used, describing when these frameworks should be used, explaining and detailing each standard, and most focusing on the implementation, success cases where these standards helped to avoid (or mitigated substantially) real incidents; lessons learned, with cases based on the prior scenarios, using known cases and my vast experience as Information Security Manager and CISO of great companies.

## BACKGROUND

The ISO/IEC 27000 is the most known and used framework of Information Security and Cybersecurity Managers. Being used as the most comprehensive and in-depth framework in different companies.

As this family of standards have more than 40 different standards, this chapter will focus only on the ISO/IEC 27001 which focus on the requirements and security techniques of the information security management systems on information technologies. Also, this is the unique standard eligible for the accredited certification, which is a very good manner to assess and to present to possible customers that the Information Security controls and cares are in place properly.

The NIST SP 800-53 is a set of controls focused on security and privacy and it defines its deliverable as "*catalog of security and privacy controls for federal information systems and organizations and a process for selecting controls to protect organizational operations (including mission, functions, image, and reputation), organizational assets, individuals, other organizations, and the Nation from a diverse set of threats including hostile cyberattacks, natural disasters, structural failures, and human errors. The controls are customizable and implemented as part of an organization-wide process that manages information security and privacy risk. The controls address a diverse set of security and privacy requirements across the federal government and critical infrastructure, derived from legislation, Executive Orders, policies, directives, regulations, standards, and/or mission/business needs. The publication also describes how to develop specialized sets of controls, or overlays, tailored for specific types of missions/business functions, technologies, or environments of operation. Finally, the catalog of security controls addresses security from both a functionality perspective (the strength of security functions and mechanisms provided) and an assurance perspective (the measures of confidence in the implemented security capability). Addressing both security functionality and security assurance ensures that information technology products and the information systems built from those products using sound systems and security engineering principles are sufficiently trustworthy"* (NIST, 2013).

Besides the well-known NIST SP800-53, NIST had also published on 2014 the Cybersecurity Framework (CSF) as a response for the Executive Order (13636) of the United States President, which directed NIST to develop a framework to reduce the Cybersecurity risks of critical infrastructure, based on the period standards, guidelines and best practice.

## MAIN FOCUS OF THE CHAPTER

Privacy and Information Security are discussed and studied around the world, and still with a subjective concept of privacy, as basically described by Elmaghraby & Losavio: *"the legal and social concepts of a citizen's "right to privacy" are entangled with the challenge of cyber security (...) legal/social concept of privacy addresses confidential aspects of life, control of one's own public profile and a life free of unwarranted interference"* (Elmaghraby & Losavio, 2014).

Also, the countries laws are being adapting to meet the privacy demand of the population. European Union started the privacy law with the GDPR which is *"the prime example of a discipline to regulate data usage and protection across a sovereign state federation such as the European Union (EU)"* (Tamburri, 2019).

Based on a subjective concept, which depends on individual will; an appropriate use of standards may not properly address the privacy needs. Besides the variety of existing standards and frameworks. Additionally, the information Security program must be aligned with the strategic planning of the company. Corroborating, Hernandez, explain that an *"appropriate information technology investment decisions must be made that are in alignment with the mission of the business. Information technology is no longer a back-office accounting function in most businesses, but rather is a core operational necessity to the business, which must have the proper visibility to the board of directors and management's attention of the program"* (Hernandez, 2013).

In the sequence follows the detailed analysis of each most used cybersecurity frameworks.

## ISO/IEC 27000:2013

The ISO/IEC 27001 (2013a), the most known and used standard by information security professionals, lists a set of controls and topics, among which are:

- **Terms and definitions:** Although this section has just a link to the ISO/IEC 27000 standard, a set of definition and terms are very important to the definition of the information security program. An easy way to test how important it is doing a pool with the information security department asking them: "in just one phrase, what is information?" to a set of information security professional. Probably you may receive different answers, like: "Information is a set of data"; "Information is the most valuable asset of the company"; "Information is the base of the knowledge". This are samples of answers I received of my information security team. Although, many of the information security professionals may have many years of experience, the concept of information is different, even to information security professionals. So, how the information security professional may execute your work properly, if even a formal definition of information is not clear to who are supposed to protect the it. Defining properly the terms are very important to be aligned with the information security team and their objectives;

- **Leadership**: The top management commitment is crucial to the information security program. Considering that most of the controls to be implements will use more resources (financial, time or labor) and it will concur with strategic or even different department objectives, the top management commitment will ensure that the proper prioritization and the resources needed will be available whenever necessary, regardless of the competition for resources. The leadership commitment also will help the support phase, when all the company will support the information security program implementation. It can be achieved through an awareness campaigns, communication and reports;

- **Planning**: Since the resources are available, a planning phase is important to be executed. Usually, when facing the Cyber Risks for the first time, it is natural the initiative to start executing and trying to manage all the possible risks. Although it is natural, it is not a best practice. The planning contemplates the risk management to define the prioritization in a sustainable manner, how to manage the risk and how to respond to them. Also, the planning phase helps on the definition of the information security objectives and the way to achieve them;

- **Documentation**: ISO/IEC 27001 may be a good strategy to have an information security certification and to do so, it is important to have all the information and documentation ready to be audited. Documentation controls includes the creation of the policy and the updating process. As the controls, procedures and process may change, the documentation must be updated to these changes;

- **Performance Evaluation**: The information security program performance must be evaluated and reported to the company top management team. This is very important to keep their commitment, report any possible issue on this implementation and also to define and have their approval to the risk response. Besides the report to the leadership, periodical audits (internal and external) are necessary to maintain the impartiality and transparency of the program;

- **Lessons-learned**: Besides these controls, lessons-learned and the continuous improvement must be in place to ensure that any new or different situation can be answered promptly and correctly.

The Appendix attached on the ISO/IEC 27001 (ISO/IEC, 2013a) list the controls and objectives of the controls, aligned with the ISO/IEC 27002 (ISO/IEC, 2013b), which is code of practice for information security controls helping information security managers to implement a complete information security management system. Usually, the information security managers use the Appendix as a summary of the controls that must be implemented. When a question comes up about how to implement the control or about the scope, the ISO/IEC 27002 is used as reference.

Actually, the Appendix lists the 114 controls divided in 14 clauses linked with the sections of the ISO/IEC 27002 (ISO/IEC, 2013b):

- A.5 Information security policies (2 controls);
- A.6 Organization of information security (7 controls);

- A.7 Human resource security (6 controls);
- A.8 Asset management (10 controls);
- A.9 Access control (14 controls);
- A.10 Cryptography (2 controls);
- A.11 Physical and environmental security (15 controls);
- A.12 Operations security (14 controls);
- A.13 Communications security (7 controls);
- A.14 System acquisition, development and maintenance (13 controls);
- A.15 Supplier relationships (5 controls);
- A.16 Information security incident management (7 controls);
- A.17 Information security aspects of business continuity management (4 controls);
- A.18 Compliance (8 controls);

As mentioned by Gordon, *ISO 27001 is designed to be vendor and technology agnostic. As such, it looks for the information security management to address the relevant risks and components in a manner that is appropriate and adequate based on risks.*(Gordon, 2016)

ISO 27018 was the first international set of privacy controls, focused on cloud computing, defining a code of practice for protection of PII in public cloud, acting as PII processors.

Although, most of the controls listed on this are based on other standards standard (ISO/IEC, 2018a), mainly the ISO/IEC 27002:2013, this standard brings new concepts dedicated to the Privacy, being subdivided in five principles:

- *Consent: CSPs must not use the personal data they receive for advertising and marketing unless expressly instructed to do so by the customers. In addition, a customer should be able to employ the service without having to consent to the use of her personal data for advertising or marketing.*
- *Control: Customers have explicit control over how CSPs are to use their information.*
- *Transparency: CSPs must inform customers about items such as where their data resides. CSPs also need to disclose to customers the use of any subcontractors who will be used to process PII.*
- *Communication: CSPs should keep clear records about any incident and their response to it, and they should notify customers.*
- *Independent and yearly audit: To remain compliant, the CSP must subject itself to yearly third-party reviews. This allows the customer to rely upon the findings to support her own regulatory obligations.*(Gordon, 2016)

An extension of the ISO/IEC 27001 certification is the ISO/IEC 27701, which focus on the requirements to maintain secure the Personally Identifiable Information (PII). An extension of the ISO/IEC 27001 certification is the ISO/IEC 27701 (ISO/IEC, 2019), which focus on the requirements to maintain secure the Personally Identifiable Information (PII). It is ISO/IEC 27001 extension, enhancing controls to maintain privacy. The ISO/IEC 27701 helps on the implementation of the Privacy Information Management System (PIMS), although the ISO/IEC 27000 helps on the implementation of the Information Security Management System (ISMS).

The ISO/IEC 27000 family is a very complete standard, starting with the strategic, tactical and operational controls, and it has been used by many companies as a starting point of the InfoSec program.

Additionally, it may be used to certificate your company and present to the market that the information security controls are in place properly.

Even with the distrust by many professionals about the line of thought on this certifications, as this is a very common standard used and it may be applied to compare different companies and help your company to decide which company you should sign a new contract, or just to define the trust relationship your company may set with.

ISO/IEC 27001 is the most common framework for cybersecurity and information security. So, for the next frameworks, lets focus on the definition and them on the differences between the framework itself and the ISO/IEC 27001.

## NIST SP 800-53

This publication has 256 controls, divided in 18 families. Each family is also identified by the two-character identifier, for example, AC for Access Control and AT for Awareness and Training. This identifier helps the Information Security Professional to easily identify the control. For instance, using just CM-5 to identify the "Access Restriction for Change" Control of the Configuration Management Family (Table 1).

*Table 1. NIST SP 800-53 Family Controls (NIST, 2013)*

| ID | Family | ID | Family |
|---|---|---|---|
| AC | Access Control | MP | Media Protection |
| AT | Awareness and Training | PE | Physical and Environmental Protection |
| AU | Audit and Accountability | PL | Planning |
| CA | Security Assessment and Authorization | AS | Personnel Security |
| CM | Configuration Management | RA | Risk Assessment |
| CP | Contingency Planning | AS | System and Services Acquisition |
| IA | Identification and Authentication | SC | System and Communications Protection |
| IR | Incident Response | SI | System and Information Integrity |
| MA | Maintenance | PM | Program Management |

Every 256 control are detailed on the Appendix F included on NIST SP 800-53 describing:

- **Control**: describing what the organization should carry out to implement this control;
- **Supplemental guidance**: explaining why it is important to implement it and also the related controls. This information is very useful to leverage the efforts to implement two different controls;
- **Control Enhancements**: which describe other activities or controls which may improve the security level with this control. Sometimes, during the risk assessment, some specific control may be considered as a high potential risk, which may require any additional cares. In the NIST SP 800-53, these cares may be listed on the own control;
- **References**: Listing any additional references;

- **Priority and Baseline Allocation**: a proposed classification of the priority used to help the Information Security Professional to decide which Control are critical.

Besides the proposed priority definition and the controls by themselves, one very important deliverable of the NIST SP 800-53 is that it provides a very extensive and holistic view of the information security controls and also the risk management. Thus, defining a Risk Management Framework helps the Information Security Professional to define which controls are critical in the situation and which control has lower criticality and so, to spend controls resources to provide a more secure environment, based on the company context.

This framework proposes a step-by-step process to implement the controls based on their methodology to prioritization, which consists of 6 steps described on the NIST SP800-53 as:

- *"Step 1: Categorize the information system based on a FIPS Publication 199 impact assessment;28*
- *Step 2: Select the applicable security control baseline based on the results of the security categorization and apply tailoring guidance (including the potential use of overlays);*
- *Step 3: Implement the security controls and document the design, development, and implementation details for the controls;*
- *Step 4: Assess the security controls to determine the extent to which the controls are implemented correctly, operating as intended, and producing the desired outcome with respect to meeting the security requirements for the system;29*
- *Step 5: Authorize information system operation based on a determination of risk to organizational operations and assets, individuals, other organizations, and the Nation resulting from the operation and use of the information system and the decision that this risk is acceptable; and*
- *Step 6: Monitor the security controls in the information system and environment of operation on an ongoing basis to determine control effectiveness, changes to the system/environment, and compliance to legislation, Executive Orders, directives, policies, regulations, and standards".* (NIST, 2013)

Taking the ISO/IEC 27000 as reference, there are many similarities of the controls proposed by this framework. Focusing on the controls that are different or do not have directly correlation with ISO/IEC 27000, this chapter lists this correlation on Table 5/ Appendix A (Appendix H on the NIST SP 800-53 publication). There are 104 controls without a direct correlation and 29 controls which the ISO/IEC 27000 control does not fully satisfy the intent of the NIST control.

Focusing on the NIST families with the greatest discrepancy in comparison to ISO/IEC 27000, the set has the families System and Communications Protection SC (with 31 controls), System and Information Integrity SI (12 controls) and Program Management PM (11 controls) (NIST, 2013). The complete list of the missing controls is presented on Table 7/Appendix A on the chapter. The consolidate amount of the missing control is detailed on the Table 2.

Although *"the goals of information security are confidentiality, integrity, and availability (CIA)"*(Clarke, 2012), a superficial analysis of the numbers of the table, highlights that the family "System and Information Integrity" is the family with the most discrepancy relative amount of controls. This analysis must not conclude that ISO / IEC does not assure properly the information integrity, or that these information security goals have any problem due the missing controls.

*Table 2. Quantity of NIST SP 800-53 Controls compared with ISO/IEC 27001 Controls*

| Family Control | Not ISO/IEC correlated control | Amount of Control on NIST | Relative Percentage |
|:---:|:---:|:---:|:---:|
| SI | 12 | 17 | 71% |
| SC | 31 | 44 | 70% |
| PM | 11 | 16 | 69% |
| CA | 5 | 9 | 56% |
| IR | 5 | 10 | 50% |
| MA | 3 | 6 | 50% |
| AU | 7 | 16 | 44% |
| IA | 4 | 11 | 36% |
| SA | 8 | 22 | 36% |
| AC | 8 | 25 | 32% |
| AT | 1 | 5 | 20% |
| CM | 2 | 11 | 18% |
| RA | 1 | 6 | 17% |
| MP | 1 | 8 | 13% |
| PS | 1 | 8 | 13% |
| PL | 1 | 9 | 11% |
| PE | 2 | 20 | 10% |
| CP | 1 | 13 | 8% |

In fact, taking a better and deep analysis, the SI family controls without a correspondent on ISO 270002 and based on the Appendix F on the NIST SP 800-53, there are very important, technical and specific issues, as organized below and extracted from the NIST SP 800-53:

- **Information System Monitoring Control:** Although "*prevention is better than cure*" (Duca, 2018) because of the costs to fix any cyberattack consequences and impacts, the monitoring is a necessary control. A proper monitoring and response process will mitigate the impacts of any attack and that's why many of the companies nowadays are investing on Security Operation Center. This control defines that the organization:
  - *Monitors the information system to detect:*
    - § *Attacks and indicators of potential attacks in accordance with [Assignment: organization-defined monitoring objectives]; and*
    - § *Unauthorized local, network, and remote connections;*
  - *Identifies unauthorized use of the information system through [Assignment: organization-defined techniques and methods];*
  - *Deploys monitoring devices:*
    - § *Strategically within the information system to collect organization-determined essential information; and*

§ *At ad hoc locations within the system to track specific types of transactions of interest to the organization;*

○ *Protects information obtained from intrusion-monitoring tools from unauthorized access, modification, and deletion.*

- **Security Function Verification Control:** Many information security professionals take care of the implementation, leaving the efficiency of the process with a lower priority. This control defines that the information system:

  ○ *Verifies the correct operation of [Assignment: organization-defined security functions];*

  ○ *Performs this verification [Selection (one or more): [Assignment: organization-defined system transitional states]; upon command by user with appropriate privilege; [Assignment: organization-defined frequency]];*

  ○ *Notifies [Assignment: organization-defined personnel or roles] of failed security verification tests; and*

  ○ *[Selection (one or more): shuts the information system down; restarts the information system; [Assignment: organization-defined alternative action(s)]] when anomalies are discovered.*

- **Software, Firmware, and Information Integrity Control:** A good process or tool to identify any change on the information security system are crucial to identify any substantial cyber-attack. It is very important that this control must be in place with a good monitoring and response process. This control defines that:

  ○ *The organization employs integrity verification tools to detect unauthorized changes.*

- **Spam Protection Control:** There is nothing more annoying than SPAM. Not only due the loss of time with unproductive e-mails, but with the possibility of phishing, which is an attack via e-mail. This control defines that the organization:

  ○ *Employs spam protection mechanisms at information system entry and exit points to detect and take action on unsolicited messages; and*

  ○ *Updates spam protection mechanisms when new releases are available in accordance with organizational configuration management policy and procedures.*

- **Information Input Validation Control:** In fact, every input must be validated, whether coming from an user or a system. This prevent the most common and widely user attack: Injections (OWASP, 2020). This control defines that:

  ○ *The information system checks the validity of [Assignment: organization-defined information inputs].*

- **Error Handling Control:** It is a day by day scenario which the information security officer is inquired about developers accessing logs or production environment to debug any possible error. One of the risks that the information security officer should consider is that the error messages are not listing the necessary information, but also any critical or confidential information, like passwords, user credential, etc. Besides the internal risk, there is the possibility to provide to an attacker additional information due a misconfigured error handling page, which may make easier the cyber-attack discovery phase. This control defines that *information system:*

  ○ *Generates error messages that provide information necessary for corrective actions without revealing information that could be exploited by adversaries; and*

  ○ *Reveals error messages only to [Assignment: organization-defined personnel or roles].*

- **Information Handling and Retention Control:** Being compliance with the law is mandatory to cybersecurity professionals as defined by the (ISC) with the code of ethics that all the CISSP

(Certified Information System Security Professional) are subject (Gordon, 2015). This control defines that:

- ○ *The organization handles and retains information within the information system and information output from the system in accordance with applicable federal laws, Executive Orders, directives, policies, regulations, standards, and operational requirements.*

- **Predictable Failure Prevention Control:** This control is not related with cybercrime (instead of a DDoS attack – Distributed Denial of Service), keeping the business process working is essential to the company survival. This control defines that the organization:

  - ○ *Determines mean time to failure (MTTF) for [Assignment: organization-defined information system components] in specific environments of operation; and*

  - ○ *Provides substitute information system components and a means to exchange active and standby components at [Assignment: organization-defined MTTF substitution criteria].*

- **Non-Persistence Control**: Advanced Persistent Threats (APTs) are very common and specific attack, which may exploit a window of opportunity. Defining a non-persistent policy will decrease it. This control defines:

  - ○ *The organization implements non-persistent [Assignment: organization-defined information system components and services] that are initiated in a known state and terminated [Selection (one or more): upon end of session of use; periodically at [Assignment: organization- defined frequency]].*

- **Information Output Filtering Control:** Very similar to Information Input Validation Control, but instead of protecting the input, this control is protection the output, which is commonly used to identify if an application is susceptible to an injection attack. This control defines that:

  - ○ *The information system validates information output from [Assignment: organization - defined software programs and/or applications] to ensure that the information is consistent with the expected content.*

- **Memory Protection Control:** A cyber-attacker aims to gain privilege to access indiscriminately the computer memory, so, the attacker will be able to exfiltrate any confidential data, or access credential information which he may use to gather the confidential information of any other source. The memory protection control helps mitigate these risks, not allowing non-authorized software to access restrict memory address. This control defines that:

  - ○ *The information system implements [Assignment: organization-defined security safeguards] to protect its memory from unauthorized code execution.*

- **Fail-Safe Procedures Control:** Together to the monitoring process, the fail-safe procedure assures the proper response to a failure (purposeful or not), leading the system to a safe state. This control defines that:

  - ○ *The information system implements [Assignment: organization-defined fail-safe procedures] when [Assignment: organization-defined failure conditions occur].*

Also, considering that the other NIST SI controls has relationship with the A5, A6, A18, A12, A14, A16 domains, this may be inferred that the core of this family are spread on the other domains, leaving only more technical items, either due to technological improvements or any more specific issues.

Also, analyzing in details each of the other controls, these characteristic behaviors occur on many of the remaining controls, which are regarding technical care implementation, for instance, controls on concurrent session control (AC-10), data mining protection (AC-23), re-authentication (IA-11), among any others. Additionally, on Appendix J on the NIST SP800-53, there are a list of privacy controls (Table 3), which are based on the Fair Information Practice Principles (FIPPs), also focused on PII protection.

*Table 3. List of Privacy Controls of Appendix J part of the NIST SP 800-53 (NIST, 2013)*

| ID | PRIVACY CONTROLS |
|---|---|
| **AP - Authority and Purpose** | |
| AP-1 | Authority to Collect |
| AP-2 | Purpose Specification |
| **AR - Accountability, Audit, and Risk Management** | |
| AR-1 | Governance and Privacy Program |
| AR-2 | Privacy Impact and Risk Assessment |
| AR-3 | Privacy Requirements for Contractors and Service Providers |
| AR-4 | Privacy Monitoring and Auditing |
| AR-5 | Privacy Awareness and Training |
| AR-6 | Privacy Reporting |
| AR-7 | Privacy-Enhanced System Design and Development |
| AR-8 | Accounting of Disclosures |
| **DI - Data Quality and Integrity** | |
| DI-1 | Data Quality |
| DI-2 | Data Integrity and Data Integrity Board |
| **DM - Data Minimization and Retention** | |
| DM-1 | Minimization of Personally Identifiable Information |
| DM-2 | Data Retention and Disposal |
| DM-3 | Minimization of PII Used in Testing, Training, and Research |
| **IP - Individual Participation and Redress** | |
| IP-1 | Consent |
| IP-2 | Individual Access |
| IP-3 | Redress |
| IP-4 | Complaint Management |
| **SE - Security** | |
| SE-1 | Inventory of Personally Identifiable Information |
| SE-2 | Privacy Incident Response |
| **TR - Transparency** | |
| TR-1 | Privacy Notice |
| TR-2 | System of Records Notices and Privacy Act Statements |
| TR-3 | Dissemination of Privacy Program Information |
| **UL - Use Limitation** | |
| UL-1 | Internal Use |
| UL-2 | Information Sharing with Third Parties |

There are many similarities of these controls and the controls listed on the Appendix A part of NIST SP 800-53, considering their contents and structure. Considering NIST SP 800-53 and ISO/IEC 27000 as reference to any information security program is essential to these program successes and hey must be harmonized and complement each other.

## NIST Cybersecurity Framework

*"The Framework focuses on using business drivers to guide cybersecurity activities and considering cybersecurity risks as part of the organization's risk management processes. The Framework consists of three parts: the Framework Core, the Implementation Tiers, and the Framework Profiles"*(Barrett, 2018). The parts are:

- **Framework Core**: This part provides the set of activities and controls to achieve the desired cybersecurity risk level. Basically, this set of activities are organized in functions. Each Function are subdivided in Categories which are also subdivided in Subcategories. Each Subcategories has an Informative References. NIST framework defines these 5 Functions as:
  - ◦ *Identify – Develop an organizational understanding to manage cybersecurity risk to systems, people, assets, data, and capabilities. The activities in the Identify Function are foundational for effective use of the Framework. Understanding the business context, the resources that support critical functions, and the related cybersecurity risks enables an organization to focus and prioritize its efforts, consistent with its risk management strategy and business needs. Examples of outcome Categories within this Function include: Asset Management; Business Environment; Governance; Risk Assessment; and Risk Management Strategy.*
  - ◦ *Protect – Develop and implement appropriate safeguards to ensure delivery of critical services. The Protect Function supports the ability to limit or contain the impact of a potential cybersecurity event. Examples of outcome Categories within this Function include: Identity Management and Access Control; Awareness and Training; Data Security; Information Protection Processes and Procedures; Maintenance; and Protective Technology.*
  - ◦ *Detect – Develop and implement appropriate activities to identify the occurrence of a cybersecurity event. The Detect Function enables timely discovery of cybersecurity events. Examples of outcome Categories within this Function include: Anomalies and Events; Security Continuous Monitoring; and Detection Processes.*
  - ◦ *Respond – Develop and implement appropriate activities to take action regarding a detected cybersecurity incident. The Respond Function supports the ability to contain the impact of a potential cybersecurity incident. Examples of outcome Categories within this Function include: Response Planning; Communications; Analysis; Mitigation; and Improvements.*
  - ◦ *Recover – Develop and implement appropriate activities to maintain plans for resilience and to restore any capabilities or services that were impaired due to a cybersecurity incident. The Recover Function supports timely recovery to normal operations to reduce the impact from a cybersecurity incident. Examples of outcome Categories within this Function include: Recovery Planning; Improvements; and Communications.* (Barrett, 2018).
- **Implementation Tiers**: This framework not only lists the activities to implement and administer the cybersecurity risk program, but also provides a specific tool to measure the Cybersecurity Risk. This tool measures the implementation of the activities in 4 Tiers, since the Tier 1, with the

partial implementation, till the Tier 4, with an adaptative implementation. Basically, NIST defines the Tiers as:

- *Tier 1 – Partial: (…) Organizational cybersecurity risk management practices are not formalized, and risk is managed in an ad hoc and sometimes reactive manner. Prioritization of cybersecurity activities may not be directly informed by organizational risk objectives, the threat environment, or business/mission requirements.*
- *Tier 2 – Risk Informed: (…) Risk management practices are approved by management but may not be established as organizational-wide policy. Prioritization of cybersecurity activities and protection needs is directly informed by organizational risk objectives, the threat environment, or business/mission requirements.*
- *Tier 3 – Repeatable: (…) The organization's risk management practices are formally approved and expressed as policy. Organizational cybersecurity practices are regularly updated based on the application of risk management processes to changes in business/mission requirements and a changing threat and technology landscape.*
- *Tier 4 – Adaptive: (…) The organization adapts its cybersecurity practices based on previous and current cybersecurity activities, including lessons learned and predictive indicators. Through a process of continuous improvement incorporating advanced cybersecurity technologies and practices, the organization actively adapts to a changing threat and technology landscape and responds in a timely and effective manner to evolving, sophisticated threats. "* (Barrett, 2018).

Although this may be very similar to maturity model (like Capability Maturity Model – CMM), this tool does not measure the implementation maturity, but it provides a tool to identify the major risk and the functions which has a better controls implementation. Additionally, some companies use this Tiers (or a similar Tiers) to compare their cybersecurity program implementation with their competitors and also creating a benchmark. This is a very powerful tool to justify investments on cybersecurity projects.

- **Framework Profiles**: The framework profile is the link between the functions, activities, controls and any other cybersecurity topic, with the strategic and company risk tolerance. This process is based on the Tiers grade, considering the current status with the objective status, defining on this step a roadmap of the cybersecurity activities. As the NIST SP800-53 (NIST, 2013), this framework helps with a step-by-step implementation map, being different in some steps:
  - Step 1: Prioritize and Scope. On this step the company identify exactly, what are the most valuable asset and also aligned with the business strategic definition;
  - Step 2: Orient. With the scope defined, it is important to consolidate the regulation applied and use external sources to identify threats and vulnerabilities on the environment;
  - Step 3: Create a Current Profile; This step is responsible for mapping and measuring the framework profile;
  - Step 4: Conduct a Risk Assessment. Based on the previous step deliverable (possible threats and current profile), the risks are assessed.
  - Step 5: Create a Target Profile. Based on the risk assessment and the current profile, a target profile is created.

○ Step 6: Determine, Analyze, and Prioritize Gaps. Since the current and the target profile are determined, the gaps between then may be identified and also may be prioritized considering the risk assessment executed.

○ Step 7: Implement Action Plan. Now, with the gap mapped and prioritized, it is possible to start the implementation.

On the Appendix A of the "Cybersecurity framework for critical infrastructure" (Barrett, 2018) document, there is a summary table of the Functions, and also a summary table with each subcategory and an Informative Reference, lists the other standards with the same control. Like the NIST SP 800-53, comparing with the ISO/IEC 27000, which is the most known framework, there are many similarities. Comparing the ISO/IEC27000 and this Cybersecurity Framework - CSF (NIST, 2018), the Table 4 presents 25 controls that there is no direct relationship with ISO/IEC 27000.

*Table 4. Outstanding Controls on ISO / IEC 27000 when compared to NIST CSF*

| Control ID | Function | Category | Control |
|---|---|---|---|
| ID.BE-2 | IDENTIFY (ID) | Business Environment (ID.BE): The organization's mission, objectives, stakeholders, and activities are understood and prioritized; this information is used to inform cybersecurity roles, responsibilities, and risk management decisions. | The organization's place in criticalinfrastructure and its industry sector is identified and communicated |
| ID.BE-3 | IDENTIFY (ID) | Business Environment (ID.BE): The organization's mission, objectives, stakeholders, and activities are understood and prioritized; this information is used to inform cybersecurity roles, responsibilities, and risk management decisions. | Priorities for organizational mission, objectives, and activities are established and communicated |
| ID.GV-4 | IDENTIFY (ID) | Governance (ID.GV): The policies, procedures, and processes to manage and monitor the organization's regulatory, legal, risk, environmental, and operational requirements are understood and inform the management of cybersecurity risk. | Governance and risk management processes address cybersecurity risks |
| ID.RA-3 | IDENTIFY (ID) | Risk Assessment (ID.RA): The organization understands the cybersecurity risk to organizational operations (including mission, functions, image, or reputation), organizational assets, and individuals. | Threats, both internal and external, are identified and documented |
| ID.RA-4 | IDENTIFY (ID) | Risk Assessment (ID.RA): The organization understands the cybersecurity risk to organizational operations (including mission, functions, image, or reputation), organizational assets, and individuals. | Potential business impacts and likelihoods are identified |
| ID.RA-6 | IDENTIFY (ID) | Risk Assessment (ID.RA): The organization understands the cybersecurity risk to organizational operations (including mission, functions, image, or reputation), organizational assets, and individuals. | Risk responses are identified and prioritized |
| ID.RM-1 | IDENTIFY (ID) | Risk Management Strategy (ID.RM): The organization's priorities, constraints, risk tolerances, and assumptions are established and used to support operational risk decisions. | Risk management processes are established, managed, and agreed toby organizational stakeholders |
| ID.RM-2 | IDENTIFY (ID) | Risk Management Strategy (ID.RM): The organization's priorities, constraints, risk tolerances, and assumptions are established and used to support operational risk decisions. | Organizational risk tolerance is determined and clearly expressed |
| ID.RM-3 | IDENTIFY (ID) | Risk Management Strategy (ID.RM): The organization's priorities, constraints, risk tolerances, and assumptions are established and used to support operational risk decisions. | The organization's determination of risk tolerance is informed by its role in critical infrastructure and sector specific risk analysis |

*continues on following page*

*Table 4. Continued*

| Control ID | Function | Category | Control |
|---|---|---|---|
| PR.IP-7 | PROTECT (PR) | Information Protection Processes and Procedures (PR. IP): Security policies (that address purpose, scope, roles, responsibilities, management commitment, and coordination among organizational entities), processes, and procedures are maintained and used to manage protection of information systems and assets. | Protection processes are continuously improved |
| DE.AE-1 | DETECT (DE) | Anomalies and Events (DE.AE): Anomalous activity is detected and the potential impact of events is understood. | A baseline of network operations and expected data flows for users and systems is established and managed |
| DE.AE-3 | DETECT (DE) | Anomalies and Events (DE.AE): Anomalous activity is detected and the potential impact of events is understood. | Event data are aggregated and correlated from multiple sources and sensors |
| DE.AE-4 | DETECT (DE) | Anomalies and Events (DE.AE): Anomalous activity is detected and the potential impact of events is understood. | Impact of events is determined |
| DE.AE-5 | DETECT (DE) | Anomalies and Events (DE.AE): Anomalous activity is detected and the potential impact of events is understood. | Incident alert thresholds are established |
| DE.CM-1 | DETECT (DE) | Security Continuous Monitoring (DE.CM): The information system and assets are monitored to identify cybersecurity events and verify the effectiveness of protective measures. | The network is monitored to detect potential cybersecurity events |
| DE.CM-2 | DETECT (DE) | Security Continuous Monitoring (DE.CM): The information system and assets are monitored to identify cybersecurity events and verify the effectiveness of protective measures. | The physical environment ismonitored to detect potentialcybersecurity events |
| DE.CM-7 | DETECT (DE) | Security Continuous Monitoring (DE.CM): The information system and assets are monitored to identify cybersecurity events and verify the effectiveness of protective measures. | Monitoring for unauthorized personnel, connections devices, and software is performed |
| RS.CO-4 | RESPOND (RS) | Communications (RS.CO): Response activities are coordinated with internal and external stakeholders (e.g. external support from law enforcement agencies). | Coordination with stakeholders occursconsistent with response plans |
| RS.CO-5 | RESPOND (RS) | Communications (RS.CO): Response activities are coordinated with internal and external stakeholders (e.g. external support from law enforcement agencies). | Voluntary information sharing occurswith external stakeholders to achievebroader cybersecurity situationalawareness |
| RS.IM-2 | RESPOND (RS) | Mitigation (RS.MI): Activities are performed to prevent expansion of an event, mitigate its effects, and resolve the incident. | Response strategies are updated |
| RC.IM-1 | RECOVERY (RC) | Improvements (RC.IM): Recovery planning and processes are improved by incorporating lessons learned into future activities. | Recovery plans incorporate lessons learned |
| RC.IM-2 | RECOVERY (RC) | Improvements (RC.IM): Recovery planning and processes are improved by incorporating lessons learned into future activities. | Response strategies are updated |
| RC.CO-1 | RECOVERY (RC) | Communications (RC.CO): Restoration activities are coordinated with internal and external parties (e.g. coordinating centers, Internet Service Providers, owners of attacking systems, victims, other CSIRTs, and vendors). | Public relations are managed |
| RC.CO-2 | RECOVERY (RC) | Communications (RC.CO): Restoration activities are coordinated with internal and external parties (e.g. coordinating centers, Internet Service Providers, owners of attacking systems, victims, other CSIRTs, and vendors). | Reputation after an event is repaired |
| RC.CO-3 | RECOVERY (RC) | Communications (RC.CO): Restoration activities are coordinated with internal and external parties (e.g. coordinating centers, Internet Service Providers, owners of attacking systems, victims, other CSIRTs, and vendors). | Recovery activities are communicated to internal stakeholders and executive and management teams |

Different of the NIST SP 800-53, which are technical controls, this controls are more procedures and governance controls, for instance: *"IB.BE-3 Priorities for organizational mission, objectives and activities are established and communicated"*, or the *"RC.CO-3 Recovery activities are communicated to internal stakeholders and executive and management teams"*. Analyzing the list of outstanding controls, based on the Functions, the Table 5 presents the missing controls.

*Table 5. Missing Controls Summary*

| Function | Quantity of missing control |
|---|---|
| DETECT (DE) | 7 |
| IDENTIFY (ID) | 9 |
| PROTECT (PR) | 1 |
| RECOVERY (RC) | 5 |
| RESPOND (RS) | 3 |

The Identify and Detect functions are the main topics that are missing on the ISO/IEC 27001, and drill-downing this analysis we identify that Risk Management, with 6 controls missing, is the main topic, just the topic detailed and explained as to be me the base of the identification, classification and prioritization of every effort, project and activities to mitigate the cyberattacks. To handle with risk management, there ISO/IEC published on 2018 the ISO/IEC 31000.

Additionally, regarding the Recovery Function, there is the ISO/IEC 22301 (ISO/IEC, 2019) which, similar to the ISO/IEC 27001, certificates companies, but on the Business continuity, ensuring that the company may respond to an critical incident in a proper way. Nowadays, considering NIST CSF, NIST SP 800-53 and ISO/IEC 27000 as reference to any information security program is essential to these program successes.

## SOLUTIONS AND RECOMMENDATIONS

Considering the scenario explained on previous topic, with a subjective definition of privacy and a variety of standards and frameworks; the information security professional may be confused to choose and apply the correct standard /framework, also considering the need to be aligned with the company strategy.

Adam Gordon said: *"All entities face uncertainty, and the challenge for management is to determine how much uncertainty to accept as it strives to grow stakeholder value"* (Gordon, 2015). So, to face this challenge, a good risk management methodology is key to maintain the malleability to fit every possible situation and also ensure the proper information security performance, even though it is a twenty-year old standard/framework.

This chapter explains the main concepts of the nowadays most used standard/frameworks, focusing on the risk management methodologies, their difference and contributing with a practical view of the application of these standards/frameworks.

## FUTURE RESEARCH DIRECTIONS

The summary of the most researched and used framework are listed on this chapter, with highlight to the risk management methodology. Adam Gordon mentioned the Australian Standard definition: of risk management framework as "*a set of components that provide the foundations and organizational arrangements for designing, implementing, monitoring, reviewing and continually improving risk management throughout the organization*" (Gordon, 2015).

Based on this definition, a future and natural extension is the expansion of the analysis of the other risk management framework or different arrangement, design of implementation methodologies, for instance, the use of ISO/IEC 31000 (ISO/IEC, 2018), The Risk IT Framework (ISACA, 2009).

Other future research is the applicability of these standard/framework on different scenarios and company sectors, consolidating or refuting the results currently found. Another future research could change the proposed method with the use of different point of analysis, such as the applicability of the threat assessment, analyzing the technical threats instead of the risk per se.

## CONCLUSION

Nowadays, many countries are defining and approving laws to normalize the privacy cares that every company should have to protect the personal information. Additionally, the cyberattacks successful rate are increasing daily. Not only the successful rate but the complexity to detect and respond to an cyberattack. Considering this scenario, it is impossible to predict the future of the Cybercrimes or the consequences of the new privacy laws. It is a constant "cat and mouse" game, where each enhancement has consequences the adversary enhancement.

As a cybersecurity professional, responsible for maintaining and ensure the right level of cybersecurity cares and resilience, define a strategic and the methodology of a cybersecurity implementation program is an extremely difficult task (Herculean task). The use of the well-known and tested frameworks and tools may help this professional.

Use a well-known and testes standard as ISO/IEC 27000 family may help the cybersecurity professional to start the implementation which may also be easily audited and certificated by an independent and external entity, granting a good sign of progress and determine the controls that need a special improvement. Additionally, using the other two standards will improve considerably the security level. Although NIST SP 800-53 are very technical controls, still, they are very important controls that need to be observed by the Security Officer and cybersecurity professional. Considering the NIST Cybersecurity Framework, they are very focused on the controls necessary to the cybersecurity environment, being more update to the actual risks and cyber-attacks.

These frameworks list a set of procedures and governance controls that are note listed on the ISO/IEC 27000, which will help the professional to have a more holistic view of all the necessary controls.

Should consider all of these frameworks, knowing them and every detail, but start the implementation of only one of them. Usually, it is a best practice to start with ISO, but each of them has many technical implementation cares that define and exemplifies the Security Officer day by day.

## REFERENCES

Barrett, M. (2018). Framework for improving critical infrastructure cybersecurity. *Proceedings of the Annual ISA Analysis Division Symposium*, *535*, 9–25.

Clarke, G. E. (2012). *CompTIA Security+ Certification Study Guide (Exam SY0-301) (Official CompTIA Guide)*. McGraw-Hill.

Duca, S. (2018). *Cybersecurity: Why prevention is better than the cure*. Retrieved March 1, 2020, from The CEO Magazine website: https://www.theceomagazine.com/business/innovation-technology/cybersecurity-why-prevention-is-better-than-the-cure/

Elmaghraby, A. S., & Losavio, M. M. (2014). Cyber security challenges in smart cities: Safety, security and privacy. *Journal of Advanced Research*, *5*(4), 491–497. doi:10.1016/j.jare.2014.02.006 PMID:25685517

Gordon, A. (2015). *Official (ISC)2 Guide to the CISSP CBK* (4th ed.). CRC Press. doi:10.1201/b18257

Gordon, A. (2016). *The Official (ISC)2 Guide to the CCSP CBK* (2nd ed.). Sybex.

Hernandez, S. (2013). *Official (ISC)2 Guide to the CISSP CBK Press Book 11* (3rd ed.). CRC Press.

ISACA. (2009). *The Risk IT Framework*. Information Systems Audit and Control Association.

ISO/IEC. (2013a). ISO / IEC 27001: Information technology — Security techniques — Information security management systems — Requirements (p. 30).

ISO/IEC. (2013b). ISO / IEC 27002: Information technology — Security techniques — Code of practice for information security controls (p. 99).

ISO/IEC. (2018). *ISO / IEC 31000:2018: Risk Management - Guidelines*.

ISO/IEC. (2019). *ISO / IEC 22301: Security and resilience — Business continuity management systems — Requirements*.

ISO/IEC. (2019). *ISO / IEC 27018: Information technology — Security techniques — Code of practice for protection of personally identifiable information (PII) in public clouds acting as PII processors .*

ISO/IEC. (2019). *ISO / IEC 27701: Security Technics - Extension for privacy information management — Requirements and guidelines*.

NIST. (2013). NIST Special Publication 800-53: Security and Privacy Controls for Federal Information Systems and Organizations. *NIST SP-800-53r4*, 400+. doi:10.6028/NIST.SP.800-53r4

NIST. (2018). Framework for Improving Critical Infrastructure Cybersecurity - CSF. v 1.1.

OWASP. (2020). Retrieved March 1, 2020, from OWASP website: https://owasp.org/www-project-top-ten/

Tamburri, D. A. (2019). Design principles for the General Data Protection Regulation (GDPR): A formal concept analysis and its evaluation. *Information Systems*, *91*, 101469. doi:10.1016/j.is.2019.101469

## KEY TERMS AND DEFINITIONS

**Advanced Persistent Threat (APT):** This is a specific type of cyber-attack, where the attacker uses different type and methodology of attacks and usually these attacks are directed and aim a specific target.

**CISSP (Certified Information System Security Professional):** This is one of the most known information security certificates issued and maintained by (ISC).

**Cyber-Attack:** Any attack that use computer, internet, or any digital device.

**Framework:** This is a set of tools and/or procedures organized and catalogued to be prepared to produce or build something, for instance, cybersecurity framework is a set of tools or procedures organized and cataloged to build a cybersecurity program.

**Phishing:** This is a specific attack, where the attacker sends a malicious e-mail, containing a malicious program embedded or a link to a site hosting the malicious program. Usually, this e-mail has a very curious content, trying to entice the reader to click or open the file.

**Risk:** A relationship between probability and impact or consequence of a threat or a situation. It may be positive or negative.

**Risk Management:** A methodology to identify, measure, classify, and compare risks.

*Previously published in the Handbook of Research on Cyber Crime and Information Privacy; pages 498-522, copyright year 2021 by Information Science Reference (an imprint of IGI Global).*

# APPENDIX

*Table 6. Version of the Appendix H of the NIST SP800-53 listing the NIST controls relationship with the ISO/ IEC 27000 controls, highlighting the outstanding controls*

| ID | Control | ISO/IEC 27001 Controls |
|---|---|---|
| AC-1 | Access Control Policy and Procedures | A.5.1.1, A.5.1.2, A.6.1.1, A.9.1.1, A.12.1.1, A.18.1.1, A.18.2.2 |
| AC-2 | Account Management | A.9.2.1, A.9.2.2, A.9.2.3, A.9.2.5, A.9.2.6 |
| AC-3 | Access Enforcement | A.6.2.2, A.9.1.2, A.9.4.1, A.9.4.4, A.9.4.5, A.13.1.1, A.14.1.2, A.14.1.3, A.18.1.3 |
| AC-4 | Information Flow Enforcement | A.13.1.3, A.13.2.1, A.14.1.2, A.14.1.3 |
| AC-5 | Separation of Duties | A.6.1.2 |
| AC-6 | Least Privilege | A.9.1.2, A.9.2.3, A.9.4.4, A.9.4.5 |
| AC-7 | Unsuccessful Logon Attempts | A.9.4.2 |
| AC-8 | System Use Notification | A.9.4.2 |
| AC-9 | Previous Logon (Access) Notification | A.9.4.2 |
| **AC-10** | **Concurrent Session Control** | **None** |
| AC-11 | Session Lock | A.11.2.8, A.11.2.9 |
| **AC-12** | **Session Termination** | **None** |
| AC-13 | Withdrawn | --- |
| **AC-14** | **Permitted Actions without Identification or Authentication** | **None** |
| AC-15 | Withdrawn | --- |
| **AC-16** | **Security Attributes** | **None** |
| AC-17 | Remote Access | A.6.2.1, A.6.2.2, A.13.1.1, A.13.2.1, A.14.1.2 |
| AC-18 | Wireless Access | A.6.2.1, A.13.1.1, A.13.2.1 |
| AC-19 | Access Control for Mobile Devices | A.6.2.1, A.11.2.6, A.13.2.1 |
| AC-20 | Use of External Information Systems | A.11.2.6, A.13.1.1, A.13.2.1 |
| **AC-21** | **Information Sharing** | **None** |
| **AC-22** | **Publicly Accessible Content** | **None** |
| **AC-23** | **Data Mining Protection** | **None** |
| AC-24 | Access Control Decisions | A.9.4.1* |
| **AC-25** | **Reference Monitor** | **None** |
| AT-1 | Security Awareness and Training Policy and Procedures | A.5.1.1, A.5.1.2, A.6.1.1, A.12.1.1, A.18.1.1, A.18.2.2 |
| AT-2 | Security Awareness Training | A.7.2.2, A.12.2.1 |
| AT-3 | Role-Based Security Training | A.7.2.2* |
| **AT-4** | **Security Training Records** | **None** |
| AT-5 | Withdrawn | --- |
| AU-1 | Audit and Accountability Policy and Procedures | A.5.1.1, A.5.1.2, A.6.1.1, A.12.1.1, A.18.1.1, A.18.2.2 |
| **AU-2** | **Audit Events** | **None** |

| ID | Control | ISO/IEC 27001 Controls |
|---|---|---|
| AU-3 | Content of Audit Records | A.12.4.1* |
| AU-4 | Audit Storage Capacity | A.12.1.3 |
| **AU-5** | **Response to Audit Processing Failures** | **None** |
| AU-6 | Audit Review, Analysis, and Reporting | A.12.4.1, A.16.1.2, A.16.1.4 |
| **AU-7** | **Audit Reduction and Report Generation** | **None** |
| AU-8 | Time Stamps | A.12.4.4 |
| AU-9 | Protection of Audit Information | A.12.4.2, A.12.4.3, A.18.1.3 |
| **AU-10** | **Non-repudiation** | **None** |
| AU-11 | Audit Record Retention | A.12.4.1, A.16.1.7 |
| AU-12 | Audit Generation | A.12.4.1, A.12.4.3 |
| **AU-13** | **Monitoring for Information Disclosure** | **None** |
| AU-14 | Session Audit | A.12.4.1* |
| **AU-15** | **Alternate Audit Capability** | **None** |
| **AU-16** | **Cross-Organizational Auditing** | **None** |
| CA-1 | Security Assessment and Authorization Policies and Procedures | A.5.1.1, A.5.1.2, A.6.1.1, A.12.1.1, A.18.1.1, A.18.2.2 |
| CA-2 | Security Assessments | A.14.2.8, A.18.2.2, A.18.2.3 |
| CA-3 | System Interconnections | A.13.1.2, A.13.2.1, A.13.2.2 |
| CA-4 | Withdrawn | --- |
| **CA-5** | **Plan of Action and Milestones** | **None** |
| **CA-6** | **Security Authorization** | **None** |
| **CA-7** | **Continuous Monitoring** | **None** |
| **CA-8** | **Penetration Testing** | **None** |
| **CA-9** | **Internal System Connections** | **None** |
| CM-1 | Configuration Management Policy and Procedures | A.5.1.1, A.5.1.2, A.6.1.1, A.12.1.1, A.18.1.1, A.18.2.2 |
| **CM-2** | **Baseline Configuration** | **None** |
| CM-3 | Configuration Change Control | A.12.1.2, A.14.2.2, A.14.2.3, A.14.2.4 |
| CM-4 | Security Impact Analysis | A.14.2.3 |
| CM-5 | Access Restrictions for Change | A.9.2.3, A.9.4.5, A.12.1.2, A.12.1.4, A.12.5.1 |
| **CM-6** | **Configuration Settings** | **None** |
| CM-7 | Least Functionality | A.12.5.1* |
| CM-8 | Information System Component Inventory | A.8.1.1, A.8.1.2 |
| CM-9 | Configuration Management Plan | A.6.1.1* |
| CM-10 | Software Usage Restrictions | A.18.1.2 |
| CM-11 | User-Installed Software | A.12.5.1, A.12.6.2 |
| CP-1 | Contingency Planning Policy and Procedures | A.5.1.1, A.5.1.2, A.6.1.1, A.12.1.1, A.18.1.1, A.18.2.2 |
| CP-2 | Contingency Plan | A.6.1.1, A.17.1.1, A.17.2.1 |
| CP-3 | Contingency Training | A.7.2.2* |
| CP-4 | Contingency Plan Testing | A.17.1.3 |
| CP-5 | Withdrawn | --- |

| ID | Control | ISO/IEC 27001 Controls |
|---|---|---|
| CP-6 | Alternate Storage Site | A.11.1.4, A.17.1.2, A.17.2.1 |
| CP-7 | Alternate Processing Site | A.11.1.4, A.17.1.2, A.17.2.1 |
| CP-8 | Telecommunications Services | A.11.2.2, A.17.1.2 |
| CP-9 | Information System Backup | A.12.3.1, A.17.1.2, A.18.1.3 |
| CP-10 | Information System Recovery and Reconstitution | A.17.1.2 |
| CP-11 | Alternate Communications Protocols | A.17.1.2* |
| **CP-12** | **Safe Mode** | **None** |
| CP-13 | Alternative Security Mechanisms | A.17.1.2* |
| IA-1 | Identification and Authentication Policy and Procedures | A.5.1.1, A.5.1.2, A.6.1.1, A.12.1.1, A.18.1.1, A.18.2.2 |
| IA-2 | Identification and Authentication (Organizational Users) | A.9.2.1 |
| **IA-3** | **Device Identification and Authentication** | **None** |
| IA-4 | Identifier Management | A.9.2.1 |
| IA-5 | Authenticator Management | A.9.2.1, A.9.2.4, A.9.3.1, A.9.4.3 |
| IA-6 | Authenticator Feedback | A.9.4.2 |
| IA-7 | Cryptographic Module Authentication | A.18.1.5 |
| IA-8 | Identification and Authentication (NonOrganizational Users) | A.9.2.1 |
| **IA-9** | **Service Identification and Authentication** | **None** |
| **IA-10** | **Adaptive Identification and Authentication** | **None** |
| **IA-11** | **Re-authentication** | **None** |
| IR-1 | Incident Response Policy and Procedures | A.5.1.1, A.5.1.2, A.6.1.1, A.12.1.1 A.18.1.1, A.18.2.2 |
| IR-2 | Incident Response Training | A.7.2.2* |
| **IR-3** | **Incident Response Testing** | **None** |
| IR-4 | Incident Handling | A.16.1.4, A.16.1.5, A.16.1.6 |
| **IR-5** | **Incident Monitoring** | **None** |
| IR-6 | Incident Reporting | A.6.1.3, A.16.1.2 |
| **IR-7** | **Incident Response Assistance** | **None** |
| IR-8 | Incident Response Plan | A.16.1.1 |
| **IR-9** | **Information Spillage Response** | **None** |
| **IR-10** | **Integrated Information Security Analysis Team** | **None** |
| MA-1 | System Maintenance Policy and Procedures | A.5.1.1, A.5.1.2, A.6.1.1, A.12.1.1, A.18.1.1, A.18.2.2 |
| MA-2 | Controlled Maintenance | A.11.2.4*, A.11.2.5* |
| **MA-3** | **Maintenance Tools** | **None** |
| **MA-4** | **Nonlocal Maintenance** | **None** |
| **MA-5** | **Maintenance Personnel** | **None** |
| MA-6 | Timely Maintenance | A.11.2.4 |
| MP-1 | Media Protection Policy and Procedures | A.5.1.1, A.5.1.2, A.6.1.1, A.12.1.1, A.18.1.1, A.18.2.2 |
| MP-2 | Media Access | A.8.2.3, A.8.3.1, A.11.2.9 |
| MP-3 | Media Marking | A.8.2.2 |
| MP-4 | Media Storage | A.8.2.3, A.8.3.1, A.11.2.9 |

| ID | Control | ISO/IEC 27001 Controls |
|---|---|---|
| MP-5 | Media Transport | A.8.2.3, A.8.3.1, A.8.3.3, A.11.2.5, A.11.2.6 |
| MP-6 | Media Sanitization | A.8.2.3, A.8.3.1, A.8.3.2, A.11.2.7 |
| MP-7 | Media Use | A.8.2.3, A.8.3.1 |
| **MP-8** | **Media Downgrading** | None |
| PE-1 | Physical and Environmental Protection Policy and Procedures | A.5.1.1, A.5.1.2, A.6.1.1, A.12.1.1, A.18.1.1, A.18.2.2 |
| PE-2 | Physical Access Authorizations | A.11.1.2* |
| PE-3 | Physical Access Control | A.11.1.1, A.11.1.2, A.11.1.3 |
| PE-4 | Access Control for Transmission Medium | A.11.1.2, A.11.2.3 |
| PE-5 | Access Control for Output Devices | A.11.1.2, A.11.1.3 |
| **PE-6** | **Monitoring Physical Access** | None |
| PE-7 | Withdrawn | --- |
| **PE-8** | **Visitor Access Records** | None |
| PE-9 | Power Equipment and Cabling | A.11.1.4, A.11.2.1, A.11.2.2, A.11.2.3 |
| PE-10 | Emergency Shutoff | A.11.2.2* |
| PE-11 | Emergency Power | A.11.2.2 |
| PE-12 | Emergency Lighting | A.11.2.2* |
| PE-13 | Fire Protection | A.11.1.4, A.11.2.1 |
| PE-14 | Temperature and Humidity Controls | A.11.1.4, A.11.2.1, A.11.2.2 |
| PE-15 | Water Damage Protection | A.11.1.4, A.11.2.1, A.11.2.2 |
| PE-16 | Delivery and Removal | A.8.2.3, A.11.1.6, A.11.2.5 |
| PE-17 | Alternate Work Site | A.6.2.2, A.11.2.6, A.13.2.1 |
| PE-18 | Location of Information System Components | A.8.2.3, A.11.1.4, A.11.2.1 |
| PE-19 | Information Leakage | A.11.1.4, A.11.2.1 |
| PE-20 | Asset Monitoring and Tracking | A.8.2.3* |
| PL-1 | Security Planning Policy and Procedures | A.5.1.1, A.5.1.2, A.6.1.1, A.12.1.1, A.18.1.1, A.18.2.2 |
| PL-2 | System Security Plan | A.14.1.1 |
| PL-3 | Withdrawn | --- |
| PL-4 | Rules of Behavior | A.7.1.2, A.7.2.1, A.8.1.3 |
| PL-5 | Withdrawn | --- |
| PL-6 | Withdrawn | --- |
| PL-7 | Security Concept of Operations | A.14.1.1* |
| PL-8 | Information Security Architecture | A.14.1.1* |
| **PL-9** | **Central Management** | None |
| PS-1 | Personnel Security Policy and Procedures | A.5.1.1, A.5.1.2, A.6.1.1, A.12.1.1, A.18.1.1, A.18.2.2 |
| **PS-2** | **Position Risk Designation** | None |
| PS-3 | Personnel Screening | A.7.1.1 |
| PS-4 | Personnel Termination | A.7.3.1, A.8.1.4 |
| PS-5 | Personnel Transfer | A.7.3.1, A.8.1.4 |

| ID | Control | ISO/IEC 27001 Controls |
|---|---|---|
| PS-6 | Access Agreements | A.7.1.2, A.7.2.1, A.13.2.4 |
| PS-7 | Third-Party Personnel Security | A.6.1.1*, A.7.2.1* |
| PS-8 | Personnel Sanctions | A.7.2.3 |
| RA-1 | Risk Assessment Policy and Procedures | A.5.1.1, A.5.1.2, A.6.1.1, A.12.1.1, A.18.1.1, A.18.2.2 |
| RA-2 | Security Categorization | A.8.2.1 |
| RA-3 | Risk Assessment | A.12.6.1* |
| RA-4 | Withdrawn | --- |
| RA-5 | Vulnerability Scanning | A.12.6.1* |
| **RA-6** | **Technical Surveillance Countermeasures Survey** | **None** |
| SA-1 | System and Services Acquisition Policy and Procedures | A.5.1.1, A.5.1.2, A.6.1.1, A.12.1.1, A.18.1.1, A.18.2.2 |
| SA-2 | Allocation of Resources | None |
| SA-3 | System Development Life Cycle | A.6.1.1, A.6.1.5, A.14.1.1, A.14.2.1, A.14.2.6 |
| SA-4 | Acquisition Process | A.14.1.1, A.14.2.7, A.14.2.9, A.15.1.2 |
| SA-5 | Information System Documentation | A.12.1.1* |
| SA-6 | Withdrawn | --- |
| SA-7 | Withdrawn | --- |
| SA-8 | Security Engineering Principles | A.14.2.5 |
| SA-9 | External Information System Services | A.6.1.1, A.6.1.5, A.7.2.1, A.13.1.2, A.13.2.2, A.15.2.1, A.15.2.2 |
| SA-10 | Developer Configuration Management | A.12.1.2, A.14.2.2, A.14.2.4, A.14.2.7 |
| SA-11 | Developer Security Testing and Evaluation | A.14.2.7, A.14.2.8 |
| SA-12 | Supply Chain Protections | A.14.2.7, A.15.1.1, A.15.1.2, A.15.1.3 |
| **SA-13** | **Trustworthiness** | **None** |
| **SA-14** | **Criticality Analysis** | **None** |
| SA-15 | Development Process, Standards, and Tools | A.6.1.5, A.14.2.1, |
| SA-16 | Developer-Provided Training | None |
| SA-17 | Developer Security Architecture and Design | A.14.2.1, A.14.2.5 |
| **SA-18** | **Tamper Resistance and Detection** | **None** |
| **SA-19** | **Component Authenticity** | **None** |
| **SA-20** | **Customized Development of Critical Components** | **None** |
| SA-21 | Developer Screening | A.7.1.1 |
| **SA-22** | **Unsupported System Components** | **None** |
| SC-1 | System and Communications Protection Policy and Procedures | A.5.1.1, A.5.1.2, A.6.1.1, A.12.1.1, A.18.1.1, A.18.2.2 |
| **SC-2** | **Application Partitioning** | **None** |
| **SC-3** | **Security Function Isolation** | **None** |
| **SC-4** | **Information In Shared Resources** | **None** |
| **SC-5** | **Denial of Service Protection** | **None** |
| **SC-6** | **Resource Availability** | **None** |
| SC-7 | Boundary Protection | A.13.1.1, A.13.1.3, A.13.2.1, A.14.1.3 |

| ID | Control | ISO/IEC 27001 Controls |
|---|---|---|
| SC-8 | Transmission Confidentiality and Integrity | A.8.2.3, A.13.1.1, A.13.2.1, A.13.2.3, A.14.1.2, A.14.1.3 |
| SC-9 | Withdrawn | --- |
| SC-10 | Network Disconnect | A.13.1.1 |
| **SC-11** | **Trusted Path** | **None** |
| SC-12 | Cryptographic Key Establishment and Management | A.10.1.2 |
| SC-13 | Cryptographic Protection | A.10.1.1, A.14.1.2, A.14.1.3, A.18.1.5 |
| SC-14 | Withdrawn | --- |
| SC-15 | Collaborative Computing Devices | A.13.2.1* |
| **SC-16** | **Transmission of Security Attributes** | **None** |
| SC-17 | Public Key Infrastructure Certificates | A.10.1.2 |
| **SC-18** | **Mobile Code** | **None** |
| **SC-19** | **Voice Over Internet Protocol** | **None** |
| **SC-20** | **Secure Name/Address Resolution Service (Authoritative Source)** | **None** |
| **SC-21** | **Secure Name/Address Resolution Service (Recursive or Caching Resolver)** | **None** |
| **SC-22** | **Architecture and Provisioning for Name/Address Resolution Service** | **None** |
| **SC-23** | **Session Authenticity** | **None** |
| **SC-24** | **Fail in Known State** | **None** |
| **SC-25** | **Thin Nodes** | **None** |
| **SC-26** | **Honeypots** | **None** |
| **SC-27** | **Platform-Independent Applications** | **None** |
| SC-28 | Protection of Information at Rest | A.8.2.3* |
| **SC-29** | **Heterogeneity** | **None** |
| **SC-30** | **Concealment and Misdirection** | **None** |
| **SC-31** | **Covert Channel Analysis** | **None** |
| **SC-32** | **Information System Partitioning** | **None** |
| SC-33 | Withdrawn | --- |
| **SC-34** | **Non-Modifiable Executable Programs** | **None** |
| **SC-35** | **Honeyclients** | **None** |
| **SC-36** | **Distributed Processing and Storage** | **None** |
| **SC-37** | **Out-of-Band Channels** | **None** |
| SC-38 | Operations Security | A.12.x |
| **SC-39** | **Process Isolation** | **None** |
| **SC-40** | **Wireless Link Protection** | **None** |
| **SC-41** | **Port and I/O Device Access** | **None** |
| **SC-42** | **Sensor Capability and Data** | **None** |
| **SC-43** | **Usage Restrictions** | **None** |
| **SC-44** | **Detonation Chambers** | **None** |

| ID | Control | ISO/IEC 27001 Controls |
|---|---|---|
| SI-1 | System and Information Integrity Policy and Procedures | A.5.1.1, A.5.1.2, A.6.1.1, A.12.1.1, A.18.1.1, A.18.2.2 |
| SI-2 | Flaw Remediation | A.12.6.1, A.14.2.2, A.14.2.3, A.16.1.3 |
| SI-3 | Malicious Code Protection | A.12.2.1 |
| **SI-4** | **Information System Monitoring** | **None** |
| SI-5 | Security Alerts, Advisories, and Directives | A.6.1.4* |
| **SI-6** | **Security Function Verification** | **None** |
| **SI-7** | **Software, Firmware, and Information Integrity** | **None** |
| **SI-8** | **Spam Protection** | **None** |
| **SI-9** | **Withdrawn** | --- |
| **SI-10** | **Information Input Validation** | **None** |
| **SI-11** | **Error Handling** | **None** |
| **SI-12** | **Information Handling and Retention** | **None** |
| **SI-13** | **Predictable Failure Prevention** | **None** |
| **SI-14** | **Non-Persistence** | **None** |
| **SI-15** | **Information Output Filtering** | **None** |
| **SI-16** | **Memory Protection** | **None** |
| **SI-17** | **Fail-Safe Procedures** | **None** |
| PM-1 | Information Security Program Plan | A.5.1.1, A.5.1.2, A.6.1.1, A.18.1.1, A.18.2.2 |
| PM-2 | Senior Information Security Officer | A.6.1.1* |
| **PM-3** | **Information Security Resources** | **None** |
| **PM-4** | **Plan of Action and Milestones Process** | **None** |
| **PM-5** | **Information System Inventory** | **None** |
| **PM-6** | **Information Security Measures of Performance** | **None** |
| **PM-7** | **Enterprise Architecture** | **None** |
| **PM-8** | **Critical Infrastructure Plan** | **None** |
| **PM-9** | **Risk Management Strategy** | **None** |
| PM-10 | Security Authorization Process | A.6.1.1* |
| **PM-11** | **Mission/Business Process Definition** | **None** |
| **PM-12** | **Insider Threat Program** | **None** |
| PM-13 | Information Security Workforce | A.7.2.2* |
| **PM-14** | **Testing, Training, and Monitoring** | **None** |
| PM-15 | Contacts with Security Groups and Associations | A.6.1.4 |
| **PM-16** | **Threat Awareness Program** | **None** |

*Table 7. Complete list of the missing controls, comparing ISO/IEC 27000 and NIST CSF*

| Control ID | Control |
|---|---|
| AC-10 | Concurrent Session Control |
| AC-12 | Session Termination |
| AC-14 | Permitted Actions without Identification or Authentication |
| AC-16 | Security Attributes |
| AC-21 | Information Sharing |
| AC-22 | Publicly Accessible Content |
| AC-23 | Data Mining Protection |
| AC-25 | Reference Monitor |
| AT-4 | Security Training Records |
| AU-2 | Audit Events |
| AU-5 | Response to Audit Processing Failures |
| AU-7 | Audit Reduction and Report Generation |
| AU-10 | Non-repudiation |
| AU-13 | Monitoring for Information Disclosure |
| AU-15 | Alternate Audit Capability |
| AU-16 | Cross-Organizational Auditing |
| CA-5 | Plan of Action and Milestones |
| CA-6 | Security Authorization |
| CA-7 | Continuous Monitoring |
| CA-8 | Penetration Testing |
| CA-9 | Internal System Connections |
| CM-2 | Baseline Configuration |
| CM-6 | Configuration Settings |
| CP-12 | Safe Mode |
| IA-3 | Device Identification and Authentication |
| IA-9 | Service Identification and Authentication |
| IA-10 | Adaptive Identification and Authentication |
| IA-11 | Re-authentication |
| IR-3 | Incident Response Testing |
| IR-5 | Incident Monitoring |
| IR-7 | Incident Response Assistance |
| IR-9 | Information Spillage Response |
| IR-10 | Integrated Information Security Analysis Team |
| MA-3 | Maintenance Tools |
| MA-4 | Nonlocal Maintenance |
| MA-5 | Maintenance Personnel |
| MP-8 | Media Downgrading |
| PE-6 | Monitoring Physical Access |

| Control ID | Control |
|---|---|
| PE-8 | Visitor Access Records |
| PL-9 | Central Management |
| PS-2 | Position Risk Designation |
| RA-6 | Technical Surveillance Countermeasures Survey |
| SA-2 | Allocation of Resources |
| SA-13 | Trustworthiness |
| SA-14 | Criticality Analysis |
| SA-16 | Developer-Provided Training |
| SA-18 | Tamper Resistance and Detection |
| SA-19 | Component Authenticity |
| SA-20 | Customized Development of Critical Components |
| SA-22 | Unsupported System Components |
| SC-2 | Application Partitioning |
| SC-3 | Security Function Isolation |
| SC-4 | Information In Shared Resources |
| SC-5 | Denial of Service Protection |
| SC-6 | Resource Availability |
| SC-11 | Trusted Path |
| SC-16 | Transmission of Security Attributes |
| SC-18 | Mobile Code |
| SC-19 | Voice Over Internet Protocol |
| SC-20 | Secure Name/Address Resolution Service (Authoritative Source) |
| SC-21 | Secure Name/Address Resolution Service (Recursive or Caching Resolver) |
| SC-22 | Architecture and Provisioning for Name/Address Resolution Service |
| SC-23 | Session Authenticity |
| SC-24 | Fail in Known State |
| SC-25 | Thin Nodes |
| SC-26 | Honeypots |
| SC-27 | Platform-Independent Applications |
| SC-29 | Heterogeneity |
| SC-30 | Concealment and Misdirection |
| SC-31 | Covert Channel Analysis |
| SC-32 | Information System Partitioning |
| SC-34 | Non-Modifiable Executable Programs |
| SC-35 | Honeyclients |
| SC-36 | Distributed Processing and Storage |
| SC-37 | Out-of-Band Channels |
| SC-39 | Process Isolation |
| SC-40 | Wireless Link Protection |

| Control ID | Control |
|---|---|
| SC-41 | Port and I/O Device Access |
| SC-42 | Sensor Capability and Data |
| SC-43 | Usage Restrictions |
| SC-44 | Detonation Chambers |
| SI-4 | Information System Monitoring |
| SI-6 | Security Function Verification |
| SI-7 | Software, Firmware, and Information Integrity |
| SI-8 | Spam Protection |
| SI-10 | Information Input Validation |
| SI-11 | Error Handling |
| SI-12 | Information Handling and Retention |
| SI-13 | Predictable Failure Prevention |
| SI-14 | Non-Persistence |
| SI-15 | Information Output Filtering |
| SI-16 | Memory Protection |
| SI-17 | Fail-Safe Procedures |
| PM-3 | Information Security Resources |
| PM-4 | Plan of Action and Milestones Process |
| PM-5 | Information System Inventory |
| PM-6 | Information Security Measures of Performance |
| PM-7 | Enterprise Architecture |
| PM-8 | Critical Infrastructure Plan |
| PM-9 | Risk Management Strategy |
| PM-11 | Mission/Business Process Definition |
| PM-12 | Insider Threat Program |
| PM-14 | Testing, Training, and Monitoring |
| PM-16 | Threat Awareness Program |

# Chapter 23
# National Cybersecurity Strategies

**Regner Sabillon**

*Universitat Oberta de Catalunya, Spain*

## ABSTRACT

*This chapter studies the phases to unify our national cybersecurity strategy model (NCSSM) in any nation cyber strategy that is either under development or improvement stages. This methodology consists of developing international cybersecurity strategies, alliances, and cooperation with different stakeholders at all possible levels. The research evaluated the best practices of 10 leading countries and five intergovernmental organizations in terms of developing effective cybersecurity strategies and policies. The authors also assessed a series of cybersecurity best practices that can be aligned with cyber governance and cyber law when countries wish to develop or enhance national cyber strategies. Furthermore, they propose guidelines to audit the national cyber strategies by utilizing their cybersecurity audit model (CSAM). CSAM could be considered for conducting cybersecurity audits in any nation state in pursuance of reviewing and measuring the cybersecurity assurance, maturity, and cyber readiness and to detect the needs to increase cyber awareness to defend and protect critical cyber assets.*

## INTRODUCTION

A study from Luiijf et al. (2013) was conducted to research about the the structure, sections and elements of nineteen National Cybersecurity Strategies (NCSS) from these countries [Australia, Canada, Czech Republic, Estonia, France, Germany, India, Japan, Lithuania, Luxembourg, Romania, The Netherlands, New Zealand, South Africa, Spain, Uganda, The United Kingdom - UK (2009 and 2011) and The United States of America (USA)]. Most NCSS in this research, embraced a holistic approach for cyberspace, and all nations have considered international threats and risks in cyberspace. Most NCSS are focusing on societies, more specifically citizens, businesses, public sector and government. Subsequently, the authors proposed a structure for developing NCSS that encompasses an executive summary, an introduction, a strategic national vision on cybersecurituy, existing NCSS' relationships with other strategies

DOI: 10.4018/978-1-6684-3698-1.ch023

at the national and international level and legal frameworks, any guidance principles, the definition of cybersecurity objectives, an inventory of tactical actions and a glossary.

As reported by NATO (2013), cyber operations indicate the employment of cyber capabilities with the primary purpose of achieving objectives in or by the use of cyberspace, and under international laws States may be responsible for the conduction of cyber operations by their organs including non-state actors.

For several years, there have been four notorious domains in warfare: Air, Sea, Space and Land. With the information era booming, a new domain was added which is now Cyberspace. Lemieux (2015) reserached several events that led to the consolidation of cyber domains as part of modern warfare studies. Network-Centric Warfare (NCW) was conducive during the US military dominance during the 1991 Gulf War, commanders took advantage of NCW to maintain their forces informed at all times regarding situational awareness, troop movement and always outmaneuvering enemy forces. Henceforth, these battlefield experiences were observed and explored by Russia and China for further acceptance into their own military operations.

The US Department of Defense - DOD (DOD, 1991) published the *Joint Publication 3-0: Operations* which included 'Information' as the fifth warfighting domain to join the existing Air, Sea, Space and Land domains. The DOD (1996) declassified the *National Military Strategy for Cyberspace Operations (NMS-CO)* where information was escalated to the cyberspace domain.

Many nations are straighten out their cyber capabilities in cyberspace by proposing, creating, implementing and continuously updating a National Cybersecurity Strategy, policy or programme. Sabillon et al. (2016) described a cybersecurity policy as the instrument developed by nations to communicate and express those aspects that want a state to protect in cyberspace. North Atlantic Treaty Organization - NATO (2019) introduced a repository with NCSS and legal documents for 81 countries [13 for Africa, 11 for Americas and The Caribbean, 19 for Asia and Oceania and 38 for Europe] and The European Union Agency for Cybersecurity (ENISA, 2019) maintains the ENISA NCSS map for the 28 member states of the European Union (EU) and for the 4 member states of the European Free Trade Association (EFTA) that lists the implementation date and the number of objectives of each NCSS . International Telecommunication Union (ITU) (2016) highlights that 72 out 193 member states have published a National Cybersecurity Strategy but the majority of countries now have a NCSS (ITU, 2019). According to the Global Cybersecurity Index GCI 2018 v3 (ITU, 2019), 58% of the United Nations members have a NCSS in place with Europe and countries from the Commonwealth of Independent States (CIS) with the highest numbers of nations with NCSS, while the Africa region has the lowest indicator (14 out of 44 countries with a NCSS).

## NATIONAL CYBERSECURITY STRATEGIES (NCSS)

A cybersecurity policy is an instrument designed by nations to communicate and express selected aspects that want a state to protect cyberspace. It is a statement which embodies the stance of a nation to bind strongly to citizens, their rights and duties; now in a stage of the widespread reality of society where instant information, mobility and social networks are the norm of its operation. This perceptibility of cyberspace requires a renewed understanding of the relationships with others and with the nations. Given the background, cybersecurity in a state policy formalizes a decision that a country now declares as a digital territory – and it has extended where similarly will exercise sovereignty, knowing that virtual space is shared with other nations and possess a national synergy (Sabillon et al., 2016).

Our primary research was aimed to study national security strategies in ten countries from five different continents, study policy-making considerations from five global intergovernmental organizations and describe the most current cybersecurity frameworks. The fundamental research had five parts. Part I reviewed the main features of national cybersecurity strategies in Australia, Canada, Israel, Japan, Malaysia, Norway, South Africa, The Netherlands, The United Kingdom and The United States of America. Part II examined the national security strategy perspectives from intergovernmental organizations like United Nations (UN), International Telecommunication Union (ITU), European Union (EU), the Organisation for Economic Co-operation and Development (OECD) and the North Atlantic Treaty Organization (NATO). Part III highlighted eleven cybersecurity frameworks that are in use globally. Part IV introduced a proposal of the National Cybersecurity Strategy Model (NCSSM) and all its components. And in Part V, we reviewed the international cooperation and knowledge transfer of the existing national strategies (Sabillon et al., 2016).

## THE NATIONAL CYBERSECURITY STRATEGY MODEL (NCSSM)

We introduce a National CyberSecurity Strategy Model (NCSSM) that is based on our previous research (Sabillon et al., 2016). The NCSSM (Figure 1) contains eight pillars that are in constant interaction and it includes certain input features to become effective. Therefore, specific outcomes are in need to be assessed continually due to the changing nature of cyberspace. According to Greiman (2015), including the comparison of national cybersecurity strategies, and then our research is based on main components of any national strategy, goals, action plans, involved agencies and future developments to consolidate and expand the strategies

Our Model was designed on the recommendations that the ITU, NATO, OECD and EU introduced to include key aspects, stakeholders, components and pillars of any NCSS.

### Input

This section requires a clear definition of the scope of the national cybersecurity strategy. Ideally, a clear understanding in terms of protecting critical information infrastructure must be achieved.

Mission, Vision, Objectives and Goals of the national cybersecurity strategy are identifiable at this stage.

### The Pillars

Pillar 1: Cybersecurity Culture is the main pillar that supports the other pillars. How citizens and society apply the use of cyber security measures

Pillar 2: Stakeholders definition and engagement: A national agency will be in charge of the NCSS creation and implementation. All stakeholders must be identified with clear roles and responsibilities.

Pillar 3: Capacity Building: All necessary measures must be taken to ensure protection from cyber threats, risks and vulnerabilities. Baseline security requirements for each sector must be defined including a minimum set of cyber security measures. Specific cybersecurity standards and frameworks are selected. A cadre of cybersecurity professionals must be recruited.

*Figure 1. The National CyberSecurity Strategy Model (NCSSM)*

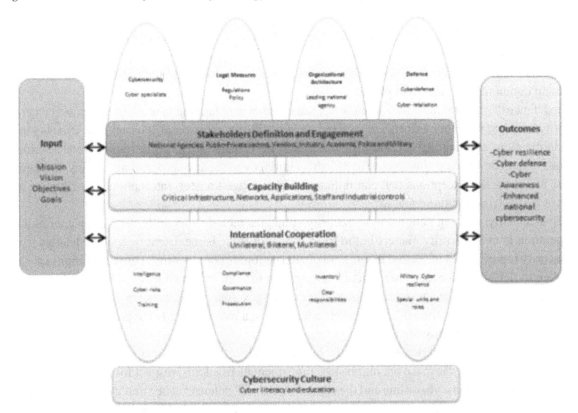

Pillar 4: International Cooperation: Countries need to be involved with the cybersecurity policy making leaders including developed nations and intergovernmental organizations due to the international nature of cyber threats.

Pillar 5: Cybersecurity: This pillar helps to achieve a strong cybersecurity framework and work in harmony with all different stakeholders to ensure jurisdiction. Procedural measures include accountability, risk management, security policing, compliance and assurance. Lastly, the technical measures are aligned with core systems and networks in terms of administration, identifying cyber threats, inspections, IT health monitoring and audits.

Pillar 6: Legal Measures: Countries must engage in creating modern laws, policies to fight and prosecute cybercrime. Develop cyberlaw capacity including police, private sector, judicial and legislative branches.

Pillar 7: Organizational Architecture: This pillar is fundamental to define the NCCS coordinator and the different agencies that participate at the national level. Participating agencies are responsible to lead cybersecurity activities in all industries and sectors. A National CERT is defined

Pillar 8: Defense: Military forces and national security agencies are prepared to develop some kind of military cyber capability in protecting defense networks, cyber warfare activities, enabling network centric warfare or manage cyber warfare strategies.

## Outcomes

Valid outcomes of NCSS must be continually evaluated using key performance indicators and objective performance metrics.

Cyber defense, Awareness, Cyber resilience and Enhancement of national cybersecurity output are the main components in this final phase.

In defance of, many nations have already implemented or are planning to implement a national cybersecurity strategy, very little efforts are targeted towards the contribution of international cybersecurity standardization, defining jurisdiction in international cyberspace or the contribution from developed nations to help developing countries to establish an initial cybersecurity programme, policy or strategy. There are just a few exceptions that can initiate the knowledge transfer, international cooperation and lessons learn sharing in these areas.

Consequently, existing national cybersecurity strategies include very little details for international cooperation in cybersecurity matters but in most cases this topic is inexistent or country leaders in cybersecurity topics are not interested in this kind of international cooperation. A consistent approach must be taken to defining a broader international cooperation to fight cybercrime, coordinate cybersecurity efforts and initiate a more aggressive approach for cyber governance and cybersecurity policy-making.

Nations like the USA, the UK and the Netherlands have a more consistent approach to international cooperation in cybersecurity matters.

The United States of America developed the *International Strategy for Cyberspace* that consists of core principles to support cyberspace operations like fundamentals freedoms, respect for property, safeguard privacy, protection from cybercrime and the right of cyber self-defense[1]. The strategy intends to provide knowledge transfer to build cybersecurity capacity, to continually develop and share cybersecurity best practices, to enhance the ability to fight cyber criminality and to develop relationships with policy makers.[2]

The United Kingdom promoted an international dialogue at the London Conference on Cyberspace for the sake of developing international norms in cyberspace and The Netherlands through their national Cyber Security Council wish to collaborate with other countries to strengthen its international orientation. The Dutch Cyber Security Council wishes to expand the international network collaboration to develop national views.

## THE CYBERSECURITY AUDIT MODEL (CSAM)

The CyberSecurity Audit Model (CSAM) is a comprehensive model that encloses the optimal assurance assessment of cybersecurity in any organization and it can verify specific guidelines for Nation States that are planning to implement a National Cybersecurity Strategy (NCS) or want to evaluate the effectiveness of its National Cybersecurity Strategy or Policy already in place. The aim of this model is to introduce a cybersecurity audit model that includes all functional areas, in order to guarantee an effective cybersecurity assurance, maturity and cyber readiness in any organization or any Nation State that is auditing its National Cybersecurity Strategy (NCS).

## Guideline Assessment

The guideline assessment only applies to the Nation States domain. The guidelines are evaluated for cybersecurity culture, National Cybersecurity Strategy (NCS), cyber operations, critical infrastructure, cyber intelligence, cyber warfare, cybercrime and cyber diplomacy.

## Evaluation Scorecard

The control, guideline and sub-control evaluation is calculated after the audit has been completed. The evaluation consists in assigning scores and ratings for each control, guideline and sub-control.

We calculate the final cybersecurity maturity rating of the Nation States domain by using the following criteria. The score can be mapped to a specific maturity level:

Immature (I): 0-30
     The Nation State does not have any plans to manage its cyberspace. A National Cybersecurity Strategy (NCS) or Policy is inexistent.

Developing (D): 31-70
     The Nation State is starting to focus on national cybersecurity. If technologies are in place, the Nation State needs to focus on key areas to protect cyberspace.

Mature (M): 71-90
     While the Nation State has a mature environment. Improvements are required to the key areas that have been identified with weaknesses.

Advanced (A): 91-100
     Nation State has excelled in national cybersecurity and cyberspace practices. There is always room for improvement. Nation State could become an international leader and help other Nation States with cybersecurity and cyberspace matters.

## Auditing a National Cybersecurity Strategy using the CSAM

The CSAM has a specific domain "Nation States" and a sub-domain "Cyberspace" to audit the Cyber function at a national, state, province or territory level.

The Cyberspace sub-domain verifies controls in the cyber culture, National Cybersecurity Strategy, Cyber operations, critical infrastructure, cyber intelligence, cyber warfare, cybercrime and cyber diplomacy areas in Table 1.

*Table 1. Cybersecurity Maturity Rating of the Nation States Domain*

| Cybersecurity Audit Model (CSAM) | | | | | |
|---|---|---|---|---|---|
| Domain | 1-Nation States | | | | |
| Sub-Domain: 1.1 Cyberspace | Ratings | | | | Score |
| | I | D | M | A | |
| 1.1.1 Cybersecurity Culture | ☐ | ☐ | ☐ | ☐ | |
| 1.1.2 National Cybersecurity Strategy | ☐ | ☐ | ☐ | ☐ | |
| 1.1.3 Cyber Operations | ☐ | ☐ | ☐ | ☐ | |
| 1.1.4 Critical Infrastructure | ☐ | ☐ | ☐ | ☐ | |
| 1.1.5 Cyber Intelligence | ☐ | ☐ | ☐ | ☐ | |
| 1.1.6 Cyber Warfare | ☐ | ☐ | ☐ | ☐ | |
| 1.1.7 Cybercrime | ☐ | ☐ | ☐ | ☐ | |
| 1.1.8 Cyber Diplomacy | ☐ | ☐ | ☐ | ☐ | |
| **Final Cybersecurity Maturity Rating** | ☐ | ☐ | ☐ | ☐ | |

## Overall Nation State CyberSecurity Readiness (NSCSR)

The CyberSecurity Readiness rating can be classified for any Nation State as follows:

Immature (I): 0-30

The Nation State does not have any plans to manage its cyberspace. A National Cybersecurity Strategy or Policy is inexistent. The Cybersecurity readiness is inexistent at this level.

Developing (D): 31-70

The Nation State is starting to focus on national cybersecurity. If technologies are in place, the Nation State needs to focus on key areas to protect cyberspace. The Cybersecurity readiness is developing at this stage.

Mature (M): 71-90

While the Nation State has a mature environment. Improvements are required to the key areas that have been identified with weaknesses. The Cybersecurity readiness is at a mature level.

Advanced (A): 91-100

Nation State has excelled in national cybersecurity and cyberspace practices. There is always room for improvement. Nation State could become an international leader and help other Nation States with cybersecurity and cyberspace matters. The Cybersecurity readiness is at an advanced level, but the Nation State must continually update its cybersecurity strategy at all times.

One of the most comprehensive guidelines (ITU, 2018) to develop a NCSS was recently designed for global cybersecurity leaders including the Commonwealth Secretariat (ComSec), the Commonwealth Telecommunications Organisation (CTO), Deloitte, the Geneva Centre for Security Policy (GCSP), the

Global Cyber Security Capacity Centre (GCSCC) at the University of Oxford, the International Tele-communication Union (ITU), Microsoft, the NATO Cooperative Cyber Defence Centre Of Excellence (NATO CCD COE), the Potomac Institute for Policy Studies, RAND Europe, The World Bank and the United Nations Conference on Trade and Development (UNCTAD). And the guide also focuses on seven areas for good practice: Governance, Risk management in national cybersecurity, Preparedness and resilience, Critical infrastructure services and essential services, Capability and capacity building and awareness raising, Legislation and regulation and Internal cooperation.

We strongly recommend that Domain 1 from our CyberSecurity Audit Model (CSAM) could be considered to plan and conduct partial or comprehensive cybersecurity audits of any NCSS in development, implementation, monitoring and evaluation phases.

## CONCLUSION AND FUTURE RESEARCH

This chapter has fixated on analyzing our research regarding the creation, policy making, structure, implementation, sustaining and auditing national cybersecurity strategies and the cyber domain for nations.

The substance of the national strategies varies widely and each country structures the strategy based on their needs related to fight cybercrime, critical infrastructure protection, stakeholders engagement, cybersecurity awareness, cyber resilience, cyber intelligence gathering, cyber attacks alertness and eradication, cyber incident response, cybersecurity research and development, cyber police organization, communication, military involvement, law and judiciary collaboration, cyber governance and international cooperation.

As a result of our research, we present 'The National CyberSecurity Strategy Model (NCSSM)' that contains eight pillars: Cybersecurity Culture, Stakeholders definition and engagement; Capacity Building; International Cooperation; Cybersecurity; Legal Measures; Organizational Architecture; and Defense. The Model involves specific input features and the outcome is measured in terms of cyber defense, cyber awareness, cyber resilience and national cybersecurity.

We also included Domain 1: Nation States of our CyberSecurity Audit Model (CSAM) that evaluates cybersecurity culture, NCCS, cyber operations, cyber critical infrastructure, cyber intelligence, cyber warfare, cybercrime and cyber diplomacy. Some countries have a higher level of maturity than others when dealing with cyberspace, cybersecurity and national cybersecurity strategy policy-making. These leading countries have to recognize the importance of international cooperation, alliance development to fight cybercrime, rule cyberspace and knowledge transfer of cybersecurity strategy matters.

The impediments of our study is that Domain 1: Nation States and Subdomain 1.1: Cyberspace from our CyberSecurity Audit Model (CSAM) have not been validated in a single Nation or State. Hereinafter, future testing will enhance the model architecture by engaging potential Nation States that may be interested in auditing their national cyberspace and strategy. Future studies will require to focus on the development of international standards and regulations to tackle cybercrime, to expand international cooperation in cybersecurity and national strategies. The challenges to overcome are to secure nations, keep peace in cyberspace while creating dynamic cybersecurity strategies.

# REFERENCES

Australian Government. (2013). *Defence white paper 2013*. Canberra: Department of Defence, Commonwealth of Australia. Retrieved from http://www.defence.gov.au/whitepaper/2013/docs/wp_2013_web.pdf>

Australian Government. (2016). *Australia's Cyber Security Strategy*. Canberra: Department of the Prime Minister and Cabinet, Commonwealth of Australia. Retrieved from https://www.pmc.gov.au/sites/default/files/publications/australias-cyber-security-strategy.pdf

Benoliel, D. (2015). Towards a Cyber Security Policy Model: Israel National Cyber Bureau Case Study. *North Carolina Journal of Law & Technology*, 435–486. https://scholarship.law.unc.edu/cgi/viewcontent.cgi?referer=https://www.google.ca/&httpsredir=1&article=1283&context=ncjolt

Bodeau, D., Boyle, S., Fabius-Greene, J., & Graubart, R. (2010). *Cyber Security Governance, MITRE*. Retrieved from https://www.mitre.org/sites/default/files/pdf/10_3710.pdf

Boyce, R. (2001). *Vulnerability Assessment: The Pro-Active Steps to Secure your Organization, SANS Institute*. Retrieved from https://www.sans.org/reading-room/whitepapers/threats/vulnerability-assessments-pro-active-steps-secure-organization-453

Canadian Government. (2010). *Canada's Cybersecurity Strategy for a Stronger and More Prosperous Canada*. Ottawa: Her Majesty the Queen in Right of Canada. Retrieved from http://publications.gc.ca/collections/collection_2010/sp-ps/PS4-102-2010-eng.pdf

Canadian Government. (2013). *Action Plan 2010-2015 for Canada's Cybersecurity Strategy*. Ottawa: Her Majesty the Queen in Right of Canada. Retrieved from https://www.securitepublique.gc.ca/cnt/rsrcs/pblctns/ctn-pln-cbr-scrt/ctn-pln-cbr-scrt-eng.pdf

CERT Division. (2017). *CSIRT Frequently Asked Questions, Carnegie Mellon University*. Retrieved from https://www.cert.org/incident-management/csirt-development/csirt-faq.cfm

Department of Defense. (2015). *Resilient Military Systems and the Advanced Cyber Threat. Defense Science Board*. Office of the Under Secretary of Defense for Acquisition, Technology and Logistics.

Department of Homeland Security. (2012). *Vulnerability Assessment and Management, NICSS*. Retrieved from https://niccs.us-cert.gov/workforce-development/cyber-security-workforce-framework/vulnerability-assessment-and-management

Donaldson, S., Siegel, S., Williams, C., & Aslam, A. (2015). *Enterprise Cybersecurity: How to Build a Successful Cyberdefense Program Against Advanced Threats*. Apress. doi:10.1007/978-1-4302-6083-7

Elran, M., & Siboni, G. (2015). Establishing an IDF Cyber Command. *The Institute for National Security Studies Insight, 719*, 1-3. Retrieved from https://www.inss.org.il/uploadImages/systemFiles/No.719-MeirandGabiforweb.pdf

European Network and Information Security Agency. (2012). *National Cyber Security Strategies: Practical Guide on Development and Execution*. Heraklion: ENISA. Retrieved from https://www.enisa.europa.eu/activities/Resilience-and-CIIP/national-cyber-security-strategies-ncsss/national-cyber-security-strategies-an-implementation-guide/at_download/fullReport

European Union. (2013). *Cybersecurity Strategy of the European Union: An Open, Safe and Secure Cyberspace*. Brussels: European Commission. Retrieved from http://eeas.europa.eu/policies/eu-cyber-security/cybsec_comm_en.pdf

European Union Agency for Cybersecurity – ENISA. (2019). *National Cyber Security Strategies (NCSSs) Map*. Retrieved from https://www.enisa.europa.eu/topics/national-cyber-security-strategies/ncss-map

Financial Executives International – FEI. (2014). *Financial Executives, Cyber Security & Business Continuity, Canadian Executives Research Foundation (CFERF)*. Retrieved from https://www.feicanada.org/enews/file/CFERF%20studies/2013-2014/IBM%20Cyber%20Security%20final3%202014.pdf

Financial Industry Regulatory Authority – FINRA. (2015). *Report on Cybersecurity Practices*. Retrieved from https://www.finra.org/sites/default/files/p602363%20Report%20on%20Cybersecurity%20Practices_0.pdf

Foresite. (2016). *Quick guide to common Cybersecurity Frameworks*. Retrieved from https://www.foresite.com/blog/quick-guide-to-common-cybersecurity-frameworks/

Greiman, V. (2015). Cyber Security and Global Governance. In *Proceedings of the 14th European Conference on Cyber Warfare & Security*. Hattfield: University of Hertfordshire.

International Telecommunication Union (ITU). (2012). *National Cybersecurity Strategy Guide*. Retrieved from http://www.itu.int/ITU-D/cyb/cybersecurity/docs/ITUNationalCybersecurityStrategyGuide.pdf

International Telecommunication Union (ITU). (2018). *Guide to Developing a National Cybersecurity Strategy: Strategic Engagement in Cybersecurity*. Geneva: International Telecommunication Union ITU. Retrieved from https://www.itu.int/dms_pub/itu-d/opb/str/D-STR-CYB_GUIDE.01-2018-PDF-E.pdf

International Telecommunication Union (ITU). (2019). *Global Cybersecurity Index (GCI) 2018*. Geneva: International Telecommunication Union ITU. Retrieved from https://www.itu.int/dms_pub/itu-d/opb/str/D-STR-GCI.01-2018-PDF-E.pdf

ISACA. (2013). *Transforming Cybersecurity*. Rolling Meadows: ISACA.

ISACA. (2014). *Implementing the NIST Cybersecurity Framework*. Rolling Meadows: ISACA.

ISACA. (2015). *Cybersecurity Fundamentals*. Rolling Meadows: ISACA.

Japanese Government. (2013). *Japan's Cybersecurity Strategy: Towards a World Leading, Resilient and Vigorous Cyberspace*. Tokyo: Information Security Policy Council. Retrieved from https://www.nisc.go.jp/eng/pdf/cybersecuritystrategy-en.pdf

Kaspersky Lab. (2015). *Top 10 Tips for Educating Employees about Cybersecurity, AO Kaspersky Lab*. Retrieved from http://go.kaspersky.com/rs/kaspersky1/images/Top_10_Tips_For_Educating_Employees_About_Cybersecurity_eBook.pdf

Lee, R. (2015). *The Sliding Scale of Cybersecurity, SANS Institute*. Retrieved from https://www.sans.org/reading-room/whitepapers/analyst/sliding-scale-cyber-security-36240

Lemieux, F. (2015). Current and emerging trends in cyber operations: Policy, Strategy and Practice. Palgrave Macmillan's Studies in Cybercrime and Cybersecurity. New York: Palgrave Macmillan. doi:10.1057/9781137455550

Lindsay, J. (2013). Stuxnet and the limits of Cyber Warfare. *Security Studies*, *22*(3), 365–404. doi:10. 1080/09636412.2013.816122

Luiijf, E., Besseling, K., & de Graaf, P. (2013). Nineteen national cyber security strategies. *International Journal of Critical Infrastructures*, *9*(1/2), 3–31. doi:10.1504/IJCIS.2013.051608

Malaysia Government. (2006). National Cyber Security. Purtrajaya: Minister of Science, Technology and Innovation. *ICT Policy Division*. Retrieved from http://www.cybersecurity.my/data/content_files/46/1235. pdf?diff=1392970989

Ministry of Economic Affairs and Communication. (2017). *2014-2017 Estonia Cybersecurity Strategy, ENISA*. Retrieved from https://www.enisa.europa.eu/topics/national-cyber-security-strategies/ncss-map/ Estonia_Cyber_security_Strategy.pdf

National Cyber Security Alliance. (2017). *Stay Safe Online, NCS*. Retrieved from https://staysafeonline. org/ncsam/

National Institute of Standards and Technology - NIST (2017). *Framework for Improving Critical Infrastructure Cybersecurity, version 1.1*. NIST.

National Institute of Standards and Technology – NIST. (2017). *NIST Special Publications SP*. Retrieved from https://csrc.nist.gov/publications/PubsSPs.html

NATO Cooperative Cyber Defence Centre of Excellence – CCDCOE. (2019). *Cyber Security Strategy Documents*. Retrieved from https://ccdcoe.org/library/strategy-and-governance/

Netherlands Government. (2014). *National Cyber Security Strategy (NCSS)2: From awareness to capability. Den Haag: National Coordinator for Security and Counterterrorism, Minister of Security and Justice*. Retrieved from https://www.enisa.europa.eu/activities/Resilience-and-CIIP/national-cyber-security-strategies-ncsss/NCSS2Engelseversie.pdf

North American Electric Relaibility Corporation – NERC. (2010). *Security Guideline for the Electricity Sector: Identifying Critical Cyber Assets, NERC*. Retrieved from <www.nerc.com/docs/cip/sgwg/ Critcal_Cyber_Asset_ID_V1_Final.pdf

North Atlantic Treaty Organization. (2012). *National Cybersecurity framework manual*. Retrieved from https://ccdcoe.org/uploads/2018/10/NCSFM_0.pdf

North Atlantic Treaty Organization. (2013). *The Tallinn manual on the international law applicable to cyber warfare*. Cambridge University Press.

Norway Government. (2013). *Cyber Security Strategy for Norway*. Oslo: The Ministry of Government Administration, Reform and Church Affairs. Retrieved from https://www.regjeringen.no/globalassets/ upload/FAD/Vedlegg/IKT-politikk/Cyber_Security_Strategy_Norway.pdf

Organisation for Economic Co-Operation and Development – OECD. (2012). *Cybersecurity Policy Making at a Turning Point, OECD.* Retrieved from http://www.oecd.org/sti/ieconomy/cybersecurity%20 policy%20making.pdf

PCI Security Standards Council. (2014). *Best Practices for implementing a Security Awareness Program, PCI DSS.* Retrieved from https://www.pcisecuritystandards.org/documents/PCI_DSS_V1.0_Best_Practices_for_Implementing_Security_Awareness_Program.pdf

Pricewaterhouse Coopers - PwC. (2016). *PwC's Board Cybersecurity Governance Framework, PwC.* Retrieved from https://www.pwc.com/ca/en/consulting/publications/20160310-pwc-reinforcing-your-organizations-cybersecurity-governance.pdf

Proaño, R., Saguay, C., Jacome, S., & Sandoval, F. (2017). Knowledge based systems as an aid in information systems audit. *Enfoque UTE, 8*(S1), 148-159. doi:10.29019/enfoqueute.v8n1.122

Sabillon, R. (2018). A Practical Model to Perform Comprehensive Cybersecurity Audits. *Enfoque UTE, 9*(1), 127–137. doi:10.29019/enfoqueute.v9n1.214

Sabillon, R., Cavaller, V., & Cano, J. (2016). National Cyber Security Strategies: Global Trends in Cyberspace. *International Journal of Computer Science and Software Engineering, 5*, 67-81.

Sabillon, R., Serra, J., Cavaller, V., & Cano, J. (2016). Cyber Warfare: Challenges within the Cyber Domain. *European Journal of Public Order and National Security., 3*(4), 7–16.

Sabillon, R., Serra, J., Cavaller, V., & Cano, J. (2017). A Comprehensive Cybersecurity Audit Model to Improve Cybersecurity Assurance: The CyberSecurity Audit Model (CSAM). *2nd International Conference on Information Systems and Computer Science (INCISCOS 2017),* 253-259. 10.1109/INCISCOS.2017.20

Sabillon, R., Serra, J., Cavaller, V., & Cano, J. (2019). An Effective Cybersecurity Training Model to Support an Organizational Awareness Program: The Cybersecurity Awareness TRAining Model (CATRAM). A Case Study in Canada. *Journal of Cases on Information Technology, 21*(3), 26–39. doi:10.4018/JCIT.2019070102

Sabillon, R., Serra-Ruiz, J., Cavaller, V., & Cano, J. (2017). A Comprehensive Cybersecurity Audit Model to Improve Cybersecurity Assurance: The CyberSecurity Audit Model (CSAM). *2017 Second International Conference on Information Systems and Computer Science (INCISCOS)*, Quito, Ecuador. 10.1109/INCISCOS.2017.20

SANS Institute. (2017). *SANS Forensics Whitepapers, SANS Institute.* Retrieved from https://digital-forensics.sans.org/community/whitepapers

Shackleford, D. (2015). *Who's using Cyberthreat Intelligence and how?* SANS Institute. Retrieved from https://www.sans.org/reading-room/whitepapers/analyst/cyberthreat-intelligence-how-35767

South Africa Government. (2012). *South Africa National Cyber Security Policy Framework.* Pretoria: Minister of State Security. Retrieved from http://www.cyanre.co.za/national-cybersecurity-policy.pdf

The Organisation for Economic Co-operation and Development. (2012). *Cybersecurity Policy Making at a Turning Point: Analysing a New Generation of National Cybersecurity Strategies for the Internet Economy*. Paris: OECD Publishing. Retrieved from http://www.oecd.org/sti/ieconomy/cybersecurity policy making.pdf

Trusted Computing Group. (2013). *Architect's Guide: Cybersecurity*. Retrieved from https://www.trustedcomputinggroup.org/wp-content/uploads/Architects-Guide-Cybersecurity.pdf

UN Institute for Disarmament Research. (2013). *The Cyber Index: International Security Trends and Realities*. Geneva: UNIDIR 2013. Retrieved from https://www.unidir.org/files/publications/pdfs/cyber-index-2013-en-463.pdf

UN Institute for Disarmament Research. (2017). *The United Nations, Cyberspace and International Peace and Security: Responding to Complexity in the 21ˢᵗ Century*. Geneva: UNIDIR. Retrieved from https://www.unidir.org/files/publications/pdfs/the-united-nations-cyberspace-and-international-peace-and-security-en-691.pdf

United Kingdom Cabinet Office. (2011). *The UK Cyber Security Strategy - Protecting and promoting the UK in a digital world*. London: UK Cabinet Office. Retrieved from https://www.gov.uk/government/uploads/system/uploads/attachment_data/file/60961/uk-cyber-security-strategy-final.pdf

United Kingdom Cabinet Office. (2014). *The UK Cyber Security Strategy - Report on progress and forward plans*. London: UK Cabinet Office. Retrieved from https://www.gov.uk/government/uploads/system/uploads/attachment_data/file/386093/The_UK_Cyber_Security_Strategy_Report_on_Progress_and_Forward_Plans_-_De___.pdf

United States Computer Emergency Readiness Team - US-CERT. (2017). *Cybersecurity Framework, US-CERT*. Retrieved from https://www.us-cert.gov/ccubedvp/cybersecurity-framework

United States of America Government. (2003). *The National Strategy to Secure Cyberspace*. Washington, DC: The White House. Retrieved from https://www.us-cert.gov/sites/default/files/publications/cyberspace_strategy.pdf

United States of America Government. (2011). *International Strategy for Cyberspace: Prosperity, Security, and Openness in a Networked World*. Washington DC: The White House. Retrieved from https://www.hsdl.org/?view&did=5665

United States of America Government. (2017). The President's National Infrastructure Advisory Council (NIAC). In *Securing Cyber Assets: Addressing Urgent Cyber Threats to Critical Infrastructure*. Washington, DC: Homeland Security. Retrieved from https://www.dhs.gov/sites/default/files/publications/niac-securing-cyber-assets-final-report-508.pdf

U.S. Department of Energy. (2007). *IT Security Architecture*. Retrieved from https://energy.gov/sites/prod/files/cioprod/documents/DOE_Security_Architecture.pdf

U.S. Department of Homeland Security. (2016). *Cybersecurity*. Retrieved from https://www.dhs.gov/topic/cybersecurity

## ADDITIONAL READING

Choi, Y. (2018). *Selected Readings in Cybersecurity*. Cambridge Scholars Publishing.

## KEY TERMS AND DEFINITIONS

**Critical Infrastructure:** The most important infrastructure or related services to provide basic sustenance to citizens like water, utilities, electricity, and internet connection.

**Cybersecurity Culture:** Manifestations of cybersecurity matters for any nation-state.

**National Cybersecurity Policy:** National instrument designed by nations-states to communicate and express selected aspects that want a state to protect cyberspace.

## ENDNOTES

[1]   United States of America Government, International Strategy for Cyberspace: Prosperity, Security, and Openness in a Networked World (Washington D.C: The White House 2011), Ch. 1, 5.

[2]   United States of America Government, International Strategy for Cyberspace: Prosperity, Security, and Openness in a Networked World, 10-15.

*Previously published in Cyber Security Auditing, Assurance, and Awareness Through CSAM and CATRAM; pages 84-102, copyright year 2021 by Information Science Reference (an imprint of IGI Global).*

# Chapter 24
# Network and Data Transfer Security Management in Higher Educational Institutions

**Winfred Yaokumah**
https://orcid.org/0000-0001-7756-1832
*Pentecost University College, Ghana*

**Alex Ansah Dawson**
https://orcid.org/0000-0002-6728-4357
*Kwame Nkrumah University of Science and Technology, Ghana*

## ABSTRACT

*This chapter explored communications security through the use of an empirical survey to assess the extent of network and data transfer security management in Ghanaian higher educational institutions. Network security management controls consist of monitoring of networks, posture checking, network segmentation, and defense-in-depth. Data transfer security management includes encryption, media access control, and protection of data from public networks. Data were collected from information technology (IT) personnel. The ISO/IEC 21827 maturity model for assessing IT security posture was used to measure the controls. Overall, the result showed that the institutions were at the planned stage of communications security management. In particular, network monitoring, defense-in-depth, and the protection of data from public networks were the most applied controls. Conversely, posture checking was the least applied control. Higher educational institutions need to review their communications security plans and better manage network and data transfer security controls to mitigate data breaches.*

DOI: 10.4018/978-1-6684-3698-1.ch024

## INTRODUCTION

The increasing number of data breaches in higher educational institutions, coupled with high complexity of emerging network technologies, poses a challenging environment for security professionals and systems administrators to put in place adequate protection on campus networks (Custer, 2010; HEISC, 2014). Computer networks and data transfer technologies have evolved significantly (Choras, 2013). Data transfer technologies encompass the breadth of digital data flows both within an organization and between external entities across network infrastructures. Digital data flow includes transfer of data, voice, video, and the associated signalling protocols. Securing information flow traversing networks requires effective network infrastructure management (HEISC, 2014). Therefore, systems administrators need to learn, understand, and know how to configure networking software, protocols, services, and devices; deal with interoperability issues; install, configure, and create interfaces with telecommunications software and devices; and troubleshoot systems effectively. Information security professionals must understand and analyze security features and fully recognize vulnerabilities that can arise within each of the systems components and then implement appropriate countermeasures (Harris, 2013).

There have been reports on increasing numbers of security incidents in the recent times (Koch et al., 2012). According to the Verizon's annual report, 76% of data breaches were carried out through network intrusion (Verizon, 2013). There have also been a significant number of reported incidents in connection with the widespread adoption of social media (Benjamin & Chen, 2012; Chandramouli, 2011). The rapid pace of data breaches can be attributed to the growing number of network users, human vulnerabilities, the vulnerabilities in applications and operating systems, and the complexity of network infrastructures that connect several devices. As emerging technologies proliferate, organizations have become increasingly vulnerable to cyber-attacks (Pfleeger & Caputo, 2012). In particular, higher educational institutions have been experiencing data breaches in the recent times due mainly to vulnerabilities in the campus network infrastructure. Many security incidents occur over the networks as a result of inadequate management of networks and data transfer services.

Information technologies have changed the way in which higher education is delivered (Martínez-Argüelles, Castán, & Juan, 2010). Higher educational institutions use and store large volumes of data, including personal information of employees and students, sensitive institutional business data, and faculty research data. But the practices to design and institute strong and effective controls to safeguard data are often at odds with higher education's values of collaboration, openness, and sharing (Coleman & Purcell, 2015; Custer, 2010). Notwithstanding, higher educational institutions must protect sensitive and critical data (Gregory & Grama, 2013). A recent study points to the growing number of cyber-attacks on colleges and universities (Garg, 2016); heightening concern among students, parents, alumni, and donors regarding the security of the personal information these institutions store, process and transmit. According to a survey conducted by Symantec, 10% of all the reported data breaches involve the education sector (Symantec, 2014). A rather current statistics show that 35% of all data breaches come from the educational institutions (Garg, 2016). This alarming phenomenon is making information security a growing concern for higher educational institutions (Gregory & Grama, 2013).

While the effect of data breaches usually focuses on the harm to affected individuals, data breaches affect the institution experiencing the breach. Depending on the nature of the breach, potential direct financial costs of a data breach may include legal representation, fines, and the expense of notifying affected individuals (Grama, 2014). In particular, higher educational institutions may face reputational consequences and consumer confidence, which can result in a loss of alumni donations and a reduction in the number of students choosing to apply to or attend the institution (Grama, 2014). Therefore, how to establish sound and effective management of campus network security in colleges and universities has become crucial (Huang & Jiao, 2014). Security professionals and systems administrators in higher educational institutions have to effectively manage security on campus networks and data transfer services to mitigate the risks.

The purpose of this study is to explore communications security (network and data transfer security) through the use of empirical survey to assess the extent of network and data transfer security management of campus networks in Ghanaian higher educational institutions and to provide some strategies for protecting campus information resources. The study assesses the extent to which higher educational institutions manage campus networks and the data traversing the networks. Network and data transfer security management fall under the broad classification of communications security management (ISO/IEC27002, 2013). As classified by ISO 27002 (2013), network security includes monitoring of wired and wireless networks, performing posture checking, segmentation of networks, and implementing defence-in-depth, while data transfer security entails encryption, media access control, control of exchanged data, and protecting data from public networks.

## BACKGROUND

### Higher Education and Information Security

Higher educational institutions amass astounding collection of information which is available in digital forms and accessible through a campus-wide technology infrastructure. For example, the universities and colleges in Ghana have deployed large information technology infrastructure including networks, operating systems, and data resources to support teaching, learning, and research activities (Yaokumah, Brown, & Adjei, 2015). These institutions have systems such as employee records, students' records, payroll, and enterprise resource planning (ERP) systems normally used by businesses. In addition, Ghanaian universities have from the scholarly information held in library collections to the administrative information stored in structured databases, faculty research, and instructional materials. The situation is more profound by the emerging trends in online and virtual universities, where academic programs are using technologies and methodologies different from the traditional classroom method of course delivery. This results in merging of voice, virtual reality, streaming video, and data traffic into a common digital infrastructure; providing the mesh of connectivity through wired and wireless connectivity on campuses; and the increasing mission-critical reliance on the Internet. Thus, higher educational institutions are regularly uploading study materials and research findings over the Internet for the speedy propagation of information (Kumar & Kumar, 2014). These data are central to learning, outreach, scholarship, and administrative functions of higher education.

Colleges and universities normally provide open academic environment for learning and hence accommodate a wide array of mobile phones, laptops, and other mobile devices that students, faculty, administrative staff, and visitors use on campus or gain access to campus networks remotely (Patton, 2015). This exposes campus networks to various attacks. But good information security practices are essential to reducing risk; safeguarding data, information systems, and networks; and protecting the privacy of the higher education community. However, recent reports mention that in 2015 some leading universities including Pennsylvania State University (PSU), Washington State University, Harvard University, Johns

Hopkins University, the University of Virginia (UVA), and the University of Connecticut have suffered cyber-attacks with considerably damage (Garg, 2016).

Accordingly, the higher educational sector including educational institutions in the developing countries present unlimited threats related to data breaches. The reasons and motives behind data breaches are many and varied. There is a very high number of data moving electronically on campus networks owing to increasing students' numbers. There is unlimited exchange of data among academic departments, administration, and academic registries. In addition, high usage of mobile devices for storing contents, ranging from personal information to research data, creates an environment for intentional as well as unintentional data beaches. According to Poll (2015), nearly 86% of college students use smart phones regularly and students, professors and research fellows receive millions of unsolicited requests for sensitive information. Theft of expensive technical know-how and hiring of people within the education system for espionage - are all growing concerns. Thus, without proper security management, the threat can get out of hands, turning an actual incident into a very expensive and stressful aftermath remedial process (Garg, 2016).

## Network Security

Network Security is defined as the process of taking physical and software preventative measures to protect the underlying network infrastructure from unauthorized access, misuse, malfunction, modification, destruction, or improper disclosure, thereby creating a secure platform for computers, users, and programs to perform their permitted critical functions within a secure environment (SANS Institute, 2013). Network security involves the use of technologies and the processes to design, build, manage, and operate a secure network (SANS Institute, 2013). Managing and operating a secure network ensures protection of information in networks and its supporting information processing facilities. Performing these activities will involve network monitoring, posture checking, network segmentation, and putting in place defense-in-depth measures.

## Network Monitoring

Network monitoring describes a system that constantly monitors a computer network for network usage pattern and performance and hence notifies the network administrator of any abnormality (Downing, 2013). Network exploits take advantage of software flaws in the systems that operate on local area networks (LANs), Bluetooth, and wireless fidelity (WiFi) or cellular networks. Network exploits can often succeed without any user interaction, making them especially dangerous when used to automatically propagate malware. With special tools, attackers can find users on a WiFi network, hijack the users' credentials, and use those credentials to impersonate a user online (US GAO, 2012). Network, server and client misconfiguration offers another avenue for hacking. Network elements, such as routers and gateways, come with a default administrator password, passwords that often never change. Hackers with access to a router can cause all traffic through it to be sent through their own servers, allowing "man in the middle" attacks (US GAO, 2012). Similarly, misconfigured servers can allow hackers to disable or modify websites, inserting code of their own. Such codes are usually intended to steal data from associated databases (Schneider, 2012). But network monitoring can identify internal security threats, virus infection, user activities, network connections, degrading hardware, low drive space, and whether the security settings are meeting compliance requirements (Downing, 2013).

## Posture Checking

Posture checking deals with performing penetration testing and network vulnerability assessment. Penetration testing is the process of attempting to gain access to computing resources without having knowledge of authentication credentials to the system (SAINT, 2016; SANS Institute, 2006). Vulnerability testing places emphasis on identifying areas on the network that are vulnerable to a computer attack (SANS Institute, 2006). Penetration tools include packet manipulation tools and password cracking tools. These are also tools that the attacker uses to gain unauthorized access to systems. Packet manipulation tools allow a penetration tester or attacker to create and send all types of specially crafted transmission control protocol/Internet protocol (TCP/IP) packets in order to test and exploit network-based security protections such as firewalls and intrusion detection systems/intrusion prevention systems (IDS/IPS), while the password cracking tools are used to detect and obtain weak passwords (SANS Institute, 2006). Vulnerability scanners have the ability to exploit multiple vulnerabilities on different hardware and software platforms; can detect the vulnerability and further verify whether the vulnerability can be exploited by an attacker (SANS Institute, 2006). As best practice, all network controls should be routinely validated by an authorized external third party through penetration testing and vulnerability assessment.

## Network Segmentation

One way to protect confidential and critical systems is to segregate networks along physical or logical lines by grouping information services, users and information systems on networks (ISO/IEC27002:2013). Using virtual LANs (VLANs) to separate systems creates an additional layer of security between regular network and most sensitive systems. This method is often utilized in order to protect data centers, credit card processing systems, and other systems considered to be sensitive or mission critical (HEISC, 2014). Network segmentation improves security; the systems administrators can have a better access control over the network by limiting access to sensitive data (ISO/IEC27002, 2013). An attacker who gains unauthorized access to a network segment would be limited to that segment and might not able to gain further access to the entire network (Reichenberg, 2014).

## Defense-in-Depth

A sound network control strategy employs the concept of defense-in-depth to provide optimal security. Defense-in-depth is a security measure that builds layers of defenses to protect digital critical assets (Edge, 2010). Layering is implemented in the physical security plan as well as policy and administration (Edge, 2010). It can be implemented with multiple security controls. For example, firewalls at the network perimeter limit the traffic that is allowed in and out of the network. The IDS/IPS devices detect and prevent traffic that is suspicious or known to be malicious (Schneider, 2012). In addition, internal network isolation limits the visibility of network traffic to devices and users by department or role (HEISC, 2014). To provide additional layer of protection, strong passwords can be enforced for all network computers as computers run host-based firewalls and antivirus software. Certain sensitive network traffic can be encrypted so that it cannot be intercepted. All of these controls are combined together to provide a layered or in-depth defensive strategy (HEISC, 2014).

## Data Transfer Security

Data transfer security entails maintaining the security of information being transferred within an organization and with any external entity (ISO/IEC27002, 2013). Providing data transfer security involves encryption of data in transit, controlling access to media, and protection of data from public networks.

### Encryption

With the purpose of maintaining the confidentiality of data, encryption can be used to transform data into a form unreadable by persons without a secret decryption key (US-CERT, 2013). Its main purpose is to ensure privacy by keeping the information hidden from anyone for whom it is not intended, even those who can see the encrypted data (US-CERT, 2013).. For example, people may encrypt files on their storage devices to prevent an attacker from reading them. Encryption of certain network traffic is an essential network control. All confidential or sensitive information leaving the network should be encrypted with proven encryption algorithms. Authentication protocols that transmit passwords or encryption keys over the network should also be encrypted (US-CERT, 2013). Secure sockets layer (SSL) is a common encryption protocol used for web traffic (HEISC, 2014).

### Media Access Control

Hindering intrusion of unwanted users gaining access to the network is essential to maintaining a secure environment. Impeding such attacks involves creating barriers and blocking unauthorized entry, but establishing boundaries for legitimate users by limiting access to network resources (Edge, 2010). Network security devices consist of security functions that are used to manage networks. These devices include firewall, intrusion prevention/detection systems (IPS/IDS), data loss prevention (DLP) and content security filtering functions such as anti-spam, antivirus or URLfiltering (Schneider, 2012). Moreover, wireless devices contain security features to prevent unauthorized access. However, wireless networks have many security issues. Hackers have found wireless networks relatively easy to break into, and even use wireless technology to crack into wired networks (Kumar & Gambhir, 2014). Therefore, networks should be managed and controlled to protect information in systems and applications. Security mechanisms, service levels and management requirements of all network services should be identified and included in network services agreements, whether these services are provided in-house or outsourced (ISO/IEC27002:2013).

### Protect Data From Public Networks

Data interception can occur when an attacker is eavesdropping on communications originating from or being sent to a mobile device (US GAO (2012). Electronic eavesdropping is possible through various techniques, such as man-in-the-middle attacks - when a mobile device connects to an unsecured wireless fidelity (WiFi) network and an attacker intercepts and alters the communication; and WiFi sniffing - occurs when data are sent to or from a device over an unsecured (i.e., not encrypted) network connection, allowing an attacker to record the information (US GAO, 2012). But with communication monitoring technologies, all information within the enterprise can be filtered, recorded, or even blocked in order to reduce the occurrence of data leakages (Mei-Yu & Ming-Hsien, 2013).

## METHOD

This study explored communications security through the use of a survey questionnaire to assess the extent of network and data transfer security management of campus networks. The population of the study was the 182 higher educational institutions (public and private universities, colleges of education, polytechnics, and tutorial colleges) accredited by the National Accreditation Board of Ghana (NAB, 2016). Higher educational institutions can be grouped under colleges and universities. Sixty higher educational institutions located within three capital cities of Ghana form the selected samples for the study. One hundred and eighty anonymous survey questionnaires were sent (3 questionnaires to each institution) to the security practitioners, systems administrators, and IT managers working in the selected institutions. The survey instrument (see Appendix), which was based on ISO/IEC 27002 (2013) framework, was adopted from Higher Education Information Security Council for measuring communications security (network and data transfer security) in higher education (HEISC, 2013). The questionnaire consisted of network security management (4 items), data transfer security management (4-items), and 3 items of demographical data (institution type, experience, and job function). Apart from the demographic data, all the items on the questionnaire used a 6-point Likert scale (*not performed = 0, performed informally = 1, planned = 2, well defined = 3, quantitatively controlled = 4, and continuously improving = 5*).

The ISO/IEC 21827 (2008) maturity model was employed to measure the responses because of its particular focus on IT security management. The metrics measure the level of management of information systems security. The description of the scale on the metrics were: *Not performed* - no security controls or plans are in place; *performed informally* - the base security practices of the control areas are generally performed on an ad hoc basis, there is also general agreement within the organization that identified actions that should be performed and are performed when required, but the practices are not formally adopted, tracked, and reported on; *planned* - the base requirements for the control areas are planned, implemented, and repeatable; *well defined* - security processes used are documented, approved, and implemented organization-wide; *quantitatively controlled* - security processes are measured and verified; and *continuously improving* - standard processes are regularly reviewed and updated and improvements reflect an understanding of and response to vulnerability's impact (ISO/IEC 21827, 2008).

The data collected were coded and analyzed using Statistically Package for Social Scientists (SPSS). Firstly, the Cronbach's alpha reliability coefficient which measures the internal consistency of the items on the questionnaire was computed: the network security of 4 items gave a coefficient of .836 and the data transfer security also with 4 items gave an alpha of .869. Thus, the coefficients were within the acceptable range of 0.7 or above, according to Hair et al. (2014). Secondly, descriptive statistics were used to ascertain the network security, data transfer security, and the individual items of the controls.

## MAIN FOCUS OF THE CHAPTER

The data analysis ascertained the practitioners' perspectives on network and data transfer security management of their campus networks. The data analysis has been divided into three parts; a) assessing network security management, b) assessing data transfer security management, and c) assessing the overall communications security. Out of the 180 survey questionnaires sent to the security practitioners, systems administrators, and IT managers working in 60 higher educational institutions, 80 responses were returned from 39 of the institutions. This represents 44.4 percent response rate. Table 1 shows the characteristics of the respondents. The vast majority, 57.5% of the respondents had 1 to 5 years experience as IT managers and network administrators in their respective institutions. This may be explained as most of the higher educational institutions are less than ten years old.

*Table 1. Characteristics of respondents*

| Respondents | Frequency | Percentage |
|---|---|---|
| Job Functions | | |
| IT Manager/IT Specialist | 36 | 45.0 |
| Systems/Network Administrator | 44 | 55.0 |
| Years of Experience | | |
| 1-5 years | 46 | 57.5 |
| 6-10 years | 28 | 35.0 |
| 11-15 years | 6 | 7.5 |

$N = 80$

## Network Security Management

Firstly, the study assessed the extent to which higher educational institutions protected the campus networks. The network security controls that were measured included monitoring of wired and wireless networks, posture checking, network segmentation, and defence-in-depth. Overall, network security management stood at 48.8 percent. This indicated that the institutions were at the planned stage of network security management (see Table 2).

Figure 2 shows the levels of network security management. With regards to network monitoring, the respondents were asked whether their institutions had controls in place to continuously monitor wired and wireless networks for detecting unauthorized access. The results indicated that on average the institutions were at the level of 59.6% of monitoring their campus networks. Network monitoring ensures the network reliability of the internal network, thereby increases user productivity (Downing, 2013). As such, systems administrators need to monitor traffic on every device (smart phones, cell phones, servers, desktops, routers, switches) connected to the wired and wireless networks on real-time bases and setup automatic discovery on the network to detect devices that are connected, removed or whose configuration settings have changed. Any device that was not registered should be denied access to connect to the campus networks. Moreover, the administrators can use network access control (NAC) to verify whether devices connecting to the network are running antivirus software. NAC can prevent access to the network until antivirus software is installed and any identified vulnerabilities on the equipment are resolved (Hedrick & Grama, 2013).

Moreover, the participants were asked whether they performed vulnerability test to assess the current antivirus software, firewall enabled, open ports, operating system (OS) patch levels of devices and all the devices connected to the network. In Figure 1, the result indicated that the level of posture checking was 41%. The intent of posture checking was to find security weaknesses in computer systems, networks or applications and to ensure that detected vulnerabilities in the system were fixed correctly. For universities to know the resilience of their critical network systems, data residing and traversing their networks to attacks, security activities must include posture checking (performing penetration testing and vulnerability assessment). It is through assessment processes that the administrators can identify security holes and configuration issues, while maintaining system integrity and resilience. Thus, it is often necessary to regularly audit and assess the systems to ensure adherence to university-wide security policy. To achieve this, there are several free and commercial vulnerability and exploitation tools that university system administrators can use to assess the health of their networks could include Nmap, Retina, SAINT, Metasploit, CORE IMPACT, and Nessus. At best, higher educational institutions should engage external qualified penetration tester on an annual basis to ensure that security controls are working effectively (HEISC, 2014).

*Table 2. Network security management*

| | Network Security Management | NP (%) | PI (%) | PL (%) | WD (%) | QC (%) | CI (%) | Mean | ML (%) | SD |
|---|---|---|---|---|---|---|---|---|---|---|
| 1 | Monitoring wired and wireless network | - | 15.0 | 25.0 | 22.5 | 22.5 | 15.0 | 2.98 | 59.6 | 1.302 |
| 2 | Posture checking | - | 40.0 | 37.5 | 7.5 | 7.5 | 7.5 | 2.05 | 41.0 | 1.211 |
| 3 | Network segmentation | 7.5 | 7.5 | 47.5 | 30.0 | 7.5 | - | 2.22 | 44.4 | .968 |
| 4 | Defence-in-depth | - | 22.5 | 32.5 | 22.5 | 15.0 | 7.5 | 2.52 | 50.4 | 1.211 |
| | Levels of Network Security Management | 1.88 | 21.25 | 32.63 | 20.63 | 13.13 | 7.5 | 2.44 | 48.8 (PL) | .965 |

Not Performed (NP – 0%); Performed Informally (PI – 20%); Planned (PL – 40%); Well Defined (WD – 60%); Quantitatively Controlled (QC – 80%); Continuously Improving (CI – 100%); ML - Management Level, $N$=80

Also, respondents were asked whether they have segmented the network architecture to provide different levels of security based on their information classification. The result revealed that the level of network segmentation stood at only 44.4%. But the universities can benefit from improved security and enhanced performance from network segmentation. For example, in the university, finance and human resources units can have their own subnet because of the sensitive nature of the data they process and store (Reichenberg & Wolfgang, 2014). Similarly, the faculty, students, alumni, and other personnel can have their own different subnets. The WiFi security controls could also be isolated from all other internal networks in order to help maintain the confidentiality and integrity of the wired network (HEISC, 2014). In this case, wireless users could not be able to access resources on wired networks (HEISC, 2014)). Doing this would limit security breaches on campus networks.

Moreover, participants were asked whether they had their servers protected by more than one security layer (firewalls, network IDS, host IDS, application IDS). The result showed that the level of defense-in-depth was a little over 50%. This level of defense-in-depth implementation signified the need for system administrators and security personnel in the universities to put in place stronger defense-in-depth strategies on their computers, servers, and wired and wireless networks which would make it more difficult for attackers to defeat the complex and multi-layered defense system to penetrate university networks. The components of defense-in-depth to be considered should include installation and updates of antivirus software, firewalls, anti-spyware programs, intrusion detection and prevention systems, multiple-factor authentication, and biometric verification systems. Hedrick and Grama (2013) investigated the extent of implementation of firewalls, intrusion detection systems (IDS), access control lists, network access control, and data loss prevention in educational institutions. The study found that firewalls and intrusion prevention systems (IPS) continued to be the most widely used security technology across campuses. In particular, firewalls were used to protect external connections (89% of the institutions studied) and high-security servers and networks (87% of the institutions studied) (Hedrick & Grama, 2013). The institutions used IPS to monitor network traffic for malicious activities and to actively prevent attempted intrusions. IPS solutions should be implemented on external Internet connections and in high-security areas to block malicious intrusion (Hedrick & Grama, 2013).

*Figure 1. Level of network security management*

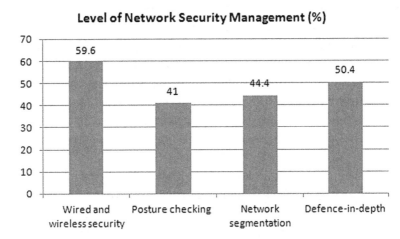

## Data Transfer Security Management

Secondly, the study assessed the extent to which higher educational institutions protect the data traversing their campus networks. Overall, data transfer security practices stood at 44.8% (see Table 3), indicating that the institutions were at the planned stage on data transfer security management. Observably, data transfer security management has been lower than network security management (which was 48.8%).

*Table 3. Data transfer security management*

| | Data Transfer Security Management | NP (%) | PI (%) | PL (%) | WD (%) | QC (%) | CI (%) | Mean | ML (%) | SD |
|---|---|---|---|---|---|---|---|---|---|---|
| 5 | Encryption | 7.5 | 22.5 | 32.5 | 15.0 | 22.5 | - | 2.22 | 44.4 | 1.242 |
| 6 | Media access control | 7.5 | 32.5 | 15.0 | 30.0 | 15.0 | - | 2.12 | 42.4 | 1.236 |
| 7 | Protect exchanged information | 7.5 | 32.5 | 7.5 | 45.0 | - | 7.5 | 2.20 | 44.0 | 1.316 |
| 8 | Protect data from public network | 7.5 | 25.0 | 15.0 | 22.5 | 30.5 | - | 2.42 | 48.4 | 1.348 |
| Levels of Data Transfer Security Management | | 7.5 | 28.13 | 17.5 | 28.13 | 17.0 | 1.88 | 2.24 | 44.8 (PL) | 1.090 |

Not Performed (NP – 0%); Performed Informally (PI – 20%); Planned (PL – 40%); Well Defined (WD – 60%); Quantitatively Controlled (QC – 80%); Continuously Improving (CI – 100%); ML - Management Level, *N*=80

This is an indication that the institutions are paying more attention to network security than data transfer security.

In particular, the respondents were asked to indicate their institution's use of appropriate and vetted encryption methods to protect sensitive data in transit. Encryption protects data at rest and in transit. Figure 2 shows the level of encryption at 44.4%, indication the need to encourage the use of encryption software to encrypt sensitive data of their devices and when sent across the network. Data encryption prevents anyone without a decryption key from being able to read the data (Beaudin, 2015). Principally, university community uses smart phones and other mobile devices to store and transmit sensitive data (personal and financial information, intellectual property), mobile data should be encrypted on these devices and when sent across to other devices for protection from potential theft. Even sensitive email messages can be encrypted using public keys. Most email clients have a feature to easily perform this task. The person receiving the message will be able to decrypt it.

Moreover, the respondents were asked whether their institutions have controls in place to protect, track, and report status of media that has been removed from secure organization sites (media access control). The result shows a score of 42.4%. In addition, the level of protection exchanged data stood at 44%, when the respondents were asked whether they had policies and procedures in place to protect exchanged information from interception, copying, modification, misrouting, and destruction. Finally, when asked whether the respondents have a process in place to ensure that data traversing public networks is protected from fraudulent activity, unauthorized disclosure, or modification, the result shows a score of 48.4%.

In order to manage and improve data transfer security, higher educational institutions could adopt some measures. Higher educational institutions could put in place mobile device and acceptable use policies. There is also the need for security education to address basic security literacy (Kaspersky & Furnell, 2014). Training and awareness programs for the university community (faculty, staff, students, alumni, contractors) must focus on how users should protect themselves on the campus and public networks. The faculty should be taught and use Virtual Private Network (VPN) when sending sensitive data among themselves or with other research institutions. VPN creates a private network through public networks and routes data securely to the recipients. Training programs should cover basic security practices such as how to turn off sharing, how to enable firewall to block unauthorized access to their devices. They should be taught how to use Hyper Text Transfer Protocol Secure (HTTPS) and Secure Sockets Layer (SSL). HTTPS is the protocol that ensures data sent between the browser and the website is encrypted and SSL establishes an encrypted link between a web server and a browser. Also, running up-to-date anti-virus software could help protect systems connected to unsecured network.

## Communications Security Management

Finally, the study assessed the maturity of the higher educational institutions' overall communication security management. Table 4 and Figure 3 show that the overall level of network and data transfer security practices, among all the institutions, was 46.8% (Level 2), which is the *planned stage* of maturity. This stage indicates that the base requirements for the networks and data transfer security controls are planned, implemented, and repeatable. Specifically, less than 5% of the institutions had no network and data transfer security controls or plans in place; about 25% had the base security practices of network and data transfer control areas generally performed on an ad hoc basis; and about 26% had the base requirements for the network control areas planned, implemented, and repeatable. Moreover, 25% had network and data transfer security processes documented, approved, and implemented campus-wide; about 15% had network and data transfer security processes measured and verified; about 5% have standard processes to regularly reviewed, updated and improve processes to response to vulnerability's impact.

Ideally, for higher educational institutions to attain the highest level of communications security, they should be at Level 5 (continuously improving). At this level, higher educational institutions would have implemented standard processes that would be regularly reviewed and updated. Also, improvements to communications security controls would reflect an understanding of, and response to, a vulnerability's impact through the process of a measured and verified (e.g., auditable) security assessment. In addition, at this level, communications security controls would have been documented, approved, and implemented institution-wide.

*Figure 2. Level of data transfer security management*

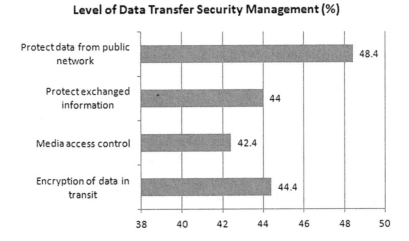

*Table 4. Network and data transfer security management*

| Network and Data Transfer Security Management | NP (%) | PI (%) | PL (%) | WD (%) | QC (%) | CI (%) | Mean | ML (%) | SD |
|---|---|---|---|---|---|---|---|---|---|
| Levels of Network Security Management | 1.88 | 21.25 | 32.63 | 20.63 | 13.13 | 7.5 | 2.44 | 48.8 (PL) | .965 |
| Levels of Data Transfer Security Management | 7.5 | 28.13 | 17.5 | 28.13 | 17.0 | 1.88 | 2.24 | 44.8 (PL) | 1.090 |
| Overall communications Security Management | 4.69 | 24.69 | 25.7 | 25.07 | 15.07 | 4.69 | 2.34 | 46.8% (PL) | .986 |

Not Performed (NP – 0%); Performed Informally (PI – 20%); Planned (PL – 40%); Well Defined (WD – 60%); Quantitatively Controlled (QC – 80%); Continuously Improving (CI – 100%); ML - Management Level, *N*=80

*Figure 3. Level of network and data transfer security management*

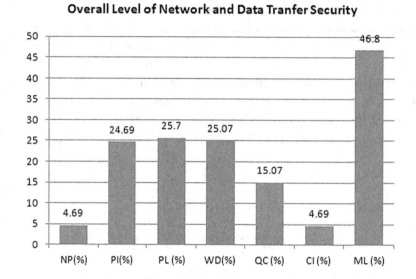

## SOLUTIONS AND RECOMMENDATIONS

Higher educational institutions have become the target of cyber attacks, which has been evident in several recent reported cases of data breaches (Garg, 2016; Symantec, 2014). This study used a survey to gain deeper understanding of network security (wired and wireless network monitoring, posture checking, network segmentation, and defence-in-depth) and data transfer security (encryption of data in transit, media access control, protection of exchanged information, and protection of data from public networks) management in Ghanaian higher educational institutions.

The results of the study showed that network and data transfer security were not adequately managed in Ghanaian higher educational institutions. The overall level of network and data transfer security practices among all the institutions stood at 46.8% (Level 2), which is the *planned stage* of maturity. This stage indicated that the base requirements for network and data transfer security controls were planned, implemented, and repeatable. With regards to the eight individual network and data transfer security controls assessed, apart from two controls, the level of management of all the other controls fell below 50%. In particular, monitoring of wired and wireless networks for an unauthorized access was about 60%, whereas protection of critical assets by more than one security layer (defence-in-depth) was about 50%. On the contrary, all the remaining measures fell below 50%. The lowest score recorded was posture checking (41%). Considering the level of data breaches in higher educational institutions, these levels of network and data transfer security management are inadequate. Consequently, higher educational institutions need to review their communications security management plans and implement a more secure network and data transfer security controls.

There are some implications of this study. First, higher educational institutions need to invest in monitoring systems to continually monitor the campus networks for unauthorized access (PWC, 2015). Network monitoring systems monitor an internal network for problems and pre-emptively identify issues such as virus infection, low drive space, and degrading hardware. This can reduce the impact these problems can have on the institutions' productivity (Beaudin, 2015). Second, higher educational institutions can deploy the necessary standards-based authentication, digital signatures (public-key encryption), directory services, and network management systems necessary for inter-institutional collaboration and resource sharing across the network to prevent unauthorized access to sensitive data in transit.

Third, implementing a strategy of defense-in-depth could defeat or discourage all kinds of attacks. Firewalls, intrusion detection systems, well trained users, policies and procedures, strong password, and good physical security are examples of some of the effective security plans that can be put in place. Each of these mechanisms by themselves is of little value but when implemented together will provide an effective security. Fourth, access to wireless and wired networks should be strictly restricted to authenticated faculty members, staff, students, and other authorized persons only. Moreover, all users must be made to change passwords periodically; systems should be deployed to encrypt passwords; and two or three-factor authentication methods can be instituted before access is allowed into campus networks. Fifth, systems administrators and security personnel need to employ standard information security frameworks and best practices to ensure data security.

## CONCLUSION

The findings of this study will be useful to IT systems administrators, IT security personnel, and IT auditors by gaining insight into network and data transfer security environment of the campus communications security. The study also showed some disparities in the management of network security between higher educational institutions in developing country, Ghana and that of the developed nations (Hedrick, 2013; PWC Report, 2015). These differences can be useful for benchmarking, which may inform IT strategic planning and management. However, the study had a limitation of low response rate. This is usually the case as evidence suggested that when collecting data of sensitive nature, the researcher should expect very low response (Kotulic & Clark, 2004).

Future research will involve replicating the study in other organizations so as to compare, benchmark, and gain insight of the broader network and data transfer security environment. Moreover, this study focussed on network and data transfer security, which were considered as technical security measures. However, data breaches happened as a result of human behavior (performing risky activities, non-compliance to security policies). As such, multi-disciplinary study including behavioural science theories will be needed to explain user bahavior. Thus, combining behavioural science with communications security (including intrusion prevention, protocol and behavior analysis, application control, vulnerability management, network segmentation, encryption and other defenses) may provide insightful results.

## REFERENCES

Beaudin, K. (2015). College and university data breaches: Regulating higher educaiton cybersecurity under state and federal law. *The Journal of College and University Law, 41*(3), 657–694.

Benjamin, V., & Chen, H. (2012). *Securing cyberspace: Identifying key actors in hacker communities. IEEE International Conference on Intelligence and Security Informatics (ISI)*, Arlington, VA. 10.1109/ISI.2012.6283296

Chandramouli, R. (2011). *Emerging social media threats: Technology and Policy Perspectives. Second Worldwide Cybersecurity Summit.* London, UK: WCS.

Choras, M. (2013). Comprehensive approach to information sharing for increased network security and survivability. *Cybernetics and Systems: An International Journal, 44*(6-7), 550–568. doi:10.1080/019 69722.2013.818433

Coleman, L., & Purcell, B. M. (2015). Data breaches in higher education. *Journal of Business Cases and Applications, 15,* 1–7.

Custer, W. L. (2010). Information Security Issues in Higher Education and Institutional Research. *New Directions for Institutional Research, 1,* 46. Doi:10.1002/ir.341

Downing, M. (2013). *The Importance of Network Monitoring.* Retrieved from http://www.animate.com/the-importance-of-network-monitoring/

Edge, I. E. (2010). Employ five fundamental principles to produce a SOLID, secure network. *Information Security Journal: A Global Perspective, 19*(3), 153-159. doi:10.1080/19393551003649008

Grama, J. (2014). *Just in time research:Data breaches in higher education.* Retrieved from https://net.educause.edu/ir/library/pdf/ECP1402.pdf

Gregory, W. H., & Grama, J. (2013). *Information Security (Research Bulletin).* Louisville, CO: EDU-CAUSE Center for Applied Research. Retrieved from http://www.educause.edu/ecar

Hair, J. F. J., Hult, G. T. M., Ringle, C., & Sarstedt, M. (2014). A primer on partial least squares structural equation modeling (PLS-SEM). *Long Range Planning, 46,* 328. doi:10.1016/j.lrp.2013.01.002

Harris, S. (2013). *All-In-One CISSP Exam Guide* (6th ed.). McGraw Hill.

Hedrick, G. W., & Grama, J. (2013). *Information Security.* Retrieved from https://library.educause.edu/resources/2013/6/information-security

HEISC. (2014). *Information Security Guide - Communications Security.* Retrieved from https://spaces.internet2.edu/display/2014infosecurityguide/Communications+Security

Higher Education Information Security Council (HEISC). (2013). *Information Security Program Assessment Tool.* Retrieved from http://www.educause.edu

Huang, N., & Jiao, Z. (2014). On campus network security system of college and university. *Journal of Emerging Technologies in Web Intelligence, 6*(4).

ISO/IEC 21827. (2008). *Information technology - Security techniques - Systems security engineering - Capability maturity model (SSE-CMM).* Retrieved from http://www.iso.org/iso/catalogue_detail.htm?csnumber=44716

ISO/IEC 27002. (2013). *Information technology Security techniques - Code of practice for information security controls.* Retrieved from http://www.iso.org/iso/catalogue_detail?csnumber=54533

Kaspersky, E., & Furnell, S. (2014). A security education Q&A. *Information Management & Computer Security, 22*(2), 130–133. doi:10.1108/IMCS-01-2014-0006

Koch, R., Stelte, B., & Golling, M. (2012). *Attack Trends in Present Computer Networks. 4th International Conference on Cyber Conflict (CYCON)*, Tallinn, Estonia.

Kotulic, A. G., & Clark, J. G. (2004). Why there aren't more information security research studies. *Information & Management, 41*(5), 597–607. doi:10.1016/j.im.2003.08.001

Kumar, G., & Kumar, K. (2014). Network security – an updated perspective. *Systems Science & Control Engineering, 2*(1), 325–334. doi:10.1080/21642583.2014.895969

Kumar, U., & Gambhir, S. (2014). A literature review of security threats to wireless networks. *International Journal of Future Generation Communication and Networking, 7*(4), 25–34. doi:10.14257/ijfgcn.2014.7.4.03

Martínez-Argüelles, M. J., Castán, J. M., & Juan, A. A. (2010). Using the critical incident technique to identify factors of service quality in online higher education. *International Journal of Information Systems in the Service Sector, 2*(4), 57–72. doi:10.4018/jisss.2010100104

Mei-Yu, W., & Ming-Hsien, Y. (2013). Enterprise information security management based on context-aware RBAC and communication monitoring technology. *Mathematical Problems in Engineering*, 1–11. doi:10.1155/2013/569562

National Accreditation Board of Ghana (NAB). (2016). *Number of accredited tertiary institutions in Ghana per category as at September 2016*. Retrieved from www.nab.gov.gh

Oblinger, D. G. (2015). *Ten reasons to tackle the top 10 IT issues*. Retrieved from http://er.educause.edu/articles/2015/1/ten-reasons-to-tackle-the-top-10-it-issues

Patton, M. (2015). Battling data breaches: For higher education institutions, Data Breach Prevention is More Complex than for Industry and Business. *Community College Journal, 86*(1), 20–24.

Pfleeger, S. L., & Caputo, D. D. (2012). *Leveraging behavioral science to mitigate cyber-security risk*. MITRE Technical Report 12-0499. Bedford, MA: MITRE Corporation.

Poll, H. (2015). *Pearson student mobile device survey 2015*. Retrieved from http://www.pearsoned.com/wp-content/uploads/2015-Pearson-Student-Mobile-Device-Survey-College.pdf

PWC Report. (2015). *The Global State of Information Security Survey 2015*. Retrieved from http://www.pwc.com/gx/en/issues/cyber-security/ information-security-survey/download.html

Reichenberg, N. (2014). Improving Security via Proper Network Segmentation. *Security Week*. Retrieved from http://www.securityweek.com/improving-security-proper-network-segmentation

Reichenberg, N., & Wolfgang, M. (2014). Segmenting for security: Five steps to protect your network. *Network World*. Retrieved from http://www.networkworld.com

SAINT. (2016). *Vulnerability management, penetration testing, configuration assessment and compliance*. Retrieved from http://www.saintcorporation.com

SANS Institute. (2006). *Penetration testing: Assessing your overall security before attackers do*. Retrieved from https://www.sans.org/reading-room/whitepapers/ analyst/penetration-testing-assessing-security-attackers-34635

SANS Institute. (2013). *Network security resources.* Retrieved from https://www.sans.org/network-security/

Schneider, D. (2012). The state of network security. *Network Security, 2*(2), 14–20. doi:10.1016/S1353-4858(12)70016-8

Symantec. (2014). *Internet Security Threat Report 2014.* Retrieved from http://www.symantec.com

United States Computer Emergency Readiness Team (US-CERT). (2013). *Security tip. Understanding Encryption.* Retrieved from https://www.us-cert.gov/ncas/tips/ST04-019

US GAO. (2012). *Information security: Better implementation of controls for mobile devices should be encouraged.* Retrieved from http://www.gao.gov/products/GAO-12-757

Verizon. (2013). *The 2013 data breach investigations report.* Retrieved from www.verizonenterprise.com

Yaokumah, W., Brown, S., & Adjei, P. O. (2015). Information technology governance barriers, drivers, IT/Business alignment, and maturity in Ghanaian universities. *International Journal of Information Systems in the Service Sector, 7*(4), 66–83. doi:10.4018/IJISSS.2015100104

*Previously published in Network Security and Its Impact on Business Strategy; pages 1-19, copyright year 2019 by Business Science Reference (an imprint of IGI Global).*

## APPENDIX

## Information Security Management Survey Instrument

The purpose of this study is to assess the level at which network and data transfer security measures have been put in place on campus networks in Ghanaian higher educational institutions and to provide strategies for protecting information resources.

Please, use the scale below to assess the level of network and data transfer security management in institution.

*Table 5. ISO 21827 International Standards Scale for Measuring Maturity Levels*

| Code | ISO 21827 | Definitions |
|------|-----------|-------------|
| 0 | Not Performed | There are no security controls or plans in place. The controls are nonexistent. |
| 1 | Performed Informally | Base practices of the control area are generally performed on an ad hoc basis. There is general agreement within the organization that identified actions should be performed, and they are performed when required. The practices are not formally adopted, tracked, and reported on. |
| 2 | Planned | The base requirements for the control area are planned, implemented, and repeatable. |
| 3 | Well Defined | The primary distinction from Level 2, Planned and Tracked, is that in addition to being repeatable the processes used are more mature: documented, approved, and implemented organization-wide. |
| 4 | Quantitatively Controlled | The primary distinction from Level 3, Well Defined, is that the process is measured and verified (e.g., auditable). |
| 5 | Continuously Improving | The primary distinction from Level 4, Quantitatively Controlled, is that the defined, standard processes are regularly reviewed and updated. Improvements reflect an understanding of, and response to, vulnerability's impact. |

## Profile of Respondent

Please indicate your response to the following questions by checking the appropriate boxes.

1. What is your current job title?
   a. Information Security Officer (CISO)
   b. Chief Information Officer (CIO)
   c. IT Manager /IT Specialist
   d. Internal Auditor
   e. Network Adminstrator
2. How many years of experience do you have at your current position?
   a. 1-5 Years
   b. 6-10 Years
   c. 11-15 Years
   d. 16-20 Years
   e. Over 20 Years

## Network Security

Please, indicate your reaction to each of the following statements by marking the checkbox that represents the level at which your institution has put in place the following network security measures.

*Table 6.*

| Description of Items | | | | | | | |
|---|---|---|---|---|---|---|---|
| NTSEC1 | My institution continuously monitors our wired and wireless networks for unauthorized access. | 0 | 1 | 2 | 3 | 4 | 5 |
| NTSEC2 | My institution has a process for posture checking, such as current antivirus software, firewall enabled, OS patch level, etc., of devices as they connect to your network. | 0 | 1 | 2 | 3 | 4 | 5 |
| NTSEC3 | My institution has segmented network architecture to provide different levels of security based on the information's classification. | 0 | 1 | 2 | 3 | 4 | 5 |
| NTSEC4 | Internet-accessible servers are protected by more than one security layer (firewalls, network IDS, host IDS, application IDS, etc). | 0 | 1 | 2 | 3 | 4 | 5 |

0. Not Performed 1. Performed Informally 2. Planned 3. Well Defined 4. Quantitatively Controlled 5. Continuously Improving

## Data Transfer Security

Please, indicate your reaction to each of the following statements by marking the checkbox that represents the level at which your institution has put in place the following data transfer security measures.

*Table 7.*

| Description of Items | | | | | | | |
|---|---|---|---|---|---|---|---|
| DTSEC1 | My institution use appropriate and vetted encryption methods to protect sensitive data in transit. | 0 | 1 | 2 | 3 | 4 | 5 |
| DTSEC2 | Controls are in place to protect, track, and report status of media that has been removed from secure organization sites. | 0 | 1 | 2 | 3 | 4 | 5 |
| DTSEC3 | My institution has policies and procedures in place to protect exchanged information (within my organization and in third-party agreements) from interception, copying, modification, misrouting, and destruction. | 0 | 1 | 2 | 3 | 4 | 5 |
| DTSEC4 | My institution has a process in place to ensure data traversing public networks is protected from fraudulent activity, unauthorized disclosure, or modification. | 0 | 1 | 2 | 3 | 4 | 5 |

0. Not Performed 1. Performed Informally 2. Planned 3. Well Defined 4. Quantitatively Controlled 5. Continuously Improving

# Chapter 25
# Conceptualizing the Domain and an Empirical Analysis of Operations Security Management

**Winfred Yaokumah**

https://orcid.org/0000-0001-7756-1832

*Pentecost University College, Ghana*

## ABSTRACT

*Operations security management integrates the activities of all the information systems security controls. It ensures that the entire computing environment is adequately secured. This chapter conducts an in-depth review of scholarly and practitioner works to conceptualize the domain of operations security management. Drawing upon the existing information systems security literature, the chapter classifies operations security management into 10 domains. Following, the chapter performs an empirical analysis to investigate the state-of-practice of operations security management in organizations. The findings show that the maturity level of operations security management is at the Level 3 (well-defined). The maturity levels range from Level 0 (not performed) to Level 5 (continuously improving). The results indicate that operations security processes are documented, approved, and implemented organization-wide. Backup and malware management are the most applied operations security controls, while logging, auditing, monitoring, and reviewing are the least implemented controls.*

## INTRODUCTION

Operations security management is the day-to-day activities involved in ensuring that people, applications, computer systems, computer networks, processes, and the entire computing environment are properly and adequately secured (Gregory, 2010). It pertains to the activities that take place while keeping computing environment up and running in a secured and protected manner (Harris, 2013; Shaqrah, 2010). Operations security management integrates the activities of all the information systems security

DOI: 10.4018/978-1-6684-3698-1.ch025

controls (Henrya, 2011). To attain a high level of operations security organizations need to put in place appropriate measures that will ensure that the routine security activities are carried out in a controlled manner (Prabhu, 2013). These activities may include documenting operating procedures; ensuring that changes to information assets are carried out efficiently; protecting information resources from malware and other threats; performing backups and ensuring timely availability of information; and carrying out logging, auditing, monitoring, and reviewing user activities (Prabhu, 2013). In order to keep up with these tasks, operations security personnel (network administrators, system administrators, and database administrators) need in-depth understanding of the domain of operations security. This knowledge will help them to fully implement and adequately handle the day-to-day operations security challenges.

However, there seems to be varying views as to what constitutes the domain of operations security. According to Gregory (2010), operations security includes security monitoring, vulnerability management, change management, configuration management, and information handling procedures. Harris (2013) considers operations security as the activities involved in ensuring that physical and environmental security (such as temperature and humidity control, media reuse and disposal, and destruction of media containing sensitive information) concerns are addressed. Moreover, the International Information System Security Certification Consortium's (ISC²) Body of Knowledge (CBK, 2017) extends operations security to cover operational support of highly available systems, fault tolerance, and mitigation of security-related cyber attacks. Also, ISO/IEC 27002 (2013) defines the scope of operations security as consisting of security procedures, roles and responsibilities; management of security in the third-party products and services; securing systems and data from malware activities; backup of data to safeguard against data lost and system corruption; and logging, monitoring, auditing, and reviewing of system activities.

Considering these different perspectives, there is the need to identify, classify, and clarify the domain of operations security for better implementation and management of operations security controls in organizations. Therefore, the objectives of this chapter are: (a) to conduct a review of scholarly and practitioner works to conceptualize the domain of operations security management, and (b) to perform an empirical analysis to ascertain the level of operations security management in organizations based on ISO/IEC 27002:2013 framework. Information security programs will be successful when measured with IT security maturity models (McFadzean, Ezingeard, & Birchall, 2011). These models are based on international standards and best practices. Information security maturity models consist of structured set of elements that describe levels of security improvement (maturity). They are often used as tools for measuring the performance of security programs in organizations (Stevanović, 2011).

Therefore, this chapter's empirical analysis of operations security management is based on the information security control objectives defined by the International Organization for Standardization/ International Electrotechnical Commission - security techniques - code of practice for information security management (ISO/IEC 27002:2013 framework). This framework is a widely accepted information technology security techniques and contains 14 security control clauses with a total of 35 main security categories and 114 controls (ISO/IEC 27002:2013, 2013). In particular, the objectives of this chapter will be achieved by answering the following three research questions:

1.  What is the domain of operations security management?
2.  What is the maturity level of operations security management in Ghanaian organizations?
3.  Are there any significant differences among the organizations with regard to the levels of operations security management?

## BACKGROUND

### Context

Legal and regulatory compliance required organizations to protect critical and sensitive data of their customers. Computer Security Institute (2011) reported that organizational information security has improved by 64% owing to regulatory compliance efforts. Compliance with legal requirements, such as Sarbanes-Oxley (SOX) for financial reporting and governance, impacted the management of information systems security (Brown & Nasuti, 2005). The Health Insurance Portability and Accountability Act (HIPPA) required healthcare organizations to "safeguard the confidentiality, integrity, and availability of electronic protected health information" (Hoffman & Podgurski, 2007, p. 7). Also, the Federal Information Security Management Act (FISMA) required all U.S. federal agencies and international banking industry to develop, document, and implement a program that would provide information security for the systems that support their operations and assets (Pabrai, 2006).

Developing countries enacted laws and regulations to protect information resources. A recent Data Protection Act 843 of Ghana was aimed at protecting the privacy and personal data of individuals (Data Protection Act, 2012). Moreover, the Electronic Transaction Act 772 of Ghana (Electronic Transactions Act 772, 2008) focused on developing "a safe, secure and effective environment for the consumer, business and the government to conduct and use electronic transactions" (p. 6). Despite these regulatory compliance efforts, a recent study found a decline in fundamental security practices (PWC, 2015). For example, a recent report ranked Ghana second in Africa and seventh in the world with respect to Internet related crimes (Joy Online, 2013). The report also indicated that about 82 cyber crimes occurred in Ghana every month - on average about 1000 crimes occurred in a year (Joy Online, 2013).

### Empirical Work

According to Harris (2013), operations security can be achieved through configuration settings, performance monitoring, fault tolerance, and accounting and verification management. Operations security management practices are based on the fundamental security concepts of need-to-know (users have only the information required to perform specific duties), least privilege (users have the fewest or lowest number of privileges required to accomplish their duties), separation of duties (high-value or high-risk tasks required two or more different individuals to complete), and job rotation (moving users through a range of job assignments) (Gregory, 2010). According to ISO/IEC27002 (2013), operations security tasks could be achieved through performing operational procedures and responsibilities; managing security in third-party systems; malware protection; backup and restoration; and logging, monitoring, auditing, and reviewing.

### Operational Procedures and Responsibilities

Operational procedures and responsibilities ensure protected operations of information processing facilities (ISO/IEC27002, 2013). It includes documentation of operating procedures, change management, capacity management, and separation of development and testing from operational environments. Change management involves changes to the organization, business processes, information processing facilities, and systems that can affect information security. Capacity management is the monitoring, tuning, and projections made of future capacity requirements to ensure that required system performance is sustained. To reduce the risks of unauthorized access or changes made to the operational environment, system development, testing, and operational environments should be segregated (ISO/IEC27002, 2013).

Concerning security roles and responsibilities, senior executives of the organization have legal obligations, compliance and regulatory requirements to ensure that resources are protected, safety measures are in place, and security mechanisms are tested to guarantee that required level of protection is maintained (Harris, 2013). In order to achieve this, organizations have to consider threats, including disclosure of confidential data, theft of assets, corruption of data, interruption of services, and destruction of the physical or logical environment (Harris, 2013). Moreover, it is important that organizations maintain security configuration standards for information systems and segregation of security duties to ensure that unintentional or unauthorized modifications of information systems can be detected.

Information security is an important concern for not only the senior executives. The users have critical role and responsibility to play by following security policies and procedures to safeguard information. Human aspects of information security should be taken into consideration as ignorance, negligence, mischief, resistance, and lack of information security awareness on the part of users can have adverse effect on the security of the organizational data (Safa, von Solms, & Furnell, 2016). In a study that assessed major information security risks within the health care sector, Deursen, Buchanan, and Duff (2013) enumerated the main risks to patients' health records: staff leaving data unattended to in their offices, staff sharing passwords with others, and staff sending emails containing personal patient data to wrong addressees.

## Security in Third-party Systems

In today's interconnected business world, more data is generated and shared with business partners and suppliers. Internet security (Zolait, Ibrahim, & Farooq, 2010) and database outsourcing become threats nowadays because they pose substantial security and privacy risks (Evdokimov, Fischmann, & Günther, 2010). It is important that the third-party and other stakeholders protect organizational data. Recent study reported that organizations do not pay much attention to third-party security (PWC, 2015). The study investigated whether organizations perform appropriate protections of vendors to ensure their ability to safeguard information. It further assessed whether organizations conduct ongoing monitoring to ensure that the third-party is protecting organizational sensitive data (PWC, 2015). From the results, only 50% of the organizations performed risk assessments on third-party vendors; 50% conducted an inventory of all third parties that handle personal data of employees and customers; and only 54% have a formal policy requiring third parties to comply with their privacy policies (PWC, 2015).

The third party systems, particularly the cloud computing, though have the benefits of scalability, cost reduction, portability, flexibility, and availability, are also faced with serious security issues (Bachlechner et al., 2014; Karadsheh, 2012). Concerns were raised over unauthorised access to third party cloud based systems - which can cause large scale exposure of organizational private data (Scanlon, Farina, & Kechadi, 2015). Thus, the need for due diligence in the selection of a trusted cloud service provider (Tang & Liu, 2015) and the establishment of appropriate security policies, service level agreement and compliance for enhancing cloud security (Karadsheh, 2012). Accordingly, it is crucial organizations put processes in place to assess and monitor third-party compliance with security requirements.

## Malware Protection

Malware protection is important to ensure that information resources are protected (ISO/IEC27002:2013) from destruction and damage. Malware is "a program that is covertly inserted into another program with the intent to destroy data, run destructive or intrusive programs, or otherwise compromise the confidentiality, integrity, or availability of the victim's data, applications, or operating system" (Souppaya & Scarfone, 2013, p. 2). Malware can gather the user's sensitive information, gain read or write access to the user's files, activate the device's microphone or camera to secretly record information, or even upload files to specific locations (US GAO, 2012). On the contrary, in the area of computer forensics, Ramalho (2014) noted that malware can be used as a means of obtaining digital evidence.

The frequency of malware incursions has heightened the need for security awareness and education, law enforcement, and installation of current security software (Martin & Rice, 2011). Fake anti-virus attacks are the current trend for malware distribution by which the attackers disguise malware as legitimate anti-virus software and convince users to install it (Kim, Yan, & Zhang, 2015). But, Nissim et al., (2015) developed a method that can detect malicious non-executable files (such .pdf, .docx) containing malware which users may mistakenly consider less suspicious or malicious. Therefore, users' ability to exhibit malware avoidance behaviours require repeated trainings (Dang-Pham & Pittayachawan, 2015). Also, organizations should implement mechanisms to detect, quarantine, and eradicate known malicious codes on all its computing systems, including workstations, servers, and mobile computing devices.

## Backup and Restoration

Data loss as a result of malware activities and system crashes represents a significant threat to individuals and organizations. Therefore, taking regular backups ensures protection against loss of data (ISO/IEC27002:2013). According to Mbowe et al. (2014), security breaches of sensitive information remained a difficult problem to solve owing to the increasing number of malware programs. In a study, Computer Security Institute (2011) found that 97% of the 234 respondents had installed anti-virus software to protect organizational data. Conversely, the study reported that malware infection accounted for 67.1 percent of all security attacks (Computer Security Institute, 2011). Accordingly, Menard et al. (2014) recommended a cloud-based backup solution as a sufficient backup alternative. Jarraya and Laurent (2010) proposed a novel Peer-to-Peer (P2P) reliable and secure backup system that utilizes the hard disk space attached to the Internet to implement a distributed backup service.

Additionally, the frequency of data backup process should be consistent with the availability requirements and the restore procedures should be routinely tested to ensure the integrity of the backup. Similarly, a study found that a very large proportion of discarded computer disks were potentially exposed to the possibility of a compromise of sensitive information (Jones, Dardick, Davies, Sutherland, & Valli, 2009). Moreover, Kljun, Mariani, and Dix (2016) found that a fifth of all computers are not backed up, and a quarter of most important files and a third of most important folders could not be (fully) restored in the event of computer failure.

## Logging, Monitoring, Auditing, and Reviewing

A log is a record of events that occur within an organization's computing systems arising from network activities, application software, and operating systems (Kent & Souppaya, 2006). The purpose is to record events and generate evidence (ISO/IEC27002:2013, 2013). The evident can help in troubleshooting, optimizing system and network performance, identifying security incidents and policy violations, and recording of user actions (Kent & Souppaya, 2006). Logs can provide data useful for investigating attacks, fraud, and inappropriate system usage (Kent & Souppaya, 2006). Data logging on networks helps in detecting and troubleshooting faults (Connolly, 2010). In particular, website log data can be used to reconstruction the website (Shieh, 2012). It can reveal user's behaviour (Arshad & Ameen, 2015) and provide trends in the use of information systems (Park & Lee, 2013).

Organizations can monitor the workforce as their activities are logged when interacting with organizational computing facilities (Alampay & Hechanova, 2010). Transaction logs can provide evidence of usage patterns of resources (Avery & Tracy, 2014). Besides, data logging over an extended period can help diagnose intermittent faults (Connolly, 2010), provide evidence for accountability (Vance, Lowry, & Eggett, 2013), and enhance intrusion detection and problem identification (United States Patent and Trademark Office [USPTO], 2009). Therefore, processes should be put in place to automatically log the utilization of information system resources and routinely monitor logs to detect unauthorized and anomalous activities. Accordingly, logging facilities and log information should be protected against tampering and unauthorized access (ISO/IEC27002:2013, 2013).

## IT Maturity Models

Various IT maturity models exist for measuring the performance of IT security and related processes. Notable among them are ISO/IEC 21827, the Control Objectives for Information and Related Technology (COBIT), and the Capability Maturity Model Integration (CMMI). ISO/IEC 21827 is an international standard based on the Systems Security Engineering Capability Maturity Model (SSE-CMM) developed by the International Systems Security Engineering Association (ISO/IEC 21827:2008, 2008). It is a standard metrics that captures security engineering practices generally observed in the industry. The metrics measures the development, operation, maintenance and decommissioning activities; management, organizational and engineering activities; system, software, hardware, and human factors; system management, operation and maintenance; and acquisition, system management, certification, accreditation and evaluation (ISO/IEC 21827:2008, 2008).

The COBIT maturity model, developed by IT Governance Institute, consists of set of best practices for IT governance and management. It ensures that IT sustains business goals, optimizes IT investment, and manages IT-related risks and opportunities (ITGI, 2010). Similarly, the CMMI is aimed at providing guidance for improving organization's processes and ability to manage the development, acquisition, and maintenance of products or services, focussing on systems engineering, software engineering, integrated product and process development, and supplier sourcing (Software Engineering Institute, 2002). Table 1 shows the maturity levels contained in ISO/IEC 21827:2008 model, which can be mapped to both COBIT maturity model and that of CMMI. However, the models differ with respect with their area of focus. Essentially, COBIT focuses on assessing the maturity of IT governance processes; CMMI model measures the maturity of software processes, and ISO/IEC 21827:2008 focuses on IT security management. Hence, ISO/IEC 21827:2008 maturity model is suitable for this study.

*Table 1. Scales for measuring IT maturity levels*

| Maturity Scale | | International Standards for Measuring IT Maturity | | | |
|---|---|---|---|---|---|
| Level | (%) | ISO 21827 | COBIT | CMMI | Definition/Meaning |
| 0 | 0 | Not Performed (NP) | Non-Existent (NE) | Non-Existent (NE) | • No security controls or plans in place.<br>• The controls are non-existent. |
| 1 | 20 | Performed Informally (PI) | Ad-hoc and Initial (AI) | Ad-hoc (AD) | • Base practices of the control areas are generally performed on an ad hoc basis.<br>• There is general agreement within the organization that identified actions that should be performed, and they are performed when required.<br>• But the practices are not formally adopted, tracked, and reported on. |
| 2 | 40 | Planned (PL) | Repeatable but Intuitive (RI) | Repeatable (RE) | • The base requirements for the control areas are planned, implemented, and repeatable. |
| 3 | 60 | Well Defined (WD) | Defined Process (DP) | Defined and Implemented (DI) | • In addition to Level 2, the processes used are documented, approved, and implemented organization-wide. |
| 4 | 80 | Quantitatively Controlled (QC) | Managed and Measurable (MM) | Managed (MA) | • In addition to Level 3, the processes are measured and verified (e.g., auditable). |
| 5 | 100 | Continuously Improving (CI) | Optimized (OP) | Optimized (OP) | • In addition to Level 4, standard processes are regularly reviewed and updated.<br>• Improvements reflect an understanding of and response to vulnerability's impact. |

# METHOD

## Research Methodology, Population and Samples

This chapter conducted a review of scholarly and practitioner literature to conceptualize the domain of operations security management. Following, the chapter utilized quantitative research methodology with a cross-sectional survey research approach (Malhotra & Grover, 1998) to assess the level of maturity of operations security management among industry sectors. Four hundred and eighty questionnaires were sent to information security officers, chief information officers, IT managers, IT specialists, and Internal Auditors who were familiar with their organizations' security environment by post, by email and by self delivery in 56 organizations drawn from five major industry sectors in three large regional capitals of Ghana. The industry sectors include (a) government public service institutions, (b) public utility companies (water, electricity, and telecommunication), (c) financial institutions, (d) educational institutions, (e) healthcare institutions, and others (manufacturing, oil and gas, IT, etc). The survey instrument was adopted from Higher Education Information Security Council (HEISC, 2013). It was modified to focus on operations security controls of the widely-accepted ISO/IEC 27002:2013 framework.

## Instrument Reliability

The questionnaire consisted of operations security management (with five controls of 20 items) (see Table 2) and a section for demographic data. Apart from the demographic data, all the items on the questionnaire used a 6-point Likert scale (*Not performed = 0, Performed informally = 1, Planned = 2, Well defined = 3, Quantitatively controlled = 4, and Continuously improving = 5*). The scale generated continuous data on all the items. The demographic data consisted of industry sector, job title, and the number of years of experience on the current job. The inter-organizational security program maturity was measured using ISO/IEC 21827 maturity model. The collected data were coded and analyzed using Statistically Package for Social Scientists (SPSS).

Firstly, the Cronbach's alpha reliability coefficient which measures the internal consistency of the items on the questionnaire was computed. Table 2 shows that the coefficients were within the acceptable range of 0.7 and above as according to Nunnuly (1978). Secondly, descriptive statistics using the mean and percentages was conducted to ascertain the information security maturity levels of the operations security controls and the individual security measures of the controls. Moreover, the Cross-tab was used to compare the organizations. Thirdly, with the intent of comparing and benchmarking the inter-organizational information security maturity levels, analysis of variance (ANOVA) was employed to analyze the significance differences among the organizations by their type.

*Table 2. Instrument reliability*

| Variables | No. of Items | Reliability Coefficient (Cronbach's Alpha) |
|---|---|---|
| Administrative Management | 4 | .785 |
| Security in Third-Party Products and Services | 4 | .739 |
| Malware Management | 2 | .747 |
| Backup and Restoration | 2 | .765 |
| Logging, Monitoring, Auditing and Reviewing | 8 | .891 |

*N = 223*

## MAIN FOCUS OF THE CHAPTER

This section conceptualizes the domain of operations security management based of the previous works. It follows with empirical analysis to assess the state-of-practice (maturity levels) of operations security management.

### Proposed Domain of Operations Security Management

Figure 1 identifies and classifies operations security into ten domains as follows:

- Resource Protection
- Access Management
- Malware Management
- System Availability Management
- Administrative Management
- Configuration and Change Management

- Business Continuity Management
- Incident Management
- Vulnerability Management
- Records Management

## Resource Protection

Resource protection is the set of activities to protect the organization's resources. These resources include facilities (such as electricity, fire alarms, communications lines, and temperature controls), hardware (such as computers and network devices), software (such as source code and intellectual property), and documentations (processes, procedures, and instruction manuals).

## Access Management

Access management consists of security policies, procedures, and controls that determine how and who should access information (Gregory, 2010). It includes user account provisioning, managing privilege accounts, password management, and review of access rights.

## Malware Management

Malware management is the use of software (referred to as anti-malware) to block, detect, and clean malicious and unwanted software on a computer system. Malware is often classified as viruses, worms, and Trojan Houses. Viruses self-replicate and insert copies of themselves into other programs or data files. Viruses can be activated by user interaction with infested files through activities such as opening a file or running a program. Unlike viruses, worms are self-contained programs that normally execute themselves without user interaction (Souppaya & Scarfone, 2013). Trojan Horses are the type of malware that disguise themselves and hide within the user's legitimate file (US GAO, 2012). Data loss as a result of malware activities represents a significant threat to individuals and organizations. Therefore, installing anti-virus, anti-rootkit, anti-spyware, anti-spam, and firewalls can ensure protection against data loss.

## System Availability Management

This is the process of ensuring that critical systems are continuously available (Negi & Pandey, 2012) to authorized users. Several measures are available to make systems resilient to failures. These include fault tolerance (duplication of components such that failure of one component will not result in the failure of the entire system), clustering (a group of two or more systems operate functionally as a single logical unit such that the system continues to operate if one of the systems fail), failover (switching over to a passive system when the active system fails), and replication (data transmission from one storage system to a counterpart storage system).

## Administrative Management

This involves management oversight and control over all activities related to the protection of organizational information assets. Management control and oversight responsibilities include establishing and enforcing security policies, risk assessment, security training and awareness, allocating resources, auditing, monitoring, and reviewing.

## Configuration and Change Management

Configuration management is the process of recording configuration changes that take place in a computing environment (Gregory, 2010). It aims at systematically controlling and monitoring the changes that have incurred in the configuration of systems during the entire lifetime (Gasparotti, 2013). Change management is a management process whereby each proposed change in an environment is formally planned and reviewed by peers and stakeholders prior to making the change (Gregory, 2010). It aims at improving stability and reducing unscheduled downtime in an environment (Gregory, 2010). Change management is carried out together with configuration management to record approved changes to systems (Gregory, 2010).

*Figure 1. Conceptualizing the domain of operations security management*

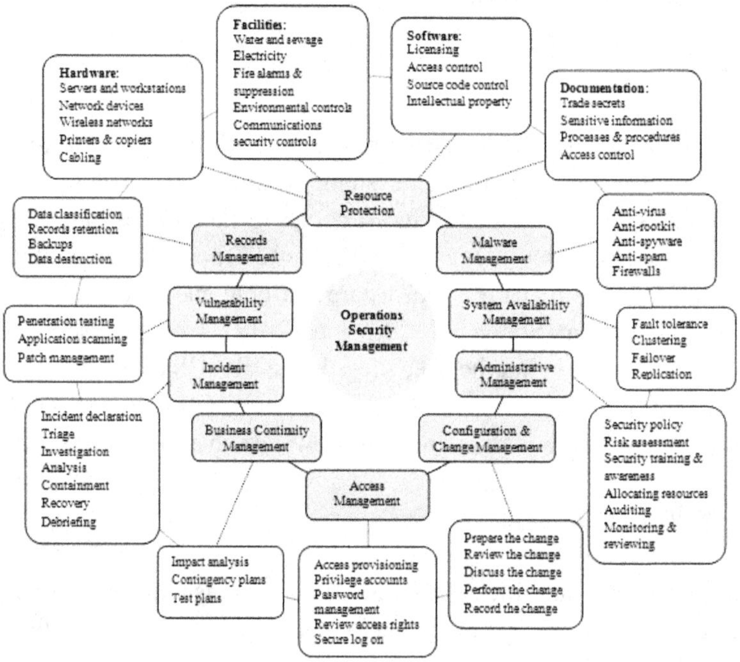

## Business Continuity Management

The increasing levels of business disruptions and disaster events have created the need for business continuity management (Asgary, 2016). A potential threat to business continuity management is globalization (Ee, 2014). Business continuity is a management activity where analysis is performed to better understand the risks associated with potential disasters and the steps that can be taken to reduce the impact of a disaster should one occur. Organizations will implement high-resilience systems that will permit critical business functions to continue operating even when a disaster strikes (Gregory, 2010). Business continuity management involves continuity planning (set of activities required to ensure continuation of critical business processes when a disaster occurs) and disaster recovery planning (set of activities concerned with assessment, salvaging, repairing, and restoration of damaged facilities and assets that support critical business processes) (Gregory, 2010). It also includes business impact analysis (catalog of all organization's important business processes and the criticality of each), contingency planning, and test plans (Gregory, 2010).

## Incident Management

The objective of information security incident management is to provide a quick, efficient and organized response in case a security incident occurs. An incident is an unexpected event that results in an interruption of normal operations (Gregory, 2010). It aims at providing sufficient information regarding the event and ensures that such an incident do not occur (Finat, 2014). An incident can be managed systematically as follows: a) incident declaration (declaration of security incident when a policy violation has occurred), b) triage (search for clues that will hopefully lead to a root cause of the incident and the ability to apply corrective measures), c) investigation (closer study of information that may lead to the cause of the incident), d) analysis (deeper study of the information that is directly related to the incident), e) containment (measures to halt the incident and to prevent its spread), f) recovery (restoring the system to its pre-incident condition), and g) debriefing (reflecting on the incident and the organization's response to it in order to learn from the incident activities) (Gregory, 2010).

## Vulnerability Management

Vulnerability management is the process of identifying weaknesses in systems and then acting to mitigate those weaknesses (Harris, 2013). Vulnerability is an inherent characteristic of any system (hardware or software). Its identification and management are essential for improving the system's resilience (Agarwal, 2015). Vulnerabilities in systems can be discovered through penetration testing, application scanning, and patch management. Penetration testing is a technique that mimics the actions of a hacker who scans a system or network for opened ports and services. Application scanning is the process of performing security tests on an application in order to find vulnerabilities in the application code itself. Patch management is a process that manages the installation of patches on systems (Gregory, 2010).

## Records Management

Activities under records management involve data classification (establishing data sensitivity levels and handling procedures) and records retention (how long information must be kept). It also includes backups (making sure information is not lost due to system failure or malfunction) and data destruction (how information should be safely discarded when no longer needed) (Gregory, 2010).

## RESULTS OF EMPIRICAL DATA ANALYSIS

This section begins by presenting the characteristics of the respondents. It is followed by the assessment of operations security maturity levels using ISO/IEC 21827 maturity scale. Following, the significant differences in the levels of operations security management among Ghanaian organizations were verified.

## Characteristics of the Respondents

Out of the 480 survey questionnaires sent to the participants, 223 were returned, yielding a 46.5 percent response rate. Of this total, 17.6% of the respondents (corresponding to 40 participants) were from Educational Institutions (University colleges, polytechnics, universities), 10.8% of the respondents (corresponding to 24 participants) were from Public Utility Companies (Water, Electricity, Telecom), 24.3% (corresponding to 54 participants) were from Financial Institutions, 16.2% (corresponding to 36 participants) were from Government Public Service, 13.5% (corresponding to 30 participants) were from Health Care Institutions, and 17.6% were from other organizations (IT Companies, Oil and Gas, Manufacturing, etc).

The vast majority of the respondents (120 in total or 53.1%) who participated in the study were IT managers (specialists), who had the responsibility of managing and performing IT security functions in their various organizations. Thirty-three respondents (representing 14.9%) were chief information officers. Thirty information security officers (representing 13.5%), fifteen internal auditors (also representing 6.7%) also took part in the study. Twenty five (representing 11.2%) were other IT personnel (i.e., IT consultants) also participated in the study. For the number of years respondents had worked on the current job position, over 22.9% had 1-5 years of experience, 35.4% had 6 to 10 years experience, 37.7% had 11 to 15 years experience, and 4% had 16 to 20 years experience.

## Assessing Operations Security Maturity Levels

Operations security controls that were measured composed of operational procedures and responsibilities, security in third-party products and services, malware protection, data backups, and logging and monitoring activities. Frequency distributions of the operations security controls and the individual security measures were measured using percentages, the mean and the standard deviation. Following, a crosstab was used to assess the levels of maturity of operations security management within the organizations:

- **Operational Procedures and Responsibilities:** To measure the level of operational procedures and responsibilities, participants responded to the extent to which their organizations maintained security configuration standards for information systems (IS) and applications; tested, authorized, and reported changes to information systems; segregated duties to ensure unintentional or unauthorized modification of information was detected; and how production systems were separated from other stages of the development life cycle. The results show that the level of operational procedures and responsibilities is at maturity Level 3 (mean = 3.04 or 60.8%) (see Table 4). This is an indication that the organizations' security operational procedures and responsibilities are well-defined. This suggests that security operational procedures and responsibilities processes used in the organizations are documented, approved, and implemented organization-wide;

*Table 3. Sample characteristics*

| Respondents | No. of Participants Responded | Percent (%) |
|---|---|---|
| **Industry Sector** | | |
| Education Institution | 40 | 17.6 |
| Public Utility Company | 24 | 10.8 |
| Financial Institution | 54 | 24.3 |
| Government | 36 | 16.2 |
| Health Care | 30 | 13.5 |
| Others (IT Companies, Oil and Gas, Manufacturing, etc.) | 39 | 17.6 |
| **Job Function** | | |
| Information Security Officers | 30 | 13.5 |
| Chief Information Officers | 33 | 14.9 |
| IT Manager /IT Specialists | 120 | 53.1 |
| Internal Auditors | 15 | 6.7 |
| Others | 25 | 11.2 |
| **Experience (Years)** | | |
| 1-5 | 51 | 22.9 |
| 6-10 | 79 | 35.4 |
| 11-15 | 84 | 37.7 |
| 16-20 | 9 | 4.0 |

$N = 233$

- **Security in Third-party Products and Services:** With regard to management of security in third-party products and services, the participants responded to the degree to which their organizations had agreements with external IS services that met the organization's specific security requirements; put processes in place for assessing that external information system providers complied with security requirements; monitored the external information system services providers' compliance with security controls; and that the external information system service agreements were executed and routinely reviewed. From Table 4, the majority of the respondents (33.8%) reported that security in third-party products and services are generally at the stage of *well-defined*. Overall, the level of maturity is a little above Level 3 (mean = 3.14 or 62.4%). This level portrays that processes used in managing security in third-party products and services are documented, approved, and implemented organization-wide;
- **Malware Protection:** Moreover, regarding *malware protection*, the respondents assessed the degree to which their organizations put in place mechanisms to detect, quarantine, and eradicate known malicious code on information systems (including workstations, servers, and mobile computing devices) and eradicated known malicious code transported by electronic mail, the web, or removable media. From Table 4, malware protection recorded a mean of 3.08 (61.6), depicting maturity Level 3. Among the five security controls of operations security management, the vast majority of the respondents reported that their organizations malware protection is quantitatively

controlled (37.8%). Information security processes are quantitatively controlled when the organizational security processes are being measured and verified (e.g., auditable);

- **Data Backup:** Likewise, the respondent assessed the extent to which data backup processes were consistent with the availability requirements and that system restore procedures were routinely tested. The results show that the maturity level is above Level 3, which has the mean of 3.32 (66.4%). Apparently, backup processes recorded the highest maturity among all the five controls of operations security management;
- **Logging, Monitoring and Reviewing:** Moreover, regarding logging and monitoring, the respondent assessed the extent to which their organizations: Put in place processes to monitor the utilization of key system resources and to mitigate the risk of system downtime; performed security-related activities that automatically logged system events; and implemented processes to routinely monitor logs to detect unauthorized and anomalous activities. Logging, monitoring and reviewing processes also included records log reviews; securing log data to prevent unauthorized access and tampering; regularly reviewing administrative and operative access to audit logs; use of file-integrity monitoring tools to alert personnel of unauthorized modification; and processes to ensure synchronization of system clocks with an authoritative source. Logging and monitoring security measures recorded the lowest maturity level among all the five controls of operations security management. It had a mean of 2.93 (58.6%), indicating the maturity level below Level 3.
- **Overall Operations Security Management:** Overall, the organizations' maturity level of operations security management was approximately at Level 3 (*well-defined*) with a mean score of 3.06 (*SD* = .808). As can be observed from Table 4, 4.1% of the organizations operations security management are *performed informally*, 17.6% are *planned*, 51.4% are *well defined*, 25.7% are *quantitatively controlled*, and only 1.4 are *continuously improving*.

*Table 4. Levels of operations security management*

| Information Security Controls | Levels in Percentages (%) | | | | | | Mean | ML (%) | SD |
|---|---|---|---|---|---|---|---|---|---|
| | NP | PI | PL | WD | QC | CI | | | |
| Security Procedures and Responsibilities | 1.4 | 4.1 | 18.9 | 44.6 | 27.0 | 4.1 | 3.04 | 60.8 | .954 |
| Security in third-party Products and Services | 1.4 | 4.1 | 21.6 | 32.4 | 33.8 | 6.8 | 3.14 | 62.4 | 1.048 |
| Malware Management | - | 8.1 | 21.6 | 28.4 | 37.8 | 4.1 | 3.08 | 61.6 | 1.040 |
| Backup and Restoration | - | 4.1 | 10.8 | 43.2 | 32.4 | 9.5 | 3.32 | 66.4 | .935 |
| Logging, Monitoring and Review | 1.4 | 6.8 | 21.6 | 37.8 | 32.4 | - | 2.93 | 58.6 | .967 |
| Maturity of Operations Security Management | - | 4.1 | 17.6 | 51.4 | 25.7 | 1.4 | 3.06 | 61.2% (WD) | .808 |

Not Performed (NP – 0%); Performed Informally (PI – 20%); Planned (PL – 40%); Well Defined (WD – 60%); Quantitatively Controlled (QC – 80%); Continuously Improving (CI – 100%); ML - Maturity Level, N=223

Observably, the majority of the organizations have their operations security management maturity at the *planned* and *well defined* stages (see Table 5). It is interesting to note that apart from Education Institutions (15%) and Public Utility Companies (12.5%), no other organization's operations security management is at the *low level* maturity (*not performed* and *performed informally*). Also, the Government Public Services had 91.7% (PL and WD) and Financial Institutions had 61.1%, which are the *moderate level of maturity*. Comparing the organizations, the results show that only 22.5% (QC and CI) of Education Institutions are at the *high level* maturity, 37% for Public Utility Company, 38.9% for Financial Institutions, 8.3% for Government public service, 50% for Health Care, and 7.7% of other organizations. Thus, the maturity of operations security management is higher within Financial and Healthcare institutions than all other organizations, with Government Public Services recorded the lowest maturity levels.

*Table 5. Maturity levels of operations security controls*

| Level | Maturity Scale | Industry Sectors (Frequency and Percentages) | | | | | |
|---|---|---|---|---|---|---|---|
| | | Education Institution | Public Utility Company | Financial Institution | Government | Health Care | Others |
| 0 | Not Performed (NP) | - | - | - | - | - | - |
| 1 | Performed Informally (PI) | 6 | 3 | 0 | 0 | 0 | 0 |
| | | 15.0% | 12.5% | .0% | .0% | .0% | .0% |
| 2 | Planned (PL) | 10 | 6 | 6 | 9 | 0 | 9 |
| | | 25.0% | 25.0% | 11.1% | 25.0% | .0% | 23.1% |
| 3 | Well Defined (WD) | 15 | 6 | 27 | 24 | 15 | 27 |
| | | 37.5% | 25.0% | 50.0% | 66.7% | 50.0% | 69.2% |
| 4 | Quantitatively Controlled (QC) | 9 | 9 | 18 | 3 | 15 | 3 |
| | | 22.5% | 37.5% | 33.3% | 8.3% | 50.0% | 7.7% |
| 5 | Continuously Improving (CI) | 0 | 0 | 3 | 0 | 0 | 0 |
| | | .0% | .0% | 5.6% | .0% | .0% | .0% |
| | No. of Respondents | 40 | 24 | 54 | 36 | 30 | 39 |

- **Individual Operations Security Measures:** Further analysis of the individual operations security measures reveals interesting findings. The majority of the security measures fall below the stage of *well defined* (mean of 3.0 or 60%). In particular, only seven (7) operations security measures attain maturity Level 3 and above, falling within 61.6% and 64.0% (mean values of 3.08 and 3.20) (see Table 6). The highest operations security measures put in place is that the organizations ensure that external information systems services providers' compliance with security controls is monitored (64.0%). Moreover, many of the organizations ensure that data backup process is frequency consistent with the availability data security requirements (63.0%). However, it can be seen that as large as 6.8% of the organizations studied do not have external service providers' compliance with security measures. In addition, routine review of external information systems service agreements (54.8%) and file-integrity monitoring tools to alert security personnel of unauthorized modifications (54.6%) occupied the lowest levels of operations security measures.

## Inter-Organizational Operations Security Management

The previous section assessed the maturity levels of operations security management. This section verifies whether there are significant differences in the levels of operations security management among the organizations. Analysis of variance (ANOVA) was employed to test six null hypotheses in turn. For each hypothesis, descriptive statistics is conducted to ascertain the mean, standard deviation and 95% confidence intervals for the independent variables and the organization type: Education Institutions, Public Utility Company, Financial Institutions, Government, Health Care, and Others (IT, Oil and Gas, Manufacturing, etc.).

*Table 6. Operations security control measures*

| No | | Operations Security Controls/Measures | NP (%) | PI (%) | PL (%) | WD (%) | QC (%) | CI (%) | Mean | ML (%)) | SD |
|---|---|---|---|---|---|---|---|---|---|---|---|
| **Operational Procedures and Responsibilities** | | | | | | | | | | | |
| | 1 | Maintains security configuration standards for information systems (IS) and applications. | 2.7 | 9.5 | 24.3 | 32.4 | 21.6 | 9.5 | 2.89 | 59.8 | 1.207 |
| | 2 | Changes to IS are tested, authorized, and reported. | 1.4 | 9.5 | 23.0 | 35.1 | 25.7 | 5.4 | 2.91 | 58.2 | 1.096 |
| | 3 | Segregation of duties to ensure unintentional or unauthorized modification of information is detected. | 1.4 | 10.8 | 18.9 | 33.8 | 28.4 | 6.8 | 2.97 | 59.4 | 1.143 |
| | 4 | Production systems are separated from other stages of the development life cycle. | 2.7 | 12.2 | 21.6 | 27.0 | 27.0 | 9.5 | 2.92 | 58.4 | 1.264 |
| **Security in Third-Party Products and Services** | | | | | | | | | | | |
| | 5 | Agreements for external IS services specify appropriate security requirements. | 2.7 | 13.5 | 17.6 | 33.8 | 20.3 | 12.2 | 2.92 | 58.4 | 1.286 |
| | 6 | Processes are in place for assessing that external IS providers comply with security requirements. | 1.4 | 9.5 | 21.6 | 28.4 | 25.7 | 13.5 | 3.08 | 61.6 | 1.232 |
| | 7 | External IS services providers' compliance with security controls is monitored. | 6.8 | 6.8 | 17.6 | 24.3 | 23.0 | 23.0 | 3.20 | 64.0 | 1.457 |
| | 8 | External IS service agreements are executed and routinely reviewed. | 2.7 | 5.4 | 35.1 | 35.1 | 35.1 | 5.4 | 2.74 | 54.8 | 1.070 |
| **Protection Against Malware** | | | | | | | | | | | |
| | 9 | Methods are used to detect, quarantine, and eradicate known malicious codes on IS including workstations, servers, and mobile computing devices. | 2.7 | 5.4 | 31.1 | 24.3 | 32.4 | 4.1 | 2.91 | 58.2 | 1.121 |
| | 10 | Methods are used to detect and eradicate known malicious code transported by electronic mail, the web, or removable media. | - | 17.6 | 21.6 | 32.4 | 24.3 | 4.1 | 2.76 | 55.2 | 1.129 |
| **Backup and Restoration** | | | | | | | | | | | |
| | 11 | Data backup process is frequency consistent with the availability requirements. | - | 6.8 | 14.9 | 44.6 | 24.3 | 9.5 | 3.15 | 63.0 | 1.013 |
| | 12 | Routinely tests the restore procedures. | 1.4 | 10.8 | 23.0 | 33.8 | 24.3 | 6.8 | 2.89 | 57.8 | 1.138 |

*continues on following page*

*Table 6. Continued*

| No | | Operations Security Controls/Measures | NP (%) | PI (%) | PL (%) | WD (%) | QC (%) | CI (%) | Mean | ML (%)) | SD |
|---|---|---|---|---|---|---|---|---|---|---|---|
| | | **Logging, Monitoring, and Auditing** | | | | | | | | | |
| | 13 | Processes are in place to monitor the utilization of key system resources and to mitigate the risk of system downtime. | 2.7 | 4.1 | 17.6 | 41.9 | 23.0 | 10.8 | 3.11 | 62.2 | 1.114 |
| | 14 | Security-related activities are automatically logged. | - | 12.2 | 23.0 | 28.4 | 24.3 | 12.2 | 3.01 | 60.2 | 1.206 |
| | 15 | Processes are in place to routinely monitor logs to detect unauthorized and anomalous activities. | 1.4 | 5.4 | 23.0 | 35.1 | 27.0 | 8.1 | 3.05 | 62.0 | 1.206 |
| | 16 | Records log reviews. | 1.4 | 8.1 | 24.3 | 33.8 | 24.3 | 8.1 | 2.96 | 59.2 | 1.124 |
| | 17 | Steps are taken to secure log data to prevent unauthorized access and tampering. | 2.7 | 9.5 | 17.6 | 29.7 | 39.2 | 1.4 | 2.97 | 59.4 | 1.118 |
| | 18 | Regularly reviews administrative and operative access to audit logs. | - | 9.5 | 20.3 | 35.1 | 20.3 | 14.9 | 3.11 | 62.2 | 1.173 |
| | 19 | File-integrity monitoring tools are used to alert personnel to unauthorized modification. | 5.4 | 8.1 | 23.0 | 23.0 | 20.3 | 4.1 | 2.73 | 54.6 | 1.158 |
| | 20 | Processes in place to ensure synchronization of system clocks with an authoritative source. | 4.1 | 9.5 | 21.6 | 33.8 | 27.0 | 4.1 | 2.82 | 56.4 | 1.171 |

N=223, NP- Not Performed, PI- Performed Informally, PL - Planned, WD - Well Defined, QC - Quantitatively Controlled, CI - Continuously Improving, ML - Maturity Level

The following hypotheses were tested:

$H_1$: *There are no significant differences among organizations regarding the level of managing security procedures and responsibilities.*

$H_2$: *There are no significant differences among organizations regarding the level of managing security in the third-party products and services.*

$H_3$: *There are no significant differences among organizations regarding the level of malware management.*

$H_4$: *There are no significant differences among organizations regarding the level of backup management*

$H_5$: *There are no significant differences among organizations regarding the level of logging and monitoring management*

$H_6$: *There are no significant differences among organizations regarding the level of operations security management*

One of the assumptions of a one-way ANOVA is that the variances of the groups being compared should be similar. As such, the Levene's test of homogeneity of variance was tested for similar variances. Levene's *F* Statistic has a significance value of $p < .05$, indicating that the assumption of homogeneity of variances was not met. Therefore, the variances in the levels of information security management among the organizations were statistically significantly different. A post hoc test (Games-Howell *post-hoc*) of multiple comparisons was conducted to determine which organizations are significantly and statistically different. The results of the ANOVA analyses are presented in Table 7.

*Hypothesis H₁* proposed that the level of operations *security procedures and responsibilities* is the same among the organizations. A one-way ANOVA was conducted to test significant differences among the organizations. Table 7 shows the mean and standard deviation of the organization types: Education Institutions was 2.30 ($N = 40$; $SD = .92$); Public Utility Companies was 3.22 ($N = 24$; $SD = .84$); Financial Institutions was 3.26 ($N = 54$; $SD = .51$); Government Public Service was 2.73 ($N = 36$; $SD = .44$); Health Care was 3.73 ($N = 30$; $SD = .51$), and other organizations (IT, Oil and Gas, Manufacturing) was 2.42 ($N = 39$; $SD = .75$). A one-way ANOVA shows (see Table 8) that there was at least one significant difference between the organizations ($N = 233$; $F (5, 217) = 17.567$; $p < .05$). The results indicated statistical significant differences in the level of operations *security procedures and responsibilities* among the organization types. As a result, the null hypothesis was not supported and therefore rejected. Table 8 shows a significant difference between the Education Institutions (46.0%) and Public Utility (64.4%), Financial Institutions (65.2%), Health Care Institutions (74.6%). Moreover, significant differences can be observed between Government Public Services (54.6%) and Financial Institutions (65.2%), Health Care Institutions (74.6%). Observably, the Public Utility, Financial Institutions, and Health Care Institutions outperform Education Institutions. Also, Financial Institutions and Health Care outperform Government Public Service.

*Hypothesis H₂* proposed that the level of *managing security in third-party products and services* is the same among the organizations. Table 7 shows the mean and standard deviation of the organization types: Education Institutions was 2.39 ($N = 40$; $SD = 1.19$); Public Utility Companies was 2.78 ($N = 24$; $SD = .96$); Financial Institutions was 3.50 ($N = 54$; $SD = .84$); Government Public Service was 2.77 ($N = 36$; $SD = .52$); Health Care was 3.63 ($N = 30$; $SD = .55$), and other organizations (IT, Oil and Gas, Manufacturing) was 2.65 ($N = 39$; $SD = .77$). A one-way ANOVA shows (see Table 8) that there was at least one significant difference between the organizations ($N = 233$; $F (5, 217) = 13.289$; $p < .05$). This indicated statistical significant differences in the level of *managing security in third-party products and services* among the organization types. Consequently, the null hypothesis was not supported and therefore rejected. Table 8 shows that Educational Institutions (47.8%) differ significantly from Financial Institutions (70.0%) and Health Care Institutions (72.6%); Public Utility (55.6%) differs significantly from Health Care Institutions (74.6%); and Financial Institutions (70.0%) differ significantly from Public Utility (55.6%). Therefore, Financial Institutions and Health Care Institutions perform better than Educational Institutions and Public Utility organizations.

*Hypothesis H₃* also proposed that the level of *malware protection* is the same among the organizations. A one-way ANOVA was conducted to test the hypothesis that *malware protection* do no differ significantly among the organizations. The mean and standard deviation of the organization types were: Education Institutions was 2.14 ($N = 40$; $SD = 1.07$); Public Utility Companies was 2.88 ($N = 24$; $SD = 1.11$); Financial Institutions was 3.03 ($N = 54$; $SD = .88$); Government Public Service was 2.79 ($N = 36$; $SD = .78$); Health Care was 3.40 ($N = 30$; $SD = .93$), and other organizations (IT, Oil and Gas, Manufacturing) was 2.81 ($N = 39$; $SD = .92$) (see Table 7). A one-way ANOVA shows that there was at least one significant difference between the organizations ($N = 233$; $F (5, 217) = 7.006$; $p < .05$) (see Table 8). Accordingly, the null hypothesis was not supported and therefore rejected. Table 8 shows the mean and significant differences in the levels of *malware protection:* Educational Institutions (42.8%) differ significantly from Financial Institutions (67.8%) and Government Public Service (54.8%) also differs significantly from Health Care Institutions (68.0%). As can be observed from the table, Financial Institutions outperform Educational Institutions and Health Care Institutions outperform Government Public Service.

*Table 7. Differences in inter-organizational operations security management*

| Security Controls | Organizations/ Institutions | N | Mean | SD | ML(%)/ (Ranking) | Maturity Level * | Organizational Differences (Post Hoc – Games Howell) |
|---|---|---|---|---|---|---|---|
| Security Roles, Responsibilities, Procedures & Security | Education Institution | 40 | 2.30 | .92 | 46.0 (6) | PL (2) | Educational -> Public Utility, Financial, Health Care. Government -> Financial, Health Care. |
| | Public Utility Company | 24 | 3.22 | .84 | 64.4 (3) | WD (3) | |
| | Financial Institution | 54 | 3.26 | .94 | 65.2 (2) | WD (3) | |
| | Government | 36 | 2.73 | .51 | 54.6 (4) | WD (3) | |
| | Health Care | 30 | 3.73 | .51 | 74.6 (1) | QC (3) | |
| | Others | 39 | 2.42 | .75 | 48.4 (5) | PL (3) | |
| Third-Party Security | Education Institution | 40 | 2.39 | 1.19 | 47.8 (6) | PL (2) | Educational -> Financial, Health Care. Public Utility -> Health Care. Financial -> Public Utility. |
| | Public Utility Company | 24 | 2.78 | .96 | 55.6 (3) | WD (3) | |
| | Financial Institution | 54 | 3.50 | .84 | 70.0 (2) | WD (3) | |
| | Government | 36 | 2.77 | .52 | 55.4 (4) | WD (3) | |
| | Health Care | 30 | 3.63 | .55 | 72.6 (2) | WD (3) | |
| | Others | 39 | 2.65 | .77 | 53.0 (5) | WD (3) | |
| Malware Protection | Education Institution | 40 | 2.14 | 1.07 | 42.8 (6) | PL (2) | Educational -> Financial, Government -> Health Care. |
| | Public Utility Company | 24 | 2.88 | 1.11 | 57.6 (3) | WD (3) | |
| | Financial Institution | 54 | 3.03 | .88 | 60.6 (2) | WD (4) | |
| | Government | 36 | 2.79 | .78 | 55.8 (5) | WD (3) | |
| | Health Care | 30 | 3.40 | .93 | 68.0 (1) | WD (3) | |
| | Others | 39 | 2.81 | .92 | 56.3 (4) | WD (3) | |
| Backup & Restoration | Education Institution | 40 | 2.74 | .99 | 54.8 (5) | WD (3) | Educational -> Financial. Financial -> Government. Government -> Health Care. |
| | Public Utility Company | 24 | 3.06 | .97 | 60.2 (3) | WD (3) | |
| | Financial Institution | 54 | 3.39 | .82 | 67.8 (1) | WD (4) | |
| | Government | 36 | 2.67 | .52 | 53.4 (6) | WD (3) | |
| | Health Care | 30 | 3.30 | .65 | 66.0 (2) | WD (4) | |
| | Others | 39 | 2.85 | 1.08 | 57.0 (4) | WD (3) | |
| Logging, Monitoring, & Auditing | Education Institution | 40 | 2.46 | 1.04 | 49.2 (6) | PL (2) | Educational -> Financial, Health Care. Financial -> Government. |
| | Public Utility Company | 24 | 2.88 | .91 | 57.6 (4) | WD (3) | |
| | Financial Institution | 54 | 3.45 | .73 | 69.0 (1) | WD (4) | |
| | Government | 36 | 2.65 | .62 | 53.0 (5) | WD (3) | |
| | Health Care | 30 | 3.25 | .83 | 65.0 (2) | WD (3) | |
| | Others | 39 | 2.95 | .58 | 59.0 (3) | WD (3) | |
| Overall: Operations Security | Education Institution | 40 | 2.41 | .90 | 48.2 (6) | PL (2) | Educational -> Financial, Health Care. Health Care -> Government. |
| | Public Utility Company | 24 | 2.94 | .86 | 59.8 (3) | WD (3) | |
| | Financial Institution | 54 | 3.38 | .67 | 67.6 (2) | WD (3) | |
| | Government | 36 | 2.70 | .44 | 54.0 (5) | WD (3) | |
| | Health Care | 30 | 3.44 | .59 | 68.8 (1) | WD (3) | |
| | Others | 39 | 2.76 | .77 | 55.2 (4) | WD (3) | |

Not Performed (NP – 0%); Performed Informally (PI – 20%); Planned (PL – 40%); Well Defined (WD – 60%); Quantitatively Controlled (QC – 80%); Continuously Improving (CI – 100%); N=233. * Nearest to maturity scale point, *N*=223

*Hypothesis H₄* proposed that the level of *backup management* is not different among the organizations. Table 7 shows the mean and standard deviation of the organization types: Education Institutions was 2.74 ($N = 40$; $SD = .99$); Public Utility Companies was 3.06 ($N = 24$; $SD = .97$); Financial Institutions was 3.39 ($N = 54$; $SD = .82$); Government Public Service was 2.67 ($N = 36$; $SD = .52$); Health Care was 3.30 ($N = 30$; $SD = .65$), and Other organizations (IT, Oil and Gas, Manufacturing) was 2.85 ($N = 39$; $SD = 1.08$). A one-way ANOVA shows (see Table 8) that there was at least one significant difference between the organizations ($N = 233$; $F (5, 217) = 5.003$; $p < .05$). Hence, the null hypothesis was not supported and therefore rejected. Observably, Educational Institutions (54.8%) differ significantly from Financial Institutions (67.8%), Financial Institutions (67.8%) differ significantly from Government *Public Service* (53.4%), and Government Institutions (53.4) differ significantly from Health Care Institutions (66.0%). Evidently, Financial Institutions outperform Educational Institutions and Government Institutions. Also, Health Care Institutions outperform Government Public Service.

*Hypothesis H₅* proposed that the level of security logging and monitoring is different among the organizations. Table 7 shows the mean and standard deviation of the organization types: Education Institutions was 2.46 ($N = 40$; $SD = 1.04$); Public Utility Companies was 2.88 ($N = 24$; $SD = .91$); Financial Institutions was 3.45 ($N = 54$; $SD = .73$); Government Public Service was 2.65 ($N = 36$; $SD = .62$); Health Care was 3.25 ($N = 30$; $SD = .83$), and Other organizations (IT, Oil and Gas, Manufacturing) was 2.95 ($N = 39$; $SD = .58$). A one-way ANOVA shows (see Table 8) that there was at least one significant difference between the organizations ($N = 233$; $F (5, 217) = 9.381$; $p < .05$). As a result, the null hypothesis was not supported and therefore rejected. Noticeably, Educational Institutions (49.2%) differ significantly from Financial Institutions (69.0%) and Health Care Institutions (65.0%). Again, Financial Institutions (69.0%) differ significantly from Government Public Service (53.0%). Obviously, Financial Institutions outperform Educational Institutions and Government Public Service. Likewise, Health Care Institutions outperform Educational Institutions.

*Hypothesis H₆* proposed that the overall level of *operations security* is the same among the organizations. Table 7 shows the mean and standard deviation of the organization types: Education Institutions was 2.41 ($N = 40$; $SD = .90$); Public Utility Companies was 2.94 ($N = 24$; $SD = .86$); Financial Institutions was 3.38 ($N = 54$; $SD = .67$); Government Public Service was 2.70 ($N = 36$; $SD = .44$); Health Care was 3.44 ($N = 30$; $SD = .59$), and Other organizations (IT, Oil and Gas, Manufacturing) was 2.76 ($N = 39$; $SD = .77$). A one-way ANOVA shows that there was at least one significant difference between the organizations ($N = 233$; $F (5, 217) = 14.181$; $p < .05$). This indicated statistical significant differences in the level of *operations security* among the organization types. As a result, the null hypothesis was not supported and therefore rejected. The results show that Educational Institutions (48.2%) differ significantly from Financial Institutions (67.6%) and Health Care Institutions (68.8%). Also, Health Care Institutions (68.8%) differ significantly from Government Public Service (54.0%). Overall, Financial Institutions and Health Care Institutions outperform Educational Institutions. Moreover, Health Care Institutions outperform Government Public Service.

*Table 8. Significant differences between and within organizations using ANOVA*

| Hypotheses | Variables | | Sum of Squares | df | Mean Square | F | Sig. | Result |
|---|---|---|---|---|---|---|---|---|
| $H_1$ | Security Roles, Responsibilities, Procedures & Security | Between Groups | 54.280 | 5 | 10.856 | 17.567 | .000 | Not supported |
| | | Within Groups | 134.101 | 217 | .618 | | | |
| | | Total | 188.381 | 222 | | | | |
| $H_2$ | Third-Party Security | Between Groups | 47.497 | 5 | 9.499 | 13.289 | .000 | Not supported |
| | | Within Groups | 155.118 | 217 | .715 | | | |
| | | Total | 202.614 | 222 | | | | |
| $H_3$ | Malware Protection | Between Groups | 31.157 | 5 | 6.231 | 7.006 | .000 | Not supported |
| | | Within Groups | 193.022 | 217 | .890 | | | |
| | | Total | 224.179 | 222 | | | | |
| $H_4$ | Backup & Restoration | Between Groups | 18.599 | 5 | 3.720 | 5.003 | .000 | Not supported |
| | | Within Groups | 161.360 | 217 | .744 | | | |
| | | Total | 179.960 | 222 | | | | |
| $H_5$ | Logging, Monitoring, & Auditing | Between Groups | 29.179 | 5 | 5.836 | 9.381 | .000 | Not supported |
| | | Within Groups | 134.992 | 217 | .622 | | | |
| | | Total | 164.171 | 222 | | | | |
| $H_6$ | Overall: Operations Security | Between Groups | 32.128 | 5 | 6.426 | 14.181 | .000 | Not supported |
| | | Within Groups | 98.329 | 217 | .453 | | | |
| | | Total | 130.457 | 222 | | | | |

$N = 233$

## SOLUTIONS AND RECOMMENDATIONS

Operations security management integrates the activities of all the other information systems security controls (Henrya, 2011). Previous studies noted the multifaceted nature of operations security management (Gregory, 2010; Harris, 2013; ISC2 CBK, 2017; ISO/IEC 27002:2013, 2013). However, few studies attempted to specify its domain for better understanding and effective management of the entire computing environment. In this chapter, ten domains of operations security management were identified. Each control of the domain was presented and discussed along with its sub-themes and countermeasures.

Following, an assessment was conducted to ascertain the maturity levels of some key domain controls of operations security management and their sub-themes (managing operational procedures, roles and responsibilities; security in third-party products and services; malware protection; data backup; and logging and monitoring activities). The study found that operations security maturity was 61.2%, which represented the maturity Level 3 (*Well-Defined*). This level suggested that operations security processes and controls were documented, approved, and implemented organization-wide. Though this level provided reasonable level of protection, ISO/IEC 27002 (2013) noted that for sustained information security, higher levels of security would be required. For example, Level 4 suggested that information security processes were measured and verified (e.g., auditable), while Level 5 (the highest level of maturity) ensured that standard processes were regularly reviewed and updated in response to vulnerability's impact. Ideally, organizations should improve operations security processes to Level 5 in order to sustain improved information security.

Among the operations security controls, backup was the most implemented security measures. Conversely, logging, monitoring, auditing, and reviewing were the least implemented measures of operations security management. The majority of the respondents reported that in their organizations malware protection was quantitatively controlled (Level 5). Logging and monitoring recorded the lowest maturity level of the mean of 2.93 (below Level 3). In terms of individual operations security measures, the highest security measures put in place were: (a) ensuring that external information systems services providers' compliance with security controls and (b) data backup processes were consistent with the organizations' data security requirements. In terms of organizational performance, the maturity of operations security management was higher within Financial and Healthcare institutions than all other organizations. The Government Public Services recorded the lowest maturity levels. A further analysis was conducted to determine the significant differences among the organizations. Consistently, among the hypotheses tested for significant differences, Financial and Health Care Institutions significantly differed from Educational Institutions and Government Public Service.

## FUTURE RESEARCH DIRECTIONS

This chapter is a preliminary study toward series of in-depth studies on information security management in organizations. The current study is limited to operations security management, although there are other security controls. However, the choice is because operations security is the centre of all information security activities (Henrya, 2011). Another limitation is that, even within the domain of operations security management identified in the chapter, only some of the measures (managing operational procedures, roles and responsibilities; security in third-party products and services; malware protection; data backup; and logging and monitoring activities) were used in the empirical analysis. Therefore, future works will include assessing other controls within the operations security domain, including incident management, vulnerability management, and business continuity management.

## CONCLUSION

For the need of integrating and better understanding of the domain of operations security, this chapter classified operations security into ten domains based on the analysis of existing scholarly and practitioner literature. Each domain has been presented and discussed with its sub-themes and appropriate security measures. This categorization would assist operations security personnel in their day-to-day activities of protecting the organization's information assets. Moreover, the chapter assessed the maturity of operations security controls and the inter-organizational information security levels. The evaluation provided information about how well operations security controls were applied in organizations. This could serve as a benchmark for making security investments decisions. The study further provided the basis for comparing inter-organizational security measures, the results of which might be useful for benchmarking performance. This might lead to competitiveness and general improvement in information security management. Finally, the findings of this chapter could be used by organizations as the basis for improving operations security in particular and information security in general.

## DISCUSSION QUESTIONS

1.  Why should organizations apply the following information security concepts when implementing operations security
    a.  Need-to-know
    b.  Least privilege
    c.  Separation of duties
    d.  Job rotation.
2.  Identify the threats to operations security and discuss the countermeasures.
3.  What measures should an organization take to in order improve the maturity of its operations security?
4.  Given the proposed domain of operations security management as in Figure 1, explain two major activities/tasks (under the following list) operations security personnel should perform to keep their computing environment continuously secured.
    a.  Resource protection
    b.  Access management
    c.  Malware management
    d.  System availability management
    e.  Administrative management
    f.  Configuration and change management
    g.  Business continuity management
    h.  Incident management
    i.  Vulnerability management
    j.  Records management

## REFERENCES

Agarwal, J. (2015). Improving resilience through vulnerability assessment and management. *Civil Engineering and Environmental Systems*, *32*(1/2), 5–17. doi:10.1080/10286608.2015.1025065

Alampay, E. A., & Hechanova, R. M. (2010). Monitoring employee use of the Internet in Philippine organizations. *The Electronic Journal on Information Systems in Developing Countries*, *40*(5), 1–20. doi:10.1002/j.1681-4835.2010.tb00287.x

Arshad, A., & Ameen, K. (2015). Usage patterns of Punjab University Library website: A transactional log analysis study. *The Electronic Library*, *33*(1), 65–74. doi:10.1108/EL-12-2012-0161

Asgary, A. (2016). Business continuity and disaster risk management in business education: Case of York University. *AD-Minister*, (28): 49–72. doi:10.17230/ad-minister.28.3

Avery, S., & Tracy, D. G. (2014). Using transaction log analysis to assess student search behavior in the library instruction classroom. RSR. *Reference Services Review, 42*(2), 320–335. doi:10.1108/RSR-08-2013-0044

Bachlechner, D., Thalmann, S., & Maier, R. (2014). Security and compliance challenges in complex IT outsourcing arrangements: A multi-stakeholder perspective. *Computers & Security, 40*, 38–59. doi:10.1016/j.cose.2013.11.002

Brown, W. C., & Nasuti, F. (2005). Sarbanes-Oxley and enterprise security: IT governance - what it takes to get the job done. *Information Systems Security, 14*(5), 15–28. doi:10.1201/1086.106589 8X/45654.14.5.20051101/91010.4

Bulgurcu, B., Cavusoglu, H., & Benbasat, I. (2010). Information security policy compliance: An empirical study of rationality-based beliefs and information security awareness. *Management Information Systems Quarterly, 34*(3), 523–548. doi:10.2307/25750690

Computer Security Institute. (2011). *The 2010 / 2011 CSI Computer Crime and Security Survey*. Retrieved from www.GoCSI.com

Connolly, C. (2010). A review of data logging systems, software and applications. *Sensor Review, 30*(3), 192–196. doi:10.1108/02602281011051362

Data Protection Act. (2012). *Protecting the privacy of the individual and personal data*. Retrieved from http://www.dataprotection.org.gh/data-protection-act

DBIR. (2013). *The 2013 Data Breach Investigations Report*. Retrieved from http://www.verizonenterprise.com/DBIR/

Deursen, N. V., Buchanan, W. J., & Duff, A. (2013). Monitoring information security risks within health care. *Computers & Security, 37*, 31–45. doi:10.1016/j.cose.2013.04.005

Ee, H. (2014). Business continuity 2014: From traditional to integrated business continuity management. *Journal of Business Continuity & Emergency Planning, 8*(2), 102–105. PMID:25416371

Electronic Transactions Act 772. (2008). *Ghana's Electronic Transaction Act 772*. Retrieved from www.unesco.org

Evdokimov, S., Fischmann, M., & Günther, O. (2010). Provable security for outsourcing database operations. *International Journal of Information Security and Privacy, 4*(1), 1–17. doi:10.4018/jisp.2010010101

Finat, C. (2014). Information security management incidents in research - development. *Romanian Review Precision Mechanics, Optics & Mecatronics, (45)*, 137-141.

Gasparotti, C. (2013). Importanţa managementului configuraţiei, cu Exemplificare în domeniul instalaţiilor navale. *Review of Management & Economic Engineering, 12*(4), 41–52.

Gregory, P. (2010). *CISSP Guide to Security Essentials*. Cengage Learning. Course Technology. Retrieved from https://www.cengage.com/c/cissp-guide-to-security-essentials-2e.../9781285060422

Harris, S. (2013). *All-In-One CISSP Exam Guide* (6th ed.). McGraw Hill.

HEISC. (2013). *Information Security Program Assessment Tool.* Retrieved from http://www.educause. edu/library/resources/information-security-program-assessment-tool

Hoffman, S., & Podgurski, A. (2007). Securing the HIPPA security rule. *Journal of Internet Law, 10*(8), 1–11.

ISC2 CBK. (2017). *The (ISC)2 Body of Knowledge.* Retrieved from https://www.isc2.org/Certifications/ CBK

ISO/IEC 21827:2008. (2008). *Information technology - Security techniques - Systems Security Engineering - Capability Maturity Model (SSE-CMM).* Retrieved from http://www.iso.org/iso/catalogue_detail. htm?csnumber=44716

ISO/IEC 27002:2013. (2013). *Information technology Security techniques - Code of practice for information security controls.* Retrieved from http://www.iso.org/iso/catalogue_detail?csnumber=54533 ISO/IEC

ITIL. (2010). *Benefits of standard IT governance frameworks.* Retrieved from http://www.itil-officialsite. com

Jarraya, H., & Laurent, M. (2010). A secure peer-to-peer backup service keeping great autonomy while under the supervision of a provider. *Computers & Security, 29*(2), 180–195. doi:10.1016/j.cose.2009.10.003

Jones, A., Dardick, G. S., Davies, G., Sutherland, I., & Valli, C. (2009). The 2008 analysis of information remaining on disks offered for sale on the second hand market. *Journal of International Commercial Law & Technology, 4*(3), 162–175.

Joy Online. (2013). *Cyber crime: Ghana 2nd in Africa, 7th in the world.* Retrieved from http://edition. myjoyonline.com/pages/news/201307/110530.php

Karadsheh, L. (2012). Applying security policies and service level agreement to IaaS service model to enhance security and transition. *Computers & Security, 31*(3), 315–326. doi:10.1016/j.cose.2012.01.003

Kent, K., & Souppaya, M. (2006). *NIST Special Publication 800-92: Guide to Computer Security Log Management - Recommendations of the National Institute of Standards and Technology.* Retrieved from csrc.nist.gov/publications/nistpubs/800-92/SP800-92.pdf

Kim, D. W., Yan, P., & Junjie Zhang, J. (2015). Detecting fake anti-virus software distribution webpages. *Computers & Security, 49,* 95–106. doi:10.1016/j.cose.2014.11.008

Kljun, M., Mariani, J., & Dix, A. (2016). Toward understanding short-term personal information preservation: A study of backup strategies of end users. *Journal of the Association for Information Science and Technology, 67*(12), 2947–2963. doi:10.1002/asi.23526

Kolkowska, E., & Dhillon, G. (2013). Organizational power and information security rule compliance. *Computers & Security, 33,* 3–11. doi:10.1016/j.cose.2012.07.001

Malhotra, M. K., & Grover, V. (1998). An assessment of survey research in POM: Form constructs to theory. *Journal of Operations Management, 16*(4), 407–425. doi:10.1016/S0272-6963(98)00021-7

Martin, N., & Rice, J. (2011). Cybercrime: Understanding and addressing the concerns of stakeholders. *Computers & Security, 30*(8), 803–814. doi:10.1016/j.cose.2011.07.003

Morrow, B. (2012). BYOD security challenges: *Control and protect your most sensitive data. Network Security*, *5-8*. doi:10.1016/S1353-4858(12)70111-3

Negi, M., & Pandey, D. K. (2012). High availability using virtualization. *International Transactions in Applied Sciences*, *4*(2), 195–200.

Nissim, N., Cohen, A., Glezer, C., & Elovici, Y. (2015). Detection of malicious PDF files and directions for enhancements: A state-of-the art survey. *Computers & Security*, *48*, 246–266. doi:10.1016/j.cose.2014.10.014

Nunnally, J. C. (1978). *Psychometric theory* (2nd ed.). New York, NY: McGraw-Hill.

Pabrai, U. A. (2006). Rules and regulations: The impact of compliance on IT. *Certification Magazine*, *8*(3), 38–40.

Park, M., & Lee, T. (2013). Understanding science and technology information users through transaction log analysis. *Library Hi Tech*, *31*(1), 123–140. doi:10.1108/07378831311303976

Prabhu, P. R. (2013). *ISO/IEC 27001:2013: Insight on Operations Security & Communications Security Domain*. Retrieved from https://wings2i.wordpress.com/2013/10/31/isoiec-270012013-insight-on-operations-security-communications-security-domain/

Ramalho, D. S. (2014). The use of malware as a means of obtaining evidence in Portuguese criminal proceedings. *Digital Evidence and Electronic Signature Law Review*, 11.

Report, P. W. C. (2015). *The Global State of Information Security Survey 2015*. Retrieved from http://www.pwc.com

Safa, N. S., Von Solms, R., & Furnell, S. (2016). Information security policy compliance model in organizations. *Computers & Security*, *56*, 70–82. doi:10.1016/j.cose.2015.10.006

Scanlon, M., Farina, J., & Kechadi, M. (2015). Network investigation methodology for BitTorrent Sync: A Peer-to-Peer based file synchronisation service. *Computers & Security*, *54*, 27–43. doi:10.1016/j.cose.2015.05.003

Shaqrah, A. A. (2010). The influence of internet security on e-business competence in Jordan: An Empirical Analysis. *International Journal of Technology Diffusion*, *1*(4), 13–28. doi:10.4018/jtd.2010100102

Shieh, J. (2012). From website log to findability. *The Electronic Library*, *30*(5), 707–720. doi:10.1108/02640471211275747

Software Engineering Institute. (2002). *Capability maturity model integration for software engineering*. Retrieved from ftp://192.58.107.24/pub/documents/02.reports/pdf/02tr028.pdf

Souppaya, M., & Scarfone, K. (2013). *NIST Special Publication 800-83 Revision 1 (2013). Guide to Malware Incident Prevention and Handling for Desktops and Laptops*. Retrieved from http://nvlpubs.nist.gov/nistpubs/SpecialPublications/NIST.SP.800-83r1.pdf

Stevanović, B. (2011). Maturity models in information security. *International Journal of Information and Communication Technology Research*, *1*(2), 44–47.

Tang, C., & Liu, J. (2015). Selecting a trusted cloud service provider for your SaaS program. *Computers & Security*, *50*, 60–73. doi:10.1016/j.cose.2015.02.001

Thielens, J. (2013). Why API are central to a BYOD security strategy. *Network Security*, 5-6. doi:10.1016/S1353-4858(13)70091-6

United States Patent and Trademark Office (USPTO). (2009). *Network and AIS audit, logging, and monitoring policy.* Retrieved from www.uspto.gov/about/vendor_info/current_acquisitions/sdi_ng/ocio_6011_09.pdf

US GAO. (2012). *Information Security: Better implementation of controls for mobile devices should be encouraged.* Retrieved from http://www.gao.gov/products/GAO-12-757

Vance, A., Lowry, P. B., & Eggett, D. (2013). Using accountability to reduce access policy violations in information systems. *Journal of Management Information Systems*, *29*(4), 263–289. doi:10.2753/MIS0742-1222290410

Willison, R., & Warkentin, M. (2013). Beyond deterrence: An expanded view of employee computer abuse. *Management Information Systems Quarterly*, *37*(1), 1–20. doi:10.25300/MISQ/2013/37.1.01

Wu, M., & Yu, M. (2013). Enterprise information security management based on context-aware RBAC and communication monitoring technology. *Mathematical Problems in Engineering*, *2013*, 1–11. doi:10.1155/2013/569562

Zolait, A. H., Ibrahim, A. R., & Farooq, A. (2010). A study on the Internet security and its implication for e-commerce in Yemen. *International Journal of Technology Diffusion*, *1*(3), 34–47. doi:10.4018/jtd.2010070102

## KEY TERMS AND DEFINITIONS

**Access Management:** Activities organizations carry out to control users' access to computer systems, networks, and facilities (buildings, rooms, workspaces). It also includes the tasks users are permitted to perform when access is granted.

**Backup:** The process of making a copy of important information from a computer system to another device for recovery or archival purposes.

**Business Continuity Management:** When an unexpected event occurs, organizations must recover and restore work to normal operations. This involves measures that are taken to reduce or prevent the effect of a disaster.

**Change Management:** The processes involved when changes to computing environment are formally planned and reviewed before the changes are implemented.

**Configuration Management:** Activities to monitor and set up the configuration of computer systems and software applications so that they can perform the needed functionality.

**Malware Management:** The use of software (known as antimalware) to block, detect, and clean malicious and unwanted software on a computer system.

**Operation Security:** The day-to-day activities that ensure that computer systems, networks, applications, and the entire computing environment are secured and protected.

**Resource Protection:** Security measures and processes that are put in place to protect information assets and resources, including facilities, hardware, software, networks, documentation, and records.

**Vulnerability Management:** The process of identifying weaknesses in systems and putting in place measures to mitigate the threats that may exploit the weaknesses.

*Previously published in the Handbook of Research on Technology Integration in the Global World; pages 304-330, copyright year 2019 by Information Science Reference (an imprint of IGI Global).*

# Chapter 26
# Challenges in Securing Industrial Control Systems Using Future Internet Technologies

**Mirjana D. Stojanović**

🆔 https://orcid.org/0000-0003-1073-5804

*Faculty of Transport and Traffic Engineering, University of Belgrade, Serbia*

**Slavica V. Boštjančič Rakas**

🆔 https://orcid.org/0000-0002-0551-3070

*Mihailo Pupin Institute, University of Belgrade, Serbia*

## ABSTRACT

*This chapter explores challenges in securing industrial control systems (ICS) and Supervisory Control And Data Acquisition (SCADA) systems using Future Internet technologies. These technologies include cloud computing, fog computing, Industrial internet of things (IIoT), etc. The need to design specific security solutions for ICS/SCADA networks is explained. A brief overview of cyber vulnerabilities and threats in industrial control networks, cloud, and IoT environments is presented. The security of cloud-based SCADA systems is considered, including benefits and risks of SCADA migration to the cloud, challenges in securing such systems, and migration toward fog computing. Challenges in securing IIoT are addressed, including security risks and operational issues, key principles for securing IIoT, the functional security architecture, and the role of fog computing. Authors point out current standardization activities and trends in the area, and emphasize conclusions and future research directions.*

DOI: 10.4018/978-1-6684-3698-1.ch026

## INTRODUCTION

Over the past thirty years information and communication technologies (ICT) have been introduced in the Industrial Control Systems (ICSs) and particularly Supervisory Control and Data Acquisition (SCADA) networks. This implied adoption of open communication standards like Ethernet, Transmission Control Protocol/Internet Protocol (TCP/IP) suite and a variety of wireless standards. Consequently, the problem of increased susceptibility to different forms of cyber security threats appeared, which was verified by a number of successful attacks on worldwide ICS/SCADA systems (Stouffer, Pillitteri, Lightman, Abrams, & Hahn, 2015; Ogie, 2017; Schwab & Poujol, 2018). The need for specific security solutions, tailored to the requirements of industrial control networks, has been recognized as a critical issue from the very beginning.

Nowadays, we are facing with proliferation of the Future Internet technologies, including cloud computing, fog computing, Internet of Things (IoT), mobile computing, big data processing and analytics. The IoT concept is rapidly evolving in different directions. Thus, the Industrial Internet of Things (IIoT) encompasses interconnected sensors, actuators, and other devices networked together with computers' industrial applications, and it represents an essential building block of the Industry 4.0 model (H. Xu, Yu, Griffith, & Golmie, 2018). Energy Internet, also known as the Internet of Energy (IoE) represents a wide area network (WAN), which integrates different types of energy resources, storage and loads, and enables peer-to-peer energy delivery on a large scale (Cao et al., 2018; Bostjancic Rakas, 2020). Heterogeneous IoT (HetIoT) extends the IoT concept to support a variety of heterogeneous wireless technologies and many different applications in daily life and industry (Qiu, Chen, Li, Atiquzzaman, & Zhao, 2018).

Although these technologies bring substantial benefits for the industry regarding information and economic efficiency, cyber security remains a crucial risk factor, which is even more distinct than when using traditional Internet technologies.

Apart from industry efforts (Howard, 2015; Nugent, 2017; Byers, 2018; Aleksandrova, 2019), only a few academic research papers systematically surveyed security issues in ICS/SCADA systems using Future Internet environments (Sadeghi, Wachsmann, & Waidner, 2015; Sajid, Abbas, & Saleem, 2016; Stojanovic, Bostjancic Rakas, & Markovic-Petrovic, 2019).

There are many open issues regarding cyber security of industrial control systems in the Future Internet environments, from the system's level (network security architectures, risk management, security policy implementation), through specific solutions (intrusion detection and prevention systems, encryption, authentication mechanisms), development of dedicated test environments, to definition of security policies that are applied during operational lifecycle. The main objective of this chapter is to emphasize challenges in securing ICS/SCADA systems in such new environments, particularly cloud computing, fog computing and/or IIoT.

The rest of the chapter is structured as follows. The background section explains the reasons for designing specific security solutions for ICS/SCADA networks and presents a brief overview of cyber vulnerabilities and threats in industrial control networks, cloud and IoT environments. In the following section, security of cloud-based SCADA systems is considered, including benefits and risks of SCADA migration to the cloud environment, challenges in securing such systems and migration toward fog computing environment. Further, challenges in securing IIoT are analyzed, including a brief comparison of IoT and IIoT requirements, security risks and operational issues, key principles for securing IIoT, the functional IIoT security architecture and the role of fog computing. The next section addresses standardization efforts in the area. The chapter ends with emphasizing the future research directions and concluding remarks.

## BACKGROUND

Although the incorporation of the Internet technologies in industrial networking has reduced the boundary between ICS/SCADA and enterprise networks, they still have basically different requirements, which naturally cause differences in network design as well as security objectives and solutions (Galloway & Hancke, 2013; Markovic-Petrovic, Stojanovic, & Bostjancic Rakas, 2019). Namely, for general-purpose infrastructures, primary focus is the balanced protection of the confidentiality, integrity and availability of data (the so-called CIA triad), which gives the highest priority to data confidentiality. The infrastructure of industrial control systems assumes the same triad, but with the reversed order of priorities (AIC), which means that the most important item is availability. This difference is essential in terms of defining security policies and selecting security mechanisms, with the key objective to preserve availability of all systems that constitute critical infrastructure 24 hours, 7 days a week (24/7 service). The ultimate goal is to achieve required performance of a real-time system, operating on the 24/7 basis under conditions in which regular behavior coexists with system failures, environmental conditions, human errors, and cyber attacks.

ICS/SCADA networks are characterized by regular traffic patterns and a limited set of telecommunication protocols (Galloway & Hancke, 2013; Mantere, Sailio, & Noponen, 2013). The most important features that affect design of specific security solutions are discussed below.

**Traffic Properties:** ICS/SCADA network traffic is characterized by throughput stability, periodic patterns, clear statistics of packet size, predictable flow direction, and expected connection lifetime. Significant increase of throughput may point to some forms of cyber attacks, failures, or operating errors. Periodic traffic prevails in control networks due to transmission of data samples in regular intervals. Aperiodic events may occur due to change of state or alarm conditions, but may also indicate some forms of attacks. Most of the systems at the fieldbus level send packets without buffering due to severe delay requirements. A clear packet size statistics is created, and the average packet size represents a good indicator of regular behavior or anomaly. Flow direction indicates which system initiates the connection. After connection establishment, data amount sent from one system to another is predictable with large probability.

**Delay Requirements:** Packet transfer delay and packet inter-arrival times from all network nodes are meaningful data for anomaly detection in ICS/SCADA networks. This is a consequence of real-time operating requirements. Response time should typically be less than the sample time of collected data. The most stringent requirements are at the fieldbus and controller network levels. Response time requirements are usually in the range of 250 microseconds to 1 millisecond whereas less stringent processes require response times in the range of 1 to 10 milliseconds. Application layer poses lower delay requirements, typically up to 1 second.

**Updates and Order of Events:** Updates should be performed on a regular basis, because the data is only valid in its assigned time period. The order of updating is important for sensor data concerning monitoring of the same process or correlated processes. The order of data arrival to the control center plays an important role in presentation of process dynamics and influences decision making.

**Protocols:** Each industrial control network implements a precisely defined set of protocols. The appearance of new protocols indicates serious changes in the network. Protocols are typically configured statically, in a way that guarantees the best network performance. Among a range of standard and vendor-specific communication protocols the most widespread are Modbus, Distributed Network Protocol (DNP3), International Electrotechnical Commission (IEC) 60870-5 series, IEC 60870-6 series and IEC 61850 series. The majority of protocols are created or extended to operate over TCP/IP networks. In addition, most of the current fieldbus protocols are Ethernet-based. A comprehensive survey and taxonomy of ICS/SCADA protocols can be found in the literature (Gao et al., 2014; Galloway & Hancke, 2013).

## Cyber Vulnerabilities and Threats in Industrial Control Networks

Cyber vulnerabilities in industrial control networks can be exploited from outside sources, such as terrorists, hackers, competitors, or industrial espionage, or from inside attacks, frequently caused by dissatisfied employees, third-party vendors, or site engineers (Yang et al., 2014). Human errors, negligence equipment failures and natural disasters may also affect ICS/SCADA vulnerabilities.

One of the most common sources of vulnerabilities refers to *resource limitations*. Physical devices are simple and designed to efficiently perform limited operations. For that reason, they often do not have memory and processing resources to carry out security functions. Real-time control systems typically suffer from poor authorization and authentication mechanisms, and they neither record login attempts nor make distinction between human users (Goldenberg & Wool, 2013).

*Legacy systems* represent another source of vulnerabilities. For example, former SCADA systems were isolated from public networks; for that reason only physical security was a concern rather than cyber security.

Attacks on ICS/SCADA systems can be classified in several ways. Moris and W Gao (2013) identify four classes of ICS attacks, namely reconnaissance, response and measurement injection, command injection and denial of service (DoS). *Reconnaissance attacks* aim to discover information about a network and to identify the equipment characteristics. *Response and measurement injection* refer to attacks where packets which contain sensor reading values are being captured, modified and forwarded. Similarly, *command injection attacks* insert false control and configuration commands into a control system. *Denial of Service* (DoS) attacks attempt to stop the proper functioning of some portion of the ICS or to disable the entire system. These attacks may target the cyber system or the physical system.

Maglaras et al. (2019) also distinguish four categories of ICS cyber attacks: key-based attacks, data-based attacks, impersonation-based attacks and physical-based attacks. *Key-based attacks* denote grabbing secret keys that are used by consumers and suppliers for registration and authentication. *Data-based attacks* refer to unauthorized change of data, and include a number of attacks such as modification attack, data integrity attack, repudiation attack, etc. *Impersonation-based attacks* try to impersonate a trusted individual or company in an attempt to gain access to sensitive data. Examples of such attacks are man-in-the-middle (MITM) attack, eavesdropping attack, replay attack and redirection attack. *Physical-based attacks* manipulate the physical properties of devices to cause sensors and embedded devices to malfunction. Examples of such attacks are differential attack, malware attack, collusion attack, and inference attack.

Ghosh and Sampalli (2019) emphasize the fact that attacks can occur at all layers of SCADA network, from the supervisory level to the field instrumentation level. They classify cyber attacks on SCADA systems into *attacks on hardware*, *attacks on software*, and *attacks on network connections*, and present a comprehensive review of the most widespread attacks on SCADA networks.

## Cyber Vulnerabilities and Threats in Cloud Environment

Besides cyber security threats that are present in the traditional computing platforms and networks, cloud computing copes with a number of additional vulnerabilities (Hari Krishna, Kiran, Murali, & Pradeep Kumar Reddy, 2016). They include:

- Attacks by other customers.
- Shared technology issues.
- Malfunctions of provider's or customer's security systems.
- Flawed integration of provider's and customer's security systems.
- Insecure application programming interfaces.
- Data loss or leakage.
- Insider attacks.
- Account or service hijacking.
- Legal and regulatory issues.

Besides, vulnerabilities depend on the type of cloud service. For example, Infrastructure as a Service (IaaS) is susceptible to most of the threats that are well known from the traditional information and communication systems (Chavan, Patil, Kulkarni, Sutar, & Belsare, 2013). Besides, customers are responsible for securing their applications, because all of them are running on the virtual machines, which act like "black boxes" for the provider. Platform as a Service (PaaS) is particularly susceptible to shared technology issues, because of different security settings for various kinds of resources and potential data leakage (Sandikkaya & Harmanci, 2012). On the other side, Software as a Service (SaaS) typically requires only a web browser and the Internet connection. Similarly to web service, it is predominantly susceptible to data security and confidentiality (Soufiane & Halima, 2017). The other common issues refer to data backup, data access, storage locations, availability, authentication, etc.

## Cyber Vulnerabilities and Threats in IoT Environment

The general architecture of IoT can be structured into three layers, namely the perception layer, network layer and application layer. Each of these layers is susceptible to different forms of cyber attacks (Kamble & Bhutad, 2018).

Perception layer is responsible for perceiving the physical properties of things and relies on several sensing technologies such as wireless sensor networks (WSNs), radio frequency identification (RFID), near field communication (NFC), etc. This layer is susceptible to cyber threats such as unauthorized access to tags, node capture attacks, tag cloning and false data injection attacks.

Network layer processes the data received from the perception layer and forwards processed data to the application layer through various wireless and wired network technologies. The most common cyber security threats encompass spoofing attack, sinkhole attack, sleep deprivation attack, different forms of DoS attacks and insecure protocols.

Application layer uses the data obtained from the underlying layer and provides the required tools for developers to implement a variety of IoT applications. It mainly relies on cloud computing and big data analytics; hence, it is susceptible to all threats that are typical for the cloud computing environment.

## SECURITY OF CLOUD-BASED SCADA SYSTEMS

There are two main ways to support SCADA applications in cloud computing environment, as indicated in Figure 1 (Stojanovic et al., 2019).

The first way assumes that SCADA application is executed on company's premises. Control functions of SCADA application are isolated in the controller network, while SCADA application is connected to public cloud services that allow visualization of processes, reports and remote access at corresponding work stations (Human Machine Interface, HMI).

The second way, which is suitable for distributed applications, assumes that SCADA application is executed in the cloud, and is remotely connected (using WAN links) to the control center. Such applications are typically implemented on private and hybrid cloud infrastructures.

*Figure 1. Support of SCADA applications in cloud computing environment*

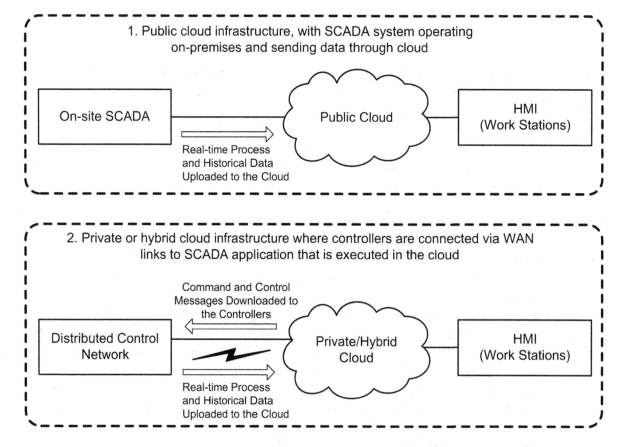

Re-hosting, refactoring and revising are the three migration scenarios of SCADA system to the cloud, with respect to service selection (Church et al., 2017). Re-hosting is the fastest and the simplest scenario, which assumes installing the existing SCADA applications in the cloud, based on IaaS. Refactoring and revising assume re-engineering to take benefit of cloud computing capabilities, primarily scalability and reliability. Refactoring refers to simple modification of particular features. For example, implementation of resource control allows adding resources when the application is intensively used and releasing resources when they are not needed. Revising assumes larger modifications at the application core. For example, PaaS database can be used for modification of application to provide multiple contracts for the offered SaaS. This requires replacement of the existing SCADA applications with cloud-based SaaS solutions.

## Benefits and Risks

When discussing benefits and risks of cloud-based SCADA systems, a distinction should be made between public and private cloud infrastructures.

With public cloud, benefits mainly refer to improving economic efficiency. On-demand access and lease of resources allows for savings in purchasing, installing and maintaining ICT equipment, as well as technical staff, needed for ICT resource maintaining. Other benefits include:

- Enhanced scalability, because users can simply purchase additional resources on a virtual cloud server, with no need of installing and maintaining the additional hardware.
- Ubiquitous access to information located on a cloud server, which makes the collaboration on projects more efficient.
- Simplified upgrade of the existing applications and deployment of new ones through re-hosting, refactoring and revising.

The use of public cloud services increases risks regarding quality of service (QoS) and cyber security. The user cannot control the network performance; even servers' locations are unknown to their users. Hence, there is a risk that QoS requirements will not be met. Probably the most challenging issue is increased and/or unpredictable delay, since it can obstruct the real-time SCADA operation and cause serious consequences to the industrial process. Besides, the problems of availability and reliability exist in every system in the public cloud.

SCADA systems using public cloud services suffer from the same cyber security risks as the other systems integrated into cloud. Still, there are a number of threats in the public cloud environment that might make SCADA systems more vulnerable:

- Due to sharing an infrastructure with unknown outside parties, such systems are more exposed to cyber threats such as command/response injection, DoS and distributed DoS (DDoS) attacks, as well as MITM attacks.
- Insecure network connections between SCADA systems and the cloud increase the risk of jeopardizing the whole industrial process by outside attackers.
- Some of widespread SCADA-specific application layer protocols lack protection, particularly in terms of authentication and encryption mechanisms.
- The use of commercial off-the-shelf solutions potentially increases the cyber security risk.

The situation is different with private cloud infrastructure, which may bring technical benefits in addition to cost reduction and improving the overall economic efficiency. Experimental results from a study on private cloud-based electric power SCADA system indicated technical feasibility of the professional private cloud solution (Chen, Chen, & Gan, 2015). Such a system meets the requirements of power grid operations, while some QoS parameters such as network load rate are even better than those of the traditional, non-cloud solution. Similarly, it is easier to secure private cloud, by applying proper security architecture, which is completely managed by the cloud owner.

## Challenges in Securing Cloud-Based SCADA Systems

According to Stojanovic et al. (2019), security solutions concerning public cloud infrastructure should address the challenges related to:

- Information input/output.
- Shared storage and computational resources.
- Shared physical infrastructure.

**Information Input/Output:** The main requirement is to avoid exposing the critical control infrastructure to the Internet. When using public cloud services, push technology should be exploited to move data to the cloud rather than pull technology. Push technology (also known as server push) is a method of Internet-based communication where the sender or central server initiates transaction request. In contrast, pull/get technology assumes that the transaction request is initiated by the receiver or client. With push technology, there are no open network ports on the control infrastructure, and SCADA applications stay isolated in the controller network.

**Shared Storage and Computational Resources:** SCADA owner cooperating with a cloud service provider (CSP) should be informed how the computational resources are managed for different cloud-based applications, including QoS guarantees, guarantees for network access, fault-tolerance strategy, etc.

**Shared Physical Infrastructure:** There is a need to secure cloud infrastructure locations, as well as communication links that connect the cloud infrastructure to the rest of the communications infrastructure. Besides, SCADA owner should be able to inspect and audit the locations from which SCADA application will be served.

When selecting the CSP and assessing maturity of the offered cloud service, a number of criteria should be taken into account, including service identification and specification, technical characteristics, business conditions, etc. It should be noted that the leading cloud service providers are working toward the "Industry cloud", i.e., cloud solutions that will meet the needs of industrial systems in terms of QoS and security requirements.

The most efficient way to protect SCADA system connected to the public cloud is to establish precise service level agreement (SLA) that fulfills the required criteria. Different approaches are possible to establish end-to-end SLA-based communication services (Bostjancic Rakas & Stojanovic, 2019). A possible SLA structure, derived from generic templates presented in works of Stojanovic et al. (2010) and Stojanovic et al. (2013), is illustrated in Figure 2. The SLA encompasses the following parts: service identification, service specification, business part, technical part and reporting.

*Figure 2. A possible structure of the SLA between SCADA owner and CSP*

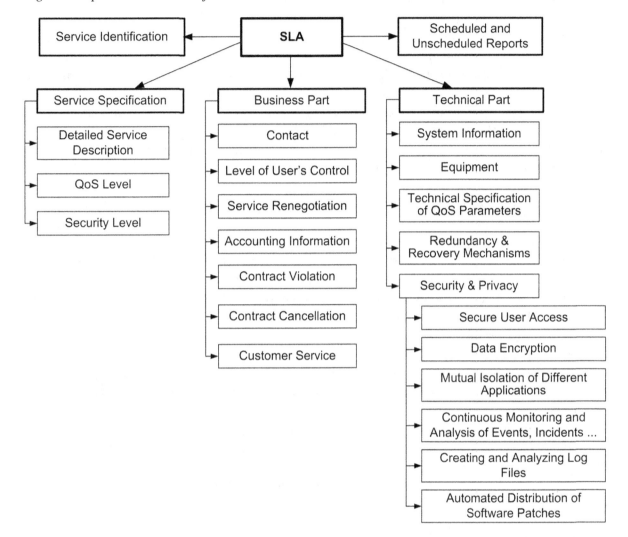

Service identification refers to the service package offered by the CSP.

Service specification encompasses detailed service description, QoS level and security level.

Business part includes contact information, the level of user's control regarding changes of the CSP infrastructure, service renegotiation capabilities, accounting information (pricing, charging and billing), consequences for both the user and the CSP in the case of contract violation, contract cancellation conditions, and customer service. Taking into account real-time operation of SCADA utility, consistent and reliable customer service should assure readiness to take immediate corrective actions of all vulnerabilities identified.

Technical part includes all relevant technical characteristics of the service such as system information, equipment specification, QoS parameters, redundancy and recovery mechanisms, as well as security and privacy. Security and privacy may refer to: secure user access; data encryption; mutual isolation of information originating from different applications; continuous real-time monitoring and analysis of events, incidents, suspicious activities and anomalies; capabilities to create and analyze log files;

means to detect intrusions in real-time; ability to generate responses to detected attacks; and automated distribution of software patches.

Reporting part assumes provisioning scheduled and unscheduled reports that satisfy business needs.

Securing the private cloud infrastructure is much simpler, since all solutions are responsibility of the network owner. Defense-in-depth strategy is recommended, i.e., "Layering security mechanisms such that the impact of a failure in any one mechanism is minimized" (Stouffer et al., 2015, p. 3). This strategy includes appropriate security policies, employing demilitarized zone (DMZ) network architecture to prevent direct traffic between the corporate and SCADA networks, as well as security mechanisms such as smart access control, firewalls, intrusion detection and prevention systems, antivirus software, deploying security patches on a regular basis, etc.

## Migration to Fog Computing Environment

Principally, fog computing extends cloud computing and services to the edge of network. Therefore, end users, fog and cloud together constitute a three layer system architecture (Mouradian et al., 2018).

Stojanovic et al. (2019) propose a fog-based architecture that includes ICS/SCADA components. Hence, the end users layer includes field devices, smart energy meters, line sensors, and may also include IIoT devices. This layer is connected with the fog layer by means of wired or wireless local area networks (LANs). The fog layer consists of one or more fog domains, each comprised of fog nodes, i.e., industrial controllers, switches, routers, embedded servers, etc. Fog nodes provide integration with the cloud layer, routing and switching, data storage and sharing, real-time analytics, outage management, controller functions, wireless access, etc. The fog layer and the cloud layer communicate via WAN connections.

Tom and Sankaranarayanan (2017) propose an IoT-based SCADA integrated with fog for power distribution automation system. Fog computing is used to perform real-time streaming analysis, in order to control consumer utilization, manage outages, control power quality and to maintain pole transformers. At the same time, low bandwidth utilization and delay are preserved when taking immediate control actions.

In terms of ICS/SCADA requirements, fog computing introduces the following benefits in comparison to cloud computing (Byers, 2018; Stojanovic et al., 2019):

- Distributed network architecture.
- LAN-based communication with ICS/SCADA components.
- Large number of server nodes.
- Low delay.
- Low bandwidth cost.
- Mobility and location awareness.
- High security.

With fog computing, security operates locally, using the same corporate ICT policy, controls, and procedures as in traditional ICS/SCADA system. Such a concept inherently improves cyber security in comparison to cloud computing environment. Yet, fog computing includes the virtualization and can still be affected by the similar threats like cloud. This implies that security solutions for fog-based and cloud-based SCADA systems are basically similar. The emphasis is on the techniques such as authentication, access control in fog nodes, intrusion detection and protecting privacy (Khan, Parkinson, & Qin, 2017).

## CHALLENGES IN SECURING INDUSTRIAL IoT SYSTEMS

The starting point for securing IIoT is a comparison with the IoT technology, because IoT and IIoT are two parallel technologies with the same standard protocols, interfaces and intelligence. However, they have different operational processes, principles, users, and goals. The main novelties that IIoT introduces in comparison to IoT are as follows:

- IIoT aims to achieve maximum efficiency and seamless workflow in any industrial process, while IoT focuses on optimizing consumption, personal comfort, and control of expenses.
- IIoT is mainly focused on monitoring production and business environmental parameters, while IoT is used to automate everyday household processes.
- IIoT architecture is designed to meet requirements of hard real-time industrial applications, with very high reliability and availability. Besides, IIoT equipment must be able to cope with extreme environmental conditions such as high variations of temperature, volume pressure, harmonic motions, at distant locations.
- Multidimensional interoperability assumes open standards which allow creating a cooperative environment with various protocols, data sets, enterprise resource planning (ERP) systems, and integration with the existing legacy operational technologies.
- High scalability assumes a widespread IIoT network of controllers, robots, and other equipment, thousands of new sensors and putting in place non-IoT devices.

### Cyber Security Threats and Risks

IIoT needs robust security and privacy mechanisms, such as encrypted and agile system architectures, specialized chipsets, authentication and real-time intrusion detection. The following threats are particularly relevant in view of IIoT: insecure web, mobile and cloud interfaces, privacy concerns, poor physical security, insecure software/firmware, insufficient authentication and authorization, insecure network connections, lack of encryption at the transport layer, etc.

Sajid et al. (2016) identify specific threats to the SCADA systems in IoT-cloud environments as follows: advanced persistent threats, lack of data integrity, MITM attacks such as spoofing and sniffing, replay attacks and various forms of DoS attacks. Cyber attacks on the IIoT system may cause not only performance deterioration and uncertainty, but also safety issues for persons, the environment, and the equipment, as well. In addition, the data collected during industrial manufacturing and production is often highly confidential, which makes IIoT systems attractive targets for attackers.

Similarly to IoT, the concept of IIoT assumes a layered hierarchy together with related security risks at each layer:

- Local area networks collect and locally process data from connected objects at the lowest layer. The main security risks refer to lack of authentication and security in sensors equipment.
- Data is transmitted to the cloud via gateways. The main security risks include lack of security in protocols and gateways.
- Data is stored and processed in the cloud. Appropriate platforms are used as well as specific algorithms such as big data analytics. The main risk factor is lack of data security.

- Interfacing between platforms and end users for monitoring may cause security risks due to lack of secure communication protocols.

The consequences of successful attack reflect in a number of operational issues such as: equipment damage, unforeseen operational concerns, endangered personal safety and regulatory issues. Security risks and operational issues in IIoT are summarized in Figure 3.

*Figure 3. Security risks and operational issues in IIoT*

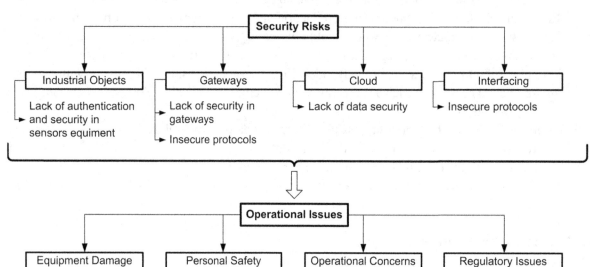

## Key Principles of IIoT Security

Key principles for securing IIoT rely on currently available good practices and the existing security standards. Following is a brief description of those principles.

*Securing All IIoT System's Parts before Integration:* Since IIoT applications are usually built with the existing ICS devices, they inherit security flaws or even the lack of security of such devices. Many of interconnected devices still use customized protocols or gateways (developed without sufficient security care) instead of universal protocols such as Open Platform Communications Unified Architecture (OPC UA). The OPC UA security architecture includes concepts such as trusted information (AIC triad) and access control (Foundation, O.P.C., 2018).

*Network Segregation:* This method has been a best practice in networking for a long time. It assumes dividing large networks into several separate logical networks, as well as developing and enforcing policies for controlling the communications between specific hosts and servers. Security tools that surround each network efficiently isolate and monitor network activities, thus preventing policy violations. An example of IIoT network segregation is implementation model based on layered databuses (Industrial Internet Consortium [IIC], 2019), as illustrated in Figure 4. Databus is a logically connected space, which implements a common set of templates (data models, protocols, security) for communication between endpoints. At the lowest layer, smart machines use databus for local control, automation and real-time analytics. Second layer encompasses systems, which use another databus for supervisory control and monitoring. Merging such systems into a "system of systems", at the third layer, enables complex and scalable applications for control, monitoring and analysis. The highest layer of this model, industrial Internet, is based on cloud computing.

*Figure 4. An example of IIoT network segregation by layered databuses (adapted from IIC, 2019)*

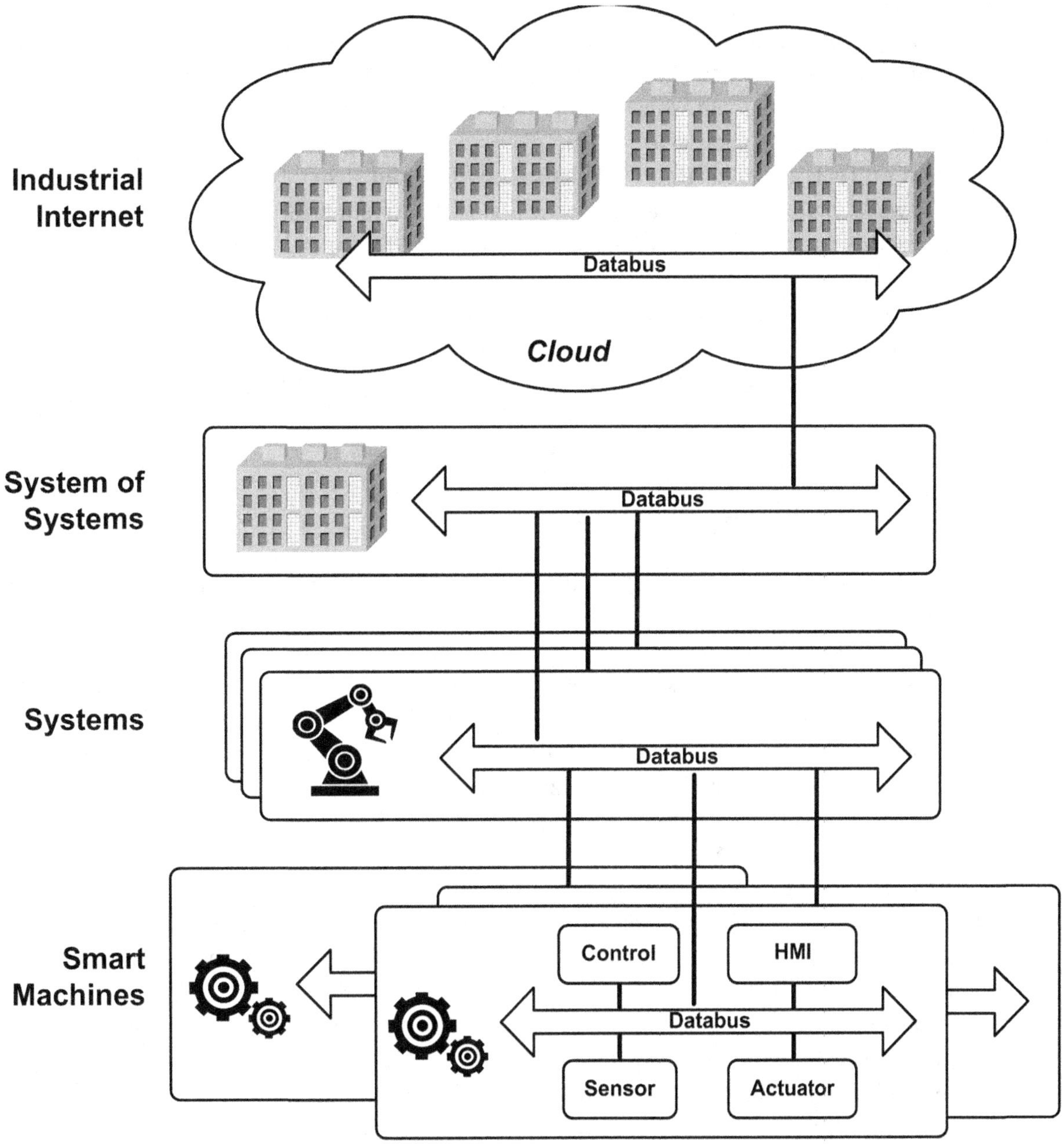

**Continuous Monitoring and Analysis:** This process assumes permanent monitoring and analysis of the network activities, in order to detect and identify anomalies and suspicious activities (Sajid et al., 2016). Analysis of log records plays an important role in troubleshooting, anomaly detection, network forensics, etc. Memory dump analysis enables detection of known and unknown malicious activities that are present within the memory of an operating system. Network traffic analysis is performed in order to detect network traffic anomalies, including malicious activities. It may encompass behavioral analysis (e.g., protocol procedures, traffic intensity, etc.) and/or traffic pattern analysis, which can be performed on per-packet basis or per-flow basis.

**Attribution of Cyber Attacks:** Disclosure of the attacker's identity and/or location directly concerns regulatory issues, particularly when attacks are launched from another country, because it poses questions concerning the authority to investigate and prosecute the cyber crime (Cook, Nicholson, Janicke, Maglaras, & Smith, 2016; Maglaras et al., 2019).

**Application of Tools for Detecting Malicious Activities and Proxy Solutions**: Detecting tools encompass firewalls, intrusion detection and prevention systems, antivirus software, etc. Proxy solutions, such as packet filtering and access control, are used to build a protection layer around vulnerable or legacy components.

**System's Maintenance:** The quality of system design predominantly influences its security level. Vulnerability tests are useful in detecting, e.g., unknown errors in cloud systems. They should be performed in regular intervals, because new threats are being revealed through analysis over time. Besides, distribution of software updates and patches on a regular basis is mandatory, particularly for the third-party software, which is typically used by IoT-cloud SCADA systems.

## Functional IIoT Security Architecture

The functional architecture of IIoT security is illustrated in Figure 5 (IIC, 2016). It encompasses the following building blocks:

- **Endpoint Protection:** This block implements security on edge and cloud devices. Its main functions encompass physical and cyber security, as well as an authoritative identity.
- **Communications and Connectivity Protection:** This block uses the endpoint authoritative identity to implement authentication and authorization mechanisms, by means of strong cryptographic techniques and the information flow control techniques.
- **Security Monitoring and Analysis:** This block is responsible for keeping the system secure by permanent monitoring and analyzing its state.
- **Security Configuration and Management:** New vulnerabilities and threats call for updates of policies, firmware and software; therefore, the security features of an IIoT system must be configurable and manageable.
- **Data Protection:** The common data protection function supports previously described building blocks, by protecting all types of data, i.e., inactive data at the endpoints (data-at-rest), data that is processed and transmitted at communication layer (data-in-motion), data collected in monitoring and analysis, as well as the system configuration and management data.
- **Security Model and Policy:** Security model coordinates the work of all functional elements and determines the way of implementation of security and the associated policies.

*Figure 5. The functional IIoT security architecture: building blocks (adapted from IIC, 2016)*

Security Configuration and Management
Security Monitoring and Analysis
Communications and Connectivity Protection
Endpoint Protection
Data Protection
Security Model and Policy

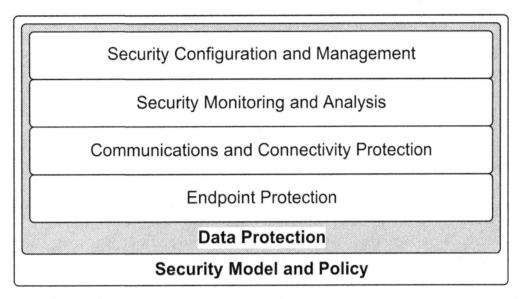

Figure 6 presents a detailed functional structure of endpoint protection block, as well as communications and connectivity protection block.

*Figure 6. Functional structure of endpoint protection and communications & connectivity protection*

Endpoint
Communications and Connectivity
Security Model and Policy
Data Protection (Data-at-Rest)
- Physical Security
- Root of Trust
- Identity
- Integrity Protection
- Access Control
- Monitoring and Analysis
- Configuration and Management
- Physical Security of Connections
- Communicating Endpoints Protection
- Cryptographic Protection
- Information Flow Protection
- Network Monitoring and Analysis
- Network Configuration and Management
Data Protection (Data-in-Motion)
Security Model and Policy

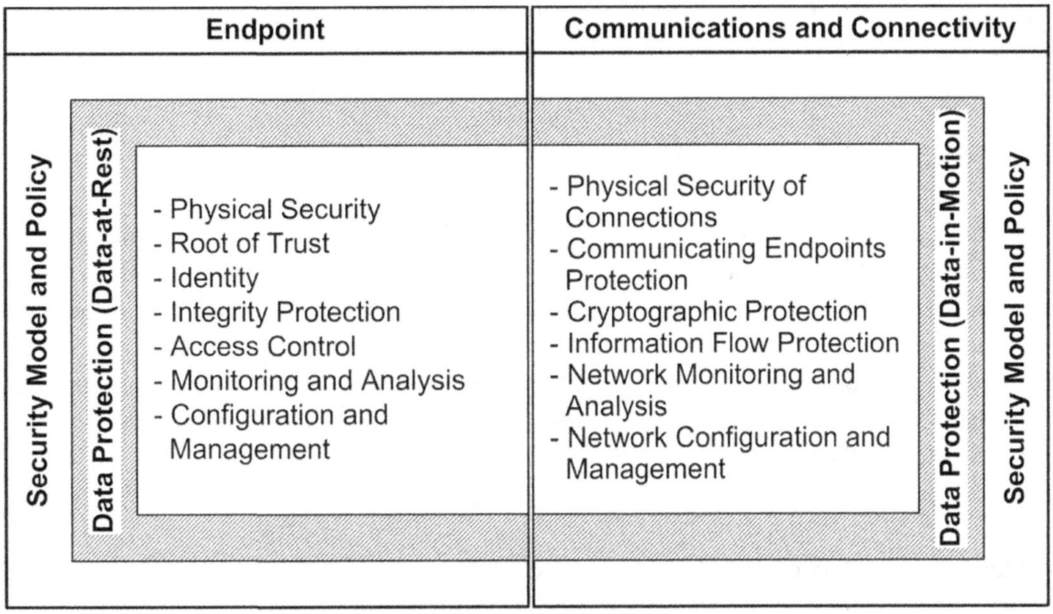

Apart from physical security, the endpoint protection includes definition of the root of trust, definition of the unified endpoint identity, integrity protection, access control, monitoring and analysis, as well as endpoint configuration and management.

Communications and connectivity protection includes physical security of connections, protection of communicating endpoints, cryptographic protection, information flow protection, network monitoring and analysis (intrusion detection, network access control, protocol analysis, log analysis), as well as network configuration and management (network segregation, cryptographic protection of communication parameters, configuration of gateways and firewalls).

## The Role of Fog Computing in Securing IIoT

Middleware support is needed between the industrial environment and cloud services, because most of industrial processes have stringent delay and security requirements. Fog can be observed as a prospective middleware for different industrial scenarios such as mining, smart grid and power industry, transportation, waste management, food industry, agriculture, etc. (Aazam, Zeadally, & Harras, 2018).

The benefits of fog computing for IIoT encompass delay reduction, agile response (in terms of data analysis and decision making), cost effectiveness and the increased security (Butun, Sari, & Österberg, 2019). Securing fog nodes, which act as gateways between IIoT network and the cloud, should encompass access control, authentication, AIC triad and protection of privacy.

Zhou et al. (2019) have shown that fog computing can provide efficient DDoS mitigation in the IIoT network. They propose a distributed attack mitigation scheme that assumes traffic analysis at multiple dispersed locations and assigns the appropriate virtualized network computation functions. The scheme has a three-level architecture (field, fog and cloud levels), where each level performs the functions corresponding to its processing capabilities. Performance evaluation has demonstrated advantages of such a method in terms of detection accuracy and timeliness.

## STANDARDIZATION EFFORTS

The importance of critical infrastructure protection resulted in intensive efforts of national and international standardization bodies to adopt standards, recommendations, directives and guidelines concerning security of industrial control systems. The objective of this section is to point to current standardization activities and trends regarding application of the Future Internet technologies in ICS/SCADA networks, rather than to provide a comprehensive review of standards. Surveys of current security standards and recommendations for ICS/SCADA systems can be found in the literature (Gao et al., 2014; Zhou, Xu, Wang, & Chen, 2017; Ghosh & Sampalli, 2019).

Relevant documents can be broadly classified into three groups:

1. General standards concerning cyber security of ICT systems.
2. Common standards and guidelines for ICS/SCADA protection.
3. Specific directives concerning ICS/SCADA in particular industrial sectors.

Table 1 summarizes the most representative standards and other documents with respect to the indicated classification.

*Table 1. Representative standards and other documents concerning ICS/SCADA cyber security*

| Type of Standard | | Publisher & Document ID | Title | Year |
|---|---|---|---|---|
| General-purpose standard concerning cyber security | | • ISO/IEC 27001 | Information security management systems - Requirements | 2013 |
| | | • ISO/IEC 27002 | Code of practice for information security controls | 2013 |
| | | • ISO/IEC 270017 <br> • ITU-T X.1631 | Code of practice for information security controls based on ISO/IEC 27002 for cloud services | 2015 |
| | | • ITU-T X.1361 | Security framework for the Internet of things based on the gateway model | 2018 |
| | | • ITU-T X.1362 | Simple encryption procedure for Internet of things (IoT) environments | 2017 |
| | | • ETSI TS 103 645 | Cyber security for consumer Internet of Things | 2019 |
| | | • IETF RFC 8576 (Informational) | Internet of Things (IoT) security: State of the art and challenges | 2019 |
| Common standard for ICS/ SCADA protection | | • NIST SP 800-82 Rev. 2 (Stouffer et al., 2015) | Guide to industrial control systems (ICS) security | 2015 |
| | | • NIST SP 500-299 | NIST cloud computing security reference architecture (draft) | 2013 |
| | | • ISA/IEC 62443 series | Security for industrial automation and control systems | Multi-part |
| | | • IIC:PUB:G4:V1.0:PB: 20160926 (IIC, 2016) | Industrial Internet of Things volume G4: Security framework | 2016 |
| Specific standard concerning ICS/ SCADA in: | Electric power industry | • IEC 62351 series | Security for industrial automation and control systems | Multi-part |
| | | • IEEE 1402-2000 | IEEE guide for electric power substation physical and electronic security | 2000 |
| | | • IEEE P2023 | Standard for digital transformation architecture and framework | Up-coming |
| | Oil and gas industry | • API 1164 | Pipeline SCADA Security | 2009 |
| | | • AGA-12 series | Cryptographic protection of SCADA communications | Multi-part |
| | Water and wastewater treatment | • ANSI/AWWA G430-14 | Security practices for operation & management | 2014 |

General standards concerning cyber security of ICT systems must be taken into account when designing and developing each security system. There are many general standards and recommendations, which are being approved by leading international standardization bodies such as International Organization for Standardization (ISO), International Telecommunication Union - Telecommunication Standardization Sector (ITU-T), Internet Engineering Task Force (IETF), American National Standards Institute (ANSI), European Telecommunications Standards Institute (ETSI), etc.

The ISO/IEC 27000-series comprises information security standards, published jointly by the ISO and the IEC, which provide best practice recommendations on information security management. The ISO/IEC 27001 is an information security management system standard (the last revision was published in October 2013), which specifies a systematic approach to managing sensitive company information so that it remains secure. Certification to ISO/IEC 27001 is possible but not mandatory; some organizations implement the standard in order to benefit from the best practice it contains. In addition, ISO/IEC 27002 is a popular, internationally-recognized standard of good practice for information security. It is relevant to all types of organization, i.e., any organization that uses information technologies. ISO/IEC 27017 standard complements the ISO/IEC 27002 by providing guidelines on the information security of cloud computing. This standard is also adopted by the ITU-T (recommendation X.1631).

The ITU-T approves recommendations in all areas of cyber security, including security architectures, models and frameworks; security management, security policy and policy mechanisms; security assessment and evaluation criteria; intrusion detection; security services; security mechanisms; layered network security; security protocol standards; next generation networks; service-specific security standards, etc. Security related work is covered by the ITU-T X-series and Y-series of recommendations. Thus, cloud computing security is addressed by the X-1600 series of recommendations. IoT security is covered by recommendations X.1361 and X.1362, which specify security framework for the IoT based on the gateway model and encryption procedure for IoT environments, respectively.

The IETF work on the Internet cyber security is organized into 22 active working groups, which cover all relevant areas of network and protocol security, as well as security management. The work on IoT security is still in the research phase. In April 2019, the IETF issued the Request for Comments (RFC) document, which presents an overview of important IoT security aspects (Garcia-Morchon, Kumar, & Sethi, 2019).

The ANSI partnered with the Internet Security Alliance (ISAlliance) and others to coordinate the work in the area of ICT cyber security.

The main areas of ETSI's work related to security cover mobile/wireless communications, emergency telecommunications, information technology infrastructure, smart cards, fixed communications, and security algorithms. In December 2012, the European Commission (EC) and the ETSI launched the Cloud Standardization Coordination (CSC) initiative, which includes cloud computing interoperability and security. In February 2019, ETSI released the first globally applicable standard for consumer IoT security (ETSI TS 103 645).

Among organizations that adopt or will adopt common standards and guidelines for ICS/SCADA protection, the most relevant are the U. S. National Institute of Standards and Technology (NIST), the International Society of Automation (ISA) and the IIC.

The NIST provides standards for the wide spectrum of technologies, from the smart electric power grid and electronic health records to atomic clocks, advanced nanomaterials, and computer chips. The NIST special publication (SP) 800-82 (Stouffer et al., 2015) provides guidelines on how to secure ICS/SCADA and other control systems, regarding their performance, reliability and safety requirements. The "NIST Cloud Computing Program" was launched in November 2010, and includes Cloud Computing Security Working Group, which works on defining the cloud computing security reference architecture (NIST SP 500-299). The work on IoT security is conducted within the "NIST Cybersecurity for IoT Program", which started in November 2016, and includes cybersecurity framework, cybersecurity framework profile for manufacturing, security systems engineering, cloud security, etc.

The ISA99 standards development committee approves standards for industrial automation and control systems security. This original and ongoing ISA99 work is adopted by the IEC in producing the IEC 62443 series of standards. The IIoT security challenges have led to the establishment of the ISA99 Working Group 9, which is focused on the IIoT cybersecurity. The objective of this working group is to explore the applicability of the well known IEC 62443 series of industrial standards to IIoT systems, including general categories of IIoT devices within industrial automation and control systems (Leander & Causevic, 2019).

The IIC has been founded in 2014 as a global non-profit partnership of industry, government and academia. It aims to help the organizations to utilize technologies that are necessary to speed up the deployment of the industrial Internet by identifying, assembling, testing and promoting best practices. The IIC's Security Working Group is responsible for a common security framework for the industrial Internet, comprising security model and policy, data protection, endpoint protection (edge-cloud), communications and connectivity protection, security monitoring and analysis, as well as security configuration and management. The first document describing the IIoT security framework has been published in 2016 (IIC, 2016). It should be noted that standard security certifications and measures still do not exist for the fog computing. The IIC will also address this issue, since it has merged with the former OpenFog Consortium in 2019.

Specific directives concerning ICS/SCADA security refer to particular industrial sectors such as the electric power industry, oil and natural gas industry, water and wastewater treatment. Most standardization efforts are carried out in the electric power sector.

IEC 62351 is a standard developed for handling the security of multiple IEC series of ICS/SCADA protocols, including IEC 60870-5 series, IEC 60870-6 series, IEC 61850 series, etc. The main security objectives include authentication of data transfer through digital signatures, authenticated access, prevention of eavesdropping, playback and spoofing, and intrusion detection capabilities.

The Institute of Electrical and Electronics Engineers (IEEE) defines a guide for electric power substation physical and electronic security (IEEE 1402-2000), which identifies and discusses security issues related to human intervention during the construction, operation, and maintenance of electric power supply substations. In 2019, the IEEE has initiated the work on the IEEE P2023, standard for digital transformation, which poses new and complex challenges in information systems and technology, process automation, cloud computing, robotics, and artificial intelligence. The standard aims to provide architecture and framework, which address scalability, systems and interfaces, security and privacy challenges for digital transformation applications.

The American Petroleum Institute (API) has issued the standard API 1164, which refers to pipeline SCADA security and addresses access control, communication security (including encryption), information distribution classification, physical issues (including disaster recovery and business continuity plans), operating systems, network design, data interchange between enterprise and third-party support/customers, management systems, and field devices configuration and local access. Additionally, the API has issued two documents related to security issues in oil and gas industry. The first document represents security guidance for the oil and gas facilities, and covers operational regulations, standards, and recommended practices, which relate to facility design and safety, environmental protection, emergency response, and protection from theft and vandalisms. The second document describes security vulnerability assessment methodology for the petroleum and petrochemical industries and contains a methodology for evaluating the probability and consequences of terrorist attacks against refineries and petrochemical facilities.

The American Gas Association (AGA) has issued standard AGA-12, which provides cryptographic protection for SCADA communications, including encryption policy; retrofit link encryption for asynchronous serial communications; protection of networked systems; and protection embedded in SCADA components.

American Water Works Association (AWWA), in cooperation with the ANSI, published the ANSI/ AWWA G430-14 standard, concerning security practices for operation and management. This standard describes critical requirements for establishing and operating a protective security program for a water, wastewater, or reuse utility. Topics covered include commitment to security, security culture, defined security roles and employee expectations, vulnerability assessment, resources dedicated to security and security implementation, access control and intrusion detection, contamination detection, monitoring and surveillance, and information protection and continuity.

## FUTURE RESEARCH DIRECTIONS

Securing ICS/SCADA systems in the Future Internet environment is an open research topic. When deciding to utilize Future Internet technologies, each company/organization should provide answers to the following questions:

1. How are models and dynamics of migration toward Future Internet environments affected by cyber security risk?
2. How industrial control systems can be secured in these new environments, i.e., what security solutions are right with respect to aforementioned priorities concerning availability, integrity and confidentiality?
3. How will investments in security affect the overall company's costs?
4. Are all security solutions ICS/SCADA-specific or solutions for general-purpose information systems can be used to some extent?

The answer to the first question is that gradual migration will probably be the best choice for most of the companies. The second question poses a number of problems that should be solved at different levels: starting from the system's level (network security architectures, definition and implementation of security policies), through multi-pronged approach that combines mechanisms such as access control, protocol analysis, endpoint security and encryption, to particular security mechanisms like intrusion detection and prevention systems, secure protocols or live forensics. The third question calls for consistent application of security risk management and the associated cost-benefit analysis. Although different qualitative and quantitative approaches, methods and tools for risk assessment in industrial control environment can be found in the literature, only a few of them deals with the Future Internet environment. The fourth question is related to the previous one, regarding security investments. This applies especially for the defense against ICS/SCADA-specific cyber security threats and securing specific communication protocols in such systems. Still, a number of general-purpose security solutions may be applicable, original or upgraded to suit the requirements of industrial networks.

Among many open leads in the area, the following are the most important:

• A precise taxonomy of cyber vulnerabilities and threats in industrial control networks is needed, particularly related to cloud, fog and IIoT environments. Additional work is also needed on the attribution of cyber attacks on critical infrastructures.

- All IIoT participants must design and integrate security into their components and systems before building them. In other words, chips, boards and software should have security built in from the beginning, and attested to the right level of security before implementation.
- One of the key features of IIoT is the integration between the machines and the humans who run them. New entry points will be introduced into the reference model to increase connectivity. These new capabilities introduce cyber security considerations that will need to be addressed.
- Special attention should be paid to development of appropriate test environments for new security solutions, including testbeds, datasets and attack models.
- Significant research efforts are needed to address risk assessment, because risk management takes the outputs of the risk assessment process to consider the options for risk mitigation and finding the trade-offs among overall costs, benefits, and risks of using Future Internet technologies in the industrial environment.
- The ongoing work on cyber security standardization should be intensified. In particular, there is a need for developing specific security standards for the other industrial sectors apart from electric power industry.

## CONCLUSION

Future Internet technologies bring a lot of benefits to the industrial sector, particularly in terms of seamless connectivity, improved scalability, efficient system configuration and maintenance, and improving the overall economic efficiency. However, cyber security problems may pose limitations to the migrations of ICS/SCADA systems toward Future Internet environments.

First, public and private cloud architectures can both be the right choice for ICS/SCADA. Although the use of public cloud services brings a number of economic benefits, it requires a careful risk analysis and gradual migration. Another issue concerns the choice of cloud service provider. A properly defined SLA represents a starting point for provisioning of secure public cloud services with the required QoS level. Migration to fog computing can mitigate risks regarding cyber security and fulfillment of stringent delay requirements. The private cloud infrastructure may bring substantial technical benefits in terms of QoS and security, in addition to cost savings and increased business opportunities.

Second, different operational processes, principles, users, and objectives of the IoT and IIoT cause the need for different security solutions. The main issue comes from the fact that IIoT applications are usually assembled with the existing ICS/SCADA equipment; hence, they bring in security issues of such equipment. For that reason, one of the key requirements for IIoT participants concerns integrating security solutions into their components and systems. Besides, introducing new entry points to the IIoT system, in order to increase connectivity, may increase cyber security risk.

Finally, intensive standardization efforts are needed in the area, including the work toward specific standards concerning particular industrial sectors as well as the cross-cut standards and guidelines.

## ACKNOWLEDGMENT

This research was supported by the Ministry of Education, Science and Technological Development of Serbia [grant number TR 32025 and grant number TR 36002].

# REFERENCES

Aazam, M., Zeadally, S., & Harras, K. A. (2018). Deploying fog computing in Industrial Internet of Things and Industry 4.0. *IEEE Transactions on Industrial Informatics, 14*(10), 4674–4682. doi:10.1109/TII.2018.2855198

Aleksandrova, M. (2019). Industrial IoT security: How to protect smart manufacturing. Retrieved October 8, 2019, from https://easternpeak.com/blog/industrial-iot-security-how-to-protect-smart-manufacturing/

Boštjančič Rakas, S. (2020). Energy Internet: Architecture, emerging technologies and security issues. In M. Stojanovic, & S. Bostjancic Rakas (Eds.), *Cyber security of industrial control systems in the Future Internet environment*. Hershey, PA: IGI Global.

Boštjančič Rakas, S., & Stojanović, M. (2019). A centralized model for establishing end-to-end communication services via management agents. *Promet – Traffic & Transportation, 31*(3), 245-255.

Butun, I., Sari, A., & Österberg, P. (2019). Security implications of fog computing on the Internet of Things. In *Proceedings of the International Conference on Consumer Electronics* (pp. 1-6). New York: IEEE. 10.1109/ICCE.2019.8661909

Byers, C. (2018). Fog computing for industrial automation. Retrieved October 8, 2019, from https://www.controleng.com/articles/fog-computing-for-industrial-automation/

Cao, Y., Li, Q., Tan, Y., Li, Y., Chen, Y., Shao, X., & Zou, Y. (2018). A comprehensive review of Energy Internet: Basic concept, operation and planning methods, and research prospects. *Journal of Modern Power Systems and Clean Energy, 6*(3), 399–411. doi:10.100740565-017-0350-8

Chavan, P., Patil, P., Kulkarni, G., Sutar, R., & Belsare, S. (2013). IaaS cloud security. In *Proceedings of the 2013 International Conference on Machine Intelligence and Research Advancement* (pp. 549-553). New York: IEEE.

Chen, Y., Chen, J., & Gan, J. (2015). Experimental study on cloud computing based electric power SCADA system. *ZTE Communications, 13*(3), 33–41.

Church, P., Mueller, H., Ryan, C., Gogouvitis, S. V., Goscinski, A., & Tari, Z. (2017). Migration of a SCADA system to IaaS clouds – a case study. *Journal of Cloud Computing: Advances, Systems, and Applications, 6*(11), 1–12.

Cook, A., Nicholson, A., Janicke, H., Maglaras, L., & Smith, R. (2016). Attribution of cyber attacks on industrial control systems. *EAI Transactions on Industrial Networks and Industrial Systems, 3*(7), 1–15.

Foundation, O. P. C. (2018). *Practical security recommendations for building OPC UA applications* (White Paper). Retrieved August 1, 2019, from https://opcfoundation.org/wp-content/uploads/2017/11/OPC-UA-Security-Advise-EN.pdf

Galloway, B., & Hancke, G. P. (2013). Introduction to industrial control networks. *IEEE Communications Surveys and Tutorials, 15*(2), 860–880. doi:10.1109/SURV.2012.071812.00124

Gao, J., Liu, J., Rajan, B., Nori, R., Fu, B., Xiao, Y., ... Chen, C. L. P. (2014). SCADA communication and security issues. *Security and Communication Networks, 7*(1), 175–194. doi:10.1002ec.698

Garcia-Morchon, O., Kumar, S., & Sethi, M. (2019). Internet of things (IoT) Security: State of the Art and Challenges. *IETF RFC 8576 (Informational)*. Retrieved October 8, 2019, from https://www.rfc-editor.org/search/rfc_search.php

Ghosh, S., & Sampalli, S. (2019). A survey of security in SCADA networks: Current issues and future challenges. *IEEE Access: Practical Innovations, Open Solutions, 7*. doi:10.1109/ACCESS.2019.2926441

Goldenberg, N., & Wool, A. (2013). Accurate modeling of Modbus/TCP for intrusion detection in SCADA systems. *International Journal of Critical Infrastructure Protection, 6*(2), 63–75. doi:10.1016/j.ijcip.2013.05.001

Hari Krishna, B., Kiran, S., Murali, G., & Pradeep Kumar Reddy, R. (2016). Security issues in service model of cloud computing environment. *Procedia Computer Science, 87*, 246–251. doi:10.1016/j.procs.2016.05.156

Howard, P. D. (2015). *A security checklist for SCADA systems in the cloud*. Retrieved October 8, 2019, from https://gcn.com/articles/2015/06/29/scada-cloud.aspx

Industrial Internet Consortium (IIC). (2016). Industrial Internet of Things Volume G4: Security Framework. Document IIC:PUB:G4:V1.0:PB:20160919. Retrieved October 8, 2019, from https://www.iiconsortium.org/pdf/IIC_PUB_G4_V1.00_PB.pdf

Industrial Internet Consortium (IIC). (2019). The Industrial Internet of Things Volume G1: Reference Architecture, Version 1.9. Retrieved October 8, 2019, from https://www.iiconsortium.org/pdf/IIRA-v1.9.pdf

Kamble, A., & Bhutad, S. (2018). Survey on Internet of Things (IoT) – security issues & solutions. In *Proceedings of the Second International Conference on Inventive Systems and Control (ICISC 2018)*, (pp. 307-312). New York: IEEE. 10.1109/ICISC.2018.8399084

Khan, S., Parkinson, S., & Qin, Y. (2017). Fog computing security: A review of current applications and security solutions. *Journal of Cloud Computing: Advances, Systems, and Applications, 6*(19), 1–22.

Leander, B., & Causevic, A. (2019). Applicability of the IEC 62443 standard in Industry 4.0/IIoT. In *Proceedings of the 14th International Conference on Availability, Reliability and Security*, (Article 101, pp. 1-8). Canterbury, UK: ACM. 10.1145/3339252.3341481

Maglaras, L., Ferrag, M. A., Derhab, A., Mukherjee, M., & Janicke, H. (2019). Cyber security: From regulations and policies to practice. In A. Kavoura, E. Kefallonitis, & A. Giovanis (Eds.), *Springer Proceedings in Business and Economics. Strategic innovative marketing and tourism* (pp. 763–770). Cham, Switzerland: Springer International Publishing. doi:10.1007/978-3-030-12453-3_88

Mantere, M., Sailio, M., & Noponen, S. (2013). Network traffic features for anomaly detection in specific industrial control system network. *Future Internet, 5*(4), 460–473. doi:10.3390/fi5040460

Markovic-Petrovic, J. D., Stojanovic, M. D., & Bostjancic Rakas, S. V. (2019). A fuzzy AHP approach for security risk assessment in SCADA networks. *Advances in Electrical and Computer Engineering, 19*(3), 69–74. doi:10.4316/AECE.2019.03008

Morris, T., & Gao, W. (2013). Classifications of industrial control system cyber attacks. In *Proceedings of the 1st International Symposium for ICS & SCADA Cyber Security Research* (pp. 22-29). Leicester, UK: British Computer Society.

Mouradian, C., Naboulsi, D., Yangui, S., Glitho, R. H., Morrow, M. J., & Polakos, P. A. (2018). A comprehensive survey on fog computing: State-of-the-art and research challenges. *IEEE Communications Surveys and Tutorials, 20*(1), 416–464. doi:10.1109/COMST.2017.2771153

Nugent, E. (2017, November/December). How cloud and fog computing will advance SCADA systems. *Manufacturing Automation, 32*(7), 22–24.

Ogie, R. I. (2017). Cyber security incidents on critical infrastructure and industrial networks. In *Proceedings of the 9th International Conference on Computer and Automation Engineering* (pp. 254-258). New York: ACM. 10.1145/3057039.3057076

Qiu, T., Chen, N., Li, K., Atiquzzaman, M., & Zhao, W. (2018). How can heterogeneous Internet of Things build our future: A survey. *IEEE Communications Surveys and Tutorials, 20*(3), 2011–2027. doi:10.1109/COMST.2018.2803740

Sadeghi, A.-R., Wachsmann, C., & Waidner, M. (2015). Security and privacy challenges in industrial Internet of Things. In *Proceedings of the 52nd ACM/EDAC/IEEE Design Automation Conference* (pp. 1-6). New York: IEEE. 10.1145/2744769.2747942

Sajid, A., Abbas, H., & Saleem, K. (2016). Cloud-assisted IoT-based SCADA systems security: A review of the state of the art and future challenges. *IEEE Access: Practical Innovations, Open Solutions, 4*, 1375–1384. doi:10.1109/ACCESS.2016.2549047

Sandikkaya, M. T., & Harmanci, A. E. (2012). Security problems of Platform-as-a-Service (PaaS) clouds and practical solutions to the problems. In *Proceedings of the IEEE 31st Symposium on Reliable Distributed Systems* (pp. 463-468). New York: IEEE. 10.1109/SRDS.2012.84

Schwab, W., & Poujol, M. (2018). The state of industrial cybersecurity 2018. Retrieved October 8, 2019, from https://ics.kaspersky.com/media/2018-Kaspersky-ICS-Whitepaper.pdf

Soufiane, S., & Halima, B. (2017). SaaS cloud security: Attacks and proposed solutions. *Transactions on Machine Learning and Artificial Intelligence, 5*(4), 291–301. doi:10.14738/tmlai.54.3194

Stojanovic, M., Bostjancic Rakas, S., & Acimovic-Raspopovic, V. (2010). End-to-end quality of service specification and mapping: The third-party approach. *Computer Communications, 33*(11), 1354–1368. doi:10.1016/j.comcom.2010.03.024

Stojanovic, M., Kostic-Ljubisavljevic, A., & Radonjic-Djogatovic, V. (2013). SLA-controlled interconnection charging in next generation networks. *Computer Networks, 57*(11), 2374–2394. doi:10.1016/j.comnet.2013.04.013

Stojanović, M. D., Boštjančič Rakas, S. V., & Marković-Petrović, J. D. (2019). SCADA systems in the cloud and fog environments: Migration scenarios and security issues. *FACTA UNIVERSITATIS Series: Electronics and Energetics, 32*(3), 345–358.

Stouffer, K., Pillitteri, V., Lightman, S., Abrams, M., & Hahn, A. (2015). *Guide to industrial control systems (ICS) security (NIST Special Publication 800-82 Rev. 2)*. Gaithersburg, MD: U.S. National Institute of Standards and Technology. doi:10.6028/NIST.SP.800-82r2

Tom, R. J., & Sankaranarayanan, S. (2017). IoT based SCADA integrated with fog for power distribution automation. In *Proceedings of the 12th Iberian Conference on Information Systems and Technologies* (pp. 1-4). New York: IEEE. 10.23919/CISTI.2017.7975732

Xu, H., Yu, W., Griffith, D., & Golmie, N. (2018). A survey on Industrial Internet of Things: A cyber-physical systems perspective. *IEEE Access: Practical Innovations, Open Solutions, 6*, 78238–78259. doi:10.1109/ACCESS.2018.2884906

Yang, Y., McLaughlin, K., Sezer, S., Littler, T., Im, E. G., Pranggono, B., & Wang, H. F. (2014). Multi-attribute SCADA-specific intrusion detection system for power networks. *IEEE Transactions on Power Delivery, 29*(3), 1092–1102. doi:10.1109/TPWRD.2014.2300099

Zhou, L., Guo, H., & Deng, G. (2019). A fog computing based approach to DDoS mitigation in IIoT systems. *Computers & Security, 85*, 51–62. doi:10.1016/j.cose.2019.04.017

Zhou, X., Xu, Z., Wang, L., & Chen, K. (2017). What should we do? A structured review of SCADA system cyber security standards. In *Proceedings of the 4th International Conference on Control, Decision, and Information Technologies* (pp. 605-614). New York: IEEE. 10.1109/CoDIT.2017.8102661

## ADDITIONAL READING

Bellavista, P., Berrocal, J., Corradi, A., Das, S. K., Foschini, L., & Zanni, A. (2019). A survey on fog computing for the Internet of Things. *Pervasive and Mobile Computing, 52*, 71–99. doi:10.1016/j.pmcj.2018.12.007

Campos, J., Sharma, P., Jantunen, E., Baglee, D., & Fumagalli, L. (2016). The challenges of cybersecurity frameworks to protect data required for the development of advanced maintenance. *Procedia CIRP, 47*, 222–227. doi:10.1016/j.procir.2016.03.059

Cherdantseva, Y., Burnap, P., Blyth, A., Eden, P., Jones, K., Soulsby, H., & Stoddart, K. (2016). A review of cyber security risk assessment methods for SCADA systems. *Computers & Security, 56*, 1–27. doi:10.1016/j.cose.2015.09.009

Dotson, C. (2019). *Practical cloud security*. Sebastopol, CA: O'Reilly Media.

Hariri, R. H., Fredericks, E. M., & Bowers, K. M. (2019). Uncertainty in big data analytics: Survey, opportunities, and challenges. *Journal of Big Data, 6*, article 44, 1-10.

Kamal, M. (2019). ICS layered threat modeling. SANS Institute – Information Security Reading Room. Retrieved October 8, 2019, from https://www.sans.org/reading-room/whitepapers/ICS/ics-layered-threat-modeling-38770

Knowles, W., Prince, D., Hutchison, D., Disso, J. F. P., & Jones, K. (2015). A survey of cyber security management in industrial control systems. *International Journal of Critical Infrastructure Protection*, *9*, 52–80. doi:10.1016/j.ijcip.2015.02.002

Lamba, V., Simková, N., & Rossi, B. (2019). Recommendations for smart grid security risk management. *Cyber-Physical Systems*, *5*(2), 92–118. doi:10.1080/23335777.2019.1600035

Lin, H., Yan, Z., Chen, Y., & Zhang, L. (2018). A survey on network security-related data collection technologies. *IEEE Access: Practical Innovations, Open Solutions*, *6*, 18345–18365. doi:10.1109/ACCESS.2018.2817921

Stojanovic, M., Acimovic-Raspopovic, V., & Bostjancic Rakas, S. (2013). Security management issues for open source ERP in the NGN environment. In M. Khosrow-Pour (Ed.), *Enterprise resource planning: Concepts, methodologies, tools, and applications* (Vol. II, pp. 789–804). Hershey, PA: IGI Global. doi:10.4018/978-1-4666-4153-2.ch046

## KEY TERMS AND DEFINITIONS

**Cloud Computing:** A method of using remote servers hosted on the Internet to store, manage, and process data.

**Cloud Service Provider (CSP):** A third-party company that offers cloud services (software as a service, platform as a service, infrastructure as a service, etc.) to business and/or residential customers.

**Cyber Security Risk:** Exposure to harm or loss resulting from data breaches or attacks on information and communication systems.

**Endpoint:** In the context of Industrial Internet of Things, a component that has computational capabilities and network connectivity.

**Fog Computing:** An architecture that uses edge devices to perform a large amount of computation, storage and communication, locally and routed over the Internet.

**Gateway:** In the context of Industrial Internet of Things, a device that bridges the edge of an IIoT system to the cloud.

**Industrial Internet of Things (IIoT):** A system of interconnected sensors, actuators, and other devices networked together with computers' industrial applications.

**Service Level Agreement (SLA):** A contract between the service provider and the customer, which defines provider's responsibilities in the sense of quality of service guarantees, performance metrics, measurement methods, tariffs and billing principles, as well as penalties for both the user and the provider in the case of contract violation.

*Previously published in Cyber Security of Industrial Control Systems in the Future Internet Environment; pages 1-26, copyright year 2020 by Information Science Reference (an imprint of IGI Global).*

# Chapter 27
# Security Framework for Supply–Chain Management

**Kathick Raj Elangovan**
*Concordia University, Canada*

## ABSTRACT

*In recent times, cyber-attacks have been a significant problem in any organization. It can damage the brand name if confidential data is compromised. A robust cybersecurity framework should be an essential aspect of any organization. This chapter talks about the security framework for cyber threats in supply chain management and discusses in detail the implementation of a secure environment through various controls. Today, a systematic method is used for handling sensitive information in an organization. It includes processes, people, and IT systems by implementing a risk management method. Distinct controls dedicated to different levels of domains, namely human resources, access control, asset management, cryptography, physical security, operations security, supplier relations, acquisition, incident management, and security governance are provided. Companies, contractors, and any others who are part of the supply chain organization must follow this security framework to defend from any cyber-attacks.*

## BACKGROUND

Cybersecurity threats pose a significant risk to any organization. According to 2018 average time to detect a breach takes up to 197 days (Ponemon, 2018) This can impact business, brand name, reputation, and revenue. To address this issue in supply chain-based organization and to enhance the cybersecurity, a security framework implementation is developed. A supply chain is a system of organizations, people, activities, information, and resources involved in moving a product or service from supplier to customer (Wikipedia, 2019a). The framework focuses on process, business drivers, people, and IT systems management by implementing a risk management approach.

DOI: 10.4018/978-1-6684-3698-1.ch027

## Setting the Stage

Cybercriminals infiltrate into an organization to steal sensitive information. Cyber breach is the worst nightmare in the Information Technology world. A few impacts are damage to the brand name, litigation, financial losses, and data theft (Ponemon, 2018). As of 2016 cyber-attack have caused loss of around $ 450 billion to the international economy and it's on the rise every year. The primary motivation in attack scenario as shown in Figure 1. Cybercrime-related attacks top the charts when it comes to the different motivation behind the attacks (Appendix 1).

*Figure 1. Attack coverage*
*Source: (Passeri, 2018)*

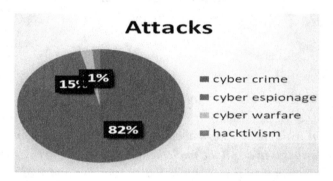

## SOLUTION APPROaCH

In recent days, the cyber-attacks towards supply chain management (SCM) have been very successful. Attackers target a weak or less secure member in a supply chain to gain access to the organization. Some of the weaker networks are mentioned below in Figure 2. one of the main reasons for the successful attack is no awareness about security in the organization and its vendors and everyone in the supply chain. Attackers use this to phish emails of the employees and send malware to infect the machines and infiltrate into the network to steal sensitive information. Attackers can request ransoms by encrypting essential data for an exchange of decryption key.

To fix these cyber risks, a security framework is required. A pure knowledge of security concerns, business processes distinct from the use of technology is needed. Every organization has its unique methods and tools to achieve the results reported by its framework. However, in this paper, This Paper propose one single security framework that must be followed by the organization and the companies in its supply chain. As described in Figure 3, The framework will follow five continuous and concurrent function or can be called a cybersecurity life cycle (Identity, Protect, Detect, Respond, Recover) (NIST, 2019). This process is used to identify, assess and manage cybersecurity risk in the environment proactively.

*Figure 2. Weak networks in SPM*

*Figure 3. Cyber security life cycle*

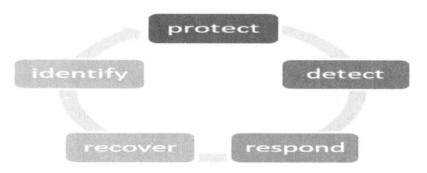

## Identify

Organizations must develop knowledge of their environment to manage cybersecurity risk to systems, data, assets, and capabilities. To adhere to this function, it is necessary to have complete clarity towards physical and digital assets and their defined roles, responsibilities and its interconnections. Understanding the risk factors are necessary to create policy and procedures to control the risks.

## Protect

This function must be used to develop and implement relevant protection and defense during or to prevent a cybersecurity event. To adhere to this, the organization should control physical and digital asset access and provide adequate awareness session to the employees. The process is to maintain baseline settings of network operations, secure sensitive information and suitably repair the incident and deploy necessary security technologies to protect the organization.

## Detect

During a security breach in the organization must have relevant controls for identifying security detections or events. This function promotes the use of continuous monitoring tools such as (Security Incident Events Management) SIEM, (Intrusion Detection System) IDS to detect any anomaly detections in the network. Policies must be created in the framework on the usage of these monitoring systems to prevent security incidents in the organizations.

## Respond

If a security incident happens, the organization must possess the capability to hold the impact. To adhere, this function must be used to create a successful security response mitigation plan and perform all necessary steps to fix the incident at priority. The response plans must be documented and tested at a specified interval to check its capability.

## Recover

This function must be used to develop a business recovery plan to restore services that were damaged due to a security incident. The recovery plan must be active to perform the business restoration and document the learned lesson in the updated business strategy record. Prioritizing the recovery activity is an essential factor when it comes to timely recovery of services.

## TECHNOLOGY CONCERNS

To create this distinct security framework, several security guidelines, global policies, best practices that are described in several security frameworks such as ISO 27000 K, NIST, PCI DSS, COBIT, HIPAA, and SOC as shown in Figure 4 are used. This framework is built towards domain-specific security so the framework can provide a strong semantics for understanding, managing, and remediating cybersecurity risk to all stakeholders in the organization. It can help to identify and prioritize the action for overcoming cybersecurity risks, and it is an excellent tool for aligning policy, business, and technological strategies for managing that risk (International Organization for Standards, n.d.; NIST, 2019; PCI Security Council, n.d.; NIST, n.d.). Using this framework cybersecurity risks across the entire organization, companies and partners in the supply chain can be managed. The purpose of this framework is not to replace an existing framework; preferably it can be used to overlay into the current process of the organization to find the security gaps.

Companies from around the world have embraced the use of the NIST Framework, including Amazon a leader in online supply chain management process, JP Morgan Chase, Microsoft, Boeing, Intel, Bank of England, Nippon Telegraph and Telephone Corporation, and the Ontario Energy Board (PCI Security Standards Council, n.d.; NIST, n.d.). ISO 27K is the internationally recognized standard that stipulates the requirements for an ISMS (information security management system). As of 2017, there are around 39000 companies that are ISO 27k certified (International Organization of Standardization, 2018) Any company that handles client credit cards or payment card data must accomplice with the mandated PCI DSS framework to be protected from any data breach. Any company that handles customer healthcare and customer healthcare insurance related industries should follow accomplice HIPAA to be protected from fraud and theft. Control Objectives for Information and Related Technology (COBIT) is a framework developed in the mid-90s by ISACA, an autonomous organization of IT governance experts. This framework started primarily with concentrating on overcoming technical risks in organizations and has now evolved recently with COBIT 5 to introduce the alignment of IT with business-strategic intentions. It is the most commonly adopted framework to obtain compliance with Sarbanes-Oxley rules (SOX).

*Figure 4. Cybersecurity framework*

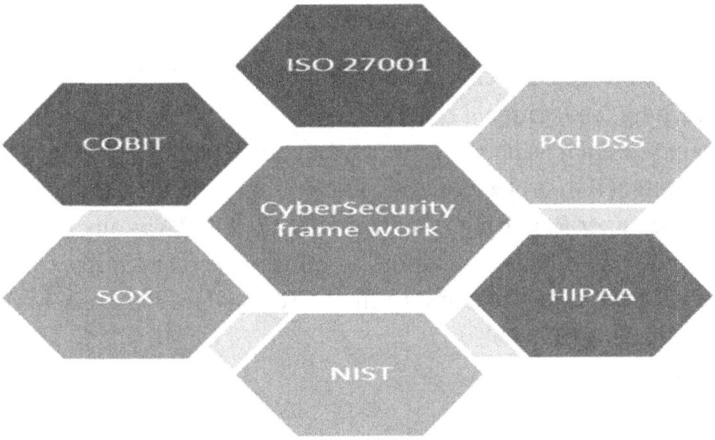

## TECHNOLOGY COMPONENTS AND FRAMEWORK IMPLEMENTATION

As mentioned earlier this framework will have a domain-specific control-based design for implementation of the security. The domains taking part in the security framework are Human resource, Asset Management, Access management, Cryptography, physical Security, Communication and operations security, Supplier relationships, systems acquisition and Maintenance, Information security and Incident management, Compliance and governance as mentioned in Figure 5. This framework will provide cybersecurity requirements in each domain to find gaps in the supply chain management organization. This framework must be followed by all the companies, vendors, consultants that belong to the supply chain. This method will help find the necessary business service where security needs to be prioritized.

## HUMAN RESOURCE SECURITY

The primary objective of human resource security is to ensure that proper background verification is done and audited at several intervals. The various reasons why it's necessary are listed below:

- Disclosure of criminal convictions.
- To identify if the employee has a history of alcohol/drug abuse.
- Improved quality of the applicants.
- Reduce incidents and losses to the organization.

*Figure 5. Security domains*

The background verification mainly checks for the employee's address, identity, education, previous employment, drug screening, and criminal checks.

The pre-employment screening is done by agencies that must be FCRA (Fair Credit Reporting Act) compliant. This act is designed to protect individuals by promoting the accuracy and fairness of information in the files of Consumer Reporting Agencies (CRA). A CRA is any company that gathers and provides information about individuals to creditors, employers, and landlords. Companies that perform pre-employment screening are also governed by the FCRA, as are the employers that utilize CRA's background services (Wikipedia, 2019b).

Five important steps of FRCA

- Purpose: Purpose of BGC must be notified.
- Disclosure: In a written document, the employee must be informed about the BGC condition.
- Authorization: Before BGC initiation written consent must be obtained from the employee.
- Certification: Summary of consumer rights.
- Adverse action: Proper adverse action must be taken during the contrary employment decision

To guarantee that employees, contractors and third-party users exit the organization, or change responsibilities within the organization, in an orderly manner. Responsibilities for implementing the change in employment or employment termination should be precisely determined and specified. The organization must achieve and support a system or set of procedures to efficiently handle the quitting of employees or the withdrawal of designated duties for employees and contractors including other third-party users. A method must also be included for the removal of assigned contracts resulting from a change in employment status for employees, contractors and other third-parties. The organization should guarantee that valuable operational skills or knowledge have been transferred to other resources before the separation of the employee or contractor (Biswas, 2013). The control framework listed in Table 1 must be implemented throughout the supply chain to avoid any breach related to Human Resources.

## Framework Control

Some most commonly used software in Human resource domains are solutions provided by ADP.

*Table 1. Security control framework for human resources*

| S.NO | Control Requirement | Evidences Required for Control Requirement |
|------|--------------------|--------------------------------------------|
| 1 | Supplier Chain Management Company background checks as per Background check policy shall be completed for every employee working in the company, vendors, consultants and all contractors | HR confirmation on completion of the Background check for employees and associates |
| 2 | All the employees in the company, vendors, consultants and all contractors must be screened as per the client mandatory Background check (example: Criminal Background Verification, reference checks, drug screening etc.) before commencing the employment. | The client required Background checks completion report for all employees and associates working in company, vendors, consultants and all contractors |
| 3 | All the employees (company, vendors, consultants and all contractors) working for the client must be required to adhere to the client specific non - disclosure/ confidentiality agreement. | 1. List of all the associates working for the client (company, vendors, consultants and all contractors). 2. Electronic Copies of the client (Non-Disclosure Agreement) NDA's signed by associates (company, vendors, consultants and all contractors) working for the client. |
| 4 | All employees (company, vendors, consultants and all contractors) shall complete all client mandated security awareness training as agreed with the client | Training trackers and completion records of all employees (company, vendors, consultants and all contractors) |
| 5 | Employees (company, vendors, consultants and all contractors) moving or quitting shall return all assets that belong to the company including a). confidential documents stored on portable storage media or in paper formats. (eg: process documents, Technical procedure documents etc.) b). all electronic equipment (eg: laptops, tablets mobiles) | 1. Off boarding process documents. 2. Latest off Boarding account tracker. 3. acknowledgements of assets returned/ return receipts returned by the employee. |
| 6 | Employees shall not share user passwords among themselves. | Number of past (last six months) security incidents involving password sharing |
| 7 | The employee shall adhere to acceptable usage of client resources (email, internet and client provided storage etc.) | Some past (last six months) security incident involving misuse of client provided resources. |
| 8 | The employee shall not share company or client confidential data with unauthorized individuals working within or outside the company | Some past (last six months) security incidents involving unauthorized information sharing of company or client confidential data. |

## Access Control Security

Access control is a system or mechanism that controls access through the authorization or revocation of rights to logical or physical assets within an organization. The objective is to regulate who can view what and how a resource s utilized in an organization. There are two types of security:

- Physical access: which controls access to buildings, campuses, (Offshore Dedicated Centre) ODC's, IT assets.
- Logical access: which control access to computer systems, data and system files.

The primary process of the access control is to provide identity authentication and authorization of employees with the use of passwords, security tokens, biometrics. Organizations also use multifactor authentication for a layered defense. The main reason is to avoid the risk associated with unauthorized access into an organization. It is one of the fundamental elements of a security program. Organizations must have procedures that must define access to computer systems, networks, files, and sensitive data (International Organization for Standardization, n.d.; PCI Security Standards Council, n.d.). Access management, or identity management, can also be thought of as Access control. Access control discusses elements to manage access to information assets and facilities. The controls are concentrated on the protection against accidental loss or damage, threats, overheating etc. It requires documented control policies and procedures, removal, registration and review of user access rights, including physical access, network access and the control of privileged restriction of access to program source code.

Few vital values to have in mind when designing access controls are:

- Ensure controlled access to services based on rights and privileges allotted to the specified user.
- Employees have the right level of access to execute their jobs effectively and no more beyond that point.
- Perspectives and views ensure that third party viewers and clients cannot view or modify implicit and critical memory locations.
- The system must allow for and aid audits and the tracing the exploitation of services.
- The system must also provide an intuitive and hierarchical interface to change the rights of users whenever required
- It must adhere to and fortify the regulatory requirements of the organization.

The control framework listed in Table 2 must be implemented throughout the supply chain to avoid any breach related to Access control.

## Framework Control

Some famous software in the market for identity access management are from IBM, one login etc.

## Asset Management Security

The assets are nothing but any hardware or software that is owned by the organization. An asset is described as "Any item of commercial value owned by a corporation.". There must be a basic understanding of asset types and their business context. The organization should identify such interdependencies and obtain a relevant plan for the indirect "enablers" that are needed to optimize the use of physical assets. also, organizations that are profoundly dependent upon physical assets should similarly understand that losses in the management of other asset types may have an intense result on the overall performance of their organizational, physical assets and their performance. Organizations should acknowledge that every asset will need to be managed in a holistic and regulated manner.

- Human assets: the knowledge, behaviour and competence of the workforce hold a significant impact on the performance of every physical asset.
- Financial assets: financial resources are needed for infrastructure expenses, development, support and materials
- Information assets: quality data and information are essential to produce, optimize and execute an asset management plan.

- Intangible assets: the organization's status and vision can have a notable influence on operating strategies, infrastructure investment, and associated costs.

*Table 2. Security control framework for access control*

| S.NO | Control Requirement | Evidences Required for Control Requirement |
|---|---|---|
| 1 | Every employee in the organization shall be given a unique ID and password to access systems. | 1.List of all associate in the organization<br>2. List of all associates with access to the client organization. |
| 2 | A process for terminating the access privileges of associates on the client systems shall be established to ensure:<br>a) Authentication details and access privileges are revoked promptly on all systems to which the user has access.<br>b) Login credentials (User ID, digital certificate, or user name) are deactivated.<br>c) Access profiles/accounts deleted. | 1.Up to date process document for access deprovisioning.<br>2. Up to date movers and leavers.<br>3. Client acknowledgements (email proof). |
| 3 | The policy of separation responsibilities shall be observed while requesting access to the client organization. (e.g. developers must not have access to production network) | 1. Logical Access request, process documents, sample forms and email to the client.<br>2. Current associate logical access list with assigned roles details.<br>3. Segregation of Duties (SOD) Matrix. |
| 4 | Client allocated ID's shall not be used by scripts or automatically invoked programs. A separate ID with no interactive login permissions shall be used for any such purposes. Whenever such ID's shall be used, this shall be documented, and a client approval sought. | 1. List of accounts that are being used by scripts or automatically invoked programs (e.g. Batch jobs) and evidenced that associates are not using them for logging.<br>2. Email approval obtained from the client for the use of any ID's by script or automatically invoked programs. |
| 5 | All the systems including servers owned by the organization must be administered by system admins and should be a complaint to organization security policies w.r.t. Antivirus, unique user ID administration through Microsoft Active Directory, patch management and Operating system hardening. | 1. Inventory of all the machines in the organization and its vendors.<br>2. The evidence is demonstrating system compliance to organizations information security policy. |
| 6 | Additional controls shall be applied to special access privileges on the organization, and its vendor's systems include(e.g., "root" in UNIX, "Administrator" in windows etc.):<br>a) define the scope of special access privileges.<br>b) restricting the use of special access privileges to narrowly defined circumstances.<br>c) require a manager or higher approval for the use of special access privileges. | 1. List of all special access privilege accounts.<br>2. Manager approval emails.<br>3. Privileged access review/ reconciliation reports. |
| 7 | All employee access to the folders tools etc. shall be documented and reviewed periodically as per the project configuration management plan | 1. UpToDate approved configuration management plan.<br>2. Access review reports or organization audit results. |
| 8 | The authorized organization representative shall approve user ID creation for all associates in the chain. | 1. User ID creation process document and form/emails to the client.<br>2. Client approval for user ID creation. |
| 9 | Shared user ID's on the organization shall not be used unless special circumstances apply. Whenever such user ID needs to be assigned this shall be documented, approval sought from an authorized representative and subject to additional controls. | 1. List of all shared user ID's on client systems.<br>2. Process for Management of shared User ID's.<br>3. Client approval is obtained for the use of shared ID's. |
| 10 | Associates using tokens to authenticate to client network/ systems shall be advised to<br>a) Keep passwords for access to tokens confidential (i.e. to avoid making them visible to others by writing them down or disclosing them to others)<br>b) Protect tokens against loss, theft and misuse (e.g. avoid sharing with unauthorized individuals)<br>c) Report if the token has been lost or stolen. | 1. Inventory list of all the client provided tokens.<br>2. Notifications (e.g.: email) to client for last / stolen tokens. |

An organization should be in a place within the company to recognize the physical, information based or environmental assets it owns, and be able to maintain and defend them properly. Significant factors to acknowledge when developing an asset data management approach include:

- Inventory (information on what assets you own & where they are)
- Ownership/responsibility (Information on who is accountable for each asset)
- Importance (Information on how significant every asset is in relative to other assets)
- Organize acceptable-use practices for information and assets.
- Establish regulatory systems for the labelling of information about any asset and its dependant assets.
- Organize the return of asset procedures (policy or plan for employee exit procedure?)
- Protection for Assets (is each asset appropriately protected?)

Asset management is typically collecting a detail of organizations hardware and software inventory. It involves a process to secure the assets by creating a list to continuously use the captured data of the asset to minimize any risk associated. IT Asset management follows the IT asset life management cycle as shown in Figure 6. Lifecycle is a systematic process. It starts with strategic planning on what kind assets are required for the organization, how to procure them. The second step is to deploy the procured asset into the organization and perform the process to maintain it and support the asset if the case of any troubleshooting requires. After the end of life, the asset is retired or sent to disposal. Every organization has a complete process for this management life cycle. To make sure that asset management has no weak spots and to retaliate any breach, the control framework from Table 3 must be implemented.

*Figure 6. Asset management life cycle*

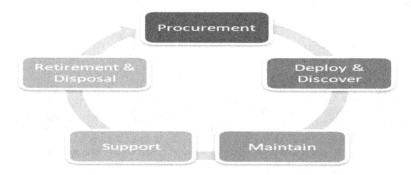

## Framework Control

Software named Maximo from IBM is one of the most famous asset management software's in the industry. Manage engine from Zoho Corp is an emerging solution for IT asset management in the market. These software's can be used to track asset inventory, scan and register assets and maintain integrity of the system.

*Table 3. Security control framework for asset management*

| S.NO | Control Requirement | Evidences Required for Control Requirement |
|------|--------------------|--------------------------------------------|
| 1 | All assets in the organization or all client-provided assets shall be recorded in an inventory that shall be:<br>a) Signed off by the client or Senior Manager.<br>b) Protected against unauthorized change.<br>c) Kept UpToDate and copied to a secure location regularly.<br>e) independent review has to be done. | 1. The client asset inventory (Hardware and software) in the internal inventory system.<br>2. Periodic review evidence. (e.g., emails or system logs) |
| 2 | All assets in the organization or client provided assets shall be handled as per information security requirements contractually agreed with the client | 1. Evidence that all client is classified as per company or client classification policy.<br>2. Access granting and authorization evidence (emails or system logs)<br>3. Copy of acceptable usage policies of the client.<br>4. Associate's acknowledgement of the client's acceptable usage policy.<br>5. Notification to the client on lost or damaged assets. |
| 3 | All information shall be classified as per the organization classification policy or the client classification policy as agreed with the client. | 1. UpToDate approved configuration management plan with asset classification details.<br>2. Sample documents (e.g., project plans, design documents etc.) with the classification label evident. |
| 4 | Upon contract termination, asset reallocation or decommissioning all client data shall be returned or securely destroyed | 1. System-generated requests raised.<br>2. Asset disposal tracker/register.<br>3. Secure disposal logs (e.g., disk wipe reports/ logs)<br>4. client email confirmation on return of client data. |

## Cryptography Security

Cryptography is the analysis and construction of protocols that would stop any third party from viewing private communication between two respective parties. In this digital age, cryptography has developed to address the encryption and decryption of any private communications over the internet and computers, a branch of network and cybersecurity, in a way far more complicated than anything the world of cryptography had observed ere the appearance of computers. Cryptographic algorithms must satisfy four main factors:

- **Confidentiality**: Protection of data from unauthorized subjects.
- **Integrity**: Preventing any unauthorized subjects from modifying the data and preventing authorized subjects from making any unauthorized modification.
- **Non-Repudiation**: This function guarantees that the subject of any event or activity can't deny that the incident ever occurred.
- **Authentication**: This function verifies that the claimed identity is valid authentication.

Cryptographic cybersecurity aims to make sure the encryption system follows all the above four criteria because the strength of encryption not only depends on computer programs but also human behavior. Some well-known encryption algorithms are AES, DES, RSA. Encryption is often a computationally intense process and may deteriorate the performance of infrastructure if not achieved optimally. Be sure to determine the administration requirements of end users and enterprise services before implementing any encryption mechanism. One must develop an implementation strategy, complete test plans, gather requirements and deploy the following best practices of products, and efficiently maintain ongoing encryption solutions. This security control framework in Table 4 will help to implement the cryptographic function and where to implement it around the organization and its supply chain to maintain encryption related security.

## Framework Control

Several companies such as Microsoft, Symantec and McAfee have their own software for the purpose of full disk encryption.

*Table 4. Security control framework for cryptography*

| S.NO | Control Requirement | Evidences Required for Control Requirement |
|---|---|---|
| 1 | Cryptography shall be used to<br>a) Protect the confidentiality of sensitive information at rest and in transit (e.g., VPN, Email encryption etc.) that is subjected to contractual, legal and regulatory related encryption requirements (e.g., Payment card industry security standard (PCI DSS), US Health Insurance Portability and Accountability Act (HIPAA)).<br>b) Encrypt all data residing on associates system. | 1. Evidence that the sensitive data is encrypted at rest and in transit (e.g., VPN to connect to client network)<br>2. Evidence that all company laptops used in the account have data encryption software installed (e.g., bit locker software, Full disk encryption software's) |
| 2 | The strength of encryption (encryption algorithm, Key length) used to encrypt data at rest and in transit shall be as per organization or client mandated standards. | The encryption algorithm and key length details (e.g., AES 128/256, 3 DES 168 Bit) |

## Physical Environment Security

The term physical security relates to actions taken to protect buildings, systems, and associated infrastructure upon threats linked with their physical environment. Physical safeguards are usually ignored but are very critical in protecting data. Physical security, over the decades, has grown sequentially more challenging for organizations. Technology environments presently provide more requirements for contingencies due to increase in the vulnerabilities. USB drives, tablets, laptops and smartphones allow for information to be stolen or lost because of their probability. Physical security is the protection of software, hardware, personnel, data and networks from physical events and actions that could cause severe damage to an organization and its supply chain. It includes protection from the flood, fire, natural disasters, theft, burglary, terrorism and vandalism. Physical security is often neglected, and its importance is underestimated in favor of more technical threats such as hacking, malware, and cyber espionage. Despite, breaches of physical security can be carried by brute force and little or no technical expertise on the role of an attacker. Several controls such as surveillance, security guards, biometric, turnstiles, access controls, walls, fences are part of security hardening. Physical security steps should be adequate to deal with foreseeable threats and should be examined regularly for their functionality and effectiveness.

Physical security controls and preserves sources in the form of technical, administrative and physical controls. Access control systems, auditing systems and intrusion detection systems are examples of some technical controls. Few examples of administrative controls are facility design, site location, building construction, employee controls and emergency response. Physical control examples include the varieties of building materials utilized and securing perimeters including locks, fencing and guards.

Deterrence, detection then delay, denial are some controls used for defending the environment. Efforts to secure physical resources should be prevented using gates, fences and guards around the organization. Vaults and locked doors guarding physical assets through denial. Physical Intrusion detection systems (IDS) and alarms are the subsequent lines of protection and caution first responders if a violation is discovered. If attackers approach their target, security measures such as a remote lock on a computer must delay the suspect from obtaining assets until police or guards arrive.

It is not enough for controls to be present to manage the physical environment, there must also be a constantly evolving strategy put in place that utilizes these controls. The organization needs to build a team that is accountable for planning and designing a physical security program. The security team should continuously develop the program using the defense in depth approach. This security framework in Table 5 provides strong control check over the above implementations so that any breach related physical security can be mitigated.

## Framework Control

There are several companies that exist to provide physical security solutions for its various aspects, like Aventura Turnstiles which provides access control, (NEC, Telpo, Cognitec) which provides biometric verification implementations, and SECURITAS which provides security personnel as a subscription/contract-based service.

*Table 5. Security control framework for physical environment*

| S.NO | Control Requirement | Evidences Required for Control Requirement |
|---|---|---|
| 1 | Physical access to facilities that support or enable client infrastructure shall be protected against unauthorized access as agreed with the client | 1. List of current associates in the organization and at vendor end and list of user ID's enabled on the access control system.<br>2. Evidence of periodic physical access reviews conducted by the account (e.g., emails, system logs etc.) and discrepancies (if any) corrected.<br>3. Physical access entry exits logs as per retention period agreed with the client. |
| 2 | All physical and environmental security requirements as agreed in the contract with the client shall be implemented. | Depending upon the applicability:<br>1. CCTV camera retention logs as per client agreed retention period.<br>2. Logs for the materials that come Inside and goes outside the facility.<br>3. Mobile phone, paper or handbag submission at the entry of the organization.<br>4. Delay door alarm activation status.<br>5. dedicated security guard's deployment around the premises.<br>6. Visitor entry and exit logs with approvals as per client agreed retention periods.<br>7. Fireproof safe for storage of physical backup tapes. |

## Communication and Operations Security

Communications Security' emphasizes the security of the network and its services through controls such as network service level agreements, segregation of networks and other network security controls which are suitable to the organization. Simultaneously it also guides in safeguarding the information in transit through controls such as policies, procedures and controls for transfer of information and agreements to ensure secure transfer of information between two entities involved in the organization (Kapersky, 2017). The scope and complexity of security operations will differ among organizations based on resource levels and risk tolerance. Still, each of its' critical areas must be addressed in some manner to help relieve familiar omnipresent risks. The most critical phase of operations security is that the operations themselves need to be reliable, repeatable and performed consistently. below are some controls that are constructed by reviewing assess the confidentiality, integrity, and availability of the operations.

- **Operational Plans and Responsibilities**: Examine documentation and assess administration regarding capacity management, change management and separation of development, testing and the production environments.
- **Malware Detection and Prevention Controls**: Examine their level of effectiveness in the organization.
- **Data Backup Plan**: Decide whether backup methods and procedures are sufficient for both off and on backup management.
- **Logging and Auditing**: Evaluate whether they are implemented efficiently so that security evaluations can be conducted to detect unauthorized access, record user activities and tampering.
- **Installation of Operational Software**: Assure the organization meets licensing conditions.
- **Implementation**: A regular vulnerability management program to be implemented to test infrastructure for known vulnerabilities that can be exploited and assure that there is an active process in place to control and manage remedial actions.
- Setup a pipeline to prepare organizations for audits to reduce risk of interruptions.

Operations security helps the organization to place appropriate controls to ensure everyday activity is carried out in a secure and controlled manner. It includes ensuring changes to information assets are carried out efficiently, documenting operating procedures the information assets are protected from malware, and vulnerabilities & other threats, controls to assure the backup is executed efficiently to assure timely availability of information, l monitoring and logging of employee actions and guaranteeing continuous development through Information security systems audit & mitigations. In a nutshell, this security framework in Table 6 will help the organization and its partners in the supply chain to place the security controls which are specific to Operations security and communication network security and to protect the information which is in transit.

## Framework Control

Examples of various companies/software that provide protection from the issues are as follows:

- Malware detection and removal - Symantec, McAfee
- Encryption of data transferred over the network - Sophos, Cisco, Juniper

- Backup - Veritas, McAfee
- Security Incident and Events Management - IBM QRadar, Manage Engine Event log analyzer.
- Vulnerability Detection and Management: GFI Events manager, Nessus, Netsparker
- Data loss Prevention - Symantec, McAfee, Sophos

*Table 6. Security control framework for communication and operations*

| S.NO | Control Requirement | Evidences Required for Control Requirement |
|---|---|---|
| 1 | Malware protection software and up to date OS patches shall be installed on the systems that are exposed to malware including<br>a) Servers<br>b) Computer devices (e.g., desktops, laptops and mobile devices) | 1.Latest Antivirus software and signature compliance reports for the workstations and servers used in the account.<br>2. Latest patch compliance reports for the workstations and servers used in the account. |
| 2 | Client mandated hardening standards shall be implemented and monitored for continued compliance | 1. Copy of the client provided hardening standard.<br>2. Evidence of hardening validation review on systems, devices and servers |
| 3 | Organization hardening standards shall be implemented and monitored for continued compliance. | Evidence of last system compliance validation review on systems, devices and servers |
| 4 | Adequate and appropriate network level segregation (via VLANs, Firewalls etc.) shall be in place as agreed with the client | 1. Up to date network diagrams.<br>2. Firewall rule base.<br>3. Details on switch ACLs. |
| 5 | All data backup on physical media shall be secured as per company or client agreed policies | 1. Backup tape movement and review logs.<br>2. Evidence that fireproof safe is in place for tape storage. |
| 6 | Before the network (e.g., firewall) and system changes being applied to the company environment:<br>a) Change requests shall be documented.<br>B) Changes shall be approved by an approving authority.<br>C) The potential business impacts of changes shall be assessed.<br>d) Changes shall be tested to ensure vulnerabilities have not been introduced. | 1. List of major system and network changes done in the last six months.<br>2. Evidence that the change management process has been adhered to including documentation, approval, review, testing, impact analysis and roll back plan creation. |
| 7 | Data backup shall be:<br>a) Performed using dedicated backup management software to strengthen the security of information backup.<br>B) Recorded in a log, which includes details about data backed up, the date and time of the backup, the backup media used and its physical location. | 1. Data backup and restoration schedule.<br>2. Latest sample backup and restoration logs.<br>3. Tapes movement and review logs (if applicable).<br>4. Fireproof safe for tape storage (if applicable).<br>5. Backup encryption logs. |
| 8 | System devices (CCTV, Firewalls) and servers shall synchronize their clocks to the centralized network time protocol (NTP) server. | 1. The evidence is confirming that the systems are deriving their time and date settings from the NTP servers.<br>2. Screenshot of sample workstations, devices and servers reflecting the correct system date and time of the NTP server. |
| 9 | Security event logging shall be in place for the systems used in the organization. | Evidence that the security event logging is enabled on the systems used in the organization and its vendors. (e.g., reports, screenshots) |
| 10 | Periodic security event/ log reviews shall be performed for critical systems (e.g., manual or by SIEM solution) as contractually agreed with the client. | Periodic manual log review reports or system generated reports (SIEM reports) |
| 11 | Security event logs must be protected and retained according to the company or client mandated retention standards. | 1. Evidence that security logs stored are tamper-free (i.e. no unauthorized modification or deletion is possible)<br>2. Oldest log as per the company or client mandated log retention policy |
| 12 | Vulnerability scanning and penetration testing of systems, equipment and network devices shall be performed to help:<br>a) Identify known technical vulnerabilities<br>b) Determine the extent to which they are exposed to threats.<br>C) Prioritize the remediation of vulnerabilities. | Evidence that a vulnerability assessment and penetration testing is conducted at least annually. |

*continues on following page*

*Table 7. Continued*

| S.NO | Control Requirement | Evidences Required for Control Requirement |
|---|---|---|
| 13 | Firewall configuration of the account shall be reviewed regularly to ensure that:<br>a) Each firewall rule Is approved and signed off by the business organization.<br>B) Expired or unnecessary rules are removed.<br>C) Conflicting rules are resolved. | Evidence that a firewall rule base review is conducted at least annually. |
| 14 | Organization or client approved software shall only be installed on systems used by the account. | 1. List of client approved software.<br>2. Microsoft SCCM reports for the software installed on the account workstations and servers. |
| 15 | Associates shall maintain client systems as per documented and approved methods of v<br>a) Administering users(e.g., adding new business users, updating access privileges, and revoking user access privileges)<br>b) Monitoring key security-related events (e.g., system crashes, unsuccessful login attempts of unauthorized users and unsuccessful changes to access privileges)<br>C) Identifying potential security | 1.Uptodate and approved standard operating procedures for system maintenance as agreed with the client organization.<br>2. Evidence is supporting compliances to the SOP's for maintaining client systems. |

## Supplier Relations Security

Supplier relationship management (SRM) is the system of strategically planning and managing of all interactions with third-party organizations that supply goods and services to an organization. In use, SRM involves creating closer, more sustainable relationships with essential suppliers to realize and uncover the original value and decrease the chance of failure.

Supplier relationship management is the enterprise-wide well-organized assessment of suppliers' capabilities and assets concerning overall business determination, the strategy of what actions to involve in with different suppliers, and execution and planning of all communications with suppliers, systematically across the relationship life cycle. The SRM focus to develop a two-way mutual beneficial relationship with its partners to deliver a significant level of innovation that could be gained by acting independently or through purchasing transaction agreement.

Since multiple parties are involved risk involved is also higher in this domain. The control framework mentioned in Table 7 must be implemented throughout the supply chain to avoid any breach related to supplier relationships.

## Framework Control

*Table 7. Security control framework for supplier relations*

| S.NO | Control Requirement | Evidences Required for Control Requirement |
|---|---|---|
| 1 | Sound information security practices shall be ensured in all supplier relationships within the account | 1. List of all suppliers used by the account.<br>2. Client approval for usage of suppliers.<br>3. Security clearance by Information Security or Governance team prior onboarding the suppliers.<br>4. Copy of the supplier agreement with the client and company information security requirement.<br>5. Evidence of a periodic security review.<br>6. Sample copies of client mandated NDA's signed by sub-contractors. |
| 2 | All company and client mandated security requirements shall be complied with when the supplier further outsources its services to another organization. | 1. Copy of the agreement signed between the supplier and the organization to which services have been outsourced containing the company and client information security requirements. |

## System Acquisition, Development, and Maintenance

Mergers and acquisitions have become very common in organizations. The security framework ensures that information security is implemented to software systems within an organization and that security is included within the policies after any acquisition or mergers. This method helps restrict errors, loss, and the misuse of organizations information. To guarantee that security is an essential element of information systems over their entire lifecycle, including those that contribute services over public networks. The framework mainly focuses on how securely the source code is developed, its review practices, security of source code production environment, how change management is carried out in the new organization, access control review and how vulnerability assessments are carried out. This framework notified in Table 8, guides the organization and its supply chain to avoid any breach related to any new system acquisitions and mergers.

## Framework Control

Change management software's: INTELEX, fresh service

## Information and Incident Management Security

Real-time incidents in the organization are captured, managed, recorded and analyzed. This process is called incident management. It tries to give a sound and complete view of any security issues within an organization. A security incident can be in any form such as intrusion attempt to compromise or data theft. Strict policy violations process must be in place to avoid any such attempts. The organization must have a solid response plan to tackle any security incident and must have a dedicated team to monitor the process so every incident can be recorded and fixed by the deadline. This security framework from Table 9, guides the organization and its supply chain to avoid any breach related to incident management.

*Table 8. Security control framework for system acquisition, development and maintenance*

| S.NO | Control Requirement | Evidences Required for Control Requirement |
|---|---|---|
| 1 | Source code development shall follow secure coding and code review practices | 1. Secure coding guidelines.<br>2. Code review checklist.<br>3. Samples of the code review performed and closure of discrepancies (if applicable) |
| 2 | Organization production data shall not be used in non-production environments. | Evidence that test data is being used in client non-production environments |
| 3 | Changes to client business applications shall be:<br>a) Performed by a formal documented in the change management process.<br>b) Reviewed to ensure that they do not adversely affect intended functionality or compromise security controls. | 1. Change management process document.<br>2. Sample recent changes and relevant evidence in line with the change management process. |
| 4 | The system development methodology shall require that:<br>a) Program coding shall be reviewed by a systems development manager to ensure that system function as intended and to confirm that security weakness (e.g. those related to hardcoded passwords, SQL/LDAP injection attacks, cross-site scripting). | 1. Sample code review reports.<br>2. Evidence is confirming that testing is performed in a non-production environment.<br>3. Segregation of duties matrix (SOD) |
| 5 | The application source code used in development environments within the company network shall be protected by<br>a) Preventing unauthorized changes to development environments. (e.g., by using access control software)<br>b) Applying strict version control over systems development software (e.g., by using configuration management recording access in the log) | 1. List of associates with access to a development environment.<br>2. Evidence that periodic access review is performed.<br>3. Reports confirming strict version control over development software.<br>4. Screenshot of anti-malware solution deployed within the development environment. |
| 6 | Sensitive business information used for testing or development purpose within client environment shall be protected by<br>a) Prohibiting the use of personally identifiable information (i.e. information that can be used to identify a person)<br>b) Using client prescribed methods. | 1. Evidence that no personally identifiable information is used to test or development environments.<br>2. Evidence that data sanitization has been done in a test or development environment.<br>3. Authorization emails for data exporting in to test or development environments.<br>4. List of associates with access to test and development environment and evidence of periodic reconciliation of the same |
| 7 | Secure coding being developed for the client shall be tested to determine the effectiveness of security controls before delivery of the code including<br>a) Vulnerability assessments (to identify weakness in software and security controls)<br>b) Penetration testing (e.g., using a black box or grey box, white box testing to simulate attack) | 1. Vulnerability assessment reports for the application developer.<br>2. Penetration test report.<br>3. Any other automatic or manual application security test reports. |
| 8 | Post implementation reviews shall cover fulfilment of business requirements (including information security) | Client email confirmation on the successful implementation of business and information security requirements. |

# Framework Control

Examples of IT Incident management software's in the market are ZOHO's manage engine, OMNIGO and ConnectWise.

*Table 9. Security control framework for incident management*

| S.NO | Control Requirement | Evidences Required for Control Requirement |
|------|--------------------|--------------------------------------------|
| 1 | There shall be a process for managing individual information security incidents which include:<br>a) Identifying and reporting information security incidents to the company security incident management team and the client as agreed in the contract.<br>b) Responding to information security incidents (e.g., escalation to the information security incident team) | 1. Security incident response plan with details including but not limited to security incident types and severity levels, client contracts, company contacts and SLA's for incident reporting.<br>2. Notifications to the client and internally within the company for past security incidents.<br>3. Evidence that all corrective and preventive controls resulting from the security incident have been successfully implemented. |

## Governance and Compliance Security

Governance and compliance describe the regulatory compliance standards related to the organization and its internal control and business processes. The organization and its supply chain must adhere to these standards (Da Veiga & Eloff, 2007). A secure framework must include communication processes, risk controls and governance methods for maintaining compliance (Biswas, 2013).

By considering the above process, a security framework is created and has to be implemented in the organization and its supply chain. For added granularity, the specifics of the process are as follows:

- Address uncertainty and hence ensure that company objectives are achieved.
- Realize regulatory compliance obligations as specified and visualize them on a global viewpoint throughout the enterprise.
- Detect, prevent and secure potential risks within the enterprise.
- Incrementally build on the design, control and access specifications, alongside the organisations control framework.
- Implement risk management both in business strategizing and everyday operations
- Comply with the appropriate regulations and standards when designing or improving infrastructure.
- Increase the signification of stakeholder decisions by improving both awareness and accountability criteria within the company.
- Put data consolidation protocols into place for easy review procedures and future prevention protocol generation.

Solidify the following of protocol implicitly in the organization by decreasing the active input required from the end-user (be it employee or client). Controls mentioned in Table 10, guides the organization to maintain strict compliance and governance in place.

## Framework Control

The company LogicGate provides various solutions to prevent and manage Governance and compliance security.

*Table 10. Security control framework for governance and compliance*

| S.NO | Control Requirement | Evidences Required for Control Requirement |
|------|---------------------|--------------------------------------------|
| 1 | There shall be documented standards/procedures for monitoring information security compliance for the account which shall cover:<br>a) Identifying the additional information security compliance obligations that are derived from the client contract, legislation and regulations | 1. The account handbook that identifies and documents any additional information security requirements form the client contract and any other legal and regulatory requirements.<br>2. The copy of the client contract/ MSA and all associated security schedules and policies.<br>3. Last internal audit reports and closure status of findings (if any) |
| 2 | The account shall ensure that an internal audit is conducted of the information security requirements as mandated client agreement | Last internal audit closure report |

## CURRENT CHALLENGES FACING THE ORGANIZATION

Some of the impediments facing the implementation of security frameworks are

- Lack of trained staff
- Lack of budget
- Lack of integration among tools

**Lack of Trained Staff**: There is a tremendous shortage of highly skilled cybersecurity professionals. In a survey by Intel, 82 percent of respondents accepted to a lack of cybersecurity skills in their corporation, 71 percent of respondents citing this deficiency accounting for primary and assessable damage. There is direct damage to the company due to the shortage of cybersecurity skills.

**Lack of Budget**: A Kaspersky survey confirms that there is a broad world decline in the amount spent for cybersecurity from $25.5 million in 2016 to $13.7 million till 2017 (Kaspersky, 2017). No organization must compromise when it comes to cybersecurity. ROI (Return of Investment) must be calculated appropriately by the chief security officer for implementing successful cybersecurity program.

**Lack of Integration Among Security Tools**: Cyber Security faces many challenges, and this is one of its main issues. Organizations use many types of security software. How is it useful if the security software doesn't talk to each other since each has its' own vendors striving to achieve their individual goals? SIEM correlation cannot help much in advanced security.

To build a security program that does not possess the above stated issues, a domain-specific control-based security architecture is required

## SOLUTIONS AND RECOMMENDATIONS

This Framework is not a "Canada only" framework. Stakeholders of the private sector made it clear of the origin that global alignment is necessary to evade duplication and confusion of effort or even conflicting expectations in the global enterprise ecosystem. This framework is built in reemphasizing the needs of the now multinational environment of business. The framework's strategy recognizes and implements international standards and organization security formats. This structure can be implemented in any supply chain organization in any country.

NIST, and all the other security frameworks adopted here, has been holding regular discussions with many nations and regions, making noteworthy internationalization advancement. NIST is actively involved with international standards-developing organizations to encourage the adoption of approaches consistent with the Framework (NIST, 2018; NIST, n.d.). Implementing a unified security framework is a tedious process in an organization and its supply chain. But this framework is created in such a way that it can be implemented over an existing security framework of the organization. Establishing this Security control involves the coordination and cooperation of the entire organization. This security framework would give much-needed confidence in mitigating risks in the organization. Confidence in fewer chances of failure would ensure non-wastage of precious economic resources. The right approach would unquestionably do the company well in the new enterprise of the global supply chain market.

## REFERENCES

Biswas, P. (2013). *ISMS Information Security Management System*. Retrieved from https://isoconsultantpune.com/

International Organization for Standards. (n.d.). *ISO/IEC 27000 family - Information security management systems*. Retrieved from https://www.iso.org/isoiec-27001-information-security.html

International Organization of Standardization. (2018). *THE ISO Survey of Management System Standard Certifications – 2017 – Explanatory Note*. Retrieved from https://isotc.iso.org/livelink/livelink/fetch/-8853493/8853511/8853520/18808772/00._Executive_summary_2016_Survey.pdf?nodeid=19208898&vernum=-2

Kapersky. (2017). *From Shaking Their Hands to Paying Off Their Debts: Third party Cybersecurity Failures Cost Businesses the Most*. Retrieved from https://www.kaspersky.com/about/press-releases/2017_third-party-cybersecurity-failures-cost-businesses-the-most

NIST. (2018). *NIST Cyber Security Framework Question and Answers*. Retrieved from https://www.nist.gov/cyberframework/questions-and-answers

NIST. (2019). *Marks Fifth Anniversary of Popular Cybersecurity Framework*. Retrieved from https://www.nist.gov/news-events/news/2019/02/nist-marks-fifth-anniversary-popular-cybersecurity-framework

NIST. (n.d.). *Cyber Security Framework*. Retrieved from https://www.nist.gov/industry-impacts/cyber-security

Passeri, P. (2018). *July 2018 Cyber Attacks Statistics*. Retrieved from https://www.hackmageddon.com/2018/09/07/july-2018-cyber-attacks-statistics/

PCI Security Standards Council. (n.d.). *PCI Security*. Retrieved from https://www.pcisecuritystandards.org/pci_security/

Ponemon. (2018). *Calculating the Cost of a Data Breach in 2018, the Age of AI and the IoT*. Retrieved from https://securityintelligence.com/ponemon-cost-of-a-data-breach-2018/

Veiga, A. D., & Eloff, J. H. P. (2007). An Information Security Governance Framework. *Information Systems Management, 24*(4), 361–372. doi:10.1080/10580530701586136

Wikipedia. (2019b). *Fair Credit Reporting Act*. Retrieved from https://en.wikipedia.org/wiki/Fair_Credit_Reporting_Act

Wikipedia. (2019a). *Supply Chain Management*. Retrieved from https://en.wikipedia.org/wiki/Supply_chain

## KEY TERMS AND DEFINITIONS

**Acceptable Usage Policy:** An acceptable use policy, acceptable usage policy or fair use policy, is a set of rules applied by the owner, creator or administrator of a network, website, or service, that restrict the ways in which the network, website or system may be used and sets guidelines as to how it should be used.

**Access Control List (ACL) in Switches:** It can control the traffic entering a network. Usually, ACLs reside in a firewall router or a router connecting two internal networks. When you configure ACLs, you can selectively admit or reject inbound traffic, thereby controlling access to your network or specific resources on your network.

**COBIT:** COBIT is a good-practice framework created by international professional association ISACA for information technology management and IT governance. COBIT provides an implementable "set of controls over information technology and organizes them around a logical framework of IT-related processes and enablers.

**Full Disk Encryption:** It is a technology which protects information by converting it into unreadable code that cannot be deciphered easily by unauthorized people. Disk encryption uses disk encryption software or hardware to encrypt every bit of data that goes on a disk or disk volume.

**HIPAA:** HIPAA (Health Insurance Portability and Accountability Act of 1996) is United States legislation that provides data privacy and security provisions for safeguarding medical information. The law has emerged into greater prominence in recent years with the proliferation of health data breaches caused by cyberattacks and ransomware attacks on health insurers and providers.

**Master Service-Level Agreement:** A master service agreement, or MSA, is a contract reached between parties, in which the parties agree to most of the terms that will govern future transactions or future agreements.

**Network Time Protocol (NTP):** The Network Time Protocol is a networking protocol for clock synchronization between computer systems over packet-switched, variable-latency data networks.

**NIST:** The National Institute of Standards and Technology is a physical sciences laboratory, and a non-regulatory agency of the United States Department of Commerce. Its mission is to promote innovation and industrial competitiveness.

**Non-Disclosure Agreement:** It is a legal contract between two parties that outlines confidential material, information, knowledge that parties wish to share with one another for certain purpose but wish to restrict access to third parties.

**PCI DSS:** The Payment Card Industry Data Security Standard is an information security standard for organizations that handle branded credit cards from the major card schemes. The PCI Standard is mandated by the card brands and administered by the Payment Card Industry Security Standards Council.

**Penetration Testing:** It is an authorized simulated cyber-attack on a computer system, performed to evaluate the security of the system.

**Security Incident:** A security incident is an event that may indicate that an organization's systems or data have been compromised or that measures put in place to protect them have failed. In IT, an event is anything that has significance for system hardware or software and an incident is an event that disrupts normal operations.

**Security Incident Event Management (SIEM):** It is software that provides real-time analysis of security alerts generated by applications and network hardware.

**Security Tokens:** A security token is a physical device used to gain access to an electronically restricted resource. The token is used in addition to or in place of a password. It acts like an electronic key to access something.

**Standard Operating Procedure (SOP):** It is a set of step-by-step instructions compiled by an organization to help workers carry out complex routine operations. SOPs aim to achieve efficiency, quality output and uniformity of performance while reducing miscommunication and failure to comply with industry regulations.

**System Centre Configuration Manager (SCCM):** It is a systems management software product developed by Microsoft for managing large groups of computers running Windows NT, Windows Embedded, macOS (OS X), Linux, or UNIX.

**Virtual Private Network:** A virtual private network extends a private network across a public network and enables users to send and receive data across shared or public systems as if their computing devices directly connected to the private network.

**Vulnerability Assessment:** It is the process of identifying, quantifying, and prioritizing the vulnerabilities in a system.

*Previously published in the Handbook of Research on Interdisciplinary Approaches to Decision Making for Sustainable Supply Chains; pages 533-555, copyright year 2020 by Business Science Reference (an imprint of IGI Global).*

## APPENDIX

## Types of Hackers

Not every hacker is evil. the word, "hacker," is usually used about cybercriminals, but a hacker can be anyone, regardless of their purposes, who use their knowledge of computer to break into a system or network bypassing security measures. Hacking itself is not a criminal activity unless the hacker is jeopardizing a system without the owner's approval. Several government agencies and organizations employ hackers to help them secure their systems. Hackers are differentiated into three types:

- White hat
- Grey hat
- Black hat

## Black Hat Hackers

Black hat hackers use their knowledge to steal data by bypassing all the security protocols. They create malware to gain access to the network. Their motivation is to take confidential information from the organization. They are involved in cyber espionage and ransomware attacks. They not only steal but they also try to modify and destroy data.

## White Hat Hackers

White hat prefers to utilize their skills for good rather than a crime. They are also called as "ethical hackers." An organization or work pay them for them to find out security vulnerability and fix the issue. They perform the attack vectors with permission from the organization to conduct a vulnerability assessment and penetration testing.

## Grey Hat Hackers

Grey Hat are neither white or black. They are a combination of both. The grey hat accesses a network or system with our owner's knowledge. If any issues are detected, they inform the problem to fix it or grant assistance for a specific fee. They are not malicious, and they don't exploit known vulnerabilities instead try to discover new. Still, this is considered illegal because the hacker did not get the consent from the owner before the attack.

*Although the term hacker tends to invoke adverse inferences when associated to, it is significant to recognize that all Hackers are not equal. If white hat hackers failed to seek out vulnerabilities and threats diligently, the black hat could find it and start exploiting it for criminal activities by collecting sensitive data.*

# Chapter 28
# Cybersecurity Incident Response and Management

**Regner Sabillon**
*Universitat Oberta de Catalunya, Spain*

## ABSTRACT

*This chapter presents a systematic literature review on best practices regarding cybersecurity incident response handling and incident management. The study identifies incident handling models that are used worldwide when responding to any type of cybersecurity incident. The authors highlight the importance of understanding the current cyber threat landscape in any incident response team and their standard operations procedures. The chapter provides guidelines for building a cybersecurity incident team in terms of incident categorization, capabilities, tasks, incident cost calculation, and metrics.*

## INTRODUCTION

Following the devastating Internet effects of the "Morris Worm" in 1988, the Defense Advanced Research Projects Agency (DARPA) assigned the Software Engineering Institute of the Carnegie Mellon University with the mission to set up a security center for emergencies – this center was lately named the CERT Coordination Center (CERT/CC). The CERT Division (Computer Emergency Response Team) of the Software Engineering Institute (SEI) has been a pioneer in providing resources to create and implement Computer Security Incident Response Teams (CSIRT) and Incident Management resources against global cybersecurity threats and vulnerabilities. According to the National Institute of Standards and Technology-NIST (2012), an event is any observable occurrence in a system or network, an adverse event is a negative consequence and a computer security incident is a violation or imminent threat of violation of acceptable use policies, standard security practices or computer security policies.

A recent study from Hathaway et al. (2015) about Cyber Readiness Index (CRI) 2.0, the CRI 2.0 methodology evaluated the cyber readiness of 125 countries by assessing the national cybersecurity commitment and maturity. The analysis included more than seventy indicators across seven basic elements: national strategy, incident response, e-crime and law enforcement, information sharing, investment in research and development (R&D), diplomacy and trade, and defense and crisis response.

DOI: 10.4018/978-1-6684-3698-1.ch028

The Cybersecurity incident response capability can be organized and achieved as a national agency (National Computer Security Incident Response Team - CSIRT) or a military unit, or through the development of an organizational team like the Computer Emergency Response Team (CERT).

## INCIDENT HANDLING MODELS

According to ISACA (2012), Incident Management is the capability to effectively manage unexpected disruptive events with the objective of minimizing impact and maintaining or restoring normal operations within defined time limits. Subsequently, Incident response is considered as a subset of incident management as the operational capability of incident management that identifies, prepares, responds to incidents to controls to control and limit damage; provides forensic and investigative capabilities; maintaining, recovering and restoring normal operations based on the service level agreements (SLAs).

According to Oriyano et al. (2020), an incident is defined as any violation or impending of the security policy. Existing corporate security policies clearly define what events are considered cyber incidents, contain procedures and guidelines for responding to cyber incidents and define clear course of action to deal with detection and response to security incidents.

Table 1 shows the most relevant incident handling and management models:

*Table 1. Cybersecurity incident handling and management models*

| Name of the model | Phases |
|---|---|
| Donaldson et al. (2015): Incident Response Process | Identify, investigate, collect, report, contain, repair, remediate, validate, report conclusions and resume normal IT operations |
| CREST (2014): Cyber security incident management capability | Prepare, respond and follow up |
| NIST (2012): The Incident Response Life Cycle | Preparation; detection & analysis, containment; eradication & recovery and post-incident activity |
| ISACA (2012): Incident Management Life Cycle | Planning and preparation; detection, triage and investigation; containment, analysis, tracking and recovery; postincident assessment and incident closure |
| SANS (2011): Incident handling step-by-step | Preparation, identification, containment, eradication, recovery and lessons learned |
| ISO/IEC 27035 (2011): Information Security Incident Management | Plan and prepare; detection and reporting; assessment and decision; responses and lessons learnt |
| ENISA (2010): Incident handling process | Report, registration, triage, incident resolution, incident closure and post-analysis |
| Kennedy (2008): Modified small business approach for incident handling | Develop a security policy, protect computer equipment, keep data safe, use Internet safely, protect the network, secure line of business applications and training |
| CERT/CC (2003) Incident handling life-cycle process | Report, analyze, obtain contact information, provide technical assistance, coordinate information & response and provide resolution |

While some incident handling models have similar phases, others combine certain elements in conjoined phases but in the end, any specific model must be able to mitigate and eradicate the cybersecurity incident in order to avoid additional cyber threats.

## THE EVERCHANGING CYBERTHREAT LANDSCAPING

The cybersecurity threat landscape is always morphing and evolving due to the constant proliferation of new technologies. Furthermore, cybercriminals are continually launching cyberattacks that tend to grow in sophistication, by adopting new anti-forensics techniques and by using procedures to avoid cybercrime detection and tracing.

McAffee estimates that the cybercrime industry has an annual worldwide revenue of $ 400 billion, with a conservative estimate in global losses of $ 375 billion and a maximum reaching the $ 575 billion. The Internet economy can generate annually between $ 2 trillion and $ 3 trillion and cybercrime takes 15% and 20% of the Internet created value. Nevertheless, most cybercrimes are never reported to avoid further financial losses, damage to corporate reputation and credibility.

ISACA and RSA reported on its global cybersecurity survey that phishing, malware and social engineering were the three most frequently occurring cyberattacks in organizations during 2015. The same study highlighted the motivation behind the cyberattacks; financial gain was the top motivator for cybercriminals, followed by service disruption and data theft. Describing a typical cybercriminal stereotype and its motives is almost impossible, mostly because cybercrime agents act based on one or several motives. Some motives entail curiosity, fun, satisfaction, publicity, manipulation, destruction, revenge, ego gratification, hacktivism, nationalism, radicalism, religion, politics, and financial benefit.

According to ENISA Threat Landscape (2016), the top cyber threats that are increasing in comparison to the previous annual report are malware, web based attacks, web application attacks, Denial of Service (DoS), insider threats, exploit kits, information leakage, ransomware and cyber espionage. The emerging technologies that are considered in the latest report include cloud computing, mobile computing, Cyber Physical Systems (CPS), Internet of Things (IoT), Big Data, Network Virtualization and Software Defined Networks (SDN/5G).

## CYBER INCIDENT CATEGORIZATION

According to NIST (2012), the incident prioritization is one the most critical decision when it comes to handling incidents. There are relevant factors that will help prioritize how a cybersecurity incident is handled (Table 2):

Functional Impact: Business applications that are a target will normally impact organization's functionality; affecting at some point the user's productivity. Incident handlers also need to analyze what are the future consequences if the functional impact of the incident cannot be contained.

Information impact: This factor depends on how the confidentiality, integrity and availability of the information are being affected. Sensitive information leakage and data theft are some examples of privacy breach.

Recoverability: The number of hours and resources to recover from an incident will determine the recoverability level.

The government of Canada (2013) created the Cyber Incident Management Framework (CIMF) which intends to provide a national approach to the management and coordination of future or current cyber threats or cybersecurity incidents. The CIMF contains the Canadian Cyber Incident Response Centre (CCIRC) impact severity matrix to help categorize cyber incidents based on information disclosure, economic, well-being, health and safety, public confidence and essential services. The matrix severity levels range from very low to the catastrophic level which is very high.

*Table 2. Functional, information and recoverability impact categorization of incidents*

| Functional Impact | Information Impact | Recoverability effort |
|---|---|---|
| None: No effect to business | None: No information was compromised | Regular: Time to recover is achievable with current resources |
| Low: Minimal effect | Privacy breach: Sensitive information was accessed or exfiltrated | Supplemented: Time to recover is achievable with extra resources |
| Medium: A critical service is not operating | Proprietary breach: Unclassified information was accessed or exfiltrated | Extended: Time to recover is not predictable; additional help is needed |
| High: Some critical services are not delivered | Integrity Loss: Sensitive or proprietary information was modified or deleted | Not Recoverable: Unable to recover from cyber incident |

(NIST 800-61 Rev 2, 2012)

## BUILDING THE CYBERSECURITY INCIDENT RESPONSE TEAMS

Kaplan et al. (2015) argue that the main objective of an incident response plan is to manage a cybersecurity incident by limiting damage, increasing the confidence of external stakeholders, and reducing costs and recovering times. In order to achieve this objective, it is required to have a clear decision making, strong coordination and accountability skills and a superior collaboration with third-party agents.

ISACA (2013) highlights that a CSIRT should cover specific key capabilities and services:

- Security incident analysis
- Intelligence assessment
- Incident resolution
- Security investigations
- Forensic evidence collection
- Coordination tasks and collaboration with external stakeholders
- Conduct proactive advice including alerts, warnings, vulnerability assessments, training and user cybersecurity awareness

A CSIRT is a group comprised of staff with advanced cybersecurity skills that is formed to deal with incident handling. A CSIRT can be recognized by other names or acronyms like Cyber or Computer Incident Response Team (CIRT); Cyber or Computer Emergency Response Team (CERT); Cyber or Computer Incident Response Capability (CIRC); Cyber or Computer Emergency Response Capability (CERC); Security Incident Response Team (SIRT); Security Emergency Response Team (SERT); Security Incident Response Capability (SIRC); Security Emergency Response Capability (SERC); Incident Response Team (IRT); Emergency Response Team (ERT); Incident Response Capability (IRC) or Emergency Response Capability (ERC).

NIST (2012) recommends a series of key tasks in order to organize a cybersecurity incident handling capability:

- Establish a formal incident response (IR) capability: Organizations must be able to respond effectively when cybersecurity defenses are breached.
- Implement an incident response policy: Having the IR policy in place assures the basis of the incident response program.
- Develop an incident response plan according to the incident response policy: The IR plan presents a roadmap for the implementation of the IR program based on the IR policy. The plan should include short- and long-term goals and program metrics.
- Implement IR procedures: IR procedures sustain detailed steps for dealing with cybersecurity incidents.
- Create clear policies and procedures related to sharing information about incidents:
- Provide the required information about incidents to the appropriate organizations: The organization should share communication about specific incidents with the media, law enforcement and the required security agencies.
- Outweigh the necessary factors when choosing the IT team model: Evaluate advantages and disadvantages of the most convenient team structure model based on the organization's resources and needs.
- Recruit staff with the appropriate skills for the IR team: Critical technical, teamwork and communications skills are fundamental for any CERT or CSIRT.
- Identify internal groups that may support the IR capability: The expertise of other internal groups or units are required to rely on such groups to fulfill the IR mission
- Decide which IR services will be offered: The main focus is to offer IR services but, in some cases, additional services can be available like security awareness, training and cybersecurity advisory services.

## CALCULATING A CYBER INCIDENT COST

Calculating the losses of cyberattacks implying a Dollar value is very difficult, there are direct losses affecting certain environments but there are also indirect financial losses like the downtime of end users not being productive due to certain consequences of the cybersecurity incident dealing with loss of network connectivity, unavailable servers, corrupted data, limited access to applications or inaccessible IT services.

Ditrich (2002) developed an effective incident cost analysis that involves answering several questions to calculate the security incident cost:

1. People involved responding to or investigating the incident?
2. Number of hours these people spent?
3. Number of people that did not work because of the incident?
4. How many hours of productive time they did lose?
5. What is the hourly rate of this staff?
6. What is the overhead percentage that the employer pays for the employees?

Another option is the Incident Cost Analysis Modeling Project (I-CAMP), that was introduced in 1997 and the second edition (I-CAMP II) that was updated in 2000 with a goal to design a cost analysis model for IT related incidents. For the initial I-CAMP study, 13 American universities did participate in this study and in the I-CAMP II, 5 additional universities joined the study. These universities were located in eastern, western and central US States which had a strong history of information technology development and use. This model estimates time and cost with an average of 48 hours per incident and the cost depends of the staff involved in the investigation. To calculate the total cost per incident, it is required to add employee benefits, indirect costs and a median cost of +/- fifteen percent.

Bottom line is to create a proper cybersecurity incident cost model for your organization using the criteria listed above.

## APPROACHES TO MEASURE AND AUDIT OF CSIRTs

As new cyber threats evolve on a daily basis, it becomes necessary the evaluation and measure of operations, growth and maturity of CSIRTs. At this time, there are not any specific standard set of benchmarks for the assessment of CSIRT operations.

Several organizations are working to develop CSIRT evaluation metrics and benchmarks (Table 3). Organizations like the Organisation for Economic Co-operation and Development (OECD), the European Network and Information Security Agency (ENISA), the CSIRT Metrics Special Interest Group, The CSIRT Development and Training team in the Carnegie Mellon University Software Engineering Institute's CERT Division, George Mason University, Hewlett-Packard, Dartmouth University, the Forum of Incident Response and Security Teams (FIRST) and the Center for Internet Security.

## CONCLUSION AND FUTURE RESEARCH

Organizations of all sizes are mostly aware that the cyber threat landscape keeps growing and can target any size company at any time. Cybersecurity incidents can impact business financial, legal, regulatory, operation and reputational. It is vital for any organization to align the cybersecurity agenda with business priorities by implementing an incident management plan. A CSIRT must have a well-defined incident service catalog that separates reactive services, proactive services and cybersecurity quality management services.

Future research for incident management must target incidents in cloud computing, in industrial systems, IoT, and to develop new incident handling approaches against emerging cyber threats.

In addition, the standardization and benchmarks needs further research to assess the incident detection, containment, remediation, recovery and restoration phases. The effectiveness can be measured based on CSIRT processes, satisfaction, performance against goals, incident management and avoidance of incident re-occurrence.

*Table 3. CSIRT evaluation metrics and benchmarks initiatives*

| Organizations | CSIRT evaluation metrics and benchmarks initiatives | Key features |
|---|---|---|
| Organisation for Economic Co-operation and Development (OECD) | Guidance for improving the comparability of statistics produces by Computer Security Incident Response Teams (CSIRTs) – 2015 | • Understanding CSIRT data, statistics and statistical indicators<br>• Main uses of CSIRT statistics<br>• Measuring CSIRT capacity<br>• Improving cybersecurity incident statistics |
| European Network and Information Security Agency (ENISA) | Deployment of baseline capabilities of National Governmental CERTs (2012) | • Cybersecurity incident service portfolio<br>• National and cross-border cooperation<br>• n/g CERT maturity model and services |
| CSIRT Metrics Special Interest Group (SIG) - Forum of Incident Response and Security Teams (FIRST) | Metrics SIG (2016) | • Seeking approaches for benchmarking and/or improving the CSIRT processes and metrics to provide effective incident management quantification<br>• Help to refine, align, and test metrics, as well as to suggest additional improvements for standardizing CSIRT practices within the community |
| CSIRT Development and Training team in the Carnegie Mellon University Software Engineering Institute's CERT Division | Incident Management Capability Metrics (2007) | • Protection phase metrics<br>• Detect phase metrics<br>• Respond phase metrics<br>• Sustain phase metrics |
| George Mason University, Hewlett-Packard, Dartmouth University | Improving CSIRT Skills, Dynamics, and Effectiveness (2013) | • Conduct contextual performance analysis and cognitive task analysis<br>• Provide measurement criteria for improvement |
| Center for Internet Security | The CIS Security Metrics (2010) | Incident management:<br>• Cost of Incidents<br>• Mean Cost of Incidents<br>• Mean Incident Recovery Cost<br>• Mean-Time to Incident Discovery<br>• Number of Incidents<br>• Mean-Time Between Security Incidents<br>• Mean-Time to Incident Recovery<br><br>Vulnerability management:<br>• Vulnerability Scanning Coverage<br>• Percent of Systems with No Known Severe Vulnerabilities<br>• Mean-Time to Mitigate Vulnerabilities<br>• Number of Known Vulnerability Instances<br>• Mean Cost to Mitigate Vulnerabilities |

# REFERENCES

Big Ten Academic Alliance. (1997). Incident Cost Analysis and Modeling Project. *CIC Chief Information Officers*. Retrieved from https://www.btaa.org/docs/default-source/technology/icampreport1.pdf?sfvrsn=0

Big Ten Academic Alliance. (2000). Incident Cost Analysis and Modeling Project I-CAMP II. *CIC Chief Information Officers*. Retrieved from https://www.btaa.org/docs/default-source/reports/icampreport2.pdf?sfvrsn=0

Campbell, T. (2003). *An Introduction to the Computer Security Incident Response Team (CSIRT): Set-Up and Operational Considerations. Global Information Assurance Certification (GIAC) Paper*. SANS.

Center for Internet Security - CIS. (2010). *CIS Security Metrics v1.1.0*. Retrieved from https://benchmarks.cisecurity.org/tools2/metrics/CIS_Security_Metrics_v1.1.0.pdf

Cichonski, P., Millar, T., Grance, T., & Scarfone, K. (2012). *Computer Security Incident Handling Guide: Recommendations of the National Institute of Standards and Technology*. NIST Special Publication 800-61 Revision 2. Gaithersburg: U.S. Department of Commerce.

CREST. (2014). Cyber Security Incident Response Guide. *CREST International*. Retrieved from https://crest-approved.org/wp-content/uploads/2014/11/CSIR-Procurement-Guide.pdf

CSIRT Metrics Special Interest Group – SIG. (2016). Metrics SIG. *FIRST SIG*. Retrieved from https://www.first.org/global/sigs/metrics

Dittrich, D. (2010). Developing an Effective Incident Cost Analysis Mechanism. *Symantec Connect*. Retrieved from http://www.symantec.com/connect/articles/developing-effective-incident-cost-analysis-mechanism

Donaldson, S., Siegel, S., Williams, K., & Aslam, A. (2015). *Enterprise cybersecurity: How to build a successful cyberdefense program against advanced threats*. Apress. doi:10.1007/978-1-4302-6083-7

Dorofee, A., Killcrece, G., Ruefle, R., & Zajicek, M. (2007). *Incident Management Capability Metrics*. SEI, Carnegie Mellon University. Retrieved from https://resources.sei.cmu.edu/asset_files/TechnicalReport/2007_005_001_14873.pdf

European Network and Information Security Agency - ENISA. (2010). *Good Practice for Incident Management*. ENISA.

European Network and Information Security Agency - ENISA. (2012). *Deployment of baseline capabilities of National Governmental CERTs*. ENISA.

European Network and Information Security Agency - ENISA. (2016). *ENISA Threat Landscape 2015*. ENISA.

Government of Canada. (2013). *Cyber Incident Management Framework for Canada*. Author.

Hathaway, M., Demchak, C., Kerben, J., McArdle, J., & Spidalieri, F. (2015). *Cyber Readiness Index 2.0 – A plan for cyber readiness: a baseline and an index*. Potomac Institute for Policy Studies.

International Organization for Standardization - ISO. (2011). *ISO/IEC 27035 Information Technology – Security tecniques- Information security incident management". International Organization for Standardization*. ISO.

ISACA. (2012). *Incident Management and Response*. Rolling Meadows: ISACA White Paper.

ISACA. (2013). *Advanced Persistent Threats: How to manage the risk to your business*. Rolling Meadows: ISACA Cybersecurity Nexus.

ISACA. (2016). *State of Cybersecurity: Implications for 2016. An ISACA and RSA Conference Survey*. Retrieved from https://www.isaca.org/cyber/Documents/state-of-cybersecurity_res_eng_0316.pdf

Kaplan, J., Bailey, T., O'Halloran, D., Marcus, A., & Rezek, C. (2015). *Beyond Cybersecurity: Protecting your digital business*. John Wiley & Sons. doi:10.1002/9781119055228

Kennedy, G. (2008). *Security Incident Handling in Small Organizations*. SANS Institute.

Killcrece, G. (2005). *Incident Management*. Software Engineering Institute, Carnegie Mellon University.

Kral, P. (2012). *Incident Handler's Handbook*. The SANS Institute.

McAffee. (2014). Net Losses: Estimating the Global Cost of Cybercrime. *Center for Strategic and International Studies*. Retrieved from https://www.mcafee.com/ca/resources/reports/rp-economic-impact-cybercrime2-summary.pdf

Organisation for Economic Co-operation and Development – OECD. (2015). *Guidance for improving the comparability of statistics produces by Computer Security Incident Response Teams (CSIRTs)*. Retrieved from https://www.oecd.org/officialdocuments/publicdisplaydocumentpdf/?cote=DSTI/ICCP/REG(2013)9/FINA&doclanguage=en

Oriyano, S., & Solomon, M. (2020). *Hacker Techniques, Tools, and Incident Handling* (3rd ed.). Jones & Bartlett Learning.

Pethia, R. (2013). *20+ Years of Cyber (in)Security*. SEI Webinar series. Retrieved from https://www.sei.cmu.edu/webinars/view_webinar.cfm?webinarid=59067

Pfleeger, S., Tetrick, L., Zaccaro, S., Dalal, R., & Horne, B. (2013). *Improving CSIRT Skills, Dynamics, and Effectiveness*. Cybersecurity Division, George Mason University – HP- Darmouth University. Retrieved from https://www.dhs.gov/sites/default/files/publications/csd-pi-meeting-2013-day-2-pfleeger-and-tetrick.pdf

Ruefle, R., Dorofee, A., Mundie, D., Householder, A., Murray, M. & Perl, S. (2014, Sept.). Computer Security Incident Response Team: Development and Evolution. *IEEE Security & Privacy*, 16-26.

Sabillon, R., Cano, J., Cavaller, V., & Serra, J. (2016). Cybercrime and Cybercriminals: A Comprehensive Study. *International Journal of Computer Networks and Communications Security*, 4(6), 165–176.

West-Brown, M., Stikvoort, D., Kossakowski, K., Killcrece, G., Ruefle, R., & Zajicek, M. (2003). *Handbook for Computer Security Incident Response Teams (CSIRTs)*. Software Engineering Institute, Carnegie Mellon University. doi:10.21236/ADA413778

## ADDITIONAL READING

Choi, Y. (2018). *Selected Readings in Cybersecurity*. Cambridge Scholars Publishing.

## KEY TERMS AND DEFINITIONS

**Cybersecurity Event:** Things that happen in particular situation that affect cybersecurity areas.

**Cybersecurity Incident:** Critical events that compromise normal operations of cyber assets within any organization.

*Previously published in Cyber Security Auditing, Assurance, and Awareness Through CSAM and CATRAM; pages 32-44, copyright year 2021 by Information Science Reference (an imprint of IGI Global).*

# Chapter 29
# Lawful Trojan Horse

**Bruce L. Mann**
*Memorial University, Canada*

## ABSTRACT

*News outlets don't usually report on training methods in counter-cyberterrorism, particularly lawful trojan attacks. Instead they describe recent cyberterrorist attacks, or threats, or laws and regulations concerning internet privacy or identity theft. Yet Europe is looking to do just that to head-off the next major cyberattack by creating rules for how member states should react and respond. Several news outlets, for example, reported that Germany's Federal Criminal Police Office (BKA) were using a Trojan Horse to access the smartphone data of suspected individuals before the information was encrypted. Although the urge to strike back may be palpable, hacking-back can put power back into the hands of the suspect. The consensus now is that government action is preferable to hacking-back at attackers.*

## HACKING THEN AND NOW

Hacking originally implied an extraordinary computer skill to extend the limits of a computer system (Chatterjee, 2019; Merisalo, 2020). Hacking required great proficiency. Today however, code libraries and automated tools available on the Internet make it possible for anyone with the will, to intrude into a computer network. The consensus is that attackers will attack a computer network in five phases (Chatterjee, 2019; Merisalo, 2020):

### Phase 1. Reconnaissance

Reconnaissance is the first phase of hacking where the attacker collects information about the target (Chatterjee, 2019). This may include identifying the target, finding out the target's IP Address Range, Network, DNS records. Attackers are often motivated by financial gain, access to sensitive information or damage to brand, so the attacker's first goal is to identify potential targets for their mission (Merisalo, 2020). The attacker's aim is to acquire the names, positions, and email addresses of the target individual or group. The attacker may collect information about the company from LinkedIn and the corporate

DOI: 10.4018/978-1-6684-3698-1.ch029

website, map the supply chain, get building blueprints, information on security systems and available entry points. They may even visit the company building, an event or call the secretary. The attacker might set up a fake company, register domains and create fake profiles for social engineering purposes. Once the attacker determines what defenses are in place, they choose their weapon. The selected vector is often impossible to prevent or detect. It can be a zero-day exploit, a spear-phishing campaign or bribing an employee. Usually there is a minimal business impact. Finally, the attacker is ready to plan an avenue of attack.

## Phase 2. Scanning

Scanning is the second phase (Chatterjee, 2019). At this phase the attacker seeks to breach the corporate perimeter and gain a persistent foothold in the environment (Merisalo, 2020). They may have spear-phished the company to gain credentials, used valid credentials to access the corporate infrastructure, and downloaded more tools like dialers, port scanners, network mappers, sweepers, and vulnerability scanners to scan data. This activity is virtually untraceable. The attacker wants details, such as computer names, IP addresses, and user account numbers by which the attacker perpetrates the attack. The initial intrusion is expanded to persistent, long-term, remote access to the company's environment. They begin testing the network for other avenues of attack, using a couple methods, to help map the network. The attacker then needs to contact someone to see which email server is currently in use. They are looking for an automated email if possible, or based on the information gathered so far, email HR with an inquiry about a job posting.

## Phase 3. Gaining Access

Gaining access is the third phase of hacking (Chatterjee, 2019). During this phase the attacker, having finished enumerating and scanning the network, now decides to explore options for gaining access to the network. Based on data collected during Phases 1 and 2, the attacker develops a blueprint of the target network. Their goal is to expand the foothold and identify the systems housing the target data (Merisalo, 2020). The attacker searches file servers to locate password files and other sensitive data, and maps the network to identify the target environment. Using any number of options, such as a phone app, website email spoofing, or zmail, the attacker sends-off a email asking users to login to a new Google portal with their credentials. A *Social Engineering Toolkit (SET) is* also initiated for penetration testing, and an email sent with the server address to the users, masking it with *bitly* or *tinyurl* to shorten the URL and manage the links. The attacker is often impersonating an authorized user. It's difficult to spot an attacker in this phase.

## Phase 4. Maintaining Access

Maintaining access is the fourth phase of hacking (Chatterjee, 2019). Since control over access channels and credentials was acquired in the previous phases, the attacker now seeks to identify and gain the necessary level of privilege to achieve their objectives (Merisalo, 2020). The attacker has acquired multiple e-mail accounts. They begin testing the accounts on the domain. An administrator account is created based on the naming structure to blend-in. As a precaution, the attacker identifies accounts that have not been used for a long time, assuming they are either forgotten or abandoned. The attacker changes the password and elevates the privileges to administrator status to maintain permanent access to the network. No overt exploitation or attacks will occur at this time. If there is no evidence of detection, a waiting game is played letting the victim think that nothing was disturbed. With access to an IT account the hacker begins to make copies of all emails, appointments, contacts, instant messages, and files to be sorted through and used later. Finally the attacker gains access to the target data. Mail servers, document management systems and customer data are compromised.

## Phase 5. Covering Tracks

In phase 5, the attacker surreptitiously removes customer data, corrupts critical systems, and disrupts business operations, then destroys any evidence with ransomware (Merisalo, 2020), clears-out all sent-emails and server logs, and temp files (Chatterjee, 2019). Prior to the attack, the attacker changes their MAC address and runs their attacking machine through at least one VPN to cover their identity. Once access is gained and privileges have been escalated, the attacker will cover their tracksThe attacker will also look for indications of the email provider alerting the user or possible unauthorized logins under their account.

## CAREERS IN HACKING

Counter-cyberterrorism has created career opportunities for those who can scan, hack, and exploit systems to assess vulnerabilities and uncover digital evidence to assist law enforcement in solving cases (EC-Council iClass, 2019).

## Ethical Hacker Training

EC-Council offers a course called *Certified Ethical Hacker*. Ethical Hacker? What is that - a benign euphemism, or incongruous oxymoron? Perhaps more accurately labeled "penetration testing" or "pen testing", or even "white hat attacking", it is intended to teach the practice of testing a computer system, network, or web application to find security vulnerabilities that an attacker could exploit. Ethical hacking can be automated with software applications, or performed manually. Either way, the process involves gathering information about the target before the test, identifying possible entry points, attempting to break in, either digital or real trespass, and reporting the findings (EC-Council iClass, 2019). In any case, the Hacker Lab Modules include: Footprinting and reconnaissance, scanning networks, system hacking, malware threats, social engineering, denial of service attacking, sessions hijacking, hacking webservers, web applications, wireless networks, mobile platforms, and evading firewalls.

The pressure is on to maintain the instrument-driven discourse across Europe to get lawful hackers hooked-up, wired, and connected to the best instruction money can buy. But while some European countries lack the technical ability to identify state-sponsored hacker groups (Lemos, 2017), others still lack the political will to call out their sponsors (Cerulus, 2019). A new EU protocol is meant to better coordinate the response to large-scale disruptions such as *WannaCry* and *NotPetya* (Information Security Media Group, 2019). Numerous vendors, including Cloudflare, Google, Microsoft, and Symantec have moved to offer free services to help governments better defend themselves against such attacks. This chapter presents some of the main factors to consider in developing clarity of purpose for cybersecurity training, education, or awareness-raising.

## COMMON TYPES

Trojan horses are hidden from the user, activated by the user when they launch a computer application like a greeting card attached to an email. Some of the most common types of Trojan Horse software are described next (Webroot, 2019).

### Backdoor Trojan

Backdoor Trojan horse programs are increasingly popular among malware creators because of the shift in motivation from fame and glory to money and profit (Lau, 2019). *Nivdort* is a backdoor trojan. It is spread using spam emails with the purpose of stealing people's passwords. It can also download more malware onto your computer and modify system settings (Bankvault, 2019). In today's black market economy, a computer with a back door can be put to work performing various criminal activities that earn money for their controllers. Schemes such as pay-per-install, sending spam email, and harvesting personal information and identities, are all ways to generate revenue. A Backdoor Trojan allows hackers to remotely access and control a computer, often for the purpose of uploading, downloading, or executing files at will.

### Exploit Trojan

The aim of an Exploit Trojan attack is to maintain a persistent presence on the victim's network looking for meaningful information. Attackers typically use it to execute shell commands that create new user accounts. If users avoid opening spam emails and attachments, there is limited risk involved. If however, the Exploit Trojan installs itself on the computer containing valuable files, the files will likely be copied or corrupted (Brown, 2019).

BlackHole is a commercial crimeware designed to be stitched into hacked or malicious sites to exploit Web-browser vulnerabilities for the purposes of installing malware of the customer's choosing (Krebs, 2016). A majority of Paunch's customers were using the kit to grow botnets powered by *Zeus* and *Citadel* banking Trojans that were typically used in cyberheists, targeting consumers and small businesses. In October 2013, 7-year-old Dmitry "Paunch" Fedotov was arrested along with an entire team of other cybercriminals who worked to sell, develop and profit from Blackhole. He was sentenced to seven years in a Russian penal colony.

### Rootkit Trojan

Rootkit Trojans are intended to prevent the discovery of malware already infecting a system so that it can effect maximum damage. *ZeroAccess Rootkit Trojan* for example, is the latest rootkit virus to gain widespread infiltration into a huge number of computers. While traditional viruses attempt to infect and destroy as many computers in their path before they're stopped by anti-virus software, rootkits aim to keep the target system working but under the control of an outside party (Eldridge, 2019). They typically give a remote user administrative power, allowing them to manipulate files and maintain control of the target system. Once the target system is controlled by the administrator the target system becomes a "botnet," or "zombie" computer, assisting the intruder to perform fraudulent acts, downloading additional malware and opening software back doors for hackers to enter. Since rootkits execute at the same privilege level as anti-malware software, they're harder to remove; the target computer can't decide which program should have greater authority to shut down the other.

## Banker Trojan

Banker Trojan is a form of Trojan horse and can appear as a legitimate piece of software until it is installed on an electronic device. Banker Trojan targets specific personal information used for banking and other online financial transactions (Kenton, 2018). It's *modus operendi* is to redirect traffic from banking and financial websites to another website, ostensibly one to which the intruder has access. When the software is executed, it copies itself onto the host computer, creating folders and setting Registry entries each time the system is started. It searches for specific cookie files relating to personal finance, which have been stored on the computer by financial websites during an Internet visit. The Trojan horse can execute a number of operations, including running executable files, downloading and sending files remotely, stealing information from a clipboard, and logging keystrokes. It collects cookies and passwords and may remove itself from a computer when commanded.

## DDoS Trojan

A Distributed Denial of Service (DDoS) Trojan can disable a network by flooding it with requests from many different sources. Large numbers of machines are tricked into installing the DDos Trojan at which time the intruder gains control of one or all the machines remotely via a client which communicates with a master server (Munson, 2019). Bombarding the target server with traffic, the DDos Trojan has effectively made it unavailable to legitimate users. The DDoS Trojan is key to ensnaring computers into a botnet. Through this primary machine in their zombie network, hackers can direct attacks at specific companies, computers, or websites. DDos Trojan attacks are often directed at famous brand-name products and services. Those behind them may make financial demands in order to cease their activity.

*Who Can You Trust?* In January 2020, Brian Krebs reported in his tech blog *KrebsonSecurity* of a man in Georgia who operated a service designed to protect companies from crippling distributed denial-of-service (DDoS) attacks pleaded to paying a DDoS-for-hire service to launch attacks against others (Krebs, 2020). Tucker Preston, 22, pleaded guilty in a New Jersey court to one count of damaging protected computers by transmission of a program, code or command .

## Downloader Trojan

These are files written to download additional malware, often including more Trojans, onto a device. The Emotet Downloader Trojan for example, spreads by emails that lure victims into downloading a Word document, which contains macros that after executing employ PowerShell to download a malicious payload (Beek, 2017). Emotet has been observed downloading a variety of payloads, including ransomware, Dridex, Trickbot, Pinkslipbot, and other banking Trojans.

## TROJANS IN THE NEWS

A few recent examples illustrate the activity of a Trojan Horse (Webroot, 2019). For an up-to-date listing of Trojan Horse, access FANDOM (2019).

### Zeus

*Zeus*, also known as *Zbot,* is a successful Trojan banking malware package with 3.6 million infections and many variants used to carry out a number of different kinds of attack. *Zeus* is difficult to detect with older antivirus programs and older security software, as it hides itself with powerful stealth techniques. It is considered that this is the primary reason why *Zeus* trojan has become the most powerful botnet on the Internet. In 2009 *Zeus* infected 3.6 million PCs in the United States. It is perhaps most well-known for its successful hack of the U.S. Department of Transportation. Zeus shares some traits with *Wajam,* including encrypted code sections, dynamic library loading, and encrypted payloads.

In September 2011, the FBI began investigating a modified version of *Zeus Trojan* known as *GameOver Zeus (GOZ)*. It is believed *GOZ* was responsible for more than one million computer infections, resulting in financial losses of more than $100 million. In August 2012, Bogachev was indicted under the nickname "lucky12345" by a federal grand jury in the District of Nebraska on charges of Conspiracy to Participate in Racketeering Activity; Bank Fraud; Conspiracy to Violate the Computer Fraud and Abuse Act; Conspiracy to Violate the Identity Theft and Assumption Deterrence Act; and Aggravated Identity Theft (FBI, 2020). In May 2014, Bogachev was indicted in his true name by a federal grand jury in the Western District of Pennsylvania. In the same month, a criminal complaint was issued in the District of Nebraska that tied the nickname of "lucky12345" to Bogachev and charged him with Conspiracy to Commit Bank Fraud.

### Wamjam

*Wamjam* uses anti-analysis and evasion techniques such as: daily release of metamorphic variants, steganography, string and library call obfuscation, encrypted strings and files, deep and diversified junk code, polymorphic resources, valid digital signatures, randomized filenames and root certificate Common Names, and encrypted updates (Carné de Carnavale & Mannan, 2019). Wajam also implements anti-detection features ranging from disabling Windows Malicious Software Removal Tool, self-excluding its installation paths from Windows Defender, and sometimes leveraging rootkit capabilities to hide its installation folder from users.

### Password-Stealing Trojan Horse

*Wirenet* is a password-stealing Trojan notable for being among the first to target Linux and OSX users, many of whom were migrating from Windows operating systems based on perceived security flaws. Researchers from Russian security company (Doctor Web) discovered a password-stealing backdoor Trojan that targets specifically Linux and Mac OS X users (Zorz, 2012). Dubbed *Wirenet*, this Trojan records passwords entered in Firefox, Chrome, Chromium and Opera (but not Safari). *Wirenet Trojan* also operates as a keylogger, that is, it sends gathered keyboard input data to intruders. In addition, *Wirenet*

*Trojan* steals passwords entered by the user in Opera, Firefox, Chrome, and Chromium, and passwords stored by such applications as Thunderbird, SeaMonkey, and Pidgin.

The U.S. Justice Department accused more than 100 people for purchasing and using "Blackshades," a password-stealing Trojan horse designed to spy on victims through their web cameras, steal files and account information, and log victims' key strokes (Krebs, 2014). Blackshades was an effective and easy-to-use tool for remotely compromising and spying on your targets. Early on in its development, researchers at CitzenLab discovered that Blackshades was being used to spy on activists seeking to overthrow the regime in Syria. The product was sold via open hacker forums, and even included an active user forum where customers could get help configuring and wielding the powerful surveillance tool. Although in recent years, a license to Blackshades sold for several hundred Euros, early versions of the product were sold on PayPal for just $40.US.

## Mobile Banking Trojan

The Mobile Banking Trojan steals login credentials from mobile banking apps or replaces legitimate apps with malicious ones. Banking Trojans rely on impersonation. Upon launching, the Trojan shows a seemingly legitimate login page for the banking app it is masquerading, requiring the victim to enter their banking credentials or credit card details, which will then be sent to the attacker's remote server (Ying, 2019). A more advanced tactic used by some Banking Trojans involves login pages dynamically loaded from a remote server based on whatever legitimate banking apps are installed on the device. As such, the attacker only needs one banking Trojan to infiltrate a victim's device, giving them the ability to steal credentials from a range of banks.

***Who Can You Trust?*** *Citadel* was a Banking Trojan that ruled the malware scene for criminals engaged in stealing online banking passwords and emptying bank accounts. U.S. prosecutors say *Citadel* infected more than 11 million computers worldwide, causing financial losses of at least a half-billion dollars. Like most complex banking trojans, *Citadel* was marketed and sold in secluded, underground cybercrime markets. *Citadel* boasted an online tech support system for customers designed to let them file bug reports, suggest and vote on new features in upcoming malware versions, and track trouble tickets that could be worked on by the malware developers and fellow *Citadel* users alike. *Citadel* customers could also use the system to chat and compare notes with fellow users of the malware.

It was this very interactive nature of *Citadel's* support infrastructure that FBI agents would ultimately locate and identify Russian hacker Mark Vartanyan, who went by the nickname "Kolypto." The nickname of the core seller of *Citadel* was "Aquabox," and the FBI was keen to identify Aquabox and any programmers he'd hired to help develop *Citadel*. Aquabox took the bait, and asked the FBI agents to upload a screen shot of the bug they'd found. European authorities arrested alleged key players behind the development and deployment of *Citadel*. Norweigan press reported that a 27-year-old Russian man identified only as "Mark" was arrested in the Norwegian town of Fredrikstad at the request of the FBI. FBI agents had bought several licenses of *Citadel* from Aquabox. Soon the agents were suggesting tweaks to the malware that they could use to their advantage. Posing as an active user of the malware, FBI agents informed *Citadel* developers that they'd discovered a security vulnerability in the Web-based interface that *Citadel* customers were using to track or collect passwords from infected systems.

## ProRat Trojan

In a lawful intervention, a Trojan Horse like *ProRat* would infect a system, open a port on the suspect's computer to allow the Law Enforcement Agent to log keystrokes, steal passwords, control files, download and run files, format the drives, take screenshots, view system information. *ProRat* is a backdoor trojan, more commonly known as a Remote Administration Tool. As with other trojans it uses a client and server. ProRat opens a port on the computer which allows the client to perform numerous operations on the server. *ProRat* is available in a free version, and a paid version. *ProRat* is known for its server to be almost impossible to remove without up-to-date antivirus software (ProRat, 2008). ProRat has a server-creator with features that allow it to be undetected by antivirus and firewall software, and also allow it to stealthily run in the background. The software removes or disables system restore points, and displays a fake error message to mislead the victims. It is often bound with other file types, such as image files, and when the image file is viewed, the server is installed in the background, undetected if no antivirus software has been installed. *ProRat* allows many malicious actions on the suspect's machine.

## EUROPEAN STANDARDS AND THE OSI MODEL

The European Telecommunications Standards Institute (ETSI) establishes telecommunications standards for Europe. In 2015, ETSI recommended that organizations make diagrams of their computer networks to identify where potential failures in the system might occur.

*Figure 1. Illustration of hardware devices on an organization's network. The system should be able to identify if new systems are introduced into the environment that have not been authorized by enterprise personnel*
(image from Critical Security Controls for Effective Cyber Defence, ETSI 2015).

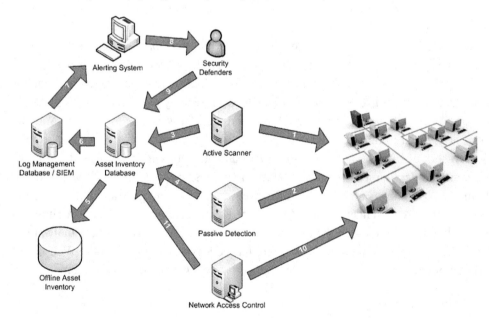

The generalized architecture for lawful interception maps quite well onto the seven packet types or layers of the Open Systems Interconnection (or OSI) model, the concepts of which are highly relevant to lawful interception (Aqsacom, 2005). The Open Systems Interconnection model (OSI model) is a conceptual model that characterizes and standardizes the communication functions of a telecommunication or computing system without regard to its underlying internal structure and technology.

## The OSI Model

The Open Systems Interconnection (OSI) reference model divides communication over a computer network into seven packet types or layers (Shieh, 2007). Examining each layer helps digital investigators construct a *modus operandi* of where digital evidence was left on a network (Casey, 2004). Digital investigators should have solid understanding of OSI Network Layers to handle network evidence.

1. Physical layer
2. Data link layer
3. Network layer
4. Transport layer
5. Session layer
6. Presentation layer
7. Application layer

### Layers 1 and 2: Physical and Data-Link

Layers 1 and 2 represent the elemental aspects of the OSI model. The Physical layer represents the electrical signaling characteristics, modulation schemes, connector pin layouts, etc. making up the networking infrastructure. Note that traditional voice interception had operated at this layer through physical wiretaps. The Data Link layer moves the IP packets or 'datagrams' between hosts. It is described by a number of protocols, including Ethernet, ATM, frame relay, Token Ring, etc (Aqsacom, 2005). Lawful interception may include retrieving information from the physical layer of a computer network because all information sent and retrieved along a computer network, passes through the physical layer. Relevant to this scenario is Casey's example wherein a suspect email was discovered to have been temporarily associated with the MAC address of another computer that belonged to an employee in the software development department of the company he worked. The MAC address is part of the data-link layer, and a source of identification of specific computer on an office-, home- or wide-area network (Casey, 2004).

### Layers 3 and 4: Network and Transport

Whereas the Network layer defines how data between hosts are to be routed to each other over one or more networks, the Transport layer establishes the connection between two hosts, creating a virtual circuit (Casey, 2004). The most common protocol operating at the Network layer is the Internet Protocol (IP) header, which contains critical information for lawful interception, such as the source and destination IP addresses. Network addresses are used to identify the hosts. Digital evidence also may be found at the network and transport layers.

The most common protocol supporting the Transport layer is the Transport Control Protocol (TCP), which assures a solid connection between hosts through data flow control, error detection, and packet reception acknowledgment. Another popular transport layer protocol is the Universal Datagram Protocol (UDP). UDP is much lighter than TCP and does not have transport acknowledgement, thus it moves packets while "hoping for the best" in their delivery to the destination. Nevertheless, UDP is useful for supporting applications such as streamed voice and video, where point-to-point (or multipoint) data transfer in layers 3 and 4 must occur fast and with a minimum of latency (Aqsacom, 2005).

## Layer 5: Session

The session layer controls the session (i.e., the connection) between computers on a network by establishing, managing and terminating the connections between a local and remote application. The OSI model made this layer responsible for "graceful close" of sessions, which is a property of TCP, and also for session check-pointing and recovery (Wikipedia, 2019). "Commands can be used to display information relating to specific sessions, provided they are still active" (Casey, 2004, p. 377). This layer controls the setup and termination of communications sessions, as well as the transfer mode of the data (simplex, half duplex, full duplex). When content is extracted from a communications link in layer 5, it is necessary to determine the transfer mode for lower level interceptions (Aqsacom, 2005).

## Layer 6: Presentation

The presentation layer is responsible for the delivery and formatting of information to the application layer for further processing or display. It relieves the application layer of concern regarding syntactical differences in data representation within the end-user systems. Layer 6 interception is closely aligned with Layer 7 Application interception; i.e., intercepted data formats from specific applications are defined through layer 6 (Aqsacom, 2005).

## Layer 7: Application

The application layer performs application services for computer application processes, and provides services to user-defined application processes, but not to the end user. For example, the application layer defines a file transfer protocol, but the end user must go through an application process to invoke the TCP/IP file transfer (Wikipedia, 2019). This layer defines how applications communicate with each other over the network. Typical applications include E-mail, file transfer, remote database queries, and remote terminal access. Some of the more common protocols operating at Layer 7 include FTP, Telnet, POP3, and HTTP. Lawful interception at the application level can reveal information exchanged by targets running such applications; however, the application data may not necessarily be readily available from network systems responsible for managing applications in layer 7, including web pages, usenet posts, email messages, and IRC logs (Aqsacom, 2005). However, application data may not be readily available from the network system responsible for managing such applications (Casey, 2004).

## PROTECTING THE GLOBAL FINANCIAL SYSTEM

In 2018 the Financial Action Task Force updated their recommendations on international standards on combating money laundering and financing terrorism and proliferation (FATF Recommendations, 2018). The Financial Action Task Force is an independent inter-governmental body that develops and promotes policies to protect the global financial system against money laundering, terrorist financing, and the financing of proliferation of weapons of mass destruction. The recommendations are recognised as the global standard for anti-money laundering and counter-terrorist financing.

The mandate of the Financial Action Task Force is to set standards and promote effective implementation of legal, regulatory, and operational measures for combating money laundering, terrorist financing and the financing of proliferation, and other related threats to the integrity of the international financial system. Financial institutions that have set-up programmes against money laundering and terrorist financing should include an ongoing employee training programme (FATF, p.77), and a financial intelligence unit that conducts both operational and strategic analysis (FATF, p.95). Operational analysis identifies specific targets (e.g. persons, assets, criminal networks and associations) to follow the trail of particular activities or transactions, and to determine links between those targets and possible proceeds of crime, money laundering, predicate offences or terrorist financing. Strategic analysis identifies trends and patterns in money laundering and terrorist financing. This information is then used to determine related threats and vulnerabilities from money laundering and terrorist financing. Strategic analysis may also help establish policies and goals for the financial intelligence unit.

### Operation Avalanche

In 2016 Operation Avalanche marked the largest-ever use of sinkholing to combat botnet infrastructures, with over 800,000 domains seized, sinkholed or blocked (Eurojust, 2017). "Sinkholing" is a research technique for redirecting the identification of the malicious command-and-control (C&C) server to law enforcement's own analysis server (Sancho & Rainer, 2019). This way, the malicious traffic that comes from each client goes straight to the research box, ready to be analyzed.

Action day for Operation Avalanche was postponed to late 2016, to allow for an identification of the perpetrators (Europol, 2016). Europol had set-up a Command Post at its headquarters in The Hague. From there, representatives of the countries involved, worked together with Europol's European Cybercrime Centre (EC3), and Eurojust officials to ensure the success of the large-scale operation. The global effort to take down the perpetrator's network involved the support of prosecutors and investigators from 30 countries. The outcome was that 5 individuals were arrested, 37 premises were searched, 39 servers were seized, and 221 servers were put offline through abuse notifications sent to the hosting providers. The victims of malware infections were identified in 180 countries (Europol, 2016).

The story began, or at least was discovered in 2012 when ransomware was detected infecting several computer systems and blocking user access. A German investigation exposed a sophisticated technical infrastructure that infected millions of private and business computer systems with banking Trojans, enabling the operators to harvest bank and e-mail passwords (Eurojust, 2017). German prosecution and law enforcement authorities approached Eurojust and Europol for support. Several operational and co-ordination meetings were held at Europol and Eurojust, with both agencies cooperating closely. These brought together a large number of Member States and third States, including the USA and Azerbaijan. Private sector partners included the German *Fraunhofer-Institut für Kommunikation, Informations-*

*verarbeitung und Ergonomie,* the Shadowserver Foundation, Registrar of Last Resort and the Internet Corporation for Assigned Names and Numbers (ICANN), INTERPOL, the Ibero-American Network for International Legal Cooperation (IberRed), which served as a liaison to Spanish-speaking countries.

## FAST FLUX NETWORKS

After dismantling the network, investigators found a Fast Flux network (Albors, 2017). "Fast Flux" is a network running several botnets that hide the domains used to download malware or host phishing websites. Fast Flux can also refer to a type of P2P network used to host both the command and control centres or proxies used by these botnets, making them difficult to find and even more difficult to dismantle. A Fast Flux network has multiple IP addresses associated with a domain name, constantly changing them in quick succession. In the case of Avalanche, more than 800,000 malicious domains used since 2009, with IP addresses being changed within periods as short as five minutes, which would initiate connections to different machines despite requesting to see the same website controlled by attackers.

There are two main types of Fast Flux networks: Single Flux and Double Flux. The Single Flux network is characterized by multiple individual nodes registering and deregistering their IP addresses as part of a DNS A (address) for a single domain name. These registrations have a very short lifespan (five minutes on average) and create a constantly changing flow of IP addresses when attempting to access a specific domain. The Double Flux network uses components and methods that adds an additional layer that makes it difficult to locate the machine actually serving the malware. In a Double Flux network, zombie computers are used as proxies, which prevent the victim from interacting directly with the servers, hosting and serving the malware, making it difficult to locate.

Several countries in Europe have proposed that law enforcement agencies should learn to hack into computers or devices to access their data. Toward that end, the European Parliament published a collective case study of hacking by law enforcement in six countries (Milt, Guteil, Liger, Heetman, Eager & Crawford, 2017). The aim of a collective case study is to combine multiple cases into a single study (Mann, 2006, p.71). The study examined the legal frameworks for hacking by law enforcement across six EU member states and three non-EU countries. The document reported on policy proposals on the use of hacking techniques by law enforcement.

## DATA PROTECTION REGULATION IN EUROPE

Europe is now covered by the world's strongest data protection rules. The General Data Protection Regulation (GDPR) came into force on May 25, 2018, and was designed to modernise laws that protect the personal information of individuals. When it comes to trespassing in Europe, 'there shall be no interference by a public authority with the exercise of this right except such as is in accordance with the law and is necessary in a democratic society in the interests of international security, public safety or the economic well-being of the country, for the prevention of disorder or crime, for the protection of health or morals, or for the protection of the rights and freedoms of others.'[1] The trouble is that when a law enforcement agent uploads a Trojan horse on a network there could be any number of consequences, either:

1. It infects a particular individual or group of individuals or specific account names, within a particular time frame, with a particular reason;
2. It infects anyone connected on the LAN for a short time, or;
3. It infects anyone by association, anywhere, anytime, for any reason.

## Network and Information Security "Culture"

The European Union Agency for Network and Information Security (ENISA) is a centre of expertise for cybersecurity in Europe. The Agency is located in Athens Greece with a branch office in Heraklion, Crete. The ENISA contributes to a high level of Network and Information Security within the European Union by developing and promoting a culture of Network and Information Security in society to assist in the proper functioning of the internal market.

## Education, Awareness-Raising, Training

According to United Nations' statistics, there are 44 countries in Europe. Each Member State has adopted a national strategy on the security of network and information systems defining the strategic objectives and appropriate policy and regulatory measures with a view to achieving and maintaining a high level of security of network and information systems. The national strategy on the security of network and information systems is intended to indicate the training, education, awareness-raising programmes on the security of network and information systems (Chapter II, Article 7 sec 1d). Moreover a Cooperation Group composed of representatives of the Member States, the Commission, and ENISA shall carry-out tasks on the basis of biennial work programmes. The Cooperation Group shall: exchange information and best practice on training, education, and awareness-raising (Chapter III, Article 2, sec 1d), and discuss the work undertaken in exercises relating to the security of network and information systems, and education programmes and training (Chapter III, Article 2, sec 3k).

## THE EUROPEAN UNION COALITION

The European Union (EU) is a political and economic coalition of 28 member states located in Europe. Together with the Council of the European Union (a.k.a. "the Council"), the European Parliament exercises the legislative function of the European Union. The European Parliament is the only parliamentary institution of the European Union that is directly elected by EU citizens. The European Union uses its leadership role to sort out disputes between member states and to resolve political crises and disagreements over controversial issues and policies. These days the stakes are high.

## United Kingdom

The United Kingdom joined what was then known as the European Communities on 1 January 1973, and left the European Union officially on 31 January 2020. It has always been a matter of concern whether the cybersecurity human resources were sufficient to meet requirements of the time (EC-Council. 2019). In their latest cybersecurity strategy, the UK government promised to increase the investment on cybersecurity from GBP 869 million to GBP 1.9 billion. U.K. planners in the National Police Chiefs'

Council have partnered with the network supplier Cisco to provide cybersecurity training to 120,000 police officers across England, Scotland, Wales, and Northern Ireland (Moore, 2018).

## Equipment Interference

In 2016, the U.K. Parliament passed the Investigatory Powers Act. Provisions in the Act permits police and intelligence agencies to carry out targeted equipment interference, that is, hacking into computers or devices to access their data and bulk equipment interference for national security matters related to foreign investigations. Material derived from equipment interference can then be used in evidence (Fact Sheet, 2015). The following year, the College of Policing in Ryton advertised for a Technical Skills Trainer in Covert Surveillance. Later that same year in November, at the Police Conference on creativity and innovation in policing, Thomas Allmark of the Northumbria Police said "the key takeaway of the conference was around digital training, some of the workshops around digital training, but also the conversations about online crime and the massive drive there needs to be within the force to adapt to that" (College of Policing, 2017).

## High Court Push-Back

In April 2018, the UK High Court ruled that the *Investigatory Powers Act* violated EU law. The government had until 1 November 2018 to amend the legislation. On 31 October 2018 the *Data Retention and Acquisition Regulations* came into force to address this ruling. These regulations increased the threshold for accessing communications data only for the purposes of serious crimes, defined as offences which are capable of being sentenced to imprisonment for a term of 12 months or more, and requires that authorities consult an independent Investigatory Powers Commissioner before requesting data. The regulations also included a loophole where rapid approval could be made internally without independent approval but with a three day expiry, and with subsequent review by the independent body. Most debates about the regulations have been about the definition of "serious crime".

## European Court Push-Back

Around the same time, the European Court of Human Rights issued judgment in three consolidated cases challenging the U.K. government's mass interception program. The judgment found deficiencies in the legal framework governing mass interception, rendering the program unlawful under Articles 8 and 10 of the *European Convention on Human Rights* (ECHR), which protect the rights to privacy and freedom of expression (ECHR, 2019).

In one case a claimant, Mandy Richards, acting in person, brought wide-ranging proceedings against 22 defendants, that included Metropolitan Police, The Army, the Department of Health, several Hospital Trusts, to mention a few. The defendants subsequently applied for an extended civil restraint order against the Claimant.

*I have, for over 18 months, asked the Police and others, where specifically appropriate to their agency, to look into reported incidents as they have occurred pertaining to malicious and unlawful interception, monitoring and manipulation of my communications and activities, unethical sharing of information, disruption to my personal and professional and political life, home intrusions, car tampering, electrical tampering, bike tampering and domestic disturbances resulting in a potentially lethal risk of harm to my person and to my health (Richards v Investigatory Powers, 2017).*

In another case, the Investigatory Powers Tribunal ruled against an application brought by Privacy International relating to the proper construction of section 5 of the *Intelligence Services Act 1994.* It held that the provision which empowered the Secretary of State to authorise "the taking … of such action as is specified in the warrant in respect of any property so specified" was wide enough to encompass computer and network exploitation or, in colloquial language, hacking of computers including mobile devices.

## France

France has been a member of the EU since 1957. In 2015 France adopted a national cybersecurity strategy. This strategy aims to accompany French society's digital transition and address the new challenges of changing uses of digital technology and the associated threats *(Ministry for Europe and Foreign Affairs, 2019).* The main emphasis in the document, "Paris Call for Trust and Security in Cyberspace", is on prevention; to prevent and recover from malicious cyber activities that threaten or cause significant, indiscriminate or systemic harm to individuals and critical infrastructure. A related overall concern is activity that damages the availability and integrity of the Internet, including interference in electoral processes through malicious cyber activity, and the potential for theft of intellectual property, including trade secrets or other confidential business information, with the intent of providing competitive advantages to companies or commercial sector.

*Legal provisions for the use of hacking tools by law enforcement in France is solely governed by the French Code of Criminal Procedure and, more specifically, the amendments of LOI no 2016-731 of 3 June 2016 strengthening the fight against organised crime, terrorism and hacker financing. The French method of raising awareness about cyber-security has been to use humour and art (Agence nationale de la sécurité des systèmes d'information, April, 2019).*

In August 2019, BBC News reported that a team of French police called "Cybergendarmes" located and destroyed a virus that had infected 850,000 computers worldwide (BBC, 2019). The anti-virus company Avast first alerted France's Digital Crime-Fighting Centre to a private server that had sent a virus called *Retadup* to hundreds of thousands of Windows-operating computers in over 100 countries but mainly in Central and South America. The virus was sent via an email offering easy money or erotic pictures. Hackers were then able to use the virus to control the computers remotely without owners realising, to create the cryptocurrency *Monero,* extort money through "ransomware" and even steal data from hospitals in Israel as well as Israeli patients. The team first tracked down where the command server for the "botnet" network, then created a replica server and used it to render the virus inactive on some 850,000 computers. The botnet operators are believed to have made millions of Euros since they set up in 2016, and are still on the run. Whereas France has developed a global approach to threats of cyberterrorism, other European countries have adopted a more conventional campaign of educational awareness.

*Figure 2. Illustration of the French method of raising awareness about cyber-security using humour and art. Translation: "I'm not falling for that. I am very cautious. I regularly change my smartphone password. One time it's 0000, another it's 1234"*
(ANSSI, 2019, my translation).

## Czech Republic

The Czech Republic has been a member state of the European Union since 2004. The Czech Republic developed an *Action Plan for National Cybersecurity* that includes education, awareness-raising, and training in information society development. Tasks defined by the Action Plan are fulfilled in cooperation and inter-operability within the meaning of Czech law, with other public institutions, and is coordinated with regards to requirements and needs of the entities responsible for the task (European Union Agency for Cybersecurity, 2019).

The planners have established a laboratory for malware impacts on the information systems detection and testing (C.3.08), and implemented a honeypot system for cyber threat detection (C.3.05). Goal F in the Action Plan for the National Cybersecurity Strategy of the Czech Republic is quite specific about training methods in counter-cyberterrorism.

### Preparing and Prosecutors

One of the most interesting initiatives in the Action Plan for the National Cybersecurity of the Czech Republic (H.4.01) is to support cybersecurity-related education of the judiciary (i.e., Judges and Prosecutors) to provide imposition and enforcement of adequate sanctions in legal disputes related to cyber issues by education of the judges and prosecutors. Another is to train cybersecurity managers in the public administration in the detection (e.g. anomalies detection), cybersecurity incidents reporting, and in other possibilities of cooperation with the NCSC (F.3.02). A third means to raise the level of education in the cybersecurity field using modern teaching methods (F.3.04).

## Preparing School-Age Students

The next few goals may be cause for concern in that they might be construed by some as indoctrinating the youth through the public education system. School student "awareness" (goal F.1.01) purports to raise cybersecurity awareness and literacy of primary and secondary school students, as well as among the large public, i.e. end users, through the intermediary of supporting initiatives, awareness campaigns, and organizing public conferences. Modernizing the school curriculum is another goal of the Action Plan (F.2.01), is to modernize the existing primary and secondary school curricula and support new university study programs designed to produce cybersecurity experts. Preparing materials for school teachers is a third goal of the National Cybersecurity Strategy of the Czech Republic (F.2.03), which means to prepare a sufficient materials for school teachers; provide the teachers with education in the cybersecurity field, and prepare a sufficient amount of school materials for students. Developing cyber-talent in students is a fourth goal of the Action Plan (F.2.06), to support, in coordination with universities, and develop student talent in the cybersecurity field.

## Preparing University Students

The Action Plan F.2.07 purports to offer cyber-internships to university students with the possibility of internship in the cybersecurity field in the Czech Republic and abroad. In accordance with F.2.08, plan administrators intend to cooperate with universities and colleges on the development of new curricula and implementation of these new programs, on creation of new "study programs" in the cybersecurity and cyber-defence fields and. In this way the Czech Republic's Action Plan means to be consistent with the ENISA's culture of Network and Information Security in society to assist in the proper functioning of the internal market. Meanwhile, some countries have taken the next step, namely: covert hackers.

## Germany

Germany has been a member state of the European Union since 1958. In March 2008 *The Register* news service reported that the German government started hiring coders to develop "white hat" malware capable of covertly hacking into terrorists' PCs. Germany's Federal Court of Justice said the practice was not covered by existing surveillance legislation (Leyden, 2007). Then in 2015, upset by a cyber hack when intruders attacked the German parliament's network, Berlin prepared to "hack back", disrupting ongoing attacks by breaking back-into the hacker's system to delete data and even destroy their system (Delcker, 2018). Berlin had revamped its tools for cyber counterstrikes, but the legislation lagged behind the changes. Then in 2016, Germany's interior minister Thomas de Maizière, detailed a wide range of measures that the German government was set to implement in response to a string of attacks.

We need a technology offensive. We must technically arm our security authorities much better than we have up to now in terms of personnel and equipment. We are planning the deployment of undercover cyber-investigators on the dark net. These will be undercover investigators who will hone in on, for example, illegal weapons trading, or communication between terrorists (Smale, 2016).

In Germany, law enforcement hacking tools are known as *Staatstrojanern*, or "State Trojans". This term essentially refers to malware that the police can use to infect targets' devices, to give them the access they need to monitor communications and conduct searches. Germany's coalition government has extended police hacking powers by slipping a last-minute amendment into a law that's nominally dealt with driving bans. The German Constitutional Court has ruled on a what the German press is calling "a new basic right", one that allows police to infiltrate a suspect's computer by using trojan horses or rootkits. Whereas police had previously only been allowed to hack people's phones and computers in extreme cases such as terrorist threats, the change now allows them to use such techniques when investigating less serious offences (Meyer, 2017). Similarly in the Netherlands, the lack of judicial oversight even extends after-the-fact.

## The Netherlands

The Netherlands has been a member state of the EU since 1958. In December 2018 Twickelerveld Intelligence and Investigations completed the 8th Edition of its course in *Counterterrorism and Applied Intelligence* (UN General Assembly, 2016). Twickelerveld is located at Schiphol Airport in Northern Holland. Module-1 of the course focuses on "Cyber Awareness and Resilience" which concerns current cyber threats. Students learn how to protect themselves from threats through demonstrations of attack schemes and campaigns, including Trojan Horses.

There is no parliamentary oversight for lawful hacking by the police in the Netherlands, except by the Secret Service. Under Article 126nba of the Code of Criminal procedure (*Kamer der Staten Generaal*, 2016), hacking can *only* be requested by the public prosecutor for investigations into crimes that are serious breaches of law, or when the investigation requires it urgently. In practice this law would allow law enforcement to access a computerised device used by a suspect, search the device with the purpose of looking at stored data, and copy the data. This article permits the interception of private information (streamed data), including password-capture and real-time monitoring of data traffic. Police hackers can influence data, by adjusting settings, turning on webcams / microphones, sabotaging or turning a device off. Moreover, the law allows law enforcement to provide itself with access to enter the computerised device in different ways, including:

- Using a vulnerability in the IT system
- Enter or intrude using a false identity or by brute force
- Use a trojan to infect the device with malware

The national law does not require ex-post supervision (after the hack) or oversight by judicial or other bodies, but assumes that ex-post oversight will take place when the case goes to trial and the evidence resulting from the investigation measures is tested in court.

## Italy

Italy has been a member of the EU since 1957. It is widely acknowledged that Italian law enforcement agencies use hacking tools in the process of criminal investigations. The technique of choice is the surreptitious installation of hidden malware known as trojan horses (Vaciago & Ramalho, 2016). Rules governing the use of government trojans with respect for individual rights was drafted in 2016 by a multi-disciplinary team of legal and technology experts, academia, law enforcement, and human rights groups.

Whereas the use of trojans are considered necessary to fight some forms of crime, often transnational, the use of cybersecurity tools should be consistent with constitutional guarantees. The law *should* establish criteria, conditions, and procedures for the use of trojans by the judiciary. However, Italian Criminal Procedure does not contain such a regulation (Civici e Innovatori, 2017).

There is a proposed requirement to notify individuals that have been the subject of invasion by such tools. Furthermore, evidence collected in a way that is outside the scope of the judge's authorisation and the punishment will not be admissible.

Moreover, case-relevant and general provisions aiming to safeguard the use of the tools have been included in the draft law (Pietrosanti & Aterno, 2017). Once an investigation has finished, the trojan must be safely removed from the target device(s), either by law enforcement or through detailed instructions.

Trojan production and use must be traceable. It is proposed that this is done through a National Trojan Registry, which would hold a 'fingerprint' of each version of the software. A trojan's source code must be deposited in a specific authority and must be verifiable with a reproducible build process. Trojans must hold an annually reviewed certificate to ensure compliance with law and technical regulation. Arguably the most extreme policy to counteract cyberterrorism may be found in Poland.

## Poland

Poland joined the European Union in 2004. Poland's Counter-Terrorism Bill would give security service unchecked power (Council of Europe: Poland, 2016). The Bill consolidates sweeping powers, including enhanced surveillance capacity, in the hands of the Internal Security Agency (ISA), with no independent oversight mechanism to prevent abuse and ensure proper accountability. The bill risks violating the rights to liberty, privacy, expression, association, peaceful assembly, and non-discrimination.

Amnesty International has also criticized the fast-track process for deliberating upon and passing the bill, and the near absence of consultation and authentic debate with civil society in that process. Article 8. 1 of the Act states that in order to recognise, prevent and combat offences of a terrorist nature, the Head of the Internal Security Agency may order the following covert activities to be undertaken, for a period no longer than three months, with regard to a person who is not a citizen of the Republic of Poland, and with regard to whom there is a fear of possible involvement in terrorist activities:

- Obtaining and recording the content of conversations by technical means, including with the use of telecommunication networks;
- Obtaining and recording the content of the image and sound of persons from premises, means of public transportation and other venues other than public spaces;
- Obtaining and recording the content of correspondence, including correspondence kept by means of electronic communication
- Obtaining and recording the data contained in it data carriers, telecommunication end devices, as well as information and tele-information systems;
- Obtaining access and controlling the content of consignments.

Article 41 introduced changes to the Telecommunication Act of 2004. By using the equipment or computer software, the Internal Security Agency may obtain access to information of which it is not an addressee by cracking or bypassing the electronic, magnetic, IT or any other safety measure, or may obtain access to the IT and communications system. The information obtained by the Internal Security Agency as a result of the security assessment conducted, remain a legally protected secret and cannot be used in the execution of the statutory tasks of the Internal Security Agency, and are subject to an immediate witnessed and recorded destruction.

Article 32b.1 refers to systems or data about the construction, functioning, and operational rules of the IT and communication systems in place, including computer passwords, access codes, and other data providing access to the system. Article 32b.1 is used to detect, prevent, or to react to terrorist events in connection with systems or data, and prosecute the perpetrators. Amnesty International has complained that the bill risks violating the rights to liberty, privacy, expression, association, peaceful assembly, and non-discrimination. Amnesty International has also criticized the fast-track process for deliberating upon and passing the bill, and the near absence of consultation and authentic debate with civil society in that process (Amnesty International: Poland, 2016).

## Spain

Spain has been a member of the EU since 1986. Spain relies on a mature legal framework for counterterrorism as a result of its long fight against the domestic terrorist group ETA. The Spanish Criminal Code specifically punishes any act of collaboration with the activities or purposes of a terrorist organization. Spain revised its penal code in 2015, empowering law enforcement agencies to prosecute individuals who glorify terrorism on social media, train remotely, operate without clear affiliation, or travel in support of non-state actors. Spain's counterterrorism capabilities, coordinated by the national Intelligence Center for Counter-Terrorism and Organized Crime (CITCO), have proven effective (U.S. Dept of State, Country Reports on Terrorism, 2016). The National Police and Civil Guard share responsibility for counterterrorism. Spain continued to implement its cybersecurity strategy to safeguard its critical information systems under the direction of the Cyber Defense Committee, charged with coordinating cybersecurity across government agencies.

## Austria

Austria has been a member state of the European Union since 1995. Austria's government has announced a plan to spend nearly €290 million over four years to combat terror (Staff, the Local, 2015). In the wake of the Charlie Hebdo attacks in Paris, the Austrian government announced the allocation of funds to combat terrorism, the funding to be used to hire new personnel trained in cybersecurity, crime fighting, and forensics. Some funding will help purchase IT upgrades, "evidence collection software. Notably, €126m will go into hiring new personnel with special skills, including specialists in cybersecurity, crime fighting and forensics. Technology investment is also planned with €34m targeting special IT technology upgrades, such as the Schengen Information System database and evidence collection software.

## Switzerland

Although Switzerland is one of only a handful of Western European countries that have not joined the European Union, the ties between Switzerland and the European Union are close. The HS Swiss' Training Security is located in Lugano Switzerland. Security Agent Training at HS Swiss specializes in the latest generation of equipment to complete the tasks. Students learn all types of logistics preparation, either pre-intervention or during the intervention, providing both organizational assessments and on-site assistance. The investigative sector is equipped with a wide range of electronic and IT tools targeted and structured to ensure the highest level of professionalism at any level of service required.

The Swiss newspaper *SonntagsZeitung* reported that the Swiss Department of the Environment, Transport, Energy and Communications is examining the use of software to listen into VOIP conversations. The Swiss Surveillance Act does not allow for Trojan horse-type surveillance, said the SunntagsZeitung, but federal criminal regulations do allow software-based wiretaps as long as they are controlled in the same manner as other surveillance equipment, it said (Staff Outlaw News, 2006).

## STRIKING BACK IN EUROPE

Although the urge to strike back against bad actors is strong in the wake of global attacks like *Mirai, WannaCry and NotPetya*, and hacking-back can put power back into victims' hands, most NATO countries agree that massive counter-attacking could constitute an act of war. Some past efforts to hack-back have foundered, in part because of concerns about collateral damage. Furthermore, hackers like to cover their tracks, by routing their attacks through other people's machines without their knowledge, in some cases, many thousands of machines (Drew, 2017; Giles, 2017). Cyber-attackers quickly adapt to conditions in which large organizations might begin hacking-back at one another, using false-flag attacks to bait one company to attack another.

The consensus response has been that government action is preferable to private companies hacking back at attackers (Lemos, 2017). For example BBC News (2019) reported that the U.S. and Taiwan has held their first joint cyber-war exercise. Taiwan's local government co-hosted the tests with the *American Institute in Taiwan*, which represents U.S. interests there. Taiwanese officials were targeted by phishing emails and texts as part of a week-long simulated cyber-war event billed as the first of its kind. The exercises involved attempts to hack into government websites by fooling workers into accepting malicious communications.

### Want to Hack a Satellite?

The U.S. Air Force will let hackers try to hijack an orbiting satellite at the Defcon Hacking Conference next year (Barrett, 2019). Selected researchers will be invited to try their ideas during a test-build six months before the 2020 DefCon Hacking Conference. The Air Force will fly the winners out to Defcon for a live hacking competition.

Some countries are using their own resources for training, others are outsourcing to private firms. All seem to want to know about the use of a Trojan Horse to collect data remotely from suspects. Trojan Horse software are malicious computer programs that pretend to be a benign application that purposefully do something the user does not expect. Trojan horse payloads can cause a variety of temporary harmful effects to permanent damage, such as logging keystrokes to steal information passwords or credit card numbers (Wikipedia, April 2008). They are distinct from viruses.

*With a Trojan horse on a compromised computer, you would be able to do whatever you wanted. That computer would be as good as your own. You would own it. Now imagine that you owned 100,000 such computers, scattered all over the world, each one running and being looked after in someone's home, office, or school. Imagine that with just one command, you could tell all of these computers to do whatever you wanted (Solomon & Evron, 2006).*

*Figure 3. The US Air Force Satellite.*
*Photo by Lockheed-Martin in Wired, 2019.*

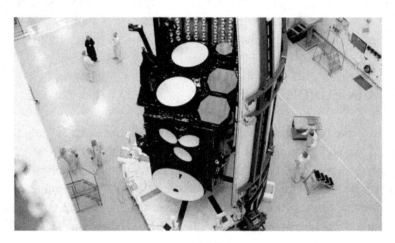

## MOVING FORWARD

Europeans are under no illusion about the need for the latest training in cyber-security. Several countries in Europe have proposed that law enforcement agencies should learn to hack into computers or devices to access their data. But *what kind of training - prevention or retaliation? Who needs the training?* The Czech Republic for example, offers a wide-range of training, education, awareness-raising to military, judges and prosecutors, college students, K-12 students, business, government. Which *tasks* should be included in the instructional unit for cybersecurity training, education, or awareness-raising? "Most lecturers will use a fairly general and unstructured approach to preparation" (Roblyer 2015, p. 5). Consider the necessary basics (e.g., typing, coding, network management), language skills, plus any physiological challenges, any gender or cultural concerns in the directions or instruction.

*Who should deliver the training - inhouse or outsource?* In the UK alone, ten universities offer masters degrees in prevention training in cybersecurity. *How should students access the training?* The EC Council offers several venues to cybersecurity training and hacking back. Hacking back can mean different things to different people: from an active defense, to destroying a hacker's infrastructure as retaliation for a cyberattack. This chapter offers lecturers the main factors associated with developing instructional materials for cybersecurity training, education, or awareness-raising.

## REFERENCES

Agence nationale de la sécurité des systèmes d'information. (2019). *Raising awareness on cyber-security through cartoons.* retrieved 3 March 2019, https://www.ssi.gouv.fr/en/actualite/raising-awareness-on-cybersecurity-through-cartoons/

Albors, J. (2017). Fast Flux networks: What are they and how do they work? *WeLiveSecurity.* Retrieved 12 March 2019, https://www.welivesecurity.com/2017/01/12/fast-flux-networks-work/

American Swiss Foundation. (2016). https://www.americanswiss.org/switzerland-and-the-european-union/

Amnesty International. (2016). *Poland: Counter-terrorism bill would give security service unchecked power.* Retrieved 17 March 2019, https://www.amnesty.org/download/Documents/EUR3742632016ENG-LISH.pdf

Aqsacom. (2005). *Lawful interception for IP networks.* White Paper. Retrieved 3 March 2019, http://www.aqsacomna.com/us/articles/LIIPWhitePaperv21.pdf

Association for Educational Communications and Technology. (2008). Definition. In A. Januszewski & M. Molenda (Eds.), *Educational Technology: A definition with commentary.* Lawrence Erlbaum.

Bankvault. (2019). *The Malware Family Most Wanted List.* Retrieved 21 March 2019, https://www.bankvault.com/locky-ransomware-is-the-3rd-most-deadly/

Barrett, B. (2019). The US Air Force will let hackers try to hijack an orbiting satellite: At the Defcon Hacking Conference next year, the US Air Force will bring a satellite for fun and glory. *Wired.* Retrieved 24 September 2019, https://www.wired.com/story/air-force-defcon-satellite-hacking/

BBC News. (2019a). *French 'cybercops' dismantle pirate computer network.* Retrieved https://www.bbc.com/news/world-europe-49494927

BBC News. (2019b). *U.S. and Taiwan hold first joint cyber-war exercise.* Retrieved 8 November 2019, https://www.bbc.com/news/technology-50289974

Beek, C. (2017). Emotet Downloader Trojan Returns in Force. *McAfee.* https://securingtomorrow.mcafee.com/other-blogs/mcafee-labs/emotet-downloader-trojan-returns-in-force/

Brown, R. (2019). *Security Breach Update: 15 March 2019.* https://tct.com.au/security-breach-update-15-march-2019/

Burack, C. (2018). German federal police use Trojan virus to evade phone encryption. *Deutsche Welle.* Retrieved 10 October 2019, https://www.dw.com/en/german-federal-police-use-trojan-virus-to-evade-phone-encryption/a-42328466

Carné de Carnavalet, X., & Mohammad Mannan, M. (2019). *Privacy and Security Risks of "Not-a-Virus" Bundled Adware: The Wajam Case.* arXiv:1905.05224v2 [cs.CR]

Casey, E. (2004). *Digital evidence and computer crime: Forensic science, computers and the Internet* (2nd ed.). Academic Press.

Cerulus, L. (2019). Europe hopes to fend off election hackers with 'cyber sanctions. *POLITICO*. Retrieved 3 March 2019, https://www.politico.eu/article/europe-cyber-sanctions-hoped-to-fend-off-election-hackers/

Chatterjee, A. (2019). Five phases of hacking. *GeeksforGeeks: A Computer Science Portal for Geeks*. Retrieved 26 February 2020, https://www.geeksforgeeks.org/5-phases-hacking/

CITCO. Intelligence Center Against Terrorism and Organized Crime: Spain (2015). First-Line practioners, retrieved 5 April 2020, https://www.firstlinepractitioners.com/practice/citco-intelligence-center-against-terrorism-and-organized-crime

Civici e Innovatori. (2017). *Rules governing the use of government trojan with respect for individual rights*. Retrieved 12 March 2019, https://issuu.com/civicieinnovatori/docs/sintesi_pdl_captatori_en

College of Policing. (2017). *Coventry, UK, video*. Retrieved 17 March 2019, https://www.college.police.uk/About/Pages/Conference_-_Everyday-innovation.aspx

Council of Europe. (2016). *Poland: On the Act of 15 January 2016 amending the Police Act and certain other Acts*. Opinion No. 839/ 2016, Adopted by the Venice Commission at its 107th Plenary Session (Venice, 10-11 June 2016), Strasbourg, 13 June 2016. Retrieved 12 March 2019, https://www.venice.coe.int/webforms/documents/default.aspx?pdffile=CDL-REF(2016)036-e

Delcker, J. (2018). A hacked-off Germany hacks back: Berlin revamps its tools for cyber counterstrikes, but legislation lags behind. *POLITICO*. Retrieved 17 March 2019, https://www.politico.eu/article/great-german-hack-back-cyber-troops-digital-attacks/

Drew, D. (2017). The 'hack back' is not a defense strategy. *IDG Contributor Network*. Retrieved 12 March 2019, https://www.csoonline.com/article/3228118/the-hack-back-is-not-a-defense-strategy.html

EC-Council. (2019). *Certified Ethical Hacker*. Retrieved 3 March 2019, https://www.eccouncil.org/programs/certified-ethical-hacker-ceh/

EC-Council iClass. (2019). *EC-Council Academic Credits Program: Turn Certification into Education with Academic Credits*. Retrieved 12 March 2019, https://iclass.eccouncil.org/ec-council-academic-credits-program/

EC-Council United Kingdom. (2019). *Training with EC-Council International Council of Electronic Commerce Consultants*. Retrieved 17 March 2019, https://www.eccouncil.org/get-certified-with-ec-council/

Eerste Kamer der Staten Generaal. (2016). *Artikel 126nba, Gewijzigd Voorstel van Wet – Computercriminaliteit III*. Retrieved 19 July 2019, https://www.eerstekamer.nl/wetsvoorstel/34372_computer-criminaliteit_iii

Eldridge, A. (2019). *The ZeroAccess Rootkit Trojan, Nerds On Call*. Retrieved 19 March 2019, https://callnerds.com/the-zeroaccess-rootkit-trojan/

Eurojust. (2017). *Operation Avalanche: A closer look*. Retrieved 3 March 2019, http://www.eurojust.europa.eu/doclibrary/Eurojust-framework/Casework/Operation%20Avalanche%20-%20A%20closer%20look%20(April%202017)/2017-04_Avalanche-Case_EN.pdf

European Parliament. (2018). *At A Glance. European Youth Event. Cyber-attacks: Not just a phantom menace*. Prepared for the European Youth Event, taking place in Strasbourg. Retrieved 12 March 2019, https://www.europarl.europa.eu/RegData/etudes/ATAG/2018/614759/EPRS_ATA(2018)614759_EN.pdf

European Telecommunications Standards Institute. (2015). *Critical Security Controls for Effective Cyber Defence*. Technical Report. Retrieved 10 October 2019, https://www.etsi.org/deliver/etsi_tr/103300_10 3399/103305/01.01.01_60/tr_103305v010101p.pdf

European Union Agency for Cybersecurity. (2019). *National Cybersecurity Strategy 2015 – 2020*. Retrieved 11 July 2019, https://www.enisa.europa.eu/about-enisa/structure-organization/national-liaison-office/news-from-the-member-states/czech-republic-national-cyber-security-strategy-2015-2020

Europol. (2016). *'Avalanche' network dismantled in international cyber operation*. Retrieved 3 March 2019, https://www.europol.europa.eu/newsroom/news/%E2%80%98avalanche%E2%80%99-network-dismantled-in-international-cyber-operation

FANDOM is an entertainment media site. (n.d.). Retrieved 17 March 2019, http://malware.wikia.com/wiki/Category:Trojan

FATF. (2018). *Recommendations*. Retrieved 17 March 2019, http://www.fatf-gafi.org/media/fatf/documents/recommendations/pdfs/FATF%20Recommendations%202012.pdf

FBI. (2020). *$3M Bounty for ZeuS Trojan Author*. U.S. Department of Justice. Retrieved 25 January 2020, https://www.fbi.gov/wanted/cyber/evgeniy-mikhailovich-bogachev

Ferguson, S. (2019). EU Seeks Better Coordination to Battle Next Big Cyberattack. *Information Security Media Group*. Retrieved 3 March 2019, https://www.bankinfosecurity.com/eu-seeks-better-coordination-to-battle-next-big-cyberattack-a-12228

General Data Protection Regulation. (2018). General Data Protection Regulation, Official Journal of the European Union, retrieved 5 April 2020, https://eur-lex.europa.eu/legal-content/EN/TXT/PDF/?uri=CELEX:32016R0679

Giles, M. (2017). Hacking Back Makes a Comeback—But It's Still a Really Bad Idea. *MIT Technology Review*. Retrieved 17 March 2019, https://www.technologyreview.com/s/609555/hacking-back-makes-a-comeback-but-its-still-a-really-bad-idea/

Guidance Software. (2007). *EnCase Forensic*. Retrieved 3 March 2019, https://www.guidancesoftware.com/products/ef_index.asp

Home Office. (2015). *Investigatory Powers Bill, Factsheet: Targeted Equipment Interference*. retrieved 12 March 2019, https://assets.publishing.service.gov.uk/government/uploads/system/uploads/attachment_data/file/473740/Factsheet-Targeted_Equipment_Interference.pdf

Information Commissioner's Office. (2007). *Data protection technical guidance determining what is personal data*. Author.

Investigatory Powers Act. (2016). http://www.legislation.gov.uk/ukpga/2016/25/contents/enacted

Kenton, W. (2018). Banker Trojan, Laws & Regulations Crime & Fraud. *Investopedia*. retrieved 19 March 2019, https://www.investopedia.com/terms/b/banker-trojan.asp

Krebs, B. (2014). Feds to Charge Alleged SpyEye Trojan Author. *KrebsonSecurity*. Retrieved 25 January 2010, https://krebsonsecurity.com/2014/01/feds-to-charge-alleged-spyeye-trojan-author/

Krebs, B. (2014). 'Blackshades' Trojan Users Had It Coming. *KrebsonSecurity*. Retrieved 25 January 2010, https://krebsonsecurity.com/2014/05/blackshades-trojan-users-had-it-coming/

Krebs, B. (2016). 'Blackhole' Exploit Kit Author Gets 7 Years. *KrebsonSecurity*. Retrieved 25 January 2010, https://krebsonsecurity.com/2016/04/blackhole-exploit-kit-author-gets-8-years/

Krebs, B. (2020). DDoS Mitigation Firm Founder Admits to DDoS. *KrebsonSecurity*. Retrieved 25 January 2020, https://krebsonsecurity.com/

Krebs, V. (2008). Social Network Analysis, A Brief Introduction. *OrgNet*. Retrieved 17 March 2019, http://www.orgnet.com/sna.html

Lau, H. (2019). Backdoor Trojan, Security Centre. *Symantec*. Retrieved 28 March 2019, https://www.symantec.com/security-center/

Lemos, R. (2017). Why the hack-back is still the worst idea in cybersecurity. *TechBeacon*. Retrieved 3 March 2019, https://techbeacon.com/security/why-hack-back-still-worst-idea-cybersecurity

Leyden, J. (2007). Germany seeks malware 'specialists' to bug terrorists. *The Register*. Retrieved 3 March 2019, https://www.theregister.co.uk/2007/11/21/germany_vxer_hire_plan/

Lockheed-Martin. (2019). Satellite. *Wired*. Retrieved 24 September 2019, https://www.wired.com/story/air-force-defcon-satellite-hacking/

Mann, B. L. (2006). Conducting formative evaluations of online instructional material. In B. L. Mann (Ed.), *Selected styles in web-based educational research* (pp. 232–242). Hershey, PA: Information Science Publishing. doi:10.4018/978-1-59140-732-4.ch016

Merisalo, T. (2020). Five phases of a cyber attack: The attacker's view. *F-Secure*. Retrieved 26 February 2020, https://blog.f-secure.com/5-phases-of-a-cyber-attack-the-attackers-view/

Meyer, D. (2017). Police get broad phone and computer hacking powers in Germany. *ZDNet CBS Interactive*. Retrieved March 3, 2019, https://www.zdnet.com/article/police-get-broad-phone-and-computer-hacking-powers-in-germany/

Milt, K., Guteil, M., Liger, Q., Heetman, A., Eager, J., & Crawford, M. (2017). Legal Frameworks for Hacking by Law Enforcement: Identification, Evaluation and Comparison of Practices, The Policy Department for Citizens' Rights and Constitutional Affairs. *European Parliament Committee on Civil Liberties, Justice and Home (LIBE)*. Retrieved 3 March 2019, https://www.europarl.europa.eu/RegData/etudes/STUD/2017/583137/IPOL_STU(2017)583137_EN.pdf

Ministry for Europe and Foreign Affairs. (2019). France and Cybersecurity. *France Diplomatie*. Retrieved 17 March 2019, https://www.diplomatie.gouv.fr/en/french-foreign-policy/defence-security/cyber-security/

Moore, M. (2018). *Cisco and UK police team up for cybersecurity training*. Retrieved 3 March 2019, https://www.techradar.com/news/cisco-and-uk-police-team-up-for-cybersecurity-training

Munson, L. (2019). The 6 Types of Trojans. *Security-FAQs*. Retrieved 19 March 2019, http://www.security-faqs.com/admin-server-dos-log-steal-and-kill-the-6-types-of-trojans.html

National Cyber and Information Security Agency. (2015). *Action Plan for the National Cybersecurity Strategy of the Czech Republic for the Period from 2015 to 2020*. Retrieved 17 March 2019, https://www.govcert.cz/download/gov-cert/container-nodeid-578/ap-cs-2015-2020-en.pdf

National Telecommunications and Information Administration, U.S. Department of Commerce. (2008). *ICANN. A statement on the Mid-Term Review of the Joint Project Agreement (JPA) Between NTIA and ICANN*. Retrieved 17 March 2019, https://www.ntia.doc.gov/ntiahome/domainname/ICANN_JPA_080402.html

Pietrosanti, F., & Aterno, S. (2017). Italy unveils a legal proposal to regulate government hacking. *Boing Boing*. Retrieved 17 March 2019, https://boingboing.net/2017/02/15/title-italy-unveils-a-law-pro.html

ProRat. (2008). Retrieved 3 March 2019, http://www.prorat.net/

Regulation of Investigatory Powers Act 2000 (c.23)

*Richards v Investigatory Powers Tribunal & Ors* [2017] EWHC 560 (QB) (24 March 2017). (n.d.). Retrieved 3 March 2019, http://www.bailii.org/ew/cases/EWHC/QB/2017/560.html

Roblyer, M. D. (2015). *Introduction to Systematic Instructional Design for Traditional, Online, and Blended Environments*. Pearson.

SS8 Networks. (2007a). *The ready guide to intercept legislation: Germany*. Retrieved 3 March 2019, https://www.ss8.com/ready-guide.php

SS8 Networks. (2007b). *United States*. Author.

SS8 Networks. (2007c). *The ready guide to intercept legislation: Germany*. Retrieved 12 March 2019, https://www.ss8.com/ready-guide.php

Sancho, D., & Link, R. (2019). *Sinkholing botnets, A Trend Micro Technical Paper*. Retrieved 17 March 2019, https://www.trendmicro.com.tr/media/misc/sinkholing-botnets-technical-paper-en.pdf

Shieh, C. (2007). *OSI Model, DoD Model and the TCP/IP Protocol Suite*. Retrieved 3 March 2019, http://bit.kuas.edu.tw/~csshieh/teach/np/tcpip/index.html

Smale, A. (2016). *Germany proposes tougher measures to combat terrorism*. Retrieved 12 March 2019, https://www.nytimes.com/2016/08/12/world/europe/germany-antiterrorism-measures.html

Solomon, A., & Evron, G. (2006). The world of botnets. *Virus Bulletin*. Retrieved 3 March 2019, http://www.virusbtn.com

Staff. (2006). *Swiss government may tap VoIP calls, OUT-LAW News*. Retrieved 12 March 2019, http://www.out-law.com/page-7379-theme=print

Staff. (2015). *Austria's €290m plan to fight terror, The Local*. Retrieved 3 March 2019, https://www.thelocal.at/20150121/austrias-290m-plan-to-fight-terror

UN General Assembly. (2016). *The right to privacy in the digital age*. A/C.3/71/ L.39/Rev.1, pp. 2-3. Retrieved 17 March 2019, https://www.un.org/Docs/journal/En/20161117e.pdf

US Dept of State. (2016). *Country Reports on Terrorism*. Retrieved 12 March 2019, https://www.state.gov/j/ct/rls/crt/2016/272231.htm

Vaciago, G., & Ramalho, D. (2016). The use of Trojans and other types of malware as means of obtaining evidence in criminal proceedings. *Digital Evidence and Electronic Signature Law Review, 13*, 88-96. Retrieved 3 March 2019, https://journals.sas.ac.uk/deeslr/article/viewFile/2299/2252

VICE on HBO. (2017). *How Israel Rules the World of Cybersecurity*. Retrieved 12 March 2019, https://www.youtube.com/watch?v=ca-C3voZwpM

Virtual World News. (2007). *Age Play Report Prompts UK Investigation of Second Life Pedophilia*. Retrieved 3 March 2019, http://www.virtualworldsnews.com/2007/10/age-play-report.html

Webroot. (2019). *Types of Trojan Horse software*. Retrieved 3 March 2019, https://www.webroot.com/us/en/resources/tips-articles/what-is-trojan-virus

Wikileaks. (2008). *Skype and SSL Interception letters: Bavaria–Digitask*. Retrieved 12 March 2019, https://www.wikileaks.org/leak/bayern-skype-interception.pdf

Wikipedia. (2008). *Fourth Amendment to the United States Constitution*. Retrieved 17 March 2019, https://en.wikipedia.org/wiki/Fourth_Amendment_to_the_United_States_Constitution

Wikipedia. (2008). *Trojan horse*. Retrieved 3 March 2019, https://en.wikipedia.org/wiki/Trojan_horse_%28computing%29

Wikipedia. (n.d.a). *OSI model*. Retrieved 17 March 2019, https://en.wikipedia.org/wiki/OSI_model

Wikipedia. (n.d.b). *TCP/IP model*. Retrieved 17 March 2019, https://en.wikipedia.org/wiki/TCP/IP_model

Ying, T.-M. (2019). The evolution of mobile banking trojans. *Symantec*. Retrieved 19 March 2019, https://medium.com/threat-intel/the-evolution-of-mobile-banking-trojans-608625c79143

Zorz, Z. (2012). Cross-platform Wirenet Trojan targets Mac and Linux users. *HelpNetSecurity*. Retrieved 12 April 2019, https://www.helpnetsecurity.com/2012/08/30/cross-platform-wirenet-trojan-targets-mac-and-linux-users/

## ENDNOTE

[1]    Article 8, European Convention for the Protection of Human Rights and Fundamental Freedoms.

*Previously published in Applying Internet Laws and Regulations to Educational Technology; pages 1-40, copyright year 2020 by Information Science Reference (an imprint of IGI Global).*

# Chapter 30
# Modeling a Cyber Defense Business Ecosystem of Ecosystems:
## Nurturing Brazilian Cyber Defense Resources

**Edison Ishikawa**
*University of Brasília, Brazil*

**Eduardo Wallier Vianna**
iD https://orcid.org/0000-0003-3914-7352
*University of Brasília, Brazil*

**João Mello da Silva**
*University of Brasília, Brazil*

**Jorge Henrique Cabral Fernandes**
*University of Brasília, Brazil*

**Paulo Roberto de Lira Gondim**
*University of Brasília, Brazil*

**Ricardo Zelenovsky**
*University of Brasília, Brazil*

## ABSTRACT

*Providing cyber defense in a country is complex. It involves ensuring the security of various products and services that are part of a global supply chain. In this complex scenario, the challenge is the development of a cyber defense business ecosystem that, reaching a minimum level of maturity, guarantees the security of products and services in cyberspace. This work proposes a cyber defense business ecosystem of ecosystems (BEoE) model with two ecosystems that must be created or fostered, the human resources training ecosystem and the product and service homologation and certification ecosystem. These two cyber defense ecosystems are key to the sustainable growth of an entire chain of production and sourcing of cyber defense goods and services. The proposed model allows the Cyber Defense BEoE to evolve, so that different actors (companies and government agencies) with different levels of maturity in defense and cybersecurity may emerge. In this way, a country's Cyber Defense BEoE may be able to provide products and services at different levels of security for its defense system.*

DOI: 10.4018/978-1-6684-3698-1.ch030

## INTRODUCTION

We live in a world that is increasingly dependent upon information and communication technology (ICTs), in which electro-digital controls are embedded in diverse products, services and systems that we use in our everyday lives. This technology and its controls contain known and unknown vulnerabilities, which put people, businesses, societies, and states at risk. In other words, ICTs are a fundamental need in order to maintain our way of life and our wellbeing. Knowledge of the vulnerabilities, and how to manage them, is essential to survival in cyberspace (FERNANDES; MEIRA, 1998).

Brazil faces an elevated dependence upon technology as compared to industrialized countries, in basically every ICT area, from electrical energy systems, through nanomaterial, semiconductors, memory, microprocessors, network and transceiver wiring, modems, switches, routers, firewalls, filmware, software, operational systems, programming language and even cryptographic algorithms (FERNANDES, 2013a). We also depend upon standards, use doctrines, operation, maintenance, and evolution of ICT systems that are not entirely matched to our conditions.

All future scenarios projected for Brazil indicate the intensification of ICT use in society, industry and government. Thus, in the absence of policies that reduce technological dependence, the country will surely lose sovereignty (FERNANDES, 2013c). In other words, the control of the chain of production, operation, maintenance and evolution of ICTs is directly related to National Development and Defense.

If the automation of information and communication is the foundation for industrial development and national defense, and if the country is tending to become less independent and less sovereign, public policies should be created to revert this situation (FERNANDES, 2013c).

Within this context, the following question should be asked: Is the cyber defense of a State tied to the success of the National Productive/Economic Cyber Defense Sector that it sustains?

This article seeks to build and test a Business Ecosystem of Ecosystems (BEoE) model to be applied to a productive/economic sector, that of cyber defense. The text explores a new approach by adapting the concept of Business Ecosystems, which is normally applied within a company in order to launch economic development of a sector with the participation of government, the productive sector, academia, and society. It is worth noting that that which is taking form is not just a game of connecting mismatched parts, but rather a joint construction involving all interested parties with the goal of creating space for consensus, which can then be followed by the erection of institutions, relations and functions of a productive/economic sector to be called the Cyber Defense Sector (FERNANDES, 2012b).

The concept of a productive/economic sector as "BEoE of Brazilian Cyber Defense" comprised of various Business Ecosystems allows comprehension of the context in which Brazilian Cyber Defense is embedded, facilitating recognition of possible connections with diverse actors and chains of production that: either exist or should be created or should be fostered within the Ecosystem.

In order to understand the construction of this model so that a space for consensus may be created between all institutional spheres involved, the chapter suggests the following route: section 2 is a bibliographical inventory on Business Ecosystems; followed by section 3 which presents the work method; next, section 4 proposes a BEoE model applied to a productive/economic sector; section 5 maps the Cyber Defense BEoE according to the model proposed in section 4; and finally, section 6 presents a few final considerations.

## THE CONCEPT OF BUSINESS ECOSYSTEMS

The concept of Business Ecosystems has evolved over time. Originating from the analogy with biological ecosystems, described as an evolving and dynamic system with competition between different species and same species for natural resources, responding to internal and external disturbances in a complex manner, in a chaotic process, seeking balance (WRI 2000, KAUFFAMAN, 1995).

Rothschild (1990) compared the economic system of capitalism to a live ecosystem, noting that phenomena such as competition, specialization, cooperation, exploration, learning, and growth, among others are also important in business, the only difference is the rate of change, being much faster in economy.

Another analogous concept, but with a wider scope, proposed by Mitleton-Kelly (2003), is that of the social ecosystem. In this ecosystem each organization is a complete participant that influences and is influenced by the social ecosystem made up of the diverse relationships between businesses, consumers, suppliers as well as economic, cultural and legal institutions. If a business or institution does not fulfill its role within the ecosystem it may close or go extinct.

However, the concept most applied to the business ecosystem is that of Moore (1996). Initially, Moore defined the business ecosystem as an economic community made up by consumers, leading producers, competitors and other stakeholder*s* in which the leading producers play a key role in the process of co-evolution of the system. Yet, in Moore (1998) the concept of business ecosystem evolved into an evenly matched system in which all actors make decisions in a decentralized and self-organized manner.

Iansiti and Levien (2004) emphasize that the participants of a business ecosystem, like those of biological ecosystems, are a large number of loosely interconnected participants that depend upon one another for their mutual effectiveness and survival. According to the authors cited, the success of a business ecosystem depends upon three factors: productivity, robustness (capacity to survive internal and external changes) and the capacity to create ecosystems and opportunities for new businesses, requiring behavioral changes that reduce protectionism and increase cooperation. Iansiti and Levien (2004b) also identify four roles that organizations may assume within a business ecosystem: keystone are just a few organizations that are classified as drivers or facilitators which have a big impact upon the entire system, ecosystem explorers, which make up the ecosystem's business body, dominators and niche players, actors which pull resources from the system but do not behave in a reciprocal manner. They stress that the objective of a business ecosystem is to supply innovation while a natural ecosystem solely seeks survival. As well as the fact that it is a corporate perspective of an ecosystem based on external actors (stakeholder*s*), in other words, more weight is put on the environment in which the business is found.

In 2006, Moore theorized the emergence of a third form of economic organization, that of ecosystematic organization. Such that modern business thinking should be based upon three pillars: markets, hierarchies (businesses) and ecosystems, which implies a need to test new foundations for competitive policy, regulation and antitrust suits. However, thinking continues to be centered upon the company's business. Moore states that the most interesting business ecosystem work comes from developing countries, where part of the resources necessary to create a business ecosystem does not exist and has to be built, in contrast to highly industrialized states in which all supplies can be considered existent and available (PRAHALAD, 2004). In this case, the ecosystem is stretched for the generation of wealth and to put an end to poverty. Prahalad's perspective is also corporate.

Articles on the subject of Business Ecosystems focus mainly on business within a company. Studies that adopt a wider approach to Business Ecosystems, like that of Rothschild (1990), treating the economy as a Business Ecosystem, are less common.

This work concentrates on modeling a productive/economic sector as a BEoE, in other words, modeling an economic/productive sector made up of diverse ecosystems. This approach of applying the business ecosystem to cyber defense as a System of Systems (SoS) is perfectly aligned with the type of complex systems to increase synergy between diverse systems to reach a common objective (Jamshidi 2008).

## RELATED WORK

Bauer and van Eeten (2009) developed a framework to study the co-evolution of cybercrime and cyber-security markets and its influence upon Information and Communication Technology (ICT) ecosystem. The study does not model cybersecurity as a business ecosystem, but rather examines stakeholder incentives to promote security and influence in the ICT ecosystem.

Das (2015) presents a view on the elements that make up a Cybersecurity Ecosystem and how they relate, seeking to identify risks in the case of security breaches of an organization's information.

Flóres et all (2016) propose a business ecosystem model for Colombian Cybersecurity, highlighting cybersecurity as a strategic component of national security. The difference is that the proposed model is based upon existent ecosystem actors and the proposed model in this article seeks to identify actors that need to be created or incentivized in order for the cyber defense ecosystem to grow in a sustainable and synergistic manner.

Goel (2017) presents a framework to build cyber defense capacities, integrating public, private, and academic sectors and society in an interdisciplinary manner in India. The strategy being the creation of Cyber Defense Business Ecosystem Clusters in each Indian state, involving the sectors cited above in order to create and adopt an array of Better Policies, which contribute to consciousness, education, security and cyber advances in all Indian cities.

Islam (2019) focuses on the socio-technical perspective of Cybercrime and Cybersecurity Ecosystems, emphasizing the importance of the human actor in the business model of the ecosystems cited.

Huang (2019) suggests the need for more active and proactive responses to cyberattacks given the fact that the dark web has become a business ecosystem that offers well-organized services.

The World Bank (2019) made public a report in reference to its Global Cybersecurity Capacity Program that had the goal of assisting some developing countries, selected through activities and technical assistance, to develop cybersecurity capacities seeking to reinforce these countries' cybersecurity ecosystem.

The studies cited confirm an evolving importance of the concept of Cybersecurity Business Ecosystems, which go from pertaining solely to business ecosystems of a company to adopting a holistic view that involves all actors of a country. In this context, this work presents a cyber defense view of a BEoE, which can be extended to a Cybersecurity BEoE, and applied to Brazil.

## METHODOLOGY

A Cyber Defense BEoE proposal was necessary in order to contextualize the projects *Escola Nacional de Defesa Cibernética* (ENaDCiber) and *Sistema de Homologação e Certificação de Produtos e Serviços de Defesa Cibernética* (SHCDCiber). The existence of cyber threats and individuals or organizations behind and countering such threats naturally brings about the creation of business ecosystems, perhaps incomplete or immature, but that make up a cyber defense ecosystem. In order to gather the requirements for the projects cited it was necessary to conceptualize that which would not be a simple business ecosystem but rather a complete cyber defense meta-ecosystem, made up of diverse independent but complete and mature ecosystems, as well as the relationships between these diverse business ecosystems and the ENaDCiber and SHCDCiber ecosystems, in order to foster and cultivate the economic sustainability of this Business Ecosystem of Ecosystems.

In order to elaborate the ENaDCiber and SHCDCiber projects, a multidisciplinary team of consultants was formed of specialists from diverse areas, academia, government and industry. Through the interaction of these specialists a conceptual map of a Cyber Defense Ecosystem of Ecosystems was developed, with the human resources formation business ecosystems (symbolized by ENaDCiber) and that of sourcing (symbolized by SHCDCiber) in place.

The Cyber Defense BEoE was used in the 2nd Conference on *Defesa Cibernética na Defesa Nacional (DCDN)*. The 2nd DCDN Conference had the objective of eliciting and validating the requirements for the projection of a National Cyber Defense School (ENaDCiber) and a System of Homologation and Certification of Products and Services for Cyber Defense (SHCDCiber). One of the courses of the DCDN Conference had the goal of presenting the architecture of the Brazilian Cyber Defense Ecosystem of Ecosystems for critique and suggestions. This course sought to validate the Cyber Defense Ecosystem of Ecosystems, focusing on the need for an Ecosystem of Ecosystems model from which the need to form human resources for the operationalization of the Ecosystem of Ecosystem could be identified. In this way, the manner in which an Educational System relates to other actors within the Cyber Defense Ecosystem of Ecosystems was discussed. It was considered that this Educational System is part of the Ecosystem of Ecosystems and that it must potentialize this Ecosystem of Ecosystems and the Ecosystem of Ecosystems requires interaction with the Educational System, creating synergy between all components of this system (Gestalt). In this way, the course discussed the Management and Evolution of the Cyber Defense Ecosystem, Professional Development, Promotion and Formation of Networks, as well as International Participation in the proposed Ecosystem of Ecosystems. It was considered that, in some way, this complex Educational System to generate Human Resources for the Cyber Defense Ecosystem of Ecosystems would have to be built, operationalized and managed by the ENaDCiber. Thus, the participants agreed that the proposed BEoE was adequate to be used as one of the documents to base the ENaDCiber upon.

The National Defense Strategy in effect at that time was considered during the mapping of the stakeholder*s* and the coordination of the DCDN Conference: mobilization, capacitation, and democratization (BRASIL, 2008). Thus, the discussion included the presence of stakeholders from these three areas, represented by the State, Academia, and Civil Society (Industry and NGOs) respectively, which were invited to participate on the issues discussed in the Conference.

For the coordination of the DCDN Conference a focal group strategy was utilized, consisting in an interview carried out by a moderator, in a non-structured and natural mánner, with a small group of respondents (CRESWELL, 2012). The main objective of focal groups is to gain a deeper view by listening to a group of people from the "target market" talk about problems that interest the researcher. The value of the strategy is in the unexpected results that generally result from an open group discussion and the confirmation of hypothesis and thesis formed in secondary studies. Experienced researchers consider focal groups to be the most important process of a qualitative study (CRESWELL, 2012).

*Figure 1. National Defense Strategy and ENaDCiber*

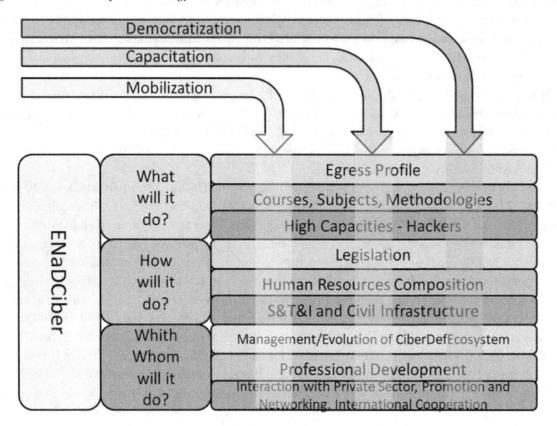

In Figure 1, the existence of 9 focal groups can be observed, all related to the Education System, represented by ENaDCiber, for the formation of HR for the Cyber Defense Ecosystem of Ecosystems. Of the focal groups, the Focal Group on Management/Evolution of the Cyber Defense Ecosystem of Ecosystems stands out as the group that validated the project.

Complementing Figure 1, in order to guarantee that not only the principles of the National Defense strategy be applied for the formation of the Focal Groups, but that the guidelines of the National Defense Strategy also orient the ENaDCiber Project in order for its Educational System to have more efficient results, the three vectors were also discussed in the following manner (Figure 2):

- Mobilization, focusing upon the sustainable evolution of the Cyber Defense Ecosystem of Ecosystems seeking the qualification, differentiation, need and offer of qualified human resources, products, services and cyber defense systems;
- Acquisition of adequate human resources as demanded by Cyber Defense, seeking excellence in acquisition, in order for the Cyber Defense Ecosystem of Ecosystems to be able to supply human resources, products, services and systems for cyber defense that meet the needs of conformity, homologation and certification established by the Homologation System;
- Democratization of the Cyber Defense Ecosystem of Ecosystems, characterized by attainment/ sourcing with transparency. Therefore the need to establish objectives (focus), select objective and effective second criteria, and effectiveness in hiring.

*Figure 2. Mapping the principles of the National Defense Strategy with the guidelines of the ENaDCiber*

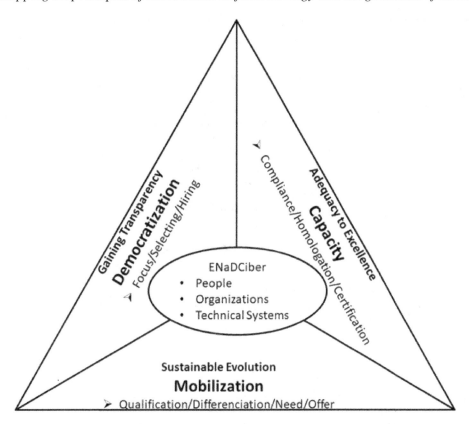

To put this Cyber Defense BEoE Model into the context of the Cyber Defense Education System, the continual process in the Figure 3 processes diagram was used. This process sought to orient the work, contextualizing it and outlining the scope of discussion in order to promote the consolidation and incorporation of successive contributions into diverse documents that were elaborated, all concomitantly. It is important to note this process was iterative and incremental, and that the information produced through learning with the execution of the project increased in quantity and quality with each cycle, emphasizing that all teams learning in this process was fundamental for the quality of the end result.

The activities that made up the process and the input produced for further activities are explained below.

The elaboration of the discussion paper "Cyber Defense BEoE" allowed for visualization of the context in which the ENaDCiber, the Cyber Defense Educational System is embedded. This facilitated the contemplation of possible relationships with diverse Ecosystems mapped by the BEoE. This BEoE allowed the mapping of capacities that should be included in cyber defense, and in light of these capacities, the definition of areas in which the ENaDCiber should act, creating a more complete, clear and consistent view of the Education System and thus, of the documents elaborated by the project.

The activity to elaborate the "Overview of the National Cyber Defense School" discussion paper presented a preliminary view of the Education System that the ENaDCiber should construct, foster and manage. This paper was an attempt to put together a first draft of this Education System. It is an initial platform upon which questions were raised and studies on viability carried out. This view is built upon assumptions raised by various stakeholders in seminaries and workshops carried out beforehand and seeks

*Figure 3. Mapping the Process for elaborating ENaDCiber*

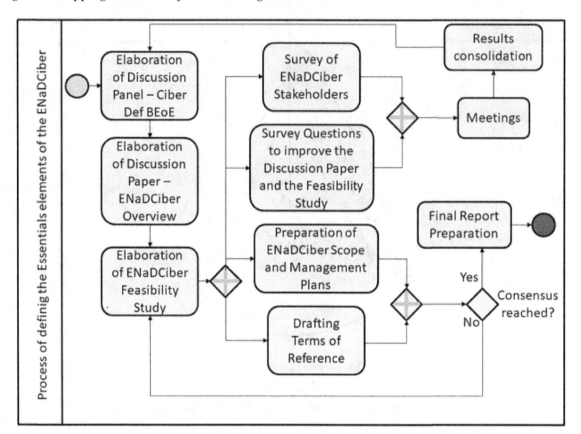

to attend to diverse needs for instruction (capacitation), research and extension that the school would need to offer to the Cyber Defense BEoE. Obviously, these assumptions as well as the Cyber Defense BEoE were reevaluated or modified, bringing a substantial evolution of this view along the course of the work.

The elaboration of the ENaDCiber Feasibility Study sought to gather that which exists similar to a Cyber Defense Educational System. Based on the information gathered, the Cyber Defense BEoE and the ENaDCiber Overview, the Feasibility Study investigated strategies to make the school viable, in accordance with the Overview, establishing lines of action, advantages and disadvantages.

Based upon the Cyber Defense BEoE, in the ENaDCiber Overview and in the ENaDCiber Feasibility Study, two activities were carried out, the survey of ENaDCiber stakeholders and the survey questions that need to be discussed in order to better define the objectives of the school.

Beyond the DCDN Conference, it is worth noting the Hacker Gathering - Discussion on the ENaDCiber in which the national hacker community raised diverse questions and suggestions for the School.

## ECOSYSTEM MODEL PROPOSAL

Business Ecosystems were conceptualized in order to structure a business' chain of production. A business that owns products or services needs to map diverse actors that participate in the business and in its relationships so that a business ecosystem with potential for sustainable growth can develop. However, the development of a state's entire economic/productive sector is not the development of a few products and services, but rather the development of an array of organizations (in industry, the state, academia, and society in general) belonging to this sector, in order to produce products, services, systems, human resources, regulation and demand in the sector seeking development.

The greatest difficulty in the cyber defense sector is that it permeates diverse global chains of production. It is very difficult for a nation to fabricate a cyber product that does not contain some component fabricated externally. Whether it's a chip, a software module, or a service. Beyond the vulnerabilities that may exist due to flaws in development, intentional flaws may be embedded in the components, which can make the effort to create a secure cyber system useless. It is within this context of an economy with globalized production, in which domination of various production chains is sought on the national or regional level in the attempt to guarantee cybersecurity that the Cyber Defense BEoE model is being developed (FERNANDES, 2013b).

Obviously, in the context of a globalized world, the domination by one nation of an entire chain of production in the cyber sector may be technically and economically unfeasible. Existent capacities must be studied, necessary capacities that are lacking must be developed, all of which must be integrated with other trustworthy chains of production in order to develop secure systems. Sharing chains through productive partnership with trustworthy nations and companies would boost not only the national economy, but also that of friendly nations. Thus the need for a Cyber Defense BEoE model that serves as a basis for other cyber defense projects.

This model structures the BEoE as a combination of Business Ecosystems (or meta-ecosystem). Each Business Ecosystem is defined by a conceptual map establishing a value network that defines the very ecosystem. Within this value network are the stakeholders, input, products and the relationships within the chain of production. Each Ecosystem, in turn, interacts with other ecosystems, bringing about a view of a BEoE that can be nurtured for the development of a productive/economic sector. The Ecosystem represented by the yellow ellipse is an attractor, an ecosystem that enables, potentializes or feeds on other ecosystems. Figure 4 shows the layout of this model.

## Brazilian Cyber Defense Ecosystem of Ecosystems Design

To try to visualize the activities of a new area of knowledge and all that this involves, this new area must first be mapped. This section therefore seeks to provide resources so as not to leave out any important requirement of that which is being referred to as a Cyber Defense BEoE.

Therefore, it is fundamental that other areas that interface with cyber defense be situated, like the security gained through the association of a hierarchy of external and internal controls of a system. In relation to security within cyberspace, the regulation ISO/IEC 27032- Guidelines for Cybersecurity (ISO, 2012), in alignment with the "spirit" of security of information inherent to family 2700, define cybersecurity (cyberspace security) as the preservation of confidentiality, integrity, and availability of information in cyberspace. Additionally, other properties, such as: authenticity, responsibility, non-repudiation, and trustworthiness, can also be included in this context. Figure 5, besides exemplifying a type of relationship between cybersecurity and other types of security, points out a series of important activities directly intertwined with cyber defense (VIANNA, 2015).

*Figure 4. Business Ecosystem of Ecosystems (BEoE)*

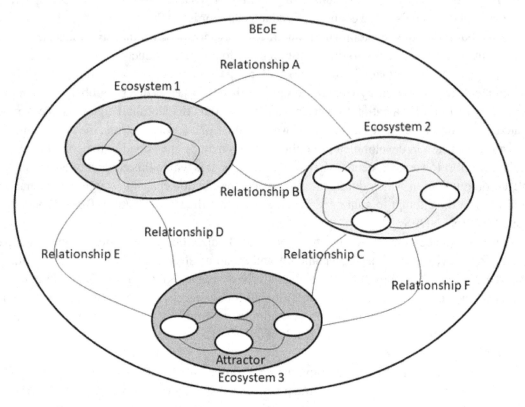

*Figure 5. Relationships between cybersecurity and other types of security Source: Vianna (2015)*

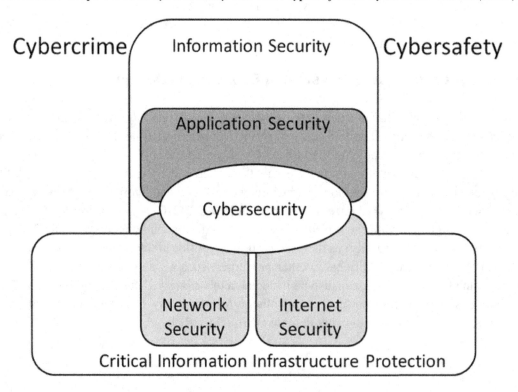

According to Moore (1996) a business ecosystem is a network that encompasses a company and its respective suppliers, clients, and other partners, in a virtuous cycle of production and added value, focusing constantly upon the aspects of interdependence and cooperation.

To define a potential cyber defense BEoE with all its components is a complex task, because it is a system of systems in evolution, growing, that is not yet complete. In other words, its existence needs to be formalized and its construction completed. In light of this, it needs to be nurtured and built. In order to do so the desired type of SoS to be fostered or generated needs to be identified: in extremely simplified terms, the Cyber Defense BEoE would be a SoS made up of the Brazilian state or Brazilian society and its integrants, being public institutions, companies, people (individually or collectively) integrated into a favorable environment (political, economic, military, scientific-technological and psychosocial (juridical, social, cultural, educational and psychological)) in order to establish a virtuous cycle of production and added value in the production of products and services for cyber defense, for critical infrastructure and to guarantee the security of defense products produced by the Defense Industrial Base (DIB) (FERNANDES, 2012a).

*Figure 6. Simplified schematic representation of the Cyber Defense BEoE with its most representative ecosystems, some relationships, and a nucleus of ecosystems necessary for boosting the BEoE as a whole*

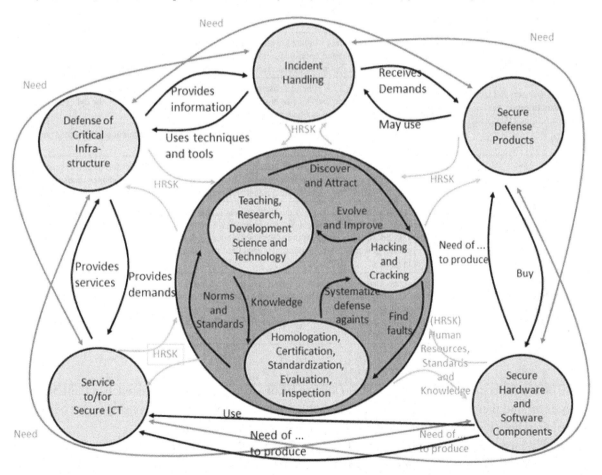

Beginning with this generic definition of a Cyber Defense BEoE, with the objective of nurturing or creating one, the various business ecosystems that make it up must be identified. These ecosystems, some existent and others that need to be created, are all interdependent and their relationships need to be fostered in order to have a synergistically positive BEoE. Figure 6 shows a schematic representation of the Ecosystem of Ecosystems, with a central nucleus of attractors as the basis upon which it is sustained and business ecosystems that can be leveraged by this nucleus of attractors. Table 1 describes each business ecosystems of Figure 6.

*Table 1. Cyber Defense BEoE*

| Business Ecosystems | Description |
|---|---|
| Analysis and management of computer security incident response (CSIR) | This is a known business ecosystem. It includes companies that produce products and services (incident and prevention equipment, antivirus, training courses, consulting for deployment teams, firewalls), its suppliers and customers (government and private institutions. |
| Reliable ICT services and reliable services for ICT | Reliable equipment, software and facilities are not a total guarantee of safety. We must ensure that the business process generates safe products and services. With regard to outsourcing, we need to hire reliable outsourced services. In this case it is necessary to ensure safe processes of every subcontractor. |
| Cyber defense for critical infrastructure | Electrical power and distribution plants, water supply, telecommunications infrastructure, financial systems, etc. are potential targets for cyberattacks. Cyber defense products and services constitute this very specialized business ecosystem. |
| Reliable defense products, services and systems | From vehicles to supersonic airplanes, every war machine has a built-in computer. Also, they are connected to a command and control system. All this equipment have known and unknown cyber weaknesses. Industries that make cyberattack proof equipment are another business ecosystem. |
| Reliable hardware and software for consumer products | This is the largest market for cyber defense products. Requiring low level security certification, but able to leverage all other cyber defense business ecosystems due to its size. Also, the cyber defense products and services for this ecosystem must be affordable to every citizen. |
| Cracking | This ecosystem is formed by criminals who sell their cyber services to criminal organizations and even pariah states through the black market. |
| Hacking | This is an unusual community, hard to characterize due to its diversity. It is composed of people with unusual skills that act in the cyber defense white market. Other cyber defense business ecosystems depend on their skills. They usually are unidentified people who interact with the world virtually. |
| Certification and homologation of cyber defense products, services and systems | This business ecosystem is composed of institutions, laboratories, human resources, legal requirements, standards, specifications and political will to enforce the buying and selling of reliable certified products, services and systems within the cyber defense market. The governments buying and regulation power is fundamental to the growth of this business ecosystem and to the cyber defense market in general. |
| Human Development (research, education, training and retention of human resources) | This business ecosystem consists of public and private education and training institutions and its personnel, human resources to be formed, and companies that will hire these specialized people. This ecosystem is fundamental to the cyber defense business meta-ecosystem because the other business ecosystems need human resources in quantity and quality to offer products, systems and services at a needed scale and price. |

To better understand the need for a Cyber Defense BEoE, to understand the existence of their business ecosystems and their constituents such as their actors, inputs, outputs and relationships, it is necessary to explain where it originates from. This is the purpose of this subsection.

From a naive perspective, initially, the BEoE of Cyber Defense was not a meta-ecosystem, just an ecosystem. In this ecosystem, the first computers did not communicate with each other and few people were able to program them. They were highly specialized and reliable people who worked in safe environments such as academia (universities), government agencies and large companies. In this environment, the concern was with the performance of its products and not safety. Likewise, the Internet, which allowed computers to communicate by making heterogeneous networks compatible, emerged in the academic and research environment in defense, in which researchers were looking for more efficient ways of sharing knowledge and cooperation. In other words, it was a reliable and safe environment. Figure 7 shows the concept map of the actors, inputs, outputs and relationships of this ecosystem in a simplified way.

*Figure 7. Concept map of a naive cyber ecosystem*

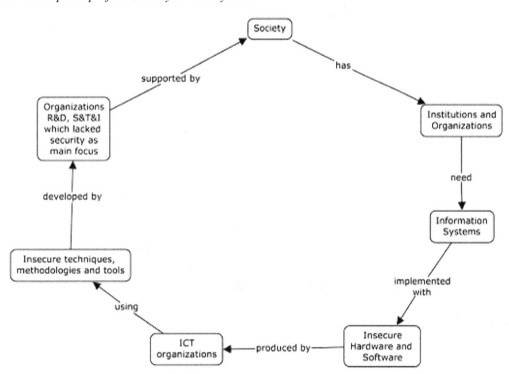

However, these technologies and tools have undergone an exponential growth in their use, expanding far beyond the borders of the safe environments for which they were designed. In this way, a totally vulnerable ecosystem was formed in a hostile environment. It didn't take long for this ecosystem to become a hostile environment. Figure 8 shows the emergence of two new actors (in yellow), previously unknown to the ecosystem, and new relationships (in blue) are being formed. Hackers attack Information Systems, which cause damage to institutions and organizations, which in turn generate demands on society for measures to protect society. To protect itself, society began to create laws for the cyber world and intelligence agencies tried to identify those responsible for cyber harm.

In this environment without malice a new actor appears, the crackers for whom the system is totally vulnerable, and as a consequence an unnecessary actor enters the scene in trusted environments to oppose crackers, the public security intelligence agencies.

*Figure 8. Concept map of an imbalanced cyber ecosystem*

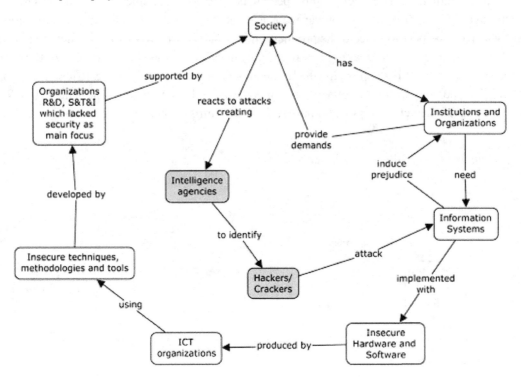

Identifying hackers (hackers will be explained in subsection 5.7) and crackers is not easy. In addition, society is increasingly dependent on information systems for its survival. For this reason, new actors have emerged in an attempt to protect what was inherently unsafe, giving rise to the first business ecosystem with added value to the Cyber Defense BEoE, the computer security incident response business ecosystem (CSIR), briefly described in the next subsection.

## Computer Security Incident Response (CSIR) Business Ecosystem

The CSIR business ecosystem is the most well-known part of the Cyber Defense BEoE, and the most visible one, since it exists and is a component of the Information and Communications Security ecosystem. Such an ecosystem encompasses companies that produce CSIR products and services (incident detection equipment, incident prevention equipment, antivirus, training courses, consultancy for the deployment of CSIR teams, firewalls etc.), customers (governmental and private organizations) and other partners, including actors (e.g., human resources training institutions and organizations) for the approval and certification of their products and services. Figure 9 shows the concept map of CSIR.

Although CSIR aims at preventing or supporting cyber threats, new ones have emerged, and the circumvention of its passive line of defense leads to severe damage to society or the state. Such threats may not reach the network; they can be previously embedded in proprietary closed source systems, or emerge through other less conventional means. The systems addressed control critical infrastructures, such as hydroelectric plants, communications satellites, water supply etc, and this vulnerability became clear after the attack of Stuxnet virus to a system based on SCADA software, widely used for industrial

*Figure 9. Concept map of the business ecosystem for the management and handling of Computer Security Incident Response (CSIR) with its main actors and relationships*

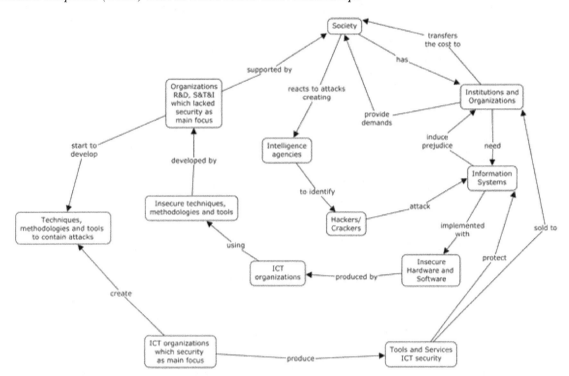

cyber controls, which included critical infrastructures (FALLIERE, 2011). The discovery of this type of vulnerability alerted to the need for a totally different approach to the attack, thus opening space for a new cyber defense business ecosystem, i.e., the cyber defense ecosystem for critical infrastructures, described in the subsection 5.9.

## A Cyber Defense Business Ecosystem for Critical Infrastructure

Failures in critical infrastructure systems are not acceptable, since they cause severe damage to the society, unlike conventional information systems. Therefore, the business ecosystem for critical infrastructure also includes CSIR business ecosystem, which, alone, is not enough. For example, a company's website may be connected to the Internet, but the critical infrastructure under its responsibility may not, and still behaves differently from what had been specified due to some exploited vulnerability that is not a network incident, but probably a cyber one.

This business ecosystem, however, incurs high costs for replacing highly specialized proprietary legacy systems. Since such a substitution is often not feasible, systems that monitor and check whether the behavior of a specific critical infrastructure follows its specifications must be developed. In a second step, more secure systems must be designed with the use of unsafe components from the market, and, in the long run, safe systems must be created with the use of safe components, as shown in the concept map of Figure 10. In other words, this business ecosystem must produce robust systems in the long term, but ensure security in unsafe legacy systems.

*Figure 10. Concept map of the Business Ecosystem for secure critical infrastructures*

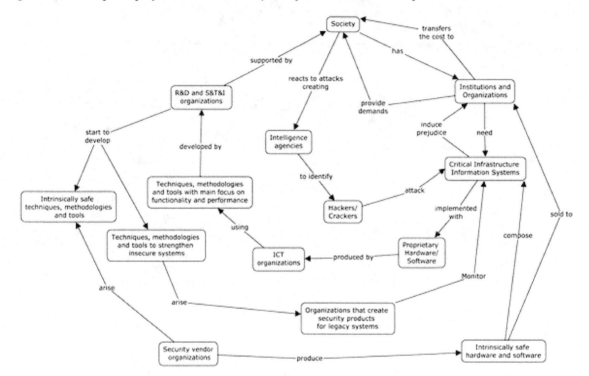

## The Secure Defense Products Business Ecosystem

The defense products of the Brazilian Defense Industrial Base that incorporate cyber systems do not yet have the necessary requirements for meeting all cyber defense needs. Apart from the needs reported in previous ecosystems, defense systems must be prevented from being remotely destroyed through signals transmitted by some means of communication.

However, any component of a defense product can have purposely hidden access for remote destruction, thus hampering the avoidance of the attack. It appears a defense product can have hundreds of thousands of components with this undesirable capability, and the challenge is to approve and certify them as safe, but this alone is not enough. Such secure components can purposely cause failures, hence, remote destruction, which leads us to the first case, i.e., the system must also be homologated and certified as safe.

The same problem occurs with the entire stack of software, hardware and communications protocols used by defense products. Almost all defense products have vulnerable components, i.e., any car or truck has an embedded computer as a fundamental part of its operation - this same component is found in military vehicles, and many components are not manufactured in their home country. Moreover, a country may not have all the technology or resources necessary for their production.

The assurance that defense products are not vulnerable is difficult. The problem is not restricted to them - since components and systems used in military vehicles are also necessary for the functioning of national transport systems, their sales cannot be prevented, which may be unsafe to a country. However, the automotive segment is not the only problem; the same occurs with components used in cellular telephony and in any product that incorporates some computational processing. The problem of defense products is prior to the homologation and certification of security of a system as a whole, and also regards the way of manufacturing a defense product component.

For most countries, self-sufficiency in this area is not economically viable. Mastering the technology of some critical components and their manufacture requires significant investments in S,T&I (Science, Technology and Innovation) and time, and the risks are very high. A solution is to encourage a multinational effort towards the creation of such a business ecosystem of dual products, i.e., for both civil and military use. After all, a market is willing to pay for products of minimum guarantee, e.g., cars not in danger of being disabled remotely, or cell phones improperly monitored. The ecosystem also includes R&D (Research and Development) activities of protocols and cryptographic algorithms, as well as active defense devices, which react after the avoidance of or support to hostile actions. Figure 11 displays a simplified concept map of the ecosystem with only the most apparent value chain highlighted.

*Figure 11. Concept map of the secure Defense Products business ecosystem*

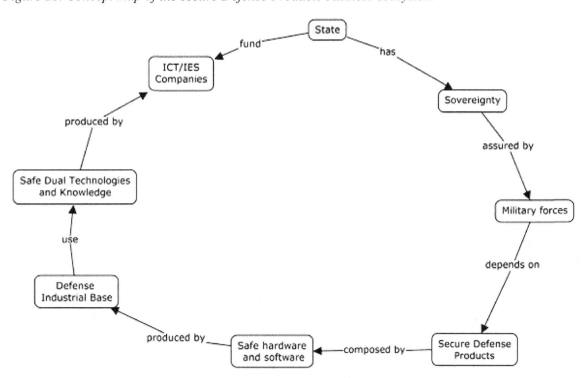

## A Secure Business Ecosystem of Services for Secure ICT

Secure equipment, software and facilities are not sufficient if organizational processes are not secure - such processes must generate secure ICT products and services. Figure 12 shows a conceptual map of this business ecosystem. For example, in the CSIR area, social engineering proof processes must avoid shoulder surfing (the act to get someone password watching the typing over their shoulders). Regarding outsourcing, safe outsourced services must be hired, and the processes of outsourced companies must be also safe. An example of a service is a backup to be performed according to norms and standards that guarantee its safety. Again, an important partner of this business ecosystem is presented, i.e,, the homologation and certification business ecosystem for secure services, explained in the next subsection.

*Figure 12. Conceptual map of the business ecosystem of secure services for ICT*

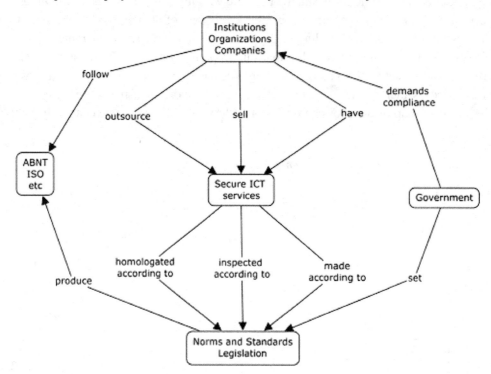

## A Secure Hardware and Software Production Business Ecosystem for Civilian Systems

This business ecosystem can be derived from the dual of the defense products business ecosystem. The current techniques and processes employed for the production of secure hardware and software systems and components are insufficient. However, all the technology and processes for the creation of safe defense products can also be applied to consumer electronics, which intensively uses hardware and software with no guarantee they are safe. The difference is the scale is much larger, i.e., the products can be manufactured on a global scale, and the challenge to make all such production chains secure requires international cooperation, or trust among nation-states, which is still far from the reality. However, some sectors in this ecosystem demand safer systems (e.g., banking automation, with internet banking, electronic commerce, among others), which can invest and offer safer products and services. Figure 13 shows the concept map of this business ecosystem.

*Figure 13. Concept map of the business ecosystem for the production of secure hardware and software for civilian systems*

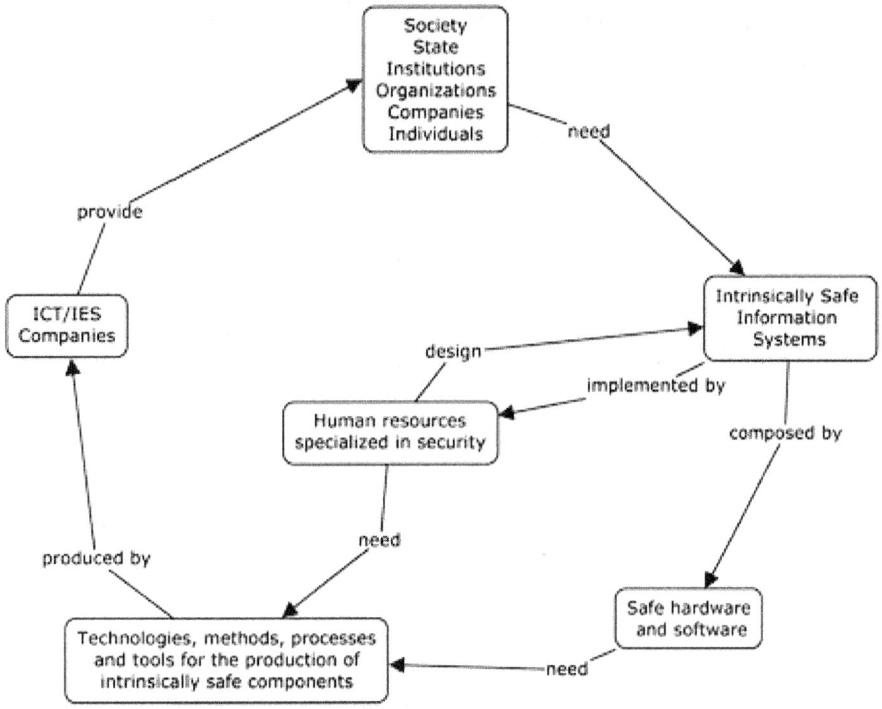

## Hacking and Cracking Business Ecosystem

Many challenges for the obtaining of secure cyber systems are still unknown. This business ecosystem involves professionals working on both sides, i.e., preventing vulnerabilities and creating or discovering them. Moreover, a black market negotiates newly discovered vulnerabilities (for which no defense or detection is provided – they are known as zero-day exploit) for criminal activities, and a gray market promotes purchases of such vulnerabilities by some governments to be used in their intelligence activities. Therefore, the core here is dedicated and highly trained human resources. Attracting individuals with such a profile (classified as hackers) to the defense is a priority, and keeping them, as well as preventing them from being co-opted into the cyber crime underworld (so as not to become crackers) are crucial. A business ecosystem subsidized by the government and that provides working conditions for those individuals, keeps them motivated and enables their contributions to the defense through research and training of new talents must be designed.

This business ecosystem, shown in Figure 14, was classified as an attractor, since it promotes changes and challenges for the entire cyber defense business meta-ecosystem.

*Figure 14. Concept map of the hacking and cracking business ecosystem*

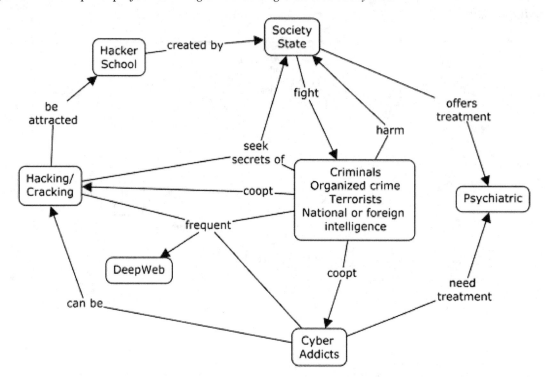

## Cyber Defense Education, Research and Extension Business Ecosystem

This is a business ecosystem that cannot be reduced to a National School of Cyber Defense that acts in a conventional way. For a cyber defense ecosystem to create a virtuous cycle of value generation and aggregation, the school must be part of a cyber defense teaching, research and extension system, which also fosters activities in other educational systems and institutions, at all levels. Such a cyber defense education system cooperates with all organizations involved in the cyber defense value chain, whether nationally or internationally; it must also follow the state-of-the-art, in line with national needs and realities, and attract talents to cyber defense (see Figure 15).

This ecosystem is an attractor, since it supplies Human Resources quantitatively and qualitatively towards a feasible Cyber Defense BEoE regarding scale and costs.

## Business Ecosystem for the Certification and Homologation of Cyber Defense Products and Services

Perhaps the latter business ecosystem is the missing input for the cyber defense BEoE to establish a virtuous cycle of value generation and aggregation. It is an attractor, since it generates demands for products, services and systems for the BEoE.

The business ecosystem of the homologation and certification system for cyber defense products (SHCDCiber) is based on the very concept of cybernetics, which has given rise to cyber products and services, with a focus on communication and control. Cyber defense products are, by definition, cyber

*Figure 15. Concept map of the cyber defense education and research business ecosystem*

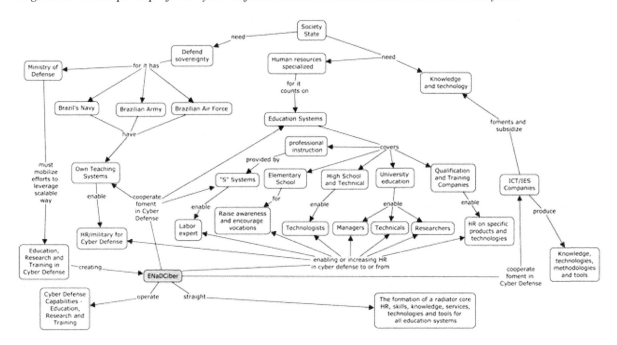

products that include hardware and software components. Cyber defense services are also enabled by hardware and software products, and cyber products are demanded by society towards their meeting of information, communication and control needs, and can be attacked by crackers. Due to this risk, such products must be safe, and the State must provide both a specific level of security, supported by an institutional environment composed of ministries and armed forces, an operational strategy that links Universities, research centers and certification bodies in general, and a sustainability strategy that maintains the system. The State coordinates and provides the basis for the system according to above-described elements. The homologation and certification system builds a normative basis and accredits laboratories and certification bodies towards the system's approvals and certifications. Figure 16 displays the concept map of SHCDCiber business ecosystem.

Below is a brief description of the creation process of this ecosystem:

1. The School trains Human Resources (HR) to work in the Cyber Defense BEoE.
2. The State and the HR trained by the school can coordinate and provide the basis for SHCDCiber according to the above-described elements.
3. SHCDCiber and the HR trained by the school can build a normative base that leverages the Cyber Defense BEoE and accredits laboratories and certification bodies towards the system's approvals and certifications.
4. The productive sector (formal and informal) and the HR trained by the school create services and products that meet the standards.
5. The State and the HR trained by the school establish policies and guidelines for the acquisition of products and services approved by SHCDCiber, thus closing the cycle.

*Figure 16. Business ecosystem for the certification and homologation of cyber defense products and services*

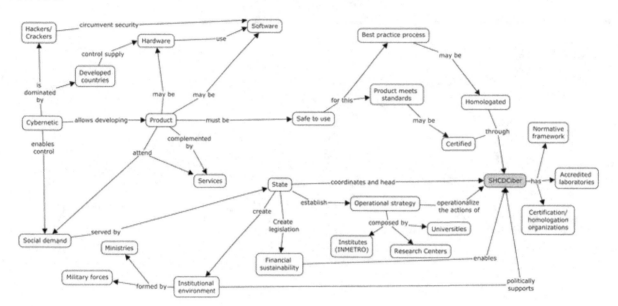

## The Evolution of the Cyber Defense BEoE

The observations collected in the DCDN Conference verified that the ENaDCiber and SHCDCiber binomial should act as a sperm factor in the transformation of the Cyber Defense BEoE - CDBEoE into a Brazilian Cyber Defense and Security System - BCDSS (Figure 17).

With this evolution, the SBDC would permit the country's greater and more complete action with respect to its information assets (understood as People, Organizations, and Technical Solutions), thus perfecting and amplifying the Brazilian capacity for cyber defense and security. This action by the country towards its Information Assets can be seen as the juxtaposition, in any point in time, of three activities:

- **Sourcing:** Identification, Selection, Hiring;
- **Suitability:** Standards, Conformity and Homologation, Certification;
- **Evolution:** Qualification/Differentiation, Identification and meeting Expectations/Needs, Identification and meeting Demand/Offer.

The country's effort, in each of these activities juxtaposed above, will occur over time. Thus, presently and in the following years, the emphasis is in *Sourcing*, because it urges the response to the market in terms of cyber defense products while still based on a relatively small substrate as compared to *Suitability* and *Evolution*. Meanwhile, with the passing of time, it is to be expected that the priority be modified. Therefore, in the mid and long term, the country will be able to invest a greater percentage of energy and resources into the *Evolution* of products for Cyber Defense and Security. This change over time is illustrated in Figure 18.

*Figure 17. ENaDCiber general objective*

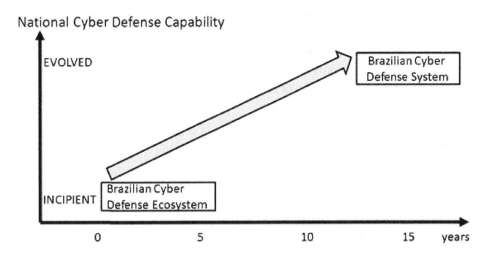

**ENaDCiber General Goal**

Catalyze the transformation of the current Brazilian Cyber Defense Ecosystem *(considered incipient)* into an *evolved and adequate* Brazilian Cyber Defense System

*Figure 18. Activity priorities for ENaDCiber*

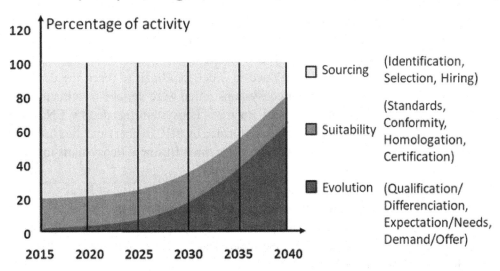

Over time, the ENaDCiber will modify its priority on Sourcing, Suitability and Evolution of Information Assets (People, Organizations, and Technical Solutions).

ENaDCiber should be open and flexible to accept future adaptations and modifications that become necessary and which may be drastically different from the characteristics seen as necessary today due to the accelerated rate of progress of science, technology, and innovation leading to unpredictability. In this way, the ENaDCiber project, due to its great technical, political and institutional complexity, should not be overly extensive in details nor should it be rigid. Rather it should be a pragmatic project that allows for the immediate application of resources available, maintaining a great ability to learn and to adapt and change direction when necessary.

Example approaches for projects carried out in complex sectors, to solve critical and urgent problems are *Innovation Hubs* in the USA; *Knowledge and Innovation Communities* in the European Union; and the National Science and Technology Institutes and Knowledge Platforms, in Brazil.

ENaDCiber should have a radically new model, innovative when compared to conventional model used in universities and military schools. It should be a new type of school and not another school within a traditional mold because the acceleration of the rate of significant change in the world (including the progress of the CT&I) requires:

- The recognition that essential contributions may stem from youth or from irreverent, questioning professionals who think creatively, "outside the box".
- The end of the argument for authority (argumentum ad baculum) and the promotion of questioning everything systematically.
- Promote, in primary and secondary education in the country, cyberattack and defense games, in an ethical manner, to motivate students to consider careers in the Cyber Defense and Security Sector.

## FINAL CONSIDERATIONS

The Objective of this work is to propose a BEoE Model as an array of Business Ecosystems to be applied with the development and nurturing of the entire productive sector of a State. Based on this BEoE model a Brazilian Cyber Defense BEoE and its evolution over time was mapped and validated.

To reach these goals, a bibliographical inventory on the subject verified that the works on business ecosystems are restricted to a company's business ecosystem, making necessary the development of the BEoE model for an economic sector that encompasses diverse business ecosystems.

This BEoE model was applied to Brazil's Cyber Defense sector, within which eight main business ecosystems were defined that need to be developed in order for Brazil to reach the desired level of sovereignty in its cyber sector. Of these eight ecosystems, three were defined as attractors, being the Acquirement and formation of Human Resources Business Ecosystem (headed by ENaDCiber), the Certification and Homologation Business Ecosystem (formed by SHCDCiber) and the Hackers e Crackers Business Ecosystem. The state should act within these three Business Ecosystems in order for the BEoE to grow in a sustainable manner.

This National Cyber Defense BEoE was validated through the application of focal group methodology, involving stakeholders from academia, industry, government, and society.

Future work, stemming from the Brazilian Cyber Defense BEoE, intends to identify capacities desired for the Cyber Defense BEoE and, from these capacities, establish Human Resource needs. Then, in response to these capacities, project ENaDCiber and SHCDCiber.

Future work also includes the application of the Cyber Defense BEoE model in order to establish a Cyber Defense SoS life cycle, with the objective of establishing strategic guidelines for obtaining cyber defense products and services.

## ACKNOWLEDGMENT

To the Brazilian Army, for financing and making this work possible. To the Brazilian Navy, the Brazilian Air Force, the representatives of the BID, the Brazilian government, academia, and Brazilian society that participated in the DCDN Conference for the completion of this work, without which this chapter could not have been carried out.

## REFERENCES

Bauer, J. M., & Van Eeten, M. J. G. (2009, November). Cybersecurity: Stakeholder incentives, externalities, and policy options. *Telecommunications Policy*, *33*(10), 706–719. doi:10.1016/j.telpol.2009.09.001

BRASIL. (2008, December). Presidency of the Republic. Decree no. 6,703, of December 18, 2008. Approves the National Defense Strategy and makes other provisions. *Official Gazette [of] the Federative Republic of Brazil*.

Creswell. (2012). Qualitative Inquiry and Research Design: Choosing Among Five Approaches. SAGE Publications, Inc.

Das, S. (2015). *The Cyber Security Ecosystem: Post-global Financial Crisis. Springer Proceedings in Business and Economics. Managing in Recovering Markets*. Springer.

Falliere, N., Murchu, L. O., & Chien, E. (2011, February). *W32 Stuxnet Dossier Version 1.4*. http://www.symantec.com/content/en/us/enterprise/media/security_response/whitepapers/w32_stuxnet_dossier.pdf

Fernandes, J. H. C. (2012a). Segurança e Defesa Cibernéticas Para Reduzir Vulnerabilidades Nas Infraestruturas Críticas Nacionais. Brasília – DF. *Centro de Estudos Estratégicos do Exército - CEEEx*. Available at: http://www.eme.eb.mil.br/ceeex/public/arquivos/nep2012/NEP_CEEEx_Jorge_Fernandes_2012.pdf

Fernandes, J. H. C. (2012b). Estudo Preliminar Para a Criação de Uma Escola Nacional de Defesa Cibernética. *Secretaria de Assuntos Estratégicos da Presidência da República - SAE e Centro de Estudos Estratégicos do Exército - CEEEx*. Available at: http://www.eme.eb.mil.br/ceeex/public/arquivos/nep2012/NEP_CEEEx_Jorge_Fernandes_2012.pdf

Fernandes, J. H. C. (2013a). *A Perniciosa Armadilha Cibernética e uma Proposta de Mobilização Nacional*. Brasília: Centro de Estudos Estratégicos do Exército - CEEEx.

Fernandes, J. H. C. (2013b, November). A Soberania Cibernética Na Zona de Paz e Cooperação Do Atlântico Sul - ZOPACAS. *Centro de Estudos Estratégicos do Exército - CEEEx*.

Fernandes, J. H. C. (2013c). *Um Sistema de Soberania Cibernética para a Projeção de Poder do Brasil em seu Entorno Estratégico. In Núcleo de Estudos Prospectivos do Centro de Estudos Estratégicos da Sétima Subchefia do Estado Maior do Exército (CEEEx/EME)*. Quartel General do Exército.

Fernandes, J. H. C., & Meira, S. R. de L. (1998) Convergent Architectures: breaking bounds among software, software development and software use towards the creation of self-sustainable systems in the cyberspace. In *Proceedings of the World Multiconference on Systemics, Cybernetics and Informatics and 4th International Conference on Information Systems Analysis and Synthesis*. Orlando, FL: International Institute of Informatics and Systemics (IIIS).

Flórez, A., Serrano, L., Gómez, U., Suárez, L., Villarraga, A., & Rodríguez, H. (2016, July). Analysis of Dynamic Complexity of the Cyber Security Ecosystem of Colombia. *Future Internet*.

Gerard Briscoe, J. O. (2010). The ABC of Digital Business Ecosystems. *Communications and the Law*.

Goel, R., & Kumar, V. (2017, June). A Public-Private-Social Ecosystem: An Interdisciplinary Framework for Cybersecurity Capacity Building. SIGMIS-CPR '17. *Proceedings of the 2017 ACM SIGMIS Conference on Computers and People Research*, 185–186.

Huang, K., Siegel, M., Pearlson, K., & Madnick, S. E. (2019, June). *Casting the Dark Web in a New Light: A Value-Chain Lens Reveals a Growing Cyber Attack Ecosystem and New Strategies for Combating It*. MIT Sloan Research Paper No. Working Paper CISL# 2019-19. Available at SSRN: https://ssrn.com/abstract=3459128

Iansiti, M., & Levien, R. (2004). Strategy as Ecolog. *Harvard Business Review*, *3*(82), 68–78. PMID:15029791

Iansiti, M., & Levien, R. (2004). *The Keystone Advantage: What the New Dynamics of Business Ecosystems Mean for Strategy, Innovation, and Sustainability*. Harvard Business School Press.

Islam, T. (2019). A Socio-Technical and Co-evolutionary Framework for Reducing Human-Related Risks in Cyber Security and Cybercrime Ecosystems. In G. Wang, M. Bhuiyan, S. De Capitani di Vimercati, & Y. Ren (Eds.), *Dependability in Sensor, Cloud, and Big Data Systems and Applications. DependSys 2019. Communications in Computer and Information Science* (Vol. 1123). Springer. doi:10.1007/978-981-15-1304-6_22

ISO. ISO/IEC 27032. (2012). Information technology -- Security techniques -- *Guidelines for cybersecurity*.

Jamshidi. (2008). Systems of Systems Engineering: Principles and Applications. CRC Press.

Kauffman, S. (1995). *At Home in the Universe: The search for the laws of self-organization and complexity*. Oxford University Press.

Mitleton-Kelly, E. (2003). *Complex Systems & Evolutionary Perspectives of Organizations: The Application of Complexity Theory to Organizations*. Elsevier.

Moore. (1996). The Death of Competition: Leadership and Strategy in the Age of Business Ecosystem. Harper Business.

Moore, J. F. (2006). Business ecosystems and the view from the firm. *Antitrust Bulletin, 51*(1).

Moore, J. F. (1998). The Rise of a New Corporate Form. *The Washington Quarterly, 21*(1), 167–181. doi:10.1080/01636609809550301

Morrar, R. (2005, August). Technological Public–Private Innovation Networks: A Conceptual Framework Describing Their Structure and Mechanism of Interaction. *Technology Innovation Management Review, 5*(8).

Prahalad, C. K. (2004, August). *The Fortune at the Bottom of the Pyramid: Eradicating Poverty Through Profits*. Wharton School Publishing.

Rothschild, M. (1990). *Bionomics: Economy as Ecosystem*. Henry Holt and Company.

Vianna, E. W. (2015). *Análise do comportamento informacional na gestão da segurança cibernética da Administração Pública Federal*. 115 f., il. [Unpublished master dissertation Dissertation]. University of Brasília. Available at: http://repositorio.unb.br/handle/10482/17832

World Bank. (2019). *Global Cybersecurity Capacity Program*. https://documents.worldbank.org/curated/en/947551561459590661/pdf/Global-Cybersecurity-Capacity-Program-Lessons-Learned-and-Recommendations-towards-Strengthening-the-Program.pdf

WRI, World Resources Institute. (2000). *World Resources 2000-2001: People and Ecosystems: The Frauing Web of Life*. Report Series.

*Previously published in the Handbook of Research on Cyber Crime and Information Privacy; pages 414-440, copyright year 2021 by Information Science Reference (an imprint of IGI Global).*

# Chapter 31
# The Challenges and Solutions of Cybersecurity Among Malaysian Companies

**Puteri Fadzline Tamyez**
*University Malaysia Pahang, Malaysia*

## ABSTRACT

*The objective of this chapter is to analyze the challenges faced by Malaysian companies in cybersecurity and to determine solution for Malaysian companies to overcome challenges in cybersecurity. The data were collected from the expert people in cybersecurity fields using interview sessions. The finding confirmed that the awareness and budget are very important in other to implement the element of cybersecurity in the company. Cybersecurity is good and desired as a protection for an organization in developing strategic planning to gain more profitability and increase the productivity of goods and services. This research will be beneficial for the organization because it will provide the solution for the company to overcome the cybersecurity issues. From this research, an organization can have potential to enhance competitiveness and understand the problem occur, then do the improvement by implementing cybersecurity.*

## INTRODUCTION

Industry 4.0 invites tremendous advantages for companies towards business sustainability. It has nine pillars altogether, namely, internet of things, big data, supply chain, cloud computing, horizontal and vertical integration, autonomous robot, addictive manufacturing, cyber security, simulation and augmented reality. However, the major challenge in facing this digitalization era is on cyber security (Jay Lee, 2016). Privacy and security of the data will always be top security measures that any organization should take. We live in a world where information are secured in digital or a cyber-form. Data from multiple sources has different formats gives difficulty for analysts to integrate the data (Ibrar, 2017). Lack of monitoring and protection against unauthorized changes or alteration will create unwanted changes

DOI: 10.4018/978-1-6684-3698-1.ch031

in data information. Most companies faces inadequate of development phase (Ibrar, 2017), thus makes it important in order to limit the risk of application related assaults or attacks.

The inadequacy of development phase as brought small and medium size enterprise (SMEs) face different risks as compared to large companies, as these organizations have limited and minimum human and monetary resources to apply information technology (IT) and cyber security systems (Heikkila, 2016). Most SMEs own traditional security mechanisms, which could not accommodate the technology of the Internets of Things (IoT) due to limited resources (Ibrar, 2017). Apart from that, they need to overcome the inadequacy of security budget and low security alertness among the workers. Lack of employee training and recovery planning has contributed to its low security alertness among employees (Heikkila, 2016). This finding further elaborates that only a few companies report on the provision of safety-related training for all employees. However, the lack of deployment process shall cause problems in managing the cyber security (Ibrar, 2017).

The inadequacy of security software's upgradability and patch ability is also one of the issues in cyber security. A number of companies usually do not put much effort in upgrading security software due to lack of resources. The low and inadequacy of physical security will allow and provide an unrecognized user to enter the data or devices using Universal Serial Bus (USB) port. This may cause companies to face many problems. Another issue is trust. Network interactions with systems that have lower standard security will invite more trust issues. Data transference is mostly carried out by wireless network, which increases the probability of miss-data problem to occur (Ibrar, 2017). This may affect in aspects of incomplete or false information. Thus, cyber security is crucial in all industries to make sure all of their data were being safely secured. This research attempts to answer the accompanying inquiry in aspects of the challenges faced by Malaysian company in cybersecurity and the solution for Malaysian companies to overcome challenges in cybersecurity.

## BACKGROUND OF STUDY

Most industries are affected by technological change and innovation or rather called industrialization revolution (Jay Lee, 2016). This revolution is due to mechanization in the first industrial revolution, the use of electricity is $2^{nd}$ industrial revolution and electronics and automation is industrial revolution 3. The revolution not only affected the production itself, but also the labour market and education system as well (Lasi, 2014). Due to development of digitalization and robotics, the industry faces the next industrial revolution, known as Industry 4.0. These new emerging technologies have a huge impact on people's education and scope of work (Katharina M., 2015).

Only qualified and highly educated workers will be able to control this technology. Digital supply chain is smart, worth-driven network that is the current path to automation and analysis in order to generate unique forms of interest and business value (Keliang Zhou, 2015). Cyber security as one of the nine pillars is exposed to external and insider cyber threats with complicated and sophisticated cyber security landscape (Wells, 2016). It is known as an activity or process, ability or capability, or state whereby information and communications systems and the information contained therein are protected from and or defended against damage, unauthorized use or modification, or exploitation" (DHS, 2014). Other than that, cyber security involves reducing the risk of malicious attack to software, computers and networks (Dan Craigen, 2014). This includes tools used to detect break-ins, stop viruses, block malicious access, enforce authentication, enable encrypted communications, and on and on. Thus, the goal of this study is twofold; to analyse the challenges faced by Malaysian companies in cyber security and to determine solution for Malaysian companies to overcome challenges in cyber security.

Cybersecurity has become a general concern for all citizens, professionals, politicians, and, more generally all decision makers. It has also become a serious concern for societies that must protect against cybersecurity attacks with both preventive and reactive measures, which imply a lot of monitoring, and must simultaneously preserve the freedom and avoid general surveillance. Cybersecurity can be defined as computer security, also known as cyber security or IT security, is the protection of computer systems from the damage to their hardware, software or information, as well as from disruption or misdirection of the services they provide (Roca et al., 2019).

Security in general includes both cybersecurity and physical security. Cybersecurity consists in ensuring three basic and essential properties of information, services, and IT infrastructures well known as the CIA triad as confidentiality, integrity, and availability (Fischer, 2016). Therefore, getting an information system means blocking unauthorized entities such as users, processes, services, machines from accessing, altering, or providing inaccessible computer data, computing services, or computing infrastructure. Other property, such as legality which means original proof of information, privacy, or protection against illegal copying may also be listed.

## LITERATURE REVIEW

### Challenges of Cyber Security

One of the challenges is there are many types of attacks against information systems. The threats are therefore numerous. The attacks can target the hardware, the network, the system, or the applications for example through the malicious actions of a malware, or even the users themselves like social engineering, phishing and others. The attacker can be an insider or an outsider. According to Roca et al., (2019), these attacks can be classified as observation attacks, perturbation attacks, and a new field known as hardware-targeted software attacks. Attacks against information systems do not usually involve the hardware layer but exploit software vulnerability. This new type of attack is especially dangerous as it makes hardware attacks possible at a distance, as opposed to classical side channel attacks. This task requires expertise at the hardware, firmware, and operating system levels.

Other types of challenge in security threat for IoT are cloning device and sensitive data disclosure (Naik, 2017). Cloning device is a foreign hardware which acts as the right device unlike in reality it is not. Bad data can quickly cause problem to the server and this require higher budget to fix. Sensitive Data Disclosure occurs when an application does not adequately protect sensitive information. Information need to be encrypted during transit as data originates from various information.

The challenge in managing cyber security is data integrity. To secure data integrity in IoT environment, it is found to be quite difficult due to the large of information and data. Data from multiple sources has variety of concepts and formats, which makes it difficult for analysts to integrate this data. Besides that, lack of monitoring and protection against unauthorized changes or alteration will make unwanted changes in data information (Ibrar, 2017). Malicious data searchers are always looking for new ways to steal the data particularly during peak hours where organizations might lack the internal capability and mechanisms to manage and secure the data (Jaime, 2016). Ransom ware attacks will affect the entire landscape of security services. It will control the entire of framework and will permit constrained access for client cooperation. From 2005 until March 2016, approximately 7600 ransom ware assaults were accounted for by Internet Crime Center.

As in many other fields, there is a well-known adage about security that says that the main threat lies between the chair and the keyboard. This adage may be exaggerated, and at the very least it deserves further study, but it must be recognized that the users are indeed sometimes a source of security problems (Fischer, 2016). Firstly, the user can be the target of the attack. In addition, the user can try to avoid using the available protection mechanisms due to the excessive complexity of use and finally the user level of education and training is too insufficient. The employee therefore not aware of the real risks or on the contrary overestimate the user. In either case, the user does not know what mechanisms are to be used when. This also can happen when the user interfaces of software systems are not well designed for the purpose of security, even if design principles that are suitable for other applicants are applied (Woodward, 2015).

On the other hand, lack of security investment among the companies and alertness among the employee also contribute to the issues in cyber security (Heikkila, 2016; Roca et al., 2019). When there is security failure caused by security attacks, organization usually do not consider it as a very serious attack that might happen again. Besides that, traditional security mechanisms are incapable to recover IoT devices as most of the devices have battery constraints and restricted assets (Yaaqob, 2017). Additionally the lack of employee training and recovery planning also contribute to the risk of cyber security (Heikkila, 2016). Empirical work reveals that only a few companies report on the provision of safety-related training for all employees.

Next is the lack of security software upgradability for protection (Yaaqob, 2017). This is due to limited resource of equipment, tools and system. Software upgradability is also costly for an organization. On one hand, most organization has lack capability to organise unstructured data (Jaime, 2016). The vast array of data makes it difficult to detect problems because the data from various sources with different formats, thus makes it difficult for the analyst to interpret and integrate the unstructured data. On the other hand, integration among the stakeholder of any industry 4.0 organization may cause obstacles in language (Lane Thames, 2017). There are many types of industry 4.0 environment such as from diverse technologies and different types of subject matter experts where only few common language are used in standard or processes that align with the company objectives and goals.

## Solutions for Cyber Security Issues

## Tools to Secure Against Cyber Threats

Rather than using several type of security protection such as antivirus, firewall, strong passwords, protecting Wi-Fi connection to secure the data, there are other few ways protect the data information and improve the level of security.

### *Digital Signature*

This is a practice that is conceivable to protect electronic data such that the original of the data, and additionally the honesty of the data, can be checked. This method of ensuring the inception and the respectability of the data is likewise called authentication. A computerized mark is just a system that can be utilized for various verification purposes. For an E-record, it comes practically near the conventional written by hand marks (Iqbal, 2016). The client can create key match by utilizing the particular crypto programming. Presently, Microsoft Internet Explorer and Netscape enable the client to make their own particular key combination. Any individual may make an application to the Certifying Authority for issue of Digital Signature Certificate.

## Encryption

This effective and imperative strategy for security in the computer system is to encode the sensitive records and messages in travel and capacity. Generally, there are four gatherings of individuals that are utilized and added, namely; the specialty of cryptography, military, discretionary corps and diarists. The military has the most sensitive part and has shaped the field (Iqbal, 2016).

## Security Audits

This practice is an effective evaluation of the security of an institution data framework by estimating on how the arrangement is going well in create up the criteria. It is to discover the vulnerabilities that an association is looking for its IT framework. A thorough audit regularly overviews the security of the structure's physical setup and condition, programming, information dealing with systems, and customer home (Iqbal, 2016).

## Cyber Forensics

Cyber forensics is the basic solution in the investigation of computerized violations. Digital legal sciences are the revelation, examination, and remaking of confirmation extricated from any component of computer frameworks, systems, media, and peripherals that enable specialists to unravel a wrongdoing (Iqbal, 2016). The primary concern with computer forensics involves imagery storage media, restoring files were deleted, finding slacks and free space, and maintain the data that being collected for prosecution purposes. Another issue is forensic networking, where it is consistent forensic in terms of the network (Sadeghil & Waidner, 2016).

## Cryptography

Cryptography is based on strong mathematical reasoning and aims to guarantee more the nature of confidentiality only. Cryptography provides tools for protection integrity and legitimacy of the message for example avoid deep amounts financial transactions are changing, to ensure not being rejected in aspects dispatchers cannot denies being the author of the message and unnamed (Roca et al., 2019). This chapter is organized into three sections:

- Cryptographic Primer is the most basic building block; such primitive permitting to encrypt or digitally sign messages;
- Cryptography Scheme usually builds primitive to provide more powerful safety goals, ensuring integrity and legitimacy of size messages;
- Cryptographic protocols rely on schemes to achieve more complex security aims, for example, to establish a safe communication channel that can be used confidential and explicit message exchange.

### Crytapanalysis

The purpose of academic cryptanalysis is to understand the threats to security of the existing primitives in order to be ahead of malicious (Roca et al., 2019). It provides an empirical measure of security thanks to a thorough and never-ending scrutiny, searching for possible weaknesses. The knowledge of state-of-the-art cryptanalysis is thus the backbone for the design of secure primitives.

## Manufacturing Risk

Manufacturing that associates with business is significantly prone to cyber security attacks due to its very nature. Collaboration with suppliers associate an increasing reliance on IoT technology to trace finished merchandise and material shipments throughout the producing method and this leaves several individual points at risk of potential attacks. Additionally, its production is heavily dependent on information, together with internal, customer, payroll, checking account, and provider data. Finally, recent international power struggles have concerned the producing business in many ways. Producing companies created up half the businesses targeted by the high-profile malware and ransom ware attacks (Shelzer, 2018). According to Jay Lee (2016), the solution is to build up an automation CPI with a time machine observing action so a virtual testing algorithm can be applying for any control activity to the framework. Cyber security requires a smart-driven approach that is used for Defence in Depth. It requires regular improvement of network and proactively response and actions to face the probable attacks.

To overcome the cyber security issues, it needs to fully apply the safety security by design (Yaaqob, 2017). The IoT systems need to moderate ransom ware during the whole lifecycle of utilization execution. This is to ensure the security verification and registration of devices in IoT networks. This is followed by educating and increasing the alertness and awareness of security issues among employees. This can be consistent through lifelong learning such as introducing the basic security concepts, practice and tools. Recuperation plans to guarantee a minimum economic loss in the case of a security failure and do the security planning for all workers. Ultimately, security policies, security risks investigation, security principles and activity models must continuously be up to date and need to monitor and maintenance regularly (Heikkila, 2016).

Security objectives, security policies, availability, integrity and confidentiality need to be clearly understood by all employees. Security principle or policy describes the responsibility of the management to security task, responsibilities and methods in implement in the security domain (Heikkila, 2016; Jaime, 2016). Apart from that, there is a need to have standard formats such as Machinery Information Management Open System Alliance (MIMOSA) databases as suggested by Jaime (2016) in order to ensure the trustworthiness of data. The security threat mechanism is known as Advanced Persistent Threat Mechanism (ATP) (Penang Skill Development Centre, 2017). This mechanism is using malware to detect sensitive data.

There are numerous risks that incorporate risky tasks, pernicious code with information uprightness to keep disclosure of unknown weaknesses vulnerabilities. Thus, it will create more troublesome for the programmers to figure out the code. Additionally, integrity mechanism is to ensure the consistency and accuracy of data while anonymity is the service of keeping and hiding data sources. It assists in guaranteeing information classification and security. Wireless communication security is to ensure the secure of configuration when communicate across wireless network and Integrity monitoring tools also can be implemented to keep the alert while completing their job duties (Yaaqob, 2017).

## METHODOLOGY

The method to collect the data in this study is a qualitative method. Observations and interviews were used as an approach to have a better knowledge regarding the topic. In addition, researchers also have use literature studies such as content analysis, case studies and phenomenological studies. The populations for this research are the company in Malaysia that applied the cybersecurity in the manufacturing companies or services while the research sample consists of top management in the Malaysian companies and professional people that are using cybersecuirty. The number of respondents depends on saturation of data from the respondents but the targeted respondents are in industries which are manager companies to answer the first research objective.

For this research, researcher was used purposive sampling method. This purposive sampling method was selected require to the characteristics of a population. For this sampling used the expert purposive samplings to provide various vary of cases relevant to a specific development or event. Other than that, researchers also have use snowball sampling to know the existing about the research studies from the acquaintances.

Interview sessions were conducted with different participants. The purpose for the interview is to obtaining specific estimation on the research topic and intended answer the question to the research topic. The interview was through telephone, email and face to face. In the interview protocol contain a headline, the description and instruction to the interviewer, crucial questions to ask, investigate for major query, transition info for the interviewer, space to record on what the interviewers are mention and the space where investigators noted a reflective note(National Center for Postsecondary, 2003).

The semi-organized interview approach was, consequently, most proper to address these issues. Despite the fact that the questioner has a prepared list of inquiries that calls interview guide, the interview procedure is adaptable and the interviewee can react openly in his/her words (Bryman, 2004). Open-inquiries in the in-depth interviews enable respondents to clarify their perspective and comprehension of supportability and economical business rehearses, without being restricted by biased classifications provided. The questioner can allow the respondents to clarify their answers (Zikmund, 2015).

Reliability and validity are from members checking and different sources. The researcher sent the transcript to the respondents in other to get the approval validation of data while different sources are from journal or past articles. The semi-structured interview data were digitally recorded and later transcribe using the denaturalized convention (Maclean, Mechthild, & Alma, 2004). Through this adaptability, thematic analysis enables detailed data exploration (Clarke, 2016). This analysis helps the researcher to discover the patterns and construct specified researcher query. For this research Atlas.ti software was applied.

## RESULTS AND DISCUSSIONS

Three participants were selected from different level managerial where two respondents are from top management and another respondent is an officer. Table 1 indicates the background of the respondents.

*Table 1. Background of Participants*

| Respondent ID | Designation |
|---|---|
| A | Head Strategic Research And Advisory Department Strategy Research Division |
| B | Branch Manager |
| C | ICT Security Officer |

## Minor Findings

## Awareness of the Importance Cyber Security in Workplace

Cyber security is a global phenomenon representing a complex socio-technical challenge for governments and private companies with the involvement of individuals. Although cyber security is one of the most important challenges faced by governments today, the visibility and public awareness remains limited. All respondents agreed on the importance of the implementation of cyber security in any organizations due to the trend of Industry 4.0.

As claimed by respondent A:

*Cyber security is important because it involves the protection of information that is accessed and transmitted via the internet or more generally through any computer network. From technology perspective, organization need to use the appropriate mix of such resources as encryption techniques, firewall, access controls and intrusion detection systems.*

This is aligned with Goutam (2015) who stated that cyber security is now considered as important part of individuals and families, as well as organizations, governments, educational institutions and our businesses. The findings of the current study is also consistent with those of Walter (2018) who found that an appropriate learning on online behaviour and system protection results decreases the vulnerabilities with safer online environment.

The average unprotected computer connected to the Internet can be compromised in moments. Thousands of infected web pages are being discovered every day. Hundreds of millions of records have been involved in data breaches. New attack methods are launched continuously. The importance of information security should be highlighted as a necessary approach to protect data and systems.

According to respondent B, *"the protection and security of employees' work and personal lives are no longer separate."*

They have been intertwined with evolving trends of social networks, the internet of things, and unlimited connectivity.

*"This is because cyber security is no longer just the responsibility of the company IT department". "It is now the responsibility of every employee, not just to protect their work assets but their personal data as well",* as stated by respondent C.

Failure to do that will make a risk or problem in the company. Other than that, the trend for cyber threat and security kept changing in an instant.

## Role of Cyber Security in Organizations

100% of respondents agreed that the role of cyber security is to protect confidentiality, and ensure integrity with availability. This is aligned with the works of Gordon (2006), who stated that cyber security is to protect the privacy of information as claimed by all of participants. Integrity is described as protecting the accuracy, reliability and validity of information. It is also to ensure that authorized users can access information on a timely basis. All the e-business models, business to business, business to consumer and business to government rely on secure transmission and storage sensitive information.

*"The role of cyber security is to establish trust so that the buyer and sellers are willing to participate in electronics transactions"* as stated by respondent A.

According to respondent B:

*The function of cyber security is to protect the assets in our organization such as intangible assets of organizations such as computer software, patents, intellectual property (IP), company information, licensing agreements, employment contracts and trade secrets are mainly stored, managed and shared on network systems.*

This is aligned with literature that states a breach of security controls by hackers or sometimes unauthorized employees which results in data privacy issues (Yaaqob, 2017). Unauthorized persons or agencies can gain access to sensitive personal information leading to identity theft and misrepresentation. Cyber security could also prevent any system failure that will cause physical damages and harm to the humans, machine, process, data and others (Ahmad et al., 2017; Goutam, 2015). This is aligned with respondent C statement that the role of cyber security is *"to secure customer data and company records"*. Organizations manage records of finances, employees, physical assets, passwords and access codes to sensitive information or to carry out specific tasks on network systems. Sensitive information must be secured from unauthorized modification or access by both employees and hackers. Knowing the crucial role of cyber security, thus, all department areas that consists of automated system, computer and networks that has information data must be protected.

## MAJOR FINDINGS

### The Challenges of Cyber Security Faced by Malaysian Companies

Cyber security which everyone is talking about has, without a doubt, become one of the most significant threats to global business in year 2018 and beyond. The characteristics of cyber-crime are a threat to all businesses regardless of size of companies. When you have an organisation that employs others, holds confidential client data, accounts, personnel files, business plans, confidential project information. If any of it is breached, it will signify that the company is vulnerable.

The challenges can be divided to five themes; namely technology, human or people, process, budget and awareness. This is based on respondent A, who claimed that, *"technology is used to support the communication that is always changing"*. Thus, with the increasing use of digital technologies such as cloud, big data, mobile, IoT and artificial intelligence with the growing connectivity of everything, come greater challenges on the level of security, compliance and data protection and regulations which should be effectively tackled.

Respondent B claimed that:

*with the growth of technology cyber threats and cyber-attacks, it has took new shapes in the form of next-generation ransom ware, web attacks and others. Scammer or hackers are always step ahead from us.*

This is accordance to the opinion of respondent C, *"the security parameter has changed."*

The second theme covers human or people, which refers to employees, employers, suppliers and customers. Organisations that do not produce user security policies or train the users in recognised good security practices will be vulnerable to many of these risks. *"Human or people need to know how to use and implement technology track or risk while using the systems"* as stated by respondent A.

This is followed by respondent B and C; *"the level of knowledge and expertise of employee are also important as it needs to ensure that the system will run smoothly."*

The present findings seem to be consistent with other research such as by Heikkila (2016), who reported that the lack of employee training qualified professionals is one of the challenges to implement learning environment that can give real access o industrial control system. Process is reported to be one of the challenges in implementing cyber security elements. This is due to the difficulty in handling the procedure of implement information security. It requires numerous stages and requires involvement of all departments in the company.

As mentioned by respondent A:

*Process means the systematic process or SOP to runs the program or systems, thus, people need to know how to use and implement the technology element track or risk when using the system.*

If users or people are not trained in securing the usage of their organisation's ICT systems or the functions of a security control, it may accidentally misuse the system, potentially compromise the security control and further affect the confidentiality, integrity and availability of the information held on the system. Hence, a proper and systematic SOP should be designed and established in certain parts of the information security in an organization. This supports literature which describes the lack of improper or unsafe operation and malicious code modifications (Heikkila, 2016).

However, in the perspectives of budget, it is also considered as a challenge in establishing cyber security system in organizations. All of the respondents agreed that implementing cyber security requires a huge amount of investment.

As stated by respondent B: *"financial or budgets also needs to be strong enough when we have information security systems in company."*

It corroborates with the findings of Heikkila (2016), who found that the lack of security investment among companies is one of the problem that is faced by companies to implement the systems.

According to respondent B and C: *"in terms of financial, the company should put priority in the information security budget under the company's strategic plan."*

This is to avoid the company from having lack of budget in aspects of security. Hackers or malware always have new ways to breach the security systems and if this happen the company will always compactible to overcome the issues if the company have stable financial. This finding is in agreement with

Jaime (2016)'s findings which showed that the malicious data seekers will always find new methods to steal the data especially during the peak hours.

There are similarities between budget by Jaime (2016) and those described by Naik (2017). Bad data can quickly cause problem to the server and requires higher budget to be fixed (Naik, 2017). Sensitive data disclosure occurs when an application does not adequately protect sensitive information. Hence, information needs to be encrypted during transit. Awareness and training program is crucial to disseminate information to all users, namely; employees, consumers, and including managers. In the case of an Information Technology (IT) security program, it should also be appropriately to communicate on security requirements and appropriate behaviour (Bada, 2015). An awareness and training program can be effective, if the material is interesting, current and simple enough to be followed. Thus, it is critical for all employees to be aware of their personal security responsibilities and the requirement to comply with corporate security policies. This can be achieved through systematic delivery of a security training and awareness programme that actively seeks to increase the levels of security expertise and knowledge across the organisation as well.

As stated by respondent B:

*Awareness is the first step that an organization needs to do in other to give knowledge to the employee"* *while respondent C claimed that, "awareness is the first protection that user can avoid from hackers' activity."*

If users are not aware of any special handling or the reporting requirements for particular classes of sensitive information, the organisation may be subjected to legal and regulatory sanctions.

## The Implementation of Cyber Security

There are several ways to implement the cyber security in the organization. In this aspect we found five themes, such as *"build a team of IT and non-IT staff which conduct top to bottom security audits, update software and systems, provide new and continuing security education, conduct risk analysis and test systems"* as agreed by all respondents.

Firstly, *"it is crucial to build a team of IT and non-IT staff"* as stated by all respondents. This team will determine the security policies.

According to all the respondents, *"conduct top to bottom security audits to review the security practices and policies of IT systems."*

Thus, it is beneficial organizations to involve all employees in the process of implementing cyber security (Bada, 2015). This theme supports the idea of Hans de Brujin (2017) who reported that if non-technical people in the organization could not understand the importance of certain policy or investment for cyber security, the process will not be well implemented.

The majority of respondents agreed that the procedure of implementation begins with *"starting with the basic elements such as accounts, passwords, workstations, and mobile devices and then work up to network hardware, then servers and applications."*

Update software and systems was not different from what other IT vendors do when the vulnerability security was discovered. As mentioned by respondent B:

*Adopts a 'push' methodology, forcing new security updates onto a user's device when they connect to the network, instead of a 'pull' methodology because we don't know when a user need their device and these updates can solve a problem.*

These finding accords with literature, where creating policies and procedures for automatic updates software and systems can help ensure the proper security measures are in place and running optimally (Shelzer, 2018).

Respondent B and C suggested that "*the company will have a good security protection if they have an advanced systems and software.*" Thus, companies must provide new and continuing security education for all employees to ensure that security policies and practices stay fresh in employees' minds and can understand any policy additions or changes.

All three respondents conclude that; "*the first thing to do is the session awareness to all staff and then setup one technical team to have specific training on cyber security.*"

The findings corroborate with Jaime (2016) works that there is a need of awareness by employees regarding the issues of information security. As respondent B suggest; "*one way can review whether the employees are demonstrate vulnerability of confidential data is to do social engineering*". This social engineering can be as simple as someone give a password to another person or it could be a user who is pulling up a website at work and surrenders passwords or other vital information that ultimately gets into the wrong hands.

Other than that, is by conducting a risk analysis to identify potential areas of weakness, failure, or compromise in workplace. All respondents found that it is "crucial *to do risk analysis which can determine on what department are critical to have security protection.*"

The three respondents also suggest that there are three processes of risk analysis conditions for its acceptance. The process of risk analysis is as follows:

1.  Firstly, "*group the results based on high, medium, and low risks in similar meaning, examine business services and categorize which ones are critical, important, or optional in implementation the system.*"
2.  Secondly, it needs to test system whether it have good impacts to the organization or not. In other to test the system "*it is important to perform regular data backups.*" This also can physically secure the information assets.

According to 50% of respondent stated that; "*all software, hardware and network need to be secured*".

This is aligned with literature Shelzer (2018) who stated that cyber security requires knowing what devices authorized and unauthorized are connected and accessing information. This knowledge will usually require a full security assessment and ongoing accountability procedure setups.

## RO2: Solutions to Overcome Challenges in Cyber Security

Type of improvement in cyber security aspects can be described as three themes which are awareness, training and budget or financial investment. It is very crucial to have awareness among all the employee and employer, a good training in other to enhance employee skills and stable financial for implement cyber security in an organization

**Theme 1:** The awareness of cyber security issues.

All organizations from large and small businesses to healthcare providers, academic institutions, and government agencies can experience data breaches or be targets of cybercrime, which can result in stolen intellectual property, theft of personal identity information, a disruption to the way do the business. A lot of campaign regarding awareness cyber security can be implemented.

For instance, *"awareness that focuses on ways to help create good cyber security awareness in the workplace which this campaign included on how to use secure methods of communication, beware of scams, minimize storage sensitive information and others"* as claimed by respondent A.

As concluded by 100% of respondents *"it is crucial to increase the level of awareness about cyber security among employees and third party."*

This is aligned with Heikkila (2016) who suggests implementing the education and increase alertness and awareness of security issues among all employees. The company needs to maintain the user awareness of the cyber risk faced by the organisation. This is because without exception, all users should receive regular refresher training or reminder on the cyber risks to the organization which are to the employee and individuals. The company also need to promote an incident reporting culture. According to Maria et al, (2015) the organization should enable establish a security culture that empowers staff to voice their concerns about the poor security practices and security incidents without fear of recrimination.

**Theme 2:** Training program.

Employees can do harm to the business by visiting infected websites, responding to phishing emails, using business email through public Wi-Fi and more. Therefore it is important for companies to offer cyber security training. Training for employee is one of the solutions for the company to overcome the challenges and problem faced in implementing the cyber security. As stated by the three respondents: *"It is crucial to increase the number of staff training."*

Top management should monitor the effectiveness of security training. This is in accordance to the findings of Shelzer (2018) who suggest establishing mechanisms in other to test the effectiveness and value of the security training provided to all staff.

*"This should be done through formal feedback by including questions in the staff survey on security training and the organization's security culture"* as stated respondent C.

Those areas that regularly feature in security reports or achieve the lowest feedback ratings should be targeted for remedial action. Respondent B added: *"Support the formal assessment of Information Assurance (IA) skills."*

Staff in security roles should be encouraged to develop and formally validate their information assurance (IA) skills through enrolment on a recognized certification scheme for IA Professionals. Some security related roles such as system administrators, incident management team members and forensic investigators will require specialist training. Training to educate staff sometimes be enough to defend against some of the most common types of attacks levelled against businesses.

**Theme 3:** Budget or financial investment

Financial is one of the resources that quite challenging in cyber security. The cost needed to implement cyber security is usually high and requires a lot of investment from the company. Other than that, budget for cyber security is a challenging process, in part due to the limited tasks. It is a series of inter-related and persistent processes (Lawrence A. Gordon, 2006). As one of the respondents stressed that,

*In terms of budget focus more on the risk department and need to allocate more investment and budget in other to face the new cyber threat.*

The companies are suggested to purchase cyber security insurance. This can help the financial costs of breaches of personal data, payment card information, and intellectual property, as well as damage to brand reputation. This tactic is to ensure they have the financial resources necessary to respond to and remediate security incidents:

*In aspect of budget the company must allocate the element of cyber security budget not in the IT depart-ment but in the earlier start project or the whole departments and in the strategic plan"* as claimed by respondent A while respondent B stated that *"the organizations can employ managed security services to make sure that cyber security programs are managed in a cost-effective manner.*

Doing so can also help ensure that companies have access to highly trained cyber security talent within their budget constraints.

**Theme 4:** Steps to secure confidential data that are being connected with the technology.

It is a well-known fact that passwords and usernames used by the majority of data users are weak (Wells, 2016). This makes it easy for hackers to get access to the information systems and compromise sensitive data of a business entity or government agency.

*"Hardware authentication is very important in other to secure the technology that have been used"* as stated by all respondents.

According to respondent B:

*Technology gurus or cyber-guru have developed a solution in the user authentication process with a new Core vPro processor that belongs to the sixth generation of processors.*

The core vPro can combine different hardware components with enhanced factors simultaneously for user identity validation purposes.

## CONCLUSION AND IMPLICATIONS

The discussion of this research was discussed based on two objectives; (1) to analyse the challenges faced by Malaysian companies in cyber security and (2) to determine solution for Malaysian companies to overcome challenges in cyber security.

It is the best practice for an organization to use the same level to judge the challenges against in-formation assets as it would be a legal, regulatory, financial or operational risk. This is achievable by incorporating information risk management information throughout the organization, which is actively supported by the board of directors, senior managers and authorized Information Assurance (IA) structure. Determining and communicating organizational attitudes and approaches to risk management is important. Thus, this study has shown that there are five challenges in the implementation of cyber security in Malaysian companies, namely; awareness, people, budget and technology.

Unfortunately, the usage by employees of organisation's Information and Communications Technologies (ICT) brings with various risks and challenges. It is critical for all employees to be aware of their personal security responsibilities and the requirement to comply with corporate security policies. This can be achieved through systematic delivery of an awareness programme that actively seeks to increase the levels of security expertise and knowledge across the organisation as well as a security-conscious culture.

Any employee may release personal or sensitive information to others. Not only that, unsatisfied users may try to abuse the system-level privileges or force other users to gain access to systems that are not permitted. Similarly, they can try to steal or physically disable the computer resources. These findings suggest that an awareness training program can be efficient if the programme is interesting, current and simpler. It was also shown that an awareness of cyber security in employee can give benefits to the organization in other to avoid cyber threats.

Ultimately, employee education and skills play major roles in running the cyber security system. Employee needs to be trained on information security to enhance the employee knowledge and the skills to secure the data. If employees are not trained to secure the usage of organisation's ICT systems or the functions of a security control, they may accidentally misuse the system, potentially compromise security control in terms of the confidentiality, integrity and availability of the information held on the system. Thus, this study has found that generally huge investment is required to implement cyber security in the company. The company should consider the budget in the early stage which stems from the strategic plan of companies.

Other than that, the increasing digital connectivity and automation practically of all processes in the business world throughout the entire value chain has led to the creation of agility. This has led to the development of a very high level of threat and significantly raises the risk of cyber security. Hardware authentication can be especially important when it comes to the Internet of Things, where the network of connected devices ensures that any device that seeks to be connected has the rights for connectivity to that particular network.

In today's world, due to the Industrial Revolution 4.0, it is essential to have information security in all aspects of operation and departments. To compete in the market situation today, it is important for companies to implement cyber security in the organization. It is time to build a better and more secured system that protects the confidential data for initiatives and better work. From the respondents' point of view, there is an urgency to strengthen cyber security in any organization. This must be considered in any company's strategic planning. However, each technology strategy has to suit to capabilities and resources available within the organization covering aspects of the capital, resources and capabilities of people to doing work. Additionally, the ability of organizational employees to carry out assigned tasks aggressively will increase mutual profit. Therefore, an advanced level of protection security is also crucial to reduce the probabilities of cyber threats and ultimately ensure the successful operation of the organization.

## REFERENCES

Ahmad-Reza Sadeghi, C. W., & Waidner, M. (2016). *Security and Privacy Challenges in.* Fraunhofer Institute for Secure Information Technology, Darmstadt, Germany.

Barbour, R. S. (2008). *Introducing Qualitative Research: A student guide to the craft of doing qualittive research.* London: Sage.

Baxter, P. (2008). Qualitative Case Study Methodology: Study Design and Implementation for Novice Researcher. *Qualitative Case Study Methodology: Study Design and Implementation, 13*(4), 544–549.

Bogdan, R. C. (2007). *Qualitative research for education: An introduction to theories and methods* (5th ed.). Boston: Pearson.

Braun, V., & Clarke, V. (2006). Using thematic analysis in psychology. *Qualitative Research in Psychology, 3*(2), 77–101. doi:10.1191/1478088706qp063oa

Brikci, N. (2007, February). *A Guide to Using Qualitative Research Methodology.* Retrieved from Google: https://cloudfront.ualberta.ca/-/media/science/research-and-teaching/teaching/qualitative-research-methodology.pdf

Bryman. (2004). *Social Research Method* (2nd ed.). Oxford, UK: Oxford University Press.

Dan Craigen, N. D.-T. (2014, October). Defining Cybersecurity. *Science Direct*, 1-9.

Deloitte. (2015). *Challenges and Solutions for the Digital Transformation and use exponential technologies.* Zurich: The Creative Studio at Deloitte.

Fischer, E. A. (2016, August 12). Cybersecurity Issues and Challenges. *Congressional Research Service*, 12.

Gizem Öğütçü, Ö. M. (2016, February). Analysis of personal information security behavior and awareness. *Science Direct, 56*, 83-93. Retrieved from https://www.sciencedirect.com/science/article/pii/S0167404815001406

Goutam, R. K. (2015). Importance of Cyber Security. *International Journal of Computers and Applications, 17.* Retrieved from https://pdfs.semanticscholar.org/5cfb/7a5bd2e6c181e8a69ebd49b1dadb795f493b.pdf

Hans de Bruijn, M. J. (2017, January). Building cybersecurity awareness: The need for evidence-based. *Science Direct, 34*, 1-7. Retrieved from https://www.sciencedirect.com/science/article/pii/S0740624X17300540

Hasnah Haron, S. N. (2017). A Hanbook for Business Research Methods. Kuala Lumpur: Pearson Malaysia Sdn Bhd.

Insight Active Learning. (2014, November 26). *Cyber Security and Related Issues: Comprehensive Coverage.* Retrieved from InsightIAS: http://www.insightsonindia.com/2014/11/25/cyber-security-related-issues-comprehensive-coverage/

Iqbal, S. (2016, May 31). On Cloud Security Attacks: A Taxonomy and Instrusion Detection and Preventation as a Service. *Science Direct*, 98-120.

Jaime, C. (2016). The challenges of cybersecurity frameworks to protect data required for the development of advanced maintenance. *Science Direct*, 223.

Jansen, C. (2016). Developing an Operating Industrial Security Services to Mitigate Risks of Digitalization. *Science Direct*, 133-137.

Jansen, D.-I. D.-P. (2016). Developing and operating industrial security services to mitigate risks of digitalization. *Science Direct*, 133-137.

Jay Lee, B. B. (2016). Introduction to cyber manufacturing. *Science Direct*, 13.

Jugder, N. (2016). *The thematic analysis of interview data: an approach used.* University of Leeds. Retrieved from http://hpp.education.leeds.ac.uk/wp-content/uploads/sites/131/2016/02/HPP2016-3-Jugder.pdf

Katharina, M. D. G. (2015). *Qualification For The Actory Of The Future*. Acta Universitatis Cibniensis – Technical Series.

Lane Thames, D. S. (2017). *Cyberrsecurity for Industry 4.0*. Springer Nature. doi:10.1007/978-3-319-50660-9

Lasi, H. F. (2014). Business & Information Systems Engineering. *Industry, 4*(0), 239–242.

Lawrence, A., & Gordon, M. P. (2006). *Managing Cyber Security Resources A cost Benefit Analysis*. McGraw-Hills Companies.

MacLean, L. M., Meyer, M., & Estable, A. (2004). Improving Accuracy of Transcript in Qualitative Research. *Qualitative Health Research, 14*(1), 113–123. doi:10.1177/1049732303259804 PMID:14725179

Manuel Dominguez, M. A. (2017). Cybersecurity training in control systems using real equipment. *Science Direct*, 12180-12184.

Maria Bada, J. R. (2015). Cyber Security Awareness Campaigns. *Research Gate, 3*, 15.

Marjo Heikkila, A. R. (2016). Security Challenges in Small- and Medium-Sized Manufacturing Enterprise. *Science Direct*, 23.

Michael Mylrea, S. N. (2017). An Introduction to Buildings Cybersecurity. *Google Scholar*, 978-982.

Naik, S. (2017). Cyber Security - IoT. *IEEE International Conference On Recent Trends in Electronics Information & Communication Technology*, 764.

National center for postsecondary improvement. (2003). *National Center for Postsecondary Improvement*. Retrieved from https://web.stanford.edu/group/ncpi/unspecified/student_assess_toolkit/sampleInterviewProtocol.html

Oliver, D. G., Serovich, J. M., & Mason, T. L. (2005). Constraints and Opportunties with Interview Transcription: Towards Reflction in Qualitative Research. *Social Forces, 84*(2), 1273–1289. doi:10.1353of.2006.0023 PMID:16534533

Paul van Schaik, D. J. (2017, October). Risk perceptions of cyber-security and precautionary behaviour. *Science Direct, 75*, 547-559. Retrieved from https://www.sciencedirect.com/science/article/pii/S074756321730359X

Penang skill development centre. (2017). *Introduction to the Industry 4.0.* Penang: Author.

Ponelis, S. R. (2015). Using Interpretive Qualitative Case Studies for Exploratory Research in Doctoral Studies: A Case of Information System Research in Small and Medium Enterprise. *International Journal of Doctoral Studies, 10*, 535–550. doi:10.28945/2339

René Waslo, T. L. (2017, March 21). *Industry 4.0 and cybersecurity.* Retrieved from Deloitte Insight: https://dupress.deloitte.com/dup-us-en/focus/industry-4-0/cybersecurity-managing-risk-in-age-of-connected-production.html

Roca, S. K.-L.-D.-V. (2019). *Cybersecurity Current Challenges and Inria's research directions.* Le Chesnay Cedex, France: Inria.

Ruggunan, D. S. (2015). Introduction to Qualitative Analysis: Thematic Analysis. *Discipline of Human Resources*, 1-38. Retrieved from http://smitg.ukzn.ac.za/Libraries/General_Docs/Introduction-to-Qualitative-Analysis.sflb.ashx

Shelzer, R. (2018, April 17). *Cybersecurity and Manufacturing: What's at Risk and How to Protect Your Facility.* Retrieved from Global Electronic Services, Inc: https://blog.gesrepair.com/cybersecurity-and-manufacturing-whats-at-risk-and-how-to-protect-your-facility/

Veal. (2006). *Research Methods for Leisure and Tourism* (3rd ed.). Harlow, UK: Pearson Education.

Wells, J. C. (2016). Cyber-physical security challenges in manufacturing systems. *Manufacturing Letters*, 74-77.

Woodward, P. A. (2015, July 20). Cybersecurity vulnerabilities in medical devices: a complex environment and multifaceted problem. *US National Library of Medicines National Institute of Health, 305*-316. Retrieved from https://www.ncbi.nlm.nih.gov/pmc/articles/PMC4516335/

Yaaqob, I. (2017). The rise of ransomware and emrging security challenges in the Internet of Things. *Science Direct*, 453-454.

Yulia Cherdantseva, P. B. (2016, February). A review of cyber security risk assessment methods for SCADA systems. *Science Direct, 56*, 1-27. Retrieved from https://www.sciencedirect.com/science/article/pii/S0167404815001388

Zhang, Z. (2016). Social media security and trustworthiness. *Science Direct*, 1-11.

Keliang Zhou, T. L. (2015). Industry 4.0: Towards Future Industrial. *Science Direct*, 2147 - 2152.

Zikmund, W. (2015). *Business Research Methods* (16th ed.). Fort Worth, TX: Dryden.

*Previously published in Industry 4.0 and Hyper-Customized Smart Manufacturing Supply Chains; pages 103-125, copyright year 2019 by Business Science Reference (an imprint of IGI Global).*

# Index

## D

## E

## F

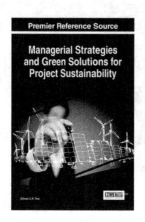

# IGI Global Author Services

Providing a high-quality, affordable, and expeditious service, IGI Global's Author Services enable authors to streamline their publishing process, increase chance of acceptance, and adhere to IGI Global's publication standards.

## Benefits of Author Services:

- **Professional Service:** All our editors, designers, and translators are experts in their field with years of experience and professional certifications.

- **Quality Guarantee & Certificate:** Each order is returned with a quality guarantee and certificate of professional completion.

- **Timeliness:** All editorial orders have a guaranteed return timeframe of 3-5 business days and translation orders are guaranteed in 7-10 business days.

- **Affordable Pricing:** IGI Global Author Services are competitively priced compared to other industry service providers.

- **APC Reimbursement:** IGI Global authors publishing Open Access (OA) will be able to deduct the cost of editing and other IGI Global author services from their OA APC publishing fee.

## Author Services Offered:

**English Language Copy Editing**
Professional, native English language copy editors improve your manuscript's grammar, spelling, punctuation, terminology, semantics, consistency, flow, formatting, and more.

**Scientific & Scholarly Editing**
A Ph.D. level review for qualities such as originality and significance, interest to researchers, level of methodology and analysis, coverage of literature, organization, quality of writing, and strengths and weaknesses.

**Figure, Table, Chart & Equation Conversions**
Work with IGI Global's graphic designers before submission to enhance and design all figures and charts to IGI Global's specific standards for clarity.

**Translation**
Providing 70 language options, including Simplified and Traditional Chinese, Spanish, Arabic, German, French, and more.

## Hear What the Experts Are Saying About IGI Global's Author Services

"Publishing with IGI Global has been **an amazing experience** for me for sharing my research. The **strong academic production** support ensures quality and timely completion." – **Prof. Margaret Niess, Oregon State University, USA**

"The service was **very fast, very thorough, and very helpful** in ensuring our chapter meets the criteria and requirements of the book's editors. I was **quite impressed and happy** with your service." – **Prof. Tom Brinthaupt, Middle Tennessee State University, USA**

**Learn More or Get Started Here:**

For Questions, Contact IGI Global's Customer Service Team at cust@igi-global.com or 717-533-8845

www.igi-global.com

Publisher of Peer-Reviewed, Timely, and
Innovative Academic Research Since 1988

## IGI Global's Transformative Open Access (OA) Model:
# How to Turn Your University Library's Database Acquisitions Into a Source of OA Funding

Well in advance of Plan S, IGI Global unveiled their OA Fee Waiver (Read & Publish) Initiative. Under this initiative, librarians who invest in IGI Global's InfoSci-Books and/or InfoSci-Journals databases will be able to subsidize their patrons' OA article processing charges (APCs) when their work is submitted and accepted (after the peer review process) into an IGI Global journal.

## How Does it Work?

**Step 1:** **Library Invests in the InfoSci-Databases:** A library perpetually purchases or subscribes to the InfoSci-Books, InfoSci-Journals, or discipline/subject databases.

**Step 2:** **IGI Global Matches the Library Investment with OA Subsidies Fund:** IGI Global provides a fund to go towards subsidizing the OA APCs for the library's patrons.

**Step 3:** **Patron of the Library is Accepted into IGI Global Journal (After Peer Review):** When a patron's paper is accepted into an IGI Global journal, they option to have their paper published under a traditional publishing model or as OA.

**Step 4:** **IGI Global Will Deduct APC Cost from OA Subsidies Fund:** If the author decides to publish under OA, the OA APC fee will be deducted from the OA subsidies fund.

**Step 5:** **Author's Work Becomes Freely Available:** The patron's work will be freely available under CC BY copyright license, enabling them to share it freely with the academic community.

**Note:** *This fund will be offered on an annual basis and will renew as the subscription is renewed for each year thereafter. IGI Global will manage the fund and award the APC waivers unless the librarian has a preference as to how the funds should be managed.*

## Hear From the Experts on This Initiative:

"I'm very happy to have been able to make one of my recent research contributions *freely available* along with having access to the *valuable resources* found within IGI Global's InfoSci-Journals database."

— **Prof. Stuart Palmer,**
Deakin University, Australia

"Receiving the support from IGI Global's OA Fee Waiver Initiative *encourages me to continue my research work without any hesitation.*"

— **Prof. Wenlong Liu,** College of Economics and Management at Nanjing University of Aeronautics & Astronautics, China

**For More Information, Scan the QR Code or Contact:**
IGI Global's Digital Resources Team at eresources@igi-global.com.